W9-ANB-745

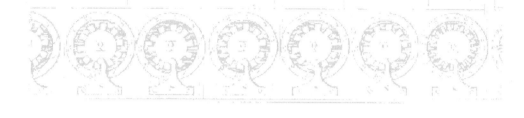

2nd edition

ENCYCLOPEDIA OF

PHILOSOPHY

3

volume

2nd edition

ENCYCLOPEDIA OF
PHILOSOPHY

DONALD M. BORCHERT
Editor in Chief

MACMILLAN REFERENCE USA
An imprint of Thomson Gale, a part of The Thomson Corporation

THOMSON

GALE

Detroit • New York • San Francisco • San Diego • New Haven, Conn. • Waterville, Maine • London • Munich

Encyclopedia of Philosophy, Second Edition

Donald M. Borchert, Editor in Chief

For permission to use material from this product, submit your request via Web at http://www.gale-edit.com/permissions, or you may download our Permissions Request form and submit your request by fax or mail to:

Permissions
Thomson Gale
27500 Drake Rd.
Farmington Hills, MI 48331-3535
Permissions Hotline:
248-699-8006 or 800-877-4253 ext. 8006
Fax: 248-699-8074 or 800-762-4058

LIBRARY OF CONGRESS CATALOGING-IN-PUBLICATION DATA

Encyclopedia of philosophy / Donald M. Borchert, editor in chief.—2nd ed.
   p. cm.
     Includes bibliographical references and index.
     ISBN 0-02-865780-2 (set hardcover : alk. paper)—
     ISBN 0-02-865781-0 (vol 1)—ISBN 0-02-865782-9 (vol 2)—
     ISBN 0-02-865783-7 (vol 3)—ISBN 0-02-865784-5 (vol 4)—
     ISBN 0-02-865785-3 (vol 5)—ISBN 0-02-865786-1 (vol 6)—
     ISBN 0-02-865787-X (vol 7)—ISBN 0-02-865788-8 (vol 8)—
     ISBN 0-02-865789-6 (vol 9)—ISBN 0-02-865790-X (vol 10)
     1. Philosophy–Encyclopedias. I. Borchert, Donald M., 1934-

B51.E53 2005
103–dc22

                2005018573

This title is also available as an e-book.
ISBN 0-02-866072-2
Contact your Thomson Gale representative for ordering information.

Printed in the United States of America
10 9 8 7 6 5 4 3 2 1

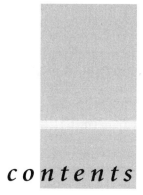

contents

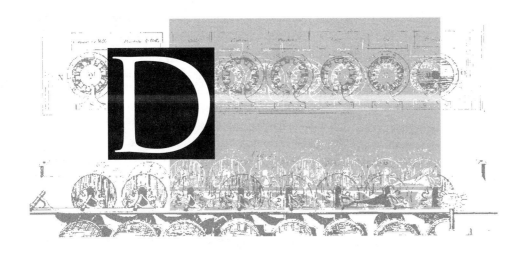

DETERMINABLES AND DETERMINATES

The terminology of "determinables and determinates" existed in scholastic philosophy, but the modern use of these terms originated with the Cambridge (U.K.) philosopher and logician W. E. Johnson, who revived the terminology in his *Logic* (1921). Johnson said, "I propose to call such terms as colour and shape *determinables* in relation to such terms as red or circular which will be called *determinates*." Some other determinables are size, weight, age, number, and texture. The terminology has since passed into philosophical currency and is now used to mark both the relation between determinate and determinable qualities and the relation between the corresponding words.

The chief features of this relation that Johnson and his successors have found interesting are:

(1) It is logically distinct from the relation of genus to species. The denotation of a species term is marked off within the denotation of a genus term by the possession of properties known as differentia. The species is thus to be construed as formed by the conjunction of two logically independent terms, either of which can, depending on the purposes at hand, be construed as genus or differentia. For example, the species term *man* is defined as the conjunction of the terms *rational* and *animal*. However, the determinate term *red* is not definable by conjoining the determinable term *color* with any other independent term. To put this point another way: Whereas we can say, "All humans are animals which are rational," no analogous statement can be made beginning, "All red things are colored things which are." Any term that could fill the gap would have to be synonymous with *red*. Red things do not possess some trait other than their redness that, when conjoined with their coloredness, makes them by definition red. Both the genus-species relation and the determinable-determinate relation are relations of the less specific to the more specific; but in the former case the specification is provided by some property logically independent of the genus, whereas in the latter case the determinate cannot be specified by adding additional independent properties to the determinable.

This characteristic has been emphasized by Johnson, John Cook Wilson, A. Prior, and John R. Searle; and it is this feature that chiefly justifies the introduction of this terminology as an addition to the traditional arsenal. Attempts have been made—by Searle, for example—to give a rigorous formal definition of the determinable relation utilizing this feature; but it is not clear to what extent they have succeeded.

(2) Determinates under the same determinable are incompatible. For example, the same object cannot be simultaneously red and green at the same point; and a man six feet tall cannot be simultaneously five feet tall. It might seem that counterexamples could be produced to this point since, for example, an object can be both red and scarlet, and red and scarlet are both determinates of color. However, such counterexamples are easily disposed of on the basis of the fact that scarlet is a shade of red, and hence red is a determinable of scarlet.

We must distinguish the relation in which red stands to scarlet from the relation in which color stands to either red or scarlet. Both are cases of the determinable relation, but they are significantly different. We may think of color terminology as providing us with a hierarchy of terms, many of which will stand in the determinable relation to each other as the specification of shades progresses from the less precise to the more precise. But at the top of the hierarchy stands the term *color,* which we may describe as an absolute determinable of all the other members of the hierarchy, including such lower-order determinables as "red" and their determinates, such as "scarlet."

Our original point can then be restated by saying that determinates under the same determinable are incompatible unless one of the determinates is a lower-order determinable of the other. In the literature of this subject, the counterexamples are usually avoided by saying that any two exact determinates—for example, exact shades of color—are incompatible. However, it is not clear what *exact* is supposed to mean in this context.

(3) Absolute determinables play a special role vis-à-vis their determinates. This role may be expressed by saying that, in general, for any determinate term neither that term nor its negation is predicable of an entity unless the corresponding absolute determinable term is true of that entity. For example, both the sentence "The number seventeen is red" and the sentence "The number seventeen is not red" sound linguistically odd because numbers are not the sort of entities that can be colored. Lacking the appropriate absolute deter-

minable, neither a determinate term nor its negation is true of the entity in question.

To have a convenient formulation of this point, we may say that the predication of any determinate term or its negation of an object *presupposes* that the corresponding absolute determinable term is true of that object. We define presupposition as follows: A term A presupposes a term B if and only if it is a necessary condition of A's being either true or false of an object x that B is true of x. Thus, in short and in general, determinates presuppose their absolute determinables. No doubt certain qualifications would have to be made to account for the operation of this principle in a natural language. For example, perhaps what is presupposed by *red* is more accurately expressed by *colorable* rather than by *colored.*

Aside from the intrinsic interest of these distinctions, they have proved useful in other areas of philosophy. John Locke's very puzzling discussion of primary and secondary qualities can be illuminated by pointing out that he fails to make sufficient use of the distinction between determinable and determinate qualities. When, for example, he says the primary qualities of a material body are inseparable from it in whatever state it may be, he clearly does not mean that a body must have this or that determinate shape or size as opposed to some other shape or size, but rather that it must have the absolute determinables of the primary qualities: It is a necessary condition of something's being a material object that it have some shape or other, some size or other, and so on.

Again, it is useful to point out that absolute determinables are closely related to categories. The notion of a category (or at least one philosophically important notion of a category) is the notion of a class of objects of which a given term can be significantly predicated. Thus, for example, correlative with the notion of *red* is the notion of things that can significantly be called red; these things are the members of the category associated with *red.* But a necessary condition of something's being a member of the class of things that can be significantly called "red" is that the absolute determinable of *red* must be true of that thing since, as we saw above, determinates presuppose their absolute determinables. Because a category (of the sort we are considering) is always a category relative to a certain term, and because a determinate term presupposes its absolute determinable, the absolute determinables provide a set of necessary conditions for category membership relative to the determinate terms.

Where the absolute determinable provides not only a necessary but also a sufficient condition of predicability of the determinate term, the absolute determinable will simply denote the members of the category associated with the determinate term. Thus, assuming *colored* (or *colorable*) is the only presupposed term of *red,* the category associated with *red,* and with any other determinate of *color,* is only the class of objects that are (or could be) colored.

See also Categories; Locke, John; Negation; Primary and Secondary Qualities; Prior, Arthur Norman; Properties; Searle, John.

Bibliography

Johnson, W. E. *Logic,* 3 vols. Cambridge, U.K.: Cambridge: University Press, 1921–1924.

Körner, S., and J. R. Searle. "Determinables and the Notion of Resemblance: Symposium." *PAS,* Supp. (1959): 125–158.

Prior, A. "Determinables, Determinates, and Determinants." *Mind* 58 (1949): 1–20, 178–194.

John R. Searle (1967)

DETERMINABLES AND DETERMINATES [ADDENDUM]

The relation between determinates and determinables has certain interesting formal and modal features. It is controversial whether these features are to be explained in terms of something more basic or whether they are primitive.

Formally speaking, the determinate-determinable relation is transitive, asymmetric, and irreflexive. Because *scarlet* is a determinate of *red* and *red* is a determinate of *color, scarlet* is a determinate of *color.* Because *scarlet* is a determinate of *red, red* is not a determinate of *scarlet.* And nothing is a determinate of itself.

Modally speaking, three features are worthy of note. First, if anything has some property, *p,* then it also has every property, *q,* of which *p* is a determinate. Thus, of necessity, scarlet things are red and colored. Second, the relation guarantees the exclusion of codeterminates. Nothing can have two determinates under a single determinable (provided the determinates are not themselves determination related). Thus, nothing can be both scarlet and crimson, because both are codeterminates of color. Third, and more controversially, any object with a determinable property must have a property that is a determinate of that property. Furthermore, there must be an exactly determinate property under every determinable.

It may be that the modal and formal structure of the determinate-determinable relation is brute, but two theories suggest otherwise. According to David M. Armstrong (1997), codeterminates under a single determinable are partially identical. Having five grams of mass just consists in having one gram of mass five times over. So, the exclusion relation is neatly explained by appeal to familiar facts about identity. Nothing can be five grams of mass and one gram of mass for the same reason that no room can have exactly one lectern and exactly five lecterns. However, the notion of partial identity for properties, as opposed to individuals, remains unclear.

Sydney Shoemaker (1984, 1998) holds that properties are individuated by the causal powers they bestow on objects that instantiate them. This theory of properties provides a ready explanation of the nature of the determinate-determinable relation: The powers endowed by a determinable property are a proper subset of the powers endowed by a determinate of that property (2001). For example, *scarlet* bestows the power to trigger scarlet detectors as well as red and color detectors. Some of the modal and formal features of the relation are then explicable simply by appeal to set theory, with its transitive, asymmetric, and irreflexive relation of proper subsethood. For example, if anything is scarlet, then it is also red, because if anything has the set of causal powers endowed by *scarlet,* then it has every subset of the causal powers in that set, and one of those subsets corresponds to *red.* The exclusion of codeterminates requires another explanation, however, which appeals to the individuation of powers. If an object were both scarlet and crimson, it would have incompatible causal powers, that is, it would be disposed to act in contradictory ways in the identical circumstances.

This reduction of the determinate-determinable relation would be more satisfying were the causal theory of properties that underwrites it less controversial. Among the more surprising consequences of the theory is that the laws of nature are strictly metaphysically necessary. Moreover, the theory is not perfectly general, but applies only to certain properties. The causal relation itself, along with purely formal properties like self-identity, cannot be correlated with a unique set of powers, but such noncausal properties may nevertheless stand in determinate-determinable relations.

One other characteristic is worthy of note: Determinates and determinables do not compete for causal efficacy. If a scarlet patch sets off a red detector, it is appropriate both to say the detector was triggered by the red and that the detector was triggered by the scarlet. The overdetermination here is harmless, which raises the possibility that the relation may be appropriated by nonreductive physicalists seeking a way to preserve the causal efficacy of the mental in a physical world; perhaps physical properties are determinates of mental determinables (Yablo 1992).

The fit is not quite right, however. To repeat the point made earlier, the determinate-determinable relation is not the genus-species relation, nor is it merely one of greater and lesser generality. A perfectly determinate shape may be realized in different materials, but the conjunctions of that shape with different types of material do not form further determinates of shape. Likewise, mental properties may still admit multiple physical realizations even if they are perfect determinates of thought (Funkhouser).

See also Armstrong, David M.; Properties; Set Theory; Shoemaker, Sydney.

Bibliography

Armstrong, David M. *A World of States of Affairs.* New York: Cambridge University Press, 1997.

Funkhouser, Eric. "The Determinate-Determinable Relation." Forthcoming, *Nous.*

Shoemaker, Sydney. "Causal and Metaphysical Necessity." *Pacific Philosophical Quarterly* 79 (1998): 59–77.

Shoemaker, Sydney. "Causality and Properties." In *Identity, Cause, and Mind: Philosophical Essays.* New York: Cambridge University Press, 1984.

Shoemaker, Sydney. "Realization and Mental Causation." In *Physicalism and Its Discontents,* edited by Carl Gillett and Barry Loewer. New York: Cambridge University Press, 2001.

Yablo, Stephen. "Mental Causation." *Philosophical Review* 101 (1992): 245–280.

Troy Cross (2005)

DETERMINISM, A HISTORICAL SURVEY

Determinism is the general philosophical thesis that states that for everything that ever happens there are conditions such that, given them, nothing else could happen. The several versions of this thesis rest upon various alleged connections and interdependencies of things and events, asserting that these hold without exception.

There have been many versions of deterministic theories in the history of philosophy, springing from diverse motives and considerations, some of which overlap considerably. We shall consider these in the order in which they have been historically significant, together with certain alternative theories that philosophers have proposed. There are five theories of determinism to be considered, which can for convenience be called ethical determinism, logical determinism, theological determinism, physical determinism, and psychological determinism.

ETHICAL DETERMINISM

ADVOCATES. It seemed to Socrates that every man always chooses what seems to him best, that no man can set as the object of his choice something that seems evil or bad to him. Plato had much the same view, arguing that no man who knows what is good can possibly choose anything else. They drew the obvious corollary that wrongdoing or the pursuit of evil must always be either involuntary or the result of ignorance.

A thirsty man, for example, might choose to drink from a certain cup in ignorance of the fact that it contains poison, or, knowing its contents, he might be forced to drink from it. But he could not, knowing that it contained poison and that this would bring upon him a great evil, voluntarily drink from it. Socrates and Plato thought that similar reasoning applies to any choice whatsoever. Hence, the Socratic doctrine that virtue is knowledge and vice ignorance. If one knows the good, he automatically seeks it; if one seeks something else, it can only be because he is pursuing an apparent, but specious, good—in other words, because he is ignorant of what is in fact good. An obvious corollary to this, and one that was drawn by Plato, is that the best commonwealth would be one governed by philosophers—that is, by men who know the good and can intellectually distinguish it from its counterfeits.

It is evident that in this ethical intellectualism, which is so central to Platonism, there is a theory of determinism. Men's voluntary actions are invariably determined by an apparent good; hence, all their actions are determined by this, if by nothing else. Philosophers who have been convinced by this teaching have nevertheless without exception insisted that it enhances rather than debases man's freedom. Freedom, they have maintained, is precisely the determination of the will by what is good. To have one's will or choice determined by what is bad is to be enslaved; to have it determined by something less than the highest good is, to that extent, to be less than perfectly free. Thus, Plato described the wicked tyrant, who pursues what is evil because he is ignorant of the true good, as enslaved and an object of pity.

René Descartes believed that no man who knew his true "end" or highest good could reject it in favor of something less and maintained that man's freedom consisted precisely in knowing that good and being thereby determined to seek it. St. Thomas Aquinas spoke similarly, with qualifications, concerning man's knowledge of his true "end" or highest good. Gottfried Wilhelm Leibniz similarly took for granted the fact that God could not possibly be guided by anything except the true good, which he must surely know, and that in creating a world, for example, he therefore could not create any but the best possible world. Still, Leibniz maintained, this is no derogation of God's freedom; on the contrary, it is the most perfect freedom to have one's will thus determined.

OPPONENTS. Aristotle rejected this theory of ethical determinism, mostly because it conflicts with what he took to be the evident fact of incontinence. It seemed clear to him that sometimes a man's desires or appetites are in conflict with his reason, precisely in the sense that he desires something bad even while knowing that it is bad, which is the very essence of incontinence. John Locke took the same position. A drunkard, Locke pointed out, well knows that his use of spirits is bad for him, but the mere knowledge of this cannot be depended upon to extinguish his desire for them.

Most contemporary thinkers incline to the same view. The moral and intellectual determination of men's choices and the consequent impossibility of genuine incontinence are no longer considered a plausible view by very many. Nevertheless, it is not easy to see just what is wrong with it. Surely, men do prefer the better to the worse in some sense—not what is absolutely better, perhaps, but what at least seems better; otherwise, why would any man choose it? It is the very nature of things bad to be shunned, and that is precisely why they are called bad.

Perhaps the real issue here is the more general opposition between rationalism and voluntarism. If one assumes the primacy of man's reason and supposes his will, or what the Greeks called his appetite, to be naturally subordinate to it, then the Socratic thesis of the determination of the will by the reason is difficult to refute. If, on the other hand, one presupposes the primacy of man's will or appetite and assumes the intellect to be at least sometimes subordinate to the will, then there is no difficulty in accounting for incontinence. Furthermore, there have been many philosophers—for example, Benedict (Baruch) de Spinoza, Thomas Hobbes, and William James—who have insisted that all it means to describe

something as good is that it is the object of one's will—that is, of his desire or interest. If this is so, then the Socratic thesis becomes utterly trivial. It amounts to saying nothing more than that the object of a man's will is always an apparent good—that is, something that is the object of his will. This is certainly true but not significant.

LOGICAL DETERMINISM

Very early in the development of Western philosophy it occurred to certain thinkers that logic alone suggests that men's wills are fettered, that nothing is really in their power to alter. This thesis was developed by Diodorus Cronus and others of his school, whom Aristotle sometimes referred to as "the Megarians," and more importantly by the highly influential school of the Stoics. Such views were associated by the ancients with the idea of fate, an idea that has, however, the same implications as certain forms of determinism with respect to human freedom. Thus, if no man's destiny is in any degree up to him, if everything that he ever does is something he could never have avoided, then in the clearest sense it is idle to speak of his having a free will. The Stoics thought that the most elementary consideration of logic shows this to be true.

The consideration in question is simply the supposition that every statement whatsoever is true or, if not true, false. This ultimately came to be expressed in the dictum *tertium non datur,* meaning that no third truth-value, besides true and false, can be assigned to any statement. If this is so, then it must hold for statements about the future as well as any others, for statements about individual men's future actions and even for statements or propositions that are never asserted. It must also, of course, apply to statements believed by the gods. The last idea eventually became very important when the belief in an omniscient and infallible god became theological dogma.

What apparently led certain ancients, such as Chrysippus, Posidonius, and the Stoics generally to take the idea of logical determinism seriously was a consideration of signs, omens, and portents, which were then widely believed in. If there are signs from which it can be discovered what is going to happen, especially what a certain man is going to do at a certain time, and if, moreover, such signs are vouchsafed to men by gods, then it seems that such predictions must unavoidably, in the fullness of time, be fulfilled. Any such prediction that was not fulfilled could not have been true when made, contradicting the supposition that it was true. If such a prediction must be fulfilled, then it seems to follow that it is not within anyone's power to confute it. The extension of this thought to all actions of all men leads quite naturally to the view that no man's actions are ever free or that nothing any man ever does was ever avoidable, it having always been true that he was going to do whatever he eventually did.

ARISTOTLE'S OPINION. A penetrating discussion of this problem is contained in some much disputed passages of Aristotle's *De interpretatione*. Aristotle there considers the question whether every true proposition, asserting that a certain event has occurred at a certain time, was true before the event in question took place and whether every false proposition, asserting that a certain event has occurred at a certain time, was false before the event failed to take place at that time.

Suppose, for example, a naval battle took place yesterday. This would seem to entail that it was already true, prior to yesterday, that it was going to occur. If anyone had said a thousand years earlier that such a battle was going to occur that day, then it would seem that his prediction was true, and if anyone had denied it a thousand years earlier, then the events of that day would have shown him to have been wrong. Aristotle, however, seemed reluctant to make this seemingly obvious inference. He suggested that it is inconsistent with the fact that men sometimes deliberate about whether to make certain things happen and with the belief all men have that it is sometimes up to them whether the events about which they deliberate will occur. If it is true a thousand years before a naval battle occurs that it is going to occur on a certain day, then whether or not anyone actually makes the prediction, it is difficult to see how, when that day arrives, it can still be up to the naval commander whether the battle will occur or what point there could be in anyone's deliberating about whether to precipitate it. The same difficulty arises if one supposes it to have been false a thousand years earlier that a naval battle would later occur. Aristotle therefore seems to suggest that some propositions—namely, those which assert or deny the future occurrence of certain deliberate actions of men or of events which are dependent upon these—are sometimes neither true nor false until the actions have either occurred or failed to occur.

SUBSEQUENT CONTROVERSY. This whole question was highly vexing to the early thinkers who followed Aristotle. It was even more troublesome to the Scholastics, many of whom felt bound to affirm the freedom of the human will but also bound to affirm that God knows from the beginning of time everything that will ever hap-

pen in his creation. Most of the Stoics, whose philosophy was highly fatalistic anyway, embraced the view of logical determinism or fatalism, while many of the Epicureans, who from moral considerations had always set themselves against any theories of fatalism, sometimes defended the view that statements about the future need not be either true or false and hence could not be known in advance even by the gods.

Diodorus Cronus was perhaps the most polemical of the early advocates of logical determinism. His fundamental principle, which is obviously a very strong one, was that it always follows from the fact that something *has* happened that it was *going* to happen and, hence, that it was true that it was going to happen before it did happen. Applying this seemingly incontestable dictum, Diodorus concluded that nothing is ever possible except what actually happens, from which it follows that it is never within any man's power to do anything except what he actually does.

Among the problems to which this conclusion gave rise was one called "the idle argument," which states that there is never any point in any man's ever taking any precautions or making any preparations. If, for example, a man is ill, then it follows from Diodorus's principle that he is either going to recover or he is not going to recover. If he is going to recover, then he will recover whether or not he summons a physician; similarly, if he is going to perish, then he will perish whether or not he summons a physician. Hence, there is no point in his summoning a physician in either case because the outcome is already inevitable. The philosopher Chrysippus sought to resolve this evident absurdity by inventing the notion of "condestinate" facts, facts whose truths are dependent upon one another. Thus, it may be true that a man is going to recover from his illness and also true that he is going to recover only if he summons a physician, from which one cannot conclude that he will recover whether or not he summons a physician. The two facts are, in this case, "condestinate."

CONTEMPORARY ANALYTICAL DISTINCTIONS. Contemporary philosophers have for the most part tried to resolve the problems of logical determinism by distinguishing between modal concepts, such as necessary, impossible, and so on, and the nonmodal concepts of true and false and by refusing to make certain inferences from one kind of concept to the other. Thus, from the fact that something happens of necessity, it follows that it happens, and from the fact that it is impossible for something to happen, it follows that it does not happen. The reverse of these inferences cannot be made, however; something might happen without being necessary, and something might fail to happen without being impossible. This permits one to say without contradiction that it is true, without being necessary, or false, without being impossible, that a certain man is going to perform a certain action.

The difficulty that some writers have found in this seemingly obvious solution is that "necessary" and "impossible," as applied to human actions, do not mean logically necessary and impossible. (As Gilbert Ryle and others have noted, the only things that can be logically necessary or impossible are propositions, not events or actions.) When the ancients described an event or action as necessary, they simply meant that it was unavoidable, and when they described it as impossible, they meant that it was not within the power of an agent to bring it about. This is still what men mean by such locutions. It is surely not obvious how an action can be avoidable on the supposition that it has been true from the beginning of the world that it would be performed by a certain man at a certain time and place, and it is not obvious how it can be within the power of an agent to perform a given action on the supposition that it is eternally false that he will. Still, as critics of this line of thought have forever pointed out, we must take for granted that men are often able to do many things which they never do and to forgo many things which they do all the time. It is perhaps just this that has always been at issue.

Following the suggestions of Aristotle, some contemporary philosophers, such as Charles Hartshorne, have maintained that predictions concerning a man's future voluntary actions are always false, the truth being expressed only by a statement to the effect that he might and might not perform them. Others have argued that such predictions are neither true nor false when made, though they eventually become either true or false. In this connection Ryle has suggested that "correct" and "incorrect," as applied to predictions of this sort, are more like verdicts than descriptions and thus convey more the idea of "fulfilled" and "unfulfilled" than of "true" and "false." It would be always wrong to call a prediction fulfilled as long as it is a prediction, and similarly, Ryle suggests, it is misleading to speak of predictions as having been true. Ryle and others have also noted the error of thinking of predictions as the causes of the events they predict, though essentially the same error was pointed out by St. Augustine and many of the Scholastics, who noted that God's prescience is never by itself the cause of anything.

Perhaps the most significant upshot of this whole problem, however, has been the considerable contemporary philosophical discussion concerning the status of future things, particularly future contingent or undetermined things. Do they exist "in the future," awaiting only the lapse of time in order to become present, or do they have the more nebulous status sometimes referred to as possible existence? Ryle has suggested that predictive statements are not true or false in the same way that statements about past things are, precisely because the things to which they ostensibly refer do not have the same determinate existence, and that some descriptive statements therefore cannot make sense until the things ostensibly described really do exist. He thus compares certain predictive statements, such as the statement that a given man is going to cough at a certain future time, with statements about "past" things which might have been but never were—for example, certain automobile accidents that were prevented. All these suggestions have raised some of the most vexatious questions in contemporary metaphysics, and they are very far from being resolved.

THEOLOGICAL DETERMINISM

With the development of Christian theology there arose the concept of a God who is, among other things, perfectly good, omniscient, and omnipotent and upon whom, moreover, the entire world and everything in it, down to the minutest detail, are absolutely dependent for existence and character. This idea is obviously loaded with possibilities for deterministic theories, and there have been many philosophers and theologians who have developed them into extensive systems, some of which have formed the basis for theological doctrines having an extremely wide and abiding influence.

MORAL DETERMINATION OF GOD'S WILL. If, for example, we consider first the absolute goodness of God, it seems incongruous not only to think of him as choosing or by his action inflicting evil, but equally of his being able to choose, inflict, or even permit evil. Since, moreover, the world is the result of his act of creation, it seems to follow that it is the only world that was ever possible, being of necessity the best that was possible. Many of the Stoics affirmed this conception, identifying the world or "nature" with God or Zeus and also with fate. The world, they thought, is the only possible world, and nothing in it could be different from what it is. It is nevertheless good, and so the aim of a wise man should simply be to find and accept his place in it. Spinoza's philosophy contains essentially the same idea. In the first book of his *Ethics* he affirms that nothing in nature is contingent, that there is no free will in God, and, hence, that things could not have been produced by God in any other manner, though Spinoza was led to these conclusions by considerations other than the mere goodness of God.

Perhaps it was Leibniz who tried hardest to reconcile the moral determinism implied by God's absolute goodness with the existence of alternative possibilities. Leibniz distinguished two senses of necessity, which he called absolute and hypothetical. Given the absolute goodness of God, he said, then the world that exists must be the only possible world, because it is of necessity the best possible one. But this is only on the hypothesis that God is good; hence, the exclusive necessity of this world is only hypothetical. In the absolute sense, not taking into account God's goodness, this world is only one of many possible worlds, contrary to what Spinoza maintained. Something is necessary in an absolute sense only if its negation involves a contradiction, and in this sense neither God's acts nor men's are necessary. The actions of men are necessary only in the sense that there is a sufficient reason for them, as for everything else. This is consistent with their being free, considered in themselves, Leibniz thought, since in no absolute sense are they necessary.

It is doubtful, however, whether Leibniz's distinctions supply more than a verbal solution to the problem of theological determinism. One can grant that this must be the only possible world given the hypothesis that it is the creation of an absolutely good creator and thus agree that apart from that hypothesis it is not the only possible world. But as soon as one affirms God's goodness, which traditional theology considered beyond doubt, then it is difficult to see in what sense alternative worlds are still "possible." Leibniz's concept of hypothetical necessity has nevertheless had the most far-reaching significance in the subsequent development of the ideas of determinism and free will, for it became a cornerstone for generations of later philosophers, like David Hume, in their attempted reconciliations of physical and psychological determinism with free will.

DIVINE OMNISCIENCE AND DETERMINISM. The omniscience of God has likewise seemed to many thinkers to imply the inevitability of everything that happens. The philosophical arguments involved in this kind of determinism, resting on the idea that all truths are eternal, are essentially the same as those which led Diodorus and others to assert fatalism, but the addition of the premise that there is a being who knows all truths

from the beginning of time gives these arguments an especially powerful appeal to the imagination.

St. Augustine. An omniscient being knows everything. St. Augustine and virtually every other theologian who contributed greatly to the development of Christian thought assumed without question that God, as thus conceived, must know in advance every action that every man is ever going to perform, including, of course, every sin he will ever commit. If this is so, then the question arises of how men can behave otherwise than God knows they will—how, for example, a man can forgo those sins that God, when he created the man, knew he would commit. The strongest concise way of expressing this point is to say that (1) if God knows that I shall perform a certain act at a certain time and (2) if I am nevertheless able to forgo that act when the time for performing it arrives, then (3) it follows that I am at least able to confute an item of divine knowledge, whether or not I actually do so. That conclusion, of course, is absurd. The second premise, accordingly, must be false if the first is true.

Carneades, a pre-Christian defender of human self-determination and freedom, maintained that even Apollo could not know in advance what men were going to do. Such a view, however, seemed so inconsistent with the notion of omniscience that hardly any Christian thinker entertained it. St. Augustine, in considering this question independently of the idea of God's power, maintained that God's foreknowledge constitutes no threat whatsoever to man's free will. God, according to St. Augustine, foresees all events because they are going to occur; they do not occur just because he has foreseen them. Thus, he compared God's prescience to a man's memory. The fact that someone remembers an event does not render that event necessary or involuntary, and the same is true with respect to God's foreknowing an event. Again, St. Augustine pointed out, there is no difficulty in the notion of God's foreknowing that someone will be happy, from which one can hardly conclude that such a man must therefore be happy against his will. And whether or not we do anything else voluntarily, it can hardly be denied that we *will* things voluntarily, and this constitutes no reason why God should not know what we are going to will. Many of the other events God foreknows are things that, as God knows, depend upon our wills for their happening, from which it follows that they are both foreknown and willed—that is, voluntary. Most of the apparent difficulties in reconciling divine prescience with human freedom seemed to St. Augustine to evaporate in any case as soon as one comprehends the nature of God's eternity. The distinctions of "before" and "after," which are essential to the formulation of this kind of theological determinism, have no application to God, according to St. Augustine. His eternity is not an everlastingness but, rather, an existence that is altogether independent of time. God therefore sees the whole of history in a manner similar to that in which we view the present, and from this point of view one is not easily tempted to suppose that God's knowledge imposes any determination on things to come.

SUBSEQUENT VIEWS. St. Augustine's reflections on this problem have for the most part been followed by subsequent thinkers. St. Thomas Aquinas, for example, similarly emphasized the eternity of God's vision and argued that God's knowledge is not by itself the cause of anything. Boethius, in *The Consolation of Philosophy,* defended the same view, adding numerous analogies to increase the plausibility of his arguments. Thus, he noted, a sign shows that to which it points without thereby producing it. In the same way God knows what will come to pass, but his knowing does not cause anything to happen. Again, a man might at one and the same time see another man walking and the sun rising; yet the man's walking can be voluntary, whereas the sun's rising is not. This, Boethius maintained, is the manner in which God views all things from the perspective of eternity. Boethius was thus led to his famous definition of eternity as "the simultaneous and complete possession of infinite life." In such a conception there is no suggestion of succession in time, and God must thus see all things in a manner similar to that in which we view things spread out in a given moment.

This Augustinian solution to the problem, echoed so often in the subsequent history of thought, has not been without dissenters, however. In the fourteenth century Peter Aureol reaffirmed what he took to be the arguments of Aristotle, maintaining that propositions concerning particular future contingent events, such as men's acts of free will, cannot be either true or false. This would seem to imply, of course, that God cannot foreknow them, but Peter Aureol seemed reluctant to draw that heterodox conclusion. He observed that God's foreknowledge does not make anything true or false and is to that extent consistent with the lack of either truth or falsity in some such propositions. He apparently did not observe that in order to be known by God, a proposition must nevertheless be true when foreknown, since God obviously cannot know something to be true that is in fact neither true nor false. William of Ockham expressed similar doubts but, unlike Peter Aureol, was unwilling to reject either the law of excluded middle or the doctrine of divine omniscience. God, according to William of Ockham, is omniscient and

hence knows all future contingent events. In the case of any disjunction to the effect that a given contingent event either is going to occur at a given time or is not going to occur at that time, God knows which of the mutually inconsistent propositions is true since he is omniscient. It follows that one of them is true and the other one false. But, according to this thinker, no one knows how this is possible, and no philosophical arguments, such as St. Augustine's, can render it really intelligible. Ockham's position thus consisted essentially of simply affirming what he thought was required by both logic and faith and refusing to render either intelligible in terms of the other.

The attempts of St. Augustine and many others to reconcile God's omniscience with the indetermination of men's actions were entirely rejected by the eighteenth-century American theologian Jonathan Edwards, who maintained that divine prescience imposes the same necessity upon things as does predestination, a doctrine that had been taught by St. Augustine. Foreknowledge, Edwards agreed, does not cause those things that are foreknown, but it nonetheless renders them certain and therefore inevitable. Indeed, such foreknowledge could not exist if determinism were not true, for there can be no certainty with respect to any contingent things. To say that things are foreknown with certainty by God and are nevertheless contingent and thus uncertain struck Edwards as an evident absurdity.

Similar doubts are expressed, among contemporary philosophers, by Charles Hartshorne. Hartshorne has defended indeterminism and free will, and defending also the belief in God, he has proposed an exceedingly interesting revision of the idea of omniscience. An omniscient being, according to him, is one who knows everything that it is possible to know. There can, however, be no antecedent truth with respect to particular future free actions of men other than that they might and might not occur. God, accordingly, cannot know whether they will be performed until the time for the performance arrives. He is nevertheless omniscient, since only those things that are inherently unknowable are unknown to him. It is significant and rarely noted that this is precisely the position taken by St. Thomas Aquinas with respect to God's omnipotence. God, according to St. Thomas, is omnipotent not in the sense that he can do anything whatsoever but, rather, that he can do anything that it is possible to do.

DIVINE POWER AND PREDESTINATION. It was earlier noted that the three chief sources of theological determinism are God's presumably unlimited goodness, knowledge, and power. It is undoubtedly the third of these alleged attributes that has been the richest source of such theories. Even St. Augustine, although he defended human freedom on other grounds, felt obliged to relinquish it in the light of his conception of God's power. Thus arose the doctrine of predestination and all the baneful consequences it has wrought in the history of Christendom.

A man's power, St. Augustine thought, is nothing in comparison to that of his maker. Indeed, a man is helpless to do anything except sin unless he is assisted by the power and grace of God—"God worketh in us both to will and to do." Adam, our first ancestor, was, to be sure, free and, hence, free not to sin, but he sinned anyway and thereby cast the entire race of men into a morass of sin from which it is unable to lift itself by its own power. God as well as the blessed are unable to sin, but men are unable to avoid it. Accordingly, no man can be saved by the exercise of his own will, which can lead him only to damnation. He can be saved only by being chosen by God.

The same opinions were promulgated by Martin Luther and John Calvin, particularly in Luther's dispute with Desiderius Erasmus and Calvin's dispute with the Arminians on the issue of man's free will; they formed a considerable part of the theological basis of the Protestant Reformation. Both Luther and Calvin stressed the power, sovereignty, and righteousness of God, subordinating to these the belief in his love and mercy. God, according to Luther, does not merely foreknow what will happen. He foreknows, purposes, and does everything according to his eternal, changeless, and infallible will. To affirm any power or freedom on man's part, particularly any freedom to perform meritorious actions, seemed to both Luther and Calvin to compromise the power of God and even to set men in competition with him. Without God's grace everything we do is evil and therefore determined. It is not within any man's power to do any good thing. Even actions which would otherwise be right and proper, such as acts of charity, are, according to Luther, without merit if not accompanied by faith and prompted by grace. Luther thus compared the human will with the will of a beast of burden, which is ridden by either God or Satan. If ridden by God, it goes where God wills, and if by Satan, where Satan wills; in neither case, however, does it choose the rider. The riders, God and Satan, vie over who shall control it. Such views as these were once, of course, the source of persecutions and upheavals, but they are rarely enunciated with seriousness now, even by theologians, for the idea of divine power no longer has the reality in men's minds that it once had.

PHYSICAL DETERMINISM

Modern theories of determinism were inspired mainly by the development of physical science, particularly in the seventeenth and eighteenth centuries. Scientists then discovered that the motions of the heavenly bodies were not only regular but also "obeyed" certain laws that could be expressed with mathematical exactness. Gradually, the whole approach to the study of nature, which had been philosophical, speculative, and heavily influenced by Aristotle, gave way to observation, experiment, and the search for laws. The idea slowly took hold that all things in nature, men included, behave according to inviolable and unchanging laws of nature. In the philosophical tradition there was a great deal that made this idea plausible, reasonable, and almost inevitable. Theories of determinism were about as old as philosophy. The rise of physical science only prompted philosophers to revise somewhat the content of deterministic theories to which they were already thoroughly accustomed. They more or less ceased thinking of human actions and other events as determined by moral considerations or by an eternal and immutable God and began thinking of them as determined by eternal and immutable laws of nature.

THE EPICUREANS. Of course, this idea was by no means new. The view that everything is composed of matter or, more precisely, of minute and impenetrable atoms or invisible material particles had been elaborated by Leucippus and Democritus before the Christian era and had been perpetuated in the teachings of the Epicureans for centuries. Such a conception of nature gave rise to the idea that if everything that happens is resolvable into the motions and combinations of atoms, then men's behavior, too, must be reducible to and understandable in terms of the motions of atoms. The early atomists assumed that this must be true even of men's thoughts and desires, since, according to them, even the "soul" is composed of atoms. The behavior of atoms, in turn, was thought to be a function of their speed, direction of motion, and sometimes their shapes. Atoms changed the direction of their motion simply by being struck by other atoms. Material bodies arose from the combination of atoms into groups or clusters and perished as a result of their dispersion. The atoms themselves, however, were individually indestructible and indivisible.

The Epicureans who took over this theory of nature were not long in discovering its implications with respect to human freedom. These philosophers were concerned mostly with discovering the means to the attainment of the highest good for man, which they took to be happiness and freedom from pain. It would be idle, however, to work out the means for the attainment of this if men had no freedom to choose those means. If the theory of atomism were true, then it would seem that what became of a man and whether he attained a good life were simply matters of how physical bodies and, ultimately, the atoms of which all bodies are composed behaved, and no man would have any hand in what became of him. The Epicureans accordingly modified the theory by claiming the atoms to have the power of occasional spontaneous motion, which they referred to as the capacity to swerve. Ordinarily, an atom would change its direction only by being driven from its path by impact with another atom, but occasionally, they maintained, an atom alters its path spontaneously, without any cause for this change at all. This enabled the Epicureans to maintain that there is an element of contingency and uncertainty in nature, that not everything is determined by physical laws, and that men can therefore intelligibly be thought of as free to some extent or, in modern terms, as having free will. The Epicureans' opponents never tired of waxing merry with the doctrine of the swerve, however. Indeed, that doctrine did enable the Epicureans to avoid determinism, but there appeared to be nothing else in its favor, and it seemed, moreover, to be plainly irrational.

HOBBES'S MATERIALISM. Perhaps the best example of physical determinism in modern philosophy is the system of Thomas Hobbes. His philosophy represents a thoroughgoing attempt to interpret human nature according to the basic presuppositions of the science of bodies—that is, physics—and although it is no longer novel, it is probably fair to say that the generations of thinkers since Hobbes who have shared his aim and purpose have not significantly modified or improved upon his fundamental ideas. Modern materialistic theories differ from Hobbes's basic system only in details and mode of expression and share equally with it such purely philosophical merits and defects as it may possess.

Hobbes denied the existence of any immaterial soul or spirit in men, maintaining, as do some contemporary materialists, such as J. J. C. Smart, that ideas, sensations, and all psychological processes are motions or modifications of matter in the brain. From this it at once follows that human behavior is the behavior of matter and is to be understood according to the same general principles that we apply to matter. The idea that men might be the original sources of their own voluntary motions or that acts of will might arise without causes was rejected as unintelligible; nothing, Hobbes said, "taketh a beginning from itself." Whatever happens, whether in the realm of

human behavior, human thought, or elsewhere is caused and hence causally determined by changes of material particles. Voluntary actions are therefore no less necessitated than anything else.

Hobbes nevertheless insisted that such complete physical determinism is consistent with human liberty, for he defined liberty as simply the absence of external restraint or impediment and, hence, as something that even inanimate things can possess. He said that, properly understood, liberty is simply the "absence of all the impediments to action that are not contained in the nature and intrinsical quality of the agent." Hobbes concluded that any unobstructed moving body can be considered free. The unobstructed water of a flowing stream, for example, descends freely, though it is not at liberty to ascend or to flow across the riverbed. It is part of the "nature and intrinsical quality" of water to flow downward, and it flows freely.

Hobbes interpreted human nature according to such analogies. All voluntary human action, he thought, is caused by the alternate operation of the general motives of desire and aversion, which he took to be similar to, and, indeed, varieties of, physical forces. The proximate or immediate cause of a voluntary motion is an act of the will, but an act of the will is never free in the sense of being uncaused. It is caused by some kind of desire or aversion. Deliberation was described by Hobbes as an alternate succession of contrary appetites, a kind of vacillation between competing impulses, in which the appetites are of such approximately equal force that neither immediately overcomes the other. Deliberation ceases when one of them comes to outweigh and thus to prevail over the other. An "act of will," accordingly, is simply the "last appetite"—that is, the desire or aversion upon which one finally acts. To speak of an agent's act of will as "free" would be equivalent to saying that the agent is able to perform it if he wills to perform it, and this Hobbes dismissed as an "absurd speech." To say a man is free to do a given action means only that he can do it if he wills—that is, that his will or "last appetite" is sufficient to produce that action—but it is obviously nonsense to speak of an act of will itself being free in any such sense. Any other sense of freedom, however, seemed to Hobbes inherently incoherent. It is, for example, a fairly common conception of liberty among the advocates of free will that a free agent is one who, when all things necessary to produce a given action are present, can nevertheless refrain from that action. This, according to Hobbes, is equivalent to saying that conditions might be sufficient to produce a given effect without that effect's occurring, which is a contradiction.

It is noteworthy that Hobbes, though he claimed all human behavior to be physically determined and necessitated, did not conclude that men are not responsible for their actions. In this his theory represents an important departure from some of his predecessors. The Epicureans took for granted that behavior that is physically determined is unfree, and they therefore denied, in the face of their own presuppositions, that all human behavior is physically determined. But Hobbes maintained that a voluntary act is simply one that is caused by an act of will. It is rendered no less voluntary by the fact that acts of will are caused. Generations of philosophers, while for the most part rejecting Hobbes's materialism, have nevertheless followed him in this and in his conception of liberty. Arthur Schopenhauer, for example, declared it nonsense to ask whether acts of will are free, giving the same reason that Hobbes had given; defined freedom as the absence of impediments and constraints; and, like Hobbes, found no incongruity in speaking of inanimate bodies, such as a flowing stream, as acting freely. In the twentieth century Moritz Schlick, A. J. Ayer, and many others made the point that freedom is not opposed to causation but to constraint. The significance of these ideas is enormous, for they appear to offer the means of once and for all reconciling the apparent opposition between determinism and freedom, thus dissolving the whole problem of free will. Many philosophers are still convinced that this insight is entirely correct and that there really is therefore no problem of free will.

PSYCHOLOGICAL DETERMINISM

Most philosophers since Socrates, and even those before him, have, unlike Hobbes, distinguished between men's minds and their bodies, taking for granted that men are not just collections of material particles. Descartes distinguished minds and bodies as two entirely distinct substances whose essential properties are utterly different. Most philosophers since have rejected much of Descartes's philosophy but have nevertheless preserved the distinction between minds and bodies. In contemporary philosophy minds and bodies are not often described as distinct substances, but an absolute distinction is nevertheless often drawn between "psychological" predicates and verbs, on the one hand, and "physical" ones, on the other, and this amounts to much the same thing. Because of this, most modern theories of determinism, as applied to human behavior, can suitably be called theories of psychological determinism. Most of these theories are in

complete agreement with Hobbes's concept of free and voluntary behavior as the unconstrained and unimpeded behavior that is caused by an act of will, a motive, or some other inner event. The only significant difference is that acts of will and other inner causes are conceived of as psychological or mental events within the mind of the agent rather than as modifications of matter in his brain.

CARTESIAN INDETERMINISM. Descartes stands out in modern philosophy as a defender of free will, which is conceived of as indeterminism with respect to the voluntary operations of the mind. In his *Meditations* he described such freedom as infinite, meaning that no limitation whatsoever is put upon the mind's power of choice. His theory was essentially that willing consists of assenting or dissenting to some conceived object of choice or to some proposition. By the understanding one is enabled to entertain certain propositions, but understanding by itself neither affirms nor denies, neither chooses nor rejects. This role is reserved for the will. Accordingly, human understanding can be of limited scope, as it is, without in any way limiting the freedom of the will. The understanding sometimes represents things in an obscure and confused manner, sometimes even falsely, as in the case of various illusions and deceptions, but it sometimes represents them clearly and distinctly. Intellectual error results from the precipitous use of the will—that is, from assenting to things that are not clearly and distinctly perceived by the understanding. Moral error results from a similar unrestrained use of free will—that is, from men's assenting to or choosing objects that are only speciously good, without a clear and distinct apprehension of their true worth. Thus, error is always avoidable. To know what is true, attain genuine knowledge, and choose rightly, one needs only to confine the assent of the will to what is clearly and distinctly perceived by the understanding as true or good. God cannot therefore be blamed for men's errors. He endowed men with understanding adequate for the perception of truth and with a will that is absolutely unlimited in its freedom to accept what is true and reject what is doubtful or false.

This way of conceiving of the human will has provided what is virtually a standard solution to the problem of moral evil—that is, to the problem of reconciling the occasional turpitude of men with the presumed goodness of their creator—but beyond that hardly any philosophers have agreed with it. Probably no other indeterminist, for example, has described the freedom of the human will as unlimited. The theory was also quickly subjected to criticism on epistemological grounds. With great perception Spinoza, for example, challenged the basic distinction between the understanding and the will. It is quite impossible, Spinoza said, to have a clear and distinct understanding of some truth without at the same time assenting to it. The perception of truth is one and the same thing with the knowledge of it, and one cannot therefore have a true idea without at the same time knowing that he has a true idea.

Much more important, however, were the implications of Descartes's idea of a "free" will, conceived of as a will that is not determined by anything else. It appeared to imply that men's choices are completely random and capricious, utterly mysterious and inexplicable. In fact, this has always been the overwhelming stumbling block for all theories of indeterminism, whether in the Epicurean notion of spontaneous swerves of atoms or Descartes's notion of uncaused assents, dissents, and choices. If such things are really free in the sense of being causally undetermined and if human behavior is to be explained in terms of such things, then human behavior itself would have to be random, capricious, and utterly inexplicable. Since, however, human behavior does not appear to be exactly what these theories suggest, there has always been a powerful incentive to reject indeterminism in favor of some conception of determinism that does not do violence to men's conceptions of liberty.

Innumerable philosophers have thought that this is accomplished in the manner suggested by Hobbes—that is, by conceiving of a voluntary action as one that is caused by such an inner event as volition, motive, desire, choice, or the like; conceiving of an involuntary action as one that is caused by some state or event external to the agent; and then defining a free action not as a causally undetermined one but as one that is not involuntary or constrained. This kind of determinism has been advocated by so many philosophers, including many contemporary writers, that it would be tedious to list them. The basic idea was suggested by Aristotle, although Aristotle did not discuss the problem of free will as such. It was lengthily defended by John Locke, who was, however, aware of some of the difficulties in it, which he never entirely resolved except by enormous equivocations. Probably the most famous classical defense of it was presented by David Hume, who is still thought by many to have solved the problem of free will.

LOCKE'S THEORY OF LIBERTY. Locke, like Descartes, distinguished between a man's mind and his body and described both as substances. Changes in a man's body, including voluntary motions, are, he thought, all caused, but the causes are within the mind in the case of volun-

tary motions. Unlike Descartes, however, Locke did not suppose that anything within the mind is causally undetermined, nor did he think it necessary to suppose this in order to preserve the belief in human freedom, which he thought misleading to label "freedom of the will."

Locke defined liberty or freedom as "a power in any agent to do or forbear any particular action, according to this determination or that of the mind, whereby either of them is preferred to the other." One acts freely, then, provided he is acting according to the preference of his own mind, and this is perfectly consistent with his action's being causally determined. It might, for instance, be determined by that very preference. Locke also defined freedom as "being able to act or not to act, according as we shall choose or will," and this again, far from implying that free actions are uncaused, implies that they are caused by the agent's choice or will. In the light of this, Locke, like Hobbes, dismissed the question whether men's wills are free as "improper" or meaningless, like asking whether a man's sleep is swift or whether virtue is square. Liberty, he said, is something that can be possessed only by agents, not by their wills.

That an action can be perfectly voluntary and nevertheless unavoidable was, Locke thought, borne out by clear examples. Suppose, for instance, that a man went to a certain room because there was someone he had a strong desire to see and suppose that while he was there conversing with him, someone secretly bolted the door behind him so that he could not leave. Now, Locke pointed out, his action of remaining in the room, entirely in accordance with his own preference and desire, would not cease to be voluntary just because he could not, unbeknown to him, leave if he wanted to.

One acts voluntarily and freely, then, in doing what one wills, prefers, or chooses. Locke distinguished, however, between desires or preferences and volitions, noting that men can prefer certain things they can by no means will. Thus, a man might prefer to fly than to walk, but he cannot will it. Locke defined a volition as "an act of the mind knowingly exerting that dominion it takes itself to have over any part of the man, by employing it in, or withholding it from, any particular action." Elsewhere he defined a volition as "an act of the mind directing its thought to the production of any action, and thereby exerting its power to produce it." A volition, then, is a psychological act that sometimes figures causally in the production of voluntary motion. It is itself causally determined by the mind, and the mind, in the determination of its volitions, is, Locke thought, causally determined by the satisfaction of doing or continuing a given action or by feeling uneasy in doing or continuing it.

There is, then, throughout Locke's involved, tortuous, and sometimes equivocating discussion the general presupposition that determinism is true and that indeterminism is irrational and unintelligible. The philosophical problem, as he understood it, is simply that of showing that determinism is compatible with what all men believe concerning human liberty. He seemed to believe that once certain crucial concepts, such as "voluntary," "free," and the like, are rightly defined and understood, the problem of free will would evaporate.

HUME ON FREEDOM AND NECESSITY. The defining of the concepts was, in any case, precisely what David Hume set out to do in his celebrated discussion of liberty. According to Hume, all men have always been of the same opinion on this subject, believing both that men are free and that all their actions are causally determined. There is therefore no philosophical problem of free will, and the whole dispute, he thought, has heretofore been purely verbal in character, involving only confusions in the meanings of words.

It was a fundamental point of Hume's philosophy that causation is essentially constant succession, that there is no necessary connection between causes and their effects. Causes, therefore, do not compel the occurrence of their effects; they only precede them. The question of whether human actions are caused, then, is simply the question of whether there is anything with which they are constantly joined. Hume claimed that no one has ever been in any doubt about this. Throughout history certain actions have always been associated with certain motives with the same constancy and regularity that one finds between any causes and their effects. Human actions are caused, then, in the same way that everything else is caused.

Far from concluding from this, however, that no human actions are free, Hume concluded the opposite, for he considered it the very nature of a free action that it springs from the motive of the agent. He therefore defined freedom as being able to act according to the determinations of one's own will—that is, of one's motives—a definition that presupposes that one's free actions are caused. One's actions are not unfree if they are caused but if they are caused by something other than the determinations of one's own will.

Nor does this conception of liberty, according to Hume, vitiate a man's responsibility for what he does. On the contrary, responsibility depends upon the causation of actions by motives. All laws are based on rewards and punishments and thus rest on the assumption that men's motives can be relied upon to have a regular influence on their behavior. There would be no point in appealing to such motives as fear and hope if nothing could be predicted from their operation. Justice, moreover, requires such an operation of motives, for no man can be a fit object of punishment if his actions are in no way traceable to his motives. Indeed, if one could not rely upon the constant and predictable operation of motives, all intercourse with one's fellows would be hazardous or impossible. One could not even invite a guest to his table with any confidence of not being robbed by him, for the knowledge of his honesty and friendliness would in that case provide no assurance. Sometimes, to be sure, men are robbed or murdered when they had every reason to expect otherwise; however, men are also sometimes destroyed by earthquakes and the like when they had no reason to expect it. No one concludes from this that earthquakes are without any causes. Determinism, then, does not imply that all human behavior is predictable in the most straightforward sense of the term, for many unpredictable things are nevertheless causally determined. A man might not know why his watch has stopped and might not have been able to predict that it was going to stop, but this is only because the cause is hidden from him. He does not suppose that there was no cause at all. Similarly, a normally genial man might on occasion be peevish, but this is only due to some cause—some intestinal disorder, for instance—that is hidden from others and perhaps even from himself.

The important question for Hume, then, was not whether all human actions are causally determined, since all men have always been convinced that they are, or whether any human actions are free, since all men have always been of the same opinion on this, too. It is simply the question of how these two beliefs, so universally shared, can both be true, and Hume found the answer to this in analyzing what is meant by saying that one's action may be caused and also free.

DETERMINISM AND RESPONSIBILITY. What is essentially Hume's argument has been repeated by other philosophers and is still vigorously pressed by many of them. There have nevertheless always been doubters who have contended that this is a superficial conception of liberty, that the actions of a causally determined agent can be "free" only in a technical sense that does not at all correspond with the notion of freedom that men in fact have and that moral responsibility requires. A genuinely free action, according to this point of view, is not merely one that is in keeping with one's preferences, desires, and volitions, but one that is avoidable or, in C. D. Broad's terminology, "substitutable." To say that a given action was free means at least, according to these writers, that the agent could have done otherwise given the very conditions that obtained, not just that he could have done otherwise if something within him had been different. This thought was expressed by Immanuel Kant, who rendered it in the formula "ought implies can." What Kant had in mind was that whenever one rightly judges that a given agent is morally obligated to perform a certain action, he must logically presuppose that the agent can perform it—not just that he can if he wants, prefers, or wills to, but that he can in some absolute sense. This kind of freedom has been aptly called "categorical," as opposed to the "hypothetical" freedom defended by Hume and others, for it is a freedom both to do and to forbear doing a certain action under the same set of conditions.

The difficulty in deterministic theories that all these critics have felt can perhaps be illustrated with an example. Suppose that a given man is often motivated to steal and that in accordance with determinism he always does steal when, prompted by that motive, his efforts to do so meet with no impediment. According to the determinist theory, these actions are then free and voluntary, and he is responsible for them. Suppose further, however, still in keeping with determinism, that he has no control over the occurrence of this motive, that it arises, let us suppose, as a result of an abominable background and deprivation in his youth, that, in short, he is the product of precisely those influences that nourish and perpetuate that motivation. One's inclination may be to say that even given such a background, he did not have to become a thief, but that would not be in keeping with the thesis of determinism. According to that thesis, it was causally determined and, hence, inevitable and unavoidable that he should become whatever he is. It follows from these suppositions, then, that he cannot help being whatever he is and performing just the actions he does perform. We can indeed still say that if he were not the kind of man he is or if he were motivated otherwise than he is or if something had been different, he could then act otherwise than he does; however, any point to ascribing this merely hypothetical kind of freedom to him seems to vanish when we add, as the determinist must, that nothing could have been different, that he could not have been any other kind of man, that he could not have been motivated differently, and that, hence, he could not have acted otherwise than he did.

It was with this sort of thing in mind that Kant, contrary to what he acknowledged to be the requirements of reason, postulated what he called a "causality of freedom" and insisted that the theory of determinism cannot be applied to men. Their freedom, he thought, must be categorical or such that their actions are not entirely determined by factors over which they have no control. The same point was pressed by G. W. Fichte, Thomas Reid, Samuel Clarke, and William James, and among contemporary writers it has been eloquently urged by C. A. Campbell and many others. It was essentially the point that was skillfully made by Henry Mansel in his criticisms of J. S. Mill's determinist theories. Mill defended a theory that was in all basic respects identical with Hume's—that causation is constant conjunction; that men, when acting voluntarily, always act in accordance with their strongest desires or aversions; that justice, morality, and the administration of laws all require such causal determination of behavior, and so on. Mansel argued that when pressed to its ultimate conclusions, this theory did not differ in its consequences from what he called "Asiatic fatalism," or the view that all men are helpless to do anything except what they actually do. Mill denied this by arguing that although one's actions are determined by his will, his will by his desires, his desires by his motives, and his motives by his character, his character is itself amenable to his will. Mill did not, however, succeed in explaining how, according to his theory of determinism, a man's character, which he evidently thought of as the ultimate determinant of his conduct, could be "amenable" to or within the control of his "will," which is merely the expression of his character.

"HARD" AND "SOFT" DETERMINISM. William James is among the relatively few philosophers who, impressed by the kind of argument Mansel directed against determinism, have defended a theory of outright indeterminism or chance. He was, like the Epicureans, led to do so by what he thought were the requirements of morals. Determinism, he said, implies that the world we have is the only possible world and that nothing could have been other than it was; he declared this to be incompatible with the reasonableness of regret and other basic moral sentiments. In the course of his argument he drew a very useful distinction between what he called "hard" and "soft" determinism. By soft determinism he meant all those theories, like those of Hobbes, Hume, and Mill, which affirm that determinism is true and then, by means of what he considered sophistical and contorted definitions, somehow manage to preserve a semblance of certain moral notions like liberty, responsibility, and so on that, according to James, are plainly obliterated by any theory of determinism. Hard determinists, on the other hand, are those who affirm what their theory entails—namely, that no man can help being what he is and doing what he does and that moral distinctions are therefore irrational and ought never to be applied to men or anything else.

There have been relatively few defenders of hard determinism, most philosophers preferring instead to try reconciling determinism with morals. Certain materialist philosophers of the French Enlightenment, such as Baron d'Holbach, are exceptions, for they did maintain that men are only helpless products of an impersonal nature who govern neither themselves nor anything else but are simply carried along to whatever destinies the circumstances of their lives inflict upon them. Arthur Schopenhauer sometimes defended the same thought, emphasizing the irrational forces that govern human behavior. The American lawyer Clarence Darrow applied this hard determinism in courts of law with the most devastating effect, saving many men from the gallows not by pretending they were legally innocent but by the simple and eloquent plea that they could not help being what they were and doing what they had done. Among contemporary philosophers the claim that men are not morally responsible, as an implication of determinism, has been vigorously defended by John Hospers, and many others have pointed out the dubious character of soft determinism. The standard "solution" to the problem of free will, embodied in the writings of Hume, Mill, and many others, is as a result no longer considered to be as obvious as it once was, and a decreasing number of philosophers are now willing to speak blithely of free and voluntary behavior's being caused by motives, desires, volitions, and the like.

DETERMINISM AND MODERN PSYCHIATRY. Contemporary psychiatrists are for the most part highly impatient with theories of human freedom, particularly the theories with which philosophers are familiar. Whether all or most human behavior is causally determined is, after all, an empirical question of fact, and psychiatrists profess to know with considerable assurance not only that it is but to some extent what the causal factors are, particularly in cases of deviant behavior. Philosophers have largely been content to speak in general terms of motives, volitions, desires, and the like as the springs of action, but psychiatrists speak of specific unconscious fears, defenses, and hostilities. One finds in their writings, in fact, an extensive and elaborate terminology for the identification and description of hitherto undreamed of forces that are supposed to be the real determinants of

behavior, including certain typical human behavior that both the learned and unlearned have long been accustomed to thinking of as rational, deliberate, and free. Philosophical speculations on the problem of free will have, as a result, come to appear rather superficial to many of those who are familiar with psychiatry.

Hospers's opinion. Perhaps no contemporary philosopher has done more toward viewing these problems in the light of modern psychiatry than John Hospers. One can, according to this writer, agree with the philosophers who maintain that freedom is opposed not to causality but to restraint and compulsion and also think of human behavior as being typically caused by human desires and even volitions. He nevertheless advances impressive empirical evidence, drawn from typical cases of the kind long familiar to psychiatry, to show that our very desires, volitions, and even deliberations are the product of unconscious forces, compromises, and defenses that are not only not within our control but whose very existence is usually unsuspected by those—all of us—who are their victims; that they were for the most part implanted in us in our earliest years, to which our memory does not even extend; and that our after-the-fact explanations or reasons for our behavior are mostly illusions and wishful thinking. "It is not," Hospers claims, "as if man's will were standing high and serene above the flux of events that have moulded him; it is itself caught up in this flux, itself carried along on the current." Spinoza compared a man with a conscious stone which thinks it moves freely through the air only because it does not know the cause of its motion, and Baron d'Holbach compared him with a fly riding on a heavy wagon and applauding itself as the driver. Hospers similarly says that a man is "like the hands on the clock, thinking they move freely over the face of the clock," a comparison that is particularly apt in the light of the psychiatrists' claim that the forces that move us lie within us and are normally deeply hidden.

Philosophers almost entirely agree that if a man's behavior is the effect of a neurosis or inner compulsion over which he has no control and of which he usually has no knowledge, then in a significant sense he is not morally responsible, and in any case he certainly is not free. The most common illustration of this is kleptomania. What is philosophically significant about kleptomania is that its victim does act according to his own volition and desire but that the volition and desire are themselves the product of a neurosis. The profound significance of Hospers's view lies in his claim, which with considerable justification he believes is empirically supported by psychiatry, that virtually all significant behavior is of the same order as kleptomania and other familiar compulsions, having its sources in the unconscious. The issue is accordingly not a philosophical one but an empirical one. It is simply whether, in fact, as Hospers graphically expresses it, "the unconscious is the master of every fate and the captain of every soul." His defense of this claim is an array of fairly typical cases that are quite well understood by psychiatrists—the compulsive gambler who always plays until he loses, the man who inwardly loves filth and so washes his hands constantly, the mother who lets her child perish of illness on the train because she "must get to her destination," and so on. In case histories like these, Hospers believes, we can, if we are honest and sophisticated, see our own lives and conduct partially mirrored and perhaps begin to have some inkling of the unconscious, deeply hidden but powerful forces that almost entirely determine what we are and what we do. If Hospers is right and if psychiatrists do actually know what they confidently claim to know—and it would be very rash to suggest that they really do not—then the problem of determinism versus free will is not, as Hume thought, resolved in a way that accommodates both views. It is, rather, solved, and it is solved on the side of hard determinism with all the enormous and, to some minds, shocking implications that theory has for morals and law.

THE THEORY OF SELF-DETERMINATION. The great difficulty of indeterminism, as previously noted, is that it seems to imply that a "free" or causally undetermined action is capricious or random. If one's action is strictly uncaused, then it is difficult to see in what sense it can be within the control of an agent or in any way ascribable to him. The difficulty with determinism, on the other hand, is that it seems to render every action ultimately unavoidable. The implications of determinism do not therefore significantly differ from those of pure fatalism.

It is partly in order to meet both of these difficulties that some philosophers have defended a theory of self-determination or agency. The essential elements of all such theories are that men are the sources or causes of their own actions; that their being the source or cause distinguishes those bodily motions that are actions from those that are not, the latter being caused by something other than themselves; and that free actions are those that an agent performs or produces but that he is not caused by anything else to perform or produce. This theory thus distinguishes "action," or "agency," as a basic philosophical category, treating actions as different in kind from

other events and as not in any way describable in terms of the latter.

The theory of self-determination is most fully and clearly set forth by Thomas Reid in his *Essays on the Active Powers of Man,* though he does not call his theory by that name. The basic idea, however, was, according to Cicero's essay *On Fate,* advocated by Carneades. It has also been defended by G. W. Fichte and Samuel Clarke. Aristotle seems to have had some such conception in mind when he spoke of men and other animals as self-moved, and Kant also seemed to when he ascribed to men a special causality of freedom and distinguished this sharply from ordinary causality. Perhaps its best-known advocate among contemporary philosophers is C. A. Campbell, who ascribes a "creative activity" to "selves"—that is, to minds or persons—and argues that men are capable of originating their own actions in opposition to the inclinations of their characters.

Carneades on causality and freedom. Carneades, in trying to resolve the problems begotten by the Epicurean theory of uncaused swerves of atoms, on the one hand, and the fatalism of their opponents, on the other, suggested that the idea of being uncaused is ambiguous, like the idea of something's being empty. When one describes a vessel as empty, one does not ordinarily mean that it is absolutely empty—that it does not contain even air, for example. One means only that it does not contain oil or wine or whatever one might expect. Similarly, when one says that a man's action was uncaused, one does not mean that it was without any cause at all but only that it had no antecedent cause. This is compatible with its having been caused by the agent himself. Carneades noted, moreover, that the Epicureans themselves ascribe the power of motion to atoms, giving no account or cause of why they should be in motion other than that it is their nature to move. Why, then, may not men be thought of as having a similar original power of motion without supposing that some antecedent force must set them going? When men act freely, he thought, they are simply the sources of their own behavior, which is therefore caused, though not caused by anything external to themselves. One acts unfreely when one is caused to act as one does by some antecedent and external force. This way of viewing the matter, Carneades suggested, does not imply any fatalism, nor does it imply that a man's actions are random, like the swerves of the atoms. To say that a man is the cause of his own action does not imply that he was unable to cause any other action, nor does it imply that his action was uncaused.

Reid's theory. Reid developed many arguments against determinism, which he sarcastically called "the glorious system of necessity," but his own positive theory is remarkably similar to that of Carneades. Reid argued that determinism is inconsistent with a whole range of beliefs that are shared by all mankind and maintained that we have far more reason for adhering to these than for affirming any philosophical theory with which they are inconsistent. In particular, he maintained that determinism is incompatible with deliberation, with morality, and with the pursuit of ends. When, for example, a man deliberates about some possible course of action, he assumes that the proposed end, as well as the means to its attainment, is within his power to accept or reject—that is, that it is up to him whether the end shall be sought and if so, how. Without this belief he could not deliberate. The belief itself, however, is incompatible with determinism, for determinism entails that no act that is performed was avoidable and that in this sense it is never up to any man what he does. Again, all men believe that a basic distinction can be made between acts that are blameworthy, praiseworthy, and neither. Determinism, however, implies that every act that is performed is ultimately unavoidable and, hence, that no such basic distinction can be made. Finally, all men believe they can pursue, sometimes over a long period of time, certain ends that they have previously conceived. This implies, however, that their actions in pursuit of such ends are within their own power and control, which is inconsistent with determinism.

Reid therefore defined the liberty or freedom of a moral agent as "a power over the determinations of his own will," a definition that contrasts interestingly with Hume's definition of freedom as "a power of acting or not acting according to the determinations of the will." In rejecting determinism, Reid did not, however, affirm that human actions are uncaused. On the contrary, he maintained that nothing happens without a cause, that everything that changes is changed either by some other thing or by itself. Not all causes, then, are antecedent and external causes. Some things, such as men, are sometimes the causes of their own behavior. Indeed, Reid took this to be the very reason for calling a man an agent—namely, that he is a being who acts, not merely one that is acted upon. To speak of an agent being caused to act by something other than himself was for Reid a contradiction, so that acting and acting freely amount to the same thing, whereas the idea of a necessary agent amounts to a contradiction.

It is evident that Reid employed the concept of causation differently from Hume. A cause, he said, is not merely some change that always accompanies another. It is always something that has the power to produce a change, whether in itself or in something else, and no man can define it beyond this. In fact, he maintained that no man would even understand any philosophical definition of a cause if he did not first have the idea of causation from the awareness of himself as an agent. There is, then, no reason why men may not be the original causes of their own voluntary actions, which is precisely what all men believe themselves to be. This way of viewing the matter permits us to say that determinism, defined as the thesis that everything that happens is the result of some antecedent cause or causes, is false and, further, that nothing occurs without any cause whatsoever. Reid's philosophy thus overcomes the chief difficulties of both determinism and simple indeterminism. It accomplishes this, however, only by introducing what many philosophers have thought to be an enormous difficulty of its own—namely, understanding how anything can be the cause of its own changes. One is reminded of Hobbes's dictum, "Nothing taketh a beginning from itself." Alexander Bain pressed this difficulty in both Reid's and Samuel Clarke's philosophies, maintaining that it rendered their claims quite unintelligible, and Patrick Nowell-Smith has made the same point against C. A. Campbell's similar views. The idea of something's being self-moved in the sense understood by Carneades, Reid, Clarke, and Campbell is obviously entirely unlike any concept of physics. Accordingly, Nowell-Smith has suggested that it should be understood in the way such physical concepts as self-regulating, self-propelled, self-starting, and the like are understood, thus rendering it less esoteric. It was Reid's view, however, that this seeming difficulty is only a fact, that all men really do consider themselves to be the causes of their own voluntary actions in a sense in which no inanimate things are ever causes, and that we should be guided in our opinions not by what this or that system of philosophy requires but by what the common sense of mankind universally affirms.

THE "STRONGEST MOTIVE." It is fairly common to suppose that a man invariably acts—in fact, must act—in response to his "strongest motive" and that voluntary behavior is therefore always causally determined by such motives. Philosophical determinists frequently fall into this line of thought, sometimes substituting "strongest desire" for "strongest motive," though it is now less common than it once was. It is well illustrated in one of Alexander Bain's discussions of the free will controversy, in which he writes that "in the absence of prohibition, [an agent's] decision follows the strongest motive; being in fact the only test of strength, of motive on the whole." Again, Bain notes that "any supposition of our acting without adequate motive leads at once to a self-contradiction; for we always judge of strength of motive by the action that prevails" and, further, that the action that follows upon deliberation "testifies which motive has in the end proved the strongest."

It is to the credit of Thomas Reid, with whose writings Bain was familiar, that he exhibited both the source of the considerable persuasiveness of such reflections as these and at the same time their fallaciousness. The reason this kind of claim has seemed so compelling to so many philosophers is that it has functioned as an analytic statement or one that is rendered true by definition of the concept of a "strongest motive." As such, it sheds no light whatsoever on any fact of human nature and leaves entirely unanswered the question of whether voluntary actions are really caused.

What, Reid asked, is the test of whether the motive that is strongest is the one acted upon? It is simply the motive that prevails. The claim that a man acts upon his strongest motive therefore means, Reid noted, only that he acts upon that motive upon which he acts, which is hardly a significant philosophical claim. If, however, we apply any other criterion for distinguishing which motive is strongest, then there is nothing at all to suggest that we always act on our strongest motives. On the contrary, it is a fairly common experience to feel strongly motivated to do something from which we nevertheless refrain from purely rational considerations, for example, or perhaps from moral ones. The temptation here, of course, is to say that the fact that one refrains from a given action only shows that some contrary motive is "stronger," but this indicates that we are again using as our concept of the strongest motive the motive that prevails and saying nothing more than that a man acts upon the motive upon which he acts.

Reid, however, went further than this by denying that motives can be likened to forces and that varying "strengths" can be ascribed to them in the first place. A motive, he said, is not a cause but a rational consideration of a reason. As such, it is something purely abstract, which has "strength" or "weakness" only in the sense of expressing wisdom, prudence, or the opposites. A "conflict of motives" is nothing at all like the conflict of opposing forces, one of which overcomes the other by superior force. It is more to be likened to the conflicting pleas of contending attorneys. One of these can be

"stronger" or have more "force" or "weight" than the other only in the sense that it is more reasonable and persuasive. When, accordingly, we speak of rational or intelligible considerations as having "force," "weight," or "strength," we are not using these notions in the sense they have for physics but as metaphors borrowed from physical nature. It is, Reid thought, largely from mixing these literal and metaphorical meanings that some persons are led into theories of determinism and into supposing that human nature bears a greater resemblance to inanimate bodies than it actually does.

CONTEMPORARY PROBLEMS

The problems of determinism are still very lively in philosophy and have recently gained powerful momentum from detailed philosophical analyses of peripheral questions. Most current philosophical discussion bearing on the problem of free will is not aimed directly at whether men have free will, but at a whole host of questions that have been begotten by this long controversy. Ludwig Wittgenstein's reflections have made it evident, for example, that philosophers do not even know what it means to call something an action in the first place or just how some of men's bodily motions qualify as actions while others do not. It is an elementary distinction that is constantly made by common sense, but philosophers have thus far been unable to analyze it. Obviously, as long as this ignorance prevails, there is little point in discussing whether men's actions are ever free. Certain recent writers, such as Arthur Danto, have suggested that the concept of an action is basic and unanalyzable and that it corresponds to nothing that is found in physical science. Previous generations of philosophers often took for granted that an action is a bodily motion caused by some such inner episode as a volition, motive, desire, or choice, but these terms are now used with much greater care.

Gilbert Ryle, in his *The Concept of Mind*, declared volitions to be a fabrication of philosophy, corresponding to nothing that has ever existed, and since his devastating critique of this whole notion there has been great reluctance among scholars even to employ the word. The concepts of desire, motive, choice, and kindred notions have been similarly subjected to criticism, so that fewer philosophers are still willing to speak blithely of them as causes. A. I. Melden, for example, maintained that no particular motive can be described at all independently of the action of which it is allegedly the cause and that its connection with an action is therefore a logical one, not, as Hume and so many others supposed, a causal one. Moreover, Melden pointed out that if an action is conceived of as a bodily motion together with its motive in order to distinguish actions from bodily motions that are not actions, then it is plainly impossible to explain any action in terms of its motive, as philosophers were once so ready to do.

The interpretation of statements expressive of human ability as either disguised or incomplete conditional statements has likewise been considerably unsettled by the precise and detailed analyses of J. L. Austin. In his celebrated essay "Ifs and Cans" this writer maintained that statements involving the locution "I can" cannot possibly require, for their complete sense, the addition of some such hypothetical as "if I choose" but are, instead, to be understood in some absolute sense. Accordingly, they do not, as so many philosophers since Hume have supposed, express the idea of a causal condition at all. "I could have if I had chosen," is similarly claimed by Austin to express a past indicative rather than a conditional despite its grammatical form, for it normally expresses the idea of having had an opportunity or ability rather than the idea of a causal connection between one's choice and one's action. In statements involving the locution "I shall if I choose," the word *shall*, according to Austin, is normally expressive of an intention rather than a simple future tense and thus also differs essentially from other conditionals in the future tense. Such painstaking analyses as Austin's, although not pursued with the explicit aim of supporting or disconfirming any theories of determinism or free will, have nevertheless considerably weakened some of the strongest defenses of determinism since so many of them have more or less presupposed that statements expressive of human ability, which are so central to any discussion of free will, are simply disguised statements of causal conditions and thus are not only consistent with, but actually imply, a theory of determinism for the very understanding of them.

The highly refined and critical inquiries of contemporary philosophy have brought into further question the whole concept of the will. Is willing to do something an act, for instance, or not? If it is, then how does it shed any light on the concept of acting? If it is not, then how does an action differ from any other bodily change having an inner psychological cause? Clearly, no difference is marked merely by applying different names to such things. Furthermore, if there are such things as acts of will, do they or do they not require antecedent causes? If not, then why should any action require an antecedent cause? If so, then how are deliberate or willed actions to be distinguished from simple compulsions?

Closely associated with the notion of the will is that of intending. Doing something intentionally is now seldom thought of as merely undergoing some change as the result of an inner intention, intentions currently being thought of more in the manner in which Reid described motives—namely, as reasons and purposes having a rational content. Again, it is fairly common practice among contemporary philosophers to distinguish sharply, as Reid did, between the causes of an action and the reasons for it. If this is a real distinction, then it follows that whether some human acts are reasonable and intelligible is quite independent of whether they are caused, and there is no absurdity in describing an action as both free, in the sense of being avoidable and not the effect of antecedent conditions, and rational. This line of thought has raised anew the whole problem of understanding purposeful behavior. Men often do certain things in order to achieve certain results, and this appears to distinguish human behavior from the behavior of inanimate things in a fundamental way. When philosophers were more eager than they are now to interpret human behavior within the framework of determinism, many of them assumed that purposeful behavior was simply behavior that is caused by purposes, desires, or intentions, but this conception harbors the same difficulties as the volitional conception of action that Ryle, Melden, and others have so severely criticized. If one is acting in acting purposefully and if action can be distinguished from such other bodily behavior as digestion, perspiration, and the like only in terms of concepts like purpose, desire, or intention, then one can hardly explain purposeful activity as action that is caused by one's purpose, desire, or intention. The connection is conceptual rather than causal. Desires, purposes, and intentions are, moreover, desires for this or that, purposes or intentions to do this or that, and their objects or aims may never be realized. Thus, they are what we sometimes call "intentional" concepts, and there seems to be nothing that completely corresponds to them in the realm of physical science. No inanimate thing, for example, can without metaphor be spoken of as behaving as it does in response to its desire for something which perhaps never has and never will exist, and no engineer who spoke in that manner of even the most sophisticated machine would ever suppose that he had thus given a causal explanation of anything.

More and more philosophers are inviting attention to certain fundamental differences between the way men view the past and the future. The future, some have wanted to suggest, is a realm of possibilities in a sense in which the past is not. This idea is at least as old as Aristotle's philosophy, but the renewed interest in whether men's actions might be free in some sense not countenanced by determinism has quickened interest in it. It is, for example, sometimes contended that there is a fundamental difference between finding that something is true and making something become true, a contention that renders the concept of action more fundamental than it was once supposed to be and raises anew the question of what is meant by acting freely.

The question, then, of whether determinism is true or of whether men have free will is no longer regarded as a simple or even a philosophically sophisticated question by many writers. Concealed in it is a vast array of more fundamental questions, the answers to which are largely unknown.

See also Aristotle; Arminius and Arminianism; Augustine, St.; Austin, John Langshaw; Ayer, Alfred Jules; Bain, Alexander; Boethius, Anicius Manlius Severinus; Broad, Charlie Dunbar; Calvin, John; Carneades; Causation; Chance; Chrysippus; Clarke, Samuel; Descartes, René; Determinism and Freedom; Determinism and Indeterminism; Determinism in History; Determinism, Theological; Diodorus Cronus; Edwards, Jonathan; Epicureanism and the Epicurean School; Erasmus, Desiderius; Fichte, Johann Gottlieb; Hobbes, Thomas; Holbach, Paul-Henri Thiry, Baron d'; Hume, David; James, William; Kant, Immanuel; Laws of Thought; Leibniz, Gottfried Wilhelm; Locke, John; Luther, Martin; Mansel, Henry Longueville; Mill, John Stuart; Peter Aureol; Plato; Platonism and the Platonic Tradition; Posidonius; Rationalism; Reid, Thomas; Responsibility, Moral and Legal; Ryle, Gilbert; Schlick, Moritz; Schopenhauer, Arthur; Smart, John Jamieson Carswell; Socrates; Spinoza, Benedict (Baruch) de; Thomas Aquinas, St.; Time; Voluntarism; William of Ockham.

Bibliography

The literature on determinism and free will is so vast that only a sampling can be given here.

A good though not recent critical history of the controversy is outlined in Alexander Bain's *Mental and Moral Science* (London, 1872), Book IV, Ch. 11. More recent general studies include Sidney Hook, ed., *Determinism and Freedom in the Age of Modern Science* (New York: New York University Press, 1958), which is a collection of papers by contemporary philosophers, and Sidney Morgenbesser and James Walsh, eds., *Free Will* (Englewood Cliffs, NJ: Prentice-Hall, 1962), which brings together carefully selected discussions from classical and modern writers and is intended mainly for students. A widely read but superficial discussion of the problem is contained in D. F. Pears, ed.,

Freedom and the Will (New York: St. Martin's Press, 1963), which is in part the transcription of a series of discussions by contemporary philosophers most of whom are connected with Oxford University.

ETHICAL DETERMINISM

The ethical determinism associated with Plato and Socrates is a theme of Plato's *Protagoras* and *Gorgias,* and certain elements of this theory are treated rather unsatisfactorily in his *Hippias Minor.* Aristotle discusses the theory and related problems in the *Nichomachean Ethics,* Book VII, Ch. 2.

LOGICAL DETERMINISM

The most frequently cited reference in discussions of logical determinism is the ninth chapter of Aristotle's *De Interpretatione.* Among the many more recent discussions of the problems arising from those passages are A. N. Prior's "Three-Valued Logic and Future Contingents," in *Philosophical Quarterly* 3 (1953): 317–326; R. J. Butler's "Aristotle's Sea Fight and Three-Valued Logic," in *Philosophical Review* 64 (1955): 264–274; G. E. M. Anscombe's "Aristotle and the Sea Battle," in *Mind* 65 (1956): 1–15; Richard Taylor's "The Problem of Future Contingencies," in *Philosophical Review* 66 (1957): 1–28; R. Albritton's "Present Truth and Future Contingency," ibid.: 29–46; and C. Strang's "Aristotle and the Sea Battle," in *Mind* 69 (1960): 447–465.

One of the best sources for the ancients' views on both determinism and fatalism and the only source for some of them is Cicero's *De Fato,* translated by H. Rackham for the Loeb Classical Library (London, 1942). The problem of fatalism, conceived of essentially as it was by ancient philosophers, has been extensively discussed in recent literature—for example, in Gilbert Ryle's provocative essay "It Was to Be," which is Ch. 2 of his *Dilemmas* (Cambridge, U.K.: Cambridge University Press, 1954), and by A. J. Ayer, "Fatalism," the concluding chapter of his *The Concept of a Person* (New York: St. Martin's, 1963). Richard Taylor's "Fatalism," in *Philosophical Review* 71 (1962): 56–66, was followed by many critical discussions by various British and American authors in subsequent issues of the same journal and in *Analysis* 23 (1962) and 24 (1963), and in the *Journal of Philosophy* 61 (1964) and 62 (1965).

THEOLOGICAL DETERMINISM

Leibniz's claim that God could create no world except the best one possible and the implications he drew from this are found in his *Discourse on Metaphysics* and his *Theodicy.* St. Thomas Aquinas's opinions on the moral determination of God's will are set forth in the *Summa Theologiae,* Part I, Q. 19, especially Articles 9 and 10.

The question whether determinism and fatalism follow from the conception of God as an omniscient being has been discussed by countless authors. St. Augustine's views, for example, are reproduced in a selection titled "On Free Will," in Morgenbesser and Walsh, op. cit., and also in *The City of God,* Book XI, Ch. 21. Boethius's famous treatment of the problem is given in *The Consolation of Philosophy,* Book V. St. Thomas Aquinas discusses it in the *Summa Theologiae,* Part I, Q. 14, Article 13. His views and the views of various other Scholastics are given in Frederick Copleston's excellent *History of Philosophy,* Vols. II–III (London, 1950–1953). An extensive defense of theological determinism and predestination on various grounds is given by Jonathan Edwards in his famous *Freedom of the Will,* edited by P. Ramsey (New Haven, CT: Yale University Press, 1957). Charles Hartshorne's rather novel and perceptive reconciliation of free will with certain theological presuppositions is found in Ch. 3 of his *Man's Vision of God* (Chicago: Willett Clark, 1941). Although some of the foregoing sources raise the question of predestination, this doctrine, developed specifically as an implication of God's power, is more fully developed in St. Augustine's *Treatise on the Predestination of the Saints,* in the Nicene and Post-Nicene Fathers, first series, Vol. V, edited by Philip Schaff (New York, 1902); see also Augustine's *Enchiridion on Faith, Hope and Love,* edited by Henry Paolucci (South Bend, IN: Regnery/Gateway, 1961). Martin Luther's uncompromising denial of human free will is set forth in his polemic with Erasmus, under the title *Discourse on Free Will,* translated by Ernst F. Winter (New York: Ungar, 1961). John Calvin's defense of the same doctrine can be found at the close of the third book of his *Institutes of the Christian Religion.*

PHYSICAL DETERMINISM

The materialism of the Epicureans and the manner in which they tried to reconcile this with free will are beautifully exhibited in Lucretius's *On the Nature of Things*; an excellent source for earlier Epicurean arguments is Cicero's *De Fato.* Thomas Hobbes's materialism and arguments in favor of determinism are most fully expressed in *On Human Nature.* A more readily available source of Hobbes's important writings on this question is a paperback book of selections edited by Richard S. Peters, *Body, Man and Citizen* (New York: Collier, 1962). Arthur Schopenhauer, though he was not a materialist, defended a theory very similar to that of Hobbes in his *Essay on the Freedom of the Will,* translated by K. Kolenda (New York: Liberal Arts Press, 1960).

PSYCHOLOGICAL DETERMINISM

Most discussions of determinism and free will in modern philosophy have been within the framework of psychological determinism, which assumes that human behavior has its origins in psychological causes of various kinds. Descartes's defense of free will within this context is expressed in the fourth of his *Meditations* and also in *The Principles of Philosophy,* Part I, Sections 32–39. John Locke's extremely vacillating but influential discussion is found in *Essay concerning Human Understanding,* Book II, Ch. 21, where he discussed at length the idea of power. The classic attempt to reconcile determinism and liberty was achieved by David Hume in Section 8 of his *Enquiry concerning Human Understanding.* A defense along similar lines has been given, among numberless others, by C. J. Ducasse, in Ch. 11 of *Nature, Mind and Death* (La Salle, IL: Open Court, 1951). A now famous essay expressing essentially the same view was written by Dickinson Miller under the name R. E. Hobart and titled "Free Will as Involving Determinism and Inconceivable without It," in *Mind* 43 (1934): 1–27. J. S. Mill defended Hume's theory in his *Examination of Sir William Hamilton's Philosophy,* the relevant excerpts from which are reprinted in Morgenbesser and Walsh, op. cit.

Problems of moral responsibility are involved in almost every discussion of determinism and are central to most of them. Immanuel Kant's treatment of the problem and his defense of the idea of a causality of freedom are given in his *Critique of Pure Reason,* under the section "Transcendental Dialectic," particularly in his discussion of the third "antinomy," and, more fully, in his *Critique of Practical Reason.* C. D. Broad's influential and highly elaborate analysis, "Determinism, Indeterminism and Libertarianism," appears in his *Ethics and the History of Philosophy* (London: Routledge, 1952) and has been reprinted in Morgenbesser and Walsh, op. cit. Problems of determinism and responsibility are discussed by several authors in Hook, op. cit., particularly in the essays by Paul Edwards, "Hard and Soft Determinism," and John Hospers, "What Means This Freedom?" Both authors vigorously defend determinism and the claim that determinism and moral responsibility cannot be reconciled with each other.

William James's essay "The Dilemma of Determinism," in which the distinction between hard and soft determinism was first made, is included in almost all of the many collections of his popular essays. Most modern and contemporary writers who have defended deterministic theories have also defended some version of soft determinism, though they have seldom used the term itself. Examples, in addition to most of those already mentioned, are Patrick Nowell-Smith, in the last two chapters of his *Ethics* (Baltimore: Penguin, 1954), and A. J. Ayer, in Ch. 12 of his *Philosophical Essays* (London: Macmillan, 1954).

The most thoroughgoing defense of the theory of self-determinism was given by Thomas Reid, in his *Essays on the Active Powers of Man,* of which there have been many editions. A contemporary defense of what is essentially the same theory is given by C. A. Campbell, in Ch. 9 of *Selfhood and Godhood* (London, 1957). The same book contains an appendix in which the opinions of Patrick Nowell-Smith are subjected to a most thoroughgoing criticism. A similar concept is defended by Richard Taylor in "Determinism and the Theory of Agency," in Hook, op. cit. The same theory underlies Taylor's "I Can," in *Philosophical Review* 69 (1960): 78–89, reprinted in Morgenbesser and Walsh, op. cit. Another article that indirectly suggests such a view is Arthur Danto's "What We Can Do," in *Journal of Philosophy* 60 (1963): 435–445. Determinism is also attacked at great length in Konstantin Gutberlet, *Die Willensfreiheit und ihre Gegner* (Fulda, Germany, 1893), and in Ch. 9 of M. Maher, *Psychology* (London, 1940). These two works are written from a Catholic point of view.

A. I. Melden's *Free Action* (London, 1961) offers fairly elaborate and penetrating analyses of a wide range of concepts that have always been central to the free will controversy, such as those of wants, motives, actions, and so on; although the author does not try to prove directly that men have free will, he attacks the bases of certain widely held determinist theories. Gilbert Ryle's *The Concept of Mind* (London: Hutchinson, 1949) contains a chapter, "The Will," which amounts to a devastating critique of the idea that voluntary actions are caused by volitions. J. L. Austin's "Ifs and Cans," which is included among his *Philosophical Papers,* edited by J. O. Urmson and G. J. Warnock (London: Oxford University Press, 1962), is a painstaking inquiry into what is meant by saying of an agent that he could have done otherwise; although it is directed at claims made specifically by G. E. Moore and Patrick Nowell-Smith, it actually attacks the foundations of theories that have been widely held for over a century.

A detailed and annotated bibliography of works on determinism and free will can be found in Paul Edwards and Arthur Pap, eds., *A Modern Introduction to Philosophy*, 2nd ed. (New York: Free Press, 1965).

Richard Taylor (1967)

DETERMINISM, THEOLOGICAL

Theological determinism or predestination is the belief that events are determined or necessitated by God. One form of the traditional belief insists that owing to his omnipotence, God controls the occurrence of things. Another form asserts that his omniscience, making possible his foreknowledge of future events, affects the occurrence of such events. There are also nontraditional forms. Throughout the history of Islamic and Jewish philosophy, the debate over predestination was central.

When Islamic philosophy emerged in Baghdad in the ninth century CE, the religious and intellectual circles in the city had been witnessing a heated debate over the issue of predestination (*al-qadar*). There were three main Islamic views at the time: events in the universe, including human actions, are not predestined (Mu'tazila); all such events are predestined (Jabriyya); some aspects of such events are predestined, whereas others are humanly "acquired" (Ash'ariyya). In treating this issue, Muslim philosophers tried to reconcile Greek rationalism with Islam.

Abū Yūsuf al-Kindī (c. 801–873) and Abū'l-Walīd Ibn Rushd (Averroes, 1126–1198) denied predestination. They interpreted the Islamic revelations to assert that God does not, for example, control human actions. They both believed that at the moment God desires or wills something to happen, it happens. However, neither God's power nor his knowledge necessitates that he desire or will everything that happens to happen. If one reads Ibn Rushd carefully, though, one discovers that for him, God determines all events, because his omnipotence means that he fulfills all possibilities. Such fulfillment includes that of the natures of things and the laws that govern them. The conduct of any being is consequent upon its nature and its laws. In some of his writings, Ibn Rushd also stresses that God's knowledge of things is the cause of those things.

Abū al-Naṣr al-Fārābī (870–950) and Abū'Alī al-Husayn ibn Sīnā (Avicenna, 980–1037) adhered to neoplatonic tendencies, according to which everything necessarily follows from God's nature. Even God's nature itself is necessitated to act in certain ways. There is no room for God's will or choice, let alone the will or choice of any other being. This is despite the fact that al-Fārābī and Ibn Sīnā speak of God's omnipotence and omniscience, and even of human free will. However, they do not use these terms in the traditional sense. "Omnipotence," for example, is the ability to fulfill all possibilities, and omniscience is knowledge of universals.

Abū Ḥāmid al-Ghazālī (1058–1111) attacked such philosophical views in his famous work *The Incoherence of Philosophers* (1184). He considered such ideas non-Islamic and classified some of them, for example, God's inability to know particular events, as heretical. In the absence of such knowledge, reward and punishment, which are essential to Islam, become meaningless, especially in light of the Islamic concept of God's absolute justice.

Reward and punishment did not pose a problem for al-Kindī, because he believed that human beings have free will and that God knows particular events. Therefore, reward and punishment are not in conflict with his justice. The other three philosophers mentioned were not concerned about the issue either. For them, God does not reward and punish people. According to al-Fārābī and Ibn Sīnā, following death, bodies eventually disintegrate and souls become close to or distant from God, based on their degree of knowledge. Their closeness is their reward; their distance is their punishment. Reward and punishment are necessary consequences of the souls' conduct in life. To Ibn Rushd, there is no reward and punishment after death. The bodies disintegrate and the individual souls merge with the universal soul.

Moses Maimonides (1135–1204) asserts the Judaic belief that the human soul is intrinsically free, and agrees with the Greek and Muslim philosophers that matter is the source of natural evil. Thus, he absolves God from moral and natural evil, and justifies reward and punishment for the former, because God does not predetermine human action. However, God can intervene under certain circumstances. Maimonides was criticized by many Jewish thinkers for his rational approach to Judaism, which they feared denies some of its basic ideas, for example, that God wills whatever happens according to his knowledge of the natures of things.

See also al-Fārābī; al-Ghazālī, Muhammad; al-Kindī Abū-Yūsuf Ya'qūb ibn Isḥāq; Averroes; Avicenna; Determinism, A Historical Survey; Islamic Philosophy; Jewish Philosophy; Maimonides; Universals, A Historical Survey.

Bibliography

Fakhry, Majid. *A History of Islamic Philosophy*. 2nd ed. New York: Columbia University Press, 1983.

Hourani, George F. "Averroes on Good and Evil." In his *Reason and Tradition in Islamic Ethics*, 249–269. Cambridge, U.K.: Cambridge University Press, 1985

Inati, Shams. *The Problem of Evil: Ibn Sina's Theodicy*. Binghamton, NY: Global, 2000.

Shams Inati (2005)

DETERMINISM AND FREEDOM

Determinism is the family of theories that takes some class of events to be effects of certain causal sequences or chains, more particularly certain sequences of causal circumstances or causally sufficient conditions. One of these theories, universal determinism, associated with much science and philosophy, concerns the class of all events without exception. Another theory concerns physical events. Determinism in a third and important sense is human determinism. It is the theory that our choices and the many other antecedents of our actions, and the actions themselves, are effects of certain causal sequences. Lesser theories, usually associated with Freud and given no philosophical attention to speak of, concern themselves with particular sorts of conscious or otherwise mental causes of choices and actions, notably early sexual desires.

There are various relations between these four determinisms, depending on how they are additionally characterized. The most important relation, perhaps, is that universal determinism entails human determinism. That is not to say, however, that human determinism cannot be asserted, supported, or proved independently of universal determinism.

It is explicit or implicit in any of the above theories that the events in question are effects as more or less standardly conceived. An effect is an event such that an identical event follows every counterpart of the causal circumstance in question, or an event such that because the circumstance occurred, the event was in a stronger sense necessitated or had to happen (Sosa and Tooley 1993). A theory of our choices and actions, in contrast, that has to do with effects so-called—say, for example, effects conceived as events preceded by merely necessary conditions, or events merely made probable by antecedents—would not ordinarily be taken as a determinism. Indeed, weaker ideas of effects have often enough been introduced by philosophers precisely in order to avoid something else explicit or implicit in deter-

minisms—that they may be inconsistent with or pose a challenge to beliefs in human freedom.

HUMAN DETERMINISM

This entry's concern will be with human determinism. It involves three large problems or enterprises.

The first is the formulation of a conceptually adequate theory. Human determinism has traditionally been thought about without reference to the philosophy of mind. Still, an adequate treatment of it must rest on a theory of the mind that is conceptually adequate: clear, consistent, and something like complete. Also, it must surely be that the theory of the mind, perhaps in what it rejects, say a puzzling power of originating choices, should be consonant with the philosophy of mind generally (Priest 1991, Heil 1998, Lowe 2000, Crane 2001).

The second problem with human determinism is its truth, whether or not this is considered in relation to universal determinism. The third problem is what can be called the human consequences for our existence of a human determinism. Is there in fact the consequence that we are not free? The philosophy of determinism and freedom, except in the philosophy of science and philosophical ruminations by scientists, has mainly concerned itself with this problem of consequences.

If these three problems are not the only ones that have been raised about determinism and freedom (Adler 1958), they have become the main ones (Kane 2002; Campbell, O'Rourke, and Shier 2004; Clarke 1995).

The formulation of a conceptually adequate theory is simple in terms of a truly physicalist or materialist philosophy of mind—one that takes conscious or mental events to have only or nothing but physical properties, however additionally conceived. In this case, human determinism becomes part of physical determinism. However, relatively few philosophies of mind are truly physicalist. Anomalous Monism, to mention one, is fairly typical in denying "nothing-but materialism" (Davidson 1980).

All other determinist theories face considerable problems of formulation. They encounter the problem of actually characterizing their primary subject matter—conscious or mental events. There is also the problem of the psychoneural relation, traditionally called the mind-body problem. If mental events are taken not to be in space, how can they be lawlike correlates or effects or causes? Further difficulties include the avoidance of epiphenomenalism, the nineteenth-century doctrine that actually makes conscious antecedents no part of the causation or explanation of our actions.

It is my view, seemingly now shared with most philosophers of determinism and freedom in the early twenty-first century, that despite these difficulties a conceptually adequate theory of human determinism can be formulated. This used to be doubted (Austin 1961, P. F. Strawson 1968).

Is any theory of human determinism true? A conceptually adequate theory has the support of much ordinary rationality, philosophy, and much science. It is notable that the ordinary philosophy of mind has no indeterminism in it. This most flourishing part of philosophy, much of it concerned with exactly the explanation of behavior, contains nothing at all of origination, an uncaused or uncausing initiation of choices and actions. Contemporary neuroscience, as distinct from philosophizing by retired neuroscientists and the like, plainly proceeds on the assumption of a human determinism. A reading of any of the main textbooks of neuroscience confirms this (Kandel et al. 1991) It is worth remarking, about what was called ordinary rationality, that in the end, which may be a long way down the line, it sits in judgment on science itself. That is to say, first of all, that inconsistency is not an option.

DENIALS OF HUMAN DETERMINISM

Despite these considerations, many or most of us do not take human determinism to be true. We deny or more likely doubt it. There may be an explanation of this, as distinct from a ground or justification, in our culture, at any rate European and North American culture.

One familiar ground used for this denial or doubt has been interpretations of quantum theory—applications to the world of the formalism or mathematics in which this part of physics can be said actually to consist. According to these interpretations, there are things at a microlevel of reality that are not effects. These things, well below the level of neural events in the brain, the events of ordinary neuroscience, are taken as made probable by antecedents but not necessitated by them. They are not chance events in the sense of being events of which it is true in advance that they are as likely not to occur as to occur. However, each one is certainly a chance event in that its actual occurrence or existence, no matter the antecedent probability, is such that there exists no causal explanation to be found for it. This is a matter of what is in the world, not our capabilities of knowing it.

Perhaps there is no strong consensus within science as to the truth of such indeterminist interpretations of quantum theory, despite an inclination in that direction. Something of the same sort may be true within physics

itself. It is notable that outstanding treatments of the question in the philosophy of science may be agnostic (Earman 1986, 2004).

Opposition to indeterminism, some of it by philosophers, is strengthened by the fact, too often glossed over, that no satisfactory interpretation of quantum theory's application to reality has ever been achieved, although the theory is now getting on for a century old. It is possible to try to explain an ascendancy of an indeterminist understanding of quantum theory, say among other philosophers who would not tolerate contradiction, obscurity, and mystery elsewhere, by the fact of a cultural and institutional ascendancy of science in general and physics in particular. It is unclear to me why indeterminist interpretations have persisted within physics in the absence of any direct and univocal experimental evidence (Bohm and Hiley 1993, van Frassen 1991, Bub 1997).

One opposition to the idea that indeterminist interpretations of quantum theory prove or indicate the falsehood of determinism has to do with the supposedly undetermined things. Are they in fact events, which is to say things that happen; perhaps understood as ordinary things having properties at or for a time (Kim 1973)? Determinism has no concern with anything other than events. Numbers or propositions or other abstract objects, for example, are not part of its subject matter of effects. It does not say five is an effect. A reading of accounts of quantum theory quickly establishes that it is not clear that the things denied to be effects, about which there is real and wide disagreement, are indeed things asserted to be effects by a determinism. Some of these have been probabilities, features of a calculation, and waves in abstract mathematical space.

There is another uncertainty about any undetermined microevents, assuming such real events to exist. What is their relation to macroevents, and in particular to the neural events ordinarily taken to be in some intimate connection with such conscious or mental events as choices? Does the microdeterminism issue in macrodeterminism? Does it "translate up"? Or does the microdeterminism, instead, "cancel out" (Weatherford 1982)?

It is difficult indeed to resist the proposition that there is no indication at all of macroindeterminism in the physical world. Taken together with the previous uncertainty about amplification, this appears to issue in a kind of dilemma. Either microindeterminism if it exists does not translate up, in which case it does not matter to the problem with which we are concerned—or, because it would translate up if it existed, and there is no macrodeterminism, it follows that microindeterminism does not exist.

Answers or attitudes with respect to the question of the truth of a determinism do indeed affect responses to the third problem, that of the consequences of human determinism. Someone inclined to the truth of determinism may then be inclined, partly as a result of the further inclination that we have some freedom or others, to the response that we must have a freedom that goes with determinism. Still, the problem of the human consequences of determinism can be considered on its own, as usually it has been by philosophers.

Traditionally those consequences have been taken as having to do with freedom or free will, moral responsibility, and the justification of punishment. The central question is whether determinism is compatible or consistent with free choices and actions, with holding people responsible for and crediting them with responsibility for actions, and with imposing justified punishments on people and rewarding them. Compatibilists, who can be traced back at least to the seventeenth century (Hobbes 1839), answer yes. Incompatibilists, with Hobbes's great adversary in their history, answer no (Bramhall 1844).

The stock in trade of compatibilists has been the conception of freedom as voluntariness. That, in a rudimentary account, is the conception of a free and responsible action as in accordance with the desire of the person in question rather than against his or her desire. It is the conception, they say, that issues in the seemingly indubitable judgment that a man chained to the wall is not free, and that a woman whose life is under real and immediate threat by someone with a gun is not free.

The stock in trade of incompatibilists has been the idea of freedom as origination. This, in a rudimentary account, is the conception of a free action as one that the person was not caused to perform, but which was up to the person or in his or her control. This is the conception, incompatibilists say, that is familiar to all of us in that most common thing in our lives: holding people responsible for things. We hold people responsible only, as we say, when they are not literally caused to do what they do, but have a choice. We take a man to have been free exactly when he could have done otherwise than he did.

DEALING WITH OBJECTIONS TO HUMAN DETERMINISM

The rudimentary conception of freedom as voluntariness, as well expressed as the absence of ordinary constraint or compulsion, has been enriched in order to deal with objections. One objection was that people in the grip of an addiction are not acting against their own desire for heroin, but nonetheless are not free. A response

in defense of compatibilism has been that voluntariness consists in someone's acting according to a desire that they desire to have. There is the possibility, indeed, of thinking of a hierarchy of desires (Frankfurt 1971).

Other objections, or perhaps the reaction that both the rudimentary and the amended ideas of voluntariness do not do justice to the fullness of our reactions to people in their actions, may call up other developments. A free choice or action, it may be said, is not only in accordance with the desired desire of the agent rather than against it, but grows out of the personality, character, history, and indeed the very being of the person. Who can object, compatibilists ask, to the idea that such a choice or action, so autonomous, is what we take to be a free and responsible one?

The conception of freedom as origination has also been given much attention, again in response to objections, usually about obscurity. It has long been insisted that an originated decision, although not a standard effect, is not merely that. It is not merely a chance or random event. Hobbes's adversary Bramhall in the seventeenth century explained originated choices and actions as owed to the elective power of the rational will. It has become common to try to explain such choices by assigning them to what is called agent causation as against standard causation (Chisholm 1976, O'Connor 1995). Agent causation, whatever else is said of it, does not give rise to effects that had to happen or were necessitated. Other attempts to further clarify origination are in terms of teleology, in particular that the occurrence of choices and actions are somehow explained by their goals (O'Connor 1995), and in terms of a mixture of determined and undetermined events (Kane 1985, 2002), and in terms of reasons rather than causes (Ginet 1990).

It is clear that a determinism can be true and there can still be voluntary choices and actions. There is full compatibility. There is nothing in a theory of determinism that rules out choices and actions being according to someone's desire. Determinism is evidently never the theory that all choices and actions are against the wills of the agents. Compatibilism, indeed, is best seen as based on the proposition that free choices and actions have certain causes, causes somehow internal to rather than external and somehow opposed to the agent.

It is equally clear that if a decent theory of determinism is true, there can be no originated choices and actions. There is clear incompatibility. An originated choice or action, by rudimentary definition, is an event that is in a standard sense uncaused. The question of whether determinism is compatible with freedom has been the question of whether our freedom consists in voluntariness or origination, not the question of whether determinism is compatible with origination.

HUME, KANT, AND COMPATIBILISM

To come to the principal arguments of the two traditions of philosophers, Hume was typical of compatibilists in maintaining that anyone who actually thinks of what he or she means in speaking of a free and responsible action will immediately see that it is an unconstrained or uncoerced one—a voluntary one. What is needed is no more than some self-reflection, unconfused by religion or the like (Hume 1955).

Kant, although in fact not an incompatibilist, certainly not an ordinary incompatibilist, was as positive in declaring that to think of one's idea of a free and responsible action is not to think merely of one that was necessitated in a certain way. To go along with Hume and suppose otherwise, he said, is to engage in no more than a little quibbling with words (Kant 1949). With these philosophers, there was already a kind of stalemate about determinism and freedom.

Near the beginning of the twentieth century, it was taken as established, by some, that compatibilism was proved by a simple consideration. If a person acted freely on some occasion, it was true that the person could have acted otherwise. But, it was said, the latter means that the person would have acted differently if he or she had chosen differently, which is consistent with determinism (Moore 1912). By the mid-twentieth century, however, it became clear to some that "could have acted otherwise" is inconsistent with determinism (Austin 1961).

Subsequent twentieth- and indeed twenty-first-century compatibilists, undaunted by the failure of their predecessors to prove it, have somehow stuck to the conviction that our common idea of freedom, our common idea of what is necessary for moral responsibility and right punishment, is voluntariness (Ayer 1973, Magill 1997). One further contention is that the idea of origination, despite the seemingly clear rudimentary description of it, is actually incoherent, and so the field is left to the tolerably clear ideal of voluntariness (G. Strawson 1986).

Another compatibilist argument, widely discussed, begins from a thought experiment about moral responsibility (Frankfurt 1969). What it amounts to is the idea of a person subject to the control of a neuroscientist with some apparatus who will secure that the person will act in a certain way if it happens that the person is not on the way to doing so. Those are the causal facts. Suppose, however, that the person actually is on the way to and absolutely committed to doing A—wants it, wants to want it, and so on. It remains true, given the neuroscientist in the background, that he cannot do anything else. But it is clear, surely, that he is morally responsible for A. It follows, we are told, that freedom does not require being able to do otherwise than we do in a strong sense—it does not require origination and is not itself origination. Other recent compatibilist argumentation has been the elaboration of the idea of voluntariness by seeing its growth and extent in terms of evolution (Dennett 2003). Our human freedom is favorably contrasted with the lesser freedom of other animals.

Twentieth-century incompatibilists gave much attention to an argument well-developed from its beginning in Kant's philosophy (van Inwagen 1986). Here we have it that a free action is one that is up to us. Suppose now that an action is subject to determinism—the effect of a causal sequence, a series of lawlike connections leading back to some causal circumstance prior to the birth of the agent. Can such an action be up to us? The answer given is that it can only be up to us if the lawlike connections and the first causal circumstance are within our control—which definitely they are not. Hence free actions cannot be effects of certain causal sequences but must be originated.

Given the unbroken history of the philosophical debate on determinism and freedom until recently, must there be a presumption that either compatibilism or incompatibilism is true? Can that respectful attitude survive certain troublesome questions and alternatives?

If you reflect on the compatibilist case of the desiring and committed agent but with the neuroscientist around the corner, or indeed on any of many cases, say the simple one of the man chained to the wall, one thing you must be persuaded of is that there certainly is *an* idea of freedom—voluntariness. Quite as clearly, if you reflect on the incompatibilist case of the agent about whom it is supposed that a causal circumstance before his birth was not up to him, one thing you must allow is that there is *an* idea of freedom such that he does not have it—origination.

Does it follow from either speculation, however, that each of us has *only* the idea of freedom in question? That we all have and use only that single settled idea? That is exactly what is intended by each speculation, exactly what it is supposed to prove.

To ask the question, perhaps, is to become at least worried. Recall the first agent doing what he wants and responsible although in the toils of the neuroscientist. Is it just the philosophers who can readily think that there still *is* a sense in which he is not free—he cannot do otherwise in a sense of the words inconsistent with determinism? And is it just the philosophers who can readily think of the second agent, who indeed does not have a causal circumstance in the distant pas in his control, that there still *is* a clear sense in which his action may indeed be in his control? It may be wholly in accord with his desires and character and his whole existence, not pushed on him by anyone else or anything else or any conflict within him. Do we not have and use both conceptions?

What may lead someone to assent to one of the two speculations, and to either compatibilism or incompatibilism, is of course the proposition that freedom either is or is not compatible with determinism. That is a logical or necessary truth, is it not? Well, it is a truth only on a certain ordinary assumption or presupposition. The presupposition of course is that freedom is one thing, that we in general have only one idea of freedom. Evidently this presupposition needs thinking about, and it has been thought about in additional ways.

DEFENSES OF COMPATIBILISM

An original defense of compatibilism prepared the way by making more explicit the fact that determinism is not best seen as raising a question of consistency or inconsistency, but rather as affecting attitudes directed at certain facts or propositions having to do with moral responsibility—and also such personal and nonmoral attitudes as gratitude and resentment (P. F. Strawson 1968). Subsequently it was proposed that determinism affects more attitudes than these, including the important attitude to the future that is hope and the important attitude to inquiry and conclusions that is confidence.

It was argued that it is plain that we are all subject to two kinds of hope, one for an open future where all has not been fixed by the past, one for a future in which we get what we want, maybe a whole kind of life. To this attitudinal argument, a behavioral one was subsequently added. What we secure by enacting and benefiting from bills of rights and political liberty is evidently an absence of compulsion. What we punish for in part is an action of which we take it that it could have been otherwise despite the past, and we have the same thought in various personal relations (Honderich 1988, 1993).

Such considerations also bear nearly as sharply on weaker positions to which compatibilists and incompatibilists may be retreating. These positions are that voluntariness is our more important conception of freedom

(Dennett 1984, 2003), the freedom more worth having, or that origination has these recommendations (Kane 1985, 2002).

THE WIDER DEBATE

The ensuing wider debate—wider than compatibilism and incompatibilism—has included the idea that our being free requires origination but our being responsible requires only voluntariness (Fischer 1994). A different inquiry into what is called autonomy also accepts that we do not have to choose between compatibilism and incompatibilism (Mele 1995). It has been argued, against compatibilism's way of saving our responsibility from determinism, that we must give up our real idea of responsibility (Pereboom 2001). There has been the more radical contention that ascribing freedom and responsibility to people is a matter of attitudes that do not depend on objective facts or propositions at all (Double 1991, 1996).

Against another thought, that of giving up the set of attitudes inconsistent with determinism and taking satisfaction in the set of consistent ones, it has been argued that despite the truth of determinism we must maintain the illusion that we have the power of origination (Smilansky 2000). The thought of giving up the inconsistent attitudes and being satisfied by the others has also been followed by another radical idea. It is that roughly our attitudes to ourselves previously associated with origination can survive acceptance of determinism, and so must be owed to something else entirely different. This could be the nature of our consciousness, or the explanatory nature of certain causal lines of events within sequences of causal circumstances (Honderich 2002).

It is too early to say, but it may be that a consensus is emerging that determinism and freedom can no longer be the protracted and tired battle between compatibilism and incompatibilism. It is not possible to conjecture about the outcome of an alternative discussion.

See also Action; Causation: Metaphysical Issues; Determinism, A Historical Survey; Freud, Sigmund; Hobbes, Thomas; Hume, David; Kant, Immanuel; Philosophy of Mind; Quantum Mechanics; Responsibility, Moral and Legal; Strawson, Peter Frederick.

Bibliography

Adler, M. J. *The Idea of Freedom.* New York, 1958; Westport, CT: Greenwood, 1973.

Albert, D. *Quantum Mechanics and Experience.* Cambridge, MA: Harvard University Press, 1992.

Austin, J. L. "Ifs and Cans." In his *Philosophical Papers*, edited by J. O. Urmson and G. Warnock. Oxford: Clarendon, 1961.

Ayer, A. J. *The Central Questions of Philosophy*. London, 1954; New York: Morrow, 1975.

Bohm, D., and B. Hiley. *The Undivided Universe*. London: Routledge, 1993.

Bramhall, John. *The Works of John Bramhall*. Oxford: John Henry Parker, 1844. Originally published in Dublin, 1675.

Bub, J. *Interpreting the Quantum World*. Cambridge, U.K., and New York: Cambridge University Press, 1997.

Campbell, Joseph Keim, Michael O'Rourke, and David Shier. *Freedom and Determinism*. Cambridge, MA: MIT Press, 2004.

Chisholm, R. M. "The Agent as Cause." In *Action Theory*, edited by Myles Brand and D. Walton. Dordrecht, Netherlands: Reidel, 1976.

Clarke, R. "Freedom and Determinism." In *Philosophical Books*. Oxford: Basil Blackwell, 1995.

Crane, Tim. *Elements of Mind: An Introduction to the Philosophy of Mind*. Oxford: Oxford University Press, 2001.

Davidson, Donald. "Mental Events." In his *Essays on Actions and Events*. Oxford: Clarendon, 1980.

Dennett, Daniel. *Elbow Room: The Varieties of Free Will Worth Wanting*. Cambridge, MA: MIT Press, 1984.

Dennett, Daniel. *Freedom Evolves*. New York: Viking, 2003.

Double, R. *The Non-Reality of Free Will*. Oxford: Oxford University Press, 1991.

Double, R. *Metaphilosophy and Free Will*. Oxford: Oxford University Press, 1996.

Earman, John. *A Primer on Determinism*. Dordrecht, Netherlands: D. Reidel, 1986.

Earman, John. "Determinism: What We Have Learned and What We Still Don't Know." In *Freedom and Determinism*, edited by J. Campbell, M. O'Rourke, and D. Shier. Cambridge, MA: MIT Press, 2004.

Fischer, J. M. *The Metaphysics of Free Will*. Cambridge, MA: Blackwell, 1994.

Frankfurt, H. "Alternate Possibilities and Moral Responsibility." *Journal of Philosophy* 66 (1969): 829–839.

Frankfurt, H. "Freedom of the Will and the Concept of a Person." In *Free Will*, edited by G. Watson, 81–95. Oxford: Oxford University Press, 1982.

Ginet, C. *On Action*. Cambridge, U.K.: Cambridge University Press, 1990.

Heil, John. *Philosophy of Mind: A Contemporary Introduction*. Oxford and New York: Routledge, 1998.

Hobbes, Thomas. *The English Works of Thomas Hobbes*. Vol. 5, edited by W. Molesworth. London: London, J. Bohn, 1839. Originally published in 1650.

Honderich, T. *A Theory of Determinism: The Mind, Neuroscience, and Life-hopes*. Oxford: Clarendon, 1988.

Honderich, T. *How Free Are You?* Oxford: Oxford University Press, 1993; 2nd ed., 2002.

Hume, David. *An Enquiry concerning Human Understanding*. Edited by L. A. Selby-Bigge. Oxford, 1955.

Kandel, E. R. R., J. H. Schwartz, and T. J. Jessell. *Principles of Neural Science*. New York: Elsevier, 1991.

Kane, R. *Free Will and Values*. Albany: SUNY Press, 1985.

Kane, R. *The Oxford Handbook of Free Will*. Oxford and New York: Oxford University Press, 2002.

Kant, Immanuel. *Critique of Practical Reason*. Translated by L. W. Beck. Chicago: University of Chicago Press, 1949. Originally published in 1788.

Kim, J. "Causation, Nomic Subsumption, and the Concept of Event." *Journal of Philosophy* 70 (1973): 217–236.

Lowe, E. J. *An Introduction to the Philosophy of Mind*. Cambridge, U.K.: Cambridge University Press, 2000.

Magill, Kevin *Freedom and Experience*. London and New York: St. Martin's Press, 1997.

Mele, Alfred. *Autonomous Agents*. Oxford: Oxford University Press, 1995.

Moore, G. E. *Ethics*. Oxford: H. Holt, 1912.

O'Connor, T. *Agents, Causes and Events*. Oxford: Oxford University Press, 1995.

Pereboom, Derk. *Living without Free Will*. Cambridge, U.K.: Cambridge University Press, 2001.

Priest, Stephen. *Theories of the Mind*. London: Penguin, 1991.

Smilansky, Saul. *Free Will and Illusion*. Oxford: Clarendon, 2000.

Sosa, E., and M. Tooley, eds. *Causation*. Oxford: Oxford University Press, 1993.

Strawson, G. *Freedom and Belief*. Oxford: Clarendon, 1986.

Strawson, P. F. "Freedom and Resentment." In his *Studies in the Philosophy of Thought and Action*. Oxford: Oxford University Press, 1968.

van Frassen, Bas. *Quantum Mechanics: An Empiricist View*. Oxford: Clarendon, 1991.

van Inwagen, P. *An Essay on Free Will*. Oxford: Clarendon, 1986.

Weatherford, Roy. *The Implications of Determinism*. London: Routledge, 1982.

Ted Honderich (1996, 2005)

DETERMINISM AND INDETERMINISM

Determinism is a rich and varied concept. At an abstract level of analysis, Jordan Howard Sobel (1998) identifies at least ninety varieties of what determinism could be like. When it comes to thinking about what deterministic laws and theories in physical sciences might be like, the situation is much clearer. There is a criterion by which to judge whether a law—expressed as some form of equation—is deterministic. A theory would then be deterministic just in case all its laws taken as a whole were deterministic. In contrast, if a law fails this criterion, then it is indeterministic and any theory whose laws taken as a whole fail this criterion must also be indeterministic. Although it is widely believed that classical physics is deterministic and quantum mechanics is indeterministic, application of this criterion yields some surprises for these standard judgments.

FRAMEWORK FOR PHYSICAL THEORIES

Laws and theories in physics are formulated in terms of dynamical or evolution equations. These equations are taken to describe the change in time of the relevant variables characterizing the system in question. Additionally, a complete specification of the initial state referred to as the initial conditions for the system and/or a characterization of the boundaries for the system known as the boundary conditions must also be given. A state is taken to be a description of the values of the variables characterizing the system at some time t. As a simple example of a classical model, consider a cannon firing a ball. The initial conditions would be the initial position and velocity of the ball as it left the mouth of the cannon. The evolution equation plus these initial conditions would then describe the path of the ball.

Much of the analysis of physical systems takes place in what is called state space, an abstract mathematical space composed of the variables required to fully specify the state of a system. Each point in this space then represents a possible state of the system at a particular time t through the values these variables take on at t. For example, in many typical dynamical models—constructed to satisfy the laws of a given theory—the position and momentum serve as the coordinates, so the model can be studied in state space by following its trajectory from the initial state (q_o, p_o) to some final state (q_f, p_f). The evolution equations govern the path—the history of state transitions—of the system in state space.

However, note that there are important assumptions being made here. Namely, that a state of a system is characterized by the values of the crucial variables and that a physical state corresponds to a point in state space through these values. This cluster of assumptions can be called the faithful model assumption. This assumption allows one to develop mathematical models for the evolution of these points in state space and such models are taken to represent (perhaps through a complicated relation) the physical systems of interest. In other words, one assumes that one's mathematical models are faithful representations of physical systems and that the state space is a faithful representation of the space of physically genuine possibilities for the system in question. Hence, one has the connection between physical systems and their laws and models, provided the latter are faithful. It then remains to determine whether these laws and models are deterministic or not.

LAPLACEAN DETERMINISM

Clocks, cannon balls fired from cannons, and the solar system are taken to be paradigm examples of deterministic systems in classical physics. In the practice of physics one is able to give a general and precise description of deterministic systems. For definiteness the focus here is on classical particle mechanics, the inspiration for Pierre Simon Laplace's famous description:

> We ought to regard the present state of the universe as the effect of its antecedent state and as the cause of the state that is to follow. An intelligence knowing all the forces acting in nature at a given instant, as well as the momentary positions of all things in the universe, would be able to comprehend in one single formula the motions of the largest bodies as well as the lightest atoms in the world ... to it nothing would be uncertain, the future as well as the past would be present to its eyes. (Translation from Nagel 1961, pp. 281–282)

Given all the forces acting on the particles composing the universe along with their exact positions and momenta, then the future behavior of these particles is, in principle, completely determined.

Two historical remarks are in order here. First, Laplace's primary aim in this famous passage was to contrast the concepts of probability and certainty. Second, Gottfried Wilhelm Leibniz (1924, p. 129) articulated this same notion of inevitability in terms of particle dynamics long before Laplace. Nevertheless, it was the vision that Laplace articulated that has become a paradigm example for determinism in physical theories.

This vision may be articulated in the modern framework as follows. Suppose that the physical state of a system is characterized by the values of the positions and momenta of all the particles composing the system at some time t. Furthermore, suppose that a physical state corresponds to a point in state space (invoking the faithful model assumption). One can then develop deterministic mathematical models for the evolution of these points in state space. Some have thought that the key feature characterizing this determinism was that given a specification of the initial state of a system and the evolution equations governing its states, in principle it should be possible to predict the behavior of the system for any time (recall Laplace's contrast between certainty and probability). Although prima facie plausible, such a condition is neither necessary nor sufficient for a deterministic law because the relationship of predictability to determinism is far too weak and subtle.

Rather, the core feature of determinism is the following condition: "Unique evolution: A given state is always followed (and preceded) by the same history of state transitions." This condition expresses the Laplacean belief that systems described by classical particle mechanics will repeat their behaviors exactly if the same initial and boundary conditions are specified. For example, the equations of motion for a frictionless pendulum will produce the same solution for the motion as long as the same initial velocity and initial position are chosen. Roughly speaking, the idea is that every time one returns the mathematical model to the same initial state (or any state in the history of state transitions), it will undergo the same history of transitions from state to state and likewise for the target system. In other words, the evolution will be unique given a specification of initial and boundary conditions. Note that as formulated, unique evolution expresses state transitions in both directions (future and past). It can easily be recast to allow for unidirectional state transitions (future only or past only) if desired.

UNIQUE EVOLUTION

Unique evolution is the core of the Laplacean vision for determinism (it lies at the core of Leibniz's statement as well). Although a strong requirement, it is important if determinism is to be meaningfully applied to laws and theories. Imagine a typical physical system s as a film. Satisfying unique evolution means that if the film is started over and over at the same frame (returning the system to the same initial state), then s will repeat every detail of its total history over and over again and identical copies of the film would produce the same sequence of pictures. So if one always starts *Jurassic Park* at the beginning frame, it plays the same. The tyrannosaurus as antihero always saves the day. No new frames are added to the movie. Furthermore, if one were to start with a different frame, say a frame at the middle of the movie, there is still a unique sequence of frames.

By way of contrast, suppose that returning s to the same initial state produced a different sequence of state transitions on some of the runs. Consider a system s to be like a device that spontaneously generates a different sequence of pictures on some occasions when starting from the same initial picture. Imagine further that such a system has the property that simply by choosing to start with any picture normally appearing in the sequence, sometimes the chosen picture is not followed by the usual sequence of pictures. Or imagine that some pictures often

do not appear in the sequence, or that new ones are added from time to time. Such a system would fail to satisfy unique evolution and would not qualify as deterministic.

More formally, one can define unique evolution in the following way. Let S stand for the collection of all systems sharing the same set L of physical laws and suppose that P is the set of relevant physical properties for specifying the time evolution of a system described by L: A system $s \in S$ exhibits unique evolution if and only if every system $s' \in S$ isomorphic to s with respect to P undergoes the same evolution as s.

TWO CONSTRUALS OF UNIQUE EVOLUTION

Abstracting from the context of physical theories for the moment, unique evolution can be given two construals. The first construal is as a statement of causal determinism, that every event is causally determined by an event taking place at some antecedent time or times. This reading of unique evolution fits nicely with how a number of philosophers conceive of metaphysical, physical, and psychological determinism as theses about the determination of events in causal chains, where there is a flow from cause to effect that may be continuous or have gaps. The second construal of unique evolution is as a statement of difference determinism characterized by William James as "[t]he whole is in each and every part, and welds it with the rest into an absolute unity, an iron block, in which there can be no equivocation or shadow of turning" (1956, p. 150). This reading of unique evolution maintains that a difference at any time requires a difference at every time.

These two construals of unique evolution are different. For example, consider a fast-starting series of causally linked states (Sobel 1998) where every state in the series has an earlier determining cause, but the series itself has no antecedent deterministic cause (its beginning—the first state—is undetermined by prior events or may have a probabilistic cause) and no state in the series occurs before a specified time. The principle that every event has an earlier cause would fail for a fast-starting series as a whole though it would hold for the events within such a series. This would be an example where causal determinism failed, but where difference determinism would still hold.

However, the causal construal of unique evolution is unsatisfactory. Concepts like *event* or *causation* are vague and controversial. One might suggest explicating causal determinism in terms of the laws L and properties P, but concepts like *event* and *cause* are not used in most physical theories (at least not univocally). In contrast, unique evolution fits the idea of difference determinism: any difference between s and s' is reflected by different histories of state transitions. This latter construal of unique evolution only requires the normal machinery of the theoretical framework sketched earlier to cash out these differences and so avoids controversies associated with causal determinism.

DETERMINISM IN CLASSICAL MECHANICS

Most philosophers take classical mechanics to be the archetype of a deterministic theory. Prima facie Newton's laws satisfy unique evolution. After all, these are ordinary differential equations and one has uniqueness and existence proofs for them. Furthermore, there is at least some empirical evidence that macroscopic objects behave approximately as these laws describe. Still, there are some surprises and controversy regarding the judgment that classical mechanics is a deterministic theory.

For example, as Keith Hutchinson (1993) notes, if the force function varies as the square root of the velocity, then a specification of the initial position and velocity of a particle does not fix a unique evolution of the particle in state space (indeed, the particle can sit stationary for an arbitrary length of time and then spontaneously begin to move). Hence, such a force law is not deterministic. There are a number of such force functions consistent with Newton's laws, but that fail to satisfy unique evolution. Therefore, the judgment that classical mechanics is a deterministic theory is false.

NEWTONIAN GRAVITY. One might think that the set of force functions leading to violations of unique evolution represents an unrealistic set so that all force laws of classical mechanics really are deterministic. However, worries for determinism await one even in the case of point-particles interacting under Isaac Newton's force of gravity, the paradigm case of determinism that Laplace had in mind.

In 1897 the French mathematician Paul Painlevé conjectured that a system of point-particles interacting only under Newton's force of gravity could all accelerate to spatial infinity within a finite time interval. (The source of the energy needed for this acceleration is the infinite potential well associated with the inverse-square law of gravitation.) If particles could disappear to "spatial infinity," then unique evolution would break down because solutions to the equations of motion no longer would be guaranteed to exist. Painlevé's conjecture was

proven by Zhihong Xia (1992) for a system of five point-masses.

Though provocative, these results are not without controversy. For example, there are two interesting possibilities for interpreting the status of these particles that have flown off to spatial infinity. On the one hand, one could say the particles have left the universe and now have some indefinite properties. On the other hand, one could say that the particles no longer exist. Newton's mechanics is silent on this interpretive question. Furthermore, are events such as leaving the universe to be taken as predictions of Newton's gravitational theory of point-particles, or as indications that the theory is breaking down because particle position becomes undefined? Perhaps such behavior is an artifact of a spatially infinite universe. If the universe is finite, particle positions are always bounded and such violations of unique evolution are not possible.

DIAGNOSIS. Other failures of unique evolution in classical mechanics can be found in John Earman's (1986) survey. What is one to say, then, about the uniqueness and existence theorems for the equations of motion, the theorems that appear so suggestive of unique evolution? The root problem of these failures to satisfy unique evolution can be traced back to the fact that one's mathematical theorems only guarantee existence and uniqueness locally in time. This means that the equations of motion only have unique solutions for some interval of time. This interval might be short and, as time goes on, the interval of time for which such solutions exist might get shorter or even shrink to zero in such a way that after some period solutions cease to exist. So determinism might hold locally, but this does not guarantee determinism must hold globally.

DETERMINISM IN SPECIAL AND GENERAL RELATIVITY

Special relativity provides a much more hospitable environment for determinism. This is primarily due to two features of the theory: (1) no process or signal can travel faster than the speed of light, and (2) the space-time structure is static. The first feature rules out unbounded-velocity systems, while the second guarantees there are no singularities in space-time. Given these two features, global existence and uniqueness theorems can be proven for cases like source-free electromagnetic fields so that unique evolution is not violated when appropriate initial data are specified on a space-like hypersurface. Unfortunately, when electromagnetic sources or gravitationally interacting particles are added to the picture, the status of unique evolution becomes much less clear.

In contrast, general relativity presents problems for guaranteeing unique evolution. For example, there are space-times for which there are no appropriate specifications of initial data on space-like hypersurfaces yielding global existence and uniqueness theorems. In such space-times, unique evolution is easily violated. Furthermore, problems for unique evolution arise from the possibility of naked singularities (singularities not hidden behind an event horizon). One way a singularity might form is from gravitational collapse. The usual model for such a process involves the formation of an event horizon (i.e., a black hole). Although a black hole has a singularity inside the event horizon, outside the horizon at least determinism is okay, provided the space-time supports appropriate specifications of initial data compatible with unique evolution. In contrast, a naked singularity has no event horizon. The problem here is that anything at all could pop out of a naked singularity, violating unique evolution. To date, no general, convincing forms of hypotheses ruling out such singularities have been proven (so-called cosmic censorship hypotheses).

DETERMINISM IN QUANTUM MECHANICS

In contrast to classical mechanics philosophers often take quantum mechanics to be an indeterministic theory. Nevertheless, so-called pilot-wave theories pioneered by Louis de Broglie and David Bohm are explicitly deterministic while still agreeing with experiments. Roughly speaking, this family of theories treats a quantum system as consisting of both a wave and a particle. The wave evolves deterministically over time according to the Schrödinger equation and determines the motion of the particle. Hence, the particle's motion satisfies unique evolution. This is a perfectly coherent view of quantum mechanics and contrasts strongly with the more orthodox interpretation. The latter takes the wave to evolve deterministically according to Schrödinger's equation and treats particle-like phenomena indeterministically in a measurement process (such processes typically violate unique evolution because the particle system can be in the same state before measurement, but still yield many different outcomes after measurement). Pilot-wave theories show that quantum mechanics need not be indeterministic.

DETERMINISTIC CHAOS

Some philosophers have thought that the phenomenon of deterministic chaos—the extreme sensitivity of a vari-

ety of classical mechanics systems such that roughly even the smallest change in initial conditions can lead to vastly different evolutions in state space—might actually show that classical mechanics is not deterministic. However, there is no real challenge to unique evolution here as each history of state transitions in state space is still unique to each slightly different initial condition.

Of course, classical chaotic systems are typically considered as if there is no such thing as quantum mechanics. But suppose one considers a combined system such that quantum mechanics is the source of the small changes in initial conditions for one's classical chaotic system? Would such a system fail to satisfy unique evolution? The worry here is that, since there is no known lower limit to the sensitivity of classical chaotic systems, nothing can prevent the possibility of such systems amplifying a slight change in initial conditions due to a quantum event so that the evolution of the classical chaotic system is dramatically different than if the quantum event had not taken place. Indeed, some philosophers argue that unique evolution must fail in such circumstances.

However, such sensitivity arguments depend crucially on how quantum mechanics itself and measurements are interpreted as well as on where the cut is made distinguishing between what is observed and what is doing the observing (e.g., is the classical chaotic system serving as the measuring device for the quantum change in initial conditions?). Although considered abstractly, sensitivity arguments do correctly lead to the conclusion that quantum effects can be amplified by classical chaotic systems; they do not automatically render one's classical plus quantum system indeterministic. Furthermore, applying such arguments to concrete physical systems shows that the amplification process may be severely constrained. For example, investigating the role of quantum effects in the process of chaos in the friction of sliding surfaces indicates that quantum effects might be amplified by chaos to produce a difference in macroscopic behavior only if the fluctuations are large enough to break molecular bonds and are amplified quickly enough.

BROADER IMPLICATIONS

Finally, what of broader implications of determinism and indeterminism in physical theories? Debates about free will and determinism are one place where the considerations in this entry might be relevant. One of the most discussed topics in this regard is the consequence argument, which may be put informally as follows: If determinism is true, then our acts are consequences of laws and events in the remote past. But what went on before we were born is not up to us and neither are the laws up to us. Therefore, the consequences of these laws and events—including our present acts—are not up to us. Whether or not the relevant laws satisfy unique evolution is one factor in the evaluation of this argument.

What of broader philosophical thinking about psychological determinism or the thesis that the universe is deterministic? For the former, it looks difficult to make any connection at all. One simply does not have any theories in the behavioral sciences that are amenable to analysis under the criterion of unique evolution. Indeed, attempts to apply the criterion in psychology do not lead to clarification of the crucial issues (Bishop 2002).

With regards to the universe, it has been common practice since the seventeenth century for philosophers to look to their best scientific theories as guides to the truth of determinism. As one has seen, the current best theories in physics are remarkably unclear about the truth of determinism in the physical sciences, so the current guides do not appear to be so helpful. Even if the best theories were clear on the matter of determinism in their province, there is a further problem awaiting their application to metaphysical questions about the universe as a whole. Recall the crucial faithful model assumption. In many contexts this assumption is fairly unproblematic. However, if the system in question is nonlinear—that is to say, has the property that a small change in the state or conditions of the system is not guaranteed to result in a small change in the system's behavior—this assumption faces serious difficulties (indeed, a strongly idealized version of the assumption, the perfect model scenario, is needed but also runs into difficulties regarding drawing conclusions about the systems one is modeling). Since the universe is populated with such systems—indeed, it is likely to be nonlinear itself—one's purchase on applying the best laws and theories to such systems or the universe as a whole to answer the large metaphysical question about determinism is problematic.

See also Determinism, A Historical Survey; Determinism in History; Philosophy of Physics; Quantum Mechanics.

Bibliography

Relevant Historical Material on Determinism:

James, William. "The Dilemma of Determinism." In *The Will to Believe and Other Essays in Popular Philosophy, and Human Immortality*. New York: Dover Publications, 1956.

Laplace, Pierre Simon de. *A Philosophical Essay on Probabilities*. Translated by Frederick Wilson Truscott and Frederick Lincoln Emory. New York: Dover Publications, 1951.

Leibniz, Gottfried Wilhelm. "Von dem Verhängnisse." In *Hauptschriften zur Grundlegung der Philosophie*. Vol. 2, edited by Ernst Cassirer and Artur Buchenau. Leipzig, Germany: Meiner, 1924.

Nagel, Ernst. *The Structure of Science: Problems in the Logic of Scientific Explanation*. New York: Harcourt, Brace, and World, 1961.

Sobel, Jordan Howard. *Puzzles for the Will: Fatalism, Newcomb and Samarra, Determinism and Omniscience*. Toronto: University of Toronto Press, 1998.

Laplace's vision expressed in the modern framework of physical theories, as well as discussions of chaos, prediction, and determinism, may be found in:

Bishop, Robert C. "On Separating Predictability and Determinism." *Erkenntnis* 58 (2) (2003): 169–188.

Bishop, Robert C., and Frederick M. Kronz. "Is Chaos Indeterministic?" In *Language, Quantum, Music: Selected Contributed Papers of the Tenth International Congress of Logic, Methodology, and Philosophy of Science, Florence, August 1995*, edited by Maria Luisa Dalla Chiara, Roberto Giuntini, and Federico Laudisa. Boston: Kluwer Academic, 1999.

Hobbs, Jesse. "Chaos and Indeterminism." *Canadian Journal of Philosophy* 21 (1991): 141–164.

Stone, M. A. "Chaos, Prediction, and Laplacean Determinism." *American Philosophical Quarterly* 26 (1989): 123–131.

There are a number of able discussions of problems for determinism in physical theories. The following all discuss classical physics; see Earman (1986, 2004) for discussions of determinism in relativistic physics:

Earman, John. "Determinism: What We Have Learned and What We Still Don't Know." In *Freedom and Determinism*, edited by Joseph Keim Campbell, Michael O'Rourke, and David Shier, 21–46. Cambridge, MA: MIT Press, 2004.

Earman, John. *A Primer on Determinism*. Dordrecht, Netherlands: D. Reidel, 1986.

Hutchinson, Keith. "Is Classical Mechanics Really Time-Reversible and Deterministic?" *British Journal for the Philosophy of Science* 44 (1993): 307–323.

Xia, Zhihong "The Existence of Noncollision Singularities in Newtonian Systems." *Annals of Mathematics* 135 (3) (1992): 411–468.

Uniqueness and existence proofs for differential equations are discussed by:

Arnold, V. I. *Geometrical Methods in the Theory of Ordinary Differential Equations*. 2nd ed. Translated by Joseph Szücs; edited by Mark Levi. New York: Springer-Verlag, 1988.

For a discussion of deterministic versions of quantum mechanics, see:

Bohm, David. *Causality and Chance in Modern Physics*. London: Routledge and Paul, 1957.

Cushing, James T. *Quantum Mechanics: Historical Contingency and the Copenhagen Hegemony*. Chicago: University of Chicago Press, 1994.

Possible consequences of determinism for free will in terms of the consequence argument may be found in:

Kane, Robert, ed. *The Oxford Handbook of Free Will*. New York: Oxford University Press, 2001.

Van Inwagen, Peter. *An Essay on Free Will*. Oxford, U.K.: Clarendon Press, 1983.

For a discussion of difficulties in applying determinism as unique evolution to psychology, see:

Bishop, Robert C. "Deterministic and Indeterministic Descriptions." In *Between Chance and Choice: Interdisciplinary Perspectives on Determinism*, edited by Harald Atmanspacher and Robert C. Bishop. Thorverton, U.K.: Imprint Academic, 2002.

Elements of the faithful model assumption have received some scrutiny in recent physics literature. In particular, there is evidence that perfect models are not guaranteed to describe system behavior in nonlinear contexts:

Judd, Kevin, and Leonard A. Smith. "Indistinguishable States I: Perfect Model Scenario." *Physica D* 151 (2001): 125–141.

Judd, Kevin, and Leonard A. Smith. "Indistinguishable States II: Imperfect Model Scenarios." *Physica D* 196 (2004): 224–242.

Smith, Leonard A. "Disentangling Uncertainty and Error: On the Predictability of Nonlinear Systems." In *Nonlinear Dynamics and Statistics*, edited by Alistair I. Mees. Boston: Birkäuser, 2001.

Robert C. Bishop (2005)

DETERMINISM IN HISTORY

Philosophical reflection upon history has always been impressed by the limited extent to which individuals and groups seem to be able to mold events to their purposes. In the case of some events at least, there seems to be an inexorable necessity—an inevitability or unavoidability—about what happens. The "necessity" of historical events, however, has been asserted by historians and philosophers of history in at least three fundamentally different senses.

SENSES OF DETERMINISM

FATE AND PROVIDENCE. The first sense is the notion that events are "fated" to occur, a notion familiar to Greek as well as Oriental thought. The central concept is of an agency external to the historical process itself, sometimes, but not always, personified, determining events somewhat in the way a human agent may be said to determine, through his will, what happens in a process he monitors and manipulates. It is generally assumed, however, that the means by which fated events are brought about lie outside the mechanism of ordinary causal connection: they are "transcendent." This clears the way for a characteristic expression of fatalism—the assertion that what is fated will occur no matter what we do to try to prevent it. To many critics, such a claim has appeared unintelligible.

For historical events are surely, in some sense at least, constituted by what we do. A revolution, for example, could hardly occur if nobody revolted. The fatalist claim thus looks self-contradictory. What fatalism really denies, however, is the preventive efficacy of anyone's actions prior to the fated event, a refinement that leaves the claim coherent, if unbelievable. Nor is the doctrine necessarily involved in the incoherence of representing prior actions as both within our power to have performed otherwise and, at the same time, fated in their turn. For fatalism, unlike some other forms of historical determinism, has generally been asserted selectively. It is the doctrine that certain things will necessarily come to pass, not that everything happens necessarily.

Many theological philosophies of history are fatalistic in the indicated sense because of the role they assign to the will of God in their accounts. Unlike most of their pagan predecessors, however, these accounts generally make some attempt to rationalize and even to moralize interventions hitherto conceived as arbitrary, and usually also as menacing. In this way a fatalistic conception of history becomes "providential." Theological interpretations, of course, leave little for philosophers to argue about; for the workings of Divine Providence can be discerned only through some extrarational insight or source of revelation. And as G. W. F. Hegel complained about providential theories generally, the overarching purpose or plan is usually conceded, even by those who claim insight into it, to be partly "concealed from our view." Some theological interpretations have tried to meet this sort of objection by identifying the workings of providence, tentatively at least, with certain standing conditions and even with historical laws. A comparison between Reinhold Niebuhr's twentieth-century *Faith and History*, with its confidence in the "providential structure of existence," and Bishop Jacques Bénigne Bossuet's seventeenth-century *Discourse on Universal History*, which still envisages God ruling the course of empire by "decree," is instructive in this connection. Yet even Niebuhr confessed in the end that, to a finite human mind, both the plan and mode of operation of God in history remain mysterious.

HISTORICAL INEVITABILITY. Any attempt to make fate or providence immanent in the ordinary processes of history is a move toward a second major conception of the necessity of historical events, one often referred to in contemporary discussion as the doctrine of "historical inevitability." In this conception, the course of history has a necessary overall direction, whether it be attributed to an active but impersonal "force," a nisus toward some ultimate goal, or a "dynamic" law of development. The necessary direction of history has been variously conceived by various philosophers. Thus the Greeks tended to envisage it as cyclical and repetitive, while most philosophers of the Enlightenment found an equally simple but linear pattern of inevitable progress. According to Giambattista Vico, history traces a spiral path as civilization after civilization, each in its own unique way, follows the curve from heroic age to neobarbarism. According to Hegel, the spiral proceeds dialectically toward the actualization of a potential human freedom, each regress contributing to an ultimate spiritual synthesis. Just how deterministic such interpretations of history's direction were actually intended to be is, in fact, a disputable matter. Almost none assert that every historical event happens necessarily; the claim is usually limited to the main trend or the more significant events. And many speculative theorists do not seem to claim even that much. Oswald Spengler, for example, in his *Decline of the West* left the origin, by contrast with the development, of historical cultures unaccounted for; Hegel's lectures on the philosophy of history can be interpreted as having held that the stages of freedom succeed each other only with "rational," and not with "natural" necessity; and Arnold Toynbee's *Study of History* discovered historical "laws" so accommodating that they appear to be compatible with an almost indefinite number of exceptions.

Yet the discovery of inevitability is generally taken to be a major goal of speculative theories of history. And historians themselves often refer to "underlying tides and currents" (A. L. Rowse) or "great social forces" (E. P. Cheyney) in a way which seems to call for a more literal interpretation than the references they also occasionally let slip to the "fate" or "destiny" of historical individuals. Recent polemical works like K. R. Popper's *The Poverty of Historicism* (Boston: Beacon, 1957) and Isaiah Berlin's *Historical Inevitability* (London: Oxford Univ. Press, 1955) certainly assume that the doctrine of inevitability is still a live option for many people. Like fatalism, it is regarded by its critics as morally and politically dangerous. But it has also been subjected to a logical and conceptual critique, the major complaint of which is that insofar as historical inevitability is asserted on empirical grounds, the notion of "necessity" is employed in a way that is scientifically indefensible. According to Popper, inevitability theories confuse genuine laws, which assert conditional and hypothetical necessities, with statements of historical *trends,* which are not necessities, but facts. Laws license prediction whenever the conditions specified in their antecedent clauses are satisfied. The lack of corresponding empirical justification for the social

"prophecies" obtained by merely extrapolating trends is often obscured by the "force" metaphors characteristically used in describing them.

A speculative theorist who wished to claim metaphysical rather than scientific status for his conclusions might perhaps remain unmoved by such considerations. Yet almost all inevitability theorists at some point cite empirical evidence; and in the nineteenth century particularly, such theories were often thought to provide models for social science itself. The belief that the extrapolation of trends is a scientifically respectable procedure, Popper observed, may well be traceable to the fascination that untypical sciences like astronomy have had for philosophers of history. The temptation is to say that if eclipses can be predicted by projecting the observed behavior of the solar system, then revolutions and the like ought similarly to be predictable by projecting the tendencies of the social system. Such reasoning ignores the fact that the cyclical "direction" of the solar system is not just observed; it is explained. And the explanation is in terms of initial conditions obtaining, together with laws of motion that are conditional and hypothetical. The same could be said of the so-called directional law of evolution in biology, which is sometimes cited as a paradigm for linear theories of historical inevitability. No corresponding attempt is usually made to derive the alleged necessity of observed historical trends from more fundamental considerations. For to represent the large-scale pattern as "resultant" in such a way, especially if the relevant initial conditions included individual human actions, might undermine the thesis of unavoidability.

SCIENTIFIC DETERMINISM. The notion of explaining historical trends in terms of the operation of scientific laws brings us to a third generic conception of necessity in history, the "scientific" sense. To put it most simply, an event might be said to be determined in this sense if there is some other event or condition or group of them, sometimes called its cause, that is a sufficient condition for its occurrence, the sufficiency residing in the effect's following the cause in accordance with one or more laws of nature. The general assertion of historical determinism then becomes the assertion that for every historical event there is such a sufficient condition. Whether, in consequence, history manifests a unitary pattern or direction is a further and separate question.

Race and climate. Many historical determinists who would claim to be "scientific" in the above sense have gone a step further. Like the inevitability theorists, they have sought a simple clue to the historical process, in this case in causal factors of a limited range. Typical of such single-factor theories are those that fasten on certain biological or psychological conditions, such as the alleged racial characteristics of certain groups, or on features of the physical environment, such as topography, climate, soil, or natural resources. The writings of Joseph Arthur de Gobineau and of Houston Stewart Chamberlain, with their concept of Aryan superiority, are notorious examples of the first of these, although few serious attempts have been made to write detailed and scholarly histories (rather than propaganda) on their principles. The search for geographical determinants, on the other hand, has a reputable record going back at least to Baron de Montesquieu and Jean Bodin, and it received classic expression in the work of Henry Thomas Buckle in the nineteenth century and of Ellsworth Huntington in the twentieth. Both types of theory, however, oversimplify the diversity of history. It is one thing to point out that civilizations originated in river valleys or that the decline of Rome was accompanied by race-mixing. It is quite another—even if some features of events can properly be ascribed to such factors—to say that all significant historical change is determined by geographical or biological causes.

Social causes. Racial and environmental interpretations locate the explanatory factors outside the course of historical events themselves. Social interpretations offer single-factor accounts that seek causes in one kind of historical condition by contrast with others. According to Karl Marx, for example, the explanation of political, religious, legal, and other "ideological" features of a society is to be found in that society's mode of economic life and in the relations of production that its human elements consequently take up toward each other. In extreme forms of the theory at least, a one-way causal relation is asserted to hold at any time between economic and noneconomic factors, as well as between economic conditions at different times. Such an economic interpretation of history, with its more variable explanatory factor, has a far richer potential than racial or environmental ones for explaining the details of historical change. As with all single-factor theories, however, any attempt to defend its monistic causal claims generally either fails to carry conviction or runs afoul of a basic distinction between sufficient (determining) and merely necessary (conditioning) conditions. Thus, in a crude but revealing lapse, often cited, Friedrich Engels argued that because a man cannot engage in politics, science, religion, and art if he lacks the basic material conditions of life, the latter *determine* the former.

Multiple-factor theories. More considered statements of single-factor theories try to provide for a degree of interaction between the chosen factor and others. This leaves the difficult problem of explaining the sense, if any, in which the special factor is the fundamental one. It also leaves the problem—which bedeviled inevitability theories as well—of the relation between large-scale social causes and effects and the actions of participating individuals. "Great man" theories like Thomas Carlyle's are rightly out of fashion, but it is difficult to deny the historical importance of a Vladimir Lenin or a Napoleon Bonaparte. Georgii Valentinovich Plekhanov's classical Marxist discussion of this problem, in *The Role of the Individual in History,* adopts the uneasy compromise that individual causes can make a difference to a historical outcome, but only to its less significant features or to its timing. Such legislation as to the "spheres of influence" of various sorts of conditions, all conceded to be necessary, often seems highly arbitrary; and under pressure, single-factor theories tend to develop into "interpretations" only in the sense of directing attention to one factor in historical change that is deemed especially noteworthy, often for pragmatic reasons. The claim that historical events are determined then ceases to have any special connection with the claims made for the chosen factor. It reverts simply to the assertion that for every event there is a sufficient condition, no matter how disparate the causal elements that may sometimes be required to constitute it.

In the broad sense thus indicated, the contention that historical events are all determined may seem quite unproblematic. And when one considers the thoroughly causal language of historical accounts, the contention may seem also to be in accordance with historical practice. It is true that what historians actually call a cause is seldom itself a sufficient condition. But it is generally assumed by determinists that its claim to be a cause depends upon its completing a sufficient set of such conditions, some of which may not have been overtly specified. Yet the assumption of scientific determinism in history has been disputed on a number of grounds, the three set forth below being among the most frequently cited. These arguments have a common feature: all claim that this assumption contradicts others that the historian normally and properly makes. In consequence, the notion is represented as importing an incoherence into historical thinking as a whole.

OBJECTIONS TO DETERMINISM

CHANCE. It has been objected, first, that history is a realm in which events sometimes occur "by chance"—it being assumed that what happens by chance cannot happen of necessity. Certainly, historians often report what happened in such terms. And chance has been regarded by some of them almost as a principle of historical interpretation. Thus J. B. Bury, in his *Later Roman Empire,* represented the success of the barbarians in penetrating the Roman Empire as due to a succession of coincidences—the "historical surprise" of the onslaught of the Asiatic Huns, which drove the Goths west and south; the lucky blow that killed a Roman emperor when the Goths engaged a Roman army that just happened to be in their way; the untimely death of that emperor's talented successor before he had arranged for the assimilation of those tribesmen who had settled within the imperial border; the unhappy fact that the two sons who subsequently divided the empire were both incompetent, and so on. Bury's example does at least afford a strong argument against the notion that history is a *self*-determining system—one of the assumptions of the doctrine of historical inevitability. It illustrates the intrusion of nonhistorical factors into the historical process—an untimely death, for example—Bury's awareness of which led him to object to any search for what he called "general" causes. Bury's example makes clearer, too, the inappropriateness of a science like astronomy as a model for social and historical explanation. For the solar system, unlike human society, is virtually isolated from such external influences. This makes it possible for us to make astronomical predictions without taking into account anything but the description of the state of the system itself at any time and to predict accurately for long periods ahead. In history the situation is very different. The sufficient conditions of historical events are seldom to be found in other historical events.

But does the admission of chance, as Bury described it, count against the whole doctrine of historical determinism in the scientific sense? In support of their claim that it must, historical indeterminists sometimes cite parallels in physical inquiry. Modern subatomic physics, for example, whether correctly or not, has often been said to be indeterministic precisely because it regards certain aspects of the behavior of single electrons as matters of chance. Yet it may be questioned whether any of the contingencies, accidents, or unlucky "breaks" mentioned by Bury were matters of chance in the physicist's sense. For there is no reason to think of any of them as uncaused. What is peculiar about them is that they occur (to use a common phrase) at the intersection of two or more relatively independent causal chains. But there is nothing in such coincidences, determinists will maintain, that enables us to say that what occurs at the "intersections"

could not be deduced from prior statements of conditions and appropriate laws, provided we took all the relevant conditions into account.

In practice, of course, a historian may not be in a position to explain why a given coincidence occurred; at least one relevant chain—the biological one leading to the emperor's death, for example—may be beyond the scope of his kind of inquiry. What happened may consequently be represented by him as something unforeseen—perhaps even as the intrusion of the "irrational" into the course of events. Here the notion of chance is extended from the paradigm case where an event is said to have no cause at all to one where the cause is simply unknown because nonhistorical.

The notion is commonly extended further (as Bury's example illustrates) to events whose causes, although not beyond the range of historical inquiry, are beyond the immediate range of the historian's interests—the appearance of the Huns, for example. This makes it misleading to define "chance event" in history, as some have done, as an event that has historical effects but lacks historical causes. The causes of the invasion of the Huns simply lie outside the story the historian is telling. The judgment that a historical event happened by chance is thus a function of what the historian (and his readers) are concerned about. (This also covers the case where "by chance" seems chiefly to mean "unplanned.") It follows that, from one standpoint, an event may properly be judged to be a chance occurrence, while from another it clearly could not be: the activities of the Huns, for example, were scarcely a matter of chance from their own standpoint. Speculative philosophers of history, if they aim to take the additional standpoints of God or "History" into account, will obviously have further problems when deciding whether something was a chance occurrence. The issues thus raised are doubtless of considerable interest for a general account of the logic of historical narration. It is difficult to see, however, that they have any important bearing on the acceptability of historical determinism.

NOVELTY. A second consideration often advanced against the determinist assumption is that history is a realm of novelty and that its course must therefore remain not only unforeseen but unforeseeable, even if we take into account the broadest possible range of antecedent conditions. The fact that what the historian discovers is often surprising is thus held to have an objective basis in human creativity, from which periodically there emerge events and conditions with radically novel characteristics. Such "emergence," it is often claimed, rules out the possibility of scientific prediction before the event because prediction is necessarily based on laws and theories that relate types of characteristics already known. In this connection it is interesting to note a "proof" offered by Popper that some historical events at least are unpredictable in principle. If we accept the common assumption that some historical events are dependent in part on the growth of human knowledge, Popper pointed out, then it is logically impossible that we should be able to predict them before they occur. For ex hypothesi, one of their conditions must remain unknown to us.

Confronted by such an argument, determinists would want to make clear that, as they conceive it, determinism does not entail predictability, even though it has, unfortunately, sometimes been defined in terms of predictability. An event can be determined even though it is not known to be so. Popper himself did not regard the argument cited above as counting against historical determinism; indeed, his own statement of it strongly suggested that the unpredictability of the events in question actually follows from their being determined in a certain way, that is, by a set of conditions that are less than sufficient in the absence of as yet unattained human knowledge. All that is required by the doctrine of determinism, however, is that events *have* sufficient conditions, whether or not they can be known before the fact. It would thus be better, perhaps, to define the notion in terms of explicability rather than predictability. Determinists often point out that the emergent characteristics of natural things can be explained in the scientific sense, although they could not have been predicted before they first emerged. In his "Determinism in History," Ernest Nagel cited the emergence of the qualities of water out of a combination of hydrogen and oxygen. These are emergent and novel in the sense of not being possessed by the original elements and not being deducible from information about the behavior of these elements in isolation. Yet we have been able to frame laws governing the emergence of these originally novel attributes under specifiable conditions that allow us to deduce and now even to predict the attributes.

A likely reply is that whereas the emergence of the characteristics of water is a recurring, experimentally testable phenomenon, the emergence of novelty in the course of history is not. At least some historical events and conditions, it may be said, are unique and hence not subject to scientific explanation even after the fact. In considering this rejoinder, however, it is important not to misunderstand the claims of scientific determinism. For these do not include the deducibility in principle of the occurrence of historical events "in all their concrete actuality." Only events as historians represent them in their narratives are said to be so deducible. And their descriptions of events, it will be argued, are necessarily phrased in terms that apply, although not necessarily in the same combinations, to events at other times and places.

It may of course be doubted that we shall ever actually discover the determining conditions of such historical novelties as Alexander's use of the phalanx, Caesar Augustus's imperial policy, or the organization of the medieval church, under descriptions as highly detailed as historians customarily apply to them—a problem scarcely touched by the consideration, advanced by Nagel, that social science has sought, with some measure of success, to discover the conditions under which men act creatively. Yet determinists will regard these as merely "practical" difficulties, not bearing on the basic issue. That issue, they will maintain, is whether the novelties that can be recognized by historical inquiry are such as to rule out their subsumability under laws "in principle." Unless historians' knowledge can be said to go beyond any description of such novelties in terms of a unique conjunction of recurring characteristics, the argument from historical novelty will be deemed to have missed its mark.

In fact, this further, and highly debatable claim is one that some historical theorists would be quite prepared to make. They would point out, for example, that we can *listen* to Wolfgang Amadeus Mozart's music and *read* Isaac Newton's scientific writings—two examples of creativity cited by Nagel—and, by thus enjoying direct acquaintance with radical historical novelty, discover more than could be conveyed by any description in terms of recurring characteristics. Ordinary historical knowledge of novel military tactics, imperial policies, or institutional organizations, they would maintain, would similarly go beyond what could be expressed without reference, either explicitly or implicitly, to named individuals, groups, or periods. They would consequently represent historical narrative as employing concrete universals—like "Renaissance" or "Gothic"—as well as abstract ones. And since scientific laws can be framed only in terms of abstract universals, they would claim that warranted assertions of novelty expressed in terms of concrete universals do undermine the assumption of determinism.

FREEDOM. A third and even more common argument against accepting a determinist view of historical events turns on the claim that history is a realm not only of chance and novelty but of human freedom. The subject matter of history, it is sometimes said, is not mere "events" but human "actions," in a distinctive sense quite familiar to plain men who deliberate and decide what to do. If the historian is not to misrepresent such a subject matter, the argument goes, then he must take seriously the notion of choosing between alternatives. As Johan Huizinga expressed it, in his "Idea of History" (in *The Varieties of History*, edited by Fritz Stern), "the historian must put himself at a point in the past at which the known factors still seem to permit different outcomes. If he speaks of Salamis, then it must be as if the Persians might still win." In *Historical Inevitability*, Isaiah Berlin gave a further and even more familiar reason for adopting the standpoint of "agency." "If determinism were true, …" he wrote, "the notion of human responsibility, as ordinarily understood, would no longer apply." For an ascription of responsibility requires the assumption that the agent was "in control," that he could have acted otherwise than he did. Historical accounts, in other words, like the moralistic ones plain men ordinarily give of their own and others' actions, presuppose "freedom of the will." And this is held to be incompatible with the assumption of determinism.

Few philosophical problems have been discussed as exhaustively (or as inconclusively) as the problem of freedom of the will, and it is quite impossible in this context to do justice to the subtleties involved. There are, however, two chief ways of handling the present objection. Historical determinists can try to explain away the problem of freedom by arguing that, although moralistic accounts properly regard historical agents as free, the sense in which they must do so is quite compatible with the deterministic assumption. Libertarians, correspondingly, can try to give an account of historic causation that does not rule out an action's being both caused and undetermined. For historians, either of these ways out of the difficulty would presumably be more acceptable than the outright denial of the legitimacy of either moral appraisal or causal explanation in historical accounts. For, with no obvious sign of strain, historians generally offer both.

The determinist case often turns on the contention that the sense of freedom involved in attributing responsibility to a moral agent is not the "could have done otherwise" of absolute indeterminism; that sense implies only that the agent would have done otherwise if certain antecedents—his circumstances or his character, for example—had been a little different. Indeed, it is often argued that the test of whether the agent is really "in control," and hence responsible, is whether he acts differently on another occasion when the conditions have been changed—say, by his having been praised or blamed, rewarded or punished. It is therefore not the agent's freedom in the sense of his action's being uncaused that is at stake. The determinist, in arguing this way, conceives himself, furthermore, as accepting, not rejecting, the notion that the moral categories the historian uses are those of the plain man. What is denied is that the "ordinary" sense of "free" is the unconditional "freedom of the will" of the metaphysicians. As for Huizinga's claim that the historian must think of the agent's problem as if there were real possibilities open to him, this would be regarded as a purely methodological point. What is brought out thereby is the applicability to actions of a concept of understanding that requires us, quite properly, to view them in relation to what the agents thought about their situations, including any illusions they may have had about them.

Many libertarians might accept the latter contention. But most would surely repudiate the claim that responsibility requires freedom only in a sense compatible with determinism. To ascribe responsibility to a person whose actions necessarily follow from antecedent events, Berlin declared, is "stupid and cruel," and he meant rationally incoherent, not just foolish. In a sense alleged to be central to our notion of responsibility, such a person could *not* have done otherwise. Must a libertarian who takes such a stand, then, abandon the possibility of explaining actions causally? Some, at least, would say, No, provided we recognize that the term *cause,* when applied to human actions, bears a special sense. Thus, according to R. G. Collingwood, the causes (in a distinctively historical sense) of "the free and deliberate act of a conscious and responsible agent" are to be sought in the agent's "thought" about his situation, his reasons for deciding to act (*Essay on Metaphysics*). What a libertarian will deny is that any combination of such "rational" causes that excludes the agent's decision to act—since the latter falls into the historian's explanandum, not his explanans—is a sufficient condition of his action. Such causes become "effective," it might be said, only through an agent's deciding to act upon them. Yet when he does so, reference to them as his "reasons" will explain what he did in the sense of making it understandable. What such reference will not and need not do is explain his action in the sense of showing its performance to be deducible from sufficient antecedent conditions.

It is generally agreed that the conflict between historical determinists and indeterminists cannot be resolved by the offering of proofs or disproofs. Modern scientific determinists, in any case, seldom state their position dogmatically. According to Nagel, for example, all that can be claimed is that the principle of determinism has "regulative" status as a presupposition of the possibility of scientific inquiry—a principle that must therefore govern the scientific study of history as well. What is particularly interesting about theories of rational causation is the conceptual foundation they offer for denying that the principle of determinism is a necessary presupposition even of seeking explanations when the subject matter is human action: they show at least the conceivability of explanatory inquiry on libertarian principles. It must be conceded, however, that few contemporary philosophers regard indeterminism as an acceptable assumption to carry into historical or social investigation.

See also Berlin, Isaiah; Bodin, Jean; Bossuet, Jacques Bénigne; Buckle, Henry Thomas; Carlyle, Thomas; Chamberlain, Houston Stewart; Chance; Collingwood, Robin George; Determinism, A Historical Survey; Determinism, Theological; Determinism and Freedom; Determinism and Indeterminism; Engels, Friedrich; Gobineau, Comte Joseph Arthur de; Hegel, Georg Wilhelm Friedrich; Lenin, Vladimir Il'ich; Marx, Karl; Montesquieu, Baron de; Nagel, Ernest; Newton, Isaac; Niebuhr, Reinhold; Paradigm-Case Argument; Philosophy of History; Plekhanov, Georgii Valentinovich; Popper, Karl Raimund; Providence; Spengler, Oswald.

Bibliography

For examples of determinist or near-determinist views of history, see H. T. Buckle, *A History of Civilization in England* (London, 1899) or E. Huntington, *Mainsprings of Civilization* (New York, 1945). The works of various speculative and single-factor theorists mentioned above may also be consulted: Patrick Gardiner's *Theories of History* (Glencoe, IL, 1959) contains relevant extracts from the works of Vico, Hegel, Marx, Plekhanov, Buckle, Tolstoy, Spengler, Toynbee, Croce, and Collingwood. For a contemporary attack on deterministic views, of both the scientific and metaphysical kinds, see Isaiah Berlin, *Historical Inevitability* (London: Oxford University Press, 1954) and the reply offered by E. H. Carr in *What Is History?* (London, 1961). For a moderate defense of the deterministic assumption against such attacks, see Ernest Nagel, "Determinism in History," *Philosophy and Phenomenological Research* 20 (1960): 291–317. The viability of indeterministic historical and social scientific inquiry is argued for in Alan Donagan, "Social Science and Historical Antinomianism," *Revue Internationale de Philosophie* 11 (1957): 433–449. The role of the individual in history is discussed in Sidney Hook, *The Hero in History* (New York: John Day, 1943). Johan Huizinga's "Idea of History" is included in English translation in *The Varieties of History,* edited by Fritz Stern, pp. 290–303 (New York: Meridian, 1956). The claim that historians use "cause" in a special sense is developed by R. G. Collingwood in *An Essay on Metaphysics* (Oxford: Clarendon Press, 1940), which should be read in conjunction with his *The Idea of History* (Oxford: Clarendon Press, 1946).

W. H. Dray (1967)

DEUSSEN, PAUL
(1845–1919)

Paul Deussen, the German philologist and philosopher, was the son of a Protestant clergyman in the village of Oberdreis in the Westerwald. He received a thorough classical training in the old secondary school of Pforta, where he developed a close friendship with Friedrich Nietzsche. Both Deussen and Nietzsche enrolled in the theological faculty at the University of Bonn, but Nietzsche soon shifted to classical philology and followed his teacher Ritschl to Leipzig. Deussen remained in Bonn for four semesters, then also shifted to classical philology and earned his doctorate at Berlin in 1869 with a dissertation on Plato's *Sophist*. After a brief period of teaching in secondary schools, he became the tutor for a Russian family in Geneva in 1872. There he intensified his study of Sanskrit, began a study of the Indian philosophical classics, and became an enthusiastic follower and interpreter of Arthur Schopenhauer (after having long resisted Nietzsche's enthusiastic endorsements). In 1881 he qualified to lecture in Berlin under Eduard Zeller on the basis of his work *The System of the Vedanta,* and became an extraordinary professor in 1887. Appointed full professor in Kiel in 1889, he retained this post until his retirement.

Deussen's major work, on which he labored for more than twenty years, was the *Universal History of Philosophy,* consisting of two large volumes in six parts. The first volume was devoted to Indian thought and the second to the thought of the West from the Greeks to Schopenhauer, with a section on the philosophy of the Bible.

For Deussen the history of philosophy was a discipline indispensable not only for the understanding of life but for its religious interpretation as well. Its task was to strip off the "mythical vestments" or "hulls" of the various philosophical and religious systems in order to discover the single unified truth that all share.

This unified, permanent truth was made clear in the philosophy of Immanuel Kant as completed by Schopenhauer, but it also embraced insights from the Vedanta, Plato's doctrine of Ideas, and Christian theology. Schopenhauer, Deussen said, had "freed the essentials of

Kant from the weight of traditional misunderstanding" and offered "the completion of a unified doctrine which is grounded in experience, internally coherent in its metaphysics, and which appears, in its practical part, as a Christianity renewed throughout its whole depth on scientific foundations, and which will become, and for the predictable future remain, the foundation of all human scientific and religious thought" (*Geschichte der Philosophie,* Vol. 1, Part 1, p. 22). Rightly understood, Schopenhauer was the *philosophus Christianissimus* (the most Christian philosopher). The affirmation of the will to live is the egoism of our natural existence; its denial is "disinterested righteousness, the love of man, and the willingness to sacrifice for great causes—all great, heroic, overindividual striving and creating" (*Erinnerungen an Friedrich Nietzsche,* p. 105). But the divine, in this synthetic conception, cannot be understood theistically. The highest Being is beyond all personality, and all will eventually confess, "I believe in one living, but not one personal God."

Deussen was one of the early interpreters of Jakob Boehme (1897). He edited a critical edition of Schopenhauer in fourteen volumes (Munich, 1911), and he founded the Schopenhauer Society and edited its yearbook from 1912 until his death.

See also Boehme, Jakob; Continental Philosophy; History and Historiography of Philosophy; Indian Philosophy; Kant, Immanuel; Nietzsche, Friedrich; Plato; Schopenhauer, Arthur.

Bibliography

Deussen's chief work was *Allgemeine Geschichte der Philosophie, mit besonderer Berücksichtigung der Religionen,* 2 vols. (Leipzig: F. A. Brockhaus, 1894–1917); Vol. I, Part 2 was translated by A. S. Geden as *The Philosophy of the Upanishads* (Edinburgh: T. and T. Clark, 1908). *Die Elemente der Metaphysik* (Aachen: J. A. Mayer, 1877), was translated by C. M. Duff as *The Elements of Metaphysics* (London, 1894).

Deussen was the first Western philosopher to include Eastern thought in a general history of philosophy in any scientific way. Among his publications in this field are *Das System des Vedanta* (Leipzig: F. A. Brockhaus, 1883), translated by Charles Johnston as *The System of the Vedanta* (Chicago: Open Court, 1912); *Die Sūtra des Vedānta,* translated from the Sanskrit (Leipzig, 1887), translated by H. Woods and C. B. Rumble as *The Sutras of the Vedanta with the Commentary of Cankara* (New York, 1906); *Sechzig Upanishads des Veda,* which he translated from the Sanskrit (Leipzig: F. A. Brockhaus, 1897); *Vier philosophische Texte des Mahâbhâratam* (Leipzig: F. A. Brockhaus, 1906); *Bhagavadgītā. Der Gesang des Heiligen* (Leipzig, 1911); and

Die Geheimenlehre des Veda (Leipzig: F. A. Brockhaus, 1907–1909.

Three volumes of an autobiographical nature are *Mein Leben* (Leipzig, 1927); *Erinnerungen an Friedrich Nietzsche* (Leipzig: F. A. Brockhaus, 1901); and *Erinnerungen an Indien* (Leipzig: Lipsius and Tischer, 1904). Bound together with the *Erinnerungen an Indien* is a lecture, "On the Philosophy of the Vedanta in Its Relations to Occidental Metaphysics," delivered and first published in Bombay in 1893.

On Deussen, see "Erinnerungen an Paul Deussen," which is Vol. 20 of *Jahrbuch der Schopenhauergesellschaft* (1920).

L. E. Loemker (1967)

DEUSTUA, ALEJANDRO O.
(1849–1945)

Alejandro O. Deustua, the Peruvian educator, aesthetician, and philosopher, was born in Huancayo. He was a professor at the University of San Marcos, rector of the University, and director of the National Library in Lima. Deustua contributed greatly to the development of Peruvian education at all levels. His philosophical writing was done at an advanced age. It reflected the influence of K. C. F. Krause and Henri Bergson.

Running through the thought of Deustua are the polar ideas of liberty and order. Their interplay extends to a philosophy of civilization, but it is most clear in his major interest, aesthetics. It may be introduced through his definitions of beauty and art. Beauty is "a conciliation of liberty and nature, through the mediation of an ideal order created by the imagination." Since an internal image is not sufficient, external forms are created by art, which is the "graceful expression of the conciliation between nature and liberty, a conciliation imagined by the artist and translated by means of adequate or expressive forms."

The element of nature is furnished by human sensibility, including sensation and emotion. Liberty is found in absence of resistance, which in turn allows development from within to take place. It belongs to spirit and is paramount in that function of spirit called imagination, which is defined not as imaginal but as creative. Liberty is manifest only in an order, and it is fully realized only in an order entirely of its own making, an artistic order or harmony. This order is created by the imagination, using sensuous elements and acting in close relation with emotion. Harmony is a unity in variety: aesthetic pleasure is opposed to monotony and to excessive complexity. Types of harmony are symmetry and rhythm. Related to these are an outward order of parts and whole in space, characteristic of classical art, and an inward order of causes or purposes in time, characteristic of romantic art. When liberty is realized in order, the result is grace.

In addition to beauty there are several other types of value, to all of which imagination can contribute in one degree or another. These values may in turn contribute to the aesthetic experience, but they fall below beauty in freedom. Logical truth is characterized by demonstrative necessity. Economic value is subject to the imperative of desire, in contrast to the disinterestedness of aesthetic experience. Although moral value presupposes a free agent, it requires that the will submit to duty and law. Religious revelation and myth are aesthetic in nature; but they demand submission to the divine will. Only in the aesthetic sphere is liberty sovereign, unbound by orders or norms external to it. For this reason, aesthetic value is "the value of values."

See also Aesthetics, History of; Beauty; Bergson, Henri; Imagination; Krause, Karl Christian Friedrich; Latin American Philosophy; Liberty.

Bibliography

WORKS BY DEUSTUA

"Las ideas de orden y libertad en la historia del pensamiento humano" (The ideas of order and liberty in the history of human thought). *Revista universitaria* (Lima), 1917–1922.

Estética general (General aesthetics). Lima: E. Ravago, 1923.

Estética aplicada. Lo bello en el arte: escultura, pintura, música (Applied aesthetics: the beautiful in art: sculpture, painting, music). Lima: Americana, 1935.

WORKS ON DEUSTUA

Salazar Bondy, Augusto. *La filosofía en el Perú* and *Philosophy in Peru*. Washington, DC, 1954. This is a single book, in both Spanish and English, published by the Pan American Union. The Spanish text is on pp. 35–40 and the English on pp. 77–82.

Arthur Berndtson (1967)

DEWEY, JOHN
(1859–1952)

The American philosopher, educator, and social critic John Dewey was born in Burlington, Vermont. A shy youth, he enjoyed reading books and was a good but not a brilliant student. He entered the University of Vermont in 1875, and although his interest in philosophy and social thought was awakened during his last two years there, he was uncertain about his future career. He taught classics, science, and algebra at a high school in Oil City,

Pennsylvania, from 1879 to 1881 and then returned to Burlington, where he continued to teach. He also arranged for private tutorials in philosophy with his former teacher, H. A. P. Torrey. Encouraged by Torrey and W. T. Harris, the editor of the *Journal of Speculative Philosophy* who accepted Dewey's first two philosophical articles, Dewey applied for the graduate program at the newly organized Johns Hopkins University. He was twice refused fellowship aid, but he borrowed $500 from an aunt to begin his professional philosophical career.

The external events of Dewey's Vermont years were relatively unexciting, and there is very little to indicate that he would become America's most influential philosopher and educator as well as one of the most outspoken champions of social reform. Yet the New England way of life left a deep imprint on the man and his thought. His modesty, forthrightness, doggedness, deep faith in the workings of the democratic process, and respect for his fellow man are evidenced in almost everything that he did and wrote.

Under the imaginative guidance of Daniel Gilman, the first president of Johns Hopkins, the university had become one of the most exciting centers for intellectual and scholarly activity. Dewey studied with C. S. Peirce, who taught logic, and with G. S. Hall, one of the first experimental psychologists in America. The greatest initial influence on Dewey, however, was G. S. Morris, whose philosophical outlook had been shaped by G. W. F. Hegel and the idealism so much in vogue on the Continent and in England.

Dewey was an eager participant in the controversies stirred up by Hegelianism. He dated his earliest interest in philosophy to a course in physiology that he took during his junior year at the University of Vermont, where he read T. H. Huxley's text on physiology. Dewey discovered the concept of the organic and developed a sense of the interdependence and interrelated unity of all things. He tells us that subconsciously he desired a world and a life that would have the same properties as had the human organism that Huxley described. In Hegel and the idealists, Dewey discovered the most profound philosophical expression of this emotional and intellectual craving. From this organic perspective, which emphasized process and change, all distinctions are functional and relative to a developing unified whole. The organic perspective could be used to oppose the static and the fixed and to break down the hard and fast dichotomies and dualisms that had plagued philosophy.

Dewey's writings during his Hegelian period are infused with an evangelical spirit and are as enthusiastic as they are vague. Whatever issue Dewey considered, he was convinced that once viewed from the perspective of the organic, old problems would dissolve and new insights would emerge. Long after Dewey had drifted away from his early Hegelianism, his outlook was shaped by his intellectual bias for a philosophy based on change, process, and dynamic, organic interaction.

After completing his doctoral studies at Johns Hopkins with a dissertation on the psychology of Immanuel Kant, Dewey joined Morris at the University of Michigan in 1884. He remained there for the next ten years, with the exception of one year (1888) when he was a visiting professor at the University of Minnesota. At Michigan, Dewey worked with G. H. Mead, who later joined Dewey at Chicago. During his years at Michigan, Dewey became dissatisfied with pure speculation and sought ways to make philosophy directly relevant to the practical affairs of men. His political, economic, and social views became increasingly radical. He agreed to edit a new weekly with a socialist orientation, to be called *Thought News*, but it never reached publication. Dewey also became directly involved with public education in Michigan. His scientific interests, especially in the field of psychology, gradually overshadowed his interest in pure speculation. He published several books on theoretical and applied psychology, including *Psychology* (New York, 1887; 3rd rev. ed., 1891), *Applied Psychology* (Boston, 1889), and *The Psychology of Number and Its Applications to Methods of Teaching Arithmetic* (New York, 1895). The latter two books were written with J. A. McLellan.

Dewey's appointment in 1894 as chairman of the department of philosophy, psychology, and education at the University of Chicago provided an ideal opportunity for consolidating his diverse interests. In addition to his academic responsibilities, Dewey actively participated in the life of Hull House, founded by Jane Addams, where he had an opportunity to become directly acquainted with the social and economic problems brought about by urbanization, rapid technological advance, and the influx of immigrant populations. Dewey mixed with workers, union organizers, and political radicals of all sorts. At the university, Dewey assembled a group of sympathetic colleagues who worked closely together. Collectively they published the results of their research in a volume of the Decennial Publications of the University of Chicago titled *Studies in Logical Theory* (Chicago, 1903). William James, to whom the book was dedicated, rightly predicted that the ideas developed in the *Studies* would dominate the American philosophical scene for the next twenty-five years.

Shortly after Dewey arrived in Chicago, he helped found the famous laboratory school, commonly known as the Dewey School, which served as a laboratory for testing and developing his psychological and pedagogic hypotheses. Some of Dewey's earliest and most important books on education were based on lectures delivered at the school: *The School and Society* (Chicago, 1900) and *The Child and the Curriculum* (Chicago, 1902). When Dewey left Chicago for Columbia in 1904 because of increasing friction with the university administration concerning the laboratory school, he had already acquired a national reputation for his philosophical ideas and educational theories. The move to Columbia, where he remained until his retirement in 1930, provided a further opportunity for development, and Dewey soon gained international prominence. Through the Columbia Teachers College, which was a training center for teachers from many countries, Dewey's educational philosophy spread throughout the world.

At the time that Dewey joined the Columbia faculty, the *Journal of Philosophy* was founded by F. J. E. Woodbridge, and it became a forum for the discussion and defense of Dewey's ideas. There is scarcely a volume from the time of its founding until Dewey's death that does not contain an article either by Dewey or about his philosophy. As the journalistic center of the country, New York also provided Dewey with an opportunity to express himself on pressing political and social issues. He became a regular contributor to the *New Republic*. A selection of Dewey's popular essays is collected in *Characters and Events*, 2 vols. (New York, 1929).

Wherever Dewey lectured he had an enormous influence. From 1919 to 1921, he lectured at Tokyo, Beijing, and Nanjing, and his most popular book, *Reconstruction in Philosophy* (New York, 1920), is based on his lectures at the Imperial University of Japan. He also conducted educational surveys of Turkey, Mexico, and Russia. Although he retired from Columbia in 1930, he remained active and wrote prolifically until his death. In 1937, when Dewey was seventy-eight, he traveled to Mexico to head the commission investigating the charges made against Leon Trotsky, during the Moscow trials. After a careful investigation, the commission published its report, *Not Guilty* (New York, 1937). In 1941 Dewey championed the cause of academic freedom when Bertrand Russell—his arch philosophical adversary—had been denied permission to teach at the City College of New York, Dewey collaborated in editing a book of essays protesting the decision.

Although constantly concerned with social and political issues, Dewey continued to work on his more technical philosophical studies. M. H. Thomas's bibliography of his writings comprises more than 150 pages. Dewey's influence extended not only to his colleagues but to leaders in almost every field. The wide effects of his teaching did not depend upon the superficial aspects of its presentation, for Dewey was not a brilliant lecturer or essayist, although he could be extremely eloquent. His writings are frequently turgid, obscure, and lacking in stylistic brilliance. But more than any other American of his time, Dewey expressed the deepest hopes and aspirations of his fellow man. Whether dealing with a technical philosophical issue or with some concrete injustice, he displayed a rare combination of acuteness, good sense, imagination, and wit.

EXPERIENCE AND NATURE

The key concept in Dewey's philosophy is experience. Although there is a development from an idealistic to a naturalistic analysis of experience and different emphases in his many discussions of the concept, a nevertheless coherent view of experience does emerge. In his early philosophy Dewey was sympathetic to the theory of experience developed by the Hegelians and the nineteenth-century idealists. He thought of experience as a single, dynamic, unified whole in which everything is ultimately interrelated. There are no rigid dichotomies or breaks in experience and nature. All distinctions are functional and play a role in a complex organic system. Dewey also shared the idealists' antipathy to the atomist and subjectivist tendencies in the concept of experience elaborated by the British empiricists. But as Dewey drifted away from his early Hegelian orientation he indicated three major respects in which he rejected the idealistic concept of experience.

First, he charged that the idealists, in their preoccupation with knowledge and knowing, distorted the character of experience. Idealists, Dewey claimed, neglected the noncognitive and nonreflective experiences of doing, suffering, and enjoying that set the context for all knowing and inquiry. Philosophy, especially modern philosophy, had been so concerned with epistemological issues that it mistook all experience as a form of knowing. Such bias inevitably distorts the character of both man's experience and his knowing. Man is primarily a being who acts, suffers, and enjoys. Most of his life consists of experiences that are not primarily reflective. If we are to understand the nature of thought, reflection, inquiry, and their role in human life, we must appreciate their emer-

gence from, and conditioning by, the context of nonreflective experience. There is more to experience, Dewey believed, than is to be found in the writings of the idealists and, indeed, in the writings of most epistemologists.

The second major departure from his early idealism is to be found in Dewey's rejection of the idea of a single unified whole in which everything is ultimately interrelated. In this respect, he displayed an increasing sympathy with the pluralism of the British empiricists. He insisted that life consists of a series of overlapping and interpenetrating experiences, situations, or contexts, each of which has its internal qualitative integrity. The individual experience is the primary unit of life.

The third shift is reflected in Dewey's increasingly naturalistic bias. The Hegelians and the nineteenth-century idealists did have important insights into the organic nature of experience, but they had overgeneralized them into a false cosmic projection. Dewey discovered in the new developing human sciences, especially in what he called the anthropological-biological orientation, a more careful, detailed, scientific articulation of the organic character of experience.

Dewey thought of himself as part of a general movement that was developing a new empiricism based on a new concept of experience, one that combined the strong naturalistic bias of the Greek philosophers with a sensitive appreciation for experimental method as practiced by the sciences. He was sympathetic with what he took to be the Greek view of experience, which considers it as consisting of a fund of social knowledge and skills and as being the means by which man comes into direct contact with a qualitatively rich and variegated nature. But Dewey was just as forceful in pointing out that this view of experience had to be reconstructed in light of the experimental method of the sciences. One of his earliest and clearest discussions of the nature of experience as an organic coordination is to be found in "The Reflex Arc Concept in Psychology" (*Psychological Review*, Vol. 3, 1896).

Dewey's interest in developing a new theory of experience led many critics to question the exact status of experience within nature, and some objectors charged him with excessive anthropomorphism. Sensitive to this type of criticism, Dewey, particularly in *Experience and Nature* (Chicago, 1925; 2nd ed., New York, 1929), attempted to deal with this criticism and to sketch a metaphysics, "the descriptive study of the generic traits of existence."

Nature, according to Dewey, consists of a variety of transactions that can be grouped into three evolutionary plateaus, or levels. Transaction is the technical term that Dewey used to designate the type of action in which the components and elements involved in the action both condition and are conditioned by the entire coordination. The elements of a transaction play a functional role in the developing coordination. The three plateaus of natural transactions are the physicochemical, the psychophysical, and the level of human experience. There are no sharp breaks or discontinuities within nature. But there are distinctive characteristics of the different levels of natural transactions that are reflected in their patterns of behavior and in their consequences. From this perspective, human experience consists of one type of natural transaction, a type that has been the latest to evolve. The distinguishing characteristics of this level of natural transaction are to be located in the type of language, communication, and social living that humans have developed. Experience is all-inclusive in the sense that man is involved in continuous transactions with the whole of nature, and through systematic inquiry he can come to understand the essential characteristics of nature. Some of the more specific areas of Dewey's philosophy can be investigated against this panoramic view of experience and nature.

ART AND EXPERIENCE

The ideas contained in Dewey's *Art as Experience* (New York, 1934) provided a surprise for many readers. Popular versions of his philosophy had so exaggerated the role of the practical and the instrumental that art and aesthetic experience seemed to have no place in his philosophical outlook. More perceptive commentators realized that Dewey was making explicit a dimension of his view of experience that had always been implicit and essential to an understanding of his philosophy. The meaning and role of art and aesthetic quality are crucial for understanding Dewey's views on logic, education, democracy, ethics, social philosophy, and even technology.

Dewey had persistently claimed that knowing, or more specifically, inquiry, is an art requiring active experimental manipulation and testing. Knowing does not consist of the contemplation of eternal forms, essences, or universals. Dewey argued that the "spectator theory of knowledge," which had plagued philosophy from its beginnings, is mistaken. He also objected to the sharp division between the theoretical sciences and the practical arts that had its explicit source in Aristotle and had influenced so much later philosophy. Dewey maintained that Aristotle's analysis of the practical disciplines is more fruitful for developing an adequate theory of inquiry than is his description of the theoretical sciences of knowing. Not only is inquiry an art, but all life is, or can be, artistic. The so-called fine arts differ in degree, not in kind, from the rest of life.

Dewey also gave a prominent place to what he called immediacy, pervasive quality, or aesthetic quality. This immediacy is not restricted to a special type of experience but is a distinctive feature of anything that is properly called "*an* experience." The primary unit of life, we have mentioned, is *an* experience, a natural transaction of acting, suffering, enjoying, knowing. It has both temporal development and spatial dimension and can undergo internal change and reconstruction.

But what is it that enables us to speak of an individual experience? Or, by virtue of what does an experience, situation, or context have a unity that enables us to distinguish it from other experiences? Dewey's answer is that everything that is an experience has immediacy or pervasive quality that binds together the complex constituents of the experience. This immediacy or pervasive quality can be directly felt or had. But this qualitative dimension of experience is not to be confused with a subjective feeling that is somehow locked up in the mind of the experiencer. Nor is it to be thought of as something that exists independently of any experiencer. These qualities that pervade natural transactions are properly predicated of the experience or situation as a whole. Within an experiential transaction we can institute distinctions between what is subjective and what is objective. But such distinctions are relative to, and dependent on, the context in which they are made. An experience or a situation is a whole in virtue of its immediate pervasive qualities, and each occurrence of these qualities is unique. As examples of such pervasive qualities, Dewey mentions the qualities of distress or cheer that mark existent situations, qualities that are unique in their occurrence and inexpressible in words but capable of being directly experienced. Thus, when one directly experiences a frightening situation, it is the situation that is frightening and not merely the experience.

These pervasive, or "tertiary," qualities are what Dewey calls aesthetic qualities. Aesthetic quality is thus an essential characteristic of all experiences. Within an experience, the pervasive quality can guide the development of the experience, and it can also be transformed and enriched as the experience is reconstructed. Aesthetic quality can be funded with new meaning, ideas, and emotions. A situation that is originally indeterminate, slack, or inchoate can be transformed into one that is determinate, harmonious, and funded with meaning; this type of reconstructed experience Dewey called a consummation. Such experiences are reconstructed by the use of intelligence. For example, when one is confronted with a specific problematic situation that demands resolution, one can reconstruct the situation by locating its problematic features and initiating a course of action that will resolve the situation. Consummations are characteristic of the most mundane practical tasks as well as the most speculative inquiries. The enemies of the aesthetic, Dewey claimed, are not the practical or the intellectual but the diffuse and slack at one extreme and the excessively rigid and fixed at the other. The type of experience that philosophers normally single out as aesthetic is a heightened consummation in which aesthetic qualities dominate.

Dewey viewed human life as a rhythmic movement from experiences qualified by conflict, doubt, and indeterminateness toward experiences qualified by their integrity, harmony, and funded aesthetic quality. We are constantly confronted with problematic and indeterminate situations, and insofar as we use our intelligence to reconstruct these situations successfully we achieve consummations. He was concerned both with delineating the methods by which we could most intelligently resolve the conflicting situations in which we inevitably find ourselves and with advocating the social reforms required so that life for all men would become funded with enriched meaning and increased aesthetic quality.

LOGIC AND INQUIRY

Early in his career, Dewey started developing a new theory of inquiry, which he called instrumental or experimental logic. Dewey claimed that philosophers had lost touch with the actual methods of inquiry practiced by the experimental sciences. The function of instrumental logic is to study the methods by which we most successfully gain and warrant our knowledge. On the basis of this investigation, instrumental logic could specify regulative principles for the conduct of further inquiry.

The central themes of Dewey's conception of logic were outlined in *Studies in Logical Theory* (Chicago, 1903), applied to education in *How We Think* (Boston, 1910), and further refined in *Essays in Experimental Logic* (Chicago, 1916). Dewey also wrote numerous articles on various aspects of logic, but his most systematic and detailed presentation is in *Logic: The Theory of Inquiry* (New York, 1938), in which he defines inquiry as "*the controlled or directed transformation of an indeterminate situ-*

ation into one that is so determinate in its constituent distinctions and relations as to convert the elements of the original situation into a unified whole" (p. 104). By itself, this definition is not sufficient to grasp what Dewey intends. But his meaning can be understood when the definition is interpreted against the background of what we have said about the individual experience or situation and the way in which it is pervaded by a unifying quality.

We find ourselves in situations that are qualified by their indeterminateness or internal conflict. From the perspective of the experiencer or inquirer, we can say that he experiences a "felt difficulty." This is the antecedent condition of inquiry. Insofar as the situation demands some resolution, we must attempt to articulate the problem or problems that are to be solved. Formulating the problems may be a process of successive refinement in the course of the inquiry. The next logical stage is that of suggestion or hypothesis, in which we imaginatively formulate various relevant hypotheses for solving the problem. In some complex inquiries we may have to engage in hypothetico-deductive reasoning in order to refine our hypotheses and to ascertain the logical consequences of the hypothesis or set of hypotheses. Finally, there is the stage of experimental testing in which we seek to confirm or disconfirm the suggested hypotheses. If our inquiry is successful, the original indeterminate situation is transformed into a unified whole. Knowledge may be defined as the objective of inquiry. Knowledge is that which is warranted by the careful use of the norms and methods of inquiry. When "knowledge" is taken as an abstract term related to inquiry in the abstract, it means warranted assertibility. Furthermore, the knowledge gained in a specific inquiry is funded in our experience and serves as the background for further inquiry. By reflecting on this general pattern of inquiry, which can be exhibited in commonsense inquiry as well as the most advanced scientific inquiry, we can bring into focus the distinctive features of Dewey's logic.

First, this pattern of inquiry is intended to be a general schema for all inquiry. But the specific procedures, testing methods, type of evidence, and so on, will vary with different types of inquiry and different kinds of subject matter. Second, a specific inquiry cannot be completely isolated from the context of other inquiries. The rules, procedures, and evidence required for the conduct of any inquiry are derived from other successful inquiries. By studying the types of inquiry that have been most successful in achieving warranted conclusions, we can abstract norms, rules, and procedures for directing further inquiry. These norms may themselves be modified in the course of further inquiry. Third, all inquiry presupposes a social or public context that is the medium for funding the warranted conclusions and norms for further inquiry. In this respect, Dewey agrees with Peirce's emphasis on the community of inquirers. Inquiry both requires such a community and helps to further the development of this community. Dewey attempted to relate this idea of a community of inquirers to his view of democracy. The essential principle of democracy is that of community; an effective democracy requires the existence of a community of free, courageous, and open-minded inquirers. Fourth, inquiry is essentially a self-corrective process. To conduct a specific inquiry, some knowledge claims, norms, and rules must be taken as fixed, but no knowledge claim, norm, or rule is absolutely fixed; it may be criticized, revised, or abandoned in light of subsequent inquiry and experience.

Dewey's theory of inquiry as an ongoing self-corrective process and his view of knowledge as that which is warranted through inquiry both differ radically from many traditional theories of inquiry and knowledge. Dewey thought of this theory as an alternative to the views of those philosophers who have claimed that there is an epistemological given that is indubitable and known with certainty. According to this epistemological model, some truths are considered to be absolutely certain, indubitable, or incorrigible. They may be considered self-evident, known by rational insight, or directly grasped by the senses. On the basis of this foundation, we then construct the rest of our knowledge. From Dewey's perspective, this general model that has informed many classical theories of knowledge is confused and mistaken. There are no absolute first truths that are given or known with certainty. Furthermore, knowledge neither has nor requires such a foundation in order to be rational. Inquiry and its objective, knowledge, are rational because inquiry is a self-corrective process by which we gradually become clearer about the epistemological status of both our starting points and conclusions. We must continually submit our knowledge claims to the public test of a community of inquirers in order to clarify, refine, and justify them.

DEMOCRACY AND EDUCATION

Dewey is probably best known for his philosophy of education. This is not a special branch of his philosophy, however, for he claimed that all philosophy can be conceived of as the philosophy of education. And it is certainly true that all the concepts we have discussed inform his thinking about education. He returned again and again to the subject of education, but the essential elements of his position can be found in *My Pedagogic Creed* (New York, 1897), *The School and Society* (Chicago, 1900), *The Child and the Curriculum* (Chicago, 1902), and especially in his comprehensive statement in *Democracy and Education* (New York, 1916).

It is essential to appreciate the dialectical context in which Dewey developed his educational ideas. He was critical of the excessively rigid and formal approach to education that dominated the practice of most American schools in the latter part of the nineteenth century. He argued that such an approach was based upon a faulty psychology in which the child was thought of as a passive creature upon whom information and knowledge had to be imposed. But Dewey was equally critical of the "new education," which was based on a sentimental idealization of the child. This child-oriented approach advocated that the child himself should pick and choose what he wanted to study. It also was based on a mistaken psychology, which neglected the immaturity of the child's experience. Education is, or ought to be, a continuous reconstruction of experience in which there is a development of immature experience toward experience funded with the skills and habits of intelligence. The slogan "Learn by Doing" was not intended as a credo for anti-intellectualism but, on the contrary, was meant to call attention to the fact that the child is naturally an active, curious, and exploring creature. A properly designed education must be sensitive to this active dimension of life and must guide the child, so that through his participation in different types of experience his creativity and autonomy will be cultivated rather than stifled.

The child is not completely malleable, nor is his natural endowment completely fixed and determinate. Like Aristotle, Dewey believed that the function of education is to encourage those habits and dispositions that constitute intelligence. Dewey placed great stress on creating the proper type of environmental conditions for eliciting and nurturing these habits. His conception of the educational process is therefore closely tied to the prominent role that he assigned to habit in human life. (For a detailed statement of the nature and function of habit, see *Human Nature and Conduct*, New York, 1922.) Education as the continuous reconstruction and growth of experience also develops the moral character of the child. Virtue is taught not by imposing values upon the child but by cultivating fair-mindedness, objectivity, imagination, openness to new experiences, and the courage to change one's mind in the light of further experience.

Dewey also thought of the school as a miniature society; it should not simply mirror the larger society but should be representative of the essential institutions of this society. The school as an ideal society is the chief means for social reform. In the controlled social environment of the school it is possible to encourage the development of creative individuals who will be able to work effectively to eliminate existing evils and institute reasonable goods. The school, therefore, is the medium for developing the set of habits required for systematic and open inquiry and for reconstructing experience that is funded with greater harmony and aesthetic quality.

Dewey perceived acutely the threat posed by unplanned technological, economic, and political development to the future of democracy. The natural direction of these forces is to increase human alienation and to undermine the shared experience that is so vital for the democratic community. For this reason, Dewey placed so much importance on the function of the school in the democratic community. The school is the most important medium for strengthening and developing a genuine democratic community, and the task of democracy is forever the creation of a freer and more humane experience in which all share and participate.

ETHICS AND SOCIAL PHILOSOPHY

In order to understand Dewey's moral philosophy, we must again focus on his concept of the situation. Man is a creature who by nature has values. There are things, states of affairs, and activities that he directly enjoys, prizes, or values. Moral choices and decisions arise only in those situations in which there are competing desires or a conflict of values. The problem that a man then confronts is to decide what he really wants and what course of action he ought to pursue. He cannot appeal to his immediate values to resolve the situation; he must evaluate or appraise the situation and the different courses of action open to him. This process of deliberation that culminates in a decision to act is what Dewey calls "valuation." But how do we engage in this process of valuation? We must analyze the situation as carefully as we can, imaginatively project possible courses of action, and scrutinize the consequences of these actions. Those ends or goods that we choose relative to a concrete situation after careful deliberation are reasonable or desirable goods. Our choices are reasonable to the extent that they reflect our developed habits of intelligence. Choices will be perverse or irrational if they are made on the basis of prejudice and ignorance. Dewey is fully aware that there are always practical limitations to our deliberations, but a person trained to deliberate intelligently will be prepared to act intelligently even in those situations that do not

permit extended deliberation. When we confront new situations we must imagine and strive for new goals. As long as there is human life, there will always be situations in which there are internal conflicts that demand judgment, decision, and action. In this sense, the moral life of man is never completed, and the ends achieved become the means for attaining further ends. But lest we think that man is always striving for something that is to be achieved in the remote future, or never, Dewey emphasized that there are consummations—experiences in which the ends that we strive for are concretely realized.

It should be clear that such a view of man's moral life places a great deal of emphasis on intelligence. Dewey readily admitted his "faith in the power of intelligence to imagine a future which is a projection of the desirable in the present, and to invent the instrumentalities of its realization." It should also be clear that ethics conceived of in this manner blends into social philosophy. Valuation, like all inquiry, presupposes a community of shared experience in which there are common norms and procedures, and intelligent valuation is also a means for making such a community a concrete reality. Here, too, ends and norms are clarified, tested, and modified in light of the cumulative experience of the community. Furthermore, it is the objective of social philosophy to point the way to the development of those conditions that will foster the effective exercise of practical intelligence. The spirit that pervades Dewey's entire philosophy and finds its perfect expression in his social philosophy is that of the reformer or reconstructor, not the revolutionary. Dewey was always skeptical of panaceas and grand solutions for eliminating existing evils and injustices. But he firmly believed that with a realistic scientific knowledge of existing conditions and with a cultivated imagination, men could ameliorate the human condition. To allow ourselves to drift in the course of events or to fail to assume our responsibility for continuous reconstruction of experience inevitably leads to the dehumanization of man.

PHILOSOPHY AND CIVILIZATION

Dewey presented a comprehensive and synoptic image of man and the universe. The entire universe consists of a multifarious variety of natural transactions. Man is at once continuous with the rest of nature and exhibits distinctive patterns of behavior that distinguish him from the rest of nature. His experience is also pervaded with qualities that are not reducible to less complex natural transactions. Thus, Dewey attempted to place man within the context of the whole of nature. In addition, Dewey was sensitive to the varieties of human experience. He sought to delineate the distinctive features of different aspects of experience, ranging from mundane practical experience to the religious dimension of experience. Within the tradition of philosophy Dewey may be characterized as a robust naturalist or a humanistic naturalist. His philosophy is both realistic and optimistic. There will always be conflicts, problems, and competing values within our experience, but with the continuous development of "creative intelligence" men can strive for and realize new ends and goals.

This synoptic view of man and the universe is closely related to Dewey's conception of the role of philosophy in civilization. Philosophy is dependent on, but should attempt to transcend, the specific culture from which it emerges. The function of philosophy is to effect a junction of the new and the old, to articulate the basic principles and values of a culture, and to reconstruct these into a more coherent and imaginative vision. Philosophy is therefore essentially critical and, as such, will always have work to do. For as the complex of traditions, values, accomplishments, and aspirations that constitute a culture changes, so must philosophy change. Indeed, in pointing the way to new ideals and in showing how these may be effectively realized, philosophy is one of the means for changing a culture. Philosophy is continually faced with the challenge of understanding the meaning of evolving cultures and civilizations and of articulating new projected ideals. The motif of reconstruction that runs throughout Dewey's investigations dominates his conception of the role of philosophy in civilization. He epitomized the spirit of his entire philosophical endeavor in his "plea for casting off of that intellectual timidity which hampers the wings of imagination, a plea for speculative audacity, for more faith in ideas, sloughing off a cowardly reliance upon those partial ideas to which we are wont to give the name facts." He fully realized that he was giving philosophy a more modest function than had been given by those who claimed that philosophy reveals an eternal reality. But such modesty is not incompatible with boldness in the maintenance of this function. As Dewey declared, "a combination of such modesty and courage affords the only way I know of in which the philosopher can look his fellow man in the face with frankness and humanity" (*Philosophy and Civilization*, p. 12).

See also Aesthetic Experience; Aesthetic Qualities; Aristotle; Experience; Harris, William Torrey; Hegel, Georg Wilhelm Friedrich; Hegelianism; Huxley, Thomas Henry; Idealism; James, William; Kant, Immanuel; Mead, George Herbert; Naturalism; Peirce, Charles Sanders; Philosophy of Education, History of; Pragma-tism; Value and Valuation; Woodbridge, Frederick James Eugene.

Bibliography

The most exhaustive bibliography of John Dewey's writings is M. H. Thomas's *John Dewey: A Centennial Bibliography* (Chicago: University of Chicago Press, 1962). This excellent guide includes a comprehensive listing of Dewey's writings, translations and reviews of his works, and a bibliography of books, articles, and dissertations about Dewey.

A less comprehensive bibliography of Dewey's writings can also be found in *The Philosophy of John Dewey*, edited by P. A. Schilpp (Evanston, IL: Northwestern University Press, 1939).

The following secondary sources are helpful as general introductions to Dewey's life and philosophy. Richard J. Bernstein, *John Dewey* (New York: Washington Square Press, 1966) focuses on the concept of experience and nature. George R. Geiger, *John Dewey in Perspective* (New York: Oxford University Press, 1958) stresses the role of aesthetic experience as the key to Dewey's philosophy. Sidney Hook, *John Dewey: An Intellectual Portrait* (New York: Day, 1939) captures both the spirit and letter of Dewey as a man, social reformer, and philosopher. Robert J. Roth, S.J., *John Dewey and Self-Realization* (Englewood Cliffs, NJ: Prentice-Hall, 1962) shows the importance and meaning of religious experience for Dewey.

Richard J. Bernstein (1967)

DEWEY, JOHN [ADDENDUM]

John Dewey has undergone an extraordinary renaissance of scholarly and public concern with his thought. Dewey (1859–1952) was encyclopedic in both his interests and achievements. The full and startling range of his written reflections is now apparent with the completed publication of his *Works* in a critical edition of thirty-seven volumes. Commentaries and critical interpretations have followed apace.

In the mediated public mind, prior discussion of Dewey's thought for the most part was devoted to his work on education, both in theory and practice. Unfortunately, these discussions of Dewey's approach to pedagogy and to schooling as an institution in a democratic society were often disconnected from his metaphysics, aesthetics, and social and political philosophy. This interpretive mishap is now being rectified with the appearance of many perceptive studies of Dewey's thought, including his previously neglected thoughts on religion and logic.

Fundamentally, John Dewey is an unregenerate philosophical naturalist, one for whom the human journey is constitutive of its own meaning and is not to be rescued by any transcendent explanations, principles of accountability, or posthumous salvation. Obviously, this position is both liberating and baleful, in that it throws us back on our own human resources, for better and for worse. In effect, we are responsible for our actions, for the course of human history, and we are called upon to navigate between the shoals of supine obeisance and arrogant usurpation. In *A Common Faith* (1934), Dewey warns of the danger to human solidarity when we do not accept this responsibility. "Weak natures take to reverie as a refuge as strong ones do to fanaticism. Those who dissent are mourned over by the first class and converted through the use of force by the second."

Leaving no philosophical stone unturned, Dewey addresses the pitfalls and possibilities of the human condition from a wide array of vantage points. His central text is *Experience and Nature,* in which he probes the transactions of the human organism with the affairs of nature. These transactions are to be understood and diagnosed as experiential oscillations between the "precarious" and the "stable." The settings for this trenchant discussion include communication, mind, art, and value. In retrospect, Dewey offered that he should have titled this work *Culture and Nature,* an appropriate reconsideration, for it is helpful to read Dewey as a philosopher of culture, with an eye toward his grasp of human institutions, social, political, and educational.

Since the 1980s the focus of commentaries on the work of Dewey has been directed to his social and political philosophy, particularly his writings between 1927 and 1935, namely, *The Public and Its Problems, Individualism Old and New,* and *Liberalism and Social Action.* Although Dewey's thought was indigenous to American culture, it is nonetheless remarkable that themes found in Marxist and existentialist traditions are present in these writings, cast differently but equally telling. Of special note is the renewed admiration for Dewey's philosophy of community and his deep grasp of the complex relationships of individuals in communities. For Dewey the irreducible trait of human life is found in the activity of face-to-face communities. Their quality is the sign of how we are faring, humanly. At the end of *Human Nature and Conduct,* he writes a message for his time and for our time as well.

Within the flickering inconsequential acts of separate selves dwells a sense of the whole which claims and dignifies them. In its presence we put off mortality and live in the universal. The life of the community in which we live and have our

being is the fit symbol of this relationship. The acts in which we express our perception of the ties which bind us to others are its only rites and ceremonies.

See also Existentialism; Feminism and Pragmatism; Marxist Philosophy; Social and Political Philosophy.

Bibliography

WORKS BY DEWEY

Works of John Dewey. Edited by J. A. Boydston. Carbondale: Southern Illinois University Press, 1969–1990. Divided into Early Works (5 vols.), Middle Works (15 vols.), and Later Works (17 vols.). This is a critical edition.

The Correspondence of John Dewey, 1871–1952. Edited by Larry A. Hickman. Charlottesville, VA: InteLex Corporation, 1999–2005. Vol. 1 (1871–1918), 1999. Rev. ed. 2001, 2005; Vol. 2 (1919–1939), 2001. Rev. ed. 2005; Vol. 3 (1940–1952), 2005.

The Essential Dewey. 2 vols. Edited by Larry A. Hickman and Thomas Alexander. Bloomington: Indiana University Press, 1998.

The Philosophy of John Dewey. Edited by J. J. McDermott. Chicago: University of Chicago Press, 1981. Complete selections from Dewey's major writings.

WORKS ON DEWEY

Campbell, J. *Understanding John Dewey.* Chicago: Open Court, 1995. The most intelligent and accurate interpretation of Dewey's thought overall.

Hickman, L. A. *John Dewey's Pragmatic Technology.* Bloomington: Indiana University Press, 1990.

Hickman, L. A., ed. *Reading Dewey: Interpretations for a Postmodern Generation.* Bloomington: Indiana University Press, 1998.

Martin, Jay. *The Education of John Dewey—A Biography.* New York: Columbia University Press, 2003.

Rockefeller, S. C. *John Dewey: Religious Faith and Democratic Humanism.* New York: Columbia University Press, 1991.

Schilpp, P. A., and L. E. Hahn, eds. *The Philosophy of John Dewey,* 3rd ed. La Salle, IL: Open Court, 1989. Contains a bibliography of Dewey's publications with entries and corrections until 1989.

Shook, John R. *Dewey's Empirical Theory of Knowledge and Reality.* Nashville, TN: Vanderbilt University Press, 2000.

Sleeper, R. S. *The Necessity of Pragmatism: John Dewey's Conception of Philosophy.* New Haven, CT: Yale University Press, 1986. An insightful presentation of the relationship between Dewey's thought and major currents in contemporary philosophy.

Welchman, J. *Dewey's Ethical Thought.* Ithaca, NY: Cornell University Press, 1995.

Westbrook, R. *John Dewey and American Democracy.* Ithaca, NY: Cornell University Press, 1991. A synoptic and especially perceptive book on Dewey's social thought.

John J. McDermott (1996)
Bibliography updated by John J. McDermott (2005)

DIALECTIC

The term *dialectic* originates in the Greek expression for the art of conversation (διαλεκτικὴ τέχνη). So far as its great variety of meanings have anything in common, it is perhaps that dialectic is a method of seeking and sometimes arriving at the truth by reasoning, but even this general description, which to fit the variety of cases is so vague as to be valueless, fails to do justice to the Hegelian and Marxist notion of dialectic as a historical process. However, among the more important meanings of the term have been (1) the method of refutation by examining logical consequences, (2) sophistical reasoning, (3) the method of division or repeated logical analysis of genera into species, (4) an investigation of the supremely general abstract notions by some process of reasoning leading up to them from particular cases or hypotheses, (5) logical reasoning or debate using premises that are merely probable or generally accepted, (6) formal logic, (7) the criticism of the logic of illusion, showing the contradictions into which reason falls in trying to go beyond experience to deal with transcendental objects, and (8) the logical development of thought or reality through thesis and antithesis to a synthesis of these opposites. Meaning (2) is notably still current, and the term is often used in a pejorative sense.

In the following discussion the different kinds of dialectic will be elucidated in their historical order.

SOCRATES AND HIS PREDECESSORS

Dialectic perhaps originated in the fifth century BCE, since Zeno of Elea, the author of the famous paradoxes, was recognized by Aristotle as its inventor (Diogenes Laërtius, *Lives* VIII, 57). Aristotle presumably had Zeno's paradoxes in mind, as they are outstanding examples of dialectic, in the sense of refutation of the hypotheses of opponents by drawing unacceptable consequences from those hypotheses. For example, it is unacceptable that Achilles never overtakes the tortoise; therefore, the hypothesis that leads to this conclusion must be rejected. Insofar as this method relies on the law of formal logic known as *modus tollens* (if *p* implies *q*, and *q* is false, then *p* is false), Zeno was a pioneer of logic, but there is no evidence that he could formulate the law itself; it was left to Aristotle later to state explicitly the principles that underlie this kind of dialectic, and thus to create the science of formal logic.

Dialectic as the use of such indirect logical arguments to defeat an opponent seems to have been used by Zeno for serious philosophical purposes, but it later

became, in the hands of the Sophists, a mere instrument for winning a dispute. For example, the Sophist Protagoras claimed that he could "make the worse argument appear the better"; such an aim belongs rather to rhetoric than to logic or philosophy. This degenerate form of dialectic was named "eristic" by Plato (for example, in *Sophist* 231E) and others, from the word ἔρις (strife). Eristic came to make deliberate use of invalid argumentation and sophistical tricks, and these were ridiculed by Plato in his dialogue *Euthydemus*, which takes its name from an actual Sophist who appears in it as a user of eristic arguments. Aristotle, too, thought the Sophists worth answering in his book *De Sophisticis Elenchis* (Sophistical refutations), although he sharply distinguished eristic from dialectic, dialectic being for him a respectable activity.

If, however, the lost work of Protagoras did begin, as several subsequent writers attest, with the claim that on every subject two opposite statements (λόγοι) could be made, and if the book continued with a content of statement and counterstatement, then Protagoras deserves to be considered the ancestor of the medieval or of the Hegelian dialectic rather than the father of eristic.

Socrates stands in contrast to the Sophists. Unlike them, he professed to be seeking the truth. But he was not above winning the argument, and what is called the *elenchus* was a major element in dialectic as practiced by him, if we are to accept as accurate the presentation of him in Plato's earlier dialogues. The Socratic *elenchus* was perhaps a refined form of the Zenonian paradoxes, a prolonged cross-examination that refutes the opponent's original thesis by getting him to draw from it, by means of a series of questions and answers, a consequence that contradicts it. This is a logically valid procedure, for it corresponds to the logical law "if *p* implies not-*p*, then not-*p* is true (that is, *p* is false)." Dialectic seems to have been, for Socrates, literally the art of discussion, a search for truth by question and answer; but the definition of a concept is the sort of truth that was typically sought by him, and he supplemented his *elenchus* with another technique, later called epagoge (ἐπαγωγή) by Aristotle. This consisted in leading the opponent on to a generalization by getting him to accept the truth of a series of propositions about particular cases. It may now be seen why, in discussing dialectic, Aristotle says "there are two innovations that may justly be ascribed to Socrates: epagogic arguments and universal definition" (*Metaphysics* M 4, 1078b). For Aristotle had a different conception of dialectic, and since *elenchus* goes back to Zeno, the two features he mentions are the only contributions made by

Socrates to dialectic as Aristotle understood it. The Socratic irony, or pretense not to know anything and not to be conducting a refutation, was a personal feature of Socrates' dialectic and contributed nothing to later developments.

PLATO

In the middle dialogues of Plato there occurs a development of the notion of dialectic beyond what we take to be typical of the historical Socrates. Even though Socrates is the protagonist, the views he is portrayed as putting forward are presumably those of Plato. Dialectic is regarded there as the supreme philosophical method, indeed the highest of human arts: it is "the coping-stone, as it were, placed above the sciences" (*Republic* 534E). In the *Cratylus* Plato had described the dialectician as "the man who knows how to ask and answer questions" (390C), and this view of dialectic as question and answer is the Socratic element that forms the single thread running through his altering conceptions of the method. Furthermore, dialectic always had the same subject matter: it sought the unchanging essence of each thing. But the kind of reasoning that Plato regarded as involved in dialectic seems to change: In the middle dialogues it was some kind of operation on hypotheses, whereas in the later ones (for example, *Phaedrus* and *Sophist*) there is, instead, an emphasis on division (διαίρεσις) as a method. Division in effect consists of a repeated analysis of genera into species, of more general notions into less general ones, as a way of arriving at a definition when no further division is possible. This process is complemented by the opposite process of synthesis or collection (συναγωγή).

Although Plato always spoke of dialectic in an extremely favorable manner, his discussion of it in *Republic* VI–VII marks a high point, as it is there made to be the distinguishing feature in the education of the philosopher-kings and is to be concerned eventually with the supreme Form, that of the Good. It is to reach certainty and overcome the need for hypotheses (*Republic* 511B). But the elevation of the sentiments expressed is matched by suitable vagueness as to the exact process involved, and the interpretation of the few words that are at all precise has been greatly disputed.

It may seem that if dialectic is a process of discussion, then it cannot be of any use for private thought. For Plato, however, there was no difference between the two: "Thought and speech are the same thing, but the silently occurring internal dialogue of the soul with itself has been specially given the name of thought" (*Sophist* 263E; see also *Theaetetus* 189E). However, Plato's most impor-

tant pupil, Aristotle, was already taking a different view of the nature of thought and hence assigning a merely secondary role to dialectic: "Deception occurs to a greater extent when we are investigating with others than by ourselves, for an investigation with someone else is carried on by means of words, but an investigation in one's own mind is carried on quite as much by means of the thing itself" (*De Sophisticis Elenchis* 169a37). Dialectic was no longer to be the method of science.

ARISTOTLE

The practice of dialectic was probably a major activity in Plato's Academy, to which Aristotle belonged from 367 BCE until Plato's death in 347. Aristotle's *Topics* was apparently intended as an aid to this dialectical debate. It is a handbook for finding arguments to establish or demolish given positions, or *theses,* such as "Every pleasure is good," and while the particular theses used as examples in the *Topics* are no doubt borrowed from the debates in the Academy, the methods provided for dealing with them are completely general, that is, applicable to any thesis of the same form. The *Topics* is therefore the first systematic account of dialectic, and Aristotle indeed boasted that prior to his own treatment of the subject "it did not exist at all" (*De Sophisticis Elenchis* 183b36), and criticized the Sophists for giving teaching that was unsystematic (ἄτεχνος). His own trend toward generality and system had the effect that in the *Topics* Aristotle discovered many basic principles of formal logic, including some in the propositional calculus and in the logic of relations, but he hardly reached an explicit formal statement of them. A large part, at least, of this work was written before his discovery of the (categorical) syllogism, a type of argument for which he developed, in his *Analytics,* an elaborate system—the earliest system of formal logic—that superseded dialectic as a theory of demonstration. But even if Aristotle's formal logic developed as an alternative to his dialectic, it may still have arisen out of dialectic in some sense, since it has been argued that he discovered the syllogism as a result of reflection on Plato's method of division.

The distinguishing feature of dialectic for Aristotle was not so much the type of reasoning as the epistemological status of the premises. Reasoning is dialectical if its premises are opinions that are generally accepted by everyone or by the majority or by philosophers; if the premises merely *seem* probable, or if the reasoning is incorrect, then it is "eristic." Aristotelian dialectic is thus quite respectable; it has even been called a "logic of probability," a name that could be misleading because dialectic does not in fact involve inductive reasoning. However, dialectic is not good enough, Aristotle believed, to be a method of acquiring knowledge proper, or science. For that we require demonstration, which is valid reasoning that starts out from true and self-evident premises. The value of dialectic, according to Aristotle, is threefold: It is useful for intellectual training, for discussions with others based on their own premises, and for examining the unprovable first principles of the sciences. "Dialectic, being a process of criticism, contains the path to the principles of all inquiries" (*Topics* 101b3).

STOICS AND MEDIEVALS

Euclides of Megara (a contemporary of Plato) and his successors in that town were logicians of note, and the Megarian tradition in logic was continued by the Stoics. The Stoic logic was known as dialectic, perhaps because the initiators of their tradition had an interest in the Zenonian paradoxes and related reasoning. Under the headship of Chrysippus, who lived from 280 to 206 BCE, the Stoic school reached its zenith, and it was still going strong four centuries later. A saying is recorded from this period, that "if the gods had dialectic, it would be the dialectic of Chrysippus" (Diogenes Laërtius, *Lives* VII, 180). By "dialectic" the Stoics primarily meant formal logic, in which they particularly developed forms of inference belonging to what we now call the propositional calculus. But they applied the term *dialectic* widely: for them it also included the study of grammatical theory and the consideration of meaning-relations and truth. This widened scope, reflecting the special interests of the early Stoics, remained typical of the school; it was accepted by Cicero and perhaps overemphasized by Seneca, who wrote that dialectic "fell into two parts, meanings and words, that is, things said and expressions by which they are said"—διαλεκτική *in duas partes dividitur, in verba et significationes, id est in res quae dicuntur et vocabula quibus dicuntur* (*Epistulae Morales* 89, 17).

In the Middle Ages "dialectic" continued to be the ordinary name for logic: for example, the first medieval logical treatise was the *Dialectica* of Alcuin. But the word *logica* was also used; in fact, Abelard wrote a *Dialectica* and more than one *Logica*. As the works of Plato and Aristotle became known, the Scholastics took over various conceptions of dialectic, and the medieval disputation, by which university degree examinations were conducted, can be regarded as a remote descendant or revival of the debates in the Platonic Academy. The disputants maintained theses and antitheses, arguing mainly in syllogisms; the most significant difference from

ancient practice was that the class of unacceptable consequences now included those propositions that were inconsistent with divine revelation.

KANT AND HIS SUCCESSORS

In his *Critique of Pure Reason* (A61, B85) Immanuel Kant asserted rather sweepingly that the actual employment of dialectic among the ancients was always as "the logic of illusion (*Logik des Scheins*)." He explained that he applied the term to logic as a critique of dialectical illusion. He titled the second division of his Transcendental Logic "Transcendental Dialectic." This new kind of dialectic was concerned with exposing the illusion of transcendental judgments, that is, judgments that profess to pass beyond the limits of experience; but the illusion can never, he thought, be dispelled entirely, as it is natural and inevitable.

Although Kant, in his Transcendental Dialectic, had set out the antinomies of pure reason as four sets of thesis and antithesis, he did not call his resolution of the antinomies a synthesis. It was his successor Johann Gottlieb Fichte who, in his *Grundlage der gesamten Wissenschaftslehre* (Jena and Leipzig, 1794), first introduced into German philosophy the famed triad of thesis, antithesis, and synthesis. In this he was followed by Friedrich Schelling, but not in fact by G. W. F. Hegel. Fichte did not believe that the antithesis could be deduced from the thesis; nor, on his view did the synthesis achieve anything more than uniting what both thesis and antithesis had established.

HEGEL AND HIS SUCCESSORS

Hegel is commonly supposed to have presented his doctrines in the form of the triad or three-step (*Dreischritt*) of thesis, antithesis, and synthesis. This view appears to be mistaken insofar as he did not actually use the terms; and even though he evinced a fondness for triads, neither his dialectic in general nor particular portions of his work can be reduced simply to a triadic pattern of thesis, antithesis, and synthesis. The legend of this triad in Hegel has been bolstered by some English translations that introduce the word *antithesis* where it is not required.

However, there is indeed a Hegelian dialectic, involving the passing over of thoughts or concepts into their opposites and the achievement of a higher unity. But if it is a process that arrives at a higher truth through contradictions, it does not constitute a new conception of dialectic. Hegel actually showed his awareness of the traditional notion by paying tribute to "Plato's *Parmenides*, probably the greatest masterpiece of ancient dialectic."

And even the doctrine that dialectic is a world process—not merely a process of thought but also found in history and in the universe as a whole—was not wholly new, but goes back to Heraclitus and the Neoplatonist Proclus. Here again Hegel, with his interest in the history of philosophy, was aware of his predecessors. What seems to be genuinely new in Hegel's view of dialectic is the conception of a necessary movement. Dialectic was said to be "the scientific application of the regularity found in the nature of thought." The "passing over into the opposite" was seen as a natural consequence of the limited or finite nature of a concept or thing. The contradictions in thought, nature, and society, even though they are not contradictions in formal logic but conceptual inadequacies, were regarded by Hegel as leading, by a kind of necessity, to a further phase of development.

Hegel has had an enormous influence not only on willing disciples but even on thinkers nominally in revolt against him, such as Søren Kierkegaard. One of the most important offshoots of the Hegelian dialectic was the Marxist dialectic, in which, of course, "matter" was substituted for Hegel's "spirit."

See also Abelard, Peter; Aristotle; Chrysippus; Cicero, Marcus Tullius; Dialectical Materialism; Diogenes Laertius; Fichte, Johann Gottlieb; Greek Academy; Hegel, Georg Wilhelm Friedrich; Hegelianism; Heraclitus of Ephesus; Infinity in Mathematics and Logic; Kant, Immanuel; Kierkegaard, Søren Aabye; Marxist Philosophy; Medieval Philosophy; Neoplatonism; Plato; Proclus; Protagoras of Abdera; Schelling, Friedrich Wilhelm Joseph von; Socrates; Sophists; Stoicism; Zeno of Elea.

Bibliography

GENERAL DISCUSSIONS

For general discussions of dialectic, see Paul Foulquié, *La dialectique* (Paris, 1949); Eduard von Hartmann, *Über die dialektische Methode* (Berlin, 1868; 2nd ed. 1910); Karl Dürr, "Die Entwicklung der Dialektik von Plato bis Hegel." *Dialectica* 1 (1947); and Jonas Cohn, *Theorie der Dialektik* (Leipzig, 1923).

SOCRATES AND HIS PREDECESSORS

On Zeno, see H. D. P. Lee, *Zeno of Elea* (Cambridge, U.K., 1936); G. E. L. Owen, "Zeno and the Mathematicians," in *PAS* 58 (1957–1958): 199–222; and John Burnet, *Early Greek Philosophy* (London, 1892; 4th ed., 1930). For the period before Socrates as a whole, see Burnet's *From Thales to Plato* (London, 1914). For criticisms of the Sophists, see Plato, *Euthydemus,* and Aristotle, *De Sophisticis Elenchis,* translated by W. A. Pickard-Cambridge in *The Works of Aristotle,* Vol. 1 (Oxford, 1928). On this whole phase of dialectic, see the extremely reliable work of William and Martha Kneale, *The Development of Logic* (Oxford: Clarendon Press, 1962), Ch. 1.

PLATO

The most helpful book on Plato's use of dialectic is Richard Robinson, *Plato's Earlier Dialectic* (Ithaca, NY: Cornell University Press, 1941; 2nd ed., Oxford: Clarendon Press, 1953), but the word *earlier* occurs in its title because it contains no examination of the methods of division and synthesis that appear in some of Plato's later dialogues. For the original descriptions of the Platonic dialectic, see the Dialogues of Plato, *passim* (in any translation), but above all the *Republic,* Books VI–VII, especially 510–540 in the standard numbering. See also James Adam, *The Republic of Plato,* Vol. II (Cambridge, U.K., 1902; reissued, 1963), pp. 168–179; Richard Lewis Nettleship, *Lectures on the Republic of Plato* (London: Macmillan, 1901), pp. 277–289; Julius Stenzel, *Studien zur Entwicklung der Platonischen Dialektik von Sokrates zu Aristoteles* (Breslau, 1917; 2nd ed., 1931), translated by D. J. Allan as *Plato's Method of Dialectic* (Oxford: Clarendon Press, 1940; reissued, New York: Russell and Russell, 1964); Francis M. Cornford, "Mathematics and Dialectic in the *Republic* VI–VII," in *Mind* 41 (1932): 37–52, 173–190; R. S. Bluck, "ὑποθέσεις in the *Phaedo* and the Platonic Dialectic," in *Phronesis* 2 (1) (1957): 21–31; D. W. Hamlyn, "The Communion of Forms and the Development of Plato's Logic," in *Philosophical Quarterly* 5 (1955): 289–302; Georges Rodier, "Les mathématiques et la dialectique dans le système de Platon," in *Archiv für Geschichte der Philosophie* 15 (1902): 479–490, and his "L'évolution de la dialectique de Platon," in *Année philosophique* (1905): 49–73; D. S. Mackay, "The Problem of Individuality in Plato's Dialectic," in *University of California Publications in Philosophy* 20 (1937): 131–154; and Juan A. Nuño Montes, *La dialéctica platónica* (Caracas, 1962).

ARISTOTLE

For the original account, see Aristotle, *Topica,* translated by W. A. Pickard-Cambridge in *The Works of Aristotle,* Vol. I (Oxford, 1928). The most accessible scholarly discussion of this phase is Ernst Kapp, *Greek Foundations of Traditional Logic* (New York: Columbia Press, 1942). Important treatments of the controversial issues involved are Friedrich Solmsen, *Die Entwicklung der Aristotelischen Logik und Rhetorik* (Berlin, 1929), his "The Discovery of the Syllogism," in *Philosophical Review* 50 (1941): 410–421, and his "Aristotle's Syllogism and Its Platonic Background," in *Philosophical Review* 60 (1951): 563–571; and Paul Wilpert, "Aristoteles und die Dialektik," in *Kant-Studien* 68 (1956): 247–284. There is also Livio Sichirollo, *Giustificazioni della dialettica in Aristotele* (Urbino, 1963).

STOICS AND MEDIEVALS

For a discussion of Stoic use of dialectic, see Benson Mates, *Stoic Logic* (Berkeley: University of California Press, 1953). For a general account of the medieval phase and references to particular works, see William and Martha Kneale, op. cit., Ch. 4. For the postmedieval rejection of dialectic, see Duane H. Berquist, "Descartes and Dialectics," in *Laval théologique et philosophique* 20 (2) (1964): 176–204.

KANT AND HIS SUCCESSORS

Kant and his successors are discussed in Graham H. Bird, *Kant's Theory of Knowledge* (London: Routledge and Paul, 1962); John E. Llewelyn, "Dialectical and Analytical Opposites," in *Kant-Studien* 55 (1964): 171–174; and Richard Kroner, *Von Kant bis Hegel,* 2 vols. (Tübingen, 1921–1924).

HEGEL AND HIS SUCCESSORS

For general discussions of the Hegelian phase, see K. R. Popper, "What Is Dialectic?," in *Mind* 49 (1940): 403–426, reprinted in Popper's *Conjectures and Refutations* (London: Routledge, 1963); Sidney Hook, "What Is Dialectic?," in *Journal of Philosophy* 26 (1929): 85–99, 113–123, his *From Hegel to Marx* (London, 1936), and his "Dialectic in Social and Historical Inquiry," in *Journal of Philosophy* 36 (1939): 365–378; and Siegfried Marck, *Die Dialektik in der Philosophie der Gegenwart,* 2 vols. (Tübingen, 1929–1931). On dialectic in Hegel, see John M. E. McTaggart, *Studies in the Hegelian Dialectic* (Cambridge, U.K., 1896); G. R. G. Mure, *An Introduction to Hegel* (Oxford: Clarendon Press, 1940); and above all, John N. Findlay, "Some Merits of Hegelianism," in *PAS* 56 (1955–1956): 1–24, and his *Hegel: A Re-examination* (London: Allen and Unwin, 1958), and a valuable chapter by him on Hegel in *A Critical History of Western Philosophy,* edited by D. J. O'Connor (London, 1964). See also Gustav E. Mueller, "The Hegel Legend of Thesis-Antithesis-Synthesis," in *Journal of the History of Ideas* 19 (1958): 411–414; Carl J. Friedrich, "The Power of Negation: Hegel's Dialectic and Totalitarian Ideology," in *A Hegel Symposium,* edited by D. C. Travis (Austin: University of Texas, 1962), pp. 13–35; and Walter Kaufmann, *Hegel* (New York, 1965). On Marx, see Harold B. Acton, *The Illusion of the Epoch: Marxism–Leninism as a Philosophical Creed* (London: Cohen and West, 1955).

Roland Hall (1967)

DIALECTICAL MATERIALISM

Marxism-Leninism is the name given to the form of Marxist theory that was accepted and taught by the Russian and Chinese Communist parties and the Communist parties associated with them. Marxism-Leninism is both a view of the world as a whole and of human society and its development. The view of human society is called historical materialism, the name bestowed upon it by Friedrich Engels. The view of the world as a whole is called dialectical materialism, a title devised by G. V. Plekhanov, the Russian Marxist, and first used by him in an article published in 1891. Marxist-Leninists regard dialectical materialism as the basis of their philosophy and generally begin comprehensive expositions of that philosophy with an account of it. One might say that dialectical materialism constitutes the logic, ontology,

and epistemology of Marxism-Leninism, and historical materialism its ethics, politics, and philosophy of history. Sometimes, however, the term *dialectical materialism* is used for the fundamentals of Marxism-Leninism as a whole. When dialectical materialism is thus conceived, the natural sciences are the working-out of dialectical materialism in the nonhuman sphere and historical materialism its working-out in the sphere of human society. But these slight differences do not affect the content of the theory.

MARX'S MATERIALISM

Approving references to materialism are prominent in Karl Marx's writings, especially in the early works. In *The Holy Family* (1845), for instance, he argued that one branch of eighteenth-century French materialism developed into natural science and the other branch into socialism and communism. Thus he regarded "the new materialism," as he called it, as a source of the social movement that he believed was destined to revolutionize human life. Materialism, as Marx understood it, was very closely connected with social criticism and social development. One aspect of materialism that Marx supported was its rejection of idealist attempts to undermine and belittle sense experience. He held that there is something dishonest and irresponsible in philosophies which deny that sense experience reveals the existence of an independent material world; hence his view of knowledge was realist, both on philosophical and moral grounds. In taking this view he was much influenced by Ludwig Feuerbach. Like Feuerbach, Marx rejected speculative philosophy, or metaphysics, as we should call it today, on the ground that the truth about the world and society can only be discovered by the use of empirical scientific methods. In a broad sense of the term, therefore, Marx was a positivist, in that he denied the possibility of any knowledge of the world that is not based on sense experience. Hence, Marx's view of the world was naturalistic and opposed to any form of religion or supernaturalism. Again under the influence of Feuerbach, Marx held that belief in God, in an afterlife, and in heaven and hell cannot be rationally justified, but may be explained (indeed, explained away) in terms of the unfulfilled needs and hopes of men whose lives are frustrated by an oppressive social order. Marx held, too, that men are not immaterial souls conjoined with material bodies. In his view, psychophysical dualism is a relic of supernaturalism and must be rejected with it. Marx did not systematically develop this view as part of a philosophical argument but took it as the basis of his view, expressed in *The Holy*

Family and in *The German Ideology* (1845–1846), that repression of the instincts and natural desires is bad. Marx, therefore, thought that thinking is inseparable from acting and that scientific advance and practical improvement are in principle bound up with one another. Marx's materialism, therefore, is very wide in scope, combining empiricism, realism, belief in the use of scientific methods pragmatically conceived, rejection of supernaturalism, and rejection of mind-body dualism. Animating these aspects of his view is the conviction that they support and justify the socialist diagnosis of social ills and the prediction that a communist form of society must come.

Marx was very much influenced by the philosophy of G. W. F. Hegel. For example, in *The Holy Family* he borrowed almost verbatim some arguments from Hegel's *Encyclopedia* against abstract and unrealistic thinking, and his earliest, unfinished sketch of his theory of man and society, the so-called *Economic and Philosophical Manuscripts* (1844), was both a critique of political economy and a critique of the philosophy of Hegel. Marx's interest in Hegel continued throughout his life. In a letter to Engels in 1858 Marx wrote that he had been looking at Hegel's *Logic* and would like, if he had time, to write a short work setting out what was wrong and what was valuable in Hegel's method. Later, in the Preface to the second edition of Volume I of *Capital*, Marx referred to "the rational kernel" of Hegel's dialectical method and said that in *Capital* he had "toyed with the use of Hegelian terminology when discussing the theory of value." This sentence does not indicate a very strong attachment to Hegel's dialectic, for "toyed with" (*kokettierte sogar hier und da*) is appropriate to a superficial liaison, and the word *terminology* (*Ausdrücksweise*) might be meant to contrast with the substance of what is being said. But although Marx was as much opposed to the speculative element in Hegelianism as any professed positivist could have been, he was deeply influenced by the Hegelian dialectical method. Jean Hippolyte has shown in his *Études sur Marx et Hegel* (Paris, 1955) how very closely the structure of *Capital* is linked with Marx's earlier, more consciously Hegelian writings, so that some of the Hegelian substance persists, although the Hegelian terminology is less apparent. One important Hegelian legacy is the view that social development takes place through struggle and opposition. Another is that the transition from one important form of society to another is by means of sudden leaps rather than by merely gradual stages. Thus Marx considered that different social laws applied at different historical epochs. Again, Marx shared Hegel's aversion to abstraction and his predilection for

total views, but in this he was at one with Auguste Comte as well as with Hegel. These views of Marx's, however, related to the theory of human society. He showed little inclination to linger over questions of ontology. There is a reference in Volume I of *Capital* to the "law discovered by Hegel in his *Logic,* that at a certain point what have been purely quantitative changes become qualitative," and at this point Marx said that some chemical changes take place in accordance with this law. However, Marx left it to Engels to pursue the matter.

ENGELS AND DIALECTICAL MATERIALISM

Engels took up the law of quantity and quality in his *Herr Eugen Dühring's Revolution in Science* (1878), generally known as *Anti-Dühring*, which had appeared as a series of articles in the Leipzig *Vorwärts* in 1877. Engels's work was directed against Eugen Dühring, a well-known non-Marxist socialist and publicist, who had vigorously criticized some Hegelian features in Marxist writers as being speculative, metaphysical, and unscientific. Thus Engels, like Marx, felt called upon to defend the Hegelianism of his youth, although, again like Marx, he claimed to have purged it of its speculative and idealist elements. In the Preface to the second edition of *Anti-Dühring* (1885) Engels stated that he had read the whole of the manuscript to Marx before it was printed and that Chapter 10 of Part II (on economics and its history) had been written by Marx himself and abridged by Engels. This chapter has no direct relevance to dialectical materialism and thus has some significance as an indication of Marx's own interests.

PHILOSOPHY OF NATURE. Engels apologized in a general way in the preface to the second edition of *Anti-Dühring* for inadequacies in his knowledge of theoretical natural science, although he retracted nothing. He also spoke with approval of "the old philosophy of nature." By this he meant a philosophical examination of the phenomena of the natural world claiming to be more fundamental and general in scope than the particular researches of individual men of science. Such inquiries were more frequent at a time when the term *philosopher* was applied to philosophers and scientists alike and the role of the natural scientist was less definitely specified than it became in the nineteenth and twentieth centuries. Engels alluded to Hegel's contributions to the philosophy of nature in the second main triad of the *Encyclopedia* and called attention in particular to Section 270 in which Hegel criticized Isaac Newton's theory of forces. Hegel, like Johann Wolfgang von Goethe and Friedrich Schelling (and William Blake), was highly critical of Newton's cosmological theories, and Engels believed that Hegel, at any rate, was being justified by subsequent researches. It should be noted, therefore, that Engels had no objection to the practice of philosophizing about the nature of the physical world but, on the contrary, was consciously reviving an older, and apparently abandoned, intellectual tradition. By doing this, he introduced into the Marxist theory of nature one of its most characteristic features: the claim that the specialized sciences of nature need to be supplemented by a unified philosophy of nature and that as they develop, the natural sciences are constantly verifying the views first propounded by Hegel in his *Logic* and in his *Encyclopedia.*

From 1873 onward Engels had been studying the natural sciences with a view to writing a comprehensive work on the dialectical characteristics of the material world. Part of what he did was incorporated into *Anti-Dühring,* but much of his more detailed work remained unpublished until 1925, when an edition of the surviving manuscripts was published by the Marx-Engels Institute in Moscow under the title *Dialectics of Nature.* This edition was found to be faulty in various ways, and corrected versions were subsequently published and translated. The work contains, inter alia, an essay on electricity (a subject much favored by Schelling and other romantics), in which Engels says that the basic thought of Hegel and Michael Faraday is the same; an attack on parapsychology as "the shallowest empiricism" and a proposal that it be rejected outright on general grounds of theory; notes on infinite series and infinite numbers, which he takes to prove that the world is both infinite and contradictory; and sketches for an attack on Ludwig Büchner and other nonsocialist, nondialectical materialists popular during the second half of the nineteenth century. Engels's criticism of Büchner is particularly interesting since, among a series of passages probably intended to document *Anti-Dühring,* there is a quotation from Büchner's *Kraft und Stoff* in which, while attacking supernaturalism and idealist philosophy, Büchner wrote: "It is needless to observe that our expositions have nothing in common with the conceptions of the old 'philosophy of nature.' The singular attempts to construe nature out of philosophy instead of from observation have failed, and brought the adherents of that school into such discredit that the name 'philosopher of nature' has become a bye-word and a nickname." Engels regarded this as an "attack on philosophy" and accused Büchner of "shallow materialist popularisation." Engels made his own attitude quite clear by appending passages from Hegel's "Philosophy of Nature."

ENGELS ON MARXIST MATERIALISM. After Marx's death in 1883 Engels was occupied in editing the unpublished parts of *Capital,* but in 1886, in some articles that appeared in the Social Democratic journal *Die Neue Zeit,* he turned his attention once more to fundamental philosophical issues. These articles were published in 1888 in book form under the title *Ludwig Feuerbach and the Outcome of Classical German Philosophy.* In this work Engels set out to explain what sort of materialism Marxist materialism is and to show how it is related to the Hegelian philosophy. Engels renewed his support for the dialectical structure of Hegel's philosophy, although, of course, he rejected its idealist aspects. There is an account of Engels's epistemology, in which a pragmatistic point of view is emphasized.

Mind and matter. According to the argument of *Ludwig Feuerbach* there are two and only two fundamental but opposing philosophical alternatives: idealism, according to which mind is primary in the universe and matter is created by, or dependent upon, mind; and materialism, according to which matter is the primary being and mind the subordinate and dependent feature of the world. It will be seen that in stating this view Engels extended the term *idealism* beyond its usual philosophical meaning to comprise not only such views as George Berkeley's immaterialism and Hegel's absolute idealism but also any form of theism. Thus, in Engels's classification, St. Thomas Aquinas and René Descartes would both be regarded as idealists because they both held that an immaterial deity created the material world. It should be noted that in this view mind is held to be secondary but not nonexistent. Engels took the widely held natural-scientific point of view that there was once a time when only matter existed and that mind evolved from it and must remain dependent upon it. He did not hold the theory of reductive materialism, according to which mind is just a form of matter.

Knowledge and perception. In *Ludwig Feuerbach* Engels also gave a brief account of knowledge and sense perception. He considered that in sense perception the material things in the neighborhood of the percipient's body are somehow "reflected" in his brain "as feelings, instinct, thoughts, volitions." Engels recognized that the theory that in perception the immediate object of awareness is a "reflection" could lead to agnosticism or idealism, for a skeptic could question whether we can ever know of the existence of material things at all if all that we directly apprehend are reflections of them. This, indeed, is a line of thought that Berkeley developed in criticizing John Locke's theory that it is ideas, not physical things, that are directly apprehended. Engels's answer was that what must dispel any such doubts is "practice, viz. experiment and industry." His discussion is vague, but he appears to have thought that skeptical doubts about the existence of material things are rendered untenable by a consideration of what we do to and with things. A skeptic's or idealist's practice belies his theories. Furthermore, Engels held that the truth of scientific theories about the material world is established by the power they give men to manufacture new substances and things and to bring the forces of nature under human control. "If we are able to prove the correctness of our conception of a natural process by making it ourselves, bringing it into being out of its conditions and using it for our own purposes into the bargain, then there is an end of the Kantian incomprehensible 'thing-in-itself'" (*Ludwig Feuerbach*, pp. 32–33). Engels appears to have conflated the problem of our perception of the external world with the problem of how scientific laws are established, but it is clear that he believed that the notion of practice can help to solve them both. In the Preface to *Ludwig Feuerbach* Engels printed for the first time, under the title *Theses on Feuerbach*, some jottings made by Marx in 1845. The doctrine of the philosophical importance of practice is stated in these theses, particularly in the first, second, fifth, and eleventh. One of the things that Marx appears to have been asserting in them is that perception is a deed or activity of the perceiving corporeal man and not merely a passivity of an immaterial mind. In 1892, in the introduction to some chapters from *Anti-Dühring* published separately under the title *Socialism: Utopian and Scientific*, Engels developed this view, arguing that perception is a more or less successful action on the world.

Attack on "vulgar materialists." Another feature of Engels's materialism is its opposition to the theories of those whom he called in *Ludwig Feuerbach* "vulgarising pedlars," and who, in later Marxist philosophy, are called "vulgar materialists." These were a group of German writers and lecturers, of whom Büchner was one, who argued that materialism was the inevitable consequence of natural science in general and of physiology in particular. Engels objected that they wasted too much time arguing that God does not exist. He also objected that they identified thought with brain processes. Furthermore, they failed to recognize the social, indeed the socialist, implications of materialism. But primarily he objected that theirs was a mechanical materialism. A consideration of this objection brings us to a central feature of Engels's dialectical materialism.

By mechanical materialism Engels meant the type of materialism current in the eighteenth century, when the most highly developed natural science was mechanics. According to this view, all the most complex phenomena of nature, including life and mind, can be reduced to the arrangement and rearrangement of material particles. The most complex beings can be nothing but arrangements of the ultimate simple ones, so that chemical combination, life, mind, and thought are no more than increasingly elaborate applications of mechanical principles. According to Engels, in saying that everything is reducible to the interaction of forces, the vulgar materialists were anachronistically upholding this eighteenth-century view, whereas the natural sciences of the nineteenth century, in developing chemistry and biology, went beyond those of the eighteenth century. In merely mechanical mixtures the original components remain side by side with each other, but in chemical combinations new substances result from the joining of their ingredients. The theory of biological evolution showed that new forms of life have emerged from the simpler forms, not merely more complex ones.

Mechanical materialism itself is a form of what Engels, following Hegel, called the "metaphysical" attitude of thought. Engels's source in Hegel is the phrase "the former metaphysics," by which Hegel referred to the philosophical method used by Christian Wolff and others in the eighteenth century in trying to prove important truths about the world and the human soul by the use of definitions and axioms and allegedly strict deductions. Engels agreed with Hegel that this quasi-mathematical method was inappropriate in philosophy and added that it was inappropriate in science too. In *Anti-Dühring* Engels said that in the metaphysical mode of thinking, "things and their mental images, ideas" are regarded as isolated and fixed; things either exist or do not exist; and positive and negative exclude one another. But this, he held, is to overlook the changefulness and interconnections of things. Collecting distinct items of information and neglecting the aspect of process helped natural science to get started but was only a preliminary stage toward grasping the world in all its interconnections, processes, beginnings and endings, and contradictions. Mechanical materialism is a fruit of metaphysical thinking. Metaphysical thinking was, in the Hegelian philosophy, and then in the writings of Marx, superseded by dialectical thinking; and this was, in Engels's view, another way of saying that mechanical materialism must be superseded by dialectical materialism. Engels believed that nineteenth-century biology and chemistry had developed along lines that Hegel had foreseen and required. In particular, he referred to passages in Hegel's *Logic* and *Encyclopedia* according to which a fuller understanding is gained when the category of mechanism is left behind and replaced by the higher categories of life. In Hegel's "Philosophy of Nature," to which Engels's *Dialectics of Nature* so often refers, the mechanical forms are succeeded by physical ones that include "chemical process" and electrical phenomena, and these by "the organic." It is this sequence that provided the framework for Engels's philosophy of nature.

Engels on dialectics. Since dialectical thinking is, in Engels's view, opposed to metaphysical thinking, it is thinking that attempts to grasp things in their interrelationships and in the totality to which they belong, in the process of change, of being born and of dying, in their conflicts and contradictions. Furthermore, it is thinking that recognizes the emergence of novelty and that sees such emergences as sudden, even catastrophic. Dialectical thinking, he also held, was becoming more and more apparent as the natural sciences progressed. Scientific discoverers were dialecticians without knowing it.

CONTRADICTIONS IN NATURE. In *Anti-Dühring* Engels expounded his dialectical philosophy of nature in some detail. Dühring had criticized the Hegelian elements of Marx's thought. In particular he had argued that contradiction is a logical relationship and that it is absurd to suppose that it can be a relationship between things or events in the natural world. In Part I, Chapter 12 of *Anti-Dühring* Engels endeavored to defend the dialectical theory against this objection. First, he said that the view that there could be no contradictions in nature rests upon the assumption of "the former metaphysics" that things are "static and lifeless." Then he argued that when we consider things in movement and in their effects upon one another, the dialectical view has to be adopted. "Movement itself," he wrote, "is a contradiction: even simple mechanical change of place can only come about through a body at one and the same moment of time being both in one place and in another place, being in one and the same place and also not in it. And the continuous assertion and simultaneous solution of this contradiction is precisely what motion is." Engels also maintained that what is true of mechanical change of place is "even more true of the higher forms of motion of matter, and especially of organic life and its development." Engels had argued in Part I, Chapter 8 that in absorbing and excreting nutriment living matter at each moment is "itself and at the same time something else." Engels also held that there are real contradictions in "higher mathematics," where straight lines and curves may be identical. (He probably had in mind Section 119 of Hegel's *Encyclope-*

dia.) Similarly, Engels said that the square root of minus one is not only a contradiction but "a real absurdity."

Engels's claim that movement is in itself contradictory is based on a passage from Hegel's *Science of Logic* in which it is argued that it is not sufficient, if something is to move, for it to be *here-now* and then, after that, *there-then,* for this would merely be for it to be at rest first in the one place and then in the other. For it to move, Hegel concluded, a body must be "here and not here in the same now" and must "be and yet not be in the same here" (*Science of Logic,* Book II, Sec. 1, Ch. 2, C). Hegel was discussing Zeno, who had argued that since movement is contradictory, what is real cannot move. Hegel in this passage accepted Zeno's arguments that movement is contradictory, but unlike Zeno concluded that since there is movement, movement "is an existing contradiction." Hegel's views on contradiction are difficult to understand and have been interpreted in various ways. If intended to argue that contradictory propositions could both be true, that "both *p* and not-*p*," then he was wrong and so was Engels in following him. For it can be proved that from any pair of contradictory propositions any conclusion we like can be deduced and hence that if contradictories are true, *anything* can be true. In this logical sense the term *contradiction* has its appropriate use in thought or discourse, as Dühring had argued. In saying that something both is and is not in the same place at the same time, that it is true both that it is in *P* at time *t* and that it is not in *P* at time *t*, the whole negating force of the word *not* is lost. Either, then, Hegel's philosophy has no value or he must have meant by "contradiction" something different from what formal logicians mean by it. It is likely enough that it is the second alternative that is correct. In attacking Dühring, Engels seems to have committed himself to the first alternative. He adopted a speculative, nonempirical thesis, for whereas movement is something that can be observed in natural things and events, contradiction is not observable in them. What Engels did in his argument about contradiction in the nature of things was to provide one of Zeno's paradoxes with a merely verbal, and indeed absurd, "solution."

It appears that Engels's doctrine on this matter is now being reinterpreted or abandoned. This process began with an article on Zeno's paradoxes by the famous Polish logician Casimir Ajdukiewicz. When this article appeared in Poland in 1948, dialectical materialists were forced to take account of his arguments. In order to do so they granted that "contradiction" does not mean "logical contradiction" when applied to what exists in nature. This view is adopted by the Russian authors of *The Fun-*

damentals of Marxism-Leninism: Manual (English translation, Moscow, no date, but later than 1960), who write: "Contradictions due to incorrect thinking should not be confused with objective contradictions existing in objective things. Although the word 'contradiction' is the same in both cases, it means different things" (pp. 99–100).

QUANTITY AND QUALITY. Another dialectical law of nature that Engels made much of in his *Anti-Dühring* is that according to which certain of the changes in nature take place suddenly and abruptly rather than by gradual accretion. The simplest instances of this sort of change are the changes of water into ice as its temperature is lowered to the freezing point and into steam as its temperature is raised to the boiling point. The ice and steam do not come into existence gradually and pari passu with the gradual lowering and raising of the temperature, but appear all at once as soon as the freezing or boiling point has been reached. Other examples of the principle were given by Engels: the sudden transformation of one chemical substance into another in the course of chemical combination; the melting points of metals; the transformation of mechanical motion into heat; the necessity for a sum of money to exceed a certain amount before it can become capital; the fact, reported by Napoleon, that whereas two Mamelukes were more than a match for three Frenchmen, a thousand Frenchmen were more than a match for fifteen hundred Mamelukes. One very general idea in all this is that gradual alterations in the quantity of something are not necessarily accompanied by a merely gradual alteration in its characteristics. Apart from this, Engels had in mind the evolutionary scheme of development from simpler forms of matter, like gases, to more distinctive and varied forms, like the many kinds of solids, plants, and animals. This development is not a mere rearrangement of otherwise unchanging particles or elements but is the emergence of new features out of the old, even though the later qualities could not have emerged unless the earlier and simpler ones had first existed. The emerged qualities, however, are not reducible to those from which they have emerged. The point at which changes in a single quality transform it into a new one Engels called a "nodal line." He also said that there is a "leap" from one quality to another.

Once again Engels was following Hegel very closely. The account in *Anti-Dühring* is based upon Sec. 108 of the *Encyclopedia* and Book I, Division 3, Chapter 2, *B* of the *Science of Logic*, where Hegel discussed the category of "measure." In these passages Hegel tried to show the part played by proportion in the constitution of things. He gave the examples of water turning, at critical points or nodal lines, into ice or steam, and of chemical combinations and constant proportions, which Engels and Marx repeated later. He also instanced birth and death, the acquisition of new properties by numbers as the series of natural numbers develops, and the acquisition of new features by the notes of a musical scale. He gave a moral example, based on Aristotle, of slight changes that turn virtues into vices, carelessness into crime, and so on. He even gave a political example, borrowed from Baron de Montesquieu, of the relation of a type of constitution to the population of a state. In the *Encyclopedia* Hegel also referred to the ancient Greek puzzles about the point at which a man becomes bald or at which a number of grains of wheat become a heap. Interesting as these examples are, they are extremely disparate. The grains of wheat example is partly a question of how many grains we shall *call* a heap, and this is to some extent a matter of decision. The concepts of a heap or of baldness are rather vague. The examples of a series of gradual physical changes succeeded by a total transformation of quality are clearly of interest to Engels because of the analogy to revolutionary social change by contrast with gradual alteration. Undoubtedly the social examples had impressed Hegel, who had called attention to the gradual steps that lead up to an explosive revolutionary break in the Preface to the *Phenomenology of Mind,* where he wrote: "This gradual disintegration which did not alter the general look and aspect of the whole is interrupted by the sunrise which, in a single flash, brings to view the form and structure of the new world."

In itself, whether there are or are not nodal lines and constant proportions in the physical world would seem to have no logical connection with the way in which the social order changes, unless, indeed, it is held that human society really is, or is reducible to, physical events—and this is in conflict with Engels's general rejection of reductive materialism. If, then, this law is not an expression of a view that is inconsistent with Engel's main view, it would seem to serve an almost animistic purpose. Sudden revolutionary change, he seems to be suggesting, is a fundamental character of the universe as a whole, so that when we urge revolution, we have the universe behind us. That the view at any rate serves this purpose may be seen from Joseph Stalin's subsequent impatience with it. When socialism is established, it is natural for the socialist leaders not to wish to think in terms of their own disappearance and of the emergence of still further social revolutions. Hence, Stalin, in his famous article on linguistics, wrote scornfully of "comrades who have an infatuation for explosions."

INTERPENETRATION OF OPPOSITES. In addition to the law of transformation of quantity into quality, Engels mentioned two other laws of dialectics, the law of the interpenetration of opposites and the law of the negation of the negation. The first of these laws was already touched upon in the exposition of the theory of contradictions in nature and of the deficiencies of the metaphysical point of view. Although Engels mentioned it in the *Dialectics of Nature,* he did not discuss it as such, and in *Anti-Dühring* his emphasis was on the other two laws, to each of which he devoted a chapter. The law of the interpenetration of opposites (which was later called the law of the unity and struggle of opposites) seems to have been intended to provide an explanation of why there is any change or development at all. An idea behind it is that in the absence of all tension everything would remain exactly as it is, since there would be nothing to provoke any change. Change takes place because the world does not consist of isolated, self-sufficient, independent particulars, but of opposing forces overcoming or being overcome. Contradiction, or opposition, is in this view the motive force both of natural and of human history.

NEGATION OF THE NEGATION. The law of the negation of the negation was more specifically emphasized by Engels. He was able to quote from a passage in Marx's *Capital* in which it is said that when, as a result of competition between capitalists, the few remaining giant capitalist enterprises find themselves confronted by a poverty-stricken proletariat, the latter will rise and expropriate the former, the expropriators will be expropriated. "Capitalist production," wrote Marx, "begets, with the inexorability of a Law of Nature, its own negation. It is the negation of the negation." According to Engels in *Anti-Dühring,* the law of the negation of the negation is "an extremely general—and for this reason extremely comprehensive and important—law of development of nature, history and thought, a law which … holds good in the animal and plant kingdoms, in geology, in mathematics, in history and in philosophy." The law is illustrated, according to Engels, by every case in which a plant has seeds that germinate and result in the growth of further plants. "But what is the normal life-process of this plant? It grows, flowers, is fertilised and finally once more produces grains of barley, and as soon as these have ripened the stalk dies, is in its turn negated. As a result of this negation of the negation we have once again the original grain of barley, but not as a single unit, but ten, twenty or thirty fold" (*Anti-Dühring,* p. 152). One idea in this very famous passage is that out of what looks like death and destruction there arises something better and more vari-

ous. (Engels in fact wrote of "qualitatively better seeds which produce more beautiful flowers.")

In his early book *The Poverty of Philosophy* (1847) Marx had quoted the Latin phrase *mors immortalis,* that is, "deathless death," and Engels similarly regarded progress as taking place through continual destruction and amplified renewal. What holds for plants obviously holds for animals. Geology illustrates the law, too, for it describes "a series of negated negations, a series arising from the successive shattering of old and depositing of new rock formations." The same law appears in mathematics. A is negated by $-A$, and "if we negate that negation by multiplying $-A$ by $-A$ we get A^2, i.e., the original positive magnitude but at a higher degree, raised to its second power" (*Anti-Dühring,* p. 153). Engels even found the law operating in the history of philosophy. In early philosophy, he held, there is a simple, natural form of materialism according to which matter is the source of everything. This form of materialism was negated by idealism, which rightly showed that mind is not the same as matter, but wrongly held that matter is dependent upon mind. In its turn, idealism is negated by "modern materialism, the negation of the negation," which contains in itself two thousand years of philosophical development. Engels believed that in "modern materialism," that is, dialectical materialism, philosophy as previously understood is destroyed and yet preserved in the positive sciences.

This law, like the law of the transformation of quantity into quality, draws together some extremely disparate types of being. Is it likely, indeed, does it make sense to say, that the same principle is exemplified in a rule for operating on algebraical symbols and in the relationship of natural materialism, idealism, and dialectical materialism? One instance of the law that has given rise to much discussion is that of the grain of barley. What is it that negates what, and what is comprised in the negation of the negation? This problem was discussed by the Russian Marxist G. V. Plekhanov in his *The Development of the Monist View of History* (1895), in which he defended Engels's view against the criticisms of another Russian, N. K. Mikhailovskii, who had made fun of the idea that, as he put it, "oats grow according to Hegel." In his account of Engels's argument, Mikhailovskii took it that it is the stalk which negates the seed, and Plekhanov accused him of misquotation and asserted that it is the whole plant which does the negating. Plekhanov argued further that Engels's account of this botanical negation of the negation was supported by an authoritative textbook of botany, Philippe Van Tieghem's *Traité de botanique* (Paris,

1891), which had recently appeared. The whole discussion is entertaining but ludicrous. For the main difficulty about the law of the negation of the negation is that it can be made to fit almost anything by carefully choosing what are to count as the negating terms. The prime interest in the law is that it is intended to give support to the view that human progress is by means of destruction that leads to better things.

ENGELS'S PHILOSOPHICAL LEGACY. Engels was deeply interested in the advances of the sciences and believed that as a result of them nineteenth-century materialism had to be very different from earlier types of materialism. But Engels was drawn in two different directions. On the one hand, he sought to establish a naturalistic, scientific view of the world, and this led him in the same direction as the positivists. On the other hand, he was attracted by Hegel's dialectical method and by the romantic dream of a philosophy of nature, and this led him to regard the positivist outlook as thin and unadventurous. Like Marx, he deplored the conservative social tendencies of Auguste Comte and considered Hegel by far the better philosopher. Nevertheless, Engels did adopt one important positivist thesis, the thesis that knowledge of the world can be obtained only by the methods of the special sciences, so that all that can survive of philosophy is logic and the philosophy of the sciences. Thus, at the beginning of *Anti-Dühring* he wrote: "What still independently survives of all former philosophy is the science of thought and its laws—formal logic and dialectics. Everything else is merged in the positive science of nature and history." It should be noted that Engels here used the very adjective "positive" that had been formerly used by Comte de Saint-Simon and Comte. Although the positivists said nothing of "dialectics," Engels's point of approach from Hegelianism to positivism was his claim that the positive sciences make use of the dialectical method. But Engels, as we have seen, searched the sciences for examples of the dialectic and so applied his terms that he could not fail to find them there. This association of a positivist view of philosophy with what positivists would describe as a "metaphysical" view of the sciences was to remain a permanent feature of dialectical materialism.

Engels also bequeathed a problem about the nature of logic. Was formal logic disproved or rendered nugatory by the dialectical logic that was coming to fruition in the nineteenth century? In holding that there are existent contradictions Engels seemed willing to go against formal logic, but he also thought that formal logic would remain as a part of philosophy alongside dialectics. His position was complicated by the fact that in *Dialectics of Nature* he

criticized formal logic as being "metaphysical" in the Hegelian sense already considered. As a result, controversy among exponents of dialectical materialism about the status of formal logic—by which they generally mean traditional Aristotelian logic—has been constantly renewed.

LENIN'S CONTRIBUTIONS

Lenin's great political achievements, as well as his deep philosophical interest, secured a respectful acceptance for his own philosophical views. And there is some appropriateness in the fact that Lenin's name, rather than Engels's, accompanies that of Marx in the name of the whole doctrine of Marxism-Leninism, since Lenin absorbed and reemphasized Engels's views before superseding him as a founding father.

Lenin's main contributions to dialectical materialism are the doctrine of *partiinost* ("party spirit" or "partisanship"), his elaborations of the Marxist theory of knowledge and of matter, and his renewed emphasis upon dialectics.

"PARTIINOST." Lenin briefly formulated the doctrine of *partiinost* as early as 1895, in the course of a controversy with the nonorthodox Marxist reformer Peter B. Struve, who had said that philosophical views were not a matter of controversy between parties but could be shared by members of opposing parties. Lenin wrote that *partiinost* is included in materialism and that no genuine adherent of materialism could remain uncommitted to the proletarian cause. In this particular context Lenin seems to have been thinking primarily of historical materialism; it is clear from his later writings, however, that he thought that the Marxist should never approach philosophical theories with detachment but should adopt or reject them in the light of their effects on the attainment of socialism. There are several points to be noted in Lenin's view. In the first place he held that dialectical materialism is not merely a theory but a form of action for the establishment of socialism. Thus, a dialectical materialist is necessarily a socialist, and his view of the world is inseparable from his efforts to promote the proletarian cause. In the second place, Lenin held that a socialist intellectual cannot be indifferent to philosophical matters. He is not a complete socialist unless he is a materialist, and a materialist of the right kind. Hence, the leaders of the socialist movement must always be on the alert to protect its doctrines against contamination by philosophical idealism. (This last is a doctrine that Stalin strictly enforced.) A fourth point on which Lenin laid great stress is that idealism is fundamentally supernaturalistic, however tenuous the connection between certain forms of it and religion may appear to be on the surface. In attacking idealism, wherever and however it appears in the socialist literature, what is really being attacked is religion and the antisocialist class forces that uphold it.

The doctrine of *partiinost* derives from Marx's and Engels's theory of ideologies. Ideologies, in their view, are systems of ideas whose function is to defend and to justify the class interests of those who believe in them and teach them, and philosophical systems are ideologies in this sense. Bourgeois ideologies serve to promote bourgeois interests, and the way to criticize them is not primarily by intellectual refutation—this will have little or no effect as long as bourgeois class interests remain—but by unmasking the motives behind them. This view is supported by the Marxist doctrine of the unity of theory and practice. In writing a philosophical book a man is taking part in the social struggle, and in a society divided into classes he is of necessity promoting or endeavoring to promote some class attitude. Lenin considered that Marxists, who understand what is going on in the ideological sphere, should do deliberately and consciously what is so often done unknowingly. This attitude was powerfully expressed in his *Materialism and Empirio-Criticism* (1909). Lenin thought that certain members of the Russian Social Democratic party were spreading what were essentially idealist philosophical views, and he set out to put them right. These Marxists (false Marxists, as Lenin thought) were adopting, under the title of empiriocriticism, the phenomenalist theories of Ernst Mach and Richard Avenarius. In doing so, according to Lenin, they were adopting a cryptoidealist philosophy that could weaken the Marxist movement by dissipating its materialism. "Marx and Engels," wrote Lenin, "were partisans in philosophy from start to finish; they were able to detect the deviations from materialism and concessions to idealism and fideism in each and every 'new tendency'" (p. 352). Thus, *Materialism and Empirio-Criticism* was largely a diatribe intended to crush a view held to be dangerous to the party.

KNOWLEDGE AND MATTER. Lenin's *Materialism and Empirio-Criticism* is not only a partisan polemic but also the book in which Lenin expounded his views about knowledge and the nature of matter. It was pointed out above that some Russian social democrats had taken up ideas from the writings of Mach and Avenarius. Mach and Avenarius had tried to put forward as consistently empiricist a view as possible. Mach sought to eliminate from physics all notions that were not capable of direct or indirect verification in sense experience, and Avenarius sought for the terms in which the simplest and most economical explanations can be given. They both concluded that fundamentally the statements of science are statements of what people do experience or will experience and that scientific laws state how such experiences are correlated with one another. To the most elementary of these experiences Mach gave the name "sensations," and empiriocriticism amounted to phenomenalism, the view that material things are actual or possible sensations. Mach's theory of scientific knowledge is not unlike that of the idealist philosopher George Berkeley, who also sought to eliminate from the body of scientific knowledge any conceptions that could not be referred to sensations, or "ideas" (as he called sensations). Mach recognized the similarity between his view of science and that of Berkeley but pointed out that his view differed from Berkeley's in that he did not hold, as Berkeley did, that sensations were produced by God.

Lenin made the most of the fact that Mach's phenomenalist theory had affinities with that of Berkeley. Berkeley, Lenin said, was honest about his religious aims, whereas "in our time these very same thoughts on the 'economical' elimination of 'matter' from philosophy are enveloped in a much more artful form." Lenin objected that these phenomenalistic views run counter to our everyday practice, in which we come across material things and act upon them. We might call this the argument from common sense. He also objected that the theory that the material world is an orderly correlation of sensations is incompatible with the well-established scientific theory that there was once a time when matter existed but beings capable of having sensations did not. Berkeley, if he had known of this argument, could have countered it by saying that God could somehow have experienced the material world. If Mach had taken this course, Lenin claimed, he would have revealed his idealism.

Having rejected idealism and phenomenalism, Lenin had to give his own account of the material world and of our knowledge of it. He adopted Engels's theory that in perception material objects are "reflected" in the percipient and produce "copies" there. From this it would seem that the material world is much as we see and hear it to be, and Lenin seems to have emphasized this. Plekhanov, following Herrmann von Helmholtz, had argued that sensations are not exact copies of objects outside us but that they possess the same structure and might more accurately be termed "symbols" or "hieroglyphs." Lenin claimed, however, that Helmholtz's view undermines its materialist basis, "for signs or symbols may quite possibly indicate imaginary objects, and everybody is familiar with the existence of such signs and symbols" (p. 239). Lenin did not see that a similar objection applies to "copies" or "reflections" as well, for unless we have independent knowledge of that from which the copy is made, we cannot know that it is a copy. Furthermore, Lenin held (*Materialism and Empirio-Criticism*, Ch. 5, Sec. 7) both that sensations copy what is in the physical world and that what is in the physical world is shown by science to be very different from what it appears to be. Thus, he wrote that sensations of red reflect "ether vibrations" of one frequency and sensations of blue, "ether vibrations" of another frequency, but he did not say how sensations can copy or be like the vibrations. Elsewhere he said that it is "beyond doubt that an image cannot wholly resemble the model" and went on to say that "the image inevitably and of necessity implies the objective reality of what it 'images'" (p. 240). By putting "images" in quotation marks, he seems to have been denying its literal force, and by saying that the images "cannot wholly resemble the model," he raised doubts about what it was he really meant to assert.

The basic thing that Lenin wanted to say about the nature of matter was that it exists objectively and independently; therefore, he actually defined matter as "that which, acting upon our sense-organs, produces sensations." This would apply to Berkeley's God as well as to material objects. Still, Lenin called this his "philosophical" account of matter, contrasting it with the "scientific" conception of matter, which changes as scientific knowledge advances. In Lenin's view, the philosophical conception of matter remains unaffected as the scientific view of it changes from atomist theories to theories of electromagnetism. In *Materialism and Empirio-Criticism* Lenin argued, probably correctly, that the electromagnetic theory of matter is no less materialistic than atomic theories. Indeed, he held that it is in closer accord with dialectical materialism. "Modern physics is in travail," he wrote, "it is giving birth to dialectical materialism" (pp. 323–324). Like Engels, he was attracted to theories of matter that "dissolve" the rigid substances and hard atoms of the older views. He believed that such theories were substituting dialectical concepts for metaphysical and mechanistic ones.

DIALECTICS. In 1894, in *What the "Friends of the People" Are*, Lenin quoted approvingly from Engels's *Anti-Dühring*. In *Materialism and Empirio-Criticism* he frequently referred to dialectics, without, however, making it the center of his discussion. But while he was in exile in Switzerland during World War I, he renewed his study of philosophy, particularly of its dialectical aspects. His *Philosophical Notebooks* (first published in 1933) show the wide extent of his reading during those years, particularly his detailed study of Hegel's *Science of Logic,* in which he noted some germs of historical materialism. Lenin's reading of this book led him to conclude that it was not so much opposed to materialist modes of thought as had previously been supposed. On the one hand, Lenin approved of the Marxist commonplace that Hegel's system is materialism turned upside down. On the other hand he wrote that in the final chapter of the *Science of Logic,* on the Absolute Idea, there is scarcely a mention of God and that "it contains almost nothing that is specifically *idealism,* but has for its main subject the dialectical method" (*Collected Works,* Moscow, 1961, Vol. 38, p. 234). It is apparent from Lenin's notes that his respect for the *Science of Logic* increased as he read it. Not only did he conclude that it transcended idealism but also that idealism itself has virtues. Two notes in particular may be referred to. Among his comments on Hegel's *Lectures on the History of Philosophy* he said: "Intelligent idealism is closer to intelligent materialism than stupid materialism" (p. 276). And at the end of a short paper titled "On the Question of Dialectics," written in 1915, he wrote that idealism "is a *sterile flower* undoubtedly, but a sterile flower that grows on the living tree of living, fertile, genuine, powerful, omnipotent, objective, absolute human knowledge" (*Philosophical Notebooks,* p. 363). Many of Lenin's jottings in his *Notebooks* are of this character, in marked contrast to the rancorous anti-idealism of *Materialism and Empirio-Criticism,* in which any approach toward idealism is regarded as treachery. Perhaps it is of significance that the one thesis common to Berkeley and Lenin is the thesis that nothing is substantial that is not active.

MAO ZEDONG (MAO TSE-TUNG)

Mao Zedong's writings on dialectical materialism are referred to here mainly because of the political eminence of their author. Apart from his poems, his writings are mostly on political subjects, and his chief excursions into philosophy are two short articles written in 1937, "On Practice" and "On Contradiction." It has been suggested that Mao has introduced an empiricist element into dialectical materialism, but this is not borne out by a study of these two writings. In the first, it is true, Mao stated that knowledge begins with sense perception in practical contexts, passes on to rational knowledge, which enables the world to be "molded" for human purposes, and then leads to more rational knowledge at a higher level. It is not clear from the article whether the author was thinking of induction or of the testing of hypotheses or of both. But it is clear that, in Mao's view, in passing to this higher level "a leap" is made. In thus utilizing the law of the transformation of quantity into quality Mao was asserting that certain sorts of rational knowledge are different in kind from sense knowledge, and this can hardly be described as empiricism.

In "On Contradiction" Mao Zedong argued that in a contradiction each contradictory aspect "finds the presupposition of its existence in the other aspect and both aspects co-exist in one entity." As examples of this he mentioned life and death, above and below, misfortune and good fortune, landlords and tenant-peasants, bourgeoisie and proletariat, imperialists and colonies. He also argued that "each of the two contradictory aspects, according to given conditions tends to transform itself into the other," and as examples of this he cited the revolutionary proletariat becoming the rulers instead of the ruled, peace and war, landlords becoming landless tenants and landless tenants becoming smallholders.

It is easy to see the incongruities in both sets of examples. The opposition between life and death, for instance, is different from those between above and below and misfortune and good fortune, for there is nothing intermediate between life and death, whereas between above and below there is the relation of being at the same level and between good and bad fortune there is the condition of having neither the one nor the other. As to the second set of examples, the transformation of revolutionaries into rulers is not a logical transformation, but something that sometimes happens and sometimes does not. The example of peace and war is trivial. Mao wrote: "War and peace transform themselves into each other. War is transformed into peace; for example, the First World War was transformed into the postwar peace. … Why? Because in a class society such contradictory things as war and peace are characterised by identity under certain conditions." We know, of course, that wars end and that peace is often followed by war, but nothing is added to this by saying that a contradictory aspect transforms itself into its opposite, as if peace were one entity and war another. These writings of Mao Zedong's are, in fact, mainly concerned with immediate practical issues and contribute little to the philosophy from which they derive. It was in Soviet Russia that dialectical materialism was most fully elaborated after Lenin died.

See also Aristotle; Avenarius, Richard; Berkeley, George; Blake, William; Communism; Comte, Auguste; Descartes, René; Dühring, Eugen Karl; Engels, Friedrich; Faraday, Michael; Feuerbach, Ludwig Andreas; Goethe, Johann Wolfgang von; Hegel, Georg Wilhelm Friedrich; Helmholtz, Hermann Ludwig von; Historical Materialism; Idealism; Infinity in Mathematics and Logic; Lenin, Vladimir Il'ich; Locke, John; Logical Paradoxes; Mach, Ernst; Marx, Karl; Marxist Philosophy; Materialism; Matter; Mikhailovskii, Nikolai Konstantinovich; Negation; Newton, Isaac; Phenomenalism; Plekhanov, Georgii Valentinovich; Saint-Simon, Claude-Henri de Rouvroy, Comte de; Schelling, Friedrich Wilhelm Joseph von; Socialism; Thomas Aquinas, St.; Wolff, Christian; Zeno of Elea.

Bibliography

MARXIST WORKS

Marx

"Oekonomische–philosophische Manuskripte." In *Marx-Engels Gesamtausgabe*, edited by D. Riazanov and V. Adoratski. Berlin, 1927–1932. Division I, Vol. III. Translated by Martin Milligan as *Economic and Philosophic Manuscripts of 1844*. Moscow and London, 1959.

"Theses on Feuerbach," appended to *The German Ideology*. Edited by R. Pascal. London, 1938.

Misère de la philosophie. Brussels and Paris, 1847. Translated by H. Quelch as *The Poverty of Philosophy*. Chicago, 1910.

Marx and Engels

Die heilige Familie. Frankfurt, 1845. Translated as *The Holy Family*. Moscow and London, 1956.

Die deutsche Ideologie. Edited by V. Adoratski. Vienna, 1932. Translated as *The German Ideology*, edited by R. Pascal. London, 1964.

Engels

Herr Eugen Dührings Umwälzung der Wissenschaft. Leipzig, 1878. Translated by E. Burns as *Herr Eugen Dühring's Revolution in Science*. London, 1934.

Die Entwicklung des Sozialismus von der Utopie zur Wissenschaft. Zürich, 1883. Translated by E. Aveling as *Socialism: Utopian and Scientific*. London, 1892.

Ludwig Feuerbach und der Ausgang der klassischen deutschen Philosophie. Stuttgart, 1888. Translated as *Ludwig Feuerbach and the Outcome of Classical German Philosophy*. London, 1935.

Dialektika Prirody. Moscow, 1925. Translated as *Dialectics of Nature*, with an introduction by G. B. S. Haldane. London, 1940; new translation, London, 1954.

Plekhanov

Selected Philosophical Works. Moscow and London, 1961. Vol. I.

K Voprosu o Razvitii Monisticheskago Vzglyada na Istoriyu. St. Petersburg, 1895. Translated by Andrew Rothstein as *In Defense of Materialism: The Development of the Monist View of History*. London, 1947.

Lenin

Materializm i Empiriokrititsizm. Moscow, 1908. Translated by A. Fineberg as *Materialism and Empirio-Criticism.* Moscow and London, 1948.

"Karl Marx." In his *Collected Works.* Moscow and London, 1960–. Vol. 21, 1964.

Filosofskie Tetradi. Moscow, 1933. Translated as *Philosophical Notebooks,* in his *Collected Works.* Moscow and London, 1960–. Vol. 38, 1962.

Others

Cornforth, Maurice. *Dialectical Materialism,* 3 vols. London, 1954.

Kedrov, B. M. *Classification of Sciences. Book I: Engels, His Predecessors.* Moscow, 1961.

Stalin, Joseph. *Dialectical and Historical Materialism.* First published as Chapter 4 of Stalin's *History of the Communist Party of the USSR.* Moscow, 1939.

WORKS BY NON-MARXISTS

Acton, H. B. *The Illusion of the Epoch: Marxism-Leninism as a Philosophical Creed.* London, 1955.

Acton, H. B. "Karl Marx's Materialism." *Revue internationale de philosophie* nos. 45–46 (1958): 265–277.

Bochenski, J. M. *Der sowjetrussische dialektische Materialismus (Diamat).* Bern and Munich, 1950. Translated by Nicolas Sollohub as *Soviet Russian Dialectical Materialism.* Dordrecht, Netherlands, 1963.

Hook, Sidney. *Reason, Social Myths, and Democracy.* New York: John Day, 1950. Contains an excellent discussion of Engels's dialectical laws.

Joravsky, David. *Soviet Marxism and Natural Science.* London, 1961. Important on "mechanism" and the relation of dialectical materialism to positivism.

Jordan, Z. A. *Philosophy and Ideology. The Development of Philosophy and Marxism-Leninism in Poland since the Second World War.* Dordrecht, Netherlands, 1963.

Paul, G. A. "Lenin's Theory of Perception." *Analysis* 5 (1938): 65–73.

Wetter, Gustav. *Der dialektische Materialismus: seine Geschichte und seine Systeme in der Sowjetunion.* Vienna and Freiburg, 1953. Translated by Peter Heath from the fourth German edition as *Dialectical Materialism. A Historical and Systematic Survey of Philosophy in the Soviet Union.* London, 1958. Discusses Marx, Engels, Plekhanov, Lenin, and later Soviet writers.

H. B. Acton (1967)

DIALECTICAL MATERIALISM [ADDENDUM]

The term *dialectical materialism,* commonly used to describe the philosophy of Karl Marx, is suggested by certain statements of Marx, but was not a term that he himself used. In the afterward to the second German edition of *Capital,* Marx says, "My dialectic method is not only different from the Hegelian, but is its direct opposite" (1996a, p. 1:19). For Georg Wilhelm Friedrich Hegel, the Idea is an independent power, a "demiurge," for which the real world is an external, phenomenal form. For Marx, "the ideal is nothing else than the material world reflected by the human mind, and translated into forms of thought" (19).

SPECIES BEING

Marx does not here directly call his method "materialist," however. In his early *Economic and Philosophic Manuscripts of 1844* he rejects the antithesis of materialism and idealism as terms usually applied to separate individuals, for a social ontology of the human being. The human being is a *species being*—that is, a being that is not just a member of a species, as are individual animals, but one that takes the life of the species as an object of concern. The animal "is one with its life activity," whereas the human being "makes his life activity itself the object of this will and of his consciousness" (1996b, p. 3:276). (No doubt Marx, in his disparagement of individualism as animalistic, underestimated the extent to which such animals as gorillas, chimps, whales, and so on create real communities comparable to those of humans.) Rather than take human consciousness as a given, and then relate it in some way to the body, Marx explains human consciousness as the result of the way in which human individuals relate to their species. "[I]t is only because he is a species-being that he is a conscious being" (276). So he concludes in general terms that go beyond the opposition of materialism and idealism that "*just as* society itself produces *man as man,* so is society *produced* by him.… Thus *society* is the complete unity of man with nature—the true resurrection of nature—the accomplished naturalism of man and the accomplished humanism of nature" (278).

In his first thesis on (Ludwig Andreas) Feuerbach, Marx says that for "all previous materialism" things are regarded as objects of contemplation, and so the active side of human practice "was set forth abstractly by idealism" (1996d, p. 5:3). In the third thesis he rejects "the materialist doctrine that men are products of circumstances and upbringing." Instead, he asserts "the coincidence of the changing of circumstances and of human activity or self-change," which is "revolutionary practice" (4). The problem with Feuerbach's materialism is that he conceives of the individual in isolation, and of the species as only "an inner, mute, general character which unites the many individuals *in a natural way,*" whereas "the essence of man is no abstraction inherent in each single individual. In its reality it is the ensemble of the social relations" (4).

Language is the initial form of human species consciousness. Language is not primarily a mode of expressing the brain activity of the separate individual, but a vehicle of the social intercourse or species being that constitutes distinctively human consciousness. "[L]anguage is practical, real consciousness that exists for other men as well, and only therefore does it also exist for me" (1996c, p. 3:44). While consciousness presupposes the activity of the brain, it exists primarily outside of the individual's head in the linguistic interchange between human beings. Language-mediated consciousness is the direct presence of the species to the individual while at the same time the individual is always creatively reproducing the species in new forms. "Consciousness is, therefore, from the very beginning a social product, and remains so as long as men exist at all" (44). In distinguishing such socially mediated human consciousness from animal consciousness Marx supposes a nonreductivist, emergentist, or "dialectical" materialist conception of the relation of conscious activity to the brain. Brain activity is nature presupposed by human social activity but then dialectically transformed and uplifted or "resurrected" by it. This is Hegel's dialectical sublation (aufhebung).

LABOR AND THE CUNNING OF REASON

This relational conception of the human individual is given specific expression in the different historical forms of social existence and in terms of different levels of analysis within these social forms. At the most basic level, and within every social form of existence, socially related individuals transform the natural world and "humanize" it through "labor." In *Capital* Marx again compares human conscious activity with that of animals, "[W]hat distinguishes the worst architect from the best of bees is this, that the architect raises his structure in imagination before he erects it in reality" (1996a, p. 35:188). Thus, the idea, purpose, or goal has primacy in relation to the materials of labor. Marx approvingly cites Hegel's own idealist analysis of the labor process in his *Logic of Hegel*, where he writes, "Reason is just as cunning as she is powerful. Her cunning consists principally in her mediating activity, which, by causing objects to act and re-act on each other in accordance with their own nature, in this way, without any direct interference in the process, carries out reason's intentions" (1968, 350). Thus, Marx directly incorporates Hegel's demiurge, the Idea, into his analysis of human labor. There are certainly material things or complexes of things, tools, and materials involved in the labor process. But thanks to the "cunning of Reason," those ideal constructions of language that constitute the presence of the species to the individual, the human agent powerfully channels the forces of nature in ways that lead to the intended goal.

Human activity is mediated by historically evolved systems of tools, material and ideal, spiritual, or cultural. While consciousness is extended through language and other means of communication (such as books, newspapers, and the Internet), practical activity on the natural environment is not merely the activity of the physical body, but of the body extended by tools. Naturalism and reductive materialism abstracts the human individual from his or her intrinsic connection to humanly produced tools and reduces the individual to the naked body alone. The human being for Marx is not "the naked ape" (Morris 1967) but the ape who wears clothes and extends his or her natural existence by humanly produced organs of thought and action existing outside of the biological organism. These organs of thought and action constitute the presence to the individual of the being of the species and are in turn objects for the individual's creative and transformative thought and action.

ALIENATION OF SPECIES BEING

Whereas in other social systems the social connections tying individuals to one another are evident on the surface of social life—as in the direct communal relations in early societies, or as the personal relations of master and slave, lord and serf—in capitalism the social relations are hidden, while the seemingly separate individual comes to the forefront of empirical awareness. Here is the historical basis of those separate, abstract individuals of both idealist and materialist philosophies that Marx attributes to the alienation of human individuals from one another. In capitalism the social relations that essentially underlie the activity of individuals take the specific existential form of separate individuals exchanging their products and labor in the market. In appearance individuals confront other individuals existing outside of them, competing with them, and serving as means to the achievement of their goals, as they are to the others. In essence there is a holistic system of division of labor that makes possible the highly specific activities of each individual and requires their interdependence. It is this underlying social interdependence that constitutes the reality of communism that progressively emerges in specific ways within the womb of capitalism. Marx's employment of the dialectical categories of essence and existence, or reality and appearance, reflects his adoption of Hegel's dialectical logic.

FETISHISM OF THE COMMODITY

The product of labor in this context has a dual nature. It is an individual object of some kind that can be described in its own terms: an automobile or a software program embodying the current state of technology and specific skills of the workers who produced it. At the same time it has an economic value that cannot be explained by its material qualities and that enables it to be equated somehow with a qualitatively different object:

> A commodity is therefore a mysterious thing, simply because in it the social character of men's labour appears to them as an objective character stamped upon the product of that labour; because the relation of the producers to the sum total of their own labour is presented to them as a social relation, existing not between themselves, but between the products of their labour. (Marx 1996a, pp. 35:82–83)

Materialists and idealists battle interminably over the explanation of this and other mysteries of philosophy because they preserve the standpoint of the independent, separate individual that gives rise to them. Behind the mystery of economic value is the social nature of human labor, the fact that each product embodies a certain proportion of the combined labor of society. Because the people whose interdependent labor is responsible for the product have organized themselves as separate, disconnected individuals, their underlying social connection takes the form of a mysterious, nonmaterial property of their products. In the value form of the commodity spirit and matter confront one another as irreducible opposites: for the "value-relation between the products of labour … [has] absolutely no connection with their physical properties and with the material relations arising therefrom" (Marx 1996a, p. 5:83). Consequently, "[t]here it is a definite social relation between men, that assumes, in their eyes, the fantastic form of a relation between things" (83).

This complex relationship produces the "fetishism" (Marx 1996a, p. 5:83) of the products of labor when they become commodities. The combined power of human beings appears before them as an external power ruling over them—the market and the quasi-omnipotent power of money. The mystery of the nonmaterial characteristics of the product can ultimately be explained in one of two ways: (1) As the expression of the social relations between the producers, seen in essentially cooperative activities that belie the capitalist form of private ownership. This is

the kind of social-historical and dialectical "materialism" that Marx espouses. (2) Or it can be approached by reference to "the mist-enveloped regions of the religious world," in which "the productions of the human brain appear as independent beings endowed with life, and entering into relation both with one another and the human race" (83). Marx thought that Hegel's idealism, for all its advances over previous materialism, did not escape this religious, other-worldly, appearance of alienated human activity.

See also Communism; Marx, Karl.

Bibliography

Marx, Karl. "Capital, Vol. 1." In *Marx, Engels, Collected Works.* Vol. 35. New York: International, 1996a.

Marx, Karl. "Economic and Philosophic Manuscripts of 1844." In *Marx, Engels, Collected Works.* Vol. 3. New York: International, 1996b.

Marx, Karl. "The German Ideology." In *Marx, Engels, Collected Works.* Vol. 5. New York: International, 1996c.

Marx, Karl. *The Logic of Hegel.* New York: Oxford University Press, 1968.

Marx, Karl. "Theses on Feuerbach." In *Marx, Engels, Collected Works.* Vol. 5. New York: International, 1996d.

Morris, Desmond. *The Naked Ape: A Zoologist's Study of the Human Animal.* New York: McGraw-Hill, 1967.

James M. Lawler (2005)

DIALECTIC IN ISLAMIC AND JEWISH PHILOSOPHY

In these closely related traditions dialectic is primarily associated with the science of *kalām*, commonly translated as "theology," but literally meaning "word," "speech," or "discussion." *Kalām* began in the eighth century as an intellectual defense of Islam against external critics and quickly developed into an internal debate over doctrinal issues concerning the legitimacy of political authority, the necessary conditions of religious belief, predestination and free will, the ontological status of the Qur'ân, and the relation of God's attributes to His essential Unity. *Kalām* was subsequently appropriated by Arabic-speaking Jews living in the Islamic realm, who shared some of its concerns and employed its distinctive techniques and formulas in the defense and systematic explanation of their own faith.

Kalām in general is marked by its dual reliance on revelation and reason. The *kalām* theologians, or *mutakallimūn*, took scripture as their primary data but employed rational argumentation to produce the most robust and coherent interpretations thereof. This distinguished them on the one hand from traditionalists and literalists who saw logical disputation and interpretation as leading to heresy, and on the other hand from the Greek-influenced Islamicate philosophers, or *falāsifa*, who were more fully committed to the demands of reason and thus wary of their theological brethren's residual dogmatism. *Kalām*'s method of reasoning and argumentation was dialectical in at least two respects. The first recalls the Aristotelian concept of dialectic, insofar as the *mutakallimūn* based their arguments on merely probable or generally accepted beliefs—specifically, the revealed truths of Islam or Judaism—rather than rationally self-evident first principles or premises that necessitated consent. The *falāsifa*, who appropriated Aristotle's hierarchical distinction between dialectic and demonstration, considered this approach insufficiently rigorous. While their own adoption of the demonstrative syllogism held out the prospect of certitude, they saw the *mutakallimūn* as hobbled by the questionable epistemic status of their faith-based premises. However, the *falāsifa* did not reject dialectic altogether. They generally recognized its value as a propaedeutic for honing intellectual skills, as well as a tool for communicating crucial truths to those unequipped for philosophical discourse. The *mutakallimūn*, for their part, remained dubious about the philosophers' claims to apodictic certainty.

The second sense in which *kalām* was dialectical recalls certain aspects of the Socratic method. First, it was dialogical: It typically took a question and answer form, in effect presupposing the existence of an intellectual adversary to drive the discourse forward. Its method was thus parasitic: The *mutakallimūn* tended to establish their own conclusions indirectly, by teasing out inconsistencies or internal contradictions in the opponent's position. This strategy often involved the use of dilemmas, where the adversary would find himself trapped between two unacceptable consequences that could be avoided only by adopting the questioner's position. The *mutakallimūn* commonly fashioned their arguments with an eye to the specific concerns, presuppositions, and methods of their opponents as well, advancing internal critiques of their adversaries to refute them on their own terms. Ironically, their assault on the *falāsifa* in the eleventh and twelfth centuries, which effectively brought an end to the classical period of Islamic philosophy, required the instrumental adoption of Aristotelian logic, specifically, the demonstrative syllogism.

Although the presence of dialectical methods within the Islamic and Jewish traditions is often attributed directly to Greek influences, a number of contemporary scholars and historical figures have made the case that versions of these argumentative strategies in fact predate exposure to Christian, Greek, or Syriac sources.

See also Aristotle; Dialectic; Islamic Philosophy; Jewish Philosophy.

Bibliography

Black, Deborah L. *Logic and Aristotle's Rhetoric and Poetics in Medieval Arabic Philosophy*. Leiden, Netherlands: E. J. Brill, 1990.

Haleem, Muhammad Abdel. "Early Kalam." In *History of Islamic Philosophy*, edited by Seyyed Hossein Nasr and Oliver Leaman. London: Routledge, 1996.

Ess, Josef van. "The Logical Structure of Islamic Theology." In *Logic in Classical Islamic Culture*, edited by G. E. von Grunebaum. Wiesbaden, Germany: O. Harrassowitz, 1970.

Ess, Josef van. *Theologie und Gesellschaft im 2. und 3. Jahrhundert Hidschra: Eine Geschichte des religiösen Denkens im frühen Islam*. 6 vols. Berlin: Walter de Gruyter, 1991–1996.

Gardet, Louis. "La dialectique en morphologie et logique arabes." In *L'ambivalence dans la culture arabe*, edited by Jean-Paul Charnay. Paris: Éditions Anthropos, 1967.

Gardet, Louis. "'Ilm al-kalam." In *Encyclopedia of Islam*, Vol. III, edited by H. A. R. Gibb et al. Leiden, Netherlands: E. J. Brill, 2003.

Leaman, Oliver. "Logic and Language in Islamic Philosophy." In *Companion Encyclopedia of Asian Philosophy*, edited by Brian Carr and Indira Mahalingam. London: Routledge, 1997.

Stroumsa, Sarah. "Saadya and Jewish *kalam*." In *The Cambridge Companion to Medieval Jewish Philosophy*, edited by Daniel H. Frank and Oliver Leaman. New York: Cambridge University Press, 2003.

Watt, W. Montgomery. *Islamic Philosophy and Theology: An Extended Survey*. 2nd ed. Edinburgh, Scotland: Edinburgh University Press, 1985.

Wolfson, Harry Austryn. *The Philosophy of the Kalam*. Cambridge, MA: Harvard University Press, 1976.

Wolfson, Harry Austryn. *Repercussions of the Kalam in Jewish Philosophy*. Cambridge, MA: Harvard University Press, 1979.

Peter S. Groff (2005)

DICTIONARIES

See *"Philosophy Dictionaries and Encyclopedias" in Volume 10*

DIDEROT, DENIS
(1713–1784)

Denis Diderot, the French encyclopedist, philosopher, satirist, dramatist, novelist, and literary and art critic, was the most versatile thinker of his times and a key figure in the advancement of Enlightenment philosophy.

LIFE

Born in Langres, son of a master cutler, Diderot was a brilliant student in the local Jesuit schools. He was sent to college in Paris and received his master's degree at the age of nineteen. Afterward, he refused to adopt a regular profession and, when his allowance was cut off, lived for many years in poverty and obscurity. His great ambition was to acquire knowledge. In this he was eminently successful, for he emerged from this period of self-education with an excellent command of mathematics and considerable proficiency in the Greek, Italian, and English languages. He first came into public notice as a translator of English works—a history of Greece, the earl of Shaftesbury's *Inquiry concerning Virtue and Merit* (1745), and Robert James's *Medicinal Dictionary* (1746–1748). He was secretly married in 1743; and his wife bore him a number of children, all of whom died in childhood except a daughter, Angélique, who lived to perpetuate the memory of her distinguished father.

In 1746 he published his first original work, the bold and controversial *Pensées philosophiques*. In that year, too, he became associated with the *Encyclopédie*, the greatest publishing venture of the century, of which he soon became editor-in-chief, with the aid of Jean Le Rond d'Alembert for the mathematical parts. This enterprise was his chief occupation and source of income until 1772. The boldness of his thought, in spite of the dexterity with which he attempted to conceal it, met almost instant opposition, resulting in the seizure of manuscripts, censorship, and temporary suppression. Only a man of Diderot's indomitable courage and determination could have brought the project to a successful conclusion.

In 1749, while manuscripts for the *Encyclopédie* were being prepared for the printer, Diderot published his *Lettre sur les aveugles* (Letter on the blind), in which he questioned the existence of purpose or design in the universe. For this and other suspect works he was seized by the police and spent a few uncomfortable months in the prison of Vincennes. His reputation in his parish as a materialistic atheist was catching up with him. The subsequent *Lettre sur les sourds et muets* (Letter on the deaf and dumb; 1751), equally original, was mild enough to

escape persecution. His *Pensées sur l'interprétation de la nature* (Thoughts on the interpretation of nature; 1754) was both a plea for strict adherence to the scientific method and an exposition of results of that method, including definite evidence in support of evolutionary transformism.

After the official suspension of the *Encyclopédie* in 1759, Diderot prudently withheld his most important philosophical works for the use of posterity. The *Rêve de d'Alembert* (D'Alembert's dream), written in 1769, and the *Réfutation de l'ouvrage d'Helvétius* (Refutation of Helvétius) first became public in the nineteenth century. *Le neveu de Rameau* (Rameau's nephew), a scathing satire of eighteenth-century society, and the novels *La religieuse* (The nun) and *Jacques le Fataliste* (Jacques the Fatalist), which saw the light of day only after the French Revolution, as well as various short stories and dialogues, were all of ethical import. Two bourgeois dramas, *Le fils naturel* (The natural son; 1754) and *Le père de famille* (The father of the family; 1758), accompanied by critical essays, could, however, be safely published, though the *Paradoxe sur le comédien* (The Paradox of the actor), important for its aesthetic insights, was withheld. Diderot's *Salons,* replete with brilliant criticism of art and literature, were also published posthumously, although in manuscript copy they formed an important part of Friedrich Grimm's *Correspondance littéraire,* written only for foreign consumption. Diderot knew that his ideas were too advanced for his own generation, but he maintained the conviction that he would some day be appreciated at his true value.

When, in 1772, his long labors on the *Encyclopédie* were ended, Diderot set off for St. Petersburg by way of Holland and spent some months in 1773 in intimate conversations with Catherine the Great. Persuaded of his merit through Grimm, she had not only paid in advance for his library (he desperately needed the money as a dowry for his daughter) but also gave him a salary as its custodian until his death. Baron d'Holbach's *System of Nature* (1770), frankly atheistic and materialistic, had sharply drawn the line between atheism and deism, and both Catherine and Frederick II took the side of the less revolutionary Voltaire. Since Diderot supported Holbach in this controversy, his political *Observations* on Catherine's plan to recodify Russian law were deemed too radical and suppressed by his royal patron.

Returning to France in 1774, Diderot spent the remaining years of his life in semiretirement, enjoying at least a semblance of domestic felicity. His letters to his mistress, Sophie Volland, form, next to Voltaire's, the most interesting correspondence of the century. His final work, the *Essai sur les règnes de Claude et Néron* (Essay on the reigns of Claudius and Nero; 1778–1782), was a eulogy of Stoic virtue, as illustrated by Seneca, and also a reply to charges of treachery and immorality made against Diderot in the *Confessions* of Jean-Jacques Rousseau, his former friend and coworker.

Diderot died in Paris six years after Voltaire and Rousseau, with whose names his is inextricably linked as a leader of the French Enlightenment.

GENERAL PHILOSOPHICAL ATTITUDES

Diderot's philosophy was remarkably undogmatic. He advocated the open mind and believed that doubt was the beginning of wisdom and often its end; he continually questioned his own theories and conclusions, developed extreme theses, or paradoxes, in ethics and aesthetics, and decided that "our true opinions are those to which we return the most often." Nevertheless, after passing briefly through a period of deistic belief (a deist, he finally concluded, was a man who had not lived long enough—or wisely enough—to become an atheist), he became an unabashed and enthusiastic materialist and developed a theory of materialism much less vulnerable than that of his forebears. His main contribution was a philosophy of science that looked far into the future and upon which his aesthetic and ethical theories were firmly and inseparably founded.

SENSATIONALISM. Like Voltaire, Rousseau, and Étienne Bonnot de Condillac, Diderot was early preoccupied with the theory of sensationalism. At weekly dinners with the latter two, John Locke's psychology was thoroughly discussed. Between Diderot and Condillac influence was undoubtedly mutual. But Condillac, having taken holy orders and being therefore more circumspect, worked out a more systematic and more abstract philosophy and left it to Diderot to direct French sensationalism into definitely materialistic channels.

Diderot's philosophical thought was clarified by his constant distrust of abstractions. Abstractions, he declared in *Rêve de d'Alembert,* are linguistic signs, which are useful in speeding up discourse and upon which the abstract sciences are built; but as symbols emptied of their ideas, they are obstacles to clear thinking. Those who use abstractions must have constant recourse to examples, thus giving them perceptibility and physical reality. The mind is nothing but the brain functioning;

the will is the latest impulse of desire and aversion. The naming of things is purely conventional.

Diderot's early philosophical publications were especially concerned with problems of communication. His empirical mind could not be satisfied with speculative studies, such as Condillac's theoretical experiment of endowing a statue with one sense at a time. He chose rather to study the actual cases of individuals deprived of the sense of sight or the sense of hearing. His *Lettre sur les aveugles* (1749) dealt first with case histories and the problems of "reading" through touch, illustrated by the methods of Nicholas Saunderson, the blind professor of mathematics at Oxford. This first truly scientific study of blindness led to Diderot's imprisonment. The passage that provoked the authorities was an imaginary deathbed conversation, in which the blind professor, unable to appreciate the alleged perfection of the order and beauties of nature, expressed his consequent doubts as to the existence of an intelligent God. The treatise on the deaf and dumb, two years later, was also based on scientific observation, but proceeded to discuss aesthetic theories, especially the importance of gesture to communication. In his later posthumous works, sensationalism played an important role in the development of his materialistic monism.

EMPIRICISM. As early as 1748, in the libertine novel *Les bijoux indiscrets* (The indiscreet toys), Diderot showed himself a pronounced empiricist, a firm believer in the efficacy of the scientific method. In an important chapter of that work, Experience (the word meant both observed fact and experiment) figures first as a growing child, who discovers with the aid of a pendulum the velocity of a falling body, calculates the weight of the atmosphere with a tube of mercury, and with prism in hand, decomposes light. The child visibly grows to colossal stature and, like a Samson, crumbles the pillars of the Portico of Hypotheses.

Diderot's *Pensées sur l'interprétation de la nature,* taking its title and inspiration from Francis Bacon, again extolled the experimental method above purely rationalistic theory. Following the work of Pierre-Louis Moreau de Maupertuis and Comte de Buffon—and especially in studying Louis Daubenton's anatomical comparison of the foot of the horse and the hand of man—Diderot arrived at principles of transformism and natural selection that were to influence greatly his mature philosophy. He surmised that "there had never been but one animal, prototype, through differentiation, of all other animals."

The dawning of the age of biological science, he believed, would usher in the great discoveries of the future.

IMAGINATION. Observation and the classification of natural phenomena was the first and essential step, but the great scientist must perceive relationships and form hypotheses, subject to experimental verification. Diderot closely associated the poetic imagination with the scientific, both in theory and practice. This theory is clearly expounded in the first of the three "conversations" of *Rêve de d'Alembert*. This section discusses the role of analogy, which is merely the working out of the rule of three by the feeling instrument that is man. To the genius, whether poet or scientist, will come the sudden perception of a new relationship, resulting in poetic metaphor or useful hypothesis.

STYLE. Diderot's own mind worked in sudden flashes of perception. His best philosophical works are random or loosely associated thoughts or observations—or dreams. His satirical narrative, *Rameau's Nephew,* and his novel, *Jacques the Fatalist,* are apparently loosely constructed, much given to dialogue, with digressions and intercalated stories after the manner of Laurence Sterne. They follow the pattern of general conversation, in which one idea gives birth to another, and so on, until the thread is difficult to retrace. The theory of associationism was firmly based, however, on his theories of sensationalism and memory (to be discussed below).

SCIENTIFIC BACKGROUND. Diderot's inquisitive and encyclopedic mind equipped him admirably to comprehend the great advances that the sciences were making in the middle of the century. From mathematics he turned to chemistry and for three years studied assiduously under Guillaume-Francois Rouelle, forerunner of Antoine Lavoisier. He was well acquainted with the work of the Dutch biologists Niklaas Hartsoeker and Bernard Nieuwyntit, who laid the foundations for the still unknown science of genetics. He was familiar with Abraham Trembley's experiments with the freshwater polyp, and with Joseph Needham's discovery of Infusoria, in apparent proof of the theory of spontaneous generation. These experiments influenced his development of the concepts of the sensitivity of matter and the essential identity of its organic and inorganic forms.

As translator of Robert James's *Medicinal Dictionary,* Diderot was well informed in the science of medicine. Characteristically, he sought (in vain), before writing his *Lettre sur les aveugles,* to be admitted to an operation for cataract, and he consorted with doctors, many of whom were contributors to the *Encyclopédie.* While in prison at Vincennes, the recently published first three volumes of Buffon's *Natural History* received his careful scrutiny, and from all possible sources he collected case histories of injuries to, and surgical operations on, the brain.

By 1769, when he composed *Rêve de d'Alembert,* Diderot was adequately prepared to develop an original philosophy of science, a monistic theory that has been described as naturalistic humanism and dynamic, or "energetistic," materialism, which far surpassed the mechanistic theories of his forebears, from Lucretius to Julien Offray de La Mettrie, and foreshadowed Charles Darwin. In this work, first published in 1830, Diderot showed himself at once a great and an imaginative philosopher and writer. In its pages, his mature philosophy, presented fantastically but seriously, was best illustrated.

MATERIALISM—MATTER IN MOTION

Diderot adopted the Heraclitean theory of flux. The universe, for him, was a single physical system, obeying the immutable laws that René Descartes assigned to matter in motion; it was dynamic or "becoming," rather than static or created. Unlike Descartes, however, Diderot followed John Toland in believing that motion was not added but was essential to matter. He gave the idealistic monad of Gottfried Wilhelm Leibniz a positive content. Diderot maintained that not only are bodies affected by external force but that the atom contains internal forces, a form of kinetic or potential energy. All things carry with them their opposites; being and not-being are part of every whole. "Living," he wrote, "I act and react as a mass; dead, I act and react in the form of molecules. Birth, life, decay, are merely changes of form." No knowledge was gained, no solution reached, in postulating a Creator or supernatural agency to account for material phenomena. All change, including the transformation of the universe from chaos to order, was to be explained by the interaction of the elementary material particles. What man perceives as order is simply his apprehension of the laws of motion as enacted by material bodies.

SENSITIVITY OF MATTER. An additional and very important hypothesis upon which Diderot's construction was built was the sensitivity of all matter, both inorganic and organic. By postulating both motion and sensitivity as inherent in matter, he felt that the entire range of natural phenomena (both physical and mental) and the full variety of experience could be adequately explained. All that nature contains is the product of matter in motion, subject to the processes of fermentation produced by heat; through eons of time growth, increasing complexity, and specialization have occurred.

Diderot believed that there were no inexplicable gulfs between the various kingdoms. The known facts concerning the inorganic, the organic, plant, animal, and man, were like islands jutting out of a sea of ignorance. As the waters receded through scientific investigation, the missing links would be discovered. "How d'Alembert differs from a cow," he admitted, "I cannot quite understand. But some day science will explain." He nevertheless attempted to trace the development of his friend, from the earth mold to mathematician, from the unconscious through the subconscious to the conscious life.

BIOLOGY AND EVOLUTION

During Diderot's lifetime the biological sciences were in their infancy. The scope and profundity of his insights are therefore all the more amazing. When scientific facts failed him, he had recourse to hypotheses that he was convinced would some day be verified. It was in consideration of this conviction that he presented his mature philosophy as a dream, a dream that, with the passage of time, can truly be called prophetic.

The crucial problem that confronted Diderot was to account for the emergence and behavior of the living individual. The coordinated behavior and continuous identity that characterize the organism seemed to transcend any possible organization of discrete material particles. It was difficult to see how merely contiguous material parts could form an organic whole capable of a unified and purposeful response to its environment. Traditionally, the existence of unique species and individuals was explained by recourse to supernatural design and metaphysical essence.

Contemporary science offered Diderot a choice between preformation, a Lucretian theory accepted at times by La Mettrie, and epigenesis, which explained organic formation in terms of juxtaposition and contiguity. Diderot rejected preformation, and in support of epigenesis he developed the concept of molecular combinations endowed with specialized functions and organic unity. In *Rêve de d'Alembert,* Diderot employed the image of a swarm of bees in an attempt to bridge the gap between contiguity and continuity in the production of a whole that is qualitatively unique and different from the sum of its parts. He pointed out that although the swarm consists simply of numerous separate individuals in physical contact, it does, as a whole, possess the characteristic of purposeful, unified behavior that is associated with the individual organism. It is possible to mistake the swarm of thousands of bees for a single animal. The unity of the organism is derived from the life of the whole, and Diderot thus affirmed the continuity of the kingdoms and refuted the metaphysical principle of essences. A half century later the discovery of the organic cell and the principles of cell division confirmed his views.

Diderot found support for his theories in the embryological ideas that he had gathered from his reading, especially of Albrecht von Haller's *Elements of Physiology,* and from Dr. Bordeu, his friend and the protagonist in the conversations of *Rêve de d'Alembert.* In the conversation with d'Alembert, which gives rise to the dream, Diderot attempts briefly to trace d'Alembert from the parental "germs." He then describes how, under the influence of heat, the chicken develops within the egg. Excluding all animistic hypotheses, he declares that this development "overthrows all the schools of theology; … from inert matter, organized in a certain way and impregnated with other inert matter, and given heat and motion, there results the faculty of sensation, life, memory, consciousness, passion, and thought."

HEREDITY. Diderot's conviction of the importance of hereditary factors constitutes the main argument of his refutation of Claude-Adrien Helvétius's work *On the Mind,* in which education and law, purely environmental factors, were proposed exclusively as causes of the development of a moral society. Diderot agreed with Bordeu ("organs produce needs, and reciprocally, needs produce organs") on the Lamarckian principle of the inheritability of acquired characteristics. Moreover, he clearly stated his belief that the individual recapitulates the history of the race and that certain hereditary factors may crop up after many generations.

To explain how parental factors are inherited (cells and genes were as yet unknown), Diderot resorted to a hypothesis of organic development through a network or bundle of threads (or fibers or filaments), which strongly suggested the nervous system. Any interference with the fibers produced abnormalities, or "monsters." (He was one of the first to seek to understand the normal through the abnormal, both in embryology and psychology.) In his careful description, in *Rêve de d'Alembert,* of the embryological differentiation between the male and female sex organs, he was led to surmise that man is perhaps the "monster" of the woman, and vice versa. His theories clearly foreshadow not only the phenomena of recessive genes but also the fundamental role of chromosomes. One of his chief arguments against design in the universe was nature's prolific production of "monsters," most of which were too ill adapted to their environment to survive. Their elimination was the closest he came to the principle of natural selection.

MATTER AND THOUGHT

Diderot believed that once it is granted that sensitivity is a property of matter and that matter thereby develops increasing complexity and specialization, it then follows that thought can best be understood as a property of that highly complex and specified material organ, the brain. He accepted Bordeu's theory of the individual life of the various bodily organs. All were linked, however, through the nervous system to the central organ, which, depending upon circumstances and temperaments, exerted more or less control over them. Personal identity, the unified self, was thus assured by the nervous system, and the brain played the role of both organ and organist.

MEMORY. Self-awareness, however, depends entirely on the remembering function of the human brain. Quite characteristically, Diderot assigned a neural mechanism to Locke's theory of the association of ideas. In his investigations of the physical substrata of memory, he read all he could find on the anatomy of the brain and injuries to the brain and consulted doctors and specialists in brain surgery. A number of case histories were reported in *Rêve de d'Alembert*. In the preliminary conversation with d'Alembert, however, he used La Mettrie's metaphor of vibrating strings and harmonic intervals to explain the association of images and memory, the passage from sense perceptions to comparisons, reflection, judgment, and thought. Memory furnishes the continuity in time, the personal history that is fundamental to self-consciousness and personal identity. In Diderot's mind, memory was corporeal, and the self had only material reality. He thus attempted to give psychology a scientific, physiological basis, which was further developed in the nineteenth and twentieth centuries.

In the midst of notes taken mostly from his reading and published later as the *Éléments de physiologie*, Diderot included an eloquent passage in support of his theory: "I am inclined to believe that all we have seen, known, perceived, or heard—even the trees of a great forest ... all concerts we have ever heard—exists within us and unknown to us." He could still see in his waking hours the forests of Westphalia, and could review them when dreaming—as brilliantly colored as if they were in a painting. Moreover, "the sound of a voice, the presence of

an object ... and behold, an object recalled—more than that, a whole stretch of my past—and I am plunged again into pleasure, regret, or affliction."

DREAMS AND GENIUS. The concept of the greater or lesser control exerted by the central organ over the other organs of the body was applied by Diderot not only to dreams but also to the phenomenon of genius. In sleep, control is relaxed and anarchy reigns. A random recall in the central organ may then be referred to the subordinate organ, or the procedure may be reversed, from organ to brain. In dreams, random combinations may be formed and dragons created. Only personal past experience is available, however, for such imaginings. The one impossible dream is that the dreamer is someone else.

Applied to genius, the explanation of which was of great concern to Diderot and an important aspect of *Rameau's Nephew*, the concept of central control ran into difficulties. In the early *Pensées philosophiques*, in opposition to Blaise Pascal, he championed the strong emotions as the chief source of the good, the true, and the beautiful. Later, his acquaintance with David Garrick led him to write a paradox on the acting profession, in which he claimed that the great actor, with complete command of his emotions, makes his audience laugh or weep by coolly calculated gesture and intonation; he must register the emotions, but not feel them at the same time. In *Rêve de d'Alembert* he explained that dominating control by the center produced wise and good men but that genius was the result of the strongest emotions under almost complete control, a theory that could be illustrated by the horseman, Hippolytus, in firm command of the most spirited horses that Greece produced. In Diderot's hands, genius was not a mere talent produced, as Helvétius had claimed, by education and chance, but a psychophysiological phenomenon, and in that respect akin, when central control is lost, to madness.

ETHICS

The fundamental principles of Diderot's ethics may be found most readily in *Rêve de d'Alembert*. Will and liberty (free will) he described as senseless terms, abstractions that obscured the facts. The will of the waking man is the same as that of the dreamer: "the latest impulse of desire and aversion, the last result of all that one has been from birth to the actual moment." "There is only one cause ... and that is a physical cause." But Diderot clearly distinguished between fatalism and determinism. Man is not, like the lower animals, a prey to the bombardment of the senses. The self, the brain with its properties of memory and imagination, intervenes between the external stimulus and the act.

Diderot was tempted, but refrained from writing a treatise on ethics. Many critics have attributed this failure to the moral dilemma posed by his determinist convictions. It is more probably that he felt his ideas were too advanced for the age and society in which he lived. Moral problems were foremost in his mind throughout his career. A letter of 1756 stated clearly his deterministic beliefs. Heredity played a dominant role, for some, happily, are endowed with moral or socially acceptable propensities, while others, unfortunately, are not. Moral monsters must be eliminated, but in general, man is modifiable. *Rameau's Nephew* is, among other things, the story of the dilemmas that confront moral man in an immoral society, in which honesty is not necessarily the best policy.

Diderot's imaginary *Supplément au voyage de Bougainville* (1796) describes and extols the primitive customs of Tahiti. Unlike Rousseau's, Diderot's "primitivism" was not a plea for a return to a less civilized society. Not nature or natural law, but the fundamental laws of nature, were uppermost in Diderot's mind. The conventions of modern society, it seemed to him, unnecessarily restricted the basic biological needs of man. Before Sigmund Freud, he sensed the dangers of sexual repression, a theme developed in the final section of *Rêve de d'Alembert* and fundamental to his novel *La religieuse*. Celibacy, in his view, led too often to mental or sexual aberration. He ended his Tahitian tale, however, with the admonition that, though we should try to change bad, or "unnatural," laws, we must obey the laws that our society has imposed.

Diderot frankly admitted his enjoyment of sensual pleasures—books, women, pictures, friends, and toasting his toes before a fire. But in the preface of *Le père de famille*, addressed to the princess of Nassau, he declared that "he who prefers a voluptuous sensation to the conscience of a good act is a vile man." He felt certain that through education and knowledge we could recognize what was good, and that virtue, or beneficence, was the one and only path to happiness. There are intimations in his works of a belief that the good and wise man, in a corrupt society, should at times rise above a bad law, a theme illustrated in his last play, *Est-il bon? Est-il méchant?*

Toward the end of his life, in his praise of Seneca, he extolled the Stoic concept of virtue as its own reward. He summed up his natural, humanistic ethics in a brief pronouncement: "There is only one virtue, justice; one duty, to be happy; one corollary, neither to overesteem life nor fear death."

AESTHETICS

In the theory and practice of the arts dependent on the imagination—literature, music, and the fine arts—Diderot also introduced innovations. His approach to the theory of Beauty was through the perception of relationships and the arts of communication. An unusual perception of relationships, through analogy and associative memory, was the mark of the genius, whether scientist or poet. The artist first experiences an emotional or aesthetic stimulus strong enough to fire his imagination. A second moment of enthusiasm, which comes from the ability to communicate his vision through his special technique, sounds, colors, lines, or words, is essential, however.

His *Encyclopédie* article "Beau" (1751) gave evidence of a thorough acquaintance with French and English aestheticians. That same year he launched out on his own in his *Lettre sur les sourds et muets*. Here he discussed the importance of gesture and expression in communication. The great actor is one who paints in gestures what he expresses in words, just as the great poet paints in sounds and rhythms what he means in words. Likewise, the beauty of a painting depends on its inner rhythm and structure. The sublime in painting and poetry is derived from the emotions imparted through the harmonies of sound and color, the wedding of sense and sound. Poetry, he declared, is therefore essentially untranslatable.

ART AND MORALITY. A strong moralistic tone pervaded Diderot's aesthetic theories and criticism. The painter must have morals as well as perspective. The bourgeois drama, a genre that he originated and illustrated, though not very successfully, should compete with the law in persuading us to love virtue and hate vice.

There was more than a touch of sentimentality in the art criticisms of the *Salons*, which he wrote biennially from 1759 to 1781. For a period, the bourgeois pathos of Jean-Baptiste Greuze held a strong appeal for him. A notable connoisseur of the arts, he was not, however, fooled. He recognized the masterly compositions of François Boucher, but condemned his allegorical subjects and depiction of the loves of the gods. Pierre Teilhard de Chardin's use of color, he knew, was far superior to that of Greuze, though his subject matter was too often "ignoble." Yet Teilhard de Chardin taught him that painting was not, as the classical theorists long held, the imitation of beautiful nature. He stood in awed amazement before

Teilhard de Chardin's painting of the skate and called it magic.

CRITICISM. Diderot created modern art criticism as a literary art. The *Salons*, especially of 1765 and 1767, still make fascinating reading and contain the best of his literary criticism. That he was himself a great writer is now at last being generally recognized. First and foremost, he was a master of dialogue; written for the ear, his dialogues are artistic transpositions of reality. His dislike of abstractions made him an early champion of realism. He never ceased to admire Molière and Jean Racine—and William Shakespeare—but believed that the theater was destined to follow new paths. His romantic spirit was revealed by his advocacy of strong emotions and his streak of sentimentality. He therefore foreshadowed the romantic-realistic revolt against classicism, delayed in France until the nineteenth century by the political revolution.

Diderot's trinity was truth, goodness, and beauty. In his aesthetic order, first place was given to that which was both useful and agreeable; second, to the merely useful; and third, to the purely agreeable. Since the essence of the arts was not subject matter, but the perception and communication of relationships, he felt it was advantageous to add a moral subject, the useful, to technical beauty.

SOCIETY AND POLITICS

Diderot made his *Encyclopédie* a major weapon for upsetting the social and political institutions of the Old Regime. In the first volume his article "Autorité politique" boldly proclaimed, before Rousseau's *Contrat social*, that sovereignty resided in the people, who alone should determine how and to whom it should be delegated. There, too, appeared the first discussion of the "general will." In an often vain effort to evade censorship, he chose out-of-the-way places, sometimes seemingly harmless definitions of terms, to point out the danger that lay before both the state and the church unless they were strictly separated.

In his *Observations* on the instructions of Catherine II to her deputies in the recodification of Russian law, he was even more forthright: "The only true sovereign is the nation," he wrote; "there can be no true legislator except the people." He also chided Catherine for submitting political institutions to religious sanction: "Religion is a support that in the end almost always ruins the edifice." He did not hesitate to call her a tyrant and refuted her arguments in favor of benevolent despotism. Her suppression of his manuscript was so thorough that parts of it were coming to be known only in the twentieth century.

Rameau's Nephew was a sweeping satire of French eighteenth-century society, especially of the often ignorant and very wealthy general tax collectors, who, with their hordes of parasites, were a menace to the development of the arts, as well as powerful enemies of the *Encyclopédie*. In a dialogue with Diderot, the parasitic nephew of the great Jean-Philippe Rameau defended his debasement and moral corruption, quite shocking to his moralistic interlocutor, as the only means of satisfying the pangs of hunger in a thoroughly corrupt society. Throughout Diderot's works—in his dramas, his short stories and novels, in his art and literary criticism, as well as in his social and political theories—his sympathies were with the Third Estate.

Because he was forced to withhold his best and most forthright works for publication by future generations, the growth of Diderot's fame has been a very slow process. Rousseau declared that it would take two centuries for the realization that he was the great genius of his century. His first enthusiasts were also men of genius, Johann Wolfgang von Goethe, Honoré de Balzac, Charles-Pierre Baudelaire, and Victor Hugo.

It can hardly be a cause for wonder that Diderot is receiving special attention in Marxist societies and that many excellent editions and translations have come from Marxist presses. Yet it was to the scientist and philosopher in Friedrich Engels, rather than the social economist, that Diderot's work most greatly appealed. His philosophical determinism was in no sense economic determinism; his sturdy bourgeois qualities give small comfort to Marxist sociology; and his views of the importance of hereditary traits are in sharp opposition to behavioristic theory. He would seem to qualify most readily as a naturalistic humanist.

See also Alembert, Jean Le Rond d'; Atheism; Buffon, Georges-Louis Leclerc, Comte de; Clandestine Philosophical Literature in France; Condillac, Étienne Bonnot de; Darwin, Charles Robert; Deism; Descartes, René; Doubt; Empiricism; Encyclopédie; Engels, Friedrich; Enlightenment; Ethics, History of; Freud, Sigmund; Goethe, Johann Wolfgang von; Helvétius, Claude-Adrien; Holbach, Paul-Henri Thiry, Baron d'; La Mettrie, Julien Offray de; Lavoisier, Antoine; Leibniz, Gottfried Wilhelm; Locke, John; Lucretius; Marxist Philosophy; Materialism; Maupertuis, Pierre-Louis Moreau de; Pascal, Blaise; Rousseau, Jean-Jacques; Scientific Method; Seneca, Lucius Annaeus; Sensationalism; Stoicism; Teilhard de Chardin, Pierre; Toland, John; Voltaire, François-Marie Arouet de.

Bibliography

WORKS BY DIDEROT

Oeuvres complètes. 20 vols, edited by J. Assézat and M. Tourneux. Paris: Garnier, 1875–1877.

Oeuvres, edited by A. Billy. Paris, 1935. Essential works in one volume.

Correspondance, edited by G. Roth. Paris, 1955–.

Le rêve de d'Alembert, edited by Jean Varloot. Paris, 1962.

English Translations

Diderot's Early Philosophical Works. Translated and edited by Margaret Jourdain. Chicago and London: Open Court, 1916.

Dialogues. Translated and edited by Francis Birrell. New York: Brentano, 1927.

Diderot, Interpreter of Nature; Selected Writings. Translated and edited by Jean Stewart and Jonathan Kemp. London: Lawrence and Wishart, 1937. Best translations of *Rêve de d'Alembert,* etc.

Rameau's Nephew and Other Works. Translated by Jacques Barzun and Ralph H. Bowen. Garden City, NY: Doubleday, 1956.

Jacques the Fatalist and His Master. Translated by J. Robert Loy. New York: New York University Press, 1959 and 1961.

Selected Writings. Translated and edited by Lester G. Crocker. New York: Macmillan, 1966.

Diderot: Political Writings, edited by John Hope Mason and Robert Wokler. New York: Cambridge University Press, 1992.

WORKS ON DIDEROT

Anderson, Wilda. *Diderot's Dream.* Baltimore: Johns Hopkins University Press, 1990.

Blum, Carol. *Diderot: The Virtue of a Philosopher.* New York: Viking Press, 1974.

Bonneville, Douglas A. *Diderot's Vie de Seneque: A Swan Song Revised.* Gainesville: University of Florida Press, 1966.

Bremner, Geoffrey. *Order and Chance: The Pattern of Diderot's Thought.* Cambridge, U.K.: Cambridge University Press, 1983.

Cabeen, D. C., ed. *A Critical Bibliography of French Literature.* Vol. IV. Syracuse, NY: Syracuse University Press, 1951. Especially valuable for researchers.

Clark-Evans, Christine. "Charles de Brosses and Diderot: Eighteenth-Century Arguments concerning Primitive Language, Particular Natural Languages and a National Language." *History of European Ideas* 16 (1–3) (1993): 183–188.

Creech, James. *Diderot: Thresholds of Representation.* Columbus: Ohio State University Press, 1986.

Crocker, Lester G. "Diderot as Political Philosopher." *Revue Internationale de Philosophie* 38 (1984): 120–139.

Crocker, Lester G. *Diderot's Chaotic Order: Approach to Synthesis.* Princeton, NJ: Princeton University Press, 1974.

Crocker, Lester G. *The Embattled Philosopher.* East Lansing: Michigan State College Press, 1954. Good general introduction to Diderot's life and works.

Davis, Colin. "Backward, Forward, Homeward: Encounters in Ithaca with Kant and Diderot." In *Proximity: Emmanuel Levinas and the Eighteenth Century,* edited by Melvyn New. Lubbock: Texas Tech University Press, 2001.

Dynnik, M. A. "On the Esthetics of Diderot." *Soviet Studies in Philosophy* 3 (1964–1965): 48–53.

Edmiston, William F. *Diderot and the Family: A Conflict of Nature and Law.* Saratoga, NY: Anma Libri, 1985.

Eisenberg, Jose. "The Theater and Political Theory in Rousseau and Diderot." *Kriterion* 41 (101) (2000): 86–108.

Fellows, Otis E. et al., eds. *Diderot Studies.* Geneva: Librairie Droz, 1949–. Critical essays and monographs in English and French by contemporary scholars. Five volumes had been published as of 1965.

France, Peter. *Rhetoric and Truth in France: Descartes to Diderot.* London: Clarendon Press, 1972.

Holt, David K. "Denis Diderot and the Aesthetic Point of View." *Journal of Aesthetic Education* 34 (1) (2000): 19–25.

Ibrahim, Annie. "The Life Principle and the Doctrine of Living Being in Diderot." *Graduate Faculty Philosophy Journal* 22 (1) (2000): 107–122.

Lough, John. *Essays on the "Encyclopedie" of Diderot and d'Alembert.* London: Oxford University Press, 1968.

Luxembourg, Lilo K. *Francis Bacon and Denis Diderot, Philosophers of Science.* New York: Humanities Press, 1967.

Niklaus, Robert. "Denis Diderot: Search for an Unattainable Absolute of Truth." *Ultimate Reality and Meaning* 3 (1980): 23–49.

Pucci, Suzanne L. *Diderot and a Poetics of Science.* New York: Peter Lang, 1986.

Rey, Roselyne. "Diderot and the Medicine of the Mind." *Graduate Faculty Philosophy Journal* 22 (1) (2000): 149–159.

Richards, Joyce A. *Diderot's Dilemma: His Evaluation Regarding the Possibility of Moral Freedom in a Deterministic Universe.* New York: Exposition Press, 1972.

Schmidt, James. "The Fool's Truth: Diderot, Goethe, and Hegel." *Journal of the History of Ideas* 57 (4) (1996): 625–644.

Simon, Julia. *Mass Enlightenment: Critical Studies in Rousseau and Diderot.* Albany: State University of New York Press, 1995.

Strugnell, Anthony. *Diderot's Politics: A Study of the Evolution of Diderot's Political Thought after the Encyclopedie.* The Hague: Nijhoff, 1973.

Vasco, Gerhard M. *Diderot and Goethe: A Study in Science and Humanism.* Geneva: Slatkine, 1978.

Waldauer, Joseph L. *Society and the Freedom of the Creative Man in Diderot's Thought.* Geneva: Droz, 1964.

Wilson, Arthur M. *Diderot: The Testing Years (1713–1759).* New York: Oxford University Press, 1957. Best biography to date and best critical studies of early works. The first of two volumes.

Norman L. Torrey (1967)
Bibliography updated by Tamra Frei (2005)

DIKĒ

Dikē is the old Greek word for "law, justice." By the fourth century BCE it was largely replaced by its cognate *dikaiosynē,* Plato's cardinal virtue, justice.

In early Greece (Homer, Hesiod), *dikē* ranges in meaning from a specific claim by one party to a dispute, to a judgment or settlement, or to the personified force or goddess Justice/Law. In Homer's *Iliad*, the trial scene on Achilles's shield (18.497–508) depicts the elders (as judges) in a competition to see who can propose the straightest *dikē* (the best judgment/settlement). In Hesiod's *Works and Days* animals eat one another, but Zeus gave humans *dikē*—law, judicial process—which is far better (276–280), and *Dikē* sits beside her father Zeus and punishes those who corrupt the judicial process with crooked *dikē* (256–262).

The sixth-century lawgiver Solon promotes *dikē*—law-abiding conduct—as part of a general program of *eunomia* (good order, law and order). He also speaks of his legislation as providing a straight *dikē* (judicial process) for every Athenian. For the fifth-century thinker Heraclitus, *dikē* becomes a cosmic force of order and balance. Heraclitus's *dikē* is not static, however, but—as in a lawsuit—a balance of opposing forces, so that, as he says paradoxically, *dikē* is *eris* (strife).

Fifth-century tragedians regularly see *dikē* as a cosmic force, justice, largely in the sense of punishment or retribution. All the characters in Aeschylus's *Oresteia* claim to seek *dikē*—justice—primarily in the sense of punishment or revenge for previous wrongs, though in some passages the chorus suggest a larger sense of justice as cosmic and social order. Plato's *Protagoras* pictures the sophist Protagoras telling a story in which the gods give *dikē*, law or justice, together with *aidōs* (respect) to all humans; he concludes from this that *dikē* is necessary for the survival of human society.

Through the fifth century, *dikē* in all its meanings—from judicial process to cosmic force—remains something external to human beings. Not until the fourth century does Plato make justice a personal virtue of individuals, and then it is no longer *dikē* but *dikaiosynē* (see especially *Republic*, Book IV).

See also Justice; Plato.

Bibliography

Gagarin, Michael. "*Dikē* in the *Works and Days*." *Classical Philology* 68 (1973): 81–94. Argues that in the beginning meanings of *dikē* are restricted to the realm of law and the legal process.

Havelock, Eric A. *The Greek Concept of Justice.* Cambridge, MA: Harvard University Press, 1978. Argues that in a preliterate, oral culture, justice is primarily procedure.

Lloyd-Jones, Hugh. *The Justice of Zeus.* 2nd ed. Berkeley: University of California Press, 1983. Broad discussion of divine justice—often seen as equivalent to *dikē*—in Greek literature.

The works of Hesiod, including his poem *Works and Days*, are available in the Penguin series and several other translations.

Michael Gagarin (2005)

DILTHEY, WILHELM
(1833–1911)

The German philosopher and historian Wilhelm Dilthey was born in Biebrich on the Rhine, the son of the preacher to the Duke of Nassau. He studied theology and philosophy in Heidelberg and Berlin and combined both of these interests in his early work on the ethical and hermeneutical writings of Friedrich Schleiermacher. Dilthey's first major publication, a volume on the life of Schleiermacher, appeared in 1870 while he was teaching in Kiel. In 1871, Dilthey received a professorship in Breslau (now Wrocklaw, Poland). It was around this time that he met Count Yorck of Wartenburg, and their friendship produced an intellectual correspondence about the nature of life and the meaning of history that has inspired thinkers such as Martin Heidegger and Hans-Georg Gadamer. In 1882, Dilthey was called back to Berlin to fill the chair that George Wilhelm Friedrich Hegel had once held. The University of Berlin and the Prussian Academy would be the locus of his world for almost thirty years, until his death in 1911. This is the period in which he published most of his writings about the human sciences (*Geisteswissenschaften*), a covering term for both the humanities and social sciences. These writings consider how the human sciences contribute to the understanding of life and history.

CRITIQUE OF HISTORICAL REASON

Dilthey saw his overall project as a Critique of Historical Reason examining the conditions that make possible the respective cognitive results of the natural and the human sciences. Although influenced by both Immanuel Kant and Hegel, he rejected the transcendental and formal limits of the former and the metaphysical absolutes of the latter. His task was to translate the insights of idealism into a more open empirical approach to what it means to experience reality.

Although the natural sciences are about nature and the human sciences about history, this does not justify hypostatizing history as a spiritual domain separate from nature. The spiritual life of human beings is conditioned—but not determined by—natural processes. Even when human beings set themselves free purposes, the realization of these purposes requires that the laws of nature be obeyed. In Book 1 of his *Introduction to the Human Sciences* (1883), Dilthey grants the human sciences a relative cognitive independence from the natural sciences. Yet he assigns the human sciences a greater reflective scope in that they express more aspects of human experience. They not only ascertain what is—as do the natural sciences—but also make value judgments, establish goals, and prescribe rules.

For the human sciences, theory is always framed by practical considerations instigated by historical life. Therefore, philosophical reflection about their conditions of possibility makes it necessary to regress behind the logical and epistemological foundations of the natural sciences to establish the more encompassing life-nexus of all human experience. This reflective turn initiated in Book 2 of the *Introduction to the Human Sciences* and worked out in the posthumously published drafts for Book 4, shows the human sciences to have an important advantage over the natural sciences in that they preserve some of the intuitive access to the reality of experience as it is lived. The natural sciences merely construct a phenomenal or ideal world that abstracts from the overall nexus of life so that human beings stand as impartial intellectual observers of this abstractly represented nature.

By contrast, the world that is formed by the human sciences is the historical-social reality in which human beings participate. It is a fuller world that is accessible not merely as conceptually mediated cognition (*Erkenntnis*), but also as immediate knowledge (*Wissen*) found in lived experience. Conceptual cognition is representational and objectifying. Lived experience provides a prerepresentational self-presence that involves a direct knowing. Any state of consciousness is implicitly present to itself in what Dilthey calls "reflexive awareness" (*Innewerden*). This does not require an explicit consciousness of being conscious—such an act of self-consciousness would be more than reflexive, namely, reflective. At the basic level of reflexive awareness there is not yet a self as an object of reflection.

According to Dilthey, there is no self underlying consciousness. Instead, the self arises out of consciousness as the correlate of the world. Within the nexus of consciousness as a function of life, reflection can differentiate between facts of inner perception and facts of outer perception, thereby producing a distinction between self and world. This world is not a product of an inference, but is felt primarily through resistance to the practical impulses of the will. Rather than grounding the objectivity of the

world on a transcendental "I think," Dilthey claims that its reality is given in the reflexive awareness of the relation between efficacy and resistance involved in willing. Through this expanded reflexive awareness, the life-nexus in which the self participates discloses things and other selves that can resist its will. These modes of reflexive awareness are as basic to Dilthey's theory of hermeneutical understanding (*Verstehen*) as the transcendental and empirical ego were to Kant's theory of intellectual understanding (*Verstand*). Whereas Kant sought an explanative mode of understanding for natural phenomena by deriving them from the most general laws of scientific cognition, Dilthey seeks to understand the meaning of things in terms of their own inherent context. Hermeneutical understanding provides a kind of situated understanding that receives its bearings from the reflexive awareness of lived or prescientific experience.

DESCRIPTION AND STRUCTURAL UNDERSTANDING

In 1894, Dilthey published another important work, the *Ideas for a Descriptive and Analytic Psychology* (Dilthey 1977). Here he works out the implications of his philosophical views about lived experience for psychology as a human science. Hitherto, psychology had been treated as a kind of natural science that synthetically constructs mental phenomena from atomistic elements such as sense-data by using hypothetical laws of association. This assumes that psychic life comes in discrete states that must be connected. Dilthey argues, however, that psychic life presents itself as a continuum in which states are already connected. It is the task of psychology to attempt to describe this general nexus of psychic life and to analyze specific states on its basis.

Dilthey's descriptive and analytic psychology has three main parts. The first delineates the general structural systems of consciousness that can be differentiated at the levels of cognition, feeling, and volition. The cognitive system relates the acts of perception, imagination, and memory on the basis of which we conceptually represent the world. The felt and instinctual aspects of consciousness can be related to form a distinct structural system whereby we coordinate the value of things. A volitional structural system functions to link and rank the purposes we set. A cross-sectional analysis of any lived experience will manifest aspects of each of these three functional structures. Indeed, the structural systems manifest a degree of interdependence belying the traditional hierarchical assumption that the cognitive level is fundamental and that feeling and willing merely respond to what has been perceived. Thus we do not perceive impressions of sense unless there is a felt interest in them and the will is stirred enough to attend to them.

The second main part of psychology as a human science traces the development of psychic life. It examines how psychic structures are defined and articulated over time. Here Dilthey stresses the importance of treating each phase in the teleological development of a psychic life-course as having its own inherent worth. Every phase has its immanent purposiveness and is to be treated as a kind of epoch. Although an epochal phase may contribute to its successor, it should never be treated as a mere means. The values of childhood, for example, should never be sacrificed for the goals of adulthood.

The third, concluding part of Dilthey's descriptive and analytic psychology integrates these structural and developmental approaches by showing how an acquired psychic nexus is gradually produced and informs future experiences. The acquired psychic nexus becomes the individualized framework according to which each self tends to specify its own experiences. It provides a historicized apperceptive mass that influences what will be perceived. It is like an implicit worldview that can regulate further experiences and actions.

Dilthey initially formulated his conception of the acquired psychic nexus as part of an effort to understand artistic creativity. In his 1887 essay "The Imagination of the Poet: Elements for a Poetics" (Dilthey 1985), Dilthey argues that what distinguishes artists from other human beings is the capacity to articulate their acquired psychic nexus in typical ways. In ordinary life, our experience and behavior reflect contingent local conditions as well as our acquired psychic nexus. Playwrights and novelists can establish fictional contexts that limit the extent to which characters will be distracted by local contingencies. By more adequately reflecting the acquired psychic nexus of their creators, the actions of fictional characters can also address more general aspects of life. The literary imagination produces typical situations and characters that help focus the meaning of human existence. Individuals manifest creativity when the perspective that informs their acquired psychic nexus becomes more than regulative, but constitutively typical.

The self-givenness of reflexive awareness and the self-presence of lived experience provide an implicit kind of understanding of life that psychological description and literary expression can make explicit. The inherent connectedness of consciousness renders it unnecessary to introduce hypothetical explanative links into the foundation of psychology. On this basis, Dilthey claims that the natural sciences are mainly about causal explanation and the human sciences about description and structural understanding. But this contrast is not absolute. Sometimes natural sciences must be content with description and interpretation, and sometimes human sciences cannot rely on general descriptions to account for significant details and must appeal to hypotheses. The difference is that the natural sciences tend to begin with explanative hypotheses, whereas the human sciences may end up with explanative hypotheses.

HERMENEUTICS

Unlike the natural sciences, the human sciences do not abstract from ordinary life, but analyze it. Analysis is compatible with understanding because, unlike abstraction, it need not isolate things from their overall context. The hermeneutical task of analysis is to enable us to recognize the whole in its parts and the parts in the whole. There is always this circularity in coordinating parts and wholes when reading a text. Hermeneutics as a human science reflects on what it means to apply the art of exegesis from texts to the experience of life in general.

The essay "The Rise of Hermeneutics," published in 1900 (Dilthey 1996), represents an important phase in Dilthey's development. Here he begins to sketch out a position that would define his final work. While he does not abandon the project of describing and analyzing lived experience, he came to view description and analysis as limited in their ability to capture the full meaning of life. The inner connectedness of our own experiences may provide a kind of self-understoodness or self-evidentness (*Selbstverständlichkeit*), but we do not achieve real self-understanding (*Selbstverständnis*) until we have manifested ourselves objectively. To truly understand ourselves is to be able to see ourselves as others see us.

One of the most revealing ways in which we manifest ourselves is through linguistic expression and communication. But Dilthey defines hermeneutics as the theory of interpreting *all* human manifestations, including actions that are not intended to communicate. The range of objectifications needing interpretation is broad. It includes impersonal theoretical judgments, abstract mathematical formulas, concrete poetic expressions of lived experience, personal correspondence, journal entries, works of art, historical monuments and archives, and political deeds and their aftereffects. They are important because only that which is publicly accessible and has been objectified in a common medium can produce determinate meaning.

The work that best articulates this hermeneutical approach to the human sciences is *The Formation of the Historical World in the Human Sciences* (1910). This most mature formulation of Dilthey's Critique of Historical Reason revisits many of the themes of the *Introduction to the Human Sciences*. The human sciences form the historical world, not by producing it, but by giving it a multifaceted discursive shape. Determinate meaning will never be found by confronting the course of history monolithically. The human sciences can give a cognitive form to various strands of history that we knowingly participate in. They allow use to analyze the overall stream of history and direct it, as it were, into a variety of structural systems in which selected currents can be examined for specific interacting forces.

Some of these historical structures had already been identified in the *Introduction to the Human Sciences* as cultural and social organizational systems. Cultural systems were conceived as purposive systems that bring individuals together to achieve certain voluntary goals. These purposive systems are not limited to the goals of high culture—the sciences, the arts, and religion—for they also include economic and social cooperation. Dilthey distinguished these cultural systems from institutional structures which make up the external organization of society. Institutions such as families, tribes, and nation-states are also interactive, but not primarily voluntary. We do not choose our parental family but are born into it. One of the advances of *The Formation of the Historical World* is that all these historical structures are no longer subsumed under the concept of "purposive system." Dilthey introduces the covering term "productive system" (*Wirkungszusammenhang*) to capture the ways in which the forces of historical life can become structurally organized. The efficacy of history is to be understood in terms of productivity before any causal or teleological account is given. The carriers of history, whether they be individuals, cultures, institutions, or communities, can all be considered as productive systems capable of exerting influence, and in some cases, realizing purposes. Each productive system of history should be approached as being centered in itself.

Individuals too are productive systems when they appropriate new impressions into their acquired psychic nexus: They cognize the present on the basis of past evaluations and future goals. The productivity of the psychic nexus lies in the ways the cognitive, evaluative, and volitional aspects of experience interact. As productive systems, individuals are centered in themselves, but far from self-sufficient. They are also dependent on other more inclusive productive systems. In the *Introduction to the Human Sciences*, Dilthey was unwilling to conceive these larger systems as subjects or carriers of history. In *The Formation of the Historical World* he qualifies his opposition to transpersonal subjects by treating them as logical rather than real subjects—they are now considered co-carriers of history. Although individuals cooperate in terms of cultural systems and other encompassing productive systems, they never engage more than a part of themselves to any of such systems and therefore cannot be defined by them. Yet the engagement can become so intensive that an individual can put his or her stamp on its mode of productivity. As a consequence, more than the agreed-upon functions of a cultural system will be achieved. For instance, in relation to the classical conventions established by Joseph Haydn (1732–1809) and Wolfgang Amadeus Mozart (1756–1791), a composer such as Ludwig van Beethoven (1770–1827) charts a new course. As a consequence, more than the expected purposes of the system will be achieved. In addition to accommodating new purposes, productive systems provide a meaning framework for expressing a variety of human values.

Dilthey states that he is not offering a philosophy of history that would establish a final purpose of human history. This is because he does not find any justification for the belief that there is a law of overall historical development. Yet there is good reason to think that there can be lawlike development within specific productive systems. Dilthey's theory of history is meant to provide the critical tools to articulate history into the productive systems that can provide an orderly understanding of history. Today, Dilthey's approach would be considered a philosophy of history of the critical rather than of the more traditional speculative kind.

THE CATEGORIES OF THE HUMAN SCIENCES

Whereas Kant's *Critique of Pure Reason* defined the categories or fundamental concepts of the natural sciences, Dilthey set out to explicate the categories of the human sciences. He distinguishes between formal and real categories. Formal categories relate to all experience, whether it be prescientific or scientific. They arise from elementary operations of thought such as comparing, differentiating, and relating that bring out what is inherent in experience. The formal categories of unity and plurality, identity and difference are shared by the natural and human sciences.

Real categories organize the content of experience more concretely. The natural and human sciences both organize their subject matter in terms of formal part-whole relations and locate them in space and time. In temporal location we can see a transition from the formal to the real. For the natural sciences, time is an infinite form that unfolds uniformly. For the human sciences, time is a finite structure that projects the future based on what is remembered from the past. The time of the human sciences is a lived reality and can be articulated in ways that allow us to understand historical development and the productive force of cultural systems.

Causality is a real category of the natural sciences. While Dilthey does not rule out its applicability to the events that are recounted in human history, he makes it clear that for the understanding of history, the Aristotelian categories "of agency and suffering, of action and reaction" are more appropriate (Dilthey 2002, p. 219). They express how human beings experience the productive force of the historical world and allow them to conceive purposiveness as an agency that stems from within and causality as a force coming from without.

Among the real categories that are distinctive for the human sciences, the three most important are value, purpose, and meaning. From the perspective of value, life is judged as a multiplicity of prized moments that can be juxtaposed. From the perspective of purpose, everything in a life-course tends to be subordinated to some future moment. According to Dilthey, the category of meaning can overcome the juxtaposition and subordination of value and purpose. Meaning articulates the connectedness of life on the basis of the relation between past and present. It is the main category of historical thought and is assigned to memory.

We resort to memory when we orient our experience to the past. On the private level, Dilthey had articulated meaning in terms of the workings of the acquired psychic nexus. At the public level, Dilthey now explicates meaning in terms of Hegel's concept of "objective spirit." Objective spirit stands for what the spirit of the past has left behind in the present and has preserved in objective form. It is the most basic framework for orienting us to the past. Objective spirit is the tradition-based sphere of commonality in which we grow up. The language we inherit, the conventions adopted, and the customs learned are all aspects of objective spirit that shape our childhood experiences. "Everything in which spirit has objectified itself contains something that is common to the I and the Thou. Every square planted with trees, every room in which chairs are arranged, is understandable to

us from childhood because human tendencies to set goals, produce order and define values in common have assigned [them] a place…" (Dilthey 2002, p. 229).

Objective spirit represents the initial framework of reference for elementary understanding, not unlike the way a dictionary serves as our first resource when a word in a sentence is not understood. Objective spirit is the common historical medium by which we orient elementary understanding. But when problems arise in understanding that a common reference cannot resolve, we must resort to what Dilthey calls "higher understanding." Higher understanding attempts to account for cases when the normal convergence between an expression and the meaning it expresses is lacking. Instead of merely appealing to objective spirit as the common background for locating meaning, higher understanding can consider more specialized contexts to determine meaning. Thus, if an unclear sentence is uttered by an economist we can consult professional handbooks. Similarly, social circumstances, industrial conditions, and market forces can be considered when some economic claim is not fully intelligible.

Although higher understanding often concentrates on more restricted productive systems as focal contexts, it will at the same time seek to extract more general results. The universality aimed at by higher understanding may be in the form of an inductive generalization or it may be that of a larger context. Thus the attempt to understand a line of poetry in relation to the poem as a whole is also an act of higher understanding. Here again the attempt is to move from common meaning to universal significance. The important breakthrough for Dilthey is that he no longer requires the understanding of human products to be related back to the psyches of their producers. Although the possibility of referring a work of art to its creator is not ruled out, it is far from being the primary source of its understanding. Indeed, a great work of art can take on a life of its own and can become itself a productive nexus generating an ever deeper meaning over time, as Gadamer has also argued.

Historical understanding, however, requires the move from universality back to individuality. It is appropriate for higher understanding to turn into what Dilthey calls a "re-experiencing," where individual contributions to the productivity of life do count. To re-experience meaning is not to reproduce the state of mind of an author, but to understand an author better than he understood himself. This is achieved by the contextualizing and structural explication of life-situations made possible by the human sciences.

REFLECTION ON LIFE

It is never enough to consider an individual life by itself. As Dilthey writes: "The limit of biography lies in the fact that general movements find their point of transition in individuals" (Dilthey 2002, p. 269). Drawing on his own struggles to complete a second volume of the life of Schleiermacher, Dilthey concludes that a biographer cannot fulfill his task without also having broached universal questions about life and history. Notwithstanding the problematic status of biography, Dilthey considers autobiography an especially instructive mode of history because here "the work of historical narrative is already half done by life itself" (Dilthey 2002, p. 222). The narrative produced is never a simple copy of an actual life-course, but a retrospective judgment that depends on the way an individual reflects on his or her life. Here history is not just a human science but has reflective philosophical import.

In the later writings Dilthey often speaks of anthropological reflection as crucial for obtaining a unity of perspective on life. The sciences are radically pluralistic and cannot provide a comprehensive outlook or worldview (*Weltanschauung*). A worldview is not merely a cognitive picture of the world. It goes deeper in expressing a specific stance (*Stellung*) toward concrete life-concerns (*Lebensbezüge*) as well as to life as a whole. An individual's stance toward life can develop into a reflective worldview on the basis of certain more general moods (*Stimmungen*). These moods are more than states of mind; they orient us to the world in ways that anticipate what Heidegger says about moods as modes of attunement in *Being and Time*.

Worldviews have been articulated in literary, religious, and philosophical works. Philosophers have conceptualized worldviews metaphysically. Dilthey analyzes three main types of such metaphysical formulations: naturalism, the idealism of freedom, and objective idealism. Naturalism as found in Democritus, Thomas Hobbes, and others reduces everything to what can be cognized and is pluralistic in structure; the idealism of freedom as found in Plato, Kant, and others insists on the irreducibility of the will and is dualistic; objective idealism as found in Heraclitus, Gottfried Wilhelm Leibniz, and Hegel affirms reality as the embodiment of a harmonious set of values and is monistic. The three types of metaphysical worldviews are incommensurable in that each is reductive in some way. No metaphysical formulation can have more than relative success. But this conclusion does not make Dilthey a relativist, for he rejects all metaphysics as speculative. Metaphysical systems attempt to arrive at universal determinations that transcend experience. All that is humanly possible is to probe reality on the basis of life-experience and to seek a more limited reflective universality.

The influence of Dilthey's thought and writings is manifold. Husserl considered Dilthey's *Ideas for a Descriptive and Analytic Psychology* (Dilthey 1977) a genial anticipation of his own phenomenological psychology and credits a meeting with Dilthey as leading to his interest in questions concerning understanding in the human sciences. Heidegger's lecture courses from 1919 through 1925 are filled with declarations of Dilthey's importance for understanding history and make extensive use of such Diltheyan terms as "life-nexus" and "life-concern." Max Weber applies Dilthey's distinction between explanation and understanding to sociology and extends Dilthey's reflections on typicality to his theory of ideal types. Herbert Marcuse's early work on Hegel is indebted to Dilthey's highly original approach to Hegel in his *Jugendgeschichte Hegels*. Georg Lukács's Marxist counterpart to this is *Der junge Hegel*.

Dilthey's work continues to play a significant role in the development of hermeneutics. While critical of the Schleiermacher-Dilthey tradition, Gadamer's hermeneutics represents an extension of Dilthey's effort to relate interpretation to the productivity and efficacy (*Wirkung*) of history. In France, the underlying influence of Dilthey's views on understanding and objective spirit can be seen in the writings of Raymond Aron, Jean-Paul Sartre, Lucien Goldmann, and Paul Ricoeur. In Spain, Ortega y Gasset had called Dilthey the most important philosopher of the second half of the nineteenth century, with the result that Dilthey was widely translated into Spanish before any other language. Now extensive translations into English, French, Italian, Chinese, Japanese, and Russian are also becoming available.

See also Gadamer, Hans-Georg; Hermeneutics; Philosophy of History.

Bibliography

WORKS BY DILTHEY

Briefwechsel zwischen Wilhelm Dilthey und dem Grafen Paul Yorck von Wartenburg, 1877–1897. Halle (Saale), Germany: M. Niemeyer, 1922. Famous correspondence about the nature of life and history.

Descriptive Psychology and Historical Understanding. Translated by Richard M. Zaner and Kenneth L. Heiges, with an introduction by Rudolf A. Makkreel. The Hague: Martinus Nijhof, 1977.

Dilthey's Philosophy of Existence. Translated by William Kluback and Martin Weinbaum. New York: Bookman Associates, 1957. Mainly about the theory of worldviews.

Das Erlebnis und die Dichtung: Lessing, Goethe, Novalis, Hölderlin. Leipzig, Germany: Teubner, 1922. Influential literary essays, two of which are translated in *Poetry and Experience.*

Essence of Philosophy. Translated by Steven A. Emery and William T. Emery. Chapel Hill: University of North Carolina Press, 1954.

Gesammelte Schriften, edited by Karlfried Gründer and Frithjof Rodi. 24 vols. Göttingen, Germany: Vandenhoeck & Ruprecht, 1914–2004.

Selected Works, edited by Rudolf A. Makkreel and Frithjof Rodi. Vol. 1, *Introduction to the Human Sciences* (1989). Vol. 3, *The Formation of the Historical World in the Human Sciences* (2002). Vol. 4, *Hermeneutics and the Study of History* (1996). Vol. 5, *Poetry and Experience* (1985). Princeton, NJ: Princeton University Press.

WORKS ON DILTHEY

de Mul, Jos. *The Tragedy of Finitude: Dilthey's Hermeneutics of Life.* Translated by Tony Burrett. New Haven, CT: Yale University Press, 2004. A reconstruction of Dilthey's ontology of life, highlighting the interpretive character of human existence, contingency, and narrativity.

Ermarth, Michael. *Wilhelm Dilthey: The Critique of Historical Reason.* Chicago: University of Chicago Press, 1978. A comprehensive account of Dilthey's thought with a good historical background.

Makkreel, Rudolf A. *Dilthey: Philosopher of the Human Studies.* Princeton, NJ: Princeton University Press, 1975, 1992. A developmental examination of Dilthey's philosophy that focuses on its relation to Kant's first and third Critiques and highlights the role of reflection and judgment in historical understanding.

Makkreel, Rudolf A., and John D. Scanlon, eds. *Dilthey and Phenomenology.* Washington, DC: Center for Advanced Research in Phenomenology and University Press of America, 1987. Exploration of Dilthey's relation to phenomenology by ten international scholars.

Owensby, Jacob. *Dilthey and the Narrative of History.* Ithaca, NY: Cornell University Press, 1994. A topical study focusing on Books 4–6 of the *Introduction to the Human Sciences.*

Revue Internationale de Philosophie 57 (4) (2003). Issue featuring a collection of essays edited by Rudolf Makkreel, including essays by Jean Grondin, Hans Ineichen, Matthias Jung, Makkreel, Sylvie Mesure, Jos de Mul, Tom Rockmore, and Frithjof Rodi.

Rodi, Frithjof, ed. *Dilthey-Jahrbuch für Philosophie und Geschichte der Geisteswissenschaften.* Vandenhoeck & Ruprecht, 1983–2000. Many volumes have special themes such as the relation between Dilthey and the early Heidegger.

Rodi, Frithjof, and Hans-Ulrich Lessing, eds. *Materialien zur Philosophie Wilhelm Diltheys.* Frankfurt am Main: Suhrkamp, 1984. A collection of classical essays on Dilthey by such thinkers as Scheler, Landgrebe, Bollnow, Plessner, Marcuse, Misch, Habermas, and Gadamer.

Rodi, Frithjof. *Das strukturierte Ganze: Studien zum Werk von Wilhelm Dilthey.* Göttingen, Germany: Hubert & Co., 2003.

A series of essays stressing the structured nature of life and experience, and the importance of articulation and expression for Dilthey.

Rudolf A. Makkreel (2005)

DINGLER, HUGO
(1881–1954)

Hugo Dingler, the German philosopher of science, was the most important representative of Continental operationism, as distinguished from the operationalism of the American physicist P. W. Bridgman. Dingler was also a main contributor to *Grundlagenforschung* (research on the foundations of the exact sciences). After studying under such teachers as David Hilbert, Edmund Husserl, Felix Klein, Hermann Minkowski, Wilhelm Röntgen, and Woldemar Voigt at the universities of Erlangen, Munich, and Göttingen, Dingler received a Ph.D. in mathematics, physics, and astronomy in 1906 and became *Privatdozent* in 1912. He was appointed professor at the University of Munich in 1920 and at the Technische Hochschule in Darmstadt in 1932. In 1934 he was dismissed on charges of philosemitism. He later resumed teaching but soon rebelled again against the political situation, and eventually he was put under the continuous watch of a Gestapo agent "who unfortunately"—as Dingler told the present writer—"was not gifted for philosophy and did not profit from my compulsory daily lessons." Such difficulties in the German political situation during Dingler's life contributed to the lack of awareness of his work, despite his some twenty books and seventy essays in exceptionally clear German. Perhaps a more decisive factor was Dingler's independence of all the main schools and trends in contemporary philosophy of science—positivism and empiricism, Neo-Kantianism, phenomenology, intuitionism, and formalism.

From the juvenile *Grundlinien einer Kritik und exakten Theorie der Wissenschaften, insbesondere der mathematischen* (Essentials of a critique and rigorous theory of the sciences, especially of the mathematical ones; Munich, 1907) to the posthumous *Die Ergreifung des Wirklichen* (The grasping of reality; Munich, 1955), Dingler's main concern was to give a new answer to the Kantian question "How is exact science possible?" He regarded arithmetic, analysis, geometry, and mechanics as the exact sciences par excellence; he called them "mental" (*geistige*), meaning that they cannot be derived from experience and must be synthesized operationally from a few univocal ideas used as "building stones" (*Bausteine*). In this way scientific inquiry was to be made continuous with every-day life and viewed in terms of practical activity. The operational reconstruction of the foundations of science was to abolish the field of foundations as an independent territory open to philosophical disagreement or mystification. Dingler came to consider the given itself, as expressed in protocol, or basic, sentences, as a highly complicated kind of result.

To prevent any residues of previous theories from entering into the operational reconstruction, we must start from a "zero situation" in which we suppose only that the world is "simply there" and that we can operate on it. This is a methodological principle, not a metaphysical denial of reality: it is a voluntary suspension of rational processes which can be brought about at any moment. After 1907, under Husserl's influence, Dingler labeled the zero situation "the standpoint of freedom from presuppositions." In 1942 he described it as *das Unberührte,* the intact or untouched—"that which has not yet been operated upon."

The first univocal step out of the zero situation consists in entertaining an idea in which the sheer relation of difference (with equality and similarity as its special cases) is present, and is applied (*anwendet*) only once, as in the idea "something distinct without further specification," that is, the idea of an entity as distinguished from all the rest, as standing out from a background. This idea is not the description of anything existing in the world but rather is the first requirement for any such description. All we can say about it is that it is present and limited; we can then specify it as constant or variable, and in either case we can also give special attention to its limits. In this way we reach a purely qualitative fourfold scheme which precedes the concepts of number, space, and time. To this scheme correspond four rules of operation, which afford the starting points of the exact sciences: (1) something distinct without further specification, and constant, for arithmetic; (2) the same, but variable, for analysis (more generally for the doctrine of time and variables); (3) the same, but constant, considered with respect to its limits, for geometry; and (4) the same, but variable, considered with respect to its limits, for kinematics and mechanics.

By means of complications of this basic scheme Dingler was able to operationally derive and prove the axioms of the exact sciences and to construct their whole fabric. This painstaking and original construction is to be found chiefly in *Philosophie der Logik und Arithmetik* (1931), *Die Grundlagen der Geometrie* (1933), *Die Methode der*

Physik (1938), and *Lehrbuch der exakten Naturwissenschaften* (1944).

See also Bridgman, Percy William; Continental Philosophy; Hilbert, David; Husserl, Edmund; Operationalism; Philosophy of Science.

Bibliography

WORKS BY DINGLER

Works on "Grundlagenforschung"
Philosophie der Logik und Arithmetik. Munich, 1931.
Geschichte der Naturphilosophie. Berlin, 1932. A history of the development of the idea of *Grundlagenforschung* in experimental science.
Die Grundlagen der Geometrie. Stuttgart, 1933.
Die Methode der Physik. Munich, 1938.
Lehrbuch der exacten Naturwissenschaften. Berlin, 1944. Only thirty copies printed. Parts reprinted with Italian translation and a commentary by Enrico Albani in *Methodos* 7 (1955): 277–287, and 8 (1956): 29–30, 122–137, 191–199.

Other Works
Metaphysik als Wissenschaft und der Primat der Philosophie. Munich, 1926.
Das System. Munich, 1933.
Das Handeln im Sinne des höchsten Zieles. Munich, 1935.
Von der Tierseele zur Menschenseele. Leipzig, 1941.
Grundriss der methodischen Philosophie. Füssen, 1949. A crystal-clear summary of Dingler's main views, but of lower technical quality than his main treatises.

Essays
"Methodik statt Erkenntnistheorie und Wissenschaftslehre." *Kant-Studien* 41 (1936): 346–379.
"Über die letzte Wurzel der exakten Naturwissenschaften." *Zeitschrift für die gesamte Naturwissenschaft* 8 (1942): 49–70.
"Das Unberührte. Die Definition des unmittelbar Gegebenen." *Zeitschrift für die gesamte Naturwissenschaft* 8 (1942): 209–224.
"Die philosophische Begründung des Deszendenztheorie." In *Die Evolution der Organismen,* edited by Gerhard Hebener. Jena, Germany, 1943.

WORKS ON DINGLER

Benini, Giorgio. *I concetti fondamentali della filosofia metodica di Hugo Dingler.* Unpublished dissertation, Catholic University of the Sacred Heart, Milan, 1953.
Ceccato, Silvio. "Contra Dingler, pro Dingler." *Methodos* 4 (1952): 223–265, with English translation 266–290 and reply by Dingler, 291–296, translated into English 297–299.
Kramps, Wilhelm. *Die Philosophie Hugo Dinglers.* Munich, 1955. The main study.
Kramps, Wilhelm, ed. *Hugo Dingler Gedenkbuch zum 75. Geburtstag.* Munich: Eidos, 1956. Contains 14 essays by various authors and a bibliography.
Sandborn, Herbert. "Dingler's Methodical Philosophy." *Methodos* 4 (1952): 191–220.

Ferruccio Rossi-Landi (1967)

DIODORUS CRONUS
(b. 4th century BCE)

Diodorus Cronus was born in Iasus, a port town in Caria (a region in the southwestern part of Asia Minor). He inherited his nickname 'Cronus' (old fogy) from his teacher Apollonius. All else that is known about his life must be inferred from anecdotal evidence, connecting him to Athens, where Zeno of Citium studied dialectic with him (cf. Diogenes Laertius 7.25), and to Alexandria, where he is acquainted with the physician Herophilus (cf. Sextus Empiricus, *Pyrrh. Hypotyp.* 2. 245) and where Callimachus mentions him in one of his *Epigrams* (cf. Diogenes Laertius 2.111) suggesting that Diodorus was known in the town. He may have died in Alexandria, some time after 290 BCE.

Since our sources attribute no writings to him, he probably left nothing written. Yet the reports on him show that he was an extremely influential figure in the generation that saw the founding of the Hellenistic schools of philosophy. He belonged to a philosophical sect known as the Dialecticians; these Dialecticianswere a school distinct from the Megarians. The name Dialecticians was not, as assumed in the older literature, another name for the Megarians (Sedley 1977). In physics, Diodorus was an atomist; he is said to have called atoms "partless" (Sextus Empiricus, *Adv. Math.* 9.363). One consequence of his atomism is that there are, according to him, no objects that move, only objects that have moved (Sextus Empiricus, *Adv. Math.* 9.363).

Diodorus's greatest impact was in the field of logic where, together with his pupil Philo the Dialectician, he seems to have laid the foundations of propositional logic. With Philo, he engaged in a controversy about the truthcriteria for the conditional; Philo favored a truth-functional analysis of the conditional, claiming that the conditional is true if and only if it is not the case that its antecedent is true and its consequent false (cf. Sextus Empiricus, *Adv. Math.* 8.113–114), Diodorus gave a different account: According to him, a conditional is true if and only if it was not possible and is not possible that its antecedent is true and its consequent false (cf. Sextus Empiricus, *Adv. Math.* 8.115–117).

Diodorus's repute as a logician, even to the present day, derives from his Master Argument, mentioned by several authors but reported explicitly only in Epictetus (cf. Epictetus, *Diss.* 2.19.1–5). Diodorus claimed that the following three propositions are incompatible: (1) Every past truth is necessary, (2) nothing impossible follows from what is possible, and (3) there is something possible that neither is nor will be true. Diodorus used (1) and (2) to argue for the falsity of (3), hence for a notion of possibility that defines the possible as that which is or will be true. Here again we find him contradicted by Philo, who defines the possible as that which, by the intrinsic nature of the proposition, is receptive of truth (cf. Boethius, *De interpretatione* ii, 234,10–235, 9). The Master Argument became a bone of contention for Hellenistic logicians; it is still a matter of controversy how exactly Diodorus thought he could deduce the falsity of (3) from (1) and (2).

See also Atomism; Epictetus; Hellenistic Thought; Logic, History of; Megarians; Possibility; Zeno of Citium.

Bibliography

TESTIMONIA
The testimonia on Diodorus are now conveniently brought together in Volume 1 of G. Giannantoni's *Socratis et Socraticorum reliquiae* (Naples: Bibliopolis, 1990, pp. 414–435). Yet notice that in the account of the Master Argument in Epictetus, a line has been omitted from the text in Giannantoni's collection, so that only the first of the three propositions is quoted in full. The testimonia on Diodorus can also be found in K. Döring, *Die Megariker* (Amsterdam: Grüner, 1972).

WORKS ABOUT DIODORUS CRONUS
Gaskin, R. *The Sea Battle and the Master Argument.* Berlin/New York: de Gruyter, 1995. Contains an extensive bibliography.

Prior, A. N. "Diodoran Modalities." *Philosophical Quarterly* 5 (1955): 205–213.

Sedley, D. "Diodorus Cronus and Hellenistic Philosophy." *Proc. Cambridge Philological Society* N. S. 23 (1977): 74–120. A pioneering study.

Vuillemin, J. *Necessity or Contingency: The Master Argument.* Stanford: CSLI Publications, 1996. Originally published in French as *Nécessité ou contingence*, 1984.

Weidemann, H. "Diodors Meisterargument und der Aristotelische Möglichkeitsbegriff." *Archiv für Geschichte der Philosophie* 69 (1987): 18–53. Discusses extensively most of the literature up to the mid-1980s.

See also the four articles by H. Weidemann, R. Gaskin, M. J. White, and N. Denyer on the Master Argument in *Logical Analysis and History of Philosophy* 2 (1999) 189–252. The articles are as follows: H. Weidemann, "'Aus etwas Möglichem folgt nichts Unmögliches'. Zum Verständnis der zweiten Prämisse von Diodors Meisterargument," 189–202; R. Gaskin, "Tense Logic and the Master Argument," 203–224; M. J. White, "The Lessons of Prior's Master Argument," 225–238; and N. Denyer, "The Master Argument of Diodorus Cronus: A Near Miss," 239–252.

Theodor Ebert (2005)

DIOGENES LAERTIUS

(c. 200 CE)

Diogenes Laertius is the author of *Compendium of the Lives and Opinions of Philosophers*, the only general book on philosophers and their philosophy that has been transmitted from classical antiquity. Diogenes is known from this work only—nothing is known about his life—and his date can only be fixed by the dates of the latest personalities mentioned in his text (second century CE), and because he seems to have written prior to the rise of Neoplatonism (c. 250 CE). His work was dedicated to a woman interested in Platonism (bk. 3 § 47).

Diogenes's work belongs to a type of ancient literature (often called *Diadocha* or *Successions*) in which accounts of the lives of philosophers were arranged as series of biographies so that teacher and student followed one another within each major philosophical school.

Diogenes's text is divided into ten sections, or "books":

1: Introduction and various "wise men," including Thales.

(2–7: The Ionian Tradition)

2: The Ionian physicists, Socrates, and the minor Socratic schools down to the early third century BCE.

3: Plato.

4: The Academy down to Clitomachus (late second century BCE).

5: Aristotle and the Peripatetics down to Lyco (late third century BCE).

6: Antisthenes and the Cynics down to the end of the third century BCE.

7: Zeno and the Stoics down to at least Chrysippus (late third century BCE), and in the missing end of the book perhaps even down to the first century CE.

(8–10: The Italic Tradition)

8: Pythagoras and his early successors; Empedocles.

9: Heraclitus; the Eleatics; the Atomists, Protagoras and Diogenes of Apollonia; Pyrrho.

10: Epicurus.

Diogenes's book is basically a compilation of excerpts from numerous sources; in the biographical sections he often tells which sources he is using, whereas the philosophical sections contain few such references.

The book is also uneven. Some lives contain nothing but anecdotes and aphorisms, whereas others are mainly doxographical reports; some have long, detailed sections on philosophy, whereas others have short, superficial sections. Diogenes is unlikely to have read many philosophical works. However, in book 10 he has preserved four long, original writings by Epicurus, which constitute the most important evidence for Epicurus's philosophy from before the period of Cicero. However, his many references to his predecessors give an impression of the Hellenistic tradition of philosophical biography. Because Diogenes seems to have had a predilection for old documents, he has preserved the testaments of four peripatetics and a number of book catalogs.

Most of Diogenes's biographies include a number of items such as birth, parents, name, appearance, relationship to other philosophers, travels, lifestyle, and circumstances of death, yet they are presented in no particular order. The dominating element in the biographies is the use of anecdotes. In antiquity it was impossible to find documentary evidence concerning a deceased person, unless that person was a famous public figure or had left written works. Often literary works were exploited without regard to the fact that the content of a fictional work is unlikely to apply to the life of its author. Therefore, Diogenes's factual information must be viewed with some skepticism: Notice that most of his dates are taken from a Hellenistic poem.

Diogenes's biographies may have been written with less artistic skill than, for example, Plutarch's; however, they are not unlike other ancient accounts of the lives of philosophers.

Diogenes devotes much space to present the doctrines of the major philosophical schools: Book 3, § 48–109, is a general introduction to the study of the *Corpus Platonicum*; as an account of Plato's philosophy it may be inadequate, but it resembles other Platonic writings of the second century CE. The section on Aristotelian philosophy (bk. 5, § 28–34) is far less satisfying, but all three parts seem to go back to the Hellenistic period. Book 7, § 38–160, is the most comprehensive account of Stoic philosophy from antiquity, the section on logic is especially important. The survey of the Skeptic tropes (bk. 9, § 79–105) is shorter than in Sextus Empiricus but otherwise comparable. The three Epicurean letters and his forty "Principal Doctrines" in book 10 are crucial to what is known about Epicurus; when Diogenes places these aphorisms at the end of his book, he indicates that he considers them a culmination of philosophical wisdom.

For the pre-Socratic philosophers, Diogenes has used a "doxographical" source similar to other accounts in late antiquity; ultimately, it derives from Aristotle and Theophrastus. In the case of Pythagoras, Diogenes presents two excerpts from Aristotle and from Alexander Polyhistor (first century BCE), thus presenting a much earlier expression of Pythagoreanism than is found in other sources from late antiquity.

Diogenes was no philosopher, but he has preserved much of philosophical significance. He seems to have had no influence in antiquity, but since Walter Burley's *On the Life and Manners of the Philosophers* (early fourteenth century), the Latin translation by Ambrosius Traversarius (1432), and the *editio princeps* of the Greek text in 1533, Diogenes has been the most important single source for the lives and often for the doctrines of ancient philosophers. Until around 1800, Diogenes was the main model for historiography of philosophy.

See also History and Historiography of Philosophy.

Bibliography

TRANSLATIONS

Diogène Laërce Vies et doctrines des philosophes illustres, edited by Marie-Odile Goulet-Cazé. Paris: La Pochothèque, 1999. French translation.

Lives of Eminent Philosophers. Translated by R. D. Hicks. London: W. Heinemann; New York: Putnam, 1925. English translation.

Vitae Philosophorum. Vols. 1 and 2 edited by M. Marcovich; vol. 3, *Indices*, edited by H. Gärtner. Leipzig/Munich, Germany: Bibliotheca Teuneriana, 1999–2002. Greek translation. A new Budé edition by T. Dorandi, in preparation, will become the standard edition of the future.

STUDIES

Giannantoni, G., ed. *Diogene Laerzio. Storico del pensiero antico*. Naples: Bibliopolis, 1986.

Haase, W., and Temporini, H., eds. *Aufstieg und Niedergang der Römischen Welt*. Berlin and New York: W. de Gruyter, 1992. (Part) II volume 36 (parts) 5–6 contains various studies in several languages.

Mejer, Jørgen. *Die Ueberlieferung der Philosophie im Altertum*. Copenhagen: Det Kongelige Danske videnskabernes selskab, 2000. Contains an extensive bibliography.

Mejer, Jørgen. *Diogenes Laertius and His Hellenistic Background*. Wiesbaden, Germany: Steiner, 1978.

Jørgen Mejer (2005)

DIOGENES OF APOLLONIA
(5th century BCE)

Diogenes of Apollonia was a Greek philosopher belonging to the last generation of the pre-Socratics (fl. around 440–430 BCE.) His native town was either Apollonia on Crete or, more probably, Apollonia on the Pontus. Nothing is known for certain about his life. It has been debated whether he wrote only one book called, in English, *On Nature* or, as Simplicius reported (in *On Aristotle's "Physics"* 151, 20), four (*On Nature, Meteorology, On the Nature of Man, Against the Sophists*). All the existing fragments seem to come from *On Nature*. His work had an effect in Athenian intellectual life toward the end of the fifth century BCE, and his influence is detectable also in some treatises of the Hippocratic corpus and in the Stoic doctrine of *pneuma* (literally breath; in Stoic philosophy, the mixture of the two active elements, fire and air, and the sustaining cause of all bodies.)

His philosophy was termed "eclectic" already by Theophrastus, and most modern commentators agree with this assessment. Theophrastus listed Anaxagoras, Leucippus, and Anaximenes as the main influences on Diogenes, and to this list we should certainly add Heraclitus. Diogenes' philosophical doctrine has three prominent aspects: his monism, the teleological traits in his cosmology, and his theory of cognition. Most of the pre-Socratic philosophers working after Parmenides adopted a pluralist ontology. Diogenes, on the contrary, returned to the monism of his Ionian predecessors. He argued that if the proper nature of apparently different types of matter were not the same, then these different types of matter could not causally interact with one another, and we could not explain such phenomena as the nutrition and growth of living organisms, in which apparently different types of matter transform into each other. Therefore, the four elements and the other types of matter of our world must have differentiated from the same primordial stuff, must retain their underlying identity, and must ultimately return to what they differentiated from (Diels and Kranz [DK], B2). Apparent things exist for a limited time, whereas the basic stuff is "an eternal and deathless body" (DK, B7). Yet it is not a passive substrate, but is "strong" and determines how things are formed from it and return to it (DK, B8, B7). Because it is active and eternal, it can also be considered a god.

Diogenes continued by arguing that the basic stuff must be intelligent. He wrote, "For without intelligence it could not have been divided up in such a way as to hold the measures of all things, of winter and summer and night and day and rains and winds and nice weather, along with the rest, which, if one is willing to consider them intelligently, one will find disposed in the finest possible way" (DK, B3). Scholars have disagreed how thorough Diogenes' teleology, as expressed in this fragment, is. According to Willy Theiler, Diogenes is a full-blown teleologist and the immediate source of the teleological views that Xenophon ascribed to Socrates in his *Memorabilia*. Others have doubted that Diogenes' conception is original and that it is genuinely teleological. Diogenes' argument certainly differs from later, explicitly teleological views in that it remains unclear whether the action of the intelligent principle is directed at some well-defined goal or goals. It also differs from classic statements of the argument from design, with which it has sometimes been associated, in that Diogenes did not argue for the existence of an intelligent causal principle, but sought to show that the ultimate causal principle, the existence of which he established on independent grounds, must also be intelligent.

Diogenes identified the bearer of intelligence with air. He argued that because humans and animals live by breathing, air must be what brings life and intelligence to them (DK, B4). If so, the air, which inheres in, and steers, all things, must be the intelligent causal principle at the cosmic level too. Moreover, the qualitative differences of air explain the differences between species and individuals (DK, B5).

Diogenes' most original contribution was a detailed description of the system of veins, which originate in the head and through which blood and air to all parts of the body. Sensation is produced when air from the outside acts on the air in the sense organs which then reaches the head through the veins. The quality of the air and the veins determine the sharpness of perception. Air mixed with blood produces thought, and we feel pleasure when the appropriate mixture of air and blood pervades the whole body.

See also Pneuma; Stoicism.

Bibliography

Barnes, Jonathan. *The Presocratic Philosophers*. 2nd ed. London: Routledge and Kegan Paul, 1982.

Diels, Hermann, and Walther Kranz. *Die Fragmente der Vorsokratiker*. 7th, rev. ed. Berlin: Weidmann, 1954.

Kirk, G. S., J. E. Raven, and Malcolm Schofield. *The Presocratic Philosophers*. 2nd ed. Cambridge, U.K.: Cambridge University Press, 1983.

Laks, André. *Diogène d'Apollonie: La dernière cosmologie présocratique*. Lille, France: Presses universitaire de Lille, 1983.

Theiler, Willy. *Zur Geschichte der teleologischen Naturbetrachtung bis auf Aristoteles*. 2nd ed. Berlin: De Gruyter, 1965.

Gábor Betegh (2005)

DIOGENES OF SINOPE
(4th century BCE)

Diogenes of Sinope, who lived in the fourth century BCE, was the prototype of the Cynics, who probably were so called from Diogenes' Greek nickname, the Dog (*kuon*; adjective form, *kunikos*). Tradition held that on coming to Athens in exile, he was influenced by Antisthenes' teaching; Diogenes' ascetic distortion of Socratic temperance gives some point to Plato's supposed remark that he was a "Socrates gone mad."

It is not easy to recover the philosopher from, on the one hand, the lurid fog of anecdotal tradition that represents the stunts of an eccentric tramp at Athens and Corinth defacing conventional human standards—as he or his father, Hicesias, was supposed to have defaced in some way the currency of Sinope—or, on the other, the idealized legend that grew after his death. But doxographic traces (for example, Diogenes Laërtius, VI.70–73) and, indeed, the tradition as a whole presuppose a serious teacher who, in disillusioned protest against a corrupt society and hostile world, advocated happiness as self-realization and self-mastery in an inner spiritual freedom from all wants except the bare natural minimum; and who, in a bitter crusade against the corrupting influence of pleasure, desire, and luxury, extolled the drastic painful effort involved in the mental and physical training for the achievement of a natural and inviolable self-sufficiency.

The anecdotes illustrate Diogenes' philosophy in action. Since for Diogenes virtue was revealed in practice and not in theoretical analysis or argument, the stories of, for example, his embracing statues in winter and his peering with a lantern in daytime for a human being, the tales of his fearless biting repartee and criticism of notables such as Alexander, however embroidered or apocryphal, correctly reflect his pointed teaching methods, which encouraged the development of a new didactic form, the *chreia*, or moral epigram. Some exaggeration here is due to the "dog-cynic" shamelessness pedagogically employed to discount convention, and some is no doubt inherent in the uncompromising extremes of Diogenes' doctrines.

He is credited with tragedies illustrating the human predicament and with a *Republic*, which influenced Zeno the Stoic, that was notorious for its scandalous attack on convention. His famous remark that he was a citizen of the world is more probably antinational than international, for he was concerned with the individual rather than the community. Diogenes sought to make any man king, not of others, but of himself, through autonomy of will, and his own life was his main philosophical demonstration to this end.

See also Antisthenes; Cynics; Diogenes Laertius; Hellenistic Thought; Plato; Zeno of Citium.

Bibliography

WORKS ON DIOGENES OF SINOPE

Crönert, W. *Kolotes und Menedemos.* Leipzig, 1906.

Diogenes Laërtius. *Lives,* VI. 20–81.

Dudley, D. R. *History of Cynicism.* London, 1937.

Höistad, R. *Cynic Hero and Cynic King.* Uppsala, Sweden, 1949.

Sayre, F. *The Greek Cynics.* Baltimore, 1948.

I. G. Kidd (1967)

DIOGENES THE CYNIC

See *Diogenes of Sinope*

DIONYSIUS THE PSEUDO-AREOPAGITE

See *Pseudo-Dionysius*

DIRECT REALISM

See *Realism*

DISCOURSE ETHICS

"Discourse ethics" refers to an approach to moral theory developed by Jürgen Habermas. It is a reconstruction of Immanuel Kant's idea of practical reason that turns on a reformulation of his categorical imperative: Rather than prescribing to others as valid norms that I can will to be universal laws, I must submit norms to others for purposes of discursively testing their putative universality. "Only those norms may claim to be valid that could meet with the approval of all those affected in their capacity as participants in practical discourse" (Habermas, 1990, p. 66). Normative validity, construed as rational acceptability, is thus tied to argumentation processes governed by a principle of universalization: "For a norm to be valid, the consequences and side effects of its general observance for the satisfaction of each person's particular interests must be acceptable to all" (p. 197). Furthermore, by requiring that perspective taking be general and reciprocal, discourse ethics builds a moment of empathy or

"ideal role-taking" into the procedure of practical argumentation.

Like Kant, Habermas distinguishes the types of practical reasoning and the corresponding types of "ought" connected with questions concerning what is pragmatically expedient, ethically prudent, or morally right. Calculations of rational choice furnish recommendations relevant to the pursuit of contingent purposes in the light of given preference. When serious questions of value arise, deliberation on who one is and wants to be yields insight into the good life. If issues of justice are involved, fair and impartial consideration of conflicting interests is required to judge what is right or just. Again like Kant, Habermas regards questions of the last type, rather than specifically ethical questions, to be the proper domain of theory. (Thus, discourse ethics might properly be called discourse morality.) This is not to deny that ethical discourse is rational or that it exhibits general structures of its own; but the irreducible pluralism of modern life means that questions of self-understanding, self-realization, and the good life do not admit of universal answers. In Habermas's view, that does not preclude a general theory of a narrower sort, namely a theory of justice. Accordingly, the aim of his discourse ethics is solely to reconstruct the moral point of view from which questions of right can be fairly and impartially adjudicated.

By linking discourse ethics to the theory of communicative action, Habermas means to show that our basic moral intuitions are rooted in something deeper and more universal than particularities of our tradition, namely in the intuitive grasp of the normative presuppositions of social interaction possessed by competent social actors in any society. Members of our species become individuals in and through being socialized into networks of reciprocal social relations. The mutual vulnerability that this interdependence brings with it calls for guarantees of mutual consideration to preserve both the integrity of individual persons and the web of their interpersonal relations. In discourse ethics respect for the individual is built into the freedom of each participant in discourse to accept or reject the reasons offered as justifications for norms, and concern for the common good is built into the requirement that each participant take into account the needs, interests, and feelings of all others affected by the norm in question. Hence, the actual practice of moral discourse depends on forms of socialization and social reproduction that foster the requisite capacities and motivation.

See also Habermas, Jürgen; Justice; Kant, Immanuel; Practical Reason.

Bibliography

Habermas, J. *Justification and Application: Remarks on Discourse Ethics.* Translated by C. Cronin. Cambridge, MA: MIT Press, 1993.

Habermas, J. *Moral Consciousness and Communicative Action.* Translated by C. Lenhardt and S. Nicholsen. Cambridge, MA: MIT Press, 1990.

Rehg, W. *Insight and Solidarity: The Discourse Ethics of Jürgen Habermas.* Berkeley: University of California Press, 1994.

Thomas McCarthy (1996)

DISPOSITIONAL THEORIES

See *Response-Dependence Theories*

DISTANT PEOPLES AND FUTURE GENERATIONS

Only recently have philosophers begun to discuss the question of whether we can meaningfully speak of distant peoples and future generations as having rights against us or of our having corresponding obligations to them. Answering this question with respect to distant peoples is much easier than answering it with respect to future generations. Few philosophers have thought that the mere fact that people are at a distance from us precludes our having any obligations to them or their having any rights against us. Some philosophers, however, have argued that our ignorance of the specific membership of the class of distant peoples does rule out these moral relationships. Yet this cannot be right, given that in other contexts we recognize obligations to indeterminate classes of people, such as a police officer's obligation to help people in distress or the obligation of food producers not to harm those who consume their products.

Of course, before distant peoples can be said to have rights against us, we must be capable of acting across the distance that separates us. Yet as long as this condition is met—as it typically is for people living in most technologically advanced societies—it would certainly seem possible for distant peoples to have rights against us and us corresponding obligations to them.

By contrast, answering the above question with respect to future generations raises more difficult issues. One concerns whether it is logically coherent to speak of future generations as having rights now. Of course, no one who finds talk about rights to be generally meaningful should question whether we can coherently claim that future generations *will* have rights at some point in the future (specifically, when they come into existence and are no longer future generations). But what is questioned, since it is of considerable practical significance, is whether we can coherently claim that future generations have rights now when they do not yet exist.

Let us suppose, for example, that we continue to use up Earth's resources at present or even greater rates, and as a result, it turns out that future generations will face widespread famine, depleted resources, insufficient new technology to handle the crisis, and a drastic decline in the quality of life for nearly everyone. If this were to happen, could persons living in the twenty-second century legitimately claim that we in the twenty-first century violated their rights by not restraining our consumption of the world's resources? Surely it would be odd to say that we violated their rights more than one hundred years before they existed. But what exactly is the oddness?

Is it that future generations generally have no way of claiming their rights against existing generations? While this does make the recognition and enforcement of rights much more difficult (future generations would need strong advocates in the existing generations), it does not make it impossible for such rights to exist. After all, the recognition and enforcement of the rights of distant peoples is also a difficult task, but obviously such rights can exist.

Perhaps what troubles us is that future generations do not exist when their rights are said to demand action. But how else could persons have a right to benefit from the effects our actions will have in the distant future if they did not exist just when those effects would be felt? Our contemporaries cannot legitimately make the same demand, for they will not be around to experience those effects. Only future generations could have a right that the effects our actions will have in the distant future contribute to their well-being. Nor need we assume that, for persons to have rights, they must exist when their rights demand action. Thus, to say that future generations have rights against existing generations, we can simply mean that there are enforceable requirements upon existing generations that would benefit future generations or prevent harm to them.

Most likely what really bothers us is that we cannot know for sure what effects our actions will have on future generations. For example, we may, at some cost to ourselves, conserve resources that will be valueless to future generations who may develop different technologies. Or, because we regard them as useless, we may destroy or deplete resources that future generations will find to be essential to their well-being. Nevertheless, we should not allow such possibilities to blind us to the necessity of a social policy in this regard. After all, whatever we do will have its effect on future generations. The best approach, therefore, is to use the knowledge we have and assume that future generations will also require those basic resources we now find to be valuable. If it turns out that future generations require different resources to meet their basic needs, at least we will not be to blame for acting on the basis of the knowledge we have.

Assuming then that we can meaningfully speak of distant peoples and future generations as having rights against us and us corresponding obligations to them, the crucial question that remains is exactly what rights they have against us and what obligations we have to them. While the answer to this question obviously depends on a substantial social and political theory, the expectation is that the rights and obligations that morally bind us to distant peoples and future generations will be quite similar to those that morally bind us to near people and existing generations.

See also Bioethics; Environmental Aesthetics; Environmental Ethics; Genetics and Reproductive Technologies; Philosophy of Technology; Responsibility, Moral and Legal; Rights.

Bibliography
Elfstrom, G. *Ethics for a Shrinking World.* New York: St. Martin's Press, 1990.
Hardin, G. *Promethean Ethics.* Seattle: University of Washington Press, 1980.
Partridge, E. *Responsibilities to Future Generations.* Buffalo, NY: Prometheus Books, 1981.

James P. Sterba (1996)

DIVINE COMMAND THEORIES OF ETHICS

The general perspective on ethics known as theological voluntarism usually appears in philosophical discussions in the specific form of divine command theories. As its title suggests, theological voluntarism is the view that ethics depends, at least in part, on God's will. In divine command theories the dependency is spelled out in terms of commands by God that express the divine will. The Hebrew Bible portrays God as establishing norms for human conduct by giving commands. Though some of them pertain exclusively to the regulation of religious rituals, others such as the prohibitions of murder and theft

clearly have ethical content. Since the Hebrew Bible counts as authoritative scripture for all three of the major monotheistic religions, divine command theories are a live option within Jewish, Christian, and Islamic traditions.

As the historical research of Janine M. Idziak (1979) shows, many Christian thinkers have exercised this option. St. Augustine, St. Bernard of Clairvaux, St. Thomas Aquinas, and St. Andrew of Neufchateau claimed that divine commands determine the ethical status of particular actions when they dealt with issues in biblical exegesis. John Duns Scotus and William of Ockham endorsed divine command theories. Both Martin Luther and John Calvin advocated an ethics of divine commands. John Locke and William Paley are among the modern philosophers who argued for divine command theories. Søren Kierkegaard's *Works of Love* (1847/1995) contains a divine command theory. In short, over a period of many centuries divine command ethics has attracted support from major figures in both Catholic and Protestant branches of Christianity.

A strong cumulative case for the importance of God's will in ethics can be constructed from within a Christian worldview. As Kierkegaard emphasized, a central element in such a case comes from the Christian New Testament. It is a striking feature of its distinctive ethics of love (*agape*) that love is commanded. In Matthew's Gospel the command is stated in response to a lawyer's query. Jesus says, "You shall love the Lord your God with your whole heart, with your whole soul, and with all your mind. This is the greatest and the first commandment. The second is like it: You shall love your neighbor as yourself" (Matthew 22:37–39). Similar commands are endorsed or stated by Jesus in the other three Gospels. If Jesus is God the son, as traditional Christians believe, such commands derive from and express the will of God. Thus, the ethics of agapeistic love advocated in the New Testament can plausibly be interpreted as having its source in a divine command.

During the final third of the twentieth century a revival of interest in divine command ethics took place among philosophers of religion. Most of the philosophers who wrote on the subject in this period understood divine command theories to be accounts of the realm of moral deontology. This domain of ethics studies topics related to duty; its main concepts are requirement (obligation), permission (rightness), and prohibition (wrongness). Edward R. Wierenga (1989) proposes a causal divine command theory according to which by commanding actions God brings it about that they are obligatory and by forbidding actions God brings it about that they are wrong. Robert Merrihew Adams (1999) advocates a theory in which an action's being obligatory consists in its being commanded by God and an action's being wrong consists in its being contrary to a divine command. Stated in general terms, the principle of obligation of a divine command theory of the type favored by these philosophers asserts that actions are obligatory if and only if, and just because, they are commanded by God. And the principle of wrongness of such a theory claims that actions are wrong if and only if, and just because, they are prohibited by God.

Adams argues that divine commands do not account for ethical goodness and related axiological characteristics. In his theistic Platonism God plays the role of the Form of the Good; God is the paradigm or standard of goodness. Other things are good in virtue of bearing a relation of resemblance to God. For Adams (1999), ethical goodness thus depends on God, but not on God's will or commands.

Philosophers who contribute to the revival of divine command ethics devote a good deal of time and energy to defending divine command theories against criticism. Perhaps the most famous objection has roots that trace back to a question Socrates raises in the *Euthyphro*. Altering it a bit to allow for the difference between Greek polytheism and monotheism, one may imagine a Socratic gadfly asking: Does God command truth-telling because it is obligatory, or is truth-telling obligatory because God commands it? No matter which way questions of this sort are answered, a difficulty for divine command ethics emerges.

If one supposes that God commands truth-telling because it is obligatory, one contradicts the claim of divine command theorists that truth-telling is obligatory because it is commanded by God. In other words, this response forces one to conclude that the obligatoriness of truth-telling is independent of God's commands. But if one insists that truth-telling is obligatory because God commands it, which is what divine command theorists are committed to doing, then one must confront a difficulty that was eloquently formulated by Ralph Cudworth in *A Treatise concerning Eternal and Immutable Morality* (1731/1976). As he notes, divine command theorists are committed to the view that lying rather than truth-telling would be obligatory if it were commanded by God.

However, divine command theorists can accept Cudworth's (1731/1976) point with equanimity if they embed their divine command account of moral deontology in an axiological theory that, like the theistic Platonism espoused by Adams, makes ethical goodness independent of God's will and commands. Understood in this way, goodness is determined by God's immutable nature and character; it is a matter of who and what God is. God's essential nature, which is paradigmatic of goodness, will then constrain what God can command. Hence, it is open to divine command theorists to hold that it is impossible for God to command lying and so is impossible for lying to be obligatory. This view is consistent with granting that lying would be obligatory if, *per impossible*, God were to command it.

Certain forms of divine command ethics can be shown to stand up well under philosophical scrutiny. Divine command accounts of obligation and wrongness deserve to be regarded as respectable options in ethical theory if the larger theistic worldviews of which they are components are themselves philosophically defensible.

See also Moral Principles: Their Justification; Religion and Morality.

Bibliography

Adams, Robert Merrihew. *Finite and Infinite Goods: A Framework for Ethics*. New York: Oxford University Press, 1999. Argues for a divine command theory within an ethical framework of theistic Platonism.

Cudworth, Ralph. *A Treatise concerning Eternal and Immutable Morality* (1731). New York: Garland, 1976. Classic source of objections to divine command ethics.

Idziak, Janine M., ed. *Divine Command Morality: Historical and Contemporary Readings*. New York: Edwin Mellen Press, 1979. Collects informative selections from writings by both defenders and critics of divine command ethics.

Kierkegaard, Søren. *Works of Love* (1847). Translated and edited by Howard V. Hong and Edna H. Hong. Princeton, NJ: Princeton University Press, 1995. Contains a divine command account of Christian agapeistic ethics.

Mouw, Richard J. *The God Who Commands*. Notre Dame, IN: University of Notre Dame Press, 1990. Defends divine command ethics within a theological perspective.

Quinn, Philip L. *Divine Commands and Moral Requirements*. Oxford, U.K.: Clarendon Press, 1978. Defends divine command ethics within a philosophical perspective and sets forth rigorous formulations of several versions of divine command theory.

Quinn, Philip L. "Divine Command Theory." In *The Blackwell Guide to Ethical Theory*, edited by Hugh LaFollette. Oxford, U.K.: Blackwell, 2001. Outlines a cumulative case, most of which is internal to Christianity, that lends support to divine command ethics.

Wierenga, Edward R. *The Nature of God: An Inquiry into Divine Attributes*. Ithaca, NY: Cornell University Press, 1989. Presents and defends a causal divine command theory.

Philip L. Quinn (2005)

DŌGEN

(1200–1253)

MAJOR WORKS OF DŌGEN

Dōgen was the founder of Sōtō Zen Buddhism and helped introduce to medieval Japan many features of Chan Buddhist theory and practice that developed during the Song dynasty in China. His major works include the *Shōbōgenzō* (Treasury of the true dharma-eye), a collection of sermons composed in vernacular Japanese from 1231 until the end of his life; the *Shōbōgenzō Zuimonki* (Miscellaneous talks), another collection of vernacular sermons compiled from 1234 until 1238; the *Eihei Kōroku* (Recorded sayings at Eiheiji Temple), a collection of sermons in Chinese compiled from 1236 to 1252; the *Fukanzazengi* (Universal recommendation for Zazen practice), a concise summary of his views on meditation composed in 1233; and the *Eihei Shingi* (Monastic rules at Eiheiji Temple), a collection of six essays dealing with monastic rules and regulations composed from 1237 to 1249.

Dōgen is often referred to as the leading philosopher in Japanese history. His writings on many Buddhist topics reflect an approach to religious experience based on a more philosophically oriented level of analysis than is found in the writings of most thinkers in Zen, which is known as a "special transmission outside the scriptures, without reliance on words and letters." Dōgen has been a major influence on modern Japanese philosophy, especially representatives of the Kyoto School such as Nishida Kitarō, Nishitani Keiji, and Abe Masao, and has been compared with a wide range of classical and modern Western philosophers and religious thinkers ranging from Aristotle and St. Thomas Aquinas to Martin Heidegger, Friedrich Nietzsche, and Jacques Derrida.

DŌGEN'S LIFE AND TEACHINGS

Some of Dōgen's major philosophical ideas emphasize that philosophy of religion must reflect personal experience of transient existence based on an awareness that the ultimate reality of the universal Buddha-nature is not beyond but is conditioned by impermanence. Impermanent reality is characterized by a fundamental unity of being-time (*uji*) in that all beings occur as temporal manifestations and time is manifested through each aspect of existence. Dōgen maintains that religious practice, or training, and spiritual realization, or the attainment of enlightenment, occur simultaneously and are inseparable in the experience of liberation known as "the casting off

of body-mind" (*shinjin datsuraku*) that is achieved through the methods of zazen meditation and kōan interpretation, which are equally conducive to realization. He also stresses that the naturalist dimension of being-time and impermanence-Buddha-nature is expressible through poetry and aesthetics, but reminds that karmic causality or moral conditioning and retribution are inherent to, rather than outside of, the attainment of enlightenment.

Much of Dōgen's emphasis on impermanence is based on his own experiences. According to the traditional accounts Dōgen was born into an aristocratic family at a time when Japan was beginning to be plagued by repeated civil warfare. He experienced profound sorrow at an early age as his father and mother died by the time he was seven. It is said that when Dōgen saw the smoke rising from incense and vanishing during his mother's funeral, he was deeply moved by an awareness of the inevitability of death and the pervasiveness of ephemeral reality.

The orphaned Dōgen decided to renounce secular life in pursuit of the Buddhist dharma. At first, he studied on Mount Hiei outside the capital city of Kyoto in the dominant Japanese Tendai church, in which the central doctrine was an affirmation of "original enlightenment" (*hongaku*) or the inherent potentiality of all beings to attain the primordial Buddha-nature. However, at the age of thirteen Dōgen had a fundamental "doubt" about the doctrine of original enlightenment: If everyone is already enlightened in that they possess the Buddha-nature, he thought, then what is the need for sustained meditative practice as required by the Buddha's teaching?

Unable to resolve this doubt in Japan, Dōgen traveled to China, where the contemplative path of Zen had become the dominant movement. At first, Dōgen was disappointed in the laxity of the Chinese Chan monks, who failed to inspire him. Then, on the verge of returning to Japan unfulfilled, he met the teacher Rujing, who insisted on an unrelenting approach to meditation. Under the guidance of his new mentor Dōgen attained an awakening experience of the casting off of body-mind, or a continuing process of liberation from all intellectual and volitional attachments, which signified the resolution of his doubt about the necessity of continuously renewed training.

Before his breakthrough experience Dōgen apparently presumed the conventional dichotomies between past, present, and future, now and then, life and death, impermanence and nirvana, time and eternity, and finitude and Buddha-nature. He thought that human beings were bound to a realm of death and impermanence and that enlightenment was beyond this realm. However, in casting off body-mind he realized that a single moment encompasses the unity of practice and attainment, so that practice is not before—nor does it lead up to—enlightenment and enlightenment is not a teleological goal reached only at the end of practice. Rather, as Dōgen writes in the *Shōbōgenzō*, "[p]ractice and realization are identical. Because one's present practice is practice in realization, one's initial negotiation of the Way in itself is the whole of original realization.… As it is already realization in practice, realization is endless; as it is practice in realization, practice in beginningless" (Dōgen, *Dōgen Zenji Zenshū*, vol. 2, pp. 546–547).

On returning to Japan, in 1233 Dōgen established the Sōtō sect at Kōshōji temple in the Kyoto area, but because of sectarian disputes with Tendai and other Zen factions he eventually moved in 1243 to the remote, pristine mountains of Echizen (now Fukui) Province, where Eiheiji temple was constructed. According to Dōgen's writings of the late period, every action generates a retributive consequence, and only authentic repentance and acknowledgment of one's guilt can offset the effects of evil karma. Still, by emphasizing the moment-to-moment cause-and-effect process of karmic retribution—which is inseparable from nirvana as part of the Bodhisattva's commitment to compassion—Dōgen is consistent with his earlier philosophy of being-time.

A central feature of aesthetic realization is Dōgen's use of poetic language, especially elaborate metaphors and philosophical wordplay, to convey emotional fulfillment that enhances rather than opposes the enlightenment experience of detachment from worldly, materialistic concerns. One of Dōgen's most eloquent poems was written near the end of his life as he returned from Echizen to the capital city for medical care. Making the journey to see Kyoto for the first time in ten years, but for what would prove to be the last time, Dōgen wrote in the five-line, thirty-one-syllable *waka* form:

Like a blade of grass,
My frail body
Treading the path to Kyoto,
Seeming to wander
Amid the cloudy mist on the mountain path.

(Heine 1989, p. 85)

See also Buddhism—Schools: Chan and Zen.

Bibliography

WORKS BY DŌGEN

Dōgen. *Dōgen Zenji Zenshū*, Edited by Kōdō, Kawamura, et al., 7 vols. Tokyo: Shunjūsha, 1988–1993.

Dōgen. *Dōgen's Pure Standards for the Zen Community*. Translated by Taigen Dan Leighton and Shohaku Okumura. Albany: SUNY Press, 1996.

Dōgen. *Dōgen's Extensive Record: A Translation of the Eihei Kōroku*. Translated by Taigen Dan Leighton and Shohaku Okumura. Boston: Wisdom, 2004.

Dōgen. *Dōgen Zenji's Shōbōgenzō* (The Eye and Treasury of the True Law). Translated by Nishiyama Kōsen and John Stevens. 4 vols. Sendai, Japan: Daihokkaikakum, 1975.

WORKS ON DŌGEN

Abe, Masao. *A Study of Dōgen: His Philosophy and Religion*. Edited by Steven Heine. Albany: SUNY Press, 1992.

Bielefeldt, Carl. *Dōgen's Manuals of Zen Meditation*. Berkeley: University of California Press, 1988.

Faure, Bernard. "The Daruma-shū, Dōgen, and Sōtō Zen." *Monumenta Nipponica* 42 (1) (1987): 25–55.

Heine, Steven. *A Blade of Grass: Japanese Poetry and Aesthetics in Dōgen Zen*. New York: Peter Lang, 1989.

Heine, Steven. *Dōgen and the Kōan Tradition: A Tale of Two Shōbōgenzō Texts*. Albany: SUNY Press, 1994.

Kim, Hee-Jin. *Dōgen Kigen—Mystical Realist*. Tucson: University of Arizona Press, 1975.

LaFleur, William R., ed. *Dōgen Studies*. Honolulu: University of Hawaii Press, 1985.

Tanahashi, Kazuaki. *Moon in a Dewdrop: Writings of Zen Master Dōgen*. Translated by Robert Aitken, et al. San Francisco: North Point Press, 1985.

Steven Heine (2005)

DOGMA

The Greek word of which "dogma" is a transliteration means "that which seems good." It was applied by Greek authors to the decrees of public authorities and to the tenets of various philosophical schools. In English the word can be used for any fixed and firmly held belief on any subject, but it usually suggests that the belief is a condition, or at least a sign, of belonging to either a secular or (more frequently) a religious group. The word can also imply that the belief rests on a special—often divine—authority; that any member of the group who attenuates or changes the belief is thereby a "heretic"; and that heresy is a moral, and perhaps also legal, offense that merits the strongest condemnation (and perhaps also punishment).

The clearest example of religious dogma in ancient philosophy comes from Plato. In the *Republic* (376Eff.) he lays down two "ways in which God is to be spoken of" (*tupoi theologias*). The first is that God is good and the cause of good alone; the second is that God is true and incapable of change. In the *Laws* (887E–888D) he actually uses "dogma" to mean a correct "belief" about the gods. Everyone must believe that the gods are concerned with human affairs and that they cannot be appeased by sacrifice. Those who reject these beliefs must be duly punished by the state.

The primary sense of "dogma" is the one it has acquired in Christianity. Other religions have their distinctive tenets, but Christianity alone deserves attention on three grounds. First, its dogmas are far more numerous and complex than those of other faiths: Judaism requires only the recitation of the *Shema*, and Islam requires only assent to the *Kalima*. (Both these short creeds affirm the unity of God.) Second, Christian dogma has had many important points of contact with Western secular philosophy. Third, Christian theologians have given to the word *dogma* itself a technical, precise significance. (There is nothing that can properly be called dogma in the religions of the East. The eightfold path of Buddhism is a nontheistic way of salvation, not a creed. In Hinduism there are many divergent views of God and the Absolute, but none of them is "orthodox.")

All the main Christian bodies are agreed that dogma is essentially the formulation of belief on the basis of the Scriptures. God revealed himself both in the events to which the Bible testifies and in the biblical interpretation of them. The role of dogma is to express the meaning of this revelation in conceptual terms.

All would also agree that dogma does not add to the revelation that was complete with the apostles. Dogma merely makes explicit what is implicit in apostolic teaching. Hence, St. Vincent of Lérins affirms that the development of dogma is an "advance" (*profectus*), not a change (*permutatio*). Although a dogma can always be restated in a form that is either more exact per se or more comprehensible to a particular audience, its substance is immutable.

This point is clearly made by Hans Küng in his important book on the second Vatican Council, *The Council and Reunion* (London, 1961). On the one hand, "dogmatic definitions express the truth with infallible accuracy and are in this sense unalterable (as against Modernism)" (p. 163). On the other hand, "one and the same truth of faith can always be expressed in a still more complete, more adequate, better formula" (p. 163).

All Christian bodies, finally, would agree that the *ultimate* object of assent is not any statement about God, but God himself. Furthermore, dogmas do not render God intelligible; they symbolize a mystery that surpasses understanding. Therefore, we cannot assent to them without the gift of faith.

However, Christians differ in their views on both the number of and the authority for dogmatic definitions. Roman Catholic theologians hold that the definitions given by twenty ecumenical councils of the church are inerrant. They further hold that the pope alone, when he speaks *ex cathedra*, is infallible in matters of faith and morals. Finally, they hold that a dogma (for example, the dogma of the Immaculate Conception) can be justified as a logical "development" even though it lacks any scriptural support.

Non-Roman Christians oppose these claims. The Orthodox church holds that only seven councils are ecumenical and inerrant. Both Martin Luther and the Anglican reformers said that all councils are capable of error. All Protestants and Anglicans agree in denying both the infallibility of the pope and the validity of dogmas that are not explicitly supported by the Bible.

From the beginning, dogma has been stated through the terms of secular philosophy. One need mention only the use made of "substance" and "relation" in the doctrine of the Trinity. Such philosophical expressions were required both to make the faith intelligible and to safeguard it against heresy. Even those Protestants who reject scholastic terminology are forced to substitute other concepts (for example, those of existentialism).

In the theology of Thomas Aquinas, and in conciliar definitions, philosophy is instrumental. The content and authority of dogma are derived wholly from revelation, although some theologians have attempted to place dogmas in the context of a speculative system that is alien to the basic principles of Christian theism. Inevitably, the dogmas then lose their original, distinctive, and (above all) supernatural significance. Thus G. W. F. Hegel and his disciples held that Christ merely exhibits in a supreme mode the natural coinherence of the finite and the infinite.

At the other extreme, some post-Kantian thinkers, while remaining in the church, have denied that dogmas state objective truths concerning God. But we are to act "as if" they were true, and in so acting we shall find that the moral life is given both a meaning and a power that it cannot otherwise possess. This reduction of dogmas to the status of pragmatic postulates is the twenty-sixth proposition condemned by the decree *Lamentabili* (1907).

Bibliography

Bettenson, Henry. *Documents of the Christian Church.* New York: Oxford University Press, 1947.

Brunner, Emil. *The Christian Doctrine of God.* Translated by Olive Wyon. London: Lutterworth, 1949. Chs. 1–11.

Journet, C. *What Is Dogma?* Translated by Mark Pontifex. London: Royal Institute of International Affairs, 1946.

Newman, J. H. *An Essay in Development.* Several editions since 1845.

H. P. Owen (1967)

DONG ZHONGSHU

(c. 179–c. 104 BCE)

Dong Zhongshu, probably the most influential Confucian scholar of the Han dynasty (206 BCE–220 CE), laid an institutional basis for the Confucian orthodoxy and for the recruitment of able scholars as government officials through the examination system. He was an expert in the Gongyang commentary of the Confucian classic *Spring and Autumn,* and he gave the classic a new interpretation that combines the ethical and political teachings of Confucius with the supernatural view of the metaphysicians.

After having received the degree of eruditus (*boshi*) in the Confucian classics, Dong Zhongshu became a public instructor during the reign (156–140 BCE) of Emperor Jing. It has been recorded that he lectured from behind a curtain, and although he had many students, few were admitted to his presence. He was also said to have been so engrossed in his scholarly pursuits that for three years he did not even once visit his garden. As a result of his responses to the written inquiries addressed to the scholars of the realm by Emperor Wu (reigned 140–87 BCE), Dong Zhongshu attracted imperial notice and was appointed minister successively to two royal princes. However, he was not successful in his political career and spent the remaining years of his life in teaching and writing. In addition to his several memorials to the throne, he is known for his work on the *Spring and Autumn,* titled *Chunqiu Fanlu* (Copious Dew in Spring and Autumn), a curious admixture of moral and metaphysical essays in seventeen chapters. He had numerous followers and his influence lasted well beyond his lifetime.

Dong Zhongshu's main contribution as a Confucian philosopher lies in his study of the *Spring and Autumn,* which, according to him, teaches "compliance with Heaven's will and imitation of the ancients." To do so is "for the people to follow the sovereign, and for the sovereign to follow Heaven." Thus, the basic principle in government is to subject the people to the sovereign's domination, and the sovereign to Heaven's will. In Dong's concept, Heaven (*Tian*) is not the all-mighty anthropomorphic god of the ancient Chinese but the physical universe itself. Somewhat akin to the Western concept of nature, it is nevertheless endowed with intellect and purpose. The ruler, as Heaven's representative on earth, should administer his kingdom in accordance with Heaven's will. As Heaven is inherently good and benevolent, so should the sovereign be. His virtuous rule will be marked by order and harmony in the universe. On the other hand, any evil act of his will cause catastrophes (such as floods and fires, earthquakes and mountain slides) and anomalies (such as comets, eclipses, and the growing of beards on women) sent by Heaven as a warning to men. "The origin of catastrophes and anomalies," he wrote in "Copious Dew," "is traceable to misrule in the state. First, Heaven sends catastrophes to admonish the people. When this goes unheeded and no changes are made, Heaven would then frighten the people with prodigies. If men are still unawed, ruin and destruction will finally befall the empire."

Although he was an avowed monarchist, Dong Zhongshu's strange science of the catastrophes and anomalies had the effect of curbing misgovernment on the part of the ruler. The idea has so embedded itself in the minds of the Chinese people that even in more enlightened and rational times, Confucian scholar-officials found Dong's concept useful as a means of remonstrance against the ruler's misuse of despotic power. But Dong Zhongshu is remembered today chiefly for his historical role in exalting Confucianism as China's official state doctrine, which was to mold the nation for more than two thousand years from the Han dynasty to the present age.

See also Chinese Philosophy; Confucius; Ethics and Morality.

Bibliography

Chan, Wing-tsit. *A Source Book in Chinese Philosophy.* Princeton, NJ: Princeton University Press, 1963.

Fung Yu-lan. *A History of Chinese Philosophy.* Translated by Derk Bodde, Vol. 2. Princeton, NJ: Princeton University Press, 1953.

Gassmann, Robert H. *Tung Chung-shu Ch'un-Ch'iu Fan Lu: Üppiger Tau des Frühling-und-Herbst-Klassikers.* Frankfurt: Verlag Peter Lang, 1988.

Tain, Tzey-yueh. "Tung Chung-shu's System of Thought: Its Sources and Its Influence on Han Scholars." Ph.D. diss., University of California, 1974.

Liu Wu-chi (1967)
Bibliography updated by Loy Huichieh (2005)

DOSTOEVSKY, FYODOR MIKHAILOVICH
(1821–1881)

Fyodor Mikhailovich Dostoevsky was a famed Russian writer whose works reflect an intense interest in philosophical questions about the human condition. With some justification, Dostoevsky's thought has been linked with existentialism—it is unsystematic and sometimes paradoxical, and his fiction in particular is marked by a concern with the irrational in human behavior and with the burdens and blessings of free choice. In the full sweep of his writings, however—which included essays, notebooks, diaries, and letters in addition to fiction—Dostoevsky gave expression to a comprehensive Christian philosophy that cannot be classed as either existentialism or irrationalism, despite his influence on thinkers of both of those schools—the European (Friedrich Nietzsche, Albert Camus), as well as the Russian (Nikolai Berdyaev, Lev Shestov).

METAPHYSICS AND EPISTEMOLOGY

Dostoevsky's conception of the human situation is rooted most fundamentally in a traditional Christian dualism: Reality is divided into material and spiritual realms, at the intersection of which stands humanity. Matter and spirit are binary opposites for Dostoevsky, mutually exclusive in essence and attributes. And yet humans partake of both—a situation that generates metaphysical and epistemological puzzles.

As physical inhabitants of the material world, human beings are perishable entities, subject to laws of causal determination of the kind discovered by natural scientists. But as spiritual persons they are eternal and not fully determinable by natural causes. Dostoevsky's sympathies lay on the spiritual side, and accordingly the major part of his philosophizing was devoted to defending such idealist theses as the immortality of the soul (which he considered the basic tenet of Christian belief) and the doctrine of free will (the philosophical thesis with which he is most closely identified). At least six separate arguments for life after death can be found in his writings, beginning in 1864 in a lengthy diary entry on the death of his first wife—a passage of utmost importance for his philosophical outlook (Scanlan 2002, pp. 19–37). The significance of free will as a defining trait of humanity is memorably portrayed in his most pointedly philosophical work—*Notes from Underground* (1864)—in which he attacks the determinism of Nikolai Chernyshevsky and other Russian materialists, contending that human choices are radically unpredictable because people are capable of deliberately falsifying any prediction made. As Gary Saul Morson (1998) points out, the notion of an indeterminate future is central to Dostoevsky's narrative style as well as to his philosophical outlook.

The epistemological puzzle created by humanity's hybrid nature is how a spiritual soul mired in a material world, dependent on a physical brain and sensory apparatus, can fully understand either realm. At times Dostoevsky despaired of the mind's ability to comprehend reality at all, but more typically he stressed the partiality and tentativeness of human knowledge and the inability of science to fathom the human essence. He regarded reason as a limited capacity, denying that it could present conclusive proofs of such beliefs as personal immortality and the existence of God; at the same time, he accepted reason as consistent with and providing some support for those beliefs, as his own discursive arguments for them attest. In the voice of Father Zosima in *The Brothers Karamazov* (1879–1880) he also accepted mystical experience as a limited source of knowledge of reality: "Much on earth is concealed from us, but in place of it we have been granted a secret, mysterious sense of our living bond with the other world" (p. 320). Even this mysterious sense, however, tells us nothing more than that there is a "full synthesis of all being," which in the 1864 diary entry he identified with God (Proffer, vol. 1, 1973, p. 40). He did not reject the theistic notion of God as a person who created and rules the world, but he based that notion not on reason or mystical experience but solely on faith grounded in love.

ETHICS

Dostoevsky's ethical thinking was dominated by his opposition to egoism and defense of altruism as expressed in Christ's commandment to "love thy neighbor as thyself." His first major attack on egoism came in *Notes from Underground*, in the form of a devastating critique of the ethical theory (a form of enlightened egoism) espoused by Chernyshevsky and his followers. In the diary entry on the death of his first wife, Dostoevsky formulated the opposition between the Christian law of love and the egoistic force in human nature that opposed it, which he dubbed the law of personality. The struggle between these two laws, both rooted in the complex material-spiritual nature of humanity, remained central to Dostoevsky's writings—fiction and nonfiction alike—throughout his career. Despite his emphasis on free choice he did not regard freedom as the highest human value; freedom is limited morally by the Christian law of love.

As the philosophical foundation for the law of love, Dostoevsky long relied on the idea that an inborn human conscience tells people authoritatively whether an action is right or wrong. Shortly before his death, however, he reluctantly admitted that conscience does not always speak univocally and that it may itself be evil; he concluded that morality has as its ultimate ground the religious faith that accepts the law of love as Christ proclaimed and lived it. Dostoevsky interpreted the law deontologically, as commanding or prohibiting actions as good or bad in themselves regardless of their results, thus rejecting utilitarianism. He vigorously opposed the idea, powerfully dramatized in both *Crime and Punishment* (1866) and *Demons* (1871–72) that an action abhorrent in itself may be justified by supposed future good consequences.

Two other recurring ethical themes in Dostoevsky's novels, particularly *Crime and Punishment* and *The Brothers Karamazov*, are also directly related to his devotion to the Christian moral ideal. These are the notions of universal moral responsibility ("I am responsible not only for my actions but for those of everyone") and the moral value of suffering. If essentially the ethical ideal is to be Christlike, it means freely accepting responsibility for others and suffering for their good, as Christ in the atonement took upon himself the sins of all humanity.

AESTHETICS

Dostoevsky's philosophy of art was laid out most fully in a polemical essay entitled "Mr. —bov and the Question of Art" (1861), directed against the so-called civic school of Russian criticism then represented most prominently by Nikolai Dobrolyubov. Just as Dostoevsky rejected utilitarian ethics, he had no sympathy for the view that art should be judged on the basis of its usefulness in promoting the satisfaction of basic human needs, such as the needs for food, shelter, and clothing.

Dostoevsky's argument against these critics was twofold. First, they failed to understand that human beings have aesthetic as well as material needs—specifically, a need for beauty, defined broadly in classical terms as "harmony and tranquility" (Magarshack 1997, p. 125), and a need to engage in creative activity—a notion reminiscent of the play theory of art advanced by Konrad Lange and Karl Groos. Second, Dostoevsky contended that utilitarian reasoning is a poor tool for determining the value of art, regardless of what needs it serves, for

such reasoning rests on predicting the future impact of a work—something people cannot do with any confidence.

Dostoevsky did not deny that aesthetic values may have social and moral significance; beauty is not a narrowly aesthetic category for him. In *The Idiot* (1868) he describes Prince Myshkin as insisting that "beauty will save the world," presumably having in mind Beauty as producing harmony and tranquility in society (p. 382). But he vigorously denied that artists have a duty to engage in useful activity. Art, he argued, should be judged on the basis of its artistry, not its moral or social impact, and he defended the right of the artist to free scope for creativity.

SOCIAL PHILOSOPHY

A critic of Russian serfdom, Dostoevsky was drawn to European Enlightenment thinking in his youth and became active in clandestine revolutionary circles; in 1849 he was arrested and sentenced to nine years of imprisonment and exile in Siberia. He was never opposed in principle to the Russian imperial system of government, however, and upon his return to European Russia and the subsequent emancipation of the serfs in 1861 be became a champion of Russian autocracy and a severe critic of violent revolution, which he attacked most powerfully in the novel *Demons*. Through many journalistic articles, especially a long series entitled *A Writer's Diary* (1873, 1876–1881), he was an influential commentator on political, economic, and other social issues, writing from a Slavophile, nationalist perspective.

Dostoevsky's defense of autocracy was based on his conviction that the citizens of Russia willingly accepted a patriarchal hierarchy of social strata based on inequalities in talents and abilities. Such inequalities are not evils in Russia, he argued, because they are mutually acknowledged in an atmosphere of respect dictated by the Christian law of love. European political institutions designed to limit authority, he contended, were outgrowths of the history of the European states, which had their origin in the conquest of one people by another (such as the Gauls by the Franks) and were still characterized by hostility between rulers and ruled, unlike the harmony between the Tsar-father and his children that always existed in Russia. In Dostoevsky's idealized conception, an autocracy can be the freest state in the world, for its rulers need not fear their subjects.

Dostoevsky's aversion to the Russian revolutionaries extended to their economic program—socialism—because he considered it one of the great European evils threatening Russia's unique civilization. He called it, paradoxically, the height of egoism, because its appeal was to personal greed and the advancement of one's own rights against those of others. Above all, he saw socialism as destructive of human freedom: The revolutionary socialist, Dostoevsky argued, seeks the compulsory union of humanity by forcing economic change in the supposed interest of all. *Notes from Underground*, *Demons*, and *The Brothers Karamazov* all offer vivid treatments of this theme; the tale of the Grand Inquisitor in the latter novel is universally acclaimed as one of the most brilliant dramatic embodiments of philosophical ideas in world literature. Dostoevsky's remarkably prescient anticipation, in these and other works, of the aims and even the tactics of the twentieth-century Russian Bolsheviks has contributed to his reputation as a prophet.

PHILOSOPHY OF HISTORY

Scattered throughout Dostoevsky's published and unpublished writings are fragments of a nationalistic theory of world history that, although generally consonant with his ethical and religious views, has provoked much controversy because of the messianic mission it ascribed to Russia (particularly in later writings such as *A Writer's Diary*) and its seeming inconsistency with his conception of the future as radically undetermined and hence unpredictable.

In an early (1864–1865) notebook, Dostoevsky sketched three stages in the evolution of human society: (1) Primitive patriarchalism, in which humans live in unreflective community, lacking a concept of self; (2) Civilization, in which personal consciousness and egoism arise; community disintegrates and previously accepted patriarchal laws are questioned. This is a diseased condition, for it undermines faith in God and destroys the spontaneity of life; and (3) Christianity, in which there is a return to God, community, and spontaneity but on a conscious level: individuals voluntarily give themselves to others by accepting the law of love.

Dostoevsky's many discussions of national differences among peoples drew on this conception of levels of evolutionary progress. He believed that the Western European peoples, and even more the Jewish people wherever they resided, represented the diseased condition of egoism characteristic of the second stage of history. Russians, by contrast, as true Christians, are altruistic; furthermore they possess a unique trait he calls *universal responsiveness*, by virtue of which they comprehend and sympathize with the problems of all peoples of the world. The Russians, then, are the only nation firmly situated in the third stage of history—Shatov in *Demons* calls them

"the only 'god-bearing' nation" (p. 247)—and it is their mission to raise others to that level by uniting them in a single loving community. As early as 1856 Dostoevsky had coined the expression *the Russian idea* for his nation's special role in world history. More than a century later, following the collapse of the Soviet Union, the term gained new life as the rallying cry of Russian nationalists.

See also Berdyaev, Nikolai Aleksandrovich; Camus, Albert; Chernyshevskii, Nikolai Gavrilovich; Egoism and Altruism; Enlightenment; Existentialism; Materialism; Nietzsche, Friedrich; Russian Philosophy; Shestov, Lev Isaakovich.

Bibliography

PRIMARY WORKS

The Brothers Karamazov: A Novel in Four Parts with Epilogue. Translated by Richard Pevear and Larissa Volokhonsky. New York: Vintage Classics, 1991.

Complete Letters. 5 vols, edited and translated by David Lowe and Ronald Meyer. Ann Arbor, MI: Ardis, 1988–1991.

Crime and Punishment. Translated by Richard Pevear and Larissa Volokhonsky. New York: Vintage Classics, 1992.

Demons: A Novel in Three Parts. Translated by Richard Pevear and Larissa Volokhonsky. New York: Alfred A. Knopf, 1994.

The Idiot. Translated by Richard Pevear and Larissa Volokhonsky. New York: Vintage Classics, 2003.

Notes from Underground. Translated by Richard Pevear and Larissa Volokhonsky. New York: Vintage Classics, 1994.

Complete Collected Works in Thirty Volumes. Leningrad, Russia: Nauka, 1972–1990.

A Writer's Diary. 2 vols. Translated by Kenneth Lantz. Evanston, IL: Northwestern University Press, 1993–94.

SECONDARY WORKS

Bakhtin, Mikhail Mikhailovich. *Problems of Dostoevsky's Poetics,* edited and translated by Caryl Emerson. Minneapolis: University of Minnesota Press, 1984.

Frank, Joseph. *Dostoevsky.* 5 vols. Princeton, NJ: Princeton University Press, 1976–2002.

Knapp, Liza. *The Annihilation of Inertia: Dostoevsky and Metaphysics.* Evanston, IL: Northwestern University Press, 1996.

Kostalevsky, Marina. *Dostoevsky and Soloviev: The Art of Integral Vision.* New Haven, CT: Yale University Press, 1997.

Lauth, Reinhard. *Die Philosophie Dostojewskis in systematischer Darstellung ("Ich habe die Wahrheit Gesehen").* Munich, Germany: R. Piper, 1950.

Magarshack, David, ed. and tr. *Dostoevsky's Occasional Writings.* Evanston, IL: Northwestern University Press, 1997.

Morson, Gary Saul. "Dostoevskii, Fëdor Mikhailovich (1821–1881)." In *Routledge Encyclopedia of Philosophy,* edited by Edward Craig, vol. 3, pp. 114–119. London: Routledge, 1998.

Proffer, Carl R., ed. *The Unpublished Dostoevsky: Diaries and Notebooks (1860–81) in Three Volumes.* Ann Arbor, MI: Ardis, 1973–1976.

Scanlan, James P. *Dostoevsky the Thinker*. Ithaca, NY: Cornell University Press, 2002.

James P. Scanlan (2005)

DOUBLE TRUTH, DOCTRINE OF

See *Averroism*

DOUBT

To be in doubt about a proposition is to withhold assent both from it and from its contradictory. Although people sometimes withhold assent with no reason for doing so and persist in this even after conceding that they have no reason, doubt is rational only when one has a reason for it and reasonable only when the reason is a good one. Doubt may be accompanied by various feelings, but it seems unlikely that there are specific feelings uniquely associated with it; in general, the feelings associated with doubt are anxiety or hesitation, which are identified as feelings of doubt when they arise in contexts involving questions of belief. In any case, philosophers are not ordinarily concerned with psychological characterizations of a doubter's state of mind. Their attention is primarily devoted to understanding the conditions under which doubt is reasonable and to defining the limits of reasonable doubt.

EVIDENCE AND REASONABLE DOUBT

Whether it is reasonable for a person to doubt a proposition cannot always be decided solely by considering the evidence that the person possesses relevant to the proposition or, in a situation in which there is purportedly noninferential knowledge, by considering his ground for assent. Doubts that are unreasonable or absurd in one situation may be quite reasonable in another, although the available evidence or ground is the same in both cases. For example, special caution is appropriate when the penalties for error are particularly great; hence, an ordinarily acceptable basis for assent may be inadequate if much depends upon avoiding error, although the gravity of the risk does not in itself constitute evidence. Moreover, a basis for assent that would be entirely compelling in normal circumstances may be insufficient if otherwise remote possibilities of error must be taken seriously because of threats posed by a resourceful deceiver.

From the fact that someone has no reason to doubt a given proposition, therefore, it does not follow that the evidence he possesses is sufficient to render unreasonable *all* doubts concerning the proposition. It would seem quite worthwhile to explore the ways in which the reasonableness of doubt is affected by considerations other than the available evidence or ground for assent. Philosophers, however, on the whole, are interested only in very general principles that are not affected by contingencies of any sort. For this reason, perhaps, philosophical studies of doubt have usually been concerned with limiting cases in which the reasonableness of doubt depends only on the available evidence or ground for assent. In other words, they have dealt mainly with what is *indubitable*—with what it is never reasonable to doubt regardless of contextual variables of the sort described above. Accordingly, a philosopher's designation of certain propositions as *dubitable* is not generally to be understood as a denial that there are circumstances in which doubting these propositions would be absurd. The designation means only that given the evidence or ground for the propositions, there are conceivable circumstances in which doubt would be reasonable.

CONDITIONS OF INDUBITABILITY

Toward the end of the First Meditation, René Descartes invokes the distinction between what is indubitable and what, in normal circumstances, is open to no reasonable doubt. In defense of his decision to regard as dubitable many propositions which, in practice, it is unreasonable to doubt, he declares, "I cannot at present yield too much to distrust, since it is not now a question of action but only of meditation and of knowledge." In their usual concerns, individuals are not often required to decide whether a proposition is indubitable, as distinct from deciding whether there is any reason to doubt it. Questions of indubitability are theoretical: they concern only the relation between a proposition and the evidence or ground for it, and take no account of the other concrete circumstances in which a proposition is evaluated.

LIMITS OF RELEVANT EVIDENCE. When is one entitled to regard a proposition as indubitable? It might be maintained that one is not entitled to do so as long as anything which can serve as evidence relevant to the proposition remains unexamined, on the ground that when this evidence comes to be examined, it may turn out to require an alteration of belief. But by virtue of the empirical and logical connections among facts, the truth-value of any proposition affects the truth-values of an unlimited number of others: Hence, the truth-values of an unlimited number of propositions are relevant to that of any proposition and may serve as evidence concerning it. Since it is impossible to examine each of these other propositions, no proposition could ever be regarded as indubitable if it were first necessary to examine everything that may serve as evidence relevant to its truth-value. On the other hand, it seems that this impasse can be avoided only if it is possible to settle in advance the import of matters that have not been examined.

IMMEDIATE EXPERIENCE. That it is in fact possible to settle the import of matters that have not been examined may be brought out as follows. The impossibility of checking all the consequences of an empirical proposition is often cited to support the view that empirical propositions must always remain dubitable. Nonetheless, many philosophers who employ this argument concede the indubitability of so-called "basic propositions," or a person's current reports of the immediate contents of his consciousness (for example, pains, sense data, thoughts). But however fragmented and ephemeral immediate experiences may be, they are not without innumerable conditions and consequences. Like those of empirical propositions (statements of fact about the world outside immediate consciousness), the truth-values of basic propositions are connected with those of an unlimited number of other propositions which may be construed as evidence relevant to them. Hence, if a person's current reports of the immediate data of his own consciousness are indubitable, it is not because he has surveyed everything that may serve as evidence relevant to them: rather, it is because his ground for making the report is such that he cannot reasonably acknowledge that any evidence could supersede it. Indeed, it is reasonable for him to require that all evidence be interpreted so as to be consistent with his report.

INCORRIGIBILITY. When one proposition serves as evidence relevant to a second, it does so by virtue of certain other empirical or logical propositions (laws or rules) by which the two are connected. The connection may be broken or its nature altered, however, if the intermediary propositions upon which it depends are rejected or revised. Thus, the possibility of coming upon contrary evidence can be excluded by requiring that this alternative be adopted whenever necessary.

But under what conditions is it reasonable to make such a requirement of incorrigibility—to arrange that nothing count as evidence against a certain proposition? In some cases (for instance, when a mathematical proposition is supported by a well-understood proof, or when a basic proposition is grounded in immediate experience) it may seem fairly clear that the conditions are satisfied. However, philosophers have failed to provide a general account of these conditions; instead, they have usually limited themselves to identifying particular instances of their satisfaction. Some philosophers have claimed with considerable plausibility that certain elementary mathematical propositions (such as that 2 + 2 = 4) may be regarded as indubitable without proof, but they have done little to explain systematically why this should be so. With regard to empirical propositions, neglect of the problem of clarifying the conditions in which they may be accepted as indubitable has resulted in part from widespread controversy over whether the problem properly arises at all. That there are no such conditions is frequently maintained by philosophers (for example, Bertrand Russell, A. J. Ayer, C. S. Peirce, C. I. Lewis) who subscribe to certain popular epistemological doctrines—in particular, the doctrines that every empirical proposition is to be construed on the model of a scientific hypothesis, or that it is to be interpreted phenomenalistically as equivalent to an unlimited number of predictions.

LOGICAL CONTINGENCY AND NECESSITY

A more general obstacle to a sound understanding of the basis of indubitability lies in a tendency to look for it in the wrong place. A proposition is indubitable when there could be no reason to doubt it, but this impossibility is not in general inherent in the logical character of the proposition itself. Indubitability is an epistemic property that depends on the relation between a proposition and the evidence or ground for assent with which it is considered. In particular, dubitability and indubitability must not be confused with logical contingency and logical necessity. The logical contingency of a proposition does not as such entail that no one has conclusive evidence or ground for it, and a logically necessary proposition may reasonably be doubted by someone who is not in a position to appreciate its necessity and who therefore must concede the possibility that further inquiry will uncover evidence against it.

Moreover, it is a mistake to suppose that evidence for a proposition is not conclusive unless its conjunction with the denial of the proposition is self-contradictory. To be sure, a proposition is indubitable if and only if no basis for assenting to its alternative is conceivable, but something may be inconceivable even though it contradicts neither itself nor what has already been established.

CONDITIONS OF RATIONAL INQUIRY

The claim that a basis for doubt is inconceivable is justified whenever a denial of the claim would violate the conditions or presuppositions of rational inquiry. Avoidance of self-contradiction is perhaps the most familiar of these conditions, but it is not the only one. For instance, since inquiry is fundamentally an attempt to discriminate between what is to be accepted and what is to be rejected, nothing can rationally be conceived which involves denying the necessity for making these discriminations or undermining the possibility of making them.

A systematic explanation of dubitability and indubitability awaits, therefore, a general theory of the nature of rationality which illuminates the presuppositions and conditions that rationality requires. Furthermore, it awaits an account, developed from this theory, of the particular conditions in which propositions of various sorts must be regarded as indubitable if the possibility of rationality is to be preserved. Even if this were done, however, a further problem would remain. While an adequate theory of rationality would give a clear account of the conditions in which a proposition may reasonably be regarded as indubitable, it cannot of course guarantee that these conditions are correctly identified in any given case. To support the claim that a certain proposition is indubitable, it is not sufficient to understand the conditions in which such claims are justified; it is also necessary to know that the conditions are fulfilled in the particular case in question.

THE INDUBITABILITY REGRESS

A disturbing pattern of argument seems to develop, however, in considering the proposition that a given proposition is indubitable. The proposition that the conditions for the indubitability of a certain proposition have been satisfied cannot itself be regarded as beyond doubt unless the conditions for *its* indubitability have been satisfied; but the satisfaction of *these* conditions is dubitable unless …, and so on.

But acknowledging this regress does not require one to concede that it is never reasonable to regard a proposition as indubitable. Rather, the view to which the regress leads appears to be that while there are occasions on which it is reasonable to regard a proposition as indubitable, it is never altogether indubitable just which occasions these are. There is an air of paradox here, perhaps, but there is no logical difficulty. The regress does not interfere with the possibility of there being satisfactory logical relations between indubitability claims and judgments establishing that these claims are reasonable. It

only interferes with our confidence in ourselves, suggesting that there is always room for doubt as to whether we are being reasonable. Or, to put the matter a bit differently, the regress supports no more than the mordant comment that it is never reasonable to insist that the question of whether one is being reasonable is entirely closed.

See also Ayer, Alfred Jules; Descartes, René; Error; Experience; Knowledge and Belief; Lewis, Clarence Irving; Peirce, Charles Sanders; Propositions; Questions; Russell, Bertrand Arthur William; Skepticism, History of.

Bibliography

In addition to loci classici in Descartes, *Meditations on First Philosophy*; David Hume, *An Enquiry concerning Human Understanding*; and Immanuel Kant, *Critique of Pure Reason*, there are particularly interesting and relevant discussions in the following more recent works: A. J. Ayer, *The Problem of Knowledge* (London: Macmillan, 1956); C. I. Lewis, *An Analysis of Knowledge and Valuation* (La Salle, IL: Open Court, 1946); N. Malcolm, "Knowledge and Belief," in *Knowledge and Certainty* (Englewood Cliffs, NJ: Prentice-Hall, 1963); G. E. Moore, "Four Forms of Scepticism," in *Philosophical Papers* (London: Allen and Unwin, 1959); and C. S. Peirce, *Collected Papers* (Cambridge, MA, 1935).

OTHER RECOMMENDED TITLES

Buryeat, M. F., ed. *The Skeptical Tradition*. Berkeley: University of California Press, 1983.

DeRose, Keith, and Ted Warfield, eds. *Skepticism*. New York: Oxford University Press, 1999.

Fogelin, R. *Pyrrhonian Reflections on Knowledge and Justification*. Princeton, NJ: Princeton University Press, 1995.

Greco, John. *Putting Skeptics in their Place*. New York: Cambridge University Press, 2000.

Hankinson, R. J. *The Sceptics*. London: Routledge, 1995.

Klein, Peter. *Certainty: A Refutation of Scepticism*. Minneapolis: University of Minnesota Press, 1981.

Lehrer, Keith. "Why not Scepticism?" *Philosophical Forum* 2 (1971): 283–298.

Roth, Michael, and Glenn Ross. *Doubting: Contemporary Perspectives on Skepticism*. Boston: Kluwer, 1992.

Sosa, Ernest. *Knowledge in Perspective: Selected Essays in Epistemology*. Cambridge, U.K.: Cambridge University Press, 1991.

Sosa, Ernest, and Enrique Villanueva, eds. *Skepticism*. Cambridge, MA: Blackwell, 2000.

Stroud, Barry. *The Significance of Philosophical Skepticism*. Oxford: Oxford University Press, 1984.

Williams, Michael. *Unnatural Doubts: Epistemological Realism and the Basis of Scepticism*. Oxford: Blackwell, 1992; corrected edition, Princeton, NJ: Princeton University Press, 1996.

Harry G. Frankfurt (1967)
Bibliography updated by Benjamin Fiedor (2005)

DRAMA

See *Greek Drama; Tragedy*

DREAMS

Almost all of us have had dreams, yet few could say with confidence what they are, beyond agreeing that they occur during sleep and have some likeness to waking experience. Yet most people would in all probability accept the kind of definition given by philosophers, for example Plato's "visions within us, … which are remembered by us when we are awake and in the external world" (*Timaeus*, 46A) or Aristotle's "the dream is a kind of imagination, and, more particularly, one which occurs in sleep" (*De Somniis*, 462a). Indeed, such notions seem to be summarized in the *Oxford Dictionary*'s definition: "A train of thoughts, images, or fancies passing through the mind during sleep; a vision during sleep." Dreams are striking phenomena, and the more superstitious see in them signs and portents of what is to happen; even today divination by dreams has not lost its popularity. A more sophisticated way of looking at dreams is to regard them as revealing something about the sleeper, either about his physical condition or about his mental state. An example of the former can be seen in the diagnostic technique used in the temple of Aesculapius; patients seeking a cure had to sleep all night in the temple precincts and would experience a "vision" that would indicate the disease or its cure. Many writers had suggested that mental states were revealed by dreams, but there was little serious study of the idea until the work of Sigmund Freud and his followers. Freud's doctrine of the unconscious, and the way in which it is revealed in dreams and other less rational activities, is important for psychiatry; but he had little to say about the nature of dreams that is of interest to the philosopher, though the fact that they had been found worthy of study may have resulted in an increase in philosophic concern about the problems they raise.

While we are having them, dreams often appear to be as real as waking experience; children have to be told that the object of their terror "was only a dream," hence not part of the world. William James expressed this well in his *Principles of Psychology*: "The world of dreams is our real world whilst we are sleeping, because our attention then lapses from the sensible world. Conversely, when we wake the attention usually lapses from the dream-world and that becomes unreal." This similarity has led philosophers to pose the question, "How can you prove whether at this moment we are sleeping, and all our thoughts are a dream; or whether we are awake, and talking to one another in the waking state?" (Plato, *Theaetetus*, 158). In perhaps the most famous example of the difficulty of distinguishing dreams from reality, René Descartes introduced his method of universal doubt. He concluded, "I see so manifestly that there are no certain indications by which we may clearly distinguish wakefulness from sleep that I am lost in astonishment" (*First Meditation*). Descartes finally resolved his doubts in this respect by appealing to a criterion of consistency: "For at present I find a very notable difference between the two, inasmuch as our memory can never connect our dreams with one another, or with the whole course of our lives, as it unites events which happen to us while we are awake" (*Sixth Meditation*). Such a consistency criterion has been adopted by several more recent writers on the topic. Unfortunately, this will not do the task required, for consistency can only be used as a test of a particular experience by waiting to see what happens in the future. It would enable me to tell that I had been dreaming, not that I am now dreaming; for however confident I am of the reality of my surroundings, something may happen in the future that will reveal them to be part of a dream. Further, the problem remains whether any consistency discovered is a real or a dreamed one.

The failure of consistency to provide a test need not be worrying, for the times in which genuine doubt arises are normally those involving memory—I am not sure if this event actually happened or whether I dreamed it. In such a case I would normally try to remember some part of the event that would have left a mark in the physical world, and then see if there is such a trace of the event; if there is nothing, I conclude that I had dreamed the occurrence. In spite of Descartes's remark, it is rare that we are in doubt about whether we *are* dreaming. The expression "I must be dreaming" is normally used in circumstances when I am quite sure that I am not dreaming, to express surprise at some pleasant occurrence, for example the arrival of a friend whom I thought to be somewhere distant. There are times when we are aware that we are dreaming, though normally a dream presents itself as real and no questions about its genuineness arise. It seems that the conviction that one is dreaming does not come from a previous doubt within the dream about the status of the experience; it just occurs, though sometimes accompanied with a feeling of relief. But in most cases the dream convinces us that it is reality, in that no doubt or questioning arises during its course. The difference between dreams and hallucinations lies in the fact that there is nothing external to dreams with which they can be compared, no tests that can be applied. For if we did apply a test in a dream, the result would be to confirm its reality. Philosophers have sought for some mark or test that would solve this problem, but there is none available. Any suggested sign of reality could be duplicated in the dream, and if all dreams bore marks of unreality, then there could not even be confusion over the remembering of them.

It has been generally agreed that dreams are due to the workings of the imagination no longer under the control of the intellect or the senses, as can be seen from the quotations at the beginning of this article; but it would seem that in such contexts the meaning of the word "imagination" had been left vague, serving rather as an indication of puzzlement than as a solution to a problem. Some recent work by physiologists has led to the suggestion (by W. Dement and N. Kleitman) that dreaming is correlated with rapid eye movements during sleep. Such a suggestion would seem to confirm Aristotle's remark that "dreaming is an activity of the sensitive faculty, but of it as being imaginative" (459a). The use of a physiological criterion for dreams has been challenged by Norman Malcolm in his book *Dreaming* (1959), which is clearly the most important contemporary discussion of the whole topic. In the course of it he challenges virtually all the assumptions made by previous philosophers. In criticism of the physiological work, he asserts that waking testimony is the sole criterion of dreaming (p. 81). The obvious difficulties that arise from the common belief that external stimuli can cause or influence the course of a dream, or that observers can sometimes tell from bodily movements that a sleeper is having a violent dream, he dismisses by means of a definition that dreams can take place only when the subject is sound asleep and that a person who is sleeping cannot respond to external stimuli (pp. 25–26). It might be thought that Malcolm was here doing the same thing for which he criticizes the physiologists, namely introducing a new concept of dreaming, for surely the ordinary unsophisticated notion includes the possibility of our recognizing that someone asleep is having a dream, in some cases at least, as well as the possibility of the dreamer being aware that he is dreaming. If both of these beliefs are ruled out by a philosophical argument, then it would appear that the concept of dreaming held by most people has been changed in important ways. Most of the points made in the earlier part of this article would be understood by those with an unsophisticated notion of dreaming.

Malcolm's arguments are, however, powerful and subtle, and his critics, of whom A. J. Ayer is perhaps the most eminent, have found it not at all easy to refute them.

Malcolm bases his reasoning on Ludwig Wittgenstein's *Philosophical Investigations,* in particular on the dictum that "an 'inner process' stands in need of outward criteria" (I. § 580). Malcolm argues that we can come by the concept of dreaming only by learning it from descriptions of dreams, "from the familiar phenomenon that we call 'telling a dream'" (II, p. 55). To talk of "remembering a dream" is to use the word *remember* in a sense different from the normal, for there is no external criterion by which we can check our memory, as there is in the paradigm cases of remembering, that of remembering an event in the public world, which can be checked by ourselves and others. What is told sincerely on waking is the dream, because there is no other way of finding out what, if anything, occurred while the teller slept. (This can be compared with Freud's reliance on the narration of the dream, but this was essential for its use in diagnosis. Nevertheless, Freud was willing to evaluate critically the veracity of actual dream accounts on the basis of his theory or as a result of previous analysis of its dreamer. For most purposes, it made no difference whether the dream account or the dream itself was being considered; Freud's concern was with different problems.)

Yet Malcolm rejects Ayer's suggestion that this theory amounts to saying that "we do not dream, but only wake with delusive memories of experiences we have never had." Malcolm is clearly correct in stressing the importance of the report of a dream and its difference from reports of public events; what the dreamer says on waking is final. Though we must learn the use of the word *dream* in the way Malcolm indicates, this does not rule out the possibility of its use being extended by further experience, for instance, correlating dream reports with observations of the dreamer, as Dement and Kleitman have done. The trouble is Malcolm's use of the term *criterion,* which is never clearly explained, and which seems to lead him into a crude verificationism; he even talks of "the senselessness, in the sense of the impossibility of verification, of the notion of a dream as an occurrence" (p. 83). A further consequence of Malcolm's use of the dream report as a criterion for dreaming is that it becomes impossible to talk of children having dreams before they have learned to speak (p. 59). If, as Malcolm apparently wishes to maintain, words can be used only if their application can be strictly verified, then many ordinary uses will be cut out. That we now have a particular concept of some mental activity does not make it impossible that further experience will lead us to introduce a modification of it, in which case the way in which we first learned it may have no bearing on the criterion of its use. For example, many words used in the sciences are first learned in an approximate way and their criteria of application refined in the course of education. Malcolm claims that his argument applies only to words that refer to "inner" processes. What he seems to do, however, is extend Wittgenstein's argument, valid in the area Wittgenstein intended it for, beyond its legitimate sphere. The primary use of the word *dreaming* depends upon the notion of telling a dream, but this does not prevent an extended use. Peter Geach remarks that Wittgenstein mentioned in a lecture Lytton Strachey's description of Queen Victoria's dying thoughts: "He expressly repudiated the view that such a description is meaningless because 'unverifiable'; it has meaning, he said, but only through its connexion with a wider, public, 'language-game' of describing people's thoughts" (*Mental Acts*, p. 3). In fact it is only because we know what it is to dream that we can understand the difficulties raised by talk of "verifying" reports of dreams.

Ayer also criticizes Malcolm's denial that one can make assertions while asleep, but in this case with less effect. It does seem clear that the words "I am asleep" cannot be used to make a genuine assertion, because such an utterance would contradict what was asserted, just as the only possible truthful reply to the question, "Are you asleep?" is "No." An absence of reply is what would lead the questioner to assert that the man was really asleep.

In spite of Malcolm's statement (p. 66) that there is no place for an implication or assumption that a man is aware of anything at all while asleep, many would claim, and understand others' claims, that they had become aware that they were dreaming. This also implies that they were aware that they were asleep. As part of a dream narrative, such awareness could be reported by the words, "I suddenly realized that it was all a dream." Clearly, such an assertion could not be taught by ostensive means. However, there seems no reason why, having learned how to use the ordinary concept of dreaming and expressions such as "I suddenly realized that," we should not combine the two into an assertion that would be commonly understood to apply to a possible experience. Malcolm's claim that a person must be partially awake to be aware that he is dreaming (pp. 38–44) seems, as suggested above, a redefinition of the term for which no adequate reason is advanced.

Malcolm wishes to say that the problem of what dreams are is a pseudo problem; he refuses to allow that they can be called experiences, illusions, workings of the imagination, or anything else they have been thought to be by previous philosophers. Ayer concludes his criticism of *Dreaming* by maintaining that dreams are experiences and mostly illusions, and "are found to be so by the same criteria that apply to illusions in general." This remark is difficult to understand; here Malcolm's stress on the report of the dream comes into its own; in recounting it I am not claiming that these things happened. Because while dreaming there is no possibility of making assertions about my experiences to other people, to describe dreams as illusions makes no sense. Malcolm has clearly made out his case in this respect. On the other hand, it seems difficult to deny that dreams are experiences, if only because the description is sufficiently vague to cover almost any "mental" phenomena. The same may be said of talking of dreams as being composed of images; here dreaming is being used as one of the examples of mental imagery, a vague concept. In spite of Malcolm's work, the problem of the nature of dreaming is still open for philosophic discussion, but any future examination of the problem will have to take his book fully into account. Many philosophers would still wish to assert that dreams occur, that they take place during sleep, while admitting that the meaning and justification of such claims is by no means clear.

See also Aristotle; Ayer, Alfred Jules; Descartes, René; Freud, Sigmund; Imagery, Mental; James, William; Malcolm, Norman; Plato; Psychoanalysis; Unconscious; Wittgenstein, Ludwig Josef Johann.

Bibliography

HISTORICAL WORKS

Aristotle. *De Divinatione per Somnum* (*On Prophesying by Dreams*). Translated by J. I. Beare, in *Works of Aristotle*, Vol. III. Oxford: Clarendon Press, 1931.

Aristotle. *De Somniis* (*On Dreams*). Ibid.

Bradley, F. H. "On My Real World." In *Essays on Truth and Reality*. Oxford: Clarendon Press, 1914.

Descartes, René. *Meditationes de Prima Philosophia*. In *The Philosophical Works of Descartes*, Vol. I, translated by E. S. Haldane and G. R. T. Ross. Cambridge, U.K., 1934.

Freud, Sigmund. *The Interpretation of Dreams*. Edited and translated by James Strachey. New York: Basic, 1955.

Freud, Sigmund. *Introductory Lectures on Psycho-analysis*. Translated by J. Riviere. London, 1949.

James, William. *The Principles of Psychology*. New York: Dover, 1950.

Malcolm, Norman. *Dreaming*. London: Routledge, 1959.

Plato. *Theaetetus* (158A). Translated by B. Jowett. Oxford, 1871.

Plato. *Timaeus* (46A). Ibid.

Russell, Bertrand. *Our Knowledge of the External World*. London, 1949.

Sartre, Jean-Paul. *L'imaginaire. Psychologie phénoménologique de l'imagination*. Paris: Gallimard, 1940. Translated by B. Frechtman as *The Psychology of the Imagination*. London, 1949.

Wittgenstein, L. *Philosophical Investigations.* Translated by E. Anscombe. Oxford: Blackwell, 1953. Especially pp. 184, 222–223. Also relevant is Malcolm's review of this work in *Philosophical Review* (October 1954): 530–559.

ARTICLES

Ayer, A. J. "Professor Malcolm on Dreams." *Journal of Philosophy* 57 (1960): 517–535. Malcolm's reply and Ayer's rejoinder in *ibid.* 58 (1961): 294–299.

Chappell, V. C. "The Concept of Dreaming." *Philosophical Quarterly* 13 (July 1963): 193–213.

Dement, W., and N. Kleitman. "The Relation of Eye Movements during Sleep to Dream Activity: An Objective Method for the Study of Dreaming." *Journal of Experimental Psychology* 53 (1957): 339–346.

MacDonald, M. "Sleeping and Waking." *Mind* 62 (April 1953): 202–215.

Manser, A. R., and L. E. Thomas. "Dreams." *Proceedings of the Aristotelian Society* Suppl. Vol. 30 (1956): 197–228.

Putnam, H. "Dreaming and 'Depth Grammar.'" In *Analytical Philosophy,* edited by R. J. Butler. Oxford, 1962.

A. R. Manser (1967)

DRETSKE, FRED

(1932–)

Born in 1932, Fred Dretske received his PhD from the University of Minnesota. He is emeritus professor of philosophy at Stanford University and professor of philosophy at Duke University. Since the early 1970s Dretske's work has been at the center of a number of key disputes in epistemology and the philosophies of perception, mind, and consciousness. Despite their range, two basic motivations unify Dretske's writings: the need to understand the mind in relation to its environment and a steadfast naturalistic outlook on the mind and its operations.

In *Seeing and Knowing* (1969), Dretske emphasized a form of perception that he labeled "nonepistemic seeing." This is an direct relation between perceiver and object not involving any particular conceptualization of the perceived object nor requiring any particular beliefs about it. Dretske argued that the concept of nonepistemic seeing is fundamental to understanding perception and the place of the mind within the world. Without it we have no way of understanding how we can all experience the same world despite having widely divergent concepts and beliefs. Via the notion of nonepistemic seeing, we can strip away our cognitive interpretive faculties and be left with the content of perception: the *objects* of the world we perceive.

Attention to nonepistemic seeing also undercuts the old idea that seeing involves "direct acquaintance" with some mysterious mental object, from whose incorrigibly known features we can only *infer* the existence of the external world.

We might naturally ask, What is the basic enabling feature of nonepistemic seeing? The answer is that there is an internal state of the perceiver that "carries the information" about the seen object. In *Knowledge and the Flow of Information* (1981), Dretske developed a sophisticated, elaborate, and technical account of information and its role in knowledge, thought, and perception. Building on his earlier epistemological work, Dretske analyzed knowledge in terms of *informationally caused* beliefs. To take one of Dretske's famous examples (from 1970), someone at a zoo *knows* that there is a zebra in front of him if that very information is causing his belief. Whether the appropriate information is available depends on the context of its occurrence, since information is a function of the *relevant* alternative messages that a signal could deliver. If there are lots of cleverly disguised mules about, his belief may not be caused by the information that there is a zebra in front of him (since the presence of that information may depend upon how much the perceiver knows about how zebras look), and thus he may not know that there is a zebra in front of him.

Dretske's account has an infamous consequence: the denial of inferential knowledge via known entailments. If our subject knows that these (the creatures in front of him) are zebras and that it follows from *x*'s being a zebra that *x* is *not* a disguised mule, then it would seem he could infer that these are not mules and hence *know* this. But how could he know this when he is utterly unable to distinguish a painted mule from a zebra? Dretske asserted that someone could know that something is a zebra without knowing that it is not a painted mule. While the mechanics of information allow this "paradox," the general issue remains highly contentious.

How can information or content play a causal role in the world? This is a key issue for Dretske's project of naturalizing the mind, or as Dretske puts it, baking "a mental cake with physical yeast and flour." Crudely put, the problem is that all behavior appears to have purely physical explanations that need appeal not to any information but only to local causes. We know how charge, momentum, and gravity cause events; informational causation seems to be something else altogether and quite mysterious.

In *Explaining Behavior* (1988), Dretske addressed this problem via a distinction between "triggering" and "structuring" causes. If *C* is an efficient or local cause of *M*, it is a triggering cause. The structuring cause of *M* is "the processes which explain why *C* causes *M*" (p. 91). In particular, the structuring causes of behavior are the historical processes that institute the triggering causal links between information-carrying mental states and behavior. Two aspects of this sort of explanation must be distinguished. The first comprises the historical processes—evolution, learning, or design—by which some internal state comes to have an "indicator function." The second is the deployment of the indicator to modify behavior *because* of what is indicated. Dretske maintains that, while a great many states serve to carry information of one sort or another and while these states certainly do enter into causal relations, only *learning* can bring about systems in which the carried information causally explains why these states cause the behavior they do. Only in learning do "we see meanings … doing some real work in shaping behavior" ("Dretske's Replies," p. 201).

The emphasis on learning leads to obvious difficulties. It seems to imply that innate mental states cannot explain behavior (perhaps cannot even *cause* behavior and maybe cannot even exist). In *Naturalizing the Mind* (1995), Dretske, elaborating his view, allowed that evolutionary processes can produce representational mental states that do not depend on learning for their efficacy. There he distinguished *systemic* and *acquired* representational states. The former are the experiential qualities of experience. Their content is nonconceptual and fixed by biology. Systemic representation underpins nonepistemic perception. And it enables acquired representations, a form of which constitute beliefs and the other propositional attitudes. This distinction allows for a more nuanced theory of mind and forms the basis for an ambitious representational theory of consciousness. In *Naturalizing the Mind*, Dretske also develops an intriguing theory of introspection in which our self-knowledge involves a special application of mentalistic concepts to our own experience.

Dretske continues to claim that representation is essentially linked to the external environment. In his theory of consciousness, the experiential nature of mental states depends on their representational properties (and all conscious states, including such "pure" sensations as pain or tickles, are conceived of as representational). While promising a complete naturalization of the most troublesome feature of the mind, representational properties have a downside. Since representational properties are determined and constituted by relations with the environment, Dretske's views have the consequence that a newly created *duplicate* of a person would utterly lack consciousness. Many find this less than plausible.

Be that as it may, Dretske presents an elegantly unified and comprehensive theory of mind that makes our mental lives fully causal in an entirely naturalistic way. His views, in their clarity, argumentative care, and intellectual honesty, exemplify the best features of modern analytic philosophy.

See also Consciousness; Content, Mental; Introspection; Mental Causation; Perception, Contemporary Views; Philosophy of Mind; Relevant Alternatives.

Bibliography

WORKS BY DRETSKE

Seeing and Knowing. Chicago: University of Chicago Press, 1969.

"Epistemic Operators." *Journal of Philosophy* 67 (24) (1970): 1007–1023.

Knowledge and the Flow of Information. Cambridge, MA: MIT Press, 1981.

"Misrepresentation." In *Belief: Form, Content, and Function*, edited by Radu J. Bogdan. Oxford, U.K.: Oxford University Press, 1986.

Explaining Behavior. Cambridge, MA: MIT Press, 1988.

"Dretske's Replies." In *Dretske and His Critics*, edited by Brian P. McLaughlin. Oxford, U.K.: Blackwell's, 1991.

"Conscious Experience." *Mind* 102 (406) (1993): 263–283.

Naturalizing the Mind. Cambridge, MA: MIT Press, 1995.

Perception, Knowledge, and Belief. Cambridge, U.K.: Cambridge University Press, 2000.

WORKS ON DRETSKE

McLaughlin, Brian P., ed. *Dretske and His Critics.* Oxford: Blackwell's, 1991.

William Seager (2005)

DRIESCH, HANS ADOLF EDUARD
(1867–1941)

Hans Adolf Eduard Driesch, perhaps the outstanding representative of neovitalism, was born at Bad Kreuznach, Germany. His father, Paul Driesch, was a merchant in Hamburg. From 1877 Hans Driesch attended the Johanneum (a humanist gymnasium) in his native city, graduating with honors in 1886. He then studied zoology, first under A. Weismann at Freiburg, then at Munich, and finally under Ernst Haeckel at Jena, receiving his Ph.D. in 1889; his dissertation was titled "Tektonische Studien an Hydroidpolypen" (Tectonic studies of hydroid polyps).

DEVELOPMENT OF DRIESCH'S THOUGHT

Reacting to arguments advanced by G. Wolff, W. His, and A. Goette, Driesch early became skeptical of Haeckel's mechanistic interpretation of the organism. The work of Wilhelm Roux, in particular, induced him to explore the whole vitalism-mechanism issue. Driesch's first publication, *Die mathematisch-mechanische Behandlung morphologischer Probleme der Biologie* (Mathematico-mechanical treatment of morphological problems of biology; Jena, 1890), led to a break with Haeckel. Then, following Roux's example, Driesch put the embryogenetic theory of His and Weismann to an experimental test. His and Weismann had held that morphogenetic development of the living organism could be explained by assuming that a specifically organized yet invisible structure of great complexity is contained in the nucleus of the germ cell and that the gradual unfolding of this structure, through nuclear division, determines the course of every ontogeny. Roux's experiments, in 1888, had seemed to confirm this theory of "tectonic preformation." When he destroyed one of the blastomeres at the two-cell stage, the remaining one would develop into a half embryo—either the left half or the right half, depending on which blastomere had been destroyed. Driesch merely intended to provide further confirmation of these facts. But where Roux had experimented with the egg of a frog, Driesch used eggs of the sea urchin. Against all expectations he found that each blastomere of the two-cell stage of a sea urchin egg developed into a whole embryo half the normal size. This was the opposite of Roux's results and was irreconcilable with the His-Weismann theory.

While at the Marine Biological Station in Naples, from 1891 to 1900, Driesch continued his experimental investigations, confirming and reconfirming in startling ways his earlier findings, and began to formulate his own theory. Relevant to the development of his ideas was a study of Otto Liebmann's book *Analysis der Wirklichkeit* (Analysis of reality) and of the writings of Immanuel Kant, Arthur Schopenhauer, René Descartes, John Locke, and David Hume. Alois Riehl's *Kritizismus* (Criticism) provided the springboard for Driesch's own theoretical efforts. The first results were published in 1893 under the title *Die Biologie als selbständige Grundwissenschaft* (Biology as an independent basic science; Leipzig). This book was followed by *Analytische Theorie der organischen Entwicklung* (Analytic theory of organic development; Leipzig, 1894), which contains the first formulation of Driesch's own teleologically oriented embryological the-

ory. But as yet this was a theory of "preformed teleology," not a vitalistic interpretation of embryological development. Only in 1895 did it dawn on Driesch that mechanistic principles could not account for his experimental findings.

Up to this time Driesch had accepted a "machine" theory of organismic development. Now he realized that such a theory would not do. In an essay titled "Die Maschinentheorie des Lebens" (The machine theory of life; in *Biologisches Zentralblatt* 16 [1896]: 353–368) he formulated as precisely as possible the view he had held so far, a view that he did not yet regard as vitalism. His first formulation of a dynamically teleological, and therefore genuinely vitalistic, theory was published under the title *Die Lokalisation morphogenetischer Vorgänge, ein Beweis vitalistischen Geschehens* (The localization of morphogenetic processes, a proof of vitalistic developments; Leipzig, 1899). In this book Driesch introduced the concept of the "harmonious equipotential system" and the proof that such a system cannot be accounted for in terms of mechanistic principles. The publication of 1899 thus marked the end of one period in Driesch's intellectual development and the beginning of another.

Gradually his interest in experimental work ceased. He now searched the literature in the field of physiology for possible proof that a "machine" theory could provide an adequate explanation of the phenomena of life. He found none, as his two books *Die organischen Regulationen* (Organic regulations; Leipzig, 1901) and *Die "Seele" als elementarer Naturfaktor* (The "soul" as elementary factor of nature; Leipzig, 1903) show. However, the conception of the "autonomy" of life had now to be justified within the broader framework of natural science. Driesch provided this justification in a book titled *Naturbegriffe und Natururteile* (Concepts of nature and judgments of nature; Leipzig, 1904). In 1905 he published *Der Vitalismus als Geschichte und als Lehre* (*The History and Theory of Vitalism*), in which he summed up his position against a historical background. That same year he "resolved to become a philosopher." His Gifford Lectures at the University of Aberdeen in 1907–1908, published in 1908 as *The Science and Philosophy of the Organism*, provided a splendid opportunity to present his position in systematic form.

From 1908 on, Driesch was concerned exclusively with philosophical problems. In 1909 he became a *Privatdozent* at Heidelberg and in 1912 a member of the university's philosophical faculty. In 1912, also, he published his basic philosophical work, *Ordnungslehre* (Theory of order). This was followed by *Die Logik als Aufgabe* (Logic as a task; Tübingen, 1913) and, in 1917, by *Wirklich-keitslehre* (Theory of reality). These three books together—ranging as they do over the fields of epistemology, logic, and metaphysics—embody the whole of Driesch's philosophical system, but they do not mark the end of his intellectual development. In *Leib und Seele* (Body and soul; 1916) Driesch set forth his definitive arguments against every "psycho-mechanical parallelism," and in *Wissen und Denken* (Knowing and thinking; Leipzig, 1919) he clarified and expanded his epistemological position.

In 1919 Driesch accepted a chair of systematic philosophy at the University of Cologne and in 1921 assumed a similar post at the University of Leipzig. During 1922–1923 he was a visiting professor in China. In 1926–1927 he lectured in the United States and in Buenos Aires. Being out of sympathy with the Nazi regime, ideologically and politically, he was retired in 1933. Adolf Hitler could not tolerate a thinker who fervently believed that nationalism was but "an obstacle to the realization of the *one* State of God." During the time of changing appointments, Driesch became interested more and more in problems of psychology and parapsychology. Books published in 1932 and 1938 reflect this development.

DRIESCH'S PHILOSOPHY

Although known primarily as one of the leading neovitalists, Driesch was also a critical realist and an "inductive" metaphysician. His system as a whole is developed most fully and most systematically in his *Ordnungslehre* and his *Wirklichkeitslehre*.

In his Gifford Lectures Driesch had evolved the argument that the phenomena of ontogenetic development, as revealed in his own experimental work, can be explained only when we assume the existence and the efficacy of some nonmechanistic and "whole-making" factor in nature, which Driesch called *entelechy*. This entelechy, "lacking all the characteristics of quantity," is not some special kind of energy, not a "constant" or a "force." It is not in space or in time but acts into space and into time. Entelechy, Driesch confessed, is "entelechy, an elementary factor sui generis" that "acts teleologically." But even Driesch could not blind himself to the fact that such a definition of his key concept is essentially meaningless because it is defined only negatively. He therefore tried, in his *Ordnungslehre,* to show that the conception of entelechy is logically legitimate after all.

Starting with the "irreducible and inexplicable primordial fact" that "knowing about my knowledge, I know something," Driesch found in his experience "primordial

concepts of order the meaning of which I, as the experiencing subject, grasp only 'intuitively'" (*Bedeutungsschau*), and that the experience as a whole presses on toward our "seeing everything in order." The method through which this "order" is revealed is that of "positing" or "discriminating" "objects of experience." It is necessary, however, to distinguish between "positing" (*setzen*) and "implicitly positing" (*mitsetzen*). What is "posited" may, in turn, "implicitly posit" something else. The whole procedure implies that the "object" is always "my" object (since I "posit" it), not some "thing-in-itself." To postulate an "objectivity" as a reality independent of, and separated from, "my" experience would involve a fallacy. Still, we must somehow transcend this "methodological subjectivism" by attempting to obtain a complete view of the totality of experience, actual and possible. In constructing this "whole" we are to be guided by the principle of economy: Only necessary steps should be taken, for "order" is perfect only when it includes everything necessary but nothing more. Now, upon inspection, I find that the experience I have is such that I can always select some specific part of it and identify it as "this," or as A. But as soon as I have posited a "this," all the rest of my experience has become a "nonthis," and the basic principle of noncontradiction—"this is not nonthis"—emerges. Moreover, when I posit a "this" and define it as *A,* I have before me (1) the *concept A* and (2) the *judgment* "*A* is there" or "*A* exists" (at least as an object for me). But let us now assume that some particular object *A* has the discernible attributes *abcd,* whereas some other object *A'* has the attributes *acd.* The objects are clearly different, but *A* includes *A',* or "*A* implicitly posits *A'*." Thus, the posit "wolf" implicitly posits "beast of prey," and any existing wolf implicitly posits an existing beast of prey. By extension, we obtain "*A* posits *A',* and *A'* posits *a*; therefore, *A* posits *a*." The principles of logic, thus, have their basis in our intuitive experience of order. The same is true, of course, of arithmetic and geometry. In fact, it is the aim of Driesch's general theory of order to disclose all the primordial elements of order first given in basic intuition.

Among "my" experiences there are some that I "have had before"; I "remember" them. This fact opens up an entirely new dimension of experience. But given this new dimension, I can now establish a remarkable order in my experience if I regard some of the objects of my immediate experience as an indication of the "being" or the "becoming" of an *X* that behaves as if it were independent of my experience of it; that is, it behaves as if it were a self-sufficient "realm of nature" in which the bipolar "cause-effect" relationship prevails. However, since, on the one hand, the effect cannot be richer in content than is its cause but, on the other hand, the living individual is a "whole" that is more than the sum of its parts, a close scrutiny of experience led Driesch to distinguish between a "merely mechanical causality" (*Einzelheitskausalität*) and a "whole-making causality" (*Ganzheitskausalität*) that involves more than merely additive changes. In onto-genetic development, for example, a mere sum of "equipotentialities" is thus transformed into the "whole-ness" of the mature organism. "Restitution" and "adapta-tions," experimentally demonstrable, are manifestations of this "whole-making" causality. The living organism itself, in its indisputable wholeness, is the most obvious result of *Ganzheitskausalität*. Thus, vitalism finds its jus-tification within Driesch's epistemology.

At the psychological and cultural levels, "whole-mak-ing causality" predominates, and Driesch posited "my soul" as "the unconscious foundation" of my conscious experience. The "soul," therefore, is also "posited in the service of order." "My primordial knowing of the mean-ing of order and my primordial willing of order … indi-cate … a certain primordial state and dynamics of my soul." "The *working* of 'my soul' [which guides my 'actions'] and certain *states* [of my soul] are 'parallel' to 'my conscious havings.'" "This sounds very artificial," Driesch admitted, "but logic is a very artificial instru-ment." When Driesch took up this theme again, in his *Wirklichkeitslehre*, he argued that "metaphysically," "my soul and my entelechy are One in the sphere of the Absolute." And it is at the level of the Absolute only that we can speak of "psycho-physical interaction." But the Absolute, so understood, transcends all possibilities of our knowing, and it is "an error to take, as did G. W. F. Hegel, the sum of its traces for the Whole."

All considerations of normal mental life lead us only to the threshold of the unconscious; it is in dreamlike and certain abnormal cases of mental life that we encounter "the depths of our soul." And in parapsychological phe-nomena—especially in telepathy, mind reading, clairvoy-ance, telekinesis, and materialization (all of which Driesch accepted as proved facts)—we find traces of a supra-individual wholeness. More important, however, our sense of duty also points toward a supra-personal whole, which, in the course of history, is continuously evolving. "In my experience of duty I am participating in the supra-personal whole of which I am an empirical embodiment, and it is *as if* I had some knowledge about the final outcome of the development of that whole." That is to say, my sense of duty indicates the general direction of the supra-personal development. The ulti-mate goal, however, remains unknown. From this point of view, history took on its particular meaning for Dri-esch.

Throughout his work Driesch's orientation is intended to be essentially empirical. Any argument con-cerning the nature of the ultimately Real will therefore have to be hypothetical only. It starts with the affirmation of the "given" as consequent of a conjectural "ground." His guiding principle in the realm of metaphysics amounts to this: The Real that I posit must be so consti-tuted that it implicitly posits all our experience. If we can conceive and posit such a Real, then all laws of nature, and all true principles and formulas of the sciences, will merge into it, and our experiences will all be "explained" by it. And since our experience is a mixture of wholeness (the organic and the mental realms) and nonwholeness (the material world), Reality itself must be such that I can posit a dualistic foundation of the totality of my experi-ence. In fact, there is nothing—not even within the ulti-mately Real—to bridge the gap between wholeness and nonwholeness. And this means, for Driesch, that ulti-mately there is either God and "non-God," or a dualism within God himself. To put it differently, either the theism of the Judeo-Christian tradition or a pantheism of a God continually "making himself" and transcending his own earlier stages is ultimately reconcilable with the facts of experience. Driesch himself found it impossible to decide between these alternatives. He was sure, however, that a materialistic-mechanistic monism would not do.

See also Continental Philosophy; Critical Realism; Descartes, René; Haeckel, Ernst Heinrich; Hegel, Georg Wilhelm Friedrich; Hume, David; Kant, Immanuel; Locke, John; Riehl, Alois; Schopenhauer, Arthur; Vital-ism.

Bibliography

ADDITIONAL WORKS BY DRIESCH

Der Vitalismus als Geschichte und als Lehre, Leipzig, 1905. Translated as *The History and Theory of Vitalism*. London, 1914. Rev. German ed., *Geschichte des Vitalismus*. Leipzig, 1922.

The Science and Philosophy of the Organism, 2 vols. London: A. and C. Black, 1908. Translated into German as *Philosophie des Organischen*. Rev. ed., Leipzig, 1921.

Zwei Vorträge zur Naturphilosophie. Leipzig, 1910.

Die Biologie als selbständige Grundwissenschaft und das System der Biologie. Leipzig, 1911.

Ordnungslehre, ein System des nichtmetaphysischen Teiles der Philosophie. Jena, 1912; rev. ed., 1923.

The Problem of Individuality. London: Macmillan, 1914.

Leib und Seele, eine Prüfung des psycho-physischen Grund-problems. Leipzig, 1916; rev. ed., 1920; 3rd ed., 1923. Translated as *Mind and Body.* New York: Dial Press, 1927.

Wirklichkeitslehre, ein metaphysischer Versuch. Leipzig, 1917; rev. ed., 1922.

Das Problem der Freiheit. Berlin, 1917; rev. ed., Darmstadt, 1920.

Das Ganze und die Summe. Leipzig, 1921. Inaugural address at the University of Leipzig.

" Mein System und sein Werdegang." In *Die Philosophie der Gegenwart in Selbstdarstellung,* Vol. I, edited by R. Schmidt. Leipzig, 1923. One of the more than 100 articles that Driesch published.

Metaphysik. Breslau, 1924.

The Possibility of Metaphysics. London, 1924.

Relativitätstheorie und Philosophie. Karlsruhe, 1924.

The Crisis in Psychology. Princeton, NJ: Princeton University Press, 1925.

Grundprobleme der Psychologie. Leipzig, 1926.

Metaphysik der Natur. Munich, 1926.

Die sittliche Tat. Leipzig, 1927.

Biologische Probleme höherer Ordnung. Leipzig, 1927; rev. ed., 1944.

Der Mensch und die Welt. Leipzig, 1928. Translated as *Man and the Universe.* London, 1929.

Ethical Principles in Theory and Practice. London, 1930.

Philosophische Forschungswege. Leipzig, 1930.

Parapsychologie. Leipzig, 1932; 2nd ed., 1943.

Philosophische Gegenwartsfragen. Leipzig, 1933.

Alltagsrätsel des Seelenlebens. Leipzig, 1938; 2nd ed., 1939.

Selbstbesinnung und Selbsterkenntnis. Leipzig, 1940.

Lebenserinnerungen; Augzeichnungen eines Forschers und Denkers in entscheidender Zeit. Edited by Ingeborg Tetaz-Driesch. Basel, 1951. Posthumous.

WORKS ON DRIESCH

Child, C. M. "Driesch's Harmonic Equipotential Systems in Form-regulations." *Biologisches Zentralblatt* 28 (1908).

Fischel, A. Review of Driesch's Gifford Lectures, *The Science and Philosophy of the Organism,* Vol. I. *Archiv für Entwicklungs-Mechanik* 26 (1908).

Griffith, O. W. Review of *The Problem of Individuality* and *The History and Theory of Vitalism. Hibbert Journal* 13.

Haake, W. "Die Formphilosophie von Hans Driesch und das Wesen des Organismus." *Biologisches Zentralblatt* 14 (1894).

Heinichen, O. *Driesch's Philosophie.* Leipzig, 1924.

Jenkinson, J. W. "Vitalism." *Hibbert Journal* (April 1911).

Jourdain, E. B. P. Review of *Ordnungslehre. Mind* 23 (1914).

Morgan, T. H. Review of *The Science and Philosophy of the Organism,* Vol. I. *Journal of Philosophy* 6 (1909).

Oakeley, H. D. "On Professor Driesch's Attempt to Combine a Philosophy of Life and a Philosophy of Knowledge." *PAS,* n.s., 21 (1920–1921).

Oakeley, H. D. Review of *Wirklichkeitslehre. Mind* 30 (1921).

Russell, L. J. Review of *Die Logik als Aufgabe. Mind* 23 (1914).

Schaxel, J. "Namen und Wesen des harmonisch-äquipotentiellen Systems." *Biologisches Zentralblatt* 36 (1916).

Schaxel, J. "Mechanismus, Vitalismus und kritische Biologie." *Biologisches Zentralblatt* 37 (1917).

Schneider, K. C. "Vitalismus." *Biologisches Zentralblatt* 25 (1905).

Secerov, Slavko. "Zur Kritik der Entelechielehre von H. Driesch." *Biologisches Zentralblatt* 31 (1911).

Spaulding, E. G. "Driesch's Theory of Vitalism." *Philosophical Review* 15 (1906).

Spaulding, E. G. Review of *The Science and Philosophy of the Organism,* Vols. I and II. *Philosophical Review* 18 (1909).

Vollenhoven, D. H. T. "Einiges über die Logik in dem Vitalismus von Driesch." *Biologisches Zentralblatt* 41 (1921).

Wagner, A. "Neo-Vitalismus," I, II. *Zeitschrift für Philosophie und philosophische Kritik,* Ergänzungsband, 136 (1909).

William H. Werkmeister (1967)

DUALISM IN THE PHILOSOPHY OF MIND

Mind-body dualism is the doctrine that human persons are not made out of ordinary matter, at least not entirely. Every person has—or, on many versions of the view, simply is identical to—a soul. A soul is said to have little in common with human bodies and other material objects but is in one way or another responsible for a person's mental life.

Mind-body dualism is sometimes called "substance dualism," to distinguish the view from "property dualism"—the thesis that mental properties (such as being in pain, thinking of Vienna) are in some way significantly different from or independent of physical properties (such as having neurons firing in one's brain in a certain pattern). Property dualism is meant to allow for what is often called "dual-aspect theory": persons are material objects with a nonphysical, mental "aspect" but no nonphysical *parts*—that is, no immaterial soul.

The entry begins with a brief discussion of property dualism, only to set it to one side in order to examine substance dualism in detail: its varieties, the traditional objections to the view, and the most popular arguments in its favor.

PROPERTY DUALISM

Before considering ways in which mental and physical properties might be distinct or independent, one needs to know what is meant by the terms *mental* and *physical*. (The expressions *property* and *state* shall be used interchangeably; being in pain is a mental property or mental state, weighing 150 pounds is a physical property or physical state. Many different things can be in pain or have the same weight; so properties and states are, in some sense, universals.)

Phenomenal states, such as experiencing a reddish afterimage or feeling a sharp pain, are surely mental states, as are "intentional attitudes" such as believing, doubting, loving, and hating. There may be puzzles about how to classify the unconscious desires and fears probed by psychoanalysts; but otherwise, the boundaries of the mental seem fairly clear. The range of things one might mean by *physical property* is, however, broader and more problematic. A narrow reading of *physical* might include only properties that come in for explicit mention in current fundamental physics—or in an imagined "final, true physics." A more generous approach would include any property expressible given just the resources of physics, mathematics, and logic. Sufficient generosity along these lines would allow for physical properties corresponding even to infinite disjunctions of arbitrarily chosen, maximally precise microphysical descriptions (that is, "consisting of such-and-such fundamental particles arranged in precisely this way, or that way, or …").

If property dualism were simply the thesis that mental properties are not identical to physical properties, narrowly construed, the doctrine would be of little interest. Synthesizing bile is a state of the liver; reaching gale force is a state of the winds in a hurricane; and neither "synthesizing bile" nor "reaching gale force" is a term likely to appear in any fundamental physics, contemporary or idealized. If "pain" fails to show up in physics for similar reasons, the mental state it names may be no less physical than the synthesis of bile or the force of a hurricane.

Given the more generous understanding of "physical," synthesizing bile or reaching gale force might well be identical to, or at least necessarily coextensive with, a physical property—a property equivalent to all the possible ways to synthesize bile or reach gale force, described in extreme microphysical detail. Imagine a god surveying all the possible worlds it could create, with their many varieties of particles and fields and laws. Such a being could disjoin all the microphysical descriptions of livers synthesizing bile or hurricanes achieving gale-force winds and thereby define physical properties necessarily coextensive with the target biological and meteorological properties. The existence of such definitions would show that the functioning of a liver or the strength of a hurricane could not possibly come apart from the behavior of the matter constituting the liver or the air and water through which the hurricane moves. If the god could do the same for mental states, that would show that they, too, are firmly grounded in microphysical facts.

To arrive at a truly interesting version of property dualism, one might suppose that even godlike powers to exhaustively describe every possible microphysical system would fail to produce a physical property necessarily coextensive with each mental property. Many who use the term follow David Chalmers (1996) in identifying it with the following sort of thesis: For at least some mental states, it is not possible to define, in terms of microphysical properties alone, a physical property common to all individuals in that mental state, and only to them—even given the resources of arbitrarily complex definitions and infinite disjunction, and even when restricting the search to a property that is merely coextensive in worlds with the same fundamental physical properties.

Property dualism, so understood, is equivalent to the failure of a variety of supervenience—a notion first used in philosophy of mind by Donald Davidson (1970) and brought into focus by Jaegwon Kim (1990). In the technical sense of *supervene* that is relevant here, the mental properties of a thing supervene upon its microphysical properties if and only if, among all the possible individuals in all the possible worlds, there is no pair with all the same microphysical properties but different mental properties. Kim showed that if supervenience held, one could define a physical property coextensive with any mental property simply by disjoining all the sufficiently precise microphysical descriptions of possible individuals having that property.

Defining property dualism as a failure of the mental to supervene upon the microphysical seems to presuppose that the fundamental properties of anything worthy of the name "physics" will not include mental states. But, as Robert Adams (1987) and Richard Swinburne (1997) point out, if mental states really are fundamental, one might expect that experiencing particular kinds of pains or smells will have to figure in some of the most basic laws. Still, so long as the nonmental physical properties of matter could be the same while the envisaged brutely mental ones could have been different (had there been different natural laws relating the two kinds of property), there would be a failure of supervenience: The mental properties would fail to supervene upon the purely physical properties.

Unlike substance dualism, property dualism remains a respectable position within philosophy of mind, defended by Chalmers (1996) and others. It seems easy to imagine physically indiscernible zombies (animate human bodies with no consciousness) or people whose spectrum of color experiences is the reverse of one's own. If genuinely possible, these scenarios show that the mental does not supervene upon the physical.

Substance dualism is also inconsistent with supervenience. If souls lack the properties mentioned in physics, they cannot very well differ physically; but, because different people are obviously thinking different things, the dualist's souls must differ mentally.

Until the latter half of the twentieth century, a dualism of mental and physical properties was largely taken for granted, even among philosophers who called themselves materialists. The term "dualism" almost always meant a dualism of distinct substances—a practice to be followed in the remainder of this entry.

PURE DUALISM AND COMPOSITE DUALISM

Many dualists, like Plato, teach that persons are entirely immaterial; they are identical with souls and are related to their physical bodies as pilot to ship. Others—perhaps René Descartes (1984), certainly St. Thomas Aquinas (cf. Stump 2003) and Richard Swinburne (1997)—identify a person with a composite of soul and body. Among composite dualists, further differences emerge: most composite dualists ascribe one's mental properties to the soul and one's physical properties to the body. On this version of composite dualism, a person is identical with a psychophysical whole that includes the thinking soul as a part. Eric Olson (2001) has drawn attention to some of the drawbacks of this view. It suggests that the soul is the real thinker, and that a person only has mental states by courtesy. But how could something—the soul—think and not be a person? How could it think for someone else? If the composite dualist insists that the person and the soul are both thinkers and that neither is the subject of mental states in a more fundamental way than the other, then each person includes two thinkers, neither of which can distinguish itself from the other.

St. Thomas Aquinas advocated a very different sort of composite dualism (for exposition, cf. Stump 2003, Leftow 2001). Within Aquinas's Aristotelian metaphysics, "accidental forms" explain a thing's accidental properties, and a "substantial form" explains its being, or essence. Following Aristotle, Aquinas calls the substantial forms of living things "souls"; the soul of a human being is responsible for its entire complex physical and mental nature. But it is not the soul that thinks or acts, it is the whole human being—a composite of matter and the soul or form that gives the matter its distinctively human structure. Aquinas departed from Aristotle in supposing that the human soul is a "subsistent form," something that continues to exist after death while not "informing" any matter. It even manages to think in that truncated state.

The Thomistic doctrine of the soul is a borderline case of mind-body dualism—although, with Eleonore Stump (2003) and Brian Leftow (2001), one may well regard its intermediate status as a promising sign. Although body and soul are united, says Aquinas, the soul has no mental properties; it is not itself a mind. Nor is it responsible for a person's mental powers alone; it includes the physical nature of a human being as well. For present purposes, dualism will be restricted to theories like Plato's pure dualism or Swinburne's composite dualism: theories positing souls with mental states of their own, in this life.

THE SPECTRUM OF DUALISMS

One point of agreement among dualists of all stripes is that there are a great many things in the world that lack mentality of any sort; and that, associated with each human person, there is a thinking thing, a soul, not composed of the same kinds of stuff as these nonmental things. The animist and spiritualist may think of the soul as extended or composite (ghostlike, perhaps composed of "ectoplasm"); but they deny, at any rate, that it is made of stuff that can be found in objects completely devoid of mentality. To be a substance dualist, then, one must at least accept a doctrine one might call *compositional dualism*: There exist things that can think alongside things that cannot think; and the thinking things either have no parts at all, or else parts of a special kind, unique to thinking things.

One could be a compositional dualist but still be a materialist. Roderick Chisholm (1978) took seriously the hypothesis that a person might be a tiny physical particle lodged somewhere in the brain. Suppose someone claimed, in a similar spirit, that the soul is a point-sized thinking substance that has the same mass as a proton and the same charge as an electron; and that every substance with a similar mass and charge is capable of thought. This rather bizarre theory qualifies as compositional dualism—yet it seems also to be a kind of materialism. Since dualism has always been thought of as an alternative to materialism, there must be more to it than compositional dualism. The missing component is clear: The thinking thing cannot simply be a special kind of physical object, such as a new species of fundamental particle; but what is it to be "nonphysical"?

Daniel Dennett sees a fundamental incoherence in the very idea of a nonphysical soul: "A ghost in the machine is of no help in our theories unless it is a ghost that can move things around ... but anything that can move a physical thing is itself a physical thing (although perhaps a strange and heretofore unstudied kind of physical thing)" (Dennett 1991, p. 35). If one were to define *physical* as "able to produce effects in space," then of course a nonphysical soul could not interact with a body. When dualists have denied that the soul is physical, they have meant many things—but none has been so foolish as to mean that.

Every plausible version of compositional dualism implies that substances capable of thought (and their parts, if any) have some important properties in common with substances utterly incapable of thought. To call a thinking thing "nonphysical" is not to say it has absolutely nothing in common with the matter of nonsentient things; it is rather to deny that they have as much in common as one might have thought. But dualists disagree about which attributes of ordinary matter are not found in thinking substances—that is, they mean different things by "nonphysical." The result is a spectrum of dualisms.

The maximal difference a dualist might posit between soul and body would be to identify souls with necessarily existing abstract objects, outside of space and time, like numbers or Plato's Forms. Some have said that persons are to their bodies as programs are to the computers that run the programs. And, if programs are understood in a way that makes them quite independent of the particular computers running them, they become abstract objects, mathematical entities. But it is hard to take this analogy very seriously. Almost all dualists will agree that souls have this much in common with ordinary material things: They are concrete entities, existing in time, and capable of change.

René Descartes allowed at least that much similarity between souls and ordinary matter, but little more. Cartesian souls are not dependent upon the behavior of matter for their continued existence or ability to think. They have no position in space. Descartes also claimed that souls are "simple," or without parts. Since he believed that everything in space was infinitely divisible, this was another way in which souls were unlike anything made of ordinary matter (Descartes, 1984).

Few dualists are so far out along the spectrum of dualisms as Descartes, however. It has become harder to deny that the ability to think depends upon a properly functioning brain. William Hasker (1999), Charles Taliaferro (1994), and other contemporary dualists go further, denying the existential independence of souls: When an organism has a sufficiently complex nervous system, it then automatically also generates a nonphysical substance to be the subject of that consciousness—an "emer-

gent substance" that remains radically but not completely dependent upon the brain for most of its operations and even for its continued existence. Hasker, W. D. Hart (1988), and—long before them—Samuel Clarke (1738) and Hermann Lotze (1885) have insisted that souls are located in space. Hart argues that mind-body interaction could even involve the transfer of a conserved quantity between soul and body. The "psychic energy" he describes makes souls even more like paradigmatic physical things. Still, Hart's souls lack charge, mass, spin, and all other interesting intrinsic properties characterizing physical particles. Furthermore, Hart defines measurable degrees of psychic energy in terms of the propensity to sustain beliefs, not in terms of physical effects; so even this quasi-physical quantity seems grounded in the mental nature of Hart's souls rather than in any features they share with ordinary matter.

Hart's view should surely qualify as a kind of dualism—his souls are immaterial enough—and the Chisholm-inspired particle materialism should not. If, as seems likely, there is no sharp line on the spectrum of compositional dualisms between the two, then the term "dualism" is vague. As with most vague yet useful terms, the region of indeterminacy is largely unoccupied.

The less extreme dualisms are of greater philosophical interest than Cartesianism. They make souls a part of the natural order, generated by any brain sufficiently complex to subserve conscious experience. One of the worst problems of interaction (the "pairing problem," discussed in the next section) is easily solved if souls are in space. Furthermore, few, if any, of the principal arguments for dualism (including the ones surveyed below) require Cartesian souls. Less radical dualisms are safer, positing no more differences between souls and material objects than are implied by the reasons for rejecting materialism.

PROBLEMS OF INTERACTION

Most objections to dualism fall under one of three heads: problems of interaction, epistemological worries, and application of Ockham's Razor. The most commonly cited "knockdown" objection to dualism is the impossibility of causal interaction between things as dissimilar as a physical body and an immaterial soul. The obvious rejoinder is that very dissimilar things do interact. For example, particles are certainly quite unlike the fields that push them around and that are, in turn, altered when particles are introduced into them. Attempts to make the objection more persuasive come in two versions.

The "pairing objection" begins with Ernest Sosa's observation: "What pairs physical objects as proper mates for causal interaction is in general their places in the all-encompassing spatial framework of physical reality" (1984, p. 275). Consider a series of duplicate guns, each of which hits a different target. Guns and targets are exactly alike; only differences in spatial relations explain why each gun hits a different target—the target at which it is aimed. Compare guns and targets to the bodies and souls of identical twins Joe and Moe. However similar they are, only Joe's body causes experiences in Joe's soul; only decisions taken by Joe lead directly to motions of Joe's body. According to the Cartesian, there can be no differences in the spatial relations between Joe's soul and the bodies of Joe and Moe; being outside of space, the soul cannot be closer to one body than to the other. But in what other respects could Joe's soul be "closer" to Joe's body than to Moe's body, and Moe's soul closer to Moe's body than to Joe's? Descartes's souls are all equally cut off from the physical world, so no answer comes readily to mind.

The pairing objection tacitly assumes that causal laws, and the dispositions and powers of objects described by such laws, are always general—an assumption some dualists reject. John Foster (1991) and Peter Unger (2006) think that souls and bodies could have not only dispositions to react to certain types of objects and situations but also dispositions to interact in special ways with particular individuals—individuals that need not differ in any qualitative or relational way.

Dualists like Clarke (1738), Lotze (1885), Hart (1988), and Hasker (1999) are in an even stronger position, since they assume that souls fall within the same spatial coordinate system as bodies. They make the natural assumption that, if souls are to be found in space at all, they must be located within the brains with which they interact. But one still wants to know exactly what sort of region a soul is supposed to occupy. Many dualists believe souls are simple, or partless. Must a simple thing occupy a geometrical point, on pain of being divisible into at least two parts, a left and right half? Some philosophers say no. Clarke (1738) and Lotze (1885) claim that the soul is spatially extended but simple. Lotze locates the soul within the brain wherever interaction takes place—which could be many different places at once, and different places at different times. Leibniz considers a mode of spatial occupancy the Scholastics called "definitive ubeity": there is a precise region in which the soul is located, but it is not true of any subregions that it is located precisely there (Leibniz, 1981, p. 221). Although these are difficult notions, they may represent ways (or perhaps two descriptions of the same way) for a soul to occupy more than a mere point while remaining a partless unity.

A second objection to interaction alleges that the mental states attributed to souls are of the wrong sort to enter into laws governing physical phenomena. If the "qualia" of phenomenal experiences (for example, the felt redshiness of a red after-image, the sharp flavor of an acrid smell) could somehow be reduced to physical states of brains or analyzed in terms of functional roles that physical states could play, then they would pose little threat to a materialistic picture within which all causation is underwritten by laws of the sort one finds in physics. If they characterize the states of a nonphysical soul, however, they will have to be taken seriously as extra, fundamental features of the world, requiring causal explanation. Causation requires laws; but in order for the astonishing variety of phenomenal states, falling under several sense modalities, to enter into the kinds of laws familiar from the sciences, they must be susceptible of precise mathematical comparison. However, as Robert Adams points out, "[t]here is no plausible, non–adhoc way of associating phenomenal qualia in general … with a range of mathematical values.…" (Adams 1987, p. 256). Laws linking the phenomenal experiences of a soul to the physical states of a body are bound to be relatively unsystematic and staggeringly complex. Far better to suppose that phenomenal properties are merely complex physical states of the brain; and that, as such, they obey laws that can be derived from those of biology, chemistry, and, ultimately, fundamental physics.

This second interaction objection, however powerful it might be, applies not only to substance dualists but also to anyone who is a property dualist about phenomenal states. Many philosophers who are happy to suppose that persons are identical with physical objects (such as living, human bodies or brains) nevertheless heartily endorse property dualism with respect to the qualia of phenomenal states. Like substance dualists, these property dualists must admit that there are additional laws governing the production of phenomenal qualia—laws that are quite complicated and, to some extent, piecemeal. (David Chalmers, Gregg Rosenberg, and others have floated theories about the form such laws might take [Chalmers, 1996; Rosenberg, 2004.])

Property dualism remains a respectable position within contemporary philosophy of mind, with powerful arguments in its favor. In the circumstances, then, this second problem of interaction can hardly be the final nail in the coffin of substance dualism.

EPISTEMOLOGICAL WORRIES

After interaction objections, the most commonly voiced complaints about substance dualism are epistemological in flavor: Suppose persons are souls that merely happen to be associated with bodies. One cannot keep track of another's soul by keeping an eye on it, or holding it fast. How, then, does one know that souls are not constantly coming and going "behind the scenes"?

Immanuel Kant's analogy illustrates the problem: "An elastic ball which impinges upon another similar ball in a straight line communicates to the latter its whole motion, and therefore its whole state (that is, if we take account only of the positions in space)." A series of mental substances passing on "representations together with the consciousness of them" would end with one that is "conscious of all the states of the previously changed substance, as being its own states, because they would have been transferred to it together with the consciousness of them." But if we identify persons with individual mental substances, "it would not have been one and the same person in all these states" (1965 p. 342). Kant's scenario is often turned into an argument against dualism: If it were reasonable to suppose that each person is identical with a soul, then it would be reasonable to be skeptical about whether we are dealing with the same person from one minute to the next. Since this is not reasonable, neither is the supposition that a person is a soul.

The argument fails if one endorses John Locke's view (in the chapter "Of Identity and Diversity" in his *Enquiry* [1975]) that a person is not identical with a particular soul but is instead constituted by a soul, and possibly by different souls at different times. So long as the succession of souls pass on the right sorts of mental states (Locke emphasizes memories), the person survives, constituted by one soul and then another. To give this reply would require that one say, with Locke, that a person and the person's soul are distinct things, although the soul thinks whenever the person does. In that case, if a person always remains responsible for the things she has done, then one soul could justly be punished for the deeds of another soul. (Locke himself seems to have thought that, although such punishment would not be unjust, it would not be very nice, and so God can be counted on not to allow soul-switching.)

Locke's approach is surely not the only way to dispel the Kant-inspired epistemological worry. Another is simply: *to quo que*. If our knowledge of the persistence of physical objects—including human bodies—is just as vulnerable to similar skeptical doubts, then materialism has no advantage over dualism. But what sort of evidence supports the belief that a physical object observed at one time is the same as an object observed at another time—and not, say, an exact duplicate that has swapped places with the original due to random quantum-mechanical fluctuations or the whimsy of a powerful demon? Just as one can imagine one soul being replaced by a near duplicate without anyone's being the wiser, so one can imagine a physical object being replaced by a near duplicate with no readily detectable evidence that a switch was made. Does the ability to imagine such things require that one produce nonquestion-begging arguments against them if one is ever to claim knowledge of identity over time? Surely not. Is there some special problem with souls? If so, it needs more spelling out than it usually receives.

OCKHAM'S RAZOR

Some of the most frequently voiced objections to dualism—the ones based on problems of interaction and epistemological worries—may become less impressive upon examination. At least one formidable objection remains, however: that there is simply no need to believe in souls in addition to bodies; so the soul falls victim to Ockham's razor, the injunction to postulate no more entities than necessary. One has the evidence of one's own senses for a world of physical bodies. But even if property dualists are right and some psychological phenomena cannot be reduced to or exhaustively explained in terms of properties similar to those now ascribed to physical bodies and their parts, nothing would be gained by supposing that these irreducible mental properties belong to some new entity. And adding the extra entities requires many further ad hoc epicycles that undermine any explanatory value their addition might have had. For instance, one must now explain why the exercise of the soul's mental powers depends so heavily upon a properly functioning brain. Perhaps hard evidence of spirit possession, reincarnation, veridical out-of-body experiences, and the like would change the situation. But, in its absence, respect for parsimony in theory construction provides a powerful reason to reject souls.

MODAL ARGUMENTS

The two most famous styles of argument for dualism may be found, unsurprisingly, in Descartes. One is a modal argument (that is, an argument built around what is possible or necessary) from the possibility of disembodiment to the conclusion that every person actually has, or is, a soul. The other is an argument from the "unity of consciousness" to the conclusion that the subject of consciousness is a partless (and so, by Descartes's lights, nonphysical) substance. Each sort of argument has been subjected to withering criticism, however; and, despite repeated attempts to revive them, the prognosis is not good.

Some of a thing's properties appear clearly to be contingent, while others seem essential. It is possible to lose a contingent property, but not an essential one—it characterizes the thing necessarily. It is possible for me to survive the loss of my leg; so having two legs is one of my contingent properties. If it were possible for me to survive the destruction of my entire body, without acquiring new bodily parts, I would be contingently embodied. If it were not possible, then having a body would be part of my essence.

Descartes develops a modal argument in his sixth meditation: "[T]he fact that I can clearly and distinctly understand one thing apart from another is enough to make me certain that the two things are distinct. … Thus, simply by knowing that I exist and seeing at the same time that absolutely nothing else belongs to my nature or essence except that I am a thinking thing, I can infer correctly that my essence consists solely in the fact that I am a thinking thing" (1984, p. 54).

Swinburne (1997) defends a roughly similar argument. He points out that it is easy to imagine scenarios in which one survives the utter destruction of all the material parts of one's body at once, or the swapping of one body for another. There is nothing straightforwardly inconsistent in such stories, and Swinburne takes this to be strong evidence that the stories represent genuine possibilities. He also assumes, not unreasonably, that no mere material object could survive such adventures. On these assumptions, one should reason as follows: "I could survive the destruction, all at once, of all the matter in my body; my body could not survive this; so I am not identical with my body."

In the absence of a reduction of possibility to logical consistency, it is unclear where evidence for possibility could come from if not from the seeming coherence of various imagined states of affairs. So it is not unreasonable to grant that, if one can conceive of being unextended or of surviving the destruction of one's body, then this fact provides at least prima facie evidence for the possibility of these things. But prima facie evidence may be undermined, and in the arguments of Descartes and Swinburne, it is counterbalanced by the conceivability of states of affairs that are inconsistent with the possibility of the separation of person and body. Many find that they are able to imagine themselves as having nothing but extended or material parts just as easily and clearly as they can imagine persisting without parts or without a body. One can conceive of oneself as a mere organism, a brain, or even a rock. But if such things cannot possibly be unextended, or continue to exist after annihilation of their physical parts—an assumption required by the modal arguments for dualism—then one has prima facie evidence for the possibility of being identical with a thing that could not possibly survive in an unextended or disembodied state. But if some envisaged situation is possibly not possible, then it is simply not possible. So it is simply not possible that I be unextended or disembodied.

The plausibility of this widely accepted principle of modal reasoning (that what is possibly not possible is not really possible at all) may be more apparent when stated in the jargon of "possible worlds": If there is a world that is possible from our perspective (that is, from the point of view of the actual world, this other world represents a way things could have been); and if, from the perspective of that other world, some imagined state of affairs or circumstance is not possible; then that imagined state of affairs is not possible from the point of view of the actual world either—that is, it is simply not possible. Applied to the case in hand, this modal principle becomes: If, according to some possible world, I do not exist without a body in any possible world, then this remains true in the actual world—I do not exist without a body in any possible world.

If I find it just as conceivable to suppose that I am entirely physical as to suppose that I become disembodied, then I have the same sort of evidence for the possibility of each supposition. But they cannot both be possible. So the evidence from conceivability cuts both ways and cancels itself out.

There is more to be said on behalf of modal arguments for dualism, of course. Perhaps the way in which one can conceive of one's disembodiment is qualitatively better—more luminous or complete—than the way in which one can conceive of one's being a mere brain or organism. And perhaps the higher quality of the act of conception brings with it an "epistemic boost" for the possibility of the scenario thus conceived. But making a case for such a difference would require wading far into the murky waters of modal epistemology.

ARGUMENTS FROM THE UNITY OF CONSCIOUSNESS

Many dualists (such as Joseph Butler [1736], Samuel Clarke [1738], Lotze [1894], and, Hasker [1999]) would agree with Descartes about the importance of what came to be called "the unity of consciousness": an argument based on the unity of consciousness alone is "enough to show me that the mind is completely different from the body, even if I did not already know as much from other considerations" (1984, p. 59).

The unity of consciousness may be illustrated by a person who sees a book fall, hears the sound of its impact, and feels a pain in her right toe where it struck. She can immediately infer that there is something that sees the fall, hears the impact, and feels a pain. The facts of experience do not simply imply the occurrence of three events, a "seeing of a book's fall," a "hearing of an impact," and a "feeling of a pain." Events of these types could occur to three different thinking things, no one of which is able to compare the sound with the sight and the pain. What must be added to capture the additional information is that the three events all occur to one and the same individual.

Thus the unity of consciousness supports the view that whatever is the bearer of psychological properties must be a single substance capable of exemplifying a plurality of properties. Its unitary nature consists in the impossibility of its having a "division of psychological labor" among parts. If a single thinker can recognize the difference between sounds and colors, this thinker does not enjoy the ability to compare the two simply by having one part that does its seeing and another that does its hearing, even if these parts are tightly bound together. As Franz Brentano remarks, this "would be like saying that, of course, neither a blind man nor a deaf man could compare colors with sounds, but if one sees and the other hears, the two together can recognize the relationship" (1995 p. 159).

Many dualists have claimed that the unity of consciousness requires that whatever is conscious must be a unity having no parts at all. Although Brentano believed the soul to be simple, he did not think the simplicity of the soul follows immediately from the unity of consciousness alone, and he was surely right. As Brentano points out, what is not ruled out as a subject of consciousness is an extended substance that exemplifies all of its psychological properties as a whole (1987). To use Brentano's metaphor, the psychological properties could be "spread equally" over all of the parts of this extended thinking thing. None of the many arguments that have been given to rule out this possibility has met with widespread acceptance, even among dualists.

ARGUMENTS FROM THE VAGUENESS OF MATERIAL OBJECTS

Arguments for dualism often take the form of objections to any normal sort of materialism. A materialism that identified a person with a single cell or proton would be at least as incredible as dualism (absent some sort of revolution in neurophysiology). What materialists want is a view according to which a human person may be identified with a reasonably normal physical object, one that already has a place in our commonsense conception of the world—an object with natural boundaries, such as those of an organism, a brain, or perhaps even a single hemisphere of a brain. But animals and their organs belong on a spectrum that includes bushes, branches, clouds, mountains, rivers, tidal waves, and all manner of ill-behaved entities. Familiar material objects such as these exhibit vagueness or indeterminacy in their spatial and temporal boundaries. And the strategies typically implemented to resolve puzzles posed by vague objects do not seem so satisfactory when applied to oneself.

Human bodies and brains appear surprisingly like clouds upon close inspection—blurry around the edges. Many particles are in the process of being assimilated or cast off; they are neither clearly "in" nor clearly "out." The temporal boundaries of living things—their coming into existence and passing away—also display a disturbing fuzziness. No one doubts that meteorologists have considerable freedom in deciding where exactly to draw the line between a hurricane and a mere tropical storm. But organisms and brains are not unlike storms in this respect; pressure to find the first and final moments in the life of a human body or brain can only force a decision like the one made by the meteorologists.

Sharper lines will not be found by those who, with Locke, dismiss biological boundaries for persons in favor of psychological ones. Neo-Lockeans must admit that psychological continuity, like biological life, is a matter of more and less; that personalities emerge, and frequently deteriorate, only gradually.

The materialist must, therefore, allow that the spatial and temporal indeterminacies of large-scale material objects infect human persons; and that the standard strategies for coping with fuzzy objects apply to persons as well. But application of these strategies to oneself can produce a disturbing sense of vertigo. The feeling is especially intense in the temporal case.

One group of botanists could establish the convention that no acorn is an oak tree, and another that oak trees are grown-up acorns; one meteorological society could lay it down that hurricanes only begin when a tropical storm attains wind-speeds exceeding 74 miles per hour, another could choose 73. Similarly, one linguistic community could insist that persons exist at conception (twinning, they might say, is the generation of two "new" persons and the end of the first); while another community might talk as though persons come into existence as soon as twinning is impossible or differentiation of organs begins or rudimentary psychological states are detectable or the first breath is taken. Similar ranges of options lie open at the other end of life. If human persons are as much like trees and hurricanes as human bodies appear to be, such differences in usage would affect the extension of "person" and, with it, the reference of "I" in the mouths of speakers from different communities. The physical facts leave room for more than one perfectly acceptable refinement of the concept "tree" or "hurricane"; if human persons are entirely physical, the same must be true of human person.

If these refinements in the extension of "person" are to be genuine possibilities, there must already exist different physical objects corresponding to the different decisions that could be made about origins and deaths; and each of these preexisting objects must have what it takes, intrinsically, to be a conscious person. Speaking and thinking differently cannot make new physical objects spring into existence, nor can it turn objects with no phenomenal states into objects with the rich phenomenology of a human person. But then there must already be quite a few humanlike creatures located wherever a human person is located, each exactly like a person in every intrinsic respect. Although some philosophers (notably, the friends of temporal parts) have learned to live with this result, it raises dizzying possibilities. If the extension of a term like *person* is determined by present and past usage and the rule for determining the referent of *I* is something like "it refers to the person speaking," then a shift from one of the acceptable refinements of "human person" to another could render a conscious, self-referring creature no longer able to think for itself. If, instead, *I* is not tied to the actual meaning of "person" but rather refers ambiguously to each of the humanlike creatures associated with a given person, then there are many thinkers with slightly different pasts and futures, and none can tell which one he or she is (a result emphasized in Olson 1997).

The possibility of fission and fusion is a further source of indeterminacy and conventionality in spatiotemporal boundaries, one that Chisholm (1976) and Swinburne (1997) have exploited in arguments for dualism. When half of a bush is destroyed, one is tempted to say it survives; when it is merely split in two, and the halves successfully transplanted, one is tempted to say one of two things: either that there are two new bushes or that the bush survives as a scattered object, part in one place, part in another. If persons are thought to be middle-sized material objects with biological or psychological persistence conditions, similar circumstances of fission and fusion are conceivable and perhaps even physically possible. (Because a great deal of basic psychological continuity is preserved through the loss of either hemisphere, fission is probably a physical possibility on neo-Lockean accounts of personal identity.) If one takes the first approach to bushes, regarding fission as the end of the original plant, one should say the same thing about a purely physical human being.

There has been little need for precision about the fate of a divided bush. But a community of language users that felt the need could surely introduce a term for things exactly like bushes while decreeing that no such thing can survive loss of half its mass at once; another community could choose 49 percent; but neither group need fear making a mistake. Comparable freedom with respect to persons would require one to say things like, "If my linguistic community were to change its mind, either this would alter my persistence conditions—a strange power to change the nature of a physical object by talking differently—or else it would shift the referent of *I* in my mouth, rendering me no longer able to refer to myself in the first person." Neither alternative is attractive. The analogue to treating the divided bush as a scattered object would be to say that a person could be in two places at once, undergoing radically different experiences, thinking incompatible thoughts, and so on.

TENDER-MINDEDNESS AND ONTIC IGNORANCE

It is hard to apply to oneself the same strategies one would unhesitatingly use to deal with indeterminacy in the identity conditions and borders of ordinary physical objects. Chisholm and Swinburne take this discomfort as evidence that human beings are not ordinary physical objects. Stipulations about whether a person survives a certain borderline adventure are bootless if the person is in fact an immaterial substance whose identity over time is an all-or-nothing affair.

Resisting materialism because it is hard to accept that human beings are as fuzzy and conventional as ordinary physical objects will no doubt strike many philosophers as mere tender-mindedness. After all, they will insist, it should be possible for philosophy to reveal something new about persons; and surely it is more certain that human beings are material objects than that they have perfectly adequate self-conceptions. (Derek Parfit [1984] takes this approach, emphasizing the radical morals to be drawn from the vagueness of human persons.)

On the other hand, it would be high-handed to dismiss as tender-minded anyone who allows the argument from vagueness to count against materialism. If the consequences of supposing that persons are vague material objects seem incredible, this might quite properly increase the weight that can be given to other considerations in favor of dualism: arguments from theological premises, for example, or more esoteric philosophical arguments (such as those of Peter Unger, J. R. Smythies, or John Foster) that would carry greater conviction if materialism were not thought to be utterly obvious and unproblematic. All by themselves, however, the foregoing arguments from vagueness ought probably be taken to support nothing stronger than (what George Graham [1999] calls) "ontic ignorance": "I know not what manner of thing I am."

See also Mind-Body Problem; Physicalism.

Bibliography

Adams, Robert Merrihew. *The Virtue of Faith*. New York: Oxford University Press, 1987. See esp. the chapter "Flavors, Colors, and God."

Brentano, Franz. *On the Existence of God*. Dordrecht: Martinus Nijhoff, 1987 (first German edition, 1929).

Brentano, Franz. *Psychology from an Empirical Standpoint*. London and New York: Routledge, 1995. First German publication of this edition, 1924.

Butler, Joseph. *The Analogy of Religion*. London: James, John, and Paul Knapton, 1736.

Chalmers, David. *The Conscious Mind*. New York: Oxford University Press, 1996.

Chisholm, Roderick. "Is There a Mind-Body Problem?" *Philosophical Exchange* 2 (1978): 25–34.

Chisholm, Roderick. *Person and Object*. La Salle, IL: Open Court, 1976.

Clarke, Samuel. "Four Defences of a Letter to Mr. Dodwell." In *The Works of Samuel Clarke*. London: John and Paul Knapton, 1738.

Corcoran, Kevin, ed. *Soul, Body and Survival*. Ithaca, NY: Cornell University Press, 2001.

Davidson, Donald. "Mental Events." In *Experience and Theory*, edited by L. Foster and J. Swanson. Amherst: University of Massachusetts Press, 1970.

Dennett, Daniel. *Consciousness Explained*. Boston: Little, Brown, 1991.

Descartes, René. *The Philosophical Writings of Descartes*. Vol. 2. Cambridge, U.K.: Cambridge University Press, 1984.

Foster, John. *The Immaterial Self*. London and New York: Routledge, 1991.

Graham, George. "Self-Consciousness, Psychopathology, and Realism about the Self." *Anthropology and Philosophy* 3 (1999): 533–539.

Hart, W. D. *The Engines of the Soul*. Cambridge, U.K.: Cambridge University Press, 1988.

Hasker, William. *The Emergent Self*. Ithaca, NY: Cornell University Press, 1999.

Kant, Immanuel. *Critique of Pure Reason*. Translated by Norman Kemp Smith. New York: St. Martin's Press, 1965.

Kim, Jaegwon. "Supervenience as a Philosophical Concept." *Metaphilosophy* 21 (1990): 1–27.

Leftow, Brian. "Souls Dipped in Dust." In *Soul, Body and Survival*, edited by Kevin Corcoran. Ithaca, NY: Cornell University Press, 2001.

Leibniz, G. W. *New Essays on Human Understanding*. Cambridge, U.K.: Cambridge University Press, 1981.

Locke, John. *An Essay concerning Human Understanding*. Oxford: At the Clarendon Press, 1975.

Lotze, Hermann. *Microcosmus: An Essay concerning Man and his Relation to the World*. Vol. 1. New York: Charles Scribner's Sons, 1894.

Lotze, Hermann. *Outlines of Psychology*. Minneapolis: S. M. Williams, 1885.

Olson, Eric. "A Compound of Two Substances." In *Soul, Body and Survival*, edited by Kevin Corcoran. Ithaca, NY: Cornell University Press, 2001.

Olson, Eric. *The Human Animal*. New York: Oxford University Press, 1997.

Parfit, Derek. *Reasons and Persons*. Oxford: At the Clarendon Press, 1984.

Popper, Karl, and John C. Eccles. *The Self and Its Brain*. Berlin: Springer-Verlag, 1977.

Robinson, Howard. "Dualism." Available online from the Stanford Encyclopedia of Philosophy. http://plato.stanford.edu/.

Rosenberg, Gregg. *A Place for Consciousness*. New York: Oxford University Press, 2004.

Smythies, John. *The Walls of Plato's Cave*. Aldershot: Avebury Press, 1994.

Sosa, Ernest. "Mind-Body Interaction and Supervenient Causation." *Midwest Studies in Philosophy* 9 (1984): 271–281.

Stump, Eleonore. *Aquinas*. London and New York: Routledge, 2003.

Swinburne, Richard. *The Evolution of the Soul*. Rev. ed. Oxford: Clarendon, 1997.

Taliaferro, Charles. *Consciousness and the Mind of God*. Cambridge, U.K.: Cambridge University Press, 1994.

Unger, Peter. *All the Power in the World*. New York: Oxford University Press, 2006.

Dean Zimmerman (2005)

DUBOS, ABBE JEAN BAPTISTE
(1670–1742)

With his *Réflexions critiques sur la poésie et sur la peinture*, Abbe Jean Baptiste DuBos—diplomat, man of letters, member of the *Académie française*—had an essential influence on the aesthetic thought of the Enlightenment.

Réflexions critiques, published for the first time in 1719 and re-edited several times, is one of the founding texts of the new "aesthetics" that came into its own in the eighteenth century. DuBos defends a sense-based theory of aesthetic feeling that is set in motion by poetry, painting, and music. In his *Réflexions*, DuBos's successors saw, on the one hand, an aesthetic that stressed the effects of artworks on spectators and that favored the highly emotional or moving dimension of the aesthetic response to art, and, on the other hand, an attempt to base aesthetic judgment on nonrational bases—what DuBos called the "sixth sense" feeling, or the "heart." His strictly emotionalist interpretation of the "paradox" of negative feelings—which has it that the more we are afflicted by the artistic representation the more pleasure we derive from it—captured the attention of all eighteenth-century theorists of tragic emotion.

The method of the *Réflexions* aims for the "experimental," that is, it is founded on the observation of psychological, social, environmental (*climatiques*), and historical causes. In this respect, his empiricism is tinged with eclecticism, while with regard to the analysis of the mind and emotions, he belongs more strictly to the philosophical vein stemming from John Locke. In view of its subject, this work can be interpreted in somewhat anachronistic terms as a *metacriticism*; as a philosophical endeavor aimed at revealing the general principles of literary and artistic criticism. A certain theoretical distance from DuBos's aesthetic thought (the coherence of which is not always obvious at first glance) helps us to see that it tries to articulate three specific issues: the analysis of the emotional response to an artwork, the theory of aesthetic judgment, and the causes of the historical variations of genius.

1) The only aim of poetry and painting is to please and to arouse feeling by the imitation of subjects that are themselves moving. Art fills a specific need: that of the mind to be kept occupied in order to avoid tedium. The "artificial" passions art stirs have thus the emotional power of ordinary passions, without having their grievous consequences. DuBos proposes that the pleasure we derive from passions (even negative ones) comes uniquely from the emotional energy and intensity inherent in them, not from the reflective consciousness that we ourselves are not at risk or from the mere enjoyment of artistic imitation. After analyzing the nature and causes of viewers' aesthetic pleasures, DuBos explores the various means of producing these pleasures by examining the powers of artistic imitation and by comparing the relative force of different artistic forms and, within these forms, the different artistic genres. Thus, tragedy is superior to comedy, for example, just as painting (which uses "natural signs") touches us more directly than poetry (which uses the "artificial signs" of language). However, at the end of the day, absolute aesthetic primacy goes to staged tragedy, which articulates a succession of "paintings" or scenes in time and takes gradual control of our emotions.

2) Aesthetic sentiment also possesses an *evaluative* dimension; it functions as a principle of *judgment* concerning artistic and literary works; DuBos demonstrates, against the pretensions of a normative and professional criticism, that only the *sentiments* of the *public*, which become more and more assured as time goes by, can reliably decide the real merit of artworks.

3) All this analysis of emotional and evaluative modalities of the artistic experience are part of what could be called a "scientific" criticism that aims to reflect on the diverse historical "causes" (both physical and moral) that explain the *variations* in the production and reception of artistic and literary works; DuBos develops a theory of genius, the manifestations of which are essentially submitted to so-called "climatic" (including physical and environmental) conditions, while simultaneously founding a vein of historical criticism supported by a cyclical conception of history. Together these three elements sketch out an aesthetic theory that is clearly anti-rationalist, for which neither individual aesthetic responses, nor the evaluation and acknowledgment of a work's merit, nor the mechanisms of artistic and literary production, are subjected to the constraints of rules and normative prescriptions. DuBos thus holds an original place in the *Querelle des Anciens et des Modernes*: he refutes the rationalist pretensions of the "*Modernes*" while shifting the debate to the analysis of the feelings.

See also Aesthetic Experience; Aesthetic Judgment; Locke, John.

Bibliography

WORKS BY ABBE JEAN BAPTISTE DUBOS

Réflexions critiques sur la poésie et sur la peinture (1719). Paris: École Nationale Supérieure des Beaux-Arts, 1993.

WORKS ABOUT ABBÉ JEAN BAPTISTE DUBOS

Becq, Annie. *Genèse de l'esthétique française: de la raison classique à l'imagination créatrice, 1680–1814.* 2nd ed. Paris: Albin Michel, 1994.

Dumouchel, Daniel. "Le problème de Dubos et l'affect compatissant: l'esthétique du 18e siècle à l'épreuve du paradoxe tragique." In *De la sympathie sous l'Ancien Régime: discours, savoirs, sociétés,* edited by T. Belleguic and E. Van den Schueren. Québec: Presses de l'Université Laval, 2005.

Lombard, Alfred. *L'Abbé Du Bos, un initiateur de la pensée moderne.* Paris, 1913.

Saisselin, Remy G. "Ut Pictura Poesis: Du Bos to Diderot." *Journal of Aesthetics and Art Criticism* (20) (2) 1960.

Daniel Dumouchel (2005)

DUCASSE, CURT JOHN
(1881–1969)

Curt John Ducasse, philosopher and educator, was born in Angoulême, France. After attending schools in France and England, he came to the United States in 1900. He received his B.A. and M.A. degrees from the University of Washington and, in 1912, his Ph.D. from Harvard University, where he had served as an assistant to Josiah Royce. He taught philosophy at the University of Washington from 1912 until 1926, at Brown University from 1926 until his retirement in 1958, and elsewhere as visiting professor. He served as president of the Association for Symbolic Logic (1936–1938), which he had helped to found, and of other learned societies. He published extensively in all fields of philosophy.

PHILOSOPHICAL METHOD

Ducasse's views on method are worked out in detail in *Philosophy as a Science: Its Matter and Method* (New York, 1941), in his Carus lectures, published as *Nature, Mind, and Death* (La Salle, IL, 1951), and elsewhere.

He held that philosophy is a science and that it differs from other sciences not in the generic features of its method but by virtue of its subject matter, which consists of "spontaneous particular appraisals" (1941) or "standard evaluative statements" (1951) made by some person or group. The primitive problems of philosophy are to define the value predicates "good," "valid," "real," and so on, and their opposites, as used by the person or persons whose standard evaluative statements are taken as data. In the definitions will appear such terms as *necessary, fact,* and *possibility,* which are also in need of analysis, giving rise to derivative problems. Both sorts of problems are essentially semantical. Ducasse is thus squarely in the analytical tradition. However, he argued more explicitly than other contemporary analysts that a proposed analysis of a term as used in paradigm statements has the status of a hypothesis, and that it can be confirmed or disconfirmed by observing whether it is substitutable for the analysans in the paradigm statements without altering any of their standard implications.

CAUSATION

Ducasse had adumbrated the above views and had applied his method to the concept of causality in *Causation and the Types of Necessity* (Seattle, 1924). Ducasse had always regarded causality as a "fundamental category," and in subsequent works he continued to refine his original analysis.

According to Ducasse, causality is a relation between events, is essentially triadic, and is correctly defined in terms of J. S. Mill's method of difference. That "method" is not in fact a method for discovering causal connections but a description of the causal relation itself. If, in a state of affairs S, only two changes occur, one the change C at time T_1 and the other the change E at time T_2, C is the cause of E. Ducasse asserted that despite David Hume's definition of causation as regularity of sequence, Hume actually thought of it in terms of the advent of a single difference in a given state of affairs, as is proved by the way he formulated his rules for ascertaining causal connections by a *single* experiment.

Given the above definition, the supposition that some events have no cause implies a contradiction. Hence, indeterminism, the view that some events are matters of objective change, is self-contradictory, although people are "free" in the sense that, and to the extent that, they can do what they will to do.

MIND AND NATURE

In *Nature, Mind, and Death,* Ducasse went on to assert that nature is the material world, comprising all the things, events, and relations which are publicly perceptible. The mental, which is directly observable only through introspection, is not part of nature. Substances are analyzed as systems of properties and their relations. A property is a causal capacity. Thus,

> to say of carborundum that it is *abrasive* means that, under certain conditions, friction of it against certain other solids causes them to wear away. … More generally, to say that a substance S has a property or capacity P means that S is such that, in circumstances of kind K, an event of kind C, occurring in S or about S, regularly

causes an event of kind *E* to occur in or about *S*. (*Nature, Mind, and Death*, p. 165)

Since *C* and *E* may stand for either a physical or a mental event, there are four kinds of properties: physicophysical, if *C* and *E* are both physical events; physicopsychical, if *C* is physical and *E* psychical; psychophysical; and psychopsychical.

The relation of a mind, a mental substance, to "its body," a material substance, is that of causal interaction. This is an analytic truth, for by "its body" can only be meant "the body with which that mind directly interacts." Many of the usual objections to interactionism presuppose a mistaken conception of causality.

In the case of physicopsychical properties ("bitter," "blue") it is important to distinguish between the sense quality in terms of which the property is defined and the property itself. "Bitter," for example, is equivocal. As applied to quinine, it is a disposition term designating the capacity of quinine to cause a certain taste experience when one places it on one's tongue. As applied to the experience itself, it is the name of a quality. With respect to the properties of material things, Ducasse is a realist. Quinine is bitter and roses are red, in the dispositional sense, even if the properties are not being exercised. Of properties, it is false that *esse* is *percipi*. But in the case of sense qualities, it is true that *esse* is *percipi*.

Now G. E. Moore, in his "Refutation of Idealism," had argued that since we can distinguish the sensum blue that is the object of a sensation from the sensing itself, sensa might exist without consciousness of them, and they might therefore be nonmental. Against Moore, Ducasse argues in *Nature, Mind, and Death* that a sensum is not an "object" of sensation but the "content" of it. When one sees some lapis lazuli, the lapis lazuli is the object seen. But the relation of the lapis lazuli to the seeing of it when "I see some lapis lazuli" is true is not the same as the relation of blue to the seeing of it when "I see blue" is true. (Compare "I taste quinine" with "I taste bitter," or "I am jumping a ditch" with "I am jumping gracefully.") After a meticulous examination of various hypotheses on what the relation of sensa to sensing might be, Ducasse concludes that sensa are species of experience. "I sense blue" means "I sense bluely," or, alternatively, "I sense in the manner blue," just as "I am dancing a waltz" means "I am dancing waltzily (in the manner of dancing called 'dancing a waltz')." Just as a waltz could not conceivably exist apart from the dancing of it, a sensum could not exist apart from the sensing of it.

On the basis of this analysis, Ducasse submits that the basic criterion of the mental may be expressed by saying that "*if something being experienced is connate with the experiencing of it, then it is a mental primitive.*"

AESTHETICS

In *The Philosophy of Art* (New York, 1929), *Art, the Critics, and You* (New York, 1944), and many articles, Ducasse formulates and defends an emotionalist theory of art and aesthetic experience. His principal contentions are that art in the broadest sense is skilled activity; that fine or aesthetic art consists in the skilled objectification of feeling; that the fine artist judges the adequacy of the work he creates not by the degree to which it approximates to beauty but by the faithfulness with which it reflects back to him the feeling to which he attempted to give objective expression; that in the aesthetic attitude one "throws oneself open" to the advent of feelings; and that judgments of aesthetic value are relative to the taste of the critic.

PHILOSOPHY OF RELIGION

In *A Philosophical Scrutiny of Religion* (New York, 1953), Ducasse defines religion as essentially any set of articles of faith, with the observances, feelings, and so on, tied thereto, that has the social function of motivating altruism in individuals and the personal function of giving the believer inner peace and assurance. According to this definition, belief in a God or gods is not essential to religion. Ducasse himself is not a theist. He holds that orthodox theism is contradicted by the existence of evil, and that polytheism is more plausible than monotheism conceived in the orthodox manner.

PARANORMAL PHENOMENA

Throughout his career, Ducasse was interested in and wrote about the "wild facts" of mental telepathy, clairvoyance, precognition, and so on. His interest in them was manifold. If paranormal phenomena do occur, received theories about the mental and the physical must be revised to account for them. It is a gratuitous assumption that any theory capable of taming the wild facts would have to postulate supernatural entities or "spooks." It could well be as scientific as are current theories about hypnotism, which have more or less tamed the wild facts of mesmerism. One of the troubles of psychical research is the lack of a fruitful theory.

If paranormal phenomena do occur, there would be important implications for philosophy. How would philosophers have to conceive of time, causality, perception if there were such a thing as precognition?

It is a logical possibility that a mind survives the death of its body (or, to allow for reincarnation, bodies), even when due account has been taken of current science. But is there any evidence that it does? If there is, it is likely to be found by objective sifting of the reports concerning paranormal phenomena. In *A Critical Examination of the Belief in a Life after Death* (Springfield, IL, 1961), Ducasse states that the conclusion about survival seemingly warranted at present is that "the balance of the evidence so far obtained is on the side of the reality of survival," but that the evidence is not conclusive.

See also Aesthetic Experience; Art, Expression in; Causation: Metaphysical Issues; Hume, David; Logic, History of: Modern Logic; Mill, John Stuart; Moore, George Edward; Parapsychology; Reincarnation; Royce, Josiah; Sensa.

Bibliography

A complete bibliography of Ducasse's writings up to December 31, 1951, is available in *Philosophy and Phenomenological Research* 13 (1) (September 1952): 96–102. This issue also contains "Symposium in Honor of C. J. Ducasse" by seven philosophers, a biographical note, and a portrait.

For George Santayana's response to Ducasse's views on causation, "ontological liberalism," art, and properties, see *The Letters of George Santayana*, edited by Daniel Cory, 213–215, 234–235, and 287–288 (New York: Scribners, 1955). For a careful review of *Nature, Mind, and Death* by H. H. Price, see the *Journal of Parapsychology* 16 (2) (June 1952).

OTHER RECOMMENDED WORKS

Ducasse, Curt John. *Current Philosophical Issues: Essays in Honor of Curt John Ducasse.* Compiled and edited by Frederick C. Dommeyer. Springfield, IL: Thomas, 1966.

Ducasse, Curt John. *Truth, Knowledge and Causation.* London: Routledge & K. Paul; New York: Humanities P., 1969.

Vincent Tomas (1967)
Bibliography updated by Michael Farmer (2005)

DUHEM, PIERRE MAURICE MARIE
(1861–1916)

Pierre Maurice Marie Duhem was noted for his original work in theoretical physics, especially thermodynamics, and in the history and philosophy of science. He was born and studied in Paris, and at the age of twenty-five published an important book on thermodynamics. In 1887 he went to the faculty of sciences at Lille University, where he taught hydrodynamics, elasticity, and acoustics. He married but his wife soon died, leaving him with a daughter. In 1893 he moved to Rennes and in 1895 to a chair at Bordeaux University, which he held until his death. Throughout his life he was a Catholic and a conservative.

His approach to physics was systematic and mathematical, and his interest in axiomatic methods undoubtedly determined to some extent the nature of his philosophical account of scientific theories, contained mainly in his book *La théorie physique: son objet, sa structure* (*The Aim and Structure of Physical Theory*), first published in 1906. He wrote a great deal on the history of science, especially in the fields of mechanics, astronomy, and physics, largely because he believed that a knowledge of the history of a concept and of the problems it was designed to meet was essential for a proper understanding of that concept. For the scientist, the history of his subject should be not a mere hobby but an essential part of his scientific work. Duhem's most important works in this field are *Les origines de la statique*, published in 1905–1906, and *Le système du monde*, an account of various systems of astronomy, in eight volumes, published between 1913 and 1958.

SCIENCE AND METAPHYSICS

Duhem's account of physical theory is positivistic and pragmatic, having clear connections with those of Ernst Mach and Henri Poincaré. It begins with, and takes its character largely from, his views on explanation. Indeed, one might say that it begins with a dogmatic and unsupported presupposition about the nature of explanation. He says that to explain is "to strip reality of the appearances covering it like a veil, in order to see the bare reality itself."

But the sciences depend upon observation, and observation shows us no more than the appearances: it cannot penetrate to the reality beneath. This reality is the province of metaphysics; only metaphysics can explain. Science merely deals with the relations between, primarily, our sensations (or the appearance of the world to us) and, ultimately, our abstract ideas of these appearances. A physical theory is somehow an abstract representation of the relations between appearances and not a picture of the reality lurking behind them.

Thus, as far as science alone is concerned, Duhem is as antimetaphysical as Mach and more so than Heinrich Hertz. But, in general, he is not antimetaphysical at all. In a sense, metaphysics is the most important of all studies because it penetrates to the reality of things and explains the appearances; but when we are doing science, we must never import into it metaphysical aims or ideas. Science and metaphysics are both highly respectable, but they are utterly distinct and must be kept so on pain of confusion.

We may, Duhem thinks, penetrate to reality, not by the methods of science, but by pure reason. He attaches great importance to the doctrine that man is free, a statement that cannot conflict with any of the conclusions of science. His metaphysical views, which he did not work out in detail, are Aristotelian; properly understood—that is, stripped of its outmoded science—the Aristotelian physics contains an accurate picture of the cosmological order, whose appearance to human beings is studied by the sciences.

Scientists, according to Duhem, have seldom made the distinction between science and metaphysics, with the result that many theories have been seen as attempted explanations and so have been garnished with strictly superfluous "pictorial" and explanatory elements. These theories can be divided into two parts, called by Duhem "representative" and "explanatory." What is valuable in such theories, and hence what survives and what may be common to apparently different theories, is the representative part.

THE USES OF THEORIES

This conception of the representative nature of theories is linked with the various ways in which theories are useful to us. First, they promote economy by connecting large numbers of experimental laws deductively under a few hypotheses or principles; we need remember only these principles instead of a large number of laws. Second, by classifying laws systematically they enable us to select the laws we need on a particular occasion for a particular purpose. Third, they enable us to predict, that is, to anticipate the results of experiments. These are functions that can be performed by the representative parts of theories, which merely link general statements derived from observation and experiment in a practically convenient way, rather than in a way that corresponds to the underlying reality of things.

THE CONSTRUCTION OF THEORIES

Duhem's account of the way in which theories are constructed exhibits his conception of the nature of physical theories. There are four fundamental operations in their construction.

(1) Among the observable, measurable properties that we wish our theory to represent, we look for a few that can be regarded as simple and as combining to form the rest. Because they are measurable, we can represent them by mathematical symbols. These symbols have no intrinsic connection with the properties they represent: they are conventional signs for these properties. For example, temperature measured in degrees centigrade is a conventional and quantitative representation of the felt warmth and cold of sense experience.

(2) We construct a small number of principles, or "hypotheses," which are propositions arbitrarily connecting our symbols in a manner controlled only by the requirements of convenience and logical consistency. We may give as an example the definition of "momentum" as the product of mass and velocity.

(3) We combine these hypotheses according to the rules of mathematical analysis; again there is no question of representing the real relations between properties, and convenience and consistency are still our guides.

(4) Certain of the consequences drawn out by our third operation are "translated" back into physical terms. That is, we arrive at new statements about the measurable properties of bodies, our methods of defining and measuring these properties serving as a kind of "dictionary" to assist us in the translation. These new statements can now be compared with the results of experiments; the theory is a good one if they fit, a bad one if they do not.

THE NATURE OF LAWS AND THEORIES

Thus, a physical theory, for Duhem, is always mathematical and is a conventional system of linkages between propositions "representing" general statements or laws arrived at by experiment or observation. It is a device for calculating, and nothing matters except that the results of the calculations square with our observations. We might illustrate this in the following way. There are various routes by plane from city A (the known laws) to city B (the new laws), and it does not matter which route we take as long as we arrive at B: We are flying blind; the plane has no windows, and we cannot see the landscape, the sun, or even the clouds during the journey; we must not suppose that the interior of the plane resembles A or B or the country in between.

The idea that physical characteristics are analyzable into basic elements that are simple and ultimate has figured largely in empiricist and positivist accounts of the sciences. This idea involves numerous difficulties, not the least among them being that of giving any precise meaning to simplicity. Duhem avoids some of the difficulties. Because physical theories do not explain, his simple elements need not be ultimate in nature; they need not be *incapable* of further analysis. They may merely be properties that we *take to be* fundamental and that we have not succeeded in analyzing.

Duhem distinguishes between "practical facts" and "theoretical facts." A description of a phenomenon in ordinary ("observational") language states a practical fact, and its translation into the symbols of the theory states a theoretical fact. But the theoretical fact, as should now be obvious, is a "fact" only in a very odd sense; it has some kind of formal correspondence with the practical fact, but it is always an approximation or an idealization and always has many alternatives.

There is a similar relation between empirical or "commonsense" laws and scientific laws. Scientific laws state the relations between symbols that derive their meanings from the theories of which they are a part. These laws are approximations and idealizations and do not state the relations between actual physical properties. As an example, Duhem cites Boyle's law. This states the relations, not between pressures that may be felt and volumes that may be seen, but between their ideal representatives in a complex theory of gases. The same word, *pressure*, may stand for different concepts in different theories, and in its commonsense, everyday use it stands for a concept or concepts different again from all these.

A commonsense law, such as "Paper is inflammable," is correctly said to be either true or false. No scientific law, however, can be said to be true or false because every accepted scientific law has equally acceptable alternatives. None of these alternatives is any more correct than any of the others. There are two points here. To call the law we actually accept "true" is to suggest that the acceptable alternatives are false, which is misleading. Moreover, all the possible alternatives are idealizations: there is nothing of which they can be said to be strictly true. The symbols used in scientific laws are always too simple to represent completely the phenomena and their connections; hence, the laws must always be provisional.

Duhem distinguishes between observation and interpretation in a way that would now be questioned by certain philosophers. An observer looking at a spot of light on a scale *may* be merely observing this spot, or he may be doing this *and* interpreting it as the final step in measuring the resistance of a coil. Here, observing needs only attentiveness and reliable eyesight, but interpreting requires a knowledge of electrical theory as well. A boy who knew nothing whatever about electrical theory could be given the task of recording the movements of the spot on the scale; a physicist who had not seen these movements but who knew the theory and was prepared to rely on the boy could interpret the records appropriately.

It follows from Duhem's account that scientific laws and theories are not arrived at by induction. No experiment in physics involves mere generalizing from observations because the description of the experiment and its result, in the appropriate terms, involves the use of our physical symbols and, therefore, an interpretation of the phenomena depending upon the acceptance of a particular theory.

Duhem has important things to say about the testing of scientific hypotheses and theories. An empirical generalization of the form "All A's are B" can never be conclusively established, because we can never be sure that we have examined all the A's, but it may be conclusively falsified by finding one A that is not B. Thus, if we take such a generalization to be the pattern of scientific hypotheses, we must say that these hypotheses are open to conclusive refutation. But this is too simple, for a scientific hypothesis can never be tested independently of other hypotheses. This is a point that probably has to be made for any adequate account of scientific theorizing, but it is clearly an essential part of Duhem's account. For him, a hypothesis is always part of a theory, and it is used to make predictions only along with other parts of the theory and perhaps other theories. The failure of a prediction, then, indicates some inadequacy in the hypothesis in question *or* in some other hypothesis of the theory *or* in another theory that has been assumed in making the prediction, but it does no more than this to locate the inadequacy. It shows conclusively that something is wrong, but it tells us neither where to look for that something nor what we must reject or modify.

Thus, there can be no crucial experiments in physics. The pattern of a crucial experiment is this: we have two conflicting hypotheses about a given phenomenon and we design an experiment that will give one specifiable result if one hypothesis is acceptable and the other not, and another specifiable result if the other is acceptable and the first not. But hypotheses are not, as this suggests, independent and isolable. In fact, we must always confront a whole theory, of which one hypothesis is a part, with another whole theory, of which the other hypothesis is a part. It is much more difficult to devise an experiment to choose between theories, and even if we could, it might be that a theory that conflicts with the experiment could be squared with it by making minor modifications whereby it would become as acceptable as the other theory under test.

This view may be criticized on the grounds that it is logically possible to find a crucial experiment that would enable us to choose between two *theories*. Of course, a theory that conflicts with experimental results may be capable of modification so that it does not conflict, but if it then gives exactly the same deductions as its rival, it is doubtful that they can be regarded as different theories, in Duhem's view. On the other hand, if they give different deductions covering the same field, it remains logically possible to devise a conclusive experiment to choose between *these two theories*. Karl Popper objects to Duhem's view on the grounds that the only reason Duhem thought crucial experiments impossible was because he stressed verification rather than falsification. It is not clear that Popper's objection is valid, for Duhem seems to have noticed the obvious fact that the aim of a crucial experiment is to eliminate one of the theories.

Although there is much in common between Duhem's and Poincaré's accounts of scientific theories, Duhem uses this last point about theory modification in criticism of part of Poincaré's view. According to Poincaré and others, certain important hypotheses of physical theory cannot be refuted by experiment because they are *definitions*. For example, the statement that the acceleration of a freely falling body is constant really defines "freely falling"; if an experiment appears to conflict with this, the most we can say is that the body was not falling freely. Nothing we observe can compel us to reject the original statement because it is not an empirical statement. Duhem, in reply, gives a different reason why we sometimes treat scientific statements in this way. It is not that the hypotheses we treat in this way are definitions but that they cannot be tested in isolation; thus, we are usually free, in the face of an unfulfilled prediction, to keep any given hypothesis and reject some other. This does not mean that we shall never be forced to reject that given hypothesis in consequence of some other modification we make to the theory, but only that the odds are against this happening on any given occasion.

See also Continental Philosophy; Conventionalism; Explanation; Hertz, Heinrich Rudolf; Laws, Scientific; Mach, Ernst; Philosophy of Science, History of; Poincaré, Jules Henri; Scientific Method.

Bibliography

WORKS BY DUHEM

Le potentiel thermodynamique et ses applications à la mécanique chimique et à la théorie des phénomènes électriques. Paris, 1886. His first book.

Le mixte et la combination chimique. Essai sur l'évolution d'une idée. Paris, 1902.

Les théories électriques de J. Clerk Maxwell: Étude historique et critique. Paris, 1902.

L'évolution de la mécanique. Paris, 1903.

Les origines de la statique. Paris, 1905–1906.

La théorie physique, son objet et sa structure. Paris, 1906. Second edition with new appendix (1914) translated by P. P. Wiener as *The Aim and Structure of Physical Theory.* Princeton, NJ, 1954. This book contains Duhem's most important philosophical work.

Études sur Léonard de Vinci, ceux qu'il a lus et ceux qui l'ont lu. Paris, 1906–1913.

"Physics—History of." In *Catholic Encyclopedia*, Vol. 12, pp. 47–67. New York, 1911.

Le système du monde. Histoire des doctrines cosmologiques de Platon à Copernic, 8 vols. Paris, 1913–1958. An enormous historical work of considerable importance.

WORKS ON DUHEM

Agassi, J. "Duhem *versus* Galileo." *British Journal for the Philosophy of Science* 8 (1957): 237–248.

Duhem, H.-P. *Un savant français: P. Duhem.* Paris, 1936.

Frank, P. *Modern Science and Its Philosophy.* Cambridge, MA: Harvard University Press, 1949.

Ginzburg, B. "Duhem and Jordanus Nemorarius." *Isis* 25 (1936): 341–362.

Jammer, Max. *Concepts of Force.* Cambridge, MA: Harvard University Press, 1957.

Launay, L. de. "Pierre Duhem." *Revue des Deux Mondes* (1918): 363–396.

Lowinger, Armand. *The Methodology of Pierre Duhem.* New York: Columbia University Press, 1941. See also a review of this work by B. Ginzburg, *Isis* 34 (1942): 33–34.

Picard, E. *La vie et l'oeuvre de Pierre Duhem.* Paris, 1922.

Poincaré, H. "Sur la Valeur objective des théories physiques." *Revue de métaphysique et de morale* 10 (1902): 263–293.

Popper, K. R. *The Logic of Scientific Discovery.* London: Hutchinson, 1959.

Popper, K. R. *Conjectures and Refutations.* London: Routledge, 1963.

Rey, A. "La philosophie scientifique de M. Duhem." *Revue de métaphysique et de morale* 12 (1904): 699–744.

Roy, E. le. "Science et philosophie." *Revue de métaphysique et de morale* 7 (1899): 503.

Roy, E. le. "Un positivisme nouveau." *Revue de métaphysique et de morale* 9 (1901): 143–144.

Peter Alexander (1967)

DÜHRING, EUGEN KARL
(1833–1921)

Eugen Karl Dühring, the German philosopher and political economist, was born in Berlin and died in Nowawes, near Potsdam. Dühring practiced law in Berlin from 1856 to 1859, but an eye ailment, eventually leading to total blindness, forced him to abandon this career. In 1861 he took his doctorate in philosophy at the University of Berlin, with a dissertation titled *De Tempore, Spatio, Causalitate Atque de Analysis Infinitesimalis Logica.* He became university lecturer in 1863, but his feuding with colleagues and his attacks on the university led to his dismissal in 1877. From then until his death he lived the life of a private scholar. In his later years, Dühring's attacks on religion (*Asiatismus*), militarism, Marxism, the Bismarck state, the universities, and Judaism became more and more virulent. Nevertheless, he retained a small group of loyal followers who founded a journal primarily devoted to his essays, the *Personalist und Emanzipator* (1899). Three years after Dühring's death, E. Döll founded the Dühring-Bund.

Dühring's early views, expressed in his *Natürliche Dialektik,* were Kantian. Eventually, however, he came to reject Immanuel Kant's phenomena-noumena distinction, with its corollary that we do not apprehend reality as it is in itself. Dühring maintained that the mind does grasp reality directly, and that the laws of thought are in some sense also laws of being.

KNOWLEDGE AND REALITY

While denouncing metaphysics and every sort of supernaturalism, Dühring formulated a theory of reality that is no less metaphysical than that of the philosophers whom he attacked. Philosophy, according to Dühring, should aim at a comprehensive account of reality, an account that will be consonant with the natural sciences. A complete knowledge of reality is possible if we restrict ourselves to what is given, using the "rational imagination" that is the organ for philosophizing. (This constructive imagination is used also in mathematics, Dühring held.) The outcome of this activity, an activity of passion guided by the understanding, will be a coherent and comprehensive world picture. Dühring praised Arthur Schopenhauer, Ludwig Feuerbach, and Auguste Comte for their efforts in this direction.

The fundamental law that we are to use in apprehending reality is the Law of Determinate Number. This law provides an easy solution to the antinomies in which reason finds itself when seeking knowledge beyond the realm of possible experience. It states that all thinkable numbers are complete or determined, and that the notion of an infinite or undetermined number is therefore impossible. Dühring suggested that the conception of an infinity of events or of units is somehow logically contradictory, as if one were to speak of a countless number that had been counted. For the theory of reality, the consequences of Dühring's law are that the number of events in time that preceded the present moment must be finite, and so too must be the number of objects in space. The history of the universe must have had an absolute beginning, and every object that exists or has existed must be divisible into a finite number of parts. It is nevertheless possible, Dühring maintained, that time and space extend infinitely from here and now.

A "primordial being" lies beyond the first event in time, though this being can be defined only by negating the properties of objects and events in time. Still, we can say of it that it contains the "roots" of every event and object, though it does not consist of events and is not an object. History develops out of this primordial being by an evolutionary process, from the more homogeneous to the more diversified.

What is actual must be here and now. The past is no longer real. The primordial condition of being no longer exists, though its traces are still evident. The laws of the physical universe, the atoms that make up matter—these are the unchanging aspects of the world, the persistent traces of the primordial being.

CHANGE AND EVOLUTION

The evolution of the universe involves the coming into being of genuinely new forms, and there exists the possibility that further novelty will emerge with the passage of time. The coming into being of motion, and of living creatures and conscious agents, are examples of new phenomena in the transition from the original condition of the world to its present state. Productive, creative activity is an essential fact about the universe, yielding new existences, new phenomena. The laws that describe such changes are nevertheless constant. We do not clearly understand how such genuine novelty occurs, and we ought not to construct speculative hypotheses. An honest philosopher will simply confess his ignorance.

How the world may evolve in the future is also beyond our knowledge. Either natural processes will continue mechanically without ever coming to an end or, what is more probable, there will emerge something radically different. Dühring accepted the latter alternative for the reason that he believed differentiation is a basic law of nature. However, since the number of possible changes is finite, there must be either an eternal recurrence of the world process, as Friedrich Nietzsche suggested, or an end.

MIND AND CONSCIOUSNESS

Dühring's philosophy of mind is at first glance dualistic. Conscious activity is totally different from inanimate processes. The former is, however, an outcome of the clash of mechanical processes or forces. The sensation of resistance is the most basic sort of consciousness, and it reveals very clearly that its origin is the antagonism of physical forces.

While Dühring's position is positivistic in its emphasis on the limitation of human knowledge to the world described by natural science, and in its rejection of any independent philosophical knowledge of reality, he differs from some nineteenth-century positivists, such as Ernst Mach, in rejecting phenomenalism as the only valid basis for knowledge. Dühring maintained that although no disembodied spirits or souls exist, the world that is given to consciousness is one that contains not only matter and physical forces but also life and activity. Furthermore, he did not repudiate the concepts of cause and force or approve of a reductionism that would restrict intelligible discourse to phenomena, a restriction that he called "a morbid and skeptical aberration."

RELIGION

In his passionate opposition to religion and to every form of mysticism, Dühring is reminiscent of Lucretius. Religion is "a cradle of delusions," he maintained, and it is only by becoming free from its superstitions that man can become truly noble. The idea of an "other world" is a stumbling block to the proper appreciation of the real world that we encounter directly. We must find our values in this world.

Dühring's teleological optimism led him to reject Charles Darwin's theory that a struggle for existence is necessitated by the insufficiency of means to satisfy natural needs. The conditions for happiness are not impossible, he said. Even pain exists as an enhancement of our appreciation of pleasure. Only manmade institutions stand in the way of human happiness; religion is one of these institutions. Science, as carried on in the nineteenth century, is equally pernicious, since it involves "a hodge podge of superstition, skepticism and apathy."

ETHICS AND ECONOMICS

Dühring held that the feeling of sympathy is the foundation of morality. In applying this theory to the field of economics, Dühring came to a conclusion that Friedrich Engels and other Marxists have found highly objectionable. The interests of capitalist and worker, Dühring maintained, are not really opposed. By means of free competition there could be an ultimate harmony and compatibility between the two classes. Dühring's economic doctrines also supported the idea of a "national" political economy. He advocated tariff protection of national industries as a means of promoting the culture and morality of all citizens in the state. This goal could be realized most effectively when the economy of a nation was self-sufficient.

NATIONALISM AND RACISM

Dühring was an ardent German patriot, and some of the enormous popularity that his writings enjoyed in the latter part of the nineteenth century can be traced to this. He worshiped Frederick the Great. Along with his nationalistic zeal, however, Dühring betrayed a generous amount of prejudice, denouncing Jews, Greeks, and even Johann Wolfgang von Goethe, who was too cosmopolitan for Dühring's taste. Some conjecture that Nietzsche was influenced by Dühring's *Wert des Lebens*. But the joyous affirmation of life that Dühring shared with Nietzsche stands in sharp contrast to the vicious, embittered tone of many of Dühring's writings, and Nietzsche's rejection of pessimism stands on quite other grounds than that of Dühring.

See also Comte, Auguste; Continental Philosophy; Darwin, Charles Robert; Darwinism; Engels, Friedrich; Eternal Return; Feuerbach, Ludwig Andreas; Goethe, Johann Wolfgang von; Kant, Immanuel; Lucretius; Nationalism; Nietzsche, Friedrich; Positivism; Racism; Schopenhauer, Arthur.

Bibliography

PRIMARY WORKS

Kapital und Arbeit. Berlin, 1865.

Der Wert des Lebens. Breslau, 1865.

Natürliche Dialektik. Berlin, 1865.

Kritische Geschichte der Philosophie. Berlin, 1869.

Kritische Geschichte der Nationalökonomie und des Sozialismus. Berlin: Grieben, 1871.

Kritische Geschichte der allgemeinen Prinzipien der Mechanik. Berlin, 1873.

Kursus der National- und Sozialökonomie. Berlin, 1873.

Kursus der Philosophie. Leipzig, 1875. Later editions are titled *Wirklichkeitsphilosophie.*

Logik und Wissenschaftstheorie. Leipzig: Fues, 1878.

Die Judenfrage. Karlsruhe and Leipzig, 1881.

Sache, Leben und Feinde. Karlsruhe, 1882. Autobiography.

Der Ersatz der Religion durch Vollkommeneres. Karlsruhe: Reuther, 1883.

SECONDARY WORKS

Adamiak, Richard. "Marx, Engels, and Dühring." *Journal of the History of Ideas* 35 (1) (1974): 98–112.

Albrecht, G. *Eugen Dührings Wertlehre.* Jena, 1914.

Döll, E. *Eugen Dühring.* Leipzig: Naumann, 1893.

Drechsler, Wolfgang. "Herrn Eugen Dühring's Remotion." *Trames* 3 (3) (1999): 99–130.

Druskowitz, H. *Eugen Dühring.* Heidelberg: Weiss, 1889.

Engels, F. *Herrn Eugen Dührings Umwälzung der Wissenschaft.* Leipzig: Genossenschaftsbuchdruckerei, 1878. Translated by E. Burns as *Herr Eugen Dühring's Revolution in Science.* London, 1935. Commonly known as *Anti-Dühring.* Attacks Dühring's philosophy, politics, and economics.

Reinhardt, H., ed. *Dühring and Nietzsche.* Leipzig, 1931.

Small, Robin. "Nietzsche, Dühring, and Time." *Journal of the History of Philosophy* 28 (2) (1990): 229–250.

Vaihinger, H. *Hartmann, Dühring und Lange.* Iserlohn: Baedecker, 1876.

Arnulf Zweig (1967)
Bibliography updated by Philip Reed (2005)

DUMMETT, MICHAEL ANTHONY EARDLEY
(1925–)

Michael Anthony Eardley Dummett is perhaps the most important philosopher of logic of the second half of the twentieth century. Born on June 27, 1925, in London, England, Dummett completed his formal education at Christ Church, Oxford, and served for many years on the faculty of that university. A fellow of All Soul's College from 1979 to 1992, Dummett was the Wykeham Professor of Logic. His influential work has made commonplace (though not uncontroversial) the claim that philosophical matters concerning logic and truth are central to metaphysics, understood in roughly the traditional sense. Dummett has profoundly and permanently shifted the ground of debates concerning metaphysical realism.

Much of Dummett's work has taken place in the context of his commentaries on Gottlob Frege, at whose hands, Dummett claims, epistemology was supplanted by the philosophy of language as the fundamental field of philosophical investigation. Frege's reorientation of philosophy, comparable to the Cartesian installation of epistemology as the foundation of philosophical thinking, finally directed philosophers' attention to the proper focus: the relation of language to reality. Dummett is thus a leading advocate of the "linguistic turn." He is heavily influenced by Ludwig Wittgenstein's later work and by intuitionism in the philosophy of mathematics.

Dummett claims to have articulated a common structure embodied in a number of disputes pitting realists against their opponents. For example, the medieval debate over universals consisted of realists, who argued for the existence of mind-independent, objective properties, against various denials of realism (conceptualism, nominalism). Realism's claim about material objects contrasts with varieties of idealism, all of which share the general view that material objects do not exist objectively and independently of the mind. Positions that are antagonistic toward the positing of an objective, mind-independent realm are antirealistic positions. Dummett holds that the proper way to approach the dispute is to investigate what logical principles that are valid on the realistic view must be abandoned by antirealism. In particular Dummett claims that the law of bivalence, according to which every meaningful statement is determinately either true or false, is the mark of realism.

According to Dummett, the route to antirealism must be a meaning-theoretical one and thus focus on the role of the notion of truth in explicating meaning. His position on the theory of meaning has been called verificationism but, more properly, should be called neoverificationism to distinguish him from logical positivism. Dummett argues that truth, if conceived realistically, cannot be the fundamental notion of a theory of meaning—that is, if truth is conceived as satisfying the principle of bivalence. He recommends abandoning this classical notion of truth. His positive proposal can be put either of two ways: he sometimes suggests that the classical notion of truth must be replaced by a different concept of truth, one that does not include the bivalence principle; at other times he suggests that truth be replaced by verification as the central meaning-theoretical notion.

The theory of meaning is concerned with the relationships of truth, meaning, and use. Holding to a sophisticated reading of the "meaning is use" idea, Dummett argues that a theory of meaning based on the classical notion of truth cannot successfully analyze the ability of speakers to use their language. That is, the meaning of a sentence cannot be identified with—or, more weakly, connected with sufficient intimacy to—the sentence's truth conditions if truth is conceived classically, because the resultant theory of meaning attributes to a speaker a grasp of meaning that cannot be explained in terms of her possession of recognitional skills pertaining to truth, i.e., her possession of certain epistemic capacities.

Dummett's key arguments concerning this conclusion have been called the acquisition and manifestation arguments. Because some of the sentences of the language in question are undecidable (their truth or falsity cannot be recognized by means of "decision procedures"), it is inexplicable how a speaker is able to learn their truth-conditional meanings through training. Grasping the truth conditions of these sentences is beyond the ken of finite beings. Similarly, since a grasp of a sentence's meaning must be conclusively demonstrable in one's actions, it is inconceivable that a speaker could display competence in the language if this means demonstrating his or her grasp of a sentence's recognition-transcendent truth conditions. Because of this sensitivity of the theory of meaning to such epistemological concerns, Dummett concludes that the central explanatory notion of a theory of meaning cannot be epistemically unconstrained. Thus, a notion of truth requires sensitivity to the epistemic limitations of language users.

This requirement leads to an intuitionistic concept of truth, whereby bivalence fails and not all sentences can be said to possess a truth value despite being meaningful. Failure of bivalence may concern past-tense and future-tense sentences, attributions of dispositional properties to no-longer-existent objects that never displayed possession or lack of the dispositions in question, and, crucially, sentences involving unrestricted quantification over infinite domains. Further pursuit of this line leads Dummett into consideration and rejection of meaning-theoretical holism and to an emphasis on the role of logical inference in verification.

Dummett presents a compelling case for the interrelatedness of metaphysical questions and meaning-theoretical ones; in particular, he argues that notion of truth—and, concomitantly, the logic that correctly formalizes the corresponding notion of valid or truth-preserving inference—depends on a prior investigation in the theory of meaning.

Dummett's importance to philosophy lies in his demonstration of the ways in which metaphysics relates to the philosophy of logic and how those two fields in turn relate to the philosophy of language.

See also Frege, Gottlob; Idealism; Meaning; Phenomenalism; Philosophy of Language; Realism; Truth; Wittgenstein, Ludwig Josef Johann.

Bibliography

WORKS BY DUMMETT

"What Is a Theory of Meaning?" In *Mind and Language*, edited by S. Guttenplan. Oxford: Oxford University Press, 1974.

"What Is a Theory of Meaning? (II)." In *Meaning and Truth*, edited by G. Evans and J. MacDowell. Oxford: Oxford University Press, 1974.

"The Justification of Deduction." In *Truth and Other Enigmas.* Cambridge, MA: Harvard University Press, 1978.

"The Philosophical Basis of Intuitionistic Logic." In *Truth and Other Enigmas.* Cambridge, MA: Harvard University Press, 1978.

"The Significance of Quine's Indeterminacy Thesis." In *Truth and Other Enigmas.* Cambridge, MA: Harvard University Press, 1978.

Frege: Philosophy of Language. 2nd ed. Cambridge, MA: Harvard University Press, 1981.

The Interpretation of Frege's Philosophy. Cambridge, MA: Harvard University Press, 1981.

"Frege on the Third Realm." In *Frege and Other Philosophers.* Oxford: Oxford University Press, 1991.

The Logical Basis of Metaphysics. Cambridge, MA: Harvard University Press, 1991.

Frege: Philosophy of Mathematics. Cambridge, MA: Harvard University Press, 1993.

The Seas of Language. Oxford: Oxford University Press, 1993.

Michael Hand (1996, 2005)

DUNS SCOTUS, JOHN
(c. 1266–1308)

As with many of the medieval Schoolmen, little is known of the early life of John Duns, the Scot (or Scotus), a theologian and philosopher. From the record of his ordination to the priesthood by Bishop Oliver Sutton at Northampton on March 17, 1291, it is inferred that he was born early in 1266. Rival traditions, neither of which can be traced to medieval sources, link him with each of the two main branches of the Duns family in Scotland. According to one account, he was the son of Ninian Duns, a landowner who lived near Maxton in Roxburghshire, received his early schooling at Haddington, and in 1277 entered the Franciscan convent at Dumfries, where his uncle was guardian. Another popular tradition, however, states that his father was the younger son of the Duns of Grueldykes, whose estate was near the present village of Duns in Berwickshire. As a bachelor of theology, Scotus lectured on the *Sentences* of Peter Lombard at Cambridge (date unknown), at Oxford about 1300, and at Paris from 1302 to 1303, when he and others were banished for not taking the side of King Philip the Fair against Pope Boniface VIII in a quarrel over the taxation of church property for the wars with England. The exile was short, however, for Scotus was back in Paris by 1304 and became regent master of theology in 1305. In 1307 he was transferred to the Franciscan study house at Cologne, where he died the following year.

WORKS

Scotus's early death interrupted the final editing of his most important work, the monumental commentary on the *Sentences* known as the *Ordinatio* (or in earlier editions as the *Commentaria Oxoniensia* or simply the *Opus Oxoniense*). An outgrowth of earlier lectures begun at Oxford and continued on the Continent, this final version was dictated to scribes, with instruction to implement it with materials from his Paris and Cambridge lectures. A modern critical edition of the *Ordinatio*, begun by the Typis Polyglottis Vaticanis (Vatican Press) in 1950, is still in progress. Though less extensive in scope, Scotus's *Quaestiones Quodlibetales* are almost as important; they express his most mature thinking as regent master at Paris. Also authentic are the *Quaestiones Subtilissimae in Metaphysicam* on Aristotle's *Metaphysics*; some forty-six shorter disputations held in Oxford and Paris and known as *Collationes*; and a series of logical writings in the form of questions on Porphyry's *Isagoge* and on Aristotle's *Categories, De Interpretatione* and *De Sophisticis Elenchis*. The *Tractatus de Primo Principio* is a short but important compendium of natural theology; drawing heavily upon the *Ordinatio*, it seems to be one of Scotus's latest works. Like the *Theoremata*, a work whose authenticity has been seriously questioned, the *Tractatus* was apparently dictated only in an incomplete form and left to some amanuensis to finish.

THEOLOGY AND PHILOSOPHY

Like the majority of the great thinkers of the late thirteenth and early fourteenth centuries, Scotus was a professional theologian rather than a philosopher. One of the privileges accorded mendicant friars like the Franciscans and Dominicans was that of beginning their studies for a mastership in theology without having first become a Master of Arts. The philosophical courses they took in preparation were pursued in study houses of their own order and were, as a rule, less extensive than those required of the candidate for an M.A. As a consequence of this educational program their commentaries on the philosophical works of Aristotle were usually written later than those on biblical works or on the *Sentences* of Peter Lombard; also, the most important features of their philosophy are frequently found in the context of a theological question. This does not mean that they confused theology with philosophy in principle, but only that in practice they used philosophy almost exclusively for systematic defense or explication of the data of revelation. But in so doing, these theologians assumed that philosophy as a work of reason unaided by faith played an autonomous role and had a competence of its own, limited though it might be where questions of man's nature and destiny were at issue.

This critical attitude concerning the respective spheres of philosophy and theology became more pronounced around the turn of the fourteenth century. Thus, we often find Scotus not only distinguishing in reply to a particular question the answers given by the theologians from those of the "philosophers" (Aristotle and his Arabic commentators) but also pointing out what the philosophers could have proved had they been better at their profession. On the other hand, the genuine interest in the logical structure of "science" (*episteme*), as Aristotle understood the term, led to an inevitable comparison of systematic theology with the requirements of a science such as Euclid's geometry.

Paradoxically, it is in the attempt of the Scholastics to show to what extent theology is or is not a science that we find the most important expressions of their ideas of a deductive system. This is particularly true of the lengthy discussions on the nature of theology in the prologue of Scotus's *Ordinatio*. Similarly, if we look for the origin of some important and influential philosophical concepts that lie at the heart of Galileo Galilei's mechanics, we find them in the medieval discussions of "the intension and remission of forms" (that is, how qualities like hot and white increase in intensity). It was in his analysis of how a man might grow in supernatural charity, for instance, that Scotus introduced his theory of how variations in the intensity of a quality might be treated quantitatively. This key notion, developed by the Merton Schoolmen and extended to the problem of motion, made possible Galileo's description of the free fall of bodies.

Scotus was most concerned with what philosophy has to say about God and the human spirit. Though his ethical views and philosophy of nature are not without interest, Scotus was primarily a metaphysician.

METAPHYSICS

Scotus was thoroughly familiar with the writings of Avicenna, whose concept of metaphysics Scotus brought to the service of theology. Avicenna agreed with Averroes that Aristotle's metaphysics was meant to be more than a collection of opinions (*doxa*) and had the character of a science (*episteme*) or body of demonstrated truths, where "demonstration" is understood in the sense of the *Posterior Analytics*. They also agreed that this science was in great part concerned with God and the Intelligences responsible for the movement of the planetary spheres. But Averroes believed that the existence of God is proved by physics or natural science (by Aristotle's argument for a prime mover), whereas Avicenna developed a causal proof within the framework of metaphysics itself. Scotus argued that the Averroistic view subordinates Aristotle's "first philosophy" to physics when it should be autonomous. Moreover—and more important—one needs a metaphysician to prove that the "prime mover" is the First Being, and metaphysics provides more and better arguments for God's existence than this particular physical proof. Part of the difficulty with the physical proof stems from Aristotle's axiom that "whatever is moved is moved by another." Scotus did not regard this as intuitively evident or deducible from any other such principles. Furthermore, he saw numerous counterinstances in experience, such as man's free will or a body's continued motion after external force is removed.

THE TRANSCENDENTALS. Scotus saw metaphysics as an autonomous science concerned with the transcendentals, those realities or aspects of reality that transcend the physical. Its subject matter, as Avicenna rightly maintained, is being as being and its transcendental attributes. In contrast with St. Thomas Aquinas, who restricted transcendental to such notions as have the same extension as "being," Scotus treated any notion applicable to reality but not included in one of Aristotle's ten categories as transcendental. At least four classes of such can be enumerated. Being (*ens*) is the first of the transcendental notions. It is an irreducibly simple notion of widest extension that is used to designate any subject whose existence implies no contradiction. "Existence" refers to the real or extramental world. Next come the three attributes coextensive with being—"one," "true," and "good"—for to be capable of existing in the extramental world, the subject must have a certain unity and be capable of being known and being desired or willed. Third, there are an unlimited number of attributes such as "infinite-or-finite," "necessary-or-contingent," "cause-or-caused," and so on, that are coextensive with being only in disjunction. Finally, there are many other predicates whose formal notion or definition contains no hint of imperfection or limitation. These are known as pure or unqualified perfections. In addition to being (*ens*), its coextensive attributes, and the more perfect member of each disjunction, this class of transcendentals includes any attribute that can be ascribed to God, whether it pertain to him alone

(such as omnipotence or omniscience) or whether it also is characteristic of certain creatures (such as wisdom, knowledge, free will).

Disjunctive attributes. Like Avicenna, Scotus regarded the disjunctive transcendentals as the most important for metaphysics, but being Christian, he conceived these supercategories of being somewhat differently. Avicenna held that creation proceeded from God by a necessary and inevitable process of emanation, whereas for Scotus creation was contingent and dependent on God's free election. Therefore, for Scotus the less perfect member of each disjunction represents only a possible type of real being, whereas for Avicenna these possible types must all eventually be actualized, and therefore the complete disjunction is a necessary consequence of "being." Scotus expressed this difference in what might be called his "law of disjunction":

> In the disjunctive attributes, while the entire disjunction cannot be demonstrated from "being," nevertheless as a universal rule by positing the less perfect extreme of some being, we can conclude that the more perfect extreme is realized in some other being. Thus it follows that if some being is finite, then some being is infinite, and if some being is contingent, then some being is necessary. For in such cases it is not possible for the more imperfect extreme of the disjunction to be extentially predicated of "being" particularly taken, unless the more perfect extreme be existentially verified of some other being upon which it depends. (*Ordinatio* I, 39)

The task of the metaphysician, then, is to work out the ways in which the various transcendental concepts entail one another. One of the more important conclusions that will emerge from such an analysis is that there is one, and only one, being in which all pure perfection coexists. Such an infinite being we call God.

PROOF FOR GOD'S EXISTENCE. Scotus suggested that the metaphysician might use any pair of disjunctives to prove God exists (and here he seems to be in the tradition of William of Auvergne and the "second way" of St. Bonaventure). However, the one metaphysical proof he chose to work out in any detail seems to be a synthesis of what he considered the best elements of all the proofs of his predecessors. Henry of Ghent, whose writings so often served as the springboard for Scotus's own discussion of any problem, had tried to bring some order into the many proofs advanced during the Middle Ages by grouping them under two general headings, the way of causality and the way of eminence. The first drew its inspiration from Aristotelian principles, whereas the second was Augustinian in tone and stemmed from the School of St. Victor and the *Monologion* of St. Anselm. The way of causality was further divided by Henry accordingly as God is treated as the efficient, the final, or the exemplar cause of creatures.

Scotus simplified the causal approach by eliminating the exemplar cause as a distinct category. He treated it as merely a subdivision of efficiency and implied that the cause in question is intelligent and does not act by a blind impulse of nature. As for the way of eminence, it was treated not simply in terms of its Platonic or Augustinian origins but as having a foundation in Aristotelian principles as well. The proof was developed in two principal parts, one dealing with the relative attributes of the infinite being—efficiency, finality, and eminent perfection—and the second with the absolute property of his infinity. Given the infinity of God, Scotus essayed to show there can be but one such being. Each section is a concatenation of closely reasoned conclusions, some thirty-odd in all.

The argument was perhaps one of the most elaborate and detailed proofs for God's existence constructed during the Middle Ages, and apart from any intrinsic merit as a whole it is of considerable historical interest. From the time Scotus first formulated it, he subjected the proof to several revisions, mainly in the direction of greater conceptual economy and logical rigor. In what seems to be the final version (in the *Tractatus de Primo Principio*), the proof is prefaced by two chapters that represent an attempt to formalize what a Schoolman at the turn of the fourteenth century must have regarded as the basic axioms and theses of the science of metaphysics. Other interesting aspects of the argument appear in answer to possible objections to the proof. One anticipates Immanuel Kant's causal antinomy. Aristotle and his Arabic commentators maintained that the world with its cyclic growth and decay had no beginning. How, then, can one argue to the existence of an uncaused efficient cause? Scotus's solution reveals the influence of Avicenna. On the ground that whatever does not exist of itself has only the possibility of existence as something essential to itself, Avicenna argued that this holds not only of the moment a thing begins to be but of every subsequent moment as well. The true cause of any effect, then, must coexist with and conserve the effect and therefore must be distinguished from the ancillary chain of partial causes that succeed one another in time.

Scotus developed this distinction in terms of what he called an essential versus an accidental concatenation of causes. A series of generative causes such as grandparent, parent, and child, or any sequence of events such as those later analyzed by David Hume, would be causes only accidentally ordered to one another in the production of their final effect. Where an essential ordering or concatenation exists, all the causal factors must coexist both to produce and to conserve their effect. This is true whether they be of different types (such as material, formal, efficient, and final) or whether they be a chain of efficient or final causes, such as Avicenna postulated for the hierarchy of Intelligences between God and the material world. While infinite regress in accidentally ordered causes may be possible, Scotus said, the chain as a whole must be essentially ordered to some coexisting cause that guarantees the perpetuity of what is constant or cyclic about such repetitive productivity. But no philosopher postulates an infinite regress where the concatenation of causes is essential and all must coexist. One does not explain how any possible effect is actually conserved, for instance, by assuming an infinity of links upon which it depends.

Technical demonstration. How is any proof that begins with factual propositions demonstrative or scientific in Aristotle's sense of demonstrative? Are not all such premises contingent? With Avicenna obviously in mind, Scotus explained that pagan philosophers could admit that every factual proposition is necessarily true because of the deterministic chain of causes that links it to the first creative cause, God. According to pagan philosophers, this is true not only of eternal entities like primary matter or the inferior or secondary Intelligences but also of all temporal events brought about by the clockwork motions of the heavenly bodies that these Intelligences cause. Empirical explanations of temporal events are required only because the human mind is unable to trace all the intricate links of causal efficacy that make any given event a necessary and inevitable consequence of God's essential nature.

If such a theory were true, Scotus argued, it would eliminate all genuine contingency from the world and thus conflict with one of the most manifest truths of human experience, namely, that we are free to act otherwise than we do. Should one deny such an obvious fact, it is not argument he needs but punishment or perception. "If, as Avicenna says, those who deny a first principle should be beaten or exposed to fire until they concede that to burn or not to burn are not identical, so too ought those who deny that some being is contingent be exposed to torments until they concede that it is possible for them not to be tormented" (*Ordinatio* I, 39). If true contingency exists, however, it can only be because the first cause does not create the world by any necessity of nature. But if the whole of creation depends upon God's free will, then every factual or existential statement about it will be radically contingent. How, then, can any proof from effect to cause satisfy Aristotle's demand that demonstration begin with necessary premises? One could argue legitimately, but not demonstratively, from such an obvious fact as contingency. Yet, Scotus maintained, it is possible to convert the argument into a technical demonstration by shifting to what is necessary and essential about any contingent fact, namely, its possibility. For while one cannot always infer actuality from possibility, the converse inference is universally valid. What is more, Scotus added, statements about such possibilities are necessary; hence, he preferred to construct the proof from efficiency in the mode of possibility thus: Something can be produced, therefore something can be productive; since an infinite regress or circularity in essentially concatenated causes is impossible, some uncaused agent must be possible and hence actual, since it cannot be both possible and incapable of being caused if it is not actually existing.

One can argue similarly of the possibility of a final cause or of a most perfect nature. (Scotus's argument in this connection bears a curious parallel to Ludwig Wittgenstein's about simple objects in the *Tractatus Logico-Philosophicus*.) Scotus saw God as the necessary or a priori condition required to make any contingent truth about the world possible; these possibilities must be a part of God's nature, "written into him from the beginning"; as source of all possibility, he himself cannot be "merely possible." It is in God's knowledge of, and power over, these limitless possibilities that we discover what is fixed, essential, and noncontingent about not only the actual world but about all possible worlds as well. Since God is the fixed locus in which all possibilities coexist, he must be infinite in knowledge, in power, and therefore in his essence or nature. Since contradictions arise if one assumes that more than one such infinite mind, power, or being exists, there can be but one God.

THEORY OF KNOWLEDGE

After establishing the existence of an infinite being to his own satisfaction, Scotus undertook an analysis of the concepts that enter into statements about God, and in so doing he threw considerable light upon his own theory of knowledge, particularly upon how he considered notions

that transcend the level of sensible phenomena to be possible.

UNIVOCITY AND THE TRANSCENDENTALS. Some of the earlier Schoolmen like Alexander of Hales, St. Bonaventure, and Henry of Ghent fell back upon various theories of innatism or illuminationism (in which elements from St. Augustine and Avicenna were grafted upon the Aristotelian theory of knowledge) to account for such knowledge as seems to have no foundation in the data of the senses. These hybrid interpretations of Aristotle had this in common: His theory was used to explain only how general or universal concepts applicable to the visible world are abstracted from sense images. But where any notion applicable to God was involved, some illumination from a transcendent mind was thought to be required. Not only did this hold for notions obviously proper to God—such as "necessary being" and "omnipotence"—but also for such seemingly common transcendentals as "being," "true," and "good." Although the latter terms were predicated of creatures as well as of God, their meaning was not univocal. Associated with each term were two similar, and hence often indistinguishable, meanings, both simple and irreducible to any common denominator. One was believed to be proper to creatures and to be abstracted from sensible things by the aid of an agent intellect; the other was proper to God, and since it transcended in perfection anything to be found in creatures, it must be given from above. It was maintained that these innate ideas, impressed upon the soul at birth, lie dormant in the storehouse of the mind, to be recalled like forgotten memories when man encounters something analogous in sensible experience. The discovery of God in created things, then, was explained much like Plato's account of how man recalls the transcendent world of ideas.

As Aristotle's own writings became better known, however, the popularity of such theories diminished. More and more Scholastics followed Thomas Aquinas in rejecting any special illumination theory to explain man's knowledge of God, but like Thomas they failed to see that this required any modification of the traditional doctrine of the analogy of being and other transcendental terms. Scotus seems to have been the first to see the discrepancy between the two positions. He pointed out that if all of our general notions (including those of being and its transcendental attributes) are formed by reflecting upon sensible things, as Aristotle explained, then some notions such as being must be univocally predicable of God and creatures, or all knowledge of God becomes impossible. Arguing specifically against Henry of Ghent, who claimed we have either a concept of being proper to God or one common to finite creatures, Scotus insisted on the need of a third or neutral notion of being as a common element in both the other concepts. This is evident, he said, because we can be certain that God is a being while remaining in doubt as to whether he is an infinite or a finite being. When we prove him to be infinite, this does not destroy but adds to our previous incomplete and imperfect notion of him. The same could be said of other transcendental notions, such as wisdom or goodness. Indeed, every irreducibly simple notion predicable of God must be univocally predicable of the finite and created thing from which it was abstracted. Any perfection of God is analogous to its created similitude, but we conceive such a perfection as something exclusive or proper to God through composite concepts constructed by affirming, denying, and interrelating conceptual elements that are simple and univocally predicable of creatures. For even though every such element is itself general, certain combinations thereof may serve to characterize one, and only one, thing. Although such concepts are proper to God, they retain their general character and do not express positively the unique individuality of the divine nature. Hence the need for proving that only one God exists.

Scotus also held that the transcendental notion of being (*ens*) is univocal to substance and accidents as well as to God and creatures. We have no more sensible experience of substance than we do of God; its very notion is a conceptual construct, and we would be unable to infer its existence if substance did not have something positive in common with our experiential data.

THE FORMAL DISTINCTION. The concept of the formal distinction, like univocity of being, is another characteristic metaphysical thesis connected with Scotus's theory of knowledge. Though usually associated with his name, the distinction did not originate with him. It represents a development of what is sometimes called the "virtual distinction" or "conceptual distinction with a foundation in the thing." The latter is an intermediate between the real distinction and that which is merely conceptual. The difference between the morning star and evening star, for example, is purely conceptual. Here one and the same thing, the planet Venus, is conceived and named in two different ways because of the different ways or contexts in which it appears to us. The real distinction, on the contrary, concerns two or more individual items, such as Plato and Socrates, body and soul, or substance and its accidents. Though two such things may coexist or even form a substantial unity or accidental aggregate, it is

logically possible that one be separated from the other or even exist apart from the other. The Scholastics generally recognized the need of some intermediary distinction if the objectivity of our knowledge of things is to be safeguarded. How is it possible, they asked, to speak of a plurality of attributes or perfections in God when the divine nature is devoid of any real distinction? How is it possible for a creature to resemble God according to one such attribute and not another? Similarly, if the human soul is really simple, as many of the later Scholastics taught, how can it lack all objective distinction and still be like an angel by virtue of its rational powers and unlike the angel by reason of its sentient nature? All agree that it is possible for the human mind to conceive one of these intelligible aspects of a thing apart from another and that both concepts give a partial insight into what is objectively present to the thing known.

To put it another way, there is a certain isomorphism between concept and reality, in virtue of which concept may be said to be a likeness (*species*) or picture of reality. This "likeness" should not be construed in terms of the relatively simply way a snapshot depicts a scene, but perhaps something more akin to Wittgenstein's "logical picture," being based upon what shows itself in both the world of facts and our thoughts about the world. In virtue of this intelligibility of form, we can speak of *ratio* (the Latin equivalent of the Greek *logos* or the Avicennist *intentio*) either as in things or as in the mind. To the extent that this *ratio* or intelligible feature is a property or characteristic of a thing, we are justified in saying that the individual possessing it is a so-and-so. Though such *rationes* can be conceived one without the other because their definitions differ and what is implied by one is not necessarily implied by the other, nevertheless, as characteristic of a specific individual, they constitute one thing. They are not separable from that individual in the way the soul can be separated from the body, or a husband from his family. Not even the divine power can separate a soul from its powers or the common features of the individual from what is unique (his *haecceity*).

Thomas spoke of this nonidentity as conceptual, with the qualification that it does not arise merely in virtue of thinking mind but "by reason of a property of the thing itself." Henry of Ghent called it an intentional distinction, but he added that the distinction is only potential prior to our thinking about it. Scotus, however, argued that if something has the native ability to produce different concepts of itself in the mind, each concept reflecting a partial but incomplete insight into the thing's nature, then the distinction must be in some sense actual.

Put in another way, there must be several "formalities" in the thing (where "form" is understood as the objective basis for a concept and "little form" or formality as an intelligible aspect or feature of a thing that is less than the total intelligible content of a thing). Here again Scotus argued (on a line later followed by Wittgenstein) that a thing's possibilities, unlike their actualization, are not accidental but are essential to it and must have some actual basis. If a thing is virtually two things inasmuch as it is able to be grasped in two mutually exclusive ways, this nonidentity of intelligible content must be prior to our actually thinking about the thing, and to that extent it exists as a reality (*realitas*) or in other words, objectively. This nonidentity of realities, or formalities, is greatest in the case of the Trinity, where the peculiar properties of the three divine persons must be really identical with, but formally distinct from, the divine nature they have in common. This formal nonidentity holds also for the divine attributes, such as wisdom, knowledge, and love, which although really one are virtually many.

The formal distinction was also used by Scotus to explain the validity of our universal conceptions of individuals, a Scotistic thesis that influenced C. S. Peirce. Unlike the "nominalists," Scotus did not believe that the common features of things can be accounted for fully in terms of their being represented by a common term or class concept. Some objective basis for this inclusion is required, and this similarity or aspect in which one individual resembles another he called its common nature (*natura communis*). This common nature is indifferent to being either individualized (as it invariably is in the extramental world) or being recognized as a universal feature of several individuals (as it is when we relate the concept of this "nature," such as "man," to Peter or Paul). The common nature is individualized concretely by what Scotus called its thisness (haecceity), which is a formality other than the nature, a unique property that can characterize one, and only one, subject.

Scotus consequently rejected the Aristotelian-Thomistic thesis that the principle of individuation is identified somehow with matter by reason of matter's quantitative aspect. This thesis would seem to make individuality something extrinsic to the thing itself, or at least the effect of something really other than the thing itself, since matter or matter signed with quantity is really distinct from the form. The requirement of haecceity is a logical one, according to Scotus, for in practice we do not differentiate individual persons or objects because we know their respective haecceity (that is, their Petrinity, Paulinity, their "thisness," or "thatness"), but because of such accidental differences as being in different places at the same time, or having different colored hair or eyes. However, this individuating difference, he insisted, is known to God and can be known by man in a future life, where his intellect is not so dependent upon sense perception.

KNOWING AS AN ACTIVITY. Though Scotus rejected illumination in favor of what is basically an Aristotelian theory of knowledge, his teaching on the subject shows the influence of some other of Augustine's ideas, notably the active role of the intellect in cognition. Scotus's position is midway between the Aristotelian passivism (the "possible intellect" as a purely "passive potency" receives impressions from without) and Augustine's activism (the intellect as spiritual can act on matter, but matter cannot act upon the spirit or mind). Scotus believed that the so-called possible intellect actively cooperates in concept formation and other intellectual operations. This activity is something over and above that which is usually ascribed to the "agent intellect." Intellect and object (or something that is proxy for the object, such as the intelligible *species* where abstract knowledge is involved) interact as two mutually complementary principles (like man and woman in generation) to produce concepts. Since these concepts reflect only common or universal characteristics of individuals rather than what is uniquely singular about them, it cannot be the singular object itself that directly interacts with the mind, but an intelligible likeness (species) that carries information only about the "common nature" of the object and not its haecceity. The formation of such a likeness or species is the joint effect of the agent intellect and sense image working together as essentially ordered efficient causes. It is in this way that Scotus interpreted the Aristotelian distinction of agent and possible intellect.

INTUITIVE VERSUS ABSTRACTIVE COGNITION. Although the above description accounts for man's abstract intellectual knowledge, Scotus believed that the human mind is capable of intuitive knowledge as well. By this he understood a simple (nonjudgmental) awareness of an object as existing. Where abstract cognition leaves us unable to assert whether a thing exists or not, one can assert that it exists from intuitive cognition of anything. In such a case no intelligible species of the object need intervene, for the mind is in direct contact with the thing known. While most Scholastics limited intuitive knowledge to the sense level, Scotus argued that if the human intellect is capable only of abstract cognition—what can be abstracted from sense encounters in the way described by Aristotle—then the face-to-face vision of God promised to us in the afterlife becomes impossible. Consequently, our ideas of the proper object of the human intellect must be expanded to account for this.

Scotus thought that rational considerations also require us to admit some degree of intuitive power in man even if the full ambit of this power cannot be established by a philosopher. There are many primary contingent propositions of which we are absolutely certain (such as "I doubt such and such" or "I am thinking of such and such"). Since this certitude cannot be accounted for by any amount of conceptual analysis of the propositional terms, we must admit some prior simple awareness of the existential situation that verifies the proposition. This cannot be mere sensory knowledge, since the existential judgment often involves conceptual or nonsensory meanings, as in the examples given above. It is not clear that Scotus wished to assert that in this life we have intuitive knowledge of anything more than our interior acts of mind, will, and so on. This would seem to limit intellectual intuition to reflective awareness and would be consistent with his statements that we have no direct or immediate knowledge of the haecceity of any extramental object. However, he believed that in the afterlife man by his native powers will be able to intuit any created thing, be it material or spiritual, and to that extent man's mind is not essentially inferior to that of the angel. On the other hand, it is not merely because of man's lapsed state that his mind is at present limited to knowing the intelligible features of sense data but also because of the natural harmony of body and mind that would obtain even in a purely natural state.

CERTITUDE. The human capacity for certitude was also discussed, with Henry of Ghent as the chief opponent. Henry, Scotus explained, appealed to illumination, not for the acquisition of our everyday concepts about the world, since these are obtained by abstraction, but for certitude of judgment. Although the "mechanics" of the process are not fully clear, two "mental images" or species are involved, one derived from creatures, the other imparted by divine illumination from above. Since both the human mind and the sensible object are subject to change, no species or likeness taken from the sensible object and impressed upon the mind will yield invariant truth. Something must needs be added from above. Scotus made short shrift of this theory. If the conclusion of a syllogism is no stronger than its weakest premises, neither does a blending of an immutable and a mutable species make for immutability. Furthermore, if the object is so radically mutable that nothing is invariant under change,

then to know it as immutable is itself an error. By way of contrast, Scotus set out to show that certitude is possible without any special illumination. This is certainly the case with first principles and the conclusions necessarily entailed by them. Such necessary truths assert a connection or disconnection between concepts that is independent of the source of the concepts. It is not, for example, because we are actually in sense contact with a finite composite that we can assert that a "whole" of this kind is greater than a part thereof. Even if we erroneously perceive white as black and vice versa, a judgment like "white is not black" precludes any possible error because it depends only on a knowledge of the terms and not on how we arrived at that knowledge.

A second type of certitude concerns internal states of mind or actions. That we are feeling, willing, doubting are experiential facts that can be known with a degree of certitude equal to that of first principles or the conclusions they entail.

A third category concerns many propositions of natural science where a combination of experience and conceptual analysis gives us certitude. Reposing in our soul is the self-evident proposition: "Whatever occurs in a great many instances by a cause that is not free is the natural effect of that cause." Even if the terms are derived from erring senses, we know this to be true, for the very meaning of nature or natural cause is one that is neither free nor acts haphazardly. If experience reveals recurrent behavior patterns where no free intelligent agent is involved, then we are evidently dealing with a natural cause. If the same situation recurs, we can be certain at least of what *should* result therefrom. That the effect expected actually does occur depends upon two further conditions: that the natural course of events is not interrupted by some unforeseen causal factor and that God does not miraculously intervene. Even sensory perception can be analyzed critically to exclude any reasonable doubt. Conflicting sense reports produce such illusions as the stick immersed in water that feels straight yet appears to be bent. Yet there is always some self-evident principle possessed by our mind that enables us to decide which sense perceptual information is correct. Here it is the proposition "Any harder object is not broken by something soft that gives way before it." There are many areas of knowledge, then, where humans are perfectly well equipped to arrive at certitude without any special divine enlightenment.

THE DOMAIN OF CREATURES

EXEMPLAR IDEAS. Scholastics generally accepted Augustine's theory that before creatures are produced, they preexist in God's mind as archetypal ideas. Scotus differed from Bonaventure and Thomas, however, by denying that God knows creatures through such ideas. Every creature is limited and finite as to intelligible content. To make God's knowledge of a creature dependent upon this limited intelligibility of any given idea denigrates the perfection of his intellect; if there is any dependence of idea and intellect, it must be the other way round. Only the infinitely perfect essence can be regarded as logically, though not temporally, antecedent to God's knowledge of both himself and possible creatures. Since possible creatures are written into the divine nature itself, in knowing his nature God knows each possible creature, and in knowing the creature he gives it intelligibility and existence as an object of thought. Like the creative painter or sculptor who produces an idea of his masterpiece in his mind before embodying it in canvas or stone, God, if he is not to act blindly but intelligently, must have a guiding idea or "divine blueprint" of the creature that is logically prior to his decision to create it. Creatures, then, are dually dependent upon God; they depend upon his infinitely fertile knowledge for their conception as exemplar ideas, and they depend upon the divine election of his omnipotent will for their actual existence. This tendency to distinguish various "logical moments" in God, and in terms of their nonmutual entailment to set up some kind of order or "priority of nature" among them, is characteristic of much of Scotus's theological speculation and became a prime target for William of Ockham's subsequent criticism.

THEORY OF MATTER AND FORM. The hylomorphic interpretation formerly attributed to Scotus was based on the *De Rerum Principio*, now ascribed to Cardinal Vital du Four. Scotus, unlike most of his Franciscan predecessors, did not accept the view of Solomon ben Judah ibn Gabirol (Avicebron) that all creatures are composed of matter and form. He considered both angels and human souls as simple substances, devoid of any real parts, though they differ in the formal perfections they possess.

Since Scotus did not equate matter with potency (as did St. Bonaventure), nor did he consider it in any way a principle of individuation (as did St. Thomas), there was no reason to postulate it in spiritual creatures either to explain why they are not pure act like God or to account for the possibility of a plurality of individuals in the same species. Hence, against Thomas, Scotus argued that even though angels lack matter, more than one individual of the same species may exist. More important, Scotus, like John Peckham and Richard of Middleton before him, insisted that matter must be a positive entity. Peckham's view grew out of his Augustinian theory of matter as the seat of the "seminal reasons," but Scotus rejected this germinal interpretation of inchoate forms and argued that if matter is what Aristotle thought it to be, it must have some minimal entity or actuality apart from form. It is true that primary matter is said to be pure potency, but there are two types of such passive potency; one is called objective and refers to something that is simply nonexistent but that can be the object of some productive creation. Matter as the correlative of form, however, is a "subjective" potency or capacity; it is a neutral subject able to exist under different forms and hence is not really identical with any one of them. Absolutely speaking, God could give matter existence apart from all form, either accidental or substantial. In such a case, matter would exist much like a pure spirit or the human soul.

William of Ockham followed Scotus on this point, as well as in his view that the primary matter of the sun and planetary spheres is not any different from that found in terrestrial bodies, though the substantial form in question may be superior to that of terrestrial elements and compounds.

THE HUMAN SOUL AS FORM. From man's ability to think or reason, Scotus argued that the intellective soul is the substantial form that makes man precisely human. But to the extent that reason can prove the soul to be the form of the body, it becomes correspondingly more difficult to demonstrate that the soul will survive the death of the body. While the traditional arguments for immortality have probabilistic value, only faith can make one certain of this truth. On the other hand, if the soul must be a spiritual substance to account for the higher life of reason, at least one other perishable "form of corporeity" must be postulated to give primary matter the form of a human body. Though to this extent Scotus agreed with the pluriformists against St. Thomas, it is not so clear that he would postulate additional subsidiary forms. A virtual presence of the lower forms (elements and chemical compounds) in the form of corporeity would seem to suffice. The form of corporeity has dimensive quantity, that is, it is not the same in each and every part of the body, as is the human soul. The same may be said of the "souls" of plants and animals. Though the human soul has the formal perfections of both the vegetative and the animal souls, these components are not really distinct parts. A formal distinction between the soul's faculties or powers suffices to account for this.

FREE WILL. Particularly in his conception of free will, Scotus departed in many respects from contemporary positions. The will is not simply an intellective appetite, a motor power or drive guided by intelligence rather than mere sense perception. Freedom of will, in other words, is not a simple logical consequence of intelligence but is unique among the agencies found in nature. All other active powers or potentialities (*potentiae activae*) are determined by their nature not only to act but to act in a specific way unless impeded by internal or external causes. But even when all the intrinsic or extrinsic conditions necessary for its operation are present, the free will need not act. Not only may it refrain from acting at all but it may act now one way, now another. The will has a twofold positive response toward a concrete thing or situation. It can love or seek what is good, or it can hate or shun what is evil. Moreover, it has an inborn inclination to do so. But unlike the sense appetites, the will need not follow its inclination. Scotus rejected Thomas's theory that man is free only if he sees some measure of imperfection or evil in a good object and that the will is necessitated by its end (the good as such), though it is free to choose between several means of attaining it.

But Scotus saw a still more basic freedom in the will, one that Aristotle and Plato failed to recognize. Their theory of human appetites and loves can be called physical in the original sense of that term. All striving, all activity stems from an imperfection in the agent, whose actions all tend to perfect or complete its nature. *Physis* or "nature" means literally what a thing is "born to be" or become. Since what perfects a thing is its good, and since striving for what is good is a form of love, we could say that all activity is sparked by love. The peculiarity of such "love," however, is that it can never be truly altruistic or even objective. It is radically self-centered in the sense that nature seeks primarily and above all else its own welfare. If at times we find what appears to be altruistic behavior, it is always a case where the "nature" or "species" is favored at the cost of the individual. But nature, either in its individual concretization or as a self-perpetuating species, must of necessity and in all that it does seek its own perfection. This is its supreme value, and the ultimate goal of its loves. Such a theory presents a dual difficulty for a Christian. How can one maintain that "God is love" (I John 4.16) and how can man love God above all things if self-perfection is his supreme value? Thomas tried to solve the problem within the general framework of the Aristotelian system by making God

the perfection of man. In loving God as his supreme value, man is really loving himself. Love of friendship becomes possible to the extent that he loves another as an "other self." This solution had its drawbacks, for certain aspects of Christian mysticism must then be dealt with in a Procrustean way. It leaves unexplained certain facets of man's complex love life. Finally, the theory commits Thomas, as it did Aristotle, to maintain that the intellect, rather than free will, is the highest and most divine of man's powers—a view at odds with the whole Christian tradition and particularly with Augustine.

Scotus tried another tack, developing an idea suggested by St. Anselm of Canterbury. The will has a twofold inclination or attraction toward the good. One inclination is the affection for what is to our advantage (*affectio commodi*), which corresponds to the drive for the welfare of the self described above. It inclines man to seek his perfection and happiness in all that he does. If this tendency alone were operative, we would love God only because he is our greatest good, and man's perfected self (albeit perfected by union with God in knowledge and love) would be the supreme object of man's affection; it would be that which is loved for its own sake and for the sake of which all else is loved.

But there is a second and more noble tendency in the will, an inclination or affection for justice (*affectio justitiae*), so called because it inclines one to do justice to the objective goodness, the intrinsic value of a thing regardless of whether it happens to be a good for oneself or not. There are several distinguishing features of this "affection for justice." It inclines one to love a thing primarily for its own sake (its absolute worth) rather than for what it does or can do for one (its relative value). Hence, it leads one to love God in himself as the most perfect and adorable of objects, irrespective of the fact that he happens to love us in return or that such a love for God produces supreme delight or happiness in man as its concomitant effect. Third, it enables one to love his neighbor literally as himself (where each individual is of equal objective value). Finally, this love is not jealous of the beloved but seeks to make the beloved loved and appreciated by others. "Whoever loves perfectly, desires co-lovers for the beloved" (*Opus Oxoniense* III, 37). Recall the tendency to make others admire the beautiful or the sorrow felt when something perfectly lovely is unloved, desecrated, or destroyed. If the *affectio commodi* tends to utter selfishness as a limiting case, the first checkrein on its headlong self-seeking is the *affectio justitiae*. Scotus wrote:

> This affection for what is just is the first tempering influence on the affection for what is to our

advantage. And inasmuch as our will need not actually seek that towards which the latter affection inclines us, nor need we seek it above all else, this affection for what is just, I say, is that liberty which is native or innate in the will, since it provides the first tempering influence on our affection for what is to our own advantage. (Ibid., II, 6, 2)

The will's basic liberty, in short, is that which frees it from the necessity of nature described by Aristotle, the need to seek its own perfection and fulfillment above all else. Here is the factor needed to account for the generous and genuinely altruistic features of human love inexplicable in terms of the physicalist theory.

Scotus therefore distinguished between the will with respect to its natural inclinations and the will as free. The former is the will considered as the seat of the affection for the advantageous. It views everything as something delightful, useful, or a good for oneself and leads to the love of desire (*velle concupiscentiae*). As free or rational (in accord with right reason), the will is the seat of the affection for justice that inclines us to love each thing "honestly" or as a *bonum honestum*, that is, for what it is in itself and hence for its own sake. Since only such love recognizes the supreme value and dignity of a person and finds its highest and most characteristic expression when directed toward another, it is usually called the love of friendship (*velle amicitiae*) or of wishing one well (*amor benevolentiae*).

ETHICAL AND POLITICAL PHILOSOPHY

Although not primarily an ethicist, Scotus did solve enough specific moral problems from the standpoint of his general system of ethics to make it clear that his ethical system falls well within the accepted code of Christian morality of the day. Yet it does have some distinctive features, most of them growing out of the theory of the will's native liberty. Without some such theory, Scotus did not believe a genuine ethics is possible. If man had only a "natural will" (a rational or intellectual appetite dominated by the inclination for self-fulfillment), he would be incapable of sin but subject to errors of judgment. On the other hand, if the will's freedom is taken to mean nothing more than simple liberation from this inclination of nature, its actions would become irrational and governed by chance or caprice. What is needed is some counterinclination that frees man from this need to follow his natural inclination yet is in accord with right reason. This is

precisely the function of man's native freedom. Man's reason, when unimpeded by emotional considerations, is capable of arriving at a fairly objective estimate of the most important human actions in terms of the intrinsic worth of the goal attained, the effort expended, the consequences, and so on. By reason of its "affection for justice" the will is inclined to accept and to seek such intrinsic values, even when this runs counter to other natural inclinations of self-indulgence. But being free to disregard the inclination for self-indulgence and to follow the higher dictates of justice, man becomes responsible for the good or evil he foresees will result from either course of action. It is the exercise of this freedom that is a necessary, though not a sufficient, condition for any action to have a moral value.

The other requisite conditions become apparent if we consider the nature of moral goodness. An action may be called good on several counts. There is that transcendental goodness coextensive with being which means simply that, having some positive entity, a thing can be wanted or desired. But over and above this is that natural goodness which may or may not be present. Like bodily beauty, this accidental quality is a harmonious blend of all that becomes the thing in question. Actions also can have such a natural goodness. Walking, running, and the like may be done awkwardly or with a certain grace or beauty. More generally, an activity or operation of mind or will can be "in harmony with its efficient cause, its object, its purpose and its form and is naturally good when it has all that becomes it in this way" (*Opus Oxoniense* II, 40). But moral goodness goes beyond this natural goodness. "Even as beauty of body is an harmonious blend of all that becomes a body so far as size, color, figure and so on are concerned," Scotus wrote, "so the goodness of a moral act is a combination of all that is becoming to it according to right reason" (II, 40). One must consider not only the nature of the action itself but also all the circumstances, including the purpose of its performance. An otherwise naturally good action may be vitiated morally if circumstances forbid it or if it is done for an evil end.

Right reason tells us there is one action that can never be inordinate or unbecoming under any set of circumstances: the love of God for his own sake. "God is to be loved" is the first moral principle or ethical norm. This and its converse, "God must never be hated or dishonored," are two obligations from which God himself can never grant dispensation. He is the one absolute intrinsic value, which cannot be loved to excess; but "anything other than God is good because God wills it and not vice versa" (III, 19).

Scotus argued here as in the case of the divine intellect. The intelligibility of a creature depends upon God's knowing it, and not the other way around. So too its actual value or goodness depends upon God's loving it with a creative love and not vice versa. This obviously applies to transcendental goodness, which is coextensive with a thing's being, but it also holds for natural and moral goodness as well. If the infinite perfection of God's will prevents it from being dependent or necessitated by any finite good, it also ensures that creation as a whole will be good. God is like a master craftsman. For all his artistic liberty, he cannot turn out a product that is badly done. Yet no particular creation is so perfect, beautiful, or good that God might not have produced another that is also good; neither must all evil or ugliness be absent, particularly where this stems from a creature's misuse of his freedom. Nevertheless, there are limits to which God's providence can allow evil to enter into the world picture. He may permit suffering and injustice so that humankind may learn the consequences of its misbehavior and through a collective sense of responsibility may right its social wrongs.

While certain actions may be naturally good or bad, they are not by that very fact invested with a moral value; they may still be morally indifferent even when all circumstances are taken into consideration. Only hatred and the "friendship-love" of God are invested with moral value of themselves, and as the motivation for otherwise naturally good or indifferent actions they may make the actions morally wrong or good. Otherwise, the action must be forbidden by God to be morally wrong or commanded by him to be morally good. To that extent, moral goodness too depends upon the will of God. However, it is important to know that some actions are good or bad only because God commands or forbids them, whereas he enjoins or prohibits other actions because they are naturally good or bad, that is, they are consonant or in conflict with man's nature in the sense that they tend to perfect it or do violence to it. Such are the precepts of the natural law embodied in the Decalogue and "written into man's heart."

But note that what makes obedience to this instinctual law of moral value is that it be recognized and intended as something willed by God; otherwise, good as it may be naturally, the action is morally indifferent. This too is a consequence of man's native liberty, which can be bound only by an absolute value or the will of its author. To the extent that the first two commandments are expressions of the first moral principle and its converse, God can never make their violation morally right or a matter of indifference; the same does not hold of the last seven, which regulate man's behavior to his fellow man. God granted genuine dispensations from natural law, permitting polygamy to the patriarchs so that the children of God might be multiplied when believers were few. This might be permitted again if plague or war so decimated the male population that race survival was threatened. In such a case, God would reveal this dispensation to man, probably through his church.

HUMAN SOCIETY. Although Scotus wrote little on the origin of civil power, his ideas of its origin resemble John Locke's. Society is naturally organized into families; but when they band into communities they find some higher authority necessary and agree to vest it in an individual or a group, and decide how it is to be perpetuated—for example, by election or hereditary succession. All political authority is derived from the consent of the governed, and no legislator may pass laws for private advantage or that conflict with the natural or divine positive law. Private property is a product of positive rather than natural law and may not be administered to the detriment of the common good. More striking, perhaps, than Scotus's social philosophy was his theological theory (which influenced Francisco Suárez and, more recently, Pierre Teilhard de Chardin) that the second person of the Trinity would have become incarnate even if man had not sinned. Intended as God's "firstborn of creatures," Christ represents the alpha and omega not only of human society but of all creation.

Known to posterity as the "subtle doctor," Scotus is admittedly a difficult thinker. Almost invariably his thought develops through an involved dialogue with unnamed contemporaries. Although this undoubtedly delighted his students and still interests the historian, it tries the patience of most readers. His style has neither the simplicity of St. Thomas's nor the beauty of Bonaventure's, yet as late as the seventeenth century he attracted more followers than they. Like students who unconsciously mimic the worst mannerisms of their mentor, many of Scotus's disciples seemed bent more on outdoing him in subtlety than in clarifying and developing his insights, so that for both the humanist and reformer "dunce" (a Duns-man) became a word of obloquy. Yet there have always been a hardy few who find the effort of exploring his mind rewarding. Even a poet like Gerard Manley Hopkins regarded his insights as unrivaled "be rival Italy or Greece," and the philosopher C. S. Peirce considered Scotus the greatest speculative mind of the

Middle Ages as well as one of the "profoundest metaphysicians that ever lived." Even existentialists, who deplore the efforts to cast his philosophy in Aristotle's mold of science, find his views on intuition, contingency, and freedom refreshing. Scotus's doctrine of haecceity, applied to the human person, invests each individual with a unique value as one wanted and loved by God, quite apart from any trait he shares with others or any contribution he might make to society.

Despite his genius for speculation, Scotus considered speculation merely a means to an end: "Thinking of God matters little, if he be not loved in contemplation." Against Aristotle, he appealed to "our philosopher, Paul," who recognized the supreme value of friendship and love, which, directed to God, make men truly wise.

See also Alexander of Hales; Anselm, St.; Aristotle; Augustine, St.; Augustinianism; Averroes; Averroism; Avicenna; Bonaventure, St.; Galileo Galilei; Henry of Ghent; Ibn Gabirol, Solomon ben Judah; Kant, Immanuel; Locke, John; Medieval Philosophy; Peckham, John; Peirce, Charles Sanders; Peter Lombard; Plato; Richard of Mediavilla; Saint Victor, School of; Scotism; Socrates; Suárez, Francisco; Teilhard de Chardin, Pierre; Thomas Aquinas, St.; Universals, A Historical Survey; William of Auvergne; William of Ockham; Wittgenstein, Ludwig Josef Johann.

Bibliography

EDITIONS AND TRANSLATIONS

Opera Omnia, edited by L. Wadding, 12 vols. (Lyons, 1639), reprinted with L. Vivès, ed., 26 vols. (Paris, 1891–1895), contains most authentic and some spurious works, with commentaries by seventeenth-century Scotists. The seven volumes of the critical Vatican edition, edited by C. Balić and others (Vatican City, 1950–), contain only the first book of the *Ordinatio* and seven distinctions of the Oxford lectures. The edition may run to thirty or forty volumes.

For *Tractatus de Primo Principio*, see M. Mueller's edition (Freiburg im Bresgau, 1941) and new editions with English translations by Evan Roche (St. Bonaventure, NY, 1949) and Allan Wolter (Chicago, 1965); the latter is titled *Duns Scotus: A Treatise on God as the First Principle*.

Wolter's book contains translations of two questions from the first Oxford lectures; his *Duns Scotus: Philosophical Writings* (Edinburgh and London, 1962) is in Latin and English, and the paperback reprint (Indianapolis, 1964) appears without Latin. The question translated in *Free Will*, edited by S. Morgenbesser and J. Walsh (Englewood Cliffs, NJ: Prentice-Hall, 1962), is Scotus's earlier view, which he modified slightly; cf. C. Balić, "Une Question inédite de J. D. Scot sur la volonté," in *Recherches de théologie ancienne et médiévale* 3 (1931): 191–208. A translation of a question on the need for theology appears in *Medieval Philosophy*, edited by Herman

Shapiro (New York: Modern Library, 1964), and in Nathaniel Micklem, *Reason and Revelation* (Edinburgh, 1953); on Christ as alpha and omega of creation in C. Balić, *Theologiae Marianae Elementa* (Sibenik, Yugoslavia, 1933), a Latin edition, and Allan Wolter, "D. Scotus on the Predestination of Christ," in *The Cord* (St. Bonaventure, NY), 5 (December 1955): 366–372, an English translation.

STUDIES AND BIBLIOGRAPHIES

The best introduction to the vast literature of the nineteenth and twentieth centuries is O. Shäfer, *Bibliographia de Vita, Operibus et Doctrina I. D. Scoti Saecula XIX–XX* (Rome, 1955); also see A. B. Emden, *A Biographical Register of the University of Oxford to A.D. 1500*, Vol. I (Oxford, 1957), pp. 607–610, and the annual *Bibliographia Franciscana* (Rome), especially Vol. XI (1962) on.

Most general histories and studies as late as C. R. S. Harris, *Duns Scotus* (Oxford, 1927), use the inauthentic *De Rerum Principio* or other spurious works. Recommended are the following more recent histories of medieval philosophy: P. Böhner and Étienne Gilson, *Christliche Philosophie von ihren Anfängen bis Nikolaus von Cues*, 3rd ed. (Paderborn, 1954); Frederick Copleston, *A History of Philosophy*, Vol. II, Part II (Westminster, MD, 1950); Armand Maurer, *Medieval Philosophy* (New York: Random House, 1962); and Julius Weinberg, *A Short History of Medieval Philosophy* (Princeton: Princeton University Press, 1964).

See Franciscan Institute Publications, Philosophy Series (St. Bonaventure, NY): Allan Wolter, *Transcendentals and Their Function in the Metaphysics of Duns Scotus* (1946), for his metaphysics; P. Vier, *Evidence and Its Function according to Duns Scotus* (1947), and Sebastian Day, *Intuitive Cognition* (1947), for his theory of knowledge; and R. Effier, *J. D. Scotus and the Principle "Omne Quod Movetur ab Alio Movetur"* (1962), for his theory of motion and of the will.

W. Hoeres, *Der Wille als reine Vollkommenheit nach Duns Scotus* (Munich, 1962), on the will; J. F. Boler, *Charles Peirce and Scholastic Realism* (Seattle: University of Washington Press, 1963), on Peirce's relation to Scotus; and especially the volume of essays commemorating the seventh centenary of Scotus's birth, J. K. Ryan and B. Bonansea, eds., *Studies in Philosophy and the History of Philosophy* (Washington, DC: Catholic University of America Press, 1965), Vol. III, may also be consulted.

Allan B. Wolter, O.F.M. (1967)

DUNS SCOTUS, JOHN [ADDENDUM]

Perhaps the most important recent area of research in Scotus's philosophy has been in modal theory. There are two fundamental questions: To what extent does Scotus develop an understanding of modalities that is fundamentally *logical*, independent of states of affairs in the actual world? And to what extent are modal concepts dependent on divine causal activity? The two questions are distinct, in the sense that the first is about the *defini-*

tion of the various modal terms, whereas the second is about the explanation for the *fact* that there are modalities at all. If God were to cause modalities, then he would also cause the property of conceivability that is the mark of logical possibility. The first question, in particular, has important ramifications for Scotus's theory of the freedom of the will.

As always with Scotus, these questions do not admit of straightforward answers. On the first question, Scotus's modal thought has, as one modern commentator puts it, a "Janus-faced character." On the one hand, Scotus often formulates modal notions as though consistency (*repugnantia*, in Scotus's Latin) is the relevant root concept: A proposition is possible if it is consistent, impossible if it is inconsistent, contingent if its contradictory is consistent, necessary if its contradictory is inconsistent. On the other hand, however, Scotus frequently talks as though consistency requires the existence of real powers and capacities, such that, for example, "possibly *p*" is true only if there is an agent with the power to bring it about that *p*. The second of these accounts clearly owes a great deal to the Aristotelian modal notions of Scotus's predecessors, according to which, for example, something is possible if and only if it is at some time actual. Scotus's proof of God's existence exploits this second account. The real possibility of there being causes in the world (entailed by the fact that there are causes in the world) requires, given the impossibility of an infinite regress of causes, the real possibility of the existence of a first cause. But such a real possibility requires that the causal conditions for the existence of such a first cause be satisfied. Now, a first cause is, according to Scotus, one whose causal explanation is somehow internal to itself. So such a being must exist, or else the conditions for its possible existence are not satisfied.

The argument clearly reveals the problems associated with the second of Scotus's modal theories. Of far more interest in the history of philosophy is Scotus's development of the notion of what he labels "logical possibility," understood as pure consistency or conceivability. Thus, he sometimes defines *possible* as "that which does not include a contradiction," and in line with this defines *contingent* as follows: "I do not call contingent everything that is neither necessary nor everlasting, but that whose opposite could have happened when this did" (Scotus 1982, p. 85). So the contingent is that whose nonexistence does not entail a contradiction. The significance of the simultaneity claim is that contingency—and modality in general—is on this account to be thought of not temporally or diachronically but synchronically, in terms of conceivable states of affairs considered as alternatives at the same time.

Scotus uses this account to undergird his radically libertarian account of human freedom. The human will is such that it can, in exactly the same set of circumstances, determine itself to act or not to act, or to do *a* or to do not-*a*. But this account requires the notion of alternative possibilities at one and the same time. Given the other aspect of Scotus's "Janus-like character" on this issue, however, an acceptance of the synchronic notion of contingency also entails the notion of libertarian freedom. For *real* contingency—contingency in the real world, as Scotus believes to be observable—requires a real free power. Scotus uses this insight as part of his argument for the claim that the first cause (God) must be a free agent. This does not mean, of course, that every logical possibility has to correspond to some real power in the world. So the new modal theory could coherently be developed without any of the residual Aristotelian apparatus—something that occurs in the generation after Scotus, and then most notably in the work of Leibniz, on which Scotus and his followers were tremendously influential.

Modern discussions of the second modal question consciously or unconsciously reflect discussions among seventeenth-century followers of Scotus. On one rather Platonist reading of Scotus, modalities are wholly independent of God; they are preconditions that govern even divine thought and action. On another reading of Scotus, God alone determines the reality, though not the content, of modalities. If there were no God, then there would be no modalities, even though the content of the modalities is not something over which God has any control. A middle position holds that, according to Scotus, modalities cannot obtain in the absence of any other reality whatever, but that Scotus does not hold God to be necessarily the required cause of modalities. In the absence of God (a counterpossible claim canvassed by Scotus for the sake of argument), there would be modal facts if and only if there were some nonmodal facts to be the bearers of the modal facts.

Scotus is well aware of the objection that a counterpossible premise entails any conclusion. But he holds that there are, as it were, degrees of conceivability about counterpossibles. The nonexistence of God seems coherently conceivable—its self-contradictoriness is not immediately evident—and in this respect is unlike the concept of a married bachelor, or, in Scotus's essentialist example, an irrational man. Scotus holds that, on this basis, principled conclusions can be drawn from such "moderate" counterpossible premises.

THE COMMON NATURE AND UNIVERSALS

Scotus is one of the most important writers on the question of universals. D. M. Armstrong explicitly notes Scotus as taking a position on universals different from that of modern writers such as Armstrong himself. For in modern theories of universals, a universal is *numerically one* in all of its exemplifications. The ancient and medieval tradition, springing in various ways from Aristotle, Alexander of Aphrodisias, and the Neoplatonists, denies this claim about universals, and Scotus provides the fullest development and explication of the ancient tradition on this question.

The Islamic philosopher Avicenna provided the clearest distillation of the ancient tradition available to the medieval West. Avicenna, echoing a common earlier distinction, distinguished a kind-nature as such from the nature existing as a concept in the mind and the same nature existing in particulars. The kind-nature as such is the *content* of the concept. According to Avicenna, the notions of numerical unity and/or multiplicity cannot be built into the kind nature—it is neither one nor many — because the nature (humanity, for example) must be able to exist both in one thing (Socrates) and in many (all human beings). On this view, the kind-nature as such is nothing more than a theoretical construct unifying the concept, on the one hand, with the particulars on the other.

Scotus accepts the threefold understanding of nature but holds that the kind-nature as such must be more than a merely theoretical construct. The kind-nature, in the account of Avicenna, is supposed to be the *subject* of both individuality (as existent in particular substances) and of universality (as existent in the mind). Scotus reasons that something that is supposed to be the subject of individuality and universality must have some real being or entity of its own. And this means that the nature as such must have such entity. The nature as such also has a certain identity or unity—Scotus calls it a "less-than-numerical" unity, compatible with divisibility into different particulars. The nature is thus identical in all its instances, but in a nonnumerical way. And this marks the way in which the developed ancient and medieval accounts are distinct from the modern accounts of, say, Armstrong who, as he puts it, "cannot understand what this second, lesser, sort of identity is" (Armstrong 1978, p. 112), (Scotus rejects views such as Armstrong's because he does not see how a numerically singular item could be the subject of different and incompatible properties in different particulars.) In line with this argument, Scotus holds that individuation is fundamentally a matter of explaining indivisibility: An individual is not divisible in the way that a nature is; this explanation must in turn be something that is intrinsically indivisible—namely, a haecceity or thisness.

See also Alexander of Aphrodisias; Aristotle; Aristotelianism; Armstrong, David M.; Avicenna; Leibniz, Gottfried Wilhelm; Modal Logic; Neoplatonism; Platonism and the Platonic Tradition; Socrates; Universals, A Historical Survey.

Bibliography

WORKS BY SCOTUS

A Treatise on God as First Principle ("De Primo Principio"), edited by Allan B. Wolter. Chicago: Franciscan Herald Press, 1982.

Philosophical Writings: A Selection, edited and translated by Allan B. Wolter. Indianapolis, IN, and Cambridge: Hackett, 1987.

Opera Philosophica, edited by Girard. J. Etzkorn, et al. St. Bonaventure, NY: The Franciscan Institute, 1997.

Frank, William A., and Allan B. Wolter, eds. *Duns Scotus: Metaphysician*. West Lafayette, IN: Purdue University Press, 1995.

Spade, Paul Vincent, ed. *Five Texts on the Mediaeval Problem of Universals: Porphyry, Boethius, Abelard, Duns Scotus, Ockham*. Indianapolis, IN, and Cambridge: Hackett, 1994.

Wolter, Allan B., ed. *Duns Scotus on the Will and Morality*. Washington, DC: Catholic University of America Press, 1986.

WORKS ABOUT DUNS SCOTUS

Armstrong, D. M. *Nominalism and Realism*. Cambridge, U.K.: Cambridge University Press, 1978.

Bos, E. P., ed. *John Duns Scotus 1265/6–1308: Renewal of Philosophy*. Amsterdam and Atlanta: Rodopi, 1998.

Cross, Richard. *The Physics of Duns Scotus: The Scientific Context of a Theological Vision*. Oxford: Clarendon Press, 1998.

Hoffmann, Tobias. *Creatura Intellecta: Die Ideen und Possibilien bei Duns Scotus mit Ausblick auf Franz von Mayronis, Poncius und Matrius*. Münster: Aschendorff, 2002.

Honnefelder, Ludger, Rega Wood, and Mechthild Dreyer, eds. *John Duns Scotus: Metaphysics and Ethics*. Leiden, New York, and Cologne: E. J. Brill, 1996.

King, Peter. "Duns Scotus on the Reality of Self-Change." In *Self-Motion from Aristotle to Newton*, edited by Mary Louise Gill and James G. Lennox, 229–290. Princeton, NJ: Princeton University Press, 1994.

Knuuttila, Simo. *Modalities in Medieval Philosophy*. London and New York: Routledge, 1993.

Sileo, Leonardo, ed., *Methodologica ad mentem Ioannis Duns Scoti*. Rome: Antonianum, 1995.

Tweedale, Martin M. *Scotus vs. Ockham: A Medieval Dispute over Universals*. 2 vols. Lewiston, Queenstown, and Lampeter: The Edwin Mellen Press, 1999.

Williams, Thomas, ed. *The Cambridge Companion to Duns Scotus*. Cambridge, U.K.: Cambridge University Press, 2003.

Wolter, Allan B. *The Philosophical Theology of John Duns Scotus.* Edited by Marilyn McCord Adams. Ithaca, NY: Cornell University Press, 1990.

Richard Cross (2005)

DURANDUS OF SAINT-POURÇAIN
(c. 1275–1334)

Durandus of Saint-Pourçain, the scholastic philosopher and theologian, bishop, and author (*Doctor Modernus, Doctor Fundatus*), was born in Saint-Pourçain-sur-Sioule in Auvergne, France. He entered the Dominican order at Clermont at the age of eighteen, and his philosophical studies were probably completed in his own priory of Clermont. By 1303 he was assigned to St. Jacques, Paris, to study theology at the university. There, according to some historians, he was influenced by his confrere James of Metz. The first version of Durandus's commentary on the *Sentences* of Peter Lombard represents his lectures as bachelor (1307–1308). In these lectures he strongly opposed certain views of Thomas Aquinas, whom the Dominican order had in 1286 commanded its members to study, promote, and defend. At Paris the nominalistic views of Durandus were immediately attacked by Hervé Nédellec and Peter of La Palu. Consequently, between 1310 and 1313 Durandus prepared a revision of his commentary, in which he mitigated many of his previous statements and omitted the more offensive passages. However, this was neither satisfactory to the order nor in accord with his own convictions. Nevertheless, he was granted a license by the university to incept in theology, succeeding Yves of Caen. Before completing his first year as master (1312–1313), he was called to Avignon by Pope Clement V to lecture in the papal *Curia,* replacing Peter Godin. Toward the end of that year the master general of the Dominicans, Berengar of Landorra, appointed a commission of nine theologians, headed by Hervé Nédellec, to examine the writings of Durandus. The commission singled out ninety-three propositions that were contrary to Thomistic teaching. Between 1314 and 1317, Durandus was continuously attacked in Paris by Hervé Nédellec, Peter of La Palu, John of Naples, James of Lausanne, Guido Terreni, and Gerard of Bologna. He replied to these in his *Excusationes* and in his Advent disputations *de quolibet* at Avignon (1314–1316). In the first *Quodlibet* he inveighed against "certain idiots" who charged him with Pelagianism or semi-Pelagianism.

Consecrated bishop in 1317, Durandus prepared a third and final version of his commentary on the *Sentences,* now free from all control by his order. He expressed regret that the first version had been circulated outside the order against his wishes, "before it had been sufficiently corrected" by him, insisting that only this new version was to be recognized as definitive. However, while some views are closer to the "common teaching" of the schools, the final version contains much that was taken verbatim from the first draft and from the first Avignon *Quodlibet.* It is, perhaps, not surprising that the final version, completed in 1327, abounds in compromises and contradictions.

In the jurisdictional dispute between Pope John XXII and Philip VI of France, Durandus sided with the pope in the treatise *On the Source of Authority* (1328), a work that later was published by Peter Bertrandi as his own composition. However, Durandus's reply to the pope's theological opinion concerning the beatific vision (1333) was promptly submitted to a commission of theologians, who found eleven objectionable statements. The reply of "the blessed master Durandus" was later vindicated by Benedict XII. But Durandus did not live to see himself vindicated, for he died at Meaux in 1334.

In philosophical matters Durandus manifested an independence of spirit more influenced by Augustine and Bonaventure than by Aristotle and Thomas. He has often been called a precursor of William of Ockham, but the similarities are only incidental; and it is most unlikely that either philosopher influenced the other. Besides denying the Thomistic distinction between essence and existence in creatures (as did Hervé Nédellec), he rejected the reality of mental species and the distinction between agent and possible intellect. For him, only individuals exist, receiving their individuality not from matter but from their efficient cause. Thus, in the act of knowing, the possible intellect is sufficiently active of itself to grasp individual existents directly and to create universal concepts by eliminating individual differences from consideration. In theology he manifested certain nominalist and Pelagian tendencies typical of the *moderni* of his day, tendencies that were to assume a more radical form in the teaching of Ockham.

In the later Middle Ages the prestige of Durandus was considerable. In the sixteenth century his final *Commentary on the Sentences* enjoyed an extraordinarily high reputation, particularly after its first printing (Paris, 1508). At Salamanca it was one of the alternative texts in the faculty of theology, the others being the *Summa* of Thomas and the *Sentences* of Peter Lombard, and the chair of Durandus rivaled those of Thomas and John Duns Scotus.

Later writers have sometimes confused this Durandus with William Durand, Durandus Petit, or Durandus Ferrandi.

See also Aristotle; Augustine, St.; Bonaventure, St.; Duns Scotus, John; Medieval Philosophy; Pelagius and Pelagianism; Peter Lombard; Thomas Aquinas, St.; Thomism; Universals, A Historical Survey; William of Ockham.

Bibliography

WORKS BY DURANDUS

De Jurisdictione Ecclesiastica et de Legibus. Paris, 1506. Published under the name of Peter Bertrandi.

Commentaria in Quatuor Libros Sententiarum. Paris, 1508, 1515, 1533, 1539, 1547, 1550; Lyons, 1533 and 1569; Antwerp, 1567; Venice, 1571 and 1586 (Venice, 1571, reprinted by The Gregg Press, Ridgewood, NJ, 1964).

Questiones de libero arbitrio. In Prospero T. Stella, "Le 'Quaestiones de libero arbitrio' di Durando da S. Porciano." *Salesianum* 24 (1962): 450–523.

Avignon disputations *de quolibet.* In *Quolibeta Avenionensia Tria,* edited by Prospero T. Stella. Zürich, 1965.

Libellus de visione Dei. In G. Cremascoli, "Il 'Libellus de visione Dei' di Durando di S. Porziano." *Studi Medievali* 25 (1984): 393–443.

Votum de paupertate Christi et apostolorum. In Jürgen Miethke, "Das *Votum de paupertate Christi et apostolorum* des Durandus von S. Porciano." In *Vera lex historiae. Studien zu mittelalterlichen Quellen. Festschrift für D. Kurze,* 149–196. Cologne, 1993.

Kaeppeli, Th., O.P., ed. *Scriptores Ordinis Praedicatorum Medii Aevi.* Vol. I. Rome, 1970, #927–960, pp. 341–350 (a repertorium of Durandus's works, with selected bibliography; see also the supplement in ibid., vol. IV, pp. 73–74. Rome, 1993).

WORKS ON DURANDUS

Fumagalli, M. T. B.-B. *Durando di S. Porziano. Elementi filosofici della terza redazione del 'Commento alle Sentenze.'* Florence, 1969.

Glorieux, P. *Répertoire des maîtres en theologie.* Paris, 1933. Vol. I, No. 70, pp. 214–220. The bibliography is relatively complete up to 1933.

Henninger, Mark G. "Durand of Saint Pourçain (B. CA. 1270; D. 1334)." In *Individuation in Scholasticism: The Later Middle Ages and the Counter-Reformation, 1150–1650,* edited by J. J. E. Gracia, 319–332. Albany, NY, 1994.

Koch, Joseph. *Durandus de S. Porciano.* Beiträge zur Geschichte der Philosophie des Mittelalters 26. Münster, 1927.

Quétif, J., and Échard, J. *Scriptores Ordinis Praedicatorum Recensiti.* Paris, 1719. Vol. I, pp. 586–587.

Schabel, Chris, Russell L. Friedman, and Irene Balcoyiannopoulou. "Peter of Palude and the Parisian Reaction to Durand of St. Pourçain on Future Contingents." *Archivum Fratrum Praedicatorum* 71 (2001): 183–300 (including an introduction to Durand, his works, his troubles with his order, and his place in contemporary debate on future contingents).

Stella, Prospero T. "Le 'Quaestiones de libero arbitrio' di Durando da S. Porciano." *Salesianum,* Vol. 24 (1962), 450–523. Additions and corrections to Koch's work.

James A. Weisheipl, O.P. (1967)
Bibliography updated by Russell Friedman (2005)

DURATION

See *Bergson, Henri; Time*

DURKHEIM, ÉMILE
(1858–1917)

The French sociologist and philosopher Émile Durkheim was born in Épinal (Vosges). At an early age Durkheim decided not to follow the rabbinical tradition of his family. On leaving the Collège d'Épinal Durkheim went to Paris, first to the Lycée Louis-le-Grand, and then, in 1879, to the École Normale Supérieure. He was dissatisfied with what he saw as a too literary, unscientific style of education, connected with a superficial dilettantism in contemporary philosophy. On graduating in 1882, he decided to devote his career to sociology with the aim of establishing an intellectually respectable, positive science of society to replace, or at least supplement, speculative philosophy and provide an intellectual foundation for the institutions of the Third Republic. At an early stage, then, Durkheim developed a preoccupation which was to dominate his whole intellectual life—to establish a genuine science of social life, which would include a science of ethics and thus provide a reliable guide to social policy.

INFLUENCES AND INTELLECTUAL DEVELOPMENT

From 1882 to 1887 he was professor of philosophy at *lycées* in Sens, Saint-Quentin, and Troyes, during which time various intellectual influences helped him to fill out his conception of a social science. His study of Herbert Spencer instilled in him a predilection for biological models, which was most pronounced in his early work. His reading of Alfred Espinas, and later personal contact with him, led him to his central conception of the "collective consciousness" of a society and the related conviction that the laws of social life are sui generis and not reducible, for instance, to laws of individual psychology.

In "Individual and Collective Representations" (1898) he argued that we should not attempt to infer social laws from biological laws, but that the findings of biology should be compared subsequently with independently established social laws on the assumption that "all organisms must have certain characteristics in common which are worth while studying." His conception of a positive science of ethics received a powerful new impetus from a visit to Wilhelm Wundt's psychophysical laboratory in Leipzig while on a leave of absence during the school term of 1885–1886. In 1887 he was appointed *chargé de cours* at the University of Bordeaux, becoming the first to teach social science at a French university; he also taught pedagogy and thus began to develop an enduring interest in the relevance of sociology to educational questions.

In 1896 Durkheim was promoted to professor of social science at Bordeaux. In 1898 he founded and became editor of *L'année sociologique*, a journal designed to unify the social sciences and encourage specific research projects. He moved to the University of Paris as *chargé de cours* in 1902, becoming professor of education in 1906 and professor of education and sociology in 1913. The outbreak of war in 1914 moved Durkheim to write a number of pamphlets with a strongly nationalistic tone, not always easy to reconcile with the views developed in his earlier, more scholarly works.

THE COLLECTIVE CONSCIENCE

Durkheim's determination to establish an autonomous, specialized science of sociology led him to investigate the possibility of viewing human societies as irreducible, sui generis, entities. From there he was led to the central conception in his work, that of "collective representations," whose system in a given society constitutes its "collective conscience." Collective representations have both an intellectual and an emotional aspect. As examples Durkheim offered a language, a currency, a set of professional practices, and the "material culture" of a society; but he also included the phenomenon of group emotions, such as may be generated, for example, at a lynching, and which cannot be accounted for as a mere summation of the individual emotions of the several participants.

Durkheim said that collective representations are "collective" rather than "universal"; they "exist outside the individual consciousness," on which they operate "coercively." It is possible to determine collective representations directly—not merely via the thoughts and emotions of individuals—by examining their permanent expressions in, for instance, systems of written law, works of art, and literature, and by working with statistical averages.

Thus, in *Suicide* Durkheim said that the "social fact" was the statistical suicide rate, not the circumstances attending individual suicides. His treatment of the relations between collective and individual representations, however, was often obscure, and he would pass from statements about the social determinants of the suicide rate to statements like this: "Human deliberations … are often only purely formal, with no object but confirmation of a resolve previously formed for reasons unknown to consciousness." His important conception of social forces thus took on a questionable, metaphysical complexion.

NORMAL AND PATHOLOGICAL SOCIAL TYPES

The conception of "social solidarity" went with that of collective representations and provided Durkheim with a means of distinguishing social types. The simplest form of social group is the "horde," which exhibits a "mechanical" solidarity in which individuals are attached directly to the group by adherence to a common set of powerful collective sentiments. The "clan" is the horde considered as an element in a more extensive group, and the most primitive form of durable social group is the segmental society organized in clans. More complex societies exhibit "organic" solidarity with extensive division of labor: the collective conscience is weak and individuals are attached to functional groups, while the society's cohesion is to be seen in the complex interdependence of these groups.

The distinction between social types led to a conception of "normal" and "pathological" forms, which provided a basis for Durkheim's account of the practical, ethical relevance of sociology. The normal is so only relative to a given social type at a particular stage of development. It may thus be difficult to determine, particularly during transitional phases. But once we have determined it in a particular case, the normal will merge with the average, though the sociologist must also attempt to show how the normal condition of a species follows logically from its nature. Durkheim believed that we can thus distinguish between social "health" and "disease" by means of "an objective criterion, inherent in the facts themselves"; for, he argued, on Darwinian lines, the dissemination of a characteristic throughout a species would be inexplicable if we did not suppose it to be on the whole advantageous. The sociologist, like the physician, should try "to maintain the normal state."

Durkheim applied this precept in the practical conclusions he drew from his study of suicide. It is important to maintain collective sentiment against suicide, at least those types of suicide most characteristic of organic solidarity, since the general ideal of humanity is the sole remaining strong collective sentiment, and the practice of suicide offends this sentiment. He advocated making use of the special nature of societies with organic solidarity in order to counteract suicide, by strengthening occupational groups and allowing them to take a firmer grip on the lives of individuals.

Durkheim's most influential discussion of a pathological social situation concerned "anomie." Anomie is characteristic of advanced organic societies and comes about when diverse social functions are in too tenuous or too intermittent mutual contact. Anomic division of labor exhibits itself in commercial crises, conflicts between capital and labor, and the disintegration of intellectual work through specialization. In relation to individuals the result of anomie is that "society's influence is lacking in the basically individual passions, thus leaving them without a check-rein." Durkheim used this concept to explain such phenomena as the high correlation between suicide and widowhood and between the suicide rate and the divorce rate.

FUNCTION AND CAUSE

Closely connected with his position on suicide and collective sentiments is Durkheim's concept of "function" as a mode of sociological explanation. He defined "function" as a relation between a system of vital movements and a set of needs. The prime need of any social collectivity is solidarity among its members, and Durkheim's main attempts at functional explanation, as in his treatments of the social division of labor, punishment, and primitive religion, were designed to show how such institutions or practices contribute to the type of solidarity peculiar to the societies in which they occur. The function of a practice is not to be confused with any aims of its practitioners; this would be to confuse sociology with psychology. But neither did Durkheim identify the function of a practice with its cause. The function of a fact does not explain its origin or nature: that would imply an impossible anticipation of consequences. Explanations of origins require the concept of an "efficient cause," though the persistence of a practice may be explained by the fact that its function helps to maintain a preexisting cause.

The causes of social facts are always to be found in preceding social facts, in the "internal constitution of the social group," or "social milieu." This concept, Durkheim held, is what makes sociology possible, by facilitating the establishment of genuinely social causal relations. Without it there could be only historical explanation, showing how events were possible, but not how they were prede-

termined. The social milieu was defined in terms of the volume of the group, the degree of communication between its members, and their concentration. Durkheim used this last concept to explain the development of the division of labor. Greater density of population brings with it a sharpened struggle for existence between individuals and this, in turn, makes necessary a greater degree of specialization. The division of labor is thus a "mellowed dénouement" of the struggle for existence.

Durkheim regarded causation as a species of *logical* relation; it was J. S. Mill's failure to recognize this, Durkheim held, that led him to speak erroneously of a possible plurality of causes. The most important method of establishing causal relations in sociology is that of concomitant variations, which can establish a genuine "internal bond" between phenomena as opposed to a merely "external" relation.

PRIMITIVE RELIGION AND CATEGORIES OF THE INTELLECT

In his treatment of primitive religion Durkheim was more immediately interested in functional than in causal questions, though he did not distinguish these as carefully as in *The Division of Labor in Society*, using apparently interchangeable phrases like "respond to the same needs" and "depend on the same causes." He also seems to have confused questions about the function of religions with questions about their meaning and truth. All religions "hold to reality and express it"; all "are true in their own fashion; all answer, though in different ways, to the given conditions of human existence." Durkheim rejected both the animistic account of primitive religions offered by Spencer and E. B. Tylor and the naturalistic account originating with Max Müller; both went astray, he felt, in masking such religions vast systems of error. Durkheim saw totemism as the most fundamental feature of primitive religions; he tried to show that the totem symbolizes not merely the totemic principle (or "god"), but also the clan itself, and this is possible because "the god and society are only one." Religion is "primarily a system of ideas with which the individuals represent to themselves the society of which they are members, and the obscure but intimate relations which they have with it." He thus regarded the explicit content of religious ideas as relatively unimportant. The reality they express is a sociological one, concealed from the worshipers themselves.

Durkheim regarded religion as the mother of thought. The categories of the intellect, such as "class," "force," "space," and "time," originate with religion. Moreover, since the reality expressed by religion is a social one, these categories themselves originally correspond to forms of social organization and activity. Because totemism involves the idea of forces permeating both the natural and the human realms, it solves the Kantian problem of how men can apply these categories to nature. The a priori necessity of these categories is a reflection of society's coercive insistence on the ritual performances in terms of which such concepts are originally used.

See also Mill, John Stuart; Philosophy of Social Sciences; Social and Political Philosophy; Society; Sociology of Knowledge.

Bibliography

WORKS BY DURKHEIM

De la division du travail social. Paris: Alcan, 1893. Translated by G. Simpson as *The Division of Labor in Society.* Glencoe, IL, 1952.

Les règles de la méthode sociologique. Paris: Alcan, 1895. Translated by S. A. Solovay and J. H. Mueller as *The Rules of Sociological Method.* Glencoe, IL, 1950.

Le suicide. Paris: Alcan, 1897. Translated by J. A. Spaulding and G. Simpson as *Suicide.* Glencoe, IL: Free Press, 1951.

Les formes élémentaires de la vie religieuse. Paris: Alcan, 1912. Translated by J. W. Swain as *The Elementary Forms of the Religious Life.* London: Allen and Unwin, 1915; Glencoe, IL: Free Press, 1954.

Education et sociologie. Paris: Alcan, 1922. Translated by Sherwood D. Fox as *Education and Sociology.* Glencoe, IL: Free Press, 1956.

Sociologie et Philosophie. Paris: Alcan, 1924. Translated by D. F. Pocock as *Sociology and Philosophy.* Glencoe, IL: Free Press, 1953. Includes "Individual and Collective Representations."

L'éducation morale. Paris: Alcan, 1925. Translated by Herman Schnurer as *Moral Education,* edited by Everett K. Wilson. New York: Free Press of Glencoe, 1961.

Leçons de sociologie: physique de moeurs et du droit. Paris: Presses Universitaires de France, 1950. Translated by C. Brookfield as *Professional Ethics and Civic Morals.* London: Routledge, 1957. The last three books, published posthumously, contain the ideas developed in Durkheim's university lectures.

On Morality and Society: Selected Writings. Chicago: University of Chicago Press, 1973.

Durkheim and the Law. Edited by Steven Lukes and Andrew T. Steven. New York: St. Martin's Press, 1983.

Durkheim's Philosophy Lectures: Notes from the Lycée de Sens Course, 1883–1884. Edited and translated by Neil Gross, Robert Alun Jones, and André Lalande. Cambridge, U.K.; New York: Cambridge University Press, 2004.

WORKS ON DURKHEIM

Alpert, Harry. *Émile Durkheim and His Sociology.* New York: Columbia University Press, 1939.

Cladis, Mark Sydney. *A Communitarian Defense of Liberalism: Émile Durkheim and Contemporary Social Theory.* Stanford, CA: Stanford University Press, 1992.

Hall, Robert T. *Émile Durkheim: Ethics and the Sociology of Morals.* New York: Greenwood Press, 1987.

Jones, Robert Alun. *The Development of Durkheim's Social Realism.* Cambridge, U.K.; New York: Cambridge University Press, 1999.

Jones, Robert Alun. *Émile Durkheim: An Introduction to Four Major Works.* Beverly Hills, CA: Sage Publications, 1986.

LaCapra, Dominick. *Émile Durkheim: Sociologist and Philosopher.* Ithaca, NY: Cornell University Press, 1972.

Lehmann, Jennifer M. *Durkheim and Women.* Lincoln: University of Nebraska Press, 1994.

Lukes, Steven. *Émile Durkheim: His Life and Work, a Historical and Critical Study.* New York: Harper & Row, 1972.

Mestrovic, Stjepan Gabriel. *The Coming Fin de Siècle: An Application of Durkheim's Sociology to Modernity and Postmodernism.* London; New York: Routledge, 1991.

Mestrovic, Stjepan Gabriel. *Durkheim and Postmodern Culture.* New York: A. de Gruyter, 1992.

Nandan, Yash. *The Durkheimian School: A Systematic and Comprehensive Bibliography.* Westport, CT: Greenwood Press, 1977.

Nielsen, Donald A. *Three Faces of God: Society, Religion, and the Categories of Totality in the Philosophy of Émile Durkheim.* Albany: State University of New York Press, 1999.

Nisbet, Robert A. *Émile Durkheim.* Englewood Cliffs, NJ: Prentice-Hall, 1965.

Parsons, Talcott. *The Structure of a Social Action.* New York: McGraw-Hill, 1937; Glencoe, IL: Free Press, 1949.

Pickering, W. S. F. *Durkheim: Essays on Morals and Education.* London; Boston: Routledge & Kegan Paul, 1979.

Pickering, W. S. F. *Durkheim's Sociology of Religion: Themes and Theories.* London; Boston: Routledge & Kegan Paul, 1984.

Poggi, Gianfranco. *Durkheim.* Oxford; New York: Oxford University Press, 2000.

Schmaus, Warren. *Durkheim's Philosophy of Science and the Sociology of Knowledge: Creating an Intellectual Niche.* Chicago: University of Chicago Press, 1994.

Wallwork, Ernest. *Durkheim: Morality and Milieu.* Cambridge, MA: Harvard University Press, 1972.

Wolff, Kurt H., ed. *Émile Durkheim, 1858–1917; a Collection of Essays, with Translations and a Bibliography.* Columbus, OH, 1962.

Peter Winch (1967)
Bibliography updated by Michael J. Farmer (2005)

DUTY

In practical reasoning of an informal sort, the concept of duty plays a limited, relatively unproblematic role. In thinking about what to do, reasonable people try to see their wants in relation to their interests and to the interests of others; they evaluate alternatives in the light of their previous commitments and bear in mind their obligations and responsibilities. Duty is one among other factors to be taken into account. The reason is obvious: A person's duties are the things he or she is expected to do by virtue of having taken on a job or assumed some definite office. One could say (although it sounds somewhat redundant) that believing that one's duties entail doing something or other is a reason, though not a conclusive one, for doing that thing, and believing that a possible line of action would count as a neglect of duty is a reason against adopting that line of action. How much weight such considerations have depends on what duties are in question and on the agent's obligations as they affect the particular situation. Duties, then, are counted as one of the considerations that guide and constrain rational choice.

The concept of duty in theoretical ethics is quite a different matter. Some moral philosophers (F. H. Bradley would be one example, Cicero another) have concerned themselves with duties of the everyday sort, those that go with being a parent, voter, teacher, or whatever. But many philosophers use "duty" quite indiscriminately to refer to particular obligations, moral principles, or indeed to anything that is held to be a requirement of conscience. "Duty" is a technical term in ethics and the rules for its use vary from one writer to another. For the most part, these differences are of no theoretical interest, but there is one important exception, the doctrine of Immanuel Kant. His views, set forth in the *Critique of Practical Reason* and in the *Foundations of the Metaphysics of Morals*, mark a radical break with traditional ethics, and since what he takes to be the central concept of morals he calls "duty," it is worthwhile finding out what he means by it.

ORDINARY DUTIES

As noted above, ordinary duties are tasks or assignments for which a man becomes responsible as a result of holding a particular job or office. When the tasks are intricate and have to be done just right, for example, the duties of an airplane pilot, then they are spelled out in detail; thus also for tasks that are relatively simple but for which applicants are unlikely to be highly motivated or imaginative, for example, the duties of a night watchman. In contrast, the duties that go with being a parent or with the practice of a profession are not codified, and responsibility for deciding what should be done is assigned to the individual.

Someone who neglects his duties deserves blame. Censure, if reasonable, is graduated to accord with the degree of neglect and with the importance of the task. A host who fails in his duties to his guests is inconsiderate but does not deserve to be pilloried. Negligence on the part of a pharmacist or a bus driver is a more serious matter. A characteristic of duties, as distinct from other con-

straints on conduct, is that a man who is delinquent loses, at some point, his title to the office that his duties define. He is court-martialed, unfrocked, disbarred, or fired (compare the euphemism "relieved of his duties"). Ceremonial dismissals are appropriate, of course, only when the duties in question are, in a broad sense, institutional and have been formulated explicitly. Not all duties fit this pattern; a man may become unfit for an office without being declared to be so, without his dereliction being so much as noticed by anyone, including himself. Someone who fails in the duties of friendship is simply no longer a friend, no matter what he or anyone else may think.

Legal penalties attach to neglect of duties where such neglect is held to be seriously detrimental to human welfare. Where a verdict has to be reached, an offense must be clearly defined. Parents, physicians, and legislators are among those to whom the greatest measure of discretion is granted in discharging their duties. It is an odd consequence that in matters of the greatest human importance only gross and flagrant derelictions of duty are punishable by law. Of course there are extralegal sanctions, and the threat of contempt and blame, of ostracism from one's group, may be a strong incentive to duty. The penalties of social disapproval, however, are distributed in a capricious and often unreasonable way, and a man may neglect all sorts of duties and yet, given discretion and a certain amount of luck, escape criticism altogether. Appreciation of this fact is what leads those concerned with moral education to try to instill in their charges a sense of duty. The attempt succeeds to the extent that the subject becomes habitually conscientious and carries out his duties without thinking about whether he might neglect them with impunity. A more primitive stratagem is to introduce the fiction of an all-seeing Providence in the hope of making the subject believe that no lapses go unnoticed and that all who neglect their duties will, on some unspecified future date, be punished.

Since duties are required minimal performances, no special merit accrues to someone who does his duty. A hero, one who does something that is both worthwhile and hazardous, acts "beyond the call of duty." A modest hero disclaims credit by saying that he did no more than his duty required. A man may be praised for carrying out some particular duty under difficult conditions. Such praise is sometimes justified and sometimes not; the claims of any duty may on occasion be outweighed by the claims of obligation or moral principle.

Although being conscientious is a virtue, it is not the only one, and unless it is mediated by intelligence and moral sensitivity, it may do more harm than good. A man must learn, for example, how to deal with conflicting duties. If he is a jobholder, a parent, and a citizen, then he holds three offices concurrently. Even if his life is well organized, situations are likely to arise in which he has to determine which of two duties takes precedence. Such questions have to be worked out in particular cases; there is no formula or principle of ranking that can be applied. Moreover, as noted earlier, questions about duties are not independent of broad moral issues: if, as seems likely, there are offices one ought not, as a matter of moral principle, to hold, then there are duties no one ought to perform, even when called upon to do so.

KANT'S DOCTRINE

The idea of taking duty (*die Pflicht*) as the central moral concept originates with Kant. There are earlier doctrines that appear, especially when paraphrased, to be analogous, but the similarities are inconsequential in contrast with the differences. Kant himself maintained that his basic thesis is neither original nor esoteric and that, on the contrary, it is self-evident to the plain man. Everyone, he held, recognizes the difference between doing something because one wants to do it and doing something because one feels that one is morally obligated to do it. Moreover, it is universally acknowledged that only what is done from a sense of moral obligation is meritorious. Kant's theory is an exposition of what he took to be the consequences of these premises. He did not claim that the *theory* is easy and familiar. (In fact, he is often obscure and difficult to follow.) He did claim that his theory is the one philosophers must eventually accept if they are consistent and if they take seriously the intimations of the plain man.

The views Kant ascribed to common sense appear to be correct: people do not deserve credit unless they act from reasons of conscience, and we do believe that such reasons are, somehow or other, distinctive. Kant used the word *duty* (and here he diverged, at least from ordinary English usage) to refer very generally to features he took to be distinctive of conscientious conduct. At times this practice leads to rhetorical vagueness, and "duty" becomes synonymous with "whatever ought to be done." However, he also gave it a more precise sense, one that appears in the set of interdependent definitions which, taken together, provide the framework of his theory. In brief, he held that the only unqualified good is the "good will" and that to have a good will is always to act from a sense of duty.

Duty involves recognition of and submission to the "moral law" that is the "supreme principle" of morality.

Since what the moral law prescribes goes (more or less) against the grain, that is, runs counter to inclinations, the law is expressed as an imperative. The imperative is described as being "categorical" and "unconditioned," and Kant meant these modifiers to reinforce the distinction mentioned earlier: objects of desire are variable and evanescent, and thus strategies for achieving such objects are applicable under some conditions and not under others. The moral law, however, applies to everyone and is unrestricted with respect to times, places, and particular situations.

The "categorical imperative" is formulated in three ways that Kant seems to have regarded as equivalent. They are as follows: "So act that the maxim of your will could always hold at the same time as a principle establishing universal law"; "Act so as to treat humanity, whether in your own person or in that of another, always as an end and never as a means only"; "Act according to the maxims of a universally legislative member of a merely potential kingdom of ends." Apart from the question of how to collate these formulas, difficult problems of interpretation arise for each of them taken separately. Nonetheless, one can see in a general way what Kant had in mind: A man is dutiful to the extent that he is seriously concerned with being equitable and fair, with treating other people like human beings and not like machines, and with trying to govern his own behavior by standards that could be adopted by everyone.

Kant believed that the concepts of duty, the good will, and the moral law are all such as can be apprehended a priori. Part of what he meant (and what is certainly true) is that no conclusions about what ought to be done can be derived directly from compilations of facts about what people do or have done. Although Kant was much concerned with distinguishing actual laws that depend on external sanctions from the moral law that the individual imposes on himself, he characterized the moral life by means of a set of juristic metaphors. The righteous man, for example, is said to "accuse himself before the bar of his conscience." This device suggests that Kant believed the "kingdom of ends" invoked in the third version of the categorical imperative to be an ideal beyond the hope of achievement. Human inclinations are apt to be anarchic, and as duty is a kind of inner law, so conscience is prefigured as a stern magistrate.

PRE-KANTIAN DOCTRINES

It is customary to cite the Stoics as the earliest philosophers to elevate duty to the status of a first principle. As far as one can tell from their writings, however, which tend to vagueness, and from sketchy accounts of what they were reputed to believe, their views were quite different from Kant's. In fact, their word *kathēkon*, usually translated as "duty," appears to mean "what it would be suitable or fitting to do." At any rate, the supreme duty is to live "in accord with nature," but it is not clear what that entails or how, if at all, one could avoid living in accord with nature. Particular maxims have to do with ways of avoiding anxiety and frustration, a goal that Kant would have regarded as morally unworthy. The one genuine point of contact, and also the most interesting contribution of Stoic thought, is the idea that morality transcends national boundaries and class distinctions. The cosmopolitanism of the Stoics marks an advance over the views of Plato and Aristotle, both of whom thought that the demands of morality can be satisfied without taking any account of the claims of barbarians, slaves, or foreigners. On the other hand, the Stoic one-world concept ought, perhaps, to be seen not so much as a moral ideal than as an implicit recognition of the changes brought about by the conquests of Alexander and, in later writings, as an aspect of the ideology of Roman imperialism.

Theological ethics attaches importance to the concept of duty, and, in this context, what is meant is, unlike Kantian or Stoic duty, something parallel to the ordinary notion. To be a believer or a member of a congregation is to hold a particular office, often one that is defined by clearly formulated rules of conduct and ritual observance. In some religions the faithful are told that they are in some sense children of God, and to the extent that this belief is taken seriously, a set of quasi-filial duties with respect to the deity will come to seem important. Kant, despite his Pietistic background, was clearly opposed to such a view. It is crucial to his doctrine that men should regard themselves and others as adults rather than as hapless children.

Anticipations of particular Kantian theses can be made out in a number of earlier writers: Richard Cumberland, Ralph Cudworth, Samuel Clarke, and Richard Price maintained (in opposition to Thomas Hobbes) that moral duty is based on self-evident axioms and that the requirements of duty are universally binding. Jean-Jacques Rousseau had much to say about conscience, which he regarded as a sort of inner voice—one that speaks with unique authority on questions of duty. David Hume explicitly remarked on the logical gap between the concept of what is done and the concept of what ought to be done. Nonetheless, it is not clear that anyone before Kant succeeded in holding in focus the idea of a morality that is not, in some indirect way, dependent on considerations of prudence.

In his paper "Does Moral Philosophy Rest on a Mistake?" (1912), H. A. Prichard argued that traditional ethics (for example, the doctrines of Plato, Aristotle, Hume, Jeremy Bentham, and J. S. Mill) goes astray in trying to work out some general answer to the question of why it is reasonable or worthwhile to do one's duty. Prichard's point is that the question itself is the result of a confusion. That something is a duty is (or may be) a sufficient reason for doing that thing, and *if* it is, then no further reason is called for. If Prichard's historical thesis is right, and it seems quite plausible, then there is a sense in which Kantian doctrine and common sense agree and are jointly opposed to traditional ethics. Ordinary duties are not hierarchically ordered under a supreme moral principle; nor do the claims of duty (individually or collectively) provide a unique determination of morally right action. Nonetheless, and despite their untidy array, ordinary duties are "unconditioned" in that they provide us with reasons for acting such that if the reasons are accepted, there is no need for, indeed no room for, further justification.

See also Aristotle; Bentham, Jeremy; Bradley, Francis Herbert; Cicero, Marcus Tullius; Clarke, Samuel; Cudworth, Ralph; Cumberland, Richard; Distant Peoples and Future Generations; Hobbes, Thomas; Hume, David; Kant, Immanuel; Kantian Ethics; Mill, John Stuart; Modal Logic; Plato; Price, Richard; Responsibility, Moral and Legal; Rights; Ross, William David; Rousseau, Jean-Jacques; Stoicism.

Bibliography

For the Stoic conception of duty, see Cicero's *De Oficiis*, which has been translated by H. M. Poteat as *On Duties* (Chicago, 1950), and W. J. Oates, ed., *The Stoic and Epicurean Philosophers* (New York, 1940).

See also Immanuel Kant, *Critique of Practical Reason and Other Writings in Moral Philosophy,* translated by L. W. Beck (Chicago, 1949), which contains *Foundations of the Metaphysics of Morals*; H. A. Prichard, "Does Moral Philosophy Rest on a Mistake?" in *Mind* 21 (1912): 121–152, also included in his *Moral Obligations* (Oxford, 1949), pp. 1–17; G. E. Moore, *Ethics* (London: Williams and Norgate, 1912), Ch. IV; G. E. Hughes, "Motive and Duty," in *Mind* 53 (1944): 314–331; W. D. Ross, *Foundations of Ethics* (Oxford, 1947), pp. 14–27; and W. K. Frankena, "Obligation and Ability," in *Philosophical Analysis,* edited by Max Black (Ithaca, NY: Cornell University Press, 1950).

Mary Mothersill (1967)

DWORKIN, RONALD
(1931–)

Ronald Dworkin, born in Worcester, Massachusetts, has been a leading participant in debates central to legal and political philosophy in the wake of the 1960s. After graduating from Harvard Law School and clerking for legendary federal judge Learned Hand, he held a number of distinguished faculty appointments in the United States and England, including Professor of Jurisprudence at the University of Oxford.

During the early portion of Dworkin's career, social movements such as those connected with civil rights, women's equality, the environment, and the Vietnam War, confronted philosophers with the task of reassessing liberalism. Influential radicals, including Herbert Marcuse, held liberalism responsible for the injustices of the era. However, other philosophers sought to reformulate and defend liberal ideas. John Rawls was the leading figure in the reformulation of liberalism, but next to Rawls, no thinker writing in English has played a larger role than Dworkin. His work is informed by the conviction that the moral task of citizens and public officials is not to jettison liberal democracy but to make their society a more faithful realization of liberal ideals.

Dworkin argues that legal reasoning has an ineliminable moral dimension and defends a form of liberalism that regards the right to equality as the sovereign political principle. His argument about legal reasoning rejects the positivist view that the existence of laws depends ultimately on social facts that can be ascertained without resort to moral judgments. It also opposes those natural law theories that hold the legal validity of a norm to depend on its consistency with substantive justice. Dworkin's defense of liberalism rejects the radical view that liberal principles are complicit in the perpetuation of oppression. It opposes as well the conservative view that liberal ideas have a corrupting influence on society. Writing as a public intellectual, Dworkin has contributed to controversies over civil disobedience, free speech, campaign financing, affirmative action, physician-assisted suicide, abortion, and civil liberties. He has also addressed debates over constitutional interpretation in the United States, rejecting theories resting on the framer's intent and advocating interpretations informed by moral principles that protect individual rights.

The most widely discussed thesis in jurisprudence for a decade was Dworkin's *rights thesis*, defended in *Taking Rights Seriously* (1977). The thesis holds that, in almost all legal cases, one side has the legal right to win.

Dworkin criticizes H. L. A. Hart's positivist classic *The Concept of Law* (1961) for claiming that in hard cases, where legal rules do not determine which side should win, judges have discretion to render decisions as social utility dictates. Dworkin argues that Hart neglects the moral principles that underlie legal rules and constitute part of the law. Such principles help to determine the legal rights of persons whereas rights function as "trumps" that an individual holds against the government and its efforts to promote utility or some other societal good at the individual's expense. Dworkin imagines a superhuman judge "Hercules," who knows all the best moral principles underlying the settled law. Though more limited in their cognitive capacities, human judges should, and characteristically do, seek out those principles that bear on the cases they decide.

The most comprehensive statement of Dworkin's legal philosophy is in *Law's Empire* (1986). The work of judges is presented as continuous with that of legal philosophers. Both involve "constructive interpretation," a way of understanding an object in light of the best purpose it can be seen to serve. Adjudication gives a constructive interpretation of the laws within the court's jurisdiction, with the aim of deciding cases under the law. Legal philosophy gives a constructive interpretation of law more generally, with the aim of determining the strongest justification for the existence of law. Dworkin argues that the strongest justification is that law serves the ideal of integrity: treating citizens according to a single, coherent scheme of moral principles.

Notable critics of Dworkin's legal philosophy include Joseph Raz and Jules Coleman, who counter his criticisms of positivism and develop their own versions of the positivist view. Although Dworkin has proved unable to dislodge positivism from its dominant position, it is widely agreed that his work has advanced legal philosophy by forcing positivists and natural lawyers alike to refine and elaborate their views.

Dworkin's political philosophy forms an integrated whole with his legal thought. He argues that a political community cannot have legitimate authority over its members unless it treats each of them with equal concern. He elaborates by developing a theory of distributive justice in which citizens have a right to an equally valuable bundle of resources with which to pursue their own conception of the good. The choices individuals make in utilizing their resources affect the value of their holdings. Resulting economic inequalities are justifiable, as they derive from the person's own values and tastes. Dworkin argues that a suitably regulated market is indispensable for justice because markets provide the only acceptable measure of the value of the resources a person holds, namely, the opportunity costs of denying those resources to others.

Dworkin contends that equality demands that individuals be respected in the exercise of their liberties, including liberties to obtain sexually explicit materials, engage in homosexual relations, and voice publicly fascist and racist attitudes. He rejects the view that equality and liberty stand in tension. Equality is the ground for civil and political liberties; it is not a competing value. Equal respect entails that government must remain substantially neutral on questions concerning what makes a good life, leaving it up to individuals to decide such matters for themselves.

Raz formulates a liberal alternative to Dworkin, arguing that government fosters freedom not by remaining neutral on questions of the good but by supporting a social environment in which a wide variety of models of a good life are visible. John Finnis and Robert George criticize Dworkin's view of equality and liberty by invoking an account of basic human goods that derives from the conservative tradition of natural law theory. Other important critics include Rae Langton and Catharine MacKinnon, who mount feminist criticisms of Dworkin's position on pornography. G.A. Cohen rejects his theory of equal resources, arguing that market outcomes are morally arbitrary. Most sweepingly, Roberto Unger criticizes Dworkin's philosophy for rationalizing the shortcomings of liberal democracy and glossing over the need for radical changes in existing forms of democracy and the market.

Dworkin has addressed many criticisms of his work, refining and revising his views in the process. His lasting contribution is to have developed a liberal account of law and politics that is original, nuanced, and systematic.

See also Philosophy of Law; Political Philosophy, History of; Rawls, John.

Bibliography

Hart, H. L. A. *The Concept of Law*. Oxford: Clarendon Press, 1961.

WORKS ABOUT DWORKIN

Burley, Justine, ed. *Dworkin and His Critics: With Replies by Dworkin*. Malden, MA: Blackwell, 2004.

Cohen, Marshall, ed. *Ronald Dworkin and Contemporary Jurisprudence*. Totowa, NJ: Rowman and Allenheld, 1983.

WORKS BY DWORKIN

Taking Rights Seriously. Cambridge, MA: Harvard University Press, 1977.

A Matter of Principle. Cambridge, MA: Harvard University Press, 1985.

Law's Empire. Cambridge, MA: Harvard University Press, 1986.

Life's Dominion: An Argument About Abortion, Euthanasia, and Individual Freedom. New York: Knopf, 1993.

Freedom's Law: The Moral Reading of the American Constitution. Cambridge, MA: Harvard University Press, 1996.

Sovereign Virtue: The Theory and Practice of Equality. Cambridge, MA: Harvard University Press, 2000.

Andrew Altman (2005)

EARMAN, JOHN
(1942–)

John Earman is an American philosopher and professor of history and philosophy of science at the University of Pittsburgh. He is perhaps best known for contributions to the history and foundations of modern physics—especially space-time theories, and often with the question of determinism in view—and confirmation theory.

Earman completed his PhD at Princeton in 1968, under the direction of Carl G. Hempel. After brief appointments at University of California, Los Angeles, and the Rockefeller University, where he enjoyed tenure for a year before its philosophy department was disbanded in 1973, Earman spent twelve years at the University of Minnesota, where he was promoted to full professor in 1974. He moved to Pittsburgh in 1985.

SPACETIME AND DETERMINISM

A theme of Earman's earliest publications is that progress can be made on perennial philosophical problems by bringing modern physics and mathematics, thoroughly and properly understood, to bear on them. Through the late 1960s the reigning orthodoxy in the philosophy of space and time held the dispute between absolute and relational accounts to have been settled conclusively, and in favor of the relationalist, by the advent of relativity theory. Presenting Albert Einstein's theory in the language of differential geometry—the mode of presentation favored by mathematical physicists—Earman argues persuasively, in "Who's Afraid of Absolute Space" (1970), that traditional terms of debate are hopelessly ambiguous. The scientifically respectable disambiguations he devises enable him to turn orthodoxy on its head. Isaac Newton's arguments for absolute space succeed, Earman contends, and absolute kinematic quantities abound in relativistic space-times. Along with the contributions of Howard Stein, Michael Friedman, and Larry Sklar, this work helped drag the philosophy of space and time into its modern era.

As Earman aged, he aimed less to resolve perennial philosophical problems than to deploy them as a sort of dragnet in which to ensnare important issues in the foundations of physics. The philosophical problems typically emerge from this deployment considerably complicated. *A Primer on Determinism* (1986), which won the Lakatos Prize in 1989, recasts the question of whether the world is deterministic as a question about whether there are other physically possible worlds—that is, other worlds obeying the same natural laws as the actual world does—that agree with the actual world at some times but not others. Subsequent chapters subject the doctrine of determinism to trial by a variety of prominent theories. Surprising verdicts are reached: Earman declares classical Newtonian mechanics, the physics that inspired Pierre Simon de Laplace's chilling statement of determinism, indeterministic. Admitting infinite signal velocities, classical physics admits as well possible worlds that agree up to a time t, but differ afterward due to the unheralded arrival at t in one world but not the other of "space invaders" that have traveled infinitely fast from spatial infinity. More often, the jury is hung and the fate of determinism is entangled with "sticky interpretations problems [that] resist narrowly scientific solutions" (p. 197). "We can't just read off the lessons for determinism from various branches of physics, for the implications we read will depend upon judgments about the adequacy of physical theories, and those judgments will depend in turn on our views about determinism" (p. 78).

In *World Enough and Space-Time: Absolute versus Relational Theories of Space and Time* (1989) determinism probes the doctrine of absolute space Earman so energetically rescued from ill repute in the 1970s. Space-time substantivalism—the thesis that spatiotemporal relations between bodies are "parasitic on relations among a substratum of … spacetime points that underlie events" (p. 12)—is a modernization of the doctrine with an impeccable pedigree: Newton himself, Earman argues, was a substantivalist. But Earman is not. He takes the lesson of Einstein's hole argument to be that anyone committed to substantivalism about general relativistic space-times is also committed to indeterminism (compare Earman and Norton 1987). On the principle that "if determinism fails, it should fail for a reason of physics" (Earman 1989, p. 181), Earman rejects substantivalism. He does not thereby embrace relationalism: "[M]y tentative conclusion is that a correct account of space and time may lie outside the ambit of the traditional absolute-relational controversy" (p. 4). The sample tertium quid he sketches—an interpretation mediated by Leibniz algebras—was later shown itself to imply indeterminism (Rynasiewicz 1992).

The hole argument turns on the fact that if one of any pair of space-times related by a *hole diffeomorphism*—roughly, a map between space-times that is the identity outside a region h (the hole) but is nontrivial inside that region—corresponds to a world possible according to general relativity, then so does the other. Supposing that substantivalists must take space-times related by a hole diffeomorphism to differ in properties

assigned space-time points inside h, Earman and Norton (1987) conclude that substantivalists must take there to be worlds possible according to general relativity that agree at some times but not others. The hole argument launched a thousand responses. Many philosophers took exception to its accounts of reference to, or criteria for transworld identity of, space-time points, while some physicists credited the hole argument for raising interpretive questions pertinent to ongoing efforts to quantize gravity.

One way determinism might fail for a reason of (general relativistic) physics arises from space-time singularities. Space-time singularities are, roughly speaking, regions of space-time at which Einstein's equations become mathematically ill defined, so that imposing those equations is insufficient to prevent determinism-destroying emanations—Earman seems particularly worried about televisions playing Richard Nixon's "Checkers" speech—from those regions. *Bangs, Crunches, Whimpers, and Shrieks: Singularities and Acausalities in Relativistic Spacetimes* (1995) discusses singularities and other eponymous acausalities. The book's topics—chronology horizons, inflationary cosmologies, and cosmic censorship—familiar to working physicists but less evidenced in philosophy journals, reflects a tendency, appearing in the mid-1980s and accelerating thereafter, for Earman to draw his problem agenda directly from contemporary physics.

BAYESIAN CONFIRMATION THEORY

The first half of Earman's *Bayes or Bust?: A Critical Examination of Bayesian Confirmation Theory* (1992) skillfully surveys the grounds supporting Bayesian confirmation theory: for example, the perspicuity of the analyses it offers of other accounts of confirmation, and its ability to provide some sort of solution to the Quine-Duhem problem and the new riddles of induction. The second half ruthlessly undermines those grounds, for example, it finds Bayesianism incapable of addressing the problem of old evidence or accommodating changes of belief in so-called scientific revolutions. Characteristically, Earman considers the point of the exercise not to reach a verdict on Bayesianism—in the introduction he admits to a diurnal oscillation between being an "imperialistic apostle" of Bayesianism and doubting its very viability—but to uncover worthwhile problems in the course of weighing the evidence.

These problems include historical ones—how to understand Thomas Bayes's essay in the context of eighteenth-century work on probability, for example. A concern, and a knack, for matters historical informs much of Earman's work. *Hume's Abject Failure: The Argument against Miracles* (2000), his most recent book, situates David Hume's argument against miracles in a historical context. That Bayes and Hume were contemporaries licenses Earman to develop Bayesian analyses of Hume's central contentions and the notions (e.g., multiple witnessing) they involve. Although *Hume's Abject Failure* was not universally well received by Hume scholars or philosophers of religion, some of whom charged it with insensitivity to Hume's broader epistemology and with harboring too many equations, the work accomplishes its self-described aim: "not simply to bash Hume … but also to indicate how, given the proper tools, some advance can be made on these problems" (p. 4).

See also Bayes, Bayes's Theorem, Bayesian Approach to Philosophy of Science; Determinism, A Historical Survey; Space.

Bibliography
Earman, John, and J. Norton. "What Price Space-Time Substantivalism? The Hole Story." *British Journal for the Philosophy of Science* 38 (1987): 512–525

Rynasiewicz, Robert. "Rings, Holes, and Substantivalism: On the Program of Leibniz Algebras." *Philosophy of Science* 59 (1992): 572–589.

WORKS BY EARMAN

"Who's Afraid of Absolute Space?" *Australasian Journal of Philosophy* 48 (3) (1970): 287–319.

A Primer on Determinism. Dordrecht, Netherlands: D. Reidel, 1986.

World Enough and Space-Time: Absolute versus Relational Theories of Space and Time. Cambridge, MA: MIT Press, 1989.

Bayes or Bust?: A Critical Examination of Bayesian Confirmation Theory. Cambridge, MA: MIT Press, 1992.

Bangs, Crunches, Whimpers, and Shrieks: Singularities and Acausalities in Relativistic Spacetimes. New York: Oxford University Press, 1995.

Hume's Abject Failure: The Argument against Miracles. New York: Oxford University Press, 2000.

Laura Ruetsche (2005)

EBERHARD, JOHANN AUGUST
(1739–1809)

Johann August Eberhard, the German theologian and "popular philosopher," was born in Halberstadt. He studied theology at Halle, and became a preacher at Halber-

stadt in 1763 and at Charlottenburg in 1774. In 1778 Frederick II of Prussia appointed him professor of theology at Halle. Eberhard became a member of the Berlin Academy in 1786 and a privy councilor in 1805. He wrote on theology, epistemology, ethics, aesthetics, philology, and the history of philosophy.

Eberhard received a Wolffian education, but, under the influence of Moses Mendelssohn and Christian Friedrich Nicolai, he soon developed a personal point of view. As a popular philosopher, Eberhard was averse to abstract speculation and interested in natural theology, psychology, ethics, and aesthetics. He opposed enthusiasm, sentimentalism, and occultism, and favored the empirical approach.

In his *Neue Apologie des Socrates* (New Apology of Socrates; 2 vols., Berlin, 1772–1778) Eberhard denied that salvation depended on revelation, and asserted that there is no original sin and that a heathen could go to heaven. He rejected eternal punishment as a contradiction of its aim—the moral improvement of the sinner.

Eberhard's *Allgemeine Theorie des Denkens und Empfindens* (General theory of thinking and feeling; Berlin, 1776) was dominated by the thought of John Locke, and by Gottfried Wilhelm Leibniz's *Nouveaux Essais*. Like Immanuel Kant and Johann Nicolaus Tetens, Eberhard vindicated sensation against the earlier tendency to stress reason; and like Kant, Tetens, and Johann Heinrich Lambert, he developed a thoroughgoing phenomenalism. He held that sensation is passive and supported Locke's view that all ideas derive from sensation. He claimed that sensing is a transition from thinking to acting.

Eberhard held that Beauty is not an objective characteristic of things, but an adequacy of the object to the representative power of the subject (a view he called—as Kant did later—"subjective finalism"). Beauty excites this activity, and the aim of art is therefore the awakening of pleasurable passions (a doctrine rejected by Kant and later German aestheticians). The first appearance of aesthetic activity in man is represented, according to Eberhard, in children's play (a foreshadowing of Friedrich Schiller's aesthetics of play).

Eberhard, as editor of the *Philosophisches Magazin* from 1788 to 1791 and of the *Philosophische Archiv* from 1792 to 1795, published a large number of articles critical of Kant's *Kritik der reinen Vernunft*, most of them written by himself. He claimed that Kant's views were entirely derived from Leibniz, and that they were only a special kind of dogmatism. Kant answered Eberhard in his *Ueber eine Entdeckung, nach der alle neue Kritik der reinen Vernunft durch eine ältere entbehrlich gemacht werden soll* (Königsberg, 1790). It was one of the few times Kant deigned to answer unjustifiable criticism.

Bibliography

ADDITIONAL WORKS BY EBERHARD

Sittenlehre der Vernunft. Berlin, 1781.

Theorie der schonen Künste und Wissenschaften. Berlin, 1783.

Vermischte Schriften. 2 vols. Halle, 1784–1788.

Allgemeine Geschichte der Philosophie. Berlin, 1788.

Handbuch der Aesthetik. 4 vols. Halle: Hemmerde und Schwetschke, 1803–1805.

WORKS ON EBERHARD

Draeger, G. *J. A. Eberhards Psychologie und Aesthetik.* Halle, 1915.

Ferber, E. O. *Der philosophische Streit zwischen I. Kant und J. A. Eberhard.* Giessen, 1884.

Lungwitz, K. *Die Religionsphilosophie Eberhards.* Erlangen, 1911.

Nicolai, C. F. *Gedächtnisschrift auf J. A. Eberhard.* Berlin, 1810.

Giorgio Tonelli (1967)

ECKHART, MEISTER
(c. 1260–1327/1328)

Meister Eckhart, the German mystic, was born Johannes Eckhart at Hochheim in Thuringia. After entering the Dominican order at an early age, he pursued higher studies at Cologne and Paris. He became successively provincial prior of the Dominican order of Saxony, vicar-general of Bohemia, and superior-general for the whole of Germany (in 1312). During the last part of his life Eckhart became involved in charges of heresy. In 1329, twenty-eight of his propositions were condemned by Pope John XXII, eleven as rash and the remainder as heretical. Nevertheless, Eckhart was to have a lasting influence upon medieval mysticism.

Eckhart's account of God and the universe depended not only on theology and metaphysical speculation but also on his interpretation of mystical experience. Thus, he distinguished between *Deus* or God, as found in the three Persons of the Trinity, and *Deitas* or the Godhead, which is the Ground of God but is indescribable. The Godhead, through an eternal process, manifests itself as the Persons. In the same way, Eckhart distinguished between faculties of the soul, such as memory, and the *Grund* or "ground" of the soul (also called the *Fünklein, scintilla* or "spark"). By contemplation it is possible to attain to this *Grund*, leaving aside the discursive and imaginative activities that normally characterize conscious life. In doing this, one gains unity with the Godhead. Although Eckhart gave some sort of explanation for the ineffability of the Godhead (namely, that it is a pure unity and thus not describable), the main motive for his doctrine lay in a feature of mystical experience—that it involves a mental state not describable in terms of thoughts or images.

The need to give an account of contemplative knowledge led Eckhart to evolve a complex psychology. The soul operates at the lowest level, through the body; thus it has powers of digestion, assimilation, and sensation. At a higher level the soul functions through the powers of anger, desire, and the lower intellect (the *sensus communis* or "common sense," which combines what is given through the various senses in perception). At a third level the soul works through memory, will, and the higher intellect. At the fourth level it is possible in principle to know things in total abstraction, that is, as pure forms, which is therefore to know them as they preexist in God's intellect. Finally, the spark of the soul can possess a kind of knowledge in which God is known as he is.

In the development of these ideas, Eckhart certainly spoke in ways which might have offended his more orthodox contemporaries. The notion of the spark within the soul seemed to imply that the soul is uncreated. The notion of God's birth within the soul, through mystical experience, seemed to present the sacraments of the church as mere means of preparing for such experience, rather than as efficacious in themselves. Likewise, Eckhart's language of deification could easily have been construed to mean that the historical Christ has only an exemplary and symbolic value. Eckhart's teaching that God creates the world in the same "eternal now" in which the emanation of the divine Persons from the Godhead takes place could be understood as implying the eternity of the world—a doctrine that conflicts with the literal sense of biblical revelation. His statement that all creatures are a "mere nothing" could be held to imply a kind of monism. Recently, however, among Catholic historians of philosophy an attempt has been made to show that his theology is less unorthodox than the above doctrines might suggest, and as a Dominican, Eckhart certainly employed the language of Thomism.

This recent discussion serves to underline the degree to which Eckhart permitted changes and inconsistencies in the formulation of his ideas. Thus, at one time he held that the divine essence is *intelligere*, or understanding (a thesis original to Eckhart, and one which reinforced the doctrine of similarity of the soul to God), and only secondarily is God *esse*, or being. Later, however, he held, in accordance with Thomist doctrine, that God's essence is *esse.* Various other fluidities and antinomies can be detected in Eckhart's thought; these were partly caused by the shifting way in which he used key terms. For example, he asserted that God is above being and yet also, that he is being. The first use of "being" could be taken to refer to finite existence; the second use could be taken in a Thomistic sense. At times he spoke of God as both Godhead and God, and at other times he spoke of God as distinguished from the Godhead.

Although on occasion Eckhart used the term *emanation* to describe the creation of the world, he in fact adhered to an orthodox account of creation out of nothing. But he stressed the continuous creativity of God, and in this and other respects he was influenced by Augustine. Even though his language about creation could be misinterpreted to imply the eternity of the cosmos, Eckhart was at pains to evolve a two-level theory of time. In a sense all events are simultaneous for God, who is timelessly eternal (so that to speak of a temporal gap between the procession of the Trinity and the creation of the world makes no sense). Temporal concepts, however, are properly applied within the created order, and therefore the creation can be dated retrospectively. Eckhart's two-level theory of time corresponded to his two-level theory of truth. The truths that we assert are limited and partial (or, as Eckhart asserted, there is untruth in them), but there is an absolute truth which can be realized existentially, namely, the pure being of the Godhead.

The general shape of Eckhart's beliefs, if we except his doctrines of the Godhead and of the soul, was fully in accord with contemporary belief (for example, in regard to angels and purgatory). What made his sermons and teachings popular was the way in which he reiterated the need to penetrate beneath the externals of religion, while his free use of homely, striking, and sometimes paradoxical examples and similes effectively conveyed his message.

There is a remarkable parallel between some of Eckhart's central ideas and the doctrines of the Indian theologian Śankara (d. c. 820)—a parallel first expounded by Rudolf Otto. In Śankara's system, too, there is a distinction between the Absolute and God conceived as personal and a similar claim that the divine can be found within the soul. The comparison may give a clue to the reason for the shape of Eckhart's teachings. It certainly suggests that there are experiential reasons for this kind of doctrine, even though they may be complicated reasons. They seem to be as follows. The experience of the introvertive mystic includes a state of consciousness in which there is both a sense of illumination and an absence of distinction between subject and object; that is, the contemplative is not having an experience like that of ordinary perception, where the thing perceived can be distinguished from the percipient. Consequently, if the mystic connects his experience with God (whom he believes in for independent reasons), he may be inclined to speak of merging with God. But since his experience is without differentiation and since the notion of God—and especially that of a Trinitarian God—includes the idea that he has attributes, it is not unnatural, although it appears unorthodox, to treat the entity experienced by the mystic as being "beyond" God conceived personally.

Indeed, Eckhart maintained that the true aristocrat (that is, the spark or ground of the soul) reaches beyond God, to the Godhead. It is likewise natural, in the Christian context in which Eckhart lived, to interpret this simple undifferentiated unity found in the Godhead as being the basis out of which the Persons of the Trinity proceed. In this way mystical experience, for Eckhart, was connected with the God of ordinary religion. Nevertheless, Eckhart endeavored to express himself in accordance with orthodox belief, despite the difficulties that he found in trying to do justice both to his experience and to the ordinary language of theism. Certainly, he did not seriously intend to deny orthodoxy.

Despite the papal condemnation of some of his propositions, Eckhart had a wide influence. Johannes Tauler, Heinrich Suso, Jan van Ruysbroeck, and the group known as the Friends of God were in different ways indebted to his teachings and example.

See also Augustine, St.; Mysticism, History of; Mysticism, Nature and Assessment of; Otto, Rudolf; Ruysbroeck, Jan van; Suso, Heinrich; Tauler, Johannes; Thomism.

Bibliography

WORKS BY ECKHART

Meister Eckhart. 4th ed, edited by F. Pfeiffer. Göttingen, 1924. Includes sermons, treatises, and fragments.

Meister Eckhart, a Modern Translation. Translated and edited by R. B. Blakney. New York, 1957. Includes bibliographical notes and the more important writings.

Selected Treatises and Sermons, edited by J. M. Clark and J. V. Skinner. London, 1958.

WORKS ON ECKHART

Clark, J. M. *The Great German Mystics.* Oxford: Blackwell, 1949. A good introduction.

Clark, J. M. *Meister Eckhart.* London: Faber and Faber, 1958. A biography.

Gilson, Étienne. *Christian Philosophy in the Middle Ages.* New York: Random House, 1955.

Otto, Rudolf. *Mysticism East and West.* London: Macmillan, 1932.

Wulf, Maurice de. *Histoire de la philosophic médiévale.* Vol. III. Louvain, 1947.

Ninian Smart (1967)

ECONOMICS, PHILOSOPHY OF

See *Philosophy of Economics*

ECONOMICS AND ETHICAL NEUTRALITY

See *Ethics and Economics*

EDDINGTON, ARTHUR STANLEY
(1882–1944)

Arthur Stanley Eddington was an English astronomer who was educated at Owens College, Manchester, and Trinity College, Cambridge, where he was Plumian professor of astronomy from 1913 to 1944. He never married, was socially rather diffident, and lived the quiet life of a Cambridge academic. He was elected a fellow of the Royal Society in 1914 and was knighted in 1930.

Eddington was one of the most brilliant theoreticians of his day, possessing an outstanding ability to survey complex and highly ramified subjects as wholes. His report to the Physical Society (1918) on the general theory of relativity, expanded into *The Mathematical Theory of Relativity* (London, 1923), contained important original contributions to the theory. Eddington's discovery of the mass-luminosity relation in stars and his explanation of white dwarf stars, which made possible the modern theory of stellar evolution, were published in *The Internal Constitution of the Stars* (London, 1926). These two books are considered to be his most substantial contributions to physics and astronomy. His interpretation of relativity theories led him to a belief in the profound importance of epistemology for physics. At first in semipopular books on modern physics—*Nature of the Physical World* (London, 1928) and *New Pathways in Science* (London, 1935) being the most important—Eddington argued for the view that physics could be almost entirely based upon investigations into the nature of sensation and measurement. A more elaborate and purely philosophical defense of his view was given in *The Philosophy of Physical Science* (London, 1939). Formal attempts actually to produce physics as derived in this way were presented in *Relativity Theory of Protons and Electrons* (London, 1936) and *Fundamental Theory* (London, 1946), published posthumously.

Eddington's real contributions to philosophy, if any, lie in his work on the epistemology of physics. However, he also defended idealism and mysticism, and he claimed that the indeterminacy of quantum physics solved the traditional philosophical problem of free will versus determinism in favor of free will. Particularly in his semipopular writings, Eddington was betrayed into philosophical excesses and, at times, gross confusion by a play of analogy and paradox, which, while part of his equipment as an immensely entertaining and brilliant writer, also served his love of mystery and obscurantism.

SELECTIVE SUBJECTIVISM

Eddington gave to his epistemological view the two names "selective subjectivism" and "structuralism." He accepted the causal theory of perception, and with this theory Eddington's own system stands or falls. From this theory it follows, first, that we know directly only the contents of our own consciousness (sense data) and, second, that these contents cannot be claimed to resemble elements of the objective world in any qualitative way. Our sensory apparatus selects from objective reality what we are able to observe and what is therefore the material for physical knowledge, just as, to use Eddington's own analogy, a net of a certain size mesh selects fish only of a size greater than the mesh. Just as we could generalize, prior to examining any catch of fish, about the size of fish the net would yield, so we can generalize in physics prior to the results of observation, merely by reflecting upon observational procedure, especially metrical procedures.

Despite distortions, mostly qualitative, in the picture that our senses thrust upon us, we may conclude that the picture has a structure in common with the unknowables that stimulate the senses. We notice patterns of recurrence in sensation, and it is the task of physics to elaborate the structure of these patterns. In particular, the structure of pointer-reading observations should be studied, since pointer readings—being merely observed coincidences—are minimally corrupted by the qualitative veils cast by our senses. However, Eddington denied the pointer readings directly represent anything objectively real.

APRIORISM

Like Immanuel Kant, to whose system Eddington admitted that his own was distantly similar, he claimed that knowledge must conform to certain primitive rational patterns if it is to be intelligible. One of these forms of thought is that we believe in the existence of minds other than our own. The recognition of a common structure in the experience of many minds leads to a belief in an objective reality independent of these minds. There is no primitive belief in an objective reality. This route to the existence of an external world is an unobtrusive but significant part of Eddington's idealistic metaphysics.

Using the notion of structure as defined in the mathematical theory of groups, Eddington was able, out of highly generalized material from epistemology (for example, the claim that only relations between things are observable) and from the forms of thought, to build quite intricate group structures, for example, the structure found in Paul Dirac's mathematical specification of an elementary particle in an elementary state giving charge and spin. In addition to this a priori derivation of the formal structure of laws, Eddington also exploited the theory of groups in deducing a priori the basic natural constants, such as the gravitational constant and the fine structure constant, from various features of the group structure of the type of mathematics employed. In this, he compared himself with Archimedes, who deduced the nature of π from the axiom of Euclid, whereas previous determinations of its nature had relied upon merely empirical methods.

On this basis Eddington claimed that the mind fits nature into a pattern determined by the nature of the mind itself; that the discoveries made by the physicist are just what his sensory, intellectual, and metrical processes dictate that he shall find.

It is difficult not to share the general view that Eddington vastly overstated the extent to which convention enters into theory construction. Extensive criticism in this entry without more extensive elaboration of the complexities of his group structure derivations would be unjust. Some brief comments must suffice.

Eddington's view was that observation was required only for the purpose of identifying, on the one hand, the elements of the group constructed by pure mathematics with, on the other hand, the theoretical terms of, say, electromagnetism. It is far from clear where he thought the complete theoretical structure then stood from the point of view of its a priori status. If such "identification" demands that it be fully observed that the electromagnetic field is properly (that is, truly) described by Maxwell's equations, which have the group structure in question, then Eddington was requiring "observation" to add a very great deal more than he seems to have been prepared to admit.

Eddington fell into confusion that illustrates well his mistakes in general. This was his claim that the basis of the special theory of relativity may be deduced a priori because it depends on the fact that simultaneity of events at a distance from each other is not observable, that is, that it depends upon an epistemological fact. It is true that to decide a question about the simultaneity of spatially separated events, one must make assumptions as to the speed of the signals that inform one that the events have occurred. And it is also true that in the last resort these assumptions could be checked only if one could decide independently on the simultaneity of events spatially distant from each other. But this epistemological circularity is an insufficient basis for relativity theory. Moreover, further contingent facts, not deducible a priori (for example, the fact that in any inertial system light takes the same time round any closed paths of the same length, whatever their orientation) are required. Eddington claimed that the result of the Michelson-Morley experiment could have been foreseen on a purely epistemological basis. It seems quite clear that he was wrong.

IDEALISM

"To put the conclusion crudely—the stuff of the world is mind-stuff," Eddington wrote in *Nature of the Physical World*. The idealist conclusion was not integral to his epistemology but was based on two main arguments.

The first derives directly from current physical theory. Briefly, mechanical theories of the ether and of the behavior of fundamental particles have been discarded in both relativity and quantum physics. From this Eddington inferred that a materialistic metaphysics was outmoded and that, in consequence—the disjunction of materialism or idealism being assumed exhaustive—an idealistic metaphysics is required.

The second and more interesting argument was based on Eddington's epistemology and may be regarded as consisting of two parts. First, all we know of the objective world is its structure, and the structure of the objective world is precisely mirrored in our own consciousness. We therefore have no reason to doubt that the objective world, too, is "mind-stuff." Dualistic metaphysics, then, cannot be evidentially supported. (The conclusion appears to be a valid deduction from its premises.)

But, second, not only can we not know that the objective world is nonmentalistic, we also cannot intelligibly suppose that it could be material. To conceive of a dualism entails attributing material properties to the objective world. However, this presupposes that we could observe that the objective world has material properties. But this is absurd, for whatever is observed must ultimately be the content of our own consciousness and, consequently, nonmaterial. This last argument confuses, among other things, the supposition that the objective world has certain properties with the supposition of our observing that it has them.

See also Determinism and Freedom; Epistemology, History of; Idealism; Mysticism, History of; Kant, Immanuel; Popular Arguments for the Existence of God; Stebbing, Lizzie Susan; Subjectivist Epistemology.

Bibliography

ADDITIONAL WORKS BY EDDINGTON

Space, Time, and Gravitation. Cambridge, U.K.: Cambridge University Press, 1921.

Science and the Unseen World. London: Allen and Unwin, 1929.

The Expanding Universe. Cambridge, U.K.: Cambridge University Press, 1933.

WORKS ON EDDINGTON

Dingle, Herbert. *The Sources of Eddington's Philosophy.* Cambridge, U.K.: Cambridge University Press, 1954.

Stebbing, S. *Philosophy and the Physicists.* London: Metheun, 1937.

Whittaker, E. T. *Eddington's Principle in the Philosophy of Science.* Cambridge, U.K.: Cambridge University Press, 1951.

G. C. Nerlich (1967)

EDUCATION, PHILOSOPHY OF

See *Philosophy of Education, History of*

EDWARDS, JONATHAN
(1703–1758)

Jonathan Edwards, the Puritan theologian and philosopher, was born in East Windsor, Connecticut. He was the only son of Timothy Edwards, the pastor of the Congregational Church at East Windsor; his mother was the daughter of Solomon Stoddard, pastor at Northampton, Massachusetts. About the age of twelve or thirteen he wrote several essays in natural science that reveal remarkable powers of observation and deduction. "Of Insects" describes the habits of spiders. Another essay, on the rainbow and colors, shows an acquaintance with Isaac Newton's *Opticks.* Around the same time Edwards wrote a short demonstration of the immateriality of the soul. These writings are the work of a precocious mind, deeply interested in nature and finding in it the marks of a provident God.

In 1716, Edwards entered Yale, where the world of philosophy opened up to him. For a short time his tutor was Samuel Johnson, who introduced him to the new philosophical ideas coming from England, especially those of John Locke. He read Locke's *Essay concerning Human Understanding*, from which, he claimed, he derived more enjoyment "than the most greedy miser finds, when gathering up handfuls of silver and gold, from some newly discovered treasure." His precocity in philosophy is proved by his notes "Of Being" and "The Mind," both probably written before his graduation in 1720.

There followed two years of graduate study in theology at Yale, in preparation for the ministry. During this period Edwards had a profound religious experience, which he described later, in his *Personal Narrative* (1739), as having given him a new awareness of the absolute sovereignty and omnipresence of God and of complete dependence on him. Edwards's religious philosophy grew out of this transforming experience.

In 1722 he became pastor of a Scotch Presbyterian congregation in New York, but the life of study and teaching attracted him, and two years later he was back at Yale as senior tutor. In 1727 he was ordained assistant minister to his grandfather Solomon Stoddard, and when Stoddard died, in 1729, Edwards took over the Northampton parish.

For almost twenty years Edwards preached and wrote in this parish. During that time he continued his boyhood custom of jotting down his reflections, which he called "Miscellanies" or "Miscellaneous Observations." They fill nine volumes and contain 1,360 entries. These journals, most of which are still unedited, were intended to be a first draft of a monumental book provisionally titled "A Rational Account of the Main Doctrines of the Christian Religion Attempted." This proposed summa of Calvinist theology was not completed.

Edwards's pervasive theme was the Calvinist doctrine of God's sovereignty and the complete helplessness of man to effect his own salvation by good works. In a famous sermon preached in Boston in 1731, titled "God Glorified in Man's Dependence," he opposed Arminianism—a doctrine derived from the Dutch theologian Jacobus Arminius (1560–1609) and then gaining ground in the colonies—which granted to men some part in their salvation through benevolence and good works. Edwards played a vigorous role in the revivalist movement known as the Great Awakening, which swept through New England in the 1740s, reaching hysterical peaks of religious enthusiasm. His own conception of religious experience is found in *A Treatise concerning Religious Affections* (1746).

Through sternness of doctrine and lack of prudence Edwards alienated his parishioners, and in 1748 he was dismissed from his parish. His next post was the missionary parish at Stockbridge, Massachusetts, where he preached to a small group of Indians and a few whites. He had plenty of leisure to write, and a major work, *Freedom of the Will*, defining and defending his Calvinist doctrine of human freedom, appeared in 1754. The sequel, *The Nature of True Virtue* (1765), places virtue in the emotions rather than in the intellect. His last completed work, "Concerning the End for Which God Created the World," is a speculative theological work on God's purpose in creation.

At Stockbridge, Edwards began a vast synthesis of theology called *The History of the Work of Redemption*, but this was interrupted by his election, in 1757, to the presidency of New Jersey College, now Princeton University. He died at Princeton the following year.

PHILOSOPHICAL ORIENTATION

In the language of the day, Edwards was a "philosophizing divine." His primary interests were religious, and his main writings were theological. Apart from his college notes he produced no purely philosophical works. However, his theological treatises abound in philosophical reflections, all of which were intended to clarify and defend his theological positions. For him the arts, sciences, and philosophy ideally had no status separate from theology; as they become more perfect, he said, they "issue in divinity, and coincide with it, and appear to be as parts of it."

Edwards's philosophical views reflect his college training in Puritan Platonism, itself an offshoot of Cambridge Platonism and the Platonism of Peter Ramus. He attempted to synthesize with this Christian Platonism elements from the English empiricists, especially Locke,

Newton, and Francis Hutcheson (1694–1746), whose works were introduced into New England in the early 1700s. Puritan Platonism taught Edwards that the spiritual world alone is real, that the visible universe is but its shadow, created to lead the mind, under the divine illumination, to an awareness of the presence of God. Into this general idealistic philosophy he wove strands of doctrine from the empirically minded Locke and the scientist Newton, whose works were beginning to make a stir in the colonies. From Locke he took the notion that all our ideas originate in sensation; from Newton, the conception of space as the divine sensorium.

BEING

In his notes "Of Being," Edwards took up the Parmenidean thesis of the necessity of Being, arguing the impossibility of absolute nothingness on the ground that it is a contradictory and inconceivable notion. Since pure nothingness is an impossibility, he held, there never was a time when Being did not exist. In short, Being is eternal. He also established the omnipresence of Being, arguing that we cannot think of pure nothingness in one place any more than we can think of it in all places. Thus, Being possesses the divine attributes of necessity, eternity, omnipresence, and infinity. Consequently, Being is God himself.

Further attributes of Being deduced by Edwards are nonsolidity and space. Solidity, he argued, is resistance to other solids, and since there are no beings outside of Being, Being itself, or God, cannot be conceived as solid. That Being, or God, is identical with space Edwards proved by the impossibility of conceiving the nonexistence of space. We can suppress from thought everything in the universe but space itself. Hence, space is divine. Following the Cambridge Platonists and Newton, Edwards conceived of God's mind as the locus in which material things spatially exist.

NATURE OF MIND

Edwards's notes titled "The Mind" are heavily indebted to Locke. Like the English philosopher, he distinguished between two faculties of the mind, understanding and will. Understanding he defined as the faculty by which the soul perceives, speculates, and judges. Its first operation is sensation, for without the activity of the senses there can be no further mental operations. The mind needs the senses in order to form all its ideas. The objects of the senses are not real qualities of bodies but impressions and ideas given to us by God. Edwards agreed with Locke that secondary qualities, such as colors, sounds, smells, and tastes, do not inhere in bodies but are mental impressions. Every intelligent philosopher, Edwards wrote, now grants that colors are not really in things any more than pain is in a needle.

IDEALISM. Edwards went beyond Locke in applying to primary qualities, such as solidity, extension, figure, and motion, the arguments against the reality of secondary qualities. All the primary qualities, he insisted, can be reduced to resistance. Solidity is simply resistance; figure is the termination of resistance; extension is an aspect of figure; motion is the communication of resistance from one place to another. Hence, a visible body is composed not of real qualities but of ideas, including color, resistance, and modes of resistance. Resistance itself is not material; it is "nothing else but the actual exertion of God's power." Consequently, the visible universe has only a mental existence. It exists primarily in God's mind, where it was designed by a free act of the divine will. It also exists in our minds, communicated to us by God in a series of united and regularly successive ideas.

Historians have debated whether Edwards owed his idealistic philosophy to George Berkeley or to his own precocious genius. At the time he formulated it, Berkeley's works were not yet available at Yale. Although it is possible that he heard reports of Berkeley's idealism, it is more likely that he arrived independently at his idealistic conclusions.

According to Edwards, minds alone are, properly speaking, beings or realities; bodies are only "shadows of being." Goodness and beauty belong to anything in proportion to its intensity of being. Hence, minds alone are really good and beautiful; the visible world has but a shadow of these perfections. Its value is to lead the mind to the enjoyment of spiritual and divine goodness and beauty.

CREATION. The created world depends entirely on God for its existence and preservation. He freely created it, and he constantly holds it in existence, as colors are continually renewed by the light of the sun falling on bodies. The universe constantly proceeds from God as light shines from the sun. Under the activity of God the universe is a revelation of the divine mind to created minds; it is a panorama of shadows and images exhibiting the divine mind and will. Edwards, in his notebook titled *Images or Shadows of Divine Things*, described nature as a symbol of God. God, he said, revealed himself in the Bible and also in the visible universe and the souls of men, which are made in the image of God. In order to interpret correctly

the symbols of God in the created world, the mind has to be purified by a divine illumination. To Edwards there is no more sublime or delightful activity than to discover and to contemplate the traces of God in nature.

THE WILL. The second faculty of the mind described by Edwards is the will. The importance of the will lies in the fact that it is the seat of the passions or affections, the chief of which is love. According to Edwards, all the other passions originate in love and are for its sake. Love is the excellence and beauty of minds. In *A Treatise concerning Religious Affections* he argued that all human activities, especially those of religion, arise from affection. The affections, he said, are the "very life and soul of all true religion." The essence of religion lies in holy love, especially the love of God. Although Edwards's doctrine of religious experience, under the influence of pietism, gives ample scope to the emotions, and he appealed to them in his sermons, he generally maintained a Puritan sobriety of expression and avoided the sensationalism that marked the Great Awakening. He insisted that religion be centered in what he called the "gracious affections" that spring from the awareness of God and divine things.

RELIGION AND ETHICS

Religious experience is possible, according to Edwards, through a supernatural sense that the elect receive by divine grace. This new sense, which is different from the five bodily senses, gives humankind, reborn by grace, a new kind of sensation or perception by which he passively receives from God ideas and truths about divine things. By a kind of sense experience the elect enjoy an inward, sweet delight in God, which unites them to God more closely than all rational knowledge of him. The way to God is through the heart rather than through the head.

PROBLEM OF FREEDOM. Edwards regarded the will, like the intellect, as an essentially passive power, moved to action by external forces. As the intellect passively receives impressions and ideas from God, so the will is inclined to agreeable objects and repelled by disagreeable objects. The will is not a self-determining power; its actions are determined by causes. God alone is free in the sense that he can determine his own volitions. The principle of causality, according to which everything that happens has a cause, applies to the movements of the human will as it does to everything created. Of course, the will is moved not by physical causes but by motives or moral causes. These motives are presented to the will by the understanding, and the strongest of them determines the movement of the will.

Edwards opposed the Arminians of his day, who attributed to the human will an inner spontaneity and power of self-determination. In his view this kind of freedom is a divine prerogative; the human will does not have this kind of inner freedom. Its actions are determined not by being physically coerced but by being morally necessitated. A man cannot help willing as he does, given the motives presented to him. And since these motives are determined by God's providence, the movements of man's will are entirely within the divine power.

Although Edwards denied that the human will has freedom of self-determination, he granted that in a sense man is free. Like Thomas Hobbes and Locke, he defined human liberty as the ability to carry out what the will inclines man to do. Liberty is the absence of impediments to action. This denial of the essential freedom of the will harmonizes well with Edwards's Calvinist belief in the total depravity of man and in predestination.

VIRTUE. The third earl of Shaftesbury (1671–1713) and Hutcheson influenced Edwards's ethics. With them he denied that true virtue consists in the selfish pursuit of pleasure or in the utility of human actions. Rather, virtue is disinterested benevolence or affection; it is the intrinsic beauty of the dispositions of man's heart. An action is good not because it is advantageous to ourselves or to others but solely because it springs from a beautiful disposition of will. Virtue is a spiritual beauty or excellence that commends itself to us for its own sake. Any other motive for acting is based on self-love and consequently does not measure up to true virtue.

Edwards did not think that man has a natural impulse to such disinterested virtue. In his view man, owing to original sin, is totally depraved and given over to self-love. Only by the election of God and the gift of efficacious grace can man rise above his "dreadful condition" and perform truly virtuous actions. Without supernatural aid seemingly disinterested affections, such as the natural love of parents for their children, are accompanied by self-love and hence are not truly virtuous. At most they are secondary virtues or the shadows of true virtue.

Edwards was the most gifted and articulate theologian-philosopher in the New England colonies and perhaps in American history. He supported a losing cause in his defense of Puritanism, but for a while he gave it new life and spirit. The liberal theology that he combated all his life finally won the day; in the form of Unitarianism it dominated New England culture in the nineteenth century. But Edwards's powerful religious and philosophical stimulus remained. New England transcendentalists, such as Emerson, although rejecting all systematic theology and proclaiming the divinity of humankind, continued the Puritan's passionate search for the divine in the communion with nature.

See also Arminius and Arminianism; Being; Berkeley, George; Cambridge Platonists; Determinism and Freedom; Emerson, Ralph Waldo; Hutcheson, Francis; Idealism; Johnson, Samuel; Locke, John; New England Transcendentalism; Newton, Isaac; Platonism and the Platonic Tradition; Ramus, Peter; Shaftesbury, Third Earl of (Anthony Ashley Cooper).

Bibliography

WORKS BY EDWARDS

Works. 8 vols, edited by S. Austin. Worcester, MA: Isaiah Thomas, 1808–1809; reprinted in 4 vols., New York, 1844, 1847. An old but useful edition, found in some libraries.

Works. 10 vols, edited by S. E. Dwight. New York: Carvill, 1829–1830. This is the standard and best edition of Edwards's works, except for those newly edited. Vol. I contains a "Life of Edwards" by Dwight.

Representative Selections, edited by C. H. Faust and T. H. Johnson. New York: American, 1935; rev. ed. (paperback), with rev. and updated bibliography, 1962. Useful selections from Edwards's works and a good bibliography.

Images or Shadows of Divine Things, edited by P. Miller. New Haven, CT: Yale University Press, 1948.

Puritan Sage: Collected Writings of Jonathan Edwards, edited by V. Ferm. New York, 1953. Useful selection of Edwards's works.

Works, edited by P. Miller. New Haven, CT: Yale University Press, 1957–. Vol. I: *The Freedom of the Will*, edited by P. Ramsey. Vol. II: *Religious Affections*, edited by J. E. Smith. A new edition that will supersede Dwight's.

The Nature of True Virtue. Ann Arbor: University of Michigan Press, 1960. Foreword by W. Frankena. Best edition of this work.

Letters and Personal Writings. Edited by George S. Claghorn. New Haven, CT: Yale University Press, 1998.

Sermons and Discourses, 1730–1733. Edited by Mark R. Valeri. New Haven, CT: Yale University Press, 1999.

WORKS ON EDWARDS

Chai, Leon. *Jonathan Edwards and the Limits of Enlightenment Philosophy*. New York: Oxford University Press, 1998.

Daniel, Stephen H. *The Philosophy of Jonathan Edwards: A Study in Divine Semiotics*. Bloomington: Indiana University Press, 1994.

Davidson, Edward H. *Jonathan Edwards: The Narrative of a Puritan Mind*. Cambridge, MA: Harvard University Press, 1966, 1968.

Delattre, Roland André. *Beauty and Sensibility in the Thought of Jonathan Edwards: An Essay in Aesthetics and Theological Ethics*. New Haven, CT: Yale University Press, 1968.

Hatch, Nathan O., and Harry S. Stout. *Jonathan Edwards and the American Experience*. New York: Oxford University Press, 1988.

Holbrook, Clyde A. *The Ethics of Jonathan Edwards: Morality and Aesthetics.* Ann Arbor: University of Michigan Press, 1973.

Jenson, Robert W. *America's Theologian: A Recommendation of Jonathan Edwards.* New York: Oxford University Press, 1988.

Lesser, M. X. *Jonathan Edwards: A Reference Guide.* Boston, MA: G.K. Hall, 1981.

Marsden, George M. *Jonathan Edwards: A Life.* New Haven, CT: Yale University Press, 2003.

McClymond, Michael James. *Encounters with God: An Approach to the Theology of Jonathan Edwards.* New York: Oxford University Press, 1998.

McDermott, Gerald R. *Jonathan Edwards Confronts the Gods: Christian Theology, Enlightenment Religion, and Non-Christian Faiths.* New York: Oxford University Press, 2000.

McDermott, Gerald R. *One Holy and Happy Society: The Public Theology of Jonathan Edwards.* University Park: Pennsylvania State University Press, 1992.

Miller, P. *Errand into the Wilderness.* Cambridge, MA: Belknap Press of Harvard University Press, 1956. Both this and *Jonathan Edwards* (below) are first class.

Miller, P. *Jonathan Edwards.* New York: W. Sloane Associates, 1949; paperback ed., 1959.

Schneider, H. W. *A History of American Philosophy*, 11–31. New York: Columbia University Press, 1946; 2nd ed., 1963.

Schneider, H. W. *The Puritan Mind.* New York: Holt, 1930; paperback ed., Ann Arbor, MI, 1958.

Smith, John Edwin. *Jonathan Edwards: Puritan, Preacher, Philosopher.* Notre Dame: University of Notre Dame Press, 1992.

Winslow, O. E. *Jonathan Edwards, 1703–1758.* New York: Macmillan, 1940; paperback ed., 1962. Pulitzer Prize–winning biography—excellent and fascinating account of Edwards's life and times, with good bibliography.

Armand A. Maurer (1967)
Bibliography updated by Michael J. Farmer (2005)

EFFICIENCY

See *Philosophy of Technology*

EGALITARIANISM

See *Social and Political Philosophy*

EGOISM AND ALTRUISM

Why do we sometimes prefer to consult the interests of others rather than our own interests? What is the relationship between selfishness and benevolence? Is altruism merely a mask for self-interest? At first sight these may appear to be empirical, psychological questions, but it is obviously the case that even if they are construed as such,

the answers will depend on the meaning assigned to such key expressions as "self-interest," "benevolence," "sympathy," and the like. It is in connection with elucidating the meaning of such expressions that philosophical problems arise—problems that are of particular interest because we cannot understand such expressions without committing ourselves, in some degree, to some particular conceptual schematism by means of which we can set out the empirical facts about human nature. That there are alternative and rival conceptual possibilities is a fact to which the history of philosophy testifies.

The problems with which we are concerned do not appear fully-fledged until the seventeenth and eighteenth centuries. That they do not is a consequence of the specific moral and psychological concepts of the Greek and of the medieval world. In neither Plato nor Aristotle does altruistic benevolence appear in the list of the virtues, and consequently the problem of how human nature, constituted as it is, can possibly exhibit this virtue cannot arise. In the *Republic* the question of the justification of justice is indeed raised in such a way as to show that if Thrasymachus's account of human nature were correct, men would find no point in limiting themselves to what justice prescribes, provided that they could be unjust successfully—and Thrasymachus's account of human nature is certainly egoistic. But Plato's rejoinder to Thrasymachus is a statement of a different view of human nature in which the pursuit of "good as such" and the pursuit of "my good" necessarily coincide.

In the medieval world the underlying assumption is that man's self-fulfillment is discovered in the love of God and of the rest of the divine creation. So although Thomas Aquinas envisages the first precept of the natural law as an injunction to self-preservation, his view of what the self is and of what preserving it consists in leads to no special problems about the relation between what I owe to myself and what I owe to others. It is only when Thomas Hobbes detaches the doctrines of natural law from their Aristotelian framework that the problem emerges in a sharp form.

INITIAL HOBBESIAN STATEMENT

Hobbes is the first major philosopher, apart from Niccolò Machiavelli, to present a completely individualist picture of human nature. There are at least three sources of Hobbes's individualism. First, there is his reading of political experience. His translation of Thucydides reveals his preoccupation with the topic of civil war, with the struggle of one private interest against another. Second, there is Hobbes's commitment to the Galilean resolutocompositive method of explanation: To explain is to resolve a complex whole into its individual parts and to show how the individual parts must be combined in order to reconstruct the whole. To explain the complex whole of social life is, therefore, to resolve it into its component parts, individual people, and to show how individuals must combine if social life is to be reconstructed. Since the individuals in terms of whose coming together social life is to be explained must be presocial individuals, they must lack those characteristics that belong to the compromises of social life and be governed only by their presocial drives. Third, there is the detail of the Hobbesian psychology, which insists that such drives must be competitive and aggressive because of the will to power over other men that ceaselessly and restlessly drives men forward.

Thus, from all three sources arises a picture of human nature as essentially individual, nonsocial, competitive, and aggressive. From this view it follows that the apparent altruism and benevolence of individuals in many situations need to be explained; the Hobbesian explanation is simply that what appears to be altruism is always in fact, in one way or another, disguised self-seeking. Undisguised, unmodified self-seeking leads to total social war. The fear of such war leads to the adoption of a regard for others from purely self-interested motives. John Aubrey in his sketch of Hobbes in *Brief Lives* tells of an exchange between Hobbes and a clergyman who had just seen Hobbes give alms to a beggar. The clergyman inquired whether Hobbes would have given alms if Jesus had not commanded it; Hobbes's reply was that by giving alms to the beggar, he not only relieved the man's distress but he also relieved his own distress at seeing the beggar's distress. This anecdote compresses the central problem into a single point: Given that human nature is competitive and self-seeking, why and how can altruism and benevolence be treated as virtues? One's immediate response to this brief and cryptic statement of the problem may well be to inquire why—if one does not share Hobbes's premises—one should take it as given that human nature is essentially self-seeking. To this one replies by posing another question: How can any actual or possible object or state of affairs provide me with a motive, appear to me as good or desirable, unless it appears to be what will satisfy some desire of mine? If the (necessary and sufficient) condition of an object's providing me with a motive is that it satisfy some desire of mine, then it will surely be the case that all my actions will have as their goal the satisfaction of my desires. And to seek only to satisfy my own desires is surely to have an entirely self-seeking nature.

EIGHTEENTH-CENTURY RESTATEMENTS

The root of the problem lies in the apparently egoistic implications of the psychological framework within which the questions of moral philosophy have been posed by a whole tradition of British thinkers from Hobbes on. Within this framework philosophers have oscillated between two positions: the Hobbesian doctrine of altruism as either a disguise or a substitute for self-seeking and the assertion of an original spring of altruistic benevolence as an ultimate and unexplained property in human nature.

On the one side we find, for example, the earl of Shaftesbury, who argues that men are so contrived that there is no conflict, but an identity, between what will satisfy self-interest and what will be for the good of others; the practice of benevolence is what satisfies man's natural bent. Bernard Mandeville, in *The Grumbling Hive, or Knaves Turn'd Honest* (later retitled *The Fable of the Bees: or, Private Vices, Public Benefits*), argues by contrast that the only spur to action is private, individual self-seeking and that it is for the public and general good that this is so. Francis Hutcheson, who treats benevolence as constituting the whole of virtue, provides no argument to back up his view, nor does he explain why we approve of benevolence rather than of self-interest.

BUTLER. Bishop Joseph Butler's position is at once more complex and more interesting than Hutcheson's or Mandeville's. Butler believes that we have a variety of separate and independent "appetites, passions and affections." Of these, self-love is only one, and it is not necessarily opposed to benevolence. We satisfy the desire for our own happiness in part, but only in part, by seeking the happiness of others. A man who inhibits those desires of his that find their satisfaction in achieving the happiness of others will not in fact make himself happy. By refusing to be benevolent, he damages his own self-interest and disobeys the call of self-love. Cool and reasonable self-love consists in guiding our actions by reference to a hierarchy of principles; supreme among these is moral reflection or conscience, by means of which human nature is defined and the good that will satisfy it discerned. Thus, self-love itself refers us to the arbitration of conscience, which in turn prescribes that extent and degree of benevolence that will satisfy the needs of self-love.

The chief objection to Butler is likely to arise from the apparently self-enclosed character of his account. In Butler's system the harmony between self-love and benevolence appears to reign by definition rather than in fact, that is, in human nature itself. But this criticism misconstrues Butler's stand, although we can deduce from Butler's psychology empirical consequences of a testable kind that at first sight render it liable to refutation by the facts. For if Butler is correct, those who are benevolent to the required degree do not find their benevolence at odds with their self-interest. In this sense, at least, virtue and happiness may be required to coincide, and if they do not coincide, Butler's view of human nature is false. But Butler allows himself an escape clause. He concedes that in the world as we know it, the pursuit of self-interest and devotion to benevolence may not appear to coincide, but, he says, the divergence seems to exist only if we do not allow for divine providence, which ensures that the world to come will be such as to ensure that self-interest and altruistic benevolence required the same actions of us.

THEOLOGY AND THE LONG RUN

In contrast with Hobbes's view that altruistic behavior (or at least just behavior) is in our immediate interest as a means of preserving ourselves from the war of all against all and in contrast with Butler's view that benevolence and self-interest are two distinct springs of action that move us to the same actions, there is the view that benevolence is to our long-term, as opposed to our short-term, self-interest. Butler, as already noted, uses something like this view to supplement his basic position, but it is the stock in trade of a form of theological egoistic utilitarianism to be found in Abraham Tucker and William Paley.

In both writers the crucial psychological premise is that men are so constructed that they always pursue their own private and individual satisfaction. In both writers the fundamental moral rule is an injunction to universal benevolence, which is equated with the promotion of the greatest happiness of the greatest number. The problem is how, given the character of human nature, a motive can be found for obeying the fundamental moral rule. The solution is to say that God has so contrived the afterlife that only if we obey the fundamental moral rule will we in the long run, that is, in the eternal run, secure our own happiness. In Paley it is clear that we could find no good reason to be moral if God did not exist, but God's function in bridging the gulf between self-interest and morality is veiled in conventional theological terms. In Tucker's *The Light of Nature Pursued* the account of how God bridges the gulf is more explicit. God has arranged that all the happiness that men either have enjoyed or will enjoy is deposited in what he calls "the bank of the universe." By working to increase the happiness of others, I increase the amount of happiness so deposited. But by increasing the

general stock of happiness, I also increase my own happiness, for God has arranged to divide this stock of happiness into equal shares, to be allotted one to a person, and so by increasing the size of the general stock, I also increase the size of my own share. I am, as it were, a shareholder in a cosmic bank of which God is at once the chairman and the managing director.

Tucker's absurdities, though unimportant in detail, do bring out how impossible is the task of reconciling an egoistic theory of human nature with a moral theory of benevolent utilitarianism. Of such impossibilities are absurdities born; to this the secular utilitarianism of David Hume, Jeremy Bentham, John Stuart Mill, and Henry Sidgwick is as much a witness as is the theological utilitarianism of Tucker and Paley.

HUME AND THE UTILITARIANS

Hume's initial approach to the problem is as flexible and undogmatic as that of any philosopher. In the *Treatise of Human Nature* Hume poses the question why we approve and obey rules that it is often in our interest to break. He makes no assumptions of the kind found in other eighteenth-century writers (men are entirely ruled by self-interest). He merely remarks, apparently on empirical grounds, that it is often the case that self-interest would, if it were followed, lead us to disregard the rules of justice. Nor does he invoke any compensating natural regard for the interests of others. We do have some regard for the interests of others, but it varies with the closeness of their ties to us, and we have by nature no regard for the public interest as such. "In general, it may be affirm'd that there is no such passion in human minds as the love of mankind, merely as such, independent of personal qualities, of services, or of relation to oneself" (*Treatise*, Bk. III, Part II, Sec. i).

If, then, self-interest would lead us to disobey the rules of justice and if we have no natural regard for the public interest, how do the rules come into existence, and what fosters our respect for them? The crucial fact is that did we not have respect for the rules of justice, there would be no stability of property. Indeed, the institution of property could not and would not exist. Now the existence of property and its stability is to all our interests, and we are always conscious of how much we are injured by others failing to observe the rules. So we have become conscious that although our immediate and short-term benefit rests in breaking the rules on a given occasion, our long-term benefit resides in insisting upon a universal observance of the rules.

By the time Hume came to write the *Enquiry concerning Human Understanding,* he had shifted his ground. He now sees self-interest and "a tendency to public good, and to the promoting of peace, harmony, and order in society" as two independent, coexistent springs of action; he sees the independent power of sympathy and of a sense of the public good, rather than a rational view of what is of long-term benefit to self-interest, as moving us to benevolence and altruism.

BENTHAM, GROTE, MILL, SIDGWICK. The utilitarians present the problem in terms differing somewhat from those of Hume because they were more rigidly committed to a psychology derived from David Hartley, according to which only pleasure and pain ever move us to action. In this psychology both "pleasure" and "pain" are the names of sensations. Clearly in this view the only pleasure whose prospect attracts me is *my* pleasure, and the only pain the prospect of which repels me is *my* pain. It seems to follow that all action is egoistically motivated, yet all four utilitarian writers make "the greatest happiness of the greatest number" either the only criterion of action or at least a central criterion. How can so egoistically motivated an agent as the utilitarians assume consult the general happiness? That he will have to learn to do so is what Bentham takes for granted in his legal and political writings. Bentham provides for inducements that will counteract the self-interest of legislators, for example. He affirms expressly that "the only interest which a man is at all times sure to find adequate motives for consulting is his own." But in the *Deontology* he seems by contrast to take it for granted that the pursuit of *my* pleasure and the pursuit of the greatest happiness of the greatest number will always as a matter of fact coincide.

This assumption of coincidence is abandoned by John Grote, who tries to minimize the difficulties by reducing our obligation to consult the general happiness to an injunction to consult the general happiness insofar as to do so will ensure our own happiness. Yet even Grote presupposes that, for the most part and generally, my happiness and that of the greatest number will not conflict.

Mill's arguments are of two kinds. He first argues that pleasure and the absence of pain are desired by all; here what is meant is clearly that each desires his own pleasure. The proof, and the only possible proof, that pleasure is desirable is that all people desire it, and since all people do desire it, it must be admitted to be desirable. Hence, everyone must acknowledge that it is desirable to produce as much pleasure as possible, and here what is

clearly meant is that each ought to desire the pleasure of all. The fallacy in the transition from the premise that each desires his own pleasure to the conclusion that each ought to desire the pleasure of all is usually thought to reside in the transition from fact to value, but it lies, rather, in the transition from an assertion about the agent's own pleasure to conclusions about the general happiness.

However, elsewhere in *Utilitarianism* Mill faces the difficulties in such a transition explicitly. He reproduces familiar arguments in an interesting form. The feelings of sympathy that Hume stressed in the *Enquiry* reappear as a man's "feeling of unity with his fellow-creatures." A man who has this feeling has a "natural want" to live in harmony with others. It is often overshadowed by selfish emotions, but those who do possess it know that they would be worse off if they did not possess it. The reason for this conviction is that the best prospect of realizing such happiness as is attainable is a willingness to sacrifice the prospects of one's own present and immediate happiness to an ascetic devotion to altruism and benevolence. Sidgwick became conscious of the difficulties that Mill brushes aside in this account. In the *Methods of Ethics,* however, Sidgwick could find no way to make the transition from the desire for one's own pleasure to that for the general happiness, and these remain for him independent goals, as they had been for some eighteenth-century philosophers.

THE PROBLEM IN EMPIRICAL PSYCHOLOGY

The philosophers from Hobbes to Sidgwick who analyze the concepts of egoism, altruism, and sympathy often write as if they were empirical students of human nature, disputing the facts of human action and motivation. But it is more illuminating to read them as offering conceptual accounts of what it is to have a good reason for action and of what the limits upon the range of possible good reasons are. But so closely allied are conceptual and empirical issues at this point in the argument that it is not surprising to find that the would-be empirical accounts that psychologists claim to have derived from observation should sometimes turn out to be a rendering of conceptual schemes which have already been encountered in philosophy. So it is with Sigmund Freud, most strikingly in his earlier writings. The important place in Freudian theory held by the pleasure principle, the concepts of gratification and of libido, and the consequent view of socialization all lead to a theory in which the gratification of the self is primary and in which altruism and benevolence are interpreted as secondary phenomena that acquire the regard that they do because they are originally associated with forms of self-gratification. Freud's genetic account differs in detail from that given by Mill, but the form of the account is the same. Nor is this accidental; the pre-Freudian psychologies of Hartley, who influenced Mill, and of Alexander Bain, Mill's contemporary offer associationist accounts in which the genetic order is the same as it is in Freud. There is, therefore, not only the task of clarifying the concepts involved in these accounts, but also the task of settling how far the issues raised are genuinely empirical and how far genuinely conceptual. The concepts in need of clarification are of five kinds: the nature of desire; self-interest; altruism and benevolence; motives, actions, and sympathies; and the genetic fallacy.

NATURE OF DESIRE. If I want something, it does not follow that I want it because it will give me pleasure to have it or because it is a means of getting something further which will give me pleasure. It is, of course, true that if I get what I want, I have thereby satisfied one of my wants. Having any of my wants unsatisfied is certainly less satisfactory than having them satisfied, but it is not necessarily painful or even unpleasant. So it is neither true that I necessarily desire pleasure nor true that in seeking to satisfy my desires, I necessarily seek pleasure or the avoidance of pain.

Moreover, if I do something, it does not follow that I do it because I want to, let alone that I do it because I shall get pleasure from it. It has sometimes been suggested that the performance of an action is itself an adequate criterion of the agent's wanting to do whatever it is, and those who hold this view interpret such an expression as "doing what one does not want to do" when it is applied in cases of action under duress as meaning that the agent would not want to perform that particular action normally but does want to do it on this occasion rather than endure the threatened consequences of not doing it. This contention is less than self-evident. Moreover, if there is a sense of "want" such that if I do something, it is thereby true that I want to do it, that sense is a weaker and a different one from that given when I explain what I do by citing as a, or the, reason that I want to do it. For it is precisely because we have independent criteria for asserting that the agent did or did not want to do what he did that the want can be cited as an explanation for the action.

Action, desire, and pleasure, then, do not stand in so close a conceptual relationship that we cannot ask as a matter of contingent fact on any given occasion whether a man acted to get pleasure or whether he did what he did

because he wanted to or not. To understand this is a necessary preliminary to understanding the notion of self-interest.

SELF-INTEREST. What is to my interest depends upon who I am and what I want. This elementary but too often unnoticed truism underlies one of Socrates's implied answers to Thrasymachus in Plato's *Republic*. The question "Is justice more profitable than injustice?" will, as Plato makes clear, be answered differently depending upon whether it is answered by a just man or an unjust man. For what the just man wants is not what the unjust man wants. Thus, there is not a single spring of action or a single set of aims and goals titled "self-interest" that is the same in every man. "Self-interest" is not in fact the name of a motive at all. A man who acts from self-interest is a man who allows himself to act from certain motives in a given type of situation. The same action done from the same motive in another type of situation would not be correctly characterized as done from self-interest. So if I eat to sate my hunger or do my job well in order to succeed, I do not necessarily act from self-interest. It is only when I am in a situation where food is short or my rising in the world requires a disregard for the legitimate claims of others that to consult only my hunger or my ambition becomes to act from self-interest. The notion of self-interest therefore has application not to human behavior in general but to a certain type of human situation, namely, one in which behavior can be either competitive or noncompetitive. Equally, in this type of situation alone can the notions of benevolence and altruism have application. Therefore, it is to the elucidation of these that we must next turn.

ALTRUISM AND BENEVOLENCE. The question canvassed in the eighteenth century whether benevolence might not be the whole of virtue could have been raised only in an age in which the concept of virtue had been greatly narrowed or the concept of benevolence had been greatly widened or both. For in most of my dealings with others of a cooperative kind, questions of benevolence or altruism simply do not arise, any more than questions of self-interest do. In my social life I cannot but be involved in reciprocal relationships, in which it may certainly be conceded that the price I have to pay for self-seeking behavior is a loss of certain kinds of relationships. But if I want to lead a certain kind of life, with relationships of trust, friendship, and cooperation with others, then my wanting their good and my wanting my good are not two independent, discriminable desires. It is not even that I have two separate motives, self-interest and benevolence, for doing the same action. I have one motive, a desire to live in a certain way, which cannot be characterized as a desire for my good rather than that of others. For the good that I recognize and pursue is not mine particularly, except in the sense that I recognize and pursue it.

We can now diagnose one major cause of confusion in the whole discussion. All too often from Hobbes on, a special type of human situation has been treated as a paradigm of the whole moral life—that is, a situation in which I and someone else have incompatible aims and my aims are connected only with my own well-being. Of course, such situations do arise, but the clash between self-interest and benevolence that characterizes them is only one case out of many in which incompatible aims have to be resolved.

MOTIVES, ACTIONS, AND SYMPATHY. We can now understand that at the root of the confusions lies a belief in the possibility of a purely a priori characterization of human motives. From Hobbes on there has been a tradition, shared by empiricists as well as by their critics, which seeks to discuss human motivation almost entirely in the light of general conceptual considerations about desires, the passions, and pleasure and pain. What evades this tradition is not only the variety of aims and motives that can inform action, a variety to be discovered only by empirical inspection, but also the specific and particular character of certain motives.

The difficulties in the notion of sympathy, for example, are such that one cannot inquire straightforwardly whether there is or is not a sympathy for humankind as such. To say that a man acted from sympathy is always to refer to a set of particular occasions when sympathy was aroused for particular people in some particular plight. How wide the range of a man's sympathies is, is an empirical fact, and there is no conceptual limit to the possibilities. But it is a conceptual point that just as a generalized ambition can be manifested only in particular aspirations, so a generalized sympathy can be manifested only in particular acts of charity and benevolence. Now, suppose a man to perform a charitable and benevolent action; we would be wrong to suppose that we can always answer the question whether he was sympathetic to them because they were his relations (or his countrymen or his next-door neighbors) or whether he would have been equally sympathetic if they had been strangers or foreigners. A man can act out of sympathy without the range of his sympathies being determinate. Thus, the eighteenth-century question whether there is, as such, a general benevolence toward humankind implanted in human breasts is misleading.

GENETIC FALLACY. The question of innate benevolence toward humankind is also misleading because the eighteenth-century view disregards both the variety and the variability of human nature. Philosophers discuss what passions men have and not what passions they might acquire. Learning is, at best, peripheral to their inquiry; insofar as it does enter, there is another fallacy in writers from Hobbes on—that of confusing the question of what motives there were originally (for Hobbes, in the state of nature; for Freud, in early childhood) with the question of what the fundamental character of motives is now, in adult life. Because the instinctual drives and desires of young children have to be socialized, it does not follow that adult attitudes and emotions are only masks for such drives and desires. This is not to say that they cannot be such masks, but if the notion is to have any content, whether they are must be an empirical question.

See also Altruism; Aristotle; Bain, Alexander; Bentham, Jeremy; Butler, Joseph; Ethical Egoism; Freud, Sigmund; Grote, John; Hartley, David; Hobbes, Thomas; Human Nature; Hume, David; Hutcheson, Francis; Machiavelli, Niccolò; Mandeville, Bernard; Mill, John Stuart; Paley, William; Plato; Self-Interest; Sidgwick, Henry; Thomas Aquinas, St.; Thucydides; Utilitarianism.

Bibliography

Broad, C. D. "Certain Features in Moore's Ethical Doctrines." In *The Philosophy of G. E. Moore,* edited by Paul A. Schilpp, 43–57. Evanston, IL: Northwestern University Press, 1942.

Broad, C. D. *Five Types of Ethical Theory,* 161–177. London: Kegan Paul, 1930.

Brunton, J. A. "Egoism and Morality." *Philosophical Quarterly* (1956): 289–303.

Ewing, A. C. *Ethics.* London: English Universities Press, 1953. Ch. 2.

Medlin, B. "Ultimate Principles and Ethical Egoism." *Australasian Journal of Philosophy* 35 (1957): 111–118.

Moore, G. E. *Principia Ethica.* Cambridge, U.K.: Cambridge University Press, 1903; paperback, 1959.

Rashdall, Hastings. *Theory of Good and Evil,* Vol. I, 44–63. London: Oxford University Press, H. Milford, 1924.

Sharp, F. C. *Ethics.* New York: Century, 1928. Chs. 22–23.

Alasdair MacIntyre (1967)

EHRENFELS, CHRISTIAN FREIHERR VON

(1859–1932)

Christian Freiherr von Ehrenfels, the Austrian psychologist and philosopher, was born in Rodaun near Vienna. He studied at the University of Vienna under Franz Brentano and Alexius Meinong, and took his doctorate at Graz in 1885. He taught at Vienna as a *Privatdozent* from 1888 to 1896, when he became extraordinary professor at the German University of Prague. He was a full professor at Prague from 1900 until 1929. Besides his professional work, Ehrenfels wrote two essays on Richard Wagner and several plays.

GESTALT PSYCHOLOGY

In psychology, Ehrenfels is best remembered for inaugurating gestalt psychology in his article "Über Gestaltqualitäten" (1890). Starting from Ernst Mach's thesis in his *Beiträge zur Analyse der Empfindungen* (Jena, 1886), that we can sense (*empfinden*) spatial and temporal forms ("wholes," *Gestalten*), Ehrenfels argued that sensing is limited to the present but that the apprehension of a complex datum requires recollection and so seems to lack the immediacy of sensing. This is particularly evident in the case of acoustic data, but it also holds for visual data perused successively. The immediate apprehension of a melody or a figure must therefore be otherwise accounted for than by sensing. Discussing acoustic complexes, Ehrenfels showed that what is in fact apprehended differs from the complex or sum of the component elements, since these vary while the gestalt remains unchanged. This is corroborated by the fact that acoustic forms (melodies) are more easily remembered than are tonal intervals or absolute pitch. Similarly, figures do not depend for their apprehension on absolute location. This implies that gestalt qualities are positive representational contents bound up with the occurrence in consciousness of complexes consisting of separable elements. In Meinong's language (adopted by Ehrenfels in a later paper), they are "founded contents" (*fundierte Inhalte*).

Ehrenfels's notion of gestalt was essentially developed from a differential analysis of data, complex, and unity, unity being regarded as a quality. The phenomenological account of a gestalt in terms of contrast, background, and poignancy—features essential to subsequent gestalt psychology—was secondary in Ehrenfels's analysis, although he did mention such features.

Ehrenfels extended the notion of gestalt to numbers and to the field of logic. He viewed the contradiction in such concepts as that of a round square as a temporal gestalt quality of the psychic process of attempting to form a representation of the concept, an attempt that proves unfeasible. Ehrenfels also used the notion of gestalt in cases, such as phenomena of style and behavior, in which an analysis into component elements is practically impossible. In general, a gestalt is a novel and creative feature with respect to its component elements (in contrast to David Hume, who admitted only the composition of impressions or ideas and imaginative interpolation within the continuum of sensory qualities).

VALUE THEORY

Ehrenfels made important contributions to value theory and ethics. His series of articles, "Werttheorie und Ethik," although inspired by Meinong's lectures, was published before Meinong's ethical works and possessed at least partial originality. Ehrenfels's subsequent *System der Werttheorie* (1897–1898) discussed points of difference with Meinong's first publications on value theory. Ehrenfels defined value as "the relation, erroneously objectified by language, of a thing to a desire directed towards it" ("Werttheorie und Ethik," in *Vierteljahrsschrift für wissenschaftliche Philosophie*, Vol. 17, p. 89) or to a disposition of desire or feeling (ibid., pp. 209–210). "The value of a thing is its desirability" (*System der Werttheorie*, Vol. I, p. 53). Ehrenfels took value not simply as instrumental to the promotion of one's happiness but insisted that instrumental value (*Wirkungswert*) is valuable only relative to intrinsic value (*Eigenwert*). We desire the existence or nonexistence of something, and do not necessarily strive for its possession as a means to our happiness. The valuable object is not bound up with utility (*Nutzen*) but possesses a more general fittingness (*Frommen*) for us. Ehrenfels adapted the economic theory of marginal utility to explain the strength of any desires possessing a fittingness for us (*Grenzfrommen*). He thus introduced a quantitative element of valuation: Values and valuation are conditioned by the prior existence of other value objects.

In view of their dependence on emotional dispositions, values have a certain relativity, but there exists wide agreement among human beings as to the value of pleasure and pain and of certain other psychic phenomena, both in ourselves and in others. We value those valuational dispositions of others that are directed toward objects valued by us. In fact, Ehrenfels restricted intrinsic values to psychic realities.

The relativity of values is also apparent in changes in valuation brought about by various causes. Ehrenfels also distinguished trends of valuation, for which he offered a theoretical scheme. Means may turn into ends, as when the satisfaction of feelings of hunger replaces nourishment as the end of eating. By contrast, superior values may feature as ends, as when in the interest of nourishment we suppress our feelings of hunger in the presence of poisonous food. A third factor in trends of value is survival, which is best assured if the object serving it coincides with it. Ends transcending mere survival are exemplified in cultural progress, in which values become nonindividualistic. Superior nonindividualistic values are transmitted through example and suggestion, and cause further value promotion in a value milieu. Ehrenfels found reason to believe that with the increasing integration of human knowledge an upward trend toward superior values could be expected.

SOCIAL ETHICS

Ehrenfels's theory of value formed the basis for his ethics, which he subdivided into social and individual ethics. Social ethics is concerned with ethical valuation, that is, valuation of psychic (or supposedly psychic) objects that are causally related to certain actions. These objects are intrinsic values, and we demand that a plurality of individuals coincide in their valuation of them. The ultimate object of ethical valuation is not action, or its means or ends, but the desiderative and emotional disposition behind it. It is then called moral (or immoral) disposition, and its valuation moral (or immoral) valuation. (Accordingly, morality is distinguished from law and custom, which do not consider disposition.) Moral dispositions are the emotional dispositions of taking pleasure in others as intrinsic values, that is, as individuals themselves possessing a disposition toward actions serving intrinsic values, particularly the dispositions of love of one's neighbor, of humanity, of God. Such pleasure in others psychologically depends on an awareness of them in thought or in more or less vivid representation. There is a perspective of comparative closeness or distance in valuation. Among other moral dispositions are justice, constancy, and honesty, and their negative counterparts.

INDIVIDUAL ETHICS

Individual ethics is concerned with man's response, through "mystical" or "tragic elevation," to his fate as a finite body. The craving for such elevation is the source of the valuations (ethical sanction, conscience) of whatever goes to promote it. These private valuations do not strictly encompass the socioethical ones, but do as a matter of fact coincide with them. Ehrenfels's individual

ethics thus was a separate strain centering on an aesthetic desire for psychic harmony. To reach such a state, belief in God or metaphysical convictions are helpful though not indispensable.

SEXUAL AND RACIAL VIEWS

Ehrenfels's tendency to emphasize biological factors led him in later writings ("Sexuales Ober- und Unterbewusstsein," 1903–1904; *Sexualethik,* 1907; "Sexualmoral der Zukunft, 1930; cf. the earlier statement in "Werttheorie und Ethik," *Vierteljahrsschrift für wissenschaftliche Philosophie*, Vol. 17, p. 354) to question moral restraint on sexuality and to advocate greater frankness, honesty, and delicacy in marital relations. He won Sigmund Freud's praise for his pioneering work in this field. His biological tendency also led him to recommend selective breeding practices for man (cf. "Die sexuale Reform," 1903–1904) and to embrace ideas bordering on race prejudice ("Leitziele zur Rassenbewertung," 1911).

METAPHYSICS

In his *Kosmogonie* (1916) Ehrenfels contributed to metaphysics a theory of the origin of the world. Rejecting a monism that admits only the cumulative effects of accidental events, he regarded the origin of the world as the result of the interaction of two principles, a principle of chaotic disorder and a principle of psychoid unity of gestalt that, with infinite improbability but with infinite time to allow for its incipience, has been solicited by the opposing principle. Once the principle of unity has been engaged, the resulting gestalt survives because it is infinitely improbable that chaos is capable of continuous destructive action of its own even in infinite time. The gestalt principle, in turn, is credited with creativity, making for further development. Ehrenfels's cosmogony can be taken as a speculative abstraction intended to put the theory of evolution on a new footing in that it tries to give a plausible account of emerging nonrandomness in the universe.

See also Brentano, Franz; Ethics, History of; Freud, Sigmund; Gestalt Theory; Mach, Ernst; Meinong, Alexius; Metaphysics, History of; Racism; Value and Valuation.

Bibliography

WORKS BY EHRENFELS

"Über Gestaltqualitäten." *Vierteljahrsschrift für wissenschaftliche Philosophie* 14 (1890): 249–292.

"Werttheorie und Ethik." *Vierteljahrsschrift für wissenschaftliche Philosophie* 17 (1893): 26–110, 200–266, 321–363, 413–425; 18 (1894): 22–97. Five consecutive articles.

System der Werttheorie. 2 vols. Leipzig: O.R. Weisland, 1897–1898.

"Sexuales Ober- und Unterbewusstsein." *Politisch-anthropologische Revue* 2 (1903–1904): 456–476.

"Die sexuale Reform." *Politisch-anthropologische Revue* 2 (1903–1904): 970–994.

Sexualethik. Wiesbaden, 1907.

"Leitziele zur Rassenbewertung." *Archiv für Rassen- und Gesellschaftsbiologie* 8 (1911): 59–71.

Kosmogonie. Jena, Germany, 1916.

"Sexualmoral der Zukunft." *Archiv für Rassen- und Gesellschaftsbiologie* 22 (1930): 292–304.

Philosophische Schriften. Munich: Philosophia Verlag, 1982.

WORKS ON EHRENFELS

Eaton, Howard O. *The Austrian Philosophy of Values.* Norman: University of Oklahoma Press, 1930.

Meister, Richard. "Ehrenfels." In *Neue deutsche Biographie,* Vol. IV, pp. 352–353. Berlin, 1959.

Orestano, Francesco. *I valori umani* (Vols. XII and XIII of his *Opere complete*), 2 vols. Vol. I, pp. 69–102, 123–126; Vol. II, pp. 46–101. Milan, 1942.

Smith, Barry, C. F. Ehrenfels, et al, eds. *Foundations of Gestalt Theory.* Munich: Philosophia Verlag, 1988.

Varet, Gilbert. *Manuel de bibliographie philosophique.* Vol. II, p. 877, note. Paris: Presses universitaires de France, 1956.

Klaus Hartmann (1967)

EINSTEIN, ALBERT
(1879–1955)

Albert Einstein was born in Ulm, in the south German kingdom of Württemberg on March 14, 1879. Following his graduation from the Federal Polytechnical Institute (*ETH*) in Zurich in 1900 he obtained a job as a patent examiner, ("technical expert, third class") in the Swiss patent office in Bern, starting in the summer of 1902. In January 1903 he married his first wife, Mileva Maric, a fellow student of physics at the *ETH* and, with Mileva's support, continued his investigations in physics, earning a PhD from the University of Zürich in 1905.

That was Einstein's "miracle year." In 1905 Einstein published the founding papers of the special theory of relativity, including a version of the famous $E = mc^2$. Also in 1905 he developed the light quantum hypothesis to treat the photo-electric effect, a work important in the subsequent development of the quantum theory and the official basis of his 1922 award of the Nobel Prize. There were also two papers on Brownian motion he produced that year, which helped demonstrate the reality of molecules.

Einstein left the patent office in 1909, moving to Berlin in 1914 to assume the directorship of the new Kaiser Wilhelm Institute for Physics. There his marriage quickly dissolved and his wife moved back to Zürich with their two sons, Hans Albert and Eduard. Einstein had been working on extensions of relativity since 1907 and in 1916 he published an account of what he called the "general theory" of relativity, which is essentially the modern theory of gravity. It predicted the bending of light rays around the sun. When that was confirmed during the solar eclipse of 1919, Einstein became a worldwide celebrity overnight, the first scientific superstar.

Einstein's celebrity status made him a target of growing German antiSemitism. His own interest was growing in Zionist and pacifist causes. Amidst this turmoil, in 1917 Einstein became ill and was cared for by his cousin Elsa Einstein Löwenthal, recently divorced and with two daughters, Ilse and Margot. Following his own divorce in 1919, he married Elsa, whose daughters also took the name Einstein.

In the period from 1914 to 1919 Einstein's scientific work continued to flourish. He began investigations into gravitational waves and cosmology, where he reluctantly introduced the cosmological constant, which he subsequently rejected, but which has come back to represent what now appears to be substantial density and pressure associated with empty space. Einstein also worked on statistical aspects of the quantum theory, developing the coefficients of spontaneous and induced emission and absorption that provided the theoretical opening for laser technology.

In the 1920s Einstein traveled extensively in aid of science and of Zionism. His scientific contributions slowed down in this period, although he made some preliminary attempts at tying together the electromagnetic and gravitational fields geometrically in a unified field theory. He made important contributions to the quantum theory of gases, developing Einstein-Bose statistics to treat radiation as a quantum gas of indistinguishable particles. This led to his discovery of the Bose-Einstein condensation, a low temperature phenomenon displaying quantum behavior at nearly macroscopic scale. In the 1927 Solvay conference Einstein began to "debate" with Niels Bohr over the foundations of the emerging quantum mechanics.

Einstein left Germany in 1932 for the Institute for Advanced Study in Princeton. He became a United States citizen in 1940. A year earlier he had signed a letter drafted by Leo Szilard advising President Franklin D. Roosevelt of the military potential of atomic energy. Later he was an advocate for the control of atomic energy and for institutions supporting world peace. He was also a prominent critic of McCarthyism and a defender of civil liberties, as well as an outspoken opponent of racism and a defender of civil rights. Einstein died on April 18, 1955, of complications following a ruptured aortic aneurysm. His last scientific work was on the unfinished project for a unified field theory. His last phrase, written a few days before his death, was in a document with the pungent title, "Political Passions, Aroused Everywhere, Demand Their Victims."

PHILOSOPHY OF PHYSICS

Throughout his life Einstein read deeply in philosophy, where he was influenced both by David Hume and Immanuel Kant, as well as by Spinoza. His views in turn influenced the development of neo-positivism, whose more extreme doctrines he rejected in his criticism of the quantum theory. His philosophical reflections on the epistemology of science, as well as on metaphysical issues relating to space, time and causality, constitute an important chapter in twentieth century thought.

RELATIVITY. Einstein was a critic of the spatio-temporal framework of Newtonian physics, following a path marked out by Ernst Mach, who attacked Newton's introduction of "absolute" space and time not as unobservable (a fact advertised by Newton himself) but as unnecessary for doing physics. In Einstein's hands, however, Mach's critical method became a tool for positive theory construction.

Newton argued that acceleration must be absolute in order to explain inertial effects, such as the way water crawls up the sides of a rotating bucket. From absolute acceleration Newton moved (questionably, it turns out) to absolute space and time. Mach countered that inertial effects, like others, could be seen as purely relational. In particular, if one could rotate large enough masses and leave the bucket alone the same water-crawling effects would occur. This idea came to be known as Mach's Principle, which strongly influenced Einstein's development of the general theory of relativity. Sympathetic to Mach's relational conception of space and time, Einstein criticized an asymmetry built into the Newtonian framework. There space and time affect the behavior of bodies in so far as, in the absence of impressed forces, bodies move inertially, along spatially straight lines with temporally constant speeds. But there is no reciprocity. If space and time are absolute, bodies cannot affect spatio-temporal structure. Once space and time were merged into a uni-

fied spacetime, the field equations of general relativity allowed a reciprocal interplay between spacetime and matter.

The introduction of four dimensional spacetime, however, comes from the 1905 special theory of relativity. There Einstein dealt with an apparent conflict between the principle of relativity (any inertial frame is suitable for the representation of electrodynamic as well as mechanical phenomena) and the constancy of the speed of light for inertial observers. In the 1905 paper Einstein approaches this conflict by applying a technique of conceptual analysis that he learned from Mach (and from David Hume). He asks what is time and quickly shifts, epistemologically, to how one tells time in reading a clock. Telling time involves a spatially local judgment of simultaneity (where are the hands, when?); that is, it involves events in more or less the same place. What about events that happen very far apart?

The suggestion is that here one reaches the limit of applicability of the concept of simultaneity. In Mach's hands (or Hume's) one might stop here, with skepticism about the very meaningfulness of assertions of distant simultaneity. But, as Einstein commented later, although he respected Mach's hobbyhorse of seeking the limits of concepts he felt that it does not give rise to anything living. To employ conceptual analysis constructively one needs a theory. In the 1905 paper that theory is grounded on a quasi-operational definition using light signals to determine when distant events happen at the same time. Armed with that definition of simultaneity one can not only reconcile the principle of relativity with the constancy of the velocity of light, one can go on to develop a spacetime framework in which descriptions of events in different inertial frames are tied to one another by Lorentz transformations that leave the so-called spacetime "interval" invariant. Einstein had wanted to refer to this work as a theory of invariants. Ironically, Max Planck coined the term "relativity," and it stuck.

One of the conceptual innovations in special relativity is the variation of relativistic mass with velocity, which no longer appears to be a constant property of matter. This shift in the conception of *mass* prompted Thomas Kuhn and Paul Feyerabend to feature an "incommensurability" between Newtonian and relativistic physics. Einstein was unequivocally against the idea that the so-called "relativistic mass" is a proper notion at all. He rejects it as coordinate dependent and, hence, merely perspectival and thinks "the—unhappily—often mentioned concept of a mass which depends on speed is quite misleading." Instead, in keeping with his emphasis on invariance (as a touchstone for scientific objectivity), Einstein says, "It is better to use the word mass exclusively for rest mass … which is always the same, independent of the speed …" (Earman and Fine 1977, p. 538). It is worth noting that the mass term m in $E = mc^2$ denotes precisely the rest mass.

Einstein was an early supporter of logical empiricism. He was also one of its icons, in part because his positivistic analysis in special relativity seemed evident also in the general theory. In his 1916 account, Einstein defends the relativity of all motion (not just inertial) by requiring that laws of nature be expressed by equations "valid for all coordinate systems." Called general covariance, this requirement, he says, "takes away from space and time the last remnant of physical objectivity." (Einstein 1987, Vol. 6 [1996], p. 287 and 291). In support he appears to offer a straightforwardly verificationist analysis. "All our space-time verifications invariably amount to a determination of space-time coincidences." (Einstein 1987, Vol. 6 [1996], p. 287 and 291). Thus it is only space-time coincidences ("to which all our physical experience can ultimately be reduced"), that is, the coordinate systems, that the laws of nature need respect.

Recent scholarship suggests that this positivist reading is mistaken (Einstein 1987, Vol. 6 (1996), p. 287 and 291). For in these passages Einstein is probably reacting to an earlier argument of his own (called the "hole argument") posing a conflict between general covariance and determinism (Einstein 1987, Vol. 6 (1996), p. 287 and 291). The key to unraveling that argument was his recognition that, by themselves, coordinates (the bare mathematical points) have no physical significance. Significance comes from the fields of the theory, as determined from given sources by the theory's field equations. That's what makes space-time coincidences observable. Einstein later held that, in general, scientific theory determines what one can observe. Thus the positivist reading has things exactly back to front. Whereas in special relativity Einstein follows a positivist line in grounding theoretical notions (simultaneity) in what is observable, here he entheorizes the observable and takes an anti-positivist line in grounding the observable in the theory itself.

QUANTUM THEORY. Einstein made fundamental contributions to the early understanding of quantum phenomena and his ideas, which emphasized the problem of wave-particle duality, influenced all subsequent developments. However Einstein became the foremost critic of the quantum mechanics that emerged from 1926 to 1930.

His dissatisfaction is often portrayed as a last ditch longing for determinism or causality ("God does not throw dice"), as against the essentially probabilistic character of quantum physics. To be sure, although Einstein was a master at statistical physics, he was certainly troubled by a science where probability occurs fundamentally. Nevertheless his problem with the quantum theory was not about determinism alone, nor even primarily about determinism at all. In a 1930s letter to his old friend and translator, Maurice Solovine, Einstein expresses his concerns this way. "I am working with my young people on an extremely interesting theory with which I hope to defeat modern proponents of probability-mysticism and their aversion to the notion of reality in the domain of physics" (Solovine 1987, p. 91). This is a typical linkage in Einstein's thought. In almost every context in which Einstein expresses reservations about quantum indeterminism he couples it with reservations about the irrealism of the theory; that is, giving up the ideal of treating individual events, or what he referred to as real states of affairs.

As usually understood, the quantum theory does not treat real states of affairs at all, not even probabilistically. It does not tell us whether an electron is likely (even) to be here or there, spinning up or down. Quantum theory only gives the probability for finding the electron here, or finding it spinning up, if one actually measures it for that particular property. This is the irrealism that Einstein found so disturbing. That there could be laws, even probabilistic laws, for finding things if one looks, but no laws of any sort for how things are independently of whether one looks, was mysticism, a "mindless" (1987, p. 119) form of empiricism.

Einstein responded with a program just as in the development of relativity. First he set out to establish the limitations of the concepts used in the quantum domain and then he explored the possibility of transcending those limitations with a positive theory. He began by challenging the uncertainty formulas. He accepted that they limit the simultaneous, precise measurement of conjugate quantities (like position and linear momentum) but he questioned the ontological reading in which they limit what is simultaneously real. He went on to examine the rationale offered, especially by Bohr, both for the statistical character of the quantum theory and for its irrealism.

Bohr postulated an uncontrollable interaction introduced in every act of measurement that, he argued, made a statistical treatment necessary and also prevented states of affairs being defined independently of the measurement. In a series of thought experiments Einstein developed the concept of indirect measurement as a challenge to Bohr's postulate. This culminated in a 1935 paper, co-authored with his research assistants Boris Podolsky and Nathan Rosen, and composed by Podolsky. Usually referred to as *EPR* this paper involved the idea that Schrödinger dubbed "entanglement" (*Verschränkung*).

Entanglement occurs when, after quantum systems interact, certain quantities become linked among the systems. In the *EPR* case, for a pair *A, B* of previously interacting particles—now far apart—both position and momentum are so linked that determining the position of one automatically determines the position of the other, and similarly for momentum. By directly measuring, say, the position of *A* one can determine *B*'s position and apparently without any "uncontrollable interaction" or disturbance of *B*, contra Bohr's postulate. Moreover by assuming a principle of local action according to which, provided the systems are sufficiently far apart, the "reality" at *B* is not affected by the measurement carried out at *A*, it follows that the position determined for *B* must have been *B*'s all along. Thus, contrary to Bohr, one can define a coordinate of position for *B* that is independent of measurement or observation there – a real state of affairs. Unfortunately, in *EPR* it is difficult to track these considerations clearly. It appears that Einstein never saw Podolsky's text before publication. When he did he expressed misgivings that it obscured his central concerns.

EPR has been seen as suggesting the possibility of a "hidden variables" account of quantum theory, an account that would introduce simultaneous values for both position and momentum, along with other quantities, and still, somehow, respect the uncertainty relations. But Einstein, who had toyed with and abandoned a hidden variables approach in 1927, was never again interested in such an account. In the context of *EPR*, he told Schrödinger explicitly that he "couldn't care less" about simultaneous values for position and momentum (Fine 1996, p. 38). In fact Einstein thought these point-particle concepts were not appropriate for the quantum domain. He hoped to introduce different concepts and explored how they would emerge from a unified field theory. Einstein pursued that quest unsuccessfully for many years. In the end he questioned whether even a field theory would do the job and speculated about the need for a purely algebraic kind of physics, one not based on a spatio-temporal continuum. He sometimes despaired, however, that this was like trying to breathe in empty space.

GENERAL PHILOSOPHY OF SCIENCE

Einstein's attempt to develop new concepts for the quantum domain accords with his anti-inductivist principle that ideas (or concepts) are free creations. By "free" he meant both that concepts are not innate and also that they are neither given in nor logically derived from experience. The only test for scientific concepts is whether they can be organized in a logically simple system that finds fruitful empirical applications. This highlights logical simplicity as a paramount factor in theory choice. It also represents a holistic attitude to theories, gleaned perhaps from Pierre Duhem. Holism is apparent in Einstein's acute analysis of the testability of geometry where, while rejecting Henri Poincaré's conventionalist defense of Euclidean physical geometry, he ultimately agrees with Poincaré that only the whole system of physics plus geometry is testable.

Einstein's work in relativity and his project for a unified treatment of gravity and quantum phenomena shows unification as central to his scientific outlook. His study of Baruch Spinoza, whom he read and re-read over the years may have influenced this attitude (or reinforced it). Certainly realism was another central feature. This is evident in his introduction of the light quantum and in his use of the kinetic-molecular picture in treating Brownian motion. It is evident as well in his worries over the instrumentalist understanding of the quantum theory. Nevertheless he ridiculed "assertions" of realism as meaningless, like chiming "cock-a-doodle-doo." For Einstein realism was not a doctrine but rather a motivational program. The program was to develop scientific theories that describe individual events themselves, without reference to conditions of observation. That is what he believed science had always done, and with great success. It was motivational because, at the personal level, he thought individuals would have no motivation to pursue science unless they felt that in doing so they were unlocking the secrets of nature. Clearly this program conflicts with the enormously successful but irrealist quantum theory, which is why Einstein struggled to make room for the possibility, at least, of a realist reinterpretation.

Determinism (or causality—he hardly draws a distinction) is another important item in Einstein's outlook. Here, again, he did not advocate a doctrine like, "The world is deterministic." Characteristically, he favored a program to entheorize determinism; that is, to build deterministic theories. His reaction to the dilemma between determinism and general covariance posed by the hole argument shows this concern, as does his sense that the probabilistic quantum theory involves a retreat into statistics. Nevertheless, in reluctantly accepting that one might have to move to an algebraic physics, he did acknowledge that science might abandon the ideal of representing events in spacetime altogether, and hence move beyond causality (or determinism).

Einstein's views are sometimes described in terms of the philosophical "isms": holism, realism, determinism and so forth. While there can be some truth to these descriptions (provided one entheorizes them), he generally regarded philosophical positions pragmatically. He saw them as tools that may be useful at certain moments for building better scientific theories, judged by the criterion of empirical success. His sometimes strong statements for or against one of the "isms" are best be seen in the terms of the dialogism described by Mara Beller in her *Quantum Dialogue*, a dialectical view that highlights the creative role of scientific disagreement in shifting contexts. Einstein himself described it this way:

> I do not feel comfortable and at home in any of the "isms." It always seems to me as though such an ism were strong only so long as it nourishes itself on the weakness of its counter-ism; but if the latter is struck dead, and it is alone on an open field, then it also turns out to be unsteady on its feet. *So, away with the squabbling.*
>
> HOWARD 1993, P. 225

See also Quantum Logic and Probability; Relativity Theory; Space; Space in Physical Theories; Time.

Bibliography

WORKS BY ALBERT EINSTEIN

"Can Quantum-Mechanical Description of Physical Reality Be Considered Complete?" With Boris Podolsky and Nathan Rosen. *Physical Review* 47 (1935): 777–780.

The Evolution of Physics. With L. Infeld. New York: Simon & Schuster, 1938.

Relativity: The Special and General Theory. 15th ed. London: Methuen, 1938.

Ideas and Opinions. New York: Bonanza Books, 1954.

The Collected Papers of Albert Einstein. Princeton, NJ: Princeton University Press, 1987. Ongoing project that will include most of Einstein's writing and correspondence.

Letters to Solovine. Translated by Wade Baskin. New York: Philosophical Library, 1987.

Out of My Later Years. New York: Bonanza Books, 1990.

WORKS ABOUT ALBERT EINSTEIN

Beller, Mara. *Quantum Dialogue: The Making of a Revolution.* Chicago: University of Chicago Press, 1999.

Earman, John, and Arthur Fine. "Against Indeterminacy." *Journal of Philosophy* LXXIV (1977): 535–538.

Einstein Archives Online. Available from http://www.alberteinstein.info/.

Fine, Arthur. *The Shaky Game: Einstein, Realism and the Quantum Theory.* 2nd ed. Chicago: University of Chicago Press, 1996.

Howard, Don A. "Was Einstein Really a Realist?" *Perspectives on Science* 1 (1993): 204–251.

Norton, John D. "General Covariance and the Foundations of General Relativity: Eight Decades of Dispute." *Reports on Progress in Physics* 56 (1993): 791–858.

Pais, Abraham. *Subtle Is the Lord: The Science and the Life of Albert Einstein.* New York: Oxford University Press, 1982.

Ryckman, Thomas. *The Reign of Relativity: Philosophy in Physics 1915–1925.* Oxford, U.K.: Oxford University Press, 2005.

Schilpp, Paul Arthur, ed. *Albert Einstein: Philosopher-Scientist.* La Salle, IL: Open Court, 1949.

Arthur Fine (2005)

ELIMINATIVE MATERIALISM, ELIMINATIVISM

"Eliminative materialism" espouses the view that our commonsense way of understanding the mind is false, and that, as a result, beliefs, desires, consciousness, and other mental events used in explaining our everyday behavior do not exist. Hence, the language of our "folk" psychology should be expunged, or eliminated, from future scientific discourse.

Two routes have been taken to get to the eliminativist's position. The first and less popular stems from a linguistic analysis of mentalistic language. Paul Feyerabend argues that the commonsense terms for mental states tacitly assume some version of dualism. Insofar as materialism is true, these terms cannot refer to anything in the physical world. Thus they should not be used in discussing ourselves or our psychologies since we are purely physical beings.

The second and better-developed approach comes out of the philosophies of science developed by Feyerabend, David Lewis, Willard Van Orman Quine and Wilfrid Sellars. Two suppositions are important for eliminativism. (1) There is no fundamental distinction between observations (and our observation language) and theory (and our theoretical language), for previously adopted conceptual frameworks shape all observations and all expressions of those observations. All observations are "theory-laden." These include observations we make of ourselves; in particular, observations we make about our internal states. There are no incorrigible phenomenological "givens." (2) The meaning of our theoretical terms (which includes our observational vocabulary) depends upon how the terms are embedded in the conceptual scheme. Meaning holism of this variety entails that if the theory in which the theoretical terms are embedded is false, then the entities that the theory posits do not exist. The terms would not refer.

Two more planks complete the eliminative argument. (3) Our way of describing ourselves in our everyday interactions comprises a rough and ready theory composed of the platitudes of our commonsense understanding. The terms used in this folk theory are defined by the platitudes. (4) Folk psychology is a radically false theory.

In support of this position. Patricia Churchland and Paul Churchland argue that belief-desire psychology wrongly assumes sentential processing; moreover, belief-desire psychology is stagnant, irreducible to neuroscience, and incomplete. Stephen Stich argues that our very notion of belief and, by implication, the other propositional attitudes is unsuitable for cognitive science. Patricia Churchland, Daniel Dennett, Georges Rey, Richard Rorty, and others argue that our notion of consciousness is confused. They all conclude, as do other eliminativists, that folk psychology should be replaced by something entirely different and more accurate, though views differ on what this replacement should be.

Attacks on eliminative materialism generally have come from four fronts, either on premise two, premise three, or premise four of the second approach, or on the eliminativist position itself, without regard to the arguments for it. Premise two asserts meaning holism and a particular theory of reference. If that theory were false, then the eliminativist's second argument would be undermined. There are alternative approaches to reference that do not assume holism; for example, causal-historical accounts do not. If meaning is not holistic, then even if folk psychology were incorrect, the terms used in that theory could still refer, and elimination of folk psychological terms would not be warranted.

Arguments that our folk psychology is not a true theory deny premise three. Here some detractors point out that even if a completed psychology did not rely on the propositional attitudes or consciousness, that fact would not entail that those sorts of mental states do not exist; instead, they just would not be referred to in scientific discourse. Nevertheless, they could still be used as they are now, in our everyday explanations of our behavior.

Others charge that premise four is false; folk psychology might be a rudimentary theory, but it is not radically false. While agreeing that belief-desire explanations or explanations involving conscious events might not be entirely empirically adequate or complete, champions of folk psychology argue that no other theory is either. In addition, our folk psychology has developed over time, is coherent, and its status with respect to neuroscience is immaterial. These arguments are generally coupled with the claim that no other alternative, either real or imagined, could fulfill the explanatory role that the propositional attitudes play in our understanding of ourselves. And until the eliminativist's promise of a better conceptual scheme is fulfilled folk psychology is here to stay. At least some properly revised version of folk psychology would remain.

Lastly, some supporters of folk psychology argue that any eliminativist program would be fatally flawed, regardless of whatever particular arguments are given, for the very statement of eliminative materialism itself is incoherent. In its simplest form, the argument runs as follows: Eliminative materialism claims that beliefs do not exist. Therefore, if eliminative materialism were true, we could not believe it. Therefore, no one can believe eliminative materialism on pain of inconsistency.

Replies to the four sorts of attacks are ubiquitous. However, answering the first three turns on (primarily empirical) issues yet to be settled. Which theory of reference is correct, whether folk psychology is actually a theory, and what revisions are required to make it adequate depend upon facts we do not yet know about ourselves or our linguistic practices.

The last point is more conceptual. In responding to it, eliminative materialists hold that something else will replace "belief," or some instances or aspects of "belief." Call this "schmelief." It is true that eliminative materialists cannot believe that eliminative materialism is true on pain of inconsistency. But, eliminativists maintain, they can "schmelieve it." Defenders of a revised folk psychology answer that, as used in this context, "schmelief" seems to be some other intentional operator or relation, a mere revision of belief. Without better exposition of what the replacement for folk psychology will be (and how it will be radically different), we simply cannot tell what the future holds for our commonsense theory of self: simple revision, peaceful coexistence, or outright replacement.

See also Consciousness; Dennett, Daniel C.; Folk Psychology; Lewis, David; Materialism; Philosophy of

Mind; Quine, Willard Van Orman; Reference; Rorty, Richard; Sellars, Wilfrid.

Bibliography

Baker, L. R. *Saving Belief: A Critique of Physicalism.* Princeton, NJ: Princeton University Press, 1987.

Boghossian, P. "The Status of Content." *Philosophical Review* 99 (1990): 157–184.

Churchland, P. "Eliminative Materialism and the Propositional Attitudes." *Journal of Philosophy* 78 (1981): 67–90.

Feyerabend, P. "Mental Events and the Brain." *Journal of Philosophy* 60 (1963): 295–296.

Horgan, T., and J. Woodward. "Folk Psychology Is Here to Stay." *Philosophical Review* 94 (1985): 197–225.

Rey, G. "A Reason for Doubting the Existence of Consciousness." In *Consciousness and Self-Regulation,* edited by R. Davidson, S. Schwartz, and D. Shapiro, Vol. 3. New York: Plenum Press, 1982.

Rorty, R. "Mind-Body Identity, Privacy, and Categories." *Review of Metaphysics* 19 (1965): 24–54.

Stich, S. *From Folk Psychology to Cognitive Science: The Case against Belief.* Cambridge, MA: MIT Press, 1983.

Valerie Gray Hardcastle (1996)

ELIOT, GEORGE
(1819–1880)

Born Marian (or Mary Ann) Evans, George Eliot was the assumed name of the English novelist, poet, essayist, and translator. She was reared near Coventry and in her early years attended a school run by a fervent evangelical mistress. From this woman she acquired intense religious beliefs, but she gradually lost her faith. In 1842 she wrote that she thought Christian dogmas "dishonorable to God" and pernicious to human happiness. Within a few months, however, she had come to regard the dogmas in themselves as of little importance. "Speculative truth begins to appear but a shadow of individual minds, agreement between intellects seems unattainable, and we turn to the *truth of feeling* as the only universal bond of union," she wrote in a letter in October 1843; a belief in the importance of feeling remained central to her life and work.

In Coventry she had a group of friends with literary and philosophical interests, and under their influence she undertook, in 1844, a translation of D. F. Strauss's *Das Leben Jesu;* the translation was published in 1846. She went to London in 1851 to work for John Chapman as assistant editor of the *Westminster Review.* She published occasional essays and read much. Among her numerous friends in London were Herbert Spencer, to whom she was falsely rumored to be engaged, and George Henry Lewes, the philosopher and critic. Lewes was married but separated from his wife. In October 1854 Eliot and he decided to live together. They never married, but they lived a life of exemplary domesticity until Lewes's death, in 1878. On May 6, 1880, to everyone's surprise, she married John W. Cross, long a family friend. She died that same year, after a short illness.

In 1854 Eliot's translation of Ludwig Feuerbach's *Das Wesen des Christentums* was published. She also translated Benedict (Baruch) de Spinoza but did not publish the translation. Upon Lewes's urging, she tried writing fiction; her first story was published in *Blackwood's Magazine* in 1857. She was immediately successful as a writer of fiction. To her fiction—notably *Adam Bede* (1859), *The Mill on the Floss* (1860), *Silas Marner* (1861), *Middlemarch* (1871–1872), and *Daniel Deronda* (1876)—rather than to her poetry or her essays, she owed her fame and her considerable influence as a moral teacher.

Eliot's views on moral, religious, and metaphysical problems pervade and profoundly shape her writings, but they are never presented in abstract, systematic form. She had no faith in general moral principles: "to lace ourselves up in formulas," she wrote, is to repress the "promptings and inspirations that spring from growing insight and sympathy." Like Strauss, Feuerbach, and Auguste Comte, she thought of religious and metaphysical doctrines as projections and symbols of feelings, and as valuable only to the degree that the feelings they express and reinforce are valuable. Her "most rooted conviction," she told a friend in 1859, was that "the immediate object and the proper sphere of all our highest emotions are our struggling fellow-men in this earthly existence," and she declared that one of her main aims in her writing was to show that human fellowship does not depend on anything nonhuman. Christianity can foster many valuable emotions, she held, but the insistence of some Christians that all action must be for the glory of God stifles benevolence and love and directs feelings away from men. The idea of God has been beneficial only insofar as it has been "the ideal of a goodness entirely human."

Eliot thus belongs with those Victorian writers who tried, in different ways, to work out a humanistic morality capable of satisfying the deep human needs that they thought the older, religiously based morality could no longer satisfy. Her view is naturalistic and deterministic; men are seen as being as much under the dominion of the laws of nature as are other parts of the world, though the comparisons are usually with organic growth and decay rather than with purely mechanical processes. Hereditary and social influences on character are heavily emphasized, as is the effect one's repeated actions or evasions will have on one's own character and hence on one's future actions.

The morality that springs from this view is primarily one of sympathy and compassion. The complexity and obscurity of motives and the mixture of good and evil in personality and in deed are constantly displayed in the novels. It is usually difficult, Eliot suggested, to know what one ought to do in particular cases; one must rely ultimately on one's deepest feelings when these are enlightened by sympathy and by knowledge of circumstances and consequences. Wrongdoing is usually traced to stupidity, callousness, or thoughtlessly excessive demands for personal satisfaction, rather than to deliberate malice or conscious selfishness. Vice and crime are shown as eventually bringing retribution, but the reward of virtue is at best the peace that comes with acceptance of one's lot. Eliot saw quiet renunciation and patient selflessness as the chief virtue. She frequently traced the career of an unusually sensitive and intelligent person who hopes to do great things for others but after painful defeats ends by settling into a life of unheroic and routine benevolence. She suggested that this is the only feasible way of achieving lasting good. In the thought that what we do will have some good effect on future generations and we shall be remembered by them with love, she held, there was a sufficient motive to virtue and a sufficient replacement of the belief in personal immortality and personal reward.

See also Comte, Auguste; Feuerbach, Ludwig; Religion and Morality; Spinoza, Benedict (Baruch) de; Strauss, David Friedrich.

Bibliography

Two essays reprinted in George Eliot's *Essays and Leaves from a Notebook*—"Evangelical Morality: Dr. Cummings" (1855) and "The Poet Young" (1857)—are especially relevant to her moral views.

The standard biography is John W. Cross, *The Life of George Eliot*, 3 vols. (London, 1885–1887); it is composed mainly of her letters, heavily censored. *Marian Evans and George Eliot*, by Lawrence and Elisabeth Hanson (London: Oxford University Press, 1952), is more accurate and contains a good bibliography. *The George Eliot Letters*, edited by Gordon Haight, 7 vols. (New Haven, CT: Yale University Press, 1954–1955), is a masterpiece of scholarship. Two essays by R. H. Hutton, reprinted in his *Modern Guides to English Thought* (London: Macmillan, 1887), give an assessment by a younger contemporary from an orthodox Christian standpoint.

There are numerous studies of Eliot's life, intellectual development, and writings. See especially Joan F. Bennett, *George Eliot: Her Mind and Her Art* (Cambridge, U.K.: Cambridge University Press, 1948); Gordon Haight, *George Eliot and John Chapman* (New Haven, CT, and London, 1940); Barbara Hardy, *The Novels of George Eliot* (London: University of London, Athlone Press, 1959); and Leslie Stephen, *George Eliot* (London, 1902).

J. B. Schneewind (1967)

ELIOT, THOMAS STEARNS
(1888–1964)

Thomas Stearns Eliot is best known as a poet and literary critic (he received the Nobel Prize for literature in 1948), but his work in social and cultural theory has also been widely influential. His principal works of this kind are *After Strange Gods* (London, 1934), *The Idea of a Christian Society* (London, 1939), and *Notes Towards the Definition of Culture* (London, 1949).

Eliot was born in St. Louis but lived in London from 1915 on and became a British subject in 1927. He was graduated from Harvard University in 1909 and engaged in advanced studies in philosophy there, at the Sorbonne, and at Oxford until 1915. In the year 1913/1914 he served as an assistant in philosophy at Harvard, studying methodology with Josiah Royce and logic with Bertrand Russell. Eliot and Russell, despite enormous differences in political, social, and religious outlooks, became close friends. Eliot's Harvard doctoral dissertation, completed at Oxford in 1915, was published as *Knowledge and Experience in the Philosophy of F. H. Bradley* (London and New York, 1964). Francis Herbert Bradley's idealism influenced Eliot's critical doctrines, and in 1926 Eliot published an essay on Bradley, reprinted in *Selected Essays* (London, 1951). In this essay he praised especially Bradley's critique of utilitarianism: "He replaced a philosophy which was crude and raw and provincial by one which was, in comparison, catholic, civilized, and universal." But even before completing his studies, Eliot had finished some of his finest early poems, and he never produced any technical philosophical studies aside from his thesis.

In his early poetry and criticism, Eliot was a considerable innovator, but it was a main goal of his experiments to try to recover the sense of a fruitful tradition. In particular, this meant rejecting the literary theory and practice of romanticism and finding earlier sources. In a famous comment in 1921, he argued that there had been, in the seventeenth century, a major change in the English mind, which he called the "dissociation of sensibility"—the separation of feeling and thought. He came later to stress a loss of a sense of order, both internal and external, and to associate it with the decline of the Christian and classical cultural framework. To counteract this loss, the poet and critic must strive to recover a sense of the whole European tradition. At the end of this phase of his development Eliot described himself as a classicist, and he was to write henceforward as a declared and orthodox Christian.

After Strange Gods is the bridge from his mainly literary to his mainly social and cultural criticism. The book's subtitle is *A Primer of Modern Heresy.* Its argument is that modern writers, deprived of tradition, have constructed private or esoteric systems of belief, and, deprived of a common language and imagery, they have been forced to experiment. The struggle for common meanings, always difficult, is now even more difficult. This failure of communication is profoundly damaging to the whole society. The writer's task is to develop the full potential maturity of the language of his society. Paradoxically, therefore, the most creative work is that which begins from and is most aware of the full tradition and history of the language in which it is written. The loss of this tradition makes the modern writer's task overwhelmingly difficult.

In *The Idea of a Christian Society,* Eliot applied and extended this argument to social questions. He argued that the Western democracies, although nominally Christian, in fact live by quite other values. The idea of a Christian society is at best an understanding of the social ends that would deserve the name of Christian, but in the modern world there is an unusually wide gap between such ends and the main principles of social organization. Many of the driving forces of modern society—especially its false emphasis on profit, its substitution of exploitation of men and things for right use, and its general adoption of commerce as the central human concern—are in fact hostile to any Christian life in the world. It is therefore not surprising, Eliot claimed, that society is far from being Christian; what is surprising is that people retain as much Christianity as they do.

In *Notes towards the Definition of Culture,* Eliot's most substantial theoretical work, he distinguished three senses of "culture"—the culture of the individual, of the group, and of the whole society. He argued that it is false to set as the goal of the group what can be the aim of the individual alone, and to set as the goal of the whole society what can only be the aim of a group. This argument became Eliot's main theoretical justification for what is ordinarily called "minority culture," and for his critique of egalitarian doctrines in education: It is false to educate the whole society to perform the cultural tasks of a particular group. At the same time, culture in each sense is necessarily connected with culture in the other senses. The group depends on the whole way of life of the society, as social organization depends upon tradition. Likewise, the culture of the individual cannot be isolated from the culture of the group.

Eliot further emphasized the extent to which the culture of a whole society is a matter of custom and behavior and is often unconscious: It is all the characteristic interests and activities of a people, whether or not some of these are thought of as "culture" in the narrower sense. What is often called "culture"—religion, arts, laws, and intellectual activity—is the conscious expression of the total culture, the whole way of life.

It follows from this, Eliot argued, that the maintenance and extension of the conscious culture of a society cannot be delegated to an elite, a group of specialists selected by merit. However skilled an elite may be in the special activities themselves, its members will necessarily lack the continuity with the rest of the society that is ultimately necessary for the health of the conscious culture. An elite, newly selected in each generation, will inevitably lack a sense of tradition. Eliot therefore saw no alternative to the maintenance of classes in society, and in particular to the maintenance of a governing class with which the specialists will overlap and interact. The need for continuity in culture, and for a tradition as opposed to a group of specialists with unrelated skills, argues, finally, for a social conservatism that will keep a proper relationship between continuity and change. This last phase of Eliot's social thinking has been especially influential since World War II.

See also Belief; Bradley, Francis Herbert; Philosophy of Social Sciences; Social and Political Philosophy; Royce, Josiah; Russell, Bertrand Arthur William; Utilitarianism.

Bibliography

Brooker, Jewel Spears. *Mastery and Escape: T.S. Eliot and the Dialectic of Modernism.* Amherst: University of Massachusetts Press, 1994.

Childs, Donald J. *From Philosophy to Poetry: T.S. Eliot's Study of Knowledge and Experience.* New York: Palgrave, 2001.

Cooper, John Xiros. *T. S. Eliot and the Ideology of Four Quartets.* Cambridge, U.K.: Cambridge University Press, 1995.

Dale, Alzina Stone. *T.S. Eliot: The Philosopher Poet.* Wheaton: H. Shaw, 1988.

Freed, Lewis. *T. S. Eliot: Aesthetics and History*. La Salle: Open Court, 1962.

Freed, Lewis. *T. S. Eliot: The Critic as Philosopher*. West Lafayette: Purdue University Press, 1979.

Gardner, Helen. *The Art of T. S. Eliot*. London: Cresset Press, 1949.

Habib, Rafey. *The Early T. S. Eliot and Western Philosophy*. Cambridge, U.K., and New York: Cambridge University Press, 1999.

Jain, Manju. *T. S. Eliot and American Philosophy: The Harvard Years*. Cambridge, U.K.: Cambridge University Press, 1992.

Kearns, Cleo McNelly. *T. S. Eliot and Indic Traditions: A Study in Poetry and Belief*. Cambridge, U.K.: Cambridge University Press, 1987.

Leavis, F. R. *The Common Pursuit*. London: Chatto and Windus, 1952. See "Mr. Eliot, Mr. Wyndham Lewis and Lawrence" and "Approaches to T. S. Eliot."

Lockerd, Benjamin G. *Aethereal Rumours: T. S. Eliot's Physics and Poetics*. Lewisburg: Bucknell University Press; London; Cranbury, NJ: Associated University Presses, 1998.

Lucy, Seán. *T. S. Eliot and the Idea of Tradition*. London: Cohen and West, 1960.

Moody, David. A., ed. *The Cambridge Companion to T. S. Eliot*. Cambridge, U.K.: Cambridge University Press, 1994.

Rajan, B., ed. *T. S. Eliot: A Study of His Writings by Several Hands*. London; Dennis Dobson, 1947.

Roeffaers, Hugo. *Eliot's Early Criticism: Philosophical Explorations into the Sacred Wood*. Frankfurt am Main; New York: P. Lang, 1988.

Schuchard, Ronald. *Eliot's Dark Angel: Intersections of Life and Art*. New York: Oxford University Press, 1999.

Shusterman, Richard. *T. S. Eliot and the Philosophy of Criticism*. New York: Columbia University Press, 1988.

Skaff, William. *The Philosophy of T. S. Eliot: From Skepticism to a Surrealist Poetic, 1909–1927*. Philadelphia: University of Pennsylvania Press, 1986.

Spurr, David. *Conflicts in Consciousness: T. S. Eliot's Poetry and Criticism*. Urbana: University of Illinois Press, 1984.

Warner, Martin. *A Philosophical Study of T. S. Eliot's Four Quartets*. Lewiston: Edwin Mellen Press, 1999.

Williams, Raymond. *Culture and Society*. London: Chatto and Windus, 1958. Part 3, Ch. 3.

Raymond Williams (1967)
Bibliography updated by Desirae Matherly Martin (2005)

ELISABETH, PRINCESS OF BOHEMIA
(1618–1680)

Elisabeth Simmern van Pallandt was born in Heidelberg on December 26, 1618, the third child and eldest daughter of Frederick V of Bohemia and Elisabeth Stuart, daughter of James I of England. Her parents' marriage represented the rising political strength of Protestantism. In August of 1620, Elisabeth's father, Frederick, departed Heidelberg for Prague to assume the position of Emperor of the Holy Roman Empire. In November 1620, Frederick lost the battle of White Mountain and with it his empire; he was forced into exile. This event is usually taken as the onset of the Thirty Years War. In the late 1620s Elisabeth joined her parents in The Hague. There, she was tutored by the Dutch humanist Constantijn Huygens and the mathematician Johan Stampioen. She also interacted with Anna Maria van Schurman. She was accomplished in Greek, Latin, German, English and French. Throughout her life, she was involved in her family's political affairs. In 1660, Elisabeth entered the Lutheran convent at Herford in the Rhine Valley. She died on February 8, 1680, as abbess of the convent.

Several of her siblings were accomplished as well. Her older brother Charles Louis rehabilitated Heidelberg University after the Thirty Years War. Her brother Rupert was known for his chemical experiments, his soldiering, and his role in founding the Hudson's Bay Company. Her sister Louise Hollandine was an accomplished painter. Her youngest sister Sophie through her marriage became Electress of Hanover and corresponded with Leibniz and Diderot among others.

In 1643 Elisabeth began a correspondence with René Descartes that continued until Descartes's death in 1650. This exchange constitutes the whole of Elisabeth's extant philosophical work. However, record of Elisabeth's intellectual interests predates this correspondence. Edward Reynolds dedicates his *Treatise of the Passions and the Faculties of the Soule of Man* to Elisabeth, suggesting that she had seen and commented on a draft manuscript. In the 1660s the British mathematician John Pell contacted Elisabeth, through Theodore Haak, regarding her solution to Appolonius's Problem (that of finding a fourth circle whose circumference touches three given circles) undertaken in her correspondence with Descartes. In the 1670s, after Elisabeth had become abbess at Herford, she was contacted by English Quakers and corresponded with William Penn and Robert Barclay. She was also in contact with Nicholas Malebranche, Francis Mercury van Helmont, and G. W. F. Leibniz.

In the seven years of their correspondence, Elisabeth and Descartes address the full scope of philosophical inquiry. They discuss metaphysics, as well as topics in natural philosophy, including physics, geometry, and medicine. Equally, their exchange includes discussions of moral psychology, ethics, and political philosophy. Because all we have of Elisabeth's philosophical writings are her letters to Descartes, and those letters principally involve reactions to his work, it is hard to determine Elisabeth's own positions. Nonetheless, by considering the presuppositions of her questions and objections, it is possible to adduce her philosophical commitments.

Elisabeth, in her letter of May 6, 1643, begins the exchange by asking Descartes how the two really distinct substances of mind and body can causally interact with one another to effect voluntary action. That is, she poses the problem of mind-body interaction. Elisabeth's problem lies in understanding the nature of the causation at work between an immaterial substance (mind) and a material one (body). It is clear from her posing of the question, and her subsequent pressing of Descartes about his answers, that Elisabeth is willing to accept only efficient causal explanations of mind-body interaction. Insofar as she is skeptical that any such explanation can be offered of the interaction between an immaterial mind and body, she is inclined to think that the mind is material, but nonetheless has a capacity for thought.

Elisabeth's questions about mind-body interaction demonstrate her commitment to a mechanist account of the natural world and shows her to be well-versed in the varieties of mechanist accounts of causation available to adopt. This interest in natural philosophy is perhaps best reflected in Descartes's dedication to her of his *Principles of Philosophy*, the work in which he lays out his physics most clearly. It is also reflected in her remarks regarding human physiology and observed natural phenomena later in the correspondence.

In 1645, in part to help Elisabeth find some comfort from the effects of the English Civil War on her family, Descartes undertook to outline his views on moral psychology—the regulation of the passions—and the nature of the sovereign good. For him, the sovereign good consists simply in virtue, which Descartes takes to be simply a firm and constant will to do all that we judge to be the best. Once again, Elisabeth raises pointed objections. Here she is concerned with preserving the traditional tie between virtue and contentment. On Descartes's account, she charges, virtue would be insufficient for contentment. Given that our knowledge is incomplete, our best judgments would inevitably be wrong sometimes, and on those occasions we would regret our actions. Elisabeth takes this regret to be incompatible with virtue. Our incomplete knowledge also raises another problem for her, that of measuring the value of things. While Elisabeth admits the passions to be sources of value, she also recognizes that different individuals evaluate things differently. For her, the central problem of ethics is not achieving the sovereign good but rather reconciling competing evaluations of things. Her interest in the passions as sources of

value leads her to request Descartes to enumerate and describe all the passions. In response, Descartes drafted his last work, *The Passions of the Soul*. Descartes sent this portion of the correspondence, including Elisabeth's letters, to Queen Christina of Sweden when she requested his views on the sovereign good.

Elisabeth and Descartes also address the problem of reconciling free will with determinism. Whereas Descartes asserts that human freedom is consistent with divine providence, though how it is so might escape us, for Elisabeth simply asserting that the two are consistent is insufficient. In addition, Elisabeth's request that Descartes lay out some maxims for civil life results in an extended discussion of Machiavelli's *The Prince* and the obligations of a good ruler to his subjects.

See also Descartes, René; Metaphysics.

Bibliography

Descartes, René. *Oeuvres*. Vols. 3–5, edited by Charles Adam and Paul Tannery. Paris: Vrin, 1996.

Elisabeth, Princess of Bohemia. *Elisabeth, Princess of Bohemia and René Descartes: Their Correspondence*. Translated by Lisa Shapiro. Chicago: University of Chicago Press, forthcoming (expected publication in 2006).

Penn, William. *An Account of W. Penn's Travails in Holland and Germany, Anno MDCLXXVII*. London: T. Sowle, 1695 and 1714.

Reynolds, Edward. *Treatise of the Passions and the Faculties of the Soule of Man*. London: Robert Bostock, 1640. Facsimile reproduction, edited by Margaret Lee Wiley, Gainseville, FL: Scholars' Facsimiles and Reprints, 1971.

Broad, Jacqueline. *Women Philosophers of the Seventeenth Century*. Cambridge, U.K.: Cambridge University Press, 2002.

Shapiro, Lisa. "Princess Elizabeth and Descartes: The Union of Soul and Body and the Practice of Philosophy." *British Journal for the History of Philosophy* 7 (3) (1999): 503–520.

Tollefson, Deborah. "Princess Elisabeth and the Problem of Mind-Body Interaction." *Hypatia* 14 (3) (1999): 59–77.

Lisa Shapiro (2005)

EMANATIONISM

Emanationism explains the origin and structure of reality by postulating a perfect and transcendent principle from which everything is derived through a process called emanation (Greek *aporroia, probolē, proodos*; Latin *emanatio*), which is comparable to an efflux or radiation. Emanation is timeless and thus can be called a process only figuratively. It leaves its source undiminished, so that the source remains transcendent; but as the process continues, each of its products is less perfect.

In these three respects emanationism is opposed to evolutionism because evolution is a temporal process in which the principle itself is involved (immanent) and in which an increase in perfection is usually conceived. Emanationism is also opposed to creationism, according to which the principle creates the rest of reality (from which it differs absolutely), either out of nothing or by transforming a preexisting, chaotic matter into a cosmos. There is some affinity between emanationism and pantheism, except that the latter teaches the immanence of the principle in its product. Some philosophers characterize emanationism as panentheism.

Emanationism forms an important part of several philosophic and religious doctrines, though it is somewhat elusive in the latter.

PHILOSOPHIC EMANATIONISM

A theory of emanation can be found to a certain extent in the philosophy of Plato and the Old Academy as presented by Aristotle. Out of two highest principles (usually called the One and the Indefinite Dyad), ideas, in some way identified with or comprising mathematicals (numbers; geometrical entities, i.e., point, line, plane, solid) evolve; out of solids, the physical world evolves. But the nature of the process (for which Aristotle used the term *genesis*) remains unclear. The Stoa, Neo-Pythagoreanism, and Philo contributed some ideas to emanationism, but the philosophy first appears in full clarity in the system of Plotinus. His supreme principle, because it is transcendent, ineffable, and absolutely simple (One), must "overflow," just as what is mature must beget. The first product of this overflowing is intelligence (*nous*), which roughly corresponds to Plato's idea. From intelligence emanates psyche (corresponding to Plato's mathematicals) which becomes, by degrees, less and less perfect, more and more multiple. From the psyche emanates matter that, when "illuminated" by the psyche, becomes the physical world.

Often, although not always, Plotinus describes emanation as a necessary, involuntary, "natural," and therefore blameless process, somewhat like a point of absolutely intense light that emits a cone of light without any loss of its own substance. As the cone of light expands in volume, it grows dimmer, finally passing into complete darkness, on which the light produces images as on a screen. But just as the ontic status of darkness is ambiguous (Is it a minimum of light or its complete absence and therefore not its product?), so the status of matter in Plotinus is never quite clear.

The emanationism of Plotinus was taken over by all Neoplatonists, but among them, Proclus deserves particular mention. By subdividing Plotinus's emanative steps, Proclus made the process more continuous; and to the "vertical" emanation he added something like a "horizontal" one, fully articulating the realms of intelligence and psyche. From Neoplatonism, emanationism passed into the Christian, Muslim, and Jewish philosophies of the Middle Ages (Dionysius the Pseudo-Areopagite, John Scotus Erigena, Nicholas of Cusa, al-Farabi, Avicenna, Averroes, the book of Zohar), often with pantheistic or creationistic modifications. In modern times, evolutionism has obliterated the emanationist philosophy.

RELIGIOUS EMANATIONISM

In religion, emanationism appears in many Gnostic systems, most conspicuously in *Pistis Sophia* (Faith-wisdom) and in some writings of Valentinus. But in neither of these is it the exclusive principle explaining the origin of everything outside the highest principle. Furthermore, emanation appears in these writings as the result of some reflection and will. It produces, not abstract principles, as in Plotinus, but a host of mythological characters—the first products of emanation according to Valentinus are thirty Aeons—performing a cosmic drama. In addition, what remains entirely in the background in Plotinian theory becomes prominent in Gnosticism; namely, that some acts of the will, which produce emanations, are the result of error or shortcomings. The physical world is created by one of the products of emanation, the Demiurge (identified with the Mosaic creator, the Platonic divine craftsman). The Demiurge is evil himself, and his creation, the world, is an evil place in which man finds himself entrapped and from which gnosis shows the elect ones a way to salvation. Although soteriology plays some part in Plotinian theory, it does not occupy a central place in the system. According to Plotinus, the efflux is balanced by a reflux, which takes place *pari passu* with the efflux. For humankind, the enactment of this reflux remains the most important task; and every person is, by nature, capable of performing it. Gnostic emanationism is ultimately motivated by a feeling of complete hostility to and estrangement from the material world—a feeling that the emanationism of Plotinus, in spite of some ascetic and pessimistic strains, explicitly refuses to countenance.

See also al-Fārābī; Aristotle; Averroes; Avicenna; Erigena, John Scotus; Neoplatonism; Nicholas of Cusa; Pantheism; Plato; Plotinus; Proclus; Pseudo-Dionysius; Valentinus and Valentinianism.

Bibliography

Dodds, E. R. "Proclus." In *The Elements of Theology*. 2nd ed., 212–214, 230. Oxford: Clarendon Press, 1963.

Eisler, R. *Wörterbuch der philosophischen Begriffe*. 3 vols., 4th ed. 321–322. Berlin, 1927–1930.

Faggin, G. "Emanatismo." In *Enciclopedia filosofica*, 1861–1864. Venice and Rome, 1957.

Heinze, M. "Emanation." In *Schaff-Herzog Encyclopedia of Religious Knowledge*, 117ff. New York and London, 1909.

Mora, J. Ferrater. "Emanación." In *Diccionario de filosofia*, 4th ed., 400–401. Buenos Aires, 1958.

Ratzinger, J. "Emanation." In *Reallexikon für Antike und Christentum*, 1219–1228. Stuttgart, 1959.

Philip Merlan (1967)

EMANATIONISM [ADDENDUM]

The sort of philosophy that the Islamic world discovered when it came into contact with the main centers of civilization in the Middle East was neoplatonism. This represented a long tradition of philosophy that had as one of its main planks a theory of how the world is linked with its ultimate cause. Emanation is an important neoplatonic concept that provides an account of this relationship. The existence of this world and the other worlds that exist along with it are taken to flow from the ultimate cause, the One that is the cause of multiplicity, and a main difference from a normal causal relationship is that the cause and the effect are often taken to occur at the same time as each other. This is because emanation represents an eternal process, not only bringing other things into existence but also sustaining their continuing existence.

This concept was taken up with enthusiasm by most of the main Islamic philosophers, and subsequently by Jewish philosophers in the Islamic world. Emanation was often identified with grace, in that God's grace could be seen as eternally influencing lower forms of existence. The identification of the One from which everything else flows is not difficult to link with the God of Islam and Judaism, and the emphasis on the unity of the deity must have struck a chord with these two monotheistic religions. What is problematic from a theological perspective is that emanationism is different from the notion of ex nihilo creation that does seem to be mentioned in both Islamic and Jewish religious texts. On this notion of creation God decides at a particular time to create the world, so first of all there was nothing in existence except God, and subsequently the world came about through his fiat.

Yet with emanation there never was nothing except God. God eternally thinks, and from that thought the worlds are produced, and the worlds always existed because God has always existed and thought. Moreover, the notion of emanation implies that God is not aware of what comes about as a result of his thought, because anything lower than the abstract level at which he thinks is beneath his dignity to contemplate.

The language of emanationism is useful for mystical thinkers in both Sufism and kabbalah. The notion of God being in constant contact with the world and everything in existence being connected to everything else provides theoretical underpinning for an immanent view of God's relationship to his creation. God is then in a radical sense *in* the world, and everything that exists is an aspect of him, even what looks insignificant. Mystics tended to argue that it is possible to come close to God by following the emanationist process back to where it starts, with God, but this is a tortuous route that only a few adepts are likely to entirely follow. For most philosophers, however, the route to perfection only goes as high as the active intellect, the most abstract form of thought of which we are capable. Once we go beyond this form of thinking we enter into realms of the emanationist cosmology that we cannot properly grasp except in general terms.

See also Islamic Philosophy; Jewish Philosophy; Kabbalah; Neoplatonism; Sufism.

Bibliography

Frank, Daniel, and Oliver Leaman, eds. *History of Jewish Philosophy*. London: Routledge, 1997.

Leaman, Oliver. *Brief Introduction to Islamic Philosophy*. Oxford: Polity, 1999.

Leaman, Oliver. *Introduction to Classical Islamic Philosophy*. Cambridge, U.K.: Cambridge University Press, 2003.

Nasr, Seyyed H., and Oliver Leaman, eds. *History of Islamic Philosophy*. London: Routledge, 1996.

Oliver Leaman (2005)

EMERGENCE

Emergence is, broadly speaking, the fact that there are features of the world—objects, properties, laws, perhaps other things—that are manifested as a result of the existence of other, usually more basic, entities but that cannot be completely reduced to those other entities. Theories of emergence tend to fall into two basic types: ontological emergence and epistemological emergence—with conceptual emergence serving as a subcategory of the latter.

Advocates of ontological emergence consider emergent phenomena to be objective features of the world, their emergent status being independent of human existence and knowledge; advocates of epistemological emergence consider emergent features to be a result of the limited abilities of people to predict, to calculate, to observe, and to explain; and advocates of conceptual emergence consider emergent features to be a product of theoretical and linguistic representations of the world.

Emergence has considerable philosophical importance because the existence of certain kinds of ontologically emergent entities would provide direct evidence against the universal applicability of the generative atomism that has dominated Anglo-American philosophy in the last century. By generative atomism is meant the view that there exist atomic entities, be they physical, linguistic, logical, or some other kind, and all else is composed of those atoms according to rules of combination and relations of determination. The failure of various reductionist programs, especially that of physicalism, would have significant impact on this program. In addition, the various accounts of epistemological emergence pose difficulties for the long established Cartesian requirement of completely transparent access to evidential relations.

Although there is no consensus upon what counts as an emergent entity, a cluster of features tends to recur in philosophical accounts of emergence. Emergent phenomena are irreducible, they are novel, they are usually unpredictable on the basis of theory, they are often unexplainable, they frequently involve global rather than merely local properties, and an emergent entity must emerge from something. This last feature separates emergent features from those entities whose existence does not depend upon anything else, such as the objects of fundamental physics or certain abstract entities. It also allows for two distinct kinds of emergence: static or synchronic emergence within which the emergent entities exist simultaneously with the entities from which they emerge; and dynamic or diachronic emergence, within which the emergent entities temporally develop from antecedent entities. Although it is rarely stated explicitly, dynamic emergence is generally held to result from more than causal processes alone.

At one time, life and chemical compounds were considered to be good candidates for emergent features, covered by what John Stuart Mill in book III of his *A System of Logic* (1843, ch. VI, pts. 1–2) termed heteropathic laws, but with advances in molecular biology and an understanding of the chemical bond that view fell into disfavor. Perhaps as a consequence, emergence came to be viewed

with a certain degree of suspicion, apparently requiring a commitment to occult qualities that was at odds with the analytic methods of science and philosophy. It is thus ironic that emergence has reemerged as a vigorous and lively field of investigation, has shed much of its air of mystery, and plausible candidates for emergent phenomena have been discovered in fundamental areas of physics as well as in other areas of science such as complexity theory. As a result, it is important when considering emergence not to restrict one's range of examples to the widely discussed cases of mental properties.

This entry will emphasize contemporary positions on emergence, although occasional historical references will be made to illustrate conceptual continuities. For a history of the area, the reader is referred to Brian McLaughlin's 1992 survey article, "The Rise and Fall of British Emergentism."

ONTOLOGICAL APPROACHES TO EMERGENCE

One influential ontological approach to emergence uses supervenience relations to account for emergent features. An early version of this approach by James van Cleve (1990) asserted that a property P of a system is emergent if and only if P supervenes with nomological necessity but not with logical necessity on properties of parts of the system, and some of the supervenience principles linking the basal properties with P are fundamental laws. That is, once the features of the most fundamental level are fixed, so—via laws of nature—are the features of all higher levels. Advocates of supervenience approaches, especially the widely canvassed position known as Humean supervenience, generally hold that supervenience is all that is required to account for higher-level features of the world. David Lewis provided an influential statement of this position in the second volume of his *Philosophical Papers* (1986, pp. ix–xvi). Supervenience approaches usually contain the irreducibility and novelty aspects of emergence. Whether the global, unpredictability, and unexplainability features are present depends upon the type of supervenience involved.

A different ontological position, developed by Jaegwon Kim in his article "Making Sense of Emergence" (1999), begins with the idea that a higher level property P is reducible if: (a) P can be functionalized—that is, defined in terms of its causal role; (b) realizers of P can be found at a lower level; and (c) there is a lower level theory that explains how the realizers operate. In contrast, a property is emergent if it is neither a physical property nor reducible to physical properties in the sense just described. Kim's position retains the irreducibility, novelty, theoretical unpredictability, and unexplainability features of emergent phenomena but apparently has the consequence that there is little scope for their existence, except perhaps in the case of qualia or consciousness.

The novelty of emergent features is usually captured in the idea that an emergent entity E must be qualitatively different from the entities from which it emerges. A popular version of this idea asserts that a property P is emergent if it has novel causal powers not possessed by entities at lower levels. The causation involved can be horizontal (to entities at the same level), upwards (to a higher level), or downwards (to a lower level). When downwards causation is involved, one of the most difficult problems facing advocates of supervenience emergence and many other ontological accounts of emergence occurs. This is the problem of causal exclusion, of explaining how emergent features can influence lower levels via downwards causation if one subscribes to the causal closure of lower levels as, for example, do most physicalists. For if the lower level is casually closed, any downwards influence is redundant, unless causal overdetermination is allowed. A clear statement of this argument can be found in Kim's 1992 article "'Downward Causation' in Emergentism and Nonreductive Physicalism."

A third ontological approach to emergence, found in Paul Humphreys' 1997 article "How Properties Emerge," addresses this problem. It has as its core idea the view that in certain cases of dynamic emergence the original elements or their properties fuse together in a way that the identities of those elements are lost in forming the new emergent entity. This feature allows emergent phenomena to avoid the causal exclusion argument because the lower level entities no longer exist and a fortiori cannot be causal competitors to the emergent entity. The position entails the irreducibility, novelty, and holistic features of emergent phenomena, but allows their predictability and explainability. Certain holistic quantum systems possessing states of joint systems but not states of individual components seem to be examples of fusion.

EPISTEMOLOGICAL APPROACHES TO EMERGENCE

Turning to epistemological accounts of emergence, one of the oldest approaches emphasizes the essential unpredictability of emergent phenomena. It is sometimes loosely and unhelpfully characterized in psychological terms by noting that emergent phenomena are surprising. A more precise version asserts that a property P belonging to domain E is emergent relative to a domain D, where E is at a higher level than D, if it is impossible to predict the occurrence of instances of P on the basis of any ideal theory about D. Early accounts of emergence based on unpredictability can be found in Stephen Pepper's article "Emergence" (1926) and C. D. Broad's book *The Mind and Its Place in Nature* (1925).

This unpredictability approach conforms to Ernest Nagel's well-known approach to the reduction of one theory to another in chapter eleven of his *The Structure of Science* (1961). Within Nagel's account, one theory is irreducible to another if the laws of a higher level theory cannot be deduced from those of a more fundamental theory by employing bridge laws connecting the two levels. Thus, in a somewhat crude manner the essential unpredictability approach to emergence captures the idea that if biology is Nagel-irreducible to physics then biological phenomena are emergent from physical phenomena. It satisfies the novelty, irreducibility and, trivially, unpredictability aspects of emergence and also accommodates nomological emergence, the view that entities of type B are emergent from entities of type A if and only if entities of type B have type A entities as constituents and there is at least one law that applies to type B entities that does not apply to type A entities. A statement of nomological emergence can be found in the physicist P. W. Anderson's much cited 1972 article "More Is Different."

A diachronic version of the unpredictability approach to emergence is widely used within the field of complexity theory and rests on the idea of stable patterns spontaneously emerging in a system. Although these patterns are, simply in virtue of being patterns, nonlocal, they are not the result of a central organizing principle but result from local, often nonlinear, interactions between members of a population. Examples of pattern emergence abound in what are commonly termed self-organized systems, one simple example of which is the formation and maintenance of bird flocks. The general area of agent-based or individual-based models, which include many examples of self-organizing systems, is of interest to philosophy because it combines a bottom-up commitment to individualism with the dynamic emergence of higher level structures possessing the features of novelty and holism. Such models can illuminate the traditional philosophical issue of methodological individualism, an issue that divides those who hold the view that there are sui generis facts in the social sciences from the individualists who deny this.

Because the dynamic emergence of the patterns can often be modeled only via computer simulations, an important aspect of these systems is captured by Mark Bedau's concept of weak emergence (2003). A weakly emergent property P is one possessed by a structured system S, where P is incapable of being possessed by components of S, and S's possessing P is a fact that can be derived only by a step-by-step simulation of S. Despite its connection with prediction via computer simulations, weak emergence is ultimately a metaphysical rather than an epistemological account of emergence. The structure of the system places objective constraints on the possibilities of computation and complex physical and biological systems must step through their own development, thus making weak emergence a claim about the world itself.

A particularly interesting kind of weak emergence occurs when a pattern P exists independently of the nature of the specific components of the system exhibiting the pattern so that the structure is in that sense autonomous. There are connections here with the multiple realizability of higher level properties, a topic that has played an important role in arguments against reduction. One approach to emergence that explicitly considers multiple realizability is Robert Batterman's asymptotic emergence (2002). This sort of emergence involves a relation between two theories, one of which is a limiting case of the other and it is unusual in not relying on the part/whole relationship upon which most other theories of emergence are based.

CONCEPTUAL APPROACHES TO EMERGENCE

Running parallel with the issues of epistemological and ontological emergence is the phenomenon of conceptual emergence, based upon the idea that theories employed at different levels of the hierarchy employ different concepts and that these concepts require the introduction of distinctive, irreducible, predicates and relations. This approach is captured in Paul Teller's characterization: An emergent property of a whole is one that is not explicitly definable in terms of the nonrelational properties of the object's proper parts (1992). Because definability depends upon the linguistic resources available in a given language or theory, this criterion for emergence is relative to the theory or language employed and reflects a common feature of linguistic development. If psychological and sociological features, to take two examples, are ontologically emergent, one should expect the resources of explicit definability to fail and to force the invention of new vocabulary. It is not difficult to see how each of the approaches to emergence described above can necessitate this kind of linguistic innovation, and it calls into ques-

tion various enterprises of linguistic reduction. Although it is not couched in terms of emergence, the influential arguments found in Jerry Fodor's 1974 article "Special Sciences" against reduction and in favor of the autonomy of the special sciences can be construed as reasons in support of conceptual emergence.

OTHER ISSUES

In contemporary philosophy, a commitment to emergent entities is generally held to violate physicalism, the position that the world's ontology contains nothing but the ontology provided by physics. What "nothing but" means differs from one version of physicalism to another, as does what is included within the scope of physics, but the core idea is that anything not required by fundamental physics is in principle redundant, even though one may employ a nonphysicalist vocabulary for practical reasons. Thus, mental entities such as beliefs are mere façons de parler on the reductionist view, and the social sciences have no genuine subject matter of their own. Strict versions of reductionism maintain similar views about biological and chemical entities.

All three approaches to emergence—ontological, epistemological, and conceptual—tend to appeal, implicitly or explicitly, to a layered view of the world that is divided into levels, with features at higher levels emerging from those at lower levels. This appeal to levels is usually grounded in the idea that larger entities such as molecules spatially include as parts smaller constituents such as atoms, this inclusion relation resulting in the familiar hierarchy of elementary particle physics, solid state physics, chemistry, biochemistry, biology, neurophysiology, and so on. Although this levels picture serves as a natural image within synchronic emergence, it can be a seriously misleading metaphor for diachronic emergence.

There is much casual talk in the literature on emergence about the difference between aggregate features and emergent features, the latter, in contrast to the former, being more than "mere sums" of the features of their components. It has turned out not to be informative to try to precisely capture what constitutes a "mere sum" but traditionally, holism—summed up in the slogan that the whole is greater than the sum of the parts—remains a core part of what is wanted from emergent phenomena. It is preferable to replace "greater than" by "different" and if this is done one has the suggestion that a property P is emergent only if it is a property of an entire system S that is composed of subsystems $S_1, \ldots S_n$ but none of the S_i possess P. This feature is possessed by, at least, the fusion, asymptotic, weak, and nomological approaches to emergence.

The principal aim of any philosophical account of emergence should be to make emergence intelligible and nontrivial. It is a separate matter, one with which science is properly concerned, whether the universe contains any examples of emergence. It is, nevertheless, a matter of considerable interest to philosophy whether examples of ontologically emergent phenomena exist because, if they do, our universe is more than an ontologically modest combinatorial device.

See also Chaos Theory; Physicalism; Reduction; Supervenience.

Bibliography

Anderson, P. W. "More is Different." *Science* 177 (1972): 393–396.

Batterman, Robert. *The Devil in the Details: Asymptotic Reasoning in Explanation, Reduction, and Emergence.* New York: Oxford University Press, 2002.

Beckerman, Ansgar, Hans Flohr, and Jaegwon Kim, eds. *Emergence or Reduction?: Essays on the Prospects of Nonreductive Physicalism.* Berlin: Walter de Gruyter, 1992.

Bedau, Mark. "Downward Causation and Autonomy in Weak Emergence." *Principia Revista Internacional de Epistemologica* 6 (2003): 5–50.

Broad, C. D. *The Mind and Its Place in Nature.* London: Routledge, 1925.

Fodor, Jerry. "Special Sciences, or The Disunity of Science as a Working Hypothesis." *Synthese* 28 (1974): 97–115.

Holland, John. *Emergence: From Chaos to Order.* Reading, MA: Addison-Wesley, 1998.

Humphreys, Paul. "How Properties Emerge." *Philosophy of Science* 64 (1997): 1–17.

Kim, Jaegwon. "'Downward Causation' in Emergentism and Nonreductive Physicalism." In *Emergence or Reduction?: Essays on the Prospects of Nonreductive Physicalism*, edited by Ansgar Beckerman et al, 119–138. Berlin: Walter de Gruyter, 1992.

Kim, Jaegwon. "Making Sense of Emergence." *Philosophical Studies* 95 (1999): 3–36.

Lewis, David. *Philosophical Papers.* Vol. II. Oxford: Oxford University Press, 1986.

McLaughlin, Brian. "The Rise and Fall of British Emergentism." In *Emergence or Reduction?: Essays on the Prospects of Nonreductive Physicalism*, edited by Ansgar Beckerman et al, 49–93. Berlin: Walter de Gruyter, 1992.

Mill, J. S. *A System of Logic: Ratiocinative and Inductive.* London: Longmans, Green and Company, 1843.

Nagel, Ernest. *The Structure of Science.* New York: Harcourt, 1961.

Pepper, Stephen. "Emergence." *Journal of Philosophy* 23 (1926): 241–245.

Teller, Paul. "A Contemporary Look at Emergence." In *Emergence or Reduction?: Essays on the Prospects of Nonreductive Physicalism*, edited by Ansgar Beckerman et al, 139–153. Berlin: Walter de Gruyter, 1992.

van Cleve, James. "Mind-Dust or Magic? Panpsychism versus Emergentism." *Philosophical Perspectives* 4 (1990): 215–226.

Paul Humphreys (2005)

EMERGENTISM

See *Emergence*

EMERSON, RALPH WALDO
(1803–1882)

Ralph Waldo Emerson, the American author and leader of New England transcendentalism, was born in Boston, Massachusetts. His father, a locally distinguished Unitarian clergyman, died in 1811 leaving Emerson and five other children in the care of a pious mother and a very learned aunt on the father's side. From 1813 to 1817 Emerson attended the Boston Latin School; then, after four undistinguished years at Harvard, he became a schoolmaster while he continued to study extramurally at Harvard Divinity School. "My reasoning faculty is proportionally weak," he confessed in his *Journal* in 1824, on deciding to become a minister, "nor can I ever hope to write a Butler's Analogy or an Essay of Hume. ... [But] the preaching most in vogue at the present day depends chiefly on *imagination* [italics added] for its success, and asks those accomplishments which I believe are most within my grasp." Made just before he was twenty-one, this acute piece of self-analysis marks the stage in Emerson's life when he really began to understand himself and gain a genuine premonition of his future role as literary artist. For Emerson is, more than anything else, an imaginative writer. (Thus Friedrich Nietzsche, who was at an early stage influenced by Emerson—admiring his "manifoldness" and "cheerfulness"—recognized him as one of the nineteenth century's few great masters of prose.)

FORMATIVE EXPERIENCES

Unitarianism was at first the main formative influence on Emerson, but it was not the most far-reaching, and the sort of preaching he was eventually to excel in had little to do with any established church or, for that matter, with Christianity as such. A trip to Florida for health reasons, in the winter of 1826–1827, brought about a chance meeting with the aristocratic Achille Murat, whose "consistent Atheism" Emerson found combined, to his surprise, with moral perspicuity. By the late 1820s the young theological student had already got through a prodigious regimen of philosophical and occult reading that included (as the most important authors for his maturer orientations) Zoroaster, Confucius, Muḥammad, the Neoplatonists, Jakob Boehme, Gottfried Wilhelm Leibniz, Baron de Montesquieu, Jean-Jacques Rousseau, Edmund Burke, the Scottish philosophers, Emanuel Swedenborg, Johann Gottfried Herder, and—above all—Madame de Staël (the *De l'Allemagne*). Emerson's attention was being irresistibly drawn to the new cultural movement in Germany. The disturbing advances in German biblical criticism were beginning to penetrate to him via his brother William's enthusiastic letters from Göttingen (William had also met and talked with Johann Wolfgang von Goethe). Soon Emerson was absorbed in Thomas Carlyle's pioneering essays on German literature, and in Samuel Taylor Coleridge's *Aids to Reflection* (1825)—in which Emerson discovered the pseudo-Kantian distinction between "Reason" and "Understanding."

In 1829 Emerson was appointed pastor of the Second Church of Boston; shortly afterward he married Ellen Louisa Tucker. Ellen's tragic death of tuberculosis early in 1831 had a deeply anguishing and yet strangely liberalizing effect upon Emerson. He questioned himself about immortality; preached sermons that expounded embryonic versions of his own later doctrines of "self-reverence" (or "self-reliance," as he sometimes called it), "compensation," and "correspondence"; found he was bored with weekday Bible classes; and eventually gave up his pastorate.

On January 2, 1833, he sailed for Europe. This first European tour (he made two more, one in 1847–1848 and one in 1872–1873) was crucial in helping him shape into something like a whole the new philosophical outlook he had been consciously groping toward since at least 1824 and to which he ultimately gave poetic expression in his major works. During a short stay in Britain he managed to get an interview with Coleridge at Highgate, met William Wordsworth, and spent twenty-four hours with the Carlyles at Craigenputtock. Carlyle immediately became a lifelong friend.

The conversations with Coleridge and Carlyle, the two men who were to the disenchanted young American living embodiments of all that was viable in contemporary European culture, had simply the effect of confirming Emerson's old belief: As a guide to solving the problem of life's meaning, there is "really nothing external, so I must spin my thread from my own bowels." He reasoned to himself that "the purpose of life seems to be

to acquaint a man with himself" and "the highest revelation is that God is in every man." In his *Journal* entry for September 8, 1833, written while sailing back to America, Emerson included with the above affirmation of his maxim of "self-reverence" two other by then quite explicit convictions: (1) "There is a *correspondence* [italics added] between the human soul and everything that exists in the world," and (2) since "a man contains all that is needful to his government within himself," it must be that "nothing can be given to him or taken from him but always there is a *compensation* [italics added]." Here were brought together the key notions that Emerson was to elaborate for the rest of his life, first in his original transcendentalist manifesto, *Nature* (1836), and then in practically all the later works, including *Essays* (First Series, 1841; Second Series, 1844), *Representative Men* (1850), *English Traits* (1856), *Conduct of Life* (1860), *Society and Solitude* (1870), and *Letters and Social Aims* (1875).

In 1835 Emerson married Lydia Jackson, with whom, he soberly remarked to William, he had found a "quite unexpected community of sentiment and speculation." Soon he was settled in unusual domestic serenity with his wife and his mother in Concord, which remained his home for the rest of his life. Emerson's writings, his sagelike personality, and his roles as the leader of New England transcendentalism and the editor of the *Dial* gradually brought him an international reputation as perhaps America's leading man of letters.

MATURE WRITINGS

If propounded by a philosopher, Emerson's assertions concerning "correspondence" and "compensation" would demand further explication and defense. But to expect anything resembling epistemological lucidity, or even concern, in a writer like Emerson would be to approach him with misconceptions. Indeed, those who read him as one would a philosopher like Immanuel Kant, Friedrich von Schelling, G. W. F. Hegel, or even Coleridge (all of whom certainly had a great influence upon Emerson), largely miss the peculiar merits and significance of his works. For Emerson was neither a critical philosopher nor an idealist metaphysician, but an intuitive sage-poet: "In Emerson," wrote Nietzsche to Overbeck, *"we have lost a philosopher."*

Like his artistic models Michel Eyquem de Montaigne, Blaise Pascal, and the Goethe of the *Maximen und Reflexionen,* Emerson was a virtuoso of the *pensée,* in which style and content, symbol and "meaning," are inseparably conjoined. His meditations are exploratory rather than defining or definitive, and the nonpropositional, revelatory use of language with which Emerson alternately enraptures and ensnares his reader renders inappropriate the conventional task of giving a systematic conspectus of his leading ideas. The analysis to be applied to any work by Emerson is that of the literary critic rather than the philosopher. His method of exploration consists in the cumulative and often dialectical juxtaposition and attempted coalescence of *aperçus* relating to a single broad theme—"Nature," "Friendship," "Wealth," "Immortality"—usually in the form of an essay, lecture, or address. In fact, all Emerson's prose works are homiletic: They are secular sermons that differ from the sermons of his ancestors, the New England Puritan divines, largely by virtue of a greater breadth and subtlety of message and the intense personalism of their inner soliloquy.

Yet, despite the epistemological imprecision of his views, Emerson is philosophically interesting in at least two ways. First, because of the very full *Journal* he kept throughout his life, he affords an extremely well-documented record of a major writer who found it urgently necessary to struggle with philosophical ideas in order to achieve personal (and artistic) integration in an age "destitute of faith, but terrified at scepticism," as Carlyle characterized it. (The ideological perplexities of his age, moreover, lead directly to our own.) Emerson strove to discover for himself "an original relation to the universe": a kind of personal *Weltansicht* that would somehow keep vital his essentially religious sensibilities and give succor to his pressing emotional needs. Since Christianity could no longer do either of these things, he meditated upon his own experience in the light of those pieces of philosophy that seemed most accommodating. That Emerson found the Germanic philosophical tradition more to his liking than the Anglo-Saxon was the natural result of his individualism, his belief in the primacy of personality, and his closely related admiration for the hero, genius, or great man, in which he joined Johann Gottlieb Fichte, Carlyle, and Nietzsche (see especially *Representative Men*). He expressed these fundamentally anthropocentric and aristocratic orientations quite succinctly: "No object really interests us but man, and in man only his superiorities; and though we are aware of a perfect law in nature, it has fascination for us only through its relation to him, or as it is rooted in the mind."

Both Schelling and Hegel influenced Emerson in profound and clearly traceable ways—Schelling first, through Coleridge, and Hegel later, particularly through W. T. Harris and the St. Louis School of Hegelians, with whose *Journal of Speculative Philosophy* Emerson was closely associated in the late 1860s and early 1870s. The primacy of "personality," or "self-consciousness," as it was usually called, was already an established axiom with the Germans. And if the all-embracing dichotomy between mind and nature—with its innumerable manifestations in the troublemaking divisions of "reality and illusion," "religion and science," "moral law and physical law," "the eternal and the temporal," in effect, the division of "the transcendental ideal and the banal actual"—could be shown to be only an immature stage in the development of Absolute Spirit whose final blossoming would exhibit all as one: Then, indeed, there would be not only "a correspondence between the human soul and everything that exists in the world" but, even better, a coalescence.

Much in the manner of Hegel, Emerson came to see History, or God, or the Oversoul as a kind of primordial schizophrenic, originally split into mind and nature and now victoriously struggling to personal integration in and through the creative achievements of human culture. Metaphysically speaking, human culture is identical with mind's reintegration with nature. Indeed for Emerson science itself becomes the handmaiden of transcendentalism: Man's conquest of the material environment shows nature to be not alien but fully transparent to mind, and since whatever is intelligible must somehow be itself intelligence, mind and nature are in reality one. But in such a panspiritualistic universe every apparent evil can only be for the greater universal good; the "compensation" for evil lies in the ultimate self-harmony of mind. This is the tortuous metaphysical hallucination that forms the basis of Emerson's optimism. As far then as it can be discerned, his *philosophia prima* is that of the German idealists, and one sympathetic way of characterizing him would be to say that where Schelling and the rest made the fundamental mistake of attempting to give rational and systematic expression to the mythology of romanticism, Emerson put the whole thing into poetry—which was exactly where it belonged.

But Emerson's individualism had a further and more practical consequence. He could never reconcile himself to the values of a civilization that, as he saw it, was "essentially one of property, of fences, of exclusiveness"; and the incisive manner in which this dissatisfaction with the prevailing social reality found expression in his writings gives Emerson a special place in the great line of romantic critics of mass society from Rousseau to Karl Jaspers. Brilliantly critical of emergent American commercialism, which necessarily seemed to involve cultural superficiality, Emerson was particularly virulent against the species of democracy that in fact often demands only conformity to depersonalizing custom, and a consequent sacrifice of individual autonomy, of "self-reliance." He did not limit his criticism to America; *English Traits* is still, among other things, a major indictment of European cant, Philistinism, and materialism by an American.

The second reason why Emerson is philosophically interesting is his influence on philosophers. Nietzsche has been mentioned; so also should be Henri Bergson. A number of Bergson's fundamental concepts often seem in part to be systematizations of Emerson's eclectic intuitions (compare, for example, the *élan vital* with Emerson's "vital force" in the essay "Experience"); perhaps the most noteworthy is the decided interest in Emerson shown by the pragmatists William James and John Dewey.

Emerson's most pervasive influence, however, was not so much on professional thinkers or writers, but on the public, through the great popular sale of his works. His highly personal yet persuasive and accessible form of romanticism insinuated itself into the general intellectual consciousness of America, and to a lesser extent into that of Europe. "His relation to us is ... like that of the Roman Emperor Marcus Aurelius," said Matthew Arnold in *Discourses in America* (published in 1885, three years after Emerson's death); "he is the friend and aider of those who would live in the spirit."

See also New England Transcendentalism.

Bibliography

The Complete Works of Ralph Waldo Emerson in the twelve-volume Centenary Edition (Cambridge, MA: Riverside Press, 1903–1904) is the standard edition of Emerson's works. Emerson's *Journals* were originally edited by E. W. Emerson and W. E. Forbes (Boston: Houghton Mifflin, 1909–1914). A more recent version is *Journals and Miscellaneous Notebooks of Ralph Waldo Emerson,* edited by William H. Gilman and others, 3 vols. (Cambridge, MA: Belknap Press of Harvard University Press, 1960–1963). For more bibliographical details consult *Eight American Authors: A Review of Research and Criticism,* edited by Floyd Stovall (New York: Modern Language Association of America, 1956; reprinted with a bibliographical supplement extended to 1962, New York: Norton, 1963). An informed and brilliantly perceptive account of the role of German thought in Emerson's intellectual development is contained in H. A. Pochmann's *German Culture in America* (Madison: University of Wisconsin Press, 1961), pp. 153–207. Among recent studies of Emerson's mind and art, the most illuminating is Jonathan Bishop, *Emerson on the Soul* (Cambridge, MA: Harvard University Press, and London: Oxford University Press, 1965).

OTHER RECOMMENDED WORKS

Cameron, Kenneth Walter. *Emerson's Developing Philosophy: The Early Lectures (1836–1838).* Hartford: Transcendental Books, 1996.
Cameron, Kenneth Walter. *Emerson's Philosophic Path to a Vocation.* Hartford: Transcendental Books, 1996.
Emerson, Ralph Waldo. *The Vision of Emerson.* Edited with an introduction by Richard Geldard. Rockport, MA: Element, 1995.
Goodman, Russell B. *American Philosophy and the Romantic Tradition.* New York: Cambridge University Press, 1990.
Gray, Henry David. Emerson: *A Statement of New England Transcendentalism as Expressed in the Philosophy of its Chief Exponent.* New York: Ungar, 1958.
Hopkins, Vivian Constance. *Spires of Form: A Study of Emerson's Aesthetic Theory.* New York: Russell & Russell, 1965.
Jacobson, David. *Emerson's Pragmatic Vision: The Dance of the Eye.* University Park: Pennsylvania State University Press, 1993.
Levin, Jonathan. *The Poetics of Transition: Emerson, Pragmatism, and American Literary Modernism.* Durham: Duke University Press, 1999.
Lopez, Michael. *Emerson and Power: Creative Antagonism in the Nineteenth Century.* DeKalb: Northern Illinois University Press, 1996.
Porter, David T. *Emerson and Literary Change.* Cambridge, MA: Harvard University Press, 1978.
Robinson, David. *Emerson and the Conduct of Life: Pragmatism and Ethical Purpose in the Later Work.* New York: Cambridge University Press, 1993.
Van Leer, David. *Emerson's Epistemology: The Argument of the Essays.* New York: Cambridge University Press, 1986.

Michael Moran (1967)
Bibliography updated by Desirae Matherly Martin (2005)

EMOTION

Over the centuries, the emotions have proven to be a notoriously recalcitrant philosophical subject, defying easy classification and stubbornly straddling accepted philosophical distinctions. With changing conceptions of the mind and its powers, categories such as emotion, desire, appetite, passion, feeling, and sentiment come and go. The general term *the emotions* is a relatively recent arrival to the English language, first gaining prominence in the nineteenth century, long after terms such as *fear, shame,* and *joy* were in common use. Its introduction was an attempt to clump together states that were supposedly marked by a degree of "emotion," a metaphorical extension of the original sense of the word, namely, agitated motion, or turbulence. Only the vagueness of the metaphor allows it to stretch far enough to cover typically quiescent "emotions" such as being pleased or sad about something.

Probably one influence on the extension of the term is the older category of "passions," in the sense of ways of being acted upon. In many languages nearly all emotion adjectives are derived from participles: for example, the English words amused, annoyed, ashamed, astonished, delighted, depressed, embarrassed, excited, frightened, horrified, irritated, pleased, terrified, surprised, upset, and worried—and even sad (from "sated"). When people are, for example, frightened, something acts on them, that is, frightens them: typically, something of which they are aware. However, even if the terms commonly used for the various emotions suggest that the notion of passivity is central to the ordinary concept of emotion, that notion seems irreparably vague, at best reflective of a prescientific picture of a person (or, for that matter, a physical object) as acting and acted on, as doing and "suffering." Indeed, it is not obvious that the states we call emotions have anything interesting or important in common that distinguishes them from all other mental states. Some philosophers and scientists have argued that what we call "the emotions" do not belong to a "natural kind" or class, and even that the concept of emotion should be banished entirely, at least from scientific discourse. These issues will be taken up in a later section.

THE PHILOSOPHICAL TRADITION

Since William Alston published his seminal article on "Emotion and Feeling" in the first edition of this Encyclopedia, philosophical scholarship in the area has undergone tremendous growth and variation. Among the major catalysts for change in philosophical thinking about the emotions have been new developments in psychology and neuroscience. However, the medium within which this ferment has largely been taking place is linguistic and conceptual analysis. Although analytic philosophers of emotion use relatively sophisticated logical and linguistic tools, their task has not been much different from that of the many classical philosophers who attempted definitions of various emotions: for example, Aristotle in the *Rhetoric*, Descartes in *The Passions of the Soul*, Hobbes in the *Leviathan*, Spinoza in his *Ethics*, and Hume in *A Treatise on Human Nature*. Moreover, the most important outcome of the analytic thrust was a view that had been at least implicit in traditional accounts, namely, cognitivism. Although there are several varieties of cognitivism, perhaps the most influential versions hold that the various emotions are distinguished in part by the types of situation that evoke them; or, more exactly, by the types of situation the awareness of which evokes them; more exactly still, by the content of the beliefs and

other propositional attitudes that cause them. Note the importance of situational and cognitive features in Spinoza's definitions, for example:

> Fear: an inconstant pain arising from the idea of something past or future, whereof we to a certain extent doubt the issue.

> Regret: the desire or appetite to possess something, kept alive by the remembrance of the said thing, and at the same time constrained by the remembrance of other things that exclude the existence of it.

The classical philosophers contributed more than definitions, of course. For example, some declared certain emotions to be the primary or basic emotions. However, the philosophers remained armchair theorists, putting forward at best introspective or anecdotal data. The scientific advances of the nineteenth century, particularly in biology, made it possible to move beyond this.

BODILY RESPONSES AND FEELINGS: DARWIN AND JAMES

In *The Expression of Emotions in Man and Animals*, published in 1872, Charles Darwin investigated the various, mostly involuntary physiological changes, especially in the facial and skeletal muscles, which constitute the so-called "expressions" of emotions (1998 [1872]). Others broadened the investigation to include the internal visceral phenomena associated with various emotions. Still, these were thought to be investigations into mere manifestations or accompaniments of emotions. As John Dewey pointed out, "The very phrase 'expression of emotion,' … begs the question of the relation of emotion to organic peripheral action, in that it assumes the former as prior and the latter as secondary" (p. 553). It was left to the introspectionist psychologists, most notably Wilhelm Wundt and Edward Titchener, to offer a systematic account of what they regarded as "the emotions themselves," namely the subjective feeling qualities characteristic of the various emotions, an account that relied heavily on what subjects reported.

To William James, these descriptive studies of "what it is like" to feel the various emotions afforded no insight or understanding. Turning instead to the causes of these feelings, he argued, in his classic 1884 paper, "What is an Emotion?" that they were actually the felt awareness of precisely those physiological "manifestations" of emotion that Darwin and the biologists had been studying. Thus, according to James's theory (also known as the James-Lange theory), an emotion is the felt awareness of reverberations of the "bodily sounding-board," that is, of bodily reactions to something perceived or thought: reactions such as trembling, quickening of pulse, crying, running, or striking someone. It is this perception of one's own bodily responses that endows each type of emotion, such as fear, anger, and joy, with its special feeling quality. From this premise James drew the radical conclusion that emotions or emotional states were effects rather than causes of these bodily reactions. Thus common sense has it backwards: The truth is that "we feel sorry because we cry, angry because we strike, afraid because we tremble, and not that we cry, strike, or tremble, because we are sorry, angry, or fearful" (James 1884, p. 190). However, this conclusion drew on the further assumption, which James inherited from the introspectionists and from Darwin himself, that the various emotions or types of emotional state were nothing but particular feeling qualities. That is, *if* the emotions are just a subclass of feeling qualities, and *if* these feeling qualities are caused by the bodily reactions that commonsense regards as manifestations or expressions of emotion, *then* common sense has it backwards.

Whatever the merits of his arguments, the influence of James brought about a major shift in philosophical and scientific thinking about the emotions. Most important, the study of emotional feelings could no longer be regarded as a special introspective science, insulated from our general theory of human beings as biological organisms.

PHILOSOPHICAL COGNITIVISM

Opposition to the first of the Jamesian premises, which treats the various emotions as just so many feeling qualities, was a major impetus to the cognitive turn in the philosophy of emotion. However, it was above all the intentionality of emotions that put the cognitive revolution on its positive course. Starting with Anthony Kenny (1963), various authors endeavored to show that, unlike the brute physiological feeling states celebrated by James, emotions and their associated feelings had the characteristic of being *about* things and events. Thus, people sometimes are (and feel) scared of snakes or angry about the fact that their car was stolen. In this respect, emotions were thought to differ from mere bodily feelings, which, if they are about anything at all, are about bodily phenomena, rather than snakes or car thefts.

The intentionality of emotions also distinguishes them from moods, which are general response templates that are not about anything in particular, even though they may have been precipitated by the awareness of particular facts or events. In many languages the same term

may be used for both a mood and an emotion: one may be sad (or: depressed, euphoric) about something, or simply in a sad (depressed, euphoric) mood or frame of mind; or both at once. How deep the distinction between emotion and mood goes is debatable, as many so-called emotions tend to spill over from one category to the other: Initially about their original precipitant ("He's angry about the theft of his car."), they develop into a general response template ("Don't go near him, he's in an angry mood!").

Among cognitive theorists, the notion that the content of emotions takes a propositional form assumed special importance. Suppose I believe that John stole my car. I may say that my anger is about the car, about the car theft, or about what John did. However, fully parsed, my anger attribution can be logically reformulated by the phrase: I am angry about the fact that "John stole my car." Because propositions are the primary vehicles of logic and cognition, the propositional nature of emotion and its intentional objects made it easy to think of emotions in both cognitive and logical terms. It was now possible to articulate and debate what were termed the logic and structure of the various emotions and even their inferential ties to one another.

An early and forthright propositional theory is due to Robert Solomon (1976), who, with a strong emphasis on phenomenology, revived the Stoic view that emotions were themselves simply normative judgments of an urgent kind. Ronald de Sousa (1987) argued that emotions are better assimilated to perceptions. Emotions of a given type, such as fright, represent what they are about as having the corresponding property—for example, as being frightening. They also impose "determinate patterns of salience" on our thought processes: guiding our attention, our lines of inquiry, and our inferential strategies. De Sousa's view in some ways anticipates Jesse Prinz's "embodied appraisal" theory, described in the section, "Somatic Wisdom" (2004). Robert Gordon (1987) argued that most emotions are propositional attitudes that are identified by their causal relations to other propositional attitudes, especially beliefs and wishes. Most emotions are "factive," that is, about a fact (or what the subject takes to be a fact) that frustrates or satisfies a wish; others, such as being afraid or hopeful, are uncertainty emotions.

Some critics argue that propositional accounts would exclude animals and infants lacking language. This criticism would seem committed to the controversial thesis that animals without language do not have any propositional attitudes, including desires or beliefs.

Nonetheless, it would be a mistake to try to force all emotions into a propositional framework. It is hard to think of a *that*-clause that describes what love or hate is about. In some cases, what is called the same emotion (or emotion type) has both propositional and nonpropositional forms. Although one may be startled (to discover) that something is the case, one may also be startled by a sound—with no associated proposition or cognition at all. Even in the case of an emotion about a fact, it is not obvious that its content is exhausted by its propositional content.

Finally, even where propositionality is not in dispute, one may not be able to explain it in terms of standard states such as beliefs and desires. For example, to sustain the claim that fearing (hoping) that p depends on being uncertain whether p, one needs to allow for compartmentalization, for example, to distinguish between emotional and intellectual certainty; otherwise one could not account for cases where the fear (hope) that p persists despite a belief that it is not at all possible (epistemically) that p. To make such a distinction with any clarity, however, may be beyond the competency of analytic philosophy. It may require reference to the underlying neural architecture. For example, Joseph LeDoux (1998) discovered that there are distinct pathways by which the amygdala may be activated, a cortical "high road" that is cognitive, and a "low road" that bypasses the cortex and is strictly perceptual. This hypothesis nicely complements the claim that some emotional states and processes might be *modular*, that is, "hardwired" in a manner that makes them impenetrable by changes in beliefs and desires. The "quick and dirty" low road often alerts us to emergencies that our cortex "knows" do not exist. These examples suggest an analogy with perceptual illusions, which a correct belief sometimes fails to dispel.

VALENCE

Emotions are often classified by their *valence*. Theorists and laypeople tend to readily agree that emotions, or most of them, are either positive or negative. The agreement evaporates, however, as soon as they are asked, "In what respect?" One point of disagreement concerns what is being evaluated: Is it what the emotion is characteristically about that makes it positive or negative (intentional valence), or is it one's having or experiencing the emotion (experiential valence)? What it is about may be good, or something the subject appraises favorably or would wish to be the case, as in pride, delight, and hope; or it may be bad, or something the subject appraises unfavorably or would wish not to be the case, as in shame, regret, and

fear. Having or experiencing the emotion might also be judged positive or negative in any of several respects. It might be characteristically positive or negative in affect (i.e., pleasant or unpleasant), or even unconsciously aversive or attractive, and it might be beneficial or harmful, or morally good or bad. Because of such disagreements, some argue that the idea of emotional valence is of dubious value and should be abandoned.

However, it may be an important feature of emotions that they have multiple dimensions of valence. If an emotion's experiential valence is of the same sign (positive or negative) as its intentional valence—for example, an aversive emotion that is about something that is bad for you or goes against your wishes—then it is likely to promote rational decision-making and action. The actions people take to alleviate the unpleasantness or aversiveness of fear (a negative aspect of having or experiencing the emotion) tend to reduce the risk of bad things happening (a negative aspect of what the emotion is about): for example, fear of a flood leads the inhabitants to retreat to high ground, thereby averting disaster. (There are of course thrill-seekers for whom the very aversiveness of fear has a second-order attractiveness, and, within the safe confines of dramatic art, many people can enjoy the fear or "as-if" fear they empathetically experience.)

Likewise, the possible negative consequences of a decision tend to be amplified in our minds by our anticipation of regret and remorse: For example, if I buy this appealing but unreliable car, I may kick myself if anything goes wrong with it. These premonitory influences may on the whole guide us to useful behavior, in roughly the way that hunger, thirst, and sexual feelings lead us, wittingly or not, to behavior that is conducive to biological fitness. Add to this theme of doubly valenced emotions a revival of James's second premise, that emotional feelings are perceptions of bodily reactions, and we are led to the topic of the next section.

SOMATIC WISDOM

From Plato onward, European and North American philosophers have thought the regulation of emotion essential to a rational life, and a similar view was promoted even earlier in Buddhism and other Asian religions. The underlying supposition was that unregulated emotions are impediments to the rational life. However, this is compatible with the thesis held by a number of philosophers that emotions, or at least some of them, make a positive and possible indispensable contribution to rational decision-making. According to De Sousa, for example, emotions are indispensable for guiding our attention, our lines of inquiry, and our inferential strategies.

It was suggested earlier in this article that if an emotion's experiential valence matches its intentional valence, then it is likely to promote rational decision-making. A similar view has received support from findings in neurology and neuroscience, most prominently by the cognitive neuroscientist Antonio Damasio (1994) and his coworkers. Damasio's somatic marker hypothesis holds that successful and unsuccessful decision outcomes produce differing bodily responses—for example, as measured by skin conductance—and the accumulation of such responses over time leads to anticipatory bodily responses that guide future decision-making. One need not be aware (phenomenally conscious) of these responses in order for them to influence decision-making. However, a part of one's frontal cortex (functionally, the somatosensory or body-sensing cortex) must keep track of them. Most of the supporting data have come from observations of decision-making deficits in people with prefrontal damage and comparison with normal subjects in experimental gambling tasks. Additional data suggest that the capacity to recognize and to name certain emotions in others on the basis of their facial expressions also depends on the capacity to monitor one's bodily responses when observing them. Damasio's theory goes far beyond this, and some of it is controversial; but this brief statement makes it clear why Damasio thinks the aversiveness or attractiveness of undergoing certain emotions can be a premonitory influence that sometimes "knows" better than pure reason does which decision paths are likely to lead to preferred outcomes.

Prinz is probably the first philosopher to build a general theory of emotion on a broad and richly detailed account of empirical research. Although sympathetic to the somatic theories of James and Damasio, he argues that our emotional "gut reactions," unlike pains, tickles, and feelings of fatigue, are representational states. Applying Dretske's thesis that a state may be representational in virtue of having an evolved function of carrying a certain class of information, he argues that these bodily changes constitute perceptual appraisals or evaluations of our relationship to the environment with respect to well-being. He calls his view a non-propositional appraisal theory, because he holds that emotions need not involve propositional attitudes such as belief, judgments, and desires (2004).

THE NATURE OF THINGS

The classical definitions of emotions were answers to questions of the traditional Socratic form: "What is regret?" "What is fear?" and so forth. The aim was not to capture the nuances of ordinary usage, but rather to be telling us something about ourselves: to explain, as Spinoza said, "not the meaning of words, but the nature of things" (1883 [1677], p. 178). However, if this is the ambition of the philosophy of emotion, then some philosophers would reply that it is up to science and not philosophy to tell us about the nature of things. In particular, we have to look beyond the terms of ordinary language and the concepts embedded in our everyday "folk" psychology, beyond even the best philosophical attempts to regiment these terms and concepts, if we are to discover what the emotions *really* are. This appears to be a special application of a more general view in philosophy of mind, that of eliminative materialism. However, whatever the merits of that general indictment of everyday psychology and any philosophy that attempts to build on it, there may be special reasons to be skeptical of traditional philosophical thinking about the emotions in particular.

Paul Griffiths maintains that we should use biological evolutionary principles of classification to determine what emotions *really* are. Following Paul Ekman (1992), a leading innovator on the role of facial expression in emotion, Griffiths posits surprise, anger, fear, disgust, sadness, and joy as the basic emotions. These adaptive responses are *evolutionary homologues*, discrete genetically ordained behavioral syndromes that are a legacy of our shared mammalian heritage. Appearing in all cultures, these adaptive responses are associated with the same facial expressions in each culture. The classification here is by descent and homology, rather than by resemblance and analogy, which is more typical of analytic approaches. The special evolutionary status of these basic emotions is reflected in Griffith's philosophical declaration that they are *natural kinds*. That is, they are *projectible* kinds: They share causal properties that are sufficiently well correlated to sustain generalizations from known to unknown cases. However, the term *emotions* does not designate a natural class of kind, for it would serve no scientific purpose to group them with the so-called higher cognitive emotions, such as envy, regret, and shame. Predictably, this thesis has sparked controversy, just as the general thesis of eliminative materialism did two decades earlier. Prinz counters that all emotions are valenced appraisals that exploit common aversive or appetitive mechanisms. Louis Charland (2002) suggests that there is a natural kind of organism that might be called an *emoter*, in virtue of having a brain that meets certain criteria of functional organization.

NORMATIVITY AND CULTURE

Evidently all cultures have implicit rules governing at least some emotions: not just whether and how they should be expressed, but also whether and under what conditions and in what degree one should have them. In European and North American cultures, at least, emotional responses are commonly measured by standards of rationality, appropriateness, and morality. A particular instance of an emotion may be thought irrational if it is based on an irrational belief or desire. However, it is common to think an instance of emotion may be irrational even if it is not based on an irrational belief or desire; typically, because it is not suited to what it is about. We also judge instances of emotions as too little or too much, for example, in the case of grief or remorse.

It was suggested earlier that the notion of passivity, of being acted on, may be an important feature of the ordinary concept of emotion. However, it is widely assumed that people have some control over how the environment acts on them and are to some degree responsible, not only for the expression of emotion, but for their having the emotion. Aside from regulating one's exposure to eliciting situations, it is supposed that one can in many cases alter the course of the emotion—for example, by intervening cognitively to reappraise the eliciting situation. Indeed, attending to one's emotional state and labeling it may alter the state. It is plausible that when we use emotion labels in giving expression to our emotion, as in, "I'm angry!" Or "I'm in love!" We are shaping as well as describing our emotional state. Emotion kinds would thus be what Ian Hacking (1995) calls "interactive kinds," like race, ethnicity, and gender: To classify one's own state as of a particular interactive kind, or to be so classified by others, tends to alter the state and to influence one's feelings and behavior accordingly.

Social constructionists would emphasize that we are shaping our emotions to fit it into an acceptable cultural mold. The psychologist James Averill argued that the various emotion concepts are merely cultural creations that shape our assessment of certain transitory syndromes. While pretending to be passively moved to behave in certain ways, people are actively adjusting their behavior to fit these cultural categories. Although this theory is a valuable counterbalance to the widely held assumption that our emotions simply "are what they are," it would be extreme to assert that our emotion categories simply create our emotions *ex nihilo* or to deny that the categories themselves are, perhaps in some societies more than in others, flexible and open to change (Reddy 2003).

Emotions seem a particularly nuanced category, varying in uncharted ways from instance to instance. They also vary in the course they follow from moment to moment and day to day. For reasons such as these, as Iris Murdoch (1970), Martha Nussbaum (2001), and Jon Elster (1999) have emphasized, often the best way of defining an emotion type is by reference to literary examples. Literary examples also make it clear that conceptions of emotion vary over time as well as from one present-day culture to another.

The issues addressed in this section may seem hopelessly tender-minded to philosophers who prefer to focus on biological mechanisms and natural kinds. In turn, philosophers drawn to the issues of this section may find the naturalistic focus excessively narrow. What is chiefly at issue is the proper equipment to bring to philosophical thinking about emotions. Should we allow ourselves to conceive human organisms as people and to employ the full panoply of concepts, learned or biologically preordained, that appear to be indispensable for everyday social perception and understanding? Or should we lay aside these concepts and steadfastly conceive human beings only as complex biological systems?

Retaining our everyday tools of social perception, we will find normative questions, matters of passivity and freedom, and the richness and perspectivity of narrative understanding coming to the fore. Laying these tools aside, we can focus on purely naturalistic explanations of emotional phenomena and the natural kinds that enter into these explanations. Partisans of the naturalistic approach may be tempted to assert that only by laying aside the accustomed tools can we discover what emotions "really" are. Partisans of the other approach might argue that to lay down these tools of social perception is precisely to forego understanding people. One important challenge task for the philosophy of emotion will be to determine whether and how to reconcile these two approaches.

See also Alston, William P.; James, William.

Bibliography

Ben-Ze'ev, Aaron. *The Subtlety of Emotions.* Cambridge, MA: MIT Press, 2000.

Charland, Louis C. "The Natural Kind Status of Emotion." *British Journal for the Philosophy of Science* 53 (2002): 511–537.

Damasio, Antonio. *Descartes' Error: Emotion, Reason, and the Human Brain.* New York: Putnam, 1994.

D'Arms, J., and D. Jacobson. "Expressivism, Morality, and the Emotions." *Ethics* 104 (1994): 739–763.

Darwin, Charles. *The Expression of the Emotions in Man and Animals.* London: John Murray, 1872.

Descartes, Rene. *The Passions of the Soul.* 1649. In *The Philosophical Writings of Descartes.* Vol. 1. Translated by John Cottingham, Robert Stoothoff, and Dugald Murdoch. Cambridge, U.K.: Cambridge University Press, 1984.

de Sousa, Ronald. *The Rationality of Emotion.* Cambridge, MA: MIT Press, 1987.

Dewey, John. "The Theory of Emotion. (I) Emotional Attitudes." *Psychological Review* 1 (1894): 553–569.

Dixon, Thomas. *From Passions to Emotions: The Creation of a Secular Category.* Cambridge, U.K.: Cambridge University Press, 2003.

Ekman, Paul. "An Argument for Basic Emotions." *Cognition and Emotion* 6 (1992): 169–200.

Elster, Jon. *Alchemies of the Mind: Rationality and the Emotions.* Cambridge, U.K.: Cambridge University Press, 1999.

Goldie, Peter. *The Emotions: A Philosophical Exploration.* Oxford: Oxford University Press, 2000.

Gordon, Robert. *The Structure of Emotions.* Cambridge, U.K.: Cambridge University Press, 1987.

Greenspan, Patricia. *Emotions and Reasons: An Inquiry into Emotional Justification.* New York: Routledge, 1989.

Griffiths, Paul E. *What Emotions Really Are: The Problem of Psychological Categories.* Chicago: University of Chicago Press, 1997.

Hacking, Ian. *Rewriting the Soul: Multiple Personality and the Sciences of Memory.* Cambridge, MA: Harvard University Press, 1995.

Jaggar, Alison. "Love and Knowledge: Emotion in Feminist Epistemology." *Inquiry* 32 (1989): 151–176.

James, William. "What is an Emotion?" *Mind* 9 (1884): 188–205.

Kenny, Anthony. *Action, Emotion and Will.* London: Routledge, 1963.

Lazarus, Richard. "The Cognition-Emotion Debate: A Bit of History." In *Handbook of Cognition and Emotion,* edited by Tim Dalgleish and Mick J. Power. Chichester, NY: John Wiley and Sons, 1999.

LeDoux, Joseph. *The Emotional Brain: The Mysterious Underpinnings of Emotional Life.* New York: Simon and Schuster, 1998.

Lyons, William. *Emotion.* Cambridge, U.K.: Cambridge University Press, 1980.

Murdoch, Iris. *The Sovereignty of Good.* London: Routledge, 1970.

Neu, Jerome. *A Tear is an Intellectual Thing: The Meanings of Emotion.* New York: Oxford University Press, 2000.

Nussbaum, Martha. *Upheavals of Thought: The Intelligence of Emotions.* Cambridge, U.K.: Cambridge University Press, 2001.

Oatley, Keith. *Emotions: A Brief History.* Oxford: Blackwell, 2004.

Ortony, A., and T. J. Turner. "What's Basic About Basic Emotions?" *Psychological Review* 97 (3) (1990): 315–331.

Panksepp, Jaak. *Affective Neuroscience: The Foundations of Human and Animal Emotions.* New York: Oxford University Press, 1998.

Prinz, Jesse. *Gut Reactions: A Perceptual Theory of Emotion.* Oxford: Oxford University Press, 2004.

Reddy, William. *The Navigation of Feeling: A Framework for the History of Emotions.* Cambridge, U.K.: Cambridge University Press, 2003.

Roberts, Robert C. *Emotions: An Essay in Aid of Moral Psychology.* Cambridge, U.K.: Cambridge University Press, 2003.

Robinson, Jenefer. "Startle." *The Journal of Philosophy* 92 (1995): 53–74.

Rorty, Amelie. "Explaining Emotions." In *Explaining Emotions,* edited by Amélie Rorty, 103–126. Los Angeles: University of California Press, 1980.

Russell, James A. "Core Affect and the Psychological Construction of Emotion." *Psychological Review* 110 (1) (2003): 145–172.

Solomon, Robert. *The Passions.* New York: Doubleday, 1976.

Sorabji, Richard. *Emotion and Peace of Mind: From Stoic Agitation to Christian Temptation.* Oxford: Oxford University Press, 2000.

Spinoza, Benedict. *Ethics.* Translated by R.H.M. Elwes. London: George Bell & Sons, 1883.

Wollheim, Richard. *On the Emotions.* New Haven, CT: Yale University Press, 1999.

Zajonc, Robert, B. "The Interaction of Affect and Cognition." In *Approaches to Emotion,* edited by Klaus Scherer and Paul Ekman. Hillsdale, NJ: Erlbaum, 1984.

Louis C. Charland (2005)
Robert M. Gordon (2005)

EMOTIVE THEORY OF ETHICS

The term *emotivism* refers to a theory about moral judgments, sentences, words, and speech acts; it is sometimes also extended to cover aesthetic and other nonmoral forms of evaluation. Although sometimes used to refer to the entire genus, strictly speaking *emotivism* is the name of only the earliest version of ethical noncognitivism (also known as expressivism and nondescriptivism).

Classical noncognitivist theories maintain that moral judgments and speech acts function primarily to (a) express and (b) influence states of mind or attitudes rather than to describe, report, or represent facts, which they do only secondarily if at all. For example: To say "Stealing is wrong" is not primarily to report any facts about stealing but to express one's negative attitude toward it. Emotivists also deny, therefore, that there are any moral facts or that moral words like *good*, *bad*, *right*, and *wrong* predicate moral properties; they typically deny that moral claims are evaluable as true or false—at least in respect of their primary meaning. The attitudes expressed by moral judgments are held to be "conative" (that is, they have a motivational element) and not "cognitive" (that is, they are not beliefs/do not have representational content). Species of noncognitivism are differentiated by the kinds of attitude they associate with moral thought and discourse: emotivism claims that moral thought and discourse express emotions (affective attitudes, sentiments, or feelings) or similar mental states, typically of approval and disapproval, and is therefore sometimes called the "boo-hurrah" theory of ethics.

To understand emotivism, it is important to contrast it with subjectivism, the view that moral judgments and utterances represent, report, or describe someone's attitudes (for example, that we can translate "Stealing is wrong" as "I disapprove of stealing"). Noncognitivist theories deny that moral expressions of attitude take the form of report or description: They are often vague about the expressive mechanism, but it is supposed to bear a family resemblance to that of ejaculations (for example, uttering "Ouch!" to express being in pain) and performatives (for example, saying "Thank you" to express gratitude). Saying "Stealing is wrong" is therefore like saying "Boo to stealing!"

The significance of this difference is apparent, to the advantage of noncognitivism, when one examines what the strategies have to say about moral disagreements. Subjectivists must accept—whereas noncognitivists deny—that moral claims are made true or false by facts about people's attitudes. If A asserts "Stealing is wrong," and B responds "Stealing is not wrong," it is possible, from a subjectivist view, for A and B to be expressing compatible judgments—if they are reporting the attitudes of different people—and therefore not actually to be disagreeing at all. Although noncognitivism does not portray A and B as disagreeing about any fact, it does claim a "disagreement in attitude": A opposes stealing, and B does not.

According to emotivists, we engage in moral discourse in order to influence the behavior and attitudes of others. They claim, therefore, that moral utterances have a psychological function of arousing emotions in others, based on a human susceptibility to emotional influence by exposure to the emotional expressions of others. Charles L. Stevenson even identifies a statement's emotive meaning with this causal tendency.

Almost all emotivist theories acknowledge that moral judgments possess some content that is descriptive and truth-apt. Consider first "thick" evaluative terms such as the names of virtues or vices (for example, *brave*) and pejoratives (for example, *geek*); here it is easy to distinguish a descriptive meaning and an emotive meaning.

But most emotivists also ascribe descriptive content to "thin" evaluative terms like *good* and *right*. One common account of this content (Stevenson 1944, Edwards 1955, Hare 1952, Dreier 1990, Barker 2000, Gibbard 2003) is that the property predicated of an object T by *wrong*, for example, is the property for which the speaker disapproves of T. Suppose Elizabeth declares "Stealing is wrong" and disapproves of stealing because she believes it typically causes misfortune to its victims; then the descriptive meaning of her utterance is that stealing typically causes misfortune to its victims. However, this meaning is deemed secondary because (a) it depends upon the emotive meaning—the descriptive meaning of *wrong* will differ from context to context, speaker to speaker, and even occasion to occasion, according to what arouses speakers' emotions, and (b) it has little or no moral significance. A and B will argue over whether stealing is wrong if they differ in attitude toward stealing but not if they differ only with regard to which properties arouse their disapproval of stealing or over whether stealing has some particular property.

HISTORY AND DEVELOPMENT

Although suggestions of emotivism can be found throughout the history of philosophy (David Hume and other early modern sentimentalists have particularly close affinities), the emergence of the theory is usually attributed to a series of short suggestions by British philosophers in the 1920s and 1930s (Ogden and Richards 1923, Barnes 1933, A. S. Duncan Jones as reported in Broad 1933–1934, Ayer 1936); however, earlier formulations appear in German/Austrian value theory from the late nineteenth century (Lotze 1885, Windelband 1903, Marty 1908, and see Satris 1987 for this influence on Anglo-American emotivism). The British emotivists were reacting, in part, to the metaethical theory of nonnaturalism (or intuitionism) advocated by G. E. Moore, H. A. Pritchard, W. D. Ross, and others.

Moore had persuasively argued that moral words could not be defined except in terms of other moral words and inferred (invalidly, as was revealed by the discovery that nonsynonymous terms could be coreferential) that moral words could not refer to "natural" or empirical properties and that moral sentences could not describe natural or empirical facts. Any such attempted definition left out something essential. (This claim is closely related to the alleged is/ought distinction, or "fact-value gap"). Emotivists were convinced by these arguments, but some, influenced by logical positivism—the doctrine that only sentences which are empirically verifiable are meaningful—balked at the notion of "nonnatural," nonempirical moral properties and facts. In their diagnosis, the essential something that cannot be captured by any naturalistic analysis of moral language is the expression of speakers' emotions.

Emotivism found its greatest and most dedicated champion in the person of the American philosopher Charles L. Stevenson (1937, 1944) and enjoyed its heyday in the 1940s and 1950s (Nowell-Smith 1954, Edwards 1955) before being largely supplanted by forms of noncognitivism that were thought to be less vulnerable to objection (especially the prescriptivism of Hare 1952, 1963). To philosophers seeking to condemn the horrors of World War II in absolute terms, the claim that moral judgments merely express feelings appeared inadequate. Emotivism's legacy is a widespread recognition today of the significance of emotions for ethical thought, and the efforts of a number of contemporary philosophers since the 1980s—most notably Simon Blackburn (1993, 1998)—who continue to argue for its central tenets.

THE CASE FOR EMOTIVISM

The philosophical stature of emotivism has risen from a number of solidly argued foundations: the apparent failures of efforts to give naturalistic definitions of moral words or to identify natural properties as their referents, epistemological scruples about the existence of nonnatural properties, and the reliable link between moral judgment and emotion. Philosophers still vigorously disagree about whether or not it is possible to find objective referents for moral terms, however, and there are alternative explanations of the connection between moral judgment and emotion: perhaps moral words name properties that reliably arouse emotional responses in us, perhaps they name the dispositional properties of reliably arousing emotional responses, or perhaps their use conversationally communicates speakers' approval and disapproval without in any strict sense "meaning" it.

Further, many philosophers maintain that it is possible and not very unusual for people to make sincere moral judgments without feeling or expressing the relevant emotion (this discussion centers on a figure known as the "amoralist") and that emotive meaning is, therefore, not an essential element of moral judgment. Emotivists commonly respond with the claim that these are not genuine moral judgments but are made in "inverted commas"—i.e. that they merely mimic the practice of moral judgment. The case for emotivism is not bolstered by this claim, however, unless grounds can be found for accepting the "inverted commas" diagnosis that are independent of emotivist convictions themselves.

The emotivist explanation of moral language also provides simple answers to a number of puzzles in metaethics: First, it explains the fact that people are typically motivated to behave in accordance with their moral judgments. Cognitivists have some difficulty explaining this motivational connection because they identify moral judgments with beliefs. On an orthodox view, a belief is not enough to motivate action by itself; it needs to be combined with a desire or similar conative attitude. But, according to emotivism, moral judgments consist in favorable and unfavorable attitudes, and people are likely to perform the actions they feel favorably toward and likely to avoid actions toward which they feel unfavorably.

Second, emotivism explains the synthetic a priori character of moral judgment stressed by nonnaturalists: that is, that despite the fact that an empirical description of a state of affairs or action entails neither by logic nor by meaning the goodness or badness or rightness or wrongness of that state of affairs or action, its description alone nonetheless suffices for us to be confident in passing moral judgment on it. Although it may seem mysterious how anyone could know just from description of a state of affairs or action that it necessarily possesses some further, unspecified property, we have no such need for further information in order to respond emotionally.

Third, emotivism explains the supervenience of the moral on the empirical: why moral characteristics are such that if two states of affairs differ in any moral respect, they must also differ in some nonmoral or empirical respect. If a person is disposed to have a certain emotional response to some state of affairs, then he or she is disposed to have the same response to any qualitatively identical state of affairs. A person will be disposed to make the same moral judgment about two states of affairs, therefore, unless there is some difference between those states that arouses different emotions. While emotivism has an easier task offering solutions to these problems than most descriptivist theories, it must contend with noncognitivist rivals that offer similar explanatory resources.

PROBLEMS

Most of the objections to emotivism in particular are also objections to noncognitivism in general and focus on respects in which moral thought and discourse behave like ordinary, factual, truth-evaluable cognitive thought and discourse. These objections have been widely believed to refute noncognitivism of all varieties, and accordingly the emphasis in recent noncognitivist writing is on the "quasi-realist" project (Blackburn 1993) of explaining how nondescriptive thought and discourse can mimic ordinary descriptive thought and discourse. The treatment here focuses on the significance of these objections for emotivist theories.

THE EMBEDDING (OR FREGE-GEACH) PROBLEM.

Emotivism purports to tell us the meaning of moral sentences; however as P. T. Geach (1960, 1965) and John Searle (1962) have pointed out, it and other forms of noncognitivism appear to succeed at most at explaining one kind of use of simple moral sentences: their use in direct assertion (for example, saying "Stealing is wrong"). Emotivism claims the descriptive form of simple moral sentences is merely a disguise. However simple moral sentences are also given many other uses in which they also behave like descriptive sentences and for which emotivist explanations seem inappropriate or impossible. Consider embedding of simple moral sentences into complex sentences and indirect contexts: disjunctions ("Either stealing is wrong, or Robin Hood was a saint"), belief ascriptions ("Elizabeth believes that stealing is wrong"), conditionals ("If stealing is wrong, then Joe ought not take Mary's lunch"), predications of falsehood ("It is not true that stealing is wrong"), and interrogatives ("Is it true that stealing is wrong?). In each case, a speaker uses the simple moral sentence "Stealing is wrong" but does not express emotions or unfavorable attitudes towards stealing. The emotivist proposal therefore is not helpful in understanding the simple moral sentence in these uses, which is reason to doubt whether it has captured its meaning at all.

It is possible to extend the emotivist account by assigning meanings in each of these contexts, but doing so introduces a further difficulty. Consider a simple moral argument: *P1. If stealing is wrong, then Joe ought not take Mary's lunch; P2. Stealing is wrong; P3. Therefore, Joe ought not take Mary's lunch.* This looks like a standard instance of *modus ponens* and therefore a straightforwardly valid argument. But if we attribute different meanings to "stealing is wrong" as it occurs in each premise, then the argument equivocates, and the conclusion doesn't follow. (Indeed, if P2 is interpreted as a mere expression of emotion without truth value, nothing can logically follow from it). Emotivism therefore casts doubt on the possibility of drawing inferences to or from moral claims—something we do all the time.

Emotivists as early as Stevenson made use of minimalist theories of truth to argue as follows: to claim that

p is true is simply to claim that *p*, so anyone who is disposed to claim "Stealing is wrong" is entitled to claim that "Stealing is wrong is true." But as the discovery of the embedding problem postdates emotivism's heyday, we do not find solutions to it from self-identified emotivists. Contemporary noncognitivists, however, devote much attention to the problem (especially Blackburn), and there are two broad strategies available: First, if some meaning can be found for the simple moral sentence that is common to these various embeddings and is compatible with emotivism, then arguably standard logic will allow moral inferences. There are two possibilities here. (a) Some seek to identify a noncognitive content that is common to all uses of moral sentences and that plausibly can be embedded in different sentential contexts. These efforts are characteristically found outside of the emotivist tradition (particularly in the work of Hare and Allan Gibbard), and the strategy does not seem so compatible with the emotivist doctrine that simple moral sentences express emotions; (b) Emotivists can turn to the supposed secondary descriptive content of moral claims to explain moral inferences. Because these descriptive contents have truth values, there is no difficulty in forming valid arguments with them. The success of any such explanation depends on the plausibility of the emotivist's claim to have identified the truth-conditional content of the premises and conclusions of moral arguments; it is also arguable that any success must come at the cost of abandoning genuine emotivism and noncognitivism.

Second, even if it is granted that there are no truth relations between the premises of moral arguments and between the contents of moral judgments, it is arguable that there are relations of coherence or consistency between the judgments or states of mind that express those contents. Blackburn accordingly proposes and develops a "logic of attitudes," a system of norms governing the consistency of combinations of attitudes. The conditional premise P1 above, on this view, expresses approval of disapproval of Joe's taking Mary's lunch in the circumstance that one disapproves of stealing. A's attitudes are then allegedly inconsistent if A holds both this second-order attitude and the attitude of disapproval towards stealing expressed by P2 but does not also disapprove of Joe's taking Mary's lunch, the attitude allegedly expressed by P3. Accused by a number of critics of conflating logical inconsistency with pragmatic incoherence (Hale 1986, Schueler 1988, Brighouse 1990, and Zangwill 1992), Blackburn suggests that we can expand the concept of consistency to encompass pragmatic and logical forms. Critics argue that this strategy is not successful: because there is no form of merely pragmatic incoherence that exactly mimics logical inconsistency, Blackburn must claim that some apparently valid moral arguments are actually inconsistent (Hale 1993 and Van Roojen 1996), but noncognitivists have not been deterred.

REASONS AND JUSTIFICATION. Emotivism is charged with being unable to accommodate the important role of rational argument in moral discourse and dispute. Although it emphasizes moral discourse's function of influencing others' behavior, it is thought to characterize this efficacy wrongly, as similar in kind to that employed in manipulation, intimidation, and propaganda. According to emotivists, we engage in moral argumentation with the immediate aim of arousing emotions in others, and moral utterances accomplish this by direct psychological causation. Their opponents object that genuine moral discourse involves furnishing others with reasons, as rational agents, to recognize as correct and thereby accept one's moral views (Hare 1951 and Brandt 1959).

It is true that conscientious moral debaters offer factual considerations as evidence or justification for their positions, and emotivists do not deny it. According to Stevenson, moral argument can take both "rational" and "nonrational" (or "persuasive") forms. On Stevenson's view, by a "reason" for a moral judgment we mean any factual consideration that might influence someone's emotions in the direction of that judgment, and therefore "rational" means of moral argument consist in offering such considerations. Protagonists in a debate over the morality of legalized abortion, for example, might dispute the facts about its consequences. "Persuasive" argumentation, on the other hand, consists in the use of emotive language for its direct psychological effects.

One line of objection, spearheaded by Richard Brandt, observes that it is possible to be emotionally influenced by considerations that are morally irrelevant, and argues that emotivism cannot accommodate the distinction between what is morally relevant and morally irrelevant. Stevenson's reply exhibits a typical noncognitivist strategy: he insists that we can meaningfully distinguish between morally relevant and irrelevant influences on people's attitudes but that when we do so, we are making further moral (and hence emotive) judgments. To judge a consideration morally irrelevant is therefore to express disapproval of being emotionally influenced by it.

OTHER OBJECTIONS. Clearly not just any emotional response constitutes a moral judgment. Emotivists therefore distinguish moral judgments from other kinds of affective or conative reaction by appealing to a distinctive kind (or kinds) of moral emotion. Some critics object that moral approval and disapproval cannot be adequately differentiated from other kinds of affective and conative states without invoking the very moral concepts that emotivists seek to explain by them—and therefore that moral emotions are in fact cognitive attitudes. Moral approval, for example, can arguably only be adequately characterized as the attitude of judging something to be morally good. If this is correct, then emotivism puts the cart before the horse in attempting to explain moral judgments by appeal to emotional states. However, if moral attitudes are not cognitive and are simply affective or conative responses, then it is questionable whether they have the sort of first-person authority that moral judgments purport to possess. If Gary's judgment that homosexuality is morally wrong rests on nothing more than a disposition to have an unpleasant feeling when he contemplates homosexuality, then he may have as good or better reason to resist, suppress, or work to change his emotional sensibilities as he has to oppose homosexuality.

Another concern addresses whether emotivism has the resources to distinguish between accepting the negation of a moral claim and not accepting that moral claim. Believing that the next president of the United States will not be a woman is not the same mental state as not believing that the next president of the United States will be a woman; likewise it seems that accepting that abortion is not wrong is not the same mental state as not accepting that abortion is wrong. Critics charge, however, that emotivism has to explain both in terms of not feeling disapproval toward abortion.

See also Brandt, R. B.; Ethical Relativism; Ethical Subjectivism; Ethics, History of; Ethics, Problems of; Hare, Richard M.; Hume, David; Intuitionism and Intuitionistic Logic, Ethical; Logical Positivism; Moore, George Edward; Noncognitivism; Ross, William David; Searle, John; Stevenson, Charles L.; Value and Valuation.

Bibliography

Ayer, A. J. *Language, Truth and Logic.* London: Gollancz, 1936.
Barker, Stephen J. "Is Value Content a Component of Conventional Implicature?" *Analysis* 60 (2000): 268–279.
Barnes, W. H. F. "A Suggestion about Value." *Analysis* 1 (1933): 45–46.
Blackburn, Simon. *Essays in Quasi-Realism.* New York: Oxford University Press, 1993.
Blackburn, Simon. *Ruling Passions.* New York: Oxford University Press, 1998.
Brandt, Richard. *Ethical Theory.* Englewood Cliffs, NJ: Prentice-Hall, 1959.

Brighouse, M. H. "Blackburn's Projectivism—An Objection," *Philosophical Studies* 59 (1990): 225–233.

Broad, C. D. "Is 'Goodness' the Name of a Simple, Non-natural Quality?" *Proceedings of the Aristotelian Society* 34 (1933–1934): 249-268.

Dreier, Jamie. "Internalism and Speaker Relativism." *Ethics* 101 (1990): 6–26.

Edwards, Paul. *The Logic of Moral Discourse.* Glencoe. IL: Free Press, 1955.

Geach, P. T. "Ascriptivism." *Philosophical Review* 69 (1960): 221–225.

Geach, P. T. "Assertion." *Philosophical Review* 74 (1965): 449–465.

Gibbard, Allan. *Thinking How to Live.* Cambridge. MA: Harvard University Press, 2003.

Hale, Bob. "Can There Be a Logic of Attitudes?" In *Reality: Representation and Projection*, edited by J. Haldane and C. Wright. Oxford: Oxford University Press, 1993.

Hale, Bob. "The Compleat Projectivist." *Philosophical Quarterly* 36 (1986): 65–84.

Hare, R. M. "Freedom of the Will." *Proceedings of the Aristotelian Society* 25 (1951): 201–216.

Hare, R. M. *Freedom and Reason.* Oxford: Clarendon Press, 1963.

Hare, R. M. *The Language of Morals.* Oxford: Clarendon Press, 1952.

Lotze, Hermann. *Outlines of Logic and the Encyclopedia of Philosophy*, edited and translated by G. T. Ladd. Boston: Ginn, 1885.

Marty, Anton. (1908). *Untersuchungen zur Grundlegung der allgemeinen Grammatik und Sprachphilosophie.* Halle: Niemeyer.

Nowell-Smith, P. H. *Ethics.* Baltimore: Penguin Books, 1954.

Ogden, C. K., and I. A. Richards. *The Meaning of Meaning.* New York: Harcourt, 1923.

Satris, Stephen. *Ethical Emotivism.* Dordrecht: Martinus Nijhoff, 1987.

Schueler, G. F. "Modus Ponens and Moral Realism." *Ethics* 98 (1988): 492–500.

Searle, John. "Meaning and Speech Acts." *Philosophical Review* 71 (1962): 423–432.

Stevenson, Charles L. *Ethics and Language.* New Haven: Yale University Press, 1944.

Stevenson, Charles L. "The Emotive Meaning of Moral Terms." *Mind* 46 (1937): 14–31.

Urmson, J. O. *The Emotive Theory of Ethics.* London: Hutcheson, 1968.

Van Roojen, Mark. "Expressivism and Irrationality." *The Philosophical Review* 105 (1996): 311–335.

Windelband, Wilhelm. "Was ist Philosophie?" In *Präludien: aufsätze und reden zur philosophie und ihrer geschichte.* 2nd ed. Tübingen: J. C. B. Mohr, 1903

Nick Zangwill. "Moral Modus Ponens." *Ratio* 5 (1992): 177–193.

Stephen Finlay (2005)

EMPEDOCLES
(5th century BCE–after 444 BCE)

Empedocles, the Greek poet, prophet, and natural philosopher, was the originator of the doctrine of four elements that dominated Western cosmology and medical thought down to the Renaissance. Empedocles was born in Acragas (Agrigento), Sicily, in the early fifth century BCE and died sometime after 444 BCE. He played a political role in his native city, apparently as a democratic leader, was later exiled, and traveled through other Greek colonies in southern Italy. In one of his poems he describes himself as a "deathless god, no longer a mortal," surrounded wherever he goes by admiring crowds asking for advice, for prophecy, and for a "healing word" to cure them from disease (Fr. 112). A number of anecdotes illustrate his reputation for supernatural powers (including the raising of the dead), and the legend that he died by throwing himself into the crater of Etna gives us an idea of the charismatic impression he left behind in the popular imagination. Modern scholars have often found it difficult to reconcile the scientific and the religious sides of Empedocles' thought. He expounded his views in powerful hexameters, of which considerable fragments are preserved from two distinct poems, *On the Nature of Things* (*Peri Physeōs*) and *Purifications* (*Katharmoi*).

NATURAL PHILOSOPHY

Theophrastus said that Empedocles was much influenced by Parmenides and even more by the Pythagoreans. Pythagorean influence must be seen in his religious teaching and probably also in the role that he assigns to numerical proportion in the natural combination of the elements. From Parmenides he accepted the fundamental principle that nothing can arise out of nothing, nor can anything perish into nonentity. But whereas for Parmenides this meant that all motion and change must be illusory, Empedocles admits that there is real process in nature: "the mixture and separation of things mixed."

By accepting four distinct elements, or "roots of all things," in place of Parmenides' monolithic Being, Empedocles is able to explain natural change as a result of the combination, separation, and regrouping of indestructible entities. There remains, of course, something illusory about the kaleidoscopic appearance of change. Since there can be no generation or annihilation of anything real, Empedocles insists that to describe natural processes in terms of birth and becoming or death and destruction is to follow a linguistic usage which is systematically misleading (Frs. 8–12). In reality there is only the mixing, unmixing, and remixing of permanent entities.

One generation later a similar view of the discrepancy between the appearance of continual change and the reality of unchanging entities led Democritus to distinguish between primary (or true) and secondary (or conventional) sense qualities. However, there is no reason to believe that Empedocles envisaged any such distinction. He assigns the qualities of color, heat, and moisture to the elements themselves and describes the formation of compounds by analogy with the action of a painter mixing his colors. He seems not to have faced the difficult question posed by such analogies: In what does the indestructibility of the elements consist if their essential properties are those that are seen to change?

Nevertheless, the simplicity of this tetradic scheme and its direct application to the great cosmic masses of land, sea, atmosphere, and celestial fire (that is, sun, stars, and lightning) led Plato, Aristotle, and most of their successors to adopt the doctrine of four elements in variously modified forms. Empedocles himself developed the doctrine in a grandiose cosmology that can be reconstructed only in part. The four elements interact under the influence of two cosmic powers, Love (or Aphrodite), on the one hand, and Strife (or Quarrel), on the other. These powers function respectively as forces of attraction and repulsion, but they are also conceived of concretely as ingredients in the mixture. They operate as a kind of dynamic fluid, comparable in some respects to the concept of phlogiston in early modern science. The power of Love or attraction acts first by bringing like together with like—for instance, earth to earth, fire to fire—but it also assimilates the elements to one another, so that what were originally unlikes become like and are united in a new, homogeneous compound (Fr. 22). Love thus represents the power of organic unity and creative combination.

The process of world formation occurs in a cycle that may be said to begin with a totally homogeneous fusion of the elements in a primordial sphere under the exclusive influence of Love. The process of differentiation is set off when Strife makes its entry into the sphere, in accordance with some fixed periodic scheme. It would seem that the cosmic sphere is always saturated with one or the other of these powers or, more frequently, with both of them in a variable ratio; the quantity of Love present in the world varies inversely to that of Strife (Frs. 35 and 16). The life cycle of the universe thus oscillates between the poles of unity and diversity: "Now there grows to be one thing alone out of many; now again many things separate out of one; there is a double generation of mortal beings, a double disappearance" (Fr. 17). This has generally been taken to imply that the creation of things occurs twice,

first in the passage from unity under Love to complete diversity under Strife and again in the reverse process from separation of all things to total fusion. (The standard interpretation has recently been challenged by Jean Bollack, who denies that Empedocles intended a double cosmogony. See bibliography.) The present phase of the world cycle is apparently regarded as one of the increasing prevalence of Strife.

Empedocles gave some account of the structure of the heavens and also of the phenomena of earth, sea, and atmosphere which the Greeks studied under the title of meteorology, but the remains of his physical poem show an equal or greater concern with zoology and botany. In the microcosm of plants and animals he discovered the same principles of elemental mixture, harmony, and separation at work. Following up an idea of Anaximander's, he imagined several phases in the emergence of living things from the earth (in combination with other elements), plants preceding animals, and he describes earlier, monstrous forms of animal life. As in Anaximander sexual reproduction appears only in the latest phase of the development. But the details of his doctrine are obscure, and it is difficult to say how far there is any significant anticipation of the theory of evolution.

PHYSIOLOGY AND PSYCHOLOGY. Empedocles shows a keen interest in embryology and physiology, explaining the structure of the eye by analogy with that of a lantern (Fr. 84) and comparing the process of respiration (including the movement of the blood) with the siphon effect of the clepsydra or water pipe, which retains or releases fluid by means of air pressure (Fr. 100). The notion of elemental combination is specified in numerical terms for certain living tissues. Bones are formed by earth, water, and fire in the ratio 2:2:4. The blend of the elements is most equal in flesh, especially in blood (Fr. 98).

Physiology passes over into psychology without a break. (It is clear that as a doctor Empedocles would have practiced psychosomatic medicine.) Blood is the primary seat of thought and perception (Fr. 105) precisely because it is here that the elements are most equably blended. Fundamental in Empedocles' psychology, as in his physics, is the principle of like to like. We see earth with the earth that is in us, water with water, love with love, strife with strife (Fr. 109). This and other passages in Empedocles suggest a one-to-one correspondence between the corporeal elements as such and our conscious experience of them. More precisely, his view seems to be that of a radical panpsychism in which, on the one hand, all elemental bodies are endowed with thought and sensation (Frs. 102–103) and, on the other hand, knowledge itself is treated like a physical thing obeying the laws of combination, attraction, and repulsion. Thus, Empedocles announces that his own teachings, if carefully assimilated, will form part of the character and elemental composition of the student, whereas, if neglected, "they will leave you in the course of time, yearning to return to their own dear kind; for you must know that all things have intelligence and a share in thought" (Fr. 110). Hence, all our conscious thought and feeling has its direct counterpart in the elemental blend within us (Frs. 107–108), which is itself continually being altered by the stream of incoming and outgoing material (Frs. 89, 106).

RELIGIOUS TEACHING

The religious views stated in the *Purifications* are so strange and so dogmatically presented that some scholars—H. Diels and Ulrich von Wilamowitz, for instance—have supposed that this poem dates from a later, less scientific period in Empedocles' life, reflecting some religious conversion after the bitter experience of exile. Now, the *Purifications* may, in fact, have been composed later than the physical poem, but no biographical development can resolve the alleged contradiction between the scientist and the mystic in Empedocles, for the physical work also presupposes a religious point of view.

In particular, *On Nature* proclaims the immortality and preexistence of the soul (or life principle) as a special case of *ex nihilo nihil*. In Empedocles' view the Parmenidean law of conservation for all real entities guarantees the indestructibility of life in exactly the same way as it guarantees the imperishability of the elements. Hence, only fools can "imagine that men exist merely during what we call life, but that they are nothing at all before being composed or after they are dissolved" (Fr. 15; compare with Fr. 11). Since it is precisely the doctrine of immortality that is supposed to contradict the psychophysics of Empedocles, this contradiction, if it exists, must be located within the physical poem. Furthermore, the same poem implies a developed theology in the description of the primordial cosmic sphere as a "god" (*theos*, Fr. 31), in the reference to the four elements as immortal deities (*daimones*, Fr. 59; compare with Fr. 6), and in the apocalyptic pronouncement of the power of Love-Aphrodite (Fr. 17). Some readers might be inclined to discount such expressions as mere features of poetic style, but such a literary interpretation of theological language, which may be appropriate in the case of Lucretius, seems unconvincing for Empedocles, who appeals to

principles of piety and purity throughout the poem (Frs. 3–5, 110, and so on).

The religious views thus alluded to in the physical poem receive emphatic statement in the *Purifications*. Here Empedocles proclaims his own divinity and traces his career as an immortal *daimōn*, banished from the company of the other gods for some prenatal crime; passing through a series of vegetable, animal, and human incarnations; at last attaining the purified life of "prophets, poets, doctors, and leaders"; and now ready to escape from human misery altogether and return once more to the blessed fellowship of the gods. Part of the process of purification consists in the ritual abstinence from meat and certain other foods, such as beans and laurel leaves. This joining of the belief in transmigration with the religious practice of vegetarianism is distinctly Pythagorean. If one adds Empedocles' notion that birth in human form means that the *daimōn* is clothed in an alien garment of flesh (Fr. 126) as a result of a lamentable fall from bliss (Fr. 118), one has a particularly striking example of that otherworldly tendency in Greek religion that is generally known as Orphic and that exercised such a profound influence on Plato as well as on the religious thought of late antiquity.

Remote as this view may seem from the biology and physics of the poem *On Nature*, Empedocles has taken care to preserve a sense of continuity between his religious teaching and his cosmology by a number of parallels, in particular by identifying the primeval sin of the *daimōn* (for which it is punished by incarnation in the cycle of rebirth) as "reliance on Strife." The fellowship of the purified spirits is conceived by contrast as a realm of Love and affection. Thus, the precosmic sphere of the physical poem is paralleled in the *Purifications* by an account of a bygone golden age in which war and bloodshed were unknown, affection prevailed between man and beast, and Aphrodite was queen (Frs. 128–129). Although both poems (which are addressed to different audiences) probably cannot be fitted together at every point, Empedocles clearly thought of the two as compatible, perhaps as complementary views of the world of nature (or physical transformation) and the world of spirit (or divine life). As a result of his panpsychism, Empedocles was able to conceive of nature and spirit as forming two aspects of a single whole rather than as constituting two entirely distinct realms. In any case the essential structure of both worlds is characterized by the same, almost Manichaean rivalry between the beneficent force of Love and the destructive power of Strife. If one sees Love in the physical poem as the cosmic counterpart of the immortal *daimōn* and his extramundane homeland, Empedocles' whole cosmology will appear as a construction designed to find a place for the Pythagorean doctrine of the transmigrating soul within the shifting and unstable world of elemental strife that had been described by the Ionian natural philosophers.

This reconciliation of the two poems is possible only if one admits the identification of the transmigrating *daimōn* with the element of divine Love—that is, with the unifying principle of intelligent organization present within each one of us but also present throughout nature. This identification has been accepted by Francis Macdonald Cornford and by others, and there is much to be said for it. But it is only fair to add that the identification cannot be proved from the extant texts and that some responsible scholars have denied that there is any possibility of reconciling the doctrine of immortality with the physical psychology of *On Nature*.

One should note Empedocles' clear statement—the first by any Greek—of the notion of an invisible, incorporeal, nonanthropomorphic deity, characterized as a "holy mind [*phrēn*] alone, darting through the whole cosmos with rapid thoughts" (Frs. 133–134). Before Empedocles, Xenophanes had insisted that the "greatest god" must be nonanthropomorphic, but he did not specify its incorporeality. On the other hand, Anaxagoras' principle of mind is clearly noncorporeal, but it is not described as a deity. Empedocles seems to have worked the Anaxagorean principle into his own theology. The phrasing of his account of the spiritual deity recalls the verses concerning Aphrodite as well as the description of the divine sphere. All three principles—the sphere in which the elements are joined, the attractive force of Aphrodite, and the "holy mind" of the cosmos—must somehow have been related in Empedocles' theology, perhaps as three different expressions of the universal power of Love. If so, Empedocles' theology forms the direct continuation of his psychology, since (on the interpretation offered above) it is this same power of Love that figures in the human microcosm as the transmigrating *daimōn*.

See also Anaximander; Leucippus and Democritus; Parmenides of Elea; Psychology; Pythagoras and Pythagoreanism; Theophrastus.

Bibliography

Remains of the poems and other ancient evidence are in H. Diels and W. Kranz, *Die Fragmente der Vorsokratiker*, Vol. I, 6th ed. (Berlin: Weidmann, 1951), Ch. 31.

There are two major studies of Empedocles: Ettore Bignone, *Empedocle* (Turin, 1916), and Jean Bollack, *Empédocle*, 3 vols. (Paris: Les …ditions de Minuit, 1965).
See also Eduard Zeller, *Die Philosophie der Griechen*, edited by Wilhelm Nestle, Vol. I, 6th ed. (Leipzig, 1920), Part 2; John Burnet, *Early Greek Philosophy*, 4th ed. (London, 1930); F. M. Cornford, "Mystery Religions and Pre-Socratic Philosophy," in *Cambridge Ancient History*, Vol. IV (Cambridge, U.K., 1939), Ch. 15; W. K. C. Guthrie, *A History of Greek Philosophy*, Vol. II (Cambridge, U.K.: Cambridge University Press, 1962); Werner Jaeger, *Theology of the Early Greek Philosophers* (Oxford: Clarendon Press, 1947); and G. S. Kirk and J. E. Raven, *The Presocratic Philosophers* (Cambridge, U.K.: Cambridge University Press, 1957).
Special studies include J. Bidez, *La biographie d'Empédocle* (Gand, 1894); Ulrich von Wilamowitz-Moellendorff, "Die *Katharmoi* des Empedokles," in *Berlin Sitzungsberichte* (1929): 626–661; Friedrich Solmsen, "Tissues and the Soul," in *Philosophical Review* 59 (1950): 435–441; D. J. Furley, "Empedocles and the Clepsydra," in *Journal of Hellenic Studies* 77 (1957): 31–34; Charles H. Kahn, "Religion and Natural Philosophy in Empedocles' Doctrine of the Soul," in *Archiv für Geschicte der Philosophie* 42 (1960): 3–35; and E. L. Minar Jr., "Cosmic Periods in the Philosophy of Empedocles," in *Phronesis* 8 (1963): 127–145.

Charles H. Kahn (1967)

EMPEDOCLES [ADDENDUM]

The philosophy of Empedocles remains the subject of widely diverging interpretations. This is so despite the discovery of important new evidence, which, far from dousing old debates, has instead further inflamed them. The following account seeks to chart the impact of the new material on a number of these still-open questions, without, however, ignoring significant contributions made to scholarship before it. Because the assessment of this material is still in its early days, the debate on many points may yet shift in one or the other direction.

THE NEW EVIDENCE

Notwithstanding the addition of a few elements to the corpus since Diels's edition, the study of Empedocles truly entered a new era in 1999 with the publication, by Alain Martin and Oliver Primavesi, of the Strasburg papyrus of Empedocles. The papyrus, assembled from numerous smaller pieces, consists of four larger sections, called by the editors sections a, b, c and d, and a few leftover scraps. These comprise a total of seventy-four hexameter lines, some very partial, of which twenty overlap with lines already known, making the identification of the text certain. By a stroke of luck, the largest section, a, continues the thirty-five-line Fr. 17, for another thirty-four lines, and thanks to a line-numbering mark in the margin of the papyrus, we can establish that the whole of Fr. 17 section a spanned lines 232 to 300 of its book. That book, as we know from Simplicius, the Aristotelian commentator, was book I of the work he calls the *Physics*, or *On Nature*. In these new lines, Empedocles moves from the broad cosmic cycle described in Fr. 17 to assert the capacity of the six principles to generate "all things," including men and women, trees, and "long-lived gods." The elements as cosmic bodies are described next, including a possible reference to a "we"—that is, humanity—within the churning world masses, but the reconstruction of these lines is controversial, the papyrus being poorly preserved. The section ends with a ten-line address to the disciple in which Empedocles promises to put before his eyes and ears "truthful proofs of my words" by showing Love and Strife at work in all manner of living creatures.

The second-longest new passage, however, section d, is the most significant for the interpretation of Empedocles. Its importance comes from the fact that, for the first time, we can see Empedocles moving from the theme of death and reincarnation, in lines 5–9, to cosmology and the origins of life, in lines 11–18, through a one-line transition at d 10. (Notably, d 5–6 overlap with the previously known Fr. 139, linked by its source to "purifications," and where Empedocles laments "shameful deeds" for the sake of food [that is, meat-eating]. The new text shows that these deeds were wrought "with claws," presumably in an earlier incarnation; the previous text had "for my lips," a much weaker reading.) Thus, unless we are willing to imagine that section d is from a different poem than the other papyrus sections, we are forced to admit that the poem that Simplicius called the *Physics* dealt with reincarnation as well.

THE NUMBER OF WORKS

Before the papyrus, the most important development in Empedoclean scholarship was the attempt to reject the older division of the fragments and assign them all to a single work, forcefully argued by Catherine Osborne in 1987 and Brad Inwood in 1992. But if section d now stands against any neat division of the fragments between religious and scientific content, it does not directly prove that there was only one work. Here one may speak, rather, of a shift in probabilities. In favor of the thesis that there was but a single work section d shows that *Purifications* material featured in the other supposed poem, raising the possibility that when Diogenes Laertius gives both titles (*Lives of the Philosophers* 8.77, the only source where they

occur together), he might in fact be giving one long title, like Hesiod's *Works and Days*. In that respect, it is noteworthy that Diogenes gives a single line total for *both* supposed works. Further, the position of Fr. 17, well into Book I, combined with the testimony of Plutarch (who, at *De exilio* 607 c, says that Fr. 115, on the exile of the *daimōn*, was "proclaimed in the beginning of [Empedocles'] philosophy"), argues for a long opening section, or proem, on more traditional themes, as in Parmenides or Lucretius.

But against the single-work thesis there still stands the difficulty that Empedocles has two sets of addressees, the "Friends from Acragas" in Fr. 112, to whom he declares himself a god, and his single disciple Pausanias, to whom he imparts the *On Nature*. A critique of the single-work approach was made by Denis O'Brien (1969), before the discovery of the Strasburg papyrus, whereas the case for a single work has been renewed by Trépanier (2004) on the basis of the new evidence. But the debate on the number of works should not obscure the more fundamental contribution of section d to our understanding of Empedocles: the renewed emphasis it places upon the unity of his thought.

THE UNITY OF EMPEDOCLES' THOUGHT AND THE DAIMŌN

The unity of Empedocles' thought seems to be the one area of emerging consensus. This is in part the result of section d but was also a trend before the papyrus was discorvered. Yet if it now seems likelier than ever that Empedocles had only one philosophical system, this may also make the apparent also seem to drive the contradiction between the reincarnated *daimōn* —or more strongly, its immortality—and Empedocles' physics all the more potent. The contradiction seems to be the following: If the transmigrating *daimōn* is a compound of elements, then even if it could survive from one reincarnation to the next, it could not survive that phase of the cosmic cycle when Strife dominates and no stable compounds endure—at least on the traditional reading of the cycle. To deal with this, a number of alternatives have been put forth. One may downplay the apparent contradiction in various ways: (1) a developmental scheme, no longer favored, posits that Empedocles changed his mind—he wrote two poems, at different stages in his life; 2) less charitably, it has been suggested that, as a poet, Empedocles did not see a contradiction, or if he did, did not care; 3) more subtly, some propose that the *Purifications* constituted the exoteric, popular version of his philosophy, meant to thrill the crowd with promises of personal salvation, whereas the esoteric *On Nature* reinterpreted that salvation as a more stringent and impersonal elemental immortality.

Alternatively, one can try to remove the contradiction by reconciling his conception of the *daimōn* with his physics. One version of this argument identifies the *daimōn* with the first principle Love, thereby denying that is a compound but granting it immortality. Or one may allow that the *daimōn* is a compound, admitting its reincarnation but denying its survival beyond one full cosmic cycle—that is, denying it full-blown immortality. To long-lived but not immortal being one can compare the "long-lived gods" of Fr. 17. The again, some interpretations of the cosmic cycle have held that Strife, while still powerful and active, will never again have complete sway. Thus, immortality might be possible for some compounds.

THE COSMIC CYCLE

That Empedocles held a doctrine of cyclical cosmic history has been generally accepted, but the actual form it took has been the subject of a surprisingly vast debate. The traditional account was the object of several challenges in the 1960s, but also of several powerful rehabilitations, of which O'Brien (1969) is the most comprehensive. Although the traditional version stresses the symmetry of the cycle and thus the equality of Love and Strife, in most alternative versions Strife is denied any creative and hence positive role in the world. Instead of the full pendulum swing found in the traditional version, and the dual creation and destruction it implies, Love would always be creative, Strife always destructive. This view was argued at greatest length by Jean Bollack (1969). To be sure, the constructive role Love plays in Empedocles' biology is far more prominent than that of Strife, whereas in his cosmology Strife is more conspicuous. But this imbalance may be no more than a difference of depiction in the original, for, as Daniel Graham (1988) has well shown, in the passages where the two powers are described together, waxing and waning over the whole macrocosm, they are systematically portrayed as equals.

See also Diogenes Laertius; Love; Lucretius; Parmenides of Elea; Plutarch of Chaeronea; Pre-Socratic Philosophy; Simplicius.

Bibliography

WORKS BY EMPEDOCLES (1962-2004)

Bollack, Jean. *Empédocle*. 3 vols. Paris: éditions de Minuit, 1969. Reprinted by Gallimard, 1992.

Inwood, Brad. *The Poem of Empedocles* (1992). 2nd ed. with new material. Toronto: University of Toronto Press, 2001.

Martin, Alain, and Oliver Primavesi. *L'Empédocle de Strasbourg*.Berlin/New York/Strasbourg: de Gruyter, 1999.

Wright, M. R. *Empedocles. The Extant Fragments*. New Haven, CT: Yale University Press, 1981.

Zuntz, G. *Persephone*.Oxford: Oxford University Press, 1971.

WORKS ABOUT EMPEDOCLES

Barnes, Jonathan. *The Presocratic Philosophers*. 2nd ed. London: Routledge, 1982.

Cantilena, Mario, ed. *Aevum Antiquum*1(2001): Forum -Sul Nuovo Empedocle. Contains seven articles on the Stasburg papyrus; for specialists.

Curd, Patricia. *The Legacy of Parmenides: Eleatic Monism and Later Presocratic Thought*. Princeton, NJ: Princeton University Press, 1988.

Furley, David J. *The Greek Cosmologists*. Cambridge, U.K.: Cambridge University Press, 1987

Graham, Daniel W. "Symmetry in the Empedoclean Cycle." *Classical Quarterly* 38 (1988): 297–312.

Kingsley, Peter. *Ancient Philosophy, Mystery and Magic: Empedocles and the Pythagorean Tradition*. Oxford: Oxford University Press, 1983.

Kirk, Gordon S., John Raven, and Malcolm Schofield. *The Presocratic Philosophers*. 2nd ed. Cambridge, U.K.: Cambridge University Press, 1983.

Long, A. A. "Empedocles' Cosmic Cycle in the Sixties." In *The Presocratics: A Collection of Critical Essays*. 2nd ed., edited by A. P. D. Mourelatos. Princeton, NJ: Princeton University Press, 1993.

Mourelatos, Alexander P. D. "Quality, Structure and Emergence in Later Pre-Socratic Philosophy." In *Proceedings of the Boston Area Colloquium in Ancient Philosophy*. Vol. 2, edited by John J. Cleary, 127–194. New York: University Press of America, 1987.

O'Brien, Denis. *Empedocles' Cosmic Cycle*. Cambridge, U.K.: Cambridge University Press, 1969.

"Empedocles Revisited." *Ancient Philosophy* 15 (1995): 403–470.

Osborne, Catherine. "Empedocles Recycled." *Classical Quarterly* 37(1987): 24–50.

Sedley, David. *Lucretius and the Transformation of Greek Wisdom*. Cambridge, U.K.: Cambridge University Press, 1998, esp. ch. 1 "The Empedoclean Opening."

Stokes, Michael. *One and Many in Presocratic Philosophy*.Washington: Center for Hellenic Studies / Harvard University Press, 1971.

Trépanier, Simon. *Empedocles: An Interpretation*. London/New York: Routledge, 2004.

Simon Trépanier (2005)

EMPIRICISM

Empiricism is the theory that experience rather than reason is the source of knowledge, and in this sense it is opposed to rationalism. This general thesis, however, can receive different emphases and refinements; hence, those philosophers who have been labeled empiricists are united only in their general tendency and may differ in various ways. The word *empiricism* is derived from the Greek ἐμπειρία (*empeiria*), the Latin translation of which is *experientia,* from which in turn we derive the word *experience.* Aristotle conceived of experience as the as yet unorganized product of sense perception and memory; this is a common philosophical conception of the notion. Memory is required so that what is perceived may be retained in the mind. To say that we have learned something from experience is to say that we have come to know of it by the use of our senses. We have experience when we are sufficiently aware of what we have discovered in this way. There is another, perhaps connected, sense of the term *experience* in which sensations, feelings, and so on, are experiences and in which to perceive something involves having sense experiences. These are experiences because awareness of them is something that happens to us. Indeed, the suggestion of passivity is common to uses of the word. To go into refinements here would not be relevant; one need only appreciate that the statement that experience is the source of knowledge means that knowledge depends ultimately on the use of the senses and on what is discovered through them. Sense experience may be necessary for the attainment of experience, but for present purposes that is unimportant.

The weakest form of empiricism is the doctrine that the senses do provide us with "knowledge" in some sense of the word. This could be denied only by one who had so elevated a conception of knowledge that the senses cannot attain to it. Plato, for example, held at one stage that because of the changeability of the world of sense, sense knowledge lacks the certainty and infallibility that true knowledge must possess. Hence, knowledge cannot be derived from the senses, but only from some other kind of awareness of what he called Forms. The most that sense perception could do would be to remind us of this genuine knowledge. This conception of knowledge demands an infallibility that sense perception cannot provide. Normally, we do not demand such high standards of knowledge, nor do we succumb to this kind of skepticism about sense perception. The commonsense view is that the senses do provide us with knowledge of some sort, and most people, when philosophizing, adopt this kind of empiricist view.

This weak form of empiricism can be generalized into the thesis that *all* knowledge comes from experience, The extreme form of this thesis would be the claim that no source other than experience provides knowledge at all. But this formulation is ambiguous, because there could be various reasons why all that we know might be dependent in some way upon experience. One reason might be that every proposition that we know is either a direct report on experience or a report whose truth is inferred from experience. A prima facie exception to such a thesis is provided by the propositions of mathematics; they have usually been thought to be a priori, not a posteriori—that is, we can know their truth independently of experience. There have, however, been philosophers who have denied the a priori nature of mathematical propositions. J. S. Mill, for example, maintained that the propositions of mathematics are merely very highly confirmed generalizations from experience and, consequently, all propositions are either reports on experience or generalizations from experience. This view has not been widely accepted.

A second reason for maintaining that all knowledge is dependent on experience would be that we can have no ideas or concepts that are not derived from experience, that is, that all concepts are a posteriori, whether or not the truths which can be asserted by means of these concepts are themselves a posteriori. It may be that we know some propositions without having to resort immediately to experience for their validation; for their truth may depend solely on the logical relations between the ideas involved. Yet these ideas may themselves be derived from experience. If all our ideas are so derived, then knowledge of any sort must be dependent on sense experience in some way. According to this thesis, not all knowledge is derived immediately from experience, but all knowledge is dependent on experience at least in the sense that all the materials for knowledge are ultimately derived from experience. St. Thomas Aquinas was an empiricist in this sense. He thought that all our concepts are derived from experience, in that there is "nothing in the intellect which was not previously in the senses" (a doctrine supposedly derived from Aristotle). He did not think, however, that all knowledge either consists of sense experience or is inferred inductively from experience. Similarly, John Locke held and tried to show that all our ideas are derived from experience, either directly or by way of reflection on ideas of sense. He did not hold, however, that all knowledge was sense knowledge.

It is possible to argue an even more complex thesis. It may be held that while there are ideas which are not derived from experience—a priori ideas—and while there are a priori truths which may or may not involve a priori ideas, such ideas and truths only have application on the precondition that there is experience. That is to say that—for human beings at any rate—reason can function only by way of some kind of connection with experience; "pure" reason is impossible. This was, in effect, Immanuel Kant's position, and although he did not call himself an empiricist *simpliciter,* he was certainly opposed to what he called dogmatic rationalism. He held that there is no place for forms of knowledge of reality which are derived from pure reason alone.

It is possible, then, to maintain a general empiricist thesis that all knowledge is derived from experience on the grounds either that (1) all that we know is directly concerned with sense experience or derived from it by strictly experiential means, that is, learning, association, or inductive inference; or (2) all that we know is dependent on sense experience in that all the materials for knowledge are directly derived from sense experience; or (3) all that we know is dependent on sense perception in that even though we can know some things a priori, this is only in a relative sense, since the having of experience is a general precondition for being said to have such knowledge. None of these theses demand any more than the ordinary conception of knowledge. They do not demand that the knowledge in question should possess absolute infallibility so that the possibility of error is logically excluded. For none of the theses in question is essentially designed to be an answer to skepticism.

EMPIRICISM AND SKEPTICISM

Some forms of rationalism, for example, the Platonic theory already referred to, are meant to be answers to skepticism. They presuppose that an adequate reply to philosophical skepticism can be given only by showing that reason can provide forms of knowledge where error is logically excluded. The search for certainty, so intimately associated with seventeenth-century rationalism in general and René Descartes in particular, aimed at showing that knowledge is possible because there are some things about which we cannot be wrong. Empiricism can be a rival to rationalism, not just in the sense already noted—that it may reject the supposition that reason by itself, without reference to sense perception, can provide knowledge—but also in the sense that it proposes an alternate way of arriving at certainty. Empiricism, in this sense, is the thesis that the certainty required to answer the skeptic is to be found in the deliverances of the senses themselves and not in the deliverances of reason. Rationalism and empiricism, in this sense, are agreed that some such certainty must be found if skepticism is to be answered. They disagree about the sources of that certainty and about the method by which the rest of what we

ordinarily call knowledge is to be derived from the primary certainties. Whereas rationalism seeks to derive knowledge in general from certain primary axioms (the truth of which is indubitable) by means of strictly deductive procedures, empiricism seeks to build up or construct knowledge from certain basic elements that are, again, indubitable. The clearest expression of this point of view is probably to be found in twentieth-century empiricism, especially that associated with the logical positivist movement. This point of view is also found in the British empiricists of the seventeenth and eighteenth centuries, Locke, George Berkeley, and David Hume, but in their case it is overladen with other elements and other forms of empiricism, some of which have already been noted. A short historical survey may serve to pinpoint the main issues.

EMPIRICISM IN GREEK AND MEDIEVAL PHILOSOPHY

It is often said that, in one sense, Aristotle was the founder of empiricism. Certainly Thomas Aquinas believed that he had Aristotle's authority for the view that there is nothing in the intellect which was not previously in the senses. It is not clear, however, that Aristotle ever raised this question. When he spoke of the relations between reason and the senses, he was concerned with issues in the philosophy of mind rather than with epistemology. Certainly Aristotle seems to have believed that knowledge is possible outside the immediate sphere of the senses and that reason can and does furnish us with necessary truths about the world. Aristotle's place in the development of empiricism, then, remains unclear.

Perhaps the first declared empiricist was Epicurus, who maintained that the senses are the only source of knowledge. Epicurus was an extreme atomist and held that sense perception comes about as a result of contact between the atoms of the soul and films of atoms issuing from the bodies around us. By this means *phantasiae* (appearances) are set up. These are all veridical. All sensations are true, and there is no standard other than sensation to which we may refer our judgments about the world. Sensations are set up in the soul by external stimuli, and for this reason Epicurus takes them to be "given." They constitute *phantasiae* when they occur in bulk. There is no further evidence that can be adduced in order that their veridicality may be assessed, either from other sensations or from reason. This is not to say that we cannot be in error concerning objects of perception; the films of atoms may become distorted in transit or the *phantasiae* caused by them may be fitted to the wrong *prolep-*

sis (conception). The last is a kind of abstract idea built up from successive sensations; the fitting of a *phantasia* to a *prolepsis* is what corresponds to judgment in Epicurus. It would appear that what Epicurus meant by his assertion that all sensations are true was that since they are caused in us, we can go no further in seeking information; they may not make us have true knowledge of objects, but in themselves they are incorrigible. Precisely how all knowledge was to be built up from these sensations is not clear, and it has often been remarked that the axioms on which Epicurus's metaphysical system rests are far from the data of sense and are often based on more or less a priori arguments. Nevertheless, Epicurus's ideal of knowledge is one which not only depends on experience for its materials but is based on basic truths of experience.

A theory of knowledge similar in many ways to that of Epicurus may be found in St. Thomas Aquinas, although the main sources of Thomas's philosophy are to be found in Aristotle. Thomas was not a complete empiricist, for he did not think that all knowledge was derived from truths of experience. Knowledge of God, for example, could be obtained in other ways, and his existence could be proved by logical argument. Yet Thomas did think that the materials for knowledge must be derived from sense experience, and he gave an account of the mechanism by which this comes about. Roughly, when the sense organs are stimulated, there also results a change in the soul, which is the form of the body; this is a phantasm, a kind of sensory image. In order for sense perception to occur, the universal character of the phantasm must be seen as such. For this purpose, Thomas resorted to Aristotle's distinction between an active and a passive reason. The active reason has to make possible the acquisition by the passive reason of the sensible form of the object of perception by a process which Thomas— probably adapting an analogy used by Aristotle— described as the illuminating of the phantasm. The active reason reveals the sensible form of the object by abstraction from the phantasm. This form is imposed upon the passive reason, which produces a *species expressa,* or verbal concept, which in turn is used in judgment. This process is called the *conversio ad phantasmata;* all concepts are arrived at in this way, by abstraction from phantasms. Hence, in applying them to entities that cannot be objects of perception, we must do so by means of analogies of various kinds with sensible objects. Thomas's empiricism is, therefore, limited to concepts, and it is only in this limited sense that he held "there is nothing in the intellect which was not previously in the senses."

THE BRITISH EMPIRICISTS

When thinking of empiricism, one tends to think, above all, of the British empiricists of the seventeenth and eighteenth centuries.

LOCKE. John Locke was an empiricist in roughly the same sense that Thomas was, and he set the tone for his successors. His "new way of ideas," as it was called, had as its purpose "to inquire into the original, certainty, and extent of human knowledge, together with the grounds and degrees of belief, opinion, and assent." The reference to certainty makes it appear that he was concerned with skepticism or with skeptical arguments similar to Descartes's method of doubt. Locke's solution to this problem, however, was by no means consistently empiricist. His main target for attack was the doctrine of innate ideas, the doctrine that there may be ideas with which we are born or, at any rate, which we do not have to derive from sense experience. The first book of his *Essay concerning Human Understanding* is devoted to a biting attack on this doctrine. In the rest of the book he sets out a positive account of the way in which ideas are built up, explaining that by "idea" he means that which the mind "is applied about whilst thinking." Ideas may be either of sensation or of reflection upon those of sensation; there is no other source. Ideas are also classified as simple or complex, the latter being built up out of the former. The mind has a certain freedom in this process, which may lead to error. (Locke later admitted ideas of relation and general ideas alongside the simple and complex.) The second book of the *Essay* is an exhaustive account of the way in which all objects of the mind are built up from ideas of sense. In this respect, then, Locke's philosophy may be considered an attempt to show in detail the truth of the kind of view which Thomas had embraced, without accepting the same view of the mechanism whereby ideas come into being.

But Locke wanted to assess the certainty of our knowledge as well as its extent. The mind's freedom in forming complex ideas is a source of error, but in the case of simple ideas the mind, to Locke, was like a great mirror, capable of reflecting only what is set before it. Nevertheless, he did not maintain that all our ideas reflect the exact properties of things nor that all knowledge is of this character. In the fourth book of the *Essay* he asserts that all knowledge consists of "the perception of the connection of and agreement, or disagreement and repugnancy, of any of our ideas," but he goes on to distinguish three degrees of knowledge—intuitive, demonstrative, and sensitive. We can have intuitive knowledge of our own existence, demonstrative knowledge of God's existence, and sensitive knowledge of the existence of particular finite things. Intuition and demonstration bring certainty with them; they provide in effect a priori knowledge. The question of how there can be a priori knowledge of the existence of anything and how this can be a matter of the agreement or disagreement between ideas presents many problems.

These problems become acute in connection with sensitive knowledge. Locke tried to argue at one point that knowledge of the existence of particular finite things is a matter of the perception of the agreement of our ideas with that of existence. This will not do; to know that something exists is not to know merely that the idea of it fits in with the idea of existence. Hence, Locke admitted that this knowledge has not the certainty of the other two, although he insisted that it goes beyond mere probability and is commonly thought of as knowledge. He also tried to argue for the claim that we do have knowledge of sensible things, maintaining that simple ideas are caused in us in such a way that the mind is passive in receiving them. Moreover, the senses may cohere in their reports. None of these considerations really show that we do have knowledge of sensible things, and Locke admitted that they did not amount to proof.

Locke did not claim that *all* our ideas correspond to the properties of things. He felt this claim was true in the case of the so-called primary qualities, for example, bulk, figure, and motion, qualities without which, he maintained, a thing could not exist. It was not true of secondary qualities—for example, color and taste. In this case, the properties of things cause us to have ideas that are not representative of those things; the term "secondary *quality*" is thus a misnomer. Locke's denial of the real existence of secondary qualities turns on his assimilation of our ideas of them to feelings like pain. (His acceptance of primary qualities was probably influenced by the success of physics in his time and its preoccupation with these properties of things.) As for things themselves, Locke maintained that we have little or no knowledge of their real essence, only of their nominal essence—their nature as determined by the way in which we classify them. This is due to the weakness of our senses. We cannot penetrate to the real essence of things, and our ideas of substances are mostly those of powers—the powers that things have to affect us and each other. It can be seen from all this that Locke was an empiricist in a very limited sense. In his view all the materials for knowledge are provided by sense perception, but the extent and certainty of sensible knowledge is limited, while on the other hand, there is nonempirical a priori knowledge of nonsensible things.

BERKELEY. One aim of Berkeley, the second of the British empiricists, was to rid Locke's philosophy of those elements that were inconsistent with empiricism, although Berkeley's main aim was to produce a metaphysical view which would show the glory of God. According to this view, there is nothing that our understanding cannot grasp, and our perceptions can be regarded as a kind of divine language by which God speaks to us; for God is the cause of our perceptions. The *esse* of sensible things is *percipi*—they consist in being perceived and they have no existence without the mind. There exist, therefore, only sensations or ideas and spirits that are their cause. God is the cause of our sensations, and we ourselves can be the cause of ideas of the imagination.

Berkeley argued against those elements of Locke's philosophy that presupposed a physical reality lying behind our ideas. He attacked Locke's conception of substance and the distinction between primary and secondary qualities, pointing out that there was no distinction to be made between them in respect of their dependence on mind. He also attacked the doctrine of abstract ideas which Locke had held, the doctrine that we have general ideas of things abstracted from the conditions of their particular existence—Locke's theory of universals. This Berkeley did because he believed that Locke's theory might provide a loophole for asserting the existence of an idea of substance. The outcome of this was Berkeley's claim that there are no restrictions on the extent of our knowledge. We have knowledge of the existence of God and ourselves to the extent that we have notions of these spirits. We have knowledge of everything else, since the existence of everything else is a matter of its being perceived. There is nothing further beyond our ken. Even subjects such as geometry, which might be supposed to involve knowledge of nonempirical matters, had to be limited in scope in order to rule out nonempirical objects of knowledge. Thus, Berkeley maintained that there is a least perceptible size; hence, there can be no ideas of infinitesimals or points.

In addition to claiming unrestricted scope for our knowledge, Berkeley asserted that knowledge is entirely dependent on sensations for all its materials other than the notions we have of God and ourselves. Berkeley claimed that this view "gives certainty to knowledge" and prevents skepticism. At the same time it defends common sense, he argued, because it does not involve the postulation of a reality behind ideas. His view gave certainty, he held, because sensations are by definition free from error; for error can arise only from the wrong use of ideas in judgment. The certainty of our sensations is due to the fact that there can be no question whether they actually represent a reality behind them; and this is the basis of Berkeley's claim to deal with skepticism. In general, all knowledge apart from that of our own existence and of God must, for Berkeley, ultimately be derived from sense perception. With these exceptions, therefore, Berkeley was an empiricist not only in respect of the scope and materials of knowledge but also in respect of its foundations. All truths must be founded on the truths of sense experience. The relations between ideas, which Locke had found a source of knowledge, were, for Berkeley, the result of the mind's own acts.

The mind operates upon the ideas given to it, comparing or contrasting them; it does not merely record what is there. Formal disciplines like mathematics, which might be thought to turn on the relations between ideas, thus depend on the ways in which the mind arbitrarily puts ideas together. Hence, to put the matter in terms more familiar today, mathematics is as much a matter of invention as discovery.

HUME. In respect to relations between ideas Hume perhaps went back to Locke, but in other respects much of Hume's philosophy may be represented as an attempt to rid empiricism of the remaining excrescences of nonempiricist doctrine in Berkeley. As to the materials for knowledge, Hume tried to improve on his predecessors with attempts at greater precision. He distinguished first between impressions and ideas, the former being the contents of the mind in perception, the latter those in imagination, and so on. He further subdivided ideas into those of sense and those of reflection, and again, into those which are simple and those which are complex. Like Berkeley, he denied the existence of anything behind impressions, and a cardinal point of his empiricism, to which he returned again and again, was that every simple idea is a copy of a corresponding impression. The understanding is therefore limited to these mental contents. Hume's main method in philosophy was what he called the "experimental method," the reference in all philosophical problems to the discoveries of experience. In effect, the conclusions which he drew from this are the opposite of Berkeley's. They can produce only skepticism. No justification can be given for belief in the existence of the self and an external world, for example. Reason cannot justify such beliefs, for all that we are given is a bundle of impressions and ideas. Only a psychological explanation can be given to account for our having such

beliefs. Hume gives such an explanation in terms of the constancy and coherence of our impressions and ideas, and the principles of the association of ideas.

Hume's theory of knowledge is based on a distinction between two kinds of relations of ideas. In the *Treatise of Human Nature* he makes the distinction between relations that depend completely on the related ideas and those that can be changed without changing the ideas. The former, in effect, constitute necessary connections, the latter factual ones. In the later *Enquiry Concerning Human Understanding* he short-circuited the discussion by distinguishing simply between relations of ideas and matters of fact. Mathematics depends entirely on relations of ideas and is thus concerned with necessary truths, the denial of which involves a contradiction. Matters of fact may rest simply on observation, but in the causal relation Hume finds the only case of a matter-of-fact relation that can take us from one idea to another. He shows that statements of causal connection cannot be logically necessary truths, in spite of the fact that we do attach some necessity to causal connections. After a long discussion he finds the explanation for this in the fact that causes precede their effects, are contiguous to them, and are such that there is a constant conjunction between them. As a result, the mind, through custom, tends to pass from one to the other. The feeling derived from this, which is an impression of reflection, constitutes the feeling of necessity that we find in the causal connection.

Hume denied any real connection between cause and effect but tried to explain why we think that there is such. His demonstration that the causal connection is a contingent one is of the utmost importance, but his conclusions about it are skeptical. He held that there can be no real or objective justification for inference from cause to effect. He did allow, it is true, that certain rules can be provided which, when followed, will give some kind of probability to those inductive inferences which we actually do make. The aim of these rules is to make custom reliable and to avoid superstition. Hume has really no right, according to his own principles, to allow so much, and in doing so, he deserts skepticism in favor of a reductionist positivism, which seeks only to deny any necessary connection among things, while retaining belief in inductive inference. The concept of causal connection is thus in effect reduced to that of constant association of events contiguous in space and closely related in time. This is a position incompatible with his general skepticism. Apart from this, Hume's philosophy is of a piece. In Hume, then, extreme empiricism led to skepticism. Apart from relations of ideas, he held, the only *knowledge* we can have is of what we can directly observe, and any attempt to palliate this conclusion can produce only inconsistency.

In British empiricism, therefore, the gradual weeding out of anything inconsistent with empiricism, either in the form of the claim that the materials for knowledge must be derived from experience or in the form of the claim that knowledge cannot go beyond experience in its objects, resulted in skepticism about most of the things which we ordinarily claim to know. Kant proposed a reconciliation between this thesis and rationalism, maintaining that the rationalist claim of a priori knowledge about reality must be restricted to its application to experience. There is no room for a priori knowledge of anything that is not an object of experience. Pure reason can provide no real knowledge, despite the claims of rationalist metaphysicians. Such nonanalytic propositions as we do know a priori constitute principles that lay down the conditions to which experience must conform if it is to be objectively valid and not just a product of the imagination. A priori truths other than mere analytic truths have validity only in reference to experience; hence, while all knowledge is based on experience, it is not all derived from experience. This is scarcely empiricism in any recognized form, nor did Kant claim that it was; but it is a thesis that gives an important role to experience in knowledge.

One final point may be made about the British empiricists: They all employed a common method of trying to build up the body of knowledge from simple building blocks. The model for this method may have been the empirical science of the day. (Hume claimed to derive his experimental method from Isaac Newton.) The rationalists claimed more for reason and sought to reveal sources for knowledge and its materials other than experience; but they were also opposed to the empiricists in their choice of method, finding their inspiration in the method of axiomatic geometry.

JOHN STUART MILL. J. S. Mill, the main figure in nineteenth-century empiricism, followed directly in the tradition of Hume. Mill's account of our knowledge of the external world, for example, was in part phenomenalist in character; it maintained that things are merely permanent possibilities of sensation. But it was mainly an account of the way in which we come to believe in such a thing as an external world and thus followed Hume in its psychological character. In one respect, however, Mill was more radical than Hume. He was so impressed by the possibilities of the use of induction that he found inductive inference in places where we should not ordinarily expect to find it. In particular, he claimed that mathematical truths were merely very highly confirmed generalizations from experience; mathematical inference, generally conceived as deductive in nature, he set down as founded on induction. Thus, in Mill's philosophy there was no real place for knowledge based on relations of ideas. In his view logical and mathematical necessity is psychological; we are merely unable to conceive any other possibilities than those that logical and mathematical propositions assert. This is perhaps the most extreme version of empiricism known, but it has not found many defenders.

TWENTIETH-CENTURY EMPIRICISM

Empiricists in the twentieth century generally reverted to the radical distinction between necessary truths, as found in logic and mathematics, and empirical truths, as found elsewhere. Necessity is confined by them, however, to logic and mathematics, and all other truths are held to be merely contingent. Partly for this reason and partly because it has been held that the apparatus of modern logic may be relevant to philosophical problems, twentieth-century empiricists tended to call themselves "Logical Empiricists" (at least those who were connected in one way or another with logical positivism). Bertrand Russell, however, who derived something from the positivists, but who owes equally much to the British empiricists, always claimed that there are limits to empiricism, on the grounds that the principles of inductive inference cannot themselves be justified by reference to experience.

In general, twentieth-century empiricists were less interested in the question of the materials for knowledge than in that of the empirical basis for knowledge. Insofar as they considered the former question, the tendency has been, as in other matters, to eschew psychological considerations and to raise the problem in connection with meaning. All descriptive symbols, it is maintained, should be definable in terms of other symbols, except that ultimately one must come to expressions that are definable ostensively only. That is, there must ultimately be terms which can be cashed by direct reference to experience and to it alone; ostensive definition consists of giving the term together with some direct act of pointing, such that no other understanding of meaning is required. In regard to nondescriptive terms the situation is less clear, but the general tendency is to assume that the only possible source of ideas which might be called a priori is logic and mathematics. Following Russell, twentieth-century empiricists assumed that mathematical notions can be reduced to logical ones or can at least involve similar features and that logical notions are concerned only with relations between symbols and can be defined accordingly. Russell, it is true, suggested that terms such as *or* might also be defined ostensively, for example, by reference to feelings of hesitation, but this suggestion has not been generally accepted.

If the views on the question of the materials for knowledge are not clear-cut, there has not been the same indefiniteness over the basis of knowledge. Although some positivists, the so-called physicalists, have maintained that the language of physics should be taken as providing the basic truths, most philosophers of positivist persuasion have gone to direct experience for the truths on which knowledge is taken to rest. These truths are to be found in sense-datum propositions—propositions that are a direct record of experience and which are for this reason incorrigible, consisting of ostensively definable terms, that is, names of sense data. It is not clear what would constitute an example of this. (Russell, for example, suggested "Red here now," where every expression is what he called a "logically proper name," such that its reference is guaranteed.) Nevertheless, it has been assumed that all propositions except logical ones must be reducible to these "basic propositions," which are about sense data.

However, propositions about physical objects are not incorrigible. Yet to suppose that such propositions deal with entities that lie behind the immediate data of the senses and that can only be inferred from those data would be to suppose that there is a gap between us and physical objects, the crossing of which is problematic. This would allow an opening for the skeptic. An alternative view is phenomenalism, the doctrine that the meaning of our statements about physical objects can be analyzed in terms of propositions about sense data. Physical objects are logical constructions out of sense data ("logical" because the issue concerns the correct logical analysis of propositions about physical objects and not the question of how, as a matter of psychological fact, we construct our ideas of physical objects). In general, according to positivists, all propositions other than those that are logically necessary must be verifiable by reduction, either directly or indirectly, to propositions about sense data. Anything which is not so reducible is nonsense. In epistemological terms, any contingent truth that we can be said to know must be founded on and reducible to propositions concerning sense experience. Necessary truths, it is generally held, are true by convention or in virtue of the meaning of the words involved. They tell us nothing about the world as such.

This program has run into difficulties of two main kinds. First, there have been difficulties in actually carrying out the analysis demanded. It would be almost universally agreed that propositions about physical objects cannot be analyzed in terms of propositions about actual and possible sense data, since the analysis would have to be infinitely long. This is an objection of principle. Second, the criterion of verifiability tends to exclude some kinds of propositions that we ordinarily think that we understand. There have been difficulties in this respect, for example, over propositions of natural law, as well as propositions of ethics, etc. There has been widespread dissatisfaction with attempts to justify empiricism of this sort.

It should now be possible to offer some assessment of empiricism. As an answer to skepticism it claims that the certainty and incorrigibility that knowledge demands can (apart from logical truths) be found only in immediate experience and that the rest of knowledge must be built upon this. In this sense, the theory is misguided as well as unsuccessful in carrying out its program. The lack of success can be seen in the fact that eighteenth-century empiricism led to skepticism, while the twentieth-century program of reduction was very widely admitted as a failure. The attempt was misguided in that knowledge does not require this kind of certainty and incorrigibility. Skepticism is not to be answered by providing absolutely certain truths, but by examining the grounds of skepticism itself. According to our ordinary conception of knowledge, what we claim to know must be true and based on the best of reasons. But by the best of reasons is not meant proof. Experience certainly provides justification for belief in, for example, physical objects, but if this belief is to amount to knowledge, it is not necessary that the justification should amount to proof. It is futile to argue whether experience or reason alone can provide proof of what we ordinarily claim to know. No one could have knowledge of the world unless he had experiences and could reason, but this does not mean that either experience or reason by themselves could provide the kind of absolute certainty which would constitute proof. Nor is it required that they should provide proof in order that knowledge may be possible.

What of the thesis that, whether or not experience can provide certainty, all knowledge is derived from experience? In Mill's sense, that all truths, of whatever kind, receive their validation from experience, the thesis is obviously false and need be considered no further. The thesis that all the materials for knowledge are derived from experience may seem more plausible. Yet, despite the number of philosophers who have maintained this thesis, it is not altogether clear what it means. The version of the doctrine held by Locke and Thomas looks like a psychological account of the origin of our ideas; in logical dress it amounts to the view that all our concepts or all the words which we use are definable in terms of those which are ostensively definable. Whether or not there are any a priori notions outside logic and mathematics, it certainly seems implausible to say that logical and mathematical notions may ultimately be definable ostensively.

More important, the notion of ostensive definition is itself suspect. How could one understand what was going on when a noise was made, accompanied by a pointing to something, unless one knew the kind of thing which was being indicated and, more important perhaps, was aware that it was *language* that was being used? In other words, much has to be understood before this kind of definition can even begin. The notion that words can be cashed in terms of direct experience without further presuppositions is, thus, highly suspect. This is not to say that there are no distinctions to be made between different kinds of concepts or words, but merely that the distinctions in question cannot be made by means of any simple distinction between empiricism and rationalism.

There remains the Kantian point that the having of experience is a condition for any further knowledge. This would certainly be the case for creatures of our kind of sensibility, as Kant would put it. Yet the logical possibility of the possession of knowledge by nonsensitive creatures remains, whether or not any such creatures exist in fact.

See also A Priori and A Posteriori; Aristotle; Berkeley, George; Descartes, René; Epicurus; Hume, David; Kant, Immanuel; Locke, John; Logical Positivism; Logic, History of; Mill, John Stuart; Plato; Positivism; Pragmatism; Rationalism; Russell, Bertrand Arthur William; Sensationalism; Skepticism, History of; Thomas Aquinas, St.

Bibliography

EPICURUS

Bailey, Cyril. *Epicurus, the Extant Remains.* Oxford: Clarendon Press, 1926. In Greek, with English translation.

Bailey, Cyril. *The Greek Atomists and Epicurus.* Oxford: Clarendon Press, 1928.

Zeller, Eduard. *Stoics, Epicureans and Sceptics.* Translated by O. J. Reichel. London and New York: Longmans, Green, 1892.

THOMAS AQUINAS

Copleston, F. C. *Aquinas.* London: Penguin, 1955.

Thomas Aquinas, St. *Summa Theologica,* Ia, 78ff., in Vol. IV of the English translation by the Fathers of the English Dominican Province. London, 1922.

THE BRITISH EMPIRICISTS

Ayer, A. J., and Raymond Winch, eds. *British Empirical Philosophers.* London: Routledge, 1952. A collection of writings by the British empiricists.

Mill, J. S. *System of Logic.* 8th ed. London: Longmans, Green, Reader, and Dyer, 1872.

See also Immanuel Kant, *Critique of Pure Reason,* the translation by Norman Kemp Smith. London, 1953.

TWENTIETH-CENTURY EMPIRICISTS

Anderson, John, *Studies in Empirical Philosophy.* Sydney, Australia: Angus and Robertson, 1962.

Ayer, A. J. *Foundations of Empirical Knowledge.* London: Macmillan, 1940.

Ayer, A. J. *Language, Truth and Logic.* 2nd ed. London: Gollancz, 1946.

Ayer, A. J. *Philosophical Essays.* London: Macmillan, 1954.

Ayer, A. J. *Problem of Knowledge.* London: Macmillan, 1956.

Ayer, A. J., ed. *Logical Positivism.* Glencoe, IL: Free Press, 1959.

Lewis, C. I. *An Analysis of Knowledge and Valuation.* La Salle, IL: Open Court, 1946.

Price, H. H. *Thinking and Experience.* London and New York: Hutchison's University Library, 1953.

Russell, Bertrand. *Human Knowledge.* London: Allen and Unwin, 1948.

Russell, Bertrand. *Inquiry into Meaning and Truth.* London: Allen and Unwin, 1940.

For other writings dealing with Empiricism, see the bibliographies to the entries Logical Positivism; Positivism; Pragmatism; and Sensationalism.

D. W. Hamlyn (1967)

ENCYCLOPEDIAS

See *Encyclopédie;* "Philosophy Dictionaries and Encyclopedias" in Volume 10

ENCYCLOPÉDIE

Encyclopédie, or the French Encyclopedia, is a famous and controversial work of reference embodying much of what the French Enlightenment liked to call "philosophy."

PURPOSE, HISTORY, AND INFLUENCE

Begun simply as a commercial undertaking to translate and adapt Ephraim Chambers's *Cyclopaedia* (1728), the *Encyclopédie* was first entrusted to the Englishman John Mills and the German Godefroy Sellius, and then to the Abbé Gua de Malves of the French Academy of Sciences. Denis Diderot became chief editor in 1747 and, with Jean

Le Rond d'Alembert as his principal colleague, greatly expanded the scope of the enterprise. Diderot's prospectus (1750) promised, as a principal and novel feature, a description of the arts and especially the crafts in France, with numerous illustrative engravings, and was accompanied by an elaborate "Chart of the Branches of Human Knowledge," which Diderot referred to as "the Genealogical Tree of All the Arts and Sciences." This *Système figuré des connoissances humaines* was avowedly inspired by the work of Francis Bacon, whose empiricism greatly influenced the entire work. Assuming that all knowledge comes originally from sensations, the *Système figuré* subsumed all branches of learning under either memory, reason, or imagination, to which corresponded, respectively, history, philosophy, and poetry. The correlation of philosophy with reason, while history was associated merely with memory, was very characteristic of the Enlightenment.

The first volume of the *Encyclopédie*, which included d'Alembert's influential "Discours préliminaire," was published in 1751, and revealed at once that the work would be carried on in the spirit of John Locke's sensationalistic psychology and epistemology. Pierre Bayle, in addition to Francis Bacon and Locke, also served as a model and inspiration for the *Encyclopédie*, though its editors rarely found it expedient to admit the fact. The *Encyclopédie* was greatly influenced by Bayle's skepticism, while falling short of his thoroughgoing Pyrrhonism. The work went much beyond him, however, in its attention to natural science, to the nascent social sciences, to economic processes, and to social reform.

The first volume established the *Encyclopédie* at once as a work that was both controversial and indispensable. It was much more comprehensive than previous works of reference, and even included copious articles on grammar, synonyms, and gazetteer-like articles concerning countries and cities. It constantly attempted to explode vulgar errors (see the article "Agnus Scythicus"), to be as precise in definition as possible, to make exact technological explanation an accepted part of the language, to suggest social reforms (see the article "Accoucheuse") or greater civil liberties (see "Aius Locutius"), and to weaken dogmatisms. In biblical criticism (for example, see "Arche de Noé") or in articles touching upon political theory (for example, "Autorité politique") or materialism (for example, "*Âme*"), the *Encyclopédie* proved itself to be adventuresome and bold.

As a result, the *Encyclopédie* encountered much opposition and suspicion, especially from orthodox religious groups. In particular, the Jesuits, whom Diderot

and d'Alembert suspected of wanting to take over the editing of the work for themselves, delighted in exposing plagiarisms in the *Encyclopédie* and in insinuating that it was subversive. In 1752, just after the publication of the second volume, the Royal Council of State prohibited further publication, although, a few months later, this decree was tacitly rescinded. Thereafter, the *Encyclopédie* was published at the rate of a volume per year until 1757, when it had reached through the letter *G*. By this time it was evident, as Diderot himself had stated in his remarkable article "Encyclopédie" in volume five, explaining the intentions and editorial policies of the work, that the object of the *Encyclopédie* was "to change the general way of thinking."

In 1757 there commenced a long and complicated crisis that resulted in d'Alembert's retiring from his part in the editing and finally in the suppression of the work by royal decree, on March 8, 1759.

Nevertheless, through the courage and tenacity of Diderot and the publishers, and as a result of the authorities studiously looking the other way, the work continued to be written, edited, and printed in secret, pending the time when it might once more be authorized. In 1765–1766, the rest of the alphabet (ten volumes of letterpress) was published. Meanwhile, the 11 volumes of plates were also being prepared and published under Diderot's supervision, the first appearing in 1762 and the last in 1772. About 4,225 sets of the original edition were sold, the price being 980 livres (326 for the 17 volumes of letterpress and 654 for the 11 volumes of plates). Inasmuch as the purchasing power of a livre was roughly equivalent to rather more than a dollar in current (1966) purchasing power, it is evident that this was a large commercial undertaking.

Each of the first seven volumes of the *Encyclopédie* had been subjected to previous censorship, but this was impossible with the last ten volumes, because they were edited secretly. There was, therefore, a considerable risk that the government might outlaw the whole edition if the articles were too forthright on theology and politics. In the end, there was little difficulty: By 1765–1766, when the final volumes were distributed, the order of the Jesuits had been suppressed and public opinion generally was moving irresistibly toward the point of view represented by the *philosophes*. But Andre-François Le Breton, the printer and chief publisher of the *Encyclopédie*, had meanwhile surreptitiously altered many of the most controversial articles after Diderot had edited them and read the proofs. Diderot discovered this treachery in 1764, too late to undo it. The subsequent discovery of a volume of proof sheets permits a before-and-after comparison of some of the articles mutilated by Le Breton; a study of these shows that the changes were substantial. The exact number of Le Breton's alterations is not known even yet, though Diderot always remained convinced that the publisher's depredations had been extensive. In spite of the maiming of the text, however, the articles in the last ten volumes are rather more sharp and critical about religious, social, and political topics than the first seven volumes had dared to be.

One of the novel features of the *Encyclopédie* was that it identified many of its contributors, the most famous being Diderot, d'Alembert, Voltaire, Jean-Jacques Rousseau ("Économie politique" and articles on music), Baron de Montesquieu ("Goût"), François Quesnay ("Fermiers," "Grains"), Baron de L'Aulne Turgot ("Étymologie," "Existence"), Jean-François Marmontel, Baron d'Holbach, and Louis de Jaucourt. After the suppression of the work in 1759, many of the contributors (a total of 160 have been identified) discontinued their collaboration, thus greatly increasing the burden on Diderot. The *Encyclopédie* represented the greatest feat in the technology of printing and publishing up to that time. It was a symbol of the intellectual preeminence of France in the eighteenth century. But it was also the symbol of a new public philosophy; and its final publication, with editorial policies and practices consistent and unchanged, was a triumphant vindication of the energy and moral courage of Diderot and even, though to a lesser extent, of his publishers.

PHILOSOPHY IN THE ENCYCLOPÉDIE

The numerous and lengthy articles in the *Encyclopédie* concerning philosophers or schools of philosophy, from "Aristotélisme" to "Zend-Avesta," constituted in themselves a stage in the development of recording the history of philosophy. Most of these articles were written by Diderot himself. In the compilation of them, he avowedly relied upon works by Thomas Stanley and Boureau Deslandes and, very heavily, upon Johann Jacob Brucker's *Historia Critica Philosophiae* (Leipzig, 1742–1744). But Brucker's work, relaxed in style and blandly deistic, was changed by Diderot into a history of philosophy that was nervous and sometimes edgy in style and, in its implicit challenging of idealism and in its inclination toward materialism, very representative of the point of view of the Enlightenment in France. Some of the articles not written by Diderot are flabby or conformist in their thought (for example, "Aristotélisme," "Spinoza"), but Diderot's own most famous ones ("Chaldéens,"

"Cyniques," "Cyrénaique," "Éclectisme," "Éléatique," "Épicuréisme," "Hobbisme," "Leibnitzianism," "Platonisme," "Pyrrhonienne") substantiate the claim that through the *Encyclopédie* Diderot was one of the creators of the history of philosophy in France.

ONTOLOGY AND EPISTEMOLOGY. It was a favorite sport of the Encyclopedists to inveigh against "metaphysics." This criticism was primarily an expression of their dislike for the great rationalistic constructions of the seventeenth century, the systematic philosophy of René Descartes, Nicolas Malebranche, Benedict Spinoza, and Gottfried Wilhelm Leibniz. In reality, since the Encyclopedists—like the logical positivists of the twentieth century—had a theory of being and a theory of knowledge, they were more metaphysical than they acknowledged or perhaps realized. The Encyclopedists predicated a real world of brute fact, and steadfastly resisted the Berkeleian philosophy, although they were familiar with it (see d'Alembert's article, "Corps"). This real world was knowable, according to the Lockean system of epistemology, through the testimony of the senses and reflection thereon. Diderot stated, for example, in the article "Inné" that "there is nothing innate except the faculty of feeling and of thinking; all the rest is acquired." Such reference to external reality interpreted by reason, led to the great emphasis given by the Encyclopedists to *expérience,* which in the French of their day had the double meaning of experiential and experimental (see d'Alembert's article, "Expérimental").

With this empirical approach to the problems of reality and knowledge, the *Encyclopédie* contributed greatly to the strengthening of the rationale of scientific hypothesis and scientific method (see, for example, "Hypothèse"). In this respect, especially noteworthy in the articles written by d'Alembert (for example, "Cosmologie" and "Cartésianisme"), the *Encyclopédie* was a forerunner to the development of positivism. Nor were the Encyclopedists lamed by Humean skepticism. They knew David Hume personally and loved him and had read his books, but they simply overlooked the implications of Hume's philosophy in respect to their own ontology and epistemology. The sensationalistic psychology of the Encyclopedists, in combination with their view of the world, strengthened them in their faith in reason, by which it was deemed possible to know and evaluate objective reality, while making it unnecessary for them to have much faith in faith. The philosophy of the *Encyclopédie* was about as far from fideism as it is possible to be.

OPPOSITION TO RELIGIOUS DOGMATISM. The *Encyclopédie* was often accused by its enemies of favoring a philosophy of materialism. This it never did outright, yet many of its articles pointed that way, especially those that had to do with the mind-body problem (for example, "Spinosiste," "Âme"). Moreover, the Encyclopedists were constantly eager to undermine dogmatic and intolerant religious orthodoxy. This function they considered as one of their most "philosophical," and it is in this connection that they helped to establish a new historiography. The Encyclopedists often wrote as though they were historical pessimists and indeed distrustful of history: "One can scarcely read history without feeling horror for the human race," wrote Voltaire in "Idole, idolatrie." Nevertheless, in their desire to shake religious dogmatism, they used criteria of historical criticism, for example, in trying to establish the correct chronology of the Bible (see "Chronologic sacrée"), and explored the nature of historical evidence (for example, as to miracles) in a way that secularized and modernized historical techniques. (In this respect the articles "Bible," "Certitude," "Mages," "Syncrétistes," are of particular interest.) As for the philosophy of history, the Encyclopedists' convictions regarding the spread of enlightenment led to a faith in progress which became one of the conspicuous features of eighteenth-century thought.

ETHICS. The *Encyclopédie* was much concerned with ethics, especially because of its insistence, as expressed by Diderot in "Irréligieux," that "morality can exist without religion; and religion can coexist, and often does, with immorality." In ethical theory many of the articles still spoke in terms of *jus naturae*, and sometimes, as in "Irréligieux," identified this moral law as "the universal law that the finger of God has engraved upon the hearts of all." But this rather conventional ethics was constantly being blended with, or superseded by, utilitarianism. The articles in the *Encyclopédie* advanced a theory of ethics that was founded not so much in the will of God as in the nature of man. And inasmuch as man was conceived of as being by nature sociable, it logically followed that an ethic grounded in man's nature was also socially conscious and other-regardful. The *Encyclopédie* also endeavored to undermine notions of free will, teaching that man, precisely because he is modifiable and educable, is capable of virtue even in a deterministic universe (see "Liberté," "Modification," "Malfaisant").

SOCIAL AND POLITICAL THEORY. The social philosophy of the *Encyclopédie* was shaped in like manner by the conviction that man by his nature is sociable (see "Philosophe"). As a result, the *Encyclopédie* was much interested in theories of social origins, and devoted a good deal of attention to the ethnography of primitive peoples, using travel books as a principal source. The article on "Humaine espèce" is a remarkable exercise in physical anthropology; and articles such as "Laboureur," "Journalier," and "Peuple" are examples of a groping toward a recognizable sociology. Thus, the *Encyclopédie* figured importantly in the development of the social sciences, as well as in the dissemination of a utilitarian social philosophy. The *Encyclopédie* had a passion for improvement and constantly applied to institutions the criterion of social usefulness.

The *Encyclopédie* also possessed a quite clearly articulated political theory, even though it was difficult to discuss political philosophy critically in a country that was professedly an absolute monarchy and exercised censorship. This political philosophy was, as might be expected, greatly influenced by Locke. Articles such as "Droit naturel" and "Égalité naturelle" spoke of "inalienable rights" and continued, as Locke and Samuel von Pufendorf had done, to explore the implications to political philosophy of new and emerging insights into the nature of man. In articles such as "Autorité politique" and "Loi fondamentale," the *Encyclopédie* praised limited monarchy and suggested that proper government rests upon consent (see "Pouvoir"). In the article "Représentants" a theory of representative government was advanced, and numerous articles suggested the guarantee of civil liberties (for example, "Habeas corpus," "Aius locutius," "Libelle") or advocated reforms ("Impôt," "Vingtième," "Privilège"). An English writer, reviewing the *Encyclopédie* in 1768, remarked that "whoever takes the trouble of combining the several political articles, will find that they form a noble system of civil liberty."

LINGUISTIC THEORY. The *Encyclopédie* was much engrossed in theories regarding the origin of language, and devoted a great deal of space to articles on grammar and on synonyms. In part this was social philosophy, in the sense that it was hoped that such speculation would throw light upon social origins; even more, it was an early manifestation of scientific and philosophical interest in the nature of language. In articles such as "Étymologie," "Élémens de science," and "Encyclopédie," Turgot, d'Alembert, and Diderot, respectively, analyzed problems of definition, semantics, and nomenclature in the attempt to explore accurately the relationship between words, concepts, and things. The Encyclopedists were remarkable for realizing that knowledge itself depends upon the correct use of language.

AESTHETICS. Aesthetic theory was not systematically developed in the *Encyclopédie*, although there were numerous articles on belletristic subjects, especially those contributed by Jean-François Marmontel (see his article "Critique") and Voltaire. Special mention should be made of Diderot's articles "Beau" and "Beauté," which reviewed extensively the aesthetic theories current in the first half of the eighteenth century and argued that it is the perception of relationships that is the basis of the beautiful.

HUMANISM. The philosophy of the *Encyclopédie* was strongly humanistic in tone. Oriented toward science, and progressive (in the sense of believing in progress), the work was integrated by the particular philosophy of man that underlies the whole. It was a philosophy, Protagorean in savor, that made man the measure of all things. This point of view was summed up by Diderot in the article "Encyclopédie": "Man is the sole and only limit whence one must start and back to whom everything must return."

See also Aesthetics, History of; Alembert, Jean Le Rond d'; Bacon, Francis; Bayle, Pierre; Berkeley, George; Descartes, René; Diderot, Denis; Enlightenment; Epistemology; Ethics; Holbach, Paul-Henri Thiry, Baron d'; Humanism; Hume, David; Language; Leibniz, Gottfried Wilhelm; Locke, John; Logical Positivism; Malebranche, Nicolas; Metaphysics, History of; Montesquieu, Baron de; Ontology; Pufendorf, Samuel von; Rousseau, Jean-Jacques; Semantics; Spinoza, Benedict (Baruch) de; Turgot, Anne Robert Jacques, Baron de L'Aulne; Utilitarianism; Voltaire, François-Marie Arouet de.

Bibliography

EDITIONS

Encyclopédie, ou dictionnaire raisonné des sciences, des arts et des métiers, par une société de gens de lettres …, 35 vols. in folio. Paris, 1751–1780. Diderot was editor-in-chief for 17 volumes of letterpress (1751–1766) and 11 volumes of plates (1762–1772); these 28 volumes were reprinted in folio at Geneva (1772–1776). The remaining volumes consist of four volumes of *Supplément*, one volume of supplementary engravings, and two volumes of index. Other editions, all published in French, appeared at Lucca (28 vols. in folio, 1758–1771), Livorno (33 vols. in folio, 1770–1779), Yverdon (58 vols. in quarto, 1770–1780), Geneva (45 vols. in quarto, 1777–1781), and Lausanne and Berne (36 vols. in octavo, 1778–1781). Reproductions of 485 of the original engravings are available in the admirably edited and inexpensive *Diderot, Denis, Pictorial Encyclopedia of Trades and Industry*, edited by Charles C. Gillispie. 2 vols. New York: Dover, 1959.

HISTORY OF THE ENCYCLOPÉDIE

Gordon, Douglas H., and Norman L. Torrey. *The Censoring of Diderot's Encyclopédie and the Re-established Text*. New York: Columbia University Press, 1947.

Grosclaude, Pierre. *Un audacieux message. L'Encyclopédie*. Paris: Nouvelles Editions Latinos, 1951.

Kafker, Frank A. "A List of Contributors to Diderot's Encyclopedia." *French Historical Studies* 3 (1963–1964): 106–122.

Le Gras, Joseph. *Diderot et l'Encyclopédie*. Amiens: Malfère, 1928.

Lough, John. "Luneau de Boisjermain v. the Publishers of the *Encyclopédie*." *Studies on Voltaire and the Eighteenth Century* 13 (1963): 115–177.

Venturi, Franco. *Le origini dell'Enciclopedia*. Florence: U Edizioni, 1946; 2nd ed., 1963.

Wilson, Arthur M. *Diderot: The Testing Years, 1713–1759*. New York: Oxford University Press, 1957.

INTELLECTUAL AND PHILOSOPHICAL ASPECTS

Barker, Joseph E. *Diderot's Treatment of the Christian Religion in the Encyclopédie*. New York: King's Crown Press, 1941.

Delorme, Suzanne, and René Taton, eds. *L'Encyclopédie et le progrès des sciences et des techniques*. Paris, 1952.

Havens, G. R., and D. F. Bond, eds. *A Critical Bibliography of French Literature*. Syracuse, NY: Syracuse University Press, 1951. Vol. IV, *The Eighteenth Century*, pp. 139–141.

Hubert, René. *Les sciences sociales dans l'Encyclopédie*. Lille: Au Siège d'Université, 1923.

"Numéro spécial à l'occasion du 2^2 centenair de l'*Encyclopédie*." *Annales de l'Université de Paris* October 1952.

Proust, Jacques. *Diderot et l'Encyclopédie*. Paris: A. Colin, 1962. Especially valuable.

Schalk, Fritz. *Einleitung in die Encyclopädie der französischen Aufklärung*. Munich, 1936.

Schargo, Nelly. *History in the Encyclopédie*. New York: Columbia University Press, 1947.

Weis, Eberhard. *Geschichtsschreibung und Staatsauffassung in der französischen Enzyklopädie*. Wiesbaden: F. Steiner, 1956.

Arthur M. Wilson (1967)

ENERGETICISM, ENERGETISM

See *Ostwald, Wilhelm*

ENERGY

Energy, from the Greek *energeia* (*en*, in; *ergon*, work), originally a technical term in Aristotelian philosophy denoting "actuality" or "existence in actuality," means, in general, activity or power of action. In the physical sciences it is defined as the capability to do work, as accumulated work or, in the words of Wilhelm Ostwald, as "that which is produced by work or which can be transformed into work." Energy is measured in terms of units of work, to overcome a resisting force of one dyne over a distance of one centimeter. (The joule = 10^7 erg = the watt-second; the kilogram-meter = 9.81×10^7 erg. In atomic physics the unit is the electron volt; $ev = 1.6 \times 10^{-12}$ erg.

In physics, energy is either kinetic or potential. A body of mass m moving with a velocity v possesses, owing to its motion, the kinetic energy $\frac{1}{2}mv^2$, which is the work necessary to overcome the inertial resistance in accelerating the body from rest to its final velocity and which is again transformed into work if the body is brought to rest. The energy that a system of bodies possesses by virtue of the relative geometrical position of its constituent parts, if subjected to gravitational, elastic, electrostatic, or other forces, is its potential energy. If, for example, a stone is raised from the surface of the earth, the potential energy of the system stone-and-earth is increased; if an elastic spring is expanded, its potential energy increases with increase of length. The attribute "potential" thus merely characterizes the latency of temporarily stored energy and does not call into question the reality of this kind of energy. With the recognition of the principle of the conservation of energy, it became apparent that the concept of energy applies to all branches of physics and to all physical sciences. Because of the at least partial convertibility of any energy into mechanical work, the aforementioned units of work also serve as measures of such energies as thermal, electric, magnetic, acoustic, and optical. For thermal energy (heat) it proved practical also to retain as a separate unit the caloric unit of heat, the calorie (equal to 4.18×10^7 erg).

HISTORY OF THE CONCEPT

In spite of its universality, the general notion of energy as a basic concept in science is a relatively recent result of a long and intricate conceptual process. From the scientific point of view this process may conveniently be divided into five consecutive stages: (1) early conceptions of energy as a source of force, (2) the rise of the concept of mechanical work, (3) the recognition of different forms of energy, of their interconvertibility, and of the conservation of their sum total, (4) the emancipation of energy as an autonomous existent, and (5) the mathematization of energy as an integral invariant. From the philosophical point of view—that is, with respect to the ontological and

epistemological status of the concept of energy—one may speak of (1) accidental, (2) substantial, (3) relational, (4) causal, and (5) formal conceptions of energy.

ENERGY AND FORCE. Aristotle was the first to use *energeia* as a technical term in his conceptual scheme, where it often signified the progressive "actualization" of that which previously existed only in potentiality. He also seems to have formed, though in an implicit manner, the idea of energy in the sense of accumulated force or accumulation of force. Force, for him, was not only the cause of motion but also the factor determining the duration or extent of motion. In the *Physics* he formulated the fundamental law of his dynamics, which, in modern terminology, states that the velocity, D/T (distance divided by time), of a mobile is proportional to the ratio of the magnitude of the moving force, A, and the resistance, B, a relationship that he described by enumerating exhaustively all possibilities under which AT/BD remains constant (with the exception of doubling the distance, D, as well as the time, T). He argued that a given finite force cannot move a mobile over an infinite distance or for an infinite time. Aristotle thus associated with every force a capacitative limitation, or, in modern terms, an energy content.

The implications of this statement for cosmology—in particular, for the motion of the celestial spheres, which derive their eternal motion ultimately from the "first mover" in accordance with the axiom "all things that are in motion must be moved by something else"—called for further clarifications. Thus, for example, Averroes, in his "Commentary on the Physics," distinguished between the primary motive force, the *motor separatus*, and the secondary forces, the *motores coniuncti*; the latter, in direct contact with the spheres, corresponding to the medieval "intelligences," draw finite quotas of force from the inexhaustible supply of the former. By this process, according to which only finite amounts are subtracted from an infinite accumulation of force, Averroes thought he was able to explain both the eternity of celestial motion and the fact that this motion does not occur instantaneously (*in instanti*), as motion under the effect of an infinite cause should do.

Considerations of this kind, which engaged Aristotelian commentators until the times of Thomas Aquinas, show clearly that the notion of force signified not only the immediate cause of motion or acceleration but also its cumulative determination, or energy content. Thomas considered the possibility of a finite and yet invariable moving force, which, being immutable, acts always in the same manner (*vis infatigabilis*), and thus he conceived of force as a moving agent independent of and separated from a constantly rejuvenating source, a notion essential for the future conception of the universe as a clockwork in action without the need of a constant supply of additional energy. Early in the fourteenth century the nominalist Peter Aureoli, in *Liber Sententiarum,* distinguished explicitly between two different aspects of force: its velocity-determining property and its capacity of consumption, or measure of exhaustibility. His differentiation can rightfully be regarded as the first ontological distinction between force and energy.

This, of course, does not imply that allusions to particular forms of energy are not found in early scientific writings. In fact, already in the *Mechanica,* commonly ascribed to Aristotle, the notion of kinetic energy is clearly referred to when it is asked:

How is it that, if you place a heavy axe on a piece of wood and put a heavy weight on the top of it, it does not cleave the wood to any considerable extent, whereas, if you lift the axe and strike the wood with it, it does split it, although the axe when it strikes the blow has much less weight upon it than when it is placed on the wood and pressing on it? It is because the effect is produced entirely by movement, and that which is heavy gets more movement from its weight when it is in motion than when it is at rest.

MECHANICAL WORK. The modern concept of energy, as the definition shows, is a generalization of the notion of work in mechanics. The concept of work can be traced back to the principle of virtual displacements, or virtual velocities, which, in turn, has its ultimate origin in Aristotelian dynamics. Aristotle's conclusions (in *De Caelo*) concerning one single force (under whose action "the smaller, lighter body will be moved farther …; for as the greater body is to the less, so will be the speed of the lesser body to that of the greater") were soon generalized for the case of a force counteracting a load, as exemplified in simple machines such as the wheel and the axle. In particular, the study of the law of the lever, as mentioned in the *Mechanica,* in Archimedes' *On the Equilibrium of Planes,* in the writings of Hero of Alexandria, and in the *Liber Karastonis,* a Latin version of the ninth-century Arabic text by Thabit ibn Kurrah, contributed to the gradual establishment of the principle of virtual displacements for which finally, in the thirteenth century, Jordanus Nemorarius tried to give a theoretical proof. The Renaissance formulation of this law—namely, that the ratio between force and load is reciprocal to that of the

spaces (distances) traversed within the same time—as pronounced by Guidobaldo del Monte (*Mechanica,* 1577), by Simon Stevin (*Hypomnemata Mathematica,* Leiden, 1608, Book 3), and by Galileo Galilei (*Opere* 2), formed the basis for the definition of work as force times distance traversed.

Pierre Varignon, in his *Nouvelle Mécanique ou statique* (Paris, 1725), reported a letter from Johann Bernoulli, dated January 26, 1717, in which the term *energy* appears in this connection, apparently for the first time in the modern period: "For all equilibrium of forces in whatever manner they are applied to each other, whether directly or indirectly, the sum of the positive energies will be equal to the sum of the negative energies taken positively." Although some historians, referring to this letter, have ascribed to Bernoulli the definition of energy as "force times distance," a critical study of the text shows undoubtedly that he still defined energy as "force times virtual velocity." In spite of the fact that this notion and its derivative, namely, the notion of work defined as "force times distance," played at least implicitly an important part in the establishment of classical mechanics—Joseph Louis Lagrange saw in the principle of virtual velocities the fundamental basis for his *Mécanique analytique* (1788), the highlight of classical mechanics—energy considerations were rarely found in theoretical or even practical mechanics prior to the middle of the nineteenth century. Before the development of the steam engine and the rise of thermodynamics, industry had little interest in energy calculations: Force, not its integrated form, counted in the use of simple machines. The primary object of theoretical mechanics, moreover, was still celestial dynamics, where, again, energetics was of little avail. This certainly is also one of the reasons why Isaac Newton's *Principia* contains practically no reference to the concept of energy or to any of its applications.

According to Ernst Mach, in *Die Mechanik in ihrer Entwicklung* (Leipzig, 1883; translated as *The Science of Mechanics,* La Salle, IL, 1942), the delay of the development of energetics as compared with that of general mechanics stemmed from what he called "trifling historical circumstances," namely, the fact that in Galileo's investigations of free fall, the relationship between velocity and time was established before the relationship between velocity and distance, so that, as multiplication with mass shows, the notions of quantity of motion or momentum and force gained priority and were regarded as more fundamental than the concept of energy, which thus appeared as a derived conception. Whatever the reason for energetics' lagging behind Newtonian mechanics, it is an indisputable fact that the concept of energy became a subject of discussion among philosophers rather than among physicists or mechanicians.

THE MEASURE OF "FORCE." Foremost among the philosophical discussions was the controversy between the Cartesians and Gottfried Wilhelm Leibniz over whether the true measure of "force" (i.e., energy) is momentum (the product of mass and velocity) or *vis viva* (as defined by Leibniz, the product of mass and the square of velocity). René Descartes, having shown in his *Principles of Philosophy* that the (scalar) quantity of motion or momentum (the vectorial nature of this quantity was recognized only by Christian Huygens) is conserved, concluded that momentum is the measure of energy. Leibniz, in "A Short Demonstration of a Remarkable Error of Descartes" ("Brevis Demonstratio Erroris Memorabilis Cartesii," in *Acta Eruditorum*, 1689), opposed this view. Lifting a load of 1 pound, he claimed, to a height of 4 feet requires the same work as lifting 4 pounds to the height of 1 foot. Since, according to Galileo, the velocities (of free fall) are proportional to the square roots of the heights (of fall), the velocity of the first object is twice that of the second before reaching ground, or $v_1 = 2v_2$. Assuming that the "forces" (energies) are proportional to the masses (moles), Leibniz concluded that $m_1 \cdot f(v_1) = m_2 \cdot f(v_2)$, where $f(v)$ is an as yet unknown function of the velocity, v. Substituting $m_2 = 4m_1$ and $v_1 = 2v_2$ yields $f(2v_2) = 4 \cdot f(v_2)$, which shows that the unknown function is quadratic in its argument, v. What is conserved and hence is the measure of "force," Leibniz concluded, is mv^2.

This controversy between the Leibnizians, among them Johann Bernoulli, Willem Jakob Gravesande, Christian von Wolff, Georg Bilfinger, and Samuel König, and the Cartesians, among them Colin Maclaurin, James Stirling, and Samuel Clarke, was essentially only a battle of words, since the Leibnizians considered force acting on bodies traveling over equal distances and the Cartesians considered force acting on bodies during equal intervals of time, as Jean Le Rond d'Alembert in *Traité de dynamique* (1743) and Lagrange in *Mécanique analytique* (1788) made clear.

CONSERVATION OF "FORCE." The interesting aspect of the Leibnizian-Cartesian controversy is the fact that both sides argued on the basis of the conservation of their respective "measures": for the Cartesians it was the conservation of momentum, for the Leibnizians that of "living force" (kinetic energy). Both contentions, as we know today, were correct, since both measures are integrals of the equations of motion. One of the most ardent sup-

porters of Leibniz was his disciple Christian von Wolff, who in the *Cosmologia Generalis* (1731) declared: "In all the universe the same quantity of living force is always conserved." Johann Bernoulli, in the essay "De Vera Notione Virium Vivarum" (in *Acta Eruditorum*, 1735), was probably the first to treat this statement of the *conservatio virium vivarum* as a fundamental principle in mechanics. The apparent loss of "living force" in inelastic collisions was usually explained away by the hypothesis that the invisible small parts of matter gain in *vis viva* just as much as the macroscopic bodies seem to lose, a view Leibniz had already expressed in *Essai de dynamique* and reaffirmed in a letter to Samuel Clarke (Fifth Letter, August 18, 1716), where he stated that "active forces are preserved in the world" and continued: "'Tis true, their wholes (unelastic colliding bodies) lose it with respect to their total motion; but their parts receive it, being shaken by the force of the concourse. And therefore that loss of force is only in appearance. … the case here is the same, as when men change great money into small." Johann Bernoulli, in contrast, explained this apparent loss as an absorption of force required for the compression of the colliding bodies.

TRANSFORMATION OF POTENTIAL ENERGY. What Bernoulli had in mind was obviously the so-called latent force, subsequently to be called potential energy, and his is the earliest description of transformation of kinetic energy into potential. The idea of such "latent force" was soon generalized to nonmechanical processes. Already in 1738 Daniel Bernoulli, in his *Hydrodynamica, sive de Viribus et Motibus Fluidorum Commentarii*, spoke of the "latent force" of combustible coal, which "if totally extracted from a cubic foot of coal and used for the motion of a machine, would be more efficient than the daily work of eight or ten men." But the measure of this "latent living force" was still mv^2.

Strictly speaking, the notion of potential—that is, a function whose space derivatives yield the force components and which therefore equals the potential energy for a unit of mass, charge, etc.—preceded the idea of potential energy. For in 1777, Lagrange, in "Recherches sur l'attraction des spheroides homogènes" (*Mémoire de l'Académie*, Paris), calculated the potential for an arbitrary discrete distribution of mass particles, and in 1782, Pierre Simon de Laplace calculated the potential for a continuous distribution. Potentials were still spoken of as "force functions"; the term *potential function* was introduced for the first time in 1828 by George Green in his *Essay of the Application of Mathematical Analysis* and later (1840), independently, by Karl Gauss.

When, in 1788, Lagrange derived the principle of the conservation of mechanical energy, or what subsequently was generally called the "theorem of the living force," as an integral of the equation of motion, he asked himself how many such integrals exist and under what conditions. The question, however, whether a similar principle exists also for nonmechanical processes did not occur to him.

The first clear and consistent terminology of energy conceptions, still in the domain of mechanical processes, was used by the Paris school of practical mathematicians and mechanicians, not by the purely analytical school headed by Lagrange and Laplace. It was Lazare Carnot who, in his *Essai sur les machines en général* (1783; republished in 1803 in a revised and enlarged edition under the title *Principes fondamentaux de l'équilibre et du mouvement*), declared that the "living force" can manifest itself either as mv^2 or as Fd (force times distance), the second being a measure of the "latent living force." Jean V. Poncelet, in *Mécanique industrielle* (1829), finally introduced for this quantity the term *mechanical work* and stated distinctly that it is the inertia of masses that serves for the accumulation of work and thus enables the transformation of work into "living force" and vice versa. Poncelet also measured this quantity by the kilogrammeter, a unit of energy universally adopted since then.

We thus see how at the beginning of the nineteenth century the notions of work and living force and their transformability became firmly established within the confines of mechanics proper. Even the *energy* was used in this connection. In *A Course of Lectures on Natural Philosophy* (London, 1807), Thomas Young, though an adherent of the Cartesian measure of force, admitted that "in almost all cases of the forces employed in practical mechanics, the labour expended in producing any motion, is proportional not to the momentum, but to the energy which is obtained." But it took another fifty years until the term *energy* in its present meaning acquired full citizenship within the vocabulary of the physical sciences. This was brought about from quite a different quarter. It derived from the study of those phenomena where heat and chemical change are the characteristic features.

CONVERSION PROCESSES. Although Francis Bacon, in his *Novum Organum*, had already stated that "the very essence of heat, or the substantial self of heat, is motion, and nothing else," and although similar statements had been made even before the seventeenth century, the late eighteenth century, in general, interpreted heat as a fluidum, in the spirit of the phlogiston theory. Still Jean B. J.

Fourier, in his *Théorie analytique de la chaleur* (1822) declared: "Thermal processes are a special kind of phenomena which cannot be explained by the principle of motion and of equilibrium." Although Joseph Black's doctrine of latent heat accounted for the disappearance of heat on the basis of the fluidum theory, the appearance of heat, as Count Rumford's experiments, at Munich in 1796 and 1798, with the boring of cannon clearly showed, was incompatible with this theory. Having eliminated all sources from which the heat produced during the boring could have originated, Rumford concluded that "it appears to be extremely difficult, if not quite impossible, to form any distinct idea of anything capable of being excited and communicated in the manner the heat was excited and communicated in those experiments, except it be motion."

At the same time (1799) Humphry Davy performed at the Royal Institution in London his famous experiment in which two pieces of ice were rubbed together by a clockwork mechanism in a vacuum, the whole apparatus being maintained at the freezing point of water. Davy concluded that heat was "a peculiar motion, probably a vibration of the corpuscles of bodies" (*Essay on Heat, Light, and the Combinations of Light,* London, 1799). Rumford's and Davy's experiments, though in their quantitative aspects not yet fully explored, suggested the interchangeability of heat and motion and thus led to the more general idea of an interconvertibility, or "correlation," of the forces of nature, previously regarded as disparate and incommensurable.

Approaching this problem from a chemical and biological point of view, Justus von Liebig, one of the earliest investigators of the economy of living organisms, advanced the theory that the mechanical energy of animals, as well as the heat of their bodies, originated from the chemical energy of their food. Such physiological experiments as those carried out in Liebig's laboratory made possible the study of conversion processes and together with increased concern with engines and natural philosophical considerations, seem to have been responsible for the independent discoveries, between 1837 and 1847, of the principle of energy conservation. In fact, Liebig's pupil Friedrich Mohr, adopting the mechanistic view that all forms of energy are manifestations of mechanical force, wrote as early as 1837: "Besides the known fifty-four chemical elements there exists in nature only one agent more, and this is called 'Kraft' ['force']; it can under suitable conditions appear as motion, cohesion, electricity, light, heat, and magnetism."

ENERGY CONSERVATION PRINCIPLE. Robert von Mayer, a physician from Heilbronn, Bavaria, who had served on a ship in the tropics, had noted that the venous blood of his patients there was redder than it had been in Europe. He explained this difference by an excess of oxygen due to a reduced combustion of the food that provided the heat of the body. He thus concluded that chemical energy, heat of the body, and muscular work are interconvertible, an idea that he pursued upon his return by a quantitative investigation of the mechanical equivalent of heat. The first enunciation of the energy conservation principle, combined with the determination of the mechanical equivalent of heat, is found in Mayer's article "Bemerkungen über die Kräfte der unbelebten Natur" (in Liebig, ed., *Annalen der Chemie und Pharmacie,* 1842, Vol. XLII, pp. 233–240). His calculations, as explained in greater detail in his *Die organische Bewegung* (1845) were based on the difference of the specific heats of air at constant volume and at constant pressure, as measured by F. Delaroche and others, yielding, in modern units, 3.65 joule per calorie; had Mayer employed Henri Regnault's more accurate results he would have arrived at 4.2 joule per calorie, the currently accepted value. The amount of heat liberated by the expenditure of mechanical or electrical work was systematically measured by James Prescott Joule, a Manchester brewer and amateur scientist. In heating liquids by the rotation of paddle wheels, forcing water through narrow tubes, or compressing masses of air, Joule demonstrated that the expenditure of the same amount of work, irrespective of the manner in which this work was done, resulted in the development of the same amount of heat. His measurements of such conversion processes gave a firm quantitative support for the conservation principle.

The discovery of the physical principle of the conservation of energy was soon found to be in full agreement with the principal tenets of the prevailing natural philosophy, the German *Naturphilosophie,* whose early proponent, Friedrich Wilhelm Joseph von Schelling, had declared in 1799, in *Einleitung zu dem Entwurf eines Systems der Naturphilosophie,* "that magnetic, electrical, chemical, and finally even organic phenomena would be interwoven into one great association … [which] extends over the whole of nature." Mayer supported his own conclusions by the metaphysical argumentation that forces are essentially causes and "causes equal effects"; since causes are indestructible and convertible into effects, forces must likewise be indestructible and interconvertible. Even the experimentalist Joule, in an article "On the Calorific Effects of Magneto-electricity, and on the Mechanical Value of Heat" (*Philosophical Magazine,* series 3, 23 [1843]: 442), declared: "I shall lose no time in repeating and extending these experiments, being satisfied that the grand agents of nature are by the Creator's fiat indestructible." In another paper (in *Philosophical Magazine,* series 3, 26 [1845]: 382) he stated: "Believing that the power to destroy belongs to the Creator alone, I entirely coincide with Roget and Faraday in the opinion, that any theory which, when carried out, demands the annihilation of force, is necessarily erroneous." The conduciveness of the philosophical climate toward the enunciation of the energy principle can most clearly be recognized from the arguments of A. Colding, who arrived at the principle independently of Mohr, Mayer, and Joule:

> The first idea I conceived on the relationship between the forces of nature was the following. As the forces of nature are something spiritual and immaterial, entities whereof we are cognizant only by their mastery over nature, these entities must of course be very superior to everything material in the world; and as it is obvious that it is through them only that the wisdom we perceive and admire in nature expresses itself, these powers must evidently be in relationship to the spiritual, immaterial, and intellectual power itself that guides nature in its progress; but if such is the case, it is consequently quite impossible to conceive of these forces as anything naturally mortal or perishable. Surely, therefore, the forces ought to be regarded as absolutely imperishable. ("Nogle Soetninger om Kraefterne," 1843, in *Philosophical Magazine,* series 4, 27 [1864]: 56–64).

Even the classic paper of Hermann von Helmholtz, the physiologist turned physicist, "On the Conservation of Force" (*Über die Erhaltung der Kraft,* Berlin, 1847), shows clearly the impact of contemporaneous philosophy, with its renunciation of Hegelianism and its reversion to an idealistic rationalism, when it declares:

> The final aim of the theoretic natural sciences is to discover the ultimate and unchangeable causes of natural phenomena. Whether all the processes of nature be actually referrible to such—whether changes occur which are not subject to the laws of necessary causation, but spring from spontaneity or freedom, this is not the place to decide; it is at all events clear that the science whose object it is to comprehend nature must proceed from the assumption that it is comprehensible.

The requirement of referring the phenomena of nature back to unchangeable final causes was interpreted by Helmholtz as reducing physical processes to motions of material particles possessing unchangeable moving forces that are dependent on conditions of space alone. Thus, Helmholtz, starting with the eighteenth-century dynamics of bodies acting under mutual attraction, generalized the Newtonian conception of motion to the case of a large number of bodies and showed that the sum of force and tension (what we now call kinetic and potential energies) remain constant during the process of motion. Applying conventional analytical mathematics, Helmholtz proved that the principle of the conservation of living force not only can be derived from Newtonian dynamics but may also serve as an equivalent point of departure for the deduction of theoretical mechanics.

This fundamental assumption may be formulated as the principle of the impossibility of a *perpetuum mobile*. When a system of particles acting under central forces passes from one configuration to another, the velocities acquired can be used to perform some work; in order to draw the same amount of work a second time from the system, one would have to restore its initial conditions by expending on it forces or energy from outside the system. The principle now requires that the amount of work gained by the transition from the first position to the second and the amount of work lost by the passage of the system from the second configuration to the first be equal, no matter in what way or at what velocity the change has been effected; otherwise a *perpetuum mobile* could be constructed on the basis of this cycle, contrary to the principle. So far Helmholtz's reasoning is but a paraphrase of the arguments used by Sadi Carnot and Benoît Clapeyron in their foundations of the thermodynamics of heat engines. By replacing the concept of work by that of "tensions" (*verbrauchte Spannkräfte*), which are equal but of opposite sign to the work performed, Helmholtz transformed the equation between living force (kinetic energy) and work into the statement that the sum of living force and tension is a constant, the tension being a function of the instantaneous state of the system. Although prima facie an insignificant change, this reformulation of the mechanical principle of the conservation of living force through the introduction of "tensions" opened up incalculable perspectives in that it could be applied to all branches of physics, not only to mechanics proper. Moreover, the new formulation was strikingly analogous to that of the principle of the conservation of matter, or mass, an accepted axiom in physical science since the times of Antoine Lavoisier. Exploiting the adaptability of the concept of "tension" to nonmechanical phenomena, Helmholtz not only reconciled the new doctrine of heat with the theory of mechanics, heat explicitly being treated as a form of energy, but also demonstrated the validity of the conservation principle for electrodynamics and other departments of physics. The recognition that mechanical work, heat, and electricity were only different forms of one and the same physical substratum—a result that can rightfully be considered the greatest physical discovery of the nineteenth century—found its analytical vindication in Helmholtz's paper.

At first, however, Helmholtz's memoir was hardly recognized, since its argumentation was based on mathematical reasoning, which at this time was accessible to but a small number of specialists. Another fundamental obstacle in the way of a just assessment of the new truth was the indiscriminate homonymous usage of the term *force* in both its Newtonian and its Leibnizian significations. Once the semantic difficulties had been removed, the principle of the conservation of energy found general acceptance and even popularity, owing to the writings of William Thomson (Lord Kelvin). In a discourse before the Royal Institution in 1856, Thomson distinguished carefully the significance of the Newtonian notion of force from what he called "energy." The term *energy*—apart from its early usage by Bernoulli and Young—had already been used three years earlier by William Rankine in his "On the General Law of the Transformation of Energy" (*Philosophical Magazine*, series 4, 5 [1853]: 106), but only Thomson's application led to its universal acceptance. "Any piece of matter or any group of bodies, however connected, which either is in motion, or can get into motion without external assistance, has what is called mechanical energy. The energy of motion may be called either 'dynamical energy' or 'actual energy.' The energy of a material system at rest in virtue of which it can get into motion, is called 'potential energy'" (*On the Origin and Transformation of Motive Power,* 1856). In 1893, in a footnote to a reprint of his 1856 lecture (in *Popular Lectures and Addresses,* London, 1894, Vol. II), Thomson wrote: "Shortly after the date of this lecture I gave the name 'kinetic energy' which is now in general use. It is substituted for 'actual' and for 'dynamical.'" Thus Helmholtz's "tension" was renamed "potential energy," and the sum total of kinetic and potential energies, the total energy of the system, was shown to be a constant that is characteristic of the system.

These innovations, however, had still to overcome some opposition. The Rankine-Thomson designation "potential energy" was rejected by John F. W. Herschel ("On the Origin of Force," in *Fortnightly Review and*

Familiar Lectures, 1857) as "unfortunate," being too common a name for such a "great truth." Even the term *conservation* of force or energy was subjected to severe criticisms, particularly by T. H. Huxley and by Herbert Spencer in his *First Principles* (1862), on the ground that "conservation" implies a conserver and an act of conserving and therefore the assumption that without such an act, force (energy) would disappear—an idea at variance with the conception to be conveyed. But in addition to the terminology, the conception itself, particularly that of potential energy, was still a matter of debate. An interesting testimony to these difficulties is Michael Faraday's paper "On the Conservation of Force" (*Philosophical Magazine,* series 4, 13 [1857]: 225–239), in which the following problem is raised: Is there creation or annihilation of force if the distance between two gravitating bodies is changed and the attractive force varies inversely with the square of the distance? "Gravitation," Faraday continued, "has not yet been connected by any degree of convertibility with the other forms of force…. That there should be a power of gravitation existing by itself having no relation to the other natural powers, and no respect to the law of the conservation of force, is as little likely as that there should be a principle of levity as well as of gravity." Rankine's answer to Faraday's objection (*Philosophical Magazine,* series 4, 17 [1859]: 250) seems to have had little effect, for as late as 1876, James Croll, in his paper "On the Transformation of Gravity" (*Philosophical Magazine,* series 5, 2 [1876]: 242–254), attempted to solve Faraday's query with the assumption that "a stone when in the act of falling [may] be acted upon by gravity with less force at any given moment than it would be were the stone at rest at that instant."

THE EMANCIPATION OF ENERGY. Although Croll's paper is full of misconceptions, which, interestingly, were clarified in an answer by the Viennese physiologist Ernst von Brücke, "On Gravitation and the Conservation of Force" (*Philosophical Magazine,* series 4, 15 [1858]: 81–90), it was of great importance for the subsequent development of the concept of energy. It connected the notion of energy for the first time with that of space. That space and change of position are necessary conditions for energy transformations Croll tried to demonstrate by the following consideration: four possibilities of energy transformations are conceivable—a change of potential energy into kinetic, of kinetic into potential, of kinetic into kinetic, and of potential into potential. Since, however, there "is evidently no such thing in nature, so far as is yet known, as one form of potential passing directly into another form" of potential energy and the existence

of kinetic energy always implies change of position, the point is proved. Having thus associated energy with space, Croll went on to dissociate it from the material medium. "Our inability to conceive how force can exist without a material medium has its foundation in a metaphysical misconception," an idea he explained in greater detail in his book *Philosophy of Theism* (London, 1857). Croll's almost casual remarks, though scientifically rather objectionable and philosophically highly speculative, may be regarded as the earliest objection to the prevailing view, which still conceived of energy as an attribute, so to speak, of the dynamic system.

Meanwhile, James Clerk Maxwell's *Treatise on Electricity and Magnetism* (1873) appeared, opening the way for a field-theory treatment of electromagnetic phenomena. It showed, in particular, that the work necessary to build up an electromagnetic field can be regarded as equivalent to the energy produced in space with a certain density that depends on the squares of the magnitudes of the electric and magnetic fields. In the case of nonstatic fields these calculations lead to the conclusion, as was shown by J. H. Poynting in "On the Transfer of Energy in the Electromagnetic Field" (*Philosophical Transactions of the Royal Society* 175 [1885]: 343–361), that energy has to flow from one place in space to another in order to compensate for changes that occur in a particular region of space. A transfer of energy, it is true, had been associated with electricity before Poynting, but the energy flow was always considered as being confined to the conducting wires.

> But the existence of induced currents and of electromagnetic actions at a distance from a primary circuit from which they draw their energy, has led us, under the guidance of Faraday and Maxwell, to look upon the medium surrounding the conductor as playing a very important part in the development of the phenomena. If we believe in the continuity of the motion of energy, that is, if we believe that when it disappears at one point and reappears at another it must have passed through the intervening space, we are forced to conclude that the surrounding medium contains at least a part of the energy, and that it is capable of transferring it from point to point.

Thus the surrounding medium or empty space became the arena in which energy moves, and energy, disjoined from matter, was raised in its ontological status from a mere accident of a mechanical or physical system to the autonomous rank of independent existence: matter ceased to be the indispensable vehicle for its transport. Mechanics, with its restricted conception of transfer of energy by matter, could proceed only as far as Gaspard de Coriolis's notion of "energy currents," described in his *Traité de la mécanique* (1844). The complete emancipation or reification of energy could be achieved only by a theory of action-at-a-distance, such as Maxwell's theory of electromagnetism. Here energy could be labeled and traced in its motion or change of form just as a piece of matter is ticketed so that it can be identified in other places under other conditions.

The recognition of the new ontological status of energy led to a result of great philosophical importance: It strengthened the position of those who opposed the prevailing kinetic-corpuscular theory of nature, according to which all processes are reduced to motions of particles and motion is the fundamental concept for physical explanation. Referring to the demonstrated equivalence of all forms of energy, the opponents claimed that kinetic energy is only one of the forms in which this quantity appears. In their view, energy was a much more general conception than motion, a conception that should not be narrowed down to mean only energy of attraction and repulsion of gravitational or electrostatic nature or energy of various forms of motion. One of the earliest exponents of this school of "energetics" was G. Helm, who, in a treatise, *Die Lehre von der Energie* (Leipzig, 1887), revived the term *energetics,* originally coined by Rankine, to characterize his position, according to which energy is the basic physical reality responsible for all natural phenomena. Helm referred to Gustav Zeuner, Ernst Mach, Josiah Gibbs, James Clerk Maxwell, A. J. von Oettingen, and Joseph Popper as advocating similar ideas. In particular, he claimed, energy can always be broken down into two factors, an intensity and an extensity factor, which characterize the quantity of energy as well as the direction in which changes of energy take place (the intensity factor always decreases).

In spite of further expositions, Helm's ideas did not attract much attention until Wilhelm Ostwald incorporated Helm's "factorization of energy" into the second edition of his treatise on physical chemistry, *Lehrbuch der allgemeinen Chemie* (1893), as the foundation of his theory of chemical affinity. In the period between the first and second editions of his treatise Ostwald embraced the new doctrine of energetics, and with his address in 1895 to the German Congress of Naturalists at Lübeck, "The Conquest of Scientific Materialism" (*Die Überwindung des wissenschaftlichen Materialismus*), he became the principal speaker of the new movement. In his view, not only was energy the universal currency of physics, but all phenomena of nature were merely manifestations of energy and of its manifold transformations.

In "Lectures on Natural Philosophy" (*Vorlesungen über Naturphilosophie,* Leipzig, 1901) Ostwald contended that since substance is by definition that which persists under transformations or changes, energy is substance. Methodological as well as epistemological considerations, he claimed, force us to see in energy the only substance—methodologically because the alternative view, scientific materialism, has failed to give an exhaustive explanation in even a single case of natural phenomena; epistemologically because "what we hear originates in work done on the ear drum and the middle ear by the vibrations of the air. What we see is only radiant energy which does chemical work on the retina that is perceived as light... . From this point of view the totality of nature appears as a series of spatially and temporally changing energies, of which we obtain knowledge in proportion as they impinge on the body, and especially upon the sense organs fashioned for the reception of the appropriate energies." Ostwald's conception of a physical object in terms of energy, of its volume in terms of compressibility, and of its shape in terms of elasticity is one of the final stages in a development that began with John Locke's sensationalistic conception and eventually put an end to the substantial conception of matter.

The "dissolution of matter" into energy was particularly welcomed by the adherents of the monistic school of thought in their search for a unified conception of the universe. Gustave Le Bon, for instance, in his *L'evolution de la matière* (Paris, 1905), spoke of the "dematerialization of matter into energy," a philosophical conclusion that in the same year found a far-reaching and profound scientific foundation. For in a paper titled "Does the Inertia of a Body Depend upon Its Energy Content?" ("Ist die Trägheit eines Körpers von seinem Energieinhalt abhängig?" in *Annalen der Physik* 18 [1905]: 639–641), Albert Einstein showed, on the basis of the Maxwell-Hertz equations of the electromagnetic field, that "if a body gives off the energy E in the form of radiation, its mass diminishes by E/c^2," where c denotes the velocity of light. Since then the mass-energy relation, $E = mc^2$, has been of fundamental importance, particularly in nuclear physics, where P. M. S. Blackett, G. P. S. Occhialini, O. Klemperer, and others showed that the total mass of a particle can be transformed into energy.

Whereas in classical mechanics differences of energy alone were of physical significance, so that energy could be determined only up to an additive constant, in modern physics energy lost this indeterminateness and became a physical quantity of absolute magnitude. Moreover, in the theory of relativity the principles of the conservation of energy, or mass, and momentum, the latter being the basis of the Cartesian measure of "force," revealed themselves only as different aspects of one and the same conservation law, the conservation of the momentum-energy four-vector. On the basis of the Einstein equation $E = mc^2$ the problem of the source of solar (or stellar) energy could be solved, the "packing effect" in nuclear physics could be explained, and the release of nuclear energy could be predicted. Energy was released mass, and mass was frozen energy, or as Bertrand Russell, in *Human Knowledge: Its Scopes and Limits* (New York, 1948), summarized the situation: "Mass is only a form of energy, and there is no reason why matter should not be dissolved into other forms of energy. It is energy, not matter, that is fundamental in physics."

CONSERVATION AND INVARIANCE. Although the theory of relativity threw new light on the conservational aspects of energy, or mass, the relationship between conservation and invariance found its final elucidation in Emmy Noether's article "Invariant Variational Problems" ("Invariante Variationsprobleme," in *Göttinger Nachricten* [1918], pp. 235–257), which demonstrates the conservation of certain quantities (for example, the canonical energy-momentum tensor) for dynamic systems that are invariant under continuous transformations of the coordinates or, more generally, of the field functions involved. Conservation thus appeared as a consequence of symmetry properties, a fact that was in part known already from the Hamiltonian formulation of classical mechanics. In particular, if homogeneity of space and time is assumed, that is, if it is postulated that the system is invariant under translational transformations of the origins of space-coordinates and time-coordinates, then the conservation of momenta and of energy is but a mathematical consequence. The principle of the conservation of energy of a given dynamic system is therefore ultimately a consequence of the invariance (or symmetry) of the system under changes in the zero-point of the time scale, that is, a consequence of the homogeneity of time.

See also Alembert, Jean Le Rond d'; Aristotle; Averroes; Bacon, Francis; Bilfinger, Georg Bernhard; Clarke, Samuel; Descartes, René; Einstein, Albert; Faraday, Michael; Force; Galileo Galilei; Gibbs, Josiah; Helmholtz, Hermann Ludwig von; Huxley, Thomas Henry; Lavoisier, Antoine; Leibniz, Gottfried Wilhelm; Mach, Ernst; Maxwell, James Clerk; Newton, Isaac; Ostwald, Wilhelm; Peter Aureol; Philosophy of Physics; Russell, Bertrand Arthur William; Schelling, Friedrich Wilhelm Joseph von; Thomas Aquinas, St.; Wolff, Christian.

Bibliography

Duhem, P. *L'évolution de la mécanique.* Paris, 1903.

Haas, A. E. "Die Begründung der Energetik durch Leibniz." *Annalen der Naturphilosophie* 7 (1908): 373–386.

Haas, A. E. *Die Entwicklungsgeschichte des Satzes von der Erhaltung der Kraft.* Vienna, 1909.

Helm, G. *Die Energetik nach ihrer geschichtlichen Entwicklung.* Leipzig, 1898.

Hiebert, Erwin N. *Historical Roots of the Principle of Conservation of Energy.* Madison: State Historical Society of Wisconsin for the Dept. of History, University of Wisconsin, 1962.

Jammer, M. "The Factorization of Energy." *British Journal for the Philosophy of Science* 14 (1963): 160–166.

Kuhn, T. S. "Energy Conservation as an Example of Simultaneous Discovery." In *Critical Problems in the History of Science,* edited by M. Clagett. Madison: University of Wisconsin Press, 1959.

Mach, E. *Die Geschichte und die Wurzel des Satzes von der Erhaltung der Arbeit.* Prague, 1872.

Planck, M. *Das Prinzip der Erhaltung der Kraft.* Leipzig: Teubner, 1st ed., 1887; 2nd ed., 1908.

M. Jammer (1967)

ENERGY [ADDENDUM]

Force is among the most fundamental concepts in Newtonian physics. Energy became an important unifying concept in nineteenth-century physics. Energy and force take on somewhat different roles in relativity and quantum mechanics.

FORCE IN CLASSICAL PHYSICS

In classical physics, force is a vector quantity. Isaac Newton's second law of motion ($F = ma$) relates the net force (F) on a body to its mass (m) and acceleration (a) in an inertial reference frame. Newton's third law says that the force exerted by body A on body B is equal and opposite to the force that B exerts on A. To apply Newton's laws of motion in a non-inertial frame, correction factors with the dimensions of force ("pseudoforces") must be introduced, such as the Coriolis and centrifugal forces.

The constituents of a system of bodies (such as a macroscopic object) exert "internal forces" upon one another, whereas "external forces" are imposed on the system from without. By Newton's third law, the internal forces cancel. Newton's second law then applies to the system as a whole: The net external force on the system equals the product of the system's total mass (the sum of its constituents' masses) with the acceleration of its center of mass. The system of bodies therefore itself constitutes a body in classical physics.

If the net force on a body is *defined* as (or is nothing over and above) the product of its acceleration and mass, then Newton's second "law" is true *trivially*. One way to avoid this result is to take "force" as defined partially by the various force laws (gravitational, electric, magnetic, etc.). Another way is to take forces as real entities existing alongside masses and accelerations and serving as simultaneous causes of accelerations. Philosophers who believe in the reality of forces have disagreed about whether component forces or only net forces are real. If component forces are real, then a zero net force may have real nonzero components. These components apparently cannot be understood as real parts of a nonexistent whole. Perhaps the components along arbitrary axes are unreal, whereas the components given by the various force laws are real. According to Nancy Cartwright, net forces are real but components are not. Hence, there is no component gravitational force between two bodies for the gravitational force law to relate to the bodies' masses and separation. The law must concern merely those (unreal) situations where a body feels only a single influence—from one other body's mass; the law then covers the net forces in those cases.

FORCE IN MODERN PHYSICS

Henri Poincare and Hans Reichenbach distinguished differential forces (such as electric and magnetic forces) from universal forces, which cannot be shielded against and would have the same effect on any body (whatever its charge, mass, chemical constitution …) in a given spatiotemporal location. A pseudoforce is a universal force, since it reflects the reference frame's acceleration, not the character of the body affected. Phenomena cannot reveal any universal forces acting on a given body, since measuring devices would be affected in the same way. Reichenbach argued that phenomena determine the geometry of spacetime only up to a conventional choice of universal forces.

According to Albert Einstein's general theory of relativity, gravity's "effects" on a body's trajectory result not from an external force, but from spacetime's geometry. To Einstein, this was suggested by the equality of inertial and gravitational masses, rendering a body's acceleration due to gravity independent of its own mass. That is, gravity

functions as a universal force, and by adopting a non-Euclidean spacetime geometry, general relativity geometrises gravity away. Einstein's "principle of equivalence" says that in any sufficiently small spatiotemporal region, there is a reference frame in which no phenomena are attributed to gravity, and so the laws do not refer to gravity. (In the canonical example, the phenomena in an elevator falling freely in a gravitational field are explained, without appealing to gravity, in a reference frame falling with the elevator. In that frame, all phenomena are indistinguishable from those experienced in an inertial frame.) This principle thus treats gravity as a pseudoforce.

In quantum physics, a body's state can be affected even as the body passes exclusively through regions where it feels no force. This occurs in the Aharanov-Bohm effect, for example.

FIELDS OF FORCE

A force at some spatiotemporal location may be interpreted as having, apart from the affected body's charge, no causes nearer in space (time) than an appropriately charged body's being some distance away (sometime earlier). This would be (retarded) action at a distance. Although Newton regarded action at a distance as impossible, he failed to offer any local causal mechanism for gravity. Accordingly, gravity was later often interpreted as action at a distance.

Alternatively, a force may be interpreted as having an entirely *local* cause: the affected body's charge and the corresponding field at the body's spatiotemporal location. A field is a vector quantity equal at a given location to the force per unit charge that would be felt by a charged point body, were one present there. In the nineteenth century, Michael Faraday, James Clerk Maxwell, Oliver Heaviside, and Heinrich Hertz developed an electromagnetic field theory. Maxwell argued that the electric and magnetic fields are real, rather than mere mathematical devices (like the electric potential), on the grounds that fields possess energy (and momentum). According to Faraday, we can account for matter's impenetrability without positing that matter consists of hard "stuff"—namely, by positing that material objects are surrounded by short-range fields of repulsive force. Accordingly, we have no reason to believe in a solid body lying somewhere deep beneath its surrounding atmosphere of fields; Faraday speculated that matter is nothing but inertia-bearing centers of fields. Max Abraham, Wilhelm Wien, and Gustav Mie were among those who later tried to develop an "electromagnetic theory of matter," according to which bodies are just local concentrations of the electromagnetic field.

ENERGY IN CLASSICAL PHYSICS

A system's energy is a scalar quantity reflecting the amount of "work" (force accumulated over distance) needed to assemble the system. Another way of putting the point is that a system's energy is its capacity to do work. The energy of a closed system is a conserved quantity.

Energy comes in two forms: kinetic and potential. A body moving with speed v has kinetic energy (equal to ½ mv^2). A system's potential energy reflects its configuration. For example, a pair of like electric charges (which mutually repel) has greater electric potential energy insofar as the two charges are nearer (and so required more work to be squeezed together to their current separation). A system's total energy is the arithmetic sum of its various kinetic and potential energies.

Energy conservation was the great unifying principle of nineteenth-century physics. All forms of energy—whether chemical (as stored in a battery), thermal, molecular (as in a chemical bond), elastic (as stored in a spring), kinetic, electric, magnetic, or gravitational—could be interconverted according to fixed rates of exchange, providing a common currency for nature's economy. A system's energy could be calculated—and some of the system's behavior thus predicted—even if a detailed mechanical model of the system was unavailable, either because the system was too complicated (e.g., a large collection of molecules) or because its presumptive inner workings were unknown (as in the case of the aether, the space-pervading medium purportedly responsible for long-distance electromagnetic interactions).

Potential energy is ascribed to a system *as a whole* (e.g., to the *pair* of charged bodies) but is assigned no definite distribution among the system's constituents. Prior to Maxwell's electromagnetic field theory, physical law also seemed silent on the *absolute* value of the system's energy; energy *differences* alone matter to energy's conservation. That is, the system's potential energy reflects the work needed to assemble it, but since we may take any configuration as constituting the initial "raw material" out of which the system is assembled, it is arbitrary which configuration is assigned zero potential energy. The arbitrariness of energy's spatial distribution and absolute value suggested that energy is not a real substance that is spread around space and "neither created nor destroyed." It suggests, rather, that energy is just an arithmetic combination of various physical quantities (e.g., charge, velocity) that is useful for predicting a system's behavior by virtue of its maintaining a constant value.

All this was greatly affected by Maxwell's electromagnetic field theory. The retarded character of electromagnetic action results in violations of Newton's third law in nonstatic cases and, therefore, in energy nonconservation—unless there are some additional energy terms beyond those used in calculating the system's total energy in a static case. Maxwell's theory supplied corrected terms for the electric and magnetic potential energies, restoring energy conservation. These corrected terms are most naturally interpreted as ascribing energy to the electric and magnetic fields—that is, to the apparently empty space surrounding charged bodies. The field energy density at a point is proportional to the square of the field's strength there. The field's zero level, as determined by the condition in which zero force per unit charge would be felt by a test body, designates a non-arbitrary condition of zero energy. Thus, by ascribing energy to the field, we find electromagnetic potential energy to have an absolute value and a determinate distribution in space. This result suggests that energy is a real substance and that the electric and magnetic fields, by virtue of containing energy, are real.

By assuming that parcels of energy have continuing identities as they move and, moreover, that energy obeys a "continuity equation" (in that parcels of energy must travel through space along continuous paths), John Henry Poynting found an expression for the energy flux density (the rate and direction of energy flow at each location in the electric and magnetic fields). This solution, the "Poynting vector," gives results that many (such as Hertz, James Jeans, and J. J. Thomson) found counterintuitive in certain cases (as when it entails that a tremendous flow of energy circulates around a stationary magnet near an unmoving charged body). Moreover, an individual parcel of energy cannot be marked in order to follow its trajectory. Furthermore, the Poynting vector is not the unique solution to the continuity equation for energy flow. All of the solutions have counterintuitive consequences like the above. They agree on the net energy flow across a closed surface. However, they disagree on the energy flow across an open surface (i.e., a surface that fails to completely enclose a volume). These results suggested to some (e.g., Heaviside and Hertz) that energy is not a substance. Perhaps it is a property (like velocity). In that case, its possession by fields might entail their reality. Alternatively, perhaps energy is merely a theoretical fiction (as Jeans believed). In that case, energy would lack sufficient ontological status to underwrite the reality of fields. This issue is not resolved within classical physics.

ENERGY IN MODERN PHYSICS

In the special theory of relativity, energy is conserved but is not Lorentz invariant. Hence, a system's energy reflects not only its real state, but also the inertial reference frame in which we have chosen to describe it. Energy and momentum are the components of a 4-vector whose length is a Lorentz invariant quantity: the (rest) mass. That is, a system's mass appears in different inertial frames as different combinations of energy and momentum.

It is sometimes said that energy and mass are interconvertible according to Einstein's famous equation $E=mc^2$, as when a ball of gas is heated and the added thermal energy becomes additional mass. Such talk of energy's being "converted" into mass (or matter) is highly misleading, since energy and mass are radically different quantities: mass is real whereas energy is not. Mass (or matter) thus cannot be or be transformed into energy; bodies are not made of energy. Physical transformations of a closed system cannot result in the appearance or disappearance of some mass, since mass is a conserved quantity.

When we consider the ball of gas as a collection of bodies, we characterize the added heat as having boosted various molecules' kinetic energies, though not their masses. When we instead consider the gas as a single body, the kinetic energy contributed by the heat counts toward the gas's mass (which is not the sum of the masses of the gas molecules). This "conversion" of energy into mass is not a real physical transformation. It is an artifact of *our* shift from treating the gas as many bodies to treating it as a single body. As in classical physics, a system of bodies is itself a body.

In quantum mechanics, the value of a system's energy is more definite insofar as the moment at which it possesses that energy is less definite. This is a form of Werner Heisenberg's "uncertainty principle." Though the proper interpretation of this principle is controversial, it is generally held responsible for the brief departures from energy conservation required for the existence of virtual particles and states. A charged point particle's infinite self-energy also remains a source of controversy in quantum mechanics, though renormalization techniques allow it to be finessed in calculations.

See also Classical Mechanics, Philosophy of; Conservation Principle; Force.

Bibliography

Berkson, William. *Fields of Force*. New York: Wiley, 1974.

Cartwright, Nancy. *How the Laws of Physics Lie*. Oxford: Clarendon, 1983.

Einstein, Albert, and Leopold Infeld. *The Evolution of Physics*. New York: Simon & Schuster, 1951.

Faraday, Michael. "A Speculation Touching Electric Conduction and the Nature of Matter." In *Experimental Researches in Electricity*, Vol. 2, 284–293. London: Bernard Quaritch, 1844.

Hesse, Mary. *Forces and Fields*. Totowa: Littlefield, 1965.

Imry, Yoseph, and Richard Webb. "Quantum Interference and the Aharonov-Bohm Effect." *Scientific American* 260 (4) (1989): 56–62.

Jammer, Max. *Concepts of Force*. Cambridge, MA: Harvard University Press, 1957.

Jeans, James. *The Mysterious Universe*. London: Macmillan, 1932.

Lange, Marc. *An Introduction to the Philosophy of Physics*. Malden: Blackwell, 2002.

Lodge, Oliver. "On the Identity of Energy." *Philosophical Magazine* 19 (series 5): (1885): 482–487.

Maxwell, James Clerk. "Action at a Distance." In *The Scientific Papers of James Clerk Maxwell*, Vol. 2., edited by W. D. Niven. 311–323. Cambridge, U.K.: Cambridge University Press, 1890.

Maxwell, James Clerk. *A Treatise on Electricity and Magnetism*. New York: Dover, 1954.

Nahin, Paul. *Oliver Heaviside*. Baltimore, MD: Johns Hopkins Press, 2002.

Poynting, John Henry. "On the Transfer of Energy in the Electromagnetic Field." In *Scientific Papers*, 175–193. Cambridge, MA: Cambridge University Press, 1920.

Reichenbach, Hans. *The Philosophy of Space and Time*. Edited and translated by Maria Reichenbach and John Freund. New York: Dover, 1958.

Marc Lange (2005)

ENGELS, FRIEDRICH
(1820–1895)

Friedrich Engels, the intellectual companion of Karl Marx, although generally considered inferior to his colleague as a thinker, contributed more than Marx to the development of the philosophical aspects of Marxism. Indeed he was the creator of orthodox Marxism as a system based on historical materialism and on dialectics. Engels was born in Barmen in the German Rhineland. His father was a textile manufacturer who had interests in England, and Engels went there to work in a cotton mill in Manchester, first as clerk, later as manager and part owner. Engels was a man of many talents, a scholar, linguist, pamphleteer, soldier, military commentator, and businessman. He was all those things with a thoroughness and distinction that would have brought him recognition in his own right, but it was his intellectual partnership with a man of genius that brought him fame. Engels met Marx briefly in Cologne in 1842, became acquainted with him in Paris in 1844, and worked actively with him before and during the revolutionary ferment of 1848, when they wrote the *Communist Manifesto.* In 1850 Engels reluctantly returned to his business in Manchester, in part because he saw that Marx needed financial support in order to continue his researches. This help Engels gave unstintingly throughout Marx's life and for years after his death, to his surviving children. Outliving Marx by twelve years, Engels edited his friend's manuscripts, notably the two volumes of *Das Kapital* left unfinished by Marx. He also served as official interpreter of Marxist doctrine during the years when it was beginning to attain worldwide influence over workingmen's movements.

Beginning with works written during Marx's lifetime and with Marx's express approval—for example, *Anti-Dühring* (1878)—Engels emphasized the scientific, positivist component in their joint theories, which he compared with those of Charles Darwin. Engels believed that he and Marx had discovered a rigid system of historical laws that would lead with inexorable necessity to socialism. These laws, Engels held, were dialectic rather than mechanical in character. That is, instead of being like the laws previously discovered in natural science and extrapolated to social studies by men whom Engels called vulgar materialists, they were laws that took account of the contradictions in reality and of the fact that development occurred in revolutionary leaps to higher levels. Engels took from G. W. F. Hegel the doctrine, which he called the law of the interpenetration of opposites, that objective contradictions exist in reality. He enunciated the law of the transformation of quantity into quality, which asserts that change occurs abruptly, after a period of gradual progression. The last dialectical law, the negation of the negation, states that progress takes place by a series of detours, from position *A* to the opposite, position—*A*, and then back to the opposite of that position, which turns out to be position *A* "raised to a higher power." To give one of Marx's own examples, the industrial bourgeoisie generates its opposite, the miserable proletariat, which then negates bourgeois capital in a revolutionary leap to the higher stage of classless industrial society.

Engels adumbrated these theories in *Anti-Dühring* and stressed them in a special excerpt from that work, *Socialism: Utopian and Scientific* (1892), but the extent to which he carried them was not known until his *Dialectics of Nature* was published in 1925. In this work he extended materialist dialectics to the natural sciences, with results that are often held to be ludicrous, and implied that dialectics would supersede formal logic. The lengthy controversies that these questions provoked in Soviet philosophy arose, then, from the work of Engels rather than of Marx.

While it is certain that Engels stressed such questions more than Marx and that he lived on to formalize a Marxist tradition out of reverence for a friend who disliked just such formalism, one must be wary of attempts to set Engels, as a scientistic pedant, against Marx, as an existentialist or idealist. It is tempting for certain neo-Marxist philosophers, but in the end impossible, to purge Marxism of all its allegedly scientific content that has since been proven untrue and to lay all these errors at Engels's door, leaving only the "profound" (or ambiguous) speculations of the young Marx as true Marxism. For one thing, it was Engels who suggested those early speculations to Marx, in 1844. And decades later it was not Engels alone but the age and his own ambitions that led Marx to present his mature theory of history as a "scientific system" (decorated with some Hegelian flourishes). At all events, it was Marx's thought as understood by Engels that came to constitute Marxism and, in particular, Soviet dogma.

See also Communism; Dialectical Materialism; Hegel, Georg Wilhelm Friedrich; Marxist Philosophy; Marx, Karl.

Bibliography

PRIMARY WORKS

Die Entwicklung des Sozialismus von der Utopie zur Wissenschaft (Socialism: utopian and scientific). Translated by E. Aveling. New York: Scribner, 1892.

Der Ursprung der Familie, des Privateigentums und des Staats (The origin of the family, private property and the state). Translated by E. Untermann. Chicago: Kerr, 1902.

Die Briefe von Friedrich Engels und Eduard Bernstein. Berlin, 1925.

Gesamtausgabe. 12 vols. Berlin and Moscow, 1927–1935.

Herr Eugen Dührings Umwälzung der Wissenschaft (Herr Eugen Dühring's revolution in science). Translated by E. Burns. London: M. Lawrence, 1934.

Ludwig Feuerbach und der Ausgang der klassischen deutschen Philosophie (Ludwig Feuerbach and the outcome of classical German philosophy). New York: International, 1934.

Dialektik der Natur (Dialectics of nature). Translated by Clemens Dutt. New York: International, 1940.

Selected Works. 2 vols. London, 1942.

Grundsätze des Kommunismus (Principles of communism). Translated by Paul Sweezy. New York: Monthly Review, 1964.

Sochineniya, 32 vols. Moscow, 1955–.

Friedrich Engels–Paul et Laura Lafargue, Correspondance, 1868–95, 3 vols. Edited by E. Bottigelli. Paris: Editions Sociales, 1956–1959.

Selected Letters: The Personal Correspondence, 1844–1877. Edited by Fritz J. Raddatz. Translated by Ewald Osers. Boston: Little Brown, 1981.

SECONDARY WORKS

Arthur, Christopher J., ed. *Engels Today: A Centenary Appreciation.* Houndmills, U.K.: Macmillan, 1996.

Carver, Terrell. *Friedrich Engels: His Life and Thought.* New York: St. Martin's Press, 1990.

Dixon, Richard et al., trans. *Karl Marx, Frederick Engels: Collected Works.* 49 vols. New York: International, 1975–.

Hook, Sidney. *Reason, Social Myths, and Democracy.* New York: Humanities, 1950.

Lichtheim, George. *Marxism.* London: Routledge and Kegan Paul, 1964.

Meyer, Gustav. *Friedrich Engels.* 2 vols. The Hague, 1934.

Steger, Manfred B., and Terrell Carver, eds. *Engels after Marx.* University Park: Pennsylvania State University Press, 1999.

Neil McInnes (1967)
Bibliography updated by Philip Reed

ENGINEERING ETHICS

"[F]or all of its influence on our modern world, the engineering profession remains a mystery to many Americans." (ASEE *Action*). These words in President Bill Clinton's statement for Engineer's Week of 1999 capture the curious situation of engineering: its products shape the world, but engineers are virtually invisible.

The academic study of ethics and responsibility in engineering began in the United States in the mid-1970s at a time of social ferment and heightened public scrutiny of the professions. Scholars from philosophy and engineering, collaborating in workshops and conferences, teaching, and research, began to penetrate the mystery. They concentrated on engineering in the United States.

Engineering originated in France in the seventeenth century and led in France to the development of the first engineering curriculum during the eighteenth century. Subsequently, engineering took shape as an occupation elsewhere, notably in the United States, Britain, Germany, and Russia. The French curriculum, with its emphasis on mathematics, physics, and chemistry, became the model for the engineering curriculum in the United States and most other countries. Despite persisting differences among countries in the status of professions and of engi-

neers, the academic study of engineering ethics spread to a number of other countries.

Engineering ethics critically examines the behavior of engineers and engineering institutions in light of the special standards of the profession and the common standards of morality. The discipline studies engineers' actions, practices, and workplace, focusing philosophical analysis on standards and concepts such as responsibility and loyalty, to help identify ethical problems and options for resolving them.

Cases or vignettes are essential starting points for teaching and research. For example, during an economic downturn, an engineer overseeing the testing of fuel pumps for a company receives instructions to curtail the testing process. The engineer's ethical concern is that he or she will not be able to ensure the life expectancy of the pumps relied on by the company's customers.

From the latter part of the nineteenth century, engineering in the United States organized as a profession, creating engineering professional societies and promulgating technical and ethical standards. The latter incorporate ordinary morality, for example, in requiring engineers to "issue public statements only in an objective and truthful manner." They include special standards, for instance, the canon requiring engineers to act "for each employer or client as faithful agents … and avoid conflicts of interest." (Accreditation Board for Engineering and Technology [ABET] 1977, p. 1).

In the ferment of the mid-1970s engineering societies revised their codes of ethics. Unsatisfied with a commitment to "due regard" or "proper regard" for the public, almost all the societies adopted as the first canon, "Engineers shall hold paramount the safety, health, and welfare of the public in the performance of their professional duties" (Florman 1986, p. 77–78).

A great majority of engineers are employees of large business organizations where they do not easily acquire authority or visibility. Still, through their professional societies, engineers profess a commitment to serve society and continue to promulgate technical and ethical standards supporting that commitment. Ethical standards articulate values underlying the technical standards, the core values—safety, reliability, and efficiency—that are also embedded in routines of engineering practice.

The engineering workplace features complexities and intricacies of large, generally hierarchical organizations. The role of engineers in business and in other organizations is elastic. They manage a range of responsibilities from narrowly technical to managerial and, while often subordinate to managers, must cooperate with them in decision making. The major ethical challenge for engineers is to deal with these complexities (including cost constraints) as employees bound by the special ethical standards of a profession as well as by moral rules. For example, they must find ethically justified, practical options for coping with instructions to curtail testing or to drastically revise public statements.

Adding to the complexity of the engineering workplace is the legal environment, including contracts, the federal and state regulatory systems for health and safety, product liability litigation, and common-law adjudication involving expert witnesses. The legal framework both constrains engineers and generates questions about additional ethical responsibilities, for example, about the extent of their responsibilities to help formulate or implement government standards to control pollution.

Individual engineers' ethical obligations derive from requirements of morality, the obligation of everyone to exercise a reasonable standard of care, the special standards of the profession, and the duties they have as employees. All these ethical imperatives inform the exercise of practical judgment by engineers, the professionals who determine specifications for the design, development, testing, operation, maintenance, and disposal of technological products and systems.

Regarding concerns about safety, for instance, they have a duty to protect the public while avoiding injury to their employers. Engineers are thus subject to tension between the duty of loyalty to the employer (complicated by having to distinguish between interests of the company and what managers want) and the obligation to hold public safety paramount. An engineer's judgment that his or her company's environmentally damaging spill should be reported to the regulatory agency might encounter resistance challenging his or her loyalty. In handling the reporting obligation, the engineer must take due care to avoid injury to the company and to a manager perhaps more concerned with self-protection than other interests.

The moral status of loyalty and the idea of critical loyalty are central in research and teaching. Discussion focuses on a range of ways to express independent judgment, from disagreement and dissent to the extreme of whistle-blowing. Dissent, such as resisting assignment to a particular project out of safety concerns, may invoke the code of ethics as support. Disagreement and dissent require tact and sensitivity so as not to cause avoidable opposition or injury.

Whistle-blowing, that is, transmitting information outside normal channels, ruptures relationships and requires justification that trumps the harm it causes. Engineers blocked from obtaining images to assess the impact of foam debris on the space shuttle *Columbia* had justification for blowing the whistle. To help engineers perform responsibly without resorting to extreme measures, research and teaching focus on impediments to responsible conduct in organizations, for example, fear, deference to authority, and "group think."

The space shuttle *Challenger* disaster revealed another impediment: normalized deviance (Vaughan 1996). It is a form of complacency, the phenomenon of gradually accepting certain anomalous, originally unexpected occurrences that portend serious harm. As the occurrences continue without leading to actual serious harm, they come to be viewed as normal. Strategies to counter this relaxation of vigilance and other impediments to responsibility are current research subjects. This is preventive ethics, catching engineering ethics problems early before they ripen into disasters.

Canon one, the code provision that enjoins engineers to "hold paramount the safety, health and welfare of the public," (ABET 1977, p. 1) requires interpretation. Analysis begins with the question: Who is the public? Should the public include, for example, the crew on the *Columbia*, workers within the engineering workplace, or everyone who might be affected by an engineering product?

Michael Davis (1998) points out the need to determine a characteristic that identifies the relevant public, that is, the vulnerable parties who may be harmed by engineers' work. He suggests identifying members of the public by their ignorance and consequent helplessness in the face of dangers from engineers' work. On this interpretation, members of the *Columbia* crew, unaware of the extent of damage from the break off of insulation and therefore helpless to do anything about their perilous situation, were members of the public.

Analysis continues by asking: How can engineers translate the *paramountcy* provision into guidelines that are less vague? Kenneth Alpern (1983) draws attention to the importance of a standard or principle of due care that holds for everyone. Its corollary, a standard of care proportionate to the magnitude of harm and "the centrality of one's role" in producing the harm, further reduces the vagueness for engineers.

Mindful that this principle can demand moral heroism and that few people are capable of heroism, engineering ethics specialists focus on sources of support for engineers and on constructing options for responsible problem solving within the capacities of most people. In constructing options for resolving ethics problems, engineers use methods resembling those for solving design problems (Whitbeck 1996).

Further analysis of the paramountcy provision addresses another problem: managers typically balance or trade off factors, such as cost, schedule, marketing, and safety. In their deliberations, managers include safety as a factor, but only as one factor that, like others, may have to be sacrificed. Because safety is a priority for engineers, they cannot treat safety in that way. Philosophers suggest interpreting canon one as requiring engineers to meet a threshold of safety before taking a balancing approach (Harris, Pritchard, and Rabins 2005). This interpretation can help engineers hold their ground with managers.

Employers' demands for secrecy and confidentiality give rise to a cluster of specific issues concerning disclosure and withholding of information and protection of intellectual property, including trade secrets and patents. Societal interests in open circulation of knowledge (and propagation of new technology) and engineers' interests in using their knowledge to advance their careers come into conflict with the interests of firms in protecting information perceived to be economically valuable.

Employment contracts generate ethical responsibilities for engineers and their employers and figure in the balancing necessary to reconcile these interests. These contracts commonly require engineers to keep information confidential even after moving to another company. Such contracts make employers responsible for clearly specifying information to be kept confidential over a reasonable period of time. Engineers become responsible for taking due care at a new job to protect specified information for an appropriately limited time. Drawing such lines between privately owned knowledge and public knowledge is an important practical issue for engineers as well as a subject for analysis in engineering ethics.

Among problems that readily arise for engineers is conflict of interest (COI). While specifying vendors, suppliers, contractors, materials, and components, engineers must be alert to affiliations, investments, and associations they have that can threaten the reliability of their engineering judgment. Philosophical investigation has explicated the concept of COI, the harm of COI, and appropriate responses for dealing with COI. Disclosure of the investment or affiliation that threatens reliable judgment is essential to avoid deceiving and betraying the party relying on professional judgment.

Because of the impact of engineers' work and the priority of safety, it is essential for engineers to acquire a sophisticated understanding of risk and approaches to dealing with risks to humans, other creatures, and the environment. One approach to fostering such understanding is to provide engineers an overview of important perspectives on risk and critical discussion of cost-benefit analysis.

Ethics specialists consider several perspectives alongside one another, those of risk experts (specialists in defining and assessing risks, usually relying on cost-benefit analysis), government regulators, and lay people. It is part of the engineering approach to provide knowledge about risks, for example, concentrations of pollutants in water. The engineering perspective also includes an understanding of cost-benefit analysis and its limitations, an orientation toward protecting the public (similar to, but not the same as that of the government regulator), and an appreciation of lay attitudes toward risks (e.g., those imposed as contrasted with those voluntarily assumed).

Accommodating lay attitudes introduces issues associated with informed consent, that is, explicit acceptance of risks by affected parties. Recognizing that many situations in engineering make it impractical to obtain voluntary informed consent, ethics analysis considers substitutes and compensatory policies. This and other engineering ethics topics encompass problems that arise for individual practitioners but point toward engineering responsibilities of the profession as a whole because they call on the collective capabilities of the profession.

Accordingly, engineers' responsibilities regarding the environment have begun to engage U.S. engineering societies as well as ethics specialists. Some societies have added provisions to their codes of ethics that provide a distinct place in decision making for attention to environmental implications.

Engineers work increasingly in an international environment. A decision-making situation may bring into play engineering standards and government regulatory standards of different countries. The tasks of finding common ground and making adjustments among differing standards consistent with morality and the paramountcy provision are appropriate responsibilities for the profession through its professional societies. For engineering ethics research, addressing international variations in standards is an important task. Advances in international law, which have been prompted by economic globalization, may encourage such research.

As radically innovative technologies have followed rapidly one after another, especially in the decades since World War II, issues associated with emerging technologies have come to the forefront. For individuals and the profession as whole, emerging technologies present issues not only regarding potential risks but also regarding the role of engineers (and the technologies they help create) in shaping the physical, social, and cultural world.

See also Duty; Ethics and Economics.

Bibliography

Accreditation Board for Engineering and Technology (ABET). *Code of Ethics of Engineers.* 1977. Available from http://ethics.iit.edu/codes/coe/abet-a.html.

Alpern, Kenneth. "Moral Responsibility for Engineers." *Business and Professional Ethics Journal* 2 (2) (1983): 39–48.

ASEE Action. "National Engineers Week" *American Society for Engineering Education Newsletter* (February 1999): 2.

Baron, Marcia. *The Moral Status of Loyalty.* Chicago: Center for the Study of Ethics in the Professions (IIT), 1984.

Davis, Michael. *Thinking Like an Engineer.* New York: Oxford University Press, 1998.

Florman, Samuel C. "Moral Blueprints." In *Engineering Professionalism and Ethics*, edited by James H. Schaub, Karl Pavlovic, and M. D. Morris, 76–81. Malabar, FL: Robert E Krieger, 1986. Originally published in the magazine *Harper's* (October 1978).

Harris, Charles E. "Explaining Disasters: The Case for Preventive Ethics." *IEEE Technology and Society Magazine* 14 (2) (Summer 1995): 22–27.

Harris, Charles E., Michael S. Pritchard, and Michael J. Rabins. *Engineering Ethics: Concepts and Cases.* 3rd ed. Belmont, CA: Thomson/Wadsworth, 2005.

Johnson, Deborah, ed. *Ethical Issues in Engineering.* Englewood Cliffs, NJ: Prentice-Hall, 1991.

Ladd, John. "Collective and Individual Moral Responsibility in Engineering: Some Questions." *IEEE Technology and Society Magazine* 1 (2) (June 1982): 3–10.

Vaughan, Diane. *The Challenger Launch Decision: Risky Technology, Culture, and Deviance at NASA.* Chicago: University of Chicago Press, 1996.

Weil, Vivian. "Engineering Ethics." In *Science and Technology Ethics*, edited by Raymond E. Spier, 59–88. London: Routledge, 2002.

Whitbeck, Caroline. "Ethics as Design: Doing Justice to Moral Problems." *Hastings Center Report* 26 (3) (May–June 1996): 9–16.

Vivian Weil (2005)

ENLIGHTENMENT

The term *enlightenment* is generally used to designate a period in European history stretching from the 1680s to the close of the eighteenth century, but this usage is not without ambiguities and controversy. During the eighteenth century the word *enlightenment* referred not to a period but to a process, a set of activities in which individuals engaged. These activities were viewed as involving the application of what was then termed *philosophy* to a range of concerns in what would subsequently be classified as the natural sciences, the humanities, and the social sciences. It was not until the nineteenth century that *the Enlightenment* came into general usage as a designation for the historical period defined by these various projects. Attempts to specify the character of the period have tended to spur reflection on the nature and scope of those projects and activities that are claimed to characterize the age. As a result, discussions of the Enlightenment typically slide into reflections on the nature and merits of the activity of enlightenment itself.

THE HISTORY OF THE CONCEPT

At the close of his 1784 essay in the *Berlinische Monatsschrift* in response to the question "What is enlightenment?" Immanuel Kant asked whether his might be characterized as an "enlightened age." He responded, "No, but it is an age of enlightenment" (p. 35). Kant's emphasis on enlightenment as an ongoing process, rather than as an achieved state, was typical of eighteenth-century usage, which favored such formulations as "century of philosophy" (Jean Le Rond d'Alembert), "age of critique" (Kant), or "age of reason" (Thomas Paine).

The question of what the process of enlightenment involved sparked an extended discussion in German journals during the 1780s, a discussion in which Kant's response would prove to be the most famous. The German *aufklären*—a word that had been used to designate a clearing of the weather and, metaphorically, a return to consciousness after a period of sleep—had been employed since the beginning of the eighteenth century as a translation for the French *eclairer* (an important term in the works of René Descartes and Gottfried Wilhelm Leibniz) and for the English *enlighten*. More generally, the use of light as a metaphor for knowledge had a long history in Western philosophy as well as a central place in religious discourse. Hence, the particular use to which these metaphors were put during the eighteenth century by those thinkers now associated with the Enlightenment had a polemical edge: True enlightenment, it was argued, resulted from the application of reason and philosophy, rather than appeals to revelation or to the mysteries of faith. Critics could, in turn, marshal the same metaphors and argue that what was proposed as enlightenment was instead a form of spiritual darkness.

The application of the term to a particular historical period was greatly influenced by Georg Wilhelm Friedrich Hegel's lectures on the history of philosophy and the philosophy of history from the 1820s, and his usage was widely imitated in German histories of philosophy and of literature. The French term for the period—*siècle des lumières*—suggested a more elastic understanding of the period: a century of "lights" rather than a single movement. English usage followed the German, but lagged behind it, with *the Enlightenment* replacing *the Illumination* as a label for the period only in the waning years of the nineteenth century. As late as 1910 the Princeton philosopher John Grier Hibben, in the first book in English to use the term consistently, treated the term as a neologism in need of explanation. Indeed, for much of the twentieth century *age of reason* remained a widely used alternative.

The seminal historical studies of the period date from the 1930s: Ernst Cassirer's *Die Philosophie der Aufklärung* (1932/1951), Paul Hazard's *La crise de la conscience europeén* (1935/1953); and Carl L. Becker's *The Heavenly City of the Eighteenth Century Philosophers* (1932), a work whose fame rests more on the novelty of its argument than on the quality of its scholarship. Peter Gay's *The Enlightenment: An Interpretation* (1966–1969) remains the most influential of the many subsequent studies. Some scholars criticize the tendency to exaggerate the unity of the Enlightenment and emphasize the diversity of enlightenments, sometimes distinguished by their "national context" (see Porter and Teich 1981), for example, the "Scottish Enlightenment," the "Berlin Enlightenment," and the "British Enlightenment." Still others (e.g., Israel 2001) maintain that a focus on national contexts ignores the cosmopolitan character of the Enlightenment, particularly in its more radical manifestations. Since the 1970s there has been a tendency for historical discussions of the Enlightenment to turn from the focus on prominent thinkers and their works that had been the defining feature of earlier studies in favor of approaches influenced by developments in social history and histories of publishing and reading. The work of the historian Robert Darnton (1995) has been particularly influential in this regard.

THE ROLE OF PHILOSOPHY IN THE ENLIGHTENMENT

In the earliest discussions the relationship between philosophy and the Enlightenment was pervasive and unproblematic: The Enlightenment was typically defined in terms of the philosophers who were said to have articulated its ideals. Some of the early controversial literature spurred by the French Revolution traced the origins of the Revolution to the writings of François-Marie Arouet de Voltaire, Denis Diderot, and the other *philosophes*, and terms such as *philosophism* and *Illumination* figured prominently in the writings of British opponents of the Revolution and in accounts (notably Augustin Barruel's [1743–1820] *Memoirs Illustrating the History of Jacobinism* [1798]) that traced the Revolution to a conspiracy of *philosophes* and Freemasons.

A more sober analysis could be found in Hegel's *Lectures on the History of Philosophy* from the 1820s, which tended to reserve the term *Aufklärung* for the German phase of the broader movement of modern philosophy that began with Descartes. In other lecture cycles Hegel extended the term to denote the modern attempt to deduce both the laws of nature and of morality from individual consciousness. In subsequent nineteenth-century German histories of philosophy the term (sometimes divided into French and German branches) was used to refer to both rationalist and empiricist tendencies in eighteenth-century philosophy, with Kant frequently portrayed as a thinker who managed to transcend the alleged limits of the movement and thus ushered in a new epoch. The early scholarship in English was heavily influenced by this tradition, with the work of Hibben (1910) representing one of the more sophisticated versions of this approach.

Cassirer offered an even more nuanced account, viewing the Enlightenment as the pivotal phase in the broader process through which "modern philosophic thought gained its characteristic self-confidence and self-consciousness" (1932/1951, p. vi). The book's opening chapter followed d'Alembert in distinguishing the *esprit de système* (the deductive system of seventeenth-century rationalism) from the *esprit systématique*, with its emphasis on induction and empirical analysis that marked the new era. In the discussions of approaches to nature, psychology, religion, history, politics, and aesthetics that followed, Cassirer (1932/1951) portrayed the Enlightenment as a European movement in which German thinkers such as Leibniz and Gotthold Ephraim Lessing stood on equal terms with their French counterparts. While Cassirer eschewed a historical account of various "individual doctrines" in favor of a study of "the form and manner of intellectual activity itself," Hazard (1935/1953) traced the history of responses to what he characterized as a "crisis of the classical mind" (i.e., seventeenth-century rationalism). If Hazard was less certain than Cassirer that this crisis had been resolved, his account nevertheless saw the Enlightenment (though the term itself does not figure prominently in his work) as an attempt to respond to a philosophical problem: the problem of finding an alternative to religious belief as a foundation for normative judgments. In contrast, Becker (1932) held that far from providing an alternative to religious faith, the *philosophes* simply substituted one sort of faith for another, with a faith in the power of reason occupying the place previously occupied by religion.

However problematic as historical narratives, such studies capture one important feature of eighteenth-century discourse. In France figures such as Voltaire, Diderot, d'Alembert, Baron Paul-Henri Thiry d'Holbach, Claude-Adrien Helvétius, and others described what they were doing as philosophy and called themselves philosophers. Still, while accounts of "the philosophy of the Enlightenment" tend to emphasize the role of epistemological questions, the reach of the term *philosophy* during the Enlightenment was considerably more expansive. Isaac Newton published his laws of motion in a work that announced itself as a contribution to *natural philosophy* and the concerns of the American Philosophical Society, founded in Philadelphia by Benjamin Franklin in 1768, were closer to the modern natural sciences than to philosophy as it is now conceived. For much of the period, treatises on natural law provided thinkers with a context for exploring a wide range of issues in the areas of anthropology, the philosophy of language, political economy, and morality that were central concerns during the period.

The emergence of the salon and the coffeehouse spurred the growth of new forms of expression—for example, Diderot's remarkably open-ended dialogues and publications such the *Tattler* and the *Spectator*, journals edited by Joseph Addison (1672-1719) and Richard Steele (1672–1729) that aimed at improving the discourse and the mores of those who frequented coffeehouses. Many of the period's most influential works—for example, Pierre Bayle's *Historical and Critical Dictionary* (1697), Diderot's *Encyclopedia* (1751–1765), and Voltaire's *Philosophical Dictionary* (1764)—were lexicons, rather than philosophical treatises, while other important texts—including Jean-Jacques Rousseau's educational treatise *Emile* (1762) or Guillaume-Thomas-François de Raynal's influential *History of the Two Indies* (1770)—defy assimilation into familiar genres of philosophical writing.

The staggering variety of works labeled as philosophy is mirrored by the Enlightenment's conception of the vocation of the *philosophe*. The entry in Diderot's *Encyclopedia* (an abridgement of a text generally cred-

ited to the grammarian César Chesneau Dumarsais [1676–1756]) characterized the *philosophe* as an individual who is chiefly concerned with those "sociable qualities" that make individuals useful members of society, "For him, civil society is, as it were, a divinity on earth; he flatters it, he honors it by his probity, by an exact attention to his duties, and by a sincere desire not to be a useless or embarrassing member of it" (p. 510). Diderot's article on "Encyclopedia" stressed the differences between the "geniuses" of the seventeenth century, who engaged in solitary and unconstrained reflection on the nature of things, and the collaborative work of the *philosophes* of his own century, whose interest lay less in making new discoveries than in organizing and disseminating the knowledge that had already been attained by artisans and other useful members of society.

A similar view of the mission of the *philosophe* is found in the posthumously published work by the thinker who is often regarded as the last of the species: Marquis de Condorcet's *Sketch for a Historical Picture of the Progress of the Human Mind* (1793). He saw *philosophes* as "concerned less with the discovery or development of truth than with its propagation." Gathering under the banner of "reason, tolerance, humanity," they "made it their life-work to destroy popular errors rather than to drive back the frontiers of human knowledge—an indirect way of aiding its progress which was not less fraught with peril, nor less useful" (pp. 136-137).

Thus, while the Enlightenment saw the publication of works—for example, John Locke's *Essay concerning Human Understanding* (1689), David Hume's *A Treatise of Human Nature* (1739–1740), and Kant's *Critique of Pure Reason* (1781)—that are among the foundational texts of modern philosophy, the eighteenth-century *philosophe* engaged in activities that no longer occupy professional philosophers and a good many of the works that the eighteenth century classified as *philosophy*—for example, the political libels and philosophical pornography that were labeled philosophical books in the clandestine book trade—fall outside the discipline as it is now practiced. For this reason the Enlightenment invoked by philosophers and the Enlightenment studied by historians working in the area of eighteenth-century studies tend to diverge. For the former, the Enlightenment was a philosophical movement that emphasized the application of reason (defined for the most part in terms associated with modern science) to all aspects of life, a project that has been embraced by some (e.g., in Karl Raimund Popper's ideal of the "Open Society") and criticized by others (e.g., in Max Horkheimer and Theodor Adorno's

[1947/2002] account of the collapse of Enlightenment into totalitarianism). In contrast, scholars working in the area of eighteenth-century studies have tended to see the Enlightenment as a network of individuals and institutions, sometimes bound together by common interests or purposes, but in many cases diverging according to local contexts or their particular concerns and commitments.

ENLIGHTENMENT PROJECTS

THE PUBLIC USE OF REASON. As a general characterization of the movement's aims, there is much to recommend Kant's definition of enlightenment as "the freedom to make a *public use* of one's reason in all matters" (p. 36). Both the essay's demand that individuals make use of their own reason and its invocation of a cosmopolitan public sphere of readers and writers reiterated ideals that had accompanied the Enlightenment from the start. The requirement that the claims of religious, political, and other authorities be brought before what Kant called the "tribunal of reason" had, for example, been a point of honor for the deist John Toland, who opened his *Christianity Not Mysterious* (1696) by observing that he had "been very early accustom'd to Examination and Enquiry, and taught not to captivate my Understanding no more than my sense to any Man or Society" (p. 7). The idea that individuals might best carry out this project of thinking for themselves in the company of others had been central to Pierre Bayle's conception of a "republic of letters" consisting of readers and critics who were bound together, despite their separation in different countries, into a common endeavor.

The emergence of what the social theorist Jürgen Habermas termed the *public sphere*—the network of institutions, including coffeehouses, salons, Masonic lodges, and reading societies in which "private people come together as a public" (1989, p. 27)—is viewed by many historians as a defining feature of the period. Coffeehouses, particularly in England, provided a venue for the circulation and discussion of news, Parisian salons played an essential role in coordinating the activities of the *philosophes*, and the Masonic movement opened a space in which new forms of sociability, expressing the ideal of fraternal solidarity, were possible. No less significant was the emergence of an international book trade, with both legal and clandestine branches. Indeed, the most compelling evidence for the spread of enlightenment in eighteenth-century Europe may be the explosion of books and periodicals that made their way into new markets, the dramatic shift in the content of these books (with works on religious subjects eclipsed by a growing

interest in science and literature by the end of the century), and the shift in reading practices from the repeated reading of a few texts (typically devotional in character) to the successive reading of a series of books, a practice that further increased the demand for new works.

TOLERATION AND RELIGIOUS HETERODOXY. Kant's suggestion that "religious matters" were central to the concerns of enlightenment and his insistence that restrictions on the public use of reason in this area were both "harmful" and "dishonorable" aptly summarized the views of those who saw themselves as engaged in efforts at enlightenment. The initial impetus behind the Enlightenment stemmed, in part, from Protestants' revulsion at Louis XIV's (1638–1715) campaign against the Huguenot minority (culminating in his Revocation of the Edict of Nantes in 1685) and reservations regarding the policies of the Catholic monarch James II (1633–1701) in England (culminating in his removal in the "Glorious Revolution" of 1688). Such concerns were particularly evident among the political and religious exiles from France and England who gathered in the Dutch Republic at the close of the seventeenth century, where they produced tracts on religious and political questions that ranged from such classic texts as Locke's *Letter concerning Toleration* (1689)—a work that had a pervasive influence throughout Europe and the New World on discussions of the proper roles of church and state—to the infamous *Treatise of the Three Imposters*, a clandestine manuscript that pieced together bits of Benedict (Baruch) de Spinoza, Thomas Hobbes, and various materialists to argue that Judaism, Christianity, and Islam owed their origins to the attempts of "imposters" (i.e., charlatans or magicians) to gain political power.

Toleration was the common cause of all those associated with the Enlightenment. In England Protestant dissenters such as Joseph Priestley and Richard Price drew on the arguments of Locke in their campaign against the limitations on political participation suffered by those who refused to swear conformity to central articles of the Anglican faith (e.g., the doctrine of the trinity). Similar arguments could be found, at the end of the century, in Moses Mendelssohn's *Jerusalem* (1783), a treatise on the relation between civil and ecclesiastical power. In France Voltaire—profoundly influenced by the diversity of religious practices he observed during his visit to England—waged a life-long campaign in support of toleration, culminating in an effort to clear the reputation of Jean Calas, a Huguenot executed under circumstances that, for Voltaire, epitomized the corruption of justice by religious fanaticism. By the end of the period the campaign for toleration could claim such legislative achievements as Thomas Jefferson's *Virginia Statute of Religious Freedom* (1786) and Article X of the French *Declaration of the Rights of Man and Citizen* (1789).

The period was also marked by efforts at purifying Christian doctrine from what were seen as subsequent distortions and fabrications. Both Locke's *Reasonableness of Christianity* (1695) and Toland's *Christianity Not Mysterious* presented themselves as attempts to recover Christ's original teaching—which they argued contained nothing that contradicted what could be ascertained through "natural" reason—from what the more pugnacious Toland characterized as "the craft and ambition of Priests and Philosophers" (p. 96). More moderate versions of such arguments persisted to the end of the period in the so-called neologism embraced by Berlin clergy, whose sermons and writings denounced popular superstitions and religious enthusiasm as contrary to a conception of Christian doctrine and emphasized the importance of moral and civic responsibilities. Parallel efforts at reform could be found within the Ashkenazic Jewry in what came to be designated the *Haskalah* (the Hebrew term for *enlightenment*).

Projects of reform, however, easily crossed over into the advocacy of heterodoxy, with Socinian and pantheist doctrines having a broad appeal. For example, Toland's later writings, which hailed the Druids as practitioners of a "natural" religion, articulated positions that are difficult to reconcile with any established version of Christianity. The same is true for the work of Lessing, especially his *Education of the Human Race* (1777), a text that influenced Hegel's early writings. While explicit endorsements of atheism remained a minority position within the Enlightenment (Holbach's *System of Nature* [1770] was the famous notorious exception), Spinoza's writings held a particular interest for more radical free-thinkers, and various pantheist and materialist doctrines lent support to formulations in which references to the deity contributed rather little to the argument.

THE NEWTONIAN IDEAL AND THE RISE OF A SCIENTIFIC CULTURE

Though known chiefly by reputation or through popularizations, the work of Newton had a significant impact during the period. His influence was felt in England both in the increasing interest in experimental approaches to natural philosophy and in the popularity of his arguments among religious dissenters. On the Continent advocates of Newton's cosmology challenged Cartesian and Leibnizian approaches, with Newtonians eventually gaining the upper hand within the French Academy of Sciences and the Berlin Academy. Voltaire and Alembert were effective advocates of Newtonian positions before the broader reading public, as was Voltaire's mistress Émilie du Châtelet (1706–1749), a skilled translator of and commentator on Newton's work.

Attempts to extend Newton's approach to other areas were frequent, with the *Optiks* (1704) rather than the more daunting *Philosophiae Naturalis Principia Mathematica* (1687) serving as a paradigm. The study of electrical phenomena attracted a great deal of interest, with Franklin's contributions to the field enjoying a wide readership in Europe. There were also notable attempts to apply what were viewed as Newtonian approaches to moral philosophy. Hume subtitled his *Treatise of Human Nature* (1739) "an attempt to introduce the experimental method of reasoning into moral subjects," Adam Smith employed analogies to gravitational attraction in his *Theory of Moral Sentiments* (1759), and Condorcet attempted to bring mathematical approaches to bear on political decision making.

More generally, science and scientific reasoning came to enjoy an enhanced status among educated laypersons. The predictive success of Newton's laws in mapping the paths of celestial bodies—most notably Edmond Halley's (1656–1742) application of these laws to the path of the comet that now bears his name—played a role in this process, as did such practical innovations as Franklin's lightning rod. Scientific academies—both state sponsored and private—also had a significant impact in demonstrating the practical implications of scientific inquiry.

HUMAN NATURE AND CULTURAL DIVERSITY

The application of Newtonian approaches to the study of politics and society was but one example of a broader interest in the study of human nature. Accounts of the voyages of James Cook (1728–1779) and Louis-Antoine de Bougainville (1729–1811) brought reports of peoples whose social arrangements, moral practices, and views on religion differed radically from European norms and that posed significant challenges to assumptions regarding the uniformity of human nature. Theories that attempted to explain this diversity in terms of differences in modes of subsistence (hunting and gathering, pastoral, agricultural, and commercial) were particularly prominent among thinkers associated with the Scottish Enlightenment. There were also extended debates on the origin of different races (a term that had a much wider meaning during this period than it would take on during the nineteenth century) between those who, like the French naturalist Comte de Georges-Louis Leclerc Buffon, maintained that all human beings descended from a common origin and that racial differences were the result of climate, and those who, like the Swede Carl von Linné (1707–1778), argued that the different races had descended from different ancestors.

Beyond these theoretical disputes, the literature on "savage peoples"—particularly accounts of the allegedly idyllic life of the natives of the newly discovered island of Tahiti—provided a means for criticizing European society. Rousseau's *Discourse on the Origins of Inequality* (1755) and Diderot's *Supplement to Bougainville's Voyage* (begun in 1772) can serve as examples of this mode of argument, which had an influential predecessor in Baron de Montesquieu's *Persian Letters* (1721).

EFFORTS AT "IMPROVEMENT"

The political views of those associated with the Enlightenment diverged widely. Some favored constitutional monarchies (with England representing one possible model), while others placed considerable hope in the efforts of reform-minded absolutists such as Frederick II of Prussia (1740–1786) and Joseph II of Austria (1741–1790). In the wake of the American Revolution republican ideas gained supporters in both England and France.

What was more pervasive than an allegiance to any particular political ideology was a concern with what was loosely characterized as "improvement." The interest of Scottish enlighteners in the promises of commercial development was reflected in Adam Smith's *Inquiry into the Nature and Causes of the Wealth of Nations* (1776). In France Jacques Necker (1732–1804) and his protégé Condorcet wrestled with the worsening fiscal and political crises that plagued the French monarchy in its final decades. Throughout Europe various societies examined ways of improving agricultural production, fostering the growth of manufacturing, and increasing the circulation of commercial goods. For example, the Lunar Society of Birmingham—whose membership included the inventors James Watt (1736-1819) and Matthew Boulton (1728–1809), the manufacturer Josiah Wedgewood (1730–1795), and the polymaths Priestley and Erasmus Darwin—waged a wide-ranging campaign for political reform and commercial development.

Perhaps there is no more compelling testimony on the role of the Enlightenment in shaping the modern world than the emergence, since the 1940s, of critiques of the so-called Enlightenment Project that hold it responsible for the various alleged pathologies of modernity (for discussions, see Baker and Reill [2001] and Gordon [2001]). While this literature tends to be rather selective in its conception of what this alleged project involved, the diversity of charges that have been leveled against the Enlightenment speaks to the complexity of the movement and its perceived relevance for the present.

See also Addison, Joseph; Adorno, Theodor; Alembert, Jean Le Rond d'; Bayle, Pierre; Buffon, Georges-Louis Leclerc, Comte de; Cassirer, Ernst; Clandestine Philosophical Literature in France; Condorcet, Marquis de; Darwin, Erasmus; Descartes, René Diderot, Denis; Encyclopédie; Enlightenment, Islamic; Enlightenment, Jewish; Franklin, Benjamin; Habermas, Jürgen; Hegel, Georg Wilhelm Friedrich; Helvétius, Claude-Adrien; Hobbes, Thomas; Holbach, Paul-Henri Thiry, Baron d'; Horkheimer, Max; Human Nature; Hume, David; Jefferson, Thomas; Kant, Immanuel; Leibniz, Gottfried Wilhelm; Lessing, Gotthold Ephraim; Locke, John; Mendelssohn, Moses; Montesquieu, Baron de; Newton, Isaac; Paine, Thomas; Popper, Karl Raimund; Priestley, Joseph; Rousseau, Jean-Jacques; Smith, Adam; Socinianism; Spinoza, Benedict (Baruch) de; Toland, John; Toleration; Voltaire, François-Marie Arouet de.

Bibliography

Baker, Keith Michael, and Peter Hanns Reill, eds. *What's Left of Enlightenment? A Postmodern Question*. Stanford, CA: Stanford University Press, 2001.

Becker, Carl L. *The Heavenly City of the Eighteenth Century Philosophers*. New Haven, CT: Yale University Press, 1932.

Cassirer, Ernst. *The Philosophy of the Enlightenment* (1932). Translated by Fritz C. A. Koelln and James P. Pettegrove. Princeton, NJ: Princeton University Press, 1951. Originally published under the title *Die Philosophie der Aufklärung*.

Condorcet, Marie Jean Antoine-Nicolas, Marquis de. *Sketch for the Historical Progress of the Human Mind* (1795). Translated by June Barraclough. London: Weidenfeld and Nicolson, 1955. Originally published under the title *Tableau Historique des Progrès de l'Esprit Humain*.

Darnton, Robert. *Forbidden Best-Sellers of Pre-Revolution France*. New York: Norton, 1995.

Dumarsais, César Chesneau. "Philosophe." In *Encyclopèdie, ou Dictionnaire Raisonné des Sciences, Arts et des Métiers*. Vol. 8, edited by Denis Diderot and Jean Le Ronde D'Alembert (Paris, 1757).

Gay, Peter. *The Enlightenment: An Interpretation*. 2 vols. New York: Knopf, 1966–1969.

Goodman, Deena. *The Republic of Letters: A Cultural History of the French Enlightenment*. Ithaca, NY: Cornell University Press, 1994.

Gordon, Daniel, ed. *Postmodernism and the Enlightenment: New Perspectives in Eighteenth-Century French Intellectual History.* New York: Routledge, 2001.

Habermas, Jürgen. *The Structural Transformation of the Public Sphere: An Inquiry into a Category of Bourgeois Society.* Translated by Thomas Burger and Frederick Lawrence. Cambridge, MA: MIT Press, 1989.

Hazard, Paul. *The European Mind: The Critical Years, 1680–1715* (1935). New Haven, CT: Yale University Press, 1953. Originally published under the title *La crise de la conscience européen.*

Hibben, John Grier. *The Philosophy of the Enlightenment.* New York: Scribner's, 1910.

Horkheimer, Max, and Theodor Adorno. *Dialectic of Enlightenment: Philosophical Fragments* (1947). Translated by Edmund Jephcott. Stanford, CA: Stanford University Press, 2002. Originally published as *Dialektik der Aufklärung: Philosophische Fragmente.*

Israel, Jonathan I. *Radical Enlightenment: Philosophy and the Making of Modernity 1650–1750.* New York: Oxford University Press, 2001.

Jacob, Margaret C. *Living the Enlightenment: Freemasonry and Politics in Eighteenth-Century Europe.* New York: Oxford University Press, 1991.

Kant, Immanuel. "Beantwortung der Frage: Was ist Aufklärung?" In Kant, *Gesammelte Schriften.* Vol. 8, edited by Könglich Preussichen Akademie der Wissenschaften (Berlin: Walter de Gruyter, 1923).

Kors, Alan Charles, ed. *Encyclopedia of the Enlightenment.* 4 vols. New York: Oxford University Press, 2003.

Melton, James van Horn. *The Rise of the Public in Enlightenment Europe.* New York: Cambridge University Press, 2001.

Outram, Dorina. *The Enlightenment.* New York: Cambridge University Press, 1995.

Porter, Roy, and Mikulás Teich, eds. *The Enlightenment in National Context.* New York: Cambridge University Press, 1981.

Schmidt, James. "Inventing the Enlightenment: British Hegelians, Anti-Jacobins, and the *Oxford English Dictionary.*" *Journal of the History of Ideas* 64 (3) (2003): 421–443.

Schmidt, James, ed. *What Is Enlightenment?: Eighteenth-Century Answers and Twentieth-Century Questions.* Berkeley, CA: University of California Press, 1996.

Toland, John. *Christianity Not Mysterious* (1696), edited by Philip McGuinness, Alan Harrison, and Richard Kearney. Dublin: Lilliput, 1997.

James Schmidt (2005)

ENLIGHTENMENT, ISLAMIC

BEGINNINGS

The Islamic *Nahḍah* (rebirth, renaissance) started in Syria and achieved its real momentum in Egypt in the nineteenth century, then as subsequently the intellectual engine room of Islamic intellectual life. The *Nahḍah* movement represented an attempt to do two things. One was to introduce some of the main achievements of European culture into the Islamic world. The other was to defend and protect the major positive features of Arab and Islamic culture and revive them despite the assaults of European imperialism. The important features of the movement were the attempt to combine these policies and the reaction to the apparent decadence of the Arab world not by rejecting Arab culture but by purifying it and introducing it to aspects of modernity from without that were seen as acceptable from an Islamic point of view.

DEVELOPMENT

The main *Nahḍah* thinkers were Sayyid Jamāl ad-Dīn al-Afghānī (1838–1897), and Muḥammad 'Abduh (1849–1905), who in their different ways sought to confront modernity not by rejecting it nor by rejecting Islam, but by effecting some kind of synthesis. The Renaissance movement suggested that one could accept some European ideas and reject others, thus preserving tradition while adopting modernity at the same time. *Nahḍah* argued that Islam is itself a profoundly rational system of thought and has no problem in accepting science and technology. So there is no reason for Muslims to abandon their faith while at the same time accepting the benefits of European forms of modernity. Interestingly, the significance of reviving Islam or Arabism played a considerable part in the political rhetoric of the time.

The most important intellectual figure in this movement was undoubtedly al-Afghānī, who as his name suggested had close connections with Afghanistan, where part of his early education took place. He seems to have been deliberately unclear about his precise ethnic origins to prevent that from being a divisive factor in his attempts to address the whole Islamic community. At the age of around eighteen he moved to India, where he came across the modernist ideas of Sayyid Ahmad Khan (1817–1898), whom he later attacked in his *Refutation of the Materialists.* Ahmad Khan was intent on proving to the British rulers of India that Islam was a religion capable of accepting rationality, and it was this apologetical tone that al-Afghānī attacked. His arguments were not based on Islam alone; they also borrowed a great deal from what he regarded as science and philosophy. He argued that Islamic philosophy was perfectly compatible with modern science and technology and should encourage Muslims to acquire the necessary skills to resist the impact of

European imperialism. Part of the Islamic Renaissance ideology was that there should be a rebirth and rediscovery of the main intellectual and political achievements of the Islamic world during its high point.

Al-Afghānī's *Refutation of the Materialists* argues that the source of evil is materialism, the philosophical doctrine that argues that the world has developed out of a set of material preconditions. He also criticizes the theory of evolution, which he sees as denying God's role in designing the world. His critique also has a social aspect in that materialism is held to reject founding society on any common moral values, and in being critical of religion as such, and of Islam in particular. This sort of critique of what is seen as European culture has since the nineteenth century become common in the Islamic world.

The influence of his ideas was amplified by the efforts of Rashīd Riḍā (1865–1935), who founded in 1898 the journal *al-Manar* (The Lighthouse) in Cairo. The central theme of the journal was that there is no incompatibility between Islam on the one hand, and modernity, science, reason, and civilization on the other. Riḍā tended to emphasize religion and was a firm opponent of secularism, arguing that supporting modernity did not imply advocating secularism.

Muḥammad 'Abduh used his position as head of al-Azhar, the leading theological university in the Sunni Islamic world, to propound the message of the *Nahḍah* that the Islamic world should accept modernity while at the same time not rejecting Islam. The period of stagnation that he identified with the tenth to the fifteenth centuries was a time when the early scientific and philosophical progress of the Islamic cultural world came to an end and the political and religious authorities had a mutual interest in maintaining control by restricting the intellectual curiosity of those over whom they ruled so effectively. What was now needed, he argued in the nineteenth century, was reform of all the institutions of the Islamic world, while preserving the timeless truths of Islam itself. He suggested that the connection between religion and modernity, in particular between Christianity and modernity, is entirely misplaced. Christianity itself advocates belief in the transience of everyday life, by contrast with the concern for possessions and comfort so characteristic of modern industrial societies. Still, Christianity found no inconsistency in combining religion with modernity, so this need not be a worry for Muslims either.

See also Evolutionary Theory; Islamic Philosophy; Materialism; Rationality; Renaissance.

Bibliography

Hourani, Albert. *Arabic Thought in the Liberal Age, 1798–1939.* New York: Cambridge University Press, 1983.

Keddie, Nikkie R. *An Islamic Response to Imperialism: Political and Religious Writings of Sayyid Jamāl al-Dīn "al-Afghānī".* Berkeley: University of California Press, 1983.

Keddie, Nikkie, ed. *Scholars, Saints, and Sufis: Muslim Religious Institutions in the Middle East since 1500.* Berkeley: University of California Press, 1972.

Kedourie, Elie. *Afghani and 'Abduh: An Essay on Religious Unbelief and Political Activism in Modern Islam.* New York: Humanities Press, 1966.

Kurzman, Charles. *Modernist Islam, 1840–1940: A Source Book.* New York: Oxford University Press, 2002.

Oliver Leaman (2005)

ENLIGHTENMENT, JEWISH

Growing emancipation of European Jews in the eighteenth century was matched by an intellectual movement that came to be called the Jewish Enlightenment or *Haskalah.* Jews started to enter the mainstream of European society, in particular in major German cities such as Berlin, and Jewish thinkers had to accomplish two tasks. They needed to show their Gentile peers that they were just as committed to rationality as anyone else, and they needed to persuade other Jews that they should establish links with the local non-Jewish cultures in which they lived.

The main embodiment of this movement was Moses Mendelssohn, who participated fully in German philosophy and culture, and lesser thinkers were Marcus Herz (1747–1803), Salomon Maimon (1753/4–1800), and Nachmun Krochmal (1785–1840). Mendelssohn first of all emphasized the importance of mastery of the local secular language, and of the contemporary culture. But this did not imply abandoning Judaism; he argued on the contrary that one could use modern ways of argumentation to explain and justify religious systems such as Judaism. He comes to argue that Judaism is a profoundly rational religion and so highly appropriate for those committed to reason. Mendelssohn was here reacting to the widespread view that Judaism was a rule-bound and legalistic system that only those stuck in a worn-out culture would persist in following. It came to be argued in German philosophy by Kant and Hegel that Judaism was a religion essentially superseded a long time ago in the past, fossilized and unsatisfactory, and Mendelssohn and other *maskilim* (Enlighteners) argued that these criticisms were misplaced.

The basis of *Haskalah* was respect for reason, as the word suggests (*sekhel* being *reason* in Hebrew) and this was to have longstanding effects on Jewish culture. It contributed to the start of Reform Judaism in Germany, its basis being a putative rational attitude to traditional Judaism. It also played a part in the secular nature of Zionism, the idea that the Jews, like other national groups, had a right to a homeland that was based on reason not tradition. After its growth and development in Germany, *Haskalah* moved east to affect the Jewish communities there, and produced a schism between the "modernizers" and those concerned to defend tradition. The *Haskalah* raised the issue of how far a religion upheld by a minority excluded from mainstream society could survive when that minority was allowed to join that society. If it could be argued that the traditional religion was as rational as anything else in society then the intellectual presuppositions of such a change might not threaten the survival of the religion. The *maskilim* were confident that both Judaism and secular European society would benefit from a more intimate relationship, because the basis of both is reason.

See also Maimon, Salomon; Mendelssohn, Moses.

Bibliography

Arkush, Alan. *Moses Mendelssohn and the Enlightenment.* Albany, NY: State University of New York Press, 1994.

Dubin, Lois. "The Social and Cultural Context: Eighteenth-Century Enlightenment." In *History of Jewish Philosophy*, edited by D. Frank and O. Leaman. London: Routledge, 1997.

Feiner, Shmuel. *The Jewish Enlightenment.* Translated by C. Naor. Philadelphia: University of Pennsylvania Press, 2004.

Harris, J. *Nachman Krochmal: Guiding the Perplexed of the Modern Age.* New York: New York University Press, 1991.

Rotenstreich, Nathan. *Jews and German Philosophy: The Polemics of Emancipation.* New York: Schocken, 1984.

Sorkin, David. *Moses Mendelssohn and the Religious Enlightenment.* Berkeley: University of California Press, 1996.

Oliver Leaman (2005)

ENTAILMENT, PRESUPPOSITION, AND IMPLICATURE

Entailment, as used by philosophers, is a term of art that, unlike *logical consequence*, lacks a precise definition that is consistently adhered to by those who employ it. Through-out much of the twentieth century, especially its early and middle years, many philosophers connected entailment with analyticity, requiring the material conditional ⌜A ⊃ B⌝ to be analytic when A entailed B. In later years, as conceptions of analyticity became less expansive, and philosophical uses of it more restricted, the presumption that entailment was to be understood in terms of analyticity waned. However, the relationship between entailment and necessity has remained robust. Standardly, when it is claimed that A entails B, B is taken to be a necessary consequence of A in the sense that it is impossible for A to be true without B's being true. Often, though not always, B is required to be apriori deducible from A, as well. The relata, A and B, are naturally thought of as propositions, or statements—in the sense of that which is stated by an assertive utterance of a sentence. However, sometimes theorists speak of sentences themselves as entailing other sentences. In such cases, it is natural to construe the relation holding between sentences as deriving from the primary entailment relation holding between the propositions they express.

A potentially more restrictive understanding of entailment requires that when A entails B, the falsity of A is a necessary consequence of the falsity of B. When entailment is understood in this way, it is sometimes contrasted with logical presupposition: A proposition A logically presupposes a proposition B if and only if the truth of B is a necessary condition for A's being either true or false. The most widely discussed (putative) examples of logical presuppositions are so-called existential presuppositions, corresponding to uses of singular terms. (These are also sometimes called *referential presuppositions*.) For example, according to a Fregean analysis of definite descriptions, the propositions expressed by (1a) and (1b) logically presuppose the proposition expressed by (1c).

1a. The person who proved Goldbach's conjecture is brilliant.

1b. The person who proved Goldbach's conjecture isn't brilliant.

1c. One and only one person proved Goldbach's conjecture.

For Frege, singular definite descriptions are complex singular terms, and the predicate *is brilliant* designates a function that assigns truth to some individuals and falsity to others. Because the sense of *the person who proved Goldbach's conjecture* fails to pick out any individual, the function designated by *is brilliant* has no argument to operate on, and (1a) is characterized as being neither true nor false. The same is true of (1b), which is taken to be the negation of (1a). Because, for Frege, the negation function—which assigns truth to falsity, and falsity to truth—has no argument to operate on in this case, proposition (1B) is not assigned any truth value. On this analysis, the truth of the logical presupposition, (1c), is a necessary condition for (1a) and (1b) to be either true or false.

THE SEMANTICS OF FREGE AND RUSSELL

Although the compositional semantics of Frege (1891, 1892a, and 1892b) produce elegant results in cases such as this, they run into trouble when fully generalized. For Frege, *n*-place truth-functional operators designate *n*-place truth functions, and the truth value of a truth-functional compound is the value of the relevant truth function at the *n*-tuple of truth values of its sentential constituents. Hence, the argument used to show that the negation of a proposition is truth valueless if and only if the proposition negated is truth valueless can be generalized to yield the conclusion that a truth functional compound is truth valueless if and only if one of its constituents is. This result is demonstrably incorrect, as is shown by (2a) and (2b)—based on an example given by Bertrand Russell in "On Denoting" (1905). (Read *if, then,* in (2a) as material implication.)

2a. If one and only one person proved Goldbach's conjecture, then the person who proved Goldbach's conjecture is brilliant.

2b. Either it is not the case that one and only one person proved Goldbach's conjecture, or the person who proved Goldbach's conjecture is brilliant.

Far from being truth valueless, these examples are made true because no one has proved Goldbach's conjecture.

This was one of the considerations that led Russell to analyze the examples in (1) differently from Frege. On his analysis, the logical form of (1a) is (R1a), while (1b) is ambiguous between (R1bw), in which the description is said to have wide scope, and (R1bn), in which it takes narrow scope.

R1a. $\exists x \, [\forall y((y \text{ is a man } \& \, y \text{ proved Goldbach's conjecture}) \leftrightarrow x = y) \, \& \, x \text{ is brilliant}]$

R1bw. $\exists x \, [\forall y((y \text{ is a man } \& \, y \text{ proved Goldbach's conjecture}) \leftrightarrow x = y) \, \& \sim x \text{ is brilliant}]$

R1bn. $\sim \exists x \, [\forall y((y \text{ is a man } \& \, y \text{ proved Goldbach's conjecture}) \leftrightarrow x = y) \, \& \, x \text{ is brilliant}]$

When (1c) is false, (R1a) and (R1bw) are also false, but (R1bn) is true. On this analysis, (1c) is a necessary consequence of (1a), and of the reading of (1b) represented by (R1bw). However, on this reading, (1b) is not the (logical) negation of (1a). Hence, for Russell, these examples are not instances of logical presupposition.

STRAWSON'S THEORY OF PRESUPPOSITION

In "On Referring" (1950), Peter Strawson considered such cases, and presented his own analysis that included the following theses: (i) meaning is a property of expressions; referring, saying something, and being true or false are properties of uses of expressions in contexts; (ii) to give, or know, the meaning of a sentence S is to give, or know, a rule for determining the contexts in which S is used to say something true, and the contexts in which it is used to say something false; (iii) the primary referring use of a name, demonstrative pronoun, or singular definite description is one in which the term is used to refer to something that the rest of the sentence is used to say something about; the meaning of such a term, when used in this way, is a rule for determining its referents in different contexts; (iv) if a singular term b in a sentence ⌜Fb⌝ is used referringly in a context C, then ⌜Fb⌝ says something true (false) in C if and only if, in C, the referent of b has (does not have) the property that F is used to express; if b fails to refer to anything, then ⌜Fb⌝ fails to say anything true or false in C; (v) definition: S presupposes p relative to C if and only if the truth of p is a necessary condition for a use of S in C to say something true or false; and (vi) uses of ⌜The F is G⌝, ⌜All Fs are G⌝, ⌜Some F's are G⌝, ⌜No Fs are G⌝, and ⌜Some Fs are not G⌝ presuppose (in the sense of (v)) that expressed by ⌜There is at least one F⌝.

Thesis (ii) is problematic. As it stands, it does not rule out, and may even seem to suggest, that the meaning of a sentence is a function from contexts of utterance to truth values. According to a better picture, presented by David Kaplan in "Demonstratives" (1989), the meaning of a sentence is a function from contexts to propositions, where the latter determine functions from circumstances of evaluation to truth values. When this view is substituted for (ii), corresponding changes must be made in theses (iii) and (iv). Strawson's emphasis on referring as the semantic function of a singular term, plus his tendency to treat referring uses of demonstratives as prime examples of this function, suggest a reformulation of (iii) and (iv) in which all referring uses of singular terms are, in Kaplan's words, *directly referential*. (iii_K) A referring use of a singular term b, as part of a sentence S, in a context C contributes the referent of b in C to the proposition expressed by S in C; the meaning of a singular term is a rule for determining the propositional constituents contributed by uses of b to the propositions expressed by sentences containing b in different contexts. (iv_K) If a referential use, in a context C, of a singular term b in a sentence ⌐Fb⌐ refers to o, and if F is used to express the property P, then ⌐Fb⌐ expresses a proposition in C that is true (false) in a possible circumstance w if and only if o has (doesn't have) P in w, if b fails to refer to anything in C, then there is no propositional constituent corresponding to b in C, and ⌐Fb⌐ fails to express a (complete) proposition in C.

The theory of presupposition that emerges from this reconstruction of Strawson's theses is a theory of what may be called *expressive presupposition*: A sentence S expressively presupposes a proposition p relative to a context C if and only if the truth of p is necessary for S to semantically express a (complete) proposition in C. This theory provides a plausible account of examples in which a pronoun, demonstrative, or demonstrative phrase is used referringly. However, the theory produces incorrect results when extended to the range of cases mentioned in thesis (vi). Such an extension also conflicts with Strawson's expressed intentions. In *Introduction to Logical Theory* (1952), he defines presupposition as follows: A statement (proposition) S presupposes a statement (proposition) S' if and only if the truth of S' is a necessary condition for S to be true or false. Because this is a definition of logical presupposition, Strawson's adoption of it belies any clear commitment to expressive presupposition, or any systematic analysis of the examples in (vi) along directly referential lines.

This suggests a second possible reconstruction of his position. On this interpretation, his theory of presupposition is substantially the same as Frege's, without the compositional semantics, but with the stipulation that statements involving certain generalized quantifiers bear existential presuppositions. This theory is broad in scope and has been historically influential. However, its leading ideas are not original with Strawson. As a historical point, it would be a mistake to attribute to him either an account of presupposition that is systematically Fregean (logical), or an account that is systematically expressive. His major discussions include elements of both, the conflict being masked by the flawed account of meaning given in thesis (ii), and the failure to articulate the more satisfactory picture later provided by Kaplan.

PRAGMATIC PRESUPPOSITION AND CONVERSATIONAL DYNAMICS

An important advance in the study of presupposition, signaled in Stalnaker (1973, 1974) and Lewis (1979), integrates presupposition into a broader theory of conversational dynamics. The crucial observation is that sentences are used in communication to contribute to an existing conversational record, which contains background assumptions shared by conversational participants. Because of this, it is natural for speakers to develop conventional means of indicating what assumptions they are making about the conversational record to which their utterances contribute. Pragmatic presuppositions may then be understood as requirements imposed on such records by utterances. Suppose, for example, that a use of S (e.g. "It wasn't Andrew who solved the problem") requires the set of background assumptions prior to the utterance to contain a specific proposition p (that someone has solved the problem). Imagine a conversation in which p is not already among the shared background assumptions prior to the utterance of S, but conversational participants are willing to accept p as uncontroversial. What response would be reasonable in such a case? The legalistic response would be to object to the speaker's remark on the grounds that p, which was required by the utterance of S, had not already been established. The speaker could then ask whether hearers were willing to accept p, and be told that they were. After adding p to the conversational record, the speaker could repeat the original remark, and continue.

But there would be no point to this. Because hearers are ready to accept p anyway, they may as well add it to the background, and let the speaker go on without objection. In short, the most efficient response is to accommodate the speaker by updating the conversational record so that it meets the requirements of the utterance. Knowing that hearers can work this out on their own, the speaker can exploit this strategy of accommodation by uttering sentences the presuppositional requirements of which are not already satisfied by the conversational record—provided the requirements are both recognizable and uncontroversial. One virtue of this pragmatic approach is its eclecticism regarding different factors that may give rise to presuppositional requirements. As indicated in Soames (1989), logical presupposition, expressive presupposition, conventional implicature, constraints on the interpretation of anaphora, and non-conventional pragmatic facts have all been suggested as sources of pragmatic presuppositions. Further developments are found in Heim (1982, 1983) and Beaver (2001).

CONVERSATIONAL AND CONVENTIONAL IMPLICATURES

Closely related to pragmatic presuppositions, are conversational and conventional implicatures, introduced in Grice (1989) (originally delivered as the William James Lectures at Harvard in 1967). For conversational implicatures, the key insight is that the efficient and rational exchange of information by cooperative speakers is governed by maxims that include: (i) don't make your conversational contribution too weak (or too strong); (ii) don't say that which you believe to be false, or that for which you lack adequate evidence; (iii) be relevant; and (iv) avoid obscurity and ambiguity; be brief and be orderly.

Conversational implicatures are propositions that a speaker is committed to, above and beyond that which is said or asserted, by virtue of the presumption that the conversational maxims are being obeyed. According to Grice, a speaker s conversationally implicates q by saying p if and only if (a) s is presumed to be observing the conversational maxims, (b) the supposition that s believes q is required in order to make s's saying p consistent with that presumption, and (iii) s assumes that the hearers can recognize both this requirement and that s is assuming this. For example, if s assertively utters a disjunction ⌜A or B⌝, then standardly s conversationally implicates that there are non-truth-functional grounds for the assertion (because if s's grounds were truth-functional, and hence sufficient for asserting either disjunct alone, then s's utterance of the disjunction would be too weak, and hence violate maxim (i)). This shows that the simple truth-functional semantics for disjunction do not have to be complicated in order to explain why assertive utterances of disjunctive sentences standardly convey non-truth-functional information.

Another example of some philosophical significance involves the observation in Austin (1964) that it would be an abuse of language for a man who can see that there is a pig in front of him—without having to make any special investigation or to infer the presence of the pig from other propositions—to assert merely that it seems to him as if a pig is present, or that he has evidence of the presence of a pig. From this Austin concludes that such assertions would be false, and that, in a case such as the one imagined, a person can have empirical knowledge without having evidence for the proposition known. However,

as pointed out in Ayer (1967), Austin's observation does not support his conclusion. Because the speaker in the imagined situation is in a position to make the stronger claim that a pig is present, the decision to make the weaker statement instead violates Grice's maxim (i). The abuse of language here is not that of stating a falsehood, but of conversationally implicating one.

Like conversational implicatures, Gricean conventional implicatures are propositions to which the speaker is committed, despite their not being parts of what is said by the speaker's utterance. The difference between the two is that the former arise from the conversational maxims, whereas the latter are due to aspects of meaning. For example, an utterance of "She is poor but honest" conventionally implicates—in virtue of the nonassertive meaning of "but"—that there is some contrast between poverty and honesty, an utterance of "He is an Englishman, and therefore, brave" conventionally implicates—in virtue of the nonassertive meaning of "therefore"—that being brave is an expected consequence of being an Englishman, an utterance of "Mary hasn't arrived yet" conventionally implicates—in virtue of the nonassertive meaning of "yet"—that Mary's arrival is expected, and an utterance of "It wasn't Andrew who solved the problem" conventionally implicates—in virtue of the nonassertive meaning attached to the construction "It was (wasn't) NP who VPed"—that someone solved the problem. (Contrast this with "Andrew didn't solve the problem.") A significant point, developed in Karttunen and Peters (1979), is that conventional implicatures such as these may plausibly be regarded as pragmatic presuppositions. This suggests that the nonassertive meaning that generates them may be presuppositional in nature.

See also Analyticity; Austin, John Langshaw; Ayer, Alfred Jules; Frege, Gottlob; Grice, Herbert Paul; Kaplan, David; Lewis, David; Presupposition; Propositions; Russell, Bertrand Arthur William; Semantics; Strawson, Peter Frederick.

Bibliography

Austin, John L. *Sense and Sensibilia*. New York: Oxford University Press, 1964.

Ayer, A. J. "Has Austin Refuted the Sense-Datum Theory?" *Synthese* 17 (1967): 117–140.

Beaver, David. *Presupposition and Assertion in Dynamic Semantics*. Stanford CA: CSLI, 2001.

Frege, Gottlob. "Function and Concept." An address given to the *Jenaisch Gesellschaft fur Medicin und Naturwissenschaft*, January 9, 1891. Translated by Max Black in *Translations from the Writings of Gottlob Frege*, edited by Peter Geach and Max Black. Oxford: Blackwell, 1970.

Frege, Gottlob. "On Concept and Object." *Vierteljahrsschrift fur wissenschaftliche Philosophie* 16 (1892a): 192–205. Translated by Max Black in *Translations from the Writings of Gottlob Frege*, edited by Peter Geach and Max Black. Oxford: Blackwell, 1970.

Frege, Gottlob. "On Sense and Reference." *Zeitschrift fur Philosophie und philosophische Kritik* 100 (1892b): 25–50. Translated by Max Black in *Philosophical Review* 57 (1948): 207–230.

Grice, Paul. "Logic and Conversation." In *Studies in the Way of Words*. Cambridge, MA: Harvard University Press, 1989.

Heim, Irene. "On the Projection Problem for Presuppositions." In *Proceedings of the West Coast Conference on Formal Linguistics: Volume 2*, edited by M. Barlow, D. P. Flickinger and M. T. Wescoat. Stanford, CA: Stanford Linguistics Association, 1983.

Heim, Irene. *The Semantics of Definite and Indefinite Noun Phrases*. Ph.D. diss. University of Massachusetts, Amherst, 1982.

Kaplan, David. "Demonstratives." In *Themes from Kaplan*, edited by Joseph Almog, John Perry, and Howard Wettstein. New York: Oxford University Press, 1989.

Karttunen, Lauri, and Stanley Peters. "Conventional Implicature." In *Syntax and Semantics 11: Presupposition*, edited by Choon-Kyu Oh and David Dinneen. New York: Academic Press, 1979.

Lewis, David. "Scorekeeping in a Language Game." *Journal of Philosophical Logic* 8 (1979): 339–359.

Russell, Bertrand. "On Denoting." *Mind* 14 (1905): 479–493.

Soames, Scott. "Presupposition." In *Handbook of Philosophical Logic Volume IV*, edited by Dov Gabbay and Franz Guenthner. Dordrecht, Netherlands: Reidel, 1989.

Stalnaker, Robert. "Pragmatic Presuppositions." In *Semantics and Philosophy*, edited by Milton Munitz and Peter Unger. New York: New York University Press, 1974.

Stalnaker, Robert. "Presuppositions." *Journal of Philosophical Logic* 2 (1973): 447–457.

Strawson, Peter F. *Introduction to Logical Theory*. London: Methuen, 1952.

Strawson, Peter F. "On Referring." *Mind* 59 (1950): 320–344.

Scott Soames (2005)

ENTROPY

See *Philosophy of Statistical Mechanics*

ENVIRONMENTAL AESTHETICS

The term *environmental aesthetics* can apply to a variety of quite disparate sorts of cases—aesthetic appreciation of natural environments, of works of art situated in nature, of works of art—for example, landscape paintings—that are of or about nature, of works of art that take nature as their medium, and of gardens, a special category that seems to straddle the divide between culture and nature. In each case the philosophical challenge is the same: to determine the proper object and mode of appreciation. While these issues have not been definitively decided in the case of art appreciation, it remains helpful to use that example as a counterpoint against which an account of environmental appreciation can be constructed.

NATURE APPRECIATION

Nature scenes and natural items figure in our culture's most clichéd examples of aesthetic appreciation. Images of sunsets, rainbows, flowers, and baby animals are the stuff that enrich greeting card companies. But nature appreciation is also addressed by aestheticians and serious philosophers in the Western tradition. Immanuel Kant's examples of free beauty in *Critique of Judgment* (1790/1987) were natural items—flowers, birds, seashells. Beautiful items, Kant believed, provided a source of disinterested pleasure, their form alone triggering a pleasurable free play of imagination and understanding.

Nature appreciation is, of course, not confined to the beautiful. Kant's contemporary, Edmund Burke, indicates this even via the title of his 1757 work *A Philosophical Inquiry into the Origins of our Ideas of the Sublime and Beautiful* (1968). According to Burke, our attention is elicited not only by natural items that are small, lovely, and delicate, but also by those that are large, awesome, and terrifying. Surprisingly, such experiences are sought out. Kant concurs, offering the starry heavens, mountain peaks, and deep chasms as examples of the sublime. Certainly, nature is as much a repository of infinity and power as of delicacy and beauty.

Convinced that these two poles, the beautiful and the sublime, do not exhaust the grounds for aesthetic appreciation, eighteenth-century writers such as Sir Uvedale Price (1747–1829) and Richard Payne Knight (1750–1824) posited a third aesthetic category, the picturesque, situated midway between the beautiful and the sublime. Though the picturesque was initially defined as a species of beauty—that sort that would look pleasing in a picture—it soon came to be identified by an independently specified set of characteristics—roughness, sudden variation, and irregularity.

Additional factors of various sorts shape our nature preferences. Some are beliefs of which we are aware. Consider Thomas Burnet's (1635–1715) theory of the broken world. Promulgated in 1681 the theory impugned mountains as blemishes visited on the previously perfect (smooth and spherical) earth in payment for humankind's Fall. In her classic study *Mountain Gloom and Mountain Glory* (1959/1997), Marjorie Hope Nicholson documented the changes that allowed Romantic poets to embrace mountain scenery. Less accessible instincts and emotions may also affect our attitudes toward nature. In the 1970s Jay Appleton formulated prospect-refuge theory according to which we all have a hard-wired preference for the savanna-type landscapes that afforded our long-ago ancestors crucially valuable opportunities to see yet not be seen. And in addition to such shared influences, we have each accumulated a vast store of personal experiences and associations that contribute to our landscape preferences.

CONTEMPORARY PHILOSOPHICAL DEBATES

Ronald Hepburn (1972–) is often credited with ushering in the current era of environmental aesthetics with his article "Contemporary Aesthetics and the Neglect of Natural Beauty" (1996/2004). Hepburn there pinpointed two crucial differences between the aesthetic appreciation of nature and the aesthetic appreciation of art: (1) The objects of nature appreciation are often unframed and unbounded, and (2) we are often immersed *in* those objects. Hepburn's rehabilitation of nature as an object of aesthetic appreciation has been welcome and effective. But it may be that in crafting his argument, he was focused on a particular subset of examples: macroscopic rather than microscopic objects of appreciation. We can savor entire panoramas: lofty mountain ranges, vast seascapes, all the sorts of scenes Donald Crawford (1938–) calls *postcardesque*, but we can also zoom in on tiny focussed delights: an alpine flower; a polished pebble; a single, wondrous insect. These are neither unbounded nor capable of immersing us. In addressing such objects we seem to adjust our focus at will; this may well counter the standard practice of the art world where conventional modes of appreciation are in place for each type of work.

Present-day philosophers have taken up Hepburn's challenge and examined the scope or proper objects of appreciation, its theory-ladenness, and the supporting roles of association, imagination, and emotion. Arnold Berleant's (1932–) 1991 theory of engagement proposes an approach to both nature and art in keeping with Hepburn's insights. Berleant emphasizes the participatory aspect of aesthetic experience, the reciprocity of perceiver and object in the aesthetic field. By contrast, Allen Carlson (2000, 2004) has built a distinctive theory of nature appreciation by rejecting at least part of the analogy between art appreciation and nature appreciation. Carlson argues that treating nature as a set of scenes or a collection of discrete but absorbing objects (e.g., the way we treat painting or sculpture) ignores just those hallmarks that were shown by Hepburn to set nature apart as unbounded and enveloping. Yet Carlson maintains that nature appreciation must be informed by some body of theory that plays the role that art theory and the history of art play in art appreciation. Carlson proposes that science fills this void in the case of nature appreciation. Thus geology, physics, astronomy, earth science, biology, and botany can all play a role in informing our appreciation of nature.

Just as it seemed that Hepburn's proposed hallmarks characterized some chunks of nature but not others (the macro rather than the micro), so, too, it seems that Carlson's theory works best for a certain subset of cases. Viewing the Rocky Mountains or the Grand Canyon, a Yellowstone geyser or a rampaging tornado, it seems that our appreciation can only be enhanced by knowing the forces that shape these expanses and events. Science here provides knowledge of origins. It is less clear that scientific knowledge is helpful in appreciating things that are small, or ordinary, or the sites of local, ongoing, yet invisible processes. Is my aesthetic appreciation of a forest path, of red maples in fall or of a spider's web glistening with dew enhanced by knowledge of the decomposition of leaf mold, of the loss of chlorophyll, or of the extrusion of spider silk?

Carlson's theory has generated a voluminous secondary literature. Among the challenges raised is the exact nature of the theories he urges appreciators to call upon—science only, or science mingled with common sense. Other critics challenge the exclusivity of Carlson's approach, suggesting that the appeal to scientific theory is one way to appreciate nature but that it can coexist with other ways. In this vein, Noel Carroll (1993) argues for the role of emotional responsiveness, insisting that it is often appropriate for people to be emotionally moved by natural scenes and events. Emily Brady (2003) argues for an expanded role for imaginative response and distinguishes four different kinds of imaginative activity—exploratory, projective, ampliative, revelatory—that are summoned up by nature. The first is a playful examination of form and its attendant associations, the second a deliberate exercise of seeing as, the third an inventive contextualizing that takes us beyond the perceptual image, and the fourth an arrival at aesthetic truth. These, too, seem compatible with the appeal to science—for example, one might wander through a forest in spring, imagine it ablaze with fall reds and oranges, and acknowledge the mechanisms that would bring this about.

In her book *Aesthetics of the Natural Environment* (2003), Brady sorts various accounts of nature appreciation into cognitive and noncognitive camps. Since Brady basically elides the cognitive with the scientific, her taxonomy classes theories that appeal to association, imagination, emotion, or nonscientific information as noncognitivist. Thus she deems Hepburn, Berleant, and Carroll noncognitivists, along with Cheryl Foster (1998) who argues for an ineffable aspect of nature that she calls the ambient; Thomas Heyd (1956–), who champions the ascription of various narratives to natural goings on (the narrative is also how Foster labels the approach opposed to the ambient); and Yuriko Saito, who believes that nature appreciation should include a moral dimension— what she calls appreciating nature on its own terms.

The foregoing discussion has not touched on one profound, underlying problem, namely, the identification or definition of nature itself. There is good reason to think that there is no unsullied nature to be found on our planet. All nature has been intermixed with or affected by culture. Malcolm Budd (1941–) believes we are always able to abstract from such mixed cases and appreciate nature as nature even when, say, viewing an animal in a zoo (2002). The degree of mental/imaginative activity required here to arrive at an all-natural, intentional object of appreciation could be considerable. The water flowing from my kitchen faucet is natural only if I abstract away the changes wrung in the city treatment plant, or better yet, imaginatively travel back to the rainfall that was its source.

ART IN NATURE / ART FROM NATURE

This last topic of mixture lays the groundwork for considering cases where art and nature blend. The most innocuous in the continuum of such cases would be sculpture gardens and sculpture parks where works of art are simply arrayed in a natural setting. The effect would be very much that of an outdoor museum. Works of art in a sculpture garden can each be appreciated on their own. Additional insights arise from their juxtaposition.

While designers of a sculpture garden would of course take care to place each work in a setting conducive to its appreciation, there is no reason to think the arrangement could not be juggled just as curators can shuffle the order in which objects are arrayed in a museum. There is, however, one important feature that comes with outdoor exhibition. The works of art are viewed against an ever-changing background. Light and temperature are no longer controlled, as in a gallery, and the viewing experience is constantly affected by ongoing natural cycles: night and day, changing seasons, passing storms.

Additional complexities arise if the works of art exhibited outdoors connect with their setting in some way or other. One site might especially suit a given work on formal grounds. Alternatively, a work might comment on or interact with its setting. More explicit still are works that are *about* their settings. In such cases we enter the realm of site specificity, a trait made infamous by the controversy surrounding the removal of Richard Serra's (1930–) sculpture *Tilted Arc* from the site for which it was designed. Proper appreciation of site-specific works involves noting not only their formal, representational, and expressive properties but also their contextual properties. Thus the significance of Eero Saarinen's (1910–1961) *Gateway Arch* in St. Louis, Missouri, would be greatly compromised if it were not situated on the west bank of the Mississippi River marking the beginning of the western frontier brought about by the Louisiana Purchase. Nor would the work have the same significance if its legs were realigned to make the arch a portal for north–south rather than east–west travel. The environmental artist Robert Irwin (1928–) has codified four varieties of site specificity in his essay "Being and Circumstance." Irwin classifies works of art as site-dominant, site-adjusted, site-specific, and site-conditioned/determined. These four categories sort works whose meaning and purpose can be understood without reference to their site, works that make some concessions (such as placement and scale) to their site, works conceived with a specific site in mind, and finally, works that draw all their cues or reasons for being from their site.

A limiting case of the phenomenon of site specificity would be works of art that take (aspects of) their site as their medium. This would be true of some of the earthworks of the 1960s and 1970s. Michael Heizer's (1944–) *Double Negative*, Robert Smithson's (1938–1973) *Spiral Jetty*, and James Turrell's (1943–) *Roden Crater* are works that result from forceful gestures in the landscape; other environmental artists such as Andy Goldsworthy (1956–) and Michael Singer (1950–) make their art of more ephemeral stuff, taking walks and documenting them, making slight, nuanced adjustments to nature and then letting them dissipate. Both Crawford and Carlson have questioned whether the more bold types of environmental installations stand in an adversarial relation to nature as a result of creating aesthetic affronts.

GARDENS

When we turn to gardens, many of the topics already covered are still relevant. Gardens are in nature and their materials are often in large part natural. Japanese Zen gardens consisting of stones and raked sand are the most familiar counterexample to this expectation. And even more traditional gardens mix natural materials with a host of other components and features: paths, walls, benches, follies, fountains. Moreover, gardens bring to the forefront questions about *degrees* of naturalness. This has varied over garden history, with gardens that seemed utterly wild and untamed in one epoch coming later to be viewed as staid and artificial. Paradoxically, many gardens that are deemed natural in style achieve that effect through an intensive application of labor and care.

Unlike the sculpture parks and environmental works just discussed, the garden is a bona fide art form with its own history. Accordingly, Richard Wollheim's (1923–2003) notions of general and individual style take hold in gardening. Many garden styles are labeled in a way that includes a national designation—the French formal garden, the English landscape garden, the Italian villa garden, the Chinese scholar garden. This nomenclature flags the importance not only of cultural influences but also of topographical and climatological ones. (However, gardeners have always tried to trump nature with such aids as orangeries and greenhouses, trade in rare and exotic plants, breeding of entirely new species, and the bedding system—which allows several different gardens to succeed one another as the seasons unfold.) In addition to sustaining the notion of different general garden styles, the art of gardening also has practitioners whose individual style is recognizable. Thus we honor Andre Le Notre (1613–1700), Lancelot 'Capability' Brown (1716–1783), Gertrude Jekyll (1843–1932), Roberto Burle Marxe (1909–1994), and many, many more.

Garden appreciation must respond to this complexity. The sort of scientific knowledge that Carlson claims enhances our appreciation of natural scenes is also relevant to the garden—especially with regard to the plant species in place and the degree of skill or manipulation required to bring about various effects. Moreover, since all gardens are created rather than naturally occurring, their designers' intentions are always there to be retrieved. These intentions can range from trying to create a sensory delight to vastly ambitious promulgation of meanings. Not many gardens are what Mara Miller (1944–) calls grand gardens—that is, those that can claim to be great works of art. But exemplars have been produced in many different cultures. Gardens *can* convey complex meanings to those who view or walk through them. Through a judicious arrangement of plants, hardscape, topography, water features, statuary, buildings, inscriptions, and more, they can present disquisitions on matters of enduring interest and concern: politics, religion, love, war, the meaning of life, our place in the cosmos. Such gardens can sustain interpretive debates, with appreciators weighing in to defend alternative incompatible accounts of their meaning.

The sorts of garden content just discussed are pursued in much the same way that audiences track the meaning of works of art. Yet important aspects of nature appreciation also apply to gardens—especially the notions of unboundedness and surroundedness called to our attention by Hepburn. Though gardens are literally bounded, Miller (1993) has pointed out an important sense in which they cannot be controlled: since gardens are comprised of living things and are subject to natural forces, they are arenas of constant change. Plants grow; daily and seasonal cycles unfold; calamities occur. A garden designer's intentions are much less efficacious than those of other artists. The end result, as Miller puts it, is that gardens have no final form. There is no practical way to freeze a garden at a point in time and declare that to be the proper object of appreciation. In this regard, gardens truly do occupy a middle ground between nature and culture; wildness and art.

See also Burke, Edmund; Kant, Immanuel; Wollheim, Richard.

Bibliography

Appleton, Jay. *The Experience of Landscape*. London: John Wiley and Sons, 1975.

Berleant, Arnold. *Art and Engagement*. Philadelphia: Temple University Press, 1991.

Brady, Emily. *Aesthetics of the Natural Environment*. Tuscaloosa: University of Alabama Press, 2003.

Budd, Malcolm. *The Aesthetic Appreciation of Nature*. Oxford: Oxford University Press, 2002.

Burke, Edmund. *A Philosophical Inquiry into the Origins of Our Ideas of the Sublime and Beautiful*, edited by James T. Boulton. Notre Dame: University of Notre Dame Press, 1968.

Carlson, Allen. *Aesthetics and the Environment: The Appreciation of Nature, Art, and Architecture*. London: Routledge, 2000.

Carlson, Allen, and Arnold Berleant. *The Aesthetics of Natural Environments*. Ontario: Broadview Press, 2004.

Carroll, Noel. "On Being Moved by Nature: Between Religion and Natural History." In *Landscape, Natural Beauty, and the Arts*, edited by Salim Kemal and Ivan Gaskell. Cambridge, U.K.: Cambridge University Press, 1993.

Crawford, Donald. "Nature and Art: Some Dialectical Relationships." *Journal of Aesthetics and Art Criticism* 42 (1983): 49–58.

Foster, Cheryl. "The Narrative and the Ambient in Environmental Aesthetics." *Journal of Aesthetics and Art Criticism* 56 (1998): 127–137

Hepburn, Ronald. "Contemporary Aesthetics and the Neglect of Natural Beauty." In *British Analytical Philosophy*, edited by B. Williams and A. Montefiore. London: Routledge and Kegan Paul, 1996.

Kant, Immanuel. *Critique of Judgment.* Translated by Werner Pluhar. Indianapolis, IL: Hackett, 1987.

Miller, Mara. *The Garden as an Art.* Albany: State University of New York Press, 1993.

Nicholson, Margaret Hope. *Mountain Gloom and Mountain Glory: The Development of the Aesthetics of the Infinite.* Seattle: University of Washington Press, 1997.

Ross, Stephanie. *What Gardens Mean.* Chicago: University of Chicago Press, 1998.

Sonfist, Alan. *Art in the Land: A Critical Anthology of Environmental Art.* New York: E. P. Dutton, 1983.

Stephanie Ross (2005)

ENVIRONMENTAL ETHICS

Spurred by growing environmental concern in the 1960s, philosophers paid increasing attention to environmental ethics in the 1970s and 1980s. The field is dominated by dichotomies: anthropocentrism versus nonanthropocentrism, individualism versus holism, environmental ethics versus environmental philosophy, organic versus community metaphors, citizen versus consumer perspectives, scientific versus social scientific justifications, and trade-offs versus synergism.

ANTHROPOCENTRIC ENVIRONMENTALISM

Traditional Western ethics is anthropocentric, as only human beings are considered of moral importance. Because people can help or harm one another indirectly through environmental impact, such as by generating pollution, destroying marshes, and depleting resources, environmental ethics can be pursued as a form of applied ethics in an anthropocentric framework.

Some anthropocentric issues concern the nature and relative importance of values. For example, does the beauty or inspirational quality of a canyon make the canyon intrinsically valuable? If so, is that value an objective feature of the canyon or an aspect of the evaluators' subjective experience or judgment? Finally, how important to people is such intrinsic, noneconomic value compared to economic considerations? Is the canyon's

intrinsic value, assuming it has such value, sufficient to forgo its flooding to generate hydroelectricity that can power economic growth? Environmental ethics is a fertile testing ground for competing axiologies.

Environmental ethics also tests competing conceptions of the individual's relationship to society. A strictly economic approach views the individual as a consumer and directs government to regulate environmental matters to maximize the satisfaction of consumer demands. An alternative approach views the individual as a citizen concerned to promote individual excellence and to preserve and improve the community's best traditions and highest moral ideals. This dichotomy parallels that between liberalism and perfectionism in political philosophy. Just as many perfectionists would forgo the economic benefits of legal prostitution to protect the traditional family, many citizen-oriented environmentalists recommend preserving wilderness areas and species diversity to promote ideals of stewardship.

Environmental justice is primarily an anthropocentric ideal concerning the appropriate distribution of benefits and burdens among human beings affected by environmental decisions. Issues of resource depletion, nuclear waste, and population policy, for example, raise questions about intergenerational justice. Do future people have rights? Can a meaningful distinction be made between future people and possible people? Why should we care about future people if they can neither harm nor help us?

Issues of environmental justice arise when governments use cost-benefit analysis (CBA) to evaluate environmental policies. CBAs typically translate all values into monetary terms with the goal of identifying policies that maximize total social wealth. Exclusively monetary evaluations jeopardize future generations through the use of a discount rate that renders impacts 500 years from now insignificant. In addition, CBAs promote decisions that are unjust to poor people because the monetary value of items in a market economy, and therefore the total value of all such items, social wealth, depends on people's willingness to pay for things. Rich people can pay more than poor people, so the preferences of the rich are weighted more heavily in CBA than the preferences of the poor. Government policies guided by CBA therefore contravene the principle of justice that the interests of each individual person be considered equally.

Environmental racism concerns practices, in derogation of environmental justice, that subject people of non-European origin to disproportionate amounts of pollution and other negative side effects of economic development. Within most industrial countries, such people are racial minorities. Internationally, such people reside in Third World countries. In both cases, many economists reject charges of environmental racism. They claim that people of color suffer disproportionate burdens not because of racist intent but because they are too poor to pay for better conditions. This is another area of tension between economic and noneconomic anthropocentric considerations.

MORAL EXTENSIONISM

Opposed to anthropocentrism are those who consider many nonhuman animals to be worthy of moral consideration in their own right. These views extend some traditional ethical theories, such as utilitarianism and neo-Kantianism, to include nonhuman individuals. Paul Taylor (2005) advocates further extension, according equal moral consideration to every living individual, amoeba included.

Many environmental philosophers consider moral extensionism too human-centered and individualistic. It is too human-centered because it justifies valuing nonhumans on the basis of similarities to human beings, such as sentience, consciousness, or merely life itself. Human traits remain the touchstone of all value. Moral extensionism is too individualistic for environmental ethics because some matters, such as species diversity, concern collectives, not individuals. From an individualist perspective, saving ten members of a common species is better than saving one member of an endangered species, other things being equal. Environmentalists concerned with maintaining species diversity reject individualism for this reason.

They reject individualism also as ecologically unrealistic. Ecology teaches that ecosystems depend on individuals eating and being eaten, killing and being killed. For example, predators must kill enough deer to avoid deer overpopulation, which would threaten flora on which deer feed. Reduced flora threatens soil stability and the land's ability to support life. So protecting individual deer from untimely death, which valuing deer as individuals may suggest, is environmentally harmful. Such harm threatens natural ecosystems, such as wilderness areas, that foster biological evolution, which is the focus of value for some nonanthropocentric environmentalists.

Tom Regan (2005) calls holistic views "environmental fascism." Sacrificing individuals for evolutionary advance or the collective good resembles Adolf Hitler's program, especially when human beings may be among those sacrificed. Human overpopulation threatens species

diversity, ecosystemic complexity, and natural evolutionary processes, so consistent, nonanthropocentric environmental holism may be misanthropic.

Holists reply that human individuals, as well as environmental wholes and evolutionary processes, are intrinsically valuable, so individual humans should not be sacrificed to promote the corporate good. However, the casuistry of trade-offs among individuals and corporate entities of various species and kinds is not well developed by the holists. But Regan (2005), for his part, does not show how all individual nonhuman mammals, for example, can be accorded the equivalent of the human right to life without destroying wilderness areas and causing the extinction of carnivorous species.

Because they value not only nonhumans but holistic entities, many environmental philosophers believe their discipline calls for thorough review of the place of human beings in the cosmos. They reject the title "environmental ethics" in favor of "environmental philosophy" or "ecosophy" to emphasize that their views are not applications of traditional ethics to environmental problems but fundamental metaphysical orientations.

HOLISTIC ENVIRONMENTALISM

Holistic views tend to compare the environmental wholes they consider valuable in themselves with either communities or organisms. Aldo Leopold's "land ethic" (2005), for example, leans toward the community metaphor. Just as the benefits people derive from their human communities justify loyalty to the group, benefits derived from complex ecological interdependencies justify loyalty to ecosystemic wholes. J. Baird Callicott (2005) maintains that community loyalty is emotionally natural to humans, as our ancestors' survival during evolution depended on sentiments of solidarity. In this sense, ethics is based on Humean sentimentalism rather than on Kantian rationality or utilitarian calculation.

The Gaia hypothesis and deep ecology stress the similarity of holistic entities to individual organisms, thereby attempting to reconcile individualism with environmentalism. The Gaia hypothesis maintains that life on Earth operates as if it were a single organism reacting to altered conditions so as to preserve itself. This explains, for example, how Earth has maintained a relatively constant temperature over a 3-billion-year period while the energy emitted toward Earth from the Sun had increased 30 percent. Metaphorically, if Earth is alive, it is our mother because Earth's processes produce and sustain us. This metaphor justifies respect for Earth and Earth's processes analogous to respect for human mothers.

Deep ecology reflects the belief of the stoics and Benedict (Baruch) de Spinoza that reality is essentially one being. Accordingly, it questions the separateness of any individual from the environmental whole. Deep ecologists point out that the skin and other borders between individuals are really permeable membranes that connect as well as divide. Arne Naess (2005), deep ecology's founder, notes that human beings can possess the entire universe in their minds and suggests identifying one's real self with nature. Degrading nature is therefore unwise because it is a form of self-degradation. Deep ecology reconciles holistic environmental concern not only with individualism but also with individual self-concern. This metaphysical consideration is bolstered by observations about the lack of genuine fulfillment experienced by most people whose lives are dominated by consuming artifacts instead of appreciating nature.

ECOFEMINISM

Whereas the land ethic and Gaia hypothesis rely primarily on information drawn from science, other environmentalists stress social scientific information. Using the results of anthropological studies, especially of foraging (hunter-gatherer) societies, some environmentalists maintain that human life is better where people do not attempt to master nature in the human interest. Many indigenous societies practice an environmental ethic, similar to the land ethic, of reciprocal exchange with nonhuman environmental constituents such as water, sun, trees, and game animals. This enriches human life and preserves the environment.

Ecofeminists emphasize the relationship between mastering nature in the supposed human interest and the oppression of women, indigenous people, and other subordinated groups. Ecofeminists claim that much Western thinking is dominated by what they call "the master mentality," which is dualistic thinking that values one member of each dyad more than the other and relegates the inferior member to serve the superior. Such dyads include men versus women, heaven versus earth, mind versus body, reason versus emotion, culture versus nature, and progress versus stagnation. White Western men are associated with the superior member of each dyad: heaven, mind, reason, culture, and progress; whereas women, indigenous people, and other subordinated groups are associated with the inferior member: earth, body, emotion, nature, and stagnation. The master mentality thus justifies the continued subordination of women and non-Western, nonindustrialized men, because humanity in general flourishes, the masters claim, when the inferior serves the superior.

The master mentality's association of women with earth and emotion explains traditional exclusions of women from high religious offices and from professions emphasizing the use of abstract reason. The association of progress with economic growth explains Western insensitivity to the disruption of traditional patterns of life in many Third World countries. Traditional agriculture returns little money but produces a large variety of food for local consumption. It suffers in comparison with Western-inspired commercial agriculture that emphasizes remunerative monocultures when progress is associated with economic growth. The master mentality also generally undervalues work traditionally done by women because much of it is done free, whether it is childcare or tending a garden to feed the family.

Ecofeminists claim that the master mentality approach to the environment serves humanity badly. Worldwide, it marginalizes and impoverishes women and other subordinated people. Humanity would fare better if people's interactions with nature were guided more by thinking traditionally associated with women. Women tend to think more relationally, organically, and holistically than (Western) men, who favor individual rights, commercial success, and mechanistic processes. Whereas typical male patterns of thought and action precipitate ecocrises, typical female patterns ameliorate them. Empowering women can save ecosystems and species diversity.

Most anthropocentrists and nonanthropocentrists believe that in general a tension exists between protecting nature and serving humanity. Nonanthropocentric concern for nature as valuable in itself precludes actions that can make human life better, they think. This is the trade-off perspective. The synergistic perspective, by contrast, is that valuing nature for itself most often precludes action that is mistakenly undertaken in pursuit of human welfare but that is actually counterproductive. For example, the Green Revolution attempted to improve human life by mastering nature but it harmed people more than it helped them because it disrupted traditional social systems and more holistically productive agriculture, argues Vandana Shiva (1991). Like the hedonic paradox, which claims that happiness is best achieved by not seeking it directly, synergists claim that human flourishing is best achieved by nonanthropocentrically valuing nature for itself rather than by trying anthropocentrically to maximize returns from nature for human beings. The land ethic, deep ecology, and ecofeminism are compatible with environmental synergism.

Because environmental ethics/philosophy questions basic assumptions in economics, technology, metaphysics, ethical theory, moral epistemology, and gender relations, it approaches religion in its attention to the fundamental concerns of human existence.

See also Animal Rights and Welfare; Applied Ethics; Distant Peoples and Future Generations; Good, The; Intrinsic Value; Rights; Utilitarianism.

Bibliography

Callicott, J. Baird. "The Conceptual Foundations of the Land Ethic." In *Environmental Ethics: Readings in Theory and Application.* 4th ed, edited by Louis P. Pojman, 149–160. Belmont, CA: Thomson/Wadsworth, 2005.

Dobson, Andrew. *Fairness and Futurity: Essays on Environmental Sustainability and Social Justice.* New York: Oxford University Press, 1999.

Hargrove, Eugene C., ed. *The Animal Rights, Environmental Ethics Debate: The Environmental Perspective.* Albany: SUNY Press, 1992.

Leopold, Aldo. "Ecocentrism: The Land Ethic." In *Environmental Ethics: Readings in Theory and Application.* 4th ed, edited by Louis P. Pojman, 139–148. Belmont, CA: Thomson/Wadsworth, 2005.

Naess, Arne. "Ecosophy T: Deep versus Shallow Ecology." In *Environmental Ethics: Readings in Theory and Application.* 4th ed, edited by Louis P. Pojman, 192–200. Belmont, CA: Thomson/Wadsworth, 2005.

Partridge, Ernest, ed. *Responsibilities to Future Generations: Environmental Ethics.* Buffalo, NY: Prometheus Books, 1981.

Pojman, Louis P., ed. *Environmental Ethics: Readings in Theory and Application.* 4th ed. Belmont, CA: Thomson/Wadsworth, 2005. This is an excellent source of information on anthropocentric environmentalism, animal rights, biocentrism, the land ethic, deep ecology, social ecology, and ecofeminism.

Regan, Tom. "The Radical Egalitarian Case for Animal Rights." In *Environmental Ethics: Readings in Theory and Application.* 4th ed, edited by Louis P. Pojman, 65–72. Belmont, CA: Thomson/Wadsworth, 2005.

Sagoff, Mark. *The Economy of the Earth: Philosophy, Law, and the Environment.* New York: Cambridge University Press, 1988. Critiques economics and CBA.

Shiva, Vandana. *The Violence of the Green Revolution: Third World Agriculture, Ecology and Politics.* London: Zed Books, 1991.

Taylor, Paul. "Biocentric Egalitarianism." In *Environmental Ethics: Readings in Theory and Application.* 4th ed, edited by Louis P. Pojman, 117–131. Belmont, CA: Thomson/Wadsworth, 2005.

Warren, Karen J. *Ecofeminist Philosophy: A Western Perspective on What It Is and Why It Matters.* Lanham, MD: Rowman & Littlefield, 2000. A comprehensive introduction to ecofeminism.

Wenz, Peter S. *Environmental Ethics Today.* New York: Oxford University Press, 2001.

Peter S. Wenz (1996, 2005)

EPICTETUS
(55 CE–c. 135)

Epictetus became a slave of Epaphroditus, himself a freedman who was secretary to Nero. After being freed by his master, Epictetus studied with the Stoic Musonius Rufus, and he taught in Rome until Domitian banished the philosophers in 89 CE. He then established a school in Nicopolis in Epirus, a town in northwest Greece founded by Octavian to commemorate his victory at Actium. Epictetus was lame, perhaps because of his sufferings as a slave, but was a renowned teacher.

Like Socrates, Epictetus wrote nothing, but his pupil Arrian compiled a record of his oral teachings. Four books of these *Discourses* survive, together with a digest of central points known as the *Manual*. Although these works reveal that Epictetus taught his students through the careful study of Stoic doctrine (II 13.21, III 16.9–10), they also make it plain that the goal of philosophical learning is not to be an exegete of Chrysippus (I 4.6–9, I 17.13–18). In fact, the discourses themselves do not offer much exegesis, nor do they often develop heavily theorized explanations, careful distinctions, or involved arguments, as a usual philosophical treatise would. For years, scholars explained this by the hypothesis that Epictetus's teachings fit a particular genre of "diatribes"—the Greek title of the *Discourses* is *Diatribai*—but, because the evidence of such a genre is very thin, the hypothesis is no longer widely accepted.

It now seems, instead, that the discourses simply teach in the ways that Epictetus associates with his three philosophical heroes: They manifest the examining role of Socrates when Epictetus refutes unnamed interlocutors by question-and-answer; they display the rebuking and kingly role of Diogenes the Cynic when Epictetus hectors pupils and exemplifies haughty leadership; and they take on the teaching, doctrinal role of the founding Stoic, Zeno of Citium, when Epictetus offers terse, straightforward principles for the guidance of life (III 21.18–19). In all of these ways, the *Discourses* and *Manual* are concerned primarily with the concrete task of helping others live better lives.

So, when Epictetus outlines the "three topics" on which a person must train to become good, they are not abstruse philosophical matters or even the broad parts of

Stoicism, logic, ethics, and physics. Rather, he insists that one must study, first, desires and aversions; second, impulses, rejection, and in general, appropriate action; and third, infallibility in assent (III 2.1–2). He counsels that the first step is to extinguish desire—to rein in the passions and to free one to do what is appropriate (III 2.3–4, *Manual* 2). Epictetus here supposes the Stoic views that passions are defective judgments about what is good and bad for one, and that desire is an impulse for what is good. To eliminate desire, then, is to free oneself from making so many judgments of what is good and bad for one. This freedom from passionate attachments, in turn, frees one to consider coolly what is merely appropriate and act accordingly. Without passions and desires, one lives by weaker impulses, in terms of what is merely appropriate. The last topic is reserved for those who have already made substantial progress in taming their desire and managing their impulses (III 2.5).

This focused deployment of Stoic ideals without the full discussion of logic and physics recalls the Cynics, who traditionally offer the Stoic a "shortcut to virtue." Epictetus does in fact endorse a brand of Cynicism (III 22), and his Stoicism is much more austere than that of, say, Cicero's *On Duties*. Nevertheless, Epictetus is not hostile to all conventional roles and the activities appropriate to them, and he does not reject logic and physics so much as he keeps the focus away from them in the *Discourses*, to keep his pupils concentrated on bettering themselves.

Accordingly, the special features of Epictetus's Stoicism serve his practical aim of helping people, and most are probably due more to it than to any doctrinal disagreement with other Stoics. Among these features, perhaps the most prominent is the oft-repeated distinction between what is up to us and what is not. This distinction, which is highlighted in the first sentence of the *Manual*, tells one to care only for one's mind or soul. Often, Epictetus puts this by saying that our volition (*prohairesis*) is up to us (see, for example, I 1.23). Because the word *prohairesis* is common in Aristotle's ethics but not among early Stoics, who used it to pick out a limited sort of impulse, some scholars see Epictetus's concentrated concern for *prohairesis* as an especially innovative suggestion of a will, inspired by Aristotle and perhaps by debates about freedom and determinism. But this interpretation is hard to support, for the resources Epictetus uses to explain what he means by *prohairesis* do not much stretch the boundaries of earlier Stoicism, and the freedom that he connects with *prohairesis* is just the moral freedom familiar from earlier Stoicism.

Another special feature of Epictetus's Stoicism is its intensely personal theology. Stoics always locate divinity in the cosmos; they attribute the orderly workings of nature to the divine reason in which all humans have a share. Epictetus personalizes all of this. He considers the goal of living to be to follow the god or gods (I 12.5, I 30.4), and he considers himself a servant of god (IV 7.20). Moreover, he refuses the picture of servitude to a distant king: on Epictetus's view, Zeus has stationed a divinity within each of us, a "god within" (I 14.12–14, II 8.12–14).

According to this thought, which clearly reinforces the emphasis on what is up to us, we all have the resources we need to live well within us. Two additional ways in which Epictetus develops his appeals to our inner resources are among the most innovative features of his Stoicism. For one, he regularly insists that we have capacities of trustworthiness and self-respect that cannot be taken from us (see, for example, I 25.4). This appeal to personal integrity and to an ability to evaluate reflectively what is appropriate to oneself suggests the modern notion of conscience, and it clearly invokes a notion of self-respect (*aidôs*) that is distinct from what is attested for earlier Stoics. Epictetus makes another interesting departure from earlier Stoics when he insists that our notions of good and bad and the like are innate (II 11.1–8). Although earlier Stoics insist that human minds are blank slates at birth, Epictetus encourages us to take heart in our substantial inheritance from the gods.

Epictetus's Stoicism is fully realized for the purpose of encouraging others to progress as Stoics. His articulation of self-reliance has attracted many readers over the centuries, and his subtle moral psychology has deservedly found a wide audience, from the second-century emperor Marcus Aurelius to the sixth-century Neoplatonist Simplicius (who wrote a massive commentary on the *Manual*) and from the sixteenth-century neo-Stoic Justus Lipsius to the twentieth-century American prisoner of war James Stockdale.

See also Cynics; Diogenes of Sinope; Marcus Aurelius Antoninus; Simplicius; Socrates; Stoicism; Zeno of Citium.

Bibliography

WORKS BY EPICTETUS

Dissertationes ab Arriano Digestae, edited by H. Schenkl. 2nd ed. Stuttgart: Teubner, 1916.

WORKS BY EPICTETUS IN TRANSLATION

The Discourses, as Reported by Arrian, the Manual, and Fragments. 2 vols., edited and translated by W. A. Oldfather. Cambridge, MA: Harvard University Press, 1925–1928.

WORKS BY EPICTETUS IN PARTIAL TRANSLATION WITH COMMENTARY

Discourses: Book One. Translated, with an introduction and commentary, by R. F. Dobbin. Oxford: Clarendon, 1998.

WORKS ABOUT EPICTETUS

Bönhoffer, A. *Epictet und die Stoa.* Stuttgart: F. Enke, 1890.

The Ethics of the Stoic Epictetus. Translated by W. O. Stephens. New York: Peter Lang, 1996.

Long, A. A. *Epictetus: A Stoic and Socratic Guide to Life.* Oxford: Clarendon, 2002.

Eric Brown (2005)

EPICUREANISM AND THE EPICUREAN SCHOOL

The Epicureans perpetuated their founder's teaching with little change. Of Epicurus's immediate circle, the most distinguished was Metrodorus of Lampsacus (c. 330–277 BCE), who predeceased his master. Metrodorus was elevated by Epicurus to a position of eminence—he alone shared the appellation "wise" (*sophos*), and his works were regarded as authoritative statements of doctrine. He wrote on epistemology, ethics, religion, poetry, and rhetoric, and he composed polemics against Plato's *Gorgias* and *Euthyphro,* and against Democritus.

Colotes of Lampsacus, another member of the original circle, published a comprehensive refutation of other schools under the title "That the Doctrines of the Other Philosophers Actually Make Life Impossible." Our knowledge of it comes from Plutarch's *Reply to Colotes.* His other writings included attacks on Plato's *Lysis* and *Euthydemus* and on the myth of Er in the *Republic.*

Hermarchus of Mytilene (325–c. 250 BCE) was Epicurus's successor as head of the school. His chief work, in twenty-two books, was on Empedocles. He also wrote on the arts (including rhetoric), attacked Plato and Aristotle, and left a collection of letters.

Polystratus succeeded Hermarchus. Two of his works have been recovered in part from the library at Herculaneum; the better preserved is "On Unreasonable Contempt for Popular Opinion."

In the second and first centuries BCE the school continued to flourish. One member, Philonides, enjoyed the friendship of Antiochus Epiphanes (king of Syria, 175–164 BCE) and attained some standing as a mathematician. Later in the second century Zeno of Sidon lectured in Athens on logic, rhetoric, poetry, and mathematics; and he introduced into his ethical teaching many of the commonplaces of the popular moral essays developed by rival schools, including the use of moral examples drawn from literary sources. Zeno's older contemporary, Demetrius of Laconia, also composed popular moral essays and wrote on logic and poetics. These men's rivals were chiefly Stoics, and under the pressure of controversy they occasionally gave new formulations to Epicurean teaching. Whether they were concerned to any great extent with the atomic theory is uncertain; it appears that they did align themselves more closely than did their predecessors with the traditions of Greek *paideia,* perhaps for the added prestige it gave them as they spread their doctrine to the east and west. (Both Zeno and Demetrius counted Romans among their students.) Yet there were a few diehards; one of the rare schisms in the school developed over the question of whether rhetoric is an art. The use of literary embellishment as a means of persuasion was contrary to the principles of the strict Epicureans, who seem to have been influenced by Plato's *Gorgias.* Yet one group accepted epideictic oratory as a legitimate pursuit.

In the first half of the first century BCE Philodemus of Gadara (in Syria), who had attended the lectures of Zeno in Athens, founded at Naples an Epicurean group with liberal tendencies. The Epicurean library at Herculaneum has yielded extensive passages from his many writings, which included moral treatises, biographies of philosophers, a history of the philosophical schools, and such polemical works as "On the Gods" and *On Methods of Inference.* Among his followers were persons of considerable eminence, notably Piso Caesoninus, Roman consul in 58 BCE, who was his principal patron. To such as these, we may suppose, he addressed "On Wealth," "On the Management of Property," and "On the Good King in Homer." This last piece is remarkable, not so much for its concern with a political matter (Epicurus had written "On Kingship") as for its use of Homer as an authority. (The Epicureans' rejection of the traditional Greek education led them to minimize the importance of the Homeric poems and to challenge the wisdom of Homer.)

Philodemus's treatises "On Rhetoric," "On Poems," and "On Music" were orthodox to the extent of maintaining that these arts are not suitable media for philosophical teaching or moral training; yet Philodemus conceded to them a positive value as art forms. Indeed, he himself had literary pretensions and composed a number of short poems. As a philosopher he won a qualified respect from Cicero. With Siro, his colleague, he attracted to the school a group of young Latin poets, among them Vergil; there is, however, no evidence to connect the school at Naples with the Roman Epicurean Lucretius.

Under the empire the Epicureans, true to their own precept, withdrew from public view. The last conspicuous member of the school was Diogenes of Oenoanda (a town in Lycia), who about 200 CE published the wisdom of Epicurus for his fellow townsmen by having a number of Epicurean writings inscribed on a wall at the entrance to the town. Most of the texts, apparently, he composed himself; two are on natural science, the remainder on ethics. He also included some of Epicurus's sayings and a letter from Epicurus to his mother.

See also Aristotle; Empedocles; Epicurus; Homer; Leucippus and Democritus; Lucretius; Philodemus; Plato; Stoicism.

Bibliography

Our knowledge of the Epicurean school is being improved by the constant publication and reediting of the Herculaneum papyri. Most of this material can be found, with good introductions and commentaries, in the series *La Scuola di Epicuro* (Bibliopolis, Naples) and also in the journal *Cronache Ercolanesi* (Naples, 1971–). For a history of the study of the papyri see Mario Capasso, *Manuale di Papirologia Ercolanese* (Galatina: Congedo, 1991). Diskin Clay, *Paradosis and Survival: Three Chapters in the History of Epicurean Philosophy* (Ann Arbor: University of Michigan Press, 1998), contains essays on a range of topics from different periods of Epicurean philosophy.

On Metrodorus see Alfred Koerte, "Metrodori Epicurei Fragmenta," in *Jahrbücher für classische Philologie*, Supplementband 17 (1890): 531–570. (There is a 1987 facsimile reprint by Garland, New York, which also contains Vincenzo de Falco, *L'Epicureo Demetrio Lacone* [Naples, 1923].) For Hermarchus see: Francesca Longo Auricchio, *Ermarco: frammenti* (Naples, 1988).

For Polystratus see: Giovanni Indelli, *Polistrato: Sul disprezzo irrazionale delle opinioni populari* (Naples: Bibliopolis, 1971), and James Warren, *Epicurus and Democritean Ethics: An Archaeology of Ataraxia* (Cambridge, U.K., and New York: Cambridge University Press 2002), Chapter 5. On Demetrius of Laconia: de Falco (see above); Enzo Puglia, *Demetrio Lacone: Aporie testuale ed esegetiche in Epicuro* (Naples, 1988); Costantina Romeo, *Demetrio Lacone: La Poesia* (Naples: Bibliopolis, 1988). There is a commentary on Plutarch's reply to Colotes (*Adversus Colotem*) by Rolf Westman, *Plutarch gegen Kolotes* (Helsinki: Acta Philosophica Femica, 1955). See also Wilhelm Crönert, *Kolotes und Menedemos* (Leipzig, 1906).

The best introduction to Philodemus is: Marcello Gigante, *Philodemus in Italy* (Ann Arbor: University of Michigan Press, 1995). There are also useful discussions in recent editions of Philodemus's works: Dirk Obbink, *Philodemus: On Piety, Part I* (Oxford: Clarendon Press, 1996) and

Richard Janko, *Philodemus: On Poems Book 1* (Oxford, 2000). There are useful articles in Dirk Obbink, ed. *Philodemus and Poetry* (Oxford: Clarendon Press, 1995) and Voula Tsouna, "Philodemus on the Therapy of Vice," *Oxford Studies in Ancient Philosophy* 21 (2001): 233–258, is a good introduction to his ethical approach.

For Lucretius: Diskin Clay, *Lucretius and Epicurus* (Ithaca, NY: Cornell University Press, 1983) and David Sedley, *Lucretius and the Transformation of Greek Wisdom* (Cambridge, U.K., and New York: Cambridge University Press, 1998) discuss the Latin poet's use of early Epicurean works. See also: Keimpe Algra et al., eds., *Lucretius and His Intellectual Background* (Amsterdam and New York: North-Holland, 1997).

For Diogenes of Oinoanda see the edition with introduction and commentary by Martin F. Smith, *Diogenes of Oinoanda: The Epicurean Inscription* (Naples, 1996; supplementary volume, 2003).

P. H. De Lacy (1967)
Bibliography updated by James Warren (2005)

EPICURUS
(341–270 BCE)

Epicurus was born on Samos to parents who were Athenian citizens. Evidence about his philosophical debts and development must be sifted from conflicting reports arising out of the agonistic context of ancient Greek philosophical rivalry and invective. While rivals charge him with merely plagiarizing his atomism from Democritus and hedonism from the Cyrenaics, his advocates praise his singular originality, probably encouraged in this by Epicurus himself. Like Parmenides, René Descartes, and other seminal figures in philosophy, Epicurus presented himself as a solitary herald of truth, creating his system *de novo* because of the inadequacy of his predecessors and teachers. Modern scholarship tends to split the difference, seeing a variety of possible influences—Democritean atomism, Cyrenaic hedonism, Aristotelian *eudaimonism*, skeptic impeturbablilty—while fully recognizing that however much Epicurus worked within an existing framework, he is responsible for a succession of remarkably influential innovations.

LIFE AND SOURCES

Epicurus spent most of his first thirty-five years in Asia Minor. There he began formulating his doctrines and collecting important adherents before embarking for Athens where he founded the Garden in 306 BCE. Alone among the major Athenian meeting places for philosophers (the Academy, Lyceum, and Stoa), it remained an authoritative center for the study and dissemination of its founder's teachings late into the Roman period—largely, no doubt, because it alone continued to flourish as an institution with endowed property, stable traditions of teaching and doctrine, and generations of faithful advocates. It was distinguished as well by its admission of women and slaves. Epicurus's death, although physically painful, is portrayed in our sources as having been appropriately philosophical.

Diogenes Laertius (third century CE), our chief source for his writings (including his will), relates that Epicurus was the most prolific author of his time (some 300 papyrus rolls). Pitifully little survives. Diogenes himself preserves three short letters outlining Epicurus's physical theory, ethics, and explanations of celestial phenomena, though doubts exist that the last is from Epicurus's hand. *Kuriai Doxai*, a collection of excerpts quoted by Diogenes, and a parallel collection surviving in another manuscript, *Sententiae Vaticanae*, were apparently designed to remind adherents of Epicurus's key claims.

Although critical, the philosophical treatises of Cicero, written some two centuries after the time of Epicurus, offer our most articulate evidence for many Epicurean arguments. Other scattered citations are preserved, especially in Plutarch, Sextus Empiricus, Seneca, and the Aristotelian commentators, though it often is difficult to discern from them the original context and intent of his arguments. *De Rerum Natura*, by the Roman poet Lucretius (d. 50 BCE), renders into verse Epicurean atomic theory, epistemology, and social thought, relying especially on Epicurus's major treatise, *On Nature*. Badly damaged parts of *On Nature* and several works by Philodemus, an Epicurean roughly contemporary with Lucretius, were recovered in Herculaneum (1752) from the Casa dei Papiri, buried by the eruption of Vesuvius in 79 CE. New methods of reconstructing these texts are yielding important information about many facets of Epicureanism. Finally, in Oenoanda, in what is present-day southwestern Turkey, a large inscription erected by one Diogenes encapsulates several basic Epicurean doctrines.

PHILOSOPHICAL SYSTEM

Although not as insistent as the Stoics about the systematic coherence of all his philosophical doctrines, Epicurus believes that his arguments from the domains of physics, epistemology, psychology, and ethics are mutually supporting. So, for instance, a linchpin in his arguments against the fear of death is the claim that persons are material entities of the sort that no longer continue to exist upon death and are therefore no longer subject to harm. This being the case, we have no reason to fear a future state that can cause us no harm.

Such a view of persons similarly undergirds his theological claim that we have no reason to fear punishment from the gods in an afterlife. Since we do not survive our deaths, the gods can hardly mete out any post mortem punishment, even if they so wished. At the same time, the relation of his materialism to many of his other central doctrines is less immediately straightforward. Epicurus sometimes describes perceptual experiences, actions, and psychological properties in ways that, to many at least, do not look easily reducible to talk about atoms and the void, and one of the persistent problems in understanding his philosophical thought is gauging the extent to which he offers, or at least intends to offer, fully reductive material accounts of each of the primary domains of his philosophical system.

Gaps in our evidence, at least at present, preclude giving a precise accounting of his philosophical successes in coping with the demands of materialism within his general thinking. But one thing seems clear. By adopting a materialist physical theory and working through its implications, Epicurus formulates a series of questions about the material bases of perception and thought, the mechanisms of choice and avoidance, and the possibility of free agency in a world consisting of matter in motion that sets him on a path distinct from such predecessors as Plato and Aristotle. Moreover, he rejects their *polis* bound conceptions of ethics and politics and offers accounts of ethical motivation and political obligation strictly rooted in notions of individual agents and their mutual relations per se. In so doing, Epicurus and his followers develop both a professional philosophical vocabulary and ways of conceiving a broad range of philosophical issues that often appear distinctly modern. Indeed, it might be more historically precise to say that many modern ways of formulating arguments can strike one as being Epicurean— no doubt because a significant number of them in fact have their origins in ancient Epicureanism.

The philosophical challenges that Epicurus faced because of the convergence of his atomism, empiricism, hedonism, and politics of solitary individualism provided a basic conceptual framework for a whole range of thinkers who helped set the terms of modern philosophical debates. Michel de Montaigne, Thomas Hobbes, Pierre Gassendi, Robert Boyle, Jean-Jacques Rousseau, Baron d'Holbach, Jeremy Bentham, and John Stuart Mill—to name just a few who particularly felt his influence—all show basic debts across a wide variety of their theoretical concerns—debts not only to more general Epicurean philosophical preoccupations, but also in many instances to Epicurus's particular methods of argument, his specific conclusions, and, above all, to the way that he originally devised the philosophical framework and individual terms in which they came to carry on their own debates.

Epicurus himself is frank about the role of materialism in his system. He asserts that if we were not made unhappy by the fear of death or suspicions that natural phenomena depend upon meddling gods, we would have no need to inquire into nature. He therefore rejects both Aristotle's defense of purely theoretical inquiry and the Socratic claim that ethical beliefs can be examined independently of a complete understanding of nature. But this does not commit him, of course, to a rigidly pragmatic conception of scientific truth. To the contrary, he insists that just as with respect to our health, what we want is not merely the semblance of health, in our scientific theories what we want is truth, not merely some beliefs that may appear true. Extra-scientific concerns may motivate our inquiries into nature, but that does not mean that our use of evidence or our procedures themselves need be compromised.

THE FEAR OF DEATH

Given, however, that Epicurus maintains that philosophical inquiry is driven by our need to understand the sources of unhappiness, it might be helpful to turn to his analysis of these, chief among them the fear of death. In contrast to most contemporary philosophers, Epicurus argues that we have no reason to fear death because it cannot harm us in the slightest. That said, however, he thinks that most people at some level do indeed fear death and that their mental lives, along with many of their actions, are affected in unhappy ways because of what turns out to be simply an irrational and readily eliminable misconception. So for instance, we find in Epicurean texts a version of the so-called symmetry argument.

Assume for the moment the Epicurean claim that death annihilates us. Before we were conceived, we also did not exist. Yet we typically are troubled only by our post mortem nonexistence. How are we to explain this asymmetry in our attitudes to two apparently similar states of our nonexistence? Epicurus argues that whenever we think about our future nonexistence, we find it difficult to view it as the total annihilation of our consciousness and to eliminate ourselves from our conception of it in the required way. This is because whenever I

try to conceive of my death, I become a kind of conscious eyewitness to it in my imagination. I thus have the illusory experience of witnessing my ongoing annihilation, with death continually depriving me of things I value. When I look back at the time before I was conceived, however, I readily see it as the state of nothingness that it is. However explicable, holding asymmetrical attitudes to two equivalent states of our nonexistence, Epicureans argue, is irrational and we should come to view both death and the time before our conception with equal indifference.

This argument, no doubt, raises quandaries about our attitudes towards our past and future, questions about whether such general temporal attitudes apply to states that we do not consciously experience, and dilemmas about the contributions of past or future potential losses in fixing the identities of persons. It also is liable to backfire. We might instead begin viewing the time before our conception as another regrettable state of lost potentialities and thus merely duplicate our anxieties.

Epicurus's central argument against the fear of death, however, is an attempt to demonstrate that all such worries about states of our nonexistence are irrational. His claim is best illustrated by his deceptively simple observation, "When we are there, death is not, and when death is there, we are not" (*Epistula ad Menoeceum* 125). Anyone wishing to show that a state of nonexistence harms us, Epicurus insists, must show who is harmed, when the harm occurs, and how one is harmed. Although these questions make sense regarding harms to existent subjects, no meaningful conception of harm, he argues, can be applied to the nonexistent. Who is harmed by death? No one, since in death there is no longer any subject to be harmed. When are we harmed by death? At no time, since when we are alive, death is not there, and when we are dead, we are not there. How are we harmed by death? In no way, since harm, whether conceived of as deprivation or lost potential, can attach only to something that exists.

The Epicurean claim that any conception of the harm of death requires there to be an existent subject of that harm has challenged philosophers to explore and clarify the metaphysical status of the dead, the place of potential losses or deprivations in accounts of personal identity, the nature of counterfactual propositions about future and past persons, and the conception of time needed to justify the intuition that death harms us. However simple at first glance, the increasingly sophisticated literature generated in response to Epicurus's argument suggests that the verdict is hardly in.

HEDONISM

One might wonder, however, as did many of Epicurus's ancient critics, how his arguments about the harmlessness of death are compatible with another of his central claims, that pleasure is our final end. Shouldn't a hedonist fear the interruption and loss of pleasure that death threatens? To understand the particular nature of Epicurean hedonism it first must be placed in its ancient dialectical context. Epicurus argues that pleasure is our ultimate goal and the sole component of our *eudaimonia*, or happiness. He further supports his ethical hedonism with a version of psychological hedonism by appealing to a so-called cradle argument; that is, that the observation of infant behavior shows that we naturally seek pleasure and avoid pain. More surprisingly, however, Epicurus argues that the pleasures that comprise individual happiness can be specified objectively because they meet nonsubjective criteria and arise from pursuits limited by objective, natural constraints.

By way of contrast, for instance, take John Locke's account of the patient with sore eyes who prefers the pleasures of drink to those of sight and who remains the sole arbiter of his own pleasures, however self-destructive. (*Essay* 2.xxi.55). For the Epicurean, such subjectivity about pleasure and the good fails to meet the minimal demands placed on *eudaimonia* in ancient ethical arguments. So, for instance, desires are open to objective assessment, he claims, because they fall into three distinct classes. Some, for example desires for immortality or power, are incapable of being satisfied and depend on erroneous beliefs, many of which have been inculcated by society. They are therefore both unnatural and unnecessary. Moreover, since they have no natural limits and attempts to satisfy them inevitably lead to frustration, they are to be rejected as sources of unhappiness. Other desires, such as for sex or for particular types of pleasant food, are natural but unnecessary. They can be satisfied if the opportunity arises, but they are not necessary for happiness. Indeed, they can become sources of unhappy disturbance and pain if one becomes troubled by their unavailability or loss.

Finally, there are desires that are both natural and necessary. These have objective, natural limits and are easily satisfied. One needs only so much bread to satisfy one's natural and necessary desire for food, and that desire, unlike those for power or immortality, has a natural limit. By focusing on the satisfaction of natural and necessary desires and by adapting our desires to our circumstances, we can avoid the frustrations of pursuing pleasures that prove "empty." What we can hope to achieve instead is a natural state of satisfaction entirely free from both mental disturbance and bodily pain. Indeed, such a seemingly neutral condition, Epicurus insists, is the most pleasant state possible. Many have found this claim about pleasure to be paradoxical, arguing that such a state is merely intermediate between pleasure and pain. He denies, however, the existence of any intermediate states, maintaining that the lack of pain and disturbance is the highest pleasure possible.

It is easy to view this, perhaps, as a mere verbal ploy since it flies in the face of what most hedonists and nonhedonists alike have found salient about pleasure, its intensity and variability as a sensation. Epicurus, however, bolsters his argument by distinguishing *katastemmatic* from *kinetic* pleasures. Although its exact force is disputed, as is the extent to which it picks out two different types of atomic movement, this distinction seems to capture two readily identifiable, though perhaps not so readily separable, aspects of pleasure. Kinetic pleasures arise, he argues, during the process of satisfying a desire. Katastemmatic pleasures are the states of satisfaction that supervene when a desire has been satisfied. Most accounts of pleasure, Epicurus claims, make the mistake of focusing only on the pleasures of satisfying desires, when in fact the different ways one satisfies desires are simply interchangeable variants. What we value above all is the attendant state of satisfaction and the freedom from want or disturbance that it signals.

To the charge that he offers us the pleasures of a corpse, the Epicurean responds that the wise prefer no longer having an itch to the pleasures of scratching. More controversial still, Epicurus argues that the highest state of pleasure is itself complete and cannot be made more valuable by lasting longer. To his critics, this account of pleasure seems suspiciously tailor-made to his claim that death in no way harms the pleasant life. To his followers, it served as a powerful explanation of how pleasure, when properly understood, can meet the demands that our happiness be not only self-sufficient, but also complete and invulnerable to any harm at the hands of death.

THE VIRTUES AND FRIENDSHIP

An undeniable optimism about the power of reason pervades every facet of Epicurus's ethics. He thinks that reason can lead us to eliminate easily any fears based on mistaken beliefs and he lauds its sober power to focus each of our choices on our final good. Like Socrates, he denies that we can know the good and yet fail to pursue it either because of unmanageable desires or incorrigible weaknesses in our character. He does not go as far as the

Stoics in simply identifying irrational desires with mistaken beliefs, but he likewise eschews Aristotle's emphasis on the necessity of habituating desires and character in the ways of virtue. For Epicurus, the therapeutic benefit of rational argument transforms lives at any stage and in any condition. Unsurprisingly, his account of virtue is strongly cognitive. All of the virtues including justice, he insists, are a species of rational prudence, instrumentally useful in securing and maintaining a life of pleasure.

Yet while prudence, courage, and moderation arguably might be claimed as virtues useful to the hedonist, the other-regarding demands of justice seem more problematic. Surely, we might suppose, one might have prudential reasons for being unjust. Why restrict one's pleasures in the interests of others? Epicurean texts offer a panoply of arguments in defense of justice that probably work best if they are taken to have as their addressees Epicurean and non-Epicurean alike. For instance, some texts single out the fear of being caught as the key incentive in obeying laws. Such a motive for being just fits rather badly with the picture of the Epicurean who is supposed to eliminate all disturbing fears and live quietly, and who in any case, has little motive for transgressing laws given the limited range of his necessary desires. Other texts praise the psychologically calming benefits of justice—hardly a motive for the non-Epicurean searching for less tranquil experiences. The central and most lastingly influential component of Epicurus's theory of justice, however, is his account of the origins and nature of justice as a mutual contract among agents "neither to harm nor be harmed." Although not the first contractual theory in antiquity, it was the Epicurean account with its postulation of an original prepolitical state of nature that took center stage for Rousseau and his predecessors.

Interestingly, Epicurus's particular formulation of the contractual theory rejects the conventionalism of many later theorists, since he argues that contracts failing to reflect mutual usefulness no longer constrain. By placing his theory of justice in the larger context of his accounts of virtue and pleasure, he insists on the essential connection between agents' continuing interests and the contracts they have formed.

Although he denies that the virtues are valuable for their own sake, Epicurus insists that one can achieve happiness only by being virtuous. His ancient critics often doubted, however, whether purely instrumental motives were sufficient for maintaining one's commitments to virtue. A parallel problem arises in his account of friendship. Epicurus often speaks of friendship in the most extravagant terms and some later Epicureans proclaim that a hedonist can value his friends for their own sakes. But if one's motives in acquiring a friend are securely rooted in one's own pleasure, how can one maintain this seemingly altruistic commitment to friends?

Various later Epicureans struggled with the problem. Some conceded that if one properly focused on one's own pleasure, one could not treat a friend's pleasures as one's own, while others argued that friends might enter into mutually self-interested contracts to value each other's pleasures equally. A few went so far as to claim that one could come to value friendship in a way that went beyond motives of individual egoistic pleasure. All, perhaps, reflect a worry about what has come to be called the hedonist paradox. We can gain the pleasure we seek from friends only by maintaining the other-regarding values of friendship and by valuing friends' pleasures as much as our own. If we instead concentrate on our own pleasures, as hedonism seems to demand, we will undermine the very values that bring us pleasure. It is unlikely, however, that Epicureans would take this as evidence against their theory. Rather, for them, valuing friends' pleasures as much as their own represents an enlightened hedonist strategy that they need to fit, however awkwardly, within the confines of their overall theory.

INDETERMINISM, FREE WILL, AND THE MIND

Whether or not Epicurus, as many have claimed, was the first to formulate questions about determinism and free will in their modern form, it is clear that he attempts to find room in a mechanistic universe for our rational pursuit of pleasure and hence for our ability to rationally discriminate among alternative choices. Like Aristotle, he rejects logical determinism, as a threat to rational deliberation, and he denies that statements about future contingent events have truth value. Likewise, he contends that if the laws of atomic motion utterly determined everything in the universe, rational argument and choice could have no meaning and they would be robbed of their efficacy. What underwrites the manifest efficacy of reason and frees us from the bonds of both logical and mechanistic fatalism, Epicurus claims, is a slight indeterminacy or swerve in the movements of atoms at no fixed time or place. Such swerves break the bonds of necessity by interrupting the endless chains of causal interactions among atoms. Attempts at understanding the physics of these random swerves and their precise effects on human action abound. Some, for example, have seen the origins of libertarian defenses of free will in Epicurus's account, with each random swerve of atoms underwriting a free and uncaused act of human volition.

Others, worried about the plausibility of such a strict correlation between micro and macroscopic events, have postulated more infrequent effects by swerves on human actions or character generally. Still others have argued that Epicurus's account is nonreductive or emergentist in a way that defuses the randomizing effects of atomic indeterminism at the macroscopic level. Swerves break causal bonds among atoms, but without generating randomness in emergent properties, thereby insuring the efficacy of rational deliberation and action. In the face of these disagreements, a few have concluded that Epicurus's main worries are innocent of such theoretical niceties and that ascribing to him either libertarian or emergentist views is merely anachronistic. Wherever the truth ultimately lies, it is certainly the case that from the early modern period onward, Epicurus was held to be the chief ancient proponent of libertarianism. And as is often the case in the history of philosophy, the subsequent reception of one's views can be far more influential than one's actual views.

Similar difficulties arise for Epicurus's philosophy of soul or mind. On the one hand, he regularly holds out the ambition of giving a strict identity theory of mind and explicates its materiality with an array of arguments showing that materialism alone explains the mutual causal interactions between mind and body. He claims, moreover, that the mind is composed of particular types of atoms whose specific properties are directly correlated to particular mental functions; for example, the smoothness of specific atoms accounts for the quickness of thought. It was the explanatory power of such instances of Epicurean reductionism that so influenced Julien de La Mettrie and d'Holbach and set the agenda for subsequent eliminativist theorists. Yet Epicurus also emphatically insists that mental properties are real properties and not mere epiphenomena. Some have taken his robust commitment to the reality of macroscopic properties as evidence for anti-reductionism or emergentism, while others have argued that his commitment to physicalist explanation not only entails reductionism, but that reductionism is entirely compatible with his endorsement of the reality of macroscopic entities. Perhaps if our own distinctions between explicative and nonreductive physicalist theories could be more confidently drawn, a choice among these options for Epicurus would be more easily forthcoming.

KNOWLEDGE AND ATOMS

However he intended to explain the relation between atoms and our world of perceptual experience, it is clear that Epicurus thinks we can attain certain knowledge of both. Epicureans share with Plato and Aristotle a conviction that skepticism is self-refuting both in theory and practice, but they disagree markedly about the criterion for knowledge immune to skeptical attack. Epicurus's epistemology, or "canonic," begins with the emphatic assertion that all sensations are true. What guarantee their truth are the mechanisms of their production. Films or images of inconceivable speed are continually streaming from bodies and striking our senses, which function simply as passive receptors that in no way distort the information they receive. Error can occur only if we extrapolate to the world from these sensations with mistaken assumptions or judgments. This we can avoid by applying to our sensations simple concepts (*prolepseis*) that, arising naturally from repeated sensations, are preserved in memory and embodied in the ordinary meanings of words.

Distrusting Aristotelian-style logics, Epicureans elaborate inferential methods for eliminating false judgments based on what they call confirmation or disconfirmation by the senses. For most subsequent empiricists, such an attempt to skirt formal logic became a dead end. However, Epicurus's arguments in defense of empiricism, especially his materialist accounts of the mechanics of perception and concept formation, enjoyed a long philosophical run, providing basic templates for a succession of empirical theories based on effluences, sense data, and other factors. Few, however, rival his ingenious attempts to work out the actual mechanics of perception in the face of what were to become standard objections to imagist theories of thought and perception.

Armed with empirical knowledge, the Epicurean believes, we can confirm the basic principles of atomism. For instance, from our perception of motion in the world, we can infer that atoms must move—an inference for which only the existence of void offers adequate explanation. Similarly, to explain the multiplicity of things we see in the word, we must postulate an indefinite number of atomic shapes. The existence of atoms themselves is confirmed by our observation that nothing comes from nothing and that division must stop somewhere for there to be something.

Interestingly, Epicurus allows multiple and competing theoretical explanations for some natural phenomena. But he indulges no such operationalist sensibilities toward the basic principles of his atomism. Collisions, rebounds, and the compounding of atoms are the basic mechanisms of the material world. In an infinite, eternal world of atoms in continual motion, there is no room for teleology or interference from the gods, who in any case are indifferent to human concerns and, at least in some Epicurean sources, seem to have no stable constitution of their own but arise in relation to our mental conceptions of them. Atoms have the properties of shape, size, and weight. Explaining differences in atomic sizes and shapes presented Epicurus with difficult puzzles, however. Unlike later philosophers, such as Agostino Nifo, who constructed atoms from independently existing minima, Epicurus denies their physical divisibility. He postulates, instead, only conceptual divisibility, which required him, with rather mixed success, to theorize spatial and temporal quanta. His argument that atoms have weight, however, was fundamental. It changed the course of ancient atomism and gave the theory its essential shape down to the time of John Dalton.

See also Atomism; Cyrenaics; Epicureanism and the Epicurean School; Hedonism; Leucippus and Democritus; Lucretius; Philodemus.

Bibliography

WORKS BY EPICURUS

Epicurus: The Extant Remains, edited by Cyril Bailey. Oxford: Oxford University Press, 1926.

The Epicurus Reader: Selected Writings and Testimonia, edited by Brad Inwood and Lloyd P. Gerson. Indianapolis, IN: Hackett, 1994.

The Hellenistic Philosophers, edited by A. A. Long and David Sedley. Cambridge, U.K.: Cambridge University Press, 1987.

Epicurea, edited by Hermann Usener. Leipzig: Teubner, 1887.

WORKS ABOUT EPICURUS

Algra, Keimpe et al., eds. *The Cambridge History of Hellenistic Philosophy*. Cambridge, U.K.: Cambridge University Press, 1999.

Annas, Julia. *Hellenistic Philosophy of Mind*. Berkeley: University of California Press, 1994.

Annas, Julia. *The Morality of Happiness*. Oxford: Oxford University Press, 1993.

Asmis, Elizabeth. *Epicurus's Scientific Method*. Ithaca, NY: Cornell University Press, 1984.

Bailey, Cyril. *The Greek Atomists and Epicurus*. Oxford: Oxford University Press, 1928.

Clay, Diskin. *Paradosis and Survival: Three Chapters in the History of Epicurean Philosophy*. Ann Arbor: University of Michigan Press, 1998.

Englert, Walter G. *Epicurus on the Swerve and Voluntary Action*. Atlanta: Scholars Press, 1987.

Festugiere, A. J. *Epicurus and His Gods*. Oxford: Oxford University Press, 1955.

Konstan, David. *Some Aspects of Epicurean Psychology*. Leiden: E. J. Brill, 1973.

Mitsis, Phillip. *Epicurus's Ethical Theory: The Pleasures of Invulnerability*. Ithaca, NY: Cornell University Press, 1988.

Nussbaum, Martha. *The Therapy of Desire: Theory and Practice in Hellenistic Ethics*. Princeton, NJ: Princeton University Press, 1994.

O'Keefe, Timothy. *Epicurus on Freedom*. Cambridge, U.K.: Cambridge University Press, 2005.

Warren, James. *Facing Death: Epicurus and his Critics*. Oxford: Oxford University Press, 2004.

Phillip Mitsis (2005)

EPISTEMIC LOGIC

See *Modal Logic*

EPISTEMOLOGY

Epistemology attempts to explain the nature and scope of knowledge and rational belief. Its purview also includes formulating and assessing arguments for skeptical conclusions that we do not have knowledge of various kinds. In addition, epistemologists address topics that are closely related to these core concerns, including evaluations of thought processes and the relationship of science to philosophy. What follows is an overview of contemporary developments in epistemology.

THE ANALYSIS OF KNOWLEDGE

The traditional analysis of knowledge is that it is a combination of three conditions: truth, belief, and justification. The idea is that for someone to have factual knowledge, what is known has to be a fact and thus true; the person has to regard it as true, that is, believe it; and the person must have an adequate basis for believing it—that is, have sufficient justification for believing it. These conditions yield knowledge defined as a sufficiently justified true belief.

The publication by Edmund Gettier (1963) of one brief critical discussion of the traditional analysis brought about a flurry of activity in epistemology. Gettier refuted the traditional analysis by offering convincing counterexamples. He described examples in which someone forms a belief on the basis of strong justifying evidence, but the belief merely happens to be true as a result of a fortunate accident, independently of the evidence. Here is an example similar to Gettier's. Someone sees something that looks perfectly sheeplike in a nearby field.

On that basis the person justifiably believes that there is a sheep in the field. As it turns out, what the person sees is not a sheep. It is a highly realistic statue. However, the person's belief that there is a sheep in the field is true because of the fortunate coincidence that there is a real sheep hidden from view elsewhere in the field. Such a belief is clearly not a case of knowledge despite its being an instance of justified true belief. So justified true belief is not sufficient for knowledge.

Arguing that the person in the example does not have an adequate basis for believing that there is a sheep in the field seems to require taking the general position that few beliefs are justified. For if that person does not have an adequate basis and is not justified, then someone in a similar situation who actually does see a sheep would also be unjustified, given that her visual information would be no better. In almost all cases of actual knowledge of the world, there are possible, although unusual, cases in which one has the same belief on the basis of comparable reasons, yet that belief is only true in this accidental way. Therefore, responding to the Gettier cases by raising the standards for justification leads to the conclusion that we know very little.

Most epistemologists responded to Gettier's examples by seeking a fourth condition for knowledge in addition to justified true belief. Some proposed that to have knowledge, it is also required that the justification for one's belief be *undefeated*, meaning roughly that there is no truth that would undermine the justification for the belief (Klein 1976). Others have suggested that in cases of knowledge the justification does not involve a falsehood (Chisholm 1989). Still others have required that the reasons justifying a known belief be *conclusive*—roughly, reasons that would not exist unless the belief were true (Dretske 1971). Counterexamples refuted the original versions of these analyses, more complex analyses replaced the originals, and new counterexamples followed. (See Shope [1983] for a detailed summary of responses to Gettier's examples.)

Not all epistemologists accept the necessity of the three traditional conditions for knowledge. Some reject the justification condition. One proposed replacement requires a suitable causal connection between a known belief and the facts that make the belief true (Armstrong 1973, Goldman 1967). Another proposed replacement requires a known belief to vary counterfactually with the truth of that belief: if the belief were not true, it would not be believed by the same method, and if it were true, it would be believed by the same method (Nozick 1981). Others have taken the more drastic tack of denying that

any set of necessary and sufficient conditions for knowledge can be given. An alternative explanation of knowledge is that it is the most inclusive *factive* mental state (Williamson 2000). A mental state is factive if the existence of the state guarantees its truth. Unlike the traditional analysis, this approach does not imply that the concept of knowledge can be decomposed into parts.

Although epistemologists have learned much about knowledge from this research, no consensus has emerged about the solution to the problem raised by examples like Gettier's.

JUSTIFICATION: FOUNDATIONALISM AND COHERENTISM

Justification itself has been investigated intensively in the wake of the Gettier problem. A central issue underlying views about justification is the infinite-regress problem. Typically, a belief is justified because it has support from other beliefs. For example, someone might be justified in believing that there are people in the next room by inference from the justified belief that Allen, Barbara, and Carol are in the next room. The supporting beliefs garner support from still other beliefs. The belief that Allen, Barbara, and Carol are in the next room might be justified by inference from the justified belief that they said they would enter the next room and then shouted that they had done so. However, given that our minds are finite, there cannot be an infinite regress of justifying beliefs. Therefore, either there are some beliefs—*basic* beliefs—that are justified without the support of other beliefs; or our beliefs form some sort of circle or web, with each justified/rational belief getting support from other beliefs within the system; or our beliefs are not justified at all. *Foundationalism* favors the first alternative, while *coherentism* favors the second. The third alternative, that no belief has any justification, seems indefensible.

The classic foundationalist view is that a belief is justified provided that it is a basic belief or rests upon a foundation of basic beliefs. Usually, the contents of basic beliefs are taken to be propositions about the mental states of the believer. For example, when someone observes an ordinary physical object in good viewing conditions, that person's visual system produces an experiential state. This is an internal mental state of the observer, knowable by introspection. Believing about oneself that one is in this experiential state is said to be a basic belief. Beliefs of this sort are supposed to provide a secure foundation for the rest of our justified beliefs. Classic foundationalists differ about the source of the security of basic beliefs. Candidate sources include the alleged infallibility of our introspective capacities and the alleged immunity from doubt of some beliefs. According to classic foundationalism, we acquire whatever justified beliefs we can get about the external world by inference from our introspectively justified beliefs about our own states. Some foundationalists hold that only a deductive (logically necessary) connection can secure sufficient justification for knowledge, whereas others hold that inductive or explanatory relations also suffice. The question of what support is sufficiently strong for knowledge is central to the discussion of epistemological skepticism.

Some foundationalists have relaxed the requirements for basic beliefs (Chisholm 1989, Huemer 2001). The central foundationalist view is that each justified belief is basic or derives its justification from basic beliefs. This view does not require basic beliefs to be certain or infallible. A more modest level of independent support is enough to stop the regress of derived justification. Foundationalists can consistently hold that support from other beliefs gets the basic beliefs beyond this modest level. If the basic beliefs need not be maximally secure, then another departure from the classic view becomes attractive. Basic beliefs can include ordinary perceptual beliefs. For example, the belief that one sees a dog can be basic. It can gain some justification that is independent of other beliefs directly from an experience, which is visually just as though one is seeing a dog. Modest foundationalism is widely thought to be an improvement upon classical foundationalism.

Modest foundationalism has its share of critics, however. Its defenders have been challenged to explain how the basic beliefs can receive even modest support from experience (BonJour 1985). The main problem is that the best understood sort of epistemic support is the justification that is given by the premises of a strong argument for its conclusion, yet the experiences cited by modest foundationalists as providing foundational support do not seem to qualify as premises of arguments. This is because experiences are not statements, but the only kinds of things that can be premises are statements.

Coherentism is the chief rival to foundationalism (Lehrer 1974, BonJour 1985). Coherentists deny that there are any basic beliefs. The secure foundations that classic foundationalists have sought are, according to coherentists, impossible. They contend that all justified beliefs get their justification from a relation of coherence that holds among a body of beliefs. Coherentists have attempted to say what constitutes coherence, often appealing to explanatory relations among beliefs as the source of coherence. Some propose that justification arises from *reflective equilibrium*—a mutual adjustment of beliefs about particular cases and beliefs about general principles covering these cases that maximizes explanatory relationships among them (Goodman 1984).

Coherentists have been challenged to avoid the apparent implication of their theory that justified beliefs can have an implausible sort of detachment from sensory input. A body of beliefs can be internally coherent while the beliefs fail to take into account the person's experience, yet coherentism seems to imply that these cohering beliefs would be justified. Intuitively, however, such beliefs seem to be as unjustified as the beliefs formed by accepting as true everything in some well-crafted, elaborate, but fantastic story.

Not all philosophers agree that we must choose sides between foundationalism and coherentism. Several have argued that the central epistemological considerations on both sides can be reconciled (Alston 1989, Haack 1993, Sosa 1991).

JUSTIFICATION: OTHER ISSUES

In addition to formulating and assessing foundationalism, coherentism, and other theories of justification, epistemologists have addressed a variety of other questions about epistemic justification. Standard versions of foundationalism and coherentism share the presupposition that justification is determined by relations among the reflectively accessible contents of our minds—experiential states, beliefs, memories, inferences, and so on. Some philosophers, however, have opposed this *internalist* presupposition, engendering extensive discussion of the contrast between this view about justification and its *externalist* alternatives. (See Kornblith 2001 for essays on these issues.)

For internalists, justification is determined entirely by internal mental factors, whereas externalists assert that justification is at least partly determined by other things. Some internalists also require the believer to be aware of all justifying factors. A typical internalist theory is *evidentialism*, which holds that evidence held in mind determines the epistemic status of beliefs (Conee and Feldman 2004, Haack 1993). *Reliabilism* exemplifies the externalist viewpoint (Goldman 1979). Reliabilism maintains that a belief's justification is determined by a propensity to produce true beliefs of the process or mechanism leading to the belief. This reliability is not an internal factor because the truth of a belief is usually not an internal fact.

A good example to point out the difference between an internalist theory and reliabilism involves the victim of a deceptive demon. The demon induces the victim to have the experiences like those a reasonable person might have through the perception of an ordinary environment. The demon's victim forms the same external world beliefs on the basis of these experiences. It is a further part of the example that the external world of the demon's victim is not at all an ordinary environment, and so her beliefs about her external world are not true. In such an example, the processes leading to the victim's external world beliefs seem to be unreliable because they produce her thoroughly false external world beliefs. So reliabilism seems to imply that such beliefs are not justified. The belief-forming processes of the counterpart person in a normal environment are presumed to be reliable, so that reliabilism implies that this person's beliefs are justified. In contrast, according to any internalist theory, the beliefs of both the normally situated person and the demon's victim are equally well justified if the individuals are in the same internal states.

Reliabilism has been a subject of intensive critical scrutiny since its introduction. Critics contend that reliabilists cannot plausibly specify the types of belief-forming processes or mechanisms on which the theory relies (Conee and Feldman 2004). For instance, the process of forming a typical visual belief can be classified as perception, visual perception, belief acquisition while relaxed, uninferred belief acquisition, and so on, indefinitely. The problem is to specify which of these process types has to be reliable in order for the resulting beliefs to be justified. Reliabilists must specify the relevant type for all of the processes that lead to justified beliefs. Critics have also charged that beliefs resulting from a reliable process can be unjustified when accompanied by a sufficient reason to think that the process is not reliable (BonJour 1985) and that beliefs resulting from an unreliable process can be justified when accompanied by reason to think that the process is reliable.

Some theories of justification require supplements to reliability. For instance, a proper functionalist theory holds that a belief is justified when the belief results from the operation of a generally reliable cognitive system that is functioning properly in an appropriate environment. One theistic variant of this view holds that the proper function of human cognitive systems is the result of the intentions of a creator (Plantinga 1993). In a nontheistic version, proper function is determined by natural selective forces. One prominent criticism of the proper functionalist approach is that it is possible for a cognitive mechanism to function improperly but felicitously. A perceptual mechanism might accidentally happen to

work much better than it was designed to work. A resulting belief could be especially well justified by the acute perception.

Epistemologists also make comparisons between epistemic justification and ethical concepts such as obligation. Discussions of what a person is justified in believing easily slide into discussions of what the person *should* believe or is *entitled* to believe. Such talk is at least superficially similar to ethical evaluations of how a person should behave and what things the person is entitled to do. It can seem that the epistemic and ethical evaluations are fundamentally the same. However, there is some question about the applicability of ethical evaluations to beliefs. It is widely thought that what one morally should do is limited to those things that one can do. If something similar holds in epistemology, then what one should believe is limited to those things that one can believe. It apparently follows from this premise that beliefs must be under our voluntary control if we are to speak of our being justified in having them. Yet it seems that beliefs are not typically under voluntary control. Some philosophers respond by arguing that, contrary to appearances, we have sufficient control over our beliefs; some contend that it is acceptable to hold that we have justification for believing some propositions even though we are not able to control whether we believe them; and others conclude that few, if any, beliefs are justified since few, if any, are under our control. There is also concern about the connections between the epistemic justification of a belief and the moral or practical benefits of the belief. (Essays on this topic are collected in Steup 2001.)

Another widely discussed set of issues turns on a distinction between a priori justification and *a posteriori* justification. Justification of a belief is a priori when it does not derive from experience, and justification is a posteriori when it does. The leading candidates for a priori justification and knowledge are beliefs in basic truths of mathematics and logic. Other candidates include beliefs apparently made true entirely by conceptual relations, such as the belief that anything red is colored. These allegedly a priori justified propositions are, if true, necessarily true.

A priori justification seems mysterious to many philosophers, since it is difficult to understand what could justify beliefs independently of experience. A wide range of proposals has been made concerning how beliefs can have a priori justification. In the naturalistic approach a priori justification results from the operation of belief-forming processes that guarantee truth and justification (Kitcher 1980). The modal-reliability approach holds that conceptual intuitions necessarily present us with mostly truths (Bealer 2000). And a resolutely traditional approach holds that humans have a capacity for rational insight that finds truth-making, necessary connections in some thoughts (BonJour 1998).

It appears that a belief could not be a priori justified or known unless its truth is somehow abstractly guaranteed. It also appears that if there is an abstract guarantee that a belief is true, then the truth of the belief must not be merely contingent. So a priori knowledge of contingent truths would be surprising. Yet some philosophers have argued that we can have such knowledge (Kripke 1980), advancing the following kind of argument: Suppose that there is a unique tallest spy; knowing nothing about this and reasoning entirely in our armchairs, we can stipulate that the name "Stretch" refers to whoever happens to be the tallest spy, if there is one. Having done this, it seems that we can logically infer from what we have done, and thereby know a priori, the following contingent truth: if there is a unique tallest spy, then Stretch is a spy. Perhaps this knowledge would not be strictly a priori, since we would be using the experience of our introduction of the name "Stretch." Nonetheless, it seems to be a way to know a contingent truth that is at least remarkably similar to a priori knowledge.

SKEPTICISM

Many traditional skeptical arguments appeal to the possibility of error. Skeptics often point out that it is possible for us to be wrong about even our most confident beliefs about the world external to our minds, perhaps because we are under the influence of a deceptive demon or some other source of deception. Skeptics typically make the further claim that this possibility implies that we lack knowledge of even the things about the world that we most confidently believe. (Many influential essays on skepticism may be found in DeRose 1999.)

Fallibilism is the heart of one influential response to skepticism (Chisholm 1989, Pryor 2000). Fallibilism is the view that knowledge is compatible with the possibility that the same belief on the same basis is false. For example, someone who has a clear view of a tree in the front yard and believes on a normal perceptual basis that there is a tree in the front yard is subject to some possibility of error. An experience that is visually just as though one is seeing a tree could have resulted from things like the efforts of a deceptive demon. However, a typical person who sees a tree has no reason at all to think that any such odd thing is actually occurring and every reason to think that there really is a tree present. Falli-bilists hold that in such cases people often have sufficiently strong justification to know that there is a tree in the yard. According to fallibilists, a skeptical argument like the one about the possibility of error relies on setting the standard of justification for knowledge too high. We can have knowledge even though we cannot have the sort of absolute immunity from error that the skeptics wrongly associate with knowledge.

Fallibilism is not without problems. It is no easy task to explain what it is about our experiential evidence that makes it a good reason for thinking that we are in the presence of ordinary objects rather than the victims of some sort of deception. Some epistemologists contend that our justification for our external world beliefs depends upon an *inference to the best explanation* of our experiences (Vogel 1990), whereas others contend that there is something intrinsic to the character of experiences that makes them indicative of external world objects. Adequately spelling out just why our beliefs are even fallibly justified remains an unfulfilled task.

Some influential arguments for skepticism are updated versions of arguments based on possibilities of deception by dreams or demons. The newer arguments often appeal to the possibility of being a *brain in a vat*. The brain-in-a-vat arguments make use of the possibility that a fully functioning human brain, immersed in a life-sustaining vat of chemicals, receives computer-controlled neural stimulation that exactly matches the neural stimulation of an ordinary person in an ordinary environment. A premise of one brain-in-a-vat argument is that any of us might, for all we know, actually be such a brain in a vat. The argument also assumes that, since this possibility might be actual, we lack knowledge of the actual external world.

A much-discussed reply to such arguments employs a causal view of reference (Putnam). On one interpretation, the reply begins with the surprising contention that what a vat-entrapped brain would express by *I am a brain in a vat* would be a falsehood. A lifelong vat-entrapped brain would have learned the term *vat* from some computer-generated stimulations. The origin of the stimulation within the computer would have no causal connection to the brain's container of a sort that would be required for the brain's term *vat* to apply to the container. Hence, according to a causal view of reference, the brain's sentence *I am a brain in a vat* would not be true. Of course, what people in normal circumstances express by that same sentence is also false. Thus, the sentence *I am a brain in a vat* does not express a truth, whichever of these situations we are actually in. The antiskeptical reply concludes that by this use of a causal view of reference, we can justify denying the brain-in-a-vat argument's premise that, for all we know, we might be brains in a vat.

The success of this sort of antiskeptical reply is in dispute. In any event, a notable limitation of the approach is that at best it refutes skeptical arguments that rely on only some brain-in-a-vat possibilities. For instance, one possibility that is unaffected by the reply is that we recently became brains in a vat, and our term *vat* refers to the vat containing us because proper causal connections were forged in our pre-vat situation.

Skeptical arguments frequently rely on an *epistemic-closure* principle that says that if a person knows one proposition and sees that another proposition follows immediately from it, then the person knows the latter proposition, too. If someone knows an ordinary fact such as that she is seeing a table, then the closure principle implies that she could know by deduction that she is not a mere brain in a vat. Since, according to some skeptics, she cannot know that she is no brain in a vat, the skeptics conclude that she does not know anything from which she could deduce this, such as that she is seeing a table. Some philosophers have denied the closure principle in an effort to argue against this case for skepticism about knowledge of ordinary facts. Most philosophers, however, contend that some version of the closure principle must be true and any mistakes in skeptics' arguments must lie elsewhere (Hawthorne 2004).

Another response to skepticism appeals to *epistemic contextualism* (Cohen 1999, Lewis 1996). Contextualists endeavor to account for the intuitive pull of the arguments for skepticism while allowing that many of our ordinary attributions of knowledge are correct. Their central thesis is about *truth conditions* for uses of sentences including the word *know* and kindred terms. A statement of the truth conditions for a particular use of a sentence specifies the conditions that have to be realized in order for that use of the sentence to state a truth. The main form of epistemic contextualism holds that the truth conditions of particular uses of any sentence including *know*, or cognate expressions, vary with the context in which the sentence is used.

Typically, the varying aspect of the truth conditions is said to be the strength of the epistemic position that is required of the subject of the sentence for a use of *know* to apply to the subject. Usually, contextualists assert that the required strength of epistemic position varies across a range that allows, at its low end, many true sentences that attribute "knowledge" to someone. Thus, what we say is often true when, in ordinary circumstances, we classify as

"knowledge" beliefs that are based on perception, memory, testimony, and perhaps inductive generalization and inference to the best explanation. Contextualists typically also assert that some contexts, at the high end of the range of variation, are demanding enough to make true denials of "knowledge" of the external world. For instance, contextualists often claim that where issues concerning skepticism are salient, the standards for true attributions of "knowledge" are very high and that consequently, in those contexts, skeptical denials of "knowledge" are correct.

Some critics of contextualism deny that skepticism is true even when arguments for it are salient. Appealing to antiskeptical grounds such as the fallibilism discussed above, the critics contend that the arguments fail and that skepticism is wrong whether or not we are thinking about it (Conee and Feldman 2004). Other critics question the linguistic foundations of contextualism (Stanley 2004).

DEPARTURES FROM TRADITION

The philosophical study of knowledge, justification, and skepticism is the core of traditional epistemology. Some epistemologists have extended the discipline. One such extension involves connecting epistemology to scientific research about how people form beliefs and how they process information. Naturalism in epistemology is roughly the view that there is substantial overlap between epistemology and the sciences that study human cognition. Some philosophers endorse naturalism, whereas others find a reasonably clear distinction between the scientific/empirical questions about cognition and the conceptual questions at the heart of epistemology. A radically naturalistic epistemology advocates abandoning traditional epistemology and replacing it with the closest empirical discipline, cognitive psychology (Quine 1969). Few philosophers defend this extreme view. However, many urge close ties between epistemology and empirical studies of human cognition. For example, epistemologists who highlight the search for ways to improve our reasoning contend that the empirical study of how people actually reason is crucial for developing useful recommendations (Kornblith 1994). Philosophers who believe that the primary role of epistemology is to explain the concepts of knowledge, justification, and the like typically see less room for empirical input. Some advocate a less extreme form of naturalized epistemology that requires explaining central epistemic concepts in terms that they deem naturalistically legitimate.

Traditional epistemology has been largely individualistic in its emphasis on questions about knowledge and justification as they apply to individuals. However, a social epistemology has arisen that raises questions about what it is for groups to have knowledge and how social factors influence the spread and development of knowledge (Schmitt 1994, Goldman 1999).

Another approach in epistemology highlights epistemic virtues (Sosa 1991). One version of virtue epistemology is a variant on the reliabilist view discussed earlier. This approach attempts to characterize knowledge or justification in terms of epistemic virtues that yield reliably true beliefs, such as open-mindedness and a willingness to consider new evidence. In a greater departure from traditional issues, other versions of virtue epistemology propose that epistemologists replace or supplement the traditional topics with that of virtuous epistemic conduct.

EPISTEMOLOGY AND RELATED DISCIPLINES

There has been extensive and significant epistemological work done in relation to issues in the philosophy of mind. Externalism in the philosophy of mind, usually called *content externalism*, is the widely held view that environmental factors can help to determine the identity of some mental states. One simple content-externalist claim is that the content of a person's thoughts formulated with natural kind terms, such as *elm* and *water*, depends on causal connections to the kind that was actually involved in the person's learning the term. If the connection had been to a different natural kind, then the person's thoughts formulated with the same term would have included a concept referring instead to the other kind. There need not be any distinguishing feature that displays to the person which kind the person's thoughts are about.

Seemingly, if this simple content externalist theory is true, then we can know it a priori. We can know that external causes help to determine some thought contents by just considering how the reference of our natural-kind terms intuitively varies in some causally different hypothetical situations. If this is correct, then the theory appears to be incompatible with the conjunction of two plausible epistemological doctrines. One of the doctrines is that we can know the contents of our own thoughts by just giving introspective attention to them. If so, then we could combine our a priori knowledge of the simple content externalist theory with our introspective knowledge of the content of one of our thoughts that is expressible using *water*. We could infer that water is causally connected to the thought and that water therefore exists. Yet, according to a second plausible epistemological doctrine,

knowledge of our environment is not so easy. It requires empirical information. Thus, the simple content externalist theory seems to imply that either we cannot know the contents of our thoughts as easily as it otherwise seems we can, or that empirical knowledge of the existence of things in our environment is easier than it otherwise seems to be.

Critics of this line of reasoning have asked whether it can really be known, without empirical investigation, that content externalism applies to any of our concepts. The applicability of the version of content externalism described here to a concept is contingent on the existence of an appropriate causal connection between the concept and some natural kind. This dependence suggests that empirical information about the existence of a properly connected kind is needed to justify applying content externalism to our concepts. (For further discussion, see the essays in Nuccetelli 2003.)

Much that qualifies as epistemology has been done in other areas of philosophy. What follows is a brief inventory of some epistemic work in allied fields. One classic epistemological topic is the problem of induction. This is the problem of establishing whether or not people can use observation of some cases to draw justified conclusions about unobserved cases, and if this can be done, explaining when and why such inferences are reasonable. This problem has been pursued within the part of philosophy of science known as confirmation theory. Second, factual knowledge entails truth. Truth is a traditional topic in epistemology. Various theories of truth are also presented and discussed in metaphysics, the philosophy of language, and philosophical logic. Third, rational change of belief is closely related to the epistemological topic of justified belief. Rational belief change is a focus of probability theory, especially under the classification of Bayesian epistemology. Fourth, epistemological issues are often important to issues of morality and religion. Epistemic concerns pertaining to morality, such as the question of how we can know what is morally right, are usually discussed in works that are primarily about moral philosophy. Similarly, epistemic issues pertaining to God are discussed primarily in works in the philosophy of religion. Finally, in the vicinity of the border between epistemology and cognitive science there has been considerable attention devoted to the nature of purported sources of knowledge and to the ways in which they do their epistemic work. Topics here include perception, memory, intuition, and testimony.

See also A Priori and A Posteriori; Basic Statements; Classical Foundationalism; Coherentism; Contextualism;

Doubt; Epistemology, History of; Evidentialism; Experience; Illusions; Inference to the Best Explanation; Internalism versus Externalism; Introspection; Intuition; Knowledge and Belief; Knowledge and Truth, The Value of; Knowledge, A Priori; Memory; Naturalized Epistemology; Perception; Propositional Knowledge, Definition of; Rationalism; Reason; Relevant Alternatives; Reliabilism; Self-Knowledge; Skepticism, History of; Social Epistemology; Solipsism; Subjectivist Epistemology; Testimony; Virtue Epistemology.

Bibliography

Alston, William. *Epistemic Justification: Essays in the Theory of Knowledge.* Ithaca, NY: Cornell University Press, 1989.

Armstrong, David. *Belief, Truth, and Knowledge.* Cambridge, U.K.: Cambridge University Press, 1973.

Bealer, George. "A Theory of the A Priori." *Pacific Philosophical Quarterly* 81 (2000): 1–30.

Bennett, Jonathan. "Why Is Belief Involuntary?" *Analysis* 50 (1990): 87–107.

BonJour, Laurence. *In Defense of Pure Reason.* Cambridge, U.K.: Cambridge University Press, 1998.

BonJour, Laurence. *The Structure of Empirical Knowledge.* Cambridge, MA: Harvard University Press, 1985.

Chisholm, Roderick. *Theory of Knowledge.* 3rd ed. Englewood Cliffs, NJ: Prentice-Hall, 1989.

Cohen, Stewart. "Contextualism, Skepticism and the Structure of Reasons." *Philosophical Perspectives* 13 (1999): 57–89.

Conee, Earl, and Richard Feldman. *Evidentialism: Essays in Epistemology.* Oxford, U.K.: Oxford University Press, 2004.

DeRose, Keith, and Ted A. Warfield, eds. *Skepticism: A Contemporary Reader.* Oxford, U.K.: Oxford University Press, 1999.

Dretske, Fred. "Conclusive Reasons." *Australasian Journal of Philosophy* 49 (1971): 1–22.

Gettier, Edmund. "Is Justified True Belief Knowledge?" *Analysis* 23 (1963): 121–123.

Goldman, Alvin. "A Causal Theory of Knowing." *Journal of Philosophy* 64 (1967): 357–72.

Goldman, Alvin. *Epistemology and Cognition.* Cambridge, MA: Harvard University Press, 1986.

Goldman, Alvin. *Knowledge in a Social World.* Oxford, U.K.: Oxford University Press, 1999.

Goldman, Alvin. "What Is Justified Belief?" In *Justification and Knowledge,* edited by George S. Pappas, 1–24. Dordrecht: D. Reidel, 1979.

Goodman, Nelson. *Fact, Fiction, and Forecast.* Cambridge, MA: Harvard University Press, 1984.

Haack, Susan. *Evidence and Inquiry: Towards Reconstruction in Epistemology.* Cambridge, U.K.: Blackwell, 1993.

Hawthorne, John. *Knowledge and Lotteries.* Oxford, U.K.: Oxford University Press, 2004.

Huemer, Michael. *Skepticism and the Veil of Perception.* Lanham, MD: Rowman and Littlefield, 2001.

Kitcher, Philip. "A Priori Knowledge." *The Philosophical Review* 89 (1980): 3–23.

Kitcher, Philip. "The Naturalists Return." *The Philosophical Review* 101 (1992): 53–114.

Klein, Peter. "Knowledge, Causality and Defeasibility." *Journal of Philosophy* 73 (1976): 792–812.

Kornblith, Hilary, ed. *Epistemology: Internalism and Externalism.* Malden, MA: Blackwell, 2001.

Kornblith, Hilary, ed. *Naturalizing Epistemology.* 2nd ed. Cambridge, MA: MIT Press, 1994.

Kripke, Saul A. *Naming and Necessity.* Cambridge, MA: Harvard University Press, 1980.

Lehrer, Keith. *Knowledge.* Oxford, U.K.: Oxford University Press, 1974.

Lewis, David. "Elusive Knowledge." *Australasian Journal of Philosophy* 74 (1996): 549–67.

Nozick, Robert. *Philosophical Explanations.* Oxford, U.K.: Oxford University Press, 1981.

Nuccetelli, Susana, ed. *New Essays on Semantic Externalism and Self-Knowledge.* Cambridge, MA: MIT Press, 2003.

Plantinga, Alvin. *Warrant and Proper Function.* Oxford, U.K.: Oxford University Press, 1993.

Pryor, James. "The Skeptic and the Dogmatist." *Nous* 34 (2000): 517–49.

Putnam, Hilary. "Brains in a Vat." In *Reason, Truth, and History.* Cambridge, U.K.: Cambridge University Press, 1981.

Quine, W. V. O. "Epistemology Naturalized." In *Ontological Relativity and Other Essays.* New York: Columbia University Press, 1969.

Schmitt, Frederick, ed. *Socializing Epistemology.* Lanham, MD: Rowman & Littlefield, 1994.

Shope, Robert. *The Analysis of Knowledge: A Decade of Research.* Princeton, NJ: Princeton University Press, 1983.

Sosa, Ernest. *Knowledge in Perspective: Selected Essays in Epistemology.* Cambridge, U.K.: Cambridge University Press, 1991.

Stanley, Jason. "On the Linguistic Basis for Contextualism." *Philosophical Studies* 119 (2004): 119–146.

Steup, Matthias, ed. *Knowledge, Truth, and Duty: Essays on Epistemic Justification, Responsibility, and Virtue.* Oxford, U.K.: Oxford University Press, 2001.

Vogel, Jonathan. "Cartesian Skepticism and Inference to the Best Explanation." *Journal of Philosophy* 87 (1990): 658–666.

Williams, Bernard. "Deciding to Believe." In *Problems of the Self.* Cambridge, U.K.: Cambridge University Press, 1973.

Williamson, Timothy. *Knowledge and Its Limits.* Oxford, U.K.: Oxford University Press, 2000.

Earl Conee (1996, 2005)
Richard Feldman (1996, 2005)

EPISTEMOLOGY, CIRCULARITY IN

Issues concerning circularity figure prominently in epistemology, finding a place in discussions of topics ranging from the Cartesian circle, to the problem of the criterion, to knowledge of the reliability of ways of forming belief.

DESCARTES AND CARTESIAN CIRCLES

Issues of circularity arise in the works of René Descartes. In his *Meditations*, in his search for items of certain knowledge (indubitable items given even the possibility of massive deception), Descartes finds that he is certain that he is a thinking being. But what makes this certain for him? The only explanation he finds is that he clearly and distinctly perceives this fact. Furthermore, he finds that clear and distinct perception could not be the source of such certainty if such perceptions could be false. So, he tentatively concludes, whatever is clearly and distinctly perceived is true. But does he really know this general principle? Could it not be that God has caused him to err even in what he clearly and distinctly perceives? Descartes then sets off to prove that a nondeceiving God necessarily exists.

In pondering the matter, Descartes seems to commit himself to the following two claims: (1) He can be certain that whatever he clearly and distinctly perceives is true only if he is first certain that God exists and is not a deceiver. (2) He can be certain that a nondeceiving God exists only if he is first certain that whatever he clearly and distinctly perceives is true. Accepting both these claims gives rise to the Cartesian circle. The problem is that if both (1) and (2) are true, then one cannot be certain of either the general principle or the view that a nondeceiving God exists. In general, if one must first know *A* to know *B* and one must first know *B* to know *A*, then it seems that one cannot know either *A* or *B*.

A related problem for Descartes concerns his use of his clear and distinct perceptions to support the general principle that whatever he clearly and distinctly perceives is true. To support this principle, he attempts to prove there is a nondeceiving God. Yet in his reasoning, he relies on premises that have no other support than his clear and distinct perceptions. Descartes thus relies on his particular clear and distinct perceptions to prove the general principle that whatever is clearly and distinctly perceived is true. To many critics, this is an epistemically unacceptable procedure. Seeing a similarity, the Scottish philosopher Thomas Reid objected that if a man's honesty were called into question, it would be ridiculous to trust his own testimony concerning his honesty. Epistemic circularity consists in using beliefs from source *A* to support the proposition that source *A* is reliable. Descartes's use of his clear and distinct perceptions to support the principle that whatever is clearly and distinctly perceived is true exhibits just such circularity. Whether such circularity is vicious is still debated. Below are some late-twentieth-century views on the issue.

CHISHOLM AND THE PROBLEM OF THE CRITERION

Another problem of circularity, one made prominent in contemporary epistemology by Roderick Chisholm (1973), is the ancient problem of the diallelus, or wheel. The problem is that to know which particular beliefs are instances of knowledge, one must know some criterion of knowledge. But among the many contenders, which criterion is the right one? To know that some proposed criterion is the right one, one must know that it picks out only instances of knowledge. Thus, to know which criterion is right, one must already know which beliefs are instances of knowledge. Chisholm formulated the problem in terms of a pair of questions: (A) What do we know? What is the extent of our knowledge? (B) How are we to decide whether we know? What are the criteria of knowledge? The problem of the criterion arises insofar as one must know the answer to B before one can answer A, and one must know the answer to A before one can answer B. As in the case of the Cartesian circle, if this is so, then one can answer neither A nor B.

Chisholm identified three responses to these questions: skepticism, methodism, and particularism. The skeptic says that to answer A one must first answer B and to answer B one must first answer A. Therefore, the skeptic concludes, one can answer neither question. One can neither pick out instances of knowledge nor identify a criterion for it. In contrast, the methodist holds that one can answer B first and then answer A. Unlike the skeptic, the methodist believes that he can know a criterion of knowledge. He holds that one must know a criterion of knowledge to know or pick out particular instances of it. Chisholm took the empiricism of Locke and Hume to be forms of methodism. One difficulty with this sort of methodism, according to Chisholm, is that it implies that we know nothing about the external world, other minds, the past, or the future. The third approach, the one favored by Chisholm, is particularism. Unlike the methodist and the skeptic, the particularist holds that one need not know a criterion of knowledge to pick out particular instances of it. The particularist holds that he can answer A and then work out an answer to B. Chisholm took Thomas Reid and G. E. Moore to be particularists. They held that we know pretty much what we ordinarily think we know, and if some philosophical criterion implies that we do not, then so much the worse for that criterion. Thus, if some criterion implies that I do not know that there are other thinking people or that I was alive yesterday, then that criterion must be mistaken.

RECENT DISCUSSIONS OF EPISTEMIC CIRCULARITY

The problem of epistemic circularity has received much attention in recent epistemology. As noted above, the problem of epistemic circularity arises for Descartes in his use of his clear and distinct perceptions to support the general principle that whatever is clear and distinctly perceived is true. Epistemic circularity also seems to be a feature of attempts to support the reliability of such doxastic sources as memory, sense perception, introspection, intuitive reason, and induction. To support the belief that one of these sources is reliable, one must appeal, it seems, to particular beliefs that issue from that source. For example, it seems that to support the belief that perception is reliable, one must appeal to beliefs produced by perception, and to support the reliability of memory, one must appeal to some memory beliefs. To many philosophers, epistemic circularity seems vicious and epistemically unacceptable. Other philosophers argue that it is not *necessarily* vicious or unacceptable.

To focus the discussion, consider the following track-record argument for the reliability of sense perception:

At t_1, I formed the perceptual belief that p, and p is true.

At t_2, I formed the perceptual belief that q, and q is true.

At t_3, I formed the perceptual belief that r, and r is true.

And so on.

Therefore, perception is a reliable source of belief.

In this track-record argument for the reliability of perception, one reasons inductively from a wide sampling of perceptual beliefs, notes that the vast majority have been true, and concludes that perception is reliable. But how does one know that the second conjunct in each premise is true? How does one know, for example, that p is true? Let us suppose that it is known on the basis of perception. In this case, one is using perception to support the conclusion that perception is reliable. This makes the track-record argument epistemically circular. But is it therefore vicious or epistemically unacceptable?

A circular argument in which a premise is identical to the conclusion seems epistemically to carry no weight. Consider an argument of the form "p; q; r; therefore p." Arguments exhibiting this sort of circularity seem useless for conferring justification on the conclusion. If, on the one hand, one is not justified in believing the premise that p, then the reasoning does not justify the conclusion

that p. If, on the other hand, one is justified in believing the premise that p, then it seems that the conclusion that p is already justified, and the reasoning or argument does not confer any justification on the conclusion that p. A defender of the track-record argument or epistemically circular arguments may concede that arguments of this form are epistemically without weight. He may still point out that the track-record argument above does not have this defect. The conclusion that perception is reliable is not identical with one of the premises, and so the argument is not for that reason unacceptable.

Another criticism of the track-record argument is based on a view about what is required for perceptual knowledge. A critic of the track-record argument might object that perceptual knowledge epistemically depends on one's knowing that perception is reliable. On this view, perceptual beliefs amount to knowledge only in virtue of one's knowing that perception is reliable. Knowledge of the premises of the track-record argument, says the critic, depends on knowledge of the conclusion, that perception is reliable. If this is so, then the premises of the track-record argument do not make the conclusion knowledge. Rather, they derive their positive epistemic status from one's knowing the conclusion. On this view of the nature of perceptual knowledge, a track-record argument would again seem unable to yield knowledge of the conclusion.

In response, one might argue that this objection rests on a mistaken view about the nature of perceptual knowledge. Perceptual knowledge, one might argue, requires that perception be reliable, but it does not depend on one's knowing that perception is reliable. In other words, S's having perceptual knowledge that p requires that S's perceptual belief that p be reliably formed, but it does not require that S know either that perception is reliable or that his perceptual belief that p is reliably formed. One might note that young children and brute animals can have much in the way of perceptual knowledge without knowing much about perception. They might even be unable to form the metabelief that perception is reliable. Indeed, one might maintain that perceptual beliefs are instances of immediate knowledge, and that they do not depend for their justification on any other belief.

ALSTON ON EPISTEMIC CIRCULARITY

William Alston, who has addressed the issue of epistemic circularity with both subtlety and care, finds that epistemic circularity does not always render an argument useless for justifying or establishing its conclusion. In "A 'Doxastic Practice' Approach to Epistemology," he writes, "Provided I can *be* justified in certain perceptual beliefs without already being *justified* in supposing that perception is reliable, I can legitimately use perceptual beliefs in an argument for the reliability of sense perception" (1989, p. 3). Still, Alston himself worries that track-record arguments are not sufficiently discriminating. Part of the worry is that someone with clearly unreliable ways of forming beliefs could produce a track-record argument comparable to the simple track-record argument for perception given above. Imagine a crystal-ball gazer who reasons as follows:

> At t_1, I formed the belief that p on the basis of crystal-ball gazing, and p is true.
>
> At t_2, I formed the belief that q on the basis of crystal-ball gazing, and q is true.
>
> At t_3, I formed the belief that r on the basis of crystal-ball gazing, and r is true.
>
> And so on.
>
> Therefore, crystal-ball gazing is a reliable source of belief.

If the gazer is asked how he knows that p is true, he will reply that he knows it on the basis of gazing into his crystal ball. Alston worries that if we allow the use of epistemically circular arguments, then clearly unreliable sources of belief can be supported by such reasoning. In particular, it appears that the gazer's beliefs about the reliability of gazing would then be on a par with our beliefs about the reliability of perception. Alston believes that we need to try a different approach.

He argues that it is rational for us to form beliefs on the basis of certain sources such as perception and memory. The argument goes roughly as follows: (1) Many of our doxastic practices, our ways of forming beliefs, including perception and memory, are firmly established. (2) It does not seem to be in our power easily to avoid forming beliefs on the basis of these practices. (3) Moreover, even if there are alternative ways of forming beliefs, the very same problems of epistemic circularity that beset our attempts to support the reliability of our current practices would also confront these alternatives. (4) Therefore, it is rational for us to continue forming beliefs as we do, such as on the basis of perception and memory. But how does the fact that it is rational to continue to engage in these doxastic practices support the belief that they are reliable? Alston's view is that in taking it to be rational to form beliefs on the basis of our firmly established practices, I "commit" myself to judging that those ways of forming beliefs are reliable. I cannot reasonably judge that it is rational for me to form beliefs in those

ways and deny that those ways of forming beliefs are reliable.

Alston's response to the problem of circularity is controversial. Some critics object that Alston's argument from firmly established doxastic practices is itself epistemically circular. Consider the claims that memory and introspection are firmly established practices and that one cannot easily avoid forming such beliefs. That certainly is true. But how does one know that? Clearly, one knows it on the basis of memory and introspection. Again, it does seem rational to form beliefs on the basis of reason. But in arguing that it is rational for one to form beliefs in that way, one must use reason itself. It does not seem, then, that Alston's strategy of appealing to our firmly established doxastic practices avoids epistemic circularity. If the track-record argument is unacceptable because it is epistemically circular, how would Alston's reasoning be any better? Furthermore, Alston worries that some clearly unreliable ways of forming beliefs can be supported if we allow epistemically circular arguments. How, critics object, does appeal to beliefs about firmly established practices help? Could not the gazer look into his crystal ball, form the belief that gazing is firmly established, and construct an argument analogous to Alston's? In short, if one problem with track-record and epistemically circular arguments is that clearly unreliable sources can be supported by them, the same seems true about arguments that appeal to beliefs about what is firmly established.

SOSA ON EPISTEMIC CIRCULARITY

Ernest Sosa (1994) holds that epistemic circularity is unavoidable if reflection on the reliability of our sources of belief is pushed far enough. In some cases, one might be able to support the belief that one source of beliefs is reliable by appealing to beliefs from another source. But we can always ask how we know that the second source is reliable. At some point, when reflection is pushed far enough, we cannot support the reliability of our sources except by appealing to beliefs that are the output of those sources. But if epistemic circularity is ultimately unavoidable, Sosa denies that it is necessarily vicious. Suppose, says Sosa, that W includes all our ways of forming beliefs, encompassing perception, memory, reasoning, etc. Suppose further (i) that W is reliable, indeed, that in our circumstances and with our nature, it is the most overall reliable way of forming beliefs we could have; (ii) that we are right in our description of W: it is exactly W that we use W in forming beliefs; and (iii) that we believe that W is reliable. Here our belief that W is reliable is formed by means of W and is true. Sosa asks, how could we possibly improve our epistemic situation? Our belief that W is reliable is based on W itself, but Sosa does not see that there is anything epistemically vicious or unacceptable about our belief that W is reliable. Since our belief that W is reliable is formed on the basis of W, we have not avoided epistemic circularity, but in what way does our belief fall short epistemically? Recalling Descartes's initial, tentative reasoning concerning the truth of what he clearly and distinctly perceives, Sosa suggests that we might reason in a similar way for the reliability of other sources. Consider the following reasoning: (1) I know that there is a hand in front of me. (2) The best explanation for this knowledge is that I perceive the fact that there is a hand in front of me. (3) But perception could not be the source of such knowledge if it were generally unreliable. (4) Therefore, perception is not generally unreliable.

Sosa asks what is supposed to be so bad about epistemic circularity. Alston worries that if we allow epistemically circular arguments, then someone could give arguments in favor of their unreliable ways of forming beliefs that are analogous to those we might give in favor of perception and memory. Sosa grants that the crystal-ball gazer, for example, could construct arguments analogous to the track-record argument, and he notes that the gazer might also appeal to his crystal ball and "see" that gazing is a firmly established practice and thus is rationally engaged in. Sosa concedes that the gazer's belief in the reliability of his way of forming beliefs might cohere with his other beliefs and, more generally, that someone could have a coherent, yet false, view about the reliability of his sources. Yet Sosa denies that this fact puts the gazer's beliefs about the reliability of his doxastic practices on a par with our own. The fact that beliefs cohere with one another might provide some degree of epistemic justification, but for Sosa, it is not the only thing relevant to the epistemic status of belief. What makes our view about our doxastic practices epistemically superior is the fact that it was formed on the basis of reliable sources or intellectual virtues. Thus, our beliefs about the reliability of memory, introspection, perception, and reason are epistemically superior to the beliefs of the gazer about crystal-ball gazing in virtue of the fact that our beliefs are based on reliable sources or intellectual virtues, whereas the gazer's are not.

See also Alston, William P.; Belief; Cartesianism; Chisholm, Roderick; Criteriology; Descartes, René; Epistemology, History of; Hume, David; Locke, John; Moore, George Edward; Reid, Thomas; Sosa, Ernest.

Bibliography

Alston, William. "A 'Doxastic Practice' Approach to Epistemology." In *Knowledge and Skepticism*, edited by Marjorie Clay and Keith Lehrer. Boulder, CO: Westview Press, 1989.

Alston, William. "Epistemic Circularity." *Philosophy and Phenomenological Research* 47 (1) (1986): 1–30.

Alston, William. *The Reliability of Sense Perception*. Ithaca, NY: Cornell University Press, 1991.

Amico, Robert P. *The Problem of the Criterion*. Lanham, MD: Rowman and Littlefield, 1993.

Chisholm, Roderick. *The Problem of the Criterion*. Milwaukee, WI: Marquette University Press, 1973.

Cohen, Stewart. "Basic Knowledge and the Problem of Easy Knowledge." *Philosophy and Phenomenological Research* 65 (2) (2002): 309–329.

Descartes, René. *Meditations on First Philosophy*. 3rd ed. Translated by Donald Cress. Indianapolis, IN: Hackett, 1993.

Fumerton, Richard. *Metaepistemology and Skepticism*. Lanham, MD: Rowman and Littlefield, 1995.

Reid, Thomas. *Essays on the Intellectual Powers of Man*. Cambridge, MA: M.I.T. Press, 1969. Especially essay 6, chap. 5.

Sosa, Ernest. "Philosophical Scepticism and Epistemic Circularity." *Proceedings of the Aristotelian Society*, supp. vol. 68 (1994): 263–290.

Sosa, Ernest. "Reflective Knowledge in the Best Circles." *Journal of Philosophy* 94 (8) (1997): 410–430.

Van Cleve, James. "Foundationalism, Epistemic Principles, and the Cartesian Circle." *Philosophical Review* 88 (1979): 55–91.

Van Cleve, James. "Reliability, Justification, and the Problem of Induction." In *Causation and Causal Theories*. Midwest Studies in Philosophy, no. 9, edited by Peter A. French, Theodore E. Uehling, Jr., and Howard K. Wettstein. Minneapolis: University of Minnesota Press, 1984.

Noah M. Lemos (2005)

EPISTEMOLOGY, HISTORY OF

Epistemology, or the theory of knowledge, is that branch of philosophy which is concerned with the nature and scope of knowledge, its presuppositions and basis, and the general reliability of claims to knowledge. The pre-Socratic philosophers, the first philosophers in the Western tradition, did not give any fundamental attention to this branch of philosophy, for they were primarily concerned with the nature and possibility of change. They took it for granted that knowledge of nature was possible, although some of them suggested that knowledge of the structure of reality could better come from some sources than from others. Thus, Heraclitus emphasized the use of the senses, and Parmenides in effect stressed the role of reason. But none of them doubted that knowledge of reality was possible. It was not until the fifth century BCE that such doubts began to emerge, and the Sophists were chiefly responsible for them.

During the fifth century BCE human practices and institutions came under critical examination for the first time. Numerous things that had previously been thought to be part of nature were seen not to be. Thus, a general antithesis was drawn between nature and human convention or custom, and the question of where the line was to be drawn between them arose. The Sophists asked how much of what we think we know about nature is really an objective part of it and how much is contributed by the human mind. Indeed, do we have any knowledge of nature as it really is? Protagoras, for example, seems to have held, if Plato's report is to be believed, that everything is as it appears to a man, that appearances are the only reality. This is the meaning, or part of it, of his famous dictum "Man is the measure of all things." Gorgias was, if anything, more radical, claiming that there was no such thing as reality, that if there were, we could not know of it, and that even if we could know of it, we could not communicate our knowledge of it.

This general skepticism led to the beginning of epistemology as it has been traditionally known—the attempt to justify the claim that knowledge is possible and to assess the part played by the senses and reason in the acquisition of knowledge. Before Plato, Democritus, the Greek atomist, had already drawn a distinction between those properties ordinarily attributed to things which, in his view, really belong to them—for example, size and shape—and those which, as he put it, are a matter of convention (*nomos*), a function of the mind—for example, color. It was Plato, however, who can be said to be the real originator of epistemology, for he attempted to deal with the basic questions: What is knowledge? Where is knowledge generally found, and how much of what we ordinarily think we know is really knowledge? Do the senses provide knowledge? Can reason supply knowledge? What is the relation between knowledge and true belief?

THE NATURE OF EPISTEMOLOGY

Epistemology differs from psychology in that it is not concerned with why people hold the beliefs that they do or with the ways in which they come to hold them. Psychologists can, in principle, give explanations of why people hold the beliefs they do, but they are not necessarily competent, nor is it their province, to say whether the beliefs are based on good grounds or whether they are sound. The answer to these questions must be sought from those who are experts within the branches of knowledge from which the beliefs are drawn. The mathematician can give the grounds for believing in the validity of Pythagoras's theorem, the physicist can give the grounds for believing in, say, the indeterminacy principle, and an ordinary but reliable witness can provide the grounds for believing in the occurrence of an accident. Normally, when the beliefs are true and the grounds sufficient, it is permissible to claim knowledge, and whether a particular truth can be said to be known may be determined by reference to the grounds that are appropriate to the field from which the truth is drawn. The epistemologist, however, is concerned not with whether or how we can be said to know some particular truth but with whether we are justified in claiming knowledge of some whole class of truths, or, indeed, whether knowledge is possible at all. The questions that he asks are therefore general in a way that questions asked within some one branch of knowledge are not.

ROLE OF SKEPTICISM. To characterize the questions asked by the epistemologist as extremely general is not, however, sufficient. Interest in very general questions of this sort and in the nature of general concepts is typical of philosophy as a whole. What distinguishes epistemology other than the fact that its interests center on the concept of knowledge? When a philosopher asks whether something is possible, the question must be set against the consideration that this thing may not be possible. It must be set against a general skepticism concerning the matter in question. To be called upon to justify the possibility of knowledge or of certain kinds of knowledge makes sense only on the supposition that it or they may not be possible. It is no coincidence that epistemology began in the context of a form of the Sophists' general skepticism about knowledge, for until such doubts had been raised, the possibility of knowledge was bound to be taken for granted. Once the doubts had been raised, they had to be answered. How they were to be answered depended on the nature of the doubts and on the degree to which any particular philosopher was susceptible to them.

Views on the nature of knowledge. Perhaps the most characteristic form of skepticism about knowledge has been based upon the premise that we ought not to claim knowledge about anything unless we are absolutely sure about it, unless there is no possibility of our being wrong. Once given this, it is possible to point out that it is at least logically possible to be wrong about most, if not all, the things that we ordinarily claim to know. Philosophers who have been impressed by this argument have generally tried to show that there are at least some things that we can claim to know, about which we cannot be wrong. Even so, most of the things that we normally think we know cannot, on this view, be said to be known at all. This consequence can be mitigated, although not removed, if it can be shown that the things accepted as known in the strict sense give reasons for believing the things that we normally take ourselves to know. Philosophers who have taken this course have differed both on what this "certain knowledge" is and on how it is connected with what we ordinarily suppose ourselves to know. Rationalists have generally attempted to show that the primary truths that constitute this certain knowledge are related to other truths somewhat as the axioms of a formal or geometrical system are related to the theorems.

Empiricists, on the other hand, have taken the view that the truths which constitute ordinary knowledge can be constructed out of the primary truths, as a building is built up from its foundations. They have differed again on the nature of the primary truths themselves. Rationalists have looked for them among the deliverances of reason, whereas empiricists have claimed that sense experience alone can provide such truths. Other philosophers have accepted part of the skeptical argument to the extent of denying the status of knowledge to some class of truths, reserving that status for some privileged class. Plato is a case in point in that for at least part of his life he maintained that sense experience never provides knowledge at all, this being reserved for a kind of awareness of or acquaintance with a world of quite distinct entities called Forms. In respect to the world of sense experience we have only opinion or supposition. This view of sense experience has not been uncommon among philosophers.

The concept of knowledge. A quite different way of dealing with the skeptical argument would be to question the initial premise that knowledge requires absolute certainty. One would not normally claim knowledge about something unless one were sure about it, but that is very different from asserting that a man could not be said to know something unless what he claimed to know was absolutely certain. Knowledge does not actually require this; it requires only that there be the best of grounds for what is claimed. To say this is to say something about what knowledge is, about the concept of knowledge itself. Hence, the skeptical arguments and the answers to them are not entirely independent of the conceptual question about the nature of knowledge. An understanding of the concept of knowledge is a prerequisite of embarking upon any attempt to answer other epistemological questions. Most philosophers have had something to say

about the nature of knowledge, although many have taken its nature for granted. From this have stemmed a number of traditional epistemological difficulties.

GREEK PHILOSOPHY

PLATO. Plato (c. 428–347 BCE) was influenced by several views—the moral teaching and philosophical practices of his master Socrates, the views of the Sophists already mentioned, and such pre-Socratic views about the nature of reality as the Heraclitean view that the sensible world is in a state of flux and the Eleatic view that reality is one and unchanging. He came to hold that reality cannot be changing or imperfect and that it must therefore consist of a world of Forms or Ideas independent of the sensible world. The exact reasons why Plato postulated a world of Forms are not altogether clear. But probably, as Aristotle says, he was influenced by Socrates' search for the essences of, for example, moral virtues. But because justice, for instance, is never found in this world in a proper and perfect form, he postulated its separate, ideal existence in order to provide the standard by which sensible instances of justice might be judged. The Forms might be known by reason, not by the senses. Whether there was a Form for every sensible particular is arguable, with respect to Plato's earlier philosophy. However, it is clear at any rate that by the time he came to write the *Timaeus* he believed this to be the case. Thus, in the first place the Forms were probably standards or exemplars of which sensible things were imperfect copies. At the same time, however, they functioned as universals, entities meant to explain how it is possible to think generally about things of one kind and how it becomes possible to attach a meaning to common names. The fact that the Forms had to fill both these roles gave rise to certain logical difficulties which Plato himself pointed out in the dialogue *Parmenides* and which he tried to deal with in the later dialogues. The Forms were always objects of knowledge and, in his earlier thought, the *only* objects of knowledge. Sensible things were, in his view, objects of opinion only.

Knowledge and true belief. The distinction between knowledge and true belief is first made by Plato in the *Meno* in the context of another Platonic epistemological doctrine—the theory of recollection (anamnesis). In this dialogue Socrates claims to elicit from a boy without instruction the answer to a geometrical problem. Since the problem is a geometrical one, it is one that cannot be answered by an appeal to the senses. Socrates therefore claims that he is enabling the boy to recollect something that he had known in a previous existence. He maintains that it is a doctrine well known to priests and poets that the soul has long ago experienced all things in its various existences. Hence, in a sense the soul knows all things, but because it has forgotten them, it has to be reminded of them. The example suggests that Plato may intend the doctrine, at least in part, as an explanation of our knowledge of a priori truths. Indeed, in the *Phaedo* he uses the doctrine to explain how we see things as instances of the Forms: Sensible things remind the soul of what it already knows and what it cannot know from sense experience— the perfect Forms. The *Meno* does not claim so much. Indeed, Plato goes on to suggest that merely arriving at the right answer to a problem may not constitute knowledge but only true belief. Knowledge requires an ability to give the grounds (logoi) on which the answer rests. Nevertheless, Plato says, true belief may sometimes be, in its practical effects, as good as knowledge.

This distinction between knowledge and true belief is retained by Plato in later dialogues, although he is not always so charitable to belief as such. At the end of Book 5 of the *Republic* Plato begins a long argument, involving the famous similes of the sun, line, and cave to show how the soul may be drawn up by education to a true knowledge of the Forms, the final stage in the process that Plato calls dialectic. At the outset Plato makes a threefold distinction between knowledge, ignorance, and an intermediate state that he calls belief. Each of these states of mind has, he says, an object. The object of knowledge is what exists; the object of ignorance is, paradoxically, what does not exist; and the object of belief is that which is between existence and nonexistence. The last seems to be identified with the sensible world. Plato appears to think of these states of mind as forms of acquaintance with some kind of object, although the allocation of the objects in question is puzzling on any account. He rejects the identification of knowledge and belief on the grounds that belief is liable to error, whereas knowledge can never be. His conception of knowledge is thus a strict one.

Knowledge and sense perception. Plato's reasons for maintaining that we cannot have knowledge of the sensible world are that we should be in error if we attributed properties to sensible things absolutely. A thing is beautiful, heavy, or good only in relation to other things; hence, Plato concludes, nothing is really beautiful, heavy, or good except the standards of Beauty, heaviness, and Goodness themselves, and they cannot be sensible things. When we judge that sensible things are beautiful, heavy, or good, we are in error and cannot therefore be said to have knowledge.

There are two objections to this argument. First, if we realize that terms like "beautiful" are relative terms, we shall not necessarily be in error in saying that sensible things are beautiful; error will arise only if we are tempted to think that they are beautiful absolutely. Second, not all terms are relative in this way; "red," for example, is not. Perhaps Plato eventually took account of both of these points, but it seems clear that he tried to deal with the second by reference to the Heraclitean doctrine that the sensible world is in a state of flux. If this doctrine is true, it is impossible to attribute any property to sensible things unequivocally. This position is put forward in the *Cratylus* and most fully expressed in the *Timaeus*. It depends, of course, on whether the Heraclitean doctrine is true and free from unpalatable consequences. It is examined in Plato's most extensive consideration of knowledge, the *Theaetetus*, a dialogue probably written at about the same time as the *Parmenides* with its criticism of the traditional theory of Forms.

In the *Theaetetus* Socrates engages in a discussion with a young mathematician, Theaetetus, concerning the nature of knowledge. Theaetetus first answers the question "What is knowledge?" in a manner typical of the dialogues, by giving examples of knowledge, but is then prevailed upon to give the answer that knowledge is esthesis (perception or sensation; the Greek word from which it comes is ambiguous). This view is identified with that of Protagoras, the Sophist, to the effect that everything is what it seems to a man and that esthesis is of what is and must be infallible—that is, what seems to a man is so and cannot be wrong. If knowledge is esthesis, it is thus an incorrigible awareness of something purely relative to the perceiver. Socrates enlarges on this view, indicating the extent to which our judgments about empirical things are relative in this way. Finally, the point of view is made absolutely general by the introduction of the Heraclitean doctrine of the flux. The joint effect of the doctrines is that all judgments about empirical things are relative— the classic Platonic point of view. This conclusion is reinforced by reference to various versions of what has become known as the argument from illusion—an argument stating that we cannot be said to perceive the real properties of things because of the possibility of illusion or because of the causal aspects of perception itself.

Having expounded the view that all empirical judgments are relative, Socrates sets out to refute it. He refutes the pure Protagorean view that appearances are the only reality by pointing out that there are acknowledged experts in different fields of knowledge concerning objective phenomena; moreover, the Protagorean view is in essence self-refuting because no absolute truth can be claimed for it on its own terms. He refutes the Heraclitean doctrine of flux by claiming that if it were true, it would be impossible to say anything about anything, a consideration which he treats as a *reductio ad absurdum*. This section of the dialogue ends with the consideration that certain properties of things—the existence of things, their identity with themselves, and their difference from other things—are ascribable to them only as a result of a judgment by the mind. Knowledge of the sensible world cannot therefore be a simple matter of having sense impressions, of esthesis in the sense specified; it must also involve judgment by the mind.

Possibility of false beliefs. In the next section Theaetetus suggests that knowledge consists of true judgment or belief. This suggestion is eventually refuted by the consideration that it is possible to believe something truly when one's grounds are insufficient. Most of the section, however, is given up to a discussion of false belief or judgment, for Socrates wonders whether this is possible. False belief cannot be a belief in what is not, for, as Parmenides showed, there is no such thing as what is not. On the other hand, if false belief consists in erroneously taking one thing for another, it is difficult to see how it is possible, for the believer must know one or both of the things in question if he is to be in the position of taking one for the other. However, if he knows at least one of the things, how can he mistakenly take it for the other? Socrates considers various possibilities, but the only cases in which he will allow the possibility of error are those in which a man fails to recognize something correctly because he has fitted the wrong sense impression to the wrong memory impression. (It is in the context of this discussion that Socrates introduces the analogy of the wax and the seal to illustrate the nature of the mind; the mind literally receives impressions from things outside it.) Since this account will not cope with judgments like 7 + 5 = 11, where there is no question of erroneous recognition of a sensible thing, Socrates introduces another analogy, likening the mind to an aviary, with pieces of knowledge represented by the birds. A man may know something in the sense that the idea of it is in his mind as a bird is in the aviary, but he may not have it at hand. That is, he may know it implicitly but not explicitly. Even here the original difficulties recur, however. How can he mistake an explicit piece of knowledge for something else?

The difficulties in this section of the dialogue depend upon construing errors of judgment as mistakes of identity and equating knowledge with direct awareness. The mistakes allowed by Plato are not strictly mistakes of identity but mistakes in matching one thing with another, the sense impression with the memory impression. Plato

returns to the matter in the *Sophist*, where he tries to provide a new logical analysis of the nature of judgment. He distinguishes between judgments of identity and existential judgments and probably between both of these and subject-predicate judgments (as they were later called). Judgments generally assert that one thing participates in another (at least the latter being a Form), but judgments of identity and existence assert the participation of something in certain especially important Forms—those of sameness and existence. These Forms are two of a list of five to which Plato gave special attention, the others being difference, rest, and motion. To say that something is identical with another thing is to say that it participates in the Form of sameness in relation to that other thing. Mistakes of judgment can arise over whether something really participates in another thing, and to that extent the difficulties of the *Theaetetus* are resolved, although it may be questioned whether Plato has given a really adequate account of judgment.

True beliefs and logoi. In the last section of the *Theaetetus*, it is suggested that knowledge may consist of true belief together with the giving of a logos. It will be remembered that knowledge was associated with the ability to give a logos in the *Meno*. Here Socrates recounts a "dream" according to which the elements of reality are perceptible but unknowable and without a logos, whereas the compounds which are formed from them are knowable and have a logos. The notion of a logos is a vague and possibly ambiguous one, but its connection with knowledge seems to imply at least that knowledge must be expressible in propositions. Socrates rejects the "dream view" (which may possibly be attributable to Antisthenes) on the ground that knowledge of compounds would not be possible unless there was already knowledge of the elements. Propositional knowledge must depend upon a knowledge by acquaintance of something, in Plato's view presumably a knowledge of the Forms. But what is the logos which, when added to belief, may turn it into knowledge? Three suggestions are considered. First, that a logos is simply the manifestation of the judgment in speech (a possible meaning of the word) is clearly insufficient. Second, that it consists of the recounting of the elements of the thing known is insufficient in that this may not actually amount to knowledge of how the elements are put together. Third, that it consists in the identification of the thing in question is rejected on the ground of circularity, for if being said to know something requires that one know the distinguishing mark of the thing in question, the account is manifestly circular. But nothing less than this is sufficient. The dialogue therefore ends inconclusively.

It is clear that in this dialogue Plato was working toward a view of knowledge which is not too far from the ordinary one. His thought, however, was never entirely free from ambivalence in this respect, and perhaps he never entirely lost his distrust of the senses. The ideal of knowledge as a kind of apprehension of a system of Forms remained. It was the task of the philosopher to investigate this system by means of dialectic, the techniques of logical division and classification. For Plato knowledge was always a state of mind and had to be accounted for accordingly. This presupposition lies behind the inconclusiveness of the *Theaetetus*. Yet most of the traditional epistemological problems arise in the course of Plato's argument, and it is worth attention for this reason alone.

ARISTOTLE. Aristotle (384–322 BCE) was not so affected by skeptical arguments as Plato was. He does, it is true, try to answer Protagoras (*Metaphysics* Γ 5ff.), and he does so in a way very much like that of Plato in the *Theaetetus*, by pointing to the standard case in each class of judgment. Even in his early (and now fragmentary) work the *Protrepticus*, he had emphasized the necessity of an appeal to the expert in deciding issues in any particular art or science. This remained his approach throughout his life. Aristotle's preoccupations with epistemology appear in two provinces in particular—in his theory of science and in his theory of the mind and its faculties. But his approach to epistemology was not so much the attempt to justify the claim that knowledge exists as the description of what knowledge and its presuppositions are.

Universals. Like Plato, Aristotle held that knowledge is always of the universal. Insofar as we can be said to know particular things, we know them as instances of a universal; we know the universal in the particular. But it must be emphasized that for Aristotle universals are inherent in particulars; he vehemently rejects the Platonic notion of a world of separate universals or Forms. (The only exceptions to the inherence of forms in matter and God and the most divine part of us, reason in the highest sense.) Knowledge therefore depends ultimately on the soul's or mind's reception of the forms of things. The soul itself, as he made clear in *De Anima*, is not a distinct, spiritual entity but the set of faculties possessed by the body insofar as it has organs to manifest them.

Means of knowledge. Sense perception is the receiving by the sense organ, the faculty of which is the respective sense, of the sensible form of a thing, as he puts it, without its matter. He also describes sense perception as an actualizing of the potentiality that the sense organ possesses as its faculty. It is not easy to see how this account of the matter can be worked out in detail. Granted that the hand becomes hot when it touches a hot object, what happens to the eye when we perceive color? Aristotle thinks that each sense is affected in a way peculiar to it, so that each sense has its own special sense object. The eye has color, the ear, sound; and so on. In addition to the special senses, there is a common sense, which has no sense organ peculiar to it. It is a faculty of all the sense organs or at least of those which are capable of perceiving the same qualities of objects; for example, size and shape are perceptible by both sight and touch. Aristotle speaks of both the special sensibles, such as color, and the common sensibles, such as shape, as essential to the respective senses. Apart from these there are the incidental sensibles, which are the things that possess these properties. Aristotle speaks of them as incidental sensibles because if we use our eyes, we are bound to see color; it is not essential that we see a particular object—to use Aristotle's example, the son of Diares. At any given time he may be the object of our vision, but he does not have to be. Some interpreters have spoken of these incidental sensibles as perceived indirectly, but there is no warrant for this interpretation in *De Anima*. As Aristotle points out, it is possible to see indirectly that sugar is sweet if we know that what we see directly is sweet. But this is quite different from perception of the incidental sensibles.

With this rather passive account of perception Aristotle gives a more active account when he stresses the role judgment plays in perception. Indeed, in the *Posterior Analytics* he speaks of the senses themselves as discriminative capacities. It is through such judgment that perceptual errors, such as mistaking the identity of a thing, can arise. Aristotle tends to say that when a sense is concerned simply with its own special object—for instance, sight with something white—there is the least chance of error. On occasion, however, he seems to imply that here error is impossible because the reception of the form in this case is something purely passive, so that there is no question of judgment. His position is not altogether clear, and there may be some confusion in his mind on this matter.

The same combination of passive impression and active judgment can be found in Aristotle's account of such faculties as imagination and memory, and to some extent there is a parallel account of the intellect itself. The persistence of the exercise of the sense faculty after its actualization by a sense object leads to the setting up of images. But imagination cannot exist in the full sense without the exercise of some form of judgment. Likewise, memory must depend not only on having images but also on a referring to the past.

It is in the account of the intellect that the parallel with sense perception comes out most clearly. There is, first, a reception of form, in this case not sensible form but intelligible form. This corresponds to having concepts. Second, there is the combination of concepts in judgment, and it is only here that the possibility of error arises. Because the higher faculties depend for their existence on the lower, the exercise of the intellect, which is in itself nothing but a mere faculty, depends on the prior exercise of sense perception. Hence, Aristotle says, the soul never thinks without an image. Owing to the influence of St. Thomas Aquinas, this has often been interpreted as the basis of empiricism. If the issue had been raised by Aristotle, the outcome might have been this doctrine, but it is not clear that he did raise it. To say that the activities of the intellect are always dependent on the workings of the lower faculties is not in itself to say that the only ideas we can have are provided by sense experience. Finally, Aristotle distinguishes between an active and a passive intellect. The intellect thus far described is the passive intellect; the active intellect, something purely actual and without potentiality, is necessary in order to make possible the actualization of the faculties of the soul. In Aristotle's thought it is given no other function.

What knowledge is. Since knowledge is concerned with the universal—with form—any knowledge which is expressible in judgment must consist of an apprehension of an essential connection between forms. To know something about a thing is to be able to subsume it under species and genus and thus to know what is essential to it. It is matter which is responsible for what is accidental, and matter is in the last analysis—as prime matter—unknowable. To a large extent Aristotle's conception of knowledge in the full sense—that is, scientific knowledge—is coincident with Plato's. For Aristotle knowledge implies order; sense experience without this is something less than knowledge. This notion of order or organization is akin to Plato's notion of logos. Similarly, the idea that knowledge consists of classification in terms of genus and species and thus of a charting of the essential connections between forms is akin to Plato's conception of dialectic as concerned with the structure of the world of Forms.

Knowledge and definition. The connection in Aristotle's thought between knowledge and classification in terms of genus and species also entails a connection between knowledge and definition, for definition itself is in terms of genus and species. Aristotle distinguishes

between nominal and real definition, the first being designed to give knowledge of terms only, the second giving knowledge of the essence of the thing itself. The difference turns largely on the fact that giving the essence of the thing involves the explanation of its cause. Thus, Aristotle says that we think that we have knowledge in the primary sense when we can give the cause of the thing. To give the cause of a thing involves the demonstration of its essence from first principles, and this is the function of science. The first principles themselves can be known only by a form of intuition; one sees their truth in their instances. It is possible to explain the principles of one science in terms of another science, but this process must come to a stop somewhere. It is the mark of a foolish man, Aristotle says, to think that everything can be proved. Principles such as the law of contradiction, which are implied in all demonstration, can be proved only dialectically. A dialectical proof is one that starts not from necessary first principles but from what is commonly accepted. In this case the proof consists in getting the man who denies the law of contradiction to say something and then to show him that what he says implies the law; he is thus convicted by his own testimony.

Aristotle thus presents us with a concept of an ideal of scientific knowledge and gives some account of what is presupposed by it. The difference between knowledge and true belief is, in his account, presumably dependent on whether what is claimed is essentially and necessarily true, a part of science as he sees it. But Aristotle gives little in the way of a justification of the claim that knowledge is possible at all, for he clearly feels no need to do so. To that extent he is out of the main stream of epistemological thinkers.

HELLENISTIC PHILOSOPHERS. If anyone in the ancient world was an empiricist, it was Epicurus, the leading Greek atomist.

Epicurus. In the view of Epicurus (341–270 BCE) all knowledge resulted from contact with the atoms of which the soul is composed by atoms from outside. It is true that he said atoms could sometimes stimulate the soul directly without affecting the senses, providing humans with visions of the gods, but in general the senses had to be involved. Atoms affecting the sense organs produced sensations; mass stimulation of the sense organs resulted in a presentation or appearance (*phantasia*) to the soul. Sense experience in the more general sense occurs when an incoming presentation is fitted to a general conception or abstract idea, which itself results from repetition of sensations. This is the nearest thing to judgment in Epicurus's system, and this is the most usual source of error. Epicurus insists that all sensations are true and that they are the ultimate standard to which we must refer all our judgments; they admit of no other check. Since they are the ultimate standard of judgment, there is no other source for a metaphysical theory about the world. This, it has often been pointed out, does not fit in very well with the claims that Epicurus makes in order to give an atomistic picture of the world.

It is not altogether clear what Epicurus meant in saying that all sensations are true, especially since he also maintained that *phantasmata*, dreams or the delusions of the mad, are true. In the context of the atomist conception of the physical basis of perception, however, the view seems to imply a doctrine, common in the history of the subject, that anything in the mind which is caused cannot be liable to error. In reality questions of truth and falsity do not arise in such circumstances, a consideration implicit in Epicurus's statement that sensations are without a logos (not the sort of thing to involve judgment), but the conclusion that error is impossible has frequently been drawn.

Stoics. The rival Stoic school was founded by Zeno (fl. c. 300 BCE), but the main figure was, perhaps, Chrysippus (c. 280–c. 204 BCE). The Stoics were also empiricists to a large extent, although there is doubt whether at least some of the school did not admit innate ideas. The central notion of Stoic epistemology was intuition or apprehension (*katalepsis*). This, as is put by the Skeptic critic Sextus Empiricus (c. 200 CE), was their standard of truth. Like the atomists the Stoics thought that things make impressions on the soul, although they differed from the atomists over which physical processes were involved. They made no suggestion, however, that these impressions were necessarily veridical. This was true only of those impressions that were clear and distinct (*enarges*). Whenever an impression is received in the soul, the soul has to register it by a process known as assent, but there cannot be said to be knowledge until there is apprehension, until the soul is gripped by the impression (*katalepsis* literally means "gripping"). When this apprehension can properly be said to exist is clearly open to question, and this was pointed out by the Skeptics. Hence, later Stoics were forced to say that apprehensive impressions were a guarantee of truth as long as there was no objection.

Skeptics. Meanwhile, the Skeptics were making attacks upon the dogmatic schools, as they called them. The general tendency of this school was to accept the doctrine of impressions and *phantasiae*, but to maintain that there was no ground for going beyond them. Thus, it was necessary to be content with appearances and not to seek for the hidden truth about reality. The arguments against dogmatism were probably unsystematized initially, but they were gradually put into order. Probably under Aenesidemus (first century BCE) a list of ten (or eight) arguments (tropes) was drawn up. Some of these were forms of the argument from illusion, stressing the possibility of illusion and error in order to suggest that there was no reason to think that we ever gain knowledge of the real truth about things. Perceptions, they said, are always relative to the circumstances, the perceiver, and so on. Hence, no *phantasia* is a criterion of truth, and nothing else can be. A later Skeptic, perhaps Agrippa (first century CE), systematized the arguments even further by constructing general forms of skeptical argument. The final form stated that because of the earlier arguments nothing could be known in itself but only in relation to other things; however, something could be known relatively to other things only if these other things could be known absolutely. Because this had already been shown to be impossible, nothing could be known.

Some Skeptics came to see that this conclusion, put so baldly, was too dogmatic. When Arcesilaus of the Academy (the New Academy of the third century BCE) was sufficiently influenced by Skepticism to claim that knowledge was impossible, perhaps claiming Socratic practice as a precedent, the Skeptics still thought that this view was a species of dogmatism. Carneades (214–129 BCE), a later academic who tried to meet the arguments of Chrysippus of the Stoa, not only maintained that absolute knowledge was impossible but also tried to substitute a theory of probability for it. He distinguished three grades of probability in respect to perceptions: (1) the simply probable, (2) the probable and confirmed by its consistency with its concomitants, and (3) the probable, confirmed and tested for inconsistency with the system to which it belongs. The last grade is science as we ordinarily know it. But even this would have been too much for the pure Skeptic. Skepticism as a system received its fullest expression in the works of Sextus Empiricus in the second century CE.

Neoplatonists. In the third century CE Platonism was revived by Plotinus, the founder of the Neoplatonic school. This was Platonism in its more mystical aspects, although Plotinus often uses Aristotelian notions, sometimes with a Platonic twist. The soul, as opposed to the body, is given preeminence, so that perception and knowledge are made a function of the soul. The soul has its own activities, which are manifested in perception and memory; the body and its impressions are merely instruments for the soul to use. The main function of the soul qua intellect is to contemplate the Forms, above which is the supreme principle or entity, the One. Unity with the One is the soul's goal.

MEDIEVAL THOUGHT

It was Neoplatonism which, according to St. Augustine (354–430), brought about his salvation from Manichaeism in theology and skepticism in philosophy. Neoplatonism offered a supposedly positive doctrine in both metaphysics and epistemology and one which St. Augustine could largely accept, thus ignoring the other, heterodox views. St. Augustine's thought is therefore Neoplatonic in its essentials. As a result he took it for granted that knowledge—and, most importantly, knowledge of God—was possible, and he felt no further need to question this assumption. The same is true of most other medieval thinkers. Since philosophy was closely linked with theology, it was axiomatic that knowledge of God was possible in some sense, and skepticism about knowledge in general was rejected by an appeal to whatever philosophical system was thought best able to explain that knowledge. Insofar as there was argument, it was about the presuppositions and sources of knowledge, not about whether it existed.

Knowledge of a thing involves, it is commonly thought, knowledge of its general characteristics and, therefore, its subsumption under a universal. Medieval thinkers differed according to their philosophical tradition, according to whether they were Platonists or, after the Aristotelian revival in the thirteenth century, Aristotelians. But the main dispute was over theories of universals. Since the dispute had theological implication, it was heated. The argument had its source in certain questions put by Porphyry, a disciple of Plotinus, about the exact status of species and universals. These questions, the answers to which Porphyry thought were obscure, were discussed by Boethius in a commentary. The main schools of thought on the subject were the realists, conceptualists, and nominalists. Realists thought that universals had an objective existence, although their view of this existence depended on whether they were Platonists or Aristotelians. Conceptualists held that universals existed only as concepts in the mind; nominalists held that the only universal things were words. Such theories, however, were rarely found in their pure form.

REALIST THEORIES OF UNIVERSALS. The division among realists is best seen in the differences between St. Augustine and St. Thomas Aquinas (1225–1274).

Augustine. St. Augustine gave preeminence to the soul, in Neoplatonist fashion. In his view the soul has its own functions and is not directly influenced by the body. Perception is based on the impressions produced by the soul when the body is stimulated. Experience, however, involves inference, as the soul subsumes its impressions under concepts. To have such concepts is, for St. Augustine, to be aware of Forms in the Platonic sense, the one difference being that in his view the Forms are thoughts in the mind of God. Thus, universals have a real existence in the mind of God, and all knowledge, even sense knowledge, involves some awareness of God. There is an ascent from lower forms of knowledge, like perception, to higher forms, with knowledge of God at the peak.

Thomas Aquinas. The Aristotelian revival in the thirteenth century led to St. Thomas Aquinas's acceptance of a more Aristotelian point of view than Augustine's. Like Aristotle, Thomas rejected self-subsistent universals, maintaining that universality is a function of the mind. Nevertheless, there are real similarities between things because of their common form. Hence, species have more than a mere mental existence.

The Thomist theory of knowledge consists largely of an explanation of how knowledge of Forms is possible. When the senses are stimulated, the soul's potentiality is actualized; a sensory image, or *phantasma*, is set up, corresponding to the object of perception. But since the universal aspects of such objects can be apprehended only by the intellect, they must be transferred from the *phantasma* to the intellect. Indeed, *phantasmata* as such are not objects of awareness on our part. The mind is aware only of the universal aspects of things, not their particularity, which is available only to the senses. Something has to illuminate the *phantasmata* in order to make clear their universal characteristics. Thomas employs Aristotle's distinction between the active and passive intellects here. The active intellect abstracts the universal or species from the *phantasma*, and this is imposed upon the passive intellect as a concept, which is then verbalized. Concepts thus exist only as the result of an abstraction of the universal aspects of things, and the essence of Thomas's empiricism is that all knowledge depends on sense experience in this way. Even knowledge of self-evident truths, which Thomas admits, as well as knowledge of the essential nature of things, is in the last resort dependent on sense experience, and all our thoughts must be based on experience. Thomas can be looked on as the founder of empiricism in the sense that he held that all the materials for knowledge come ultimately from experience and from nowhere else. Unlike the later philosopher John Locke, however, he did not set out to justify the doctrine in detail.

CONCEPTUALIST THEORIES OF UNIVERSALS.

Although Thomas may be classed as a realist in his theory of universals because he maintained that there are objective similarities between things by virtue of their common form. He could not do so without the notion of concepts in the mind.

Abelard. Peter Abelard (1079–1142) had previously held a conceptualist theory of universals, emphasizing the extent to which universality is a function of the mind. He held that universals are really concepts (*sermones*) involved in judgments that particular things have something in common. They are arrived at by abstraction from particular things, by attending to features of things considered in themselves. Abelard even used the notion of a generic image—that is, an image not of any particular thing but, supposedly, of what is common to a whole class of things—in order to account for our ability to think of things generally. He was anxious to reject both realism and the contemporary nominalism held by Roscelin of Compiègne (d. c. 1125), who maintained that universals were just words or even names. He did not, however, deny that concepts had a basis in things. Hence, in a sense Thomist realism and Abelardian conceptualism are very much two sides of the same coin.

NOMINALIST THEORY OF UNIVERSALS.

Similar considerations apply to the great nominalist thinker of the fourteenth century, William of Ockham.

Ockham. Even Ockham (c. 1285–1349) did not quite maintain that the only universal things are words, for he held that words are conventional signs corresponding to concepts that are natural signs of things. Universality lies in the sign-significate relation, in the fact that both words and concepts can be signs of a class of things. To the question "What are universals?" Ockham initially replied that they had only a logical existence; they were meanings, the contents of the mind when thinking generally. For Ockham the term *universal* was what he called a term of second intention. A first intention is the state of mind involved in the apprehension of particular things; a second intention is that involved in the apprehension of first intentions. The term *universal* thus picks out the content of our apprehension of our first-order apprehensions of a class of things. "Redness" is not the name of an entity but

of the content of the relation which exists between the sign or concept "red" and particular red things. Ockham later took another step toward conceptualism by holding that universals had a mental, not just a logical, existence. He then held that universals are the concepts that the mind has and which are the natural substitutes for things themselves. Ockham probably took this step for reasons of economy, for in the earlier account universals were a sort of intermediary between the mind and particular things. The place given to generality remained the same, however. There was nothing general in the world; generality depended on the relationship between the mind and particular things.

The real novelty of Ockham's approach lay in his holding the view, new to medieval thought, that the mind itself could have apprehension of particular things. Thomas, for example, had denied this, holding that the mind could be concerned only with universal characteristics abstracted from *phantasmata*. The consequent gap between the mind and the senses inevitably involved a representative theory of perception; the mind was confronted only with the representatives of things. Ockham denied all this. He held that the mind could be concerned directly with the particular by means of intuitions. Intuitive knowledge is a direct knowledge of a thing or its existence. The senses provide an intuition of a thing's existence, and the intellect provides an intuition of its nature. John Duns Scotus (c. 1266–1308) had held that intuition of a particular was a necessary condition of the abstraction of the universal from it, but he had also held that this intuition must, in this life at any rate, be confused. Ockham denied this. In his view intuitions may be perfect or imperfect respectively, according to whether they are dependent merely on present experience or whether they also involve past experience. The possibility of imperfect intuitions, however, depends on the possibility of direct, perfect intuitions.

Although Ockham thought that this kind of direct knowledge does exist, he did not claim that all intuition was equally clear; clarity, moreover, was not always enough to guarantee truth. In the first respect, he claimed, as St. Augustine had done earlier, that we have clearer knowledge of our own mind than of other things. In the second he maintained that God can give us an intuition of something that does not in fact exist (a consideration which looked forward to René Descartes's suggestion that God might be a deceiver). This is not the natural course of things, however.

Much of Ockham's thought is in the Stoic tradition, and to some extent this can be said about Descartes, the first of the rationalist thinkers of the seventeenth century. By this time, however, the questioning of the accepted points of view of the Middle Ages had led to increased skepticism. Descartes's theory of knowledge is therefore in the fullest sense the beginning of that "search for certainty" whose elements were found in Plato but had not been prominent after him.

SEVENTEENTH-CENTURY RATIONALISM

DESCARTES AND CARTESIANISM. The emergence of science during the Renaissance and the disputes that it produced led to a certain skepticism about claims to knowledge and to the search for a method, like that of science, which would determine the truth once and for all. Descartes (1596–1650) was the pioneer in this new tradition, and although his roots were in the Middle Ages, he was to a large extent an innovator. Being a mathematician of distinction, he saw the solution to problems of epistemology in the systematization of knowledge in geometrical form, although he did not carry out the full program himself. This involved starting from axioms whose truth was clear and distinct. He describes the ideal method in the second chapter of the *Discourse on Method* as (1) not to accept as true anything of which we have not a clear and distinct idea, (2) to analyze the problem, (3) to start from simple and certain thoughts and proceed from them to the more complex, and (4) to review the field so thoroughly that no considerations are omitted. Of what do we have clear and distinct ideas? To deal with this problem, Descartes employs the method of doubt—a form of skepticism. This method involves setting on one side anything that can be supposed false until one arrives at something that cannot be supposed false.

That there is a goal to this skepticism is, it might be objected, prejudged, for Descartes points to the fact that he has often been deceived to suggest that he may always be deceived. This conclusion is not, however, admissible, since to establish his premises, he must at least know that he has sometimes been deceived. The truth is that Descartes has a definite conception of what knowledge must be, and most of what we ordinarily call knowledge does not fit that conception. His approach is therefore not strictly that of the general skeptic. It consists in setting on one side anything that does not possess the mark of genuine knowledge, this mark being that we should have clear and distinct ideas of the thing in question. We have a clear idea of a thing when it is open to the mind, when we are clearly aware of it; an idea is also distinct when we have a full knowledge of the nature of its object and of the

means whereby that object can be distinguished from other things. Many philosophers have believed that we do not have certain knowledge of empirical truths but that we do have it of mathematical truths. Descartes agrees to the extent that he maintains that we can have clear and distinct ideas of the objects of mathematics, but he also maintains that if God were a deceiver, he might have caused us to have false beliefs even here. Hence, it is at least a possible hypothesis that there is an archdeceiver who brings it about that I am mistaken in all my beliefs. Is there anything which is free from this contingency?

"Cogito ergo sum." The result of Descartes's inquiry into this matter is that there is at least one proposition which is indubitable in the sense that I cannot be wrong in maintaining it. This is the proposition "I think, therefore I exist" (*Cogito ergo sum*). Descartes is definite that this is not to be treated as an argument despite its form; it is an indubitable proposition. (In a sense Descartes had been anticipated in this by St. Augustine's "If I am mistaken, I exist" [*Si fallor sum*], but St. Augustine had not used the proposition for exactly the same purposes.) It is reasonably clear that I cannot deny either "I think" or "I exist" without absurdity, although this is not enough to show that the *cogito* is in any way a logical truth. Yet for Descartes it must have the kind of necessity that is generally attributed to logical truths; it must be logically impossible for the proposition to be false. Moreover, it must have content such that its truth entails the existence of something with a specific nature—namely, a spiritual or thinking substance which has certain ideas, particularly those of God and material objects. Only then can Descartes go on to justify belief in such objects.

In effect, therefore, Descartes says that I can doubt everything except that I doubt. Since doubting is a form of thinking, I cannot doubt that I think, and since thought requires a thinker, I cannot doubt the existence of myself as the thinker. It might be objected that even if there is no reason to reject this position, it has not been shown to be necessary. If I cannot doubt that I doubt, this may be a contingent matter, not a logical necessity. Once given the *cogito*, however, Descartes can go on to use it as the premise of an argument whose outcome will be the justification of our belief in a world independent of ourselves.

The status of perception. Granted that we have ideas of a world of material things, what prevents those ideas being mere figments of the imagination? Ideas in themselves are purely mental entities (although Descartes is never very clear about their exact nature); they may or may not represent the things they purport to represent.

Ideas can be innate, adventitious, or fictitious. To say that they are adventitious is to say that they come from things outside us; to say that they are fictitious is to say that they are produced by the mind itself. Innate ideas are a priori, inborn. Which ideas these are, if any, may be disputed. But, at all events, our ideas of material things are clearly not innate. Why, however, are they not merely fictitious?

To say that an idea is fictitious is not to say that it is impossible for it to be an idea of something objective. To some of our ideas perhaps nothing could possibly correspond; these would be logical impossibilities and would have no objective validity in Cartesian terms. For an idea to have objective validity, the reality in it must be caused by something that has the same reality, either formally or eminently, in itself. A machine, to use Descartes's example, may be formally the cause of a man's idea of it; his idea may be a copy of the machine, the two having the same form. But if the man conceives of the machine himself, then he or his mind is eminently the cause of his idea; the idea is not a mere copy of its cause, for the source of the idea is something higher. If, then, our ideas of material things are to be objectively valid or have objective reality, they must either be copies of actual material things or be produced by something higher. If they are produced by something higher, they were produced either by our minds or by God. To show that our ideas of material things do correspond to those material things, Descartes has to show that they are not produced in this way either by our own minds alone or by God.

Now, ideas in themselves, Descartes maintains, cannot be strictly true or false; it is the use we make of them that can be true or false. Hence, truth and error are functions of judgment. Nevertheless, we have a natural disposition to believe that our ideas are veridical. In Meditation III, Descartes points to this natural disposition and to the fact that our perceptions do not depend on the will as reason for believing in the veridicality of our perceptions, although he rejects these considerations as insufficient. In Meditation VI, however, he has recourse to the same considerations, although they must now be viewed in the context of the view that perception is a faculty of the mind plus body and does not express the essence of the mind alone, which is concerned solely with thinking. The passivity of our perceptual ideas thus seems to be invoked in order to reject the notion that our ideas of material objects could be a product of our own minds. Ideas of material objects, however, might still be caused by God. Yet if this were true and if nothing answered to those ideas, God would be a deceiver, for he would be giving us a natural disposition to believe in the existence of things which do not exist in fact. God, Descartes maintains, is not a deceiver. This point is taken as axiomatic and provides the ultimate guarantee of our belief that we do perceive an objective world.

Existence of God. The existence of God is therefore a cardinal point in the chain of argument. Descartes produces two sets of arguments designed to demonstrate his existence as a necessary truth. The first argument, in Meditation III, is based on the same considerations about the causes of our ideas as those adduced in connection with ideas of material things. The idea of God, which Descartes takes to be objectively valid, could be produced only by something having the same reality formally or eminently in it. We, being inferior creatures, could not produce it, and it could not come from any other source except God himself. Hence, there must be a God. This argument is a version of the so-called Cosmological Argument.

The other argument, to be found in Meditation V, is a version of the Ontological Argument first invoked by St. Anselm. God must through his essence possess all positive attributes in perfection. Existence is a positive attribute; hence, God must exist. It is now generally recognized that neither argument is sufficient to demonstrate the necessary existence of God. However, the necessary existence of God must be demonstrated if the argument concerning the existence of material things is to have any cogency.

If Descartes's argument for the existence of God had been sound, he would have shown that all the reality in our ideas must be in their causes. More is required if it is to be shown that our ideas are, at least in some cases, copies of their causes. This is a problem for any representative or causal theory of perception, any theory that holds that our ideas and perceptions are mental entities which are, at best, only representatives of things outside them. From Descartes's point of view there is the general consideration that God is not a deceiver; any errors or illusions to which we are subject are the results of judgments we make because of the ideas we receive. This makes it incumbent on us, if we are to avoid error, to take due account of the clarity and distinctness of our ideas. We are right in judging that our ideas correspond to their causes only if those ideas are clear and distinct.

Primary and secondary qualities. In Descartes's opinion there is a big difference between primary qualities, such as figure, magnitude, and motion, and secondary qualities, such as color. Primary qualities can be known by an intuition of the intellect (*inspectio mentis*). Our ideas of them are clear and distinct because of the part they play in mathematics, and in mathematics, therefore, the intellect can be regarded as having a proper knowledge of reality. This is not to say that we cannot make mistakes concerning the primary qualities of objects; judgment can be as liable to error here as elsewhere. However, since the ideas of them are clear and distinct, we have the assurance that in general objects do have such qualities. We have no such assurance in the case of secondary qualities. The intellect is not involved here, but since the senses were, Descartes maintains, provided only for the conservation of life, it does not matter very much whether our ideas of secondary qualities correspond to the actual qualities of objects.

It would not be generally admitted today that mathematics does provide the kind of knowledge of reality that Descartes requires. The question of the exact connection between mathematics and the world is a complicated one. Granted, however, that mathematical ideas have a precision not possessed by other ideas, it does not follow that we have a precise knowledge of any qualities of physical objects. For it remains an open question to what extent such ideas are applicable to physical objects. There is a genuine distinction between primary and secondary qualities in that the first are measurable in a way that the second are not. This, however, is not sufficient to justify the claim that knowledge of primary qualities is knowledge of reality in a way that knowledge of secondary qualities is not. In some places—for instance, *Principles*, Part IV, Section XI, and *Dioptric*, Section VI—Descartes tries to reinforce this view by arguing that since the effects in the brain caused by the stimulation of our senses possess only the properties of motion, figure, and extension, there is no means whereby we could come to apprehend any other properties of objects. There is a circularity in this argument, since its premise is that we do know of the primary qualities possessed by brain processes, whereas all ideas, being the effects of physical processes, should be in the same position.

In sum, Descartes's theory of knowledge is essentially one of a representative kind. It is based on the idea that the mind or soul, being something very different and distinct from the body, can have as its contents only ideas, which are, at best, representatives of physical things. The mind has its own activities, and its nature is to be active. Through these activities it can come to have knowledge of abstract mathematical truths. But all sense knowledge, as opposed to intellectual knowledge, can come only through the medium of ideas, and that these ideas correspond in any way to the physical objects presented to the senses is inevitably open to question. The justification of

our belief that they do depends, in the long run, on the affirmation that there is a God and that he is not a deceiver. Descartes thinks that he can demonstrate that there is a God, taking as true by definition that he is no deceiver and that our natural disposition to trust our senses is therefore justified.

Occasionalism. Since Descartes conceived of the soul and the body as distinct substances with distinct essences—that of the soul being thought and that of the body extension—he was inevitably faced with the problem of how one could act on the other. He was never very clear on this point, although he came to insist that there must be some quasi-substantial union between the two. In some places—for example, the *Dioptric*—he speaks of brain processes giving "occasion" to the soul to have sensations or ideas. Some of his followers, who thereby became known as occasionalists, took up this notion and tried to explain the apparent link between soul and body by saying that God puts ideas into the soul on the occasion of the bodily processes. Arnold Geulincx (1624–1669) said that God puts the ideas there by means of the bodily processes; Nicolas Malebranche (1638–1715) said that God acts directly on the mind on the occasion of the bodily processes. Since Malebranche had leanings toward the views of St. Augustine, he interpreted this occasionalism in terms of the Augustinian doctrine that we know all things in God.

Malebranche. In other respects Malebranche tends to follow Descartes, although often with greater emphasis. He, too, insists that we have clear and distinct ideas of figure, extension, and movement, since these qualities, being conceivable in mathematical terms, are open to the intellect. He also lays great emphasis on our liability to error in anything connected with the senses, especially if we think that the senses provide us with knowledge of things as they actually are. In one respect, however, he adds a certain sophistication to the Cartesian distinction between the ideas or sensations that arise in the mind without any intervention on our part and the judgments that we make and which depend on our will. Sometimes what we see differs from what would be expected on the basis of the sensations resulting from the stimulation of our senses. We may see a thing in its right size, for example, although the actual pattern of stimulation received in the eyes is different; alternatively, we can be subject to illusion when the conditions of stimulation are not abnormal. In such circumstances we are not generally aware of making any judgment in order to correct the sensations received. Malebranche therefore distinguishes between natural judgments, or judgments of sense, and free judgments. Free judgments depend on our will, but natural ones do not; they are, he says, a kind of complex sensation in that they do not depend on us. They are, he explains, made by God in us, in consequence of the laws of the union between soul and body. As judgments they can be true or false, but as sensations they may occur against our will and are certainly not due to our will. Malebranche is in an ambivalent position here, but his difficulties show a certain honesty.

SPINOZA. It has often been remarked that what makes the thought of Benedict (Baruch) de Spinoza (1632–1677) especially interesting is that it combines the quite different and, as generally conceived, quite disparate traditions of nominalism and extreme rationalism. In his nominalism he belongs to the tradition of William of Ockham and, more particularly, of Thomas Hobbes (1588–1679). Hobbes maintained that only names were universal. Although names were signs of images of things that constitute our conception of them, there was nothing universal in the conceptions themselves. Only the use to which names are put was universal, for they are taken as signs of many things. Hobbes used this to mount an aggressive attack on the paraphernalia of Scholasticism—essences, substance, and the like. He was a tough-minded mechanist who thought that reality consisted solely of corporeal bodies in motion.

Although he did not have the same motive, Spinoza was similarly opposed to the apparatus of Scholasticism. Indeed, he may have been influenced by Hobbes. In his *Ethics*, Part II, Spinoza held that as a result of the stimulation of our bodily senses by many things, confused, composite images arise, and it is these images that general words represent. There is no place for universals existing in things. Since these images may be set up differently in different men, "universal notions," as Spinoza calls them, may differ from man to man. The knowledge that is expressed by their means can only be confused. Spinoza is not content to leave knowledge there, however; he has the conception of knowledge of a much higher kind, and his working out of this conception is in effect the systematizing of Cartesianism. To make Cartesianism consistent, however, he had to change much in it.

Monism. Although according to Descartes's view the clarity and distinctness of an idea was a necessary condition of its truth, it was not a sufficient condition of its truth. It was always possible to raise the question of whether any particular idea did correspond to reality and, in particular, to its cause. This was a consequence of the dualism between the mind and its ideas and the physical world, a dualism inherent in Cartesianism. Spinoza replaced this dualism by a monism according to which the mental and the physical were two aspects of one thing—ultimately, God or Nature. In adopting this view, he was again carrying out the implications of Cartesianism, for Descartes had asserted that in the proper sense the concept of substance belongs only to God, for only God is self-subsistent, or *causa sui*. Hence, in Spinoza's view everything is a modification or mode of the one true substance, depending on God for its existence. The Cartesian distinction between mental and material substance becomes a distinction between the two infinite attributes of God in Spinoza's theory. Bodies are modifications of God qua extended, and minds are modifications of God qua thinking. They are not distinct things; they are merely parallel aspects of the one true substance. The order of ideas in the mind is the same as the order of things. Hence, the objects, or *ideata*, of ideas, insofar as these have reference to God, are always truly represented by them. No ideas can be absolutely false, and insofar as they refer to God, they must be true. Ideas can be considered false only from the point of view of what we ordinarily call a single human mind, not from the point of view of God.

Truth and falsity. Because everything can be deduced from the essence of God, everything is subject to necessity, and this applies to ideas as much as to everything else. There is no room in Spinoza's theory for the Cartesian distinction between ideas and the will; for him the will and the intellect are the same. Falsity cannot therefore arise from the exercise of our will in the employment of ideas. For Spinoza the exercise of the will in judgment is not something additional to having ideas, and he emphasizes that it is wrong to think of ideas as simple pictures that may or may not correspond to their objects. To have an idea of something and to make a judgment about it are one and the same, and it is by virtue of this composite conception that ideas, not only judgments, can be true or false. Considered as part of God's thinking, ideas cannot, of course, be false, for in that case they must always correspond, qua modifications of God as thinking, to the modifications of God as extended. But considered as ideas in a single human mind, they can represent their objects confusedly or inadequately. In having a confused idea of an object, we fail to see it as following necessarily from the nature of things. Such ideas, Spinoza says, are like consequences without premises.

In the *Ethics*, Part II, Definition 4, Spinoza defines an adequate idea as "an idea which, insofar as it is considered in itself without relation to an object, has all the properties or intrinsic marks of a true idea." If an idea is confused, it cannot be adequate. Therefore, truth must have an intrinsic criterion, not just the extrinsic criterion of the correspondence of an idea to its object. In other words, the clarity and distinctness that Descartes had looked to for the foundations of knowledge is the mark of every true idea. Truth and adequacy thus merge. For full truth an idea must be seen to be true, and this is possible only insofar as it is seen to follow from the nature of things. Truth, Spinoza says, is its own criterion. This is connected with another of Spinoza's epistemological views—that knowledge must ultimately be reflexive. Anyone who really knows something must know that he knows. If a man knows that something is necessarily so, he must know that he knows this, since the truth of what he knows must be manifest.

The doctrine of truth that Spinoza presents is commonly referred to as the coherence theory of truth, and it is normally associated with the doctrine of degrees of truth, knowledge, and reality. The distinctions between grades of reality that exist between the one true substance and its various modifications is paralleled by distinctions between kinds of knowledge. True knowledge, the having of adequate ideas, entails seeing things as following from the essence of God. Knowledge can be more or less inadequate or confused to the extent that a thing is not seen as following necessarily from that essence. Absolute truth consists in having adequate ideas, although every idea has some degree of truth since it must have a counterpart in the order of things. In other words, an idea, although necessarily true in some respect, has greater truth to the degree that it is adequate and to the degree that its object is seen as fitting in with the order of things. Like most versions of the coherence theory of truth, this is really not a theory of what truth is or what is meant in calling an idea or judgment true, but, rather, a theory of when or under what conditions an idea or judgment can be seen to be true. A judgment can be seen to be true if it coheres with the system of judgments that characterize reality. But coherence theorists tend to say that any judgment which can be seen to cohere with other judgments in this way is thereby "more true" than those which do not cohere. In effect, they tend to use the word *true* so that it is more or less equivalent to *verified*. A judgment that has a higher degree of verification by virtue of its coherence with other judgments is said to be ipso facto more true. The coherence theory of truth is thus a genuine epistemological theory, a theory of the conditions under which we can be said to know a proposition as true.

Kinds of knowledge. Spinoza distinguishes three grades of knowledge. Full knowledge Spinoza refers to as the third kind of knowledge and characterizes it as intuition. This kind of knowledge, he says in the *Ethics*, Part II, "proceeds from an adequate idea of the formal essence of certain attributes of God to an adequate knowledge of the essence of things." To have this knowledge is the goal of philosophy—to see things *sub specie aeternitatis*, as conforming to a kind of necessity. The right method in philosophy as set out in the *Treatise on the Correction of the Understanding* is to rid the mind of confused and inadequate ideas and to lead it to ideas which are adequate. It is significant that Spinoza calls this kind of knowledge intuition, because in its essence it consists of seeing the world as a coherent whole bound by necessary connections. Most rationalists have ended up with some such conception, and for them reason is inevitably second best. So it is for Spinoza.

What Spinoza calls reason is the second kind of knowledge, below intuition. This is best described by distinguishing it from the first kind of knowledge, which is knowledge derived from vague experience and is also called opinion or imagination. This corresponds roughly to sense experience. (Knowledge from hearsay, the fourth kind of knowledge, added in the *Treatise* to the bottom of the list, is of little importance for present purposes.) From sense experience we gain confused ideas of things without respect to their place in the general order of things. We may obtain knowledge of a similar status from signs—that is, from reading or hearing words which allow us to form ideas similar to those of the imagination. Both of these sources may lead to the setting up of the universal notions referred to earlier, notions that vary from person to person and cannot provide genuine knowledge. In the course of our experience, however, we may light upon notions that are common to all people, such notions as those of extension and other general attributes of reality. These notions Spinoza calls common notions, to be sharply distinguished from the universal notions already discussed. These common notions correspond to the ideas of primary qualities that Descartes had allowed to be clear and distinct because they were the objects of intellectual intuitions. For Spinoza, too, they provide the starting point of the sciences, and as such our ideas of them are adequate. They can be seen to be true of reality inasmuch as they reflect all-pervasive features of reality. It is for this reason that they are common to all humans; they are not subjective like the universal notions.

Reason or science thus consists in elaborating the essential features of the attributes of which we have common notions. Like Descartes, Spinoza conceived of science as based on the model of mathematics in general and geometry in particular. His conception of the right method in philosophy itself is modeled on the geometrical method. Indeed, Spinoza had tried to set out the Cartesian philosophy in a geometrical fashion according to the rules that Descartes had preached but had not practiced as well. Thus, although science, the systematization of knowledge, is ultimately derived from sense experience, it reflects the actual order of things more truly than experience does. Nevertheless, the goal of all knowledge is not just this systematization but the seeing of things as a whole, *sub specie aeternitatis*. For this reason intuition stands above reason.

Because the second and third kinds of knowledge involve adequate ideas, they cannot give rise to falsity. Sense experience alone can be the source of falsity. Through sense experience we can have only confused ideas, since ideas reflect particular modifications of reality in some finite respect, not in relation to the infinite attributes of God. Sense experience is ordinarily thought of as a passive form of knowledge, as opposed to forms of knowledge that demand the use of reason. This passivity, Spinoza thinks, is only a sign of the inadequacy of our ideas in this case. Activity on the part of the mind is, conversely, adequacy in its ideas. Spinoza points out that the human mind is part of the infinite intellect of God. Hence, "when we say that the human mind perceives this or that, we say nothing else than that God, not in so far as he is infinite, but in so far as he is explained through the nature of the human mind, or in so far as he constitutes the essence of the human mind, has this or that idea" (*Ethics*, Part II). Just as the ideas of sense experience are confused and inadequate only in relation to our mind, although when considered as God's ideas they are true, so the ideas of sense experience are passive in relation to our mind but are nevertheless part of God's active thoughts.

In sum, for Spinoza the goal of all knowledge is seeing the world as a single whole. On the way to this lies reason or science, which attempts to reveal things as subject to necessity by means of self-evident, necessary truths about things. All else, although not absolutely false, is the source of illusion. But, as in everything else in Spinoza, an adequate understanding of his theory of knowledge also involves an adequate understanding of his complete metaphysics or theory of reality. This is true of philosophers in general but never more so than in Spinoza's case.

LEIBNIZ. In many ways Gottfried Wilhelm Leibniz (1646–1716) is Spinoza with a strong dash of common sense. Spinoza's monism, especially its assertion of the necessity of things and the apparent consequence that free will is impossible, was anathema to Leibniz. In these respects Leibniz revolted against Spinoza, but in other respects he was very much like Spinoza. He, too, drew no distinction between the will and the intellect and made activity and passivity in the mind a function of the clarity and distinctness or otherwise of our ideas. Furthermore, although common sense told him that there must be a plurality of things, not just one, he had to conceive of each ultimate thing as a simple substance possessing all the properties of Spinoza's one substance.

Leibniz simple substances had to have a unity in plurality in that, although simple, each one had to be capable of reflecting the whole universe from its point of view. Since Leibniz took as axiomatic that in every true proposition the predicate is contained in the subject, everything that can be said about a substance is so because of the nature of that substance, and all the relations which it has to other things must arise from the nature of that substance and be internal to it. It is for this reason that every true substance must reflect the universe from its point of view and in this way be a microcosm of the macrocosm. The only thing, Leibniz thought, which could be both simple and capable of reflecting the universe in this way was something like the soul. In consequence, he postulated the existence of a plurality of simple substances, spiritual in nature, which he called monads. But for the monads, he said, Spinoza would be right.

Necessary and contingent truths. Since the properties of each monad were internal to it, it might be thought that Leibniz, like Spinoza, would have maintained that everything was a matter of necessity. However, although Leibniz maintained that all the properties of a substance are internal to it and thus follow from the nature of the substance, for other reasons he maintained a clear distinction between truths that are necessary in the logical sense and truths that are dependent on the facts. He was thus perhaps the first to draw a clear distinction between necessary or logical and contingent or factual truths. The first he called truths of reason, the second truths of fact. These truths had different principles as their basis. Truths of reason were dependent on the principle of contradiction, since their necessity turned on the fact that their denial would result in a contradiction. Leibniz thought that such truths, when their terms are defined, could be reduced to identical propositions of the form "A is A." The reduction to such identical propositions would therefore proceed by means of chains of definitions. Mathematical truths are of this kind, and Leibniz was one of the first to seek a basis for mathematics in logic.

Truths of fact, on the other hand, could not be justified by reduction to identical propositions; their basis had to be found in a separate principle, the principle of sufficient reason. This principle received different formulations at different stages of Leibniz's thought. Insofar as it was meant to allow for the contingency of matters of fact while providing a rationale for them, Leibniz tended to formulate the principle by reference to the choice of God. In creating this universe, God could choose from a number of possible worlds each having a different order or structure. Since, as Leibniz thought, for various different reasons, the number of monads is infinite, the number of such possible worlds is also infinite. Any contingent truth about *this* world has for its justification the fact that in choosing this world, God chose it as the best of all possible worlds. The truth remains contingent because it is dependent on God's choice, but a sufficient reason for its truth is that God chose it as part of the best of all possible worlds. At other times, however, Leibniz's appeal to God's choice has fewer theological implications. For example, in his correspondence with Samuel Clarke, he tries to refute the idea of an infinite absolute space by saying that in such a space God would have no sufficient reason for putting the universe here rather than there. This means that there would be no way of telling where the universe was and that it would, in consequence, make no sense to speak of it as being in one place rather than another. This use of the principle of sufficient reason amounts to something like the use of the verification principle by logical positivists—the meaning of a proposition lies in the method of verification.

When Leibniz maintains, however, that in every true proposition the predicate is included in the subject, he seems to undermine the distinction between truths of reason and truths of fact. For this doctrine would make all propositions into what Immanuel Kant was later to call analytic propositions or judgments, propositions that are logically necessary. In consequence, it has been maintained (for example, by Louis Couturat) that in some of Leibniz's writings the principle of sufficient reason merely states that all true propositions are analytic, whereas the principle of contradiction states that all analytic propositions are true. In fact, this is probably a consequence of Leibniz's main views rather than a statement of it. If every proposition about a substance attributes to it a property that is part of its essence, then all such propositions must be analytic even if they are to be characterized as truths of fact on other grounds.

Leibniz accepted this conclusion but tried to evade the contradiction implicit in characterizing a truth of fact as analytic by explaining that the number of properties possessed by any substance must be infinitely great, as the points of view from which a thing can be regarded are endless. We, being finite creatures, cannot complete the analysis of any given substance. Hence, we cannot know for certain whether any given attribute really does belong to it; we cannot, without completing the analysis, even know whether it is possible for this substance to possess the property; it may be a contradiction to suppose it. God, being infinite, can complete the analysis, and so for him all propositions about things are analytic or logically necessary. We, on the other hand, can know only that if a proposition is true, it is necessarily true, but we cannot know for certain whether any given proposition is true. In our judgments about the truth of propositions, we have to depend on probabilities—that is, we have to estimate what reasons are sufficient for our conclusions. Thus, for us any judgment of fact is contingent. For God contingency enters only in that he has chosen what substances there should be, which of all possible worlds should exist. For him everything thereafter is necessary. Hence, the principle of sufficient reason comes into consideration in two related ways—first, in that it guides, without determining, God's choice of a world and, second, in that it guides our decision concerning which world God has chosen.

Perception and appetition of monads. So much for the logical consequences of Leibniz's point of view. Given the metaphysical system according to which there exist, an infinite number of spiritual entities or monads, other consequences also follow. According to Leibniz, every monad has perception and appetition—the apparent passive and active features of mental life. Since everything about a monad is internal to it, these features can indeed be only apparent. Appetition is that aspect of a monad responsible for internal change and development. No monad can affect or be affected by any other monad. A perception is any property of a monad that results from its development but that may reflect changes in other monads. (This use of the term *perception* is, although influenced by Leibniz's metaphysics, clearly very general, but its use was very general throughout the seventeenth century.) What may seem to be activity on the part of one monad with respect to another is really having distinct perceptions, whereas passivity is having confused perceptions. Here Leibniz sides with Spinoza.

Self-consciousness of monads. Leibniz's criterion of a distinct idea of a thing is the ability to list the characteristics which distinguish the thing from other things. This clearly involves a degree of self-consciousness, and this is possessed only by the monads constituting the human soul. Although all monads have perceptions in that other things are represented in them, not all have apperception. To have apperception, the monad must be conscious of what is involved in its perceptions, and those perceptions must therefore be distinct. The distinction between perception and apperception means that perceptions can sometimes be unconscious. Leibniz brings forward a number of arguments in support of this view, ranging from the argument that reflection upon perceptions must come to a stop with perceptions that are not self-conscious to the argument that there must be what he calls *petites perceptions.* When we hear the roar of the sea, he argues, we are not aware of hearing each little ripple despite the fact that the waves are made up of ripples. Since the overall perception must correspond in complexity to its object, he concludes that there must be perceptions corresponding to the ripples, and these little perceptions are therefore unconscious. This is not a psychological discovery but a philosophical analysis the premises of which are open to dispute. Like Descartes, Leibniz accepts the representative theory of perception in thinking that perception consists in having ideas which are, or may be, representative of objects. If this theory is rejected, Leibniz's argument about *petites perceptions* loses much of its force.

Error in perception. Just as Leibniz sides with Spinoza in maintaining that activity and passivity are to be explained in terms of the distinctness of our ideas, so he agrees with him, against Descartes, over the explanation of error. There is no room for the individual will in Leibniz's system. Appetition is only the impulse that provides the development of the monad's perceptions; it in no way corresponds to the will. Error is merely a matter of having confused ideas, and since these are correlated with passivity, the passive aspects of mental life—sense perception and the like—are the source of error.

Innate ideas. Yet although Leibniz can distinguish between ideas of perception and ideas of reason, or the understanding, it remains true that according to his view in a sense all ideas are innate. None is literally produced by things affecting our sense organs. Yet the distinction between ideas in terms of their clarity and distinctness does mean that it is possible to say that some ideas are what Kant called a priori—in no way derived from the senses. These are ideas such as those of mathematics, and

Leibniz criticized his empiricist adversary Locke for failing to take sufficient account of these ideas. Indeed, to the empiricist principle that there is nothing in the intellect that was not first in the senses Leibniz replied, "Except the intellect itself."

Rationalism generally tends to emphasize the part played by the intellect in contradistinction to that played by the senses. It holds that real knowledge is that provided by the intellect, for only there is the certainty which knowledge requires. Moreover, it is by means of the disciplines that are peculiarly the province of the intellect that knowledge is to be obtained and preserved.

BRITISH EMPIRICISM

In general, empiricism stands in opposition to rationalism both in its views about the main source of our ideas and in its views concerning the source of true knowledge. Thus, it is often, historically speaking, a reaction against rationalism. The so-called British empiricists of the seventeenth and eighteenth centuries, however, were empiricists only in tendency. The first, Locke, was a complete empiricist concerning the source of our ideas, but he was often a rationalist in allowing other than empirical knowledge. Locke's new way of ideas, as it was called, was an attempt to show that all the materials for knowledge are derived from sense experience. Locke did not claim, however, that all knowledge was founded on experience in any other sense. George Berkeley, who carried on Locke's new way of ideas and even sharpened some of Locke's claims, especially on the subject of abstract ideas, was fundamentally a metaphysician with a special way of looking at the world. David Hume, the last of the trio, claimed to introduce the experimental method into philosophy, following in the steps of Newton, and of the three he had by far the best right to be counted an empiricist. Indeed, his empiricism led him extremely close to skepticism concerning a number of claims to knowledge; such skepticism, he believed, could be avoided only by "inattention" to philosophical issues. But all three of these philosophers were united in their opposition to any doctrine of innate ideas.

LOCKE. Book I of Locke's *Essay concerning Human Understanding* is devoted to an attack on the doctrine of innate ideas, and the positive doctrine begins only in Book II. At the outset Locke (1632–1704) had claimed that he was following the "historical plain method," the object of which was to "set down any measures of the certainty of our knowledge." This historical plain method consists in classifying our different ideas and plotting their source as a prelude to an assessment of claims to different kinds of knowledge. Despite appearances this is not a psychological method; it is a method of philosophical analysis designed to discover the logical character of different ideas. In this way Locke distinguishes between ideas of sense and ideas of reflection. Ideas of reflection result from the operation of the mind itself upon ideas of the sense. There is no other source of ideas.

Locke also distinguishes between simple and complex ideas of both kinds, complex ideas being formed by the mind in compounding simple ideas. He seems to think that what it is to have a simple idea of sense is fairly obvious; it is to be aware of a particular quality of an object mediated by a single sense. The criterion of simplicity was, however, a problem for all British empiricists. In having simple ideas the mind is passive, but some activity is allowable in the forming of complex ideas.

Primary and secondary qualities. Among simple ideas of sense Locke makes an important distinction—already implicit in Descartes and others—between ideas of primary and ideas of secondary qualities. Primary qualities, such as bulk, number, figure, and motion, are, Locke thinks, inseparable from the bodies in which they are found. Bodies could not exist without them. Secondary qualities, such as color, sound, and taste, are, on the other hand, "nothing in the objects themselves but powers to produce the various sensations in us by their primary qualities." In other words, the primary qualities of things produce sensations in our minds that are ideas of secondary qualities, but "secondary quality" is a misnomer to the extent that there is really no such quality in things. Thus, our ideas of primary qualities actually correspond to the things that produce them, whereas our ideas of secondary qualities, although produced by things, resemble nothing in those things, being purely subjective. Locke brings forward a number of arguments for this conclusion, arguments based mainly on the assimilation of our perception of secondary qualities to sensations of pain. That is, he takes the perception of, for example, warmth or color to be the same kind of thing as feeling pain.

Account of perception. He thinks of perception in general as identical with merely having sensations, and he thus fully embraces the causal theory of perception according to which perceiving is having sensations caused by things. He goes further than this in respect to primary qualities, for here he also accepts the representative theory of perception according to which our ideas represent the things that cause them. This theory, as we have seen, was the stock in trade of seventeenth-century philosophy.

Like most theorists of this pattern, Locke can give no good reason for the view that any of our ideas resemble their causes, and he cannot take the rationalist course of appealing to an intellectual intuition of some properties of things. It is a fair guess that he, like Descartes and others, was influenced by the success of physical science in maintaining that physical properties like extension—properties which are measurable—are *the* properties of things. There is also the connected fact that these properties are perceptible by more than one sense, as Aristotle had noted in his theory of common sensibles.

Modes, substances, and relations. Complex ideas may be exhaustively subdivided into ideas of modes, substances, and relations. Ideas of modes are ideas of things that depend on substances for their existence—for example, the idea of a triangle or a murder. Ideas of substances are ideas of particular things taken as existing by themselves—the complex idea of substance, he goes on to say, consists mostly of powers. Ideas of relation, finally, result from a comparison of one idea with another. Locke came to have some dissatisfaction with this classification of complex ideas, and in the fourth edition of the *Essay* he introduces a fourfold classification of ideas—simple ideas, complex ideas, ideas of relation, and general ideas. However this may be—and there is room for dissatisfaction with Locke's second classification, too—all ideas other than simple ones are in some way formed by the mind out of simple ideas.

Locke classified ideas of space, time, and number as ideas of modes. That is to say that they are ideas of entities which depend for their existence on particular things. We build up our ideas of these entities out of our ideas of particular things when seen in the appropriate relations. Kant later showed that such a view of the source of our ideas of space and time was untenable; Leibniz commented on the fact that Locke failed to take account of the a priori nature of the ideas of space and time and attributed the failure to Locke's inexperience with mathematics.

Locke maintained that our ideas of physical substances are mostly ideas of powers and that the idea of power is an idea of another mode. Since what we know of physical substances is largely due to their effects on us or on other substances, ideas of physical substances all mainly ideas of power. The effects, Locke thinks, are due to the motions of the invisible parts of things, but owing to the weakness of our senses, we are unable to perceive the nature of these causes. We have little or no knowledge of the "real essences" of things. What we do know of things is of their "nominal essences"—their nature merely in respect of the classifications into which we fit them. Such classifications may not correspond to the real nature of things. Here Locke clearly shows how much he was influenced by the physical sciences. He thought that classifications show the way to the nature of things, but that owing to the weakness of our senses, we are unable to do more than gain a general impression of the nature of those physical processes. Therefore, we have to be content with an ordering of things according to their effects rather than as they are themselves.

Theory of general words. Locke adds to the account of ideas a discussion of language and of the words corresponding to the various ideas. It is in the context of this discussion that he puts forward his theory of the meaning of general words, a theory that was to come under attack from Berkeley. This theory—that the meaning of general words is given by the general or abstract ideas to which they correspond—is in effect Locke's theory of universals. He expresses the problem by asking, "Since all things that exist are only particulars, how come we by general terms; or where find we those general natures they are supposed to stand for?" His answer is that words are general by being signs of general ideas, and we form general ideas by abstraction, "separating from them the circumstances of time and place, and any other ideas that may determine them to this or that particular existence." Thus, words become capable of representing a number of individuals by standing for an abstract idea. Locke's view is therefore a form of conceptualism in that the universal or general element lies in our ideas or concepts, not in anything nonmental. Given a liberal enough interpretation of the word *idea*, there is perhaps no great difficulty in understanding what Locke is getting at, although the implication that the meaning of words must always consist in their standing for something (in this case an abstract idea) is certainly wrong. The idea terminology is a vague one, common though it was in the seventeenth and eighteenth centuries, but most of those who employed it would have denied that ideas were simple images of things. Moreover, such an interpretation is far from consistent with much that Locke says about ideas. Nevertheless, the use of the term "abstract idea" is not without its difficulties, especially since Locke says that such ideas must represent things.

Kinds of knowledge. In his account of ideas and their classification Locke is the strict empiricist, maintaining that all ideas must be ultimately derived from simple ideas of sense, either directly or as a result of the operations of the mind upon these. His account of knowledge, given in the last book of the *Essay*, is less empiricist in

character; indeed, it owes an obvious debt to Cartesianism. He begins with the claim that knowledge is nothing but "the perception of the connexion of and agreement or disagreement and repugnancy of any of our ideas." This agreement or disagreement can be classified into four kinds: (1) identity or diversity, (2) relation, (3) coexistence or necessary connection, and (4) real existence. It is the fourth kind which presents the difficulties. How can the knowledge of the existence of a thing be a matter of the perception of the agreement or disagreement between our ideas alone? This could be so only if our knowledge of the existence of things could be a priori. Locke thinks that some knowledge of this sort can be shown to be a priori, but it is knowledge of the existence of sensible things that presents the greatest difficulties.

Locke distinguishes between three degrees of knowledge in a manner which is reminiscent of Spinoza's distinction between the three kinds of knowledge. There is, first, intuitive knowledge; second, demonstrative knowledge; and, third, "sensitive" knowledge of particular finite existences. The last Locke adds almost as an afterthought on the ground that it has by no means the certainty that belongs to the first two, although it goes beyond mere probability and is commonly thought of as knowledge. (Locke's conception of the standard to which knowledge must attain is noteworthy here.) Apart from the different degrees of certainty that are to be attached to these kinds of knowledge, they also differ in that intuitive and demonstrative knowledge can be concerned with relations between ideas (we can see that white is not black, and we can reason from one idea to another) but sensitive knowledge is concerned only with the existence of the objects of ideas. This is not to say that there cannot be intuitive and demonstrative knowledge of existence, too. Locke thinks that we have intuitive knowledge of our own existence (compare Descartes's *cogito*) and demonstrative knowledge of God's existence (by means of a version of the Cosmological Argument; Locke distrusts the Ontological Argument). But how can the existence of anything be known from ideas alone? Locke sometimes appears to say that such knowledge consists in the perception of the agreement of certain of our ideas with the idea of existence, but in general he acknowledges that more is required than this—real existence and not merely conceived existence. The difficulties here are especially evident in connection with sensible knowledge.

Existence of external world. In Book IV of the *Essay* Locke tries to justify the claim that we have knowledge of the existence of particular sensible things by showing that our ideas do correspond to the things that cause them.

Whereas complex ideas may not always correspond to things because of the part played by the mind in forming them, simple ideas receive no contribution from the mind; they are entirely passive. Unfortunately, it does not follow from this that they are necessarily veridical. He adduces further considerations, stressing the passivity of the mind in receiving ideas and the way in which the senses may cohere in their reports. None of these considerations is really sufficient, and Locke admits that they do not amount to proof. In fact, by simultaneously embracing a general empiricist approach and a representative theory of perception, Locke cannot provide a guarantee of, or even any general argument for, the veridicality of the senses. He cannot provide any independent access to the objects of perception other than that provided by the senses themselves. Like most empiricists, Locke accepts the correspondence theory of truth in that the truth of a proposition consists in its correspondence to the facts. (Truth, he says, signifies "the joining or separating of signs, as the things signified by them do agree or disagree one with another.") But he has no general warrant for the belief in the correspondence of ideas to things.

BERKELEY. The main aim of Bishop Berkeley (1685–1753), as he conceived it, was to defend common sense and religion against skepticism and atheism. But both his metaphysics and his theory of knowledge, connected as they are, can be partially regarded as attempts to rid Locke's theory of impurities. Locke's view of the world involved, besides minds and their contents (ideas), material substances, for the most part unknowable. Berkeley wished to get rid of material substances precisely because they were unknowable. In his view the existence of material objects consists only in their being perceived; their *esse* is *percipi* (their existence is to be perceived). In consequence, they must be regarded as complexes of ideas whose cause cannot be any substance underlying them but must be a spirit, the only active thing. Some of our ideas may be caused by ourselves qua spirits, but insofar as ideas have what we normally think of as an objective order, they must be caused by the supreme spirit, God. The laws of nature according to which ideas are ordered are guaranteed by God, and our ordinary way of looking at and talking about the world obscures this fact. Berkeley therefore thought that it was necessary to rid Locke's views of those elements which prevented this insight. The main issues concerned the notion of substance as the cause of our ideas, with the connected doctrine of the distinction between primary and secondary qualities. Berkeley also found fault with Locke's doctrine of abstract ideas, partly for its own sake but also because he thought it one of the main supports for the doctrine of substance. We might, that is, have an idea of substance by abstraction; it had to be shown that this was impossible.

Knowledge of the external world. At first, in the *New Theory of Vision*, a work on both optics and philosophy, Berkeley maintained that physical objects are primarily objects of touch. Vision, he asserted, could provide us with no direct perception of the distance of things, for the retina of the eye is only a two-dimensional surface. Our sensations of sight (and, like others of his time, Berkeley thought that perception fundamentally consists in having sensations) can only be of expanses of color. When we perceive things as at a distance from us, what really happens is that the visual sensations which we have suggest to us certain ideas derived originally from touch and connected with the visual sensations by experience. The *New Theory of Vision* consists largely in the working out of this theory in detail. Berkeley came to see, however, that there was no reason for making this distinction between sight and touch. All senses should be alike in these respects. Insofar as we have knowledge of what we take to be physical things, it is because we have, as the result of experience, so connected ideas that having certain sensations or ideas suggests other sensations or ideas. These ideas make up a collection that we identify as an object. Thus, for Berkeley objects are, in some sense, identical with collections of ideas.

In the beginning of the main part of his *Principles of Human Knowledge*, Berkeley flirts with the view, now known as phenomenalism, that all we mean when we say, for example, that there is a table in our study when we are not there is that if we were there, we should perceive it. But he adds as an alternative the suggestion that what we mean is that "some other spirit actually does perceive it," and this is his main view. What we ordinarily take to be things are really bundles of ideas in some spirit's mind; they have a certain stability even when we are not perceiving them because God still is. Indeed, it is God's having ideas according to a certain order that guarantees the order of our ideas.

Sensations and ideas generally (for although sensations are, strictly speaking, one species of idea, Berkeley often uses the terms interchangeably) are entirely passive. Their *esse* is *percipi*. On the other hand, spirits—God or ourselves—can be active. We cannot have ideas of spirits, although we have a notion of them, since we can understand the word *spirit* and at least know that we are the source of some of our ideas. There is no room in this for any substance's underlying our ideas, since we have no idea of such a thing. Furthermore, the special place that

Locke had given to primary qualities—that of being the properties essential to material substance—is untenable, and if what Locke said about secondary qualities is right, there are no grounds for making any distinction between them and primary qualities. They are equally dependent on the mind, so that if secondary qualities are subjective (and Berkeley accepts and adds to Locke's arguments for this conclusion), they must all be. All qualities are ideas in the mind.

Theory of universals. Berkeley's fiercest attack upon Locke was directed against his doctrine of abstract ideas. Berkeley interpreted Locke as asserting the existence of ideas or images that possess contradictory properties. The abstract idea of a triangle must be simultaneously scalene, isosceles, and equilateral. This is clearly impossible. It is doubtful whether Berkeley is right in this interpretation, but he clearly thought that if such ideas were admitted, there could be little objection to the admission of the idea of substance, too—that is, the idea of a physical but in principle imperceptible object.

In the place of abstract ideas, Berkeley introduced a theory of universals that was nominalist in character. Universals are merely particular ideas that are representative of other ideas in the same class in the way in which a particular man may be representative of other men; hence, their universality lies only in their power of representation. There is no need to assume the existence of general ideas since general words need not correspond to general ideas in order to have meaning. In other words, Berkeley challenged the theory of meaning that asserts that all words are names and refer to something—*unum nomen, unum nominatum* (one name, one thing named), as the Scholastics put it. In his view general words stand for a number of particular ideas belonging to the same class. General words are different from names in that general words represent a number of things indifferently. It must be confessed, however, that it is difficult to see clearly what, according to Berkeley's view, is involved in understanding a general word. Certainly, it involves having an idea which indifferently represents a whole class of things, but what is it to see that it does so?

Refutation of skepticism. Berkeley's general view has certain consequences. It means, for example, that important sections of mathematics have to be abandoned. There must, Berkeley believed, be a least perceptible size. Since all our ideas are ultimately derived from sensations, there can be no ideas of infinitesimals or points. For the most part, however, Berkeley considers himself to be defending common sense against the attacks of the metaphysicians. The vulgar, he maintains, believe that "those

things they immediately perceive are the real things" (that is, not imperceptible substance), but philosophers believe that "the things immediately perceived are ideas which exist only in the mind." Berkeley characterizes his own view as the joining of these two notions in that he equated real things and ideas. He thinks that given his view that ideas, which are the objects of immediate perception, are the real things, there is no room for doubt concerning the real nature of things—a doubt which Locke had expressed. Moreover, since what is immediately perceived is by definition free from error, only the wrong use of ideas in judgment can give rise to error. Error is thus a product of the imagination. Insofar as we rely upon our sense perceptions as directly given, we must be free from error. Thus, Berkeley claims, his view prevents skepticism and "gives certainty to knowledge."

Concept of knowledge. Apart from the reference to God and spirits, Berkeley is a strict empiricist not only in the sense that he believes that all the materials for knowledge are derived from sense perception (as Locke, too, believed) but also in the sense that knowledge is itself founded on sense perception. Locke was not such a complete empiricist; he thought that knowledge in the strict sense is founded on intuition and demonstration, and he made skepticism possible to a certain extent over sense perception because he thought that its veridicality could not be completely shown. According to Berkeley, knowledge derived from reasoning must ultimately be founded on knowledge based on sense perception. Sense perception, in turn, is no longer conceived of as having ideas that are produced by objects and may not always represent their causes.

Berkeley has given up the representative theory of perception with its assumption that something so underlies our ideas that they may be representative of it. His rejection of the representative theory of perception is the basis of his claim to combat skepticism. Yet, as Hume asserted, it has often seemed a claim that fails to produce conviction, because the claim that what is directly perceived is free from error is true by definition. The question of how we know when we have direct perception still remains, however. Not all ideas are objects of immediate or direct perception; some are ideas of the imagination. According to Berkeley, these are less regular, vivid, and constant than ideas of perception, and they are more "dependent on the spirit"; they can be distinguished from ideas of sense by these criteria. But are all ideas of perceptible things ideas of things immediately perceived, and if not, how do we tell which are?

In the first of the three *Dialogues between Hylas and Philonous*, Berkeley argues that by sight we immediately perceive only light, colors, and figures; by hearing, only sounds; by taste, only tastes; by smell, only odors; and by touch, only tangible qualities. Here he appears to be arguing from the premise that these things are the special or proper objects of the senses. Although it is difficult to know what, if anything, is special to sight and touch, it is easy to see what is meant in the case of the other senses. Even if we grant that we hear only sounds, taste only tastes, and smell only odors, it does not follow, however, that we cannot be mistaken about the characteristics of these objects in particular instances. Are we necessarily free from error in hearing when we hear that a sound is loud or soft?

Nor is our attribution of colors necessarily free from inference as it should be if the perception of color is immediate. What, then, really counts as an object of immediate perception? In answering this question, Berkeley is subject to the same difficulties that have beset more modern philosophers when they have sought to base the philosophy of perception on the notion of sense data. If the foundations of knowledge are found in the deliverances of the senses, there must be certain perceptions that are incorrigible in the sense that they cannot logically be subject to doubt. But what counts as incorrigible perception? Berkeley tries to answer this question by assimilating perception to having bare sensations. Sensations, however, are not the sort of thing that can be right or wrong. The mere passivity of sensation, as opposed to the will, does not show that error arises from the will. If this criticism is valid, Berkeley's theory does not satisfactorily prevent skepticism in the way that he supposes.

HUME. Locke thought that his inquiry had revealed the limitations of the understanding by showing that there are parts of nature that our senses cannot discern. Berkeley, on the other hand, thought that there was nothing which our understanding could not grasp. Sense perception gives us complete knowledge of reality, and we have in addition notions of spirits, including God. Indeed, we could regard our ideas as a sort of divine language by means of which God speaks to us, so that our senses, if viewed correctly, continually reveal the glories of God. Hume (1711–1776) agreed with Berkeley in thinking that there is nothing in nature that lies beyond the reach of our senses, but, contrary to Berkeley, Hume reached the conclusion that our understanding is very limited and that skepticism is the only reasonable attitude toward knowledge. That Hume was intentionally a skeptic has been disputed, but there is no doubt that this is the logi-cal outcome of his views. He thought that whatever Berkeley's claims, his arguments were in fact skeptical: "They admit of no answer and produce no conviction." In effect, therefore, Hume's position is that of following the principles of empiricism to their conclusion without any ancillary claim to knowledge of the inner workings of nature or of God. His conclusions are also something of a *reductio ad absurdum* of empiricism.

Nature of ideas. Hume begins by drawing a sharp distinction between impressions and ideas, impressions being the perceptions of sense and ideas the perceptions of the imagination or memory. In this he claims to be restoring the term *idea* to its original use. Every simple idea must have a corresponding impression—the idea of red, for example, resembling the impression of red—and complex ideas may be formed out of simple ideas. As with Locke, both impressions and ideas may be divided into those of sense and those of reflection, impressions and ideas of reflection being impressions and ideas of the mind's reflection on impressions or ideas of sense.

The criteria of the simplicity of an impression or idea are as much a problem here as with Locke. To have a simple impression is to have an elementary perception that cannot be further broken down into other perceptions, and this will function as a building block out of which the rest of knowledge may be constructed. Hume takes very strictly the principle that to every simple idea or perception of imagination or memory there must correspond an impression, or perception of sense, although at the very outset he admits a possible exception in the idea of a color in a series. We may have the idea of such a color from the principle of a series without ever having seen it. This possible exception, however, Hume refuses to take as important.

The principle that every simple idea must correspond to an impression is vital for a delimitation of the understanding and as a weapon against rationalism. Impressions and ideas can, however, be distinguished only by the superior force and vivacity of impressions; they cannot be distinguished in terms of their relations to physical objects or minds, for our knowledge of physical objects is derived solely from impressions, if at all. Likewise, among ideas, ideas of memory have a superior liveliness to ideas of the imagination. It is extremely doubtful whether this is always true, and this, in turn, casts doubt on any attempt to characterize remembering and imagining on empiricist lines by reference to the contents of the mind alone.

Theory of universals. Hume follows Berkeley in his theory of abstract ideas or universals. In his view there are no abstract ideas, strictly speaking; however, ideas can be particular in their nature and general in their representation. Hume's only addition to Berkeley's account is his attempt to indicate how this can happen through the association of ideas. The occurrence of one idea may dispose the mind to call up all other ideas associated with it. Hence, the understanding of a general word lies in the disposition of the mind to have the ideas of those things to which it may be applied. This is not a very plausible account in itself since the notion of understanding cannot be analyzed in terms of habits or dispositions of minds, but it is at least an attempt to tackle the problem. The solution is in accord with Hume's general approach; his account of belief is similar.

Space and time are difficult notions for an empiricist to deal with, for, as Kant pointed out, particular phenomena seem to presuppose space and time rather than vice versa. Hence, it is difficult to see how our ideas of space and time can be derived from our ideas of particular phenomena. Locke had nevertheless classified our ideas of space and time as ideas of modes. Hume attempts to deal with our perception of spatial extension and temporal duration in terms of the order in which impressions or ideas appear. But in consequence he has to admit that ultimately the impressions that are ordered in this way cannot themselves be extended or of extended objects, nor can they take time. In general, Hume's treatment of space and time is one of the more puzzling parts of his work.

Causality. Hume's greatest reputation derives from his treatment of causality, although his approach to this subject is similar to his approach to the problem of our knowledge of the external world or of ourselves. His approach is founded upon a distinction between different kinds of relation. There are "relations of ideas," which depend completely on the ideas related, and factual relations, which can be changed without changing the ideas. This is a distinction between logical and matter-of-fact relations, and it leads to a distinction between logical truths and factual truths that parallels Leibniz's. Hume is interested in the causal relation because he believes that it is the only matter-of-fact relation that can lead us from one idea to another. Causality is not a logical or a priori connection, but it is a connection. This assertion is of the utmost importance. Why, however, do we think that there is some necessity in causal connections? It cannot be a logical necessity; also, it cannot be derived from a more general necessity such as might be provided by a principle of universal causality, for Hume believes that such a principle must be contingent and that the evidence for it

must be derived from our knowledge of particular causal connections.

He therefore proposes to "beat about the neighbouring fields." He notes that we generally take a cause to be antecedent to its effect and contiguous to it in space. More important, in experience there is a constant conjunction between cause and effect. In a sense these factors provide the basis for our belief in the necessity of the causal connection. Hume takes belief to be a lively idea associated with a present impression, and here the principles of the association of ideas again play a part. What makes an idea a belief is the feeling of being determined by habit or custom to pass from the impression to the associated idea. This feeling is an impression of reflection. It is in such an impression that Hume finds the source of our idea of necessary connection between cause and effect, for the "experimental method"—the resort to experience—should show us that there is no impression of power as such. It is due to habit or custom that we pass from cause to effect, and our belief in the necessity of doing so arises from the impression of a reflection of being determined to do it.

It is important to note just what Hume has achieved here. He has not in any way justified our belief in the necessity of the causal connection; he has merely attempted to explain the origin of the belief by giving a psychological explanation, not a philosophical justification, of the belief. But he has rejected all theories of occult powers in things, so that in one sense he may be considered to have said that what we mean by calling one thing the cause of another is that it is a uniform and contiguous antecedent of another event. To this extent his account is a reductive analysis; he analyzes our notion of cause by reducing it to notions that we understand. Yet Hume can find no justification for inferring the occurrence of one event from that of another; certainly, one event does not logically imply the occurrence of the other, but what other justification is there? Hume's conception of justification fails just because he recognizes no other kind of justification except that one thing logically implies another. Although Hume is commonly said to have raised the problem of induction, he made no real attempt to solve it himself, nor could he within his framework.

Knowledge of the external world. In Hume's account of knowledge of the external world the skepticism already implicit in his account of causality comes to the fore. Like Berkeley, Hume distinguishes between the beliefs of the "vulgar" and of the "philosophical system." The vulgar believe that we are aware of perceptions only, but they also believe that some of them—our perceptions of primary and secondary qualities—have permanent existence. The philosophical system holds that there is a distinction between objects and perceptions and that only objects are permanent. Hume claims to side with the vulgar, but he sees no reason to distinguish any perception from any other. The mind is like a theater in which scenes come and go. Yet he does admit that it is natural to believe in a world of permanent objects. Reason can provide no justification of this belief, but we can give a psychological explanation of it like the account of our belief in the necessity of causality.

Our impressions have a certain coherence and constancy—that is, they fit together and recur in the same order after intervals. As a result, the imagination tends to carry on by custom or habit, and it attributes more regularity to objects of perception than they actually possess. Thus, we come to believe in a world of permanent objects, and we tend to reconcile what reason tells us of the interrupted nature of perceptions and what our imagination suggests about their regularity by a "philosophical" (as opposed to a commonsense) belief in a world of permanently existing objects. Nevertheless, a "direct and total opposition betwixt our reason and our senses" remains. Hume often speaks as if objects were just bundles of perceptions, but he has to deal with the belief that they are more than this. For such a belief he can give no justification, although he offers an explanation of its origin. In the last resort he can only recommend inattention to both our senses and our understanding. This is nothing if not skepticism.

Personal identity. Very much the same account is given of our knowledge of ourselves, a fact which may seem even more paradoxical. Once again, Hume uses the appeal to experience to indicate that we have no impression of the self. He rejects once and for all Berkeley's suggestion that we have a notion of the self. Belief in the self must therefore be parallel to belief in an external world, and Hume proceeds similarly. Belief in our identity through time must result once again from the coherence and constancy that exists between our impressions and ideas, as a result of which the imagination takes them to be impressions and ideas of a single self. Once again, however, no reason can be given for this belief, a fact that worried Hume more than his other tendencies toward skepticism. He returned to the topic in an appendix to the *Treatise of Human Nature*, but in the end he could find no way of ridding himself of his worry except a game of backgammon and a good dinner.

Account of perception. Hume rejected Lockean substance, with the result that perceptions—impressions and ideas—become the substantial entities in his ontology (as he in effect admits in *Treatise*, Book I, Part 4, Ch. 5). In retaining the terminology of perceptions, especially that of impressions, Hume clung to the skeleton of the causal or representative theory of perception. But the skeleton no longer had flesh, despite the suggestiveness of the terminology. Thus, Hume is forced to take his starting point from perceptions that are logically independent of any owner and any object. In one place he says that there is nothing objectionable in the idea of an unperceived perception—a very odd notion. From this he has to build a world that fits the common supposition that there are physical objects and persons. The premises from which Hume derives his position are unacceptable, but given them, he can provide no reason whatsoever for belief in such a world and has to say that the belief is just a product of the imagination. This is skepticism with a vengeance, but it is the logical outcome of his approach.

REID'S CRITICISM. Hume's contemporary Thomas Reid (1710–1796) thought, rightly enough, that Hume's conclusions were manifestly absurd. Finding nothing wrong with the arguments presented by Hume, he concluded that the fault must lie in the premises and proceeded to attack the whole "way of ideas" which was the source of these premises. Reid maintained that it was necessary to make a strict distinction between sensation and perception, a distinction that the doctrine of impressions and ideas blurred. Reid was quite right about this, and his account of the nature of sensation and perception is interesting for its own sake. Sensation, he said, is an act of the mind that has no object distinct from that act, its prototype being pain. Perception is a much more complicated affair, involving a conception of an object and a belief in its existence. In many cases we fail to note the distinction because most of our perceptions are accompanied by sensations. Sensations provide in themselves no basis for inference about the nature of perceived qualities of things, although things cause the sensations. Reid expresses the relation between perception and sensations by saying that the sensations suggest the perceptions; sensations are natural signs of perceived qualities. This suggestion and the sign relationship involved are not a matter of experience, for we do not experience sensations in the same way that we perceive things (to have a sensation is not to perceive anything in itself). The relationship is a natural one like, he says, that between expressions of emotions and the emotions themselves.

Whatever the worth of this account, it is certainly a completely different analysis of perception from that of other philosophers of the period. In claiming to defend our ordinary beliefs by this account against the skepticism introduced by Hume, Reid set himself up as a philosopher of common sense, a position adopted by G. E. Moore in the twentieth century. Reid did retain some of the features of British empiricism, however, especially in a distinction between original and derived perceptions, a distinction that is in some respects very similar to that between simple and complex ideas or impressions. Moore similarly employed much of the apparatus of sense data invoked by modern empiricists.

KANT

Kant (1724–1804) represents the juncture of seventeenth-century rationalism and British empiricism. Brought up in the tradition of post-Leibnizian rationalism, he was, as he put it, awakened from his dogmatic slumber as a result of a reading of Hume. His critical philosophy, as expressed in the *Critique of Pure Reason*, can be characterized as an attempt to draw the boundaries between the proper use of the understanding and the improper use of reason in making assertions of speculative metaphysics and as an attempt to show how the understanding can provide objectively valid knowledge of those things which Hume left to the imagination.

CLASSIFICATION OF JUDGMENTS. Kant bases his approach upon a twofold distinction between types of judgment. There is, first, a distinction between a priori and a posteriori judgments, the first being judgments whose truth can be known independently of experience, the second being judgments whose truth can be known only through experience. A priori judgments are pure when they involve only concepts that are themselves independent of experience. On the other hand, it is not a necessary condition of a judgment's being a priori that it should involve only such concepts. The concepts that are involved in a posteriori judgments, however, must be derived from experience, must be empirical.

The second distinction, that between analytic and synthetic judgments, is different. Analytic judgments are judgments about a thing that give no information about the thing, although they may serve to analyze or explain the concepts involved. This is because the concept of the predicate is contained, albeit covertly or obscurely, in the concept of the subject. The denial of these judgments involves a contradiction; hence, they correspond to what Leibniz called truths of reason. Synthetic judgments, on the other hand, do give information about a thing; in them the concept of the predicate is not included in that of the subject, and their denial does not involve a contradiction.

Kant now combines the two distinctions. Analytic a posteriori judgments are clearly impossible, but there is no difficulty, Kant thinks, about analytic a priori judgments or about synthetic a posteriori judgments. There remains the class of synthetic a priori judgments. It is on these, Kant thinks, that the claims for metaphysics rest, and it is these in particular that empiricists refuse to admit. Kant's program is to show whether and to what extent such judgments exist. The outcome of the program is that although metaphysics in the traditional sense is impossible, synthetic a priori judgments are admissible—first, in mathematics and, second, in the form of the presuppositions of objective experience or science. This program, which constitutes the critical philosophy, is Kant's substitute for traditional metaphysics.

SYNTHETIC A PRIORI KNOWLEDGE. The possibility of synthetic a priori knowledge means that not all knowledge about things can be derived from experience. Nevertheless, Kant thinks that all such knowledge is based on experience. It starts from what he calls intuitions, but since knowledge involves the possibility of making judgments about things, it cannot consist of intuitions alone; it must also involve concepts. To have a sensible intuition is to have a simple awareness of something by means of the senses. This awareness Kant analyzes in a way that derives much from the British empiricists. A sensible intuition consists, first, of a sensation as the content of the intuition. Its form consists of spatial or temporal extension. Hume had to admit that impressions have an order, but he drew the consequence that the impressions themselves were unextended and nontemporal when at their simplest. Kant generally argues that sensations have only intensive qualities, qualities that can vary only in degree. Nevertheless, since the intuition consists of the sensation plus the form—that is, its relations to other sensations—spatiotemporal form is something which is a necessary part of our experience. One cannot, as Locke seemed to suppose, build up ideas of extension from first impressions. Spatiotemporal form is a necessary, a priori characteristic of experience.

Since Kant, however, has assumed a theory of perception similar to the representative theory, this a priori spatiotemporal form applies only to things as they appear to us—to phenomena. It does not apply to whatever may be thought to lie behind our experiences (things-in-themselves). This fact Kant expresses by saying that spatial and temporal characteristics (and primary qualities in general) are empirically real but transcendentally ideal. The characteristics in question are not merely subjective; they are objective—valid for all men—but only in relation to phenomena, not to things-in-themselves. (Throughout, Kant's criterion of objectivity is the criterion of intersubjectivity—validity for all men; he is pointing out that from the point of view of the critical philosophy something may be objective in this sense without being a feature of something independent of the mind.)

Pure a priori intuitions. Kant goes on to argue that we have not only a sensible intuition involving a priori spatiotemporal features but also a pure a priori intuition of space and time themselves. It is by virtue of this that the science of mathematics is possible. In order to do geometry, for example, it must be possible to make constructions in space, an idea that presupposes that we have an intuition of space. (Kant insists that this is an intuition, not a concept, but his reasons for this are complex and difficult to understand.) Arithmetic similarly presupposes an intuition of time. It is for this reason that mathematical judgments are both synthetic a priori and possible. Kant took it for granted that Euclidean geometry was *the* geometry of space, so that his account provided the justification of that geometry. It has often been suggested that the discovery of other geometries has undermined his case, and to some extent it has. But Kant would still have insisted that some intuition of space is a necessary condition of the possibility of any geometry, and there is something to be said for this position. Our concepts of space and time are not concepts that can be simply abstracted from experience.

CATEGORIES OF UNDERSTANDING. Space and time, then, provide the form of all experience, just as sensation provides the content. What is given in this way must be subsumed under concepts in judgment if knowledge is to result. "Thoughts without content," Kant says, "are empty, intuitions without concepts are blind." But in itself the formation of judgments is not enough for knowledge. The judgments that we make might be just the work of the imagination, as Hume in effect supposed in considering our knowledge of the external world. What criteria, then, have to be observed in the case of objectively valid judgments? Kant's answer is that such judgments have to conform to certain principles of the understanding and that these principles are derived from the pure or formal concepts, which Kant calls categories, of the understanding. Only insofar as our judgments conform to these

principles can the judgments that we make about appearances be intersubjective, true for all men. Objectivity can be a question of this intersubjectivity alone because no valid judgments can be made about things-in-themselves. What, then, are these principles, and what are the categories?

In the section of the *Critique* known as the "Transcendental Analytic" Kant puts forward two arguments for categories. The first, the "metaphysical deduction," tries to argue for the existence of the categories directly, by finding the key to the list of categories in the traditional table of judgments provided by formal logic. To each of the traditional headings under which judgments can be classified logically, there corresponds, Kant believes, a concept that provides the principle of construction of an objectively valid judgment. The second argument the "transcendental deduction," attempts to show that the existence of categories of the understanding is a necessary condition of possible experience. The two arguments are complementary in that the transcendental deduction depends upon the metaphysical deduction for the actual list of categories, while the metaphysical deduction does not really show that categories are necessary to objective experience.

It is true that later, in discussing the principles derived from the categories, Kant brings forward specific arguments in each case, so that it might be said that the case for accepting each of these principles does not depend entirely on an acceptance of the metaphysical deduction. Yet, it is the metaphysical deduction alone that provides the guide to which categories and which principles we should seek. Today, the metaphysical deduction is almost universally rejected. There can be no validity in the attempt to derive a table of categories for objectively valid judgments from a table of judgments classified according to purely logical principles. It remains, therefore, that if the transcendental deduction is valid, it is possible to accept some categories as necessary, but apart from arguments for specific cases one cannot determine which categories are necessary by reference to any general rule.

Transcendental deduction. The argument of the transcendental deduction is very complex, and only the most general outline will be given here. First, the senses provide us with a manifold of sensations set out in space and time. Second, in order that they may form a unity, the understanding, with the aid of the imagination, has to synthesize them. The imagination helps us to see the manifold as a manifold in space, and in the form of memory it ensures that we also see it as a unity over a temporal period. Kant calls these two forms of synthesis the synthesis of apprehension and the synthesis of reproduction. Third, in the synthesis of recognition the manifold has to be given a principle of unity by subsumption under a concept, so that we see the manifold as a such-and-such. The results of this, however, could still be only subjective. In order to attain objective validity, the understanding must enable us to conceive of the manifold as united in an object. What Kant calls the transcendental unity of apperception is the awareness of experiences as part of one consciousness and as having an object, although neither the owner nor the object of those experiences can be found in the experiences as such. Objective experience presupposes these features; otherwise, the situation would be, as Hume in effect supposed, a mass of experiences whose connection with a person or objective world is merely contingent.

Fourth, the judgments we make about the manifold of experience thus unified must themselves conform to certain principles of unity. It must be possible, for example, to see certain connections within experience as that of ground to consequent, and our judgments must presuppose such connections in the things joined in them. Thus, we arrive at the idea that if objective experience is to be possible, it must conform to such categories as ground and consequent. The categories are concepts of the principles of connection of things in judgment, if that connection is to be more than a mere subjective one. They are categories because they are applicable to anything.

Transcendental judgment. The categories derived from the logical table of judgments according to the metaphysical deduction are purely formal. For example, Kant believes that the category of ground and consequent is derivable from the logical notion of a hypothetical judgment. This purely formal category of ground and consequent can be given content only by being applied to phenomena in such a way that it emerges in more material form in terms of the particular relation of ground and consequent that is applicable in the case of phenomena—that is, in terms of the relation of cause to effect. Kant formulated a doctrine of schematism to explain how we can apply the purely formal categories to experience. A schema is a kind of principle for the construction in the imagination of anything that falls under a given concept. It is that which enables us to identify a given object as an instance conforming to the concept. Thus, the schema for each of the categories can be thought of as the principle for the application of the pure category to phenomena in time. The notion of ground and consequent applied to

phenomena in time emerges, as we have seen, as the notion of cause and effect (an essentially temporal notion). It is only from these schematized categories that it is possible to derive the principles of the understanding according to which all objectively valid judgments must be viewed. These principles Kant discusses and argues for separately.

In all this Kant believes he has explained how judgments about mere phenomena can be objectively valid although they are confined to these phenomena. The judgments in question are by no means applicable to things-in-themselves, to whatever lies behind phenomena. Such notions as those of a world lying behind phenomena and of a real self that is aware of them are noumena, and as such they must be thought of as limiting concepts. To treat such concepts as if they were concepts of an ordinary kind and to use them in a systematization of knowledge, as is done in speculative metaphysics, is wrong and is liable to produce fallacies. A noumenon is merely a "nonphenomenon," and the concept of a noumenon is essentially a negative one, but reason tends to treat such concepts as positive, and from this the illusions of speculative metaphysics stem.

CRITIQUE OF METAPHYSICS. The judgments that the understanding allows us to make are conditional in that they are relative only to possible experience. Pure reason tends to assume an absolute, something unconditional, which provides the basis of the unity of all judgments of the understanding. It thus provides us with ideas whose proper use is only regulative, in that they are ideas of the goals or limits toward which the understanding may strive without being able to apply them directly to experience. To use these ideas, as speculative metaphysics does, as ideas under which we can directly subsume reality—such ideas as those of the absolute unity of the thinking subject, the absolute unity of the world in space and time, and the absolute unity of the conditions under which anything can be thought at all, the entity of entities or God—is the source of antinomies and other forms of contradiction or fallacy. Kant sets out to expound these contradictions and their resolutions in detail, but it is impossible to follow the argument here. The section of the *Critique* known as the "Transcendental Dialectic" is a critique of rational psychology, speculative cosmology, and metaphysical theology with its attempts at a demonstration of the existence of God. Although there is much other material in the *Critique*, this section essentially completes the critical philosophy in its attempt to show that the understanding can provide objectively valid knowledge of phenomena and to reveal the limitations of the proper use of the ideas of reason.

An assessment of Kant's work in the theory of knowledge is difficult to give. It contains many extraordinary insights, although their detailed development often leaves much to be desired. Above all, perhaps, it takes as its starting point the analysis of experience provided by the British empiricists, and this undoubtedly limits it.

POST-KANTIAN IDEALIST PHILOSOPHY

FICHTE. German philosophy after Kant is in many ways a commentary upon Kant's philosophy, either as further development or opposition. The idealism which was so characteristic of nineteenth-century philosophy was begun when Johann Gottlieb Fichte (1762–1814) found fault with the Kantian view of things-in-themselves that are beyond the reach of knowledge and proceeded to reject the notion on grounds similar to those which are commonly used against any causal or representative theory of perception—there can be no good reason for believing in such things. With the rejection of things-in-themselves, even as a limiting concept, we are left merely with experiences or phenomena, and it is of these that, in the idealist view, reality must consist. The general problem of idealism that Fichte thus introduced was how it was possible to distinguish among experiences those which are purely subjective and those which are really objective. The problem is how we can distinguish between what is contributed by the mind and what is not, between the self and not-self, as Fichte put it. In Kant's view objectivity was equivalent to validity for all people, but that it was at all possible to distinguish between what was due to the mind and what was not seemed guaranteed only by the existence of things-in-themselves. With the rejection of the latter, experiences and experiencer became only two sides of the same coin. For this reason the general trend of idealism was toward the coherence theory of truth—the view that experiences and judgments are true to the extent that they cohere with one another, forming a coherent system. This view was naturally associated with the doctrine of degrees of truth— that judgments have varying degrees of truth to the extent that they cohere with each other. This more or less intelligible view was, however, complicated by being involved with the view that judgments about the empirical world have a very low degree of truth because they bring with them paradox and contradiction. The sensible world is therefore only appearance, and reality must be something else.

HEGEL. The belief that the sensible world is only appearance is perhaps less marked in G. W. F. Hegel (1770–1831) than in some of his idealist successors—for example, F. H. Bradley. Hegel was influenced not only by Kant but also by Greek thought, especially by Platonist and Neoplatonist conceptions of an intelligible world of Forms with a structure of its own. Nevertheless, Hegel's relation to Kant may be roughly characterized by saying that he attempted to restore the functions of reason that Kant had forbidden. Whereas Kant had tried to justify the processes of the understanding while underlining the contradictions involved in an improper use of reason, Hegel tries to show that the understanding involves its own paradoxes, which can be resolved only by the use of reason; this, in Hegel's view, is by no means improper.

Dialectical method. Contradictions arise during the application of philosophical categories like those of the One and the many, so that the philosopher finds himself asserting both a thesis and its antithesis, in a manner similar to that expounded in Kant's antinomies. There is, Hegel thinks, a method which reason can pursue in order to resolve any such contradiction. Reason has to find a synthesis, some category that will reconcile those which produce the apparent contradiction. But the resolution may, in turn, find itself opposed to a further antithesis which demands another synthesis and so on. This method Hegel calls dialectic. According to him, it provides the key to understanding how the ideas of reason may be charted. In the end they will be seen to be dependent on the ultimate, absolute idea that provides the ground for everything else. Thus, the idea of something absolute and unconditional which Kant had rejected is restored.

It must be confessed, however, that as a method in the strict sense, Hegelian dialectic is sadly defective in that there appear to be no rules for its use. Hegel presents a series of insights, sometimes real, sometimes imaginary, into the relationships between very general and abstract philosophical ideas, like those of being and essence or consciousness, self-consciousness, and reason. Dialectic provides the architectonic according to which these relationships may be charted, and Hegel is excessively thoroughgoing in its use. The result—the Hegelian system—is a complete map of all forms of knowledge and of all philosophical ideas, constructed on a single plan. The attempt is ambitious; the ground for its validity, slender in the extreme. It would be foolish, however, to deny the incidental insights.

Theory of knowledge. Hegel's theory of knowledge may be found partly in his *Science of Logic* and partly in his *Phenomenology of Mind*. In the *Science of Logic* he explains his view of Kant, criticizing Kant's trust of the understanding and Kant's, to Hegel's own mind, undue restriction of the functions of reason. Then, through the dialectic he charts the notions most central to reason, beginning with the opposition between the categories of Being and Nothing, the synthesis of which he finds in Becoming. These are notions which reason finds indispensable for any account of the world and upon which logic must depend.

In the *Phenomenology* Hegel sets forth his view of perception most clearly. There Hegel begins by pointing out that consciousness appears to be an apprehension of what is immediate, of what *is*, which is, it appears, a confrontation of the ego with something else (as Fichte also supposed). But sense knowledge proper must involve a subsumption of this immediate consciousness under universals or concepts, and, moreover, there is no way of grasping the particular that is thus subsumed under concepts except by reference to other concepts. Proper names and even words like "this" are, in Hegel's view, general words, since they apply to a multitude of different things (Hegel here ignores or fails to appreciate the way in which they so apply); hence, they furnish us with no means of identifying a particular independently of universals. Sense knowledge thus turns out to be a mediated knowledge, a knowledge which is possible only through the medium of universals and which is not a direct knowledge of reality.

There is, however, Hegel argues, a contradiction between the fact that we take ourselves to perceive things which are unitary entities and the fact that our knowledge of them can exist only through a plurality of universals which are themselves unconnected. This contradiction is resolved only because the intellect provides us with a higher universal that constitutes the basis or condition for applying the lower-order universals in sense perception. This higher universal is force, the idea of "lawlikeness." The unity of the objects of perception is due to the lawlike connections that exist between the universals under which they are subsumed. This is something that can be discerned only by the intellect, which thus produces the synthesis of the contradictions apparent within consciousness. This, of course, does not end the matter for Hegel, as the phenomena of consciousness are equally phenomena of self-consciousness. The opposition between consciousness and self-consciousness requires a synthesis by reason.

BRADLEY. The kind of general argument that Hegel used can also be found in the English idealist Bradley (1846–1924), although he was far less attached to Hegel's method, referring to the dialectic as "the bloodless ballet of the categories." (In spite of being chronologically out of order, emphasis is placed on Bradley here because Bradley, although often difficult to understand, is generally easier than Hegel for English-speaking readers. The slight differences between Hegel and Bradley matter little in light of their essential similarity of purpose.) In his *Principles of Logic* Bradley argues that all judgments are only conditionally true in that the identification of the portion of reality which is their subject involves subsumption under universals. The judgment as a whole therefore says that some universal can be ascribed to reality only on condition that some other universal or universals may be ascribed to reality. All judgments, although categorical in that they are concerned with reality (reality being the subject of all judgments), are also hypothetical in this sense. Hypotheticals must likewise rest upon a ground; their truth is dependent upon connections within reality (Hegel's force).

In Bradley, however, there is greater emphasis on the idealism. For Bradley universals correspond to ideas, so that in judgment we are attaching an idea to reality. However, since what is known can be connections between ideas only, reality as we know it is a system of ideas joined by what he calls internal relations. A judgment is true to the extent that the ideas which it ascribes to reality cohere with the whole system of ideas. By an internal relation, as opposed to an external relation, Bradley means a relation that is more than a contingent one. The relations that form the system that constitutes what we know of reality are more than mere contingent relations, although they are not so close as to be logical entailments. All that we can know of reality apart from the ideas under which we subsume it is that it is experience; it is the bare fact of consciousness from which Hegel starts. Bradley is indeed Hegel made more palatable for English tastes.

It is only fair to add that in his most explicitly metaphysical work, *Appearance and Reality*, Bradley finds paradoxes in the notion of relations in general. The idea that two things may stand in a relation gives rise, he claims, to an infinite regress. What is relational must be set down as appearance only. It follows that judgment can never amount to absolute truth, for all judgment involves the setting of ideas in relation; all judgment, in other words, involves inference. No judgment can therefore furnish more than a limited degree of truth or be about something which has more than a limited degree of reality.

Judgments about the Absolute, the sum total of reality, may have a certain intellectual incorrigibility, since they will in effect ascribe to the absolute reality what is merely part of itself, but they cannot add up to truth itself. This is inevitable, since Bradley takes all judgment to be asserting the identity of subject and predicate, of reality and idea, while maintaining an unbridgeable gap between them—between the "that" and the "what," as he puts it. The notion of judgment therefore involves a contradiction in itself, and for this reason the understanding is condemned. Intuition or immediate awareness gives us the bare fact of experience as constituting reality. What it is unconditionally and absolutely only reason can tell us. Whereas Kant had maintained that reason can tell us nothing of what is absolute and unconditional and that only paradox can result from the attempt to make it do so, the Hegelian doctrine espoused by Bradley is that the limitations of the understanding can be seen only by going beyond its limits to what is not finite and not conditioned but absolute. The claims for reason had never been pushed so far before, nor have they been since.

SCHOPENHAUER. With Arthur Schopenhauer (1788–1860) there was a partial return to Kant. Schopenhauer thought that Hegel's dialectical method was barren because it ignored Kant's insights into the nature of reason and the understanding. Yet he retained Hegel's idealist approach. Kant's phenomena became presentations or ideas in a sense similar to Berkeley's; that is, they became subjective experiences. Schopenhauer thought that the world consists of ideas or presentations and that necessary connections judged to exist between them are, as Kant thought, merely conditional; however, Schopenhauer does not accept the paraphernalia of Kant's categories for justifying such judgments. In his view all justifications for claiming objective experience rest on the principle of sufficient reason, which takes various forms according to the form of knowledge involved. It acts as a logical ground (the *ratio cognoscendi*) in connection with logical truths, as a ground connected with the features of space and time (the *ratio essendi*) in connection with mathematical truths, and as causality (the *ratio fiendi*) in connection with ordinary empirical phenomena. Thus, the notion of causality is made to play the role of all Kant's categories in relation to empirical phenomena; causality is their only ground for necessity in this sphere. Schopenhauer finally looks to the will as the only ground for action, for moral necessity. As one class of phenomenon, action finds its explanation only in the will.

Will as the thing-in-itself. The world as idea or presentation is only one half of Schopenhauer's philosophy (his main work is titled *The World as Will and Idea*). Although he accepted the idealist framework, he thought that the demand for a thing-in-itself as the basis of all our ideas was inescapable. He finds the nature of the thing-in-itself in the will. Reality consists of the manifestations of one force, the will, which uses consciousness as an instrument for its own self-promotion. Only in art is there anything like freedom from it, for only there does the mind achieve a state akin to the contemplation of Platonic Ideas, a sort of permanency which is foreign to the general manifestations of the will.

Although the last part of Schopenhauer's thought had some influence upon the romantic movement in nineteenth-century German thought, it has not received much welcome from the mainstream of philosophers. However, Schopenhauer's theory of knowledge, contained in the part of his philosophy devoted to the world as idea, contains much of interest along lines which are, in origin, Kantian.

LATE NINETEENTH-CENTURY PHILOSOPHY

Philosophical thought in Germany during the nineteenth century tended to be either romantic or neo-Kantian. Neo-Kantian philosophy came under empiricist influences from Britain, and at the end of the century under Franz Brentano and Alexius Meinong this finally led to a return to realism, a movement that not only produced phenomenology (perhaps the dominant philosophy in Europe today) but also to some extent influenced Bertrand Russell and other realist philosophers in the English-speaking world.

BRENTANO. Brentano (1838–1917) held that the objects of psychology were mental acts. Each mental act had an immanent object—what Brentano called an intentional object—thus reviving scholastic terminology. These objects were a kind of internal accusative to the relevant act, as a judgment is to the act of judgment. They provide the content of the act. But what is the status of these objects? Clearly, the question is especially pertinent because it is possible to think of or make judgments about things that do not exist. How can a real act have an unreal object?

MEINONG. This was the problem that Meinong (1853–1920) took up. He postulated nonexistent objects to explain the possibility of our thinking, for example, of things that do not or cannot exist. Similarly, false judgments were said to correspond to what he called objectives—nonexistent states of affairs which would be facts if only the corresponding judgments were true. Objectives could not be said to exist, for they were not things, but they might subsist. From a linguistic point of view, this doctrine implied a realist theory of meaning, according to which the meaning of any expression was given by a corresponding entity. The fact that these entities were not themselves mental entities (although they gave content to what is mental) implied a return to realism in a more general sense. Objects could be real, according to Meinong, without being actual.

HUSSERL. Edmund Husserl (1859–1938), another disciple of Brentano, started from very much the same point of view as Meinong, maintaining that the proper philosophical task was to investigate the essence of mental acts and their objects. Philosophy consisted, in his view, in an inquiry into the essence of different manifestations of consciousness and the essences with which they are concerned. To study this, it was necessary to strip off all presuppositions, metaphysical or otherwise. Husserl later emphasized this aspect increasingly. He adopted the method of *epoch*—the bracketing of presuppositions—in a manner akin, as he pointed out, to the Cartesian method of doubt. This would lead to pure consciousness as the one absolute, the one firm thing, and from this the philosopher may turn back to investigate the essence of different phenomena as they appear to consciousness. Thus, in effect the initial realist point of view led back to one that was more like idealism. But this belongs, properly speaking, to the twentieth century.

J. S. MILL. Meanwhile, in Britain the predominant philosophy at the beginning of the nineteenth century was sensationalism with its attendant associationism. James Mill (1773–1836) took a radically empiricist point of view, trying to reduce perception to merely having sensations and other mental phenomena to sensations plus the ideas associated with them. His son J. S. Mill (1806–1873) brought greater sophistication to this point of view and, in so doing, led to its downfall. Like his father, J. S. Mill wished to reduce all knowledge to experience, to the association of certain ideas with basic sensations. He expressed a great admiration for Berkeley's *New Theory of Vision* and its explanation of how we come to see things as at a distance. He thought it possible to explain in a similar way how we come to think of ourselves as perceiving a permanent world of things. We have expectations that take us beyond the immediate sensations because of the

associations built up in experience between our immediate sensations and ideas of "permanent possibilities of sensation." Our ideas of material things are simply ideas of these permanent possibilities of sensation. Like Hume, Mill approaches this problem psychologically; he seeks to explain why we believe in an external world. To the extent, however, that he is inclined to add that things are simply these permanent possibilities of sensation, his view is the extreme empiricist doctrine of phenomenalism, the doctrine that all we mean by "material object" is something about our experiences.

Mill's main contributions to philosophy perhaps lie in logic, ethics, and politics. His general approach, however, is psychological, based on a conception of experience as atomistic sensations which could be linked to derivative ideas by the processes of association. Mill's general point of view is perhaps nowhere more obvious than in his account of such necessary propositions as those of mathematics. These are, in his view, simply very highly confirmed generalizations. The only necessity is psychological necessity.

Mill's view of knowledge came under attack in the latter half of the nineteenth century from many sources in Britain and elsewhere. In Britain perhaps the main attack came from the returning idealism, particularly as represented by F. H. Bradley. His main line of thought, as already discussed, was Hegelian with less emphasis on the dialectic and greater emphasis on the idealist point of view, according to which reality consists of experience organized in thought by attaching ideas to it in judgment. In *Appearance and Reality* Bradley sought to show that all features of the empirical world are only appearance and that reality must consist of a form of experience which is absolute and unitary and transcends all the contradictions of appearance. His criticism of Mill is that the pure sensory given is a myth; all the content of our knowledge must come by way of ideas—that is, through thought—and association "marries only universals." Experience in itself is nothing.

BERGSON. Criticisms of a different kind came from France and America. In France there were few philosophical developments of interest during the nineteenth century until Henri Bergson (1859–1941). Bergson was an anti-intellectualist who emphasized life against thought. Much of his approach was therefore biological. The space and time of which we are conscious, Bergson thought, are continuous; the division of it into things and processes is due to the intellect, which carries out the division according to our biological needs. Perception involves an awareness of the possible moves that our body can make in relation to an object; in contrast, sensation corresponds to a simple response to a stimulus. Like Bradley, Bergson thought that the atomistic sensations of the sensationalist were a product of intellectual analysis. There are actually no basic experiences of this sort. We perceive things as our biological needs cause us to do so. Similarly with memory; our body acts like a sieve. Without the body our mind might remember everything, and this would be both useless and even disastrous biologically. Our body saves us from this, causing us to select only that which is biologically useful.

Because of this emphasis on biological utility, there is a relativism inherent in Bergson's point of view, and it has much in common with American pragmatism as instituted by William James. Bergson went further than James in his emphasis on life, however. His starting point was a thesis about time that is really outside the scope of this article. Roughly, his view was that the time of consciousness (*la durée*) is continuous; the ideas which thought presents to us are or seem discontinuous. The continuity of consciousness must be due to an interpenetration of those ideas, and as a result, they form a developing series in which, given that each member developed from what has gone before, each member must be unique. The development itself is due to a vital spirit, and the same is true of the universe at large.

JAMES. Bergson's emphasis upon the continuity of consciousness has its counterpart in James's thesis of the stream of thought. In his *Principles of Psychology* William James (1842–1910) insisted, in opposition to the sensationalists, that there were no atomic sensations or ideas; distinct ideas are selected phases of one stream of consciousness, and these phases make up a continuity because each idea has a fringe which overlaps that of its neighbors. Thus far, however, James was content to argue that our ideas are determined by what things there are. We must, he maintained, distinguish between knowledge by acquaintance and knowledge about something (not to be confused with a somewhat similar but really different distinction made by Russell). The baby is acquainted with the universe but he has not yet selected anything from the mass of sensation with which he is confronted. Thus, he knows nothing *about* anything. James was later to go further in Bergson's direction. In *Essays in Radical Empiricism* he rejected the distinction between thought and things, embracing a thesis that is known as neutral monism, the thesis that reality consists of one stuff (in this case experience) out of which both the mental and the physical are to be constructed according to the prin-

ciples which govern each. From this continuous experience a plurality of thoughts and objects can be developed, a plurality of things related by concatenation only, as experience tells us they are. In this James set himself in opposition to his other bête noire, idealism, with its emphasis on internal relations and its denial of plurality.

PEIRCE AND DEWEY. James's special claim to fame (although some would say notoriety) is perhaps his status as the founder of pragmatism, although this, too, has Bergsonian affinities. The original source for the pragmatist point of view was C. S. Peirce (1839–1914), a rather isolated figure. A man with a great wealth of ideas, Peirce, as a nonprofessional philosopher, was to some extent outside the main stream of philosophical thought. He came to philosophy as a mathematician and scientist. He was opposed to all intuitions of the Cartesian type, largely because of his belief in the power of hypothesis and his disbelief in ultimate inexplicables. Perhaps his greatest contribution, however, lies in his theory of signs and meaning. In this connection Peirce maintained that our conception of anything is determined by our conception of the practical bearings of that thing. In sum, meaningfulness is a question of practical utility, and the meaning of any given concept or expression is given by its precise utility.

James turned this theory of meaning into a theory of truth, much to Peirce's disgust. He maintained that the test of the truth of any belief was its fruitfulness. To say that a belief is true is to say that it is good in this sense. Such is the pragmatic theory of truth.

For John Dewey (1859–1952) it is knowledge that is successful practice; propositions are merely instruments which may take us to the goal toward which experimental inquiry is directed. There is no final truth; instead, there is "warranted assertability" when the judgments which we make lead us to the abstract goal of science in accordance with scientific method.

TWENTIETH-CENTURY REALISM

The course of twentieth-century philosophy was not smooth, and it is therefore not easy to chart. No more than a sketch will be attempted here. Undoubtedly, however, the main philosophical event at the start of the century was a swing from idealism to realism. In America there were the neorealists, such as E. B. Holt, W. B. Montague, and R. B. Perry, influenced by James and his theory of neutral monism; in England there was Samuel Alexander, and in Germany there was Meinong. The most important figures in this revolution were G. E. Moore and

Bertrand Russell at Cambridge, and of these Moore was the originator in this respect.

MOORE. G. E. Moore (1873–1958) began with a criticism of Bradley. Moore thought that Bradley had not taken far enough his rejection of the view that we abstract our ideas from experience. Insisting that concepts or ideas should be regarded as the objects, the meanings, of our thoughts, Moore went on to argue that there must be propositions as the objects of beliefs. Things are merely collections of concepts and as such enter into propositions as their constituents. Propositions are what we believe when we hold any belief, true or false. This amounts to an insistence upon a distinction between any mental activity or form of awareness and its object. Moore's article "Refutation of Idealism" in his *Philosophical Studies* is founded on just this point, for he finds the refutation of the doctrine that *esse est percipi* in a distinction, somewhat after the manner of Brentano, between the act of awareness in perception and the object of awareness, between consciousness and its object. Idealists, he maintained, failed to notice the distinction.

Moore was later to give up his doctrine of propositions, for in considering the problem of false belief, he said that "there do not seem to be propositions at all, in the sense in which the theory demands them." If there were, there would have to exist something corresponding to false beliefs, and the fact of its existence would make the beliefs true, not false. Belief cannot therefore consist in a relation between ourselves and an object. The rejection of propositions in this objectively existing sense may look like the abandonment of the very foundations of his realism, and so in a sense it is. But Moore did not give up the view that we do know of a reality independent of our minds, and when he abandoned the account of false belief which implied the existence of objectively existing propositions, he nevertheless maintained categorically that we must not give up the view that truth somehow consists in correspondence with reality.

Existence of the external world. Moore sometimes said that he never doubted that we do know things about reality that we ordinarily think we know. Therefore, he was not influenced by the usual skeptical arguments against this position. In his view the real philosophical problem was to analyze what we mean when we say that we have this knowledge. Moore has generally been one who raises the difficulties about this problem rather than one who gives the answers. He has definitely maintained, however, that we do have knowledge of many different kinds of thing, and in his notorious "Proof of an External

World" (*Proceedings of the British Academy*, 1939) he gave as a good argument for the existence of such a world the fact that we can point to objects in it. Thus, he held up his hands, saying, "Here is one hand, and here is another," to prove the existence of an external world. Moore's thought moved toward the view that what requires defending is common sense, ordinary beliefs such as the belief that there are objective things, like his hand, in the world. When metaphysicians say such things as "Time is unreal," this is an affront to common sense and demands explanation. Ludwig Wittgenstein later said that the view defended by Moore was not strictly common sense, since it was a philosophical point of view. This seems correct; what Moore meant by common sense was a general realist point of view.

Account of perception. In his analyses of what we mean when we claim knowledge, however, Moore's discussion follows the lines of those which have been more influenced by skepticism. Thus, in his account of perception he brings in sense data as what we actually see or directly apprehend when we look at something. Characteristically, he distinguishes between the sense datum (the object that we actually see) and the sensation which we might be said to have of it. But in using the words "direct apprehension" and "actually seeing," he suggests that he wants that indubitability which other philosophers have sought as an answer to the skeptic. Direct apprehension cannot be of the physical object, for, he argues, when an envelope is held up, it cannot be this that we actually see, since some people may fail to identify it as such. There is room for error about the identity of the object but not, perhaps, about its color or even shape as seen, so it must be these that we actually see. Moore's main worry is about the exact relation that exists between sense data and physical objects, both of which, he thinks, certainly exist. The answer that he would like to give is that sense data are parts of the surfaces of physical objects, but the fact that different people may have conflicting views of these objects prevents him from giving this answer. The right answer and, for the same reason, the precise nature of sense data were always a puzzle to him.

It may be wondered why Moore felt it necessary to bring in sense data at all. The answer must be that for Moore there had to be things which we just know, and although we may know of the existence of physical objects, we may not be so sure of their exact qualities. Hence, the possibility of error plays a part in Moore's thought just as it has done in that of others, even if the influence of skepticism is not so explicit. Direct apprehension fills the same role in his philosophy of perception as intuition in his ethics. The notion has its parallel in the conception of knowledge employed by his Oxford contemporary John Cook Wilson and his disciples, such as H. A. Prichard. They thought the trouble with idealism lay in its failure to see that there was a distinct state of mind, knowledge, in which there was no possibility of error.

RUSSELL. Bertrand Russell (1872–1970) was first an idealist but was converted to realism by Moore. From his early study of Leibniz, Russell took the view that philosophy consists in the analysis of propositions, and his interest in logic also brought him to a concern with language. During the early 1900s he became interested in Meinong, whose realism seemed to confirm Moore in Russell's line of thought. However, he came to think that Meinong's supposition that there had to exist objects to explain our ability to think of things which do not exist in fact, such as round squares, showed, as he put it, an insufficiently robust sense of reality. Partly in response to this and partly in response to a more complex theory of meaning put forward by the mathematical logician Gottlob Frege, Russell set forth the theory of descriptions.

According to the theory of descriptions, phrases of the form "the so-and-so" are incomplete in meaning. They have no meaning (in the form of an object of reference) in themselves; to give their meaning, it is necessary to analyze the meaning of the whole sentence in which they occur. Sentences of the form "The so-and-so is *F*" are really tantamount to composite sentences including as a part the sentence asserting that something exists corresponding to the description "the so-and-so." Where nothing of the kind exists, the whole proposition is false ("proposition" here being equivalent to "statement," not the objectively existing object of beliefs). The theory of descriptions became a tool of analysis, and Russell used it in many connections.

Theory of knowledge. The main importance of the theory in epistemology is connected with Russell's distinction between knowledge by acquaintance and knowledge by description. Knowledge by acquaintance is Moore's direct apprehension, but Russell has always been more concerned with the justification of claims to knowledge than was Moore. For Russell it was important that all knowledge be founded on knowledge by acquaintance, if it was to be possible at all, for only in knowledge by acquaintance is error absolutely impossible. In *Problems of Philosophy* Russell gave a list of entities of which we have knowledge by acquaintance—sense data, memory data, the self, and universals. Of physical objects we have

only knowledge by description because here error is possible.

Russell also declares that "every proposition which we can understand must be composed wholly of constituents with which we are acquainted." (By "proposition" he meant the objectively existing entity in the early Moorean sense.) This is possible only if anything of which we have knowledge by description is reducible to things of which we have knowledge by acquaintance. Physical objects, for example, must be reduced to sense data or, since they are not always being perceived, to a combination of sense data and sensibilia—actual and possible sense data. They must, as Russell puts it, be considered as logical constructions from sense data; they are simply bundles of sense data and sensibilia.

From the logical point of view, names of physical objects are disguised descriptions, and the theory of descriptions shows that it is not necessary to suppose the existence of a special class of entities called physical objects in order to give propositions about them a meaning. What we are acquainted with when we perceive a physical object is a number of sense data; the physical object we know only by description, and any statement expressing a fact about it is a statement about a description. This statement is analyzable, so that it contains an existential proposition about something answering to that description, according to the theory of descriptions; it is, that is, about something falling under a set of universals, and these are objects of acquaintance as much as sense data are. The notion of an object of acquaintance is closely connected with that of a logically proper name, an expression that cannot fail in its reference. Descriptions can, of course, fail in that there may be nothing answering to them. With the reduction of physical objects to sense data, knowledge of physics is preserved, and this has always been a cardinal point in Russell's program. On the actual status of sense data, Russell's opinion varied, but when most impressed by physics, he made them, paradoxically enough, entities in the brain.

Logical atomism. At the beginning of World War I, when Russell had come under the influence of Wittgenstein, he held that the ultimate constituents of the universe are atomic particulars, which are terms of relations in atomic facts. All other facts were to be built up from atomic facts by the processes of logic. The atomic particulars are sense data, and the relations supply the universal element in the fact.

The theory of logical atomism is a metaphysical theory rather than an epistemological one, and this is even more obviously true of Wittgenstein's version in his *Trac-*

tatus Logico-philosophicus. Russell differs from Wittgenstein in his more explicit interest in the nature of the constituents of atomic facts, and it is clear that his choice of these constituents was determined by his desire to found all knowledge on knowledge by acquaintance. The one exception to the program that Russell found at this stage was that of mental states like belief, for he could not see how statements about beliefs could be reduced to more elementary statements. In order to deal with the problem, he has flirted with behaviorism, since if belief is analyzable only in terms of behavior, this, in turn, may conceivably be explained in terms of sense data.

Russell changed his mind over the details of his logical atomism, especially when he was influenced by the logical positivists, but the framework remained the same. His account of memory is similar to that of perception; it is founded on memory experiences only contingently related to the past, although they may have a feeling of familiarity. The memory data are objects of acquaintance, but the past itself is not. In one general respect, however, Russell acknowledges that empiricism fails—in our knowledge of the postulates on which, in his opinion, inductive inference and, therefore, science rest. Induction, he thinks, is founded on habit, and the principles implicit in such habits cannot themselves be derived from experience. Despite his belief in the limitations of empiricism, Russell never wavered in his defense of realism. He always embraced and keenly defended the correspondence theory of truth.

Nature of mathematics. Nothing has been said thus far of Russell's work on the foundations of mathematics, especially his great contribution, written with A. N. Whitehead, in *Principia Mathematica*, although this is in a sense part of his epistemology. In *Principles of Mathematics* Russell held that mathematical propositions were synthetic, but when, influenced by Frege, he embarked on the attempt to reduce mathematics to logic by deriving it from a small number of axioms containing only logical notions, he held mathematical propositions to be analytic. This is too complicated a matter for discussion here. The exact nature of mathematical propositions is still a matter of dispute, but the attempt to reduce them to logic may now be seen to be a great and splendid failure.

WHITEHEAD. It may be noted briefly that Russell's partner in *Principia Mathematica*, A. N. Whitehead (1861–1947), took a very different road in epistemology. He tried to explain the properties of things in terms of their relations to one another. In perception the mind tries to grasp—or in Whitehead's term to "prehend"—a part of the system of nature around it; it is reacting to the environment in biological fashion. There are no atomic sense data; to suppose that there are is to be liable to the "fallacy of misplaced concreteness"—the view that because science has a concept (such as that of an instant), there must be entities of this sort in experience. To some extent Whitehead's thought is in the idealist tradition, but it also contains a certain Platonism. The particulars of which nature is composed, he thought, are events; the permanent characteristics that we recognize in them are objects. The objects are, as he puts it, ingredient "into events," not into just one event but through an indefinite neighborhood of events. We do not, that is, see single things with isolated characteristics; we view them as part of a system. Whitehead's thought is, however, difficult, and little can be done to make it intelligible in a short space.

LOGICAL POSITIVISM

Wittgenstein's *Tractatus* influenced a group of philosophers in Vienna who were mainly interested in the philosophy of science after the empiricist fashion of Ernst Mach. Wittgenstein had said that to understand a proposition is to understand what it would be like for it to be true. The Vienna circle, as this group became known, wrongly interpreted this as a general criterion of significance, and so the verification theory of meaning was born. According to this theory, meaningful propositions must be either analytic or empirically verifiable. The propositions of mathematics and logic were thought to belong to the first class, and the propositions of science to the second. Metaphysical propositions, belonging to neither group, were declared meaningless.

The members of the group differed over the details of this scheme, and a progressive relaxation in its rigor gradually took place. One of the biggest problems was the status of the verification principle itself, for on the face of it it is neither analytic nor empirically verifiable. The eventual outcome for some members of the group was to view it as a recommendation only. There were also other problems. The initial aim of the movement was, above all, to lay the foundations of science. Scientific propositions had to be preserved and metaphysics excluded. It became apparent that it was difficult, if not impossible, to provide a formulation of the verification principle which fulfilled both goals.

Moritz Schlick (1882–1936), the original leader of the group, felt compelled to interpret scientific laws as rules rather than statements. Another problem lay in the meaning of the phrase "empirically verifiable." Schlick held that ultimately there had to be a direct confrontation with experience. Other members of the movement—for example, A. J. Ayer (1910–1989)—held that there had to be basic propositions which were directly and strictly verifiable (and thus absolutely incorrigible), although others could be indirectly verified by reference to these. This led to a distinction between strong and weak verification; propositions about physical objects, for example, might be only weakly verifiable, since an indefinite number of propositions about immediate experience would have to be invoked in order to verify them conclusively. In this, positivism was associated with the thesis of phenomenalism that statements about physical objects are analyzable into a collection of statements about sense experiences. The fact that such an analysis must be indefinitely long has resulted in a progressive modification of the thesis on the part of its main proponents—for instance, Ayer.

Truth. Schlick's view brought with it the correspondence theory of truth. Otto Neurath (1882–1945), on the other hand, held that this involved an attempt to go outside the web of language and ran the risk of a lapse into metaphysics. Neurath maintained that there had to be "protocol propositions"—observation reports on which science might be founded—but that these need not be reports of immediate experience. The truth of a protocol proposition was determined by its coherence with other propositions making up the language of science. Thus, Neurath embraced a coherence theory of truth. This general line was developed by Rudolf Carnap (1891–1970) into a form of conventionalism. He put forward a "principle of tolerance," maintaining that logic had no morals; verificationism thus became a proposal for the best way of developing the language of science. Whereas Schlick and the earlier Carnap had maintained that basic propositions must be about immediate experience, Neurath had maintained the thesis of physicalism that protocol propositions must be in the language of physics. In line with his relaxation of the criteria, Carnap came to accept what he called the "thing-language"—the language of the commonsense world—as the basis for scientific language. Today, positivism in its strict form is more or less a thing of the past.

Nature of science. It is noteworthy that Karl Popper (1902–1994), who was not a member of the movement but who was influenced by it and influenced it, held that the key to an understanding of science lay not in verifiability but falsifiability. He put this forward, however, not as a theory of meaning but as a criterion for the demarcation of science from metaphysics. The generalizations of science are, because of their very form, unverifiable, but they *are* falsifiable, whereas the propositions of meta-

physics are not. Popper developed these views into a thesis about science as based on the hypothetico-deductive method. The aim of science is to put forward bold hypotheses, the deductive consequences of which must be subject to rigorous testing and criticism. This view is associated with a form of skepticism, for Popper sometimes maintains that we can never *know* the truth. The best that we can do is to put forward hypotheses and subject them to rigorous tests, for this is the way in which science progresses. Truth itself is just an illusion.

CONTEMPORARY MOVEMENTS

Contemporary philosophy is in an untidy state of nonuniformity. In Europe perhaps the most prevalent philosophy is a phenomenology deriving from Husserl. This movement is also associated with existentialism, originally a reaction against the superrationalism of Hegel and, therefore, to some extent a form of irrationalism. Existentialists have added little to epistemology; they tend to take for granted the existence of an objective world, aiming only to present a picture of it and of man's place in it. Those existentialists who derive something from Husserl—for example, Jean-Paul Sartre and Maurice Merleau-Ponty—are concerned mainly with descriptions of forms of consciousness, with phenomenology as descriptive psychology.

ORDINARY-LANGUAGE PHILOSOPHY. Perhaps the most significant movement, apart from latter-day positivism and pragmatism, is the so-called ordinary-language philosophy, today most closely associated with Oxford. The leading spirit of the movement is, however, the Cambridge philosopher Ludwig Wittgenstein (1889–1951), who has had an immense influence. His work is not easy to summarize; it is in part a series of comments upon his earlier logical atomist views and the theory of meaning that it espoused. Only a small part of his work can be mentioned here. He has criticized the attempts implicit in much sense-datum philosophy to construct a private language by arguing that the results of such attempts would lack the essential conditions of a language. There would be no way of distinguishing between the occasions on which one was following a rule in applying an expression and those on which one was making a new decision so to apply it. He has also stressed the importance of bringing back terms to the language game (as he calls possible languages) that is their original home—ordinary language. This, he maintains, is perfectly in order as it is; the important thing is to examine the uses to which expressions are put, with the recognition that language is a form of life and must be treated accordingly. Among other things this has led to the recognition of truths which are necessary but not analytic, truths which he calls "grammatical." These are truths which express nonanalytic connections between concepts. The emphasis upon such truths and the arguments which lead to them on the part of followers of Wittgenstein is in a sense a partial return to Kant. (The distinction between analytic and synthetic truths in general has in any case come under fire from several quarters, especially from the American logician W. V. Quine [1908–2000]. But his emphasis on the necessity of assessing the status of propositions only within a system is something more of a move toward the idealist point of view.)

The appeal to ordinary language has been used for many purposes. Gilbert Ryle (1900–1976), for example, has used it in order to plot, as he puts it, the logical geography of mental concepts such as mind, belief, or will. He, too, has attacked the notion of sense data, and he has made and emphasized an important distinction between knowing how and knowing that. For present purposes the main importance of the appeal to ordinary language lies in its confrontation of the skeptic. The most stringent appeals to usage (rather than merely to the functions of language, as in Wittgenstein's case) have been made by J. L. Austin (1911–1960), who has emphasized the extent to which many philosophers including skeptics, have departed from our ordinary use of words. It is clear, however, as Austin in effect admitted, that an appeal to what we ordinarily say cannot settle these issues, however much it may be a good first move. Arguments are first required in favor of our ordinary way of speaking.

It has been argued, for example, that anyone who says that we never know anything but only believe or suppose it robs the concept of belief of an essential contrast with knowledge, without which it would be meaningless. This argument—the so-called argument from polar concepts—is invalid, because a philosopher can use the concept of belief as long as he has the concept of knowledge, as long as he knows what it would be like to know; he does not have to admit that anyone knows anything as a matter of fact.

Another argument is that we can never deny that we have knowledge altogether, because this would be denying the existence of the paradigm case by reference to which we have learned the meaning of the word *knowledge*. This argument—the so-called paradigm-case argument—fails, in the opinion of the present writer, because it assumes that meaning is given by the applications of a term. Whereas it might be difficult to see how we could

have come to attach meaning to a term unless we had learned some of its applications, it is not logically impossible that we should have done so. Hence, more complicated arguments are required.

This is the situation. Most philosophers would agree that if we are to be said to know a proposition p, we must believe p, p must be true, and we must have good reasons for believing in p. There is perhaps little argument over the first two conditions, although there might be some hesitation over the details. The problem is what counts as good reasons for believing in p. In the ordinary way we recognize different reasons according to the nature of the proposition involved. The skeptic denies that any of these are sufficient, and it is impossible to produce any knockdown argument which will dispose of the skeptic's claim. Each application of this claim must be assessed on its own merits, and the answer to the skeptic must therefore be a dialectical one in the Socratic sense. But the very existence of recognized forms of knowledge presupposes that there must be such knowledge. This is, however, only a presumption, not a proof.

Traditionally, and for good reason, skepticism has had biggest sway in connection with claims to knowledge of objects of perception, knowledge derived from memory, knowledge of other minds, and inductive knowledge. In each of these cases the skeptic may present too high a standard of knowledge, which cannot, in the ordinary way, be attained. But the temptation to accept such a standard may be increased by adopting certain views about the nature of—for example, perception or memory. If perception is thought of as merely having sensations or memory as merely having images or ideas in the mind, there is necessarily a gap to be crossed from our own minds if there is to be objective knowledge in these fields. Hence, the talk of knowledge of an external world, external to our own minds. With a different conception of memory or perception, in which an essential connection is recognized between memory and the past or perception and an objective world, this gap is removed. This is not to get rid of the skeptical problem at one fell swoop, since it remains a question whether and under what conditions these concepts of perception and memory can be applied. This, however, is merely the general problem of how knowledge is possible in different fields; it can be dealt with dialectically. In other words, an incorrect conceptual analysis can worsen the skeptical problem, but a correct one cannot solve it. But the presumption remains that objectivity is possible in these fields, even if it is incapable of proof. Each doubt can be alleviated only by argument; there is no overall answer. Finally, the supposition that an answer can be provided by showing that there are forms of knowledge in which error is logically excluded and which are therefore absolutely indubitable is an illusion. First, there is no indubitable knowledge; second, it is not necessary for the general possibility of knowledge that there should be. Much of the history of epistemology has depended on this illusion.

See also Abelard, Peter; Alexander, Samuel; Antisthenes; A Priori and A Posteriori; Arcesilaus; Aristotelianism; Aristotle; Augustine, St.; Austin, John Langshaw; Ayer, Alfred Jules; Bergson, Henri; Berkeley, George; Boethius, Anicius Manlius Severinus; Bradley, Francis Herbert; Brentano, Franz; Carnap, Rudolf; Carneades; Cartesianism; Chrysippus; Cosmological Argument for the Existence of God; Couturat, Louis; Descartes, René; Dewey, John; Dialectic; Duns Scotus, John; Empiricism; Epicurus; Fichte, Johann Gottlieb; Frege, Gottlob; Geulincx, Arnold; Gorgias of Leontini; Hegel, Georg Wilhelm Friedrich; Hellenistic Thought; Heraclitus of Ephesus; Hobbes, Thomas; Holt, Edwin Bissell; Hume, David; Husserl, Edmund; Innate Ideas; Intuition; James, William; Kant, Immanuel; Knowledge, A Priori; Leibniz, Gottfried Wilhelm; Leucippus and Democritus; Locke, John; Logical Positivism; Mach, Ernst; Malebranche, Nicolas; Meinong, Alexius; Merleau-Ponty, Maurice; Mill, James; Mill, John Stuart; Montague, William Pepperell; Moore, George Edward; Neo-Kantianism; Neoplatonism; Neurath, Otto; New Realism; Ontological Argument for the Existence of God; Paradigm-Case Argument; Parmenides of Elea; Peirce, Charles Sanders; Perry, Ralph Barton; Plato; Platonism and the Platonic Tradition; Plotinus; Popper, Karl Raimund; Porphyry; Pre-Socratic Philosophy; Protagoras of Abdera; Quine, Willard Van Orman; Rationalism; Realism; Reid, Thomas; Roscelin; Ryle, Gilbert; Sartre, Jean-Paul; Schlick, Moritz; Schopenhauer, Arthur; Sextus Empiricus; Skepticism, History of; Socrates; Spinoza, Benedict (Baruch) de; Stoicism; Thomas Aquinas, St.; Universals, A Historical Survey; Whitehead, Alfred North; William of Ockham; Wittgenstein, Ludwig Josef Johann.

Bibliography

For the texts of individual philosophers see the separate articles devoted to them.

INTRODUCTORY BOOKS

Ayer, A. J. *The Problem of Knowledge.* London: Macmillan, 1956.

Russell, Bertrand. *The Problems of Philosophy.* London: Williams and Norgate, 1912.

Woozley, A. D. *Theory of Knowledge.* London, 1949.

GENERAL HISTORIES

Copleston, Frederick. *A History of Philosophy.* 7 vols. London: Burns, Oates and Washbourne, 1947–1975.

Hamlyn, D. W. *Sensation and Perception.* London: Routledge and K. Paul, 1961. A history of the philosophy of perception; contains bibliography.

O'Connor, D. J. *A Critical History of Western Philosophy.* New York: Free Press of Glencoe, 1964.

OTHER RECOMMENDED TITLES

Ayers, Michael. *Locke: Epistemology and Ontology.* London: Routledge, 1991.

Buryeat, M. F., ed. *The Skeptical Tradition.* Berkeley: University of California Press, 1983.

Fine, G. "Knowledge and Belief in Republic V." *Archiv fur Geschichte der Philosophie* 60 (1978): 121–139.

Fogelin, Robert. *Hume's Scepticism in the Treatise of Human Nature.* London: Routledge and Kegan Paul, 1985.

Hankinson, R. J. *The Sceptics.* London: Routledge, 1995.

Lehrer, Keith. *Thomas Reid.* London: Routledge, 1989.

Lovejoy, Arthur O. *The Revolt against Dualism.* La Salle, IL: Open Court, 1930.

Moser, Paul K. "Epistemology (1900–Present)." In *Routledge History of Philosophy.* Vol. 10: *Philosophy of the English Speaking World in the 20th Century,* edited by John Canfield. London: Routledge, 1996.

Moser, Paul K., and Arnold VanderNat, eds. *Human Knowledge: Classical and Contemporary Approaches.* Oxford: Oxford University Press, 1987; 2nd ed., 1995; 3rd ed., 2002.

Pears, David. *Hume's System.* Oxford: Oxford University Press, 1990.

Popkin, R. *The History of Scepticism from Erasmus to Spinoza.* Berkeley: University of California Press, 1979.

Shope, R. *The Analysis of Knowing.* Princeton, NJ: Princeton University Press, 1983.

Sosa, Ernest. "How to Resolve the Pyrrhonian Problematic: A Lesson from Descartes." *Philosophical Studies* 85 (1997): 229–249.

Stroud, Barry. *Hume.* London: Routledge and Kegan Paul, 1977.

Stroud, Barry. *The Significance of Philosophical Scepticism.* Oxford: Oxford University Press, 1984.

White, Nicholas. *Plato on Knowledge and Reality.* Indianapolis: Hackett, 1976.

Williams, Bernard. *Descartes: The Project of Pure Enquiry.* Atlantic Highlands, NJ: Humanities Press, 1978.

D. W. Hamlyn (1967)
Bibliography updated by Benjamin Fiedor (2005)

EPISTEMOLOGY, HISTORY OF [ADDENDUM]

Knowledge (*'ilm*) has occupied a central place in the Islamic intellectual tradition. The religious incentive for this stems from the fact that the Islamic belief is grounded in a knowledge claim about God's existence and His revelation. The theologians (*mutakallimin*) consider knowledge as a prerequisite for religious belief (*iman*). A related question is God's knowledge of things—how God as the knower (*al-'alim*) knows particulars, which are subject to change, without change in His essence. To address this issue, Ibn Sinā had absolved God of the necessity of knowing every particular thing and event because this might introduce change in his unchanging essence. Ghazālī, in turn, accuses Ibn Sinā of denying God the ability to know particulars. The general consensus on God's knowledge of things, however, is that His knowing is a generative act in that He knows things by creating them. In this sense, God's knowledge of things does not follow their existence, which would be to attribute ignorance to God, but precedes them.

In philosophy, four major theories of knowledge have developed. The first is the concept of knowledge as abstraction (*tajarrud*). Following Aristotle, the Muslim Peripatetics define knowledge as the abstraction of the intelligible forms of things from their material properties. We know things through their intelligible forms—that is, only as universals. When the mind encounters a particular object, it abstracts its form and turns it into a conception in the mind. This, however, raises the question of whether what we know is a universal or the things themselves.

Knowledge as abstraction leads to what we might call the representational theory of knowledge, according to which knowledge is an imprint or picture (*rasm*) of actually existing things in the mind. When there is a perfect correspondence between the thing and its representation in the mind, we arrive at true knowledge.

The second theory is based on knowledge as a relation (*idafah*) between the thing known and the knower. The knower intends things in the extramental world, and this intending creates a relation between a person and his or her object of knowledge. Defended by some theologians, knowledge as relation fails to account for self-knowledge where the knower and the known are one and the same thing. When I say, for instance, that I feel pain, object and subject are the same. Otherwise, we would have to admit a relation between myself and myself.

The third theory defines knowledge as a property of the knower. Knowledge belongs to the knower as a state of the mind (*hala nafsaniyyah*). Combining elements from the above theories, this view reduces knowledge to concepts in the mind. It also seems to suggest that what the mind knows is its internal procedures rather than the things in the external world. The goal of knowledge, however, is to know things as they are, not simply as they appear to us.

The fourth theory of knowledge proposed by Suhrawardi and developed by Mullā Ṣadrā argues for what is called knowledge-by-presence (*al-'ilm al-huduri*). Suhrawardi defines knowledge as presence rather as absence or negation, as the Peripatetic term "abstraction" implies. Ṣadrā takes this point further and equates knowledge with existence (*wujud*). According to him, knowledge is a mode of existence and knowing is a cognitive act of unveiling an aspect of the all-inclusive reality of existence. This leads Ṣadrā to his celebrated defense of the unification of the intellect and the intelligible.

Bibliography

Aminrazavi, Mahdi. *Suhrawardi and the School of Illumination.* Surrey, U.K.: Curzon, 1997.

Chittick, William. *The Heart of Islamic Philosophy: The Quest for Self-Knowledge in the Teachings of Afdal al-Din Kashani.* Oxford and New York: Oxford University Press, 2001.

Rosenthal, Franz. *Knowledge Triumphant: The Concept of Knowledge in Medieval Islam.* Leiden: E. J. Brill, 1970.

Mehdi Ha'iri Yazdi. *The Principles of Epistemology in Islamic Philosophy: Knowledge by Presence.* Albany, NY: State University of New York Press, 1992.

Hossein Ziai. *Knowledge and Illumination: A Study of Suhrawardi's Hikmat al-ishraq.* Atlanta: Scholars Press, 1990.

Ibrahim Kalin (2005)

EPISTEMOLOGY, RELIGIOUS

The epistemology of religion, as practiced by philosophers, is seldom concerned with the sorts of epistemological questions that emerge on a practical level in ordinary religious life, such as how to determine the correct interpretation of a scriptural text or how to know whether someone's claim to special divine guidance is to be credited. Rather, it tends to focus on the epistemic evaluation of the most basic tenets of the religious worldview in question—the existence of God, the creation of the world and God's relation to it, and the possibility of recognizing divine action in the world and divine revelation. From the 1960s on, religious epistemology has been characterized by a marked decline of fideism, with a renewal of interest in evidentialism and an even more pronounced upsurge of what may be termed experientialism.

Fideism is best characterized as the view that one's basic religious beliefs are not subject to independent rational evaluation. It is defended by urging that religious convictions are the most basic part of a believer's world-view and thus more fundamental than anything else that might be used to evaluate them. It is also said that to evaluate religious beliefs by standards other than the internal standards of the religious belief system itself is in effect to subject God to judgment and is thus a form of idolatry. In the mid-twentieth century fideism took two main forms, existentialism and Wittgensteinian fideism. In the succeeding decades philosophical existentialism has suffered a massive decline, as has its theological counterpart, neoorthodoxy. Wittgensteinian fideism, on the other hand, arose largely in response to the positivist contention that God-talk is cognitively meaningless; with the defeat of positivism it has lost much of its relevance. Many religious thinkers, freed from the need to defend religion's cognitive meaningfulness, have felt a renewed impulse to contend for the truth of their faith. And on the other hand, critics of religion have moved readily from the contention that belief in God is meaningless to the logically incompatible assertion that it is false and/or lacking in evidential support.

Evidentialism is the view that religious beliefs, in order to be rationally held, must be supported by other things one knows or reasonably believes to be true. Evidentialist defenses of religion typically rely heavily on theistic arguments, and all of the classical arguments saw renewed interest in the late twentieth century. Versions of the ontological argument propounded by Charles Hartshorne, Norman Malcolm, and Alvin Plantinga are clearly valid, though their premises remain controversial. William Rowe's work has directed renewed attention to the Clarke-Leibniz version of the cosmological argument, and new versions of the design argument teleological argument for the existence of God, focusing on God as the source of the basic laws of nature, have been developed by Richard Swinburne and others. Even the moral argument (Robert Adams) and the argument from religious experience (Gary Gutting) have come in for renewed attention. Two new arguments, or versions of arguments, are keyed to developments in cosmology. The "kalam cosmological argument" (William Craig) uses big-bang cosmology to argue that the physical universe as a whole has a temporal beginning and thus is in need of an external cause. And the anthropic cosmological principle is used by John Leslie, among others, to support a new version of the design argument: The apparent fact that the basic laws and initial conditions of the universe are "fine tuned" for life, with no apparent scientific explanation for this fact, is taken as evidence of intelligent design. Both of these arguments benefit from their association with cutting-edge science but also in consequence become vulnerable to future changes in scientific thinking on cosmology.

Evidentialist arguments against religion take a variety of forms. Most basically, evidentialists argue that the theistic arguments are unsuccessful and that theism fails for lack of evidential support. There are various challenges to the coherence and logical possibility of the traditional divine attributes. In most cases, however, these arguments, if successful, lead to a reformulation of the attributes in question rather than to the defeat of theism as such. But by far the most active area of consideration for antireligious evidentialism has been the problem of evil; the volume of writing on its various forms, by both critics and believers, has probably exceeded that on all of the theistic arguments taken together.

Along with the renewed consideration of the various arguments there have been reflections on the requirements for a successful argument. Traditional natural theology claimed to proceed from premises known or knowable to any reasonable person (e.g., "Some things are in motion") by means of arguments any reasonable person could see to be valid. By these standards it is not difficult to show that all of the arguments fail. But the standard is clearly too high; it is difficult to find significant arguments in any area of philosophy that meet it. No doubt a good argument should not be circular or question begging, and its premises must enjoy some kind of support that makes them at least plausible. But what seems plausible, or even evidently true, to one person may not seem so to another, equally rational, person; thus, the recognition emerges that arguments and proofs may be "person-relative" (Mavrodes 1970).

Furthermore, even a good argument is not necessarily decisive by itself, so it is necessary to consider the ways in which a number of arguments, none of them in itself conclusive, can lend their combined weight to establishing a conclusion. One model for this has been developed by Basil Mitchell, who compares arguments for religious beliefs to the kinds of cumulative-case arguments found in fields such as history and critical exegesis as well as in the choice between scientific paradigms. Richard Swinburne, by contrast builds a cumulative case for divine existence using the mathematical theory of probability. While it is not possible to assign precise numerical probabilities to the propositions involved in theistic argumentation, Bayes's theorem does provide insight into the way in which evidence contributes in a cumulative fashion to the support or defeat of a hypothesis such as theism Bayesianism. In addition, John L. Mackie and Michael

Martin have developed what are in effect cumulative-case arguments for atheism.

EXPERIENTIALISM

The most significant development in the epistemology of religion during the 1980s and early 1990s was the rise of a new type of theory distinct from both fideism and evidentialism. This theory, found in the writings of Richard Swinburne, Alvin Plantinga, and William Alston, lacks a generally recognized label (the term *Reformed epistemology* properly applies only to Plantinga's version) but may be termed experientialism in view of its emphasis on the grounding of religious belief in religious experience. Experientialism differs from fideism in that it does not seek to insulate religious belief from critical epistemic evaluation: rather, it affirms that religious experience can provide a sound epistemic basis for such beliefs. Experientialism is also importantly different from the evidentialist "argument from religious experience" in the following respect: The religious experience is not first described in ontologically neutral terms and then made the basis for an inference to the existence of the religious object. On the contrary, the religious belief is grounded directly in the religious experience, without mediation by inference, just as perceptual beliefs are grounded directly in perceptual experience.

This difference is important for a couple of reasons. For one thing it is more faithful to the phenomenology of both religious and perceptual belief: in typical cases neither form of belief involves such an inference. But more important, the direct grounding of belief in experience offers better prospects of a favorable epistemic status for the resulting beliefs than does the inferential approach. This is readily apparent in the case of perceptual experience: attempts at a "proof of the external world" have been notably unsuccessful, yet only those in the grip of philosophical theory doubt that we do in fact acquire a great deal of knowledge about the world through our perceptual experience. In the same way it is at least conceivable that believers acquire knowledge of God experientially even if no compelling inferential argument from religious experience is available.

Swinburne, Plantinga, and Alston share what may be termed a weak foundationalist approach to epistemology. That is to say, they accept the distinction between "basic" beliefs, which do not derive their rational acceptability from other beliefs, and "derived" beliefs, which gain their support from the basic beliefs. But they do not accept the traditional foundationalist restriction of basic beliefs to those that are nearly or entirely immune to doubt—beliefs that are self-evident, evident to the senses, or incorrigible. Each of them, furthermore, includes some religious beliefs in the category of basic beliefs. The epistemological task, then, is to show that this inclusion is epistemically proper—to show that such religious beliefs are among our "properly basic beliefs." (The terminology is Plantinga's, but the issue is the same for all three thinkers.) Each of them approaches this issue in a different way, though the approaches are ultimately compatible. Plantinga argues, following Roderick Chisholm, that the proper approach to the question of which beliefs are properly basic is inductive: one first conducts an inventory of the beliefs one takes oneself to hold rationally, then eliminates those that derive their epistemic support from other beliefs, and those that remain will be taken as properly basic. The typical Christian believer, Plantinga thinks, will find that she considers her belief in God to be rational but does not ground it inferentially on other beliefs she holds; thus, she will conclude that this is a properly basic belief. To be sure, atheists or believers in other religions will not concur in this, but Plantinga finds this to be unproblematic: "Followers of Bertrand Russell and Madalyn Murray O'Hair may disagree: but how is that relevant? Must my criteria, or those of the Christian community, conform to their examples? Surely not. The Christian community is responsible to *its* set of examples, not to theirs" (Plantinga and Wolterstorff 1983, p. 78).

In contrast with Plantinga's "internal" justification of the rationality of belief, both Swinburne and Alston attempt to show that religious experiences should have some epistemic weight, even for those who do not share the belief system the experiences ostensibly support. Swinburne appeals to the "principle of credulity," which states that "(in the absence of special considerations) if it seems (epistemically) to a subject that x is present, then probably x is present; what one seems to perceive is probably so" (1979, p. 254). He argues that a general denial of this principle lands us in a "sceptical bog" and that there is no justification for excluding religious experience from its scope.

Alston develops a "doxastic practice" approach to epistemology (indebted to both Thomas Reid and Ludwig Wittgenstein), which holds that all socially established doxastic practices are "innocent until proved guilty"; "they all deserve to be regarded as prima facie rationally engaged in … pending a consideration of possible reasons for disqualification" (1991, p. 153). Alston's delineation of the "Christian mystical practice" and his defense of its epistemic status constitute a systematic, detailed, and highly sophisticated presentation of experientialism.

One major difficulty for experientialism is the existence of incompatible experientially grounded beliefs in different religions—in Alston's terms, the existence of a plurality of mutually incompatible mystical practices. Alston concludes that religious experience alone probably cannot resolve this ambiguity and that "the knowledgeable and reflective Christian should be concerned about the situation … [and] should do whatever seems feasible to search for common ground on which to adjudicate the crucial differences between the world religions, seeking a way to show in a non-circular way which of the contenders is correct. What success will attend these efforts I do not presume to predict. Perhaps it is only in God's good time that a more thorough insight into the truth behind these divergent perspectives will be revealed to us" (1991, p. 278).

Critics, however, have urged more far-reaching objections to the experientialist program. According to Richard Gale, the analogy between religious experience and sense perception is weak, with the dissimilarities far outweighing the similarities. He also argues that religious experience could not be cognitive—that is, could not provide independent grounds for belief in the existence of its object—and that religious objects such as God or the One are not possible objects of perceptual experience, even if they exist. Alston, on the other hand, has argued in detail that the phenomenological structure of religious experience is perceptual and that "mystical perception" constitutes a genuine species of perception along with sense perception.

See also Alston, William P.; Atheism; Bayes, Bayes' Theorem, Bayesian Approach to Philosophy of Science; Chisholm, Roderick; Clarke, Samuel; Cosmological Argument for the Existence of God; Evil, The Problem of; Existentialism; Fideism; Leibniz, Gottfried Wilhelm; Mackie, John Leslie; Malcolm, Norman; Moral Arguments for the Existence of God; Ontological Argument for the Existence of God; Philosophy of Religion; Plantinga, Alvin; Positivism; Probability and Chance; Reid, Thomas; Religious Experience; Religious Pluralism; Teleological Argument for the Existence of God; Theism, Arguments For and Against; Wittgenstein, Ludwig Josef Johann.

Bibliography
Alston, W. P. *Perceiving God: The Epistemology of Religious Experience.* Ithaca, NY: Cornell University Press, 1991.

Gale, R. M. *On the Nature and Existence of God.* Cambridge, U.K.: Cambridge University Press, 1991.

Mackie, J. *The Miracle of Theism: Arguments for and against the Existence of God.* New York: Oxford University Press, 1982.

Martin, M. *Atheism: A Philosophical Justification.* Philadelphia: Temple University Press, 1990.

Mavrodes, G. *Belief in God: A Study in the Epistemology of Religion.* New York: Random House, 1970.

Mitchell, B. *The Justification of Religious Belief.* New York: Oxford University Press, 1981.

Plantinga, A., and N. Wolterstorff, eds. *Faith and Rationality: Reason and Belief in God.* Notre Dame, IN: University of Notre Dame Press, 1983.

Swinburne, R. *The Existence of God.* Oxford: Clarendon Press, 1979.

William Hasker (1996)

EPISTEMOLOGY, RELIGIOUS [ADDENDUM]

The most significant development in religious epistemology at the beginning of the new millennium was the completion of Alvin Plantinga's trilogy on warrant and religious knowledge. Plantinga's earlier work on Reformed epistemology focuses on the question of whether religious beliefs can be justified, in the sense that they can be accepted without violating any epistemic duties. His later work is concerned with *warrant*, defined as that which, added to true belief, enables such belief to qualify as knowledge. Plantinga argues convincingly that warrant is distinct from justification and also from rationality, in any of the several senses of the latter term. His own view is most akin to reliabilism, but he argues that standard versions of reliabilism face debilitating objections, and comes out instead for a definition of warrant in terms of the proper functioning of a person's epistemic faculties.

For these faculties to function properly, they must function as they were designed to function, and they must be functioning in an appropriate environment, the kind of environment for which they were designed. (The notion of *design* seems already to bring something like a theistic assumption into play. Plantinga, however, concedes provisionally that evolution may be thought of as "designing" people's epistemic equipment, though in the end he thinks this cannot be spelled out satisfactorily.) Furthermore, a person's faculties must be such that, in those circumstances, they function reliably, so as to produce as outputs a high proportion of true rather than false beliefs. Plantinga's formal definition of warrant is: "A belief has warrant for a person *S* only if that belief is produced in *S* by cognitive faculties functioning properly (subject to no dysfunction) in a cognitive environment that is appropriate for *S*'s kind of cognitive faculties, according to a design plan that is successfully aimed at truth" (Plantinga 2000, p. 56).

Given this epistemological framework, can belief in God be warranted when this belief is held in a basic way and not derived from other held beliefs? Plantinga's answer to this is yes. He holds that there is a component in the cognitive equipment of every person that is specifically designed to produce a belief in God, given certain "inputs" that are commonly available in our ordinary environment. Such inputs would include such situations as when people contemplate the majesty of the starry heavens, find God speaking to them in the Bible, or feel disgusted because of something they did wrong. This component in thehuman cognitive makeup Plantinga calls—following John Calvin—the *sensus divinitatis* (sense of divinity). When the *sensus* does its work, and produces in someone a belief in God, it is doing exactly what it is designed to do. Furthermore, the sensus is reliable because the belief that it regularly produces—namely, a belief that there is a God—is in fact true. (Malfunction, leading to a distorted conception of God, is of course possible.) Belief in God, produced in this way, satisfies all the conditions for being warranted, and when the belief is held with sufficient firmness the believer may be correctly said to know that there is a God.

Plantinga wishes to claim warrant also for the specific doctrinal beliefs of Christianity—for the "great things of the Gospel" (Plantinga 2000, p. 80). Considerably simplified, the model he presents is as follows: God, desiring to reveal himself, has become the principal author of the Scriptures of the Old and New Testaments, which contain his message to humankind. The individual who becomes aware of the teachings of the Gospel, through reading them or otherwise hearing of them, may come to have faith in these teachings; this faith is produced by the Holy Spirit, and has both a cognitive dimension (the teachings are "revealed to our minds") and a volitional/affective dimension (they are "sealed to our hearts"). One then comes to believe these teachings in a basic way; they are not inferred from anything else one believes, but as Jonathan Edwards said, the spiritually enlightened "believe the doctrines of God's word to be divine, because they see divinity in them" (Plantinga 2000, p. 259). A somewhat surprising (and perhaps implausible) consequence of this is that the fact that these doctrines are taught in Scripture does not constitute any part of the warrant they have for the typical believer.

Plantinga argues, however, that beliefs so formed can be—and in typical cases are in fact—warranted when held in a basic way.

This model has been described on the assumption that the Christian faith is true, but that is an assumption Plantinga qua philosopher is not entitled to. Accordingly, his formal conclusion is not that belief in Christianity is warranted, but that, if Christianity is true, then belief in its truth is probably warranted. (If it is not true, then God has not endowed humans with the *sensus divinitatis*, nor is he the principal author of Scripture, nor is faith produced in believers by the Holy Spirit, as the model claims. In this case, belief in the truth of Christianity has other sorts of causes, and is probably *not* warranted.) Plantinga concludes that the de jure objection, which claims that Christian belief is unwarranted, cannot stand on its own without support from the de facto objection, that Christianity is in fact false.

As one may expect, all of Plantinga's principal claims have met with vigorous criticism. Internalist epistemologists such as Richard Fumerton regard his externalist proper functionalism as overly permissive in the beliefs it counts as warranted. Another criticism is directed at the somewhat negative and defensive character of his apologetic. Plantinga defends the propriety of holding certain kinds of basic beliefs, but this may be of little help to those (including many believers) who do not actually find themselves believing these things in a basic way. Richard Swinburne (2001), along with a number of others, has urged that Christian apologetics ought to go beyond this and present reasons that could be convincing to the inquiring nonbeliever. Plantinga, however, considers that determining the truth of Christian belief lies "beyond the competence of philosophy" (Plantinga 2000, p. 499).

See also Plantinga, Alvin.

Bibliography

Kvanvig, Jonathan, ed. *Warrant in Contemporary Epistemology; Essays in Honor of Plantinga's Theory of Knowledge.* Totowa, NJ: Rowman and Littlefield, 1996.

Plantinga, Alvin. *Warrant and Proper Function.* New York: Oxford University Press, 1993.

Plantinga, Alvin. *Warranted Christian Belief.* New York: Oxford University Press, 2000.

Plantinga, Alvin. *Warrant, the Current Debate.* New York: Oxford University Press, 1993.

Plantinga, Alvin, R. Douglas Geivett, Greg Jesson, Richard Fumerton, Keith E. Yandell, and Paul K. Moser. Symposium on *Warranted Christian Belief. Philosophia Christi* 3 (2) (2001): 327–400.

Swinburne, Richard. "Plantinga on Warrant." *Religious Studies* 37 (2) (2001): 203–214.

William Hasker (2005)

EPISTEMOLOGY AND ETHICS, PARALLEL BETWEEN

Usually, actions are taken and policies adopted to realize envisaged goals, and they are undertaken because of belief that they will probably realize the goals. Actions and policies may be criticized, then, on one of two grounds: that the goals are ill-chosen or that the belief that the actions or policies will probably achieve the goals is ill-founded. It is interesting, and perhaps indicative of the facts to be examined below, that many words of appraisal—such as "justified," "warranted," "reasonable," "right"—are used, although possibly in slightly different senses, to indicate the acceptability or unacceptability of both goals and beliefs. Moreover, such appraisals obviously have two features in common. First, the appraisal of a particular goal or belief can be made only in view of some general principle or standard; second, the standards and principles in question are not self-certifying, and their rational justification must be a serious question for a thoughtful person. The appraisal of actions and policies thus raises two questions about both goals and beliefs: What are the proper principles or standards to be used in appraisals, and what is the rational basis for regarding any principle or standard as proper?

Historically, ethics has been the philosophical discipline concerned with these two questions about goals. (However, "goals" must be taken broadly to include not only the question of ultimate values but also the question of moral obligations and moral rights.) And historically, epistemology has been the discipline concerned with the same questions about beliefs. (Again, "beliefs" must be taken broadly to go beyond mere predictions of consequences of the use of certain means to include theories, explanations, and systems of mathematical thought.)

In order to develop the parallel between ethics and epistemology, it is convenient to identify ethical and epistemological statements. Ethical statements are those that imply a statement that could be expressed by some English sentence containing essentially "is a good thing that," "is a better thing," or "is morally obligatory that" (on the assumption that "morally obligatory" does not introduce special concepts different from a phrase such as "it is

morally wrong not to"). The class of statements thus specified will be identical with the class of statements that moral philosophers have traditionally been concerned with. Similarly, epistemological statements are those that imply a statement which could be expressed by some English sentence containing essentially "It is reasonable (or warranted) for a person S to place more confidence in h than in i," in which it is understood that for h and i can be substituted expressions of the form "its being true that. …" The class of statements thus specified is identical with the class of statements that epistemologists have been concerned with. It is useful to identify as ethical terms those phrases whose occurrence in a sentence distinguish it as an ethical statement and to identify as epistemic terms those phrases whose occurrence in a sentence characterize it as an epistemological statement.

PROBLEM OF ETHICS AND EPISTEMOLOGY

Moral philosophers have not, at least qua moral philosophers, been concerned with the acceptability of particular ethical statements such as "It would be a good thing if Jones learned to play the piano." Rather, moral philosophers have attempted to arrive at acceptable universal ethical statements which could serve as standards for the appraisal of particular situations. Thus, moral philosophers have defended or criticized such statements as "Enjoyment is always a good thing, abstracted from all consideration of consequences; nothing else is so" and "An action is morally right if and only if it will produce consequences as good as those of any other action the agent could have performed instead." The formulation of such generalizations, together with the proposal of reasons in support of them, is generally called normative ethics. Like moral philosophers, epistemologists are not concerned with the acceptability of particular epistemological statements such as "It is now highly probable that viruses are the cause of some forms of cancer." Instead, they have attempted to arrive at acceptable universal epistemological statements to be used as standards in appraising particular statements. Thus, they have examined the acceptability of such statements as "If at a time t person S seems to remember that he had the experience E at an earlier time, then he is initially warranted in believing that he did have the experience E" or "If at time t person S believes the statement h about his own experience at t, then it is reasonable for S to place at least as much confidence in h as in any other statement." The formulation of statements like these and the proposal of reasons in support of them have traditionally been the main occupation of epistemologists. In order to distinguish this task from other concerns of epistemologists, we may call it epistemology proper.

SOME MINOR POINTS OF SIMILARITY. If it is morally wrong for a person to take action *A*, but he takes that action, then in the absence of any excuse we attribute to him a fault of character and say he is morally blameworthy. Similarly, if a person has good reason for believing a certain statement but he does not, then in the absence of any good excuse we attribute to him an intellectual fault and characterize him as intellectually open to criticism. (The excuse in either case might be much the same; for instance, a person might plead that he was very upset, not "himself.") It is sometimes said that the parallel extends further in another direction, that just as there are several senses of "morally obligated," so there are corresponding senses of "reasonable to believe." For instance, it is widely believed that "morally obligatory" is sometimes used to mean the act which a being omniscient about the facts of the case and about moral principles would be morally blameworthy for not doing if he were in the place of the agent; this is said to be a sense of "morally obligatory" different from that employed when a person with possibly faulty information about the facts and imperfect clarity about moral principles is said to be morally obligated to do something. Correspondingly, it is sometimes suggested that there is a sense of "reasonable to believe" in which we may say that it is reasonable for a person to believe that any statement is *true*; this sense is contrasted with the sense in which we say it is reasonable for a man to believe what is supported by the evidence he has. Whether there are such different senses in either case we must leave an open question here.

EPISTEMOLOGY REDUCIBLE TO ETHICS?

Some philosophers (R. Chisholm, for example) have thought that there is more than just a parallel between epistemology and ethics. They have thought that epistemic terms are properly defined by means of ethical terms. If this is correct, epistemological statements are complicated ethical statements, and, presumably, epistemology is a branch—doubtless a somewhat special one—of ethics. In accordance with this view, for example, the statement "It is warranted for *S* to place more confidence in *h* than *i*" might be taken to mean "For any good thing *G*, if *S* had to choose between risking it by a wager on the truth of *h* or risking it by a wager on the truth of *i*, he would be obligated to wager on *h*." If sound, this defini-

tion has the advantage of reducing the number of undefined terms in one's total system of concepts. The disadvantages of the definition are (1) that it is doubtful whether there is any useful sense of "obligated" in which the implied equivalence is true, (2) that the definition seems to be more obscure than the definiendum, and (3) that it does not seem that the meaning of "warranted belief" involves the notion of moral obligation but, conversely, that a person's being obligated to do something, in one ordinary sense, can be explained only by reference to the propositions it is reasonable for him to believe about his situation.

THEORIES OF MEANING AND VERIFICATION

If epistemology is not reducible to ethics, there is still a parallel between the higher-order questions and theories to which epistemology proper leads and those to which normative ethics leads. The discipline dealing with these epistemological questions and corresponding to the discipline of metaethics we may call metaepistemology. The central question of these disciplines, roughly, is how the statements of normative ethics and epistemology proper, respectively, can be supported, what is their "logic." The task of showing this is different, of course, from the task of producing a specific line of reasoning in support of specific ethical or epistemological principles. Can such principles be supported in the same way that propositions in the empirical and mathematical sciences can be? Whether they can be depends in part on what the meanings of the special epistemological or ethical terms are. Moral philosophers recognize three main views about the meaning of ethical terms and, correspondingly, about the ways in which ethical principles may be justified. Three very similar views have been given by epistemologists for the meaning and support of epistemological principles.

NONNATURALISM. The first view, which we may call nonnaturalism in epistemology and ethics alike, affirms two things. It affirms (1) that epistemic and ethical terms are meaningful and that epistemological and ethical statements are true or false and (2) that epistemic and ethical terms do not name observable qualities (such as color or shape) and that their meanings cannot be defined, even partially, by citing a relation between them and names of observable qualities. Epistemic and ethical terms can be explained only by way of other epistemic and ethical terms. Hence, neither epistemic nor ethical principles can be confirmed by observation in the way that principles in the empirical sciences can be. This means that when we know ethical and epistemological statements that are not analytically true (as contrasted with ones like "A person ought to do his duty" or "One cannot know something unless it is reasonable for him to believe it"), our knowledge is synthetic a priori knowledge. A clear example of this view is the theory of probability held by J. M. Keynes, who thought that "probable" is an indefinable concept and that the axioms of probability theory are a priori synthetic knowledge.

NATURALISM. The second view can be called naturalism or "definism." It agrees with the first affirmation of nonnaturalism but denies the second. It holds that epistemic and ethical terms can be explained without the use of other epistemic or ethical terms, that they can be explained exclusively by use of empirical and logical concepts. As a result it holds that nonanalytic epistemological and ethical principles have the same logical status as the principles of the empirical sciences and can be appraised ultimately by reference to the data of observation or introspection.

For example, according to one such definition of an epistemic term, the statement "It is reasonable for S to believe h" means just "S believes h." A more plausible theory defines "know" as follows: "S knows that h at time t" means that h follows logically from the propositions S believes about his own experience at t (including what he seems to remember), plus the following (enumerated) principles of inductive logic and principles about the truth or probability of memory beliefs. Examples of parallel definitions in ethical naturalism are familiar. If the second definition given were accepted, it would be an analytic proposition that the principles of deductive and inductive logic are known by everyone, just as, given a utilitarian definition of "right," the principle of utilitarianism is analytic.

Parallel to the claim of the ethical relativist that conflicting basic ethical principles may be affirmed with equal warrant by different persons or social groups, is it possible that conflicting basic epistemological principles may also be affirmed with equal warrant by different persons, even if a naturalistic analysis of epistemological terms is adopted? For instance, just as the ethical relativist may affirm that different assessments of the ethical obligation of making a promise may be made with equal warrant by different persons, may someone claim with reason that different assessments, say, of the weight of an additional observation in support of some general law may be made with equal warrant by different persons? Such questions must be left unanswered here. It is obvious, of course, that given different evidence, it may be reasonable for a person S to believe some propositions which it would be unreasonable for person S' to believe.

NONCOGNITIVISM. The third view, which may be called noncognitivism, denies the thesis common to naturalism and nonnaturalism that epistemological and ethical statements are true or false but agrees with nonnaturalism that epistemic and ethical terms cannot be defined by means of empirical and logical concepts. Noncognitivism holds, however, that epistemic and ethical terms have a function and, in a sense, ideas in meaning. Ethical terms have been assigned various functions by different writers (functions like expressing the speaker's attitudes, changing the audience's attitudes, issuing prescriptions, declaring one's principles, giving advice, entreating, urging, exhorting, and so on).

Somewhat similar proposals have been made for epistemic terms. "It is probable that h," for example, is sometimes said to be a guarded way of affirming h or a cautious way of encouraging others to believe h. Again, "it is probable that h" is suggested not to assert that the speaker believes h but to express his belief in h. A more complex suggestion is to say that "it is reasonable to believe h" declares or expresses the speaker's own somewhat guarded inclination to believe and usually, at the same time, as a result of people's conditioning in the use of the language, strengthens the beliefs of others in h.

Further, parallel to ideas in C. L. Stevenson's ethical theory, one might say that epistemic terms also have some rather indefinite descriptive meaning, perhaps to the effect that acceptance of the proposition in question would conform to generally recognized standards—the standards, perhaps, of scientists. One could say, as P. H. Nowell-Smith does in his ethical theory, that epistemic terms have various functions in various contexts and that it is a mistake to look for some single function performed by them on every occasion. It could be added that the use of epistemic words (similar to the suggested parallel to Stevenson's theory) carries special contextual implications which distinguish them from nonepistemic terms. Since the noncognitivist does not think that epistemic and ethical statements are either true or false, his view does not contain any theory about how the truth of such statements may be established, although it often contains a descriptive account of various ways in which persons do or could try sensibly, in view of the kind of statement in question, to remove their disagreements. Defenders of the noncognitive view in epistemology include R. Chisholm, Stephen Toulmin, and J. N. Findlay. Although they have been popular, noncognitive views, in epistemology and ethics alike, appear to face some difficulties. (For instance, in conditional clauses, such as "If it were known that …, then …" or "If it were a good thing to …, then …," the ethical and epistemological terms seem to be used in their normal sense, but obviously nothing is being urged or expressed. Again, whatever specific function one assigns to terms of either type, it seems possible to find affirmations which employ the terms and cannot plausibly be said to be performing that function.) Moreover, it is doubtful whether there are conclusive reasons for rejecting "definism" (naturalism) in all its possible forms.

SOME BROADER PERSPECTIVES

One feature of both ethical and epistemic terms is that even very educated people do not have any clear idea of their meaning or of how to support their applicability in, for example, the way they are able to support the assertion that someone is a bachelor. Nor is it clear how an appeal to whatever vague meaning there is could be used reasonably to require anyone, on pain of inconsistency, to accept a corresponding ethical or epistemological principle; the fact that a person rejected such a principle would always be good reason for saying that his use of the epistemic or ethical term does not correspond to the sense needed in order to require the principle. It would appear that one of the functions of moral philosophy and epistemology is, rather, to propose helpful and clarifying uses for these terms.

What would be a helpful and clarifying use for these terms must presumably be decided by a broad view of human nature and society, a view of action and the requirements of reliable prediction for the purpose of action, the need of informal social controls in a complex society, and the necessity for impartial and general rules for such control, given that human beings are for the most part intelligent, self-interested creatures. However this may be, it is likely that reflection on the functions of science (reasonable beliefs) and conscience in society may provide, in the case of science at least as well as in the case of ethics, a guide for the philosopher's reconstruction of the meaning of ethical and epistemic terms and a basis for the appraisal of epistemic and ethical principles.

It should be noted that metaethics and metaepistemology both have another part. That part is the explanation of various concepts necessary for the understanding of terms and statements of both epistemology and ethics and for an understanding of theories about how epistemological and ethical statements may be supported. Among the concepts that are epistemologically important

are "meaning," "truth," "reference," "analytic," and "a priori." Some of these concepts are also important for ethics; other concepts important for ethics are "action," "choice," "free choice," "voluntary," "intention," "motive," and so on. Both metaethics and metaepistemology, then, have branches devoted to these auxiliary concepts.

If there is a parallel between ethics and epistemology, should we go on to say that there is a parallel between ethics and science since, after all, to assert any statement in science is at least to imply that there is evidence for what is stated, that it is generally known, and so on? Is not every scientific statement, at least covertly, an epistemological statement? It seems clarifying not to go this far. Epistemological statements are of the form "It is warranted for S to believe that …," and we should note that what comes after the "that" is the sort of statement that occurs in the textbooks of science. If the meaning of this statement also has to be construed as somehow epistemological, difficulties arise.

See also Analytic and Synthetic Statements; Chisholm, Roderick; Epistemology, History of; Ethical Relativism; Ethics, History of; Keynes, John Maynard; Metaethics; Naturalism; Noncognitivism; Stevenson, Charles L.

Bibliography

Adler, Jonathan E. *Belief's Own Ethics*. Cambridge, MA: Bradford Book MIT Press, 2002.

Alston, William. *Epistemic Justification: Essays in the Theory of Knowledge*. Ithaca, NY: Cornell University Press, 1989.

Atkinson, R. F. "'Good' and 'Right' and 'Probable' in *Language, Truth and Logic*." *Mind* 64 (1955): 242–246.

Audi, Robert. *Belief, Justification, and Knowledge*. Belmont, CA: Wadsworth, 1988.

Austin, J. L. *Philosophical Papers*. Oxford: Clarendon Press, 1961. Pp. 67–71.

BonJour, Laurence, and Ernest Sosa. *Epistemic Justification: Internalism vs. Externalism, Foundations vs. Virtues*. Malden, MA: Blackwell, 2003.

Chisholm, R. "Firth and the Ethics of Belief." *Philosophy and Phenomenological Research* 51 (1) (1991): 199–128.

Chisholm, R. *Perceiving*. Ithaca, NY: Cornell University Press, 1957.

Chisholm, R. "Evidence as Justification." *Journal of Philosophy* 68 (1961): 739–748.

DePaul, Michael. *Balance and Refinement: Beyond Coherence Methods of Moral Inquiry*. New York: Routledge, 1993.

DePaul, Michael, and Linda Zagzebski, eds. *Intellectual Virtue: Perspectives from Ethics and Epistemology*. Oxford: Clarendon Press, 2003.

Fairweather, Abrol, and Linda Zagzebski, eds. *Virtue Epistemology*. New York: Oxford University Press, 2001.

Feldman, Richard. "Epistemic Obligations." In *Philosophical Perspectives 2*, edited by J. E. Tomberlin. Atascadero, CA: Ridgeview Press, 1988.

Firth, R. "Chisholm and the Ethics of Belief." *Philosophical Review* 68 (4) (1959): 493–506.

Firth, R., and R. Chisholm. "Ultimate Evidence." *Journal of Philosophy* 53 (1956): 722–739. A symposium.

Greco, John. "Virtues and Vices in Virtue Epistemology." *Canadian Journal of Philosophy* 23 (1993): 413–432.

Lewis, C. I. *The Ground and Nature of the Right.* New York: Columbia University Press, 1955. Chs. 2–3.

Sinnot-Armstrong, Walter, and Mark Timmons, eds. *Moral Knowledge?* New York: Oxford University Press, 1996.

Sosa, Ernest. *Knowledge in Perspective.* Cambridge, U.K.: Cambridge University Press, 1991.

Steup, Matthias, ed. *Knowledge, Truth, and Duty.* New York: Oxford University Press, 2001.

Toulmin, Stephen. "Probability." In *Essays in Conceptual Analysis*, edited by A. G. N. Flew. London: Macmillan, 1956.

Urmson, J. O. "Some Questions concerning Validity." ibid.

Williams, Bernard. *Ethics and the Limits of Philosophy.* London: Fontana Press, 1985.

Zagzebski, Linda. *Virtues of the Mind: An Inquiry into the Nature of Virtue and the Ethical Foundations of Knowledge.* Cambridge, U.K.: Cambridge University Press, 1996.

Richard B. Brandt (1967)
Bibliography updated by Benjamin Fiedor (2005)

EQUALITY, MORAL AND SOCIAL

The proposition "*A* and *B* are equal" may be descriptive or normative, but in either case it is incomplete without a statement of the respects in which the objects or persons compared are deemed to be equal. In instances where this appears not to be so, either the context supplies the complement or the comparison is of pure quantities, as in pure mathematics. Two objects equal in weight, or height, or value may be unequal in other respects; apart from the abstractions of mathematics and logic, no two objects could ever be said to be equal in all respects, only in all relevant respects.

Correspondingly, to say that two candidates are equal in merit would usually mean that with respect to their performances in some understood competition or examination, they deserve to be treated alike; it does not rule out treating them differently if they are unequal in other respects. Aristotle's celebrated account of justice in Book III of the *Ethics* amounts to this: No distinction ought to be made between men who are equal *in all respects relevant to the kind of treatment in question*, even though in other (irrelevant) respects they may be unequal. On the other hand, in any matter in which they are in relevant respects unequal, they ought to be treated in proportion to their relevant inequalities.

These analytical distinctions are of considerable importance in dealing with equality as a moral and social ideal. Thomas Jefferson's claim that "all men are created equal" cannot be rebutted by pointing to the obvious fact that some are taller, stronger, or more clever than others. The claim is intelligible only as a prescription, as saying that there is some respect, at least, in which no difference ought to be made in the treatment or consideration given to all men, whatever differences there might be in their qualities and circumstances.

HISTORY OF EQUALITY AS AN IDEAL

Plato preached the political equality of the sexes, Aristotle that of all free citizens; nevertheless, both laid more stress on not treating unequals equally than on any general conception of equality. Aristotle believed that some men were slaves by nature, Plato that some souls were not merely capable of higher development than others but more valuable on that account. The political egalitarianism of Pericles' Athens, described by Thucydides, was concerned only with the equality of Athenian citizens and excluded slaves and foreigners. The first generalized egalitarianism was that of the Stoics, who stressed the natural equality of all men as rational beings with an equal capacity for virtue: "Virtue closes the door to no man; it is open to all . . . the freeborn, the freedman, the slave and the king . . . neither family nor fortune determines its choice—it is satisfied with the naked human being" (Seneca).

The New Testament doctrine of the equality of all souls in the sight of God (Galatians 3:26–29) is a religious expression of a similar principle: "Ye are all one in Christ Jesus." It was profoundly modified, however, by the Augustinian doctrine of election. Men were equal only in the sense that by sin all were totally, and therefore equally, unworthy; God in his mercy extended grace to some but not to others. Thomas Aquinas qualified the equality of all men in the sight of God by the doctrine that slavery is the consequence of sin. Though there are signs of a crude social egalitarianism in some of the protest movements of the later Middle Ages, such as the Lollards and the Hussites, medieval social theory was, on the whole, antiegalitarian, deeming hierarchy to be natural both to society and to the whole universal order.

Modern egalitarianism had its beginnings in the seventeenth century. It is related in part to Calvinist doctrine, which, although it admittedly drew a sharp distinction between the saved and the damned, insisted at the same time on the equality of the elect, whether clerical or lay. This view of equality came to be associated with a theory of church government—and indirectly of secular government—that derived legitimate authority (i.e., the right of superiors to command inferiors) from the voluntary agreement of natural equals to submit to such of their number as they chose. These doctrines were given their first completely secular expression—associated with theories of natural right and social contract—by some of the Parliamentarians in the English civil war, particularly the Levelers. Colonel Rainborough's declaration in the General Council of the Army in 1647, that "the poorest he that is in England hath a life to live as the greatest he" and that no one can have a duty to obey a government that "he hath not had a voice to put himself under" is a classic expression of democratic political egalitarianism.

The idea of a natural equality of all men was a dominant theme from the seventeenth century on. Thomas Hobbes took it for granted that in the state of nature men are equal in right because roughly equal in strength and cunning. John Locke argued that by nature men are equally free, are subject only to natural law, and enjoy the same natural rights. This turns the problem of political authority and obligation into a search for reasons why free and equal men should accept the limitations of civil society. Political inequality, of ruler and ruled, must be justified as a conventional device for the better safeguarding of the rights and advantages that all men already possess but cannot securely enjoy, in a state of nature.

In eighteenth-century philosophy the idea of a natural equality of rights was reinforced by a theory of human nature, as put forth by Étienne Bonnot de Condillac and Claude-Adrien Helvétius, maintaining that all differences of character, talent, and intelligence are due to differences in environment and experience. By nature men are equal in the sense that at birth they have a limitless potentiality without natural characteristics to differentiate one from another. Consequently their diverse natures are, in fact, contingent; in principle all men are equally perfectible, given the appropriate social arrangements.

Jean-Jacques Rousseau explained social inequality by the pressures of a sophisticated way of life; in the state of nature men's needs are simple, none need rely on anyone but himself, so none can exploit another or make him subject. For Rousseau the key problem for social philosophy, to which the sovereignty of the general will could provide a solution, was to reconcile the natural equality and autonomy of men with the social condition and political authority. Without this reconciliation men cannot realize their potentiality as morally self-governing persons. Immanuel Kant offered a philosophically sophisticated version of a very similar moral position: All

human beings must be treated as ends, not merely as means; all men are equally "legislating members of the kingdom of ends," because all are equally capable of realizing the good will, the only thing in the world good in itself.

These doctrines permeated the great revolutionary movements in America and Europe at the end of the century and were made explicit in their declarations of rights. In America the doctrine of equality was a denial that any authority imposed on unwilling subjects could be legitimate merely on grounds of law or prescription; in France l'égalité repudiated privileges of prestige and opportunity based solely on noble birth. But alongside these broad popular movements were others, such as François-Noël Babeuf's Conspiracy of the Equals, which challenged economic inequalities. Protests of this kind became increasingly important in the nineteenth century, in the evolution of socialist and communist thinking.

The target of modern egalitarianism, however, is by no means solely, or even primarily, economic inequality. Such inequality is objectionable to many socialists not so much as an unequal distribution of goods but as a source of unequal power, prestige, and regard. Other forms of differentiation have been as strongly attacked—in particular, differentiation by race and color and by sex. Again, egalitarians may make very general claims, such as that in the Universal Declaration of Human Rights (adopted by the United Nations General Assembly in 1948), that "all human beings are born free and equal in dignity and rights," or they may claim, more specifically, "equality before the law" or "equality of opportunity."

This history has two noteworthy features. First, there is a recurrent theme, the idea of a universal but imprecisely defined equality; behind all differences of talents, merits, and social advantages there is some characteristically human nature by virtue of which all men are equal. Second, the focus of egalitarianism has shifted continuously, now attacking the differential treatment of barbarian and Greek, now of freeman and slave, noble and commoner, black and white, rich and poor, male and female. Egalitarianism might be said not so much to assert equality as to deny the justice of some existing inequality of treatment based on some allegedly irrelevant differences of quality or circumstance.

UNIVERSAL EQUALITY AS AN IDEAL

The notion of universal equality as an ideal is difficult to pin down. Many egalitarians have tried to argue that despite the many points of inequality, all men are alike in possessing reason, or a soul, or some other essentially human characteristic or nature, by virtue of which they stand equal. The difficulty, however, is to find an important characteristic that all men possess in *precisely the same degree*, so that whatever differences their other inequalities might justify, this fundamental equality would make them equal *qua* men. And even if one could identify such a characteristic, what would follow from it? If all men are alike in having souls, in what respect should they therefore be treated alike? After all, God is widely believed to punish wicked souls and to reward virtuous ones.

The ideal of universal equality can often be reduced to the principle that all men ought to be equally considered. This does not mean that there is any respect in which they are all alike and by virtue of which they should all be treated alike; it is rather a principle of procedure: that all men ought to be treated equally, despite all their differences, until a case has been made for saying that some particular difference between them is relevant to the matter at hand. The onus of proof rests on whoever wants to make distinctions. And up to a point this might be said to be implicit in the notion of rational decision, because it would be irrational, within a given class of cases, to treat some differently from others if no relevant grounds could be found for distinguishing between them.

Nevertheless, the principle of equal consideration does presuppose an initial commitment or decision, for it takes for granted whose interests are to count. No one claims equal consideration for all mammals—human beings count, mice do not, though it would not be easy to say why not. The Greeks made a similar distinction between themselves and barbarians, Aristotle between natural slaves and naturally free men, the slaves counting only as tools for the free men. It is not easy to see how anyone who seriously held that white men mattered but black did not could be reasoned out of this position, any more than one could argue for the equality of men and mice. Of course, many people who practice discrimination profess to believe that black men are in some way inferior to white, in intelligence, sensibility, responsibility, or some such quality, and on this account ought to be treated differently. But this is to admit the principle of equal consideration for all men, that all men count, and that an argument has to be made to justify discriminating against some among them. The man who denies that they count at all is not bound to show reasons, any more than we feel the need to show reasons for treating inanimate objects, plants, or primitive organisms, such as amoebas, according to our pleasure. Although we hesitate to inflict unnecessary pain on sentient creatures, such as mice or dogs, we are quite sure that we do not need to show good reasons for putting human interests before theirs. The boundaries of moral consideration are enlarged in practice by awakening sympathy and imagination; moral reasons presuppose an initial moral concern.

The principle of equal consideration may be more, therefore, than what is necessarily implied by the concept of rational action. The notion of acting with good reason does not in itself rule out any inequality of treatment, for it may always be possible to argue that there is some relevant difference between members of a given class. But the principle that all men should be treated as members of the class whose equality is procedurally presupposed is not necessarily implied by the notion of rational action.

However, to some philosophers universal equality has meant more than equal consideration for all men. John Plamenatz, for instance, has tied the notion closely to natural rights and has argued that there are some rights "so much more important than others that these others ought always, or nearly always, to be sacrificed to them, should the need arise" ("Equality of Opportunity," in Bryson et al., eds., *Aspects of Human Equality*, pp. 79–107). The purpose of this equality of rights is to ensure equality of freedom and opportunity: "the equal right of all men to live the kind of life that seems good to them … equality of opportunity to be oneself, to live as one pleases." This is attractive, but it hardly touches the problem of what is to be done when what pleases one man interferes or competes with what pleases another. Nor does it cope with the diversity of inclinations—can one be said to have, on a given income, an equal opportunity to become a collector of Picassos or of seashells? Or does equality of opportunity require differential provisions, so that the chance of fulfillment matches the aspiration? Does it envisage open competition or a handicap? Plamenatz has attached very great weight to the principle that every individual's view of where his own interests lie should be given equal consideration. He thus closely associates equality and freedom, denying both that one man's interest might legitimately be subordinated to another's and that anyone can be the proper judge of someone else's interest.

For some philosophers (D. D. Raphael and Gregory Vlastos, for example) the ideal of universal equality requires that the inequalities of nature be mitigated or rectified. By this view, precisely because men born with superior talents or social advantages can claim no merit on that account, it should be the aim of social policy to compensate for such advantages by differentiating between men to redress the balance. It is of course true that modern welfare states commonly do provide special amenities, such as wheelchairs for the crippled or hearing aids for the deaf, to bring naturally handicapped people up to some minimum standard of well-being. But an account in terms of meeting needs or deficiencies is more accurate than one in terms of rectifying inequalities, for the policy is not so much to remedy a handicap that one man suffers in comparison with another (wheelchairs are not meant to enable handicapped persons to compete in races with runners) as to provide conditions necessary to his well-being, understood in the light of some presupposed standard of what a good life requires. This standard will no doubt be governed by the advantages commonly enjoyed by most people in the community, so that in an affluent society a person will be taken to have more needs than in an impoverished one; however, the claim will still be grounded on his own needs and interests, not on the greater advantages enjoyed by those more fortunate.

SPECIFIC EGALITARIAN IDEALS

The demand for equality is very often directed against some specific inequalities in social arrangements. It may take the form of a protest either against distinctions based on some specific ground (for example, racial equality, sexual equality) or against discriminations in a particular field (for example, equality before the law, economic equality). Each consideration necessarily involves the other; complaints of sexual inequality imply that sex is made a ground of distinction in some fields, unspecified but understood, where it is considered by the critic to be inappropriate (for example, salaries, jobs in the public service, voting rights). On the other hand, the claim to equality before the law implies that in legal relations or in relations between persons appearing before a court, some unspecified but understood difference (perhaps of sex, or of color, or of wealth) is made a ground of distinction and ought not to be.

The meaning of these ideals changes with their context. No one means by "equality before the law" that no distinctions should be legally recognized. A social system consists necessarily of different roles, such as father, son, tenant, landlord, and congressperson, each with its own appropriate qualifications and characteristic rights and duties, established and supported by law. A system is said to be unequal only if the differences in privileges are considered unjustifiable because they are irrelevantly grounded or because the qualifications for assuming a role are unduly restrictive (for instance, if a white skin is a necessary condition for voting rights). These ideals change their focus over time. "Equality before the law" in

eighteenth-century France meant ending the disabilities of the members of the third estate as compared with the privileges of the nobles and clergy. Today it may mean abolishing racial disabilities, such as existed in South African law and with Jim Crow sanctions in the United States, or seeing that prejudice does not interfere with the administration of law. It may also mean eliminating the advantages of wealthy litigants over poorer ones, by public legal aid schemes, or making certain that no one is prevented by poverty from getting a fair trial (see Justice Hugo Black's opinion in *Griffin v. Illinois*, 351 U.S. 12, 1956).

Equality very rarely means treating everyone alike; usually it means getting rid of one system of distinctions and replacing it with another. Thus, equality of opportunity in education hardly ever means giving everyone exactly the same education; rather, it means eliminating some hitherto determining factor such as ability to pay school or university fees and substituting a test of proficiency. More ambitiously, it might aim at a system with various arrangements, each meant for an appropriate grade of intelligence or type of aptitude. Those who call this equality do so on the ground that the treatment accorded to each is equally appropriate to his needs. Thus, R. H. Tawney argued that "the more anxiously a society endeavours to secure equality of consideration for all its members, the greater will be the differentiation of treatment which, when once the common human needs have been met, it accords to the special needs of different groups and individuals among them" (*Equality*, p. 39). The greater the equality of consideration, the greater the differentiation in treatment. If the latter is not called "inequality in treatment" it is because the word *inequality* has acquired, in this sort of context, a pejorative force; "inequalities" have come to mean *indefensible* differences in treatment.

See also Impartiality; Justice.

Bibliography

HISTORY OF EGALITARIAN IDEALS

Abernethy, George L., ed. *The Idea of Equality*. Richmond, VA: John Knox Press, 1959. An anthology, from the Old Testament and Herodotus to the present. Contains bibliography.

Bouglé, Celestin. *Les idées égalitaires*. Paris: Alcan, 1899.

Lakoff, Sanford A. *Equality in Political Philosophy*. Cambridge, MA: Harvard University Press, 1964.

Locke, John. "Second Treatise on Civil Government" (1690). In *Two Treatises of Government*, edited by P. Laslett. Cambridge, U.K.: Cambridge University Press, 1960.

Rousseau, Jean-Jacques. *Discours sur l'origine et les fondements de l'inégalité parmi les hommes* (Discourse on the Origin of Inequality). Amsterdam, 1755. Various modern editions have been published.

Stephen, Sir James Fitzjames. *Liberty, Equality, Fraternity*. London: Smith Elder, 1873. A classic nineteenth-century criticism of radical and egalitarian ideals.

Thomson, David. *Equality*. Cambridge, U.K.: Cambridge University Press, 1949. Surveys the principal modern egalitarian ideals against a historical background—a useful, brief general introduction.

MORE-RECENT DISCUSSIONS

Benn, S. I., and R. S. Peters. *Social Principles and the Democratic State*. London: Allen and Unwin, 1959. Reissued as *Principles of Political Thought*. New York: Collier, 1964. See especially Chs. 5–7.

Brandt, Richard B., ed. *Social Justice*. Englewood Cliffs, NJ: Prentice-Hall, 1962. Essays by K. E. Boulding, Paul A. Freund, William K. Frankena, Alan Gewirth, Gregory Vlastos.

Bryson, L. et al., eds. *Aspects of Human Equality*. Fifteenth symposium of the Conference on Science, Philosophy, and Religion. New York: Harper, 1956. Nineteen papers on various aspects. See especially J. Plamenatz, "Equality of Opportunity."

Carritt, E. F. *Ethical and Political Thinking*. Oxford: Clarendon Press, 1947.

Hobhouse, L. T. *Elements of Social Justice*. London: Allen and Unwin, 1922.

Margolis, J. "'That All Men Are Created Equal.'" *Journal of Philosophy* 52 (13) (1955): 337–346. Argues a "fundamental and actual equality of all men."

Raphael, D. D. "Justice and Liberty." *PAS* 51 (1950–1951): 167–196.

Spiegelberg, Herbert. "A Defence of Human Equality." *Philosophical Review* 53 (2) (1944): 101–124. Interprets the concept in terms of compensation.

Williams, Bernard. "The Idea of Equality." In *Philosophy, Politics and Society*, edited by Peter Laslett and W. G. Runciman. 2nd series. Oxford: Blackwell, 1962.

Wollheim, R., and Isaiah Berlin. Symposium on "Equality." *PAS* 56 (1955–1956): 281. Reprinted in *Justice and Social Policy*, edited by F. A. Olafson. Englewood Cliffs, NJ: Prentice-Hall, 1961.

ECONOMIC AND SOCIAL EQUALITY

Dahrendorf, R. "On the Origin of Social Inequality." In *Philosophy, Politics and Society*, edited by Peter Laslett and W. G. Runciman. 2nd series. Oxford: Blackwell, 1962. A sociological approach.

Harris, R. J. *The Quest for Equality*. Baton Rouge: Louisiana State University Press 1960. "Equality" in American constitutional history and law.

Jouvenel, Bertrand de. *Ethics of Redistribution*. Cambridge, U.K.: Cambridge University Press, 1951. A critical analysis of egalitarianism.

Lampman, R. J. "Recent Thought on Egalitarianism." *Quarterly Journal of Economics* 71 (2) (1957): 234–266. Surveys economic doctrines.

Myers, H. A. *Are Men Equal?* Ithaca, NY: Great Seal, 1955. The American egalitarian tradition.

Tawney, R. H. *Equality*. Rev. ed. London: Allen and Unwin, 1952.

ADDITIONAL SOURCES

Anderson, Elizabeth. "What Is the Point of Equality?" *Ethics* 109 (2) (1999): 287–337.

Clayton, Matthew, and Andrew Williams, eds. *The Ideal of Equality*. New York: Palgrave Macmillan, 2000. Includes texts by the editors: John Rawls, T. M. Scanlon ("The Diversity of Objections to Inequality"), Tom Nagel, Derek Parfit ("Equality or Priority"), Larry Temkin, G. A. Cohen, Richard Arneson, and Ronald Dworkin. Essential contemporary texts.

Cohen, G. A. "On the Currency of Egalitarian Justice." *Ethics* 99 (4) (1989): 906–944.

Cohen, G. A. *If You're an Egalitarian, How Come You're So Rich?* Cambridge, MA: Harvard University Press, 2000.

Cohen, Joshua. "Democratic Equality." *Ethics* 99 (4) (1989): 727–751.

Cohen, Marshall, et al., eds. *Equality and Preferential Treatment: A Philosophy and Public Affairs Reader*. Princeton, NJ: Princeton University Press, 1977. Incluces essays by Tom Nagel, J. J. Thomson, Robert Simon, George Sher, Ronald Dworkin, Owen Fiss, and Alan Goldman.

Darwall, Steve, ed. *Equal Freedom*. Ann Arbor: University of Michigan Press, 1995. Includes essays by T. M. Scanlon, John Rawls ("The Basic Liberties and Their Priority"), Ronald Dworkin, Amartya Sen ("Equality of What?"), and G. A. Cohen.

Dworkin, Ronald. *Sovereign Virtue*. Cambridge, MA: Harvard University Press, 2000.

Dworkin, Ronald, et al. "Symposium on *Sovereign Virtue*." *Ethics* 113 (1) (2002): 5–143. Contains essays by Matthew Clayton, Andrew Williams, Michael Otsuka, Robert van der Veen, Marc Fleurbaey, and Ronald Dworkin.

Hurley, Susan. *Justice, Luck, and Knowledge*. Cambridge, MA: Harvard University Press, 2003.

Johnston, David, ed. *Equality*. Indianapolis: Hackett Publishing, 2000. With texts by Plato, Aristotle, the Levellers, Hobbes, Rousseau, Burke, de Tocqueville, Marx, Tawney, von Hayek, Rawls, Nozick, Sen ("Equality of What?"), Dworkin, Walzer ("Complex Equality"), Kymlicka, and Iris Young.

Kagan, Shelly. "Equality and Desert." In *What Do We Deserve?*, edited by Louis Pojman and Owen McLeod. Oxford: Oxford University Press, 1999.

Kekes, John. *The Illusions of Egalitarianism*. Cornell: Cornell University Press, 2003.

Koppelman, Andrew. *Antidiscrimination Law and Social Equality*. New Haven, CT: Yale University Press, 1996.

Nagel, Thomas. *Equality and Partiality*. Oxford: Oxford University Press, 1995.

Okin, Susan Moller. *Justice, Gender, and the Family*. New York: Basic Books, 1989.

Otsuka, Michael. *Libertarianism without Inequality*. Oxford: Oxford University Press, 2004.

Persson, Ingmar. "A Basis for Interspecies Equality." In *The Great Ape Project: Equality Beyond Humanity*, edited by Paola Cavalieri and Peter Singer. New York: St. Martin's Griffin, 1996.

Pojman, Louis P., and Robert Westmoreland, eds. *Equality*. Oxford: Oxford University Press, 1996. Includes texts by Aristotle, Hobbes, Rousseau, Hume, Babeuf and Marechal, Oppenheim, McKerlie, Temkin, Kant, Nozick, Lucas, Benn, Vlastos, Schaar, Fishkin, Westen, Galston, Rawls, Matson, Nielson, Hare, Arneson ("Equality and Equal Opportunity for Welfare"), Rakowski, Nagel, Frankfurt ("Equality as a Moral Ideal"), Pojman, Walzer ("Complex Equality"), and Vonnegut.

Rakowski, Eric. *Equal Justice*. Oxford: Oxford University Press, 1993.

Rawls, John. *A Theory of Justice*. Rev. ed. Cambridge MA: Harvard University Press, 1999 [1971].

Raz, Joseph. "Equality." Chapter 9 in his *The Morality of Freedom*. Oxford: Oxford University Press, 1986.

Roemer, John. *Equality of Opportunity*. Cambridge, MA: Harvard University, 1998.

Scheffler, Samuel. "What Is Egalitarianism?" *Philosophy and Public Affairs* 31 (1) (2003): 5–41.

Sen, Amartya. *Inequality Reexamined*. Oxford: Oxford University Press, 1992.

Shiffrin, Seana Valentine. "Egalitarianism, Choice-Sensitivity, and Accommodation." In *Reasons and Values: Themes from the Work of Joseph Raz*, edited by Philip Pettit, Samuel Scheffler, Michael Smith, and R. Jay Wallace. Oxford: Oxford University Press, 2004.

Steiner, Hillel. "Capitalism, Justice, and Equal Starts." *Social Philosophy and Policy* 5 (1987): 49–71.

Tawney, R. H. *Equality*. Rev. ed. London: Rowman & Littlefield, 1952 [1931].

Temkin, Larry. *Inequality*. Oxford: Oxford University Press, 1993.

Vallentyne, Peter. "Equality, Efficiency and Priority for the Worse Off." *Economics and Philosophy* 16 (2000): 1–19.

Van Parijs, Philippe. *Real Freedom for All: What (If Anything) Can Justify Capitalism?* Oxford: Oxford University Press, 1995.

Waldron, Jeremy. *God, Locke, and Equality: Christian Foundations in Locke's Political Thought*. Cambridge, U.K.: Cambridge University Press, 2002.

Wilkinson, T. M. "Raz on Equality." *Imprints* 3 (2) (1998): 132–155.

Stanley I. Benn (1967)
Bibliography updated by Thomas Pogge (2005)

EQUALITY, MORAL AND SOCIAL [ADDENDUM]

Equality is a potent ideal that plays a major role in a wide-range of social, political, and moral debates. Unfortunately, equality defies easy characterization, and few ideals of such significance have been so poorly understood.

EQUALITY OF WHAT?

Much debate concerns what kind of equality is desirable: income, resources, primary goods, power, welfare, opportunity, needs satisfaction, capabilities, functionings, rights, or liberties. Should the chief concern be legal, social, or political equality? These are extremely important questions, as equality of one kind fosters inequality of another. Although many assume that we should only be concerned with one kind of equality, it is arguable that various kinds of equality matter, perhaps to various degrees in different contexts.

VARIOUS KINDS OF EGALITARIANISM

Philosophers have long distinguished between formal and substantive principles of equality. It is perhaps more useful to distinguish between equality as universality, as impartiality, or as comparability. A basic principle of rationality, equality as universality reflects the view that all reasons and principles must be universal in their application. Because it applies universally, even the view that all blondes should be rich and all brunettes paupers meets this egalitarian principle.

Equality as impartiality holds that all people must be treated with disinterested fairness. Of course, positions vary dramatically regarding what constitutes treating people impartially. For example, Kantians regard impartiality as treating people as ends in themselves and never merely as means, whereas for Utilitarians it requires neutrality concerning different people's interests when maximizing the good.

Although all plausible moral theories are committed to equality as universality and impartiality, equality as comparability reflects a deeper commitment to equality. Equality as comparability is concerned with how people fare relative to others. This is a distinctive substantive view that rivals nonegalitarian positions such as Utilitarianism and libertarianism.

Another important distinction is between instrumental egalitarianism, according to which equality is valuable only insofar as it promotes some other valuable ideal, and noninstrumental egalitarianism, which holds that equality is sometimes valuable in itself, beyond the extent to which it promotes other ideals. On noninstrumental egalitarianism, any complete account of the moral realm must allow for equality's value.

Many who favor significant redistribution from the wealthy to the poor are instrumental egalitarians; they favor such redistribution only as a way of reducing suffering, aiding the worst off, fostering solidarity, or strengthening democratic institutions. Such reasons are morally significant and compatible with equality as universality and impartiality. But each is also compatible with the rejection of noninstrumental egalitarianism and equality as comparability.

Further distinctions: in person-affecting versions of egalitarianism, inequality only matters insofar as it adversely affects people; in impersonal versions, inequality can matter even when it does not adversely affect people. Similarly, deontic egalitarianism focuses on duties to address the legitimate complaints of victims of inequality by improving their situations, whereas telic egalitarianism focuses on removing objectionable inequalities as a means of improving the goodness of outcomes. Deontic egalitarianism focuses on assessing agents or actions in order to minimize the consequences of unavoidable inequalities for which no one was responsible, whereas telic-egalitarianism focuses on the goodness of outcomes in such a way that such inequalities may matter.

UNDERSTANDING EQUALITY

The notion of equality is widely assumed to be:

holistic—concerned about (in)equality between groups or societies, blacks and whites, women and men, Ethiopians and Swiss, and so on. The aim is to address the factors accounting for objectionable inequalities between different groups or societies;

simple—we all know what equality is, that where everybody has the same amount of x, for whatever x we are interested in; and

essentially distributive—concerned with how certain acts or goods are distributed among various groups; *ceteris paribus,* an equal distribution is best.

The conventional assumptions are questionable. Arguably, the notion of equality is:

individualistic—groups and societies are not the proper objects of moral concern, individuals in groups and societies are. For example, though on average whites may be richer than blacks, if inequality of wealth matters, then it matters between rich and poor blacks, as well as rich blacks and poor whites;

complex—in judging outcomes regarding inequality, many considerations seem relevant, including how much deviation there is from a state of "pure" equality, how "gratuitous" the inequality seems, or the extent to which individuals have a "complaint" regarding equality. Moreover, the size of an individual's egalitarian complaint may depend on how he or she fares relative to the average person, the best off person, or all those better off than he or she; and, in addition, one might add individual complaints, focus on the worst-off's complaints, or add everyone's complaints, but give special weight to larger complaints. On reflection, there are many distinct "aspects" of equality that underlie and influence egalitarian judgments; and

essentially comparative—equality is a relation that obtains between individuals, and the concern is for how individual's fare relative to each other.

LUCK EGALITARIANISM AND RESPONSIBILITY

Luck egalitarianism aims to rectify luck's influence in people's lives. Acknowledging the importance of autonomy and personal responsibility, luck egalitarianism holds that it is bad when one person is worse off than another through no fault or choice of his or her own. So luck egalitarians object when equally deserving people are unequally well off but not when one person is worse off than another due to his or her own responsible choices—perhaps to pursue a life of leisure or crime.

Some luck egalitarians distinguish between option luck—luck to which we responsibly open ourselves—and brute luck, luck that simply befalls us, unbidden. On this distinction, any option-luck inequalities such as those that result from people autonomously choosing to gamble or invest in the stock market are unobjectionable. By contrast, brute luck inequalities—such as those that result from some being born with less intelligence or to poorer parents or being struck down by lightning, cancer, or an accident—are objectionable.

Against luck egalitarianism, some claim that egalitarians should aid the worse off—for example lung-cancer victims or low-income earners—even if they were partly responsible for their predicament—say, because they smoked or dropped out of school. Against the option/brute luck distinction, some contend that drawing the line between them is difficult and that it is objectionable if Mary takes a prudent risk and John an imprudent one yet Mary fares much worse than John, because option luck frowns on Mary but smiles on John.

EQUALITY AND FAIRNESS

If I give one piece of candy to Andrea and two to Rebecca, Andrea might immediately protest, "Unfair!" This natural reaction suggests an intimate connection between equality and fairness. On one view, concern about equality is a matter of comparative fairness that focuses on how people fare relative to others. Specifically, concern about equality reflects the view that inequality is bad when and because it is unfair, where the unfairness consists in one person being worse off than another no more deserving.

The intimate connection between equality and fairness illuminates the relevance and limitations of luck egalitarianism's "through-no-fault-or-choice-of-their own" clause. On this view, among equally deserving people inequality is bad because it is unfair for some to be worse off than others through no fault or choice of their own. But among unequally deserving people inequality is not bad or unfair for someone less deserving to be worse off than someone more deserving even if the former is worse off through no fault or choice of his own. For example, egalitarians need not object if criminal John is worse off than law-abiding Mary, even if John craftily avoided capture and so is only worse off because, through no fault or choice of his own, a falling brick injured him.

Additionally, in some cases inequality is bad because unfair even though the worse off are responsible for their plight, as when people are worse off because they chose to do their duty or acted beyond the call of duty, in adverse circumstances not of their making. So, on reflection, luck itself is neither good nor bad from the egalitarian standpoint. Egalitarians object to luck that leaves equally deserving people unequally well off. But they can accept luck that makes equally deserving people equally well off or unequally deserving people unequally well off proportional to their deserts. Thus, luck will be approved or opposed only to the extent that it promotes or undermines comparative fairness.

ARGUMENTS AGAINST EQUALITY AND RESPONSES

Many arguments have been offered against equality. Some contend that a world in which everyone would be the same would be undesirable. On some accounts, equality conflicts with freedom because even if one had a perfectly equal outcome, one could only preserve such an outcome by preventing people from voluntarily engaging in beneficial exchanges. Some argue that equality requires that we level down the better off if we cannot benefit the worse off. For example, we might have to blind the sighted, handicap the athletically gifted or disfigure the beautiful even if no one benefited from such actions. Thus, many believe that we should accept prioritarianism, and give priority to peo-

ple the worse off they are in absolute terms, rather than egalitarianism, which focuses on people's relative positions.

Some egalitarians soundly reject the radical egalitarian position that people should be equal in all respects. Only some inequalities are normatively significant, they argue, and they are compatible with vast inequalities in other respects. Regarding freedom, egalitarians may argue that genuine freedom involves the autonomous formulation and effective implementation of a meaningful life plan commensurate with one's capacities, a prospect that is incompatible with the levels of inequality prevalent throughout much of the world. Moreover, freedom is not all that matters; fairness does, too, so some tradeoffs may be necessary between freedom and equality when they conflict.

The leveling-down objection fails against person-affecting and deontic egalitarianism. Moreover, although it applies to telic versions of equality as comparability, it also applies to other impersonal moral principles to which many are committed, like proportional justice. Egalitarians can admit that worsening conditions for the better off might be bad but that this does not show that inequality doesn't matter, merely that it isn't all that matters. Equality is not the only ideal that would have terrible implications if exclusively pursued; the same is true of justice, utility, freedom, and perfection. The main lesson of the leveling-down objection is that we must be pluralists, a point readily granted by egalitarians.

REMAINING QUESTIONS

Many questions have not been addressed. For example, does inequality matter more at high or low levels? Is it affected by variation in population size? Does it matter between societies as much as within societies? Or between different species? Should egalitarians compare whole lives, simultaneous segments of lives (say, today's elderly with today's youth), or corresponding segments of lives (today's elderly with tomorrow's elderly)? Should egalitarians be neutral regarding space and time, or does inequality's significance depend on whether societies are connected? These questions are all important, and their answers may significantly bear on our understanding of morality and equality. It is no accident that appeals to equality are ubiquitous. Equality remains a powerful human ideal.

See also Libertarianism; Utilitarianism.

Bibliography

Anderson, Elizabeth. "What Is the Point of Equality?" *Ethics* 109 (1999): 287–337.

Arneson, Richard. "Equality and Equal Opportunity for Welfare." *Philosophical Studies* 56 (1989): 77–93.

Arneson, Richard. "Welfare Should Be the Currency of Justice." *Canadian Journal of Philosophy* (2000): 497–524.

Atkinson, A. B. *The Economics of Inequality*. Oxford: Clarendon Press, 1975.

Cohen, G. A. "On the Currency of Egalitarian Justice." *Ethics* 99 (1989): 906–944.

Crisp, Roger. "Equality, Priority, and Compassion." *Ethics* 113 (2003): 745–763.

Dworkin, Ronald. *Sovereign Virtue*. Cambridge, MA: Harvard University Press, 2000.

Dworkin, Ronald. "What is Equality? Part 1: Equality of Welfare," and "Part 2: Equality of Resources." *Philosophy and Public Affairs* 10 (1981): 185–246, 283–345.

Frankfurt, Harry. "Equality as a Moral Ideal." *Ethics* 98 (1987): 21–43.

Hurley, Susan. "Luck and Equality." *Supplement to the Proceedings of The Aristotelian Society* 75 (2001): 51–72.

Kolm, S. Ch. "The Optimal Production of Social Justice" In *Public Economics*, edited by J. Margolis and H Guitton, pp. 145–200. New York: Macmillan, 1969.

Kolm, S. Ch. "Unequal Inequalities, I and II." *Journal of Economic Theory* 12 and 13 (1976): 416–42, 82–111.

Lippert-Rasmussen, Kasper. "Egalitarianism, Option Luck, and Responsibility." *Ethics* 111 (2001): 548–579.

Lucas, J. R. "Against Equality." *Philosophy* 40 (1965): 296–307.

Lucas, J. R. "Against Equality Again." *Philosophy* 52 (1977): 255–280.

McKerlie, Dennis. "Equality and Time." *Ethics* 99 (1989): 475–91.

Nagel, Thomas. *Equality and Partiality*. New York: Oxford University Press, 1991.

Nozick, Robert. *Anarchy, State, and Utopia*. New York: Basic Books, 1974.

Nussbaum, Martha, and A. K. Send, eds. *The Quality of Life*. Oxford: Clarendon Press. 1992.

Parfit, Derek. "Equality or Priority?" In *The Ideal of Equality*, edited by Matthew Clayton and Andrew Williams, pp. 81–126, New York: St. Martin's, 2000.

Rakowski, Eric. *Equal Justice*. Oxford: Oxford University Press, 1993.

Rawls, John. *A Theory of Justice*. Cambridge, MA: Harvard University Press, 1971.

Roemer, John. *Equality of Opportunity*. Cambridge, MA: Harvard University Press, 1998.

Schaar, John H. "Equality of Opportunity and Beyond." In *Nomos IX: Equality*, edited by R. Pennock and J. Chapman, pp. 228–249. New York: Atherton Press, 1967.

Scheffler, Samuel. "What Is Egalitarianism?" *Philosophy and Public Affairs* 31 (2003): 5–39.

Sen, A.K. *Inequality Reexamined*. Cambridge, MA: Harvard University Press, 1992.

Sen, A. K., with James Foster. *On Economic Inequality*. Oxford: Clarendon Press, 1997.

Temkin, Larry S. "Egalitarianism Defended." *Ethics* 113 (2003): 764–782.

Temkin, Larry S. *Inequality*. Oxford: Oxford University Press, 1993.

Temkin, Larry S. "Inequality: A Complex, Individualistic, and Comparative Notion." In *Philosophical Issues* 11, edited by Ernie Sosa and Enriquea Villanueva, 327–352. Blackwell, 2001.

Temkin, Larry S. "Justice and Equality: Some Questions about Scope." In *Social Philosophy and Policy*. Vol. 12, edited by Paul Miller, 72–104. New York: Cambridge University Press, 1995.

Tungodden, Bertil. The Value of Equality. *Economics and Philosophy* 19 (2003): 1–44.

Vallentyne, Peter. "Brute Luck, Option Luck, and Equality of Initial Opportunities." *Ethics* 112 (2002): 529–557.

Vonnegut, Kurt, Jr. "Harrison Bergeron." In *Welcome to the Monkey House*. New York: Dell, 1998.

Williams, Bernard. "The Idea of Equality." In *Philosophy, Politics, and Society*, Second Series, edited by Peter Laslett and W.G. Runciman, 110–131. Basil Blackwell, 1962.

Larry Temkin (2005)

ERASMUS, DESIDERIUS
(1466?–1536)

Desiderius Erasmus, the great Renaissance humanist and scholar, was born at either Rotterdam or Gouda in Holland, the illegitimate son of a priest. As a child he studied at Gouda, and from 1475 to 1483 he studied at Deventer with the Brethren of the Common Life, a pious, modernist-humanist order. Next, he studied at Hertogenbosch, became an Augustinian friar at St. Gregory's (near Gouda), and, in 1492, was ordained a priest. Disliking monastic life, in 1494 he became the Latin secretary to the bishop of Cambrai. The next year he went to the University of Paris to study theology, but he found both the life and the scholastic philosophy distasteful. In 1499 he went to England, where he became a close friend of the humanists John Colet and Thomas More and devoted himself to the study of the classics and sacred literature, desiring to combine the new humanistic spirit, based on the revival of interest in the classics, with Christian learning. In 1500 he returned to the Continent and devoted himself to the study of Greek. One of his first famous works was published in this period, the *Enchiridion Militis Christiani* (Handbook of a Christian soldier; 1501), an appeal for a return to the simple spirit of early Christianity.

In Belgium, in 1504, Erasmus came across a manuscript of Lorenzo Valla's *Annotationes* on the New Testament, in which Valla criticized the Vulgate (Latin) version of the Bible and set forth a critical method for arriving at a correct text of scripture. Erasmus was tremendously impressed and published an edition of Valla's work in 1505, after which he returned to England and copied the Greek New Testament from the manuscripts available to him there. He then went to Italy as a tutor to the sons of Henry VIII's doctor and took his doctorate of divinity at Turin in 1506. He lived in various Italian cities for the next three years and began publishing the famous edition of his *Adagia*, a collection of 3,000 proverbs from classical writers, at Venice in 1508. As a result of this work, he was soon recognized as the foremost scholar of northern Europe. In 1509 he returned to England and stayed with Thomas More. There, he wrote the *Moriae Encomium* (In praise of folly), a witty satire on worldly learning and activities and a presentation of simple, pious, nontheological Christianity. While in England he lectured at Cambridge on Greek and on St. Jerome's [c. 347–419] epistles. In 1514 he went to Basel, Switzerland, to assist the publisher Johann Froben (c.1460–1527) in preparing an edition of his works. While there he received a summons to return to monastic life, which he resisted strongly, and finally Pope Leo X (1475–1521) granted him a dispensation allowing him to live in the world.

In 1516 he published one of his most influential works, the Greek edition of the New Testament. Comparing various manuscripts and citations from the church fathers, he presented a more accurate text than the Vulgate, along with his own elegant Latin version and many learned and critical notes. This edition became a model and inspiration for the new learning and for critical scholarship. Theologically, its omission of an interpolated passage in I John 5:7–8, stating the doctrine of the Trinity, greatly influenced liberal reformers like Michael Servetus, and its emphasis on St. Paul and the Greek fathers strongly affected those early reformers and those who antedated the Reformation who were anxious to turn from the opulence of the Church of Rome and from the intricacies of late Scholasticism to the spirit of primitive and early Christianity.

From 1517 to 1521 Erasmus stayed chiefly in Louvain, where he was involved with the new college for the study of the sacred languages: Greek, Hebrew, and Latin. He corresponded with humanistic scholars all over the world and became, perhaps, the leading figure of the northern Renaissance. His influence was great in all Europe, especially in southern France and Spain (where he was offered a chair at the new University of Alcalá). Liberal and reformist theologians and classical scholars looked to him for inspiration. In 1521 he went back to Basel, where, with Froben, he published a long series of works on the church fathers (editions on St. Jerome, St.

Cyprian [third century], Pseudo-Arnobius [fifth century], St. Hilary [c. 315–c. 367], St. Irenaeus [c. 120 to 140–c. 200 to 203], Ambrose [339–397], St. Augustine, St. Chrysostom [c. 347–407], St. Basil [c. 329–379], and St. Origen [185?–?254]), all of which helped center attention on the theology of the early fathers rather than on that of the medieval Scholastics. His *Colloquies*, first published after 1518 and in many revised and expanded editions thereafter, is an excellent example of the revived and revitalized Latin style of the Renaissance; the several editions include biting and satirical attacks on various human institutions and beliefs, especially those connected with the church and with popular superstition.

Erasmus's merciless and witty critiques of church practices, monastic activities, Scholasticism, popular religion, and so on, as well as his scholarly efforts toward establishing the Greek text and the meaning of the New Testament and the doctrines of the early church fathers, had made him outstanding in the movement for church reform. As the reform movement became more revolutionary, however, Erasmus tried to stay aloof from the struggles. Both orthodox and reformist theologians pressed him to take a stand, while he sought means for mediation and reconciliation. When Martin Luther became more aggressive and violent in his words and actions, and when various early reformers criticized Erasmus for his refusal to join them, he, always hypersensitive to criticism, withdrew more and more.

Finally, in 1524 Erasmus spoke out against Luther in his work *De Libero Arbitrio* (On Free Will), in which he tried to show that Luther had dogmatically decided that man had no free will, even though (1) the issue was so complex that no human could really find a satisfactory solution to the problem and (2) the biblical texts were so obscure that no one could really tell what they asserted. Erasmus maintained that he preferred to recognize the inability of man to discover adequate answers to such theological problems and to rest content with the decisions of the church on such matters. Luther's furious reply, *De Servo Arbitrio* (The bondage of will; 1525), cried out against Erasmus's gentle humanistic skepticism and his willingness to accept church teachings uncritically. Christianity, Luther insisted, requires certainties, not opinions or probabilities. Salvation cannot be based on doubts. He concluded that if Erasmus wished to remain a skeptic, he should remember that *Spiritus sanctus non est scepticus* (the Holy Spirit is not a skeptic) and that judgment day is coming.

Erasmus wrote another answer, the *Hyperaspistes* (1526), and to a great extent broke with his former reform-minded friends. When the reformers took control at Basel in 1529, Erasmus left for Freiburg im Breisgau, Germany, where he stayed almost until his death (which occurred in Basel seven years later as he was preparing to return to Holland). During his last years he continued to use his vast scholarship, his pen, and his influence to bring about religious and political peace. Attacked by both the radical reformers and the conservative churchmen, he tried to find a moderate solution before both sides became so rigid that a compromise maintaining the unity of Christendom was impossible. He advocated making sufficient internal reforms within the church to satisfy the less extreme reformers. Various popes and some Reformation leaders took him seriously (Pope Paul III [1468–1549] is supposed to have wanted to make him a cardinal), while the Sorbonne theologians condemned some of his works and views. The Spanish Inquisition stamped out the influence of his followers in Iberia, and the leading reformers attacked him both as a petty, self-serving person and as a heretical religious thinker.

THOUGHT

Erasmus's ambiguous position in the religious struggles was probably the result of his peculiar nondogmatic point of view and his cautious attitude toward developments in human affairs. He claimed to advocate the "philosophy of Christ," in contrast with the various kinds of Scholastic theories put forth by the Thomists, the Scotists, the Ockhamites, and others. Their technical discussions about the nature of baptism, grace, and the freedom of the will left him entirely unmoved. Rather than take their arguments and analyses seriously and present refutations, Erasmus attempted to undermine the whole Scholastic approach with the force of his ridicule.

In place of the philosophical and theological systems of the time Erasmus set forth his "philosophy of Christ," to be arrived at by pious study rather than by disputations. This "philosophy" was supposed to represent the simple and essential message of Christianity in its spirit rather than its letter; it was a message to be lived, not to be formulated in abstract systems. It was a nondoctrinal religion, a religion without a theology, that could be approached through the early church fathers and the morality of the New Testament but not through the morass of distinctions, terminology, and theory built up in the Middle Ages. This outlook had a great impact on the most liberal reformers and the nondoctrinal mystics.

Erasmus, who was so fully aware of the foibles of man, was also extremely cautious about the genuine possibilities for reform or constructive improvement in man

and his institutions. This may account for his refusal to leave the Church of Rome (although he died without receiving the sacraments). Some have interpreted this refusal as due to personal fears, but it seems more probable that Erasmus remained within the church because he believed that it was better to preserve and improve what already existed than to risk the even greater abuses that might follow the destruction of the current order. Erasmus saw the Church of Rome as fossilized, in much the same manner that he portrayed the Jewish synagogue. On the contrary, he saw the reformers as revolutionists who, intentionally or not, were destroying the very fabric of human existence. He told Luther, "I always freely submit my judgment to the decisions of the Church whether I grasp or not the reasons which she prescribes."

He also declared, in the midst of the early Reformation struggles, "I will put up with this Church until I shall see a better." He apparently felt that, given the human condition, it was important to retain the (far from ideal) way that Christ's message had been institutionalized; at the same time he urged a revival of concern for the substance of this message and a revitalization of the church through the correction of as many abuses as possible and the encouragement of scholarly and moral efforts to recapture the original Christian spirit. Otherwise, he feared, the frail human world might be torn entirely asunder. But, for better of worse, the course of events carried the division of Christendom to a complete rupture; each side became more and more rigid and dogmatic rather than compromising on a vague or undefined Erasmian position.

INFLUENCE

Although Erasmus can hardly be classified as a professional philosopher, he influenced the course of philosophy in many ways. His humanistic scholarship greatly affected the European educational system and, both personally and through his many writings, Erasmus greatly encouraged the teaching and study of Greek, Latin, and Hebrew—the languages that were most important to intellectual achievement. The upheavals in the curricula that occurred in most of the major institutions of higher learning at that time were in large measure due to Erasmus's influence and spirit, and the study of the hitherto unknown or neglected classics of both the Greco-Roman and the Judeo-Christian worlds (many in the editions prepared by Erasmus himself) that resulted from this was the source of many new ideas and theories that became part of the intellectual revolutions of the Renaissance.

Erasmus's ridicule of Scholasticism, although hardly a philosophical refutation of either its methods or its doctrines, created the generally accepted view that the medieval approach to philosophical questions was trivial and useless. He made it difficult for many intellectuals to take seriously the views of St. Thomas Aquinas, John Duns Scotus, William of Ockham, and such later Scholastics as Francisco Suárez.

Besides teaching future generations to scoff at the achievements of the school philosophers, Erasmus also had a major role in creating the critical spirit that culminated in the Enlightenment. Through his satire, his critical scholarship, and his undogmatic spirit Erasmus popularized a critical and questioning attitude toward accepted mores, institutions, opinions, and texts that was to flourish in many forms in the next centuries, undermining confidence in almost every area of traditional achievement.

Thus, Erasmus, who was essentially conservative by nature and who shunned almost all theoretical or philosophical discussion, not even wishing systematically to oppose dogmatism with skepticism, as Michel Eyquem de Montaigne later did, was one of the most influential figures of the sixteenth century in changing the entire intellectual climate of opinion and in establishing the direction in which modern thought developed.

See also Augustine, St.; Colet, John; Duns Scotus, John; Luther, Martin; Medieval Philosophy; Montaigne, Michel Eyquem De; More, Thomas; Ockhamism; Origen; Patristic Philosophy; Reformation; Renaissance; Scotism; Servetus, Michael; Suárez, Francisco; Thomas Aquinas, St.; Thomism; Valla, Lorenzo; William of Ockham.

Bibliography

WORKS BY ERASMUS

Omnia Opera. 9 vols., edited by Beatus Rhenanus. Basel, Switzerland: N.p., 1540–1541.

Desiderii Erasmi Roterodami Opera Omnia, Emendatiora et avctiora. 10 vols., edited by Jean Le Clerc. Leiden, Netherlands: Petri Vander, 1703–1704.

The Epistles of Erasmus. 3 vols., edited and translated by Francis Morgan Nichols. New York: Longmans, Greene, 1901–1918.

Opus Epistolarum. 12 vols., edited by P. S. Allen. Oxford, U.K.: Clarendon Press, 1906–1958.

The Praise of Folly, edited and translated by Leonard F. Dean. Chicago: Packard, 1946.

Inquisitio de Fide, edited and translated by Ernst F. Winter. New York: N.p., 1961.

The "Adages" of Erasmus: A Study with Translations, edited by Margaret Mann Philipps. Cambridge, U.K.: Cambridge University Press, 1964.

The Colloquies of Erasmus. Translated by Craig R. Thompson. Chicago: University of Chicago Press, 1965.

La correspondance d'Érasme: Édition intégrale traduite et annotée d'apres l'Opus epistolarum. 12 vols., edited by P. S. Allen, H. M. Allen, and H. W. Garrod. Brussels, Belgium: Presses Académiques Européennes, 1967–1984.

The Collected Works of Erasmus. 86 vols. Toronto, Canada: University of Toronto Press, 1974–2003.

WORKS ABOUT ERASMUS

Allen, Percy Stafford. *The Age of Erasmus*. Oxford, U.K.: Clarendon Press, 1914.

Allen, Percy Stafford. *Erasmus: Lectures and Wayfaring Sketches*. Oxford, U.K.: Clarendon Press, 1934.

Bataillon, M. *Érasme et l'Espagne*. Paris: E. Droz, 1937. A two-volume Spanish-language edition translated by Antonio Alatorre was published by Fondo de Cultura Económica (Mexico City, Mexico) in 1950.

Bouyer, Louis. *Autour d'Érasme: Études sur le christianisme des humanistes catholiques*. Paris: Éditions du Cerf, 1955.

Feugère, Gaston. *Érasme: Étude sur sa vie et ses ouvrages*. Paris: L. Hachette et cie, 1874.

Froude, James Anthony. *Life and Letters of Erasmus: Lectures Delivered at Oxford 1893–4*. London: Scribner, 1894.

Haeghen, Ferdinand van der. *Biblitheca Erasmiana: Bibliographie des oeuvres d'Érasme*. 12 vols. Ghent, Belgium: C. Vyt, 1897.

Huizinga, Johan. *Erasmus and the Age of Reformation*. Translated by F. Hopman and Barbara Flower. New York: Harper, 1957.

Kaiser, Walter J. *Praisers of Folly: Erasmus, Rabelais, Shakespeare*. Cambridge, MA: Harvard University Press, 1963.

Kunze, Johannes. *Erasmus und Luther: Der Einfluss des Erasmus auf die Kommentierung des Galaterbriefes und der Psalmen durch Luther, 1519–1521*. Hamburg, Germany: Lit, 2000.

Popkin, Richard H. *The History of Scepticism: From Savonarola to Bayle*. Rev. ed. New York: Oxford University Press, 2003.

Renaudet, Augustin. *Érasme: Sa pensée religieuse et son action d'après sa correspondance (1518–1521)*. Paris: F. Alcan, 1926.

Renaudet, Augustin. *Érasme et l'Italie*. Geneva: E. Droz, 1954.

Torzini, Roberto. *I labirinti del libero arbitrio: La discussione tra Erasmo e Lutero*. Florence, Italy: L.S. Olschki, 2000.

Richard Popkin (1967, 2005)

ERIGENA, JOHN SCOTUS
(c. 810–c. 877)

John the Scot (Irishman) or Erigena (of Irish birth) was active as a scholar in the court of Charles the Bald around 850 to 870. He intervened in the debate on predestination with a controversial treatise. At the request of the emperor, he made a Latin translation of the works of Dionysius the Pseudo-Areopagite (followed later by translations of St. Maximus the Confessor [c. 580–662] and Gregory of Nyssa). The direct contact with the Greek theological tradition opened his mind for a more speculative neoplatonic interpretation of the Christian doctrine of creation than what he knew from his Latin authorities. Confronting both hermeneutic traditions with the requirements of "right reason," Erigena composed his own theophilosophical synthesis, *Periphyseon*.

Periphyseon is an attempt to understand the "division of Nature" and its "unification," thus offering a comprehensive interpretation of the Christian doctrine of creation, sin, and salvation as revealed in Genesis 1–3. Nature stands for the whole universe, encompassing both God and creation in all its divisions. It is the task of the philosopher to examine both the division of this Nature, that is, its articulation into a manifold of species from the most general to the most particular, and its unification from the utmost manifold to absolute simplicity. In the neoplatonic tradition *diairesis* (which divides a genus into specific forms) and *synopsis* (which brings a dispersed plurality under a single form) are not just two logical procedures of dialectic. They correspond to the movements of reality: the procession of multiplicity from the One and its return into the One; in Christian terms, creation and redemption.

At the start, Erigena introduces his famous fourfold division of nature, which will provide the main structure for the entire discussion. By applying the dialectical method of dividing a genus into species by differences, he presents a division that can be applied to the whole Universe, or Nature. The most fundamental difference is that between creating and being created. Applying four possible combinations of these differences one may discover the four fundamental species of Nature:

(1) That which creates and is not created

(2) That which creates and is created

(3) That which is created and does not create

(4) That which neither is created nor creates

The first species of nature is God, the uncaused cause of everything. The third species, which is diametrically opposite to the first, stands for the sensible world, comprehending the many species of animals and plants that come to be in times and places. The second species has attributes of both extremes: it is both created and creative. This is the level of the primordial ideas wherein God has from all eternity created all species (before they are manifested in time and place and individualized in matter). Finally, there is the fourth nature, which must be understood again as God. It is, however, God not as the creative cause from which all things proceed, but as the ultimate Good toward which of all things return.

In this division the divine nature is that which stands first and last. Still, God is not simply a species among many, because he "transcends everything that is or can be" and thus seems to fall outside all system. But one could as well say that God is the whole system in its unfolding and that all four divisions of nature are moments within the circular process whereby the divine nature proceeds from and returns to itself. In fact, the most fundamental distinction, that between creative nature and created nature, must itself be overcome. This is most true on the level of the primordial ideas, wherein the creator expresses in his Word his being as the being of the creatures: therefore, that nature is said to be both creative and created. As Erigena provokingly says, "God is the essence of all things" (*essentia omnium*). "It follows that we ought not to understand God and the creature as two things distinct from one another, but as one and the same" (Vol. III, 678C). In fact, this sensible world has no subsistence on its own but exists only through participation in the divine being and the primordial causes.

If the being of the creature is nothing but a participation in the being of its creator, one may also understand the creation of the world as God's creation of himself. "God is everything that truly exists because he himself makes all things and is made in all things." By creating the manifold species God reveals and makes himself known proceeding from his ineffable nature, where he is unknown even to himself. In this sense creation is revelation and the whole world must be understood as a theophany, that is, an "appearing of God." For everything that exists is nothing else but "the apparition of what is not apparent, … the comprehension of the incomprehensible, the materialization of the spiritual, the visibility of the invisible" (Vol. III, 633A). When it is said in the Christian creed that God creates "from nothing," it can only mean that God creates all things "out of the nothingness," which he is himself as transcending all beings. Only in his creatures "he begins to be."

In this cosmic process of emanation and return, human nature occupies a central place. Human nature, which comprehends body, vital powers, perception, imagination, reason, and intellect, is the "workshop of all things" (*officina omnium*), the intermediary connecting the whole universe, preventing its falling into separate sensible and intelligible realms. Apart from being created, human nature resembles the divine nature in all respects. Thus, as the divine mind, the human soul finds in itself eternal *a priori* knowledge of all created things. In the divine wisdom, however, things exist as primordial causes or substantial forms, in human knowledge as the effects of those ideal forms.

Through the Fall, however, this connatural knowledge has been lost and the soul has fallen into ignorance of itself and of the content of its ideas. Human nature turned away from the creator, dishonoring its natural dignity and making itself similar to the beasts. This irrational nature does not belong to the image of God. In his original plan God had wanted to create humans similar to angels, not divided into male and female, without needing for their multiplication a sexuality similar to that of irrational beasts. But because God had foreseen from all eternity that humans would abuse their freedom and sin, from the first moment of their temporal existence, and thus fall from the status of equality with the angels to the level of the beasts, he introduced in the creation of the human being the consequences of sin before it occurred. Thus, the sexualized fleshy body (with all what it involves as pain, passion, sickness, and corruption) was created with the original rational nature, an addition required as a remedy and a penance for sin. It will be overcome when, at the resurrection, all shall rise in a perfect, sexless, spiritual body.

A philosopher must not only explain how creatures proceed from God but also how they return "by the same stages through which the division had previously ramified into multiplicity, until it arrives at that One which remains inseparably in itself and from which that division started" (Vol. II, 526A). Erigena makes a clear distinction between the general return to God, which is the common and natural destination of the whole creation (all corporeal things will return, that is, be resolved into their incorporeal causes), and the special return, which is only reserved to rational beings, the angels and the humans. At the end all human beings, blessed and damned alike, will return to the perfection of one and the same human nature. Still, they will be individually distinguished, not by differences in nature, body, or place, but by the different access each shall be granted to God's self-revelation. Those who led a righteous life will be beatified and allowed to see God in differing gradations of his theophanies. The damned, on the contrary, will be refused access to that vision and will be eternally tormented with the "vain dreams" of those things that incited their desires while still living.

Erigena stands apart from any of his contemporaries in his original speculations on creation and redemption, showing a great confidence in the harmony of reason and revelation. Still, he only exercised a limited direct influence in the Middle Ages, where he was mostly appreciated as a translator of Dionysius. *Periphyseon* was condemned as heretical in 1225 and copies of it were burned. From a philosophical point his greatest accomplishment is his understanding of creation as the self-creation of God. This doctrine attracted the admiration of idealist philosophers such as Friedrich Wilhelm Joseph von Schelling and Georg Wilhelm Friedrich Hegel, which led to his rediscovery in the twentieth century.

See also Neoplatonism; Pseudo-Dionysius.

Bibliography

WORKS BY ERIGENA

Periphyseon = The Division of Nature. Translated by I. P. Sheldon-Williams. Montreal: Bellarmin, 1987.

Periphyseon. 5 vols. Turnhout, Belgium: Brepols, 1996–2003.

Treatise on Divine Predestination. Translated by Mary Brennan. Notre Dame, IN: University of Notre Dame Press, 1998.

WORKS ABOUT ERIGENA

Brennan, Mary. *A Guide to Eriugenian Studies: A Survey of Publications 1930–1987.* Fribourg, Switzerland: Editions Universitaires, 1989.

Carabine, Deirdre. *John Scottus Eriugena.* New York: Oxford University Press, 2000.

McEvoy, James, and Michael Dunne, eds. *History and Eschatology in John Scottus Eriugena and His Time.* Louvain, Belgium: Louvain University Press, 2002.

Moran, Dermot. *The Philosophy of John Scottus Eriugena: A Study of Idealism in the Middle Ages.* New York: Cambridge University Press, 1989.

Van Riel, Gerd, Carlos Steel, and James McEvoy, eds. *Iohannes Scottus Eriugena: The Bible and Hermeneutics.* Louvain: Louvain University Press, 1996.

Carlos Steel (2005)

EROS

See *Love*

ERROR

When we engage in discursive thought and declarative speech, we may attain various forms of success: intelligibility, precision, correctness, and so on. These felicities are best explained by contrast with the corresponding mishaps that threaten our beliefs, assertions, and especially our claims to know something. A person's thinking may be inadequate because he is ignorant, and what he says may be deficient because it is incoherent, rough, or, perhaps most important of all, downright false.

Many philosophers have been troubled in attempting to account for the occurrence of falsity in people's assertions and opinions, that is, in trying to understand how there could be such a thing as error at all. In examining these difficulties, we shall assume a man's statement is erroneous in case it is false and it reflects his belief. Thus, if a man lies, he may speak falsely, but not erroneously. We shall also assume that a person holds a false belief when he is inclined to express it in a statement that would be false. The statement would be erroneous; consequently we can say the belief it mirrors is erroneous as well.

Our inquiry will focus on a pair of famous knots:

(1) Do we believe anything when our belief is false? If a surgeon is convinced his patient will die, and he is correct, there is something he expects: the patient's demise. But if he is mistaken, there is no such event as the patient's death. Did the surgeon then expect nothing? Depicted thus, erroneous thinking seems impossible. Plato inherited this perplexity from Parmenides and finally resolved it.

(2) Granting that error can occur, is it ever voluntary? Clearly we are to blame for some of our mistakes, yet who knowingly and willingly goes in for false beliefs? This puzzle comes from René Descartes.

THE POSSIBILITY OF ERROR

Parmenides' maxim was that only being—what is—can exist. From this he argued that we cannot "know that which is-not … nor utter it; for the same thing can be thought as can be." In other words, "You will not find thought without what is, in relation to which it is uttered" (G. S. Kirk and J. E. Raven, *The Presocratic Philosophers*, Cambridge, U.K., 1957, pp. 269–278). According to Plato, the Sophists drew an incredible doctrine from these enigmas: They argued that error is asserting and believing "what is not," specifically, talking and "thinking contrary to the things that are" (*Sophist* 240C, D, F. M. Cornford translation). To state and think what is not is, however, to state and think nothing, which is not stating or thinking.

What could have led the Sophists to this paradoxical view? Naturally, it reinforced other logically quite independent doctrines of theirs regarding truth and falsity, for example, their claim that whatever seems true to any man is true for him and therefore *is* true (*Theaetetus* 161C–179C). The only direct support for their denial of error, however, derives from analogies. In *Euthydemus* (283E–288A) the stating of what is not is compared with

impossibilities such as doing but doing nothing or gesturing although there is no gesture one performs. The parallel with sense perception in *Theaetetus* (188D–189B) is renowned. If you see, hear, or touch, then there is something you perceive. To see what is not, is not seeing.

PLATO'S THEORY OF ERROR. In reply, Plato suggests alternative models that will incline us to regard falsehoods as full-fledged (though incorrect) assertions. His most promising comparison is with spelling, where misspelling is the natural counterpart to stating falsely. This analogy is central to Plato's unsuccessful third definition of knowledge in *Theaetetus* (201D–208B), and it reappears in his successful treatment of falsity in *Sophist* (242D–253, 261D–264B). We should imagine a student who tries to spell syllables and words as his teacher says them or inscribes them. When he answers, aloud or in writing, with the right letters in the right order, he uses letters to represent a thing "that is," the teacher's utterance or inscription. According to conventions of spelling, the correct sequence of letters corresponds to what the teacher said or wrote. When the student misspells, he fails to represent the teacher's utterance or inscription, and nothing corresponds to the misspelling. Does the pupil therefore spell nothing? We describe his failure more accurately by saying: "When he misspells, what he spells is not; that is, not anything said or written by the instructor." How shall we describe cases where he gets some letters right and thus represents phonetic or graphological elements of what the instructor said or wrote? Clearly he does not *spell* those elements. For suppose he answers, "w-i-n" after the instructor says "wine." It makes no sense to claim: "He misspelled the word, but he correctly spelled some sounds the teacher made." Further, if the student happens to give the correct spelling of another word (as in this case), we must realize that the other word "is not," because the teacher did not say it. All this is secondary, however; the significant point is that when he misspells, the pupil is nevertheless engaged in the activity of spelling. This suggests that incorrect statements are statements after all.

Let us develop this parallel. If we restrict ourselves to the simplest paradigms—Plato used the true statement "Theaetetus is sitting" and the false statement "Theaetetus is flying"—we notice how words in declarative speech function like letters in spelling. Individual letters may represent sounds but do not spell them. Similarly, the name "Theaetetus" stands for a thing that is, but saying the name "Theaetetus" is not stating anything. Spelling words requires you to conjoin letters of different types, consonants and vowels, in appropriate patterns. Speech, too, is fitting words together. "If you say 'lion stag horse' or any other names," Plato remarks, "such a string never makes up a statement"; but joining a noun with a verb "gets you somewhere" and of such a compound "we say it 'states,' not merely 'names' something" (*Sophist* 262B–E).

Now if you proclaim, "Theaetetus is flying," when he is not airborne, you refer by name to something that is, in the course of *stating* what is not. There is no aerial activity of Theaetetus to correspond to what you state. If you declare, "Theaetetus is sitting," and his posture is appropriate, then something corresponds to what you state. In Plato's words, the true statement "states about [Theaetetus] the things that are"; whereas "the false statement states about [him] things *different* from the things that are," and therefore states "things *that are not* as being" (*Sophist* 263B).

This correspondence theory of true and false statements may be extended to thought by our assumption that a man thinks falsely in case he is inclined to express his thought in a statement that is false. So formulated, the Platonic theory illustrates how error, even though it is believing what is not, hardly consists in believing nothing. Therefore, Sophists cannot maintain that thinking erroneously is not thinking.

Plato's account is, however, needlessly anchored to the type of counterexample he used against the Sophists. The falsehood "Theaetetus is flying" happens to be "about" an existing thing, but Plato makes this feature a prerequisite for every statement, true or false. He writes: "Whenever there is a statement, it must be about something" that exists (*Sophist* 262E; cf. 263C). Even if this ruling allows statements about things that do not exist now but did or will exist, it excludes too much. For instance, it would be impossible for me to state falsely, "There are flying saucers." By Plato's rule, saying this is not stating unless there are flying saucers for me to talk about. So if I *state* that there are flying saucers, I speak truly.

Here we should invoke Plato's orthographic model. The student does not cease to spell when upon occasion he misses every letter and thus fails to represent any sounds his teacher made. By analogy, why disqualify my utterance simply because I fail to refer to existing things? A correspondence theory still explains why it is false to state, "There are flying saucers": nothing corresponds to what is stated; that is, nothing corresponds to the existence of flying saucers, because none exist.

But the correspondence theory needs elaboration before it will transform Plato's view into a general account of correct and incorrect assertion. What "things

that are" would I depict if I conceded "Flying saucers do *not* exist"? Does the nonexistence of flying saucers correspond to what I state? How can there be such a thing? Again, what "things that are" differentiate a true subjunctive conditional, for example, "If I had watered the lawn, it would not have died," from its false contrary, "Even if I had watered the lawn, it would have died"? Does the same withered grass make one statement true and the other false?

Because of these obscurities it appears that Plato has demonstrated how incorrect belief and assertion can occur, but he has not produced an exhaustive analysis of them. Plato's demonstration shows awareness of the distinctive features of assertion, sensitivity to the differences between referring and asserting, and perspicacity about the ontological status of what a person believes; indeed, treatments of error by such twentieth-century philosophers as G. E. Moore and Bertrand Russell are not more satisfactory in these respects.

MOORE AND RUSSELL. Moore's *Some Main Problems of Philosophy*, adapted from lectures he delivered in 1910–1911, appears to contain two incompatible theories: (1) The dyadic theory, according to which believing pairs believers and propositions. "Error," writes Moore, "always consists in believing some proposition which is false" (p. 66). (2) For complicated reasons Moore later contends that "there simply are no such things as propositions" for people to believe (p. 265), and he renounces his "attempt to analyse beliefs" (p. 266). Nevertheless, he characterizes truth and falsity of beliefs as follows: "To say that a belief is true is to say that the fact to which it refers is or has being; while to say that a belief is false is to say that the fact to which it refers is not" (p. 267). In technical terminology: "To say that [a] belief is … false is to say that there is *not* in the Universe any fact to which it corresponds" (p. 277).

In his 1953 preface, Moore comments that his two theories may after all be consistent; perhaps he used the term *proposition* in different senses when he first maintained and later denied their existence as targets for believing (p. xii). Apart from this problem, fundamental questions arise concerning Moore's treatment: Are there any facts for mistaken beliefs to be about? Are they nonexistent facts "in the Universe," or perhaps existent ones outside it? Besides, the very notions of "proposition" and "fact" are notoriously obscure.

Moore hints at a different analysis when he considers a person's belief that we are now listening to a brass band. What the person erroneously believes is a "combination of us at this particular moment with the hearing of that particular kind of noise"—a combination which "simply has no being" (p. 255).

Russell's multiple relation theory, in his *Problems of Philosophy*, develops such an analysis. Concerning Othello's mistaken belief that Desdemona loves Cassio, Russell says: "The relation called 'believing' is knitting together into one complex whole the four terms Othello, Desdemona, loving and Cassio" (p. 126). This belief is mistaken because there does not exist another "complex unity, 'Desdemona's love for Cassio,' which is composed exclusively of the *objects* of the belief, ... with the relation [loving] which was one of the objects occurring now as the cement that binds together the other objects of the belief" (p. 128).

The snags in this analysis are well known. How does loving cement things? In case Desdemona is indifferent to Cassio, how does believing sew them together with loving and Othello? Can believing stitch together any collection of objects? Russell noted the last two problems in his 1918 lectures, "The Philosophy of Logical Atomism" (in *Logic and Knowledge*). He recognizes that the structure of Othello's belief requires that "loves" should "occur as a verb"; but he is afraid that admitting the syntactical unity of "Desdemona loves Cassio" is tantamount to "assuming the existence of the non-existent ... [namely,] a non-existent love between Desdemona and Cassio" (p. 225). But as Plato saw, there can be units of speech—statements—and thought without correspondents in reality.

ERROR AND VOLITION

Plato did not need to convince us that false belief is possible. But Descartes's thesis, that error is always voluntary, seems a contrived solution to an entirely gratuitous theological muddle. This appearance is deceptive.

Descartes begins his *Meditations* with a survey of dreaming, sensory illusion, and the errors they occasion; next he shows we can prove a few things for certain, including God's existence. Then he reasons: The deity "cannot have given me a faculty [of thinking] whose right employment could ever lead me astray"; however, "it seems to follow that therefore I can *never* go wrong" (*Meditation* IV, in *Descartes' Philosophical Writings*, translated by P. T. Geach and G. E. M. Anscombe, p. 93). Descartes's answer to this puzzle is that men have false beliefs, but through their own doing, not God's. Men are endowed by God with such power of will that they can assent to propositions they do not know to be true—that is, to "ideas" that are not "clear and distinct." Is God to blame for this disharmony between our limited capacity

for knowledge and our unlimited power of assenting? No, "will is just a single thing; it is incompatible with its nature that anything should be subtracted from it" (*Meditation* IV, p. 99). Besides, although we are free to, we do not have to believe propositions for which we lack conclusive proof. In order to avoid "unsuspected error," we must restrain our desire for truth and withhold assent until we know for certain. (Descartes's *Principles of Philosophy* XXIX, XXXII, XXXV, XXXIX, XLII explain these points in detail.)

Now if we put aside Descartes's theological preoccupations, and his advice that we should only believe what is obvious, at least two genuine questions arise:

(1) Do we exercise any control over our convictions and opinions, as Descartes's concept of "assenting" requires? Clearly, people may decide to make statements. Some criminals voluntarily confess their misdeeds, and others are forced, against their will, to admit guilt. How about belief? Can we choose to reject a proposition that seems most likely, according to available evidence, and believe another that seems less plausible? Perhaps not. But we often make decisions as we form our opinions, as we collect or neglect data and seek or ignore expert testimony. Men who undergo brainwashing are deprived of this control over the formation of their beliefs. The same holds, incidentally, for knowledge. It is absurd to say the investigator decided *to know* but not absurd to say he resolved *to find out* for certain who robbed the grocer. Moreover, children are compelled *to learn* things. In acquiring knowledge and forming opinions, we pursue rather obvious goals: conclusive proof and correct information.

(2) Even so, is it intelligible to suppose that people act deliberately and knowingly when they settle upon *false* beliefs? One everyday case should dispel the appearance of contradiction: I study the racing form, mull over the evidence, and conclude that Wayfarer is bound to take the handicap. I willingly commit myself to this belief by wagering my paycheck. I realize, however, that even well-grounded expectations like mine can prove erroneous. Consequently, if my horse loses, it is true to say, "I formed my erroneous belief willingly, after deliberation, with the intention of predicting the handicap winner; furthermore, I was aware that I could be mistaken." It was not my goal to be wrong, but it was within the scope of my intention. Anyone who aims at truth is prepared for falsity, just as a marksman is prepared to miss the bull's-eye. Can we say I erred "knowingly"? A man who punches another is hardly ever certain that his victim will be injured, but

from a legal standpoint he knowingly inflicts harm if he has reason to think injury might result from his blow.

There remains another type of error, fortunately quite infrequent, where such awareness is impossible. This is the unusual situation where you are convinced you know something, banish doubt from your mind, and still turn out to be wrong. Perhaps you acted deliberately and followed your inclinations in pushing your investigation until you believed you could not be wrong. But with this degree of conviction, you cannot have the least awareness that you are mistaken. Your error, then, is not fully voluntary.

See also Correspondence Theory of Truth; Descartes, René; Moore, George Edward; Plato; Russell, Bertrand Arthur William; Sophists; Volition.

Bibliography

PLATO

Plato's *Theaetetus* and *Sophist*, along with excellent commentary, are translated by F. M. Cornford in *Plato's Theory of Knowledge* (London: K. Paul, Trench, Trubner, 1935). For further analysis of Plato's theory, see Gilbert Ryle, "Letters and Syllables in Plato," *Philosophical Review* 69 (4) (1960): 431–451; D. Gallop, "Plato and the Alphabet," in *Philosophical Review* 72 (3) (1963): 364–376, and Raphael Demos, "Plato's Philosophy of Language," with comments by J. L. Ackrill, in *Journal of Philosophy* 61 (20) (1964): 595–613.

MOORE AND RUSSELL

The views of Moore and Russell can be found in G. E. Moore, *Some Main Problems of Philosophy* (London: Allen and Unwin, 1953), especially Chs. 3 and 13–16, and Bertrand Russell, *Problems of Philosophy* (London: Williams and Norgate, 1912; reset 1946), Ch. 12, and "The Philosophy of Logical Atomism," in *Logic and Knowledge*, edited by R. C. Marsh (London: Allen and Unwin, 1956). For a view opposed to those of Moore and Russell, see Alexius Meinong, *Untersuchungen zur Gegenstandtheorie und Psychologie* (Leipzig, 1904), translated by Isaac Levi, D. B. Terrell, and Roderick Chisholm as "The Theory of Objects," in *Realism and the Background of Phenomenology*, edited by R. M. Chisholm (Glencoe, IL: Free Press, 1960).

There is a brilliant discussion of the connection between negative judgments and falsity in Gottlob Frege's essay "Negation," in *The Philosophical Writings of Gottlob Frege*, edited and translated by Max Black and P. T. Geach (Oxford: Blackwell, 1952).

DESCARTES

See *Descartes' Philosophical Writings*, translated by P. T. Geach and G. E. M. Anscombe (Edinburgh, 1954). Spinoza's objections to Descartes's theory that belief necessarily involves assent can be found in the *Ethics*, Part I, Props. 29, 32, and appendix, and all of Part II; see also the lucid

analysis of Descartes and Spinoza by J. L. Evans, "Error and the Will," in *Philosophy* 38 (1963): 136–148.

OTHER RECOMMENDED TITLES

Almeder, Robert. "Recent Work on Error." *Philosophia* 27 (1999): 3–58.

Bennett, Jonathan. "Spinoza on Error." *Philosophical Papers* 15 (1986): 59–73.

Burgess, John. "Error Theories and Values." *Australasian Journal of Philosophy* 76 (1998): 534–552.

Devlin, John. "An Argument for an Error Theory of Truth." *Nous*, Supp. 17 (2003): 51–82.

Gomez-Torrente, Mario. "Vagueness and Margin for Error Principles." *Philosophy and Phenomenological Research* 64 (2002): 107–125.

Howson, Colin. "Error Probabilities in Error." *Philosophy of Science*, Supp. 64 (4): S185–S194.

Popkin, Richard. *Scepticism from Erasmus to Spinoza*. Berkeley: University of California Press, 1979.

Sievert, Donald. "Whose Fault Is It Anyway? Descartes's Doctrine That We, and Not God, Are Responsible for the Errors of the World." *Southwest Philosophy Review* 13 (1997): 33–41.

Stroud, Barry. "Explaining the Quest and Its Prospects: Reply to Boghossian and Byrne." *Philosophical Studies* 108 (2002): 239–247.

Wiland, Eric. "Psychologism, Practical Reason and the Possibility of Error." *Philosophical Quarterly* 53 (2003): 68–78.

Williams, Bernard. *Descartes: The Project of Pure Enquiry*. Atlantic Highlands, NJ: Humanities Press, 1978.

Irving Thalberg (1967)
Bibliography updated by Benjamin Fiedor (2005)

ERROR THEORY OF ETHICS

An "error theory of ethics" is the view that the ordinary user of moral language is typically making claims that involve a mistake. The concepts of ethics introduce a mistaken, erroneous, way of thinking of the world or of conducting practical reasoning. The theory was most influentially proposed by John L. Mackie in his book *Ethics: Inventing Right and Wrong* (1977). Mackie believed that ordinary moral claims presuppose that there are objective moral values, but there are no such things. Hence, the practice of morality is founded upon a metaphysical error.

Mackie's arguments against the existence of objective values are of two main kinds. One is the argument from relativity, which cites the familiar phenomenon of ethical disagreement. Another is the argument from "queerness." The moral values whose existence Mackie denies are presented as metaphysically strange facts. They are facts with a peculiar necessity built into them: their essence is that they make demands or exist as laws that "must" be obeyed. In Kantian terms, the demands made by morality are thought of as categorical, "not contingent upon any desire or preference or policy or choice." The foundation of any such demands or laws in the natural world is entirely obscure. Hence, the right response of a naturalist is to deny that there can be such things. It should be noticed that this is not supposed to be an argument against any particular morality, for instance, one demanding honesty or fidelity, but against the entire scheme of thought of which particular ethical systems are examples.

Another influential theorist whose work bears some resemblance to Mackie's is Bernard Williams, whose *Ethics and the Limits of Philosophy* (1985) equally raises the doubt that ethics cannot possibly be what it purports to be, although Williams's own arguments are more specifically targeted on the morality of duty and obligation.

Responses to the error theory have taken several forms. Both the argument from relativity and that from queerness have been queried, the former on the grounds that, even if ethical opinions differ fundamentally, this does not prevent one from being right and the others wrong, and the latter mainly on the grounds that Mackie suffered from an oversimple, "scientistic" conception of the kind of thing a moral fact would have to be. Perhaps more fundamentally, it is not clear what clean, error-free practice the error theorist would wish to substitute for old, error-prone ethics. That is, assuming that people living together have a need for shared practical norms, then some way of expressing and discussing those norms seems to be needed, and this is all that ethics requires. Mackie himself saw that ethics was not a wholly illegitimate branch of thought, for he gave a broadly Humean picture of its function in human life. Even projectivists maintain that our need to express attitudes, coordinate policies, and censure transgressions is a sufficient justification for thinking in terms of ethical demands. Ethics does not invoke a strange world of metaphysically dubious facts but serves a natural human need.

See also Mackie, John Leslie; Metaethics; Williams, Bernard.

Bibliography

Blackburn, S. "Errors and the Phenomenology of Value." In *Essays in Quasi-Realism.* New York: Oxford University Press, 1993.

Mackie, J. L. *Ethics: Inventing Right and Wrong.* Middlesex, U.K.: Penguin, 1977.
Williams, B. *Ethics and the Limits of Philosophy.* Cambridge, MA: Harvard University Press, 1985.

Simon Blackburn (1996)

ESCHATOLOGY

"Eschatology" is a doctrine or theory (*logos*) of the end (*eschaton*). "End" here can have two meanings. First, it can mean the end of each individual human life. Second, it can mean the end of the world—or, more narrowly, of the human race. In the first, the individualistic, sense eschatology is an account of the destiny that awaits each person after death. In the second, the cosmic or social, sense it is a description of a goal (*telos*) in which history will be fulfilled. This goal may be of either a this-worldly or an otherworldly kind.

The distinction between these two senses is important, for it is possible to have an eschatological doctrine in one sense without having any in the other. Plato held that the soul, being immortal, would face judgment after death, that it would receive rewards and punishments according to the goodness or badness of its earthly life, and that it would be given an opportunity to choose the condition of its next existence (*Republic* 608C to end). However, he did not believe that there was any purpose to history as a whole. Conversely, a Marxist believes in a purpose of history although he disbelieves in personal survival.

It is doubtful whether eschatology in the second sense is to be found anywhere outside Zoroastrianism and Judaism—together with the religious and philosophical systems that have drawn inspiration from them: Mithraism from the first, Christianity and Islam, and Western thought in general, from the second. According to Greek and Indian thinkers history moves in cycles. Just as the seasons recur within each solar year, so all events recur in a sequence of "Great Years." By contrast, the Persian Zend-Avesta and the Bible state that history is nonrepeatable and that it is destined for a divine fulfillment in which good will triumph over evil.

In the Bible the second sense predominates. The Old Testament contains only a few vague references to a personal afterlife. But it often refers to a future time when God will establish his everlasting reign of righteousness and peace (for example, Isaiah 11:1–9). The New Testament affirms that this divine end or goal has been reached by the exalted Christ, who defeated the powers of evil on the cross (see, for example, Acts 2:14–36; Colossians 2:8–15; Ephesians 2:11–22; Hebrews 2:5–18). Those who believe in Christ have eternal life here and now (John 3:36; 5:24). While living in "this age," this spatiotemporal order that is still subject to sin and death, they have a foretaste of "the age to come," a renewed cosmos that will be wholly subject to the will of God.

This view of history stands in contrast, first, to the Greco-Roman theory of recurrent cycles—a theory condemned by Origen and Augustine—second, to the humanistic dogma of inevitable social progress, and, third to Marxism. Although the Marxist philosophy of history owes its form to G. W. F. Hegel's dialectic, its content has often been called a secularization of Christian eschatology. Materialistic determinism would be equivalent to a personal providence, the proletariat to the "chosen people," and the "classless society" to the kingdom of God.

During the early centuries of the church most theologians taught that there will be a universal resurrection of the dead for a final judgment at the end of history, when Christ will appear again "in glory." As a result of this judgment, it was also generally taught, some, the saved, will pass to paradise, where they will enjoy the beatific vision, but others, the damned, will be punished with everlasting torment. Four comments on this scheme are necessary:

(1) One must distinguish between belief in the immortality of the soul and belief in the resurrection of the body. The first belief is derived from Plato, who held that the soul will survive in an incorporeal state. The second belief is based on biblical revelation. Thomas Aquinas held both beliefs. He considered the immortality of the soul to be rationally demonstrable. He also thought that the dogma of a bodily resurrection could be rationally justified on the ground that since soul and body constitute (as Aristotle taught) a single substance, the soul requires the body for its self-expression and beatitude. (To account for the obvious fact that the flesh decays at death, Origen proposed the theory that although the resurrected body will have the same "form" as its earthly counterpart, it will have a different "matter.")

(2) Origen maintained that all spiritual creatures—angels, humans, and devils—will be saved in a final "restoration" (apocatastasis). But although his doctrine (known as Universalism), which was shared by Gregory of Nyssa, could claim biblical support, it was attacked by Augustine and formally condemned.

(3) Even orthodox Christian Fathers (such as Irenaeus), as well as Gnostics and Montanists, were millenarians. They believed that Christ would reign on Earth for a thousand years before the end of terrestrial history. But since the fifth century millenarianism has been almost wholly confined to minor sects.

(4) Although Clement of Alexandria and Origen spoke of a fire that would purge guilty souls, the full doctrine of purgatory (as a place of temporary punishment preparatory to the beatific vision) was not developed until the Middle Ages.

In the twentieth century there was a new attempt to understand the eschatological teaching of the New Testament (especially in the light of Albert Schweitzer's thesis that Jesus expected an imminent end of history and therefore intended his moral teaching solely for an interim). On the other hand, Rudolf Bultmann attempted to "demythologize" biblical eschatology, to restate it in existentialist terms that will make it intelligible to modern man. These instances indicate a twofold revival of interest in eschatology among professional theologians.

See also Augustine, St.; Bultmann, Rudolf; Clement of Alexandria; Death; Eternity; Gregory of Nyssa; Hegel, Georg Wilhelm Friedrich; Marxist Philosophy; Origen; Plato; Thomas Aquinas, St.; Zoroastrianism.

Bibliography

Bultmann, R. *History and Eschatology, the Presence of Eternity.* Edinburgh: Edinburgh University Press, 1957.

Charles, R. H. *Eschatology.* London, 1913. The standard work on Jewish and early Christian eschatology.

Corcoran, Kevin, ed. *Soul, Body, and Survival: Essays on the Metaphysics of Human Persons.* Ithaca, NY: Cornell University Press, 2001.

Cullmann, O. *Christ and Time.* Translated by Floyd V. Filson. London, 1951. An excellent study on the New Testament.

Flew, Antony. *The Logic of Mortality.* Oxford: Blackwell, 1987.

Hick, John. *Death and Eternal Life.* New York: Harper and Row, 1976.

Penelhum, Terence. *Survival and Disembodied Existence.* New York: Humanities Press, 1970.

H. P. Owen (1967)
Bibliography updated by Christian B. Miller (2005)

ESP PHENOMENA, PHILOSOPHICAL IMPLICATION OF

See *Parapsychology*

ESSENCE

See *Definition; Essence and Existence; Universals, A Historical Survey*

ESSENCE AND EXISTENCE

It will avoid misunderstanding if the topic of essence and existence is expounded in an order other than chronological.

SEVENTEENTH-CENTURY VIEW

Thomas Hobbes and John Locke insisted that definitions are not of things but of names. In so doing, they conceived of themselves as breaking with Aristotelianism. Hobbes said that the essence of a thing is "that accident for which we give a certain name to a body, or the accident which denominates its subject"; he had earlier denied that "the definition is the essence of any thing"; and his example of an essence is that "extension is the essence of a body" (*De Corpore*, II, 8, 23).

Locke distinguished the real essence from the nominal essence; the nominal essence is the idea of the property or properties the possession of which justifies the application of a given name; the real essence is as it is understood by "those who look on all natural things to have a real but unknown constitution of their insensible parts, from which flow those sensible qualities which serve us to distinguish them one from another, according as we have occasion to rank them into sets under common denominators" (*Essay* III, 3, 17).

The mistake that Hobbes and Locke ascribed to Aristotelianism was that of confusing the meaning of an expression with the nature of the object which the expression characterizes. In the empiricist tradition this separation of questions of meaning from questions of characterization continued to be influential. One consequence is that the concept of the real essence is dropped altogether. Another is that philosophy itself becomes defined as the study of meaning, as a linguistic inquiry. But will the Lockean separation of the real and the nom-inal, from which so much of this derives, bear scrutiny? Did Aristotle commit the error ascribed to him? Is it an error?

ARISTOTLE AND THOMAS AQUINAS

For Aristotle, the essence of an object ($\tau\grave{o}$ $\tau\acute{\iota}\,\mathring{\eta}\nu\,\mathring{\epsilon}\mathring{\iota}\nu\alpha\iota$) was what finds expression in the concept that the object embodies, the concept under which it must be identified if it is to be identified as what it is. The natural response of someone trained in the empiricist tradition is to question this concept of an object. In any particular case the question "What is *this?*" can have more than one correct answer—for instance, "a coat" or "a piece of cloth." To ask further what the essence of the thing indicated is, is to miss part of the Aristotelian point, which is best brought out by considering problems of identity. If I ask whether this is the same coat that you wore last year, I am not asking the same question that I would be asking if I inquired whether this is the same cloth made up into trousers that you used to wear in the form of a coat. "The same coat" and "the same cloth" pick out different identities. When I pick out "this" as an object, I can do so only by identifying it under some description, and the object does not have a nature apart from being identified under a description. For otherwise I could not identify what was to be characterized. In other words, we cannot identify an object solely by means of pronouns like "this" or by pointing.

It might be thought a fatal objection to this view that I can apparently identify an object without knowing what it is (a case which Aristotle allows for). Suppose I pick up something in your room and simply ask, "What is this?" The range of possible answers includes "a piece of stone," "a carving," "an image of a saint." My ignorance may extend as far down the range of specificity as you please; I must still be able to find some description to add to my use of "this" or to my pointing. For if I pick it up twice, I must be able to identify it as the same object; and it is a condition of my identifying it as an object at all that I should be able in principle to pick it up, or otherwise indicate it, more than once. Possible reidentification is a necessary condition of identification. But if this is so, then I must, in picking it up, be able to characterize it, even if only as "that small colorless lump" or some such description. There is a limit to vagueness, at which such purely formal concepts as "thing" and "object" lie.

Insofar, then, as Aristotle is concerned with the minimal conditions for identifying and characterizing objects, he is justified in a view which makes understanding what something is, inseparable from understanding the meaning of the description which must be applied to it if it is to be identified as what it is. The nominal and the real cannot be entirely divorced. But Aristotle expresses all this in terms of the concepts of substance and of matter and form, and in so doing he appears to lay himself open to the Hobbes-Locke type of criticism. What Aristotle meant by τί ἦν εἶναι is the subject of disagreement among translators and commentators. Hugh Tredennick in translating *Metaphysics* 1031a15 ff.) uses "essence"; Joseph Owens invents an arbitrary phrase, "the What-Is-Being" of a thing, and explains it in terms of the being of a thing which is the being of its form. The form is the necessary and unchanging element in a thing, in contrast with the matter and the composite, which may change, and the generic characteristics, which may belong to some other species (*Doctrine of Being in the Aristotelian Metaphysics,* p. 94).

Aristotle thus made the concept, under which an object must fall if it is to be identified and characterized as what it is, express a timeless and necessary element in the nature of the object itself. And insofar as Hobbes, for example, wished to deny that this timeless and necessary element was what a definition could refer to, it would be difficult to disagree. But any further discussion of Aristotle could only proceed by analysis of the doctrine of matter and form.

What is clear is that Aristotle inherited from Plato the notion of a range of fixed and timeless Forms, natures or essences which are embodied in the changing physical world. Less pessimistic than Plato about the possibility of knowledge of the nature of particular material objects, he retained the view that what the intellect grasps is always a form which could have been embodied in other matter. The name given to the being that the intellect grasps is οὐσία, which W. D. Ross renders as *essence,* following Quintilian and Seneca, who translated it as *essentia. Essentia* comes to mean the nature of a thing, the answer to the question *quid sit.* Augustine used *substantia* and *essentia* without difference of meaning, and Boethius translated οὐσία as *substantia.* From then on the word *substantia* was used in this sense and *essentia* was reserved for a new context which was first found in explicit form in Giles of Rome. This contrast is that between essence and existence, which received its completest statement in the work of St. Thomas Aquinas.

THOMAS AQUINAS. A substance is composite; it is an essence upon which existence has been conferred. When existence is conferred on an essence, what was hitherto merely possible becomes actual. In the case of physical bodies, a form receives matter. Thus the concepts of essence and existence, potency and act, form and matter are mutually correlative. The notion of *esse* being conferred upon an *essentia* so that a substance is brought into being was foreign to Aristotle because the notion of creation was foreign to him. For Aristotle, analysis in terms of essence or substance was a way of approaching what already exists or is in the process of change. For Thomas, that anything at all exists must itself be explained. It is a purely contingent fact that any particular essence is an embodied existent. The only exception to this is God, in whom essence and existence are identical. But it does not follow that by grasping what God is, we can grasp that he is, as Anselm had supposed in his vision of the Ontological Argument. For we cannot grasp the divine essence.

MODERN VIEWS

The vocabulary of essence and existence was preserved after the seventeenth century both by late Scholasticism and by its intellectual first cousin, rationalist metaphysics. Christian von Wolff inherited, perhaps from Francisco Suárez, whose influence he acknowledged, a view of the universe as a system of essences on which God has chosen to confer existence. But his view of essence as what can be conceived as a clear and distinct idea points to the influence of René Descartes and in his version of the Ontological Argument we can see the confluence of John Duns Scotus and Gottfried Wilhelm Leibniz. Knowledge of essences is expressed in propositions which are necessary truths. But these necessary truths are truths about possibilities, and it is a contingent matter of God's will being what it is that these particular essences have been actualized.

A line of thought that is only superficially like that of rationalist metaphysics runs from Spinoza to G. W. F. Hegel. In Spinoza the essence that entails existence is that of the single substance. But this version of the Ontological Argument is only part of Spinoza's whole set of theorems determining the all-inclusive *Deus sive natura.* Hegel treated the transition from essence to existence as part of the logical play with concepts that is an essential preliminary to the world of becoming. Of course we cannot deny that being is; but that, for Hegel, is only because the assertion is so bare and empty. When we deal with the realm of becoming, we have the sharpest of contrasts between the *Was-sein* (essence) and the *Das-sein* (existence), as Friedrich von Schelling, the enemy of all clear distinctions, complained.

The notion of an essence as a fixed possibility whose character may be delimited apart from our acquaintance with the existence which embodies it was inherited from Scholasticism by Franz Brentano and Edmund Husserl, whose phenomenology is concerned with essences insofar as it is a study of what is involved in *any* act of judgment, belief, feeling, or willing, independently of the context of particular acts. The use of "essence" and "existence" by Jean-Paul Sartre is partly derived from phenomenology and partly from Scholasticism. The latter influence is apparent in the way in which Sartre uses the formula that existence precedes essence in order to deny that men are created by God. Sartre identifies such a conception of creation with the notion of God creating beings with fixed, already determinate natures who would therefore be unfree. Nothing of this appears to be entailed by Thomas's use of "essence" and "existence," but Leibniz and Wolff could be more convincingly convicted on this charge. Sartre wishes to convey by his formula that men do not have determinate natures, fixed in advance of their choices. By this he means that Smith does not have an existence determined for him which if he did not live out he would not be Smith; so it is Leibniz or Wolff, and not Thomas, whose propositions he is in fact denying.

What, then, is Sartre asserting? The contention that existence precedes essence may be interpreted as entailing various consequences, not all of which were necessarily intended by Sartre. Sartre clearly does believe that his contention not only constitutes the denial of one species of determinism, as has already been noted, but also involves the invalidity of any version of the Ontological Argument, whether Anselmian, Cartesian, or Hegelian. That is, no essence is such that it is a necessary truth that there must exist some individual embodying that essence. But unfortunately the Sartrian contention is so loosely stated that he might also be taken to imply—what he certainly would not want to imply—that there are no essences, that is, no meanings, apart from existences. This is plainly false. Many meaningful expressions do not name or denote anything that exists, many descriptions do not characterize anything that exists, as the common examples of "unicorn" and "glass mountain" make clear. The chief difficulty with the Sartrian thesis, however, is not that it plainly entails absurd consequences. It is, rather, that the thesis is stated so generally, and is so inadequately developed, that it is not at all clear what does or does not follow from Sartre's contention.

See also Aristotelianism; Aristotle; Brentano, Franz; Descartes, René; Duns Scotus, John; Giles of Rome; Hobbes, Thomas; Husserl, Edmund; Leibniz, Gottfried Wilhelm; Locke, John; Ontological Argument for the Existence of God; Ross, William David; Sartre, Jean-Paul; Schelling, Friedrich Wilhelm Joseph von; Seneca, Lucius Annaeus; Spinoza, Benedict (Baruch) de; Suárez, Francisco; Thomas Aquinas, St.; Wolff, Christian.

Bibliography

PRIMARY SOURCES

Aristotle. *Metaphysics.* Translated by Hugh Tredennick. Cambridge, MA: Harvard University Press, 1944.

Aristotle. *Metaphysics.* Edited by W. D. Ross. Oxford, 1948.

Sartre, Jean-Paul. *L'être et le néant, essai d'ontologie phénoménologique.* Paris: Gallimard, 1943. Translated by H. E. Barnes as *Being and Nothingness, an Essay on Phenomenological Ontology.* New York: Philosophical Library, 1956.

Sartre, Jean-Paul. *L'existentialisme est un humanisme.* Paris: Nagel, 1946. Translated by P. Mairet as *Existentialism and Humanism.* London: Methuen, 1948.

Thomas Aquinas. *De Ente et Essentia.* Edited by M. D. Roland-Gosselin. Le Saulchoir, 1926. Translated by Armand Mauer as *Being and Essence.* Toronto, 1949.

Thomas Aquinas. *In Metaphysicorum Aristotelis Commentaria.* Edited by M. R. Cathala. Turin: Marietti, 1935.

Thomas Aquinas. *Summa Theologica.* Ottawa, 1941–1945. Translated by the Dominicans of the English Province, 3 vols. New York, 1947.

Wolff, Christian von. *Philosophia Prima Sive Ontologia.* Frankfurt and Leipzig, 1730.

SECONDARY SOURCES

Anscombe, G. E. M., and P. T. Geach. *Three Philosophers.* Ithaca, NY: Cornell University Press, 1961. Discussions of Aristotle, Thomas Aquinas, and Frege.

Ayer, A. J. "Some Aspects of Existentialism." *Rationalist Annual* (1948).

Bobik, Joseph. *Aquinas on Being and Essence, a Translation and Interpretation.* Notre Dame, IN: University of Notre Dame Press, 1965.

Owens, Joseph. *The Doctrine of Being in the Aristotelian Metaphysics.* Toronto: Pontifical Institute of Mediaeval Studies, 1951; 2nd ed., 1957.

Alasdair MacIntyre (1967)

ESSENCE AND EXISTENCE [ADDENDUM]

There was a lively and extended debate in Islamic philosophy over the relative status of essence and existence. Avicenna argued that existence is preceded by essence, in that everything that exists only comes into existence because it is brought into existence by something else, except for the ultimate existent, God, the necessary being. Many things might exist, they have essences, but unless something brings them to existence they will remain mere essences without existence. So essence precedes existence. This view was challenged by Averroes, who argued that in an eternal universe anything that could exist would exist, and the existence of a thing is not just an attribute added onto it, but is an essential aspect of its meaning. In any case, if existence is an additional attribute, suggested Shihāb al-Dīn Yaḥyā al-Suhrawardī, then essence would have to exist before the attribute was applied for it to be an essence, and an infinite regress is started. He took this stance to show that essence precedes existence since the latter is only an idea with no reality attached to it, and it is essence that characterizes reality.

Despite Averroes's arguments, the principle that essence is the most basic concept in ontology was widely accepted in Islamic philosophy right up to the time of Mullā Ṣadrā. Mullā Ṣadrā entirely reversed al-Suhrawardī's thesis, arguing that existence is equivalent to reality. This is because existence is a necessary aspect of what it is for something to exist and so there is no regress in treating the concept as an attribute. Reality is existence, albeit manifested in a variety of different ways, and these different ways appear to one to be essences. What affects one are things that exist, and one forms ideas of essences after they impinge themselves on one, so there is no doubt that one sees here a theory in which existence precedes essence.

The significance of the debate lies in what it tells of the nature of philosophy. For Avicenna and al-Suhrawardī, philosophy is the study of the essences or ideas of things, and one then moves on to wonder whether and how far they exist. For Averroes and Mullā Ṣadrā, philosophy is a study of existing things, and as one knows more about them one knows more about their properties, but they can have no properties unless they first exist. Averroes criticized the doctrine of essentialism since it implies that something has to come from outside of something to bring it to existence, and this implies that the universe constantly requires an outside force to activate it. He saw Aristotle as arguing that the natural world consists of entities that have to have the properties they have, and that if they exist they have to exist since otherwise they would be different (i.e., nonexistent) things. Taking any other position makes the acme of Aristotelian science, the definition, vacuous, since it suggests that there are aspects of a thing (its existence) that might or might not be present, thus reducing the power of the definition.

The position that is taken on essence and existence also affects the way in which philosophy is done. An essentialist uses thought experiments in philosophy, since the imagination can rule on what notions are possible or otherwise. So Avicenna and his school accordingly used examples and potentialities to explore ideas and assess their possibility. If one's imagination cannot make sense of an idea, then that idea lacks possibility and so the state of affairs that it describes cannot exist. Those who are opposed to essentialism are critical of imagination in philosophy, since they argue that envisaging a possibility does not give one useful information about what is actually a possible existent.

See also Aristotle; Averroes; Avicenna; Islamic Philosophy; Mullā Ṣadrā; Suhrawardī, Shihāb al-Dīn Yaḥyā.

Bibliography

Leaman, Oliver. *Introduction to Classical Islamic Philosophy.* 2nd ed. New York: Cambridge University Press, 2003.

Nasr, Seyyed Hossein, and Oliver Leaman. *History of Islamic Philosophy.* 2 vols. London: Routledge, 1996.

Oliver Leaman (2005)

ESTHETICS

See *Aesthetics, History of; Aesthetics, Problems of*

ETERNAL RETURN

"Eternal return" is the doctrine that every event in the universe, in all its details and in its whole cosmic context, will recur an infinite number of times in exactly the same way that it has already occurred an infinite number of times in the past. This doctrine must be distinguished from the belief in the general periodicity of nature, according to which the main features—but not the specific details—of human and cosmic history recur.

THE PRE-SOCRATICS

The periodicity of various phenomena is a fact of daily experience; the alternation of day and night, of lunar phases and of the seasons of the year, and the rhythm of breathing and heartbeats were known to primitive people. Even the idea that cosmic history repeats itself in its general features appeared in various forms in mythological thought. Among the pre-Socratics the idea was held by Anaximander, Empedocles, and the atomists. The existing universe was regarded as a result of the differentiation of an original chaos—watery, fiery, or qualitatively undetermined—into which it would eventually return and from which a similar universe would emerge. This idea of the periodicity of worlds soon became associated with the belief that not only the general features but also the most specific details would recur in the same order that they had occurred countless times in the past. According to Eudemus of Rhodes, this was the belief of the Pythagoreans: "Everything will eventually return in the self-same numerical order, and I shall converse with you staff in hand, and you will sit as you are sitting now, and so it will be in everything else, and it is reasonable to assume that time too will be the same" (H. Diels and W. Kranz, *Fragmente der Vorsokratiker*, 58B34).

The same idea of the cyclical nature of time was present, according to Pierre Duhem, in the thought of another Pythagorean, Archytas of Tarentum, who defined time as "the interval of the universe." The length of this cosmic cycle, called the Great Year or Perfect Number, was variously estimated by different thinkers who were influenced by Pythagoreanism. For Heraclitus it was equal to 10,800 years (according to another source 18,000 years). According to the testimony of the Stoics and of Simplicius (whose reliability on this point has been doubted by Friedrich Schleiermacher, Ferdinand Lassalle, John Burnet, and G. S. Kirk), it measured the period separating two successive conflagrations in which an old world perishes and a new one is reborn.

PLATO AND ARISTOTLE

Plato associated the period of the Great Year not with a periodically recurring cataclysm but with a return of all the celestial bodies to the same relative positions. Nor did Aristotle accept a universal conflagration, which was clearly incompatible with his idea of the incorruptible celestial realm. Nevertheless he did, if we accept his authorship of the *Problemata*, uphold eternal return in its most radical form: "Just as the course of the firmament and each of the stars is a circle, why should not also the coming into being and the decay of perishable things be of such a kind that the same things again come into being and decay?" (*The Works of Aristotle*, Vol. VII, p. 916a). Aristotle realized that the circularity of becoming would imply a relativization of succession: If the Trojan War will inevitably recur, in a sense we are living "prior" to it. The author of *Problemata*, however, was reluctant to accept the ultimate consequence of the idea of cyclical becoming: "To demand that those who are coming into being should always be numerically identical, is foolish" (ibid.).

THE STOICS

The problem of cyclical becoming was faced by the Stoics, who believed that at the end of each cosmic cycle a uni-

versal conflagration (ἐκπύρωσέις) that dissolves the universe into the original fire will occur. This will coincide with the beginning of another cycle; the events of the previous cycle will then be reconstituted in all their details and in the same order. But Stoics followed Aristotle by claiming that another Socrates who will marry another Xantippe and be accused by another Meletus will not be numerically identical with the previous Socrates, since numerical identity implies an uninterrupted existence. Some younger Stoics, in conceding small differences between successive Socrateses, gave up the circularity of becoming in all but name.

PLOTINUS

A curious argument for eternal return was given by Plotinus in the *Fifth Ennead* (Book VII, Chs. 1, 2). According to Plotinus, the intelligible world contains the ideal patterns not only of genera but also of all individuals, each of which successively finds its embodiment in the realm of change. But since the supply of these patterns is finite, a time will come when the same pattern—for example, of Socrates—will have to be incarnated again, and this will be possible only in the next identical cosmic cycle. Thus the successive cycles are identical, but there is no repetition within each cycle.

JEWISH AND EARLY CHRISTIAN THOUGHT

Both Judaism and Christianity, with their emphasis on the finiteness and irreversibility of cosmic history, were strongly opposed to the doctrine of eternal return. According to both the Jewish and the Christian view, the history of the world is bounded by two unique and unrepeatable events: its beginning (the Creation) and end (the Last Judgment). Every individual human life is similarly unique.

Origen, while accepting with the Neoplatonists the eternity of the world and even metempsychosis, rejected the identity of successive cosmic cycles because such a concept was incompatible with human freedom. Nemesius (*De Natura Hominis*, Ch. 38) and St. Augustine (*De Civitate Dei*, Book XII, Chs. 11, 13) rejected the doctrine, Nemesius on the ground that the Resurrection cannot take place periodically, Augustine because the incarnation of Christ occurred only once.

MEDIEVAL THOUGHT

A decree of 1277 threatening excommunication of those who accepted the Neoplatonic idea of a Great Year lasting thirty-six thousand years demonstrates the survival of this belief into the Middle Ages. Although St. Thomas Aquinas rejected the cyclical view of time by claiming that the re-creation of numerically identical individuals would be contradictory, and as such was beyond even God's power, his view was not shared by John Duns Scotus and William of Ockham. Nicolas Bonet and François de la Marche explicitly insisted on God's power to restore any past motion, and therefore a corresponding past interval of time, since there was no difference between motion and time.

EARLY MODERN THOUGHT

Thus, at the threshold of the modern era two of the central ideas of the modern cyclical view of time were present—the reversibility of motion and the relational theory of time. The third essential ingredient of the cyclical theory—the finiteness of the material universe—was excluded by Giordano Bruno's vision of innumerable worlds and limitless space. This may explain the absence of the idea of eternal recurrence in Bruno's contemporaries despite their Neoplatonic leanings. For if the number of constituent parts of the universe is infinite, the number of possible combinations is also infinite, and recurrence of the same configuration is not inevitable.

In Isaac Newton and his successors there was an additional motive for not considering the cyclical view. They regarded time as absolute, as intrinsically irreversible, irrespective of its content. Even a complete restoration of the content of the past moment would not make this moment itself present.

René Descartes came very close to the cyclical view when he wrote that matter must successively pass through all its possible forms, but since matter to him was coextensive with infinite space, the number of its configurations was inexhaustible. Furthermore, the pagan and astrological associations of the ancient cyclical theory made it thoroughly suspect.

NINETEENTH-CENTURY VIEWS

Interest in eternal return was revived only with the development of modern cosmogony. The nebular hypothesis of Immanuel Kant (1755) and Pierre Simon de Laplace (1796) implicitly raised the question of the origin of any primordial nebula: Did it represent a truly initial stage preceded by an act of supernatural creation, or was it merely one of the countless stages in an unending cycle of successive worlds? The principle of the uniformity of nature in time, anticipated by Bruno's and Benedict (Baruch) de Spinoza's belief in the eternity of the uni-

verse, strongly favored the second answer. Although the law of entropy suggested the irreversibility of the whole cosmic process, because of its statistical character it did not exclude the general periodicity of nature. Various hypothetical mechanisms were invented to provide a "rewinding of the cosmic clock," at least on a local scale. The most popular one was that of cosmic clashes by which two stellar masses that had lost their heat could be transformed into another nebula, which would then develop into another world "ever the same in principle, but never the same in concrete results," as Herbert Spencer wrote in his *First Principles* (p. 550).

Such a new world could be the same even in concrete details only if the cosmic mass did not contain an infinite number of units. Eugen Dühring, in various writings (heavily annotated copies of which were found in Friedrich Nietzsche's library), rejected the concept of actual infinity as self-contradictory and inapplicable to the physical world.

In Nietzsche's thought the concept of a finite universe and of the discrete structure of matter implied a finite number of possible successive configurations, and therefore an inevitable recurrence of a configuration defining a state of the universe that had already occurred an infinite number of times in the past; and this recurring cosmic state must, according to the then accepted deterministic scheme, generate the series of the same events in the same order as in the previous cosmic cycles. This view, formulated by Nietzsche at the end of the fourth book of *Fröhliche Wissenschaft* (1881), became central to his philosophy. The intensely lyrical way in which this view was expressed in *Thus Spake Zarathustra* hid its intellectual origins, which are far more obvious in the posthumously published fragments of *The Will to Power* (see *The Complete Works of Friedrich Nietzsche*, Vol. XV, Ch. 2, esp. p. 430). Prior to Nietzsche only a few nineteenth-century thinkers held the same view: Louis A. Blanqui (*Éternité par les astres*, 1871), Gustave Le Bon (*L'homme et les sociétés*, 1881), Jean Marie Guyau (*Vers d'un Philosophie*, 1881). It was not held, however, by Dühring, who claimed that the continuity of space admitted an infinite number of configurations even if the number of atomic units was finite (*Cursus der Philosophie*, pp. 84–85). The same objection against eternal return was raised by Alois Riehl and Alfred Fouillée; against this view Franz Selety pointed out that concrete processes were discrete and not mathematically continuous, and therefore, he claimed, eternal recurrence was unavoidable; and G. N. Lewis claimed that the attempt at avoiding an exact recurrence by assuming a whole continuum of possible values is eliminated by the quantum theory.

Henri Poincaré, although he formulated the theorem of phases, according to which any mechanical system of a finite number of particles will in a sufficiently long time pass through a configuration infinitely close to the previous one, nevertheless dismissed the application of the theorem of phases to cosmogony in his *Leçons sur les hypothèses cosmogoniques* (p. 23) as "the dream of eternal return." C. S. Peirce (*Collected Papers*, Vol. I, pp. 498–500) held the cyclical view on the unusual ground that "since every portion of time is bounded by two instants, there must be a connection of time ringwise." Furthermore, this view was entirely incompatible with the rest of his philosophy. The arguments of Abel Rey in favor of the cyclical view were not essentially different from those of Nietzsche, since they were based on the classical corpuscular-kinetic scheme of nature.

CONTEMPORARY THOUGHT

The contemporary crisis of the classical scheme of nature makes the doctrine of eternal return extremely questionable. The doctrine was based on four fundamental assumptions: (*a*) that the universe is made up of distinct atomic units that persist through time without any intrinsic change, so that they may be identified in successive moments; (*b*) that the number of atomic units is finite; (*c*) that it is meaningful to speak of a definite "state of the universe" at each instant; (*d*) that one such particular state (embodied in a definite atomic configuration) causally determines all future states (Laplacean determinism).

Except for the thesis that the size of the universe is finite, which is favored by some cosmologists, none of these theses remains unchallenged by the recent developments in physics. The atoms of modern physics do not have the rigidity and permanence of classical atoms; and without permanent elements there can be no recurring configurations. The ontological status of "state of the universe at an instant" is challenged by the relativization of simultaneity, and the validity of rigorous determinism has been seriously questioned since the formulation of the indeterminacy principle in 1927.

Moreover, there are ambiguities and discrepancies within the theory of eternal return itself. The assumption of a completely identical repetition of cosmic situations makes the theory intrinsically unverifiable. Moreover, either the successive identical cycles are distinguished by their positions in time—which means that we surreptitiously introduce an irreversible time as their container—

or we insist on the numerical identity of the cycles. But we then have only one cosmic cycle, and it clearly becomes meaningless to speak of a "succession of cycles" or of their "repetition." Although it is self-contradictory to speak of numerical identity of genuinely successive events, the two views have often been held jointly, as by the Scotists and Nietzsche.

The eternal return is rejected by all thinkers who insist on the irreversibility of becoming, genuine novelty, and the immortality of the past. Mircea Eliade regarded the theory as a manifestation of "ontology uncontaminated by time and becoming" (*The Myth of the Eternal Return*, p. 89); Émile Myerson saw in it an attempt to eliminate becoming (*L'identité et réalité*, Ch. 8). The emotional effect of the doctrine is equally ambiguous. Thus Nietzsche's mystical ecstasy over "the ring of eternity" was tinged by a note of anxiety and even despair. Gustave Le Bon compared the recurring cosmic cycles to the labors of Sisyphus, and Miguel de Unamuno, in *The Tragic Sense of Life*, regarded the doctrine as a poor substitute for personal immortality.

See also Anaximander; Aristotle; Atomism; Augustine, St.; Bruno, Giordano; Descartes, René; Dühring, Eugen Karl; Duns Scotus, John; Fouillée, Alfred; Heraclitus of Ephesus; Kant, Immanuel; Laplace, Pierre Simon de; Lassalle, Ferdinand; Nemesius of Emesa; Neoplatonism; Newton, Isaac; Nietzsche, Friedrich; Origen; Peirce, Charles Sanders; Plato; Plotinus; Poincaré, Jules Henri; Pre-Socratic Philosophy; Pythagoras and Pythagoreanism; Riehl, Alois; Schleiermacher, Friedrich Daniel Ernst; Simplicius; Spinoza, Benedict (Baruch) de; Stoicism; Unamuno y Jugo, Miguel de; William of Ockham.

Bibliography

CLASSICAL AND MEDIEVAL

Diels, H., and W. Kranz. *Fragmente der Vorsokratiker*. 6th ed. Berlin: Weidmann, 1951.

Duhem, Pierre. *Le système du monde*. Paris: A. Hermann, 1954. Vol. I, pp. 65–85, 164–169, 275–296; Vol. II, pp. 447–461; Vol. VII, pp. 441–461. On the idea of the Great Year in Greek and medieval thought.

Mugler, Charles. *Deux thèmes de la cosmologie grecque: Devenir cyclique et la pluralité des mondes*. Paris: Librarie C. Klincksieck, 1953.

Ross, W. D., ed. *The Works of Aristotle*. Oxford, 1923. Vol. VII.

Sambursky, Samuel. *The Physical World of the Greeks*. Translated by Merton Dagut. New York, 1956. Ch. 8. On Greek cosmogony.

NIETZSCHE ON ETERNAL RETURN

The Complete Works of Friedrich Nietzsche. Translated by A. M. Ludovici. Reissued, New York, 1964. Vol. XV, Ch. 2, esp. p. 430.

Andler, Charles. *Nietzsche, sa vie et sa pensée.* 5th ed. Paris: Gallimard, 1958. Vol. II, pp. 402–424; Vol. III, pp. 284–294. Vol. II discusses mythological, Greek, and modern influences on Nietzsche.

Batault, Georges. "L'hypothèse du retour éternel devant la science moderne." *Revue philosophique* 57 (1904): 158–167.

Bois, Henri. "Le 'retour eternal' de Nietzsche." *Année philosophique* 24 (1913): 145–184.

Danto, Arthur. *Nietzsche as Philosopher.* New York: Macmillan, 1965. Ch. 7.

Heidegger, Martin. *Nietzsche.* Pfullingen, Germany: Neske, 1961. Vol. I, Ch. 2; Vol. II, Ch. 3.

Horneffer, Ernst. *Nietzsches Lehre von der ewigen Wiederkunft und der bisherige Veröffentlichung.* Leipzig, 1900.

Löwith, Karl. *Nietzsches Philosophie der ewigen Wiederkunft des Gleichen.* Stuttgart, 1956.

Schlechta, Karl. *Nietzsches grosser Mittag.* Frankfurt, 1954.

Stambaugh, Joan. *Untersuchungen zum Problem der Zeit bei Nietzsche.* Haag: Nijhoff, 1959.

Steiner, Rudolf. *Friedrich Nietzsche. Ein Kämpfer gegen seine Zeit,* 3rd ed. Dornach, 1963. Pp. 187–197. On the relation of Nietzsche to Dühring.

GENERAL

Čapek, Milič. "The Theory of Eternal Recurrence in Modern Philosophy of Science." *Journal of Philosophy* 57 (1960): 289–296.

Couturat, Louis. "De l'évolutionnisme physique et du principe de la conservation de l'énergie." *Revue de métaphysique et de morale* 1 (1893): 564–572.

Denbigh, K. G. "Thermodynamics and the Subjective Sense of Time." *British Journal for Philosophy of Science* 4 (1953–1954): esp. p. 187.

Dühring, Eugen. *Cursus der Philosophie.* Leipzig: R. Reisland, 1876.

Eliade, Mircea. *The Myth of the Eternal Return.* New York: Pantheon, 1955.

Lewis, G. N. "Symmetry of Time in Physics." *Science* 31 (1930): 569–577.

Marbe, Karl. *Die Gleichförmigkeit der Welt.* Munich, 1916. Chs. 8–11.

Meyerson, Émile. *L'identité et réalité.* 5th ed. Paris, 1951.

Peirce, C. S. *Collected Papers.* Edited by Charles Hartshorne, Paul Weiss, and Arthur W. Burks. 8 vols. Cambridge, MA: Harvard University Press, 1931–1958.

Poincaré, Henri. *Leçons sur les hypothèses cosmogoniques.* Paris: A. Hermann, 1911.

Rey, Abel. *Le retour éternel et la philosophie de la physique.* Paris: Flammarion, 1927.

Riehl, Alois. *Zur Einführung in die Philosophie der Gegenwart.* Leipzig: Teubner, 1903.

Selety, Franz. "Über Wiederholung des Gleichen im kosmischen Geschehen." *Zeitschrift für Philosophie* 5 (1914).

Spencer, Herbert. *First Principles.* 4th ed. New York: Appleton, 1896.

Weber, Louis. "L'évolutionnisme physique." *Revue de métaphysique et de morale* 1 (1893): 425–452.

Whitrow, G. J. *The Natural Philosophy of Time.* London: Nelson, 1961. Ch. titled "Cyclic Time," esp. pp. 40–41.

Zawirski, Zygmunt. *L'évolution de l'idée du temps.* Cracow, 1936. Pp. 336ff.

Milič Čapek (1967)

ETERNITY

The word *eternal* is derived from the Latin *aeternus,* a contraction of *aeviternus,* which, in turn, is derived from *aevum,* a word from the same root as the English words *ever* and *aye.* In Greek the corresponding adjectives are even more obviously connected with the notion of everlasting existence. This is the original sense of the word *eternal* and probably also the sense that is still the most common in ordinary language. But in certain philosophical contexts the notion of everlasting existence is expressed rather by "sempiternal," "eternal" being reserved for the sense of "timeless."

THE "TIMELESS PRESENT" IN SCIENCE

In English and other Indo-European languages there is a usage described by grammarians as the timeless present. When, for example, we say, "Seven is a prime number," we do not intend our use of the present tense to convey anything about the present as distinct from the past or the future. For this reason we find something very curious in the sentences "Seven was a prime number" and "Seven will be a prime number." Existential statements of a mathematical kind do not refer to the time of speaking. An assertion such as "There is a prime number between 5 and 10" could never be countered sensibly by the remark "You are out of date." For this reason the entities discussed in mathematics can properly be said to have a timeless existence. To say only that they have a sempiternal or omnitemporal existence (that is, an existence at all times) would be unsatisfactory, because this way of talking might suggest that it is conceivable they should at some time cease to exist, an absurdity we want to exclude.

Mathematics, however, is not the only study in which use of the timeless present is appropriate. The same idiom can be found in all studies that are concerned with necessary truths as distinct from matters of fact. It may occur, for example, even in empirical studies when the propositions we formulate involve the notion of necessary connection. Thus, we say "The hydrogen atom contains only one proton" because we do not wish to allow that hydrogen atoms may in the past have contained or may in the future come to contain more than one proton.

Here, however, our use of the timeless present is certainly not intended to suggest that hydrogen atoms exist out of time. What we wish to call timeless is simply the connection between being a hydrogen atom and containing a single proton. Sometimes such connections have been called eternal verities, most commonly when it has been thought they could be known a priori, as in mathematics.

GREEK THOUGHT

A different conception of timelessness appears in Parmenides' poem "The Way of Truth," where he says of the One, "It neither was at any time nor will be, since it is now all at once [ὁμοῦ πᾶν] a single whole." Since Parmenides and his pupil Zeno argued against the reality of change, we must suppose that this remark does not represent the One as existing merely for a moment but says rather that the One cannot be described in a language that employs tenses. The One exists all at once because it involves no temporal succession of earlier and later. But why should anyone talk in this way? Perhaps Parmenides accepted the religious teaching of Xenophanes, that the Whole is an everlasting god, and tried to defend it against Heraclitus's doctrine of universal flux by maintaining that the Whole is spherical in all respects—that is, temporally as well as spatially. For such a Whole could not itself be in time, and if we talk about it at all we must employ the timeless present. This is only a guess, but there is evidence to show that a conception of cyclical time order was current in the Pythagorean school with which Parmenides is said to have been connected in his youth.

From Parmenides the notion of a mode of existence that allows no distinction between past, present, and future passed to Plato, who applied it to his Forms, or Ideas. The most influential passage of his works dealing with this subject is in the *Timaeus* (37E6–38A6), where he contrasts the created world with the eternal living being, its timeless archetype.

The language of the passage is poetical, and it seems that we are not expected to take all the details seriously. In particular, Plato can scarcely have meant us to believe that time was an afterthought of the creator. Rather, we are to understand that time is to the perceptual world of becoming what eternity is to the intelligible world of being. For Plato said later (*Timaeus* 38B5), "Time was created with the heaven," and he seems to have held that it is identical with the movements of the heavenly bodies, which are commonly said to measure its passage. In many of his works Plato glorified the eternal and spoke of the temporal as something inferior, but he did not, like Parmenides and Zeno, deny the reality of time. The most he

said in this regard is that temporal things never have being but are always in a state of becoming, as Heraclitus had argued. However, this seems to be no more than a recognition that we cannot talk of temporal things in the timeless present as we talk of Forms and mathematical objects.

The connection with necessity that Plato had claimed for timeless eternity Aristotle claimed for sempiternity. For having rejected Plato's doctrine of the creation of time (*Physics* 251b14), he did not wish to say that anything was wholly severed from it. Thus, in one place he explicitly associated the objects of mathematics with the universe, which he certainly did not regard as timeless (*Nicomachean Ethics* 1112a22). In his view the objects of mathematics are eternal (ἀΐδια) but only in the sense that they exist always—that is, are sempiternal. He held that among sempiternal things there is no difference between possibility and actuality and also that there is nothing merely accidental (*Physics* 203b30, 196b10). In one place he even said that sempiternal things, insofar as they are sempiternal, are not in time, because they are not bounded by time or subject to aging and the other conditions of time (*Physics* 221b30). Apparently he had in mind not only mathematical objects, such as numbers, but also God and the sun and stars and the whole heaven. For he said elsewhere that the heavenly bodies, unlike perishable things, are not wearied by their motion. The sun is active forever, and there is no danger that it will give out, as some philosophers feared (*Metaphysics* 1050b24). Benedict (Baruch) de Spinoza may have been influenced, even if only indirectly, by Aristotle's doctrine when he used the word *aeternitas* to signify both necessity and sempiternity.

CHRISTIAN THEOLOGY

The doctrine of Plato's *Timaeus* passed into Christian theology, with emphasis on the notion of timeless *life*. As early as the St. John Gospel (8:58) there is a curious passage in which Jesus is represented as saying, "Before Abraham was I am." But it is fairly clear that the author of this gospel knew something of Greek philosophy, possibly at second hand through the works of the Jewish theologian Philo of Alexandria, and also that his narrative is no mere historical record of the life of Jesus. By the end of the fifth century there was nothing at all strange in the use of Platonic thought for the exposition of Christianity, and St. Augustine, when commenting, in his *De Civitate Dei* (xi, 21), on the sentence in Genesis "God saw that it was good," referred to the passage of the *Timaeus* cited above. In his *Confessions* (xi, 13) he wrote also of God's "ever-present eternity" and said that for God "all years stand at once" (*omnes simul stant*). A century later Boethius, in his *De Trinitate* (4), said that our "now," by running as it were (*quasi currens*), makes time and sempiternity, whereas the divine "now," by abiding, unmoved and immovable, makes eternity; in the final chapter of his *De Consolatione Philosophiae* he discussed this at greater length.

> Eternity is the complete possession of eternal life all at once—a notion that becomes clearer from comparison with things temporal. For whatever lives in time moves as something present from the past to the future, and there is nothing placed in time that can embrace the whole extent of its life at once. It does not yet grasp tomorrow, and it has already lost yesterday. And even in the life of today you do not live longer than in the transitory moment. That, then, which is subject to the condition of time, even if (as Aristotle thought of the world) it has no beginning or end and its life extends through endless time, is still not such as may be rightly judged eternal. For though its life be endless, it does not grasp and embrace the extent of it all at once [*totum simul*] but has some parts still to come. ... And so, if, following Plato, we wish to give things their right names, let us say that God is eternal, but the world everlasting.

All these notions reappeared in the Middle Ages. St. Thomas Aquinas, for example, quoting Boethius as his authority, said in his *Summa Theologiae* (I, x, 1) that there are two marks of eternity, namely, that the eternal has neither beginning nor end and that eternity contains no succession, being all at once (*tota simul existens*). This last phrase, though Thomas could scarcely have known as much, is a rendering of words Parmenides had used over seventeen centuries earlier. Not content, however, with the old distinction of time and eternity, medieval theologians sometimes spoke of *aevum*—that is, everlasting-ness—as something intermediate that was appropriate to the heavens and to angels. This was conceived by some as having a beginning but no end and by others (probably influenced in part by Aristotle's account of God and the heavenly bodies) as possessing earlier and later, but without innovation and aging. Thomas regarded the latter view as self-contradictory, since, he held, there could be no succession without aging. *Aevum* does not necessarily include earlier and later, according to Thomas, though these can be joined with it, as is the case with angels, who have changeless being as well as the capacity of change according to choice (*Summa Theologiae* I, x, 5).

CRITICISM OF THE THEOLOGICAL USE

Anyone who, like Boethius, speaks of eternity as "the complete possession of eternal life all at once seems to be running together two incompatible notions, that of time-lessness and that of life. For we can attach no meaning to the word *life* unless we are allowed to suppose that what has life acts. No doubt the word *acts* may be taken in a wide sense. Perhaps it is not essential that a living thing produce changes in the physical world. But life must at least involve some incidents in time, and if, like Boethius, we suppose the life in question to be intelligent, then it must also involve awareness of the passage of time. Purposeful action is action with thought of what will come about after its beginning. It is difficult to decide how much of this Plato was prepared to admit when he wrote the *Timaeus*. In his earlier works (for example, the *Meno* and the *Phaedo*) he tried to explain the possibility of a priori knowledge by a doctrine of reminiscence, which involves the hypothesis that before this life the human soul lived among timelessly existent Forms and contemplated them directly as in this life it sees things belonging to the realm of becoming. But he probably came to realize that there is something absurd in the suggestion that a soul can pass part of its time in a timeless realm and then at a certain date enter the temporal realm, for he appears to have dropped the doctrine of reminiscence in his later dialogues, where instead of glorifying the soul by treating it as something akin to the timeless Forms he praised it as the source of motion.

In the *Republic*, which belongs to the middle of his literary life, he spoke of God, who is presumably alive, as having created one and only one Form of each kind. But the wording of the passage (*Republic* 597C) seems to be obviously playful, and it is unlikely that Plato ever meant to suggest seriously that the Forms had been created. In the *Timaeus*, as we have seen, the Forms are said to be the timeless model used by the demiurge, or craftsman, who made the temporal world. Yet this same timeless model is said to be itself alive (*Timaeus* 37E6). Is this to be taken seriously? Unlike medieval theologians, for whom things predicated of the eternal were to be interpreted analogically, Plato maintained (*Timaeus* 29B) that discourse about the eternal is to be understood in the strict and primary sense of the words it employs.

How did the theologians come to commit themselves to talk about timeless life? The influence of Plato's style counts for a lot, but not for everything. One might say in the case of Thomas that the surprising thing is that he held to Plato's account of time and eternity though he must have known it had been criticized by Aristotle. Probably the explanation is to be found in a peculiarity of Christian doctrine. Aristotle, though a theist of a sort, not only rejected the Platonic notion of the creation of time but also maintained the sempiternity of the heavens. To a theologian who had to produce a metaphysical scheme concordant with biblical revelation (which denied the sempiternity of the cosmos) this must have made Aristotle's criticism of Plato's doctrine of eternity seem unsatisfactory. But apart from that, Plato's doctrine had the positive merit of seeming to provide for the necessity of God's existence. If it is correct, once we have admitted that we understand the meaning of the word *God* and that it involves no inconsistency, we cannot sensibly deny that God exists. Another manifestation of this theological interest in the necessity of God's existence is Anselm's ontological argument. Admittedly, this was rejected by Thomas, but for epistemological reasons concerned with the limits of our capacities, not for the assumption it involves that divinity, by definition, entails existence. On the contrary, Thomas, following Boethius, said that God's essence and existence are one.

OTHER PHILOSOPHICAL USES

In later European thought Spinoza and various idealist philosophers used the word *eternity* to describe the existence of their God or Absolute. Spinoza, for example, said in his *Ethics* (I, Definition viii), "By *eternity* I mean existence itself in so far as it is conceived necessarily to follow solely from the definition of that which is eternal. Existence of this kind is conceived as an eternal truth, like the essence of a thing, and therefore cannot be explained by means of duration or time, though duration may be conceived without a beginning or an end." Here there is no longer any verbal connection of eternity with life, but there is still a wish to maintain that something concrete exists with the timeless necessity of which we speak in mathematics. Similar assertions have been made in Indian philosophy, which does not in any way derive from Parmenides or Plato, and we must therefore suppose that they correspond to a widespread demand of religious thought. In modern times even the Pythagorean notion of a cyclical time order has again been considered seriously, by Kurt Gödel.

See also Aristotle; Augustine, St.; Boethius, Anicius Manlius Severinus; Gödel, Kurt; Heraclitus of Ephesus; Indian Philosophy; Parmenides of Elea; Plato; Spinoza, Benedict (Baruch) de; Thomas Aquinas, St.; Time; Time, Consciousness of; Xenophanes of Colophon; Zeno of Elea.

Bibliography

Brabant, F. H. *Time and Eternity in Christian Thought.* New York: Longmans, Green, 1937.

Cushman, R. E. "Greek and Christian Views of Time." *Journal of Religion* (1953): 254–265.

Festugière, A.-J. "Le sens philosophique du mot αἰών." *La parola del passato.* Fasc. 11 (1949): 172–189.

Gödel, Kurt, "A Remark about the Relationship between Relativity Theory and Idealistic Philosophy." In *Albert Einstein: Philosopher-Scientist,* edited by P. A. Schilpp. New York: Tudor, 1951.

Guitton, J. *Le temps et l'éternité chez Plotin et chez Saint Augustin.* Paris: Boivin, 1933; 2nd ed., 1956.

Guthrie, W. K. C. "Time and the Unlimited." In *A History of Greek Philosophy.* Vol. I. Cambridge, U.K.: Cambridge University Press, 1962. Pp. 336–340.

Haldane, J. B. S. "Time and Eternity." *Rationalist Annual* (1946): 33–38.

Kneale, W. C. "Time and Eternity in Theology." *PAS* 61 (1960–1961): 87–108.

Mondolfo, Rodolfo. *L'infinito nel pensiero dei Greci.* Florence: F. Le Monnier, 1934. 2nd enl. ed. published as *L'infinito nel pensiero dell'antichità classica.* Florence, 1956.

Wolfson, H. A. "Duration, Time, and Eternity." In *The Philosophy of Spinoza,* Book I. Cambridge, MA: Harvard University Press, 1934. Ch. 10.

William C. Kneale (1967)

ETERNITY [ADDENDUM 1]

Since Kneale wrote his article, many writers have argued against divine timelessness by claiming that it is inconsistent with divine omniscience. If God knows everything, they reason, he knows what time it is now. But the token of "now" in (say) "it is noon now" refers to the time at which the speaker speaks. So if one knows that it is noon now, and one knows this only if one is able to assert it truly, one exists now (see Stump and Kretzmann 1981). A variant has it that if God is always omniscient, at noon he believes that it is noon and not 1 PM, and at 1 PM that it is 1 PM and not noon. Plausibly, what a person believes is an intrinsic fact about that person. But a timeless being cannot change intrinsically: What changes intrinsically has an intrinsic property at one time that it lacks at another. Some would reply here that one can only know what is true, and if God is timeless, for him it is not noon, or any other time: it is noon for God only if some part of his life which is located at noon is temporally present, and if God is timeless, no part of his life is located at noon or is temporally present.

This raises, of course, the question of how it can be noon for us but not God. And this question leads to an argument others (e.g. Craig 2002) press, that divine timelessness is inconsistent with our ordinary view of time. We ordinarily think that the present exists and the future does not. But a timeless being's life has no future part: lives with future parts are ipso facto lives in time. If your death is still to come for a timeless being, your death lies in a future part of its life. So for a timeless being, your death is not still to come. But for you, it is still to come. Events yet to come for us must not be yet to come for a timeless being: they must already be there, in some way. And so it seems to follow that the future as well as the present exists: If all of time later than noon exists for God, it exists, period, even for us. Either divine timelessness entails the reality of the future, counter to our usual way of thinking about time, or else if God is timeless, some parts of time are real relative to some persons but not others: For us, it is (say) noon, as all of time that is later than noon does not exist, but for God, all of time later than noon exists, and so it is not noon.

Stump and Kretzmann (1981) argued (contra Kneale) that talk of timeless action makes sense and that the move to make here has been known since Aquinas. God's acts consist of atemporal intendings plus effects of these that occur at particular times. God's contribution to the acts is not located in time, but nonetheless his life can "involve some incidents in time" (Kneale). Purposeful action involves "thought of what will come about after its beginning" (Kneale), but "after" can have a sense involving causal as well as temporal precedence and can also refer to temporal effects of an atemporal intention that occur after other such effects. Stump and Kretzmann also claim that an eternal being's life endures in its own way: "timeless duration" is no contradiction, and neither is "timelessly present." Further, they argue, events in an eternal life are in a sense simultaneous with events in time: "simultaneous" does not always mean "at the same time"; in the eternal-temporal case it has a complex sense involving the coexistence of eternal and temporal presents.

Some might see Stump and Kretzmann as working out a hybrid doctrine of divine eternity, one involving neither sheer timelessness nor ordinary temporality but presentness and duration without the full range of temporal features. Such "intermediate" theories have multiplied. Craig (2002) suggests that God is timeless "before" creating and became temporal by creating. It is hard not to think this view contradictory: being over seems a paradigmatic temporal property, one only temporal events have, yet according to Craig the timeless phase of God's life is over. Padgett (1992) argues that God is "relatively timeless"—that is, in some but not all ways in time. As he

sees it, points in our time are points in the time God exists in, but length relations between these points do not exist for God. For us, noon is an hour before 1 p.m. but for God there is no definite length of time between the time we call noon and the time we call 1 p.m. Swinburne (1993) suggests that, whereas God exists in a time without definite length before he creates, once he creates, the lengths of time that exist for us exist for God.

See also Time, Consciousness of.

Bibliography

Craig, William. *God, Time and Eternity*. Dordrecht: D. Reidel, 2002.

Leftow, Brian. *Time and Eternity*. Ithaca, NY: Cornell University Press, 1991.

Padgett, Alan. *God, Eternity and the Nature of Time*. New York: Macmillan, 1992.

Stump, Eleonore, and Norman Kretzmann. "Eternity." *Journal of Philosophy* 79 (1981): 429–458.

Swinburne, Richard. "God and Time." In *Reasoned Faith*, edited by Eleonore Stump, 204–222. Ithaca, NY: Cornell University Press, 1993.

Brian Leftow (2005)

ETERNITY [ADDENDUM 2]

Islamic and Jewish philosophy emerged from a Hellenistic climate in which the universe was taken to be an everlasting emanation from a unitary source (Plotinus), so the debate that ensued among thinkers in these two traditions had to reconcile this philosophical conviction with the pronouncement of their respective revelational books: "In the beginning God created heaven and earth" (Genesis 1.1) and "God said 'be' and it is" (Qur'an 2:117). An absolute beginning linked to an initial moment of time is conflated here with the freedom of the creator to create. Plotinus never denied emanation to be free, although that freedom appropriate to the One would be vastly different from creatures: not being faced with anything—including alternatives—freedom in the One (so far as humans can grasp it) would be more like pure assent.

Al-Fārābī (d. 950), the first of the Muslim philosophers to elaborate this subject, introduced *necessity* into the founding emanation by modeling it on logical deduction: everything that is derives from a single premise. Ibn Sīnā (979–1037), "Avicenna" to Europeans and North Americans, refined this scheme to align it with the "wandering" heavenly bodies (planets)—identified as successive spheres—to create a philosophical cosmology to articulate, after a fashion, the transition from one to many. On the Muslim side, al-Ghazālī (1058–1111) countered this necessary emanation (proposed as an adaptation of the Qur'an) with the charge of *unbelief* (*kufr*), whereas Moses Maimonides (d. 1204), the Jewish thinker imbued with Islamic philosophy, took these charges and elaborated them into a strict division of creator from creatures in order to safeguard the freedom and transcendence of the creator from creation.

Thus the crucial distinction between *everlasting* and *eternal* emerges: while what always was ("everlasting") might not have been, it is impossible for the One source of all that is not to be, so the One must be said to be "eternal." By connecting *eternal* with origins and with an adequate distinction of creator from creatures (which al-Farabi's logical model failed to do), these thinkers could affirm the creator God's eternity without further exploring the issue. Timelessness will be a feature of the eternal One because time itself is created; but eternity will comprise more than timelessness (which could also be said of mathematical entities) because its reality explains the existence of the universe. This discussion can be distinguished from the question of whether the origin of the universe requires an initial moment of time; the creator God would have to be eternal even if some creatures were everlasting. One can detect a Neoplatonic concern for the origin of all things in a unitary source, here adapted to a free creator whose transcendence can be removed from any hint of anthropomorphism by the assertion of *necessary existence* (Ibn Sīnā), and by distinguishing even everlasting things that are created from their uncreated *eternal* source.

Bibliography

Burrell, David. *Knowing the Unknowable God: Ibn-Sina, Maimonides, Aquinas.* Notre Dame, IN: University of Notre Dame Press, 1986.

Frank, Daniel H., and Oliver Leaman, eds. *History of Jewish Philosophy.* New York: Routledge, 1997.

Gerson, Lloyd. *God and Greek Philosophy : Studies in the Early History of Natural Theology.* New York: Routledge, 1990.

Nasr, Seyyed Hossein, and Oliver Leaman, eds. *History of Islamic Philosophy.* New York: Routledge, 1996.

David Burrell (2005)

ETHICAL EGOISM

Generally defined as the view that one ought to do whatever and only whatever is in one's own maximum interest, benefit, advantage, or good, "ethical egoism" contrasts with (1) psychological egoism, which says that people do in fact, perhaps necessarily, act in that way; and from (2) alternative ethical theories, which claim that we have other fundamental obligations such as to act for the sake of others, even at ultimate cost to ourselves, or in ways having no necessary relation to anyone's benefit.

Egoism strikes many as cutting through pretenses and getting down to fundamentals. This appearance soon dissipates when we make essential distinctions. Foremost is that due to the classic work of Bishop Joseph Butler (1692–1752). Is "self-interest" in that theory to be understood as one's interest in certain states unique to one's own self—as distinct from certain states of other people? Or is it merely interests of one's own self—the interests one happens to have, whatever they may be? Since action is necessarily motivated by interests of the agent motivated by them, the second interpretation is trivial: Whatever we do, we are somehow interested in doing it. But the first interpretation is implausible: People are notoriously capable of sacrificing themselves—for friends, loved ones, or causes.

Ethical egoism would also be vacuous if it said only that whatever we ought to do, we ought to do it only if we are motivated to do it. Only when self-interest is construed in the narrow sense, as describing certain of our interests—those focused specifically on oneself—but not others, does it make sense to say that we ought to act self-interestedly. Then the question "Why?" arises, for we have our choice.

This brings up the question of what is the ultimate good or interest of an agent. Alas, we must leave this important issue open in the present discussion. The next question, however, is crucial. What is meant by *ethical*? Here we must distinguish between a wide sense in which *ethical* means something like "rational" and a narrower sense in which specifically moral requirements are intended. I should choose Bordeaux 1989, but that isn't a moral matter; that I should refrain from cheating is.

If ethical egoism is understood in the wider sense, it is a theory about rational behavior; and construing self-interest in Butler's second way, egoism says that a rational agent acts so as to maximize the realization of whatever she or he is interested in attaining. This highly plausible idea is noncommittal about the content of our interests.

Now turn to the moral version. Moral rules call upon us all to do or refrain from certain things, whether we like it or not. Can there be a rational egoistic morality, then?

But the interests of different persons can conflict. This leads to a problem, which becomes clear when we distinguish two possible interpretations of moral egoism:

(1) "First-person" egoism appraises all actions of all persons on the basis of the interests of the propounder alone. What Jim Jones thinks, if he is this kind of an egoist, is not only that Jim Jones ought to do whatever, and only whatever, conduces to Jim Jones's best interests—but that everyone else should, too. This is consistent, to be sure, but from the point of view of anyone except Jim or his devotees, it is evidently irrational, if they too are self-interested.

(2) "General" egoism, on the other hand, says that each person ought to do whatever is in that person's interests. If Jim is an egoist of this type, he believes that Jim ought to do whatever is in Jim's interests, but Sheila ought to do whatever is in Sheila's interests, and so on.

Serious conceptual problems arise with general egoism. Suppose that Jim's interests conflict with Sheila's: Realizing his frustrates hers. Does Jim tell Sheila that it is Sheila's duty to do what is in Sheila's interests? Or what is in Jim's interests? Or both? Every answer is unacceptable! The first is unacceptable to Jim himself: How can he, as an exclusively self-interested person, support actions of Sheila's that are detrimental to himself? The second is unacceptable to Sheila: If she is exclusively self-interested, why would she take Jim's "advice"? And the third is flatly inconsistent: For their interests to "conflict" means that they cannot both do what is in their own best interest.

A standard reply is to hold that egoism tells each of the differing parties merely to try to do what is in their interests. But this is either just wrong or turns the theory into something else: "Here, all you ought to do is try to bring about your best interests—but it doesn't matter whether you succeed!" But self-interested agents are interested in results.

Or it might be held that the good life consists not in succeeding but in striving. This turns egoism into a game, and in conflict situations, a competitive game. And games are interesting, but also very special, requiring players to abide by certain game-defining rules. True chess-players do not cheat, even if they can—cheating is not really playing the game. They want opponents to do their best, even if they themselves lose. Of course, they prefer to win, but even if they do not, the game is worthwhile. This defense lacks generality. Ethical egoism is not about games, it is about life. Some people may make life into a game, but most people do not. They want results, not just effort; in conflicts, they are not about to cheer for the other side.

So egoism seems to be self-defeating. What to do? The answer requires, first, that we utilize the vital distinction between egoism as (1) a theory of rationality—of what is recommended by reason; and (2) as a theory of morality. The latter is interpersonal, and concerns rules for groups. Such rules require that people sometimes curtail their passions and conform to the rules.

If we view egoism as a theory of rationality, then whether agent A should aim only at bringing about certain states of A is an open question. But that A should aim at bringing about only those states of affairs that A values is not: We can act only on our own values—in acting, we make them our own.

But when we turn to the subject of formulating specifically moral principles, we must attend to the facts of social life. From the point of view of any rational individual, moralities are devices for securing desirable results not attainable without the cooperation of others. To do this, mutual restrictions must be accepted by all concerned. They will be accepted only if they conduce to the agent's interests. Therefore, moral principles, if rational, must be conducive to the interests of all, those to whom they are addressed as well as those of the propounder herself. Thus, egoism leads to contractarianism: Moral principles are those acceptable to each person, given that person's own interests, if all comply. Undoubtedly, some will not; but noncompliance, as Thomas Hobbes observed, leads to war, which is worse for all.

Rational egoism, then, leads to the abandonment of moral egoism. Sensible people will condemn egotism, and regard selfishness as a vice: We do better if we care about each other, engage in mutually beneficial activity, and thus refrain from one-sided activity that tramples upon others, such as killing, lying, cheating, stealing, or raping. The core of truth in egoism leads to a fairly familiar morality, whose principles must cash out in terms of the good of every agent participating in society. Narrowly egoistic moral principles cannot do this, and thus are the first to be rejected by rational egoists—another of those fascinating paradoxes of which philosophy is full.

See also Butler, Joseph; Egoism and Altruism.

Bibliography

Baier, K. *The Moral Point of View*. Ithaca, NY: Cornell University Press, 1958. Chapter 8, sections 1–4.

Butler, J. *Sermons*. London, 1726. Preface, I, and XI.

Fumerton, R. A. *Reason and Morality: A Defense of the Egocentric Perspective*. Ithaca, NY: Cornell University Press, 1990.

Hobbes, T. *Leviathan*. London, 1651. Chapters VI, XIII–XV.

Huemer, M. "Is Benevolent Egoism Incoherent?" *Journal of Ayn Rand Studies* 3 (2002): 259–288.

Hunt, L. "Flourishing Egoism." *Social Philosophy & Policy* 16 (1999): 72–95.

Kalin, J. "Two Kinds of Moral Reasoning: Ethical Egoism as a Moral Theory." *Canadian Journal of Philosophy* 5 (1975): 323–356.

Kelley, D. *Unrugged Individualism*. Poughkeepsie, NY: Institute for Objectivist Studies, 1996.

Long, R. *Reason and Value: Aristotle vs Rand*. Poughkeepsie, NY: The Objectivist Center. 2000.

Machan, T. *Generosity*. Washington, DC: Cato Institute, 1998.

Mack, E. "Egoism and Rights." *The Personalist* (Winter 1973): 5–33

Medlin, B. "Ultimate Principles and Ethical Egoism." *Australian Journal of Philosophy* 35 (1957): 111–118.

Plato. *Republic*. Books 1, 2.

Rand, A. *Virtue of Selfishness*. Toronto: Signet. 1961.

OTHER RECOMMENDED WORKS

On virtue-theoretic treatments of self-interest, see: Annas, J., *The Morality of Happiness* (New York: Oxford. 1995); Aristotle, *Nicomachean Ethics*; Badhwar, N., "Friends As Ends in Themselves," *Philosophy & Phenomenological Research* 48 (1987): 1–23; Cottingham, J., "Partiality and the Virtues," in *How Should One Live?* (New York: Oxford University Press, 1996); Den Uyl, D., *The Virtue of Prudence* (New York: Peter Lang, 1991); Foot, P., "Morality as a System of Hypothetical Imperatives," in *Virtues and Vices* (Berkeley: University of California Press, 1978); Hampton, J., "Selflessness and the Loss of Self," *Social Philosophy & Policy* 10 (1993): 135–165; von Humboldt, W., *The Limits of State Action* (Indianapolis: Liberty Fund, 1993); Rasmussen, D., "Human Flourishing and the Appeal to Human Nature," *Social Philosophy & Policy* 16 (1999): 1–43; Schmidtz, D., *Rational Choice and Moral Agency* (Princeton, NJ: Princeton University Press, 1995).

On contractarian treatments of self-interest: Gauthier, D., *Morals by Agreement* (New York: Oxford University Press, 1986); Narveson, J., *The Libertarian Idea* (Toronto: Broadview, 2001).

Other theories with egoistic components: Mack, E., "Moral Individualism, Agent-Relativity, and Deontic Restraints," *Social Philosophy & Policy* 7 (1989): 81–111; Nagel, T., *View from Nowhere* (New York: Oxford University Press, 1986); Scheffler, S., *The Rejection of Consequentialism* (New York: Oxford University Press, 1982); Wolf, S., "Moral Saints," *Journal of Philosophy* 79 (1982): 419–439.

On the connection between psychological and ethical egoism: Dawkins, R., *The Selfish Gene* (New York: Oxford University Press, 1976); Feinberg, J., "Psychological Egoism," *Reason and Responsibility* (Belmont: Wadsworth, 2005); Nagel, T., *The Possibility of Altruism* (Princeton, NJ: Princeton University Press, 1979); Ridley, M., *The Origins of Virtue* (London: Penguin, 1998).

Jan Narveson (1996)
Bibliography updated by David Schmidtz (2005)

ETHICAL NATURALISM

Philosophical naturalism, considered in general, is not a unified doctrine but a broad label applied both to methodological stances (e.g., "The methods of philosophy are continuous with those of empirical science") and to substantive positions (e.g., "For a belief to be epistemically warranted is for it to be the product of a certain kind of causal process"). The two are often combined, as when a naturalistic interpretation of a given domain of discourse is justified as "the best explanation" of associated practices. However, the two are in principle independent. In the moral case, for example, it has been argued that a projectivist or noncognitivist interpretation gives a better explanation of moral practice than any substantive naturalism (Blackburn 1984, Gibbard 1990).

But what makes a method or interpretation naturalistic? Attempts to give an explicit definition have largely been abandoned in favor of pointing. Roughly, naturalistic methods are those followed in actual scientific research (including—according to some but not all naturalists—mathematics and social sciences as well as natural sciences). And a naturalistic interpretation of a discourse is one based upon predicates or terms that play a role in the explanatory theories that research has generated.

This characterization of naturalism is informative but incomplete. There are vigorous debates within the philosophy of science over just what the methods, concepts, or posits of contemporary science are. Moreover, interpretation based upon naturalistic terms encompasses some quite different tasks. Some examples follow, but first we should ask, Why stay within naturalistic terms at all? Science is a theoretical, descriptive/explanatory enterprise while morality is held to be essentially practical and normative. One might think, no sooner did morality emerge from the shadow of religion than philosophers began trying to push it into the shadow of science. Is it never to be allowed to stand in its own right as a distinctive domain of inquiry?

An answer of sorts is possible. Morality by its nature cannot stand entirely on its own. Moral discourse is supervenient upon the nonmoral and, specifically, the natural—two actions or agents cannot differ in their moral qualities unless there is some underlying difference in their natural qualities. This and other truisms about morality, such as "Ought" implies "can," tie moral evaluation to the natural world in ways that no ethical theory can altogether ignore. Moreover, morality presents us with various epistemic and metaphysical puzzles. We believe that we have come to possess at least some moral knowledge—but how? (See Harman 1977.) We treat moral statements as if they stated genuine propositions—but can this idea be sustained in light of the normative role of moral judgment? We freely make moral judgments, but do they have presuppositions or make claims that are incompatible with our understanding of the natural world?

Hard determinists, for example, have challenged intuitive attributions of moral responsibility by arguing that the notion of free agency they presuppose is incompatible with the world revealed by physics. And John L. Mackie is led to an "error theory" of morality by his diagnosis that moral evaluation attributes to states of the world an objective "to-be-pursuedness" that cannot be fit with any plausible empirical theory (Mackie 1977).

Immanuel Kant, for one, frankly accepted that he could see no way of reconciling the deliberative standpoint of morality with the causal perspective of science. Rational agents must, he held, postulate the compatibility of moral agency with the natural order, even though this remains inexplicable to them. But few philosophers have been willing to stop there. Empirical science affords the best-developed picture we have of ourselves and our world. Without the special authority of religion to back it up, morality inevitably becomes a focus of practical and theoretical concern.

Substantive moral naturalists in effect propose to overcome some of the mystery and potential conflict surrounding the relation of morality to our empirical self-understanding by showing just how much of morality might be found within the domain of the natural. This could be done by providing a naturalistic account of moral discourse that affords an analysis of moral terms (Lewis 1989), or permits a worthwhile revision of moral language that nonetheless can serve virtually all the same functions (Brandt 1979), or enables us to reduce moral properties to natural properties (Railton, 1993), or shows moral properties to be natural properties in their own right (e.g., thanks to their contribution to empirical explanation; see Boyd 1988, Miller 1985, Sturgeon 1985). Substantive ethical naturalism promises to explain such important features of moral discourse and practice as the applicability of notions of truth and falsity to moral claims, the supervenience of the moral upon the natural, the role of natural properties in justifying moral claims, and the possibility of semantic and epistemic access to moral notions through ordinary experience.

The first half of the twentieth century had not been kind to substantive ethical naturalism (for a brief history, see Darwall et al. 1992). Condemned by G. E. Moore (1903) for committing the "fallacy" of trying to close an "open question" by analytic means and rejected by non-factualists (emotivists, prescriptivists, etc.) for failing to capture the special relation of moral evaluation to motivation and action, naturalism fell into disuse. But by mid-century naturalism had begun to win its way back. The initial steps were taken, independently, by Philippa Foot (1958–1959) and Geoffrey Warnock (1967), who argued that one could not be competent in moral discourse unless one possessed some substantive, contentful moral concepts. Moral evaluation is distinguished from aesthetic or prudential, for example, in part because it has a certain descriptive, arguably natural content—namely, a concern with the effects of our actions on the well-being of others. If we came upon a society in whose behavioral code the key notion was *guleb*, a term applied in the paradigm case to warriors who have killed an enemy bare-handed, we would certainly mislead if we translated *guleb* as "morally good" or "just" rather than "valiant" or "courageous."

Meanwhile, Peter Geach (1965) showed convincingly that existing nonfactualist views could not account for the full grammar of moral discourse, in particular, the logical behavior of unasserted moral claims in conditionals.

Foot (1972) took the next step as well, challenging the "internalist" conception of the relation of moral evaluation to motivation that served as the basis for nonfactualism. She argued that ordinary moral agents are able to see themselves as motivated by a rationally optional concern for others. Those who lack such a concern might lack moral character, but they do not make a linguistic mistake in using the moral vocabulary.

This sort of moral "externalism" offers an alternative explanation of why moral evaluation and motivation are so intimately related, at least in paradigm cases. Concern for others is a very basic part of normal human life. An Aristotelian would say that human nature itself is social; a Darwinian would emphasize the contribution of concern for others to inclusive fitness and to the possibility of benefiting from reciprocal altruism. Speculative biology apart, it is possible to see how social norms involving concern for others, keeping promises, and so forth might emerge and be sustained in virtue of their contribution to solving various serious coordination and collective-action problems. Such norms will function best only if well internalized by a major part of the population. It should therefore be unsurprising that moral judgment is usually accompanied by a positive attitude. Moreover, it should not be forgotten that moral judgment is a species of assertion and that assertion itself involves, not only signaling a cognitive attitude of belief, but also various forms of active endorsement or encouragement, as well as associated claims of authority. Moral externalism, by drawing upon these ingredients (and others) for an alternative explanation of the evidence—such as it is—offered on behalf of internalism, has attracted a number of defenders (see, for example, Boyd 1988, Brink 1989, Railton 1986).

Another sort of naturalism, however, takes the opposite tack. It treats the purported relation to motivation as fundamental but interprets it in a subjectivist rather than nonfactualist manner. Subjectivist interpretations of moral discourse have historically faced difficulties in accommodating all the elements of an interconnected set of features of morality: the critical use of moral assessment, the nonrelativistic character of moral judgment and the possibility of genuine moral disagreement across social or cultural differences, the limits on empirical methods in resolving moral disputes, and the seemingly normative character of the relation between moral judgment and motivation. Can new forms of subjectivism succeed where others have failed?

Consider the simple subjectivist formula:

(1) Act A is morally good = A is such that one would approve of the performance of A.

Since approval is a positive attitude, (1) establishes a relationship with a source of motivational force. But is it the right relationship?

We do not typically regard our current tendencies to approve or disapprove as morally authoritative—they might, for example, be based upon hasty thinking or false beliefs. This has led naturalists to modify (1) to require that the approval be well informed and reflectively stable. (See, for example, Brandt 1979 and Firth 1952. For criticism, see Velleman 1988.)

Moreover, not all species of approval have a moral flavor. I can approve of an act because of its aesthetic or pious qualities, for example. Some naturalists therefore amend (1) to restrict the object of approval (e.g., to the set of rules one would—reflectively, informedly, etc.—approve for a society in which one is going to live [cf. Brandt 1979]). Others attempt to identify in naturalistic terms a specifically moral sort of attitude of approval or disapproval (e.g., an attitude of impartial praise or anger). Critics have argued that no noncircular characterization of this kind is possible (for a subjectivism without reductive ambitions, see Wiggins 1987).

Formulas like (1) also threaten to yield relativism. Since they introduce a necessary link to facts about motivation, moral attribution becomes tied to contingencies of individual psychology. That seems wrong, since moral evaluation purports to abstract from individual interest and motive and to prescribe universality. If one is not correspondingly motivated, that is a deficiency in oneself rather than an excusing condition or a limit on the reach of moral judgment. Each of us recognizes that he or she can in this sense be motivationally defective from a moral point of view. (But see Harman 1975 for a defense of a naturalistic moral relativism.) This has led naturalists to modify the formula away from the individualistic language of "one" or "I" and in the direction of a more inclusive "we" or "everyone" or even "normal humans" (see, respectively, Lewis 1989, Smith 1994, and Firth 1952). New problems arise. The notion of "normal human" threatens to introduce a term that itself requires naturalization—since we believe that statistically "normal" humans might be motivationally defective from a moral point of view—for example, in lacking sympathy with those from other groups. (Of course, one could at this point also embrace circularity.) If we insist that everyone approve, there is again a risk that contingencies of motivational idiosyncrasies will receive authority—this time, in preventing us from attributing moral value to states of affairs virtually all (but still not quite all) of us approve heartily on reflection. A less ambitious alternative is to replace "one" with "us" and seek moral consensus where we may. This would help explain the "outreach" function of moral discourse without altogether removing the account's relativism.

An alternative approach avoids relativism by "rigidifying" the subjectivist formula (cf. Wiggins 1987). One fixes the truth conditions of moral judgments by reference to the motivations *actually* prevalent in one's moral community (e.g., "A is such that we, with our actual motives and with full and informed reflection, would approve of it"). This secures the desirable result that changes in our motives will not in themselves change what is morally good. But it undermines some of the critical role of moral assessment in our own society (since, again, we can imagine that our actual motives are morally defective) and will have the result that those brought up in different social environments with different acquired motivations will lack a common subject matter even though they believe they are having a genuine moral disagreement (for discussion, see Johnston 1989).

No ethical naturalism has emerged that meets all the desiderata of an account of moral discourse and practice.

Nonnaturalists and nonfactualists attribute this to a mistaken starting point. But no alternative account has met all the desiderata, either. Moral naturalists have often been accused of "changing the subject"—shifting the locus of attention from the position of the agent involved in practical deliberation to that of the scientist engaged in theoretical description. But this criticism begs the question. Naturalists seek to explain, not ignore, moral experience; if they are right, the phenomena they study are the very stuff of moral thought and action.

See also Conditionals; Determinism and Freedom; Foot, Philippa; Kant, Immanuel; Mackie, John Leslie; Metaethics; Moore, George Edward; Naturalism; Philosophy of Science, Problems of; Projectivism; Supervenience.

Bibliography

Blackburn, S. *Spreading the Word.* Oxford: Clarendon Press, 1984.

Boyd, R. "How to Be a Moral Realist." In *Essays on Moral Realism,* edited by G. Sayre-McCord. Ithaca, NY: Cornell University Press, 1988.

Brandt, R. *A Theory of the Good and the Right.* New York: Oxford University Press, 1979.

Brink, D. O. *Moral Realism and the Foundations of Ethics.* Cambridge, U.K.: Cambridge University Press, 1989.

Darwell, S. et al. "Toward *Fin de siècle* Ethics." *Philosophical Review* 101 (1992): 317–345.

Firth, R. "Ethical Absolutism and the Ideal Observer." *Philosophy and Phenomenological Research* 12 (1952): 317–345.

Foot, P. "Moral Beliefs." *Proceedings of the Aristotelian Society* 59 (1958–1959): 83–104.

Foot, P. "Morality as a System of Hypothetical Imperatives." *Philosophical Review* 81 (1972): 305–316.

Geach, P. "Assertion." *Philosophical Review* 74 (1965): 445–465.

Gibbard, A. *Wise Choices, Apt Feelings.* Cambridge, MA: Harvard University Press, 1990.

Harman, G. "Moral Relativism Defended." *Philosophical Review* 84 (1975): 3–22.

Harman, G. *The Nature of Morality.* New York: Oxford University Press, 1977.

Johnston, M. "Dispositional Theories of Value." *Proceedings of the Aristotelian Society* 63 (1989): suppl., 139–174.

Lewis, D. "Dispositional Theories of Value." *Proceedings of the Aristotelian Society* 63 (1989): suppl. 113–137.

Mackie, J. L. *Ethics: Inventing Right and Wrong.* New York: Penguin, 1977.

Miller, R. "Ways of Moral Learning." *Philosophical Review* 94 (1985): 507–556.

Moore, G. E. *Principia Ethica.* Cambridge, U.K.: Cambridge University Press, 1903.

Railton, P. "Moral Realism." *Philosophical Review* 95 (1986): 163–207.

Railton, P. "Reply to David Wiggins." In *Reality, Representation, and Projection,* edited by J. Haldane and C. Wright. New York: Oxford University Press, 1993.

Smith, M. *The Moral Problem.* Oxford: Blackwell, 1995.

Sturgeon, N. "Moral Explanations." In *Morality, Reason, and Truth,* edited by D. Copp and D. Zimmerman. Totowa, NJ: Rowman and Allanheld, 1985).

Velleman, D. "Brandt's Definition of 'Good.'" *Philosophical Review* 97 (1988): 353–371.

Warnock, G. *Contemporary Moral Philosophy.* London: Macmillan, 1967.

Wiggins, D. "A Sensible Subjectivism?" In *Needs, Values, Truth: Essays in the Philosophy of Value.* Oxford: Blackwell, 1987.

Peter Railton (1996)

ETHICAL NATURALISM [ADDENDUM]

Substantive ethical naturalists believe that the ethical is natural, that is, that ethical properties are natural properties. *Strong,* or *reductive,* ethical naturalists hold that there is an interesting further question of *which* natural properties the ethical ones are, just as there is an interesting question of which chemical property water is (Railton 1986, Jackson 1997). *Weak* ethical naturalists deny this; some hold that ethical properties, though natural, are irreducible (Boyd 1988), while others are in the business of *revising* moral language (Brandt 1979).

Moore's open-question argument was advanced against strong ethical naturalism, which he claimed committed the *naturalistic fallacy.* The basic idea of the argument is that we can test *cognitive significance* to test claims of property identity. So, for example, if *good* just is *pleasure,* then "Pleasure is good" should mean the same as "Good is good," and be equally informative to speakers who understand the two statements. There are different versions of the argument, according to which test of cognitive significance is used. It looks like a good argument against those who think that such property identities are *analytic,* or follows from the meanings of the words or the concepts that they express, but not against those who think that this identity thesis is *synthetic,* like the thesis that water is H_2O (Moore 1903, Brink 1989).

But synthetic naturalism may not have all of the same philosophical attractions as the analytic version. For example, naturalists have long held that naturalism can help explain how we can acquire moral knowledge. This seems easily true of analytic naturalism (Harman 1977), but synthetic naturalists have not yet explained how their naturalism provides help in moral epistemology not available to nonnaturalists.

More striking is the fact that though it is widely known that synthetic naturalism escapes Moore's open-question argument, many still believe that the argument shows something against synthetic naturalism—a reaction that synthetic naturalists find puzzling. Nonnaturalists typically remain convinced, however, that Moore's argument illustrates how strong naturalism involves identifying ethical properties with something that they are not (Shafer-Landau 2003). And others maintain that naturalists do not really believe in ethical properties at all (Nagel 1985, McNaughton 1989).

It is not hard to see the force of these objections. If a friend tells you that he believes in God because God is love and he believes in love, you are bound to conclude that if he is really speaking literally, then he is an atheist. Whatever theists mean by saying that God is love, it is not simply that God is the relation that holds between two people when one loves the other. Naturalist theories about God seem bound to feel this way. They all seem to identify God with something else, and as a result they fail to be realist about God (Schroeder 2005).

By analogy, this can make ethical naturalism look hopeless. But that would be premature. Strong naturalism is clearly true about bachelors. Bachelors are just unmarried adult men. If your friend tells you he believes in bachelors because he believes in unmarried adult men, you will not conclude that he does not really believe in bachelors. Nonnaturalists think that ethical properties are more like God, but strong naturalists think that they are more like bachelorhood.

One salient difference between God and bachelors is that God is supposed to have features that love and other natural entities lack: omniscience and omnipotence, among others. If your friend does not believe that love is omniscient and omnipotent, then he does not believe in God. But in contrast, it is easy to see that unmarried adult men have the properties of bachelors (Schroeder 2005).

To find out whether ethical naturalism is more like naturalism about God or like naturalism about bachelors, then, we need to think about what features ethical properties have, and whether natural properties could have them. An old idea about the ethical is that ethical properties have to be related in some way to *motivation*. This is the thesis of *internalism*. Nonnaturalists have argued that natural properties could not motivate as internalism requires (Mackie 1977), but some naturalists have responded by explaining how they can (see especially Smith 1994).

More recently, nonnaturalists have insisted that internalism, even if true, is not what is special about ethical properties. Rather, they say, what is special about ethical properties is that they are *normative*. And if natural properties are not normative, it follows that ethical properties cannot be natural ones (Hampton 1998). But the evidence that natural properties cannot be normative is no better than the evidence that they cannot be ethical. If anything, it is worse. Nonnaturalists typically say that to be normative is to involve *reasons*, in some way. But if *reason* is a natural property, then natural properties could involve reasons, and hence be normative (Schroeder 2005).

A different worry about ethical naturalism is that if ethical properties are natural, then they must be highly disjunctive, and therefore uninteresting. This notion seems to force us to give up the idea that ethical discourse carves nature at its joints. This impression is reinforced by some naturalists who write at a very abstract level, such as Jackson (1997), but it is not sustained by looking in detail at most serious strong naturalist proposals. The problem is one of level of description.

A final serious objection leveled against ethical naturalism applies just as much to weak naturalism as to strong naturalism. It is that naturalism makes ethics out to be an a posteriori discipline, whereas surely ethical knowledge should be a priori (Shafer-Landau 2003). Since nonreductive naturalists hold that what makes ethical properties respectable is that they play a certain explanatory role, they may be particularly susceptible to this charge. But perhaps synthetic strong naturalism can escape it. The fact that empirical investigation was the right way to investigate what natural property samples of water have in common does not entail that empirical investigation is the right way to investigate what natural property right actions have in common. On the contrary, it seems that philosophers engage in the study of what right actions have in common all the time. Such study is ordinary normative ethical inquiry.

Bibliography

Boyd, Richard. "How to Be a Moral Realist." In *Essays on Moral Realism*, edited by Geoffrey Sayre-McCord. Ithaca, NY: Cornell University Press, 1988.

Brandt, Richard. *A Theory of the Good and the Right*. Oxford, U.K.: Oxford University Press, 1979.

Brink, David. *Moral Realism and the Foundations of Ethics*. Cambridge, U.K.: Cambridge University Press, 1989.

Hampton, Jean. *The Authority of Reason*. Cambridge, U.K.: Cambridge University Press, 1998.

Harman, Gilbert. *The Nature of Morality*. Oxford, U.K.: Oxford University Press, 1977.

Jackson, Frank. *From Metaphysics to Ethics*. Oxford, U.K.: Oxford University Press, 1997.

Mackie, J. L. *Ethics: Inventing Right and Wrong*. New York: Penguin, 1977.

McNaughton, David. *Moral Vision*. Oxford, U.K.: Basil Blackwell, 1989.

Moore, G. E. *Principia Ethica*. Cambridge, U.K.: Cambridge University Press, 1903.

Nagel, Thomas. *The View from Nowhere*. Oxford, U.K.: Oxford University Press, 1985.

Railton, Peter. "Moral Realism." *Philosophical Review* 95 (1986): 163–207.

Schroeder, Mark. "Realism and Reduction: The Quest for Robustness." *Philosophers' Imprint* 5 (1) (2005). Available from http://www.philosophersimprint.org/005001/.

Shafer-Landau, Russ. *Moral Realism*. Oxford, U.K.: Oxford University Press, 2003.

Smith, Michael. *The Moral Problem*. Oxford, U.K.: Basil Blackwell, 1994.

Mark Schroeder (2005)

ETHICAL OBJECTIVISM

See *Objectivity in Ethics*

ETHICAL PRINCIPLES

See *Moral Principles: Their Justification*

ETHICAL RELATIVISM

The term *ethical relativism* is always used to designate some ethical principle or some theory about ethical principles, but within this limitation different authors use it quite differently. Contemporary philosophers generally apply the term to some position they disagree with or consider absurd, seldom to their own views; social scientists, however, often classify themselves as relativists. Writers who call themselves relativists always accept the first and second and sometimes accept the third of the theses described as descriptive relativism, metaethical relativism, and normative relativism, respectively.

DESCRIPTIVE RELATIVISM

The first thesis, without which the others would lose interest, is that the values, or ethical principles, of indi-viduals conflict in a fundamental way ("fundamental" is explained below). A special form of this thesis, called "cultural relativism," is that such ethical disagreements often follow cultural lines. The cultural relativist empha-sizes the cultural tradition as a prime source of the indi-vidual's views and thinks that most disagreements in ethics among individuals stem from enculturation in dif-ferent ethical traditions, although he need not deny that some ethical disagreements among individuals arise from differences of innate constitution or personal history between the individuals.

FUNDAMENTAL DISAGREEMENT.
The most important and controversial part of the first thesis is the claim that diversities in values (and ethics) are fundamental. To say that a disagreement is "fundamental" means that it would not be removed even if there were perfect agreement about the properties of the thing being evaluated. (If dis-agreement is nonfundamental then it may be expected that all ethical diversity can be removed, in principle, by the advance of science, leading to agreement about the properties of things being appraised.) Thus it is not nec-essarily a case of fundamental disagreement in values if one group approves of children's executing their parents at a certain age or stage of feebleness whereas another group disapproves of this very strongly. It may be that in the first group the act is thought necessary for the welfare of the parent in the afterlife, whereas in the second group it is thought not to be. The disagreement might well be removed by agreement about the facts, and indeed both parties might subscribe, now, to the principle "It is right for a child to treat a parent in whatever way is required for the parent's long-run welfare." The disagreement might be simply about the implications of this common princi-ple, in the light of differing conceptions of the facts. There is fundamental ethical disagreement only if ethical appraisals or valuations are incompatible, even when there is mutual agreement between the relevant parties concerning the nature of the act that is being appraised.

METAETHICAL RELATIVISM

A person might accept descriptive relativism but still sup-pose that there is always only one correct moral appraisal of a given issue. Such a position has been widely held by nonnaturalists and by some naturalists (see, for example, the interest theory of R. B. Perry). The metaethical rela-tivist, however, rejects this thesis and denies that there is always one correct moral evaluation. The metaethical rel-ativist thesis is tenable only if certain views about the meaning of ethical (value) statements are rejected. For instance, if "*A* is right" *means* "Doing *A* will contribute at least as much to the happiness of sentient creatures as anything else one might do," it is obvious that one and only one of the two opinions "*A* is right" and "*A* is not right" is correct. Thus, the metaethical relativist is restricted to a certain range of theories about the meaning of ethical statements. He might, for instance, subscribe to some form of emotive theory, such as the view that ethical statements are not true or false at all but express the attitudes of the speaker. Or he might adopt the naturalist view that "is wrong" means "belongs to the class of actions toward which I tend to take up an impartial attitude of angry resentment" (held by the relativist E. A. Westermarck) or the view (suggested by the anthropologist Ruth Benedict) that the phrase "is morally good" means "is customary."

ETHICAL REASONING. At the present time metaethical relativists do not wish to rest their case solely on an appeal to what ethical statements mean; nor would their critics. The point of active debate is rather whether there is some method of ethical reasoning whose acceptance can be justified to thoughtful people with force comparable to the force with which acceptance of inductive logic can be justified. Is there any such method of ethical reasoning that can be expected in principle to show, when there is a conflict of values or ethical principles, that one and only one solution is correct in some important and relevant sense of "correct"? Metaethical relativists deny that there is any such method, and their denial may take either of two forms: They may deny that there is any method of ethical reasoning that can be justified with force comparable to that with which scientific method (inductive logic) can be justified. Or they may agree that there is such a method but say that its application is quite limited, and in particular that the fullest use of it could not show, in every case of a conflict of ethical convictions or of values, that one and only one position is correct in any important sense of "correct."

USE OF THE TERM *RELATIVISM*. Many writers, both in philosophy and in the social sciences, accept a combination of descriptive relativism and metaethical relativism. Philosophers who hold this view, however, seldom label themselves "relativists," apparently because they think the term confusing in this context. There is seldom objection to "cultural relativism" as a descriptive phrase, for it can be taken to mean that a person's values are "relative" to his culture in the sense of being a function of or causally dependent on it. But if "ethical relativism" is construed in a similar way, to mean that ethical *truth* is relative to, in the sense of being dependent on or a function of, some-

thing (for example, a person's cultural tradition), then this term is thought to be confusing since it is being used to name a theory that essentially denies that there is such a thing as ethical "truth."

One frequent confusion about what implies ethical relativism should be avoided. Suppose metaethical relativism is mistaken, and there is a single "correct" set of general ethical principles or value statements. It may still be true, and consistent with acceptance of this "correct" set of principles, that an act that is right in some circumstances will be wrong in other circumstances. Take, for instance, the possible "correct" principle "It is always right to do what will make all affected at least as happy as they could be made by any other possible action." It follows from this principle that in some situations it will be right to lie (for instance, to tell a man that he is not mortally ill when one knows he is, if he cannot bear the truth) and that in other situations it will be wrong to lie. Thus, even if metaethical relativism is false there is a sense in which the rightness of an act is relative to the circumstances or situation. The fact that the rightness of an act is relative to the circumstances in this way does not, of course, imply the truth of metaethical relativism.

NORMATIVE RELATIVISM

Neither descriptive nor metaethical relativism commits one logically to any ethical statement. The former is simply an assertion about the diversity of moral principles or values actually espoused by different persons; the latter is only a general statement about whether ethical principles are ever "correct." Nothing in particular about what ought to be, or about what someone ought to do, follows from them. Of particular interest is the fact that it does not follow that persons, depending on their cultural attachments, ought to do different things. In contrast, a person who holds to some form of what I shall call "normative relativism" asserts that something is wrong or blameworthy if some person or group—variously defined—thinks it is wrong or blameworthy. Anyone who espoused either of the following propositions would therefore be a normative relativist:

(*a*) "If someone thinks it is right (wrong) to do *A*, then it *is* right (wrong) for him to do *A*." This thesis has a rather wide popular acceptance but is considered absurd by philosophers if it is taken to assert that what someone thinks right really is right for him. It is held to be absurd because taken in this way, it implies that there is no point in debating with a person what is right for him to do unless he is in doubt himself; the thesis says that if he *believes* that *A* is right, then it *is* right, at least for him.

The thesis may be taken in another sense, however, with the result that it is no longer controversial, and no longer relativist. The thesis might mean: "If someone thinks it is right for him to do *A,* then he cannot properly be condemned for doing *A.*" This statement merely formulates the view, widespread in the Western world, that a person cannot be condemned morally for doing what he sincerely believes to be right. (In order to receive universal approval, some additions must doubtless be added to the thesis, such as that the person's thoughts about what is right must have been the product of a reasonable amount of careful reflection, not influenced by personal preferences, and so on.) The thesis is not relativist, since it is not asserted that any person's or group's belief that something is blameworthy is either a necessary or a sufficient condition of its being blameworthy.

(*b*) "If the moral principles recognized in the society of which *X* is a member imply that it is wrong to do *A* in certain circumstances *C,* then it *is* wrong for *X* to do *A* in *C.*" This principle says, in effect, that a person ought to act in conformity with the moral standards of his group. Like the preceding principle, this one has a good deal of popular acceptance, is espoused by some anthropologists, and has some plausibility; it will be discussed below.

DIFFICULTIES IN THE RELATIVIST POSITIONS

The following appear to be the most important questions about the various relativist theses: (*a*) Is descriptive relativism supported by the scientific evidence? There are methodological obstacles in the way of answering the question whether there is fundamental diversity of ethical views. Such diversity would be established by producing two individuals, or cultures, who attribute identical properties to an act but nevertheless appraise it differently. But it is not easy to be sure when one has produced two such individuals or cultures. First, it is difficult to demonstrate that an act is believed to have identical properties by individuals or groups who appraise it differently. Is theft the same thing in societies where conceptions or systems of property differ? Is incest the same thing in societies with different kinship terminologies, different ways of counting lineage, and different beliefs about the effects of incest? It is possible to question members of different cultural traditions in an abstract way so that such differences in conception are ruled out, but then it is likely that the informant will not grasp the question and that his answer will be unreliable. The second difficulty is that there is no simple test for showing that groups or individuals really conflict in their appraisals. We may know that we think it

morally wrong to do so-and-so, but it is not clear how to determine whether a Navajo agrees with us. Perhaps we have first to determine whether the Navajo language contains an expression synonymous with "is morally wrong." Or can we show that a Navajo does not think it morally wrong to do *A* by the fact that he feels no guilt about doing *A?* Or perhaps a mere conflict of *preferences* is sufficient to establish a disagreement in personal values. These questions deserve more discussion among anthropologists than they have received.

The evidence for descriptive relativism consists mostly of reports from observers about what is praised, condemned, or prohibited in various societies, usually with only scanty information on the group's typical conception of what is praised or blamed. In some instances projective methods and dream analysis have been utilized, and discussions with informants have elicited fragments of the conceptual background behind the appraisals. On the basis of such material most social scientists believe there is some fundamental diversity of values and ethical principles. Several decades ago some investigators (among them W. G. Sumner and Ruth Benedict) supposed that the extent of diversity was practically unlimited, but by the 1960s it was believed that there is also considerable uniformity (for example, universal disapproval of homicide and cruelty). One reason for believing there is considerable uniformity is that it appears that it would be difficult for a social group even to survive without the presence of certain features in its value system. (A social system must provide methods for rearing and educating the young, for mating, for division of labor, for avoiding serious personal insecurity, and so on.) Uniformity of evaluation is the rule in areas that pertain to survival or to conditions for tolerable social relationships; in other areas there are apt to be fundamental differences. Psychology adds some support to this construction of the empirical data. It offers a theory of enculturation that explains how fundamentally different values can be learned, and it also suggests how some universal human goals can set limitations to diversity among value systems.

(*b*) Does descriptive relativism support metaethical relativism? It is evident that from descriptive relativism nothing follows about what ethical statements mean or could fruitfully be used to mean. It is also evident that nothing follows about whether there is some method of ethical reasoning that can correctly adjudicate between conflicting ethical commitments, at least in some cases. Descriptive relativism may very well have bearing, however, on whether a justifiable method of reasoning in ethics (assuming there is one) could succeed in adjudicating between all clashes of ethical opinion. To be sure about this we would need to have an account of the reasonable method of ethical reflection before us. But let us take an example. Suppose we think that the only reasonable way to correct a person's ethical appraisal is to show him that it does not coincide with the appraisal he would make if he were vividly informed about all the relevant facts and were impartial in his judgment. Then suppose the descriptive relativist tells us that some people are simply left cold by the ideal of equality of welfare and that others view it as a basic human right, when both groups have exactly the same beliefs about what equality of welfare is and what its consequences would be. In this case we might be convinced that both parties were already impartial (if the views were not just typical of different social or economic classes) and that further information probably would not change their views. Doubtless much more analysis of the situation is necessary, but it is clear that given the described assumption about actual ideals and the assumption about the limitation of ethical argument, one might be led to a cautious acceptance of the view that not all ethical disputes can be resolved by this justifiable method of ethical reasoning.

(c) Are cultural and metaethical relativism necessarily committed to any form of normative relativism? Neither the cultural relativist nor the metaethical relativist is committed logically to any form of normative relativism. It is consistent to assert either of these positions and also to affirm any value judgment or ethical proposition one pleases. However, the second proposition cited under normative relativism (that a person ought to act in conformity with the moral standards of his group) at least presupposes the acceptance of cultural relativism. There would be no point in asserting this normative principle if cultural relativism were not accepted.

How strong are the arguments that can be advanced in favor of this form of normative relativism? Suppose that in X's society it is a recognized moral obligation for a person to care for his father, but not for his father's siblings (at least to anything like the same degree), in illness or old age. Suppose also that in Y's society it is recognized that one has no such obligation toward one's father or his siblings but does have it toward one's mother and her siblings. In such a situation it is hard to deny that X seems to have some obligation to care for his father and that Y seems not to have, at least to the same degree. (Some philosophers hold that there is no obligation on anyone, unless one's society recognizes such an obligation for the relevant situation.) So far, the principle seems intuitively

acceptable. In general, however, it appears less defensible, for the fact that X's society regards it as wrong to play tennis on Sunday, to marry one's deceased wife's sister, and to disbelieve in God does not, we should intuitively say, make it wrong for X to do these things. Thus, our principle seems valid for some types of cases but not for others. The solution of this paradox probably is that for those cases (like an obligation to one's father) where the principle seems acceptable, the reasons for which it seems acceptable are extremely complex and are not based simply on the fact that society has asserted that an obligation exists. When society recognizes a moral obligation, there are many repercussions that basically affect the types of responsibility the individual may have toward other members of his society. For instance, one result of a society's recognizing a son's moral obligation to care for his father is that no one else will take care of the father if the son does not. Another is that a kind of equitable insurance system is set up in which one pays premiums in the form of taking responsibility for one's own father and from which one gets protection in one's old age. So it is at least an open question whether it can seriously be claimed that the moral convictions of a society have, in themselves, any implication for what a member of the society is morally bound to do, in the way our suggested principle affirms that they do.

See also Emotive Theory of Ethics; Metaethics; Perry, Ralph Barton; Sumner, William Graham; Value and Valuation; Westermarck, Edward Alexander.

Bibliography

Aberle, D. F., et al. "The Functional Prerequisites of a Society." *Ethics* 60 (1950): 100–111.

Asch, S. E. *Social Psychology,* Chs. 12, 13. New York: Prentice-Hall, 1952. An excellent critique of the evidential basis for descriptive relativism.

Benedict, Ruth. "Anthropology and the Abnormal." *Journal of General Psychology* 10 (1934): 59–82. A graphic account of some ethnological data in support of a rather extreme type of relativism.

Brandt, R. B. *Ethical Theory,* Chs. 5, 6, 11. Englewood Cliffs, NJ: Prentice-Hall, 1959. A cautious review and assessment of the evidence.

Brandt, R. B. *Hopi Ethics.* Chicago: University of Chicago Press, 1954. An analysis of the values of the Hopi Indians with special reference to relativism. Methodologically oriented.

Firth, Raymond. *Elements of Social Organization,* Ch. 6. London: Watts, 1951. A learned survey of anthropological material by an anthropologist with leanings toward relativism.

Ginsberg, Morris. *Essays in Sociology and Social Philosophy.* Vol. I. New York, 1957. A learned survey of the evidence by a sociologist.

Herskovits, Melville. *Man and His Works,* Ch. 5. New York: Knopf, 1948. One of the most vigorous contemporary defenses of relativism by an anthropologist.

Kluckhohn, C. "Ethical Relativity." *Journal of Philosophy* 52 (1955): 663–677. A cautious assessment of the evidence by an anthropologist who stresses the uniformities of value systems.

Ladd, J. *Structure of a Moral Code.* Cambridge, MA: Harvard University Press, 1956. A fine study of the Navaho, emphasizing methodological problems.

Linton, R. "Universal Ethical Principles: An Anthropological View." In *Moral Principles of Action,* edited by R. N. Anshen. New York: Harper, 1952. An excellent statement, by an anthropologist of the middle-of-the-road position, emphasizing both uniformities and diversity.

Westermarck, Edvard A. *Ethical Relativity,* Ch. 5. New York: Harcourt Brace, 1932. A shorter defense of the relativist position, intended primarily for persons interested in philosophy.

Westermarck, Edvard A. *The Origin and Development of the Moral Ideas,* Vol. I, Chs. 1–5. London: Macmillan, 1906. One of the most influential statements of the relativist position, with encyclopedic documentation; however, it is methodologically somewhat unsophisticated.

Richard B. Brandt (1967)

ETHICAL RELATIVISM [ADDENDUM]

Accepting ethical relativism can make a big difference. Opponents often think that the doctrine arises from conceptual confusion and encourages indifference to moral enormities. Advocates think that the doctrine is an antidote to an oppressive moral imperialism that often rationalizes the more worldly forms of imperialism. Both sides can agree that ethical relativism has significant implications for how we should do normative ethics.

VULGAR AND NOT-SO-VULGAR RELATIVIST ARGUMENTS FOR TOLERANCE

A good example of debate over the normative implications of ethical relativism is Bernard Williams's (1972) criticism of "vulgar relativism," which he defined in three propositions: (1) "Right" means "right for a given society." (2) "Right for a given society" is to be understood in a functionalist sense (roughly, that conceptions of what is right are part of the social fabric). (3) It is wrong for people in one society to condemn or interfere with the values of another society. Williams pointed out that (3) employs a nonrelative sense of "right" and "wrong" excluded by (1). The vulgar relativist confusedly derives a universal

moral principle of toleration from a sense of "right" that excludes any universal principle.

Relativists might deny that they are arguing for universal toleration. Rather, they may view tolerance as a value prominent within certain kinds of moralities—ones that emphasize respect for the autonomy of individuals and peoples and that require intervention in their affairs to be justifiable to them (at least when the intervention is rational and informed). To practice such restraint is to treat individuals as ends in themselves. Moreover, relativists may be addressing those who value autonomy to persuade them in particular that the existence of apparently irresolvable moral disagreements over basic moral values and norms is an occasion for not intervening (Wong 1984).

Indeed, one of the apparently irresolvable disagreements might concern the value of autonomy itself. Some moral traditions emphasize that individuals have morally legitimate interests that ought to be protected when they come into conflict with social interests. Other traditions emphasize that individuals flourish only in relationship to others. The former will provide a central place for the value of individual rights, such as rights to choose one's vocation and rights to privacy. The latter will not, or will have to provide a different basis for such rights, probably in terms of their value to desirable relationships. Reflective and knowledgeable members of both kinds of traditions might become aware of this value difference, and some of them might conclude that members of the other tradition are not necessarily mistaken. It may be, however, that only members of an autonomy-valuing tradition, such as the traditions dominant in the industrialized countries of the West, have a reason to refrain from intervening in other traditions on the grounds that such an intervention impedes members of the other traditions from acting on their reasonable values.

The no-so-vulgar relativist argument for tolerance, then, starts from the premise of metaethical relativism—the doctrine that there can be conflicting moral judgments about a particular case that are both fully correct (Harman 1978b). This metaethical premise coheres perfectly well with a normative premise that values autonomy, and their conjunction yields the conclusion, addressed to those who value autonomy, to refrain from intervening in the affairs of other societies.

NORMATIVE RELATIVISM

There is another way in which relativism can have implications for normative theory. Gilbert Harman (1978b) defined "normative moral relativism" as the position that two people can be subject to conflicting moral demands and not be subject to some more basic moral demand that, in their situation, accounts for this. For example, some groups of people think that one ought not to cause animals needless suffering, and others do not. Normative relativism allows for the possibility that the former ought to refrain from causing animals needless suffering and that the latter are not subject to a similar constraint. Harman's path to normative relativism starts from two premises: Moral demands, when applicable, provide people with compelling reasons to act in the required way, and reasons to act are "internal." Reasons are internal if the relevant agents have available warranted practical reasoning leading to a decision to perform the relevant act, and if the practical reasoning is anchored in moral demands that the agents already accept or in other desires, intentions, and beliefs that they have. A controversial part of Harman's argument that reasons are internal is his rejection of the distinction between justifying moral reasons and motivating moral reasons. Justifying moral reasons, according to this distinction, warrant agents to do things without their necessarily being able to reason from existing desires, intentions, and beliefs to a decision to perform the actions.

IMPLICATIONS OF METAETHICAL RELATIVISM FOR DOING NORMATIVE ETHICS

Accepting metaethical relativism can shape one's conception of how to do normative ethics. Consider Harman's (1975) account of morality as constituted by the implicit agreements that structure relations among the parties. On this account, many moral disagreements must be understood as disagreements among members of a group bound together by an implicit agreement. They disagree in how to interpret the terms of their agreement or in how to solve or mitigate conflicts between different elements of their agreement. This conventionalist account of morality eliminates the possibility of resolving disagreements by appealing to ideal moral principles existing independently of any implicit agreement. Rather, people are left to work out their differences with each other in ways very much like the give-and-take of politics (Harman 1978a).

Harman applies this idea to explain why the duty not to harm others is commonly perceived to be stronger than the duty to help those in need. Everyone benefits equally from a stringent duty not to harm, but the poor and weak benefit much more from a duty of mutual aid. Since the poor and weak have much less bargaining power, the expected compromise is just what is commonly accepted: a much stronger duty not to harm. Harman's conventionalist conception of morality prompts an attitude toward moral phenomena that would be different under a robustly realistic conception of morality. Under a conventionalist conception, one comes to view the belief in a stronger duty not to harm not as based on a moral fact existing independently of social convention, but as resulting from the calculus of bargaining. If one desires to change the terms of agreement, one must engage in politics. To strengthen a duty to mutual aid, for example, one might look for points of leverage with which to strike a more advantageous bargain for the poor and weak, or one might appeal to the desires or interests of the rich and strong that go beyond narrow self-interest and are served by a stronger duty to mutual aid.

Metaethical relativism need not rest on such a purely conventionalist conception of morality as Harman's. Rather, one might hold that morality is socially invented under constraints arising from its function in human life of promoting social cooperation and from the features of human nature that make some ways of promoting social cooperation better than others (Wong 1996). The constraints might eliminate some moralities as unsuitable but nevertheless leave several acceptable moralities yielding conflicting, yet fully correct, moral judgments about particular cases. In such cases, when adherents of different and equally correct moral positions must deal with each other, a conception of morality as politics can again seem appropriate.

THE NEED FOR A MORAL VALUE OF ACCOMMODATION IN THE FACE OF SERIOUS DISAGREEMENT

The politics involved need not be unconstrained by moral values. One such value is accommodation, defined as a commitment to supporting noncoercive and constructive relations with others in spite of one's disagreements with them (Wong 1992). Such a value is likely to be present in a wide range of moralities because it is needed to manage the divisive effects of moral disagreement. Serious moral disagreement is common even in a group with relatively homogeneous moral beliefs. For example, the source of disagreement over abortion seems to be not so much a difference in ultimate moral principles held by the opposing sides, but partly a difference over the applicability of a commonly held principle requiring the protection of human life and partly a difference over the relative weight to be given to the widely held principle of protecting individual autonomy. Serious disagreement of this kind is ubiquitous, and if it always threatened to become a source of schism, no society could survive for very long without brutal repression.

Even if accommodation is necessary for managing the divisiveness of disagreement, it does not have automatic priority over the moral values that are the source of serious disagreement. Abortion opponents may accept legal abortion in the early stages of fetal development to accommodate abortion-rights advocates, but be unwilling to accept compromise on abortion in the later stages of fetal development. And they may be unwilling even if they see their disagreement with those who advocate late-term abortion as irresolvable through the use of a common reason. Ultimately, there seems to be no useful general theory that specifies when to accommodate and when not to. It is a matter of judgment in the concrete situation, and also a matter of creatively devising courses of action that both honor one's own values and accommodate others who disagree. Some abortion-rights advocates and foes, for example, have joined common ground in efforts to prevent unwanted pregnancies.

ETHICAL RELATIVISM AND THE HIGH AMBITIONS OF MODERN MORAL THEORY

Ethical relativism has a deflating effect on modern normative theory, and especially on its highest ambitions. Consider Thomas Nagel's (1979) classification of five different sources of value: first, specific obligations to other people or institutions that depend on some special relation to the person or institution in question (e.g., motherhood); second, constraints on action deriving from general rights that everyone has, such as rights to liberty of certain kinds or freedom from assault or coercion; third, utility, the effects of what one does on everyone's welfare; fourth, perfectionist ends and values, such as the intrinsic value of scientific achievements and artistic creations; and fifth, commitment to one's own projects and undertakings. On Nagel's view, each of these sources is irreducible. The typical ambition of modern normative theory, however, has been to identify some of these sources as basic and the rest as derivative. Utilitarians, for instance, typically strive to reduce all moral considerations to utility, basing the assignment of individual rights and special obligations on utility. Absent reduction of moral considerations to one source, the next highest ambition is to specify general rankings of sources of value to settle cases of conflict between the several basic values. Deontologists, for example, might strive to specify how individual rights constrain the goal of maximizing utility.

The relativist views such attempts as preaching to the converted. There is no viable reduction of all moral value to one source or even a uniquely correct ordering of several irreducible values. The sources of value reflect the disorderly diversity of what human beings value and the various ways they have of structuring their relations with one another. Relativists hold that social convention plays an ineliminable role in selecting which values a group's morality emphasizes the most and in dealing with conflicts between important values. While relativists might disagree on the degree to which moralities are constrained by independent factors such as the functions of morality or the limits of human nature, they agree that independent constraining factors cannot validate the highest ambitions of modern moral theory. Moreover, even if we descend to particular cases of conflicts between values, the relativist will argue, contrary to Nagel, that there is no uniquely correct answer as to how to resolve such cases (or at least many of these cases) without collective and individual invention (see Walzer 1983, 1987; Wong 1996). If ethical relativism is true, much, if not most, of modern normative theory is wrong-headed, and this perhaps partly explains the intensely negative reaction that the doctrine elicits from many moral philosophers.

See also Metaethics; Noncognitivism; Objectivity in Ethics; Projectivism.

Bibliography
Harman, Gilbert. "Moral Relativism Defended." *Philosophical Review* 84 (1975): 3–22.

Harman, Gilbert. "Relativistic Ethics: Morality as Politics." *Midwest Studies in Philosophy* 3 (1978a): 109–121.

Harman, Gilbert. "What Is Moral Relativism?" In *Values and Morals*, edited by Alvin I. Goldman and Jaegwon Kim. Dordrecht, Netherlands: Reidel, 1978b.

Nagel, Thomas. "The Fragmentation of Value." In his *Mortal Questions*. Cambridge, U.K.: Cambridge University Press, 1979.

Walzer, Michael. *Interpretation and Social Criticism.* Cambridge, MA: Harvard University Press, 1987.

Walzer, Michael. *Spheres of Justice: A Defense of Pluralism and Equality*. New York: Basic Books, 1983.

Williams, Bernard. *Morality: An Introduction to Ethics.* New York: Harper Torchbooks, 1972.

Williams, Bernard. "The Truth in Relativism." *Proceedings of the Aristotelian Society* 85 (1974–1975): 214–228.

Wong, David B. "Coping with Moral Conflict and Ambiguity." *Ethics* 102 (1992): 763–784.

Wong, David B. *Moral Relativity.* Berkeley: University of California Press, 1984.

Wong, David B. "Pluralistic Relativism." *Midwest Studies in Philosophy* 20 (1996): 378–400.

David B. Wong (2005)

ETHICAL SKEPTICISM

See *Emotive Theory of Ethics; Ethical Relativism*

ETHICAL SUBJECTIVISM

A subjectivist ethical theory is a theory according to which moral judgments about men or their actions are judgments about the way people react to these men and actions—that is, the way they think or feel about them. It follows that moral predicates are not possessed by actions or actors in the absence of people who pass judgments upon them or who respond to them with such feelings as admiration, love, approval, detestation, hate, or disapproval. It follows from this definition that nonpropositional or noncognitive ethical theories are not subjective, for according to them there are no moral propositions at all, and thus moral judgments cannot be propositions about people's feelings.

This definition is also intended to exclude views according to which moral judgments are judgments about how people behave; hence, views such as that "wrong" means "contrary to the accepted code of the society in which the action is performed" will not count as subjective, even if, as seems likely, statements about moral codes are statements about the prohibitory or permissory behavior of the communities possessing these codes. Although this distinction is not hard and fast (for statements about moral codes might often turn out to be statements about how the people possessing these codes think or feel), we shall maintain it in order not to trespass too far into the subject of ethical relativism, which is treated elsewhere. Elements of subjectivism can be found in so many ethical theories that it is almost impossible to give an account of them. The greatest, though not the most consistent, subjectivist was the eighteenth-century Scottish philosopher David Hume. The theory has also been popular among anthropologists, of whom Edward Westermarck was probably the most outstanding.

Subjectivist theories can provisionally be classified according to whether moral judgments are alleged to be about the speaker's thoughts or feelings, about the thoughts or feelings of some group of people, or about the thoughts or feelings of men as such.

MORAL JUDGMENTS STATE WHAT THE SPEAKER FEELS

The view that moral judgments are about the feelings of the person making the judgment—that what I mean when I say that an action is right or that a man is good is that the thought of that man or action evokes in me, personally, at this moment, a feeling of approval—has been subjected to an enormous number of objections. It has been argued that, so far from its being possible to identify moral judgments as those judgments that are about feelings of approval, it is in fact only possible to identify feelings of approval as those feelings that are evoked by the judgment that an action is right, and argued that if we feel approval of an action because we judge it to be right, our thinking that it is right cannot be identical with our approving of it. It has also been objected that if the theory is true, all I need do to settle any doubt I have concerning the rectitude of someone else's action is to introspect, and that it is very difficult, if not impossible, to be mistaken about one's feelings, although it is very easy to make a mistake about whether an action is right. More plausibly, it has been alleged that the theory implies that one can only criticize someone else's moral judgment on the ground that the other person is mistaken about how he himself feels.

Some of the worst difficulties for the theory arise from the fact that sentences offered as definitions of moral judgments contain such words as *I*, *now*, and *here*, whose reference depends upon who uses them, at what time, and in what place. From this it follows that one person's moral judgments can never be incompatible with any other person's moral judgments; the sentence "I do not feel disapproval of divorce," when used by one speaker, does not express a judgment incompatible with that expressed by the sentence "I do feel disapproval of divorce," uttered by a different speaker. It would appear, however, that when one person says, "Divorce is wrong," he does mean to say something incompatible with what someone else means when he says, "Divorce is not wrong." From the fact that moral judgments are alleged to have a covert reference to the feelings the speaker now has, it follows that if at one time he judges an action (say, Brutus's assassination of Caesar) to be right, his judgment is not incompatible with the judgment he may make at a later time when he judges Brutus's assassination of Caesar to be wrong. For according to this theory, what he meant on the first occasion was that he did not then feel disapproval of Brutus's assassination of Caesar, and what he meant on the second occasion was that he now does. Clearly there is no reason why both judgments should not be true.

G. E. Moore, in a famous argument, attempted to deduce that the subjectivist theory led to the paradoxical conclusion that the same action could be both right and wrong, and that one and the same action could change from being right to being wrong. (It is important to remember that Moore thought classes of actions—for example, marrying one's deceased wife's sister—could change from being right to being wrong, that is, that an instance of a class of actions, performed at one time, might be right, while another instance of the same class of actions, performed at a later time, might be wrong.) First, Moore argued as follows. If Jones approves of Brutus's assassination of Caesar and says Brutus was right, it follows from the theory that Brutus was right. Similarly, if Smith disapproves of Brutus's assassination of Caesar and says Brutus was wrong, then Brutus was wrong. Hence Brutus was both right and wrong to assassinate Caesar. Second, to show that Brutus's assassination of Caesar can change from being right to being wrong, all Moore thought he need do was to point out that if Jones says (at a time when he approves of Brutus's action) that Brutus was right, then according to the theory, Brutus was right; if he later comes to disapprove of Brutus's action, then, if he says Brutus was wrong, according to the theory, Brutus was wrong. If Jones can truly judge at one time that Brutus was right and at a later time that Brutus was wrong, it must follow that Brutus's action has changed from being right to being wrong.

C. L. Stevenson has criticized Moore's argument in the following manner. Although Jones can truly say that Brutus was right to assassinate Caesar and Smith can truly say that Brutus's action was wrong, neither Jones nor Smith nor anyone else can say that this action is both right and wrong. For anyone to be able to say it is both right and wrong, someone would have both to approve of it and disapprove of it. Hence, although Jones, who approves of Brutus's action, can say it is right, and Smith, who disapproves of it, can say it is wrong, neither can say it is both right and wrong. Moore's mistake, perhaps, consisted in construing the theory we are considering as maintaining that "right" is a predicate like "disapproved of by *someone*" (from which it would follow that the same action can be both right and wrong), whereas "right" is alleged to be a predicate like "disapproved of by me, the speaker," from which it follows that the same action cannot be both right and wrong, since the speaker cannot both approve and disapprove, on the whole, of one and the same action.

A free exposition of Stevenson's criticism of Moore's argument (that if the view that moral judgments are statements about the speaker's feeling is true, one and the same action can change from being right to being wrong) might take the following form. Moore supposes that if ten years ago I could truly say Brutus was right to assassinate Caesar (because at that time the thought of this action did arouse approval in me) and now I can truly say that Brutus was wrong to do this (because at this time the thought of his action arouses disapproval in me), it follows that the action must have changed from being right to being wrong. Stevenson, however, points out that the statement "Brutus's action has changed from being right to being wrong" is equivalent to the conjunction of statements "Brutus's action was right a while ago" and "Brutus's action is now wrong." Although the truth of the second of these statements is entailed by the fact that I now feel disapproval of Brutus's assassination of Caesar, the first of them is not entailed by the fact that I earlier felt approval of Brutus's assassination of Caesar. Although Moore supposes "Brutus's assassination of Caesar *was* right" to mean "I *once* approved of Brutus's assassination of Caesar," what it actually means is "I *now* approve of Brutus's erstwhile assassination of Caesar," and, ex hypothesi, "I do not now approve of Brutus's action, I disapprove of it." Moore's mistake is to suppose that the word *was* in the sentence "Brutus *was* right to assassinate Caesar" shows that the sentence is about my past approval, whereas in fact its function is to show that it is the action I am disapproving of, not my disapproval, that is past.

Although Stevenson's detailed criticisms of Moore are valid, it is possible to restate Moore's arguments in a way that avoids them. To take the second of Moore's arguments first, it would plainly be absurd for me to say that Brutus was wrong to assassinate Caesar and at the same time to say that I was correct many years ago when I judged that Brutus was right to assassinate Caesar. If I now say he was wrong, I am bound to say that when, earlier, I said he was right, I was mistaken. In regard to the first argument, although it does not follow from this subjectivist theory that anyone can say that an action is both right and wrong, it does follow that if Jones says that Brutus was right to assassinate Caesar, he is not saying anything incompatible with what Smith is saying when he says that Brutus was wrong to assassinate Caesar.

Clearly, however, Jones and Smith think they are saying something incompatible, and it is unlikely that they have such a poor understanding of how to use their own language as to be mistaken on this point. In other words, according to the subjectivist theory, if Jones says Brutus was right to assassinate Caesar, Smith can say to Jones that Brutus was wrong and at the same time agree that Jones is making a true statement when he says that Brutus was right. This is absurd. Stevenson has tried to overcome this particular difficulty by saying that although insofar as Jones and Smith are making assertions, their assertions are not incompatible with one another, they are doing something over and above asserting things—namely, Jones is trying to evoke in Smith an attitude of approval toward Brutus's action, and Smith is trying to evoke in Jones an attitude of disapproval toward Brutus's action. Hence, although their beliefs are compatible, their interests clash. Jones aims to achieve something that is incompatible with what Smith aims to achieve. A consideration of this view of Stevenson's, however, would take us away from subjectivism to a consideration of nonpropositional ethical theories.

The difficulties already mentioned may well be fatal to the type of subjectivist theory we are considering, at any rate as long as it is not bolstered by the nonpropositional theory. Moreover, there is a further difficulty that seems to settle the issue. Suppose Jones says that the death penalty for murder ought to be retained in Great Britain, and he says this because he wrongly supposes that abolishing the death penalty would lead to an increase in the number of murders. According to this kind of subjectivism, all Jones means when he says that the death penalty ought to be retained is that the thought of retaining it arouses in him feelings of approval, and since it does do this, his statement that it ought to be retained is true, however mistaken he may be about the facts of the situation. He is under no obligation to withdraw his statement, therefore, when he discovers his mistake. Again, this is absurd.

MORAL JUDGMENTS STATE THE SPEAKER'S THOUGHTS

So far we have considered the view that moral judgments are judgments to the effect that the action under judgment arouses certain feelings in the person making the judgment. It is possible, however, to think that what someone making a moral judgment is asserting is that the action or person being judged arouses in the person making the judgment certain thoughts or beliefs. The most natural view is that someone who asserts that an action is wrong is saying that the thought of the action arouses in him personally the belief that it is wrong, or in other words, that all we mean when we say that an action is wrong is that we personally think it is wrong. This view is circular because even though it offers a definition of "wrong" (that is, it maintains that "X is wrong" just means "I think X is wrong"), the word *wrong* still occurs in the definition (compare "'thoroughbred horse' means 'horse both of whose parents are thoroughbred horses'").

It is obviously impossible to get rid of the circularity by again substituting "thought wrong" for "wrong" in the definition, however many times we do it.

OBJECTIVE AND SUBJECTIVE SENSES OF "RIGHT"

It is quite commonly held that whenever one thinks one is acting rightly, one is acting rightly. Philosophers who hold this view, however, are not properly regarded as subjectivists. Clearly, if the word *right* is being used twice in the same sense when it is asserted that one is doing rightly if one does what one thinks is right, the view is contradictory. According to it, one would be acting rightly even if one did what one mistakenly thought was right: From the fact that one mistakenly thought it was right it follows that it is wrong, and from the fact that one is acting rightly if one does what one thinks is right, it follows that the act is right. Those philosophers who have held this view, however, have generally distinguished two senses of the word *right*, sometimes called an objective sense and a subjective sense, and have held that an action is right, in the subjective sense, if it is thought to be right in the objective sense. This removes both the contradiction and the suggestion that the property of being right depends on being thought to be right; the property of being subjectively right depends on the different property of being thought to be objectively right.

MORAL JUDGMENTS STATE WHAT A COMMUNITY FEELS

Next to be considered is the view that when individuals make moral judgments they are talking not about the way they themselves think or feel about the things they are judging, but of the way some group of people thinks and feels about these things. Presumably the group of people might be named by a proper name—for example, "Englishmen" or "Melanesians," or more plausibly (to avoid the difficulty that Englishmen cannot be supposed to be talking about the feelings of Melanesians and vice versa) by a descriptive phrase such as "my group" or "the community to which I belong." The theory that moral judgments are about the feelings of the speaker's own community is open to a large number of the objections to which the private reaction theory is open and a few more besides. Although two people, one of whom says a given action is right and the other of whom says that the same action is wrong, will be saying incompatible things if they belong to the same community, if they belong to different communities their statements will be perfectly compatible. Again, if a man says at one time that an action is right and at a later time that the same action is wrong, there is no need for him to withdraw his first assertion, provided that the attitude of the community to which he belongs has changed during the interval. In that case there is no reason why both his first assertion and his second assertion should not be true. It follows, too, that however ignorant or mistaken a given community may be concerning the nature of the action being morally assessed, the statement by a member of that community that the action is right will be true as long as his community does approve of it. For example, if a community disapproves of giving eggs to pregnant women because it believes that this will cause them to give birth to chickens, the statement by a member of the community that it is morally wrong to give eggs to pregnant women will be a true one, because this community really does have the feelings it is alleged to have.

Over and above these quite fatal objections, the theory that moral judgments state how members of a community feel about the actions under judgment is exposed to two difficulties, to which the view that they state how the speaker feels is not exposed. Although one might just accept the conclusion, implied by the latter theory, that one discovers a given action is right by introspection (in Hume's language, by looking inside one's breast and discovering there a sentiment of approval or disapproval), it is quite impossible to accept the view that one discovers a given action is right simply by asking other members of one's community whether they approve of it. The theory also leads to the quite unacceptable consequence that anyone who believes, for example, that most of his community approves of retaining a law against homosexuality and at the same time believes that the law against homosexuality ought to be abolished believes two logically incompatible things; for, according to this theory, what he is believing when he believes that the law against homosexuality ought to be abolished is just that most of his community would feel approval of its abolition.

A variant of this last theory would be the view that what we mean when we say that an action is right is that it is approved of by the agent's community, not the speaker's. This is more plausible because it means that instead of condemning actions performed in distant places or times because they do not accord with the moral attitudes of our community, we may praise them because they do accord with the moral attitudes of the community to which the man who performed them belonged. Hence, it appeals to a tendency in some modern moral philosophers to be rather absurdly uncritical of the moral attitudes of communities other than their own. They may

be less willing to accept this variant theory, however, when they realize that if it is true, they must be equally uncritical of the morals of their own community. It must be pointed out that according to this theory, if one says, "Introducing racial segregation into University X was wrong," one means that introducing segregation into the university was disapproved of by the community in which the action was performed. It is perfectly obvious, however, that one might perfectly well think that it was wrong and at the same time know that it was not disapproved of by the community in which it was performed. Again, this theory has the difficulty that even when a community disapproves of some practice only because the community is grossly mistaken concerning its nature (as in the case of the women and the eggs), we are still bound to say that the practice is wrong, providing the community does in fact disapprove of it.

MORAL JUDGMENTS STATE WHAT MOST PEOPLE FEEL

The objections that have already been raised against earlier types of subjectivism can be applied without much difficulty to the view that what we mean when we say an action is right is that most people approve of it. This theory does imply that any two individuals (whoever they are), one of whom condemns an action and the other of whom judges it to be right, really will be saying incompatible things, for it cannot be that most people approve of an action and at the same time disapprove of it. However, since people may change from approving of something to disapproving of it, the theory does entail that a man may judge an action to be right and later judge the same action to be wrong without having to retract his first judgment. The theory means that an action is wrong if most people feel disapproval of it, however ignorant or mistaken they may be about the nature of the action. It also means that it is impossible for a man to make up his mind concerning the rectitude of any action unless he has decided whether humankind in general would approve of it; it is obvious, however, that we can make up our minds on such questions without having the least idea what the attitude of most men would be. In view of what has already been said about the theory that what we mean when we say that an action is right is that the speaker thinks it is right, nothing need be said about the analogous views that an action is right if the speaker's community thinks that it is right, or that an action is right if most people think that it is right.

It is fairly obvious from what has been said that all subjectivist theories need to be amended, at least to exclude the possibility that the attitude of the people we are alleged to be describing when we make moral judgments is not based on ignorance or mistake. Hence, a consideration of subjectivism may lead to the view that an action is right not if it is approved of by any actual person or group of people, but only if it would be approved of by a person of a very special kind—for instance, one who, at the very least, is never ignorant of or mistaken about any relevant matter of fact concerning the action toward which his attitude of approval is directed. Hence, a consideration of subjectivism must inevitably lead to a consideration of ideal observer theories; these, however, are best treated as a variety of ethical objectivism.

See also Emotive Theory of Ethics; Error Theory in Ethics; Ethical Naturalism; Ethical Relativism; Metaethics; Moral Skepticism; Noncognitivism.

Bibliography

Boyd, Richard. "How to Be a Moral Realist." In *Essays on Moral Realism*, edited by Geoffrey Sayre-McCord, Ithaca: Cornell University Press, 1988.

Brandt, Richard. *A Theory of the Good and the Right*. Oxford: Clarendon Press, 1979.

Brink, David. *Moral Realism and the Foundations of Ethics*. Cambridge, U.K.: Cambridge University Press, 1989.

Carritt, E. F. *Ethical and Political Thinking*. Oxford: Clarendon Press, 1947.

Carritt, E. F. *The Theory of Morals*. London: Oxford University Press, 1928.

Edwards, Paul. *The Logic of Moral Discourse*. Glencoe, IL: Free Press, 1955. An acute discussion of various kinds of subjectivism.

Ewing, A. C. *The Definition of Good*. New York: Macmillan, 1947. Ch. 1.

Firth, Roderick. "Ethical Absolutism and the Ideal Observer," *Philosophy and Phenomenological Research* 12 (1952): 317–345.

Foot, Philippa. "Does Moral Subjectivism Rest on a Mistake?" *Oxford Journal of Legal Studies* 15 (1995): 1–14.

Harman, Gilbert. "What Is Moral Relativism?" In *Values and Morals*, edited by Alvin Goldman and Jaegwon Kim. Dordrecht: Reidel, 1978.

Harman, Gilbert, and Judith Thomson. *Moral Relativism and Moral Objectivity*. Oxford: Blackwell, 1996.

Hume, David. *Inquiry concerning the Principles of Morals*, edited by C. W. Hendel. New York: Liberal Arts Press, 1957. Ch. 1, Appendix I. The classical criticism of objectivism.

Hume, David. *Treatise of Human Nature*, edited by L. A. Selby-Bigge. Oxford: Clarendon Press, 1888; reprinted 1955. Bk. III, Pt. I, Secs. I–II.

Johnston, Mark. "Dispositional Theories of Value." *Proceedings of the Aristotelian Society* Suppl. (1989): 139–174.

Kant, Immanuel. *The Moral Law, or Kant's Groundwork of the Metaphysics of Morals*. Translated by H. J. Paton. London: Hutchinson, 1948.

Lewis, David K. "Dispositional Theories of Value." *Proceedings of the Aristotelian Society* Suppl. (1989): 113–137.

McDowell, John. "Values and Secondary Qualities." In *Morality and Objectivity*, edited by Ted Honderich. London: Routledge & Kegan Paul, 1985.

Moore, G. E. *Ethics*. London: Williams and Norgate, 1912. Chs. 3–4. An important criticism of subjectivism.

Plato. *The Republic*. Translated, with an introduction, by A. D. Lindsay. New York, 1907; paperback ed., 1958. Bk. I.

Price, Richard. *A Review of the Principal Questions in Morals*, edited, with an introduction, by D. Daiches Raphael. Oxford: Clarendon Press, 1948. Excellent defense of objectivism.

Ross, W. D. *The Foundations of Ethics*. Oxford: Clarendon Press, 1939. This work and the following are two modern versions of Price's theory.

Ross, W. D. *The Right and the Good*. Oxford: Clarendon Press, 1930.

Shafer-Landau, Russ. *Moral Realism*. Oxford: Clarendon, 2003.

Smith, Michael. "Dispositional Theories of Value." *Proceedings of the Aristotelian Society* Suppl. (1989): 89–111.

Smith, Michael. *The Moral Problem*. Oxford: Blackwell, 1994.

Stevenson, C. L. "Moore's Arguments against Certain Forms of Ethical Naturalism." In *The Philosophy of G. E. Moore*, edited by P. A. Schilpp. Evanston, IL: Northwestern University Press, 1942. A reply to some of Moore's criticisms.

Westermarck, Edward. *Ethical Relativity*. New York: Harcourt Brace, 1932. A well-known version of subjectivism.

Wiggins, David. "A Sensible Subjectivism." In *Needs, Values, Truth*. Oxford: Basil Blackwell, 1987.

Jonathan Harrison (1967)
Bibliography updated by Mark van Roojen (2005)

ETHICAL THEORY

See *Metaethics*

ETHICS

Ethics is the branch of philosophy that tries to understand a familiar type of evaluation: the moral evaluation of people's character traits, their conduct, and their institutions. We speak of good and bad people, the morally right or wrong thing to do, just or unjust regimes or laws, how things ought and ought not to be, and how we should live. One part of the subject, metaethics, is concerned with what such judgments mean, what, if anything, they are about, whether they can be true or false, and if so what makes them true or false. The other part of the subject, normative ethics, is concerned with the content of those judgments: What features make an action right or wrong; what is a good life; and what are the characteristics of a just society? This entry will concentrate on normative ethics, though some comments on metaethics will be unavoidable. And within normative ethics it will concentrate on general principles and foundations (what is usually called moral theory) rather than on applied ethics, the discussion of specific cases. Moral theory seeks a systematic understanding of the full range of moral convictions and disagreements and of their possible grounds.

WHAT IS MORALITY?

Morality of some kind seems to be a universal human phenomenon; it is a subpart of the broader domain of the normative, which seems also to be characteristically human. Normative questions and judgments are about what we ought to do, want, believe, or think (rather than just about what we actually do), and about the reasons for and against doing or believing one thing rather than another. Only rational beings, and probably only beings with language, are capable of normative thinking.

Many normative questions are not moral. If we ask whether we ought to believe on the basis of the available evidence that a painting is by Rembrandt, that is a normative question, but not a moral one. Moral questions are about what we ought to do and how we ought to live, not about what we ought to believe. In answering them we need to appeal to what are called practical reasons—reasons for doing or wanting something—rather than the purely evidential or theoretical reasons that determine the justification for factual or scientific belief.

But not all practical reasons and practical norms are moral, either. There are norms that tell you what you ought to do to keep your rose bushes healthy, the right way to make an omelet, or what to wear if you are going to be knighted by the queen, but these are not moral judgments. The moral is a subpart of the large normative domain of the practical.

Its further definition is the subject of controversy among different moral theories, but a rough approximation is this: Morality identifies certain norms that apply to everyone in a certain group and that should be recognized as valid for everyone by each member of the group although their separate individual aims and desires may differ and lead them into conflict with one another. In most, but not all modern moral theories, the group to which moral norms apply includes all mentally competent human beings. In such theories morality is conceived as consisting of universal norms.

Morality aims to provide us, in the practical domain, with a common point of view from which we can come to agreement about what all of us ought to do. This may be different from what each of us might want to do or want other people to do, if we looked at the question only from our own personal point of view. Morality tries to discover a more objective standpoint of evaluation than that of purely personal preference.

Much of the content of moral norms has to do with our relations to each other—how we treat each other in our individual conduct and how they are treated by collective institutions that we support. There are also moral norms and evaluations having to do with the way we conduct our own lives, norms that tell us how anyone may succeed or fail in living well. Virtues like prudence and self-control are examples of this universal but partly self-regarding aspect of morality. There are also important moral questions about our relations to the rest of the natural world, especially to other animals. But the bulk of the subject has to do with our lives as members of the human community.

Though there are ethical relativists who disagree, moral rules such as those that condemn murder, injury, lying, stealing, and betrayal and endorse kindness, honesty, and generosity are usually thought to apply universally. Whether this can be shown is one of the big questions of ethics, but such norms are not supposed to depend for their validity on the code of a particular society or group or the laws of a particular government. They are not like local codes of etiquette, taboos, or specific traffic or commercial regulations. Even the wrongness of a crime like murder does not depend on its being against the law. Rather, moral norms are supposed to be recognizable by a form of thought that is available in principle to any adult human being—even though some people may be better at it than others.

At the center of morality are standards that serve not only the interests of a particular individual who follows them but also the collective good of the community, by making it a safer place or otherwise promoting the general welfare of its members. But for those standards to do their work, most people have to adhere to them. Normative ethics tries both to identify such standards and to explain how individuals, even though their interests diverge in many respects, can be attached to universal norms that serve the common good.

OBJECTIVE REASONS OR SUBJECTIVE FEELINGS?

Most moral theories ascribe a kind of objectivity to moral judgments, because such judgments are supposed to issue from a point of view that different people can share and that enables them to arrive at agreement about what should be done, what would be wrong, what would be fair, and so forth. Even when people disagree about such things, they usually share the belief that there is a right answer to the question, though they do not agree about what it is. They do not think of their moral disagreements simply as a divergence of personal preferences.

However, there is controversy about the exact nature of the convergence of judgments that we try to reach in moral thinking and about its source. This is one of the main questions of metaethics: Are moral judgments based on universally valid reasons, which would permit them to be objectively true or false, or do they merely express widespread subjective feelings that many people share? In the latter case, while we can come to agree in these judgments, they do not make claims that are either true or false; rather, they express certain attitudes or responses—though perhaps responses on which all human beings can converge.

One of the most important defenders of the subjective alternative is the eighteenth-century Scottish philosopher David Hume (1739, 1751). He argues for the claim that moral judgments express a special type of feeling, sentiment, or attitude on the ground that this is needed to explain how moral norms, like other practical norms, are capable of motivating people to act.

For example, if someone judges that it would be wrong to leave a campsite littered with garbage, this will probably move him or her to take the trouble to clean it up before he or she leaves. If we assume further that motivation must always start from some desire or feeling of the agent, it seems to follow that morality must get its motivational force from something of that kind—for example, from a sympathetic aversion to the unhappiness of others. For how could the recognition of any truth revealed by reasoning or thought alone, without the help of a desire, have the motivational consequences of a normative judgment?

Defenders of the objective alternative usually hold a different view of motivation. They are likely to maintain that while feelings and desires are often the source of motivation, there is also a form of practical reasoning that is capable of motivating rational persons on its own, through the recognition of existing reasons alone. If you decide, after considering the effect on others, that it would be wrong to leave the campsite a mess, you recognize that you have a reason to clean it up, and that will lead you, if you are a decent person, to do so. On this view the motive is produced by recognition of the norm,

rather than the norm being the mere expression of a preexisting feeling or motive.

This opposition between the view that moral judgments express subjective feelings and the view that they express objective normative beliefs capable of being true or false has many different forms and subtle variations, but it is present everywhere in ethical theory, and in some cases it plays an important role in disputes over the normative content of morality, although it is primarily an issue of metaethics. It is also important in discussing the question whether moral standards have a universal basis, or whether they are really culturally relative. On the subjective or expressivist theory the relativist conclusion is not necessary, but it seems more of a possibility than on the theory of objective moral reasons.

MORALITY AND SELF-INTEREST

One of the great questions of ethics is whether, and if so to what extent, morality requires us to subordinate our individual self-interest to the general good. There is one view, whose most important representative is the seventeenth-century English philosopher Thomas Hobbes (1651), according to which morality does not conflict with self-interest because its requirements actually derive from self-interest in a subtle way.

Hobbes's argument is that certain rules of conduct are necessary for human beings to live at peace with one another and to enjoy the benefits of civilization, because if people do not abide by those rules they will fall into a miserable condition of insecurity and violence. They are the rules of morality, prohibiting murder, assault, theft, fraud, breach of contract, and so forth, and it is in every individual's self-interest to live in a society in which they are followed. General adherence to morality serves the collective self-interest of all the individual members of any community.

This alone is not enough, however, to show that private adherence to those rules is in the individual self-interest of each member of the community. That general adherence is in the collective interest of all does not imply that individual adherence is in the personal interest of each, because an individual cannot by his or her own conduct bring it about that others will act in the same way. What would serve the collective self-interest therefore does not necessarily coincide with what people would be led to do by their individual self-interest.

Hobbes thinks that reasoning allows us to see that collective self-interest would be served by general adherence to the rules of morality, but that individual self-interest makes it irrational to follow those rules on our own, since that would simply permit others to take advantage of us. He concludes that to bring the rule of morality into effect, it is necessary to provide all individuals with incentives guaranteeing that individual and collective self-interest will coincide. This can be done only by a system of law, enforced by a sovereign with a monopoly of force over the members of the community. Only then will it be safe for each person to follow the rules, knowing others will also follow them because it is likewise in their personal interest to do so.

According to this theory self-interest does not motivate us to abide by the requirements of morality directly. If we could get away with it, self-interest would lead us to prefer that everyone else followed the rules, while we ourselves were exempt from them. But that alternative is not available, and it would be much worse for each of us if no one followed the rules. So the uniform solution that serves all of our interests best is that everyone follow the rules and that a system of incentives be set up to ensure that no individual can do better for himself or herself by breaking them.

There are also theories descended from that of Hobbes that preserve the connection between morality and self-interest but do not rely for stability only on external incentives produced by the enforcement mechanisms of a legal system. The Canadian American philosopher David Gauthier (1986) proposes that some of the work of bringing individual and collective self-interest to coincide can be done by internalizing the moral rules, so that individuals are inhibited against breaking them even apart from the threat of punishment. Feelings of guilt, for example, are a kind of emotional self-punishment that people who have internalized the rules inflict on themselves when they break them. It is in our collective interest for each member of the community to be subject to such feelings, because a community in which the moral norms have been internalized in this way provides its members with the benefits of mutual trust and peaceful cooperation.

In views of this kind there is already a departure from the reliance exclusively on self-interest to motivate moral conduct, even though morality is thought to serve the interest of each of its adherents. But many moral theories put a much greater distance than this between morality and self-interest. In different ways, most modern accounts of morality part company with Hobbes and base the appeal of moral norms on a concern for everyone, not just for oneself. This means that morality may sometimes require the individual to sacrifice his or her own interests

for the good of others or to avoid transgressing the rights of others. That poses the question of the nature of the reasons or motives that can outweigh self-interest in these cases. If you can make a gain by harming someone else, why shouldn't you do it?

CONSEQUENTIALISM AND UTILITARIANISM

One important type of answer to this question is that everyone's life is just as important or valuable as everyone else's, and in particular your happiness is no more valuable than other people's happiness. Therefore, you have a reason to care impartially about what happens to everybody, and in your conduct should try to promote the general good and not just your own.

This depends on an important distinction between two ways in which things can be good or bad: They can be good or bad for someone, or they can be good or bad, period. If something is good for me, that obviously gives me a reason to want and promote it, but it does not obviously follow that anyone else has a reason to want and promote it, unless it is also good for him or her. But if something is simply good, period, then it is something anyone has a reason to want and promote.

Some things, like health and pleasure, are clearly good for the person who has them. And it is possible to hold the view that this is the only kind of value there is—value for someone. On this view there may be things, like the destruction of the ozone layer, that would be bad for everyone, but even that would not make it bad, period. Most ethical theories, however, hold that some of the things that are good or bad for individuals, like pleasure and pain, or happiness and unhappiness, are also good or bad without qualification—objectively good or bad, one might say. And each person has a common reason to promote what is good and to prevent what is bad in this way—not only what is good or bad for him- or herself. Some theories derive the content of morality entirely from such a conception of objective value—maintaining that morality emerges once we recognize the objective value and disvalue of the occurrence of all those things that are good or bad for individuals.

Utilitarianism is the most fully developed version of such a theory. A version of it is found in Hume; it was further developed by the English philosophers Jeremy Bentham (1798), John Stuart Mill (1863), and Henry Sidgwick (1907) and continues to be influential. Utilitarianism holds that morality is simply the specification of those forms of conduct that contribute most effectively to the greatest overall happiness for all persons—or all sentient beings—impartially considered.

The basic value on which the whole theory depends is some measure of what is good in the lives or experiences of particular individuals—what is in itself desirable for them, and therefore also objectively valuable. This may be pleasure and the avoidance of pain, happiness and the avoidance of unhappiness, the satisfaction of their desires or preferences and the avoidance of their frustration, or perhaps some other measure, depending on the particular version of utilitarianism. Whatever the measure, it must be roughly quantifiable in a way that allows comparison between persons, and addition and subtraction of the amounts of the value to determine the total that is present in complex cases involving many people with different experiences.

This measure of value is called utility (a technical term—in this context the word does not mean "usefulness"). Utilitarianism is the theory that we should act, and organize our institutions, so as to promote the maximum total amount of utility, weighing the utility that arises in the lives of all persons impartially. This is sometimes crudely expressed by the formula "the greatest good for the greatest number."

What matters, according to this view, is not the quality of our actions themselves but the utility, as measured for example by general happiness, of the overall outcome of what we do, compared with the available alternatives. For this reason utilitarianism is an example of a consequentialist moral theory. It is results that matter, not the means by which we reach them. So an important feature of consequentialism is that it does not make a fundamental moral distinction between positive and negative responsibility for good or bad outcomes.

For example, one is positively responsible for someone else's suffering if one deliberately hurts that person, but negatively responsible if one fails to save him or her from being harmed. According to utilitarianism this alone makes no moral difference between the two cases: Morality does not require merely that you not harm people; it makes you equally responsible for the prevention of harm, from whatever cause. It even requires you to cause harm if that is the most effective way to bring about the greatest overall balance of good. If there is a moral difference between harming and failing to prevent harm, it must be due to some difference in the utility of the results.

Another significant feature of utilitarianism is that what matters in determining the rightness or wrongness of actions is the total utility that results, not how it is distributed among individuals. In calculating the total we add together or aggregate quantities of utility from different lives, and the sum of many small amounts of pleasure or pain from different people's experiences may add up to much more utility than the intense pleasure or pain of one individual.

Working out the details for principles of conduct and political, social, and economic institutions depends on estimates of the likely results of the various alternatives, and combining probabilities and utilities to arrive at a measure of what is called expected utility. This is often uncertain and difficult. But the ultimate moral foundation is simple: What matters is that people should have good experiences and avoid bad ones, and the higher the overall balance of good minus bad, the better. The aim of morality is to tell us how to maximize the amount of good in the world, where good is measured objectively and impartially, so that our own personal good is no more important a part of the total than anyone else's.

RIGHTS, OBLIGATIONS, EQUALITY, AND DESERT

Some familiar aspects of ordinary moral thought do not seem to conform to the utilitarian standard. One of the most controversial issues in moral theory is whether those aspects can be explained by utilitarianism, and if not, whether we should conclude that utilitarianism is false or that those aspects must be rejected.

Apparently, counterutilitarian moral norms are those that either require or permit a course of action or policy that fails to maximize utility. One type of example is found in the large and diverse category of individual rights, which include rights against certain kinds of interference or violation by others, and rights to do what one wishes so long as one does not violate the rights of others.

For example, it seems to be widely accepted that each individual has a right not to be killed, injured, enslaved, kidnapped, or imprisoned if he or she is not hurting anyone else—even when violating one of those rights would be useful as a means to producing a large net balance of benefits overall. Even if someone else's life could be saved by forcibly taking one of your kidneys and transplanting it to him or her, this would not be morally acceptable if you did not consent to it. For another example, each of us is generally thought to have a right to devote most of our resources and attention to our own life and the lives of our friends and family, even if we could do more good overall by dedicating ourselves to the general welfare of everyone.

Other examples come from the sphere of special obligations, both those that arise from particular undertakings, like contracts and promises, and those that follow from standing conditions like citizenship and family membership. Conventional morality holds that one is obligated to keep a promise even if marginally more good than harm would be done by breaking it, that one should give special weight to the welfare of one's children, and so forth.

In ordinary moral reflection on social policy and public institutions, considerations of fairness seem to be sensitive not to the total aggregate welfare produced, but to the distribution of benefits and disadvantages among individuals. A distribution that produces greater total welfare at the cost of great inequality between rich and poor may be morally inferior to one with a lower total but less poverty and more equality of opportunity.

Finally, in thinking about the criminal law, the allocation of punishments seems to be justified not merely by what would produce the most utility, through deterrence and prevention, but also by the requirement that only those who are guilty be punished, and that the punishment deserved is proportional to the gravity of the offense. (The idea of moral desert brings up the large question of free will and moral responsibility. There are those who doubt that people can be responsible for their actions in a way that would mean they deserve punishment for wrongdoing, so that punishment can be justified only as a deterrent. But that issue is beyond the scope of this discussion.)

What these familiar moral ideas have in common is that they do not appear at first sight to interpret the right as what will maximize the overall good for individuals. They seem to rely instead on independent standards for what is right and wrong—standards that either permit or require certain types of actions even if we believe they will not produce the greatest impartial benefit. Such standards set certain moral limits on what we may do to other people and impose certain positive requirements as well, including moral requirements that must be met by the institutions of government. But they leave us morally free to lead our lives as we wish within those boundaries, without having to take the promotion of the general good into account in all our choices.

Standards of this kind (often referred to as deontological standards by contrast with the consequentialist variety) seem to require a foundation different from the impartial concern for the interests of all, which is the basis of utilitarianism. But before discussing what that foundation might be, it is necessary to consider the utilitarian response.

ACT-UTILITARIANISM AND RULE-UTILITARIANISM

Hume holds that all of morality can be accounted for by its tendency to promote utility, but that this works in two different ways. In some cases the relation of a morally good or bad act to utility is direct, as in the case of kindness or cruelty. These he describes as examples of the natural virtues and vices—types of conduct that increase or decrease utility act by act, through their direct causal effects.

But there is another set of moral requirements, which he calls the artificial virtues, where the effects on utility are not necessarily produced by each morally good act taken alone. Instead, the good effects are produced only by a general rule, convention, or practice, and it is one of the conditions of the utility of rules of this kind that they must be followed even in individual cases where the particular action they require is harmful to utility.

The utilitarian explanation of strict rights, obligations, and duties depends on this type of analysis, which is called rule-utilitarianism—by contrast with act-utilitarianism, which assesses the rightness of actions by their effects on utility taken one by one. For example, the institution of stable property rights, without which a functioning economy would be impossible, requires that property owned by one person should not be subject to appropriation by another person whenever the latter can get more utility from it than the former. A landlord has to be able to charge his or her tenants rent, even though they may need the money more than he or she does, or else no one would invest in rental property. The great utility of the general rules of property depends on their being consistently followed even in cases where violating them would advance utility, since that is the only way to ensure security and stability.

Likewise, the institution of promises has great utility because it makes it possible for people to rely on each other's future conduct and to create such reliance. But it can do so only because it is not permissible to break a promise whenever this would produce more utility than keeping it.

To some extent the utilitarian advantage of such rules can be obtained by embodying them in laws of property and contract that are enforced by the courts. But the rules also seem to have moral weight apart from such enforcement: Violation of property rights and breach of promise seem wrong in themselves, and the rule-utilitarian explanation is that they are wrong because they violate valuable institutions or conventions.

Similar explanations can be offered of why it is morally permissible for individuals to live their lives without making every decision on the basis of how they can contribute the most to maximizing utility for humanity as a whole. The reason is that so much of human happiness depends on the pursuit of personal aims and fulfilling personal relationships, and a strict requirement that every act must strive to maximize general utility would make personal projects, friendships, and commitments impossible. In other words, a world governed by strict act-utilitarianism would be a world with much lower overall utility than a world in which not every action aimed to maximize impartial utility.

These are only some examples. The rule-utilitarian strategy can be applied to a wide variety of apparent exceptions to utilitarianism, including rights of bodily integrity, the requirement that punishment be deserved, the right to freedom of speech, the special obligation of parents toward their children, and the values of political, social, and economic equality.

Still, it is not clear just how much of the apparently counterutilitarian morality of rights, obligations, and permissions can be accommodated by rule-utilitarianism in this way. For example, the Australian philosopher Peter Singer (1972, 1979), a prominent utilitarian, argues that in the very unequal world in which we live, there is no justification for the moral latitude most well-off people in rich countries assume they have to favor themselves and their friends and families, when their resources could bring so much more benefit to the destitute in impoverished countries. In Singer's view utilitarianism should be seen as a radical position that cannot be used to underpin conventional morality, but requires that it be overturned.

There is also a theoretical problem about the relation between rule-utilitarianism and moral motivation. The problem is that, if a utilitarian is attached to property rights and the obligation of promises because of the contribution of those institutions to general utility, that does not explain what his or her reason is for abiding by the rule in an individual case that clearly does not serve utility. The utilitarian may say that there is a strong moral reason to want the institution of promises to exist. But if breaking a promise in a particular case will not cause the institution to disappear, or even weaken it noticeably, and if he or she can thereby produce more benefit than harm,

why should the utilitarian's moral aim of maximizing utility not lead him or her to conclude that breaking the promise is the right thing to do in that case?

Some utilitarians are prepared to accept this conclusion. This is the act-utilitarian position, according to which laws, conventions, and practices may change the circumstances in ways that affect what acts will best promote utility, but can never make it right to do what one knows will not produce the most benefit.

Others believe that, since utility is best served if individuals have internalized a strict attachment to certain rules so that they are unwilling to break them even to promote utility, this creates an independent reason for adherence in such cases. In a sense, the utility of the rule provides a justification for the moral fiction that there is a reason to act contrary to utility in the particular case.

KANTIAN CONTRACTUALISM

The main rival to a consequentialist foundation for rights and special obligations is a theory that emphasizes the separate importance of each individual person instead of the value of maximizing the sum of benefits to the aggregate of all persons. According to this alternative the aim of morality is to find principles of conduct under which people are given equal consideration, not merely as elements in an aggregate, but as individuals. This would mean that the apparently counterutilitarian character of individual rights, for example, is real and cannot be explained away by rule-utilitarianism.

The most important representative of this type of theory is the eighteenth-century German philosopher Immanuel Kant (1785, 1788), who holds that moral principles can be identified directly by reference to a single standard, which he calls the categorical imperative. (He calls it *categorical* to indicate that its application to an individual is not conditional on what that person happens to want; the reasons provided by morality do not depend hypothetically on interests or desires, but apply categorically and unconditionally to all persons simply in virtue of their rationality.)

The categorical imperative says, roughly, that we should act only on principles that we would want everyone to act on. It is often referred to as the standard of universalizability, since it means that each of us should govern our conduct by principles that we would be willing to see followed universally. But if this test is to identify a single set of moral principles that apply to everyone, there must be a way to decide what principles we would want everyone to follow that will not give different answers for different people depending on their interests and situation. That implies that in answering the question we must try to take into account the point of view of every person simultaneously, putting ourselves in the place of each of them, and rejecting those principles that could not be accepted by everyone.

The tradition deriving from the categorical imperative is sometimes called contractualism because it identifies moral principles through an imaginary agreement: They are the principles whose adoption by everyone would not be unacceptable to anyone. The results of such a test may be much less determinate than the utilitarian standard, but it does seem to imply some major differences from utilitarianism. First, the insistence on separate acceptability to each individual will rule out justifications that depend on aggregation of small benefits across many lives to outweigh a large cost to a single individual. Second, in deciding what principles are and are not universally acceptable, the determining factor will have to be some system of priorities among the things that matter in human life, and the effects that different principles would have on each person, as measured by these values.

MODERN CONTRACTUALISM

One result will be that in the application of moral standards to social policy, there will be a direct reason to concentrate on the relief of poverty and improvement in the condition of the worst off, not merely as a means of improving the total or average welfare, as in utilitarianism. This is a feature of the American philosopher John Rawls's (1971) theory of justice.

Another result is that the justification for individual rights will be different from that offered by rule-utilitarianism. The right not to be killed, injured, or deprived of liberty even if it would promote the general welfare will depend not on the overall balance of costs against benefits for all people affected by the existence or nonexistence of such a right, but on the importance for each separate individual of the security that such a right provides, by comparison with the advantages for each individual that its absence might make possible.

The right to pursue one's personal aims, interests, and attachments rather than the general welfare in most of what one does will depend not on the effect of such a right on the general welfare, but on the importance for each person of this kind of freedom by comparison with the value for each person of the possible benefits of its general restriction.

The emphasis is on providing certain protections and basic benefits to everyone equally rather than maximizing the overall sum of benefits. This is a fundamental difference in the approach to the foundation of morality, a difference in the way in which the interests of all persons are combined from a moral point of view.

Modern successors to Kant attempt to make the standard more precise in different ways. Rawls claims that what is wrong with utilitarianism is that it does not take seriously the distinction between persons. Writing not about morality in general but about social justice, he embodies the contractualist ideal in an imaginary choice called the Original Position, in which people are supposed to choose the principles of justice for their society without knowing who they are; this forces them to choose principles that would be acceptable whoever they turned out to be. Though influenced by Rawls, T. M. Scanlon (1998), another philosopher in the contractualist tradition, proposes a different test. He maintains that to identify standards of right and wrong we must search for principles that no one seeking to arrive at common standards of interpersonal justification could reasonably reject, knowing both his or her own situation and that of others.

Unlike a consequentialist theory, the contractualist method cannot proceed simply by calculating the total expected costs and benefits of different rules of conduct or forms of political and social organization. Rather, it must evaluate the priorities among different kinds of costs and benefits, for each individual, of living under alternative rules or systems. Which principles and practices are morally acceptable will depend on these priorities, applied equally to everyone.

For example, both utilitarianism and contractualism condemn slavery, but they do so for different reasons. Utilitarianism says slavery is wrong because the total misery of slaves vastly outweighs the total benefit to slave owners. Contractualism says slavery is wrong because any reasonable person thinking about his or her own or any other life must regard the avoidance of the possibility of being a slave as having strict priority over the possibility of enjoying the advantages of being a slave owner.

DEONTOLOGY: DOING AND ALLOWING

Not everyone who believes in rights and special obligations thinks they have to be justified by either contractualism or rule-utilitarianism. The general term for these apparently nonconsequentialist parts of morality is deontology, and there is an alternative ethical tradition, called intuitionism (represented, for example, by the English philosopher W. David Ross [1930]), according to which the deontological elements of morality are fundamental. They do not derive from anything else, but they reveal themselves to reflection about what would and would not be the right thing to do in different cases.

On this view it is evident that we may not kill an innocent person to save five others (e.g., by harvesting the first person's organs for transplantation), and there is no more fundamental explanation of why we may not: It would be murder, that is all. The details of these moral requirements are sometimes complicated, but they can be discovered by exercising moral intuition in respect to real and imaginary cases that bring out the relevant distinctions.

One of the most important of these distinctions, mentioned earlier, contrasts the things we do to other people, for which we are positively responsible, and the things that happen to other people that we might have been able to prevent, for which we are only negatively responsible. If we kill an innocent person to transplant his or her organs to five others, for example, we would be positively responsible for the death of that person. But if we do not kill that person and the other five die of organ failure, we are not positively responsible for their deaths and have not violated their right to life. This means that the prohibition against murder must include some specification of the way in which one person's conduct has to be related to another person's death for it to count as wrong.

Different accounts have been offered of this relation. It might seem that what matters is whether your action causes the death or whether it is caused by something or someone else. But this turns out to be wrong in two ways. First, you may cause a death as an unavoidable side effect of something else you do, but if you were acting to save many more lives, you are not to blame. For instance, if you are the pilot of a plane that is about to crash, and you steer it from a densely populated area to a sparsely populated area, you are causally responsible for the deaths of a smaller number of people but you are not to blame, because it was a side effect of your aiming the plane away from the larger number.

Second, you may be to blame for a death that you didn't cause but could have prevented, if you deliberately failed to act to ensure that the death would occur. For example, if you let an otherwise healthy patient with asthma choke to death so that you can harvest his or her organs to save five others, you have intentionally allowed the patient's death—aimed at it even without causing it—in a way that makes the action wrong.

So the element of intention—intentionally causing or permitting someone's death either as an end in itself or as a means to something else—is an important part of wrongful killing. And rights in general have to be understood as rights against the intentional imposition of harms of various kinds.

In a morality of this kind, we are not generally responsible for preventing what is bad and promoting what is good. Morality is defined instead by a set of constraints against the intentional imposition of harm or violation of rights, plus some well-defined and limited positive obligations—like keeping our promises and taking care of our families.

Instead of deriving the content of morality from a point of view that tries to take everyone's interests into account—either a consequentialist or a contractarian point of view—intuitionism understands morality as setting a kind of boundary around each person, that protects us from intentional violation and interference by others. Positive obligations are also understood individually, as arising from the specific commitment undertaken by a promise or a contract, explicit or implied, with another person.

AGENT-NEUTRALITY AND AGENT-RELATIVITY

The difference between deontological and consequentialist moral theories can also be described in terms of a formal distinction between two kinds of principles or reasons: agent-relative and agent-neutral.

An agent-relative principle specifies what each individual should do in a way that involves an ineliminable reference to that agent himself or herself, or his or her situation—even when the principle is stated in its most general form. For example, the principles "Everyone may give priority to their own interests over those of a stranger," "Everyone should do what is best for their family," "Everyone should keep their promises," and "Everyone should refrain from killing innocent people" are all agent-relative.

The following principles, however, are all agent-neutral: "Everyone should promote the general welfare," "Everyone should promote the stability and devotion of families," "Everyone should try to minimize the breaking of promises," and "Everyone should aim to minimize the killing of innocent people." Agent-neutral principles depend on the objective value of certain kinds of happenings or states of affairs, without regard to their relation to the agent. All that matters is whether the agent is in a position to affect the occurrence or nonoccurrence of the desirable or undesirable outcome. If the value attaches to a type of action, such as murder, an agent-neutral principle would not distinguish between a murder that the agent commits and one that someone else commits and that the agent could prevent. Accordingly, the principle that everyone should aim to minimize the occurrence of murders could authorize committing one murder to prevent several others.

For this reason, deontological principles naturally take an agent-relative form. They tell each individual what he or she may, must, and must not do, without giving all individuals a common outcome or state of affairs that they must try to promote. Deontological principles are universal, but the aims they assign to each individual always depend on his or her situation and are related to him or her. This logical feature unites the three aspects of deontology: deontological prohibitions—"Don't (you) commit murder"; deontological requirements—"Keep your promises"; and deontological permissions—"You can enjoy your life instead of devoting it to the service of humanity."

The exercise of moral intuition on different cases reveals a surprisingly detailed system of deontological principles on which many people can agree and that form a large part of conventional morality. But the view that there is no systematic foundation underlying these diverse principles, that their truth cannot be explained by something more basic, leaves many moral philosophers dissatisfied.

What they want is a general foundation for deontology to rival the clarity of consequentialism. Since it seems obvious that there is always a reason to prefer better results, deontologists need to explain in a clear fashion why morality often prohibits actions that would have the best overall results and permits other actions that would not have the best overall results. If promoting the best consequences is not, as utilitarianism maintains, the governing standard of morality, then it would be good to know what is.

VIRTUE

Contractualism is the most prominent foundational alternative to consequentialism, and it works by offering an alternative interpretation of what it is to treat all persons with impartial respect. But there is another way of criticizing consequentialism, and that is to attack its foundation directly, by denying the moral authority of the impartial point of view.

The criticism goes like this: Ethics is concerned with how people should live and what they should do, and the point of view from which we should seek an answer to that question is the point of view of the individual, not an impersonal point of view that takes into account all individuals at once. Even if this yields moral requirements on how one should treat other people, they must arise from considerations about how one has reason to live one's life and what kind of person one wants to be.

One version of this approach takes as basic the question: What is the difference between a good and a bad person? Once we know the difference between a virtuous and a vicious character, we can identify the morally right thing to do as what a virtuous person would do in the circumstances. This way of understanding the subject is found in Aristotle's *Nicomachean Ethics*.

The reason we all have to care about virtue, on this view, is not an impartial concern for others, but that being a good person is an aspect of being a good human specimen—analogous to physical health and being in good physical condition. To be virtuous is to function well with respect to feelings, desires, motives, and actions, including interactions with other people. Moral virtue, like good physical functioning, is part of the good for each individual, and it has as elements the distinct virtues such as courage, temperance, prudence, generosity, honesty, and justice. Each of these is a set of motivational dispositions and dispositions to choose that lead to virtuous conduct.

Some of the virtues, like courage and temperance, are good partly because they enable the individual to pursue his or her own aims effectively. But a virtue like justice is good for the individual because people are essentially social beings and must be able to live in harmony with others. This conception of ethics leaves the content of interpersonal morality rather vague. Instead of principles of conduct, it offers a rough indication of the types of motivational and behavioral dispositions, recognizable by example in the character of virtuous individuals, to which everyone has reason to aspire, simply in order to be a good person. But at least this account, even if it does not start from impartiality, offers a kind of harmony between the interests of the virtuous individual and the interests of the community to which he or she belongs.

RESISTANCE TO IMPERSONAL MORALITY

A more skeptical challenge to the impartial standpoint comes from the English philosopher Bernard Williams (1981, 1985). He argues that impersonal moral theories, whether consequentialist or contractualist, are incompatible with the integrity of an individual life, which is found in the unconditional commitment to particular projects and particular persons. Such commitments would be impossible if impersonal values were permitted to take precedence over them.

This is most forceful as a response to utilitarianism. Even if, from an impersonal standpoint, everyone's life is just as important as everyone else's, that is simply not true from your individual standpoint, and the impersonal standpoint has no authority on its own to overrule the standpoint of the individual. Ethics is supposed to govern individual conduct, so it must find its basis in the motivation of individuals. This may include some impartial values, but it also includes much else. For most people, life gets its substance and meaning from aims and attachments that are inseparable from the personal point of view. These cannot simply be abandoned when it turns out that there is something impersonally more valuable that one could do with one's life.

Utilitarians can reply in either of two ways. They may say that in rejecting the demands of impersonal value, Williams is simply rejecting morality, and that the whole point of morality is to replace the natural selfishness of individuals with an impartial perspective. Nobody said it would be easy. Alternatively, they may emphasize the ways in which utilitarianism takes into account the point of view of the individual, since it is the source of the happiness whose maximization over all persons utilitarianism takes as the aim of morality.

However, even after we take this second point into account, it is clear that utilitarianism, including rule-utilitarianism, will under some circumstances require the radical subordination of individual aims to the general welfare. There is an important difference of opinion here over what morality can reasonably demand of us.

The conflict between Williams's objection and contractualism is less stark, but here, too, he claims that it is incompatible with the nature of basic personal commitments to subordinate them to the test of what could be universalized, or what could be reasonably agreed to by everyone as a principle of conduct. Even to say, for example, that it is permissible to devote yourself to your children because you find it acceptable that everyone should favor their own children is inconsistent with the immediate and unconditional nature of your attachment to your own children. It is, in Williams's phrase, "one thought too many." Williams's resistance to the ultimate authority of the objective, impersonal standpoint is partly inspired by the more radical resistance to impartiality of Friedrich Nietzsche (1897), the great nineteenth-century German critic of Christianity and moral universalism. Contractualists like Scanlon reply that it does not denigrate the independent force of personal attachments and projects to require that they be embedded in a moral framework that sets limits to their pursuit, since the desire to live on mutually acceptable terms with others is such an important human value that it must be allowed to shape other, more personal values.

The question of the relative weight and interaction between personal motives and the claims of impartiality in determining the content of morality is a fundamental one, and it generates continuing controversy. Uncompromising utilitarians like Singer maintain that the commonsense morality that most people accept and that strictly limits their responsibility to sacrifice their own interests and aims for those in greater need is much too undemanding. If we really take seriously the undeniable fact that other people's suffering is just as bad as our own, we will have to change our lives.

In contrast, defenders of more conventional morality hold that while it is admirable to be self-sacrificing, it is also supererogatory—that is, it is morally praiseworthy but goes beyond what is morally required. They maintain that utilitarianism, by holding people morally accountable for anything that happens for which they are negatively responsible, leaves them with an unacceptably diminished control over their lives.

These disputes pose the question of whether or to what extent the content of morality should depend on a prior assessment of the human motives available to induce people to live in accordance with its requirements. There is a division of opinion between those who think morality has to rely on preexisting motives and those who think it can create new motives, by revealing specifically moral reasons we all have to act in certain ways.

Among the first group we find Hobbes, who derives morality from redirected self-interest, and Hume who derives it from a natural moral sentiment arising from sympathy for the happiness and unhappiness of others. Among the second group is Kant, who believes that the recognition that an intention cannot be universalized will itself motivate us to refrain from acting on it. He holds that the recognition of moral principles, without an antecedent desire, is enough to create a motive.

Even if morality introduces new motives, it may be important to take into account human nature, including natural self-interest and natural personal attachments, in constructing a workable moral code. The question then becomes: How can humans who are not naturally impartial live together in a way that acknowledges that objectively none is of more intrinsic value than another?

RELATIVISM

So far this entry has discussed ethical theories that offer different accounts of morality conceived of as a single system—that is, as a set of general standards that will allow us to determine what is right or wrong for any person to do, in any society. That does not mean that the same specific actions will be morally required of everyone, since in different circumstances, different forms of conduct may satisfy or violate the same universal moral standards. For example, with overpopulation and environmental degradation, activities like deforestation and the unrestrained burning of fossil fuels, which on a small scale were once harmless, can become dangerous to future generations, and therefore wrong.

But is it also possible that the basic moral standards themselves should vary over time, or from culture to culture? The view that morality, even at the most fundamental level, is not universal but arises from local cultures or conventions that may vary is called ethical relativism. Relativism is not the view that there is a single overarching and universal moral principle, namely: "Follow the moral conventions of your culture"; nor is it the view that some other universal principle, such as utilitarianism, implies that it is always best to follow the conventions of the culture in which you find yourself. Relativism is the position that the true and ultimate source of moral standards is always a set of rules, practices, and attitudes shared by a historically situated community. While not everyone in the community will obey the rules, and some may reject them, there is often enough of a consensus about what the rules are to make it possible to identify them.

Morality, on this interpretation, is closer to etiquette or law than it is on the universalist interpretation. Naturally, there will be some overlap among moral systems—all of them can be expected to condemn murder and theft in some form, for example. But slavery, the subordination of women to their male relatives, polygamy, or homosexuality may be morally wrong in some societies and morally unquestionable in other societies, depending on the prevailing norms.

On this view it is probably a mistake to say that slavery in ancient Rome was wrong, that bullfighting in Spain is wrong, or that the subordination of women in Saudi Arabia is wrong. There is no universal, timeless standpoint from which to make these judgments. They would have to be defended from a standpoint internal to the cultures that they are about, and if that cannot be done, they should be abandoned.

That does not mean that it is impossible to criticize morally what a society does, for its conduct may sometimes violate its own moral principles. It may also sometimes be the case that there is no prevailing moral code in a particular culture, especially during periods of social transition or upheaval.

These qualifications mean that it will not always be easy for a defender of relativism to identify the standards that apply in a particular society. But relativism at least clearly rules out the attempt to appeal to universal standards. Even an internal moral critic of a society—someone who says, against the general consensus, that slavery is morally wrong—would be mistaken if he or she were making a universal claim. The critic has to be understood as trying to change the standards or as finding an inconsistency between one part of the prevailing standards and another part.

Relativism has the consequence that we must dismiss as confused certain judgments that we are strongly inclined to make, which implicitly or explicitly appeal to universally valid or objective standards in morality. They include judgments about societies other than our own, whose standards we think are mistaken, or judgments about our own society, whose present standards we think may be mistaken and may be rightly rejected by later generations.

Relativism cannot account for the apparent fact that when an individual rejects the moral standards that prevail in a culture, either from within or from outside, he or she may not be simply applying the standards of an alternative culture, but may be appealing to deeper moral reasons, such as unfairness to some members of the society or failure to give certain interests their true weight. Such arguments point to deeper and more general standards by which local conventions can be assessed.

This is connected with the question of the motivation for being moral. If morality is based on custom, the motivation for conforming to it is in a sense shallow. To be moral is to have internalized the patterns of conduct that prevail in one's surroundings. If, however, morality is not relative but universal, this means that the motives that attach us to moral norms must be deeper, and theories of the foundations of morality must try to identify them.

MORALITY AND RELIGION

There is a way of defending the universality and objectivity of moral truth different from those that have been discussed so far. That is to claim that moral standards are laid down by divine command.

If this means that nothing would be right or wrong unless God declared it to be so—that "if God does not exist, everything is permitted"—then it is not a plausible view. Even if God does command that we not kill, lie, steal, and so on, it seems more plausible to hold that he forbids those things because they are wrong, not that they are wrong because he forbids them. (A polytheistic version of this point is made in Plato's dialogue *Euthyphro*.)

Though we can understand how divine command might establish specific requirements like dietary restrictions or forms of worship—where we are obliged to follow them simply out of obedience—the ordinary standards of morality seem different: They seem to depend on the intrinsic features and effects of certain kinds of conduct rather than on something external to them. We can understand what is wrong with murder without reference to God.

On the other hand, it may be possible to preserve a version of the divine command theory by referring to the characteristics of God, as all-knowing, all-good, and loving the world and his creatures. The rules that a divine being enjoins people to obey might in that case be said to be correct in virtue of the features of God's nature that lead him to choose those rules. But it also means that he chooses them for characteristics that themselves make them correct and that he could not have commanded a different morality.

Religion is sometimes thought to play another role, as the guarantor of an incentive to be moral through divine punishment and reward in an afterlife. The afterlife also serves a direct moral purpose in allowing us to hope that the world is not fundamentally unjust and that the virtuous will be rewarded, however much they may have suffered on this earth.

However, most modern moral philosophy has not depended on religion, but has tried to interpret ethics in secular terms. Those who believe that God commands our adherence to moral standards usually hold that we use our independent understanding of those standards in forming our idea of God's will. An exception is John

Locke (1690), for whom the assumption that God gave the earth to human beings in common plays an important role in moral and political theory.

ETHICS, POLITICS, AND LAW

One of the main applications of moral theory is to evaluate political and social institutions—institutions like representative democracy or the market economy—as well as the more specific actions of government. But there are two different ways of thinking about politics from a moral point of view.

The first way is to start by identifying moral standards that apply to everything, and then to figure out what they imply for the special and complex case of political institutions and political life. This is the method favored both by utilitarianism and by the radical form of individual rights theory called libertarianism. Utilitarianism holds that the right way to evaluate anything, from an individual action to a form of government, is by reference to the value of its overall consequences for the total welfare of all persons, impartially considered. Libertarianism, on the other hand, determines the rightness or wrongness of individual actions and social institutions alike solely by reference to whether they violate or protect the natural rights of individuals not to be harmed, to exercise their freedom, and to acquire and transfer property. Because these theories hold that a single moral standard governs everything from individual conduct to the design of large social institutions, they are sometimes known as monist theories.

By contrast, other theories (sometimes called dualist—the terms are due to Liam Murphy [1999]) hold that ethics is more complicated than this and that different standards are appropriate for the regulation of different kinds of thing. According to this second approach it is a mistake to assume that the moral evaluation of institutions should derive from the same norms that govern individual conduct.

An important example of the dualist approach is Rawls's (1971) theory of justice. Rawls maintains that while private individuals should be free to pursue their own aims in life and favor their own and their families' economic interests, the basic institutions of a society must be much more impartial toward the interests of all its members. The social structure should be designed with the aim of providing equality of opportunity for all, and with the aim of reducing social and economic inequality by raising the condition of the worst-off class as much as possible. These strongly egalitarian values, according to Rawls, apply not to the personal interactions of individuals, but to the design of the common institutions, imposed and sustained by state power, that provide the unchosen public framework for their private lives.

Whether one is a monist or a dualist, politics and law are important subjects for ethical theory. Politics poses in the starkest way questions about how to combine the conflicting interests of many different people who are affected by an institution, law, or policy. It poses questions about the relations between different values—the value of life, of liberty, of prosperity, and of freedom from coercion and violation of different kinds. It poses crucial questions about the possibility of outweighing harms to some by aggregate benefits to others.

The fundamental division between consequentialist and contractualist approaches shows up here. Consequentialists will not take the protection of individual rights as basic, but will regard it as an instrumental means for the promotion of the general welfare. Contractualists, by contrast, will find reasons to limit the power of the state over the individual in a separate and untradeable concern for each individual's autonomy and inviolability, regarded not merely as an element in the general welfare whose total is to be maximized.

Followers of Hobbes will hold that the only legitimate ground for state action is the provision of goods that are in the collective self-interest of all the citizenry, such as police protection, defense, economic stability, and public health. Utilitarians, on the contrary, will also favor policies that increase the total welfare, even if it means redistributing resources from the rich to the poor. Contractarians will give priority to the protection of individual rights, securing equal opportunity, and raising the social minimum. Libertarians will favor the minimum of government needed to keep the peace, protect individual rights, and secure private property. Therefore, many familiar political disagreements have a moral dimension and require that we ask how much and what kind of consideration we owe to the interests of our fellow citizens through our common institutions.

The distinction between monist and dualist theories comes up again when we ask whether the same principles that govern the moral acceptability of political institutions inside existing states should also be applied to our relations to people in other societies, indeed to the world as a whole. If our most fundamental moral duties to everyone are the same, then the division of the world into separate societies with special responsibility for their members is a historically understandable contingency, but it may or may not be morally acceptable. On the other hand, moral standards for the world as a whole may be different from those appropriate within a particular society. The question of the moral evaluation of the overall world order is a vital and wide open question.

BOUNDARIES OF THE MORAL COMMUNITY

This entry has been discussing moral standards as if they concerned our relations to other human beings, present and future. But there are other candidates for moral consideration: most notably, other sentient creatures who are not members of our species and human organisms not yet born—embryos and fetuses. We can leave aside the value of plants and other parts of nature because it seems separate from morality, just as aesthetic value seems to be in a different category. Morality is especially concerned with how we treat one another, but it probably goes beyond this to include our treatment of beings or creatures that are sufficiently like us in relevant respects.

The first question is whether sentience itself—the capacity to have conscious experience and to feel pleasure and pain—is sufficient to bring a creature under the protection of morality. On the utilitarian theory the answer is a clear yes. Pleasure is good and pain is bad, wherever they are found, so it is right to promote the first and avoid the second in all sentient creatures.

It may be difficult to compare the quantity, quality, and value of pleasures and pains across different species, so it is not always easy to calculate what actions or policies would maximize overall utility. There may also be, in some versions of utilitarianism, forms of human pleasure or happiness that are not available to other animals, and whose value counts heavily in calculating the total to be maximized. That is maintained by John Stuart Mill in the theory of higher and lower pleasures. But many utilitarians maintain that the widely prevalent treatment of animals in factory farming and slaughter for food, as well as in much scientific experimentation, is morally unacceptable.

It is doubtful that nonhuman creatures could be excluded from moral consideration entirely, except by an ethical theory based entirely on self-interest. Since other creatures do not threaten us and cannot enter into cooperative engagements with us, we have no reasons of self-interest to adopt ways of living at peace with them.

If we accept an other-regarding consequentialist basis for ethics, animals will certainly be included under its protection, but there may be different requirements on our treatment of animals from those on our treatment of people. Avoidance of suffering is likely to be the main thing, and limits on killing or on infringement of liberty will probably depend on whether they lessen suffering.

It is less clear how contractarian theories can handle the moral status of creatures who cannot be imagined as participants even in a hypothetical agreement on standards of conduct. But perhaps this could be done through some system of imaginary representation of their interests (Scanlon [1998] discusses this issue).

The moral status of unborn humans is a different question. If we separate it from religious doctrine about when the soul enters the body, it becomes a question about whether the potential to develop into a fully conscious human being confers on an embryo or fetus some part of the moral protection due to such a being after it is born. Answers range from the position that the embryo has all the moral rights of an infant, specifically the right not to be killed, from the time of conception, when its genetic constitution is determined, to the position that it has no moral claims before the child is born alive and may therefore be disposed of at the discretion of the pregnant woman. In between are views that as the fetus develops toward viability it becomes gradually more and more difficult to justify interrupting the pregnancy deliberately—that is, the reasons for doing so have to be progressively stronger.

The difficulty of these boundary questions reveals uncertainty about the true foundations of ethics, but that is not surprising. Human morality is a constantly developing system of norms, and its philosophical investigation by ethical theory is an indispensable part of the process.

See also Applied Ethics; Consequentialism; Decision Theory; Deontological Ethics; Divine Command Theories of Ethics; Ethics, History of; Game Theory; Kantian Ethics; Metaethics; Teleological Ethics; Utilitarianism; Value and Valuation; Virtue Ethics.

Bibliography

Adams, Robert Merrihew. "A Modified Divine Command Theory of Ethical Wrongness." In *The Virtue of Faith and Other Essays in Philosophical Theology*, 97–122. New York: Oxford University Press, 1987.

Anscombe, G. E. M. *Collected Philosophical Papers*. Vol. 3, *Ethics, Religion, and Politics*. Minneapolis: University of Minnesota Press, 1981.

Aristotle. *Nicomachean Ethics*.

Bentham, Jeremy. *An Introduction to the Principles of Morals and Legislation*. London: Printed for T. Payne, 1789.

Brandt, Richard B. *A Theory of the Good and the Right*. New York: Oxford University Press, 1979.

Donagan, Alan. *The Theory of Morality*. Chicago: University of Chicago Press, 1977.

Foot, Philippa. *Virtues and Vices, and Other Essays in Moral Philosophy*. Oxford, U.K.: Blackwell, 1978.

Fried, Charles. *Right and Wrong*. Cambridge, MA: Harvard University Press, 1978.

Gauthier, David. *Morals by Agreement*. New York: Oxford University Press, 1986.

Gibbard, Allan. *Wise Choices, Apt Feelings: A Theory of Normative Judgment*. Cambridge, MA: Harvard University Press, 1990.

Hare, R. M. *Freedom and Reason*. Oxford, U.K.: Clarendon Press, 1963.

Hare, R. M. *Moral Thinking: Its Levels, Method, and Point*. New York: Oxford University Press, 1981.

Harman, Gilbert. *The Nature of Morality: An Introduction to Ethics*. New York: Oxford University Press, 1977.

Hobbes, Thomas. *Leviathan, or, The Matter, Forme, and Power of a Common-Wealth Ecclesiasticall and Civill*. London: Printed for Andrew Ckooke, 1651.

Hume, David. *An Enquiry concerning the Principles of Morals*. London: Printed for A. Millar, 1751.

Hume, David. *A Treatise of Human Nature*. 1739.

Kagan, Shelly. *The Limits of Morality*. New York: Oxford University Press, 1989.

Kagan, Shelly. *Normative Ethics*. Boulder, CO: Westview Press, 1998.

Kamm, Frances M. *Morality, Mortality*. 2 vols. New York: Oxford University Press, 1993–1996.

Kant, Immanuel. *Critique of Practical Reason*. 1788.

Kant, Immanuel. *Groundwork of the Metaphysics of Morals*. 1785.

Korsgaard, Christine M., with G. A. Cohen. *The Sources of Normativity*, edited by Onora O'Neill. Cambridge, U.K.: Cambridge University Press, 1996.

Locke, John. *Second Treatise of Government*. 1690.

Mackie, John L. *Ethics: Inventing Right and Wrong*. New York: Penguin, 1977.

Mill, John Stuart. *Utilitarianism*. London: Parker, Son, and Bourn, 1863.

Moore, George Edward. *Principia Ethica*. Cambridge, U.K.: Cambridge University Press, 1903.

Murphy, Liam. "Institutions and the Demands of Justice." *Philosophy and Public Affairs* 27 (4) (1999): 251–291.

Nagel, Thomas. *The Possibility of Altruism*. New York: Oxford University Press, 1970.

Nagel, Thomas. *The View from Nowhere*. New York: Oxford University Press, 1986.

Nietzsche, Friedrich. *The Genealogy of Morals*. New York: Macmillan, 1897.

Nozick, Robert. *Anarchy, State, and Utopia*. New York: Basic Books, 1974.

Parfit, Derek. *Reasons and Persons*. Oxford, U.K.: Clarendon Press, 1984.

Plato. *Euthyphro*.

Plato. *Gorgias*.

Quinn, Warren. *Morality and Action*. New York: Cambridge University Press, 1993.

Railton, Peter. *Facts, Values, and Norms: Essays toward a Morality of Consequence.* New York: Cambridge University Press, 2003.

Rawls, John. *A Theory of Justice.* Cambridge, MA: Belknap Press of Harvard University Press, 1971.

Rawls, John. "Two Concepts of Rules." *Philosophical Review* 64 (1) (1955): 3–32.

Ross, W. David. *The Right and the Good.* Oxford, U.K.: Clarendon Press, 1930.

Scanlon, T. M. *What We Owe to Each Other.* Cambridge, MA: Belknap Press of Harvard University Press, 1998.

Scheffler, Samuel. *Human Morality.* New York: Oxford University Press, 1992.

Scheffler, Samuel. *The Rejection of Consequentialism: A Philosophical Investigation of the Considerations Underlying Rival Moral Conceptions.* New York: Oxford University Press, 1982.

Sidgwick, Henry. *The Methods of Ethics.* 7th ed. London: Macmillan, 1907.

Singer, Peter. "Famine, Affluence, and Morality." *Philosophy and Public Affairs* 1 (1) (1972): 229–243.

Singer, Peter. *Practical Ethics.* New York: Cambridge University Press, 1979.

Smart, J. J. C., and Bernard Williams. *Utilitarianism: For and Against.* Cambridge, U.K.: Cambridge University Press, 1973.

Thomson, Judith Jarvis. *The Realm of Rights.* Cambridge, MA: Harvard University Press, 1990.

Thomson, Judith Jarvis. *Rights, Restitution, and Risk: Essays, in Moral Theory*, edited by William Parent. Cambridge, MA: Harvard University Press, 1986.

Williams, Bernard. *Ethics and the Limits of Philosophy.* Cambridge, MA: Harvard University Press, 1985.

Williams, Bernard. *Moral Luck: Philosophical Papers, 1973–1980.* New York: Cambridge University Press, 1981.

Wolf, Susan. "Moral Saints." *Journal of Philosophy* 79 (8) (1982): 419–439.

Thomas Nagel (2005)

ETHICS, DEONTOLOGICAL

See *Deontological Ethics*

ETHICS, HISTORY OF

The term *ethics* is used in three different but related ways, signifying (1) a general pattern or "way of life," (2) a set of rules of conduct or "moral code," and (3) inquiry *about* ways of life and rules of conduct. In the first sense we speak of Buddhist or Christian ethics; in the second, we speak of professional ethics and of unethical behavior. In the third sense, ethics is a branch of philosophy that is frequently given the special name of metaethics. The present discussion will be limited to the history of philosophical

or "meta" ethics, for two reasons. First, because it is impossible to cover, with any degree of thoroughness, the history of ethics in either of the first two senses. Practices and the codification of practices are the threads out of which all of human culture is woven, so that the history of ethics in either of these senses would be far too vast a subject for a brief essay. Second, although ethical philosophy is often understood in a broad way as including all significant thought about human conduct, it can well be confined within manageable limits by separating purely philosophical thought from the practical advice, moral preaching, and social engineering that it illuminates and from which it receives sustenance. This distinction, while somewhat artificial, makes sense of the common opinion that philosophy in general, and ethical philosophy in particular, was invented by the Greeks.

The central questions of philosophical ethics are: What do we or should we mean by "good" and "bad"? what are the right standards for judging things to be good or bad? how do judgments of good and bad (value judgments) differ from and depend upon judgments of value-neutral fact? But when these questions are answered, it is important to find out the differences between specific types of value judgments that are characterized by such adjectives as *useful, right, moral,* and *just.* We may therefore divide our subject matter into the search for the meaning and standards of good in general, and of well-being, right conduct, moral character, and justice in particular. Needless to say, these are not watertight compartments. Many philosophers reject sharp distinctions between them. But provisional separation of these topics, subject to reunification in accordance with particular philosophical views, will prove helpful in disentangling the various issues on which philosophers have taken opposing stands, so that the history of ethics can be seen as irregular progress toward complete clarification of each type of ethical judgment.

GREEK ETHICS

Ethical philosophy began in the fifth century BCE, with the appearance of Socrates, a secular prophet whose self-appointed mission was to awaken his fellow men to the need for rational criticism of their beliefs and practices.

Greek society of the fifth century was in a state of rapid change from agrarian monarchy to commercial and industrial democracy. The religious and social traditions that had been handed down from one generation to the next through the natural processes of social imitation and household training were brought into question by the accession to power of a commercial class, whose members were untrained in and scornful of the ancestral way of life. New rules of conduct were required by a market economy in which money counted more than noble birth and in which men had to be considered equals as buyers and sellers. Men who wished to be elected to public office, but had not been trained at home as rulers of serfs and household servants, needed a more explicit and general code of conduct than was embodied in the sense of honor and esprit de corps of the landed aristocracy. Occurring with the rapid political and social transformation of Greece, and interacting with it as both cause and effect, was the development of basic industrial arts and a scientific technology. These forces both expressed and intensified the developing interest in rational evaluation of beliefs. As Henry Sidgwick put it:

> This emergence of an art of conduct with professional teachers cannot thoroughly be understood, unless it is viewed as a crowning result of a general tendency at this stage of Greek civilization to substitute technical skill for traditional procedure…. If bodily vigour was no longer to be left to nature and spontaneous exercise, but was to be attained by the systematic observance of rules laid down by professional trainers, it was natural to think that the same might be the case with excellences of the soul. (*Outlines of the History of Ethics*, p. 21)

Early Greek thinkers drew frequent comparisons between medicine and ethics, describing ethics as the "art of living" and the "care of the soul." Socrates' motto, "A sound mind in a sound body," suggests the medical image of ethics as mental hygiene. Many thinkers took a special interest in medicine, and, recognizing the interdependence of mind and body, they practiced a rudimentary psychiatry. Alcmaeon of Croton, Empedocles, and Democritus were renowned for their psychotherapeutic skills. This biological conception of mind and soul led to a more critical and scientific approach to problems of ethical judgment. Philosophers began to search for reasons for established modes of conduct and, where no reasons were found, to suggest that action could be directed toward individual goals in defiance of tradition. The professional teachers known as Sophists, whose social role was to prepare the uncultivated nouveaux riches for positions of power in the rising democracies, employed the newfound weapon of logic with devastating effect against the code of honor of the declining aristocracy. Protagoras, Gorgias, and Thrasymachus taught methods of self-advancement and of attaining virtue. They stressed the difference between subjective values and objective facts,

arguing that good and evil are matters of personal decision or social agreement (*nomos*) rather than facts of nature (*phusis*).

SOCRATES. Socrates stood midway between the unexamined, traditional values of the aristocracy and the skeptical practicality of the commercial class. Like the Sophists, he demanded reasons for rules of conduct, rejecting the self-justifying claim of tradition, and for this reason he was denounced as a Sophist by conservative writers like Aristophanes. But unlike the Sophists, he believed that by the use of reason man could arrive at a set of ethical principles that would reconcile self-interest with the common good and would apply to all men at all times.

The central questions of ethical philosophy were raised for the first time by Socrates and the Sophists, but only Socrates realized the difficulty, bordering on impossibility, of finding adequate answers. In this respect, Socrates may be regarded as the first philosopher, in the strictest sense of the term. While the Sophists, after exposing the impracticality of traditional rules of conduct, then offered glib formulas in their place—such as "Justice is the rule of the stronger" (Thrasymachus) and "Man is the measure of all things" (Protagoras)—Socrates applied the same logical criticism with equally devastating results to both aristocratic and marketplace morality. He did not find the universal and self-evident code he searched for, but it was his memorable achievement to have revealed to humankind that without such a code its actions will lack justification and that moral perfection is therefore an ideal to which we can only approximate. Perfect clarity about what constitutes moral perfection is no more of this world than is moral perfection itself.

Our knowledge of Socrates is primarily derived from the dialogues of Plato, so it is not possible to draw a sharp line between the ideas of the two men. But since Plato's early dialogues are considerably different in style and content from those that he wrote later in life, one may take the early as fairly representative of Socrates and the late as more expressive of Plato's own thought. The chief differences discernible are the following: The more Socratic dialogues are devoted to the criticism of conventional beliefs and to the demonstration of the need for further inquiry, while the later dialogues argue for positive conclusions; the early dialogues search for definitions of ethical concepts, while the later dialogues are concerned with justifying a contemplative way of life in which pleasures of the senses are spurned in favor of pleasures of the mind; finally, the Socratic style is conversational and argumentative, while that of the later years is more didactic and abstract.

The Socrates of the early dialogues raises questions about the meaning of ethical terms, such as "What is justice?" (*Republic*), "What is piety?" (*Euthyphro*), "What is courage?" (*Laches, Charmides*), "What is virtue?" (*Protagoras*). The answers offered by others to these questions are then subjected to a relentless cross-examination (Socratic dialectic), exposing their vagueness and inconsistency.

Although Socrates did not separate judgments of value from judgments of fact, the negative results of his line of questioning suggest a distinction that was made explicit only in modern times by David Hume and G. E. Moore. In each of his discussions of ethical concepts such as courage or justice, Socrates refutes all efforts to define them in terms of ethically neutral facts. For example, when, in the *Protagoras, Laches,* and *Charmides,* courage is defined as resolute facing of danger, Socrates observes that a man who faces dangers that he would be wise to avoid is a fool rather than a hero. The generalization toward which Socrates points the way, although he does not arrive at it himself, is that ethical concepts can never be adequately defined in terms of observable facts alone. Many philosophers, beginning with the Sophists, have believed that this principle leads to ethical skepticism. Plato attempted to escape such skepticism by means of his theory of Forms, and the modern school of intuitionism proposes a similar way out. Indeed, all the ethical theories developed since Socrates may be considered as alternative explanations of the relation between facts and values, naturalistic theories stressing their interdependence and nonnaturalistic theories stressing their differences. Socrates, in demanding rational grounds for ethical judgments, brought attention to the problem of tracing the logical relationships between values and facts and thereby created ethical philosophy.

PLATO. Plato's thought may be regarded as an endeavor to answer the questions posed by Socrates. From the *Republic* on through the later dialogues and epistles, Plato constructed a systematic view of nature, God, and man from which he derived his ethical principles. The foundation of this metaphysical view was the theory of Forms, whose most succinct formulation may be found in the discussion of the Divided Line, toward the end of Book VI of the *Republic*. Plato divides the objects of knowledge into two main categories and each of these into two subcategories symbolized by unequal sections of the line. The main division is between the realm of changing, sen-

sible objects and that of unchanging, abstract forms. Knowledge of sensible objects acquired by sense perception is inaccurate and uncertain, for the object of sense, like the river of Heraclitus, is in continual flux. In contrast, knowledge of timeless forms is precise and rigorously provable. The realm of sensible objects is subdivided into shadows and images, in the lower section, and natural objects in the upper section. The realm of forms is subdivided into mathematical forms and ethical forms. At the apex of this ascending line is the Form of the Good, in relation to which all other objects of knowledge must be defined if they are to be adequately understood. Thus, ethics is the highest and most rigorous kind of knowledge, surpassing even mathematics, but it is also the most difficult to attain. Mathematics leads us away from reliance on visual images and sense perception, and ethical philosophy demands an even greater effort of abstraction. The objects of ethical knowledge are even less visualizable than geometrical forms and numbers—they are concepts and principles ultimately unified under the all-encompassing concept of the Good.

Although Plato suggests in this and other passages that ethical truths can be rigorously deduced from self-evident axioms, and thus introduces the mathematical model of knowledge that has guided many philosophers ever since, he does not employ a deductive procedure in his discussions of specific ethical problems, perhaps because he did not feel that he had yet attained an adequate vision of the Good that would supply him with the proper axioms from which to deduce rules of conduct. His actual procedure follows what he calls an ascending dialectic, a process of generalization through the give and take of conversation and the consideration of typical cases, a process designed to culminate in an intellectual vision of the structure of reality, from which, by a "descending dialectic" or deduction from general principles, particular judgments of value can be deduced. Plato's main goal in his ethical philosophy is to lead the way toward a vision of the Good.

The Socratic-Platonic ethical theory identifies goodness with reality and reality with intelligible form and thus concludes that the search for value must lead away from sense perception and bodily pleasure. This suggests an ascetic and intellectualistic way of life that is spelled out in full detail in the *Republic,* in the description of the training of the guardians. Some difference in the degree of intensity of the preference for mind over body may perhaps be discerned in the increasing severity of tone from the early dialogues to the later. In the *Protagoras* and *Symposium,* Socrates argues for rational control over the body for the sake of greater pleasure in the long run, but he does not oppose pleasure as such. In the *Symposium* the unity of body and mind is a luminous thread throughout the discussion. Love is regarded as a search for the pleasure that consists in possession of what is good, and it is shown to exist on many levels, the lowest being that of sexual desire and the highest that of aspiration toward a vision of eternity. While still under the influence of Socrates, Plato distinguishes noble pleasures from base pleasures, rather than condemning pleasure in itself. The image he draws of Socrates is of a man who eats and drinks heartily and enjoys himself on all levels of experience, but in rationally controlled proportions. Socrates enjoys the wine at the symposium as much as anyone else, but unlike the others he remains sober to the end. While the poet Agathon becomes drunk with his own rhetoric, Socrates employs richly sensual language and metaphor in a way sufficiently controlled to make a philosophical point and so remains master of his rhetoric as well as of his body.

In the extraordinarily beautiful dialogue *Phaedo,* which describes the day of Socrates' execution, the theme of superiority of soul to body is dealt with directly, as might be expected of a philosopher who is about to die. Here Socrates commits himself unequivocally to a rejection of the body and its pleasures, maintaining that a wise man looks forward to his own death, when the soul is freed from its corporeal prison. Whether this is an exact expression of Socrates' attitude toward life may, however, be doubted in view of other dialogues, such as the *Protagoras.* In any case, it is natural for a man confronting death to try to set the best possible light on it. But it was this more somber, otherworldly strain in Socrates that Plato in his later works elaborated into a mystical vision of a timeless higher world. Plato has Socrates say, in the *Philebus,* "no degree of pleasure, whether great or small, was thought to be necessary to him who chose the life of thought and wisdom" (translated by B. Jowett, New York, 1933, Para. 33).

In the *Timaeus,* where, significantly, the protagonist is no longer Socrates but the Pythagorean Timaeus, pleasure is described as "the greatest incitement to evil," and Timaeus places the "inferior soul" below the neck, separating it from the intellect. Plato's severe castigations of bodily pleasures, his sharp separation of soul from body and of the eternal from the temporal, and his mystical cosmology entail a more extreme asceticism than that preached or practiced by Socrates.

Plato's mistrust of bodily pleasure and perceptual judgment led him to take an unfavorable view of public opinion and, consequently, of democratic institutions. In the *Republic,* and still more emphatically in the *Laws,* he proposed that society be ruled by an intellectual elite who would be trained to govern in accordance with their vision of eternal forms. He proposed, in the *Laws,* a ruthless system of punishments and the propagation of ideologically useful myths that would preserve social harmony and class distinction. Yet despite his support of severe punishment for social transgressions, Plato followed Socrates in holding, in the *Protagoras, Timaeus,* and *Laws,* that evil is due only to ignorance or madness and that "no man is voluntarily bad," a paradox that Aristotle later tried valiantly to resolve.

ARISTOTLE. One might expect that Aristotle, who studied at Plato's Academy for many years, would take the same view of nature and human conduct as his mentor. But the differences between Plato and Aristotle are more fundamental than the resemblances. Although Aristotle naturally used a similar terminology and shared with Plato certain principles and attitudes expressive of the rationality of Hellenic culture, his method of inquiry and his conception of the role of ethical principles in human affairs were different enough from Plato's to establish a rival philosophical tradition. Plato was the fountainhead of religious and idealistic ethics, while Aristotle engendered the naturalistic tradition. Throughout the subsequent history of Western civilization, ethical views that looked to a supranatural source, such as God or pure reason, for standards of evaluation stemmed from the metaphysics of Plato, while naturalistic philosophers who found standards of value in the basic needs, tendencies, and capacities of man were guided by Aristotle.

Aristotle was born in Stagira, Macedonia, the son of Nicomachus, court physician to Amyntas II. He received early training in biology and physiology and in methods of careful observation and classification, a fact that may account for his later differences with Plato on the role of sense perception in the acquisition of knowledge. While Plato was guided by mathematics as a model of scientific knowledge, Aristotle modeled his system on biology, stressing the importance of observation of recurrent patterns in nature. Thus Plato's goal for philosophical ethics was to make human nature conform to an ideal blueprint, while Aristotle tailored his ethical principles to the demands of human nature.

Aristotle's ethical writings, consisting of the *Eudemian Ethics,* the *Nicomachean Ethics,* and the *Politics,* all edited by his disciples from his lecture notes, constitute the first systematic investigation of the foundations of ethics. Since the *Eudemian Ethics* is superseded by the *Nicomachean Ethics* and the *Politics* is an extension of his ethical principles to social regulation, this discussion will be confined to the ideas contained in the *Nicomachean Ethics*.

In the latter work, Aristotle's main purpose was to define the subject matter and methodology of philosophical ethics. In doing so, he both drew upon and revised the beliefs and values of the Greek society of his time. Aristotle begins his study by searching for the common feature of all things said to be good and, in contrast with Plato, who held that there is a Form of Good in which all good things "participate," Aristotle concludes that there are many different senses of "good," each of which must be defined separately for the limited area in which it applies. Each such "good" is pursued by a specific practical art or science, such as economics, military strategy, medicine, or shipbuilding. But the ends of these particular disciplines can be arranged in order of importance, so that the supreme good can be identified with the goal of the most general practical science to which the others are subordinate. On an individual level, this all-inclusive science is ethics; on a social level, it is politics. The end of ethics is personal happiness and that of politics is the general welfare, and since the good of the whole ranks above that of the part, personal ethics is subordinate to politics. However, this principle does not entail, for Aristotle, that the individual must sacrifice his interests to those of the community, except under unusual conditions such as war, because he assumed that the needs of both normally coincide.

Aristotle identifies the supreme good with "happiness," which he defines as the exercise of natural human faculties in accordance with virtue. His next task is to define virtue as a skill appropriate to a specific faculty, and he distinguishes two classes of virtues—intellectual and moral. There are five intellectual faculties, from which arise art, science, intuition, reasoning, and practical wisdom. He offers a long list of moral virtues, defining each as the mean between the extremes of either emotion or tendencies to action. For instance, courage is the mean between the excess and the deficiency of the emotion of fear, temperance is the mean between the tendencies to eat and drink too much or too little, justice is the mean with respect to the distribution of goods or of punishments. The bulk of the *Nicomachean Ethics* contains detailed analyses of the criteria of specific moral virtues. The final result of Aristotle's investigations is the definition of happiness or the good life as activity in accordance with virtue, and thus as the harmonious fulfillment of man's natural tendencies.

SUMMARY: SOCRATES, PLATO, AND ARISTOTLE. Returning to the central problems of ethical theory, one may hazard an estimation of the contributions of Socrates, Plato, and Aristotle to their clarification. Socrates was the first to recognize the importance of analyzing the meaning of good, right, just, and virtuous, and of articulating the standards for ascribing these properties. Plato charted a spiritualistic direction for finding the answers in a realm of timeless ideals, while Aristotle located the answers in the scientific study of biology, psychology, and politics. Good, for Plato, means resemblance to the pure Form, or universal model of goodness, which serves as the standard for all value judgments. Actions are right, laws are just, and people are virtuous to the degree to which they conform to the ideal model. For Aristotle, good means the achievement of the goals at which human beings naturally aim, the balanced and rational satisfaction of desires to which he gives the name "happiness." Right action, just laws, and virtuous character are the means of achieving individual and social well-being. All three philosophers agree in identifying individual good with social good and in defining moral concepts such as justice and virtue in terms of the achievement of good.

Moral responsibility. The concept of moral responsibility that acquired crucial importance in later Christian thought was only obliquely considered by Plato and more fully, although inconclusively, dealt with by Aristotle. Plato, who identified virtue with philosophical understanding, concluded that "no one does evil voluntarily," so that wrong action is always due to intellectual error. Aristotle recognized that intellectual error must be distinguished from moral vice, since the former, unlike the latter, is involuntary. In order to distinguish punishable evil from innocent mistakes, he explained vice as due to wrong desire as well as poor judgment. The will, for Aristotle, is rationally guided desire, formed by moral education and training. But since even voluntary action is determined by natural tendencies and early training, Aristotle searched for an additional factor to account for the freedom of choice necessary for moral responsibility. He thought he found that factor in deliberation, the consideration of reasons for and against a course of action. The further question, as to whether, when an agent deliberates, he has any choice of and consequently any responsibility for the outcome of his deliberation, was not considered by Aristotle and remains an unsettled issue between determinists and libertarians. In general, the concepts of free will and moral responsibility did not become matters of great concern until the rise of Christianity, when people became preoccupied with other-worldly rewards and punishments for moral conduct.

HELLENISTIC AND ROMAN ETHICS

During the two millennia from the death of Aristotle in the fourth century BCE to the rise of modern philosophy in the seventeenth century CE, the interests of ethical thinkers shifted from theoretical to practical ethics, so that little advance was made in the clarification of the meanings of ethical concepts, while, on the other hand, new conceptions of the goals of human life and new codes of conduct were fashioned. The philosophical schools of Skepticism, Stoicism, Epicureanism, and Neoplatonism that set the ethical tone of Hellenistic and Roman thought offered a type of intellectual guidance that was more like religious teaching than like scientific inquiry and paved the way for the conquests of Christianity. The popular conception of philosophy as an attitude of indifference to misfortune applies best to this period, in which philosophy and religion were nearly indistinguishable.

The subtlety of Socrates' thought is attested to by the variety of schools that developed out of his teaching. Plato and, through Plato, Aristotle probably represent the Socratic influence most completely. But the Stoics, Epicureans, and Skeptics also owed their guiding principles to Socrates. Aristippus of Cyrene, at first a disciple of Socrates, founded the school of Cyrenaicism, which followed the simple hedonistic principle that pleasure is the only good. Antisthenes, another Socratic disciple, founded the Cynic school on the apparently opposite principle that the good life is one of indifference to both pleasure and pain. The Cynics, of whom Diogenes was the most renowned, rejected the comforts of civilization and lived alone in the forests, like the dogs after whom they named themselves. Cyrenaicism developed into Epicureanism, and Cynicism into Stoicism. Soon after the death of Aristotle, Pyrrho of Elis initiated the philosophy of Skepticism, influenced by both the Sophist and the Socratic criticisms of conventional beliefs. According to Skepticism, no judgments, either of fact or of value, can be adequately proved, so that the proper philosophical attitude to take toward the actions of others is one of tolerant detachment, and toward one's own actions, extreme caution. In the second century BCE, the leaders of Plato's Academy, Arcesilaus and Carneades, adopted Skepticism, and Carneades developed a theory of probability that he applied to ethical judgments. During this period, the Peripatetic school at Aristotle's Lyceum continued the Aristotelian tradition until it merged finally with Stoicism.

EPICUREANISM. Epicurus (c. 341–270 BCE) founded one of the two dominant philosophical schools of the era between the death of Aristotle and the rise of Christianity. The other dominant school was, of course, Stoicism. These two traditions are often thought of as diametrical opposites, yet it may plausibly be argued that the differences between them were more verbal than substantial. Both views of life were fundamentally pessimistic, directed more toward escape from pain than toward the positive improvement of the human condition. Both encouraged individual withdrawal from the public arena of struggle for economic and political reform, in favor of personal self-mastery and independence of social conditions. The later Roman Stoics modified this extreme individualism and placed more stress on civic duties, but even they preached resignation to the imperfections of social organization rather than efforts at improvement.

Epicurus based his ethics on the atomistic materialism of Democritus, to which he added the important modification of indeterminism by postulating a tendency of the atoms that make up the human body—and particularly its "soul atoms"—to swerve unpredictably from their normal paths, resulting in unpredictable human actions. In this way, Epicurus thought he could account for freedom of the will. He assumed that freedom of choice of action is incompatible with the deterministic principle that all events are necessary results of antecedent causes. But this identification of freedom with pure chance seems to entail that a capricious person is more free than a rational and principled person, and such a conclusion would contradict Epicurus's own vision of moral life. For Epicurus's main difference with his Cyrenaic predecessors lay in his conviction that, by the use of reason, one could plan one's life and sacrifice momentary pleasures for long-run benefit. Like the Cyrenaics, Epicurus held that pleasure is the single standard of good. But he distinguished "natural pleasures," which are moderate and healthful, from "unnatural" satiation of greed and lust. His name for moderate and natural pleasure was *ataraxia,* gentle motions in the body that he regarded as the physiological explanation of pleasure. He proposed, as the ideal way of life, a relaxed, leisurely existence, consisting in moderate indulgence of the appetites, cultivation of the intellect, and conversation with friends, which is how Epicurus himself lived and taught in his famous garden. Two centuries later, Epicureanism was established in Rome by Lucretius (c. 99–55 BCE), whose influential poem, *On the Nature of Things,* helped to spread Epicureanism among the Roman aristocracy.

STOICISM. Stoicism was by far the most impressive intellectual achievement of Hellenistic and Roman culture prior to Christianity, providing an ethical framework within which metaphysical speculation, natural science, psychology, and social thought could flourish to such a high degree that Stoicism has not unjustly been identified in the public mind with philosophy itself, that is, with the distinctively "philosophical" attitude toward life. Like every great tradition, Stoicism evolved through many stages and thus comprehends a great variety of specific beliefs. Historians generally distinguish three main stages of its development:

(1) The early Stoa—which derived its name from the portico, or porch, on which the early Stoics lectured—whose important figures were Zeno of Cyprus, Cleanthes, and Chrysippus. Chrysippus made the most substantial contributions to Stoic logic and theory of knowledge. The early Stoics remained close to Cynicism in recommending withdrawal from community life so as to render oneself independent of material comforts, social fashions, and the opinions of one's fellow men. Their ethical goal was the achievement of apathy, the state of indifference to pleasure and pain. They considered reason to be the distinctive nature of man and proposed that one should live "according to nature" and thus according to rational principles of conduct.

With the Stoics, the concept of duty acquired a central place in ethics, as conformity to moral rules that they identified with laws of human nature. The later Roman Stoics developed this doctrine into the theory of natural law on which Roman jurisprudence was largely based. Most of the Stoics were materialists, yet imbued with natural piety, and many identified God with the Logos of Heraclitus, as a universal "fire" or energy of nature embodied in its lawlike processes. Many were fatalists, maintaining that man can control his destiny only by resigning himself to it, a principle that contrasted vividly with their emphasis on rationality and self-control. They sought to reconcile this extreme determinism with freedom and moral responsibility by means of the Aristotelian distinction between external and internal causation, thus suggesting that the free man is one who, in understanding the necessity of what befalls him, accepts it and thus freely chooses it, a solution echoed in modern thought by G. W. F. Hegel's definition of freedom as the recognition of necessity.

(2) The middle Stoics, notably Panaetius and Posidonius, brought Stoicism to Rome, shaping the doctrine to the political-mindedness of the Romans by modifying its extreme individualism and stressing the importance of social duties.

(3) The late Stoics, Seneca, Epictetus, Marcus Aurelius, and, to some extent, Cicero—who accepted only certain parts of Stoic doctrine—developed the ideal of a "cosmopolis," or universal brotherhood of man, in which all men would be recognized as having equal rights and responsibilities, an ideal that Christianity absorbed into its conception of the "City of God" and which, in the modern age, Immanuel Kant made the cornerstone of his system of ethics.

NEOPLATONISM. Epicureanism offered a way of life that was open only to the leisure class. Stoicism appealed to highly reflective men of all classes, as evidenced by the fact that the two great figures of late Stoicism were the educated slave Epictetus and the emperor Marcus Aurelius. However, both philosophical views could interest only those of a sufficiently high level of education and thoughtful temperament to place intellectual values above all others. As the Roman Empire declined, and reason seemed powerless to solve the intense economic and social problems of the empire, an atmosphere of pessimism and disaffection with reason began to prevail, a situation that Gilbert Murray described as "a failure of nerve." Interest increased in finding supernatural routes to salvation of the kind offered by various religious cults, and even in the intellectual schools the study of logic and natural science declined in favor of a search for psychological means of escape from suffering. The philosophy of Neoplatonism fashioned by Plotinus (c. 204–270) offered an intellectual road to salvation, while early Christianity paved an emotional and ritualistic highway toward the same destination. Later, these two roads converged.

Plotinus lectured in Rome and, after his death, his notes were edited by his disciple Porphyry, forming the work titled *Enneads*—so called because of its division into chapters of nine sections each. Plotinus developed one strain of Plato's thought, the ascetic mysticism of the passages on the Form of the Good in the *Republic* and the *Symposium* and the pantheistic metaphysics of the *Timaeus.* According to Plotinus, the world is a series of emanations or overflowings of the One, the ineffable and ultimate reality of which every determinate thing is a part. The One is so transcendent as to be indescribable, "the One, transcending intellect, transcends knowing." But if the One cannot be described, it can at least be negatively characterized in terms of what it is not, namely, that it is not limited by any finite properties. This negative characterization of the One was the source of Christian "negative theology," the description of God in terms of the denial of all modes of limitation.

The One emanates intelligible Forms or Platonic Ideas, out of which the World Soul produces individual souls that in turn emanate lower beings in a process that approaches, but does not quite reach, pure matter. Matter, as total formlessness, is so far from true being that it does not exist. Identifying evil with matter or formlessness, Plotinus concluded that evil does not exist in an absolute sense, but only as incompleteness or lack of good. This account of evil as having no positive existence was later adopted by Augustine and most subsequent theologians.

Since Plotinus, following Plato, equated goodness with reality and evil with unreality or distance from the One, it followed that virtue consists in purging the soul of reliance on sensual pleasures and imagery, so that it can ascend the ladder of being and return to its source in the One. The culmination of this process of purification through self-denial is the mystical experience of reunion with the One, which Plotinus describes—having experienced it himself at least four times—as "the flight of the Alone to the Alone." Thus virtue, for Plotinus as later for Augustine, is not its own reward but is a means to a metaphysical state of blessedness. In the words of the historian W. T. Jones, "Like other men of his time, Plotinus found this world a sea of troubles and a vale of tears; like them he sought to leave it; and like them he found perfect peace only in otherworldliness." How much of this view was absorbed into Christian, Islamic, and Judaic theology can hardly be overestimated, although the influence of Platonism on Judaism was mainly through Philo Judaeus (fl. 20 BCE–40 CE), an Alexandrian Jew and contemporary of Jesus, who combined elements of Stoicism with a Platonistic interpretation of Judaic theology and ethics.

(The above section on Hellenistic and Roman ethics was prepared in collaboration with Professor Richard O. Haynes of the University of Hawaii.)

MEDIEVAL ETHICS

The rise of Christian philosophy, out of a fusion of Greco-Roman thought with Judaism and elements of other Middle Eastern religions, produced a new era in the history of ethics, although one that was prepared for by Stoicism and Neoplatonism. The Stoic concern with justice and self-mastery, and the Neoplatonic search for reunion with the source of all being, were combined in early Christian philosophy with the Judaic belief in a personal God, whose commandments are the primal source of moral authority and whose favor is the ultimate goal of human life. Two sources of ethical standards, human reason and divine will, were juxtaposed in one system of ethics, and the tension between them was reflected in conflicting sectarian interpretations of theological principles.

From the second to the fourth century, Christianity spread through the Roman Empire, offering the poor and the oppressed a hope for otherworldly happiness in compensation for their earthly suffering, and thus a way of life with which the more pessimistic and intellectualist schools of philosophy could not compete. By the fourth century, Christianity dominated Western civilization and had absorbed the main ideas and values of the secular schools of thought, as well as rival religions such as Manichaeism, Mithraism, and Judaism. Having converted the masses, it was time to win over the intelligentsia, and doing this required the hammering out of an explicit and plausible system of metaphysical and ethical principles. This task was performed by the Church Fathers, Clement of Alexandria, Origen, Tertullian, Ambrose, and, most completely and authoritatively, by Augustine.

AUGUSTINE. St. Augustine (354–430), born near Carthage, the son of a pagan father and a Christian mother, was first a Manichaean and later became converted to Christianity. He rose in the church to become bishop of Hippo and helped to settle the doctrinal strife among the many Christian sects by constructing a system of theology, ethics, and theory of knowledge that soon became the authoritative framework of Christian thought, modified but not supplanted by subsequent church philosophers. Augustine's major works, *Confessions, The City of God, Enchiridion,* and *On Freedom of the Will,* wove together threads of Stoic ethics, Neoplatonic metaphysics, and the Judeo-Christian doctrine of revelation and redemption into a many-colored fabric of theology. With Augustine, theology became the bridge between philosophy and revealed religion, the one end anchored in reason and the other in faith, and ethics became a blend of the pursuit of earthly well-being with preparation of the soul for eternal salvation.

Like the Neoplatonists, Augustine rejected almost entirely the claims of bodily pleasures and community life, maintaining, as St. Paul had done, that happiness is impossible in this world, which serves only as a testing ground for reward and punishment in the afterlife. Augustine inherited the Neoplatonic conception of virtue as the purgation of the soul of all dependence on material comforts in preparation for reunion with God. Against the Stoic and Aristotelian reliance on reason as the source of virtue, Augustine maintained that such apparently admirable traits as prudence, justice, wisdom, and fortitude—the four cardinal virtues identified by Plato and stressed by Stoics and Christians—are of no moral worth when not inspired by Christian faith. With the pessimistic view of life characteristic of an era of wars, political collapse, and economic decline—a view already apparent in the Stoic, Epicurean, and Neoplatonic modes of withdrawal from social responsibilities—intensified by his personal sense of guilt and worthlessness, Augustine saw life on Earth as a punishment for Adam's original sin. "For what flood of eloquence can suffice to detail the miseries of this life?" he laments in *The City of God*.

Nature. The tension between natural and supernatural values in Augustine's ethical thought shows itself most clearly in his ambivalent attitude toward nature. Nature, as God's creation, must be unqualifiedly good. Natural evils are only apparently evil, and in the long run they contribute to the fulfillment of divine purpose. Natural evil is simply imperfection that makes variety possible and thus, when viewed on a cosmic scale, does not exist at all. On the other hand, since man must be held morally responsible for his sins, human sin cannot be so easily explained away as incompleteness that promotes the cosmic good. Moreover, it is man's bodily desires that tempt him to sin. Without the aid of divine grace, the promptings of human nature, whether impulsive or rational, lead only to vice and damnation. Augustine resolves this paradoxical view of human nature by holding that man, unlike other natural species, was endowed by his Creator with free will and thus with the capacity to choose between good and evil. Through the original sin of Adam he has chosen evil, and it is for this reason, rather than because of any flaw in his original construction, that he is irresistibly inclined to further sin.

Free will and divine foreknowledge. If Augustine's dual conception of nature is explained by his concept of free will, the latter contains new difficulties. The problem of free will is critical in Christian ethics, which emphasizes responsibility and punishment. The Greek ideal of practical reason ensuring physical and mental well-being was supplanted by the ideal of purification of the soul through suffering, renunciation, and humble obedience to divine will.

Where the practice of virtue produces well-being as its natural consequence, as in the Greek view, virtue carries with it its own reward in accordance with the causal processes of nature, so that causal necessity and moral desert are not merely compatible; they normally coincide. But in the Christian view, causal necessity and moral responsibility seem incompatible, for the choice between good and evil is made by the soul, independently of natural processes, and its reward or punishment is independent of the natural effects of human actions. Man is punished or rewarded to the degree to which he voluntarily obeys or disobeys the commands of God. In the Greek view, man suffers from the natural consequences of his mistakes, but in the Christian view, no matter what the natural consequences of his actions, he is held to account for the state of his soul. It is his motives and not his actions that count in assessment of his moral responsibility, and the primary motive is his desire for, or his turning away from, God.

Responsibility is thus transferred from the consequences of a person's actions to the state of his soul. Yet if the soul is created by God, and not subject to its temporary owner's control, then in what sense can man be said to have freedom of choice between good and evil? Augustine describes the soul that chooses evil as "defective," but if so, is not the Creator of the defective soul responsible for its deficiency? In absolution of God, Augustine argues that a defect is not a positive entity, thus not a created thing and not attributable to a creator—a terminological escape that is vulnerable to the objection that, on such grounds, a man who stabs another produces in his victim a deficiency rather than a positive state and therefore is not responsible for his "nonexistent" product.

Augustine's concept of free will is further complicated by his support of the theological principle of divine omniscience, which entails foreknowledge by God of human decisions. The term *predestination,* used by later theologians and notably by the Protestant reformers, suggests a determinism that Augustine rejects in his criticism of fatalism. For Augustine, God knows what man will choose to do and makes it possible for man to act on his free choices but does not compel him to any course of action. To the obvious question of how God can know in advance what has not been destined or causally necessitated, Augustine replies by means of his subtle analysis of time. God has knowledge, not of what we are compelled to do but of what we freely choose to do, because his knowledge is not the kind of advance knowledge that is based on causal processes but is due to the fact that, in the mind of God, we have already made our decisions. All of past and future time is spread out in the specious present of the divine mind, so that what, from our limited standpoint, would be prediction of the future is, for God, simply direct awareness of contemporaneous events.

Distinctions among ethical concepts. While Augustine's ethical writings are mainly concerned with the substantive problem of how to achieve redemption, rather than with the clarification of ethical concepts, much of his writing is philosophical in our strict sense, in that it suggests solutions to conceptual or metaethical problems of meaning and method. Augustine opposed the classical tendency to define the moral concepts of rightness and virtue in terms of individual and social well-being and interpreted moral right and virtue as obedience to divine authority. The concept of good is split into a moral and a practical sense. Good as fulfillment of natural tendencies is subordinated to eternal beatitude, the fulfillment of the aspirations of the virtuous soul. Freedom and responsibility are interpreted as internal states of the soul and as excluding, rather than (as for Aristotle) presupposing, causal necessity.

FOURTH TO THIRTEENTH CENTURIES. From Augustine in the fourth century to Peter Abelard (1079–1142) in the eleventh century, Christian, Islamic, and Judaic philosophy was dominated by Neoplatonic mysticism and preoccupied with faith and salvation. The outstanding figure of this period was John Scotus Erigena (c. 810–c. 877), whose conception of good was the Platonic one of approximation to timeless being and whose view of life as issuing from and returning to God bordered on heretical pantheism.

By the eleventh century, interest in rational philosophical speculation had revived, and even those Schoolmen like Bernard of Clairvaux (1090–1153), who continued to defend religious mysticism and denounced reliance upon reason as inimical to faith, nevertheless employed philosophical arguments to refute contrary opinions. Augustine had asserted that one must "believe in order to understand," and St. Anselm (1033–1109) took this to mean that faith is not incompatible with reason but, rather, prepares the soul for rational understanding. The main issues among philosophers of this time were the relation between faith and reason, and the nature of universals.

Abelard, however, an extraordinarily original and independent thinker whose vibrant personality reveals itself in his philosophical writings, rediscovered some of the unsolved problems of ethical philosophy. Abelard brought into clear view the distinctive features of Christian ethics implicit in Augustine's work, in particular, the split between moral and prudential concepts that sharply

separates Christian ethics from Greek ethics. Abelard held that morality is an inner quality, a property of motive or intention rather than of the consequences of one's actions, a principle that was later stressed by the Reformation and attained its fullest expression in the ethical system of Kant. A somewhat heretical corollary follows from Abelard's principle, namely that, as Étienne Gilson put it, "Those who do not know the Gospel obviously commit no fault in not believing in Jesus Christ," and it seems clear from all this that Christian faith need not be the foundation for moral rules. Abelard concluded that one can attain to virtue through reason as well as through faith.

THOMAS AQUINAS. The towering figure of medieval philosophy is, of course, Thomas Aquinas (c. 1224–1274), whose philosophical aim was to reconcile Aristotelian science and philosophy with Augustinian theology. The way to this achievement had already been prepared by the revival in western Europe of interest in Aristotle, whose thought had been preserved and elaborated by Muslim and Jewish scholars such as Avicenna, Averroes, and Maimonides and had been brought to the attention of Christendom by the commentaries of Albert the Great. It remained for Aquinas to prove the compatibility of Aristotelian naturalism with Christian dogma and to construct a unified view of nature, man, and God. This he undertook with remarkable success in his *Summa Theologiae* and *Summa Contra Gentiles.*

To a large degree, Aquinas's union of Aristotelianism with Christianity consisted in arguing for the truth of both and in refuting arguments of his predecessors and contemporaries that purported to show their incompatibility. Aristotle's ethics was relativistic, rational, and prudential; Augustinian ethics was absolutist, grounded on faith, and independent of consequences. Now one of these views is totally misguided, or else there must be room for two different systems of ethical concepts and principles. Aquinas adopted the latter alternative and divided the meaning of ethical concepts into two domains, "natural" and "theological." Natural virtues, adequately accounted for by Aristotle, can be attained by proper training and the exercise of practical reason, while theological virtues—faith, hope, and love—require faith and divine grace. Similarly, he distinguished two highest goods, or paramount goals of life, worldly happiness and eternal beatitude (which has precedence); the former is achieved through natural virtue and the latter is achieved through the church and its sacraments. Aquinas thus expressed a considerably more optimistic attitude than did Augustine toward the possibility of improving man's lot on earth through knowledge of nature and intelligent action. This helped to prepare the climate for the rebirth of natural science, whose first stirrings were felt in the thirteenth century.

Natural law. At the center of Thomistic ethics was the concept of natural law. The medieval doctrine of natural law, stemming from Aristotle's teleological conception of nature and from the Stoic identification of human reason with the Logos, was a fusion of naturalistic Greek ethics with monotheistic theology. On this view, the promptings of informed reason and moral conscience represent an inherent tendency in the nature of man, and conformity to this nature fulfills both the cosmic plan of the Creator and the direct commands of God revealed in the Scriptures. Natural law is the divine law as discovered by reason, and therefore the precepts of the church and the Bible, and scientific knowledge of the universal needs and tendencies of man, provide complementary rather than competing standards of ethical judgment. Where conflicts between science and religious authority arise, they must be due to inadequate understanding of science, since church authority and dogma are infallible.

The Thomistic unification of scientific and religious ethics in the doctrine of natural law—further elaborated in subtle detail by Francisco Suárez and other legalists—was an effective way of making room, within the religious enterprise of achieving salvation, for the practical business of everyday living in pursuit of personal and social well-being. The ideological supremacy of theology was maintained, but the doctrine of natural law purported to guarantee reliable knowledge of nature, psychology, and political economy. The weakness in this system was that it placed religious barriers in the way of scientific advance, tending to sanctify and render immune from revision whichever scientific principles seemed most congenial to theology, such as instinct theory in psychology, vitalistic biology, and geocentric astronomy.

Free will. Aquinas's account of freedom and moral responsibility was, in general form, similar to that of Augustine, maintaining the compatibility of free will with predestination or divine foreknowledge. Aquinas also maintained the compatibility of free will with causal determinism, thus dealing with the problem on the level of prudential ethics as well on as the theological level of grace and salvation. Aquinas's solution makes effective use of Aristotle's analysis of choice and voluntary action in terms of internal causality and deliberation, and it identifies free will with rational self-determination rather than with the absence of causal influences. On the other hand, Aquinas's concept of freedom is, as a result, more

relativistic than Augustine's, and, while it explains the conditions under which an agent may be held responsible for his actions—namely, the conditions of desire, knowledge, and deliberation—it does not meet the further issue of whether these faculties that determine action are within the control of the agent, that is, whether a person can freely choose the habits and desires that determine his actions. Later writers, particularly Protestant theologians, tended to interpret Augustine as stressing predestination and Aquinas as stressing free will, but it may be argued to the contrary, that Augustine's conception of free will as an inexplicable and supernatural thrust of the soul allows the agent more independence of his formed character than does Aquinas's, but by that very token, Aquinas's account is more congenial to a scientific view of man.

Subsequent scholastic philosophy, from the fourteenth to the seventeenth centuries, added little to the clarification of metaethical problems, but it probed further into the relation between intellect and will as sources of human and divine action. John Duns Scotus (c. 1266–1308), William of Ockham (c. 1285–1349), and Nicolas of Autrecourt (c. 1300–after 1350) developed the voluntaristic doctrine that the will is free in a more absolute sense than that accounted for by Aquinas, in that it is independent both of external causality and of determination by the intellect—that is, by the agent's knowledge of what is right and good. Their view in one way strengthened the case for religious faith as against scientific reason, at least in matters of ethical judgment, but, in another way, it helped stimulate an attitude of individualism and independence of authority that prepared the ground for the secular and humanistic ethics of the modern age.

EARLY MODERN ETHICS

Philosophy seems to flourish best in periods of rapid social transformation, when the conceptual framework of a culture crumbles, requiring a reexamination of basic concepts, principles, and standards of value. The sixteenth and seventeenth centuries, which saw the demise of medieval feudalism and ushered in the modern age of industrial democracy, were, like the fifth and fourth centuries BCE, a period of intense philosophical ferment. In both cases, the preceding century witnessed the demolition of traditional beliefs, while the succeeding century was one of systematic reconstruction. The development of commerce and industry, the discovery of new regions of the world, the Reformation, the Copernican and Galilean revolutions in science, and the rise of strong secular governments demanded new principles of individual conduct and of social organization.

In the sixteenth century, Francis Bacon demolished the logic and methodology of medieval Scholasticism. Desiderius Erasmus, Martin Luther, and John Calvin, while attempting to strengthen the bond between religion and ethics, undermined the elaborate structure of canon law based on the moral authority of the medieval church, and Niccolò Machiavelli dynamited the bridge between religious ethics and political science. The task of reconstruction in philosophy was performed in the seventeenth century by René Descartes, Thomas Hobbes, Gottfried Wilhelm Leibniz, Benedict de Spinoza, and John Locke.

HOBBES. Modern ethical theory began with Thomas Hobbes (1588–1679). The advent of Galilean natural science had challenged the traditional notions, supported by authority, of purpose, plan, and value in the physical world; it cast into doubt the doctrine of natural law and nullified the anthropomorphic assumptions of theology. New standards of ethical judgment had to be found, not in the cosmic plan of nature or in scriptural revelations of the divine will but in man himself, either in his biological structure, or in his agreements with his fellow men, or in the social and political institutions that he creates. Thus were born, simultaneously and to the same parent, the ethical philosophies of naturalism, cultural relativism, and subjectivism, respectively.

Born in a time of international and domestic strife, Hobbes regarded the preservation of life as the paramount goal of human action and constructed his system of ethics and political science in his major work, *Leviathan,* with the principle of self-preservation as its cornerstone. His enthusiasm for Galileo Galilei's physics and his conviction that all fields of knowledge could be modeled on this universal science (following the method of Euclid's geometry) may have suggested to him that the drive to self-preservation is the biological analogue of the Galilean principle of inertia. Hobbes conceived of man as a complex system of particles in motion and attempted to deduce ethical laws from the principle of self-preservation. He offers, however, two formulations of this principle, the first of which is his foundation of ethics, while the second is, in effect, the repudiation of ethics.

The tendency to self-preservation, according to Hobbes, expresses itself in the quest for social harmony through peacekeeping institutions and practices or, alternatively, in the aggressive drive toward power over one's fellow men. Thus he formulates his "first and fundamental" principle in two parts, the "law of nature" to the effect that "Every man ought to endeavor to peace as far as he has hope of obtaining it," and the "right of nature," that "when he cannot obtain it, he may seek and use all the helps and advantages of war." Which of these two forms of the principle of self-preservation should be applied depends, for Hobbes, on whether the agent finds, himself in a well-organized society or in a "state of nature" in which he cannot expect cooperative behavior on the part of his fellow men. Thus, the concept of ethical law applies to social agreements and commitments, while that of rights applies to the exercise of natural powers. In the state of nature one has a right to do whatever one has the power to do.

From his fundamental law of nature, Hobbes derives a number of specific rules that prescribe the means of establishing and maintaining a peaceful society, the primary means being the willingness to make or, if already made, to maintain the social contract in which individual rights or powers are surrendered to a sovereign in return for the guarantee of personal security. The state is thus the artificial creation of reasonable men, a "Leviathan" that maintains peace by means of power relinquished to it by its citizens. Once such a commonwealth has been established by contract or conquest, other general rules of conduct follow in accordance with Hobbes's theory of psychology. To restrain the natural human tendencies to envy, mistrust, self-aggrandizement, and aggression, the virtues of accommodation, gratitude, clemency, obedience to authority, and respect for the equal rights of others are recommended by "laws of nature" as effective means of ensuring social harmony.

Reason and ethical laws. Hobbes's use of the term "laws of nature" in referring to ethical principles is to be distinguished sharply from the medieval concept of natural law that he rejected. There is, for Hobbes, no moral order in the cosmos, nor any natural prompting toward justice and sympathy for others in human nature. Man, like the rest of nature, is a system of particles perpetually moving and colliding in accordance with physical laws whereby direction and intensity of motion are determined solely by preponderance of force. Yet reason plays a role in human action that distinguishes man from the rest of the world machine. Ethical rules are "precepts, found out by reason, by which a man is forbidden to do that which is destructive of his life or taketh away the means of preserving the same."

In his mechanistic physiology, Hobbes explained reason as a mechanical process in the brain consisting in the combining and separating particles that serve as representations of objects and qualities; thus, cognitive processes are a special type of physical process, governed by the same laws. But on this mechanistic view of man, it is difficult for Hobbes to account for the prescriptive character he attributes to ethical laws as distinguished from physical laws. Throughout his discussion, Hobbes vacillates between a conception of ethics as a branch of physical science that describes the behavior of human mechanisms and the quite different conception of ethics as rational advice on how to get along with one's fellow men by consciously restraining one's aggressive impulses. Both sides of the *nomos-phusis* controversy between the Sophists and Plato are represented in Hobbes's thought, and he cites both social authority and prudential reason as sources of ethical obligation. Moral virtue consists in conformity to custom and law, in opposition to the natural aggressiveness that equips a man for survival in the state of nature, yet the "precepts found out by reason" provide a natural basis for the establishment of customs and laws.

Desire and will. Hobbes's account of desire and will is designed to bridge the gap between rational directives and physical laws. He defines "good" as "any object of desire" and desire as the motion toward an object that results from physiological processes ("endeavors") within the body. To act rationally does not entail freedom to act contrary to one's physiological impulses, since rationality or deliberation is simply the mediating processes of the central nervous system. The will is not a supernatural power controlling desires but simply the last stage of deliberation that eventuates in overt action, and thus is itself a neurological process governed by laws of physics. Freedom of the will from causal influences is, for Hobbes, a senseless combination of concepts; freedom is the "absence of external impediments" to the will. It is the person who is free or unfree, and not his will, since his freedom consists in the determination of his overt actions by his will rather than by external forces. Yet this mechanistic account of the will seems in paradoxical contrast with his subjectivist account of civil law as deriving its obligatory force from the arbitrary will of the sovereign, an account that comes dangerously close to the Aristotelian and Augustinian notions of the will as a "first cause."

Naturalism and nonnaturalism. The importance of Hobbes to modern ethical theory is inestimable. In freeing ethics from bondage to revealed theology and its anthropomorphic view of nature, Hobbes brought philosophy back to the problems with which it had begun to wrestle in the time of Socrates and the Sophists, and of which it had lost sight for a millennium. At the same time, he raised the understanding of these problems to a higher level, profiting both from the Christian insight that moral principles have an obligatory force and from the refinements of scientific method introduced by Bacon, Galileo, and Descartes.

If ethics was to become a body of reliable knowledge, it must be grounded on objective laws of psychology and biology, rather than on tradition, sentiment, and church authority. On the other hand, if nature and its scientific description are ethically neutral, then ethics is to be contrasted with science and purged of references to nature, just as natural science must be purged of references to ethical values. In that case, ethical principles must be understood as subjective expressions of emotion and desire, and not as objectively verifiable laws. This dilemma has plagued philosophy ever since, and, if it was not resolved by Hobbes, at least his thought was not completely impaled on either horn but only a bit on both.

EARLY INTUITIONISTS. Reaction to Hobbes's attack on the objectivity of ethical judgment was immediate. The doctrine of natural law and its vision of nature as a moral system were defended in a new form by a group of scholars at Cambridge who became known as the Cambridge Platonists, principally Ralph Cudworth (1617–1688) and Henry More (1614–1687). They maintained that moral principles are self-evident truths, as certain and immutable as the laws of mathematics. Richard Cumberland (1631–1718) attempted to deduce all the principles of ethics from a single "Law of Nature" that later became the cornerstone of utilitarian ethics, namely, the law that all actions should promote the common good. Nicolas Malebranche (1638–1715) developed the Cartesian theory of ethics as a deductive system but gave it an Augustinian slant, attributing to God the sole power to translate knowledge of ethical truth into action. Malebranche realized that the analogy between ethics and mathematics fails to explain the connection between ethics and action, and so he made a virtue of this defect by means of his "Occasionalist" account of causality as divine intervention. Samuel Clarke (1675–1729) developed an intuitionist theory of "natural religion" similar to that of Cudworth and More, holding that the quality of right or "fitness" is an intrinsic property of actions that the mind can perceive as directly as it perceives geometrical relations.

SPINOZA. Born in the Netherlands of Jewish refugees from the Spanish Inquisition, Benedict de Spinoza (1632–1677) combined Descartes's faith in the capacity of reason to govern action with Hobbes's mechanistic theory of psychology to express a scientific vision of nature as a unified system of laws. In his *Ethics Demonstrated in the Geometric Manner* Spinoza, like Hobbes but with more formal precision, derived the principles of physics, psychology, and ethics from metaphysical axioms.

The first principle of psychology for Spinoza, as for Hobbes, is the drive to self-preservation and self-aggrandizement, corresponding to the physical principle of inertia. But Spinoza's unique achievement was to derive, as the logical corollary of this egoistic psychology, a rational, humane, and cultivated way of life. A strict determinist in his metaphysics and a thorough naturalist in his ethics, Spinoza held that every event is deducible from antecedent causes and concluded that ethical right is identical with causal necessity. The rules of conduct are therefore laws of human nature, obeyed by all but obeyed blindly by the selfish person enslaved by his passions while understood and accepted by the free man who, in achieving a vision of the necessary order of all things, experiences the "intellectual love of God" that provides both happiness and moral virtue.

While Spinoza tried more consistently than Hobbes to reduce ethics to psychology and thus to make it a branch of natural science, it has often been contended that his program was self-defeating. For if men cannot help acting in accordance with their desires, and if nothing is objectively good or bad but only appears so to those who do not understand the necessity of all events, then what sense can there be to either prudential or moral rules of conduct? Having banished values from nature, Spinoza, like Hobbes, had to relocate them in human consciousness. But then consciousness must be either a supranatural force that interrupts the causal order of nature—as it was for Descartes—or a part of nature and thus ethically neutral, in which case ethics becomes senseless; or, finally, consciousness is an illusory reflection of physical processes in the body, in which case ethics, too, is illusory. Spinoza and Hobbes vacillated between the last two alternatives although, as we have seen, Hobbes's prescriptivist account of moral right as stemming from the will of an authority may be suspected of having slipped an element of supranatural agency back into the picture.

In their social and political theories, both Spinoza and Hobbes argued for the appraisal of institutions and policies in terms of the satisfaction of human needs rather than of conformity to religious tradition. But Hobbes's conception of force as the basis of law led him to support political authoritarianism, while Spinoza's identification of value and right with rational self-interest enabled him to argue, like Locke, for representative government and maximum civil liberty.

LOCKE. John Locke (1632–1704) is generally regarded as the founder of modern utilitarianism, although his applications of utilitarian ethics to social and political theory were more influential than his analysis of standards of individual conduct. He combined the mathematical model of ethical judgment suggested by Descartes and the Cambridge Platonists with a hedonistic theory of psychology according to which pleasure is the goal of all human action and consequently is the fundamental standard of evaluation. In his *Essay concerning Human Understanding,* Locke criticizes the doctrine of innate ideas of Descartes and Leibniz, in defense of the principle that all knowledge is founded on experience; he then, somewhat paradoxically, offers an account of ethics as a deductive science in which specific rules of conduct are derived "from self-evident propositions, by necessary consequences as incontestable as those in mathematics." The appearance of paradox dissolves, however, on noting that, for Locke, the formation of the ideas of goodness and justice is due to the sensations of pleasure and pain, and thus ethical concepts are derived from experience although their logical relations are then discoverable by reflective analysis.

Locke follows Hobbes in defining good as the object of desire, but then, assuming that the only property of things which provokes desire is their tendency to produce pleasure or reduce pain, he also defines good as "what has an aptness to produce pleasure in us." Again, like Hobbes, Locke defines moral virtue as conformity to custom and law, but he differs from Hobbes in maintaining that custom and law can in turn be evaluated by the more fundamental standards of utility and natural rights. It is in terms of these more basic standards that Locke justifies representative government and civil liberty.

Locke's main contribution to the clarification of the meaning of ethical concepts was in his distinction between "speculative" and "practical" principles. Speculative knowledge is independent of action, while practical principles (including ethical principles) can be said to be believed and known to be true only insofar as they are acted upon. This distinction accounts for the obligatory force of ethical principles and eliminates the need for a supernatural agency, "free will," to translate belief into action, although it makes it difficult to explain why, if practical principles are "self-evident propositions," we do not all behave in a morally impeccable way. Like Hobbes, Locke ridicules the notion of free will as a semantic absurdity similar to the questions "whether sleep be swift or virtue square." Will is the power of the mind to decide on action, and freedom the power to carry out one's decisions, that is, to get what one wants.

MORAL-SENSE THEORIES. The seventeenth-century philosophers found the connection between self-interest and morality in the threat of punishment—divine, natural, or civil—that coerces the individual to be moral for the sake of self-interest. But it was soon noticed that this connection breaks down wherever the expected benefit to the individual of immoral conduct outweighs the likelihood of punishment and that, if morality is grounded in psychology, then human nature cannot be as aggressively self-centered as the apostles of self-preservation and pursuit of pleasure maintained.

The third earl of Shaftesbury (1671–1713) and Francis Hutcheson (1694–1746) proposed that moral obligation has its source in benevolent affections, such as love and pity, that are as natural and universal as the more aggressive tendencies ("self-affections"), such as envy, greed, and the impulse to self-preservation. Moreover, there is a "moral sense" in man that finds unique satisfaction in actions directed toward the common good. This moral sensibility turns us from the pursuit of pleasure toward the performance of duties toward others and explains our admiration of self-sacrifice independently of external reward or punishment.

Bernard Mandeville (c. 1670–1733), in *The Fable of the Bees*, defended egoistic psychology against this attack and ridiculed the concept of moral conscience as a hypocritical device for maintaining social privileges, a view later echoed by Baron d'Holbach, Karl Marx, and Friedrich Nietzsche. Bishop Joseph Butler (1692–1752), whose sermons in defense of Christian morality against the cynicism of Hobbes and Mandeville reveal extraordinary analytical power, argued that benevolence and conscience are as deeply rooted in human nature as is self-love. In adding conscience or intuition of duty to benevolence as the psychological source of moral obligation, Butler lessened the stress of earlier moral-sense theorists on emotion and gave more recognition to the role of rational judgment.

Moral-sense theory, refined further by David Hartley (1705–1757) and Adam Smith (1723–1790), who applied utilitarian ethics to economic theory, achieved its most persuasive formulation in the writings of David Hume.

HUME. David Hume (1711–1776), like Hartley and Smith, combined an emotional account of morality with a utili-

tarian theory of good. Hume's discussions of ethics in the third part of his *A Treatise of Human Nature* and, more fully, in his *An Enquiry concerning the Principles of Morals* are attempts to answer the metaethical questions of the meaning of good, right, justice, and virtue; by what standards they are attributed to persons and actions; how it is psychologically possible for men to admire and cultivate morality at the expense of self-interest; and by what rules ethical disputes can be decided in favor of one judgment against another. Despite the clarity and good sense that Hume brings to bear on these topics, his discussion shifts inadvertently from one type of question to another, particularly from questions of meaning to questions of motivation, a shift characteristic of moral-sense theories.

Hume begins his studies of ethical judgment with a search for the meanings of ethical terms. Finding no observable facts or logical relations that answer to our concepts of goodness, justice, and moral virtue, Hume concludes that the function of ethical terms is not to denote qualities or relations but to convey a "sentiment of approbation," so that their meaning is to be found in the feelings of the judge rather than in the object judged. We call things good for the same reason that we call them beautiful: because we find them agreeable. An object is good if it is immediately pleasant, or if it is a useful means for attaining something else that is pleasant. Virtues are qualities that render a person agreeable or useful to himself or to others, whether they are "natural virtues" such as talent, wit, and benevolence or "artificial virtues" like honesty and justice. While judgments as to what is useful in producing pleasure, insofar as they rest on knowledge of causal facts, are within the competence of reason, nevertheless they depend, for their distinctively ethical import, on feeling or taste, since rational knowledge alone is "not sufficient" to produce any moral blame or approbation. "Utility is only a tendency to a certain end; and were the end totally indifferent to us, we should feel the same indifference toward the means. It is requisite a certain *sentiment* should here display itself" (*Enquiry concerning the Principles of Morals,* Appendix I).

Thus, according to Hume, there are two possible grounds or standards of evaluation, utility and feeling, the one objective and subject to rational confirmation, the other subjective and personal. The objective standard, unfortunately, applies only to instrumental values and not to ultimate ends. However, the subjectivity of feelings is not cause for despair about achieving agreement on ethical judgments, since the sentiment that motivates them, the disinterested pleasure and approval that we feel in contemplating actions directed toward the welfare of others, is, for Hume as for Butler, a universal tendency in human nature.

Moral reasons and psychological motives. In common with Hobbes and Locke, who justified moral conduct by the fear of punishment, and the earlier moral-sense theorists, who explained moral obligation in terms of the benevolent affections, Hume identifies the psychological motives that influence and often prejudice moral judgments with the logical grounds or reasons for moral judgments. From the premise that, were it not for our natural benevolence, we would not care enough about moral issues to make moral judgments, Hume draws the non sequitur that the only evidence which supports such judgments lies in the feeling of approval or disapproval that motivates them.

Hume tends to equate moral virtue with the artificial quality of justice, artificial because it is required only for the protection of property rights in a society in which goods are neither too scarce nor sufficiently abundant. The importance for social harmony of strict conformity to laws renders it dangerous and undesirable to make exceptions in the name of expediency. Consequently, the utility of strict justice outweighs the utility of any possible exceptions. But Hume realized that this rather abstract utilitarian consideration can hardly explain our sense of moral obligation and our admiration for those who demonstrate high moral character. He therefore supplements this account with the notion of "disinterested interest" that resembles the rational moral sense appealed to by Butler, Richard Price, and Thomas Reid (see below).

However, Hume is not positing any occult faculty, for he explains disinterested moral approbation as a combination of the natural quality of sympathy for others (pain at witnessing another's pain) and the habit of following rules. Since natural sympathy alone would lead us into injustices and considerations of utility alone would seem to justify exceptions to general rules, we come to agree on general principles of conduct and transfer to these principles the sentiment of approbation that we originally felt toward the happiness or release from pain usually produced by following such principles. Thus arises the sense of moral duty and the capacity for disinterested approval. Here again, Hume offers a psychological description of the motivating processes that cause us to approve of moral virtue as an answer to the question of what criteria we use to judge persons and actions to be worthy of moral approval. Once this identity of psychological motive and logical ground is presupposed, it becomes impossible to distinguish between correct and incorrect moral judgments. The question as to whether action that meets with general approbation actually merits such approbation cannot even be raised, since merit has already been identified with the mere fact of approbation.

Freedom. On the issue of free will and its relation to moral responsibility, Hume argued persuasively that responsibility presupposes the causal efficacy of threat of punishment. He developed further the arguments of Hobbes and Locke that freedom is not a quality of the will but a relation between desire, action, and environment, such that a man is free when his actions are caused by his own desires and unimpeded by external restraints, a view that William James later baptized "soft determinism."

COMMONSENSE INTUITIONISM. Hume's subjective account of moral judgment was countered by the commonsense intuitionism of Thomas Reid (1710–1796) and Richard Price (1723–1791), who explained the moral sense, or conscience, that enables man to distinguish right from wrong as a combination of benevolent emotion and rational intuition. Both argued, like Butler, that moral principles are not in need of utilitarian justification but are as natural to man as self-love and desire for pleasure. Reid argued that moral qualities are as directly perceived as physical properties are and thus exist in the object judged rather than in the feelings of the subject who judges. Ethics is as much a matter of objective fact as science is, except that its principles are self-evident and can be discovered by "common sense" alone, uncorrupted by bad philosophy. Reid also defended the belief in freedom of the will as the ground of moral responsibility, arguing that we are introspectively aware of our ability to choose between good and evil independently of our desires.

THE FRENCH ENLIGHTENMENT. Ethical thought in eighteenth-century France paralleled developments in Great Britain, although the French philosophers failed to establish as strong traditions as their British contemporaries. French thought subsequent to the eighteenth century added little to moral philosophy as compared with that of Germany and Great Britain. Due to their intense involvement in political issues, the French writers placed rhetorical effectiveness above clarity and consistency as a standard of philosophical value.

Voltaire (François-Marie Arouet, 1694–1778) and Jean-Jacques Rousseau (1712–1778) led the revolt against Cartesian rationalism as well as against political and religious superstition, so transforming philosophy into ideology that *idéologue* became a popular French synonym for *philosophe*. Voltaire employed acid satire in attacking religious and philosophical obscurantism in *Candide,*

Zadig, and his *Philosophical Dictionary,* while Rousseau inaugurated the romantic style of soul-stirring emotional intensity, in place of detached analysis and rigorous argument. Denis Diderot (1713–1784) raised philosophical writing to the highest level of literary grace and subtlety since Plato, criticizing conventional morality and religious beliefs in his remarkable essay-novels *Le neveu de Rameau, Jacques le fataliste,* and *Rêve de d'Alembert.* Yet while appreciating their extraordinary intellectual qualities and the permanence of their place in Western culture, it must be noted that they provided few new concepts and principles on which later ethical philosophers could build.

Rousseau. Rousseau's celebrated exaltation of untutored human nature in his two *Discourses* attributed genial and cooperative tendencies to man's innate disposition and aggressively self-serving tendencies to the harmful influence of civilization. This coincided with the British moral-sense theorists' attacks on Hobbesian egoism. However, unlike Hume (his friend and benefactor prior to their notorious public quarrel), Rousseau considered custom and law to be arbitrary restraints on natural impulses rather than rational methods of channeling self-interest toward the common good. Whatever justification can be given for control of the individual by social institutions lay, for Rousseau, in their claim to represent the "general will," that is, the desires of the majority, independently of whether what is so desired is good. While Rousseau argued forcefully, in *The Social Contract,* for popular sovereignty and the right of revolution, he justified the use by the state of extremely repressive measures, such as the death penalty for atheism. His rather mystical notion of the state as the embodiment of the general will helped to inspire the overthrow in France of absolute monarchy in favor of representative government, yet half a century later it was employed by Johann Gottlieb Fichte, and a century after that by V. I. Lenin, in the justification of authoritarianism.

Although Rousseau's religious mysticism and his preference for feeling over rational prudence were contrary to the general tone of the Enlightenment, his most lasting contribution to ethical philosophy was his insistence that good and evil tendencies are due to social causes, a principle that he shared with baron de Montesquieu, Voltaire, and the Encylopedists. The soundness of this principle is subject to question, but there can be no doubt that it served as a useful guide in the reform of social institutions.

Montesquieu. Charles Louis de Secondat, baron de la Brède et de Montesquieu (1689–1755), in *The Spirit of the Laws* founded the relativistic conception of moral and political principles as grounded in the traditions of particular societies. The "spirit of the laws" is the system of social practices in relation to which new laws are to be evaluated. Western European governments require a division of functions and compensating checks and balances to fulfill the partly republican, partly monarchical values of European society. In treating values as historical and sociological facts, rather than as divine principles or natural laws, Montesquieu developed further the scientific approach to ethics and politics begun by Machiavelli and Hobbes.

The Encyclopedists. Denis Diderot, Claude-Adrien Helvétius (1715–1771), and baron d'Holbach (1723–1789) derived, from a materialistic theory of nature, an ethical view based on the self-centered pursuit of pleasure as the sole rational motive for action. A well-ordered society, on their view, is one in which the pursuit of personal well-being is unhindered by social authority. Insofar as there are conflicts between morality and self-interest, these are due to defects of social organization and perverse education, rather than to the moral defects of individuals. These Encyclopedists, and kindred spirits in other countries, such as the Italian legal philosopher Cesare Bonesana Beccaria, employed utilitarian moral theory in political campaigns for representative government and humane laws and punishments.

KANT AND THE GERMAN ENLIGHTENMENT. The Enlightenment attack on tradition and authority in favor of individual reason took a nonutilitarian form in the philosophy of Immanuel Kant (1724–1804). The utilitarians identified reason with practical intelligence in the pursuit of happiness. Kant, however, inherited the Cartesian and Leibnizian conception of reason as the intellectual recognition of abstract truths. In fashioning an ethical theory that became the main rival of utilitarianism, Kant combined the Augustinian emphasis, revived by Butler, Price, and Reid, on the internal sense of moral obligation with the rationalistic ideal of knowledge as a deductive system. In his *Critique of Pure Reason,* he attempted to show that the laws of science are imposed by the mind on the objects of its perceptions and can thus be known with certainty through reflection on the a priori structure of knowledge. In his *Critique of Practical Reason* he applied the same analysis to ethics, founding morality on the a priori laws with which "practical reason" regulates action. While Kant defended religious faith against the utilitarian freethinkers, he shared their view that ethics is independent of theology, and he followed the deistic tradition of interpreting God as a scientific and ethical ideal, rather than as a supernatural source of revelation and authority.

In his most influential work on ethics, *The Foundations of the Metaphysics of Morals*, Kant made the most thorough attempt by any philosopher to clarify and explain the difference between ethical principles and laws of nature. The difference lies both in our subjective sense of obligation to obey moral laws, as contrasted with laws of nature, toward which we feel no such obligation, and in the practical—that is, prescriptive—meaning of moral laws, in contrast with the "theoretical"—that is, descriptive—meaning of laws of nature. In virtue of this difference, moral rules are expressed in the imperative mood and laws of nature in the declarative mood. To account for this disparity, Kant distinguished two realms of knowledge dealing with two metaphysically distinct subject matters. Natural science, including scientific psychology, formulates laws of nature that the mind imposes on the objects of perception in accordance with the principle of causal determinism. Ethics articulates the "laws of freedom" that a rational being imposes on his own actions and expects other rational beings to recognize and obey. The justification for these rules lies in the logical fact that to be rational means to act in accordance with general rules and that moral rules are those which can be followed consistently by all rational beings. Thus, insofar as man is moral, he is rational and, in this sense, free; insofar as he is immoral, he is an irrational slave to his natural inclinations. The reward of virtue is not happiness but dignity and freedom.

Moral virtue: The supreme good. Kant's system of ethics is built on three pillars: the examination of the facts of moral experience, the analysis of the logic of ethical judgment, and the formulation of the metaphysical principles presupposed by ethical judgments, as distinct from scientific generalizations. In the first part of the *Foundations* Kant argues, like Reid, that commonsense reflection, uncorrupted by the dialectics of philosophers, informs us with unwavering certainty that duty is distinct from pleasure and utility, that moral virtue or "good will" is the supreme good to which all other values are subordinate, and that moral worth is not measured either by the consequences of a person's actions or by his natural benevolence but by the agent's intention to obey moral laws.

Categorical imperatives. In the second section of the *Foundations,* Kant attempts to explain the distinctive character of moral laws by clarifying the logical differences between three types of rules or imperatives: technical "rules of skill," prudential "counsels" as to how to achieve happiness, and moral duties. The first two, he

argues, are "hypothetical imperatives" whose directives are contingent on the desires of the agent. Naturalistic ethics mistakes counsels of prudence for moral laws because the desire for happiness is so universal that directives toward this end have the superficial appearance of unconditional laws. But the generalization that all men seek happiness is a law of nature, not a rule commanding action, and the very possibility of a moral code entails that this psychological generalization is subject to exception. For moral duty requires that the agent sacrifice his personal happiness and even the welfare of his community rather than violate a "categorical imperative."

A moral or genuinely categorical imperative is a rule that commands a type of action independently of any desired end, including happiness. Kant accepts the utilitarian account of hypothetical imperatives but argues that the peculiar obligatoriness of moral principles can be explained only by their unrestricted universality and thus by their independence of any facts of human nature or circumstance. It is not in virtue of what satisfies human needs, but in virtue of the demand of reason that action be in accordance with universal law, that we feel obligated to obey moral principles.

Universalizability criterion. To the question of whether any rule of action can qualify as a moral principle, Kant's answer was in the negative. He maintained that there is one general or "fundamental" categorical imperative from which all specific moral duties can be derived: "Act only on that maxim which you can will to be a universal law." All maxims or specific rules of conduct can be judged morally right or wrong according to this general criterion. If universal obedience to a proposed rule would contradict the very purpose of the rule, as is the case for rules that under certain circumstances permit lying, stealing, or taking life (somewhat inconsistently, Kant approved of capital punishment), then the rule cannot be part of a true moral code. In contrast, a rule such as "Do not make false promises" can in principle be followed without exception and thus qualifies as a moral duty.

This criterion of universalizability, that is, the logical or psychological possibility of requiring universal obedience to a rule of action (logical for "strict" duties and psychological for "meritorious" duties), was undoubtedly Kant's most original and important contribution to ethical theory. It expresses more precisely and unambiguously the "golden rule" to be found in all the great religions, and it has been incorporated, in one form or another, in most modern systems of ethical theory. Countless writers since Kant have attempted to reformulate the criterion of universalizability in a way sufficiently qualified to avoid reasonable objections, but without complete success.

The obvious objection to Kant's formulation is that no one would want any specific rule of action to be followed without exception. No one would want the truth to be told on occasions when unmitigated harm would result—for example, when a murderer demands to know where his intended victim is hiding. Kant's own reply to this objection is that, while one may not be psychologically inclined to tell the truth on such occasions, there is no logical contradiction in willing—that is, commanding—that it be told, come what may.

A second objection is that Kant assumes, for any rule of action, that either it or its negation must be a moral law, and yet there are few rules, if any, which we would care to have followed universally in either positive or negative form. Kant argues that, since it would be self-defeating to will that every person may make false promises when it suits his purposes, we ought to will that false promises never be made. Yet on the same reasoning one could justify all sorts of absurd laws, such as that everyone at all times wear heavy clothing, since we would not and could not will the universal prohibition of heavy clothing.

A third weakness of Kant's theory is that it provides no grounds for deciding what is right in a situation where apparent moral duties collide and one must be sacrificed in favor of another. With respect to this problem, utilitarianism seems clearly superior to Kantian ethics.

Autonomy of the will. The third part of Kant's ethical theory consists in the metaphysical account of the rational will as a source of action outside the sphere of causal determinism and thus not an object of scientific investigation. The autonomy of the will—that is, the capacity to obey laws of its own conception in defiance of natural causes—is, Kant argues, a necessary presupposition of any moral code. For if all actions were necessary effects of natural causes, then moral evaluation would be pointless. *Ought* implies *can*, that is, the obligation to do what is right entails the ability to do it and the ability not to do it. Since science rests on the regulative principle of universal determinism, there can be no scientific proof of freedom of the will. But this only shows the radical difference between science and ethics and the folly of attempting to derive ethics from psychology. Man as an object of scientific inquiry is an organic phenomenon obeying laws of biology and psychology. But man as an object of ethical evaluation is a noumenal being, free to obey or disobey the dictates of practical reason. From this dual conception of man as both inside and outside

nature, Kant derives an ideal way of life impressive in its purity and its faith in human perfectibility. Man as a rational agent is a member of a "kingdom of ends" in which he is both subject and sovereign, legislating for himself and for others. The highest goal of human life is to realize this ideal "kingdom" in individual and social practice.

NINETEENTH-CENTURY ETHICS

Nineteenth-century ethical thought became a battleground for two rival traditions. Utilitarianism, stemming from Locke, Hume, and the French Encyclopedists, dominated British and French philosophy, while idealistic ethics was supreme in Germany and Italy. Both traditions took root in the United States, with idealism appealing to the religious vision of Ralph Waldo Emerson and Josiah Royce, while utilitarianism answered to the developing faith in technology that found philosophical expression toward the end of the century in the pragmatic ethics of James and John Dewey.

UTILITARIANISM. Christian ethics based on divine authority and natural law was given a utilitarian interpretation by William Paley (1743–1805) in his *Principles of Moral and Political Philosophy.* The source of moral obligation, he agreed with Hobbes, lies in the "violent motive resulting from the command of another," while the ground of goodness is pleasure or utility. But moral duty and self-interest coincide because God, as the paramount authority, commands us through the Scriptures and the promptings of conscience to seek the general good as well as our own happiness. Moral obligation is supported both by natural pleasure in the welfare of others and by the fear of divine punishment that provides the selfish but rational person with a good reason to sacrifice his pleasure for the common good. Paley's psychological account of morality, like that of earlier moral-sense theories, failed to explain why anyone who lacks natural benevolence ought to have it. His alternative justification of morality in terms of the fear of divine punishment equally fails to explain why such punishment would be just and why a nonbenevolent nonbeliever in Christian theology can nevertheless be expected to behave morally.

Bentham. The mainstream of utilitarian thought was anticlerical. Jeremy Bentham (1748–1832) and James Mill (1773–1836) formed a political movement that helped bring about legislative reforms by criticizing social institutions in terms of their utility in producing "the greatest happiness for the greatest number." In his influential *Introduction to the Principles of Morals and Legislation,*

Bentham formulated a theory of ethics and jurisprudence remarkable for its clarity and consistency. The great appeal of Bentham's theory lay in its apparent simplicity and ease of application, although these virtues may have been more apparent than real. Bentham attempted to make ethics and politics scientifically verifiable disciplines by formulating quantitative standards of evaluation. He began with the psychological generalization that all actions are motivated by the desire for pleasure and the fear of pain: "Nature hath placed mankind under the governance of two sovereign masters, *pain* and *pleasure*. It is for them alone to point out what we ought to do, as well as to determine what we shall do. On the one hand the standard of right and wrong, on the other the chain of causes and effects, are fastened to their throne" (*Principles*, London, 1823, p. 1). From this equation between ethical obligation and psychological necessity, Bentham derived the general principle of utility that "approves or disapproves of every action whatsoever, according to the tendency which it appears to have to augment or diminish the happiness of the party whose interest is in question," happiness being understood as the predominance of pleasure over pain.

The most original but also the most dubious part of Bentham's theory is his "hedonic calculus" for measuring pleasures and pains, in computing the overall value of alternative policies. If such a procedure were feasible, ethical judgments would be as scientific as meteorological forecasts, even though both are subject to considerable error, due to the complexity of the factors involved. But Bentham's ideal of a science of ethics runs afoul of two internal difficulties, the resistance of pleasure to measurement and the impossibility of predicting the long-range consequences of actions. Aside from these internal defects, there remains the general objection that pleasure, unlike pain, is not a bodily sensation but a favorable response to an object grounded on the perception of value in the object, as Thomas Reid had argued. To conclude that an object is good from the fact that it pleases us involves the circular reasoning that it is good because it is judged to be good, a principle too vacuous to provide a guide to ethical judgment. If, on the other hand, pleasure is understood in a more narrow, technical sense as desirable bodily sensations, then Bentham's identification of happiness and welfare with pleasure is unacceptable because it reduces human experience to the level of animal existence. The plausibility of Bentham's theory may be due to the ease with which he shifts inadvertently from one of these senses of *pleasure* to the other.

Despite its theoretical defects, Benthamite utilitarianism, which was more socially oriented than that of Locke and Hume, had a salutary effect on social legislation. His analysis of pleasures into factors of intensity, duration, propinquity, certainty, fecundity, and "extent" (number of persons affected) offered reasonable criteria by which alternative social programs and laws can be evaluated and was a marked improvement over the sanctification of existing laws and customs by which Hobbes, Locke, and Hume had made the transition from self-interest to morality. But there is a missing link in Bentham's chain of reasoning that may not be reparable within the confines of his hedonistic psychology, namely, the link that should connect the desire for one's own pleasure with the willingness to consider "extent" or pleasure of others in deciding on a course of action. Is desire for the pleasure of others also a "sovereign master under which nature hath placed us?" If so, then desire for one's own pleasure cannot be sovereign as well. If not, then on what ground are we required to consider the factor of extent?

Mill. John Stuart Mill (1806–1873) recognized the defects in Bentham's formulation of utilitarianism, and in his essay "Utilitarianism" he offered a more sophisticated version that sought to incorporate the moral insights of rival ethical systems. Realizing that Bentham's emphasis on quantitative aspects of pleasure reduces pleasure to bodily sensation and tends to justify an uncultivated mode of life, Mill proposed a new factor by which pleasures could be compared, the factor of quality. Some pleasurable experiences, notably intellectual, aesthetic, and moral achievements, are qualitatively superior to the satisfaction of bodily needs: "Better to be Socrates unsatisfied than to be a fool satisfied." But like Epicurus's preference for "natural" over "unnatural" pleasures, Mill's criterion of quality introduces a standard of value other than pleasure, by which pleasure itself can be evaluated, and thus contradicts the principle of utility, that pleasure is the single standard of good.

Mill also tried to make room in utilitarian theory for the appreciation of the saintly virtues, renunciation and self-sacrifice, by arguing along Humean lines that such virtues are originally valued for their social utility but that we later become attached to them for their own sake, and that this psychological shift from appreciation of virtue as a social instrument to admiration of virtue for itself is a good tendency because it, too, is socially useful. For the appreciation of moral qualities independently of their immediate consequences ensures the social reliability of the agent and, in the long run, produces more good than harm. This utilitarian defense of moral principles rested on an optimistic belief in the generally beneficial tendencies of man. In applying it to political theory, Mill argued for democratic institutions, minimum state interference in social life, and free economic competition. Assuming a general convergence of individual and social benefit, Mill, like Hume and Bentham, left unanswered the question why, in cases of conflict, one *ought* to place public over private interest and confined himself to explaining why we admire the person who does so. Yet if the social utility of moral self-sacrifice is the only rational ground for favorable judgment of it, then it would seem to follow that each of us has reason to approve of self-sacrifice in others but not in himself. If the step from individual happiness to the greatest good for the greatest number is justified only by the long-range coincidence of the two, then whenever we are assured that they will not coincide, we have no reason to prefer public welfare to our own other than the irrational habit of doing so, a habit that, in such case, it would be wise to break. In Kantian terms, utilitarianism, even in Mill's sophisticated version, fails to provide a logical bridge between inclination and obligation, between *is* and *ought*.

Later intuitionists, beginning with Henry Sidgwick, attempted to supply this bridge by combining the Kantian theory of rational duty with the utilitarian theory of value, maintaining that we are intuitively aware of the duty to obey moral principles at the expense of self-interest but that moral principles, in turn, are justified by their utility in promoting the common good.

IDEALIST ETHICS. Kant's distinction between man as noumenon, legislating and obeying "laws of freedom," and man as phenomenon, governed by laws of nature, was incorporated into new ethical systems by later German idealists, who assimilated the phenomenal side of the distinction to a part of the noumenal side, making natural science subordinate to ethics. Johann Gottlieb Fichte (1762–1814) extended the noumenal will into a universal force that creates the material world out of its own force and expresses itself partially in the free rational will of the individual conscience but more fully in social institutions and laws. The individual thus achieves self-realization in identifying himself with the universal will and voluntarily accepting his *Beruf* (vocation) as part of the social order.

Fichte. In his early work *Wissenschaftslehre* (*Theory of Science,* 1794) Fichte enlarged Kant's ethical concept of man into a metaphysical picture of the universe. Rejecting Kant's notion of things-in-themselves, Fichte reduced reality to the projections of an absolute mind, and he reduced mind itself to will. The criterion of reality became a practical one: That is real which it is right or good to believe and to act upon (the beginning of pragmatism). Fichte went even further than Kant in stressing moral duty as the goal of life. Kant had sharply separated duty from self-interest in criticizing positions of the kind later referred to as utilitarianism, but Fichte moved full circle by reidentifying moral duty with a higher form of self-interest, the self-realization of an absolute will of which each person is a temporary embodiment. The logical problem created by Fichte's voluntaristic idealism is caused by the fact that it begins with Kant's primacy of moral good over prudential good but concludes with a form of supernatural utilitarianism in which prudential good of a higher self reappears as the ground of morality.

Fichte explained the function of the state as the regulation of conflicts among individuals in protection of their natural rights, and on this basis he supported democratic government. But he advanced the view, later elaborated by Hegel, that governmental restraints on individual action are not limitations of personal freedom but expressions of the higher freedom of the absolute will.

In *The Vocation of Man* (1800) Fichte, who had been accused of atheism, developed a less rationalistic and more religious view of human life. He identified the absolute will with the personal God of Christianity and moral duty with the vocation imposed on man by God. In his later *Addresses to the German Nation* (1808) he applied his notion of divinely ordained vocation to the German nation, which he claimed was destined to raise civilization to a higher level. The evolution of Fichte's thought from austere moralism to religious mysticism and then to chauvinistic nationalism provides an instructive example of the lengths to which thought can go in denying the basic distinctions from which it begins, such as that between self-interest and moral duty or between individual rights and social restraints.

Hegel. G. W. F. Hegel (1770–1831) developed Fichte's social basis of ethics further and in more historical terms. For Hegel value, morality, and law are among the highest forms of self-realization of absolute spirit. The Enlightenment doctrine of abstract rights is only the first stage in the development of ethical consciousness. A higher stage is reached in the Kantian sense of moral duty, which recognizes the conflict between individual rights and social responsibilities, subordinating the former to the latter. But the highest stage of self-realization of "objective mind" involves the incorporation of rights and duties in a rational system of social and political institutions which the individual citizen recognizes as the embodiment of the national will. The perfect freedom that consists in rational self-determination is achieved when individual conscience coincides with custom and law, so that will and reason, subjective motivation and objective necessity, become identical. But this is possible, according to Hegel, only in the modern age of the national state, Christian conscience, and constitutional law. In earlier stages of human history, whatever was necessary for historical progress was, for that age, necessary and therefore right, as, for example, the institution of slavery was necessary and right in ancient Greece. "World history," he declared, "is world justice."

POST-HEGELIAN THEORIES. The impact of Darwin's theory of natural evolution produced naturalistic echoes of Hegelian historical relativism in the utilitarian "survival of the fittest" doctrine of Herbert Spencer (1820–1903), the Marxist philosophy of class conflict, and the cultural elitism of Nietzsche.

Marx. Karl Marx (1818–1883) transformed Hegel's theory of the dialectical self-realization of mind into a doctrine of dialectical development of history through class conflict. In the Marxist theory, moral principles represent the sanctification of the interests of the ruling class at each stage in the development of progressively superior modes of economic organization. Marx criticized both utilitarian and Kantian ethics as variant expressions of bourgeois marketplace procedures. Subordinating rules of individual conduct to the historical imperatives of "revolutionary praxis," the *Communist Manifesto* of Marx and Friedrich Engels called for revolutionary action to achieve a classless society in which "the free development of each is the condition for the free development of all," a society that would require neither the internal repressions of conscience nor the external repressions of laws and punishments. Both morality and the state would "wither away."

Schopenhauer. Arthur Schopenhauer (1788–1860), like Fichte, located the source of both egoistic pursuit of pleasure and moral obligation in the universal will. The morality of equal rights for all represents a higher development of consciousness than that of self-interest, but a still higher stage is reached in the philosophical understanding that the will, in any form, produces illusion and suffering and that the extinction of desire is the only salvation. Schopenhauer gave the Stoic and Buddhist ethic of ascetic renunciation an idealistic metaphysical basis.

Kierkegaard. Søren Kierkegaard (1813–1855) rejected the rationalistic and socially oriented ethic of Hegel in favor of religious individualism. While, like Hegel, he regarded the conflict between self-interest (the "aesthetic attitude") and duty (the "ethical attitude") as reconciled and transcended in a higher stage of consciousness, he denied that this stage could be achieved by reason and described it as a "leap of faith" preceded by tragic anguish. As the contemporary existentialists who have rediscovered Kierkegaard have put it, "The world is absurd" because there are no objective grounds for human decisions. What is right, according to Kierkegaard, is what the individual asserts with the total commitment born of faith, but it is right only for him. Emotional authenticity rather than conformity to rules is the proper guide to action.

Nietzsche. Friedrich Nietzsche (1844–1900) proposed a less mystical but equally individualistic transcendence of moral codes. Like Hobbes and Mandeville, he regarded altruism as contrary to natural impulse and denounced moral restraint as a device created by religion to contravene the natural order of dominance of the strong over the weak. The true source of value lies in the creative self-assertion of the artist and the man of genius who produce new and positive forms of good, while moral prohibitions produce only resentment, envy, and dull conformity.

American developments. In the United States, the transcendentalists, led by Ralph Waldo Emerson (1803–1882) and the pragmatic idealist Josiah Royce (1855–1916), fashioned still other variations on the idealist theme of self-realization as the goal of human life. The transcendentalists identified the self with the creative force of nature, the "oversoul." Royce, following Hegel, defined the fully realized self as a unity of personal and community interests. All of these post-Hegelian philosophies rejected the Kantian morality of strict adherence to general rules of conduct and proposed ways of transcending the conflict between duty and self-interest through a higher mode of consciousness in which the conflict allegedly disappears.

Toward the end of the nineteenth century, William James (1842–1910) and John Dewey (1859–1952) developed the philosophy of pragmatism, in which all of human knowledge is regarded as essentially ethical. They rejected both the Kantian separation of ethics from natural science and the traditional conception of scientific knowledge as disinterested contemplation of value-neutral truths. The split between value and fact was bridged by reinterpreting both so that they became indistinguishable. James combined utilitarianism with a creative individualism similar to that of Nietzsche and the pre-scriptivism of Hobbes, by identifying the source of value with the human act of making a claim, thus bestowing value on the object claimed. Ethical judgment is a rational process of determining by empirical investigation which policies are likely to satisfy the maximum number of such claims. James defended the indeterminist concept of free will, criticizing what he called the soft determinism of Hume and Mill as a purely verbal escape from the embarrassing consequences of scientific determinism.

BRITISH IDEALISM AND INTUITIONISM. In the last quarter of the nineteenth century the vitality of idealism began to attract even the sober British intellect, and the ethics of self-realization became a powerful rival to utilitarianism through the influence of Thomas Hill Green, Bernard Bosanquet, and F. H. Bradley.

Green. Thomas Hill Green (1836–1882) introduced Oxford students to the lofty vision of idealist metaphysics. In his *Prolegomena to Ethics* (published posthumously) Green derived liberal ethical and political principles from his conception of the individual self as part of a universal and divine self. He criticized both utilitarianism and moral-sense theories for downgrading the role of reason in moral judgment and for reducing human motives to natural causes. A motive, he argued, is a goal previsioned by a rational consciousness, not an event or process in the body. Value is therefore logically prior to desire rather than a product of desire. One can desire or find pleasure only in what one has judged to be good. The source of evil must therefore be found in defects of the understanding, in the failure of the human mind to realize its identity with the universal mind. The highest good is thus as much an object of self-interest as any other, but it is the kind of self-interest that also constitutes morality.

Green was active in social and political controversies, supporting the North in the American Civil War and supporting liberal legislation in England. Green rejected laissez-faire individualism, insisting on the more positive role of government in promoting social welfare.

Green's ethical theory was sharply criticized by Sidgwick in *The Ethics of Green, Spencer and Martineau* (1902). Sidgwick argued that Green's identification of morality with higher self-interest obliterates the all-important distinction between prudence and duty and thus fails to provide a basis for moral responsibility, a defect that, as we have seen, goes all the way back to Plato.

Bosanquet. Bernard Bosanquet (1848–1923), like Green, grounded ethics and politics on idealist metaphysics. Bosanquet stressed somewhat more than Green the uniqueness of individual values while at the same time taking a Hegelian view of the state as the embodiment of objective mind. Like Green, Bosanquet actively supported liberal political causes.

Bradley. Francis H. Bradley (1846–1924), generally considered the most distinguished ethical theorist among the British idealists, criticized both utilitarianism and Kantian formalism and favored a Hegelian conception of the community as an organic unity whose needs, expressed in social institutions, transcend those of individual citizens, a conception that he applied in the defense of conservative social policies. Bradley was probably more consistent than Green and Bosanquet. If law and custom are the expression of a higher self, then only internal inconsistencies can justify reforms, and individual rights are subordinate to group or national interests. In his *Ethical Studies* (1876) Bradley supported retributive punishment on the ground (which he held to be self-evident to common sense) that punishment is unfair unless it is deserved and that moral desert is independent of social utility. He attempted to reconcile freedom with causal determinism in the notion of an all-encompassing Reality that determines itself in accordance with rational laws. Recognizing that idealism faces the problem of accounting for evil and that its traditional solution—claiming that evil does not exist—is contrary to the judgment of common sense on which Bradley himself always relied, he employed a subtle distinction between existence and reality in holding that evil, though it exists, is unreal. From the standpoint of the totality of knowledge, evil may be seen to contribute to cosmic harmony. This "solution" was later castigated by Bertrand Russell as a morally untenable justification of evil.

Sidgwick. Henry Sidgwick (1838–1900) combined the social utilitarianism of Mill with the intuitionism of Butler and Kant. In *The Methods of Ethics* (1875), a work described by C. D. Broad as "the best treatise on Moral Philosophy that has ever been written," Sidgwick raised ethical analysis to a new level of precision and logical rigor. Setting aside practical moralizing as not the business of objective philosophical analysis, Sidgwick interpreted the task of moral philosophy to be the clarification of the logic of moral judgment, a conception of philosophy that was continued by the contemporary British school of linguistic analysis.

Sidgwick held that there are just three approaches to ethics worth philosophical consideration: egoistic hedonism, utilitarianism, and intuitionism. He pointed out that neither the self-centered ethics of Hobbes and the French Encyclopedists nor the socially oriented ethics of Bentham and Mill can justify the step from psychology to ethics, that is, from the description of human motivation to judgments of moral obligation. Even those who declare that one ought to pursue one's own interests must justify their use of *ought,* and this cannot be done on the grounds of psychological facts alone. Sidgwick therefore insisted on distinguishing psychological hedonism from ethical hedonism and grounding the latter on intuition. His argument is reminiscent of Hume's claim that values cannot be deduced from facts, and it anticipates G. E. Moore's later analysis of the "naturalistic fallacy."

All three "methods of ethics" rest, according to Sidgwick, on principles held to be self-evident, and thus intuitionism is, to some extent, inescapable. The egoist must assume the self-evident rightness of pursuing one's own pleasure, and the social utilitarian must assume the rightness of maximizing the common good. Intuitionists differ from utilitarians and egoists only in holding many principles and duties to be self-evident as well, and thus they expose themselves to inevitable counterinstances. The more numerous and specific the rules claimed to be self-evident, the more subject to exception and vulnerable to disproof. Sidgwick concludes that social utilitarianism offers the correct standard of moral judgment but that this standard is in turn grounded on direct awareness of moral obligation. Thus at least one, and probably at most one, moral intuition is essential for moral judgment.

Sidgwick could not finally decide between the conflicting claims of self-interest and social utility. He leaned toward the latter as definitive of moral duty, but he recognized that one's self-interest rightly carries a special weight, other things being equal. Perhaps he would have been able to reconcile these two "intuitions" more easily had he considered utilitarianism in a somewhat weaker form, as the principle that one ought always to refrain from causing unnecessary suffering, rather than the stronger claim that one ought always to aim at maximizing happiness. For while one's own welfare seems naturally to outweigh that of others, it is very close to being self-evident to any morally sensitive person that he ought not to pursue his interests at the cost of substantial suffering to others.

It would appear from our brief glance over the history of ethics through the nineteenth century that philosophers failed to find any conclusive ethical truths and merely argued, more persuasively and with a more impressive display of learning than most, for whatever way of life and standards of conduct they happened to prefer. In some respects this impression would be justified, and it serves to remind us of the differences between scientific knowledge and ethical wisdom. The perennial character of the problems, the lack of general agreement on proposed solutions, and the return of later doctrines to principles advanced by earlier ones all contrast strikingly with the irreversible progress of scientific discovery. It has been suggested by some contemporary philosophers that the endless disputability of ethical issues is rooted in the very nature of ethical language, so that it is not a defect of philosophy to have failed to achieve general agreement on ethics. As W. B. Gallie put it (*Philosophy and the Historical Understanding,* New York, 1964), ethical concepts are "essentially contestable." It is essential to their meaning that they evoke continual disputes as to the correct standards for their application. But if we cannot find historical progress in the form of final settlement of issues, we can at least discern some degree of gradual, if irregular, advance toward greater clarity in the formulation of the issues.

On the central issue of the logical relation between facts and values, ethical theories have provided increasingly clear and sophisticated statements of two fundamental positions, naturalism and nonnaturalism (sometimes called teleology and deontology). Naturalistic theories relate values to facts by defining "good" and related concepts in terms of observable criteria, such as fulfillment of natural tendencies (Aristotle), satisfaction of desire (Hobbes and Spinoza), production of pleasure for the greatest number (utilitarianism), conduciveness to historical progress (Spencer and Marx), or efficiency of means to ends (Dewey). Nonnaturalistic theories stress the fact that the meaning of ethical terms goes beyond the observable facts on which ethical judgments are grounded, and they locate the additional component of meaning outside nature. Plato located it in a realm of abstract Forms, Christianity in the will of God, the intuitionists in the direct recognition of the quality of rightness, the moral-sense theorists in the feeling of approbation. Each of these accounts of value and moral right has revealed an additional dimension of the complex logic of ethical judgment. Naturalistic theories have brought to light various ways in which ethical judgment is grounded on the fulfillment of biological and social needs, while nonnaturalistic theories have revealed prescriptive aspects of moral concepts that are independent of prudential considerations. The main effort of twentieth-century ethical philosophy was to weave together in a consistent pattern all the threads, both naturalistic and nonnaturalistic, that constitute our philosophical heritage.

CONTEMPORARY NONNATURALISM

In much of the English-speaking world G. E. Moore's *Principia Ethica* (Cambridge, U.K., 1903) is taken to be the starting point of contemporary ethical theory. But it is important to recognize that this primacy is to a considerable degree local and distinctive of the tradition of analytical ethics. On the Continent and in Latin America the work of Max Scheler and Franz Brentano has been a preeminent influence. For much of American thought until about the mid-twentieth century, the work of John Dewey or Ralph Barton Perry provided the starting point. But, for all that, it is reasonable to begin with G. E. Moore.

MOORE. It is the critical side of Moore's work in ethics that has had the most lasting effect. His delineation of the subject matter of ethics and his very careful effort to show that any form of ethical naturalism involves a fundamental conceptual mistake—the work of the first three chapters of *Principia Ethica*—has been the part of Moore's work that has deeply affected contemporary ethical thought. However, Moore's own positive nonnaturalistic cognitivism, with its reliance on nonnatural characteristics, has found few adherents. Most philosophers—C. L. Stevenson and R. M. Hare are typical—who have been convinced that in essence Moore's case against naturalism is sound have not followed Moore's lead but have adopted some form of noncognitivism.

It was Moore's belief that if moral philosophers simply interest themselves in good conduct, they are not really starting at the beginning, for we cannot know what good conduct is until we know what goodness is. Moore's concern was with a "general enquiry into what is good." Our first question must be "What is good and what is bad?" Such knowledge of good and evil, Moore claims, is the "goal of ethical investigation"; but, he stresses, "it cannot be safely attempted at the beginning of our studies, but only at the end." First we must consider how "good" is to be defined.

Moore clearly is not interested in giving a stipulative definition of "good," and from his disclaimers in *Principia Ethica* about being interested in a merely verbal point, it would seem that he is not interested in a lexical definition either. What he is after, in seeking a definition of "good," is just this: what property or set of properties is common to and distinctive of anything that could conceivably be properly called intrinsically good, for instance, "answering to interests." Moore thinks "good" stands for a prop-

erty, and he seeks to determine what it is. Moore's answer, which he is aware will cause discontent, is that "good" is not definable. All we can finally say correctly is that good is good and not anything else. "Good," like "red," is, in the appropriate sense, indefinable. Good is a simple, unanalyzable, nonnatural characteristic. We are either directly aware of it or we are not, but there is no way of defining it or analyzing it so as to make it intelligible to someone who is not directly aware of it.

Such a radical claim on Moore's part would have little force if he could not thoroughly refute naturalistic and metaphysical theories that do purport to give the kind of characterization of intrinsic goodness that he takes to be impossible.

Moore's case against naturalism. Let us consider Moore's case against ethical naturalism. An ethical naturalist holds that moral judgments are true or false empirical statements ascribing an empirical property or set of properties to an action, object, or person. "Good" is defined in terms of this property or set of properties. But, Moore argues, we will not come to know what good is simply by "discovering what are those other properties belonging to all things which are good." Those who commit what Moore calls the naturalistic fallacy think that when they have "named those other properties they were actually defining good; that these properties, in fact, were simply not 'other,' but absolutely and entirely the same with goodness." But to identify good with any other property is to commit the naturalistic fallacy. The naturalists confuse the question of the meaning of the concept of good with the quite different question of what kinds of things are good.

In a famous argument, which has been dubbed the open-question argument, Moore points out that for whatever naturalistic value we substitute for the variable x in a proposed definition of "good," we can always significantly ask if it is good. If a man says "Happiness is good," or "Self-realization is good," or "The object of any interest is good," we can always significantly ask "Is happiness good?," "Is self-realization good?," "Is the object of any interest good?" Even though we agree, let us say, that happiness is good, it is an evident fact of language that these questions are not without significance. But they would be without significance if "good" did mean "happiness," or "self-realization," or "the object of any interest," just as it is pointless to ask if a father is a male parent or a puppy is a young dog. For whatever naturalistic definitions we offer—whatever naturalistic values replace the variable x—it always makes sense to ask if that thing is good. Since this is so, these naturalistic definitions can be seen to be inadequate.

This can be seen in another way as well. If a statement like "The satisfaction of desire is good" were a definition of the sort Moore was searching for, it would be analytic and it would be self-contradictory to assert "This satisfies desire but it is not good." For whatever naturalistic definition one proposes, however, one can assert without self-contradiction "This is *x* but it is not good," but if *x* meant the same as "good" this would be impossible, for "*X* is good" would then be analytic. But since this is possible it is clear that the proposed statement is synthetic.

Moore's influence. The above arguments of Moore's, together with his famous argument in Chapter 3 of *Principia Ethica* against Mill's alleged naturalism, have provided the background for much of the controversy in contemporary ethical theory. While few have accepted all the details of Moore's case against ethical naturalism, it has been felt by many that Moore's essential case is well taken. R. M. Hare in his *The Language of Morals* (Oxford, 1952), P. H. Nowell-Smith in his *Ethics* (Harmondsworth, U.K., 1954), and A. C. Ewing in his *Second Thoughts in Moral Philosophy* (London, 1959) try to restate these Moorean insights in such a way as to present a decisive case against ethical naturalism.

It should be noted, however, that the reception of Moore's case against naturalism, even on the part of such eminent nonnaturalists as A. N. Prior and E. W. Hall, has not been that favorable. It is generally thought now that (1) the naturalistic fallacy is not, strictly speaking, a fallacy but is at best a mistake and (2) that it is not really distinctive of naturalism but should be called the definist fallacy, that is, the belief that moral terms are capable of definition in nonmoral terms.

Criticisms of Moore. It is easy to see that someone, though at a certain price, could be a consistent ethical naturalist and that Moore's naturalistic fallacy would not really point to anything necessarily fallacious in such a naturalist's reasoning. An ethical naturalist who is also a hedonist could argue: By "intrinsic good" I am just going to mean "pleasure." This is a stipulative definition on my part and I am making no claim that it squares with ordinary usage, but it will give a clear and consistent definition of "good" that fits well with my preanalytic insight that pleasure and pleasure alone is intrinsically good. It is indeed true that on my theory "Pleasure is good" is a tautology and "Is pleasure intrinsically good?" is a self-answering question. Still, there is a normatively vital question that I can and do ask with perfect conceptual propriety. The vital open question is this: Should an indi-

vidual seek pleasure and only pleasure as the thing that, morally speaking, he ought always to do? If a man takes this position, Moore's arguments, given above, do not show anything fallacious in his thinking, that is, he has committed no formal or informal fallacy, though it can be shown by some additions to Moore's arguments that he has said something that is mistaken.

There is a further criticism of Moore that can be made with considerable plausibility. Though it is indeed true that *good* taken in isolation cannot be defined, the term *good* is in reality always used in specific contexts, with context-dependent meanings and with such riders as "good at" and "good for." But in such a context *good* can be defined. "A good car," "good teacher," "good at ballet," or even "good man" can be naturalistically defined, even though *good* sans phrase cannot. Finally, and perhaps most importantly, it has been pointed out that the open-question and noncontradiction arguments are not conclusive. At best they show why all the naturalistic definitions hitherto proposed do not work. They do not show that naturalistic definitions are impossible.

DEONTOLOGICAL NONNATURALISTS. There are other nonnaturalists who, while holding cognitive meta-ethical theories, reject Moore's ideal utilitarianism. Moore thought that Bentham and Mill were mistaken in trying to define *good* naturalistically, but that they were not mistaken in regarding good as the fundamental moral concept and were not mistaken in arguing that it is always our duty to seek to bring the greatest total good possible into being. H. A. Prichard, W. D. Ross, E. F. Carritt, and C. D. Broad all agree with Moore that intrinsic good is a unique, nonnatural quality that is indefinable and can only be known directly. But they reject Moore's claim that *right* means "productive of the greatest possible good." *Right*, they argue, is also sui generis; it is not reducible to *good* or to any teleological concept. To say "This is a right act" means, according to Ross, "This act ought to be done." Furthermore, even what makes an act right is not to be completely determined by teleological concepts. An act, even though it may be productive, everything considered, of the best consequences, may still not be the right thing to do. Even Broad, who makes the most concessions to the utilitarians of any of the deontologists (as they are called), argues that in determining what is suitable to the actual situation, we must consider both the total fittingness of the events that are relevant to the act in question and the utilities in question, and then without any precise measure of what is suitable to the situation, we must decide what we are to do. The utilitarians, including

Moore, the deontologists agree, oversimplify the situation here.

In 1909 H. A. Prichard, in his celebrated article "Does Moral Philosophy Rest on a Mistake?," set forth in perceptive but uncompromising form the deontological position. But it is W. D. Ross, taking Prichard's position as a starting point, who has been the most influential of these deontological nonnaturalists. Ross's *The Right and the Good* (Oxford, 1930) and his *Foundations of Ethics* (Oxford, 1939) present the classical statement of these views.

Prichard. In "Does Moral Philosophy Rest on a Mistake?" Prichard argued that it was an endemic mistake of moral philosophy to try to give reasons for our obligations. Moral obligation cannot be reduced to acts that ought to be done because by doing them, more good is likely to result than by doing any alternative act. We do not, Prichard contended, come to appreciate an obligation by argument, but in a particular situation we are either directly aware of what it is we ought to do or we are not. Moral philosophy cannot justify these obligations; it can only (1) help us to come to understand the nature of this immediate type of awareness and (2) help us to see through the confused attempts to exhibit the "truly rational foundations" of these obligations by showing how they are grounded in human interests.

Ross. Ross accepted the Prichardian belief that we have an intuitive insight into our obligations, but he went on from certain hints in Prichard to develop a concept of prima-facie duty. A prima-facie duty is a conditional duty of a very distinctive kind. What is meant by saying that it is "conditional" is that it is something that always would be an actual duty were it not for the fact that in certain circumstances there are more stringent moral considerations that outweigh it. But prima-facie duties are always actual duties unless such conditions obtain. Ross takes it as "self-evident that a promise, simply as such, is something that prima facie ought to be kept, and it does not, on reflection, seem self-evident that production of the maximum good is the only thing that makes an act obligatory." Like John Cook Wilson and Prichard before him, Ross takes as his data "the moral convictions of thoughtful and well-educated people." They serve as his point of departure and his check on all theorizing concerning morals.

Reasoning from this base, Ross can show that we do not always reason as utilitarian moralists would have us reason. We often have duties of special obligation that conflict with the utilitarian principle that we should always maximize good. If we carefully attend to the data of ethics—our actual moral experiences—we will note that we have prima-facie duties to fidelity, reparation, gratitude, justice, beneficence, nonmaleficence, and self-improvement. Some of these prima-facie duties are more binding than others. *Ceteris paribus,* the duty of nonmaleficence outweighs our obligation to keep a promise. But Ross stresses—as does Broad—that it is not always the case that we have a rule, a general principle, for deciding what to do when there is a conflict in prima-facie duties. Sometimes we simply have to appreciate or come to "see" what is suitable to the situation.

Criticisms of deontology. Many, though by no means all, philosophers would agree that the deontologists have shown that moral reasoning is not as simple as the classical utilitarians took it to be. But it has been thought by many that consequences play a far larger role in determining what makes an act right than the deontologists have been willing to admit. Their rather antiquated epistemology of intuitions, synthetic a priori judgments, and so forth, and their misleading use of mathematical analogies have stood in the way of an acceptance of deontology. It is, however, quite feasible to argue that such appeals are not essential to a deontological view.

It has also been repeatedly argued that a deontological position, with its list of prima-facie duties and its appeal to the convictions of the thoughtful and the well-educated, is thoroughly ethnocentric. To these objections it is reasonable to reply that most of Ross's prima-facie duties are very similar to the kind of generalities that the anthropologists Ralph Linton and Robert Redfield (among others) have claimed to be cross-culturally sanctioned "universal values." Moreover, the appeal to thoughtful and well-educated people surely need not and should not limit itself to people in one cultural circle.

Rather more important criticisms of deontology have been that it gives us no criteria for deciding what laws, practices, rules, or institutions are worthy of our acceptance. Here the kind of quasi-utilitarian reasoning concerning practices characteristic of the good-reasons approach seems to have decided advantage.

Ewing. It should be mentioned that A. C. Ewing in two closely reasoned books, *The Definition of Good* (New York, 1947) and *Second Thoughts in Moral Philosophy* (London, 1959), works out a theory that in many respects tries to find a middle ground between Moore and Ross. Ewing takes *ought* as his fundamental term, and in the second work he makes far more concessions to the naturalists and noncognitivists than in the first, without abandoning what he takes to be the core of his nonnaturalism.

PHENOMENOLOGICAL VIEWS. Moore, Ross, Broad, and Ewing are not the only nonnaturalists and intuitionists who have exerted a considerable influence on contemporary ethical thought. During a roughly comparable period, Franz Brentano, Nicolai Hartmann, and Max Scheler had a comparable influence on the Continent.

It is necessary to mention that in contemporary philosophical thought there is a fundamental cleavage that divides the English-speaking and Scandinavian countries, on the one hand, from the Continent, Latin America, and the Near East and Far East, on the other. In these latter areas of the world the influence, either direct or indirect, of the philosophers so far discussed has been slight, while the influence in intellectual circles of the philosophers to be discussed in this section and in the section on existentialism has been considerable. Even though Moore, Ross, and Ewing opposed empiricism, their techniques remained analytical, while the work of the philosophers about to be discussed is philosophy in the grand manner; that is, it is comparatively speculative and metaphysical.

Brentano. Franz Brentano's *The Origin of Our Knowledge of Right and Wrong* (Leipzig, 1889) and his later *Grundlegung und Aufbau der Ethik* (F. Mayer-Hillebrand, ed., Bern, 1952) mark the beginning of contemporary Continental ethical theory. In 1903 G. E. Moore remarked that Brentano's work more closely resembled his own than that of any writer with whom he was acquainted. Like Moore, Brentano rejected naturalistic definitions of ethical terms, regarded fundamental moral concepts as sui generis, and thought judgments of intrinsic value incapable of being proved.

To gain an adequate understanding of Brentano's ethical theory, it is essential to understand the rudiments of what he called descriptive psychology (the latter, in Edmund Husserl's hands, was to become phenomenology). Brentano classified mental phenomena into three fundamental classes: ideas and sensory presentations (images and the like), judgments, and emotions. That is to say, there are three fundamental ways in which one may be intentionally related to something. One may simply think of it, one may take an intellectual stance toward it by either accepting it or rejecting it, or one may take an emotional or attitudinal posture toward it. To do the last is a matter of loving or hating it. (Brentano, of course, uses *love* and *hate* here in a very stretched manner.) Brentano regarded emotions as intentional; he maintained that "certain feelings refer unmistakably to objects and language itself signifies this through expressions that make use of it." Moreover, emotions, like judgments but

unlike ideas, can properly be called either correct or incorrect. In this way Brentano differed radically from the emotivists.

How do we decide whether a given emotion is correct or incorrect? Here Brentano, who like Ross was a careful student of Aristotle, was very Aristotelian. We can come to understand what a correct emotion or, for that matter, a correct judgment is only by contrasting actual cases of emotions and judgments taken to be correct by experienced and thoughtful people with cases that are not so regarded.

To say that something is good—where we are talking about "intrinsic good"—is to say that it is impossible to love it incorrectly. To say that something is intrinsically evil is to say that it is impossible correctly to love whatever is in question. "Good" and "evil" are what Brentano called synsemantic terms: They do not refer to concrete particular things, either physical or mental. But such ethical concepts were, on Brentano's view, objective because of the impossibility of loving correctly whatever is hated correctly and of hating correctly whatever is loved correctly. The truth of these fundamental moral judgments is directly evident to the mature moral agent. Any question about the empirical evidence for them is as impossible as it is unnecessary.

Scheler. Max Scheler attempted to apply Husserl's phenomenological method to moral concepts. His major works in ethics, *Formalism in Ethics and the Ethics of Intrinsic Value* (Halle, 1916) and *The Nature of Sympathy* (Bonn, 1923), are among his earlier writings (*The Nature of Sympathy* is simply a second and enlarged edition of the early *Zur Phänomenologie und Theorie der Sympathiegefühle*, Halle, 1913); but his later work in philosophical anthropology, *The Forms of Knowledge and Society* (Leipzig, 1926), also has important implications for his ethical theory.

Scheler's ethics is best understood by setting it in relation to that of Kant. Scheler accepted Kant's critique of naturalistic and utilitarian ethical theories. But while he took the categorical imperative as pointing to an essential feature of morality, he thought that such Kantian formalism was incomplete. Like Husserl, Scheler believed that Kant was mistaken in limiting the a priori to the purely formal. The phenomenological method shows that we have a *Wesensschau* (an intuition of essences) in virtue of which we know certain fundamental a priori but nevertheless nonformal moral truths, such as "Spiritual values have a higher place in the scale of values than vital values, and the Holy a higher place than the spiritual."

Given this very extended sense of "a priori," it is correct to say, according to Scheler, that there are objective nonformal moral judgments which are universal, necessary, and synthetic. These moral judgments are said to have an intrinsic content that is given in our intuition of essences.

Scheler argued that there is a hierarchy of objective values, all open to our intuitive inspection. There is, he would argue, nothing subjective about this ordering. In the hierarchy of values phenomenologically given to man, we have at the top religious values, then cultural values (aesthetic, speculative, scientific, and political), and finally, at the bottom, material values (useful things, things that satisfy needs, desires, etc.). All of these values are thought to have an ethical dimension. Questions concerning moral obligation arise when there is a conflict of values. Moral obligation is that which binds us, in such a situation, to take as the order of our incentives the values as they are ordered in the value hierarchy. Scheler was, however, sufficiently Kantian to believe that the ultimate ground of moral obligation lay not in the consequences of moral acts but in the intentions of moral agents. To someone who has studied Mill, Sidgwick, or Ross, this seems like a plain confusion between the moral "grades" we would give a person and an objective consideration of what acts are morally right.

There is another aspect of Scheler's moral theory that should be mentioned, namely, his claim that love and sympathy are the sole means by which we gain an intuitive insight into moral reality. Like Brentano, he thought that these feelings had intentional objects, and like Blaise Pascal, he thought that there was a "logic of the heart"—that through the feelings we gain a type of cognition into essential value structures that can be had in no other way.

Hartmann. Nicolai Hartmann's massive work *Ethics* was published in Berlin in 1926. It shows the influence of Scheler and Husserl and is without doubt the most extensive phenomenological discussion of value in the literature. Ethics, for Hartmann, is part of a general theory of value, though, as might be expected, ethical values are the highest values. "Value" for Hartmann, as for Scheler, is a general predicate, and under it there are more specific predicates for determinate values, for instance, "beauty" is to "value" as "red" is to "colored." Values are said to be essences, and we have a direct though emotionally tinged intuition of essences. Being essences, values, like numbers, are thought by Hartmann to have an ideal self-existence (*Ansichsein*). But unlike numbers, values have a "material essence."

Like Scheler, Hartmann believes that if we will but attend patiently to our feelings, we will be able to discern, though vaguely, some hierarchical ordering of those things that are valuable. Putting aside as far as possible our theoretical preconceptions concerning values, we should reflect carefully on our actual experience until we achieve a clear and evident insight into value phenomena. This, of course, is a desideratum that will never be completely achieved, for "morally no age entirely comprehends itself." The real ethical life is "a life deeper than consciousness." But there is a capacity on the part of the human animal to appreciate the valuable, and by ever more carefully attending to this, we can attain both a clearer view and a more purified form of the moral life.

Though values are material essences, they are not, as in Plato, identical with being. Hartmann, no more than Moore or Jean-Paul Sartre, will identify what is good or what has worth with what exists. That would destroy the autonomy of ethics and obscure the nature of value. But although values are independent of existence, they are related to existence by a "tendency to reality" that Hartmann calls the ideal Ought-to-Be. We have many different values, but it always remains the case that values ought to be. The criteria for what is good or for what is valuable vary from context to context, but the ought-to-be remains the same: "The ideal Ought-to-Be is the formal condition of value, the value is the material condition of the Ought-to-Be." In contrast with the ideal Ought-to-Be there is the more practical, more directly morally relevant "Ought-to-Do." Here "ought" implies "can," and here practical moral questions arise about making something the case that is not the case.

More recent developments in Germany. Finally, a brief note is in order about more recent developments in ethics among German philosophers. Martin Heidegger, whose influence is completely overshadowing in Germany, took a dim view not only of the relevance of logic to philosophy but also of philosophical ethics. This has impeded systematic work in ethics in Germany, but nonetheless it is going on. There has been a reaction against the work of Scheler and Hartmann. O. F. Bollnow has argued for a *Situationsethik* and Richard Schattländer has contended that the Scheler-Hartmann approach is too speculative and theoretical and does not adequately handle the moral agent's question: What ought I to do? But the Scheler-Hartmann school is hardly dead, for Hans Reiner, in his *Das Prinzip von Gut und Böse* (Freiburg, 1949), gives us a detailed and vigorous restatement of such a position. Against Heidegger, he defends the philosophical importance of a general theory of value. But in an effort to blunt Heidegger's criticism that such investigations are morally and humanly irrelevant, Reiner concerns himself primarily with moral values. In his concern with moral value, he examines in some detail the problem of ethical relativism, and in this examination he stresses the importance of anthropological investigations to our understanding of morality.

NATURALISM IN AMERICA

While ethical naturalism seemed to have received its quietus in England from Moore and Ross and certainly could not be considered a major force on the Continent, in America in various forms it was, until shortly after World War II, the dominant form of ethical theory.

PERRY. R. B. Perry developed a general theory of value with specific applications to questions of normative ethics, law, politics, economics, and education in his *General Theory of Value* (Cambridge, MA, 1926) and *Realms of Value* (Cambridge, MA, 1954). "Value" is used by Perry in a very broad sense as a generic term to group together such terms as *desirable, good, worthwhile, right, beautiful, holy, obligatory,* and the like. Perry defines *value* as follows: "a thing—anything—has value, or is valuable, in the original and generic sense when it is the object of an interest—any interest." In an attempt to make his contention overtly verifiable, Perry in turn defined *interest* quasi behavioristically as "a train of events determined by expectation of its outcome." *Interest* for Perry was an umbrella term for such terms as *like, desire, preference,* and *need* and their opposites. For something to have positive value, it must be an object of a favorable interest; for something to have negative value, it must be an object of aversion, disapproval, or dislike: In short, it must be an object of negative interest.

It should be understood that this definition of *value* is not taken by Perry to be either a lexical or a purely stipulative definition. It is, rather, a reforming definition. That is to say, it is a deliberate proposal concerning the use of a term in the language, but the proposal is not simply a stipulation, for it has some antecedent basis in the usage in question. It is proposed that this use be adopted as the standard use in order to clear up what are taken to be confusions allegedly resulting from unclear and vacillating usage. By such maneuvers Perry hoped to escape from Moore's arguments concerning the naturalistic fallacy.

Such a theory, initially at least, is extremely attractive, for it holds out a promise for a genuine "normative science" and thus for some objective, if not absolute, knowledge of good and evil. It holds out the promise that we will eventually use the emerging sciences of man to gain some cross-cultural and interpersonally confirmed, and thus objective, knowledge of right and wrong.

The crucial problem for the naturalist is to show how all statements containing ethical terms can be translated into statements that do not contain such terms and are directly or indirectly confirmable or disconfirmable by empirical observation. What must be achieved to develop such a naturalism is to show the tenability of some set of naturalistic definitions of key moral terms.

Working from his initial definition of "value," Perry developed his system from the following definitions:

(1) "*X* has value" equals "*X* is the object of any interest."

(2) "*X* is bad" equals "*X* has negative value."

(3) "*X* is good" equals "*X* has positive value."

(4) "*X* is intrinsically good" equals "*X* is the object of a favorable interest for its own sake."

(5) "*X* is extrinsically good" equals "*X* is the object of a favorable interest because *X*, directly or indirectly, is the most efficient means to something which is intrinsically good."

(6) "*X* is morally good" equals "*X* is the object of interests harmoniously organized by reflective agreement."

(7) "*X* is the highest good" equals "*X* is the object of an all-inclusive and harmonious system of interests."

(8) "*X* is morally right" equals "*X* is conducive to the moral good."

(9) "*X* is morally obligatory" equals "*X* is a social demand that, of any alternative demand, is most clearly called for by the ideal of harmonious happiness."

A theory based on these definitions should, Perry would argue, provide us with a systematic account of our normative concepts and exhibit the rationale of our moral judgments. However, it would be queried by many, including many who are not intuitionists, just how it can be that all moral statements are really a subspecies of empirical statement and how they all could, even in principle, be empirically confirmed or disconfirmed. To take moral statements as empirical statements asserting that so-and-so is the case seems to miss their distinctive, dynamic, and guiding function in the stream of life.

DEWEY. For John Dewey, moral philosophy had a definite normative ethical function. Dewey wanted to criticize normative standards and hoped to indicate more reasonable moral goals. "Philosophy's central problem," he wrote, "is the relation that exists between the beliefs about the nature of things due to natural science and beliefs about values—using that word to designate whatever is taken to have rightful authority in the direction of conduct."

His basic proposal was that we should use what he called experimental intelligence in morals. This means that in moral inquiry we should use the same methodological principles we use in scientific inquiry. We should develop a scientific critique of our institutions and of the patterns of conduct designated "moral." In order to do this we must show the untenability of what Dewey took to be an unjustified but ancient philosophical preconception that injects a divorce or dichotomy between scientific knowledge, on the one hand, and moral, philosophical, or religious knowledge, on the other. There is but one kind of knowledge, with one reliable method of fixing belief, the experimental method, though this knowledge and method of fixing belief must be applied to different subject matters.

To most people, the use of the experimental method in ethics heralds a drop of any normative ethical standards. In trying to establish that this is a misconception, Dewey tried to establish a severe contextualism. A central mistake of traditional moral philosophies, both naturalist and nonnaturalist, was that of looking for one bedrock *summum bonum* or one ultimate moral criterion rather than realizing that there is an irreducible plurality of moral standards and that moral problems are fully intelligible and rationally resolvable only in a definite context. Moral standards are a part of a cultural context in which means and ends are qualitatively continuous and functionally interactive.

This reference to a continuum of means and ends leads to another main element in Dewey's moral philosophy. He argues against the specialist's conception of ethics. To hold this conception, which is traditional with philosophers as different as Plato and Russell, is to stress the distinction between intrinsic good and instrumental good and to contend that intrinsic good is the sole object of philosophical interest. This, according to Dewey, is a mistaken dichotomy rooted in the ancient Greek dichotomy between theory and practice. It is not only intellectually bankrupt but it can, Dewey argues, have vicious social consequences. It even makes for irrationalism in ethics, for given this conception, we are easily led to the assumption that while science can deal with mundane instrumental goods, the highest goods—the basic ends, namely, intrinsic goods—must be grasped by intuition, be vouchsafed by revelation, or be merely a matter of the whims of mortal will. Dewey argued that in concrete moral contexts, answers concerning means actually transform ends. In reasoning morally it is not a matter of discovering the most efficient means to attain a fixed end. If in considering the means it becomes apparent that our ends are utopian, we will, if we are behaving rationally, often give them up or modify them in view of this discovery. Here intelligence has a major role to play in morality. Ends cannot rationally be divorced from means. In fact, they are always functionally interactive. Furthermore, what is an end in one problematic situation is a means in another, and so on. There are never any actual normative goals or ends that are simply intrinsic goods. Ideals are always transformable in the light of what we discover about our world, and they are always imbedded in a network of other ideals.

Such considerations, it will surely be objected, hardly show that there are no intrinsic goods—but it could be contended that they effectively argue against Aristotelian final ends, or against the belief that in moral appraisal we can justifiably consider intrinsic goods independently of their consequences—and this, after all, is the major point Dewey wanted to establish.

Here we hardly have the metaethical concerns that are so distinctive of the work of Moore and Perry. But Dewey—though he did not call it that—also had a metaethical theory.

Dewey argued that moral judgments are judgments of practice. That is to say, they are made in problematic situations of choice in which a moral agent is trying to decide what to do. This gives them their distinctive normative or de jure force. But at the same time they remain de facto empirical statements. It is this puzzling amalgam that we must understand if we are to get clear what Dewey was claiming.

Dewey asserted that value judgments are not mere prizings and disprizings. They are predictions about the capacity or incapacity of actions, objects, or events to satisfy desires, needs, and interests. As such they are confirmable and disconfirmable. They predict that certain ends in view will satisfy certain vital impulses under certain conditions. Not everything that is desired is desirable, but those things which are desired "after examination of the relations upon which the object depends" are desirable. In short, to say of something that it is valuable, desirable, or good is to say that it is something which would be desired or approved after reflection upon its relevant causes and consequences.

Criticism of Dewey. Dewey's theory has been subject to some trenchant criticisms by Morton White and Charles Stevenson and has been staunchly defended by Sidney Hook, Gail Kennedy, and Gertrude Ezorsky. The basic considerations here are as follows: Even if *X* is desired after an examination of the causes and consequences of desiring *X*, it still does not follow that *X* is desirable or that *X* ought to be desired. However, to carry out Dewey's program of identifying moral statements as a subspecies of empirical statement, some such identity of meaning must be established.

But the admission that Dewey is wrong in claiming that moral statements are empirical statements or hypotheses is not destructive to his overall program about the place of reason in ethics. If we ask how we justify our ethical evaluations, it seems that much of Dewey's method of criticism, including much of his use of science, could still be reasonably instituted. Dewey's great failure in talking about morality was in not realizing how very different "values" and "facts" are; his great success was in seeing the extensive relevance of scientific knowledge and scientific method to the making of intelligent moral appraisals.

CONTEMPORARY NONCOGNITIVISM

Both naturalism and nonnaturalism are cognitive theories. That is to say, they regard moral utterances in the declarative form as statement-making utterances that assert the existence of certain moral facts and are thus either true or false. But first in Sweden, and later in England and America, a quite different kind of metaethical theory developed that has been called a noncognitive theory. According to this theory, moral statements do not assert moral facts; they are neither confirmable nor disconfirmable, and there is nothing to be known by "moral intuition." It is even characteristic of this view to argue that it is either mistaken or at least misleading to characterize moral utterances as true or false.

EMOTIVE THEORY. The noncognitive view, which has subsequently been called the emotive theory, received its first formulation in 1911, when the Swedish philosopher Axel Hägerström drew the outlines of such a theory in his inaugural lecture, "On the Truth of Moral Propositions." In 1917 Hägerström developed his ideas with particular attention to the concept of duty in his *Till Frågan om den Gällande Rättens Begrepp* (Uppsala, 1917). Similar statements of the emotive theory have been developed in

Scandinavia by Ingmar Hedenius and Alf Ross. Independently of its Scandinavian formulation, the emotive theory was first stated in the English-speaking world by I. A. Richards and by Bertrand Russell, but it was developed in the Anglo-Saxon world by A. J. Ayer and by Charles Stevenson. There have also been interesting if somewhat atypical statements of it by Richard Robinson, Rudolf Carnap, and Hans Reichenbach.

The emotivists were convinced that moral statements are not a subspecies of factual statement, and they were further convinced that it was impossible to derive a moral statement from a set of purely factual statements. As Hägerström put it, "There is no common genus for the purely factual and the 'ought.' By using the predicate 'ought to happen' we refer an action to an altogether different category from the factual. That an action 'ought to be done' is regarded as something which holds true altogether without reference to whether it actually is done or not." The whole notion that there is a determinate character of an action that would make a moral statement true or false is, Hägerström argues, an illusion. There is nothing there for an "unmoved spectator of the actual" to observe that would either confirm or disconfirm his moral statements. Moral statements characteristically take a declarative form, but they actually function not to assert that so-and-so is true but to express an attitude toward an action or a state of affairs.

The emotive theory developed as a *via media* between intuitionism, on the one hand, and ethical naturalism, on the other. Both of these ethical theories displayed crucial difficulties. "Nonnatural qualities" and "nonnatural relations" were obscure, fantastic conceptions, to say the least, and the notion of intuition remained at best nonexplanatory. Furthermore, it was plain that moral judgments are closely linked to one's emotions, attitudes, and conations. But, as Moore in effect showed, neither "A cup of tea before bed is good" nor such general utterances as "Pleasure is good" and "Self-realization is good" are empirical or analytic.

The function of ethical statements. The emotivists maintained that while the grammatical function of a sentence like "A swim before bed is good" is indicative, its actual logical function is much closer to that of an optative or imperative utterance, such as "Would that we could go swimming before bed" or "Swim before bed." Because of this, emotivists have claimed that it is misleading to say that ethical sentences can be used to make statements: They do not function to assert facts.

Similarly, it is a mistake to treat all words as simply functioning to describe or designate some characteristic or thing. Some words so function; but there are other words, like *nasty, saintly, graceful,* and *wise,* that function primarily or in part to express the attitudes of the utterer or to evoke reactions on the part of the hearer. The emotivists claim that *good, ought, right,* and the like are also emotive words. This gives them their normative function.

Ethical argument. Hägerström and Ayer contend that the fact that there are no moral facts carries with it the corollary that there can be no genuine moral knowledge. There are no moral facts to be learned; there is no moral information to be gained or forgotten. It makes clear sense to say "I used to know the difference between a pickerel and a pike, but by now I've forgotten it," but what is meant by "I used to know the difference between right and wrong, but by now I've forgotten it"? The word *forgotten* could hardly do its usual job here. The utterance is so deviant that without explanation and a very special context, we do not understand it. Considerations of this sort bring us to the realization that moral utterances are not used to state facts or assert truths; their essential role is a noncognitive one. They typically express emotions, attitudes, and conations and evoke actions, attitudes, and emotional reactions.

Because of this fact about the logical status of moral utterances, it always remains at least logically possible that two or more people might agree about all the relevant facts and disagree in attitude—that is, disagree about what was desirable or worth doing.

We do, however, as Ayer and Stevenson stress, give reasons for moral judgments. If I say "MacDonald did the right thing in killing Janet," it is perfectly in order to ask me to show why this is so. If I say "I don't have any reasons. There aren't any reasons, but all the same I just know that MacDonald did the right thing," I am abusing language. I am saying something unintelligible, for we cannot "just know" like that. The person who claims that an action is right must always be prepared to give reasons for his moral claim.

Ayer and Stevenson grant all that. This is indeed how we do proceed when we are being reasonable about a moral disagreement. But Ayer says: "the question is: in what way do these reasons support the moral judgments? They do not support them in a logical sense. Ethical argument is not formal demonstration. And they do not support them in a scientific sense either. If they did, the goodness or badness of the situation, the rightness or wrongness of the action, would have to be something apart from the situation, something independently verifiable, for which the facts adduced as the reasons for the moral judgment were the evidence." But this is just what

we cannot do. There is no procedure for examining the value of the facts, as distinct from examining the facts themselves.

If we cannot demonstratively prove or inductively establish fundamental moral claims, then what can it mean to say that a factual statement *F* is a good reason for a moral judgment *E*? The emotivist's answer is very simple: If *F* causes the person(s) to whom *E* is addressed to adopt *E*, to share the attitude expressed by *E*, then *F* is a good reason for *E*. It is Ayer's and Stevenson's claim that whatever in fact determines our attitudes is ipso facto a good reason for a moral judgment.

Criticisms of emotive theory. It has been argued by many moral philosophers (W. D. Falk, Richard Brandt, Errol Bedford, Paul Edwards, and Kai Nielsen, among others) that so to characterize what is meant by "a good reason" in ethics is persuasively to redefine "a good reason" in ethics. As Bedford has well argued against the emotive theory, "we do use logical criteria in moral discussion, however inexplicit, unanalyzed, and relatively vague these criteria of relevance may be." Remarks like "It doesn't follow that you ought to" or "That's beside the point" are just as common and just as much to the point in moral argument as elsewhere. There is no reason to think that these remarks about relevance differ in any essential way from their use in nonevaluative contexts. We don't just seek agreement when there is a moral dispute, but we try to justify one claim over another and we rightly reject persuasion as irrelevant to this task of justification.

Stevenson has replied that to answer in this way is in effect to confuse normative ethical inquiries with metaethical ones. *Good* and *relevant* are normative terms and have their distinctive emotive force. To say that such and such are good reasons is to make a moral statement. Making such a statement involves leaving the normative ethical neutrality of metaethical inquiry. One answer to this is that to say what is meant by "good reasons" in ethics is to mention "good reasons" and not to use them.

EXISTENTIALISM. Noncognitivism is not limited to emotivism. The existentialists do not call themselves noncognitivists, nor do they write metaethical treatises. But reasonably definite metaethical assumptions are implicit in their writings. Their contention that "men create their values," their stress on decision, commitment, and the impossibility of achieving ethical knowledge, strongly suggests a noncognitivist metaethic. We shall limit the examination here to two major figures, Albert Camus and Jean-Paul Sartre.

Camus. Unlike Sartre, Albert Camus wrote no technical philosophy, but in his *Myth of Sisyphus* (Paris, 1942), *The Rebel* (Paris, 1951), and his plays and novels he did articulate an ethical view that has been called the ethics of the absurd. To read Camus is to be immediately thrown into normative ethics via what has been called philosophical anthropology. We are immediately confronted with a picture of man and man's lot. Man is divorced from the world yet is paradoxically thrust into it. The world as we find it—given our hopes, our expectations, our ideals—is intractable. It is incommensurate with our moral and intellectual demands. Life is fragmented. We seek to discover some rational unity amidst this diversity and chaos. We discover instead that we can only impose an arbitrary unity upon it. *L'homme absurde,* as distinct from *l'homme quotidien,* sees clearly the relativity and flux of human commitment and the ultimate purposelessness of life. Yet man has a blind but overpowering attachment to life as something more powerful than any of the world's ills or any human intellectualization. But the world is ultimately unintelligible and irrational, and man's lot in the world is absurd.

Given this situation, all moral commitments are arbitrary. There is no escaping this: Reason will only show us the arbitrariness of human valuations, and a Kierkegaardian leap of faith in the face of the absurd is evasive. It is evasive because it is to consent to absurdity rather than to face up to it, recognizing it for what it is. Man's dignity comes in his refusing to compromise. His very humanity is displayed in his holding on to his intelligence and in recognizing, contra Kierkegaard, that there is no God and, contra Karl Jaspers, that there is no metaphysical unity that can overcome the absurdity of human existence.

Yet paradoxically, and some would claim inconsistently, in his novel *The Plague* (Paris, 1947), and in his essays, collected and published in English under the title *Resistance, Rebellion and Death* (New York, 1961) Camus writes with passion and conviction in defense of human freedom and intelligence. Camus's rationale for this is that we become *engagé* because we see that life has no ultimate meaning and that, finally free from a search for cosmic significance, we can take the diverse experiences of life for what they are in all their richness and variety. Yet beyond that and perhaps because of that, Camus, as a humanist, is espousing the cause of man. By this is meant, as is very evident in *Resistance, Rebellion and Death,* that Camus repeatedly defends human freedom, equality, and the alleviation of human misery and deprivation. We must become involved, but in this involvement Camus urges a reliance on human intelligence in facing the problems of men.

What might be taken to be a conflict between the more theoretical side of Camus's thought and his more directly normative ethical side comes out in his fourth "Letter to a German Friend." Camus agrees with his "German friend" that the world has no ultimate meaning, but he does not and will not conclude from this, as his "German friend" did, "that everything was equivalent and that good and evil could be defined according to one's wishes." Camus then goes on to remark that he can find no valid argument to answer such a nihilism. His only "answer" is "a fierce love of justice, which after all, seemed to me as unreasonable as the most sudden passion." Camus felt he could only resolutely refuse to accept despair and "to fight against eternal injustice, create happiness in order to protest against the universe of unhappiness." Camus concludes with a cry of the heart that while "the world has no ultimate meaning … something in it has a meaning, namely man because he is the only creature to insist on having one."

Sartre. Jean-Paul Sartre's views on man's condition are in many important respects like those of Camus, but to a far greater degree than Camus, Sartre in *Being and Nothingness* (Paris, 1943) and *Critique de la raison dialectique* (Paris, 1960) sets his ethical theorizing in the murky atmosphere of metaphysics. The promised systematic work on ethics that was to follow *Being and Nothingness* has not been forthcoming, but in one way or another all of Sartre's works are concerned with ethics. It can be said that there are two Sartres, or at least that the Sartre of *Critique de la raison dialectique* has moved from his earlier existentialism over to a kind of Marxist materialism. Here we shall for the most part (except where specifically noted) be concerned with the earlier Sartre, whose philosophical endeavor centered on his massive *Being and Nothingness.*

Sartre, like Camus, finds man's lot in the world absurd. Since there is no God, life can have no ultimate meaning and there can be no objective knowledge of good and evil. We cannot "decide a priori," or find out by investigation, what we are to do. Man in his forlornness and freedom imposes values. The choices man makes, the projects he forms for himself, and the sum of his acts constitute his values. There is no good and evil to be intuited or in any way discovered by the human animal. Man in anguish creates his values by his deliberate choices, and, to add to his anguish, in making his choices "he involves all mankind." That is to say, Sartre stresses the Kantian claim that moral judgments, in order to be moral judgments, must be universalizable, but, as Sartre adds in his lecture "Existentialism Is a Humanism" (1945), though their "form is universal ... the content of ethics is variable" and there is no rational way of justifying the acceptance of moral principles with one content rather than another.

Sartre thinks this position is simply a matter of drawing out in a nonevasive manner the implications of a consistent atheism. Only if there were a God could values have an objective justification, but without God "everything is permissible" and "as a result man is forlorn, because neither within him nor without does he find anything to cling to." In this, Sartre is surely mistaken. It does not follow that if there is no God, nothing matters, or that everything is permissible. It is not a contradiction to assert, "Though there is no God, the torturing of children is still vile," and the nonexistence of God does not preclude the possibility of there being an objective standard on which to base such judgments.

Sartre asserts flatly, in good Moorean spirit, "Ontology itself cannot formulate ethical precepts. It is concerned solely with what is, and we cannot possibly derive imperatives from ontology's indicatives." (All the same, his account of morality in *Being and Nothingness* and his account of human action relevant to morality are immersed in "the language of being.") In fact, Sartre goes on to point out that ontology and what he calls existential psychoanalysis can in a given situation constitute "a moral description, for it presents to us the ethical meaning of various human projects." This method of description—though hardly the descriptions themselves—is very like the phenomenological method practiced by Scheler and Hartmann. Yet to proceed in this way hardly constitutes a violation of the is/ought distinction, since Sartre's descriptions of moral evaluations—descriptions of man's ethical life—need not themselves be evaluative, though given the language Sartre uses, they often are.

"Man," he tells us, "pursues being blindly by hiding from himself the free project which is this pursuit." Existential psychoanalysis can reveal to man the real goal of his pursuit. Horrified by the "death of God," man attempts in his anguish to be God. He flees from his freedom—he does not wish to be a creator of values—but in what Sartre ironically calls the spirit of seriousness, he seeks to deny human subjectivity and attributes to value some independent cosmic significance. To the extent that we are caught up in this spirit of seriousness, we will try to fuse "being-for-it-self" with the brute facticity of "being-in-itself." (The odd phrase "being-in-itself" is simply the label for the self-contained reality of a thing,

while its mate, "being-for-itself," is the label for the realm of consciousness that perpetually strives to transcend itself.) But if we pursue this line, we still condemned to despair, for we "discover at the same time that all human activities are equivalent ... and that all are on principle doomed to failure." Phenomenological analysis reveals to man that though he perpetually tries to become a thing, a brute existent, the fact that he has consciousness makes this impossible. Given this ability to think and to feel, man, whether he likes it or not, is slowly led to see that without God he can have no essential nature; that is, though he may form his own projects, there is and can be no purpose to life.

It should be noted that Sartre's view of man's lot is even grimmer than Camus's, for Sartre contends that even in community with others there is no surcease from suffering and alienation, for human relations are essentially relations of conflict and estrangement.

In *Critique de la raison dialectique*, Sartre tries to work out a new kind of Marxism and a new materialist conception of man. But he wishes to integrate his existentialist conceptions into a Marxist materialism in such a way that the latter can come to have a truly "human dimension." Marxism, he argues, must purge itself of its deterministic conceptions of man and acknowledge a rational conception of human freedom. Sartre, in a reversal from *Being and Nothingness*, now argues that there is nothing intrinsic in human nature that makes conflict, war, and a reign of terror inescapable, though, like a good Marxist, he does argue that conflict is a basic factor in human history. It is scarcity, scarcity of goods and materials, that triggers human conflict. Only under these conditions of scarcity is social conflict inescapable and a rational social order impossible. Men make their own history by the choices they make in the face of problems created by history. But man remains the rider, not the horse. Human choices—human projects—are still free choices for which men remain responsible.

RECENT VIEWS ON MORAL DISCOURSE

LINGUISTIC PHILOSOPHY. As has frequently been noted, there are at least superficial resemblances between the existentialists and the otherwise very different, self-consciously metaethical theories of such linguistic philosophers as R. M. Hare, P. H. Nowell-Smith, Bernard Mayo, Alan Montefiore, and John Hartland-Swann.

There is, indeed, this much similarity between these linguistic philosophers and the existentialists. All of the former make the following contentions, all of which would be welcome to the latter:

(1) Moore was essentially right about the naturalistic fallacy. That is to say, moral statements cannot be deduced from any statement of fact, whether biological, historical, psychological, sociological, or religious.

(2) No moral choice or question of value can ever be guaranteed by logical rules.

(3) We are free, as far as language or logic is concerned, to apply evaluative or prescriptive terms to anything we wish to commend or condemn, criticize or approve, prescribe or forbid.

(4) Moral utterances are generalizable decisions, resolutions, or subscriptions.

Given that a man accepts certain moral principles, other moral principles can, together with certain factual statements, be derived from the above principles. But like Ayer and the existentialists, these linguistic philosophers hold that there must be some moral principles which are not derived from any other principles—moral or otherwise—and, being fundamental moral principles, they are not even verifiable in principle. They express moral commitments and can have no rational ground, for what is deemed worthy of acceptance ultimately depends on the very commitments (generalizable decisions, resolutions, or subscriptions) an agent is willing to make.

Many people have thought that such a view of morality is either directly or indirectly nihilistic—that both the linguistic philosophers and the existentialists espouse what is in effect an irrationalism that would undercut the very possibility of a rational normative ethic.

If we consider a reply linguistic philosophers typically make to such criticisms, we will become aware of a crucial dissimilarity between them and the existentialists and a fundamental defect in existentialist ethics.

Linguistic philosophers have frequently claimed that the existentialists have merely dramatized a logical point. That moral principles are expressions of commitment or choice, that man cannot simply discover what is good or evil or know a priori that a certain thing must be done but must "create his own values," is not a worrisome fact about the human predicament; it is a conceptual truth concerning the nature of moral discourse. It is not a fact of the human condition that man is born into a world alien and indifferent to human purposes. What is a fact is that the phrases "the universe has a purpose" and "value and being are one" are unintelligible phrases. To say "man

creates his own values" is in reality only to say in a dramatic way that a judgment of value is an expression of choice. This statement, it is argued, is not an anguished cry of the human heart but is merely an expression of a linguistic convention.

To say "If *x* is a judgment of value, then *x* is an expression of choice" is not to say "Any choice at all is justified," "Anything is permissible," or "All human actions are of equal value." These latter statements are themselves value judgments and could not follow from the above-mentioned statement, for it is not itself a statement of value but a nonnormative metaethical statement about the meaning of evaluative expressions, and, as Sartre himself stresses, one cannot derive an "ought" from an "is." In general, Hare and Nowell-Smith, as well as Ayer and Stevenson, stress the normative neutrality of metaethical statements.

Hare. R. M. Hare in two very influential books, *The Language of Morals* (Oxford, 1952) and *Freedom and Reason* (Oxford, 1963), developed a very closely reasoned metaethical analysis of the type that has been discussed. In *The Language of Morals,* Hare views moral utterances as a species of prescriptive discourse, and he feels that we can most readily come to understand their actual role in the stream of life if we see how very much they are like another form of prescriptive discourse, namely, imperatives. Imperatives tell us to do something, not that something is the case. Moral utterances in their most paradigmatic employments also tell us to do something. Imperative and moral utterances do not, as the emotivists thought, have the logical function of trying to get you to do something. Rather, they tell you to do something. Furthermore, there are logical relations between prescriptive statements, just as there are logical relations between factual statements.

Moral judgments are viewed as a kind of prescriptive judgment but, unlike singular imperatives, moral judgments (as well as all value judgments) are universalizable. Hare means by this that such a judgment "logically commits the speaker to making a similar judgment about anything which is either exactly like the subject of the original judgment or like it in the relevant respects."

Hare stresses that while almost any word in certain contexts can function evaluatively, *good, right,* and *ought* almost always so function. The evaluative functions of these terms are distinct from their descriptive functions and are an essential part of their meaning. In fact, the distinctive function of all value words is that they in one way or another commend or condemn. But while *good* is a general word of commendation, the criteria for goodness vary from context to context and are dependent on what it is that is said to be "good."

The meaning of *good* or any other value term is never tied to its criteria of application. There is nothing in the logic of our language to limit the content of a moral judgment. As far as logic is concerned, any universalizable prescription that expresses a deep concern or commitment is ipso facto a moral prescription, and we can decide without conceptual error to do anything that it is logically or physically possible to do. If we treat the resulting decision as a decision of principle, that is, a universalizable prescription, then it is a value judgment that is in good logical order. As Nowell-Smith has well put it in discussing Hare's theory, "Nothing that we discover about the nature of moral judgments entails that it is wrong to put all Jews in gas-chambers."

Criticism of Hare. Probably the most persistent dissatisfaction with Hare's theory has resulted from the belief that it makes moral reasoning appear to be more arbitrary than it actually is. To say "Nothing that we discover about the nature of moral judgments entails that it is wrong to put all Jews in gas-chambers" is, it will be argued, a reductio of such a position. Hare would reply that to argue in such a way is to fail to recognize that he is talking about entailment, and that he is simply making the point that from nonnormative statements one cannot deduce normative ones.

Hare argues that his thesis about the logical status of moral utterances does not commit him to the position that there can be no rational resolution of basic conflicts in moral principle. Returning, in *Freedom and Reason,* to a stress on decisions (though with a new attention to inclinations), Hare contends that to have a morality we must have freedom. Specifically, we must have a situation in which each man must solve his own moral problems. (This is not to moralize about what we should do but to state a logical condition for the very existence of moral claims.)

Philosophers who have criticized Hare, including someone as close to him as Nowell-Smith, have suggested that Hare still has a far too Protestant conception of moral discourse. He fails really to take to heart the Wittgensteinian claim that here, as elsewhere in human discourse, we must have public criteria for what could count as a logically proper moral claim. As F. E. Sparshott—whose book *An Enquiry into Goodness* (Chicago, 1958) deserves more attention than it has received—notes: Hare's individualism leads him to neglect the fact that a morality, any morality, will necessarily incorporate "those rules of conduct that seem necessary

for communal living." It is not the case that just any universalizable set of prescriptions can constitute a morality or a set of moral judgments.

THE GOOD-REASONS APPROACH. The last metaethical theory we shall discuss has been dubbed the good-reasons approach. Stephen Toulmin, Kurt Baier, Henry Aiken, Marcus Singer, Kai Nielsen, A. I. Melden, A. E. Murphy, and John Rawls may be taken as representative figures of this point of view. It is an approach that obviously has been deeply affected by the philosophical method that we have come to associate with the work of the later Ludwig Wittgenstein. These philosophers have centered their attention on the logic of moral reasoning. Their central question has been "When is a reason a *good* reason for a moral judgment?" Accordingly, the crucial problems center on questions concerning the nature and limits of *justification* in ethics. These philosophers agree with the noncognitivists that moral sentences are used primarily as dynamic expressions to guide conduct and alter behavior. And they would also agree with ethical naturalists that moral utterances usually, at least, also make factual assertions. But they believe that the primary use of moral utterances is not theoretical or just emotive but practical. Hare and Nowell-Smith are right in stressing that they are designed to tell us what to do.

Yet while moral utterances typically tell us what to do, language with its complex and multifarious uses does not neatly divide into "the descriptive" and "the evaluative," "the constative" and "the performative," "the cognitive" and "the noncognitive." These are philosophers' specialized terms, and they do not help us to understand and clearly characterize moral discourse but actually distort our understanding of it. There can be no translation of moral terms into nonmoral terms, and the ancient problem of bridging "the is-ought gulf" is a muddle, for there is no clear distinction between such uses of language and no single function that makes a bit of discourse normative. Some moral utterances indeed bear interesting analogies to commands or resolutions, but they cannot be identified with them. It is a mistake to think ethical judgments are like scientific ones or like the judgments of any other branch of objective inquiry; yet cognitivist metaethicists were correct, not in pressing this analogy but in maintaining that there is a knowledge of good and evil and that some moral claims have a perfectly respectable objectivity. No matter how emotive or performative moral utterances may be, when we make a moral judgment, it must—logically must—satisfy certain requirements to count as a moral judgment. In making a moral judgment, we must be willing to universalize the judgment in question, and it must be possible to give factual reasons in support of the moral claim.

The advocates of the good-reasons approach in the general tradition of the later Wittgenstein did not take it to be incumbent on the philosopher to translate moral utterances into some clearer idiom. They did not believe that there was some other favored discourse or form of life that moral discourse or morality should be modeled on. What was expected of the philosopher was that he should describe morality so as to perspicuously display the living discourse at work. In particular, philosophers should concern themselves with a conceptual cartography of the nature and limits of justification in ethics. Before we can reasonably claim that moral judgments are at bottom "all subjective" or that no moral claim can be "objectively justified," we must come to understand what can and what cannot count as a good reason in ethics and what the limits of moral reasoning are.

Toulmin. Two books, Stephen Toulmin's *An Examination of the Place of Reason in Ethics* (Cambridge, U.K., 1950) and Kurt Baier's *The Moral Point of View* (Ithaca, NY, 1958), have most single-mindedly attacked the problem of moral reasoning. They may be taken as paradigms of the good-reasons approach. Toulmin argues that moral rules and moral principles are to be justified by discovering which of these rules or principles, if consistently acted upon, will most likely lead to the least amount of avoidable suffering all around. Those social practices that probably will cause the least amount of suffering for humankind are the social practices that ought to be accepted. Classical utilitarians maintained that a moral rule is justified if it tends to produce greater happiness all around than any alternative rule, but Toulmin favors the negative formulation because (1) though it is very difficult to determine what will make people happy or what they want, it is less difficult to determine what causes suffering, and (2) it is less the function of morality to tell men what the good life is than to tell them what not to do so that their interests, including their differing conceptions of the good life, can be realized to the maximum extent. This theory about moral reasoning, while purporting to be metaethical, is very close to the normative ethical theory sometimes called rule utilitarianism.

Toulmin argues that if we examine closely the way moral reasoning is actually carried on, it will become evident that moral rules and practices are characteristically judged by roughly utilitarian standards, while many individual actions are judged by whether or not they are in accordance with an accepted moral rule or social practice. Utilitarians point out that it is of the greatest social utility that we characteristically judge moral acts in this seemingly nonutilitarian fashion. However, frequently a decision concerning how to act involves conflicting moral rules with no clear order of subordination, and in some situations there seems to be no moral rule—unless the principle of utility is taken as a moral rule—that is readily applicable. In such a situation, the thing to do is to act on a utilitarian basis when it is at all possible to make some reasonable judgment of the probable beneficial consequences to the people involved of doing one thing rather than another. If that is not possible in a given situation, then we should act as a reasonable man would act. (The concept of a reasonable man, we should not forget, is itself very much a moral concept.)

Criticism of Toulmin. There certainly are a host of objections that spring to mind concerning Toulmin's account. First, it will be said that this is normative ethics, not metaethics: It tells us what we should do, what a good reason is, and how we can justify basic moral rules. Moreover, why should we accept it? Once we see through its modish trappings, it will become apparent that it has all the difficulties attendant on classical utilitarianism.

It could be replied that though the speech is in the material mode and sounds like normative ethics, in reality it is a brief description of how moral reasoning is actually carried on. Even if this reply is accepted, there are difficulties here too, for viewed this way, Toulmin's account surely looks like an account of a basically sociological sort of how certain people in fact reason. That is to say, it appears to be an impressionistic bit of descriptive ethics and hardly a metaethical account of the logic of moral reasoning. It covertly and persuasively redefines as "moral" only a very limited pattern of reasoning—reasoning that expresses the historically and ethnographically limited views of a determinate group of people. The ethnocentric character of this linguistic analysis makes it implicitly, but surreptitiously, normative.

This contention will be rejected by many. It will be argued that moral reasoning, like any other mode of reasoning, is limited. To determine what the moral point of view is and what it is to reason morally, we need first to determine the function (purpose, overall rationale) of morality.

The function of morality, Toulmin tells us, is to adjudicate conflicting interests and to harmonize desires (that is, moderate our impulses and adjust our demands) so as to reconcile them with our fellows, in such a way that everyone can have as much as possible of whatever it is that, on reflection, he wants. Given this conception of the function of ethics, something like Toulmin's account of moral reasoning is very plausible, but it has been objected that morality has no *one* such function. Many people have ideals of human excellence that have nothing to do with such a conception of the function of ethics: Many Jews and Christians, with their ideals of the love of God, do not conceive the function of moral living in this way, and the Buddhist community with its ideals of arhatship certainly would not accept, either in theory or in practice, such a conception of the function of ethics. Morality is a much more complicated and varied activity. There are diverse and often conflicting functions of morality. Any attempt to claim one function or rationale of morality as the function or the purpose of morality so circumscribes what can count as moral considerations that its effect is unwittingly to advocate one limited moral outlook as the moral point of view.

Finally, even if Toulmin could make out a case for claiming that the function of morality, or the primary function of morality, is such as he claims it to be, one could still ask, concerning this descriptive account of morality, "Why keep it as the sole or primary function of morality?" If altering the function of morality somewhat alters the meaning of "moral," then why should we be such linguistic conservatives? What is so sacred about that function of morality and its attendant conception of morality?

Toulmin could claim that now his critic has confused normative issues with metaethical ones. The issues here are complex and lead us into the heart of current discussion about the nature of moral reasoning. Yet a strong case can be made for the contention that there is more to be said for a general approach such as Toulmin's and Baier's than has commonly been thought.

It seems evident that much contemporary thinking about ethics, while devoted to Moore's exacting standards of making perfectly clear precisely what is being claimed, is concerned not with the very general question of the meaning of *good* or, for that matter, *right* or *ought* but with the rich texture of moral reasoning. This brings once more to the foreground the kind of detailed descriptions of the moral life distinctive of such phenomenologists as Scheler and Hartmann, but given the present care for actual conceptual distinctions, we may develop a kind of linguistic phenomenology that may be of major importance to an understanding of morality. Perhaps the most exciting endeavors from this point of view have been those of Rawls, Philippa Foot, and Georg von Wright. Rawls, in a series of distinguished essays, has shown the central role of considerations of justice in moral deliberation and the way such considerations modify utilitarian

patterns of reasoning; Foot, also in a series of much-discussed essays, has shown the importance of a discussion of the virtues and the vices and has reinvigorated ethical naturalism. Wright's masterful discussion of the varieties of goodness in his *The Varieties of Goodness* (London, 1963) has contributed immensely to our understanding of morality.

See also Abelard, Peter; Albert the Great; Alcmaeon of Croton; Anselm, St.; Antisthenes; Aristippus of Cyrene; Aristotle; Augustine, St.; Averroes; Avicenna; Ayer, Alfred Jules; Bacon, Francis; Baier, Kurt; Beccaria, Cesare Bonesana; Bentham, Jeremy; Bernard of Clairvaux, St.; Bosanquet, Bernard; Bradley, Francis Herbert; Brandt, R. B.; Brentano, Franz; Broad, Charlie Dunbar; Butler, Joseph; Calvin, John; Cambridge Platonists; Camus, Albert; Carnap, Rudolf; Carneades; Chrysippus; Cicero, Marcus Tullius; Clarke, Samuel; Cleanthes; Clement of Alexandria; Cudworth, Ralph; Cumberland, Richard; Cynics; Cyrenaics; Descartes, René; Dewey, John; Diderot, Denis; Diogenes of Sinope; Duns Scotus, John; Emerson, Ralph Waldo; Empedocles; Engels, Friedrich; Epictetus; Epicurus; Epicureanism and the Epicurean School; Erasmus, Desiderius; Erigena, John Scotus; Ethics; Ethics and Morality; Fichte, Johann Gottlieb; Galileo Galilei; Gorgias of Leontini; Green, Thomas Hill; Hägerström, Axel; Hare, Richard M.; Hartley, David; Hartmann, Nicolai; Hegel, Georg Wilhelm Friedrich; Heidegger, Martin; Hellenistic Thought; Helvétius, Claude-Adrien; Heraclitus of Ephesus; Hobbes, Thomas; Holbach, Paul-Henri Thiry, Baron d'; Hume, David; Husserl, Edmund; Hutcheson, Francis; James, William; Kant, Immanuel; Kierkegaard, Søren Aabye; Leibniz, Gottfried Wilhelm; Lenin, Vladimir Il'ich; Leucippus and Democritus; Locke, John; Luther, Martin; Machiavelli, Niccolò; Maimonides; Malebranche, Nicolas; Mandeville, Bernard; Mani and Manichaeism; Marcus Aurelius Antoninus; Marx, Karl; Mill, James; Mill, John Stuart; Montesquieu, Baron de; Moore, George Edward; More, Henry; Murphy, Arthur Edward; Neoplatonism; Nicolas of Autrecourt; Nietzsche, Friedrich; Origen; Paley, William; Panaetius of Rhodes; Pascal, Blaise; Perry, Ralph Barton; Philo Judaeus; Plato; Plotinus; Porphyry; Posidonius; Price, Richard; Prior, Arthur Norman; Protagoras of Abdera; Pyrrho; Rawls, John; Reid, Thomas; Religion and Morality; Ross, William David; Rousseau, Jean-Jacques; Royce, Josiah; Russell, Bertrand Arthur William; Sartre, Jean-Paul; Scheler, Max; Schopenhauer, Arthur; Seneca, Lucius Annaeus; Shaftesbury, Third Earl of (Anthony Ashley

Cooper); Sidgwick, Henry; Skepticism, History of; Smith, Adam; Socrates; Sophists; Spinoza, Benedict (Baruch) de; Stevenson, Charles L.; Stoicism; Suárez, Francisco; Tertullian, Quintus Septimius Florens; Thomas Aquinas, St.; Voltaire, François-Marie Arouet de; William of Ockham; Wittgenstein, Ludwig Josef Johann.

Bibliography

GENERAL HISTORIES OF ETHICS

Historical and Social Context of Ethical Beliefs

Brinton, C. C. *A History of Western Morals.* New York: Harcourt Brace, 1959. A very readable history of ethical beliefs and practices.

Bruce, A. B. *The Moral Order of the World in Ancient and Modern Thought.* 4 vols. London: Hodder and Stoughton, 1899. A detailed study of the literary and religious background of ethical thought from ancient Greece to the Reformation.

Dittrich, Ottmar. *Geschichte der Ethik.* 4 vols. Leipzig: Meiner, 1926. A scholarly study of the literary and religious origins of Western ethical ideals.

Harkness, G. E. *The Sources of Western Morality.* New York: Scribners, 1954. An exploration of the ancient origins of modern ethics. Useful comparisons of primitive with Old Testament ethics and of Greek with Christian ethics.

Kropotkin, P. A. *Ethics, Origin and Development.* Translated by L. S. Friedland and J. R. Piroshnikoff. New York: Dial Press, 1924. A Marxist account of the development of ethics from primitive to modern Western society.

Lecky, W. E. H. *History of European Morals.* 2 vols. New York, 1919. A justly celebrated study of how moral values reflect, but fail to keep up with, actual practices in the Western world. Vol. I, Ch. 1, discusses modern British ethical philosophy.

Mencken, H. L. *Treatise on Right and Wrong.* New York: Knopf, 1934. Perceptive and often caustic comments on the evolution of moral ideas in philosophy and religion; a critique of authoritarianism.

Robertson, J. M. *A Short History of Morals.* London: Watts, 1920. A relativistic view of the history of ethics, stressing the sociological sources of morality.

Westermarck, Edward. *The Origin and Development of Moral Ideas.* 2 vols. London: Macmillan, 1908. A monumental work of historical and anthropological scholarship.

Histories of Ethical Philosophy

Broad, C. D. *Five Types of Ethical Theory.* London: Kegan Paul, 1930. A critical study, by a distinguished intuitionist, of the ethical systems of Spinoza, Butler, Hume, Kant, and Sidgwick.

Kautsky, Karl. *Ethics and the Materialist Conception of History.* Translated by J. B. Agnew. Chicago: Kerr, 1907. A brief sketch of the evolution of ethical thought by a noted Marxist.

MacIntyre, Alasdair. *A Short History of Ethics.* New York: Macmillan, 1966. An important discussion by a contemporary analytic philosopher.

Mackinnon, D. M. *A Study in Ethical Theory.* London: A. and C. Black, 1957. A comparison of the theories of Kant, Butler, and the utilitarians as alternatives to religious ethics.

Maritain, Jacques. *Moral Philosophy.* Translated by M. Suther. New York: Scribners, 1964. A critical evaluation of secular ethical theories from the standpoint of Catholic theology.

Martineau, James. *Types of Ethical Theory.* 2 vols. Oxford: Clarendon Press, 1898. Vol. I evaluates the metaphysical and ethical views of Plato, Descartes, Malebranche, Spinoza, and Comte. Vol. II criticizes utilitarian and moral-sense theories.

Rogers, R. A. P. *A Short History of Ethics.* London: Macmillan, 1911. A brief survey of the history of ethical theory. Incomplete but clear and readable.

Sidgwick, Henry. *Outlines of the History of Ethics.* London, 1886. A brief but illuminating discussion of the most important schools of ethical thought from ancient Greece to nineteenth-century England.

Swabey, W. C. *Ethical Theory: From Hobbes to Kant.* New York: Philosophical Library, 1961. A useful summary of several philosophical systems.

PLATO

General Expositions

Dickinson, G. L. *Plato and His Dialogues.* New York: Norton, 1932.

Field, G. X. *The Philosophy of Plato.* London, 1951.

Friedländer, Paul. *Plato.* Translated by Hans Meyerhoff. New York, 1958–1964. A multivolume work of tremendous scholarship on the cultural background of Plato's writings.

Shorey, P. *What Plato Said.* Chicago: University of Chicago Press, 1933.

Taylor, A. E. *Plato, the Man and His Work.* London, 1908.

Specialized Studies

Lodge, R. C. *Plato's Theory of Ethics.* New York: Harcourt Brace, 1928. A thorough study limited to Plato's ethical ideas.

Nettleship, R. L. *Lectures on the Republic of Plato.* New York, 1962. An extraordinarily illuminating study of Plato's most important dialogue.

Relation of Plato to Other Greek Thinkers

Burnet, John. *Platonism.* Berkeley: University of California Press, 1928. Distinguishes sharply between Socratic and Platonic views.

Cornford, F. M. *Before and After Socrates.* Cambridge, U.K.: Cambridge University Press, 1960.

Demos, R. *The Philosophy of Plato.* New York: Scribners, 1939. Rejects any systematic interpretation of Plato.

Field, G. C. *Plato and His Contemporaries.* London: Methuen, 1948.

Gould, J. *The Development of Plato's Ethics.* Cambridge, U.K.: Cambridge University Press, 1955.

Hampden, R. D. *The Fathers of Greek Philosophy.* Edinburgh: A. and C. Black, 1862.

Merlan, Philip. *From Plato to Platonism.* The Hague, 1960.

Plato's Ethics and Politics

Crossman, R. H. *Plato Today.* New York: Oxford University Press, 1939. Critical.

Fite, W. *The Platonic Legend.* New York: Scribners, 1934. Critical.

Koyré, Alexandre. *Discovering Plato.* New York: Columbia University Press, 1945. Favorable.

Levinson, R. B. *In Defense of Plato.* Cambridge, MA: Harvard University Press, 1953.

Wild, J. D. *Plato's Modern Enemies.* Chicago: University of Chicago Press, 1953. Favorable.

ARISTOTLE

Aristotle's Ethics

Gauthier, R. A. *La morale d'Aristote.* Paris, 1958.

Grene, Marjorie. *A Portrait of Aristotle.* London: Faber and Faber, 1963.

Marshall, T. *Aristotle's Theory of Conduct.* London: Unwin, 1906.

Mure, G. R. G. *Aristotle.* London, 1932.

Oates, W. J. *Aristotle and the Problem of Value.* Princeton, NJ: Princeton University Press, 1963.

Randall, J. H. *Aristotle.* New York, 1960. Chs. 11–14.

Ross, W. D. *Aristotle.* London, 1930.

Veatch, H. B. *Rational Man.* Bloomington: Indiana University Press, 1962.

Walsh, J. J. *Aristotle's Conception of Moral Weakness.* New York: Columbia University Press, 1963.

Aristotle and Other Ethical Philosophers

Cornford, F. M. *Before and After Socrates.* Cambridge, U.K.: Cambridge University Press, 1960.

Hampden, R. D. *The Fathers of Greek Philosophy.* Edinburgh: A. and C. Black, 1862.

Merlan, Philip. *Studies in Epicurus and Aristotle.* Wiesbaden: Harrassowitz, 1960.

Taylor, A. E. *Aristotle.* London, 1943.

HELLENISTIC AND ROMAN ETHICS

Epicureanism

DeWitt, N. W. *Epicurus and His Philosophy.* Minneapolis: University of Minnesota Press, 1954.

Hadzsits, G. D. *Lucretius and His Influence.* New York: Longmans Green, 1935.

Merlan, Philip. *Studies in Epicurus and Aristotle.* Wiesbaden: Harrassowitz, 1960.

Stoicism

Arnold, E. V. *Roman Stoicism.* Cambridge, U.K.: Cambridge University Press, 1911. Middle and late Stoa.

Bréhier, Émile. *Chrysippe et l'ancien Stoicisme.* Paris: Presses Universitaires de France, 1951. Early Stoa.

Brussell, F. W. *Marcus Aurelius and the Later Stoics.* New York, 1910.

Murray, Gilbert. *Stoic, Christian and Humanist.* Boston: Beacon Press, 1950.

Wenley, R. M. *Stoicism and Its Influence.* Boston: Marshall Jones, 1924.

Neoplatonism

Elsee, C. *Neoplatonism in Relation to Christianity.* Cambridge, U.K.: Cambridge University Press, 1908.

Feibleman, J. *Religious Platonism.* London: Allen and Unwin, 1959.

Pistorius, P. V. *Plotinus and Neoplatonism.* Cambridge, U.K.: Bowes and Bowes, 1952.

Switalski, B. *Neoplatonism and the Ethics of St. Augustine.* New York: Polish Institute of Arts and Sciences in America, 1946.

Whittaker, T. *The Neoplatonists.* Cambridge, U.K., 1918.

Comparisons

Hicks, R. D. *Stoic and Epicurean.* New York: Scribners, 1910.

Zeller, Eduard. *Stoics, Epicureans and Sceptics.* Translated by O. J. Reichel. London: Longmans Green, 1880.

MEDIEVAL ETHICS

General Histories of Medieval Philosophy

Copleston, F. C. *A History of Philosophy,* Vols. II and III. Westminster, MD: Newman Press, 1950–1953.

Gilson, Étienne. *Reason and Revelation in the Middle Ages.* New York: Scribners, 1938.

Gilson, Étienne. *The Spirit of Medieval Philosophy.* Translated by A. Downes. New York: Scribners, 1936.

Hawkins, D. J. B. *A Sketch of Mediaeval Philosophy.* London: Sheed and Ward, 1946.

Husik, I. *A History of Mediaeval Jewish Philosophy.* New York: Macmillan, 1916.

Augustine

Gilson, Étienne. *Introduction a l'étude de saint Augustin.* Paris: Vrin, 1943.

Switalski, B. *Neoplatonism and the Ethics of St. Augustine.* New York: Polish Institute of Arts and Sciences in America, 1946.

Erigena and Abelard

Bett, H. *Johannes Scotus Eriugena.* Cambridge, U.K., 1925.

Sikes, J. G. *Peter Abailard.* Cambridge, U.K.: Cambridge University Press, 1932. Chs. 2 and 8.

Thomas Aquinas

Copleston, F. C. *Aquinas.* London, 1955. Ch. 5.

D'Arcy, M. C. *St. Thomas Aquinas.* Dublin, 1953. Ch. 9.

Gilson, Étienne. *The Philosophy of St. Thomas Aquinas.* Translated by E. Bullough. St. Louis, 1934.

Maritain, Jacques. *St. Thomas and the Problem of Evil.* Milwaukee, WI: Marquette University Press, 1942.

Mullane, D. T. *Aristotelianism in St. Thomas.* Washington, DC: Catholic University of America, 1929.

SEVENTEENTH-CENTURY ETHICS

Hobbes

Laird, John. *Hobbes.* London: Benn, 1934.

Peters, R. S. *Hobbes.* Harmondsworth, U.K.: Penguin, 1956.

Stephen, Leslie. *Hobbes.* Ann Arbor: University of Michigan Press, 1961.

Taylor, A. E. *Hobbes.* New York, 1908.

Spinoza

Bidney, D. *The Psychology and Ethics of Spinoza.* New Haven, CT: Yale University Press, 1940.

Broad, C. D. *Five Types of Ethical Theory.* London: Kegan Paul, 1930. Ch. 2.

Hampshire, S. *Spinoza.* Harmondsworth, U.K.: Penguin, 1951. Chs. 4 and 5.

Joachim, H. J. *A Study of the Ethics of Spinoza.* London: Clarendon Press, 1901.

McKeon, R. *The Philosophy of Spinoza.* New York: Longmans Green, 1928.

Locke

Aaron, R. I. *John Locke.* Oxford: Clarendon Press, 1955.

Lamprecht, S. P. *The Moral and Political Philosophy of John Locke.* New York: Columbia University Press, 1918.

Cambridge Platonists

Cassirer, Ernst. *The Platonic Renaissance in England.* Translated by J. P. Pettegrove. Austin: University of Texas Press, 1953.

Powicke, F. J. *The Cambridge Platonists.* Cambridge, MA, 1926.

EIGHTEENTH-CENTURY ETHICS

Moral-Sense Theories

Bonar, J. *Moral Sense.* New York: Macmillan, 1930.

Raphael, D. D. *The Moral Sense.* London: Oxford University Press, 1947.

Clarke

Le Rossignol, J. E. *The Ethical Philosophy of Samuel Clarke.* Leipzig, 1892.

Butler

Broad, C. D. *Five Types of Ethical Theory.* London: Kegan Paul, 1930. Ch. 3.

Duncan-Jones, A. E. *Butler's Moral Philosophy.* Harmondsworth, U.K.: Penguin, 1952.

Shaftesbury and Hutcheson

Fowler, Thomas. *Shaftesbury and Hutcheson.* London, 1882.

Hume

Basson, A. H. *David Hume.* Harmondsworth, U.K., 1958. Ch. 5.

Broad, C. D. *Five Types of Ethical Theory.* London: Kegan Paul, 1930. Ch. 4.

Smith, Norman Kemp. *The Philosophy of David Hume.* London: Macmillan, 1941.

Stewart, J. B. *The Moral and Political Philosophy of David Hume.* New York: Columbia University Press, 1963.

Price and Reid

Raphael, D. D. *The Moral Sense.* London: Oxford University Press, 1947.

French Enlightenment

Becker, C. L. *The Heavenly City of the Eighteenth Century Philosophers.* New Haven, CT: Yale University Press, 1932.

Cassirer, Ernst. *The Philosophy of the Enlightenment.* Translated by F. Koelln and J. P. Pettegrove. Princeton, NJ: Princeton University Press, 1951.

Crocker, L. G. *Nature and Culture.* Baltimore: Johns Hopkins Press, 1963.

Halévy, Élie. *The Growth of Philosophic Radicalism.* Translated by M. Morris. New York: Macmillan, 1928.

Rouston, M. *The Pioneers of the French Revolution.* Translated by F. Whyte. Boston: Little Brown, 1926. A study of the social and political involvements of the Encyclopedists.

Kant

Broad, C. D. *Five Types of Ethical Theory.* London: Kegan Paul, 1930. Ch. 5.

Jones, W. T. *Morality and Freedom in the Philosophy of Immanuel Kant.* Oxford: Oxford University Press, 1940.

Körner, S. *Kant.* Harmondsworth, U.K.: Penguin, 1955. Chs. 6 and 7.

Lindsay, A. D. *Kant.* London, 1934.

Paton, H. J. *The Categorical Imperative.* New York: Hutchinson, 1947.

Paton, H. J. *The Moral Law, or Kant's Groundwork of the Metaphysic of Morals.* New York: Hutchinson, 1948.

Teale, A. E. *Kantian Ethics.* London: Oxford University Press, 1951.

NINETEENTH-CENTURY ETHICS

Utilitarianism

Halévy, Élie. *The Growth of Philosophic Radicalism.* Translated by M. Morris. New York: Macmillan, 1928.

Stephen, Leslie. *The English Utilitarians,* 3 vols. London: Duckworth, 1900.

German Idealism

Dewey, John. *German Philosophy and Politics.* New York: Putnam, 1942. Highly critical.

Hook, Sidney. *From Hegel to Marx.* New York: Reynal and Hitchcock, 1936.

Löwith, Karl. *From Hegel to Nietzsche.* Translated by D. Green. New York: Holt, Rinehart and Winston, 1964.

Marcuse, Herbert. *Reason and Revolution.* London: Oxford University Press, 1941.

Royce, Josiah. *The Spirit of Modern Philosophy.* New York, 1896.

Fichte

Adamson, Robert. *Fichte.* Edinburgh, 1881.

Royce, Josiah. *The Spirit of Modern Philosophy.* New York, 1896. Part I, Ch. 5.

Hegel

Findlay, J. N. *Hegel.* London, 1958. Chs. 5 and 11.

Marcuse, Herbert. *Reason and Revolution.* London: Oxford University Press, 1941.

Royce, Josiah. *The Spirit of Modern Philosophy.* New York, 1896. Part I, Ch. 8.

Stace, W. T. *The Philosophy of Hegel.* New York: Dover, 1955.

Schopenhauer

Copleston, F. C. *Arthur Schopenhauer, Philosopher of Pessimism.* London, 1947.

Mann, Thomas. *Schopenhauer.* Stockholm, 1938.

McGill, V. J. *Schopenhauer, Pessimist and Pagan.* New York: Brentano, 1931.

Nietzsche

Brinton, C. C. *Nietzsche.* Cambridge, 1941.

Copleston, F. C. *Friedrich Nietzsche.* London, 1942.

Lefebvre, Henri. *Nietzsche.* Paris, 1939.

Marx

Berlin, Isaiah. *Karl Marx.* London: Butterworth, 1939.

Hook, Sidney. *From Hegel to Marx.* New York: Reynal and Hitchcock, 1936.

MacIntyre, A. C. *Marxism, an Interpretation.* London: SCM Press, 1953.

Marcuse, Herbert. *Reason and Revolution.* London: Oxford University Press, 1941.

Tucker, R. *Philosophy and Myth in Karl Marx.* Cambridge, U.K.: Cambridge University Press, 1961.

American Transcendentalism

Pochmann, H. A. *New England Transcendentalism and St. Louis Hegelianism.* Philadelphia: Carl Schurz Memorial Foundation, 1948.

Schneider, H. W. *A History of American Philosophy.* New York: Columbia University Press, 1946.

Royce and James

Santayana, George. *Character and Opinion in the United States.* New York: Scribners, 1920.

Smith, J. E. *Royce's Social Infinite.* New York: Liberal Arts Press, 1950.

British Idealism

Pfannenstill, Bertil. *Bernard Bosanquet's Philosophy of the State.* Translated by Bert Hood. Lund, Sweden: Hakan Ohlsson, 1936.

Sidgwick, Henry. *The Ethics of Green, Spencer and Martineau.* London, 1902.

Wollheim, Richard. *F. H. Bradley.* Harmondsworth, U.K., 1959. Ch. 6.

Sidgwick

Broad, C. D. *Five Types of Ethical Theory.* London: Kegan Paul, 1930. Ch. 6.

TWENTIETH-CENTURY ETHICS

Assessments of Moore

Adams, E. M. *Ethical Naturalism and the Modern World-View.* Chapel Hill: University of North Carolina Press, 1960. Careful discussion of naturalism-nonnaturalism debate.

Broad, C. D. "G. E. Moore's Latest Published Views on Ethics." *Mind* (1961).

Field, G. C. "The Place of Definition in Ethics." *PAS* (1932). Key discussion of difficulties in Moore's conception of definition.

Frankena, W. K. "The Naturalistic Fallacy." *Mind* (1939). Classical source for discussion of naturalistic fallacy.

Hall, E. W. *Categorial Analysis.* Edited by E. M. Adams. Chapel Hill: University of North Carolina Press, 1964. Important defense of Mill against Moore.

Prior, A. N. *Logic and the Basis of Ethics.* Oxford: Clarendon Press, 1949. Crucial for history of the naturalistic fallacy.

Taylor, Paul. *Normative Discourse.* Englewood Cliffs, NJ: Prentice-Hall, 1961. Is/ought carefully discussed and a general theory of value developed along linguistic lines.

Warnock, Mary. *Ethics since 1900.* Oxford: Oxford University Press, 1960.

Wellman, Carl. *The Language of Ethics.* Cambridge, MA: Harvard University Press, 1961. Clear statement of difficulties in ethical naturalism.

Deontological Nonnaturalism

Broad, C. D. "Critical Notice of H. A. Prichard, *Moral Obligation.*" *Mind* (1950).

Broad, C. D. *Ethics and the History of Philosophy.* London: Routledge, 1952.

Broad, C. D. *Five Types of Ethical Theory.* London: Kegan Paul, 1930.

Broad, C. D. "Imperatives, Categorical and Hypothetical." *Philosopher* (1950).

Broad, C. D. "Review of Julian S. Huxley's Evolutionary Ethics." *Mind* (1944).

Broad, C. D. "Some of the Main Problems of Ethics." *Philosophy* (1946).

Broad, C. D. "Some Reflections on Moral-Sense Theories in Ethics." *PAS* (1944–1945).

Carritt, E. F. "Moral Positivism and Moral Aestheticism." *Philosophy* (1938). Less important than Prichard or Ross but still influential.

Carritt, E. F. *The Theory of Morals.* London: Oxford University Press, H. Milford, 1928.

Ewing, A. C. "The Autonomy of Ethics." In *Prospect for Metaphysics,* edited by I. T. Ramsey. New York: Philosophical Library, 1961.

Ewing, A. C. *The Definition of Good.* New York: Macmillan, 1947.

Ewing, A. C. *Ethics.* London: English Universities Press, 1953.

Ewing, A. C. *Second Thoughts in Moral Philosophy.* London: Routledge and Paul, 1959.

Hall, E. W. *Categorial Analysis.* Edited by E. M. Adams. Chapel Hill: University of North Carolina Press, 1964.

Hall, E. W. *Our Knowledge of Fact and Value.* Chapel Hill: University of North Carolina Press, 1961.

Hall, E. W. *What Is Value? An Essay in Philosophical Analysis.* London: Routledge and Paul, 1952.

Prichard, H. A. *Moral Obligation.* Oxford: Clarendon Press, 1949. Posthumously collected essays. Primary source for deontology.

Assessments of Deontological Nonnaturalism

Edwards, Paul. *The Logic of Moral Discourse.* Glencoe, IL: Free Press, 1955.

McCloskey, H. J. "Ross and the Concept of a *Prima Facie* Duty." *Australasian Journal of Philosophy* (1963).

Monro, D. H. "Critical Notice of *Second Thoughts in Moral Philosophy.*" *Australasian Journal of Philosophy* (1960).

Schilpp, P. A., ed. *The Philosophy of C. D. Broad.* New York: Tudor, 1959. Note essays by Frankena, Hare, and Hedenius and Broad's reply. Broad's work, though largely critical of other philosophers, represents a key statement of deontology.

Strawson, P. F. "Ethical Intuitionism." *Philosophy* (1949).

Assessments of Phenomenological Nonnaturalism

Hook, Sidney. "A Critique of Ethical Realism." *International Journal of Ethics* (1929).

Jensen, O. C. "Nicolai Hartmann's Theory of Virtue." *Ethics* (1942).

Schlick, Moritz. "Is There a Factual *A Priori?,*" In *Readings in Philosophical Analysis,* edited by Herbert Feigl and Wilfrid Sellars. New York: Appleton-Century-Crofts, 1949.

Walker, Merle. "Perry and Hartmann, Antithetical or Complementary?" *International Journal of Ethics* (1939).

Ethical Naturalism

Dewey, John. *Essays in Experimental Logic.* Chicago: University of Chicago Press, 1916.

Dewey, John. "Ethical Subject Matter and Language." *Journal of Philosophy* (1945).

Dewey, John. *Human Nature and Conduct.* New York: Holt, 1922.

Dewey, John. *The Problems of Men.* New York: Philosophical Library, 1946.

Dewey, John. *The Quest for Certainty*. New York: Minton Balch, 1929.

Dewey, John. *Theory of Valuation*. Chicago: University of Chicago Press, 1939.

Findlay, J. N. *Language, Mind and Value*. London: Allen and Unwin, 1963.

Findlay, J. N. *Values and Intentions*. London: Allen and Unwin, 1961.

Foot, P. R. "Goodness and Choice." *PAS*, Supp. Vol. (1961).

Foot, P. R. "Moral Arguments." *Mind* (1958).

Foot, P. R. "Moral Beliefs." *PAS* (1958).

Pepper, Stephen. *A Digest of Purposive Values*. Berkeley: University of California Press, 1947.

Prall, D. W. *A Study in the Theory of Value*. Berkeley, CA, 1921.

Reid, J. R. "The Nature and Status of Values." In *Philosophy for the Future*, edited by R. W. Sellars, V. G. McGill, and Marvin Farber. New York: Macmillan, 1949.

Reid, J. R. *A Theory of Value*. New York: Scribners, 1938.

Rice, P. B. *On the Knowledge of Good and Evil*. New York: Random House, 1955.

Stace, W. T. *The Concept of Morals*. New York: Macmillan, 1937.

Westermarck, Edward. *Ethical Relativity*. London: Kegan Paul, 1932.

Assessments of Ethical Naturalism

Ezorsky, Gertrude. "Inquiry as Appraisal: The Singularity of John Dewey's Theory of Valuation." *Journal of Philosophy* (1958).

Frankena, William. "C. I. Lewis on the Ground and Nature of the Right." *Journal of Philosophy* (1964).

Frankena, William. "Ethical Naturalism Renovated." *Review of Metaphysics* (1957).

Frankena, William. "Lewis' Imperatives of Right." *Philosophical Studies* (1963).

Frankena, William. "Obligation and Motivation in Recent Moral Philosophy." In *Essays in Moral Philosophy*, edited by A. I. Melden. Seattle: University of Washington Press, 1958.

Frankena, William. "Three Comments on Lewis's Views on the Right and the Good." *Journal of Philosophy* (1964).

Hare, R. M. *The Language of Morals*. Oxford: Clarendon Press, 1952.

Kennedy, Gail. "Science and the Transformation of Common Sense: The Basic Problem of Dewey's Philosophy." *Journal of Philosophy* (1954).

Wellman, Carl. *The Language of Ethics*. Cambridge, MA: Harvard University Press, 1961.

White, Morton. *Social Thought in America*. New York: Viking Press, 1949.

White, Morton. "Value and Obligation in Dewey and Lewis." *Philosophical Review* (1949).

(See also the works by Moore, Ross, Ewing, and Hall previously cited.)

Contemporary Noncognitivism

Ayer, A. J. *Language, Truth and Logic*. London: Gollancz, 1935.

Ayer, A. J. "On the Analysis of Moral Judgments." In his *Philosophical Essays*. New York: St. Martin's Press, 1954.

Carnap, Rudolf. *Philosophy and Logical Syntax*. London: Kegan Paul, 1935.

Cassirer, Ernst. "Axel Hägerström: Eine Studie zur schwedischen Philosophie der Gegenwart." *Goteborgs Hogskolas Arsskrift* (1939).

Edwards, Paul. *The Logic of Moral Discourse*. Glencoe, IL: Free Press, 1955.

Hedenius, Ingemar. "Etikens Subjecktivitet." In *Tro och Moral*. Stockholm, 1955.

Hedenius, Ingemar. *Om Rätt och Moral* (On Law and Morals). Stockholm, 1941.

Hedenius, Ingemar. "Values and Duties." *Theoria* (1949).

Reichenbach, Hans. *The Rise of Scientific Philosophy*. Berkeley: University of California Press, 1951.

Richards, I. A. *The Meaning of Meaning*. New York, 1933.

Richards, I. A. *Speculative Instruments*. Chicago: University of Chicago Press, 1957.

Robinson, Richard. *An Atheist's Values*. Oxford: Clarendon Press, 1964.

Robinson, Richard. "The Emotive Theory of Ethics." *PAS*, Supp. Vol. (1948).

Ross, Alf. *Kritik der sogenannten praktischen Erkenntniss*. Copenhagen, 1933.

Ross, Alf. *On Law and Justice*. Berkeley: University of California Press, 1959.

Ross, Alf. "On Moral Reasoning." *Danish Yearbook of Philosophy* (1964).

Ross, Alf. "On the Logical Nature of Propositions of Value." *Theoria* (1945).

Russell, Bertrand. *Religion and Science*. London: Butterworth-Nelson, 1935.

Schilpp, P. A., ed. *The Philosophy of Rudolf Carnap*. La Salle, IL: Open Court, 1964.

Stevenson, Charles. *Ethics and Language*. New Haven, CT: Yale University Press, 1944.

Stevenson, Charles. *Facts and Values*. New Haven, CT: Yale University Press, 1963.

Stevenson, Charles. "The Scientist's Role and the Aims of Education." *Harvard Educational Review* (1954).

Assessments of the Emotive Theory

Bedford, E. "The Emotive Theory of Ethics." In *Proceedings of the Eleventh International Congress of Philosophy*, Vol. X. Amsterdam, 1953.

Brandt, Richard. "The Emotive Theory of Ethics." *Philosophical Review* (1950).

Falk, W. D. "Goading and Guiding." *Mind* (1954).

Foot, P. R. "The Philosopher's Defense of Morality." *Philosophy* (1952).

Nielsen, Kai. "Bertrand Russell's New Ethic." *Methodos* (1958).

Nielsen, Kai. "On Looking Back at the Emotive Theory." *Methodos* (1962).

Tegen, Einar. "The Basic Problem in the Theory of Value." *Theoria* (1944).

Assessments of Existentialism

Ayer, A. J. "Albert Camus, Novelist-Philosopher." *Horizon* (1946).

Ayer, A. J. "Novelist-Philosophers: Jean-Paul Sartre." *Horizon* (1946).

Ayer, A. J. "Philosophy at Absolute Zero." *Encounter* (1955).

Beauvoir, Simone de. *The Ethics of Ambiguity.* Translated by Bernard Frechtman. New York: Philosophical Library, 1948. Important in its own right and in relation to Sartre.

Cranston, Maurice. *Sartre.* Edinburgh and London, 1962. General discussion of the range of Sartre's work. Elementary but clear.

Cruickshank, John. *Camus and the Literature of Revolt.* New York, 1959. Contains a detailed and sympathetic account of Camus's thought.

Cruickshank, John, ed. *The Novelist as Philosopher.* London: Oxford University Press, 1962.

Hochberg, Herbert. "Albert Camus and the Ethic of Absurdity." *Ethics* (1965). Important analytical criticism.

Jeanson, Francis. *Le problème moral et la pensée de Sartre.* Paris, 1947. Sympathetic and informal discussion of Sartre's moral theory.

Murdoch, Iris. *Sartre: Romantic Rationalist.* New Haven, CT: Yale University Press, 1955. Relates Sartre to English thought.

Warnock, Mary. *Ethics since 1900.* Oxford: Oxford University Press, 1960.

Warnock, Mary. *The Philosophy of Sartre.* London: Hutchinson, 1966. Challenging but sympathetic assessment of Sartre.

Wollheim, Richard. "Modern Philosophy and Unreason." *Political Quarterly* (1955).

Wollheim, Richard. "The Political Philosophy of Existentialism." *Cambridge Journal* (1953).

Linguistic Noncognitivism

Hare, R. M. "Descriptivism." *Proceedings of the British Academy* (1963).

Hare, R. M. "Universalizability." *PAS* (1954).

Hartland-Swann, John. *An Analysis of Morals.* London: Allen and Unwin, 1960.

Mayo, Bernard. *Ethics and the Moral Life.* London, 1958.

Montefiore, Alan. "Goodness and Choice." *PAS,* Supp. Vol. (1961).

Montefiore, Alan. *A Modern Introduction to Moral Philosophy.* New York: Praeger, 1959.

Nowell-Smith, P. H. "Contextual Implications and Ethical Theory." *PAS,* Supp. Vol. (1962).

Nowell-Smith, P. H. *Ethics.* London: Penguin, 1954.

Nowell-Smith, P. H. "Morality: Religious and Secular." *Rationalist Annual* (1961).

Nowell-Smith, P. H. "Review of *Freedom and Reason.*" *Ratio* (1964).

Assessments of Linguistic Noncognitivism

Binkley, Luther. *Contemporary Ethical Theories.* New York: Philosophical Library, 1961.

Castañeda, Héctor-Neri. "Imperatives, Decisions and 'Oughts.' A Logico-Metaphysical Investigation." In *Morality and the Language of Conduct,* edited by Héctor-Neri Castañeda and George Nakhnikian. Detroit, MI: Wayne State University Press, 1963.

McCloskey, H. J. "Hare's Ethical Subjectivism." *Australasian Journal of Philosophy* (1959).

McCloskey, H. J. "Nowell-Smith's Ethics." *Australasian Journal of Philosophy* (1961).

Monro, H. D. "Are Moral Problems Genuine?" *Mind* (1956).

Monro, H. D. "Critical Notice of *Freedom and Reason.*" *Australasian Journal of Philosophy* (1964).

Monro, H. D. "Impartiality and Consistency." *Philosophy* (1961).

Sparshott, F. E. "Critical Study of *Freedom and Reason.*" *Philosophical Quarterly* (1963).

Good-Reasons Approach

Aiken, H. D. *Reason and Conduct.* New York: Knopf, 1962.

Baier, Kurt. "Decisions and Descriptions." *Mind* (1951).

Baier, Kurt. *The Meaning of Life.* Canberra, 1957.

Falk, W. D. "Action-Guiding Reasons." *Journal of Philosophy* (1963).

Falk, W. D. "Goading and Guiding." *Mind* (1953).

Falk, W. D. "Morality and Nature." *Australasian Journal of Philosophy* (1950).

Falk, W. D. "Morality, Self and Others." In *Morality and the Language of Conduct,* edited by Héctor-Neri Castañeda and George Nakhnikian. Detroit, MI: Wayne State University Press, 1963.

Falk, W. D. "Moral Perplexity." *Ethics* (1956).

Falk, W. D. "Morals without Faith." *Philosophy* (1944).

Falk, W. D. "Obligation and Rightness." *Philosophy* (1945).

Falk, W. D. "'Ought' and Motivation." *PAS* (1947–1948).

Gauthier, David. *Practical Reasoning.* Oxford: Clarendon Press, 1963.

Ladd, John. "The Issue of Relativism." *Monist* (1963).

Ladd, John. "Reason and Practice." In *The Return to Reason,* edited by John Wild. Chicago: Regnery, 1953.

Ladd, John. *The Structure of a Moral Code.* Cambridge, MA: Harvard University Press, 1957.

Melden, A. I. *Rights and Right Conduct.* Oxford, 1959.

Melden, A. I. "Two Comments on Utilitarianism." *Philosophical Review* (1951).

Murphy, A. E. "Blanshard on Good in General." *Philosophical Review* (1963).

Murphy, A. E. *The Theory of Practical Reason.* Edited by A. I. Melden. La Salle, IL: Open Court, 1965.

Murphy, A. E. *The Uses of Reason.* New York: Macmillan, 1943.

Murphy, A. E., William Hay, and Marcus Singer, eds. *Reason and the Common Good.* Englewood Cliffs, NJ: Prentice-Hall, 1963.

Nielsen, Kai. "Appraising Doing the Thing Done." *Journal of Philosophy* (1960).

Nielsen, Kai. "Can a Way of Life Be Justified?" *Indian Journal of Philosophy* (1960).

Nielsen, Kai. "Conventionalism in Morals and the Appeal to Human Nature." *Philosophy and Phenomenological Research* (1962).

Nielsen, Kai. "The Functions of Moral Discourse." *Philosophical Quarterly* (1957).

Nielsen, Kai. "The 'Good Reasons Approach' and 'Ontological Justifications of Morality.'" *Philosophical Quarterly* (1959).

Nielsen, Kai. "The Good Reasons Approach Revisited." *Archiv für Rechts- und Sozialphilosophie* (1965).

Nielsen, Kai. "Is 'Why Should I Be Moral?' an Absurdity?" *Australasian Journal of Philosophy* (1958).

Nielsen, Kai. "Justification and Moral Reasoning." *Methodos* (1957).

Nielsen, Kai. "Why Should I Be Moral?" *Methodos* (1963).

Rawls, John. "Constitutional Liberty and the Concept of Justice." In *Nomos*, Vol. VI: *Justice*, edited by Carl J. Friedrich and John W. Chapman. New York: Atherton, 1963.

Rawls, John. "Justice as Fairness." *Philosophical Review* (1958).

Rawls, John. "Legal Obligation and the Duty of Fair Play." In *Law and Philosophy*, edited by Sidney Hook. New York: New York University Press, 1964.

Rawls, John. "Outline of a Decision Procedure for Ethics." *Philosophical Review* (1951).

Rawls, John. "The Sense of Justice." *Philosophical Review* (1963).

Rawls, John. "Two Concepts of Rules." *Philosophical Review* (1955).

Singer, Marcus. *Generalization in Ethics.* New York: Knopf, 1961.

Singer, Marcus. "The Golden Rule." *Philosophy* (1963).

Singer, Marcus. "Negative and Positive Duties." *Philosophical Quarterly* (1965).

Taylor, Paul. "The Ethnocentric Fallacy." *Monist* (1963).

Taylor, Paul. "Four Types of Ethical Relativism." *Philosophical Review* (1954).

Taylor, Paul. *Normative Discourse.* Englewood Cliffs, NJ: Prentice-Hall, 1961.

Taylor, Paul. "On Justifying a Way of Life." *Indian Journal of Philosophy* (1961).

Toulmin, Stephen. *An Examination of the Place of Reason in Ethics.* Cambridge, U.K.: Cambridge University Press, 1950.

Toulmin, Stephen. "Is There a Fundamental Problem of Ethics?" *Australasian Journal of Philosophy* (1955).

Toulmin, Stephen. "Knowledge of Right and Wrong." *PAS* (1949–1950).

Toulmin, Stephen. "Principles of Morality." *Philosophy* (1956).

Wright, Georg von. *The Logic of Preference.* Edinburgh: Edinburgh University Press, 1963.

Wright, Georg von. *Norm and Action.* London: Routledge and K. Paul, 1963.

Wright, Georg von. "On Promises." *Theoria* (1962).

Wright, Georg von. "Practical Inference." *Philosophical Review* (1963).

Wright, Georg von. *The Varieties of Goodness.* London, 1963.

Raziel Abelson (1967)
(Ethics through the nineteenth century)
Kai Nielsen (1967)
(Twentieth-century ethics)

ETHICS, HISTORY OF: OTHER DEVELOPMENTS IN TWENTIETH-CENTURY ETHICS

Even setting aside the rich interplay between naturalism, nonnaturalism, and noncognitivism that is one of the hallmarks of twentieth-century moral philosophy, a very rich history remains, one that is impossible to even fully summarize here. Much of the story may be found elsewhere in the present volume in discussions devoted to particular moral theories and philosophers. The present entry examines just a few of the many themes that have occupied the attention of moral philosophers working within a diversity of traditions and that have thus exercised substantial influence on the shape of moral philosophy in the twentieth century.

MORAL PRINCIPLES

Whether the number of principles governing right conduct is one, or several, or even indefinitely many is a question that has animated the development of moral philosophy over the past century. Of course, this is by no means a new problem for moral philosophy, and the responses found to it in the twentieth century are themselves shaped by earlier debates between the nineteenth-century utilitarians and their intuitionist and idealist opponents.

Indeed, the *ideal utilitarianism* developed in George Edward Moore's *Principia Ethica* (1903) can usefully be seen as a possible rapprochement between utilitarianism and more pluralistic views. Moore maintained that there was but one ultimate principle of duty that one should act so as to promote as much good (intrinsic value) as possible, and in *Principia*, he maintained this principle to be analytic. It is puzzling that Moore did not take his own Open Question Argument to tell against this identity claim, but setting that aside, Moore appears to be an archmonist about ultimate principles of right action.

If we take note of Moore's innovative and influential value theory, however, it becomes clear that Moore is in a position (assuming his view is otherwise sustainable) to accommodate many of the insights of pluralists. Two aspects of Moore's value theory are critical. First, Moore held that goodness (or intrinsic value) is not identical to any natural property. Consequently, the bearers of intrinsic value may form an ultimately heterogenous group, having nothing salient in common other than their goodness. Indeed, Moore is a pluralist about the bearers of intrinsic value. Second, Moore argued that the value of a whole need not be the same as the value of the sum of its parts; such wholes are *organic unities*.

This pluralism about the bearers of intrinsic value and the flexibility that the doctrine of organic unities affords when it comes to the value of a whole, yield a view that seems well poised to accommodate the concerns of pluralists about ultimate principles. For pluralists have long emphasized that there are seemingly many potential grounds of duty and have challenged utilitarians to show that their view could leave in tact the seeming legitimacy of many moral rules that are not directly concerned with promoting utility. For the consequentialist who identifies goodness with a specific natural property and denies the doctrine of organic unities, these are very difficult challenges to meet. For one must then show that the apparently diverse grounds of duty really all involve the (naturalistically construed) property of goodness or else explain away the appearances. And one must show that apparently legitimate moral rules (e.g., rules governing the keeping of promises) really do serve to promote goodness. To a consequentialist of Moore's stripe, however, it is always open to identify further bearers of intrinsic value to accommodate our intuitions about the diverse grounds of duty and to appeal to the doctrine of organic unities to maintain the legitimacy of accepted moral rules even when these seem to lead to a universe with very disvaluable *parts*. Indeed, it may seem that provided a sufficiently flexible theory of value, the determined consequentialist will be able to say just about anything when it comes to duty.

Shortly, Moore's consequentialism was subjected to influential critique by William David Ross. Where earlier pluralists had identified many principles of (all things considered) duty, in *The Right and the Good* (1930), Ross sought principles of *prima facie duty*. For Ross, prima facie duties were acts of a type that tend to be our duty all things considered. Moreover, if someone had a prima facie duty to wash his neighbor's car (say because he had promised to do so), then this would be an all-things-considered duty if it did not pose any conflict with other prima facie duties. Ross argued forcefully that our apprehension of certain kinds of acts as prima facie duties does not depend upon our apprehension of them as being productive of more rather than less good.

In most, or perhaps all, cases, however, an agent will have conflicting prima facie duties. How is one to determine what duty requires, all things considered? To this, Ross answered that there are no principles (or at least no principles we have any prospect of identifying and using) that would determine the answer to this question, and that the best one can do is to exercise good judgment regarding which prima facie duty is, in the circumstances, most weighty. In taking this position, Ross appears to avoid an influential argument for monism about ultimate principles to which John Stuart Mill had given powerful voice in his *System of Logic* (1843/1874). Mill had argued that there could only be one possible ultimate moral principle because any set of several principles were liable to conflict about a given case, and there would need to be

a higher principle to be an *umpire* between them. By construing principles as principles of prima facie duty and by denying that there are any principles determining final duty, Ross seems to sidestep Mill's argument.

At the same time, Ross cast serious doubt on whether the systematic advantages often credited to monism about principles (especially by the nineteenth-century hedonistic utilitarians) could really survive the death of naturalistic accounts of the good, a death that Moore's arguments were at the time widely held to have confirmed. Ross recognized that some may be dissatisfied that a system of prima facie duties leaves no clear method for determining final duty. Ross plausibly replied that his view was no worse off in this regard than was the *ideal utilitarianism* of Moore. While Ross's view provides no discernible method for determining which of several prima facie duties is most weighty, Moore's view provides no discernible method for determining which of the various goods (as well as combinations thereof) that we might produce through our action have the greatest intrinsic value. One consequence of this debate between Moore and Ross was that the debate between monists and pluralists was revealed to depend critically on views of value and moral conflict.

Despite Ross's influential case for pluralism, the two dominant normative theories of the twentieth century, utilitarianism and Kantian deontology, both hold that there is only one ultimate principle of duty though, of course, they disagree about what this principle is. A perennial challenge for such views is to explain and or to justify the seeming legitimacy of a diverse set of common moral rules. It is worth looking briefly, then, at some of the resources developed by principle monists to meet this challenge.

For the principle monist, it is critical to define some relationship between whatever principle is taken to be ultimate and more particular midlevel moral rules, such as rules against promise-breaking or against dishonesty. One possibility, discussed influentially by John Rawls in "Two Concepts of Rules" (1955) is that some rules might be constitutive of a practice while other rules serve to justify that rule-constituted practice. Thus, Rawls imagines that a utilitarian might use a consequentialist principle to justify a practice of punishment that is itself constituted by backward-looking retributive rules. For example, a practice of punishment might be constituted in part by a rule that only those who have committed a crime are to be punished (no matter how much good punishing an innocent might do) even while the practice is justified by the good it brings about. Despite what the example of punishment might seem to suggest, this distinction does not entail that the only apt justifications of rule-constituted practices are consequentialist ones. Indeed, a Kantian could claim that the justification for a practice is that it best expresses respect for the dignity of each person even while that practice is constituted by rules that do not directly concern the dignity of persons. Rawls was quick to emphasize that his distinction was not a new one. Nevertheless, his clear and forceful discussion of it led moral philosophers to more steadfastly distinguish different levels of justification.

The latter half of the twentieth century saw the careful development of a variety of views about the relationship between ultimate standards and the more particular and diverse moral rules familiar from everyday life. Many of these developments were advanced by consequentialists. One influential view was put forward by Richard M. Hare in *Moral Thinking* (1981). According to Hare, there are two distinct levels of moral thinking. One, which Hare called *intuitive moral thinking*, involves the deployment of familiar and relatively simple moral principles in deciding how to act.

Hare claimed that intuitive moral thinking is characterized by a plurality of such principles and that such principles can conflict with one another by recommending different and incompatible courses of action. When this occurs, Hare argued, we can ascend to *critical moral thinking*. Doing so requires deploying a superior principle (for Hare, a version of the principle of utility). This principle is capable of both adjudicating the conflict between rival principles at the intuitive level and (in conjunction with facts about human psychology) justifying our everyday use of intuitive moral thinking. For example, instead of trying to determine which of two conflicting intuitive principles is more weighty (as Ross advocated), we can ask directly what course of action would best satisfy the utilitarian principle. Nevertheless, our everyday use of intuitive principles is justified because (for agents like us) directly applying the principle of utility to all of our decisions would be cumbersome, costly, and error prone.

Importantly, Hare's *two-level* view of the relationship between the principle of utility and more particular moral principles differs from classic versions of rule utilitarianism as well as from other forms of *indirect utilitarianism*. On the rule utilitarian view, the rightness of an act is defined in terms of its conformity to the best (i.e., best at promoting good consequences) rules whereas for Hare, it is possible both for an act to be in conformity with intuitive principles and yet wrong as well as for an act to be violative of intuitive rules and yet right. Right-

ness is determined by the principle governing critical moral thinking.

The resources of Hare's view can be deployed not only in considering familiar moral rules, but also in considering qualities of character. For just as the principle of utility might recommend the adoption of a range of more or less simple moral rules, so, too, it might recommend the cultivation of useful character traits. Again, though, one must be careful to distinguish what principle is actually the standard of rightness or duty. For some philosophers, such as Peter Railton, the act-consequentialist principle remains the ultimate moral standard even while it recommends that we develop the kinds of character traits that will sometimes lead us to act contrary to it. Others, however, suggest that the proper way for the utilitarian to evaluate acts is by reference to the motive that leads an agent to act with motives being evaluated by reference to their consequences.

Not surprisingly, the increased attention to indirect and two-level versions of principle monism also spawned more careful criticisms. In the case of indirect theories such as rule utilitarianism, one important worry—nicely and influentially discussed by David Lyons (1935–) in *Forms and Limits of Utilitarianism* (1965)—has been that such views inevitably *collapse* into their more direct progenitors. In the case of rule utilitarianism, for example, the collapse supposedly occurs because the really best rules would recommend the very same choices and actions as would a direct application of the principle of utility. In the case of two-level theories, an important set of worries has concerned the stability of the view. Some philosophers worry whether human beings really can smoothly ride the escalator between intuitive and critical thinking more or less as circumstances warrant.

In other cases the worry is more conceptual. For if (as Hare's view seems to require) it is sometimes advisable to set aside the ultimately correct standard, then it seems possible that there could be circumstances in which it is advisable to permanently set aside (or even to banish from thought entirely) the putatively correct standard. Whether a proper standard of conduct could be *self-effacing* (to borrow a term from Derek Parfit's influential discussion in *Reasons and Persons* [1984]), has been a matter of intense dispute, especially with regard to moral standards. Some, following philosophers such as Henry Sidgwick, welcome the possibility; others see in it a deep confusion. In some cases the thought has been that moral standards are essentially deliberative tools and so must have some place in the psychology of moral agents. In other cases the thought has been that moral standards essentially play a role in interpersonal relations and so must remain *public*, where they can be appealed to, criticized, and defended.

Despite the development of new tools to defend principle monism, the last quarter of the twentieth century saw a notable (and ongoing) revival of pluralism, sometimes of a new and more radical variety. Some of this interest centered on the ways in which various values might conflict. Where Ross was cautiously skeptical of identifying principles that would systematically rank prima facie duties, some philosophers, such as Thomas Nagel (1970), began to argue that various values might be fundamentally incommensurable, perhaps because they arise or make sense only within certain standpoints or perspectives. Clearly incommensurable values would seriously complicate the prospects for reasoned and justified choice when such values conflict, and there is no general agreement on whether it would remain possible at all.

But the revival of interest in pluralism has also been inspired by careful reflection on the sheer variety of considerations that can acquire moral significance. Where Ross had countenanced a limited set of principles governing prima facie (but not final) duty, a new breed of pluralists (sometimes called particularists) seek to challenge whether there are any moral principles at all—or at least whether a proper understanding of morality must make reference to them. On such views our moral understanding is not best represented as the application of universal rules but, rather, should be seen as kind of direct appreciation of the moral relevance of the particular features before us. The advantages and liabilities of this position are still being explored and debated.

MORAL AND PERSONAL VALUE

According to a dominant view of moral value, what is of moral value should be an object of care and concern for any rational agent. This view goes back at least to Plato, and according to it, moral value is of universal appeal; one has reason to care about it no matter who one is. Though widely held this view raises a number of important questions, in part because there seem to be many values that do not necessarily have a claim on any rational person. We might call such values *personal values* to denote that whether (or perhaps how) one ought to care about them depends upon what sort of person one is. Such values are also commonly referred to as *nonmoral values*. Among the most commonly offered examples are the value we find in personal relationships, such as the value of one friend to another, the value of achieving a personal goal or project such as the goal of amassing the

world's most comprehensive collection of glass paperweights, and the value of living up to a personal ideal such as being a good marine or a good writer.

It is now widely agreed that such personal values need not be self-interested in any intuitive sense since a person's projects and concerns might be directed outward to others and to the world. Intuitively, the person whose project is to save land for a bird sanctuary is working to benefit the birds or the environment and not, at least in the first instance, herself. It is often thought that personal values depend upon the particular relationship in which a person stands to the object of value (as the value a parent finds in their child may depend on it being *their* child) or upon the particular preferences or choices the person has made (amassing those paperweights may be of importance only because the agent has come, perhaps by choice, to care about doing so).

If we accept some distinction between moral and personal value, then a number of issues arise. Since distinguishing moral and personal value raises the possibility of their coming into conflict, one must wonder whether they really do so. One view, associated with Immanuel Kant, is that personal values cease to be of value if ever their pursuit runs afoul of moral value. Consistent with this, though, one might hold that moral values themselves must make room for the pursuit of nonmoral ends and that our understanding of what moral value requires of us should be shaped by our intuitions about the reasonable pursuit of other values. Then there is the possibility that there is a genuine conflict between moral and personal values, and this raises questions about what the appropriate response to such a conflict would be. Before turning to these issues in more depth, however, it is worth pausing to ask whether they might be sidestepped.

Given the immense energy devoted to understanding the relationship between moral and personal value, it is notable that the twentieth century opened with a classic rejection of the problem. Moore argued that the tendency to distinguish moral and personal value rested on confusion and that in fact there is no such thing as personal value. Though couched as an argument against egoism, Moore's reasoning, if sound, would undermine the possibility of something being valuable to me but not to others. For Moore held that any putative claim of the form *X* is good for *A* must be resolved into a claim of absolute value (either into the claim that *X* is absolutely good and so in having *X*, *A* would have something absolutely good or else into the claim that it is absolutely good that *A* have *X*) or else into a psychological claim, such as the claim that *A* desires *X*, which Moore argues is not really a value claim at all. To be sure, Moore did not deny that many of the supposed examples of personal value are in fact valuable (if anything, he emphasized their value), but he argued that properly understood, such value must be *absolute* and so equally of value from any point of view. Few now accept Moore's argument or its conclusion. For a representative criticism see John Leslie Mackie's "Sidgwick's Pessimism" (1976); for a more recent defense of an argument that is similar in spirit to Moore's, see Brian Medlin's (1927–2004) "Ultimate Principles and Ethical Egoism" (1957).

Setting Moore's position aside, there remain a host of questions about the relationship between moral and personal value. During the heyday of Ross and his fellow intuitionists, these questions received comparatively less attention. But as Rossian pluralism receded from center stage and utilitarianism and Kantian ethics (and later virtue ethics) began to be perceived as the main alternatives, the relationship between moral and personal value became a central topic of debate for moral philosophers.

According to one influential critique initiated by Bernard Williams, some moral theories fail precisely because they do not give a proper place to personal values. In his "Critique of Utilitarianism" (1973), Williams charged that utilitarianism requires agents, in so far as they take up a moral point of view, to regard their own projects and values as of no greater importance than the values and projects of others. Indeed, the value of anyone achieving their personal aims depends not at all on whose aims they are but on what contribution they make to the overall amount of happiness in the world. However, having personal values in the first place seems to presuppose attaching some significant importance to them, and such values are part of what make us who we are.

The problem, Williams charged, is not that utilitarianism implies implausible moral verdicts but that it leaves us thinking about matters in the wrong way. And if utilitarianism asks us to treat our own values and projects as having no greater importance than anyone else's, then, as Williams put it, it amounts to an assault on our psychological health, on our *integrity*. Though officially directed at utilitarianism, Williams's argument was more broadly influential. It inspired further close attention to the character and variety of personal values and to the ways in which they are an essential element of any familiar picture of human life and agency. Some philosophers were also quick to attempt to extend Williams's point to moral theories other than utilitarianism and to take his

critique to undermine any normative theory that embodied a very strict impartiality.

As moral philosophers gave greater attention to personal values in the 1970s and 1980s, there was at the same time a great increase in the moral discussion of concrete moral problems. None received greater attention than the grave problem of hunger and poverty. In light of these developments, a new interest in the *demandingness* of morality arose. It is important to distinguish the issue of demandingness from the question whether moral requirements represent categorical or hypothetical imperatives. While the latter is a matter of whether moral requirements represent actions as good (or bad) in virtue of the ends that may be brought about by acting on them, the former is a matter of the imposition that complying with morality makes upon the other interests and concerns of the agent. A moral requirement might be categorical (requiring an agent to perform certain actions *whether they serve certain purposes or not*) and yet still not be very demanding if complying with it would not frequently or profoundly interfere with an agent pursuing other aims. Conversely, an imperative might be hypothetical and still be very demanding. While the question of whether moral requirements represent categorical or hypothetical imperatives is a matter, in some sense, of the logic of moral requirements, the demandingness of moral requirements depends crucially upon both the content of moral requirements and also upon contingent facts about the aims of the agents to whom moral requirements apply, and also the state of the world.

Demandingness has come to be such an important issue, in part because, given the state of the world, it seems likely that virtually any plausible moral theory threatens to be extremely demanding. While this may be obvious in the case of utilitarianism, it may be no less true of any moral theory that recognizes a duty to aid others in need, as virtually any plausible view must do. As philosophers such as Peter Singer in his famous paper "Famine, Affluence, and Morality" (1972) have emphasized, most people in developed countries, even those of modest means, are in a position to take actions that would save the lives of many other people simply by sacrificing what in the light of comparison seem like trivial personal goods. And yet there is no obvious stopping point to this argument, and if there is not, then morality might require us to sacrifice nearly everything—at least until circumstances change and our aid is no longer needed (which is unlikely to say the least!).

Philosophers have explored various responses to the issue of demandingness. Three will be noted here. First, for some, the problem is not with any account of morality that leaves morality demanding. Morality simply is demanding—or at least can be in a world such as ours—and if people are often unwilling to do what morality requires, this is because they do not care as much as they should about morality. As an alternative to such rigorism, many philosophers have argued that theories of morality that leave morality highly demanding are dubious for that reason. The task is then to find a plausible revision. In the case of our duties to the needy, some have suggested that those duties are less stringent when those in need are far away and unfamiliar. Others suggest that morality requires us only to do our fair share of the helping, even if this leaves many of those in desperate need without help at all. Still others argue that our duty to aid, especially when applied to those in faraway lands, is a collective not an individual one.

A third approach is to argue that morality may be very demanding but that morality should not be the sole or even dominating concern of a good person. On this view our ideal of a person is of one whose concern with morality is itself tempered by other (possibly conflicting) concerns. This last possibility shows further that the issue of demandingness must be distinguished from the question of whether moral demands are *overriding*. Just as a job might be very demanding even while only a fool would allow its demands always to override other concerns, so, too, some suspect that morality might be highly demanding but that one can also give it too high a place in one's life.

Though the view that moral value has a claim on all rational agents has been a dominant one, it has also been subjected to interesting and influential critique. In the first half of the twentieth century, much effort was made to understand what attitude is involved in the judgment that something is of moral value. Under the influence of Moore's Open Question Argument and along with the rise of the early noncognitivists, it was often thought that virtually anything could be coherently judged to have moral value. After all, if (as Moore held) moral value is not identical to any natural property, or (as the early noncognitivists maintained) to hold something to have moral value is just to take a special favorable attitude towards it, then there seems to be no conceptual bar to holding virtually anything to have moral value. In the latter half of the twentieth century, however, following the lead of philosophers such as Philippa Foot and Gertrude Elizabeth Margaret Anscombe, many moral theorists began to think that there was a necessary connection between judgments of moral value and particular human

concerns. To claim, for example, that painting two of one's toenails green is morally good is, philosophers such as Foot argued, simply unintelligible (absent some special background story) since doing so has no discernible connection to human flourishing or well being.

Once philosophers began to look to the possibility that there might be a necessary connection between moral evaluation and specific human concerns and interests, they also began to look carefully at evaluative concepts that seem clearly to implicate such a connection, such as specific virtue concepts like courage and modesty. Where the first half of the twentieth century was dominated by discussion of ethical concepts such as *good* and *right* (sometimes called *thin* ethical concepts), the latter half of the century saw steadily increasing interest in *thick* ethical concepts, such as virtue concepts, that single out specific forms of action and practical orientation as worthy of esteem.

To think that moral evaluation must somehow be directed at specific human concerns and interests is clearly consistent with the possibility that the relevant concerns are (or at least can be) universally the concerns of any rational being. Thus, one might suppose that in seeing courage as a moral value one must suppose that it is worthy of the esteem of any rational agent. As the century progressed, however, philosophers such as Alasdair MacIntyre (1981) and Williams began to argue that the very way in which we make moral or ethical evaluations is shaped by particular institutions and practices—by what we might call culture. And since these differ from place to place and time to time, it is not clear that all rational agents must even share a mode of evaluation, much less that there is some thing (*moral value*) with which all rational beings should be concerned. Indeed, for such philosophers, the very idea that moral value is that value which has a claim on any rational being is itself a (dubious) product of Enlightenment culture, with Kant receiving a large share of blame. Though such philosophers are not skeptical about moral value, they are denying a particular way of demarcating moral value from supposedly other values. If such philosophers are correct, moral values would seem to have some of the hallmarks commonly associated with personal values: they depend upon the particular position and concerns of agents.

AGENCY

It is scarcely possible to imagine a moral theory that does not depend upon claims about the nature of human or rational agency, but the degree to which moral philosophers actively look to accounts of agency in developing and defending normative theories fluctuates over time. Philosophers such as David Hume and Kant based their moral philosophy on sophisticated and original accounts of agency. By contrast, the beginning of the twentieth century saw a comparative neglect of agency. At least two factors may provide a partial explanation.

The first is that the early intuitionists, beginning with Moore, were highly interested in human agents as knowers of moral propositions or facts. If moral propositions were intuitive or self-evident, then the serious and difficult question became how human beings have such knowledge. On the surface this does not preclude a deep interest in agency (perhaps, in a Kantian vein, human beings know about the moral necessity of certain acts by knowing something about human agency). But the surrounding philosophical climate tended to eclipse this alternative. The nineteenth century saw the rapid and exciting development of psychology as an empirical science. Add to this the fact that Moore's Open Question Argument made it seem scandalous even to appear to derive moral conclusions from empirical observation. But if human agency is ultimately a matter of psychology and psychology is a matter to be settled by empirical methods, then the intuitive moral knowledge the intuitionists attributed to human beings could not be based upon knowledge of agency lest the dreaded naturalistic fallacy be committed. The second factor that may partially explain philosopher's relative neglect of agency is the fact that philosophers were busy looking elsewhere, especially to linguistic phenomena.

The latter part of the twentieth century, however, saw renewed and intense interest in the integration of normative theories with theories of agency. In part, this may be traced to the rise of Kantian ethics that treats moral principles as principles of rational willing. It was also no doubt influenced by the rise of *action theory* in the latter half of the twentieth century as well as by the renewed interest philosophers showed in problems of personal identity and by exciting work done on the issue of free will. All of these developments had the effect of drawing attention to human beings as actors with values, ideals, beliefs, emotions, evolving desires and interests, plans, habits, addictions, and more. This is quite different from looking to human beings as perceivers of value.

It is not possible to summarize all of the ways in which moral philosophy has been impacted by its renewed and increasing attention to agency. One important theme concerns the possible analogy between the interest agents are rational to take in their own future concerns and the interest agents are morally required to take in the concerns of others. We think of agents as unified across time. To reprise an example of Nagel's: If I expect that I will want to eat a persimmon next week, then I will be concerned to take the steps necessary to make this possible (even if I do not now care whether I eat a persimmon next week or care whether I come to want to eat a persimmon next week). Indeed, the ability to integrate one's desires and concerns this way is considered a hallmark of prudential rationality. In *The Possibility of Altruism* (1970), Nagel argued that, properly understood, vindicating the rationality of caring about the interests of your own future self also shows how one may vindicate the rationality of caring about the interests of others. Though he later abandoned this argument, Nagel's effort to integrate the justification of important moral norms with an account of an agent as a person persisting through time and potentially aware of other persons and their interests was of lasting importance. Philosophers such as Parfit, as well as Nagel himself, continued to develop these themes.

One such development was an increased attention to a distinction, first introduced by Nagel, between *agent relative* and *agent neutral reasons*. Though the proper way of drawing the distinction is a difficult technical matter, the intuitive heart of the distinction is between those reasons that are reasons for some agents but not for others and those reasons that are reasons no matter who you are. For example, I may have a reason to hold a birthday party for my child because it is my child. But many would doubt that you have a reason to hold a party for my child or even to help me hold one (though you might have a reason to hold a birthday party for *your* child). The reason depends on who I am. By contrast, if a stranger is about to step accidentally in front of an oncoming bus and I can pull him back, then I have a reason to do so. In this case, however, many people are inclined to agree that this is a reason anyone else has as well, or at least would have, provided only that they were in a position to do something about the matter.

The contrast between agent-relative and agent-neutral reasons is of importance in part because agent-relative reasons seem to be at play in the kinds of personal values discussed in the prior section. But many philosophers have also come to see them at work in important aspects of moral thinking, especially in the nature of *deontological* prohibitions on certain kinds of action. On one plausible interpretation, a person committed to a prohibition against, for example, killing the innocent, will care deeply about who does any killing. Though such a person may recognize any killing of the innocent to be bad, it may matter greatly to them that they not be the one doing the killing. Because many philosophers are interested in defending the rationality of such moral norms, locating their place in an account of the kinds of reasons that agents may have has become a critical question.

THE RISE OF NATURALISM IN MORAL PHILOSOPHY

For much of the twentieth century, the empirical study of moral judgment, norms, and behavior was given little attention by moral philosophers. This state of affairs is undergoing a profound reversal. The present discussion will not attempt to summarize the state of developing research, but three types of inquiry are notable.

First, the rapid development of evolutionary biology spawned renewed interest in developing accounts of how moral norms might have arisen out of a process of evolution. Of course, the suspicion that moral norms do have some such history is an ancient one, but the techniques of modern evolutionary research, including the tools of game theory and the computer simulation, have made it possible to better develop and critically assess possible explanations. Of particular interest are norms regarding helping behavior (or altruism), cooperation, and fair dealing. There are often significant differences in the use of terminology between those conducting this empirical research and those engaged in more traditional moral philosophy. For example, in discussions of the evolution of moral norms, altruistic behavior is often any behavior that in fact benefits another whereas for many traditional moral philosophers, behavior is altruistic only if it is undertaken for the sake of benefiting another. So long as these terminological issues are treated with care, however, they do not seem to present any decisive obstacles.

Another area of rapidly developing research is the application of neuroscience and cognitive science to the topic of moral judgment. While moral philosophers have long deployed hypothetical cases as intuition pumps, the recent use of brain scanning techniques appears to reveal that moral thinking about different kinds of cases involves activity in distinct brain regions. Such results are of interest not least because many moral arguments depend upon claims that different cases are analogous and so merit comparable analysis. The science involved in these studies is both complex and rapidly evolving, and many philosophers and scientists expect increasingly fine-grained and thorough results.

A third area where empirical research has blossomed and impacted moral philosophy is in the area of social psychology. Moral theories of all stripes attribute to human beings beliefs in moral principles, or acceptance of moral norms, or possession of virtuous character traits. In each case the attribution typically brings along with it an expectation that an agent of whom it is true will be appropriately motivated to act accordingly. In this way, moral theories claim that agents have certain moral outlooks and that these outlooks impact the agents' behavior. In short, moral theories make claims about agency. Whether agents really are so motivated, however, appears to many to be an empirically testable hypothesis. Using the tools of social psychology, some scientists and philosophers have begun to emphasize the degree to which human beings of all stripes seem to be influenced by what would seem to be morally irrelevant factors.

For example, one might have thought that whether a person would help a stranger would depend largely on whether that person was a good person (perhaps because they have the virtue of kindness, or because they accept some moral principle that dictates helping others). Experimental studies, however, seem to reveal that whether people help each other is highly correlated with such factors as whether they are in a good mood, a factor that most would count as morally irrelevant and as precisely the kind of thing that sound moral commitment would get round. Thus, some have suggested that certain moral theories may rest upon dubious or false presuppositions about human agency.

In each of these cases, the precise relevance of empirical findings to more familiar questions of moral philosophy is disputed and uncertain. Few, if any, researchers believe that such empirical findings straightforwardly reveal which of our moral commitments are worthy of our endorsement and which are not. Brain scans do not tell us whether a moral intuition is to be trusted or not; evolutionary accounts of the development of norms do not tell us whether those norms are morally worthy or not. At least they do not do so in any simplistic way. Neither, however, do many philosophers assume that such empirical findings are ultimately irrelevant to the familiar normative questions of moral philosophy. For many moral philosophers, the question is not whether empirical science is relevant but how so. The absence of any consensus answer to this question may be due in part to the fact that the empirical sciences in question are not yet fully developed. Perhaps as we get a better scientific picture of the nature and history of moral norms and judgment, the relevance of this picture to normative questions will become clearer. Of note as well, though, is the fact that there is no agreed-upon epistemology for settling normative questions, and unless there is, it seems unlikely that philosophers will be able to agree about the relevance of empirical studies. Indeed, one may suspect that questions of how empirical results are relevant to normative questions will itself become an important locus of dispute (if it is not so already) in assessing rival moral epistemologies. It is often remarked that Moore's writings set the stage for the development of twentieth-century moral philosophy, and in many ways, they did. But he surely would not have written this ending.

See also Anscombe, Gertrude Elizabeth Margaret; Consequentialism; Empiricism; Enlightenment; Epistemology; Foot, Philippa; Hare, Richard M.; Hedonism; Hume, David; Idealism; Intuition; Kant, Immanuel; MacIntyre, Alasdair; Mackie, John Leslie; Mill, John Stuart; Monism and Pluralism; Moore, George Edward; Nagel, Thomas; Naturalism; Parfit, Derek; Plato; Rawls, John; Ross, William David; Sidgwick, Henry; Singer, Peter; Utilitarianism; Virtue Ethics; Williams, Bernard.

Bibliography

Adams, Robert M. "Motive Utilitarianism." *Journal of Philosophy* 73(1976): 467–481.

Anscombe, G. E. M. "Modern Moral Philosophy." *Philosophy* 33 (1958): 1–19.

Brandt, R. B. "Toward a Credible Form of Utilitarianism." In *Morality and the Language of Conduct*, edited by H.-N. Castañeda and G. Nakhnikian. Detroit, MI: Wayne State University Press, 1963.

Dancy, Jonathan. *Moral Reasons*. Oxford: Blackwell, 1993.

Hare, Richard M. *Moral Thinking: Its Levels, Method, and Point*. Oxford: Clarendon Press, 1981.

Hooker, Brad. *Ideal Code, Real World: A Rule-consequentialist Theory of Morality*. Oxford: Oxford University Press, 2000.

Lyons, David. *Forms and Limits of Utilitarianism*. Oxford: Oxford University Press, 1965.

MacIntyre, Alasdair. *After Virtue: A Study in Moral Theory*. Notre Dame, IN: University of Notre Dame Press, 1981.

Mackie, J. L. "Sidgwick's Pessimism." *Philosophical Quarterly* 26 (1976): 317–327.

McDowell, John. "Virtue and Reason." *Monist* 62 (1979): 331–350.

Medlin, Brian. "Ultimate Principles and Ethical Egoism." *Australasian Journal of Philosophy*. 35 (1957): 111–118.

Mill, John Stuart. *System of Logic Ratiocinative and Inductive, Being a Connected View of the Principles of Evidence and the Methods of Scientific Investigation* (1843). 8th ed. New York: Harpers & Brothers, 1874.

Moore, G. E. *Principia Ethica*. Rev. ed., edited by Thomas Baldwin. Cambridge, U.K.: Cambridge University Press, 1903; 1993.

Nagel, Thomas. *The Possibility of Altruism*. Princeton, NJ: Princeton University Press, 1970.

Parfit, Derek. *Reasons and Persons*. Oxford: Clarendon Press, 1984.

Railton, Peter. "Alienation, Consequentialism, and the Demands of Morality." *Philosophy and Public Affairs* 13 (1984): 174–131.

Rawls, John. "Two Concepts of Rules." *Philosophical Review* 64 (1) (1955): 3–32.

Ross, W. D. *The Right and the Good*. Oxford: Oxford University Press, 1930.

Singer, Peter. "Famine, Affluence, and Morality." *Philosophy and Public Affairs* 1 (1972): 229–243.

Williams, Bernard. "A Critique of Utilitarianism." In *Utilitarianism: For and Against*, edited by J. J. C. Smart and Bernard Williams. New York: Cambridge University Press, 1973.

Williams, Bernard. *Ethics and the Limits of Philosophy*. Cambridge, MA: Harvard University Press, 1985.

Sean D. McKeever (2005)

ETHICS, TELEOLOGICAL

See *Teleological Ethics*

ETHICS AND ECONOMICS

Economics is linked to both ethics and the theory of rationality. Economics complements and intersects with moral philosophy in both the concepts it has constructed and in its treatment of normative problems.

RATIONALITY, UTILITY THEORY, AND WELFARE

At the foundation of economics lies a normative theory of individual rationality. The theory raises no questions about the rationality of ultimate ends and few questions about the rationality of beliefs. It maintains that an agent A chooses (acts) rationally if A's preferences are rational and A never prefers an available option to the option chosen. A's preferences are rational only if they are transitive and complete—that is, A can consistently rank all alternatives. If an agent's preferences are complete and transitive and satisfy some technical conditions, they can be represented by numbers. These numbers, which are arbitrary apart from their order, are "ordinal utilities." If an agent's preferences satisfy additional conditions concerning risky or uncertain alternatives, then they can be represented by a cardinal utility function. In contemporary economic theory, utility is merely an index locating alternatives in a preference ranking, not a substantive good.

Given economists' commitments to utility theory in explaining human choices, it is natural that they would look to levels of utility (preference satisfaction) as the measure of welfare. It is, however, difficult to justify identifying welfare with the satisfaction of preferences, even as a simplification. Satisfying preferences that depend on false beliefs is often harmful, whereas satisfying preferences that do not concern oneself is typically irrelevant to one's welfare. Many philosophers endorse a more nuanced identification of well-being with the satisfaction of "informed" and self-interested preferences, and they can thus employ some of the framework of normative economics. Even with these qualifications, it is questionable whether taking well-being to be the satisfaction of preferences is suitable for assessing claims to scarce resources. Should one measure the well-being of those who have learned—possibly quite rationally—not to want what they have not gotten by the satisfaction of their preferences?

Some economists propose different conceptions of well-being. Of particular contemporary interest is Amartya Sen's capability approach. In Sen's view, a capability is the ability to achieve a certain sort of "functioning": literacy is a capability; reading is a functioning. People may value capabilities for their own sake as well as for the kinds of functioning they permit; someone who stays in his or her room may still be glad to know that the door is not locked.

One advantage of more objective approaches such as Sen's is that they avoid the problems of interpersonal comparison that derive from identifying well-being and preference satisfaction. Formerly, economists such as Pigou cited diminishing marginal utility of income to argue that a more equal distribution of income would increase total welfare. This argument compares the contributions income makes to the well-being of different people.

Once one takes seriously the preference-satisfaction view of well-being, these comparisons become problematic. Lionel Robbins argued that there is no objective way to compare the extent to which A's and B's preferences are satisfied, and most (though not all) economists maintain that economic evaluations must not rely on interpersonal-utility comparisons.

EFFICIENCY AND PARETO OPTIMALITY

Efficiency has a technical meaning within normative economics. Suppose that utility is the satisfaction of preferences. Consider some allocation of resources S—S is a "Pareto Improvement" over some other allocation R if and only if it increases the utility (preference satisfaction) of at least one person without decreasing anyone's utility.

In other words, S is a Pareto improvement over R if and only if someone prefers to R, and nobody prefers R to S. S is "efficient" or "Pareto optimal" if no other allocation is a Pareto improvement over S. If S is Pareto optimal, then every alternative that satisfies someone's preferences better leads to someone else's preferences being less well satisfied. The Pareto concepts permit economists to rank some social states in terms of preference satisfaction without making interpersonal-utility comparisons.

If one is minimally benevolent and favors satisfying people's preferences, then, other things being equal, one will endorse Pareto efficiency. Moreover, it can be proved that competitive equilibria under certain idealized conditions (no externalities, no public goods, no informational limits, and so on) are Pareto efficient. Minimal benevolence then implies that competitive equilibria are (other things being equal) morally good economic states. A second theorem shows that an efficient economic outcome with any desired distribution of welfare can be attained by a competitive market, given the right initial distribution of endowments to agents. A preference-satisfaction view of well-being combined with minimal beneficence establishes the moral claims of efficiency.

Efficiency judgments capture only one moral dimension along which to assess economic policies, institutions, processes, and outcomes. Rather than pretending that efficiency judgments are conclusive or conceding that they reflect only one of a great many evaluative perspectives, economists generally regard economic evaluation as two-dimensional. In addition to questions of efficiency—with respect to which economists claim a special competence—there are also questions concerning distribution or equity, about which economists typically have little to say.

This view of economic evaluation is inadequate because the Pareto concepts have very limited applicability: Economic changes usually involve winners and losers. One way to extend the assessment of efficiency is via the notion of a potential Pareto improvement, where there are winners and losers in terms of preference satisfaction but the winners are able to compensate the losers. No compensation is actually required. Kaldor and Hicks thought that a potential Pareto improvement showed that the economic "pie" had grown larger, whereas questions about who wins and who loses concern equity not efficiency and should be left to the political process. This view is subject to technical difficulties, and the bottom line is that there is no way to judge changes that affect distributions while remaining neutral on distributive questions.

MORAL MATHEMATICS

The tools and theories of economists have contributed significantly to moral philosophy. Contemporary examples can be found in the literature on egalitarianism or on measures of freedom. The two branches of economics that have been most relevant to moral philosophy are social choice theory and game theory.

One can call any ranking of social states a "social-welfare function," and normative principles can be regarded as constraints on social-welfare functions. The Pareto principle, for example, picks out those social welfare functions that rank R over S if somebody prefers R to S and nobody prefers S to R. Economists have hoped to identify additional plausible normative principles relating individual and social welfare and from them to deduce some general method of evaluating outcomes, policies, and institutions. This framework is quite limited. Procedural matters such as fairness or due process apparently count only instrumentally. Furthermore, in investigating the implications of principles constraining acceptable relationships between individual and social values, Kenneth Arrow wound up establishing a striking impossibility theorem.

Social choice theory is the proof and interpretation of theorems concerning the aggregation of preferences, judgments, and interests. The relevance of social-choice theorems to morality depends on what is being aggregated and for what purpose. Does one seek principles for making social decisions or for carrying out social evaluations? Is one aggregating preferences or judgments? A good deal of social-choice theory, like John Harsanyi's derivation of utilitarianism, consists of formal arguments for moral conclusions, but the most important role of social choice theorems has been to reveal ambiguities and difficulties in apparently plausible moral principles. The interpretation of social-choice theorems is a subtle and complex task.

Game theory is concerned with strategic circumstances, where outcomes depend on the choices of several agents. The theory of games is particularly relevant to moral philosophy in its analysis of interaction problems of moral importance. Problems of social cooperation are often complicated, and it may be enlightening to think about recurring patterns. The most famous of these is the so-called "prisoner's dilemma," in which individuals who act in their self-interest reach a worse outcome for everyone than agents who do not. Prisoner's dilemmas vividly represent problems of social cooperation, free-riding, and public-goods provision.

Modeling interactions with game theory is a subtle task, because there are many different simple games and because simple models abstract from so much. Actual interactions, unlike prisoner's dilemmas, are rarely "one-shot" games, and game-theoretic analyses of repeated interactions are complicated and controversial. Even if game theory were in a more settled state, there would be grounds to hesitate before employing it to address ethical questions. One may have qualms about its focus on preference satisfaction and about whether the only perspective for individuals to adopt in social interactions is individual maximization. Nevertheless, some philosophers and economists such as Geoffrey Brennan, James Buchanan, David Gauthier, and Ken Binmore have used game theory to argue for views of justice.

CONCLUSION

Economists and moral philosophers share interests in rationality and in evaluating social institutions, processes, outcomes, and policies. Although the theoretical starting points of economists and moral philosophers differ, the two subjects have a great deal to offer each other. Moral philosophers who want their work to bear on social institutions, policies, and outcomes have much to learn from economists, who have studied the consequences of alternative policies and who have sought operational measures of theoretical concepts. Economists also offer moral philosophers formal and conceptual tools. At the same time, economists concerned with evaluating institutions and policies cannot avoid thinking about ethics.

See also Good, The; Utilitarianism; Value and Valuation.

Bibliography

Arrow, Kenneth. *Social Choice and Individual Values.* 2nd ed. New York: Wiley, 1963. This seminal contribution gave birth to social choice theory.

Binmore, Kenneth. *Game Theory and the Social Contract.* Cambridge, MA: MIT Press, 1998. A two-volume application of game theory to the theory of justice by a leading game theorist.

Brennan, Geoffrey, and James Buchanan. *The Reason of Rules: Constitutional Political Economy.* New York: Cambridge University Press, 1985. An application of game theoretic reasoning to problems of constitutional design.

Broome, John. *Weighing Goods.* Oxford: Basil Blackwell, 1991. A philosophical treatment of problems of rationality and well-being.

Dworkin, Ronald. *Sovereign Virtue: The Theory and Practice of Equality.* Cambridge, MA: Harvard University Press, 2000. Essays on egalitarianism that reflect the influence of economics.

Elster, Jon. *Sour Grapes: Studies in the Subversion of Rationality.* New York: Cambridge University Press, 1983. A study of the notion of rationality and of failures of rationality.

Elster, Jon, and John Roemer, eds. *Interpersonal Comparisons of Well-Being.* Cambridge, U.K.: Cambridge University Press, 1991.

Gauthier, David. *Morals by Agreement.* Oxford: Oxford University Press, 1986. An ambitious attempt to derive a theory of justice from bargaining theory.

Hardin, Russell. *Morality Within the Limits of Reason.* Chicago: University of Chicago Press, 1988. An application of game theory and rational choice theory to the defense of utilitarianism.

Harsanyi, John. "Cardinal Welfare, Individualistic Ethics and Interpersonal Comparisons of Utility." *Journal of Political Economy* 63 (1955): 309–321. A social-choice theoretical "proof" of utilitarianism.

Harsanyi, John. *Rational Behavior and Bargaining Equilibrium in Games and Social Situations.* Cambridge, U.K.: Cambridge University Press, 1977. A general development of rational-choice theory and game theory with a systematic discussion of interpersonal utility comparisons.

Hausman, Daniel, and Michael McPherson. *Economic Analysis and Moral Philosophy.* Cambridge, U.K.: Cambridge University Press, 1996. A comprehensive survey of literature on ethics and economics.

Hicks, John. "The Foundations of Welfare Economics." *Economic Journal* 49 (1939): 696–712. A classic statement of "new welfare economics" based on the compensation criterion.

Kaldor, Nicholas. "Welfare Propositions of Economics and Interpersonal Comparisons of Utility." *Economic Journal* 49 (1939): 549–552. The first presentation and application of the notion of a potential Pareto improvement.

Kolm, Serge-Christophe. *Justice and Equity.* Translated by Harold See. Cambridge, MA: MIT Press, 2002. A pathbreaking book drawing on economic concepts in addressing philosophical questions.

Little, Ian. *A Critique of Welfare Economics.* 2nd ed. Oxford: Oxford University Press, 1957. A classic discussion of the difficulties of welfare economics without interpersonal comparisons.

McClennen, Edward. *Rationality and Dynamic Choice: Foundational Explorations.* Cambridge, U.K.: Cambridge University Press, 1990. A general development of the theory of rational choice including a critique of the standard theory and the development of an alternative.

Nussbaum, Martha. *Women and Human Development.* Cambridge, U.K.: Cambridge University Press, 2001. An alternative presentation of the capability approach.

Pigou, Arthur C. *The Economics of Welfare.* London: Macmillan, 1920. The classic statement of traditional utilitarian welfare economics.

Robbins, Lionel. *An Essay on the Nature and Significance of Economic Science.* 2nd ed. London: Macmillan, 1935. A major methodological overview with a classic argument against the possibility of interpersonal comparisons.

Samuelson, Paul A. "Evaluation of Real National Income." *Oxford Economic Papers* N.S. 2 (1950): 1–29. A demonstration of the impossibility of disentangling efficiency and distributional questions.

Scanlon, Thomas. "Preference and Urgency." *Journal of Philosophy* 72 (1975): 655–670. An argument that questions of justice cannot be decided only by considerations involving preference satisfaction.

Sen, Amartya. *Inequality Reexamined.* Cambridge, MA: Harvard University Press, 1992. An introduction to Sen's more recent work on inequality, capabilities, and welfare.

Sen, Amartya. *On Ethics and Economics.* Oxford: Blackwells, 1987. A concise but demanding introduction to the subject.

Sen, Amartya, and Bernard Williams, eds. *Utilitarianism and Beyond.* Cambridge, U.K.: Cambridge University Press, 1982. An influential anthology of essays on economics and ethics with particular reference to utilitarianism.

Taylor, Michael C. *The Possibility of Cooperation.* New York: Cambridge University Press, 1987. A technical and philosophical study of game-theoretical problems of repeated interactions.

Daniel M. Hausman (2005)

ETHICS AND EPISTEMOLOGY

See *Epistemology and Ethics, Parallel Between*

ETHICS AND MORALITY

Ethics signifies an aspect of human life that can also be called *morality*. There seem only minor differences in usage between the two terms. We speak more naturally of *professional ethics* than of *professional morals* to refer to virtues and codes of behavior of specific professions. This is not, however, because the word *moral* is restricted to human beings, or rational persons, as such, because we also speak naturally of *role morality*. A somewhat more substantial difference is that some forms of behavior especially related to sexuality, such as homosexuality, abortion, and premarital intercourse, are condemned (by some) as *immoral* where *unethical* would not be used. This usage may require a notion of a natural order (possibly of a religious character) that certain actions violate, even if they do not cause harm in some other way. At the same time, *immoral* and *unethical* are often used interchangeably, and both historically and contemporaneously, both can connote wrongness in actions and vice in character.

One influential attempt to get philosophical mileage out of the distinction between morality and ethics is Bernard Williams's *Ethics and the Limits of Philosophy* (1985). Williams proposed that ethics concerns how one should live (although excluding purely egoistic answers to that question), and morality a systematic but narrower set of concerns that constitute one among many approaches to the ethical. Common usage does not support this linguistic suggestion, but the suggestion of broader and narrower ways of construing the subject with which moral philosophy deals has been influential in its own right.

What Williams refers to as *morality* is essentially Kant's view of it, although that view shares features with other philosophers, and contemporary Kantians have challenged aspects of Williams's reading of Kant. Prominent distinguishing features of the morality system, according to Williams, are the following:

(1) *Obligation is the fundamental moral notion.* However, considerations that render an action obligatory, such as its reducing the suffering of others, or involving defending an honorable person against attack, may also, in some circumstances, render an action good but not obligatory (sometimes called *supererogatory*). In *ethics*, by contrast, good actions can be those instantiating virtues, such as courage, justice, or compassion, without further assessment of the action as obligatory or supererogatory.

(2) *The source of moral demand lies within the agent's own autonomous self.* Yet most moral outlooks recognize some obligations and moral demands as arising, irreducibly, from outside ourselves, for example, from social or institutional roles we occupy, or relationships, such as familial ones, that are not simply voluntarily assumed.

(3) *Ethical assessment encompasses only that for which we are fully responsible*—that is, voluntary actions. Yet, Williams notes, we standardly treat as reflecting on an agent's ethicality responses (such as emotions and feelings) as well as actions, a dimension of the moral life especially emphasized by Aristotle and Iris Murdoch (1970). More generally, we see assessment of character, which is never entirely voluntary, as morally appropriate. Here Williams fails to note, and sometimes implies otherwise, that in the virtue tradition some degree of voluntariness is required for moral assessment. An emotional reaction or disposition over which (or over whose causal antecedents) the agent had absolutely no control whatsoever would not be a fit object of ethical assessment.

A comparable, but not equivalent, view of the difference in question here is that between universal moral requirements and the good life or personal flourishing. Like Williams's distinction between ethics or virtue and the morality system, this distinction is far from sharp.

See also Duty; Virtue Ethics; Williams, Bernard.

Bibliography

Murdoch, Iris. *The Sovereignty of Good*. London: Routledge, 1970.

Williams, Bernard. *Ethics and the Limits of Philosophy*. Cambridge, MA: Harvard University Press, 1985.

Lawrence Blum (2005)

ETHICS AND RELIGION
See *Religion and Morality*

EUCKEN, RUDOLF CHRISTOPH
(1846–1926)

Rudolf Christoph Eucken, the German philosopher of life, was born in Aurich, East Friesland. He studied philology and philosophy at the University of Göttingen; after attaining his doctoral degree, he taught several years at Frankfurt Gymnasium. In 1871 he became professor of philosophy at the University of Basel, and in 1874 at Jena, where he remained until his death. In 1908 he received the Nobel Prize in literature.

Eucken was not a systematic philosopher. He began with life as man experiences it. Life inevitably tends to organize into "systems of life" that are organic or institutional. The function of philosophy is to make the meaning of each system explicit and, by explicating each, to raise the question, Which is to be preferred? But philosophy does not merely explicate; it also helps to transform existing life systems. Men assess these explications practically, in terms of their fruitfulness for life or for a particular life system. Each man chooses a life system, but he does not choose one simply for himself. Every act of such choosing inevitably involves other men. There is no escape for any man from this social involvement.

Life is a process, an evolution; it cannot be contained within the boundaries of any philosophy or life system. The strains and stresses created when life breaks its established boundaries raises the deep need for a new philosophy or new philosophies, and inevitably men develop them. Eucken believed that every significant new philosophy is more comprehensive and clearly defined than any past philosophy.

The elaboration of new philosophies comes only through action (i.e., activism), through man's relentless affirmation of life—an affirmation which recognizes both the good and evil inherent in life. No significant philosophy is ever purely intellectualistic, for life is more than an idea or a theory. At its best, life is creative energy bursting into expression and molding past and present experience into a higher, more spiritual unity and order. For Eucken, life is neither noological nor psychological nor cosmological; its basis and meaning are to be found in man.

Life in man is self-conscious; as such, it goes beyond the subjective individual to bind together all conscious beings. Through this transcendence, it becomes the "independent spiritual life," or man reaching through action toward the absolute truth, beauty, and goodness. This "independent spiritual life" is attained only as personality is developed, but it is never a final achievement, since it is always a process that evolves as history. It is not rooted in the external world but in the soul, and it manifests itself more and more completely as the soul becomes independent of this world, self-willed yet subordinate to the ultimate trinity of truth, beauty, and goodness. These ultimates are not theoretical abstractions; they are concrete human experiences that push man beyond cosmic nature to something transcendentally spiritual.

Man has his beginning in nature, but through his soul evolves beyond it. His soul raises questions such as "Why?" and "Whence?" and opposes nature at all points. His soul seeks to become timeless and above nature, even as it feels helpless in the grasp of nature. In spite of this feeling of helplessness, it continues to seek freedom—a freedom realized through the creation of a consistent philosophy that makes possible man's physical and spiritual survival. For Eucken, thought is not something intrinsic to itself but a means, or organ, of life itself.

The need for a new philosophy, Eucken felt, arises from two social conditions—modern man's drive for a "broader, freer, cleaner life, a life of greater independence and spiritual spontaneity" and his drive for a "naturalistic culture … which limits all its activity to the world around us" (*Can We Still Be Christians?*, p. 51).

The first drive provides modern man with a basis for radically transforming classical Christianity. Man's new problems, created by science, transcend the theological and ritualistic solutions that Christianity offered for millenniums. The eternal contribution of Christianity is its religious affirmation of universal redemption. But redemption must be combined with new elements of faith (science as the true complement of religion; religious democracy, or the political equality of all religions before man; complete separation of church and state) if Christianity is to help give birth to the new spiritual philosophy needed by man.

Eucken was very critical of naturalism. A naturalistic culture imposes false limitations upon man's essential spirituality. The conception of a naturalistic culture is a result of the impact of science upon man's life—an impact that is essentially good, but dangerous if it leads to the restriction of man's potentialities to the realm of nature only. In two works, *Individual and Society* (1923) and *Socialism: An Analysis* (1921), Eucken clarified the grounds of his criticism of naturalism. The naturalistic approach opens the door to individual freedom, but it is unable to guide man in the proper use of his freedom, since it lacks an overarching conception of unity. It fails to understand the necessity of social cooperation and social cohesion. Intellectualistic idealism understands the necessity for cooperation, cohesion, and unity, but fails to understand the need for individual freedom. The only proper answer, Eucken believed, is spiritual autonomy. Autonomy gives primacy to the whole of which the individual is a part, but it never reduces him to a state of utter subordination to that whole. The individual realizes his own unique freedom through this whole.

In *Socialism: An Analysis* Eucken also offers six criticisms of socialism: It cannot give unity to the life process; it fails to understand man's need for an inner life; it makes the present the only significant moment in man's life and thus cuts him off from the past and future; by reducing men to mathematical equality, it fails to appreciate genuine cultural and spiritual differences among men; espousing no higher faith than naturalism, it reduces social life to a struggle of man against man; and by considering man in purely economic terms, it stunts and aborts his true nature.

Eucken illustrated the attainment of freedom in terms of science and the peaceful society. In science the primary objective is to give man control over nature, but this task can be accomplished only when scientists cooperate by working together. Science, in other words, is essentially social, but it accomplishes its task through the freedom to investigate that is given to scientists. The peaceful society, although not yet attained, plainly depends upon human cooperation, upon no man raising his hand against another.

However, spiritual autonomy is not possible in a naturalistic culture. It rests upon a faith that goes beyond naturalism—the spiritual belief that man can produce a better and a freer world for all of humanity. Such a belief cannot find support in external circumstances alone. It requires the presence in each man of an inner life, a life constantly struggling to attain the good.

See also Beauty; Determinism and Freedom; Naturalism; Truth.

Bibliography

WORKS BY EUCKEN

Geschichte und Kritik der Grundbegriffe den Gegenwart. Leipzig, 1878.

Die Einheit des Geisteslebens in Bewusstsein und Tat der Menschheit. Leipzig, 1888.

Der Sinn und Wert des Lebens. Leipzig, 1908. Translated by Lucy Judge Gibson and W. R. Boyce Gibson as *The Meaning and Value of Life.* London: A. and C. Black, 1909.

Grundlinien einer neuen Lebensanschauung. Leipzig, 1907. Translated by Alban G. Widgery as *Life's Basis and Life's Ideal.* London: A. and C. Black, 1911.

Können wir noch Christen sein? Leipzig, 1911. Translated by Lucy Judge Gibson as *Can We Still Be Christians?* New York: Macmillan, 1914.

Erkennen und Leben. Leipzig: Quelle and Meyer, 1912. Translated by W. Tudor Jones as *Knowledge and Life.* London: Williams and Norgate, 1913.

Sozialismus und seine Lebensgestaltung. Leipzig, 1920. Translated by Joseph McCabe as *Socialism: An Analysis.* London: T.F. Unwin, 1921.

Lebenserinnerungen. Leipzig, 1921. Translated by Joseph McCabe as *Rudolf Eucken: His Life, Work and Travels.* London: T. F. Unwin, 1921.

The Individual and Society. Translated by W. R. V. Brade. London, 1923.

WORKS ON EUCKEN

Gibson, W. R. B. *Rudolf Eucken's Philosophy of Life.* London: A. and C. Black, 1907.

Jones, W. T. *An Interpretation of Rudolf Eucken's Philosophy.* London: Williams and Norgate, 1912.

Rubin Gotesky (1967)

EUDAIMONIA

See Appendix, Vol. 10

EURASIANISM

(Classical) Eurasianism (Russian: *evraziistvo*) was an ideological-philosophical movement among Russian émigré intellectuals in the 1920s and 1930s. Its founders were the ethnologist and linguist Nikolai Sergeevich Trubetskoi, the geologist and economist P. N. Savitskii (1895–1968), the musicologist P. P. Suvchinskii (1892–1985), and the religious philosopher Georgii Vasil'evich Florovskii. Later in the 1920s major supporters and theoreticians joined the movement, including the historian G.

V. Vernadskii (1886–1967) and the philosopher Lev Platonovich Karsavin.

Eurasianism was born as a reaction to the Russian revolution and the political situation in Russia after the crisis of World War I, revolution and civil war, and the Bolsheviks' rise to power. The Eurasians were not opposed to the revolution, as it put an end to the bankrupt European tsarist regime, but were against communism, which in their view was also a typical European product. As Russians were not Europeans according to the Eurasians, Russia needed its own ideology, which would do justice to its own particular historical and cultural development.

The Eurasians' anti-European attitude manifested itself from their first joint publication, *Ischod k vostoku. Predchuvstviia i sversheniia. Utverzhdenie Evraziitsev* (Exodus to the East: Forebodings and events: An affirmation of the Eurasians; 1921). It was, in a sense, a continuation of a book published by Trubetskoi in 1920, *Evropa i chelovechestvo* (Europe and mankind). In this book Trubetskoi warned against the imminent Europeanization of the world, which was the direct result of Romano-Germanic chauvinism. The colonialist countries of western Europe considered other cultures inferior to their own culture and tried to put their stamp everywhere in the world. Russia, according to Trubetskoi, had to stand up to this pernicious influence and follow its own path.

A central concept of Eurasianism was a geographical one. The Eurasianists did not divide the enormous surface of land of the Northern Hemisphere into two (Europe and Asia), but into three parts: (Western) Europe, including Poland, the Baltic states and the Balkans, Asia—the Far East, Southwest Asia, and Southeast Asia—and in between as a separate geographical world the relatively flat area extending from the Danube estuary to the Lena River basin. It is the area that was formerly controlled by the Mongol ruler Genghis Khan (c. 1162–1227) and that roughly corresponded with the territory of the Russian tsarist regime and with that of the Soviet Union. Contrary to Europe and Asia, Eurasia is not open to the sea; it has a continental climate with hot summers and cold winters.

Eurasia is inhabited by various peoples, Slavic as well as non-Slavic or, as Trubetskoi calls them, Turanic peoples, including the Finno-Ugrians, Samoyeds, Tartars, Turkmenians, and Kalmyks. For historical and geographical reasons all these Eurasian peoples form a unity, as do their languages. Culturally and spiritually—and in this respect the Eurasians differ from the nineteenth-century Slavophiles from whom they borrowed much of their ideology—the Russians are closer to the peoples of Eurasia than to their Slavic brothers such as the Czechs and the Poles, who belong to an entirely different world: catholic Europe.

The geopolitical idea of Eurasia was for the first time realized by Genghis, who submitted the entire Eurasian territory for some 150 years to the mogul yoke. Generally, this period is considered as a time of stagnation and decline, but for the Eurasians it was the beginning of the Russian empire, triumphantly continued by the Muscovite state that, after having defeated the Mongols, was even better suited to establish the unity of Eurasia as it had a clear ideology: that of the Orthodox Church. The Eurasians considered Orthodoxy as one of the pillars of Eurasia's cultural identity. Different from the heretical rationalistic and individualistic Catholicism and Protestantism, it was based on brotherhood (*sobornost*) and therefore in an excellent position to unite all the Eurasian peoples, be they Slavic, Islamic, or heathen.

For the Eurasians the reign of Peter the Great (1672–1725), who wanted to bridge the gap between Russia and Europe and make his country one of the European powers, on a par with England and France, was disastrous for Russia's development. In particular, it led to the fragmentation of Russian society: on the one hand a Europeanized upper class, consisting of the tsar, his civil servants, and the intelligentsia; on the other hand the Russian people. Instead of stimulating cooperation between and assimilation of Russians and Turanians, the Russian monarchy aimed at enforced Russification of the Turanian peoples. Moreover, it considered the Orthodox Church primarily as a means of becoming a European power; it suppressed the independence of the church and submitted it to its own secular authority. Peter's policy was continued by the Romanovs who ruled after him. It resulted in the introduction into Russia of all kinds of notions that were strange to the Eurasianist mentality: imperialism, militarism, and capitalism by the state, and liberalism, parliamentarism, and socialism by other, progressive groups in Russian society. As the Soviet state was based on European ideas, it missed the opportunity to start a really new period, based on Russia's national character, history, and civilization. The only way to "save" Russia was to return to its roots, that meant to the spirit of its pre-Petrine past.

The Eurasians did not consider themselves utopians, but tried to start from historic and social facts. In the joint publication *Evraziistvo* (Eurasianism; 1926), which appeared when the movement was at its height, they developed the idea of a real people's party that would endorse their ideology and not that of the communists, but would leave intact many of the economic and political structures the Bolsheviks had introduced. In the 1930s the Eurasian movement gradually declined. The communist ideology proved to be much stronger than expected and in émigré circles many people were opposed to the growing contacts between members of the Eurasian movement and the Soviet regime.

Neo-eurasianism arose at the end of the twentieth century. It builds on the ideas of classical Eurasianism and the ethnogenesis theory of Lev Gumilev (1912–1992; the son of the famous poets Anna Akhmatova [1889–1966] and Nikolai Gumilev [1886–1921]). The movement holds particular geopolitical intentions and considers Eurasia as a separate civilization that under the leadership of the Russians as a young and fresh ethnos will break the dominance of the dying European ethnoses and in this way will change the political and cultural map of the world. Its main theoretician is the (nationalistic) philosopher Aleksandr Dugin (1962–), who is also the leader of the political party Partiia Evraziia (Eurasia Party).

See also Florovskii, Georgii Vasil'evich; Karsavin, Lev Platonovich; Trubetskoi, Nikolai Sergeevich.

Bibliography

Böss, Otto. *Die Lehre der Eurasier: Ein Beitrag zur russischen Ideengeschichte des 20. Jahrhunderts.* Wiesbaden, Germany: Otto Harassowitz, 1961.

Riasanovsky, Nicholas V. "The Emergence of Eurasianism." *California Slavic Studies* 4 (1967): 39–74.

Riasanovsky, Nicholas V. "Prince N. S. Trubetzkoy's 'Europe and Mankind.'" *Jahrbücher für Geschichte Osteuropas* 12 (1964): 207–220.

Shlapentokh, Dmitry V. "Eurasianism Past and Present." *Communist and Post-communist Studies* 30 (2) (1997): 129–151.

Trubetzkoy, Nikolai Sergeevich. *The Legacy of Genghis Khan and Other Essays on Russia's Identity*, edited by Anatoly Liberman. Ann Arbor: Michigan Slavic Publications, 1991.

Vinkovetsky, Ilya. "Classical Eurasianism and Its Legacy." *Canadian-American Slavic Studies* 34 (2) (2000): 125–139.

Vinkovetsky, Ilya, and Charles Schlacks, Jr., eds. *Exodus to the East: Forebodings and Events: An Affirmation of the Eurasians.* Marina del Rey, CA: Charles Schlacks Jr., 1996.

W. G. Weststeijn (2005)

EUSEBIUS
(265–339 or 340)

Eusebius, the church historian and Christian apologist, was bishop of Caesarea (Palestine) early in the fourth century. He is best known for his enthusiastic support of the emperor Constantine and for his pioneering *Historia Ecclesiastica,* intended to show how the church expanded but always remained the same because of its leaders' fidelity to tradition. Though Eusebius was essentially a historian rather than a philosopher, he did produce one work of significance for the history of philosophy. This is his *Praeparatio Evangelica* (Preparation for the Gospel), probably written between 312 and 318. It consists of fifteen books, perhaps because Porphyry's treatise, *Kata Christianon* (Against the Christians), contained the same number. Eusebius claimed that his treatise went beyond earlier works of controversy or exegesis; the novelty seems to have lain in the method of quoting passages in which philosophers contradict one another, although he obviously found materials for this technique in some of his pagan sources.

The *Praeparatio* may be outlined thus: the earliest cosmogony (I. 7–8); the earliest theology (I. 9); Phoenician theology (I. 10); Egyptian theology (II. 1); Greek mythology (II. 2–8); Greek "physical" theology (III. 1–17); Greek oracles (IV–VI), leading on to the doctrines of Greek philosophers on fate, free will, and foreknowledge (VI); Hebrew doctrines (VII–IX); the chronological priority of Hebrew learning to Greek (X); the agreements and disagreements of Greek philosophy with the Hebrew oracles (XI–XIII); and the inconsistency of Greek philosophy, culminating with a transcription of part of the treatise "On the Doctrines of Philosophers" ascribed to Plutarch (XIV–XV).

The sources used by Eusebius reflect the predominantly Platonic character of the books assembled in church libraries, especially at Caesarea, by Origen and others. Eusebius made extensive use of Plato and Philo, but not of Aristotle. His other sources include the textbooks by Arius Didymus and Pseudo-Plutarch, as well as works by eclectic Platonists of the second Christian century (Atticus, Numenius, Plutarch, Severus) and a few of their contemporaries (the Peripatetic Aristocles, the Epicurean Diogenianus, the Cynic Oenomaus). From the third century he used the treatise "On Fate" by Alexander of Aphrodisias, the school text of Plotinus (earlier than that found in Porphyry's edition), several works by Porphyry ("On Abstinence," "Letter to Anebo," "Against the Christians," "Philological Lectures," "On the Philosophy to Be Derived from Oracles," "On the Soul against Boethus," "On Statues"), and a fragment by a Christian Neoplatonist named Amelius.

His basic viewpoint is that of a Christian ecclesiastic and a historian; he has considerable sympathy for his favorite philosophers (especially Plato), but he is not really at home with them. Indeed, in his later work, *Theophania* (On the theophany), written after 337, his attitude toward philosophy is markedly hostile.

In later times the *Praeparatio* was used as a mine of philosophical quotations by such Christian apologists as Theodoret and Cyril of Alexandria (Cyril often looked up Eusebius' sources and provided slightly different quotations). It would appear that this is its principal value.

See also Alexander of Aphrodisias; Apologists; Aristotle; Cosmology; Numenius of Apamea; Origen; Plato; Plotinus; Plutarch of Chaeronea; Porphyry; Precognition.

Bibliography

WORKS BY EUSEBIUS

The best Greek texts are in *Die griechischen christlichen Schriftsteller der ersten drei Jahrhunderte,* published by the Berlin Academy from 1902 on, although the first volume needs to be reedited (see F. Winkelmann, *Die Textbezeugung der Vita Constantini des Eusebius von Caesarea,* Berlin: Akademie_Verlag, 1962). Translations include H. J. Lawlor and J. Oulton, *Eusebius: The Ecclesiastical History and the Martyrs of Palestine,* 2 vols. (London, 1928), valuable commentary; W. J. Ferrar, *The Proof of the Gospel* (*Demonstratio Evangelica*), 2 vols. (London: Society for Promoting Christian Knowledge, 1920); and E. H. Gifford, *Eusebii Pamphili Evangelicae Praeparationis Libri XV,* 4 vols. in 5 (Oxford, 1903).

WORKS ON EUSEBIUS

Full bibliography in J. Quasten, *Patrology* (Utrecht: Spectrum, 1960), Vol. III, pp. 309–345 (on the *Praeparatio,* pp. 329–331). Later titles include D. S. Wallace-Hadrill, *Eusebius of Caesarea* (London: A.R. Mowbray, 1960) and J. Sirinelli, *Les vues historiques d'Eusèbe de Césarée* (Dakar, Senegal, 1961). On early use of Eusebius' works see Pierre Canivet, *Histoire d'une entreprise d'apologétique au Ve siècle* (Paris: Bloud & Gay, 1958); R. M. Grant, "Greek Literature in the Treatise *De Trinitate* and Cyril *Contra Julianum,*" *Journal of Theological Studies* 15 (1964): 265–279.

Robert M. Grant (1967)

EUTHANASIA

Euthanasia used to refer to an easy and gentle death, but it has come to refer to methods of inducing that kind of death, or more precisely, methods of bringing about death sooner and usually with less pain and suffering. Euthanasia used to be limited to patients in the terminal stage of an illness, but it is now thought to be appropriate in some cases of nonterminal patients, for example, those in a persistent vegetative state and those suffering from an incurable and very painful chronic disease such as multiple sclerosis.

VOLUNTARY ACTIVE EUTHANASIA

Voluntary active euthanasia (VAE) is when a physician accedes to a rational *request* of an adequately informed, competent patient to be killed, for example, with a lethal intravenous injection of pentothal.

PHYSICIAN-ASSISTED SUICIDE

Physician-assisted suicide (PAS) is when a physician, at a rational *request* of an adequately informed, competent patient who plans to commit suicide, knowingly provides that patient with the medical means to commit suicide and the patient uses those means to commit suicide.

VOLUNTARY PASSIVE EUTHANASIA

Voluntary passive euthanasia (VPE) is when a physician abides by a valid rational *refusal* of treatment by an adequately informed, competent patient knowing that doing so will result in the patient dying, for example, complying with the refusal of a ventilator-dependent patient with motor neuron disease to receive further mechanical ventilatory support. Abiding by *patient refusal of hydration and nutrition* (PRHN) is another example of VPE, as is abiding by such refusals given in advance directives—either living wills or durable powers of attorney for health care—even though the patient is incompetent at the time the treatment is withheld or withdrawn.

Patients are *competent* to make a decision about their health care if they have the ability to make a rational decision. This requires both that they have no relevant mental disorder that prevents them from making a rational decision and that they have the capacity to understand and appreciate all the information necessary to make that decision. They are adequately informed when they have all the information necessary to make a rational decision. Patient competence, having adequate information, and no coercion by the health care team, are the elements of valid (informed) consent or refusal of treatment. If participation in research or donating an organ, rather than treatment, is involved, coercion by anyone invalidates consent.

Decisions by patients are *irrational* if they know the decisions will result in serious harm to them, for example, death, chronic pain, or significant disability, and they do not have adequate reasons for suffering that harm, for example, beliefs that some people, either themselves or others, will thereby avoid suffering an equal or greater

harm by that decision. Only those decisions count as irrational that result in the person suffering significant harm and for which almost no one in the person's culture would rank the benefit gained or harm avoided as providing an adequate reason. Often, however, rational people rank harms in different ways; for example, it is rational to rank several months of suffering from a chronic or terminal disease as worse than death and it is also rational to rank death as worse.

INVOLUNTARY ACTIVE EUTHANASIA

Involuntary active euthanasia (IAE) is the killing of a patient who is suffering in order to relieve that suffering but without a request from the patient to be killed. This is most likely to occur with permanently incompetent patients who are unable to make such a request.

INVOLUNTARY PASSIVE EUTHANASIA

Involuntary passive euthanasia (IPE) is allowing a suffering patient to die by ceasing treatment, in order to relieve that suffering, when the patient has neither refused that treatment nor has an advance directive refusing that treatment. This is most likely to occur with permanently incompetent patients who are unable to refuse treatment and do not have an advance directive refusing that treatment. Ceasing treatment for permanently incompetent patients who do not have advance directives refusing that treatment but who have communicated to their families that they would not want to live in this kind of condition, is usually considered to be VPE rather then IPE.

As of 2005, VAE and IAE are illegal in every state in the United States, but PAS is legal in Oregon, and many people have begun to argue for its legalization in other states. IPE is also illegal, except when continuing treatment is considered futile, but almost all those who do bioethics hold either that the definition of futility be broadened so that all treatment of patients in a persistent vegetative state be classified as futile or that some other method be established that allows discontinuing all treatment, including hydration and nutrition, for those in a persistent vegetative state when there is no religious reason for the treatment to be continued.

The United States Supreme Court has explicitly distinguished between VPE and PAS, and by consequence, VAE, holding that only the former is based on a fundamental right to be left alone. The Court correctly regards terminal sedation, that is, being sedated to unconsciousness until one dies, as VPE for those patients who have refused hydration and nutrition and whose pain and suffering cannot be controlled in other ways. VPE is approved by the American Medical Association and all other medical and legal organizations. Philosophers have attempted to provide an account of VPE that explains its almost universal acceptance. All of these attempts have identified VAE with killing and VPE with allowing to die. Two of the most common ways of distinguishing between VAE (killing) and VPE (allowing to die) are (1) acts versus omissions and (2) withholding versus withdrawing.

The philosophical distinction between acts and omissions seems a natural way to distinguish between killing and allowing to die. On this account, if a physician *does* something, for example, injects an overdose of morphine or turns off the respirator, that is an action and should count as VAE, should be considered killing, and should be prohibited. If the physician does nothing but, rather, simply fails to do something, for example, does not turn on the respirator or does not provide essential antibiotics, that is an omission and should count as VPE, should be considered allowing to die, and should be permitted. However, it seems pointless to distinguish between an authorized physician who turns a knob that stops the flow of life-sustaining antibiotics and one who omits filling the bag when it runs out of those antibiotics. Those who have used the distinction between acts and omissions to distinguish between VAE and VPE have usually concluded that the distinction has no moral significance.

The distinction between withholding and withdrawing treatment seems to have great appeal for some doctors as a way of distinguishing between killing and allowing to die. Some maintain that if patients validly refuse to start a life-saving treatment, doctors do not have a duty to force it on them and so are only allowing them to die. However, once treatment is started, if discontinuing it would lead to the patient's death, they have a duty to continue, and it is killing not to do so. Doctors are not required to force patients to go on the ventilator if they refuse, but once patients have accepted going on the ventilator, doctors have a duty to keep them on if taking them off would result in their death, even if they have had a change of mind.

As with the previous distinction between acts and omissions, there seems to be no morally significant difference between withholding and withdrawing treatment. Physicians do not have a duty to continue treatment if an adequately informed, competent patient rationally refuses to have it continued. Imagine two unconscious patients who are going to be put on a respirator; one becomes conscious *before* being put on and the other *after* being put on, but both are competent, adequately informed, and rationally refuse treatment. This accident of timing is morally irrelevant. Further, this way of distinguishing between active and passive euthanasia may create serious practical problems. Patients who had not been adequately evaluated (often at the scene of an accident) may be judged inappropriate for rescue efforts because the doctors believe that once the patient is on a ventilator they cannot legitimately withdraw it.

The inadequacy of these two attempts to distinguish between VAE and VPE has led many to doubt that there is a morally relevant distinction between them. However, closer attention to the way the distinction is actually made, both in law and medicine, shows that what was overlooked is the crucial role played by the patient. When a patient rationally and validly *refuses* what is offered, the physician is legally and morally required not to overrule that refusal. Abiding by a valid rational refusal, knowing that death will result, counts as VPE whether this involves (1) an act or an omission or is (2) withholding or withdrawing. That everyone acknowledges that a physician must abide by a valid refusal of treatment, whether this involves an action or is a case of withdrawing, explains why VPE is almost universally considered to be morally acceptable.

If a patient *requests* the physician to do something, however, the physician is not morally required to do it if in the physician's judgment it is inappropriate to do so. Physicians may accede to patient requests if they regard them as appropriate, but rarely are they required to do so. If a patient requests that a doctor do something illegal or that the doctor considers immoral, the doctor usually is not required to accede to that request. Killing patients at their rational request is illegal, and even if it were to be legalized, many physicians would still consider it to be immoral. Even granted that it is sometimes morally acceptable for physicians to kill patients at their request, it will never be legally or morally required for them to do so. This is sufficient to distinguish VAE from VPE, for it is legally and morally required for physicians to abide by the rational valid refusals of their patients.

Confusion sometimes arises because a patient's refusal is framed as a request. For example, a patient's *request* that no cardiopulmonary resuscitation (CPR) be attempted counts as a refusal of permission for CPR. Similarly, written advance directives requesting the cessation of other therapies or of hydration and nutrition, count as refusals. Any request for not starting or stopping a treatment is a refusal of treatment, and if the patient is competent and the request is rational, doctors are morally and legally required to abide by it.

Distinguishing between refusals and requests becomes more difficult when the life-prolonging treatment is provided by a device such as a pacemaker that has been implanted in the patient. Even though a pacemaker can be reprogrammed to cease functioning without any surgical procedure, some have considered the pacemaker to have become part of the person and so regard the request to turn it off as a genuine request and not as a refusal. However, the dominant view is that whether the artificial device that is keeping the person alive is inside or outside is not the important consideration. If the device can be turned off from the outside, then the patient's request can be counted as a refusal and should be honored. However, because it is not clear that the patient's request should be counted as a refusal, it is not clear whether the doctor is legally required to have the pacemaker turned off. On the other hand, if a surgical procedure is required, for example, to take out an implanted heart valve, no one would count the request to have it taken out as a refusal, and if any doctor agreed to such a request, that doctor would be regarded as having killed the patient.

Using valid refusal versus requests as the way of distinguishing VPE from VAE, while it explains the moral acceptability of VPE, does not make VAE morally unacceptable. Given present knowledge and technology, a physician can kill a patient absolutely painlessly within a matter of minutes. If there were no way for patients to shorten the time of their dying or for their pain to be controlled, VAE would seem to be clearly morally acceptable. However, PRHN, which, contrary to common belief, does not cause suffering, normally results in patients becoming unconscious within a week and dying within another week, and there is no limit on ways to control their other pain during that time. Because all proposals to legalize VAE or PAS involve at least a two-week waiting period, it seems pointless to argue for legalizing VAE or PAS, which are controversial, rather than providing education about PRHN, a form of VPE, which is already universally accepted. Failure to appreciate the available alternative of PRHN makes arguments such as those presented to the Supreme Court in The Philosopher's Brief in favor of declaring Washington and New York states prohibition of assisted suicide unconstitutional far less persuasive than they otherwise would be.

Abiding by the refusal of an advance directive of a competent patient, when that patient becomes incompetent, is also regarded as VPE. If competent patients explicitly state in advance directives that should they become permanently incompetent they want all life prolonging treatments to be discontinued, then the physician is morally required to abide by that refusal. However, some challenge this view, claiming that the views of the competent person who filled out the advance directive may not be the same as the views of the incompetent person to whom they are being applied. Some hold that advance directives need not be followed if the physician believes that the incompetent person would no longer choose to have life-prolonging treatment withdrawn. A public policy must be judged, however, in terms of the effects that this policy would have on everyone affected if all of them knew of the policy. Competent persons who fill out advance directives refusing life-prolonging treatment if they become permanently incompetent consider it distasteful and devoid of dignity to live as a permanently incompetent person, but after becoming permanently incompetent, the person, having no sense of dignity, does not view life with distaste.

If everyone knew that advance directives would not be honored in these cases, some permanently incompetent persons would live longer than they would if such advance directives were honored. This might be a positive result although it is not clear whether the incompetent person views it in that way. However, it is clear that another result of everyone knowing that their advance directives would not be honored would be anxiety, anger, and other unpleasant feelings by those competent persons who had made out such advance directives. This could result in an increase in deaths of such competent persons in order to avoid the unwanted prolongation of their lives as incompetent persons. That the public policy of honoring advance directives is likely to have better consequences than the public policy of not honoring them justifies the policy.

See also Applied Ethics; Bioethics; Medical Ethics.

Bibliography

Battin, Margaret P., Rosamond Rhodes, and Anita Silvers. *Physician Assisted Suicide: Expanding the Debate.* New York: Routledge, 1998.

Bernat, James L., Bernard Gert, and R. Peter Mogielnicki. "Patient Refusal of Hydration and Nutrition: An Alternative to Physician-Assisted Suicide or Voluntary Euthanasia." *Archives of Internal Medicine* 153 (1993): 2723–2728.

Brock, Dan W., *Life and Death* (especially pp 95–232). Cambridge, U.K.: Cambridge University Press, 1993.

Clouser, K. Danner, "Allowing or Causing: Another Look." *Annals of Internal Medicine* 87 (1977): 622–624.

Dresser, Rebecca S. and John A. Robertson. " Quality of Life and Non-treatment Decisions for Incompetent Patients." *Law, Medicine & Health Care* 17 (3) (1989): 234–244.

Dworkin, Ronald, Thomas Nagel, Robert Nozick, John Rawls, Thomas Scanlon, Thomas, and Judith Jarvis Thomson, as *amici curiae* in Supreme Court cases: Washington et al. v. Glucksberg et al. and Vacco et al. v. Quill et al. (Known as *The Philosopher's Brief*), 1996.

Gert, Bernard, *Morality: Its Nature and Justification.* Rev. ed. New York: Oxford University Press, 2005.

Gert, Bernard, Charles M. Culver, and K. Danner Clouser. *Bioethics: A Systematic Approach.* Oxford University Press, 2006.

The Hastings Center. *Guidelines on the Termination of Life Sustaining Treatments and Care of the Dying.* Bloomington: Indiana University Press, 1987.

Lynn, Joanne, ed. *By No Extraordinary Means: The Choice to Forego Life-Sustaining Food and Water.* Bloomington: Indiana University Press, 1986.

President's Commission for the Study of Ethical Problems in Medicine and Biomedical and Behavioral Research. *Deciding to Forego Life-Sustaining Treatment.* Washington, DC: Government Printing Office, 1983.

Quill, Timothy E. *Death and Dignity.* New York: Norton, 1993.

Rachels, James. "Active and Passive Euthanasia." *New England Journal of Medicine* 292 (1975): 78–80.

Rachels, James. *The End of Life: Euthanasia and Morality.* New York: Oxford University Press, 1986.

Van er Maas, Paul J. et al. "Euthanasia and Other Medical Decisions concerning the End of Life." *Lancet* 338 (1991): 669–674.

Supreme Court Decisions: Washington et al. v. Glucksberg et al. and Vacco et al. v. Quill et al., 1997.

Wanzer, Sidney J. et al. "The Physician's Responsibility Toward Hopelessly Ill Patients: A Second Look." *New England Journal of Medicine* 320 (1989): 844–849.

Weir, Robert F. *Abating Treatment with Critically Ill Patients.* New York: Oxford University Press, 1989.

Bernard Gert (2005)

EVANS, GARETH
(1946–1980)

As an undergraduate from 1964 to 1967, Gareth Evans, a British philosopher of language and mind, studied for the PPE degree (philosophy, politics, and economics) at University College, Oxford, where his philosophy tutor was Peter Strawson. In 1968, less than a year after completing his degree, Evans was elected to a fellowship at University College. He took up the position in 1969, succeeding Strawson, who had become Waynflete Professor of Metaphysical Philosophy at Oxford. During the 1970s Evans and his University College colleague John McDowell played leading roles in developing a distinctive conception of truth-theoretic semantics, drawing on the work of Strawson, Michael Dummett, and especially Donald Davidson. Their coedited collection, *Truth and Meaning: Essays in Semantics*, appeared in 1976.

While philosophy of language enjoyed a central position in Oxford philosophy of that period, Evans did not share the view (regarded by Dummett as constitutive of analytic philosophy) that philosophy of language is foundational and so takes priority over philosophy of mind in the order of philosophical explanation. He attached particular importance to the mentalistic notion of understanding, and his work on the theory of reference was set within a theory of thought and especially thought about particular objects. Evans's published work ranged over philosophy of language, metaphysics, philosophy of mind, and philosophy of psychology. In 1979 he was elected to the Wilde Readership in Mental Philosophy at Oxford. He died in August 1980, at the age of thirty-four. His book *The Varieties of Reference* (1982), incomplete at the time of his death, was edited and brought to publication by McDowell. A collection of thirteen of his papers and two shorter notes appeared in 1985, and a further note was published in 2004.

NAMES AND REFERENCE

In his first published paper, "The Causal Theory of Names" (1973/1985) Evans contrasted two theories about the reference of names: the description theory and the causal theory. Evans agreed with Kripke (1972) in rejecting the description theory of reference, which he regarded as drawing support from a flawed account of what is involved in thought directed toward a particular object. In opposition to this description-theoretic account of object-directed thoughts, Evans maintained that a subject may think about a particular object in virtue of standing in a contextual relation to it and without being able to frame any description that the object uniquely satisfies. However, Evans did not accept the causal theory of reference suggested by Kripke's remarks. In the Kripkean picture, the reference of a name is established by an initial baptism and is then passed on from earlier to later users of the name. Evans challenged this picture by highlighting the fact that a name may change its reference over time and, more generally, he argued that a bare causal connection is not sufficient to underwrite reference. As against both the description theory and the Kripkean causal theory, Evans proposed that the bearer of a name is the object that is the dominant source of the body of information that speakers associate with the name.

Many of the themes of his early paper on names—including opposition to description-theoretic accounts of object-directed thoughts, rejection of causal theories as insufficiently demanding, and appeal to the notion of information—recur in *The Varieties of Reference*, set against the historical background of Gottlob Frege and Bertrand Russell. Evans read Frege as committed to the principle that if a name has no reference, then a sentence containing the name has no truth-value and does not express a thought; a speaker using the sentence does not literally say anything. This "no reference, no thought" principle is in line with Frege's view that the semantic function of a name is to introduce an object, but it appears to rule out the possibility of names with sense but no reference, a possibility that Frege clearly allowed once his distinction between sense and reference was in place. Evans sought to reduce the tension that this reading finds in Frege's position by appealing to Frege's assimilation of the use of empty names to fictional uses of language, which express pretended senses or "mock thoughts."

Evans held that many singular terms—especially demonstratives such as "that ball" or "that vase"—conform to the "no reference, no thought" principle, and he called such expressions "Russellian" singular terms. He also held, following Russell, that definite descriptions, even though they appear superficially to occupy name positions, are not really referring expressions but rather quantifier expressions; "the F" semantically resembles "some F" and "every F." The contrast between a Russellian singular term, whose significance depends on its having a referent, and a definite description, whose significance can be grasped independently of whether it has a denotation, was fundamental for much of Evans's work on reference (Sainsbury 1985).

OBJECT-DIRECTED THOUGHT

Although *The Varieties of Reference* begins and ends with philosophy of language (returning to the topic of names and name-using practices in its final chapter), the central chapters address the issue of thoughts directed toward particular objects. According to the description theory of object-directed thoughts, thought about a perceived, remembered, heard-about, or recognized object, about an occupied place or about a present time, is a matter of the object, place, or time uniquely satisfying a descriptive condition that the thinker frames and deploys in thought. Alternative theories of *de re* (or object-directed) thought appeal to the causal relations implicated in perception, memory, and testimony and to contextual relations to places and times (Burge 1977). While Evans was opposed to the description theory, he was also concerned, here as in philosophy of language, that causal theories were liable to be insufficiently demanding. He was particularly critical of what he called "the photograph model of mental representation," according to which the causal ancestry of a mental state is sufficient to determine which object the state represents (as causal ancestry is sufficient to determine which object a photograph is an image of).

Evans's own theorizing about object-directed thoughts was guided by Russell's principle, which says that to think about a particular object, a thinker must know which object is at issue. Evans interpreted the principle as requiring discriminating knowledge, that is, the capacity to discriminate the object of thought from all other things, and this, at least initially, sounds so demanding as to make object-directed thought an extraordinary achievement. But Evans's examples of how to meet the principle make it seem more tractable: presently perceiving the object, being able to recognize it, knowing discriminating facts about it.

When a thinker meets the requirement of Russell's principle by having discriminating knowledge of a particular object, the thinker is said to have an adequate Idea of the object. In this technical use of the term, an Idea deployed in thought about an object is analogous to a concept deployed in thought about a property. Evans was particularly concerned with cases (centrally, cases of demonstrative identification) in which a thinker's Idea of an object depends on an information link between the thinker and the object, so that the Idea of the object, and thoughts in which the Idea is deployed, are information-invoking. The picture here is not that the information link contributes to the thought about the object, because the thinker frames a descriptive condition along the lines of "the object, whichever it is, that is the source of this information." It is the information link itself, and not a thought about the information link, that plays a role in making object-directed thought possible.

If, as a result of malfunction or hallucination, there is really no information link to an object, then the thinker has no adequate Idea of this information-invoking kind. A thinker who is unaware of the problem may essay a thought and yet fail to think about any particular object at all. Information-invoking thoughts (centrally, demonstrative thoughts) are object-dependent; where there is no object, there is no thought. Evans was especially interested in cases where understanding a singular term requires an information-invoking thought, and hence object-dependent thought, on the part of the hearer. For in such cases, it is possible to argue that the singular term is Russellian, that its significance depends on its having a referent.

DESCRIPTIVE NAMES

Despite the central role played by Russellian singular terms in *The Varieties of Reference*, Evans did not equate the categories of Russellian singular terms and referring expressions. In "Reference and Contingency" (1979/1985), he considered descriptive names (names whose referents are fixed by description). His example was the name "Julius," introduced with the stipulation "Let us use 'Julius' to refer to whoever invented the zip fastener [or zipper]." "Julius" behaves epistemically and modally like the definite description "the actual inventor of the zip." Evans offered "If anyone uniquely invented the zip, Julius invented the zip" as an example of a sentence whose truth can be known a priori, even though it is contingent. Evans argued that the thought expressed by the nonmodal sentence "Julius is *F*" is the same as the thought expressed by "The inventor of the zip is *F*"—a thought that can be grasped whether or not "Julius" refers to anyone. But he rejected the suggestion that descriptive names belong semantically with definite descriptions and maintained that, although the descriptive name "Julius" is not a Russellian singular term, it is still a referring expression. His argument for placing descriptive names in the category of referring expressions, alongside Russellian singular terms and separate from definite descriptions, involved two main points. First, as the introducing stipulation makes clear, the semantic contribution of "Julius" is stated using the relation of reference, no less than is the semantic contribution of a Russellian singular term ("John" refers to John). Second, even in a semantic theory for a modal language, the semantic contribution of a descriptive name, like that of a Russellian singular term, can be stated using a reference relation that is not relativized to possible worlds, but this is not generally so for definite descriptions.

INFORMATION AND NONCONCEPTUAL CONTENT

The notion of information, as Evans used it, is not the notion of what a subject believes. Indeed, Evans suggested that we should take the notion of being in an information state as a primitive notion, not to be explained in terms of belief, judgment, and reasons. Because perceptual-information states can be present in a creature that does not think or apply concepts, Evans maintained that the representational content of perceptual states is a kind of nonconceptual content. To be in states with such content (perhaps the nonconceptual content that a sound is coming from direction *d*) a creature does not need to apply, or even to possess, the concepts that we use to specify the content of the states (concepts such as those of sound and direction).

Evans held a distinctive view of the relationship between perceptual-information states and perceptual experiences according to which conscious perceptual experience requires that perceptual-information states should function as inputs to a system for thinking and reasoning. Thus, only a creature with concepts can enjoy perceptual experiences. Nevertheless, a perceiving, thinking, concept-applying creature need not possess all the concepts that would be required fully to specify the content of a perceptual experience and, in having the experience, need not employ even those concepts that are possessed. Evans allowed that the representational content of perceptual experience need not be conceptual content, and in subsequent work, the notion of nonconceptual content has played a major role in accounts of the representational content of perceptual experience (Crane 1992, Gunther 2003, Peacocke 2001).

FURTHER THEMES

Several of Evans's papers—beginning with "Identity and Predication" (1975/1985) and including "Semantic Structure and Logical Form" (1976/1985) and "Does Tense Logic Rest upon a Mistake?" (1985)—contributed to the foundations of semantics and particularly to constraints on semantic theories that show how the meanings of whole sentences depend on the meanings of their parts. In "Semantic Theory and Tacit Knowledge" (1981/1985), he connected the requirement that a semantic theory should reveal semantic structure in sentences with the idea that speakers of a language have tacit knowledge of such a theory. Evans developed a substantive account of tacit knowledge (see also Davies 1987, Peacocke 1989) and distinguished the nonconceptualized content of tacit-knowledge states from the conceptualized content of belief states.

Evans's account of the semantic properties of descriptive names, put forward in "Reference and Contingency" (1979/1985), led to developments in two-dimensional modal logic (Davies and Humberstone 1980; see also Evans 2004), and he made further use of the notion of a singular term with its reference fixed by description in seminal work on pronouns. In "Pronouns, Quantifiers, and Relative Clauses" (1977/1985) and in "Pronouns" (1980/1985), Evans developed an influential account of the semantic function of pronouns that depend for their interpretation on an earlier quantifier phrase yet without being interpretable as bound variables (Neale 1990; King 2005). Finally, "Things without the

Mind" (1980/1985) and "Molyneux's Question" (1985), along with the central chapters of *The Varieties of Reference*, have had a profound influence on subsequent work in philosophy of psychology, particularly work concerningthe perception and representation of space and, more generally, the conditions for an objective conception of a spatial world (Eilan, McCarthy, and Brewer 1993).

See also Davidson, Donald; Dummett, Michael Anthony Eardley; Frege, Gottlob; Kripke, Saul; McDowell, John; Philosophy of Mind; Proper Names and Descriptions; Reference; Russell, Bertrand Arthur William; Semantics; Strawson, Peter Frederick.

Bibliography

WORKS BY EVANS

With John McDowell, eds. *Truth and Meaning: Essays in Semantics*. Oxford, U.K.: Oxford University Press, 1976.

The Varieties of Reference. Oxford, U.K.: Oxford University Press, 1982.

Collected Papers. Oxford, U.K.: Oxford University Press, 1985.

"Comment on 'Two Notions of Necessity.' " *Philosophical Studies* 118 (2004): 11–16.

OTHER WORKS

Burge, Tyler. "Belief *de re*." *Journal of Philosophy* 74 (1977): 338–362.

Crane, Tim, ed. *The Contents of Experience: Essays on Perception*. Cambridge, U.K.: Cambridge University Press, 1992.

Davies, Martin. "Tacit Knowledge and Semantic Theory: Can a Five Per Cent Difference Matter?" *Mind* 96 (1987): 441–462.

Davies, Martin, and I. L. Humberstone. "Two Notions of Necessity." *Philosophical Studies* 38 (1980): 1–30.

Eilan, Naomi, Rosaleen McCarthy, and Bill Brewer, eds. *Spatial Representation: Problems in Philosophy and Psychology*. Oxford, U.K.: Blackwell Publishers, 1993. 2nd ed., Oxford, U.K.: Oxford University Press, 1999.

Gunther, York H., ed. *Essays on Nonconceptual Content*. Cambridge, MA: MIT Press, 2003.

King, Jeffrey C. "Anaphora." In *The Stanford Encyclopedia of Philosophy*, fall 2005 ed., edited by Edward N. Zalta. Available from http://plato.stanford.edu/entries/anaphora/.

Kripke, Saul. "Naming and Necessity." In *Semantics of Natural Languages*, edited by Donald Davidson and Gilbert Harman, 253–355. Dordrecht, Netherlands: D. Reidel, 1972.

Neale, Stephen. *Descriptions*. Cambridge, MA: MIT Press, 1990.

Peacocke, Christopher. "Does Perception Have a Nonconceptual Content?" *Journal of Philosophy* 98 (2001): 239–264.

Peacocke, Christopher. "When Is a Grammar Psychologically Real?" In *Reflections on Chomsky*, edited by Alexander George, 111–130. Oxford, U.K.: Basil Blackwell, 1989.

Sainsbury, R. M. Critical notice: *The Varieties of Reference*, by Gareth Evans. *Mind* 94 (1985): 120–142.

***Martin Davies* (2005)**

EVENTS IN SEMANTIC THEORY

It is an ancient idea that many verbs are used to describe events—things that happen, in places and at times. Frank Plumpton Ramsey introduced an important twist, in the context of distinguishing events from facts. Suppose that Aggie hit Pat. Then on Ramsey's view, the fact reported with (1)

(1) Aggie hit Pat

is the general proposition that there was a hitting of Pat by Aggie. This existential generalization, unlike any event, has no specific spatiotemporal properties. But any event of Aggie hitting Pat verifies (1). So the action report seems to mean that an event of a certain sort occurred. Though at least initially, it is not clear how to square this with the compositionality of linguistic meaning. Let the invented monadic predicate Aghipatish$_1$ be satisfied by z if and only if (iff) z was a hitting of Pat by Aggie. Then plausibly, (1) is true iff $\exists z[\text{Aghipatish}_1(z)]$. But this biconditional reveals nothing about how the meaning of (1) is determined by the constituent words. And prima facie, the logical form of (1) is Hit$_2$(**a**, **p**); where **a** and **p** are names for Aggie and Pat, respectively, and Hit$_2$ is satisfied by an ordered pair $\langle x, y \rangle$ iff x hit y. Donald Davidson (1967, 1985) shows how to represent the meaning of (1) compositionally and "eventishly," and he offers an argument for doing so. Others develop his proposal and provide independent support for it.

ADVERBIAL MODIFICATION

Let Hit$_3$ be satisfied by an ordered triple $\langle x, y, z \rangle$ iff z was a hitting of y by x, so that $\forall x \forall y \{\text{Hit}_2(x, y) \leftrightarrow \exists z[\text{Hit}_3(x, y, z)]\}$. Then (1a),

(1a) $\exists z[\text{Hit}_3(\mathbf{a}, \mathbf{p}, z)]$

which is true iff $\exists z[\text{Aghipatish}_1(z)]$, has parts corresponding to the words in (1). If we represent the meaning of (1) with (1a), we can explain the apparent synonymy of (1) with (2):

(2) There was a hitting of Pat by Aggie

But one wants to see further evidence of the alleged covert variable.

An action report can be extended as in (3–8):

(3) Aggie hit Pat softly

(4) Aggie hit Pat with a red stick

(5) Aggie hit Pat in March

(6) Aggie hit Pat with a red stick in March

(7) Aggie hit Pat in March with a red stick

(8) Aggie hit Pat softly with a red stick in March

One might be inclined to represent the meaning of (3) with $SoftlyHit_2(\mathbf{a}, \mathbf{p})$; where the invented binary predicate is satisfied by $\langle x, y \rangle$ iff x hit y softly. But if an inference from (3) to (1) is of the form $\Phi_2(\alpha, \beta)$, so $\psi_2(\alpha, \beta)$, we need some other explanation for why the truth of (3) guarantees the truth of (1). One can stipulate that $\forall x \forall y [SoftlyHit_2(x, y) \rightarrow Hit_2(x, y)]$. However, one wants to know why the corresponding English sentences are related in this fashion. Furthermore, (3) seems to be synonymous with "There was a soft hitting of Pat by Aggie," which implies (2). Such implications are reminiscent of conjunction-reduction, as in inferences like the following: $\exists x[Red(x) \& Stick(x)]$, so $\exists x[Stick(x)]$.

This invites Davidson's (1967) hypothesis that the logical form of (3) is (3a);

(3a) $\exists z[Hit_3(Aggie, Pat, z) \& Soft_1(z)]$

where $Soft_1(z)$ means that z was done softly. Furthermore, sentences like (1–8) exhibit a network of entailments. The truth of (4) or (5) also guarantees the truth of (1); (6) implies (7), which implies each of (4–6); and (8) implies each of (1–7). These facts, which illustrate that adverb-reduction is often a valid form of inference in natural language, go unexplained if we represent the meanings of (3–8) with binary predicates like *HitInMarchWithARedStick_2*. But we can explain the entailments by analyzing the adverbial modifiers as predicates conjoined with others, as in (7a);

(7a) $\exists z[Hit_3(Aggie, Pat, z) \& In_2(z, March) \& With_2(z, a red stick)]$

where $In_2(z, March)$ and $With_2(z, a red stick)$ mean that z occurred in March, and that z was done with a red stick. By analogy, "There was a red stick on the table touching the chalk" implies that there was a red stick on the table, a stick touching the chalk, a red stick, and so on.

There are also nonimplications to account for. Each of (3–5) could be true, even if (8) is false. Aggie may have hit Pat more than once, but never softly with a red stick in March. Let's suppose, though, that Aggie hit Pat exactly twice: once in March with a red stick, and once in April with a blue stick. Then (9–11) are true, like (4–6), but (12–13) are false.

(9) Aggie hit Pat with a blue stick

(10) Aggie hit Pat in April

(11) Aggie hit Pat with a blue stick in April

(12) Aggie hit Pat with a red stick in April

(13) Aggie hit Pat with a blue stick in March

The truth of (9) and (5) does not guarantee the truth of (13). Nor does the truth of (4) and (10) guarantee the truth of (12). This is what Davidson's (1967) account predicts.

If (4) and (10) are true, there were events z1 and z2, such that $Hit_3(Aggie, Pat, z1) \& With_2(z1, a red stick) \& Hit_3(Aggie, Pat, z2) \& In_2(z2, April)$. But it does not follow that there was an event z such that $With_2(z, a red stick) \& In_2(z, April)$. So (12) can be false, and likewise for (13). If we represent the meanings of (1–13) with predicates like *HitWithARedStickInApril_2*, we must add stipulations corresponding to the network of implications, and then explain why the English sentences exhibit these implications and not the others. (Note that appealing to times, instead of events, will not account for the facts. Aggie may have hit Pat simultaneously with a red stick softly and with a blue stick sharply.)

OTHER EVIDENCE

We can specify the meaning of (14) with (14a):

(14) Aggie fled after Pat fell

(14a) $\exists z\{Fled_2(\mathbf{a}, z) \& \exists w[(After_2(z, w) \& Fell_2(\mathbf{p}, w)]\}$

which is true iff an event of Aggie's fleeing occurred after an event Pat's falling. Words like *after* can thus be analyzed as devices for expressing relations between events. Perceptual reports are also relevant. In (15) as opposed to (16):

(15) Pat heard Aggie shout

(16) Pat heard that Aggie shouted

shout is untensed, and replacing *Aggie* with another name for the same individual is sure to preserve truth. Thus, one might render (15) as (15a),

(15a) $\exists z \exists w[Heard_3(\mathbf{p}, w, z) \& Shout_2(\mathbf{a}, w)]$

which is true iff there was a hearing by Pat of a shouting by Aggie. This lets us account for the ambiguity of (16), which can imply that the hearing took place in the hall or that the shout did:

(16) Pat heard Aggie shout in the hall

(16a) $\exists z \exists w[Heard_3(\mathbf{p}, w, z) \& Shout_2(\mathbf{a}, w) \& In_2(the hall, z)]$

(16b) $\exists z \exists w [\text{Heard}_3(\mathbf{p}, w, z) \ \& \ \text{Shout}_2(\mathbf{a}, w) \ \&$
$\text{In}_2(\text{the hall}, w)]$

Another kind of evidence concerns the intuitive unacceptability of certain adverbial modifications. While (18) sounds somehow wrong, (17) and (19) do not:

(17) Aggie ran for an hour

(18) Aggie ran in an hour

(19) Aggie ran to the store in an hour

If we represent the verb-phrase meanings in (17) and (19) with $RanForAnHour_2$ and $RanToTheStoreInAnHour_2$, not only do we fail to capture implications, we are left wondering why "ran in an hour" is a defective complex monadic predicate. By contrast, (17a) and (19a)

(17a) $\exists z [\text{Ran}_2(\mathbf{a}, z) \ \& \ \text{For}_2(z, \text{an hour})]$

(19a) $\exists z [\text{Ran}_2(\mathbf{a}, z) \ \& \ \text{To}_2(z, \text{the store}) \ \&$
$\text{In}_2(z, \text{an hour})]$

suggest that "for an hour," unlike "in an hour," can be part of an event description that does not provide an independent way of saying when the events described are finished. This hypothesis is confirmed by examples like (20–21):

(20) Aggie painted the walls for/in an hour

(21) Aggie painted walls for/in an hour

While (20) is fine with either modifier, (21) is not. Furthermore, with "in an hour" (20) implies an event that ended when the walls in question were covered with paint. With "for an hour" neither sentence implies that Aggie finished painting any wall.

A striking generalization about action reports of the form "Subject Verb Object," with the verb in active voice, is that such reports invariably imply that the subject of the sentence was the actor. We can invent a predicate Tih_2 satisfied by $\langle x, y \rangle$ iff y hit x; and we can imagine a language in which a homophone of (1), with *Aggie* as the subject, means that $\text{Tih}_2(\mathbf{a}, \mathbf{p})$—or equivalently, $\text{Hit}_2(\mathbf{p}, \mathbf{a})$. However, there are no such expressions in natural human languages. And while the source of this fact is a matter of debate, a great deal of evidence suggests a constraint on how grammatical relations are related to thematic relations that hold between events and their participants. In which case, event variables (and thematic relations) are introduced somehow. However, there is more than one way to introduce them.

THEMATIC ELABORATION

Let $Hitting_1$ be satisfied by z iff z was an event of hitting, ignoring tense for simplicity. Let $Agent_2$ and $Patient_2$ signify thematic relations, without worrying here about how to get beyond intuitive specifications of these relations, so that $\forall x \forall y \{\exists z [\text{Hit}_3(x, y, z)] \ \text{iff} \ \exists z [\text{Agent}_2(z, x) \ \& \ \text{Hitting}_1(z) \ \& \ \text{Patient}_2(z, y)]\}$.

This makes it easy to explain why it follows from (1) that Aggie did something, there was a hitting, and something happened to Pat. This view also preserves a sense in which the transitive verb *hit* is a binary predicate. For while the verb itself is associated with a monadic predicates of events, *hit* is also associated with two thematic relations. Correlatively, one can capture the distinction—independently motivated in many languages that mark nominative and accusative case—between intransitive verbs like *fled* that implicate action, and those that do not. Intuitively, events of falling (like deaths) are things that happen to individuals (not things done), even if such events are intended effects of actions. Besides, one can supplement Davidson's (1967) original proposal—as Davidson (1985) did—with hypotheses like the following:

$\forall x \{\exists z [\text{Fled}_2(x, z)] \leftrightarrow \{\exists z [\text{Agent}_2(z, x)] \ \& \ \text{Fleeing}_1(z)]\};$

$\forall x \{\exists z [\text{Fell}_2(x, z)] \leftrightarrow \{\exists z [\text{Patient}_2(z, x)] \ \& \ \text{Falling}_1(z)]\}.$

But there are at least two construals of such hypotheses.

One might view them as analyses of multiply unsaturated verb-meanings. From this perspective the verb *hit* is satisfied by ordered triples $\langle x, y, z \rangle$ such that z was a hitting whose Patient was y and whose Agent was x. In which case, given standard assumptions about semantic compositionality, *hit Pat* is satisfied by ordered pairs $\langle x, z \rangle$ such that z was a hitting whose Patient was Pat and whose Agent was x. Less standardly, one might say that *hit* is satisfied by events of hitting (period) and that *hit Pat* is satisfied by each event of hitting whose Patient is Pat. This is, in effect, to adopt the following hypothesis: combining *hit* with a direct object corresponds to predicate-conjunction, not predicate-saturation; and the thematic relation "being the Patient of" is expressed by a certain grammatical relation, between the verb and its object, not simply by the lexical meaning of *hit*.

Barry Schein (1993, 2002) and others argue that considerations involving plurality, along with the need for second-order quantification, favor the second perspective. On this kind of view, "Five boys ate two pizzas" has a (collective) reading according to which there some events of eating whose Agents were five boys, and whose Patients were two pizzas; where this does not imply that any one event had all five boys and both pizzas as participants. The first view fits more naturally with the following formulation of the collective reading: There was an event whose (plural) Agent was a collection of five boys, and whose Patient was a collection of two pizzas. Still, however one thinks of thematic elaboration, it both extends the scope of event analyses and highlights difficulties.

As many authors have discussed, verbs like *boil* can appear in transitive and intransitive forms, with a characteristic entailment illustrated in (22):

(22) Aggie boiled the soup; so the soup boiled

Treating the two forms as independent predicates, $Boiled_2(x, y)$ and $Boiled_1(x)$, makes the implication mysterious. So one might analyze (22) as in (23) or (24):

(23) $\exists z\{Agent_2(z, \mathbf{a})\ \&\ \exists w[C_2(z, w)\ \&\ Boiling_1(w)\ \&\ Patient_2(w, \mathbf{s})]\ \}$; so $\exists z[Patient_2(z, \mathbf{s})\ \&\ Boiling_1(z)]$

(24) $\exists z\{Agent_2(z, \mathbf{a})\ \&\ \exists w[M_2(z, w)\ \&\ Boiling_1(w)]\ \&\ Patient_2(z, \mathbf{s})\}$; so $\exists z[Patient_2(z, \mathbf{s})\ \&\ Boiling_1(z)]$

Here, $\mathbf{s}$ stands for the soup, C_2 indicates a causal relation holding between an action and some of its effects, and M_2 indicates a merelogical relation holding between processes that start with actions and end with effects of those actions. Many linguists argue that some such analysis is required, especially given the constraints on how grammatical relations are mapped to thematic relations. But specifying the requisite causal/merelogical relation has proven difficult. Moreover, (23) fails to represent Aggie and the soup as coparticipants in some event describable with an adverbial phrase; yet, if Aggie boiled the soup on Monday, both Aggie's action and the resultant boiling occurred on Monday. And given (24), a background premise is required to reveal the inference as valid: $\forall y \forall z \forall w[M_2(z, w)\ \&\ Patient_2(z, y) \rightarrow Patient_2(w, y)]$.

This raises hard questions about the individuation of actions and their relation to thematic relations. More generally, it is unclear what event variables range over, given the kinds of considerations that motivate such variables. Suppose that Aggie drank a pint of beer (and nothing else) in ten minutes. Then for those ten minutes Aggie drank beer. Let $z1$ be this event of Aggie drinking beer, and let $z2$ be the event of Aggie drinking the pint in question. Intuitively, $z1$ is $z2$; Aggie's beer drinking was none other than the drinking of that pint. In which case, $z1$ satisfies "in ten minutes" iff $z2$ does; and $z2$ does. However, if $z1$ satisfies "in ten minutes," why is "Aggie drank beer in

ten minutes" anomalous? This kind of question arises often.

Consider two billiard balls, $\mathbf{b}$ and $\mathbf{c}$, that came into contact exactly once. At that moment, $\mathbf{b}$ touched $\mathbf{c}$, and $\mathbf{c}$ touched $\mathbf{b}$. Perhaps *touched*, used in this way, does not mark its subject as an Agent, but letting Sub_2 and Ob_2 signify the relevant thematic relations, whatever they are: $\exists z[Sub_2(z, \mathbf{b})\ \&\ Touching_1(z)\ \&\ Ob_2(z, \mathbf{c})]$, and $\exists z[Sub_2(\mathbf{c}, z)\ \&\ Touching_1(z)\ \&\ Ob_2(\mathbf{b}, z)]$. One might have expected the touching of $\mathbf{c}$ by $\mathbf{b}$ to be identical with the touching of $\mathbf{b}$ by $\mathbf{c}$. But how can any one event of touching, z, be such that: $Sub_2(z, \mathbf{b})\ \&\ Ob_2(z, \mathbf{c})\ \&\ Sub_2(z, \mathbf{c})\ \&\ Ob_2(z, \mathbf{b})$? Presumably, $Sub_2(z, \mathbf{b})$ implies that $\mathbf{b}$ is the unique individual that bears the relevant thematic relation to z—and likewise for $Sub_2(z, \mathbf{c})$—since Aggie touched/lifted Pat does not mean merely that there was a touching/lifting with Aggie as one of potentially many touchers/lifters, and Pat as one of potentially many things touched/lifted.

One can avoid the false implication that $\mathbf{b} = \mathbf{c}$ by denying that event variables in semantic theories range over language-independent occurrences. However, this has implications for the relations among meaning, truth, and ontology. Another option is to elaborate further, treating notation like $Sub_2(z, \mathbf{b})$ as shorthand for claims of the form: $\exists e[R_2(e, z)\ \&\ P_2(e, \mathbf{b})]$; where e ranges over language-independent spatiotemporal particulars individuated (at least roughly) in accordance with intuitions about events, R_2 signifies a relation that holds between such particulars and their grammatical presentations, and P_2 signifies a suitable participation relation. But if z ranges over things individuated partly in terms of the grammatical relations that verbs bear to their arguments, we still face questions about the individuation of events and their relation to any thematic relations appealed to in theories of meaning.

See also Event Theory; Semantics.

Bibliography

Davidson, Donald. "Adverbs of Action." In *Essays on Davidson: Actions and Events*, edited by Bruce Vermazen and Merrill B. Hintikka. Oxford, U.K.: Clarendon Press, 1985.

Davidson, Donald. "The Logical Form of Action Sentences." In *The Logic of Decision and Action*, edited by Nicholas Rescher. Pittsburgh: University of Pittsburgh Press, 1966.

Fodor, Jerry. "Three Reasons for Not Deriving 'Kill' from 'Cause to Die.'" *Linguistic Inquiry* 1 (1970): 429–438.

Higginbotham, James. "The Logical form of Perceptual Reports." *Journal of Philosophy* 80 (1983): 100–127.

Higginbotham, James, Fabio Pianesi, and Achille C. Varzi, eds. *Speaking of Events.* New York: Oxford University Press, 2000.

Landman, Fred. "Plurality." In *The Handbook of Contemporary Semantic Theory*, edited by Shalom. Lappin. Oxford, U.K.: Blackwell, 1996.

LePore, Ernest, and Brian P. McLaughlin, eds. *Actions and Events: Perspectives on the Philosophy of Donald Davidson*. Oxford, U.K.: Blackwell, 1985.

Parsons, Terry. *Events in the Semantics of English*. Cambridge, MA: MIT Press, 1990.

Pietroski, Paul. *Events and Semantic Architecture*. New York: Oxford University Press, 2005.

Ramsey, Frank. "Facts and Propositions." *Aristotelian Society* (Supplement) 6 (1927): 153–170.

Schein, Barry. "Events and the Semantic Content of Thematic Relations." In *Logical Form and Language*, edited by Gerhard Preyer and Georg Peter. New York: Oxford University Press, 2002.

Schein, Barry. *Plurals*. Cambridge, MA: MIT Press, 1993.

Taylor, Barry. *Modes of Occurrence*. Oxford, U.K.: Blackwell, 1985.

Tenny, Carol. *Aspectual Roles and the Syntax-Semantics Interface*. Dordrecht, Netherlands: Kluwer Academic, 1994.

Thomson, Judith. *Acts and Other Events*. Ithaca, NY: Cornell University Press, 1977.

Vendler, Zeno. *Linguistics in Philosophy*. Ithaca, NY: Cornell University Press, 1967.

Paul M. Pietroski (2005)

EVENT THEORY

An event is anything that happens, an occurrence. The idea of an event began to take on a philosophical life of its own in the twentieth century, due to a reawakening of interest in the concept of change, to which the concept of an event seems inextricably tied, and to the growing use of the concept of an event in scientific and metascientific writing (see Broad 1933, McTaggart 1927, and Whitehead 1929). Interest in events has also been sparked by versions of the mind-body identity thesis formulated in terms of events and by the idea that a clearer picture of events will facilitate discussion of other philosophical issues.

Discussions of events have focused on whether there are events and, if so, what the nature of events is. Since whether there are events depends in part on what they would be like if there were any, the two issues have usually been treated together.

Some philosophers (e.g., J. J. Thomson) simply assume that there are events; others argue for that assumption. Donald Davidson has asserted that there are events (and actions) by arguing that, to explain the meanings of claims involving adverbial modifiers (e.g., "Jones killed Smith in the kitchen") and singular causal claims (e.g., "the short circuit caused the fire"), we should suppose that such claims implicitly quantify over, or posit,

actions and events (e.g., killings, short circuits, and fires). Opponents of Davidson's analyses (e.g., Terence Horgan) have argued that alternative semantic theories, which do not posit events, are able to explain the semantic features of Davidson's target sentences.

While some singular terms purporting to refer to events are proper names (e.g., "World War I"), many are definite descriptions (e.g., "the killing of Caesar by Brutus"). The semantics of singular descriptions for events has been studied by Zeno Vendler and Jonathan Bennett. Of particular interest is the distinction between perfect nominals, such as "Quisling's betraying of Norway," which refer to events (or actions or states), and imperfect nominals, such as "Quisling's betraying Norway," which refer to factlike entities. Bennett has argued that much of what is wrong in Jaegwon Kim's theory of events can be traced to confusions involving these two sorts of nominals and to expressions (e.g., "the betrayal") that are ambiguous and can refer either to events or to facts.

Most philosophers take events to be abstract particulars: particulars in that they are nonrepeatable and spatially locatable, abstract in that more than one event can occur simultaneously in the same place. Some philosophers who think this way (e.g., Lawrence Brian Lombard) take events to be the changes that objects undergo when they alter. (Others, such as Bennett, have doubts about this; others, such as Kim and David Lewis, deny it outright.) Thus, the time at which an event occurs is the (shortest) time at which the subject of that event changes from the having of one to the having of another, contrary property. Since no object can have both a property and one of its contraries simultaneously, there can be no instantaneous events.

Events inherit their spatial locations from the spatial locations, if any, of the things in which those events are changes. Events do not get their spatial locations by occupying them; if they did, then distinct events, like distinct physical objects, could not occur in the same place simultaneously. But more than one event apparently can occur at the same time and place. However, some philosophers (e.g., W. V. O. Quine) hold that events are concrete and that events and physical objects do not belong to distinct metaphysical kinds.

Though it seems clear that some events are composed of others, it is not clear what the principles are that determine when events compose more complex events. Some views of events (perhaps A. N. Whitehead's) seem compatible with there being subjectless events, events that are not changes in anything whatsoever. However, subjectless events could not be changes, for it seems absurd to suppose that there could be a change that was not a change in or of anything.

Theories about the nature of entities belonging to some metaphysically interesting kind must address the issue of what properties such entities essentially have. In the case of events, the issue is made pressing by the fact that certain theories concerning causation (e.g., Lewis's) require that judgments be made about whether certain events would occur under certain, counterfactual circumstances.

In the literature on events, attention has been given to four essentialist issues. The first is whether the causes (or effects) of events are essential to the events that have them; Peter van Inwagen has suggested that an event's causes are essential to the events that have them, while Lombard has argued that neither the causes nor the effects of events are essential to them. The second concerns the subjects of events; Bennett and Lewis suggest that the subjects of events are not essential, while Lombard and Kim argue that they are. The third is whether an event's time of occurrence is essential to it. Lombard has argued in favor of this essentialist claim, while Bennett and Lewis have argued against it. And the fourth is whether it is essential that each event be a change with respect to the properties to which it is in fact a change. Though the first three issues have received some attention, the fourth has attracted the most, due to the prominence given to debates between the defenders and opponents of Kim's and Davidson's views on the identity of events.

Theories about events typically contain, as a chief component, a "criterion of identity," a principle giving necessary and sufficient conditions for an event e and an event e' to be identical. Though there is no general agreement on this, such a principle is sought because, when it satisfies certain constraints, it becomes a vehicle for articulating a view about what it is to be an event and how events are related to objects belonging to other kinds.

Quine holds that events are the temporal parts of physical objects and thus that events and physical objects share the same condition of identity: sameness of spatiotemporal location. Kim's interest in events centers in part on the idea that they are the objects of empirical explanations. Since what is typically explained is an object's having a property at a certain time, Kim takes an event to be the exemplification of a property (or relation) by an object (or objects) at a time. This idea, combined with some others, led him to hold that an event e is the same as an event e' if and only if e and e' are the exemplifications of the same property by the same object(s) at the

same time. Kim's view has been criticized, principally by Lombard and Bennett, on the grounds that what it says about events is more plausibly seen as truths about facts. Kim's view has also been criticized by those whose intuitions concerning the identity of events more closely match Davidson's.

Davidson once proposed that events, being essentially the links in causal chains, are identical just in case they have the same causes and effects. He has since abandoned this position in favor of Quine's.

Another view that places causation at the heart of the idea of an event is due to Lewis, who has tried to construct a theory in which events have just those features that would allow them to fit neatly into his counterfactual analysis of causation. In some respects, Lewis's view is like Myles Brand's in that both are moved in part by the idea that more than one event can occur simultaneously in the same place. Lewis takes an event to be a property-in-intension of a spatiotemporal region, so that events that in fact occur simultaneously in the same place but could have had different spatiotemporal locations are distinct.

Bennett thinks that the concept of an event is not precise enough to withstand much critical examination on its own and that events should be thought to be (only) whatever they need to be in order to make constructive use of them in the discussion of other philosophical issues. Like Lewis, Bennett takes an event to be a property; but, for Bennett, the property seems to be a property-in-extension and is a particular. That is, Bennett thinks that events are tropes.

Lombard's view is, like Kim's, a variation on a property exemplification account. Lombard's version is derived from the idea of events as the changes that objects undergo when they alter, and it takes events to be the exemplifyings of "dynamic" properties at intervals of time. Such alterations are the "movements" by objects from the having of one to the having of another property through densely populated quality spaces, where each quality space is a class of contrary properties, the mere having of any member of which by an object does not imply change.

See also Bennett, Jonathan; Davidson, Donald; Kim, Jaegwon; Lewis, David; Metaphysics; Mind-Body Problem; Quine, Willard Van Orman; Thomson, Judith Jarvis; Whitehead, Alfred North.

Bibliography
Bennett, J. *Events and Their Names.* Indianapolis: Hackett, 1988.

Brand, M. "Particulars, Events, and Actions." In *Action Theory*, edited by M. Brand and D. Walton. Dordrecht: Reidel, 1976.

Broad, C. D. *An Examination of McTaggart's Philosophy.* Cambridge, U.K.: Cambridge University Press, 1933.

Davidson, D. *Essays on Actions and Events.* New York: Oxford University Press, 1980.

Davidson, D. "Reply to Quine on Events." In *Actions and Events: Perspectives on the Philosophy of Donald Davidson*, edited by E. LePore and B. P. McLaughlin. Oxford: Blackwell, 1985.

Horgan, T. "The Case against Events." *Philosophical Review* 87 (1978): 28–47.

Kim, J. "Events and Their Descriptions: Some Considerations." In *Essays in Honor of Carl G. Hempel*, edited by N. Rescher et al. Dordrecht: Reidel, 1970.

Kim, J. *Supervenience and Mind,* Chaps. 1, 3. New York: Cambridge University Press, 1993.

Lewis, D. "Events." In *Philosophical Papers,* Vol. 2. New York: Oxford University Press, 1986.

Lombard, L. B. *Events: A Metaphysical Study.* London: Routledge and Kegan Paul, 1986.

McTaggart, J. M. E. *The Nature of Existence,* Vol. 2. Cambridge, U.K.: Cambridge University Press, 1927.

Quine, W. V. O. "Events and Reification." In *Actions and Events: Perspectives on the Philosophy of Donald Davidson,* edited by E. LePore and B. P. McLaughlin. Oxford: Blackwell, 1985.

Quine, W. V. O. "Things and Their Place in Theories." In *Theories and Things.* Cambridge, MA: Harvard University Press, 1981.

Thomson, J. J. *Acts and Other Events.* Ithaca, NY: Cornell University Press, 1977.

van Inwagen, P. "Ability and Responsibility." *Philosophical Review* 87 (1978): 201–224, esp. 207–209.

Vendler, Z. "Facts and Events." In *Linguistics in Philosophy.* Ithaca, NY: Cornell University Press, 1967.

Whitehead, A. N. *An Enquiry concerning the Principles of Natural Knowledge.* Cambridge, U.K.: Cambridge University Press, 1919.

Whitehead, A. N. *Process and Reality.* Cambridge, U.K.: Cambridge University Press, 1929.

Lawrence Brian Lombard (1996)

EVIDENTIALISM

"Evidentialism" is the view about epistemic justification that identifies the extent to which a person is justified in believing a proposition with the extent to which the evidence the person has supports the truth of the proposition. Other doxastic attitudes such as withholding judgment and denying are also justified by the character of the person's evidence.

A full-scale evidentialist theory would explain what constitutes evidence, what it means to have a certain body of evidence, and what it means for a body of evidence to support a proposition to any given extent. Ordinarily, people count as evidence external things such as fingerprints and bank records. However, according to evidentialists, our fundamental evidence is constituted by our perceptual experiences, our apparent memories, and other mental states. A full-scale theory requires an account of what we have as this ultimate sort of evidence: It is unclear, for example, whether someone's unactivated memories are part of the person's current evidence. The evidential support relation to which evidentialists appeal is not a familiar logical relation. Perceptual states can support beliefs about the external world, yet there is no familiar logical relation between those states and the beliefs they support. Furthermore, one's evidence on its own does not support its distant and unnoticed logical consequences. A complete evidentialist theory would clarify the justifying connection between a body of evidence and a proposition.

Leading skeptical controversies are usefully understood to concern what sort of evidence is required for knowledge. For example, if knowledge requires complete epistemic justification, and this requires having entailing evidence, then skeptics can cogently argue that we have no such evidence for any empirical proposition and that therefore we have no empirical knowledge. On the other hand, standard skeptical arguments fail if nonentailing evidence can completely justify belief. An evidentialist theory can resolve this dispute either way.

Diverse theories of justification can be understood as evidentialist views that differ on the nature of evidence, its possession, and how it supports belief. For instance, a typical coherentist theory in effect holds that a person has her beliefs as evidence and that support by evidence consists in coherence with it. A typical foundationalist theory in effect holds that justified beliefs must include some that are defended by a foundational sort of evidence—for example, by perceptual states—and that this evidence is had by the person by being consciously accessible.

Evidentialism entirely discounts factors that figure centrally in some theories of justified belief. These factors include the intellectual pedigree of the belief, the believer's capacity or intention to fulfill intellectual duties or to exemplify cognitive virtues, and the normal functioning of the operative belief-forming mechanism. Justifying evidence for a belief might happen to arise in an irresponsibly haphazard inquiry with no attempt to fulfill any epistemic duty, as a fluke result of some abnormal cognitive activity lacking in intellectual virtue. The evidentialist view is that regardless of all this, belief is justified because the evidence possessed supports the proposition.

See also Classical Foundationalism; Coherentism; Epistemology; Skepticism, Contemporary; Skepticism, History of.

Bibliography

Chisholm, R. "A Version of Foundationalism." In *The Foundations of Knowing*. Minneapolis: University of Minnesota Press, 1982.

Feldman, Richard, and Earl Conee. "Evidentialism." *Philosophical Studies* 48 (1985): 15–34.

Feldman, Richard, and Earl Conee. *Evidentialism*. Oxford: Oxford University Press, 2004.

Goldman, Alvin. *Epistemology and Cognition*, 87–93. Cambridge, MA: Harvard University Press, 1986.

Haack, Susan. *Evidence and Inquiry*. Oxford: Blackwell, 1993.

Moser, Paul. *Knowledge and Evidence*. Cambridge, U.K.: Cambridge University Press, 1989.

Plantinga, A. *Warrant and Proper Function*, 185–193. Oxford: Oxford University Press, 1993.

Earl Conee (1996)
Richard Feldman (1996)
Bibliography updated by Benjamin Fiedor (2005)

EVIL

For most twentieth-century philosophers, intent on dividing philosophy into discrete subdivisions, the problem of evil was a matter for philosophical theology, or—more rarely—for ethics and moral psychology. The theological question is as easy to state as it is hard to answer: How is a world full of evil and suffering compatible with the existence of an omnipotent, benevolent creator? The ethical question is altogether different: How can rational beings commit evil acts? The first question has preoccupied theists since *The Book of Job;* the difficulty of finding a satisfactory answer has served many as a reason for rejecting theism. The second question has been answered in some religious traditions by the appeal to original sin, but in recent years more it has often been viewed as outside the focus of traditional philosophy. The history of modern philosophy reveals that the problems are related, and part of a larger set of questions that precedes both: Can we make sense of the lives we are given? Does human reason have the ability to find or make the world intelligible? These are not questions that are driven primarily by theological or ethical concerns, but that drive those concerns, and arguably philosophy itself.

Aristotle claimed that philosophy begins in wonder; for Schopenhauer the main subject of this wonder is the world's evil and wickedness. Even if misery were visited only on the wicked or completely outweighed by goodness, alone might well question why it should exist at all. Idle curiosity alone might inspire such questioning about why things are as they are in general; but that questioning is likely to become urgent when things go wrong. If the principle of sufficient reason is the claim that nothing happens without a reason, then there are two choices: to seek an explanation for the evils in the world or to abandon the principle of sufficient reason itself.

Orthodox thinkers have often taken the latter route, maintaining that belief is not only a matter of faith but of absurd faith. Pierre Bayle (1647–1706), the French philosopher known as "the arsenal of the Enlightenment," took this view to its logical conclusion. He thought that Manicheism, the belief that the universe is controlled by equally powerful good and evil forces, is the scientific explanation that best conforms to the data. Insofar as faith prescribes monotheism, however, Manicheism is precluded—along with any attempt at scientific explanation altogether. After all, Bayle concludes, the new Cartesian philosophy teaches that properties like color are only secondary to mathematical properties, which we do not perceive but infer. With this great a gap between experience and scientific explanation, why take the latter seriously at all?

Bayle's "theory of the incomprehensibility of all things" was the target of Leibniz's *Theodicy* (published 1710). Concerned to reconcile faith and science by proving that both were based on the principle of sufficient reason, Leibniz argued that anguish over God's seeming tolerance for evil resulted from ignorance of His ways. Ptolemaic astronomy did not challenge the work of the divine creator but rather that of the early cosmologists. Similarly, Leibniz promises, later scientific discoveries will reveal our discontent with the world to be a function of our ignorance. God has reasons we do not yet understand, but if our knowledge were as infinite as the creator's, we too could recognize this world as the best possible one.

Voltaire's *Candide* ridiculed such arguments, and Hume's *Dialogues concerning Natural Religion* demolished them. The later Kant found Leibnizian attempts to verge on blasphemy and thought the appeal to God's unknown reasons to be a mockery of suffering that required "no refutation but the abomination of anyone with the least feeling for morality" (1968). What unites their rejection of Leibniz's theodicy is the rejection of a metaphysical tradition extending back to Plato. For this rationalist metaphysics, the appearances we see appear to reflect evil and corruption; the reality behind them is truer and better than what we experience. Against this view, the more empirical outlook of Voltaire, Hume, and Kant can be seen as a moral imperative, for it implies keeping faith with the world's victims by acknowledging the reality of their suffering. But can that reality be acknowledged without entirely capitulating to it? Is it possible to maintain that evil is not essential to the world but rather an unhappy accident?

Jean-Jacques Rousseau (1712–1778) adopted just such an approach, and Kant found his solution so extraordinary that he called him "the Newton of the mind" (1942). Rousseau substituted the idea of history for the idea of original sin that had seeped into the most sober discussions of evil. Humankind was created morally neutral; a series of accidents based on minor instances of vanity and greed cascaded into the moral deterioration known as civilized society. At any particular point, we might have stopped the process, which has now gone so far that only the most radical measures hold promise of salvation. *The Discourse on Inequality* is Rousseau's diagnosis of evil, and his own replacement for the myth of the Fall; *Emile* is his recipe for a cure and the hope of salvation. The mixture of self-help manual and sacred text, science and literature is crucial: Rousseau argues that the problem of evil was so deep that it could only be approached on all fronts. Different forms of pedagogy, arts, political organization, religion, and metaphysics are all required to respond to it. Small wonder that Rousseau's plans for simultaneously reshaping individual human beings and their societies spurred the French Revolution.

The worry fueling debates about the difference between appearance and reality was not the fear that the world might be different than it seems, but rather the fear it might *not*. By acknowledging the reality of evil while maintaining that reality could be changed, Rousseau dislodged the problem of evil from the theological context in which it had been embedded.

That context is exemplified in Christian Wolff's work, which still divides evils into metaphysical, natural, and moral evils. The first evil was the imperfection in the substance(s) of which the world is made; the second was the suffering we experience through earthquakes, floods, plagues, and the like; the third was the cruelty and injustice we visit upon each other. After the mid-eighteenth century the two former evils were viewed as natural limits and natural catastrophes, devoid of significance. The only remaining evil is the moral evil committed by intentionally acting human beings. This absolves God of responsibility for evil while turning our attention to questions of ethics, psychology, history, education, and

economics. With these issues in the forefront, nineteenth-century philosophy carried on the discussion of evil. While theistic discourse receded ever farther to the margins, modern thinkers remained preoccupied with the meaning of life and the intelligibility of a world full of evil. This was true not only for philosophers sometimes considered peripheral to the canon (for example, Rousseau, Voltaire, and Schopenhauer) but also for those central to it (for example, Spinoza, Leibniz, Hume, Kant, and Hegel). Nor it is a matter of national heritage: the sober Briton John Stuart Mill could write about the problem in terms almost as vehement as Nietzsche's.

The problem of evil was no longer central in twentieth century philosophy, but it persisted in different forms, retaining the bond between ethics and metaphysics. No one would take up Hegel's project of "theodicy, a justification of the ways of God (such as Leibniz attempted in his own metaphysical manner, but using categories which were as yet abstract and indeterminate)" (1975, p. 43). In the wake of Auschwitz, every form of theodicy was viewed with suspicion. But thanks to the work of two very different twentieth-century philosophers, the problem of evil remained a major concern of philosophy. Hannah Arendt's *Eichmann in Jerusalem: A Report on the Banality of Evil* was criticized for deflating the gravity of Eichmann's crimes by calling them banal. In fact she sought to justify a world in which criminals like Eichmann are possible, by showing they are not the result of deep or demonic impulses but of mindless and not entirely intentional behavior. With this work Arendt takes up a project going back to Rousseau: Explaining the existence of evil allows us to show that it does not belong to the essence of the world, and that it may be at least partially eradicable. In thereby reducing the role of intention in moral evil, Arendt challenged a conception of evil that had dominated modern thought.

The other twentieth-century philosopher in question, John Rawls, is known for his insistence that political philosophy is independent of metaphysics, but in later works and conversations he made clear that the problem of evil was a major concern behind his work. The author of the first major English book of substantive ethics since Mill, Rawls wrote in response to two metaphysical and moral problems that ground the problem of evil: the problem of contingency and the problem of reconciliation. In *Justice as Fairness* he invokes Hegel to stress political philosophy's role in providing reconciliation. Rawls's goal is to show that a realistic utopia, in which greatest evils are eliminated, is possible; without that hope "one might reasonably ask, with Kant, whether it is worthwhile to live on earth" (1999, p. 128). Such passages encourage renewed attention to his main work, *A Theory of Justice*, the two principles of which show that human beings need not resign themselves to fate but can meet "the arbitrariness of fortune" with measures of their own (p. 102). If the problem of evil is evident in the work of two such different contemporary philosophers, it is likely to occupy major philosophers, whether theist or not, for the foreseeable future.

See also Arendt, Hannah; Aristotle; Bayle, Pierre; Cartesianism; Enlightenment; Evil, The Problem of; Hegel, Georg Wilhelm Friedrich; Hume, David; Kant, Immanuel; Leibniz, Gottfried Wilhelm; Mani and Manichaeism; Mill, John Stuart; Plato; Rawls, John; Rousseau, Jean-Jacques; Schopenhauer, Arthur; Spinoza, Benedict (Baruch) de; Virtue and Vice; Voltaire, François-Marie Arouet de; Wolff, Christian.

Bibliography

Arendt, Hannah. *Eichmann in Jerusalem: A Report on the Banality of Evil*. New York: Viking, 1963

Bayle, Pierre. *Historical and Critical Dictionary*. Translated by J. J. Knapton and P. Knapton, 1738. Reprint, New York: Garland, 1984.

Hegel, Georg Wilhelm Friedrich. *Introduction to the Lectures on the Philosophy of World History*. Translated by H. B. Nisbet. Cambridge, U.K.: Cambridge University Press, 1975.

Hume, David. *Dialogues concerning Natural Religion*, edited by J. C. A. Gaskin. Oxford: Oxford University Press, 1993.

Leibniz, Gottfried Wilhelm. *Theodicy*, edited by Austin Farrar. Translated by E. M. Huggard. La Salle: Open Court, 1985.

Kant, Immanuel. *Reflexionen. Kants Gesammelten Werken*, Band 20. Berlin: Akademie Ausgabe 1942.

Kant, Immanuel. "Über das Mißlingen aller philosophischen Versuche in der Theodizee." In *Werke*, Band 8, edited by Wilhelm Weischedel. Frankfurt/Main: Shirkamp, 1968.

Neiman, Susan. *Evil in Modern Thought: An Alternative History of Philosophy*. Princeton, NJ: Princeton University Press, 2002.

Rawls, John. *Justice as Fairness*. Cambridge, MA: Harvard University Press, 2000.

Rawls, John. *The Law of Peoples*. Cambridge, MA: Harvard University Press, 1999.

Rawls, John. *A Theory of Justice*. Cambridge, MA: Harvard University Press, 1971.

Richardson, Henry, and Paul Weithman, eds. *The Philosophy of John Rawls*. New York: Garland, 1999.

Rousseau, Jean-Jacques. *Discourse concerning the Origins of Inequality*, edited and translated by Victor Gourevitch. New York: Harper and Row, 1986.

Rousseau, Jean-Jacques. *Emile*. Translated by Allan Bloom. New York: Basic Books, 1979.

Schopenhauer, Arthur. *The World as Will and Representation*. Translated by E. F. J. Payne, Dover, 1966.

Voltaire, Francois-Marie Arouet. *Candide, Zadig, and Selected Stories*. Translated by Donald M. Frame. London: Penguin, 1981.

Susan Neiman (2005)

EVIL, THE PROBLEM OF

The problem of evil concerns the contradiction, or apparent contradiction, between the reality of evil on the one hand, and religious beliefs in the goodness and power of God or of the Ultimate on the other. In a very general classification, the religions of the world have offered three main types of solution: (1) There is the monism of the Vedanta teachings of Hinduism, according to which the phenomenal world, with all its evils, is *maya*, or illusion. A confused echo of this doctrine is heard in contemporary Western Christian Science, which affirms that "evil is but an illusion, and it has no real basis. Evil is a false belief" (Mary Baker Eddy, *Science and Health*, auth. ed., Boston, 1934, p. 480:23,24). Considered as a response to the problem of evil as stated above, this view is defective in that it redescribes the problem but does not attempt to solve it, for it leaves unexplained the evil of our suffering from the compulsive illusion of evil. (2) There is the dualism exemplified most dramatically in ancient Zoroastrianism, with its opposed good and evil deities, Ahura Mazdah and Angra Mainyu. A much less extreme dualism was propounded by Plato (*Timaeus* 30A and 48A) and is found in various forms in the finite deity doctrines of such modern Western philosophers as J. S. Mill (expounded in "Attributes," *Three Essays in Religion*, London, 1874) and Edgar Brightman (*A Philosophy of Religion*, New York, 1940, Chs. 8–10). (3) There is the distinctive combination of monism and dualism, or of an ethical dualism set within an ultimate metaphysical monism (in the form of monotheism) that has been developed within Christianity and that represents the main contribution of Western thought to the subject.

Since the terms of the problem of evil vary with the character of the religious beliefs which give rise to it, a separate study is required for each of the great religious systems. In the present article, however, the problem will be treated only in the context of the Christian tradition.

Christianity (like Judaism and Islam) is committed to a monotheistic doctrine of God as absolute in goodness and power and as the creator of the universe ex nihilo. The challenge of the fact of evil to this faith has accordingly been formulated as a dilemma: If God is all-powerful, he must be able to prevent evil. If he is all-good, he must want to prevent evil. But evil exists. Therefore, God is either not all-powerful or not all-good. A theodicy (from *theos*, god, and *dikē*, justice) is accordingly an attempt to reconcile the unlimited goodness of an all-powerful God with the reality of evil.

The kinds of evil distinguished in the literature of theodicy are (1) the evil originated by human beings (and angels), that is, moral evil or sin; (2) the physical sensation of pain and the mental anguish of suffering, which may be caused either by sin or by (3) natural evil, that is, disease, tornado, earthquake, and so forth; and (4) the finitude, contingency, and hence imperfection of all created things which some have called metaphysical evil. The last two topics will be treated in the course of discussing the others in response to the questions: "Why has an infinitely powerful and good God permitted moral evil in his universe?" and "Why has an infinitely powerful and good God permitted pain and suffering in his universe?"

THE PROBLEM OF MORAL EVIL

THE TRADITIONAL AUGUSTINIAN THEODICY. The problem of evil was a lifelong preoccupation of Augustine (354–430), and the main lines of thought that he established have been followed by the majority of subsequent Christian thinkers. Before his conversion to Christianity, Augustine was attracted by Manichaeism, a powerful contemporary religious movement with Eastern and Gnostic roots, which affirmed an ultimate dualism of good and evil in the forms of light, or spirit, and darkness, or matter. In turning from this doctrine to Christianity, Augustine rejected a final dualism in favor of belief in a good God as the sole ultimate reality, and rejected the Manichaean disparagement of matter in favor of an acceptance of the material world as reflecting the goodness of its creator.

But if the sole ultimate power is unambiguously good, what is evil and whence does it come? In answer to this question, Augustine develops two interlocking lines of thought, presenting the *privative* and the *aesthetic* conceptions of evil.

Evil as privation. Augustine counters the Manichaean conception of evil as an independent reality and power coeternal with good by his analysis of evil (derived from Plotinus, *Enneads*, I, Eighth Tractate) as the privation, corruption, or perversion of something good. Evil, he taught, has no independent existence, but is always parasitic upon good, which alone has substantival being. "Nothing evil exists in itself, but only as an evil aspect of some actual entity" (*Enchiridion*, Ch. 4). Thus, everything

that God has created is good, and the phenomenon of evil occurs only when beings which are intrinsically good (though mutable) become corrupted and spoiled.

Augustine expresses the same thought from another perspective when he equates being with goodness. God, as the highest, richest, and most intensely real being, is the supreme good, and everything that he has brought into existence is ipso facto good. For this reason the corruption that we call evil can never be complete; for if a thing becomes so vitiated in nature that it ceases to exist, the evil which is parasitic upon it must also cease to exist. Hence, there can be no wholly evil being.

How does this spoiling of God's initially good creation come about? Augustine's answer is that evil has entered into the universe through the culpable volitions of free creatures, angels and humans. Their sin consisted, not in choosing positive evil (for there is no positive evil to choose), but in turning away from the higher good, namely God, to a lower good. "For when the will abandons what is above itself, and turns to what is lower, it becomes evil—not because that is evil to which it turns, but because the turning itself is wicked" (*City of God*, XII, 6). Augustine holds that natural evils, such as disease, are divinely ordained consequences of the primeval fall of man, and thus traces all evils either directly or indirectly to a wicked misuse of creaturely freedom: "There are two kinds of evil, sin and the penalty for sin" (*Against Fortunatus*, 15).

When we ask what caused man to fall, Augustine's answer is his doctrine of deficient causation. There is no efficient, or positive, cause of evil willing. Rather, evil willing is itself a negation or deficiency, and to seek for its cause "is as if one sought to see darkness, or hear silence" (*City of God*, XII, 7). Perhaps the best way to interpret this obscure teaching is as an assertion of the inexplicability, in principle, of free volitions; for "what cause of willing can there be which is prior to willing?" (*Free Will*, III, xvii, 49). Augustine is saying that the origin of moral evil lies hidden within the mystery of human and angelic freedom. The freely acting will is an originating cause, and its operations are not explicable in terms of other prior causes.

Aesthetic conception of evil. The other main theme in Augustine is the aesthetic conception of evil, which is also derived from Plotinus (*Enneads*, III, 2, 17). According to this view, what appears to be evil, when seen in isolation or in a too limited context, is a necessary element in a universe that, viewed as a totality, is wholly good. From the viewpoint of God, who sees timelessly and as a whole the entire moving panorama of created history, the universe is good: "To thee there is no such thing as evil, and even in thy whole creation, taken as a whole, there is not" (*Confessions*, VII, 13).

The presupposition of this aesthetic view is the ancient conception, deriving from Plato (*Timaeus*, 41 B–C), which Arthur Lovejoy has called the principle of plenitude (*The Great Chain of Being*, Cambridge, MA, 1936). According to this principle, a universe in which all the varied potentialities of being are realized and which contains as many different kinds of entity as are possible (lower as well as higher, lesser as well as greater), is a better universe—one which more adequately expresses the infinite creativity of God—than would a universe which contains only the highest type of created beings. There is thus an immense hierarchy of forms of created existence, and each creature, in its own proper place in the scheme of nature, is good and glorifies its Maker. Those that are lower in the scale of being are not on that account evil; they are just different goods, contributing in their different ways to the perfection of the universe. Again, things that are transitory by nature, appearing and then perishing within the ever-changing pattern of nature's beauty, contribute, even by their death, to the perfection of the created order. As a very minor subtheme within this aesthetic conception, Augustine sometimes also uses the notion of evil as providing a contrast by which good shines the more brightly.

As an application of the principle of plenitude, Augustine holds that the universe must contain mutable and corruptible creatures, compounded of being and nonbeing. It is better that the universe should include free beings who may, and do, fall than that it should omit them. Thus, Augustine brings even moral evil within the scope of his aesthetic conception. In doing so, he employs the further principle (later invoked by Anselm, in his atonement theory) that as long as sin is exactly balanced by just punishment, it does not upset the moral harmony of the universe. "Since there is happiness for those who do not sin, the universe is perfect; and it is no less perfect because there is misery for sinners.... So, whatever a soul may choose, ever beautiful and well-ordered in all its parts is the universe whose Maker and Governor is God" (*Free Will*, III, 9, 26–27).

Influence of the Augustinian analyses. Both of these main Augustinian themes reappear in the thought of Thomas Aquinas in the thirteenth century (*Summa Theologiae*, I, 47–49).

Martin Luther and John Calvin, the Reformers of the sixteenth century, were not interested in developing a general theodicy, although they followed Augustine in his doctrine that all the evils of human life flow ultimately from the culpable fall of man.

Gottfried Wilhelm Leibniz, in his *Théodicée* (1710), employed the two Augustinian themes, the privative and aesthetic conceptions, in the course of his argument that this is the best of all possible worlds (or, more strictly, the best of all possible universes, for he uses "world" in its most comprehensive sense)—a notion pointedly satirized in Voltaire's *Candide* (1759). It is the best, not because it contains no evil, but because any other possible universe would contain more evil. The eternal possibilities of existence are individually present to the Divine Mind which, like an infallible calculating machine, surveys all possible combinations and selects the best, to which it then gives existence.

SUMMARY AND CRITICISM OF THE AUGUSTINIAN THEODICY. The traditional Augustinian theodicy in respect to moral evil asserts that God created man with no sin in him and set him in a world devoid of evil. But man willfully misused his God-given freedom and fell into sin. Some men will be redeemed by God's grace, and others will be condemned to eternal punishment. In all this, God's goodness and justice alike are manifested.

This traditional theodicy has been criticized for its accounts of the origin and of the final disposition of moral evil.

The origin of moral evil. It is urged that the notion of finitely perfect beings willfully falling into sin is self-contradictory and unintelligible (cf. Friedrich Schleiermacher, *Der christliche Glaube*, 2nd ed., Berlin, 1830–1831, par. 72). A truly perfect being, though free to sin, would in fact never do so. To attribute the origin of evil to the willful crime of a perfect being is thus to assert the sheer contradiction that evil has created itself ex nihilo.

There appears, further, to be a disharmony between this theodicy and Augustine's doctrine of predestination, which in effect sets the origin of moral evil within the purpose and responsibility of God. Augustine's doctrine (*City of God*, XI, 11 and 13, and XII, 9) refers to the fall of the angels. Calvin (*Institutes*, III, 23, 7 and 8,) has a parallel doctrine referring to the fall of man.

The assumption of the traditional theodicy that it is logically impossible for God to have created humans such that they would always freely make right moral choices has recently been attacked under the name of "the free will defense." Defining a free action as one that flows from the nature of the agent, without external compulsion, recent writers have claimed that, without logical contra-

diction, God might initially have given men a nature that would always freely express itself in right actions. (See J. L. Mackie, "God and Omnipotence," *Mind* [April 1955], and Antony Flew, "Divine Omnipotence and Human Freedom," *New Essays in Philosophical Theology,* 1955. For an important critical comment on these two articles, see Ninian Smart, "Omnipotence, Evil and Supermen," *Philosophy* [April 1961], and replies in the same journal by Flew [January 1962], and Mackie [April 1962].) Three of the questions involved in this debate are: (1) In denying that we do what we do because we are what we are, and that therefore we might have been made so that we would always freely act rightly, can we avoid equating free behavior with merely random behavior? (2) Is there any important difference between a good will that has been created ready-made as such, and one which has become steadfastly good as the outcome of a history of moral endeavor and struggle? (3) If God's primary purpose for humans is to evoke in them a free and uncompelled love and trust in relation to himself, would this purpose be frustrated by his creating people so that they cannot do other than make this response?

The final disposition of moral evil. The criticism of the eschatological aspect of the traditional Augustinian (and also, on this point, the Calvinist) theodicy has been expressed as a dilemma. If God desires to save all his human creatures, but is unable to do so, he is limited in power. If, on the other hand, he does not desire the salvation of all, but has created some for damnation, he is limited in goodness. In either case, the doctrine of eternal damnation stands as an obstacle in the way of Christian theodicy.

THE IRENAEAN TYPE OF THEODICY. Prior to Augustine and the development of his theology by the Latin fathers of the Christian church, a significantly different conception of the fall of man was prevalent among many of the Greek-speaking fathers, chief among them Irenaeus (c. 120–202). Whereas Augustine held that before his fall, Adam was in a state of original righteousness, and that his first sin was the inexplicable turning of a wholly good being toward evil, Irenaeus and others regarded the pre-Fall Adam as more like a child than a mature, responsible adult. According to this earlier conception, Adam stood at the beginning of a long process of development. He had been created as a personal being in the "image" of God, but had yet to be brought into the finite "likeness" of God. His fall is seen, not as disastrously transforming and totally ruining man's situation, but rather as delaying and complicating his advance from the "image" to the "likeness" of his Maker. Thus, man is viewed as neither

having fallen from so great a height of original righteousness, nor to so profound a depth of total depravity, as in the Augustinian and Calvinist theologies; rather, he fell in the early stages of his spiritual development and now needs greater help than he otherwise would have required. (The contrast between the Latin and Greek doctrines of the Fall is most fully presented in N. P. Williams, *The Ideas of the Fall and of Original Sin.* London, 1927.)

In much of the British theology from the mid-nineteenth to the mid-twentieth century, which has been influenced by Friedrich Schleiermacher's discussion of evil, this earlier, less dramatic conception of the Fall has been carried further. The Fall is regarded as a virtually inevitable incident in man's development as a child of God. If man is to enter into a genuinely personal relationship with his Maker, he must first experience some degree of freedom and autonomy. For only a relatively independent being can enter into a relationship of love and trust with his Creator, and man's fall is seen as a fall into this independence. It is thus analogous to the phase of disobedience which signals a young child's assertion of his own individuality in relation to his parents.

This line of thought may be carried further on the basis of the awareness in much modern theology that the "Fall" does not refer to a historical or prehistorical, but rather a mythological event. That is to say, man has never actually existed in a state of pre-Fall perfection. The Fall story is an analysis of man's present condition of estrangement from God, but not an account of how he came to be in this condition. Using our knowledge of the early state of humankind, we may say that man, as he emerged from the lower forms of life, was endowed with only dim and rudimentary conceptions of his Maker. He existed at an epistemic distance from God, which allowed him to respond to modes of divine revelation that do not coerce the human mind but which preserve man's relative autonomy. Man's existence at this epistemic distance from God constitutes his fallen estate, and from this flows the moral and spiritual cleavage and estrangement which is traditionally called "original sin." In this type of theodicy, God bears the *ultimate* responsibility for (in other words, is the necessary and knowing cause of) man's existence as a fallen creature, although, on his own level, man remains individually responsible for his personal choices and actions. Further, though the significance of this cannot be pursued here, the God who has thus created man as imperfect but perfectible has also entered into human life, in Christ, to bring about man's redemption.

THE PROBLEM OF PAIN AND SUFFERING

HUMAN PAIN AND SUFFERING. Some instances of suffering—for example, those caused by war, injustice, and the many forms of "man's inhumanity to man"—are traceable to human wrongdoing, and thus fall within the problem of moral evil. But other sources of pain, such as disease, earthquake, flood, drought, and storm, are built into the structure of the world itself. Surely, it is urged, they make it incredible that the world should have been designed by a Creator who is both perfectly good and infinitely powerful. The theist's reply is that this reasoning presupposes that God's purpose in making the world must have been to produce a hedonic paradise for man to inhabit. (This is the assumption, for example, of David Hume in his *Dialogues concerning Natural Religion, XI.*) It is assumed by the critic of Christian theodicy that the Creator's problem was analogous to that of a human being who is making a cage for a pet animal. He will naturally make it as safe and agreeable as he can, and any remaining sources of danger or discomfort are evidences of either his want of care or want of means. But the Christian conception of the divine purpose in creation differs from the one which is presumed in such a criticism. According to the Augustinian and Calvinist theologies, nature was created free from defect, and its present perils and hardships are punishments which man has brought upon himself. According to the Irenaean type of Christian theodicy, the purpose of the world is to be a place of "soul-making," an environment in which the higher potentialities of human personality may develop. To this end, it is claimed, nature is an autonomous system operating by its own laws, which men must learn to obey.

If God had created a world in which natural law were continuously adjusted for the avoidance of all pain, the more heroic human virtues would never be evoked. Indeed, a great part of our present moral language would be meaningless. There would be no such thing as "doing harm," for no one would be able to suffer any kind of injury; there would be no such thing as "doing good," for there would be no needs, deficiencies or occasions for improvement; there would be no such thing as a crime or a benefaction, an act of generosity or of meanness, of kindness or unkindness; and there would be no situations to which such qualities as courage, fortitude, loyalty, honesty, and the caring and protective aspects of love would be appropriate responses. There would thus be no occasions for moral choice. Such a world would be ill-designed to evoke many of the human traits which we value most highly. Indeed, it would seem that the "rough edges" of the world—its challenges, dangers, tasks, difficulties, and possibilities of real failure and loss—constitute a necessary element in an environment which is to call forth humanity's finer qualities.

But might not men have been created by God already possessed of these virtues? This is one of the points of contemporary debate. On the one side it is argued that, in principle, there are no limitations to an omnipotent God's capacity to create beings endowed with specific personal characteristics. On the other side it is argued that a virtue which has been formed as a result of making real decisions in real situations of moral choice is of greater value than the analogous virtue created by divine fiat, and that it is reasonable to suppose that the Creator is not content to build into men the merely ready-made and unearned qualities.

However, the discernible connection between the more heroic human virtues and the kind of world in which we live remains a very general one. It does not by any means amount to a one-to-one correspondence between each item of evil in human experience and some moral gain accruing to those who undergo it. Further, it appears that evil has crushed the human spirit as often as it has developed it, and that men have collapsed before life's challenges and opportunities as often as they have risen triumphantly to meet them. Accordingly, this type of theodicy demands completion in an eschatology. It points toward the eternal happiness of human beings in society with one another and in communion with God, which is symbolized by the "Kingdom of Heaven"; and its fuller claim is that the final fulfillment of God's purpose for his creatures in his heavenly kingdom constitutes a good so great and enduring that it justifies all the pains which have been experienced in order to reach it. (At this point, again, theodicy excludes the notion of eternal torment, for such torment could never serve any good end beyond itself, and would thus constitute precisely the kind of unredeemed evil which would make a theodicy impossible.)

A fundamental objection that is raised against this appeal to eschatology is that there is a contradiction between justifying a first-order evil, such as danger, as being required for the second-order good of courage, and then justifying the process by which courage is produced out of evil by reference to a future heavenly state in which, presumably, there will no longer be any dangers, and hence no need to have developed the virtue of courage in the first place. More generally, if heaven is free from "rough edges," how will virtues, so dearly bought in this world, survive within it?

Possibly the difficulty might be met in terms of heavenly analogues of earthly virtues, created by the development of the latter but no longer requiring the situations which evoked them; or in terms of the transmutation of a particular virtue (courage, for example) into an aspect of faith in God. However, Christian theology has not developed any definitive answer to this question.

ANIMAL PAIN. Thus far this article has been concerned with evil as it directly affects humankind in the forms of sin, pain, and suffering. There is also, however, the baffling problem of animal pain beneath the human level. Throughout the animal kingdom, one species devours another, and painful accidents and lingering diseases disable and then kill. How is this spectacle of "nature, red in tooth and claw" to be reconciled with the religious belief in an omnipotent and perfect Creator?

Certain solutions of the problem have been proposed. It is claimed that the lower animals live wholly in the present moment and lack the high-level capacities of memory, anticipation, and conscience that give rise to the human experience of suffering as distinct from the experience of physical pain; that the pain mechanism is a necessary warning device in bodily organisms that move about within a material environment; and that an animal's life, even though violently terminated, is predominantly active and pleasurable.

Solutions of a more speculative nature have been sought in two main directions. From the viewpoint of the Augustinian type of theodicy, it has been suggested that the premundane fall of Satan has had cosmic consequences, perverting the entire evolutionary process to a savage struggle for existence (see for example, C. S. Lewis, *The Problem of Pain*, pp. 122–124). The criticisms that have been made of the Augustinian account of the origin of evil apply also to this extension of it.

From another point of view, which adopts a theme of Eastern thought, it has been suggested that there may be a continuous reincarnation of souls through the levels of animal existence up to self-consciousness in human life. Thus, the pain of the animals is not wasted, but is part of a long constructive process (see Nels Ferré, *Evil and the Christian Faith*, pp. 62–65). The aspect of this suggestion that is most readily open to criticism is its entirely speculative and unverifiable character.

See also Anselm, St.; Augustine, St.; Calvin, John; Evil; Indian Philosophy; Leibniz, Gottfried Wilhelm; Lovejoy, Arthur Oncken; Luther, Martin; Mani and Manichaeism; Mill, John Stuart; Monism and Pluralism; Moral Psychology; Moral Realism; Plato; Plotinus; Punishment; Thomas Aquinas, St.; Voltaire, François-Marie Arouet de; Zoroastrianism.

Bibliography

STATEMENTS AND HISTORIES

The problem of evil is forcibly stated in J. S. Mill, "Nature," *Three Essays on Religion* (London: Longmans, 1874) and David Hume, *Dialogues concerning Natural Religion,* edited by Norman Kemp Smith, 2nd ed., X and XI (London, 1947).

For historical treatments of the attempts to meet the problem, see Julius Müller, *Die Christliche Lehre von der Sünde,* 3rd ed., 2 vols. (Breslau: Josef Max, 1849), translated by William Urwick as *The Christian Doctrine of Sin* (Edinburgh: T. & T. Clark, 1868); F. Billicsich, *Das Problem des Übels in der Philosophic des Abendlandes,* 3 vols. (Vienna, 1952–1959); Charles Werner, *Le problème du mal dans la pensée humaine* (Paris, 1944); R. A. Tsanoff, *The Nature of Evil* (New York, 1931); A. G. Sertillanges, *Le problème du mal,* Vol. I (Paris, 1948); and N. P. Williams, *The Ideas of the Fall and of Original Sin* (London: Longmans, 1927).

PLOTINUS AND AUGUSTINE

Plotinus deals with the problem in the *Enneads,* First Ennead, Eighth Tractate, and Third Ennead, Second Tractate, which appear in *The Enneads,* translated from Greek by Stephen Mackenna (London, 1917–1921). See also B. A. G. Fuller, *The Problem of Evil in Plotinus* (Cambridge, U.K.: Cambridge University Press, 1912). Augustine's main discussions of evil are in *De Libero Arbitrio, De Vera Religione,* and *De Natura Boni,* among his anti-Manichaean works, translated by J. H. S. Burleigh in *Augustine: Earlier Writings* (London and Philadelphia, 1943); and in his *Confessions,* Bk. VII, Chs. 3–5 and 12–16, and *Enchiridion,* Chs. 3–5 in *Confessions and Enchiridion,* translated and edited by A. C. Autler (London and Philadelphia: Westminster, 1955); and *De Civitate Dei,* Bk. XI, Chs. 16–18 and Bk. XII, Chs. 1–9, translated and edited by Marcus Dods (Edinburgh, 1871). See also M. L. Burton, *The Problem of Evil: A criticism of the Augustinian point of view* (Chicago and London: Open Court, 1909); Régis Jolivet, *Le problème du mal d'après saint Augustin* (Paris: G. Beauchesne, 1936).

THOMAS AQUINAS

Thomas Aquinas deals with the problem of evil in his *Summa Theologiae,* First Part, Questions 47–49, and *De Malo* (second of the Quaestiones Disputatae); see A. C. Pegis, ed., *The Basic Writings of Saint Thomas Aquinas* (New York: Random House, 1945). See also Jacques Maritain, *St. Thomas and the Problem of Evil* (Milwaukee, WI: Marquette University Press, 1942).

LEIBNIZ

Leibniz's famous work is titled *Essais de théodicée sur la bonté de Dieu, la liberté de l'homme, et l'origine du mal* (Amsterdam, 1710), translated by E. M. Huggard as *Theodicy; Essays on the Goodness of God, the Freedom of Man, and the Origin of Evil* (London: Routledge & K. Paul, 1951). For a contemporary theological critique of Leibniz, see Karl Barth, *Die Kirchliche Dogmatik* (Munich: Kaiser, 1932), Vol. 3, Part 1, par. 42,3; translated into English as

Church Dogmatics, edited by T. F. Torrance and G. W. Bromiley (Edinburgh, 1959–1960).

HELLENISTIC THEODICY

For origins, see Irenaeus, *Adversus Haereses,* edited by W. W. Harvey, 2 vols. (Cambridge, U.K., 1857), Bk. IV, Chs. 37–38, also found in A. Roberts and J. Donaldson, eds., *The Writings of the Ante-Nicene Fathers* (Edinburgh, 1867; Grand Rapids, MI, 1885), Vol. I; and A. Harnack, ed., *Epideixis* (Leipzig, 1807), translated by J. P. Smith as *Proof of the Apostolic Preaching* (Westminster, MD: Newman, 1952).

JEWISH WRITINGS

Some major Jewish writings on the problem of evil are Maimonides, *Guide of the Perplexed,* translated by M. Friedländer, 3 vols. (London: Trubner, 1881–1885), Book III, and Martin Buber, *Bilder von Gut und Böse* (Cologne: J. Hegner, 1952), translated by Michael Bullock as *Images of Good and Evil* (London: Routledge & K. Paul, 1952).

NINETEENTH-CENTURY STUDIES

The Idealist treatment of the problem is found in Josiah Royce, *Studies of Good and Evil* (New York: D. Appleton, 1898). Arthur Schopenhauer's views are in his *Parerga und Paralipomena* (Berlin: A. W. Hahn, 1851), from which T. B. Saunders has assembled and translated passages under the title "On the Sufferings of the World," in *Studies in Pessimism* (London: Sonnenschein; New York: Macmillan, 1890).

TWENTIETH-CENTURY DISCUSSIONS

The following are some modern Augustinian discussions: A. G. Sertillanges, *Le problème du mal* (Paris: Aubier, 1951), Vol. 2; Paul Siwek, *The Philosophy of Evil* (New York: Ronald, 1951); François Petit, *Le problème du mal* (Paris, 1958), translated by C. Williams as *The Problem of Evil* (New York: Hawthorne, 1959); Charles Journet, *Le mal* (Paris, 1961), translated by Michael Barry as *The Meaning of Evil* (London: G. Chapman, 1963); Mark Pontifex, "The Question of Evil" in *Prospect for Metaphysics,* edited by Ian Ramsey (London and New York: Allen & Unwin, 1961); and among Protestant writers, C. S. Lewis, *The Problem of Pain* (London: Bles, 1940); Austin Farrer, *Love Almighty and Ills Unlimited* (New York: Doubleday, 1961).

The Irenaean type of theodicy finds classic expression in Friedrich Schleiermacher, *Der Christliche Glaube,* 1st ed. (Berlin: G. Reimer, 1821), Part I, 3, and Part II, translated and edited by H. R. Mackintosh and J. S. Stewart as *The Christian Faith* (Edinburgh: T. & T. Clark, 1928). More recent writers who tend in this direction include F. R. Tennant, *Philosophical Theology,* Vol. 2, Ch. VII (Cambridge, U.K.: Cambridge University Press, 1930); William Temple, *Nature, Man and God,* Ch. XIV (London: Macmillan, 1934); and Nels Ferré, *Evil and the Christian Faith* (New York: Harper & Row, 1947); J. S. Whale, *The Christian Answer to the Problem of Evil* (London, 1939). John Hick, *God and Evil* (London: Macmillan, 1966) traces the two types of theodicy, Augustinian and Irenaean, and presents an Irenaean theodicy for today.

Some philosophical discussions are: A. C. Ewing, *Fundamental Problems of Philosophy,* pp. 247–250 (London, 1951); J. E. MacTaggart, *Some Dogmas of Religion* (London: E. Arnold, 1906), Chs. 6 and 7; C. H. Whiteley, *An Introduction to Metaphysics* (London: Metheun, 1950), Ch. 11. In addition to the articles referred to in the body of this article, see John Wisdom, "God and Evil," in *Mind* 44 (173) (1935): 1–20, and H. D. Aiken "God and Evil," in *Ethics* 68, (2) (1958): 77–97, (1949), reprinted in Aiken's *Reason and Conduct* (New York: Knopf, 1962).

More purely theological discussions occur in P. T. Forsyth, *The Justification of God* (London: Duckworth, 1916) and Karl Barth, *Die Kirchliche Dogmatik* (Munich: Kaiser, 1932), Vol. 3, Pt. 3, par. 50, translated as *Church Dogmatics,* edited by T. F. Torrance and G. W. Bromiley (Edinburgh: T. & T. Clark, 1959–1960). A book discussing Karl Barth's views on the problem of evil is Kurt Lüthi, *Gott und das Böse* (Zürich: Zwingli-Verlag, 1961).

See also C. G. Jung, *Antwort auf Hiob* (Zürich: Rascher, 1952), translated by R. F. C. Hull as *Answer to Job* (London: Kegan Paul, 1954). On the problem of animal pain, see the relevant chapters in the works cited by Ferré, Farrer, and Lewis.

John Hick (1967)

EVIL, THE PROBLEM OF [ADDENDUM]

The problem of evil concerns whether the existence of an all-powerful, all-knowing, perfectly good creator is rendered unlikely (or less likely than it would otherwise be) given the horrendous evils that afflict the world. John Hick's soul-making theodicy is perhaps the best known of the attempts to provide a plausible account of the role that evils may play in the divine plan for human life. Two other important theodicies are due to Marilyn Adams and Richard Swinburne.

In "The Problem of Hell: A Problem of Evil for Christians" (1993), Marilyn Adams discusses the problem of evil from the perspective of Christian theism, acknowledging the distinctive values of Christian theism as well its dark side, "the postmortem evil of hell, in which the omnipotent creator turns effectively and finally against a creature's good" (p. 302). As a Christian philosopher, her own view is that God's goodness to the creatures he creates is such that he will provide to each person a life that is a great good to that person on the whole. Accordingly, she rejects the traditional doctrine of an eternal hell in favor of universal salvation. In developing her view Adams carefully discusses the alternative view that some creatures so misuse their free will that God has no choice but to condemn them to an eternal life in hell, a place of constant torment whose inhabitants would be better off had they not been born.

Adams's view is that a careful look at how some people exist in the world—such as kids brought up in crack houses, or the abused—makes it simply unrealistic to suppose that each person freely chooses an evil life or a good life. She insists on seeing God as the loving, forgiving father, rather than as the vengeful lord bent on punishing those who disobey his rules. To the objection that withdrawing the threat of eternal punishment leads to moral and religious laxity, she replies that her pastoral experience as an Anglican priest suggests otherwise: "the disproportionate threat of hell produces despair that masquerades as skepticism, rebellion, and unbelief. If your father threatens to kill you if you disobey him, you may cower in terrorized submission, but you may also (reasonably) run away from home" (Adams 1999, p. 325). Because it is abundantly clear that the majority of humankind fail in this life to grow into true children of God, Adams must suppose that there are postmortem lives in which the slow progression in growth continues until all become true children of God. She also must suppose that undergoing suffering is somehow an important step to fully entering into a life with a God.

In "Some Major Strands of Theodicy" (1996) Swinburne cites certain good states of affairs—for example, enjoyment and pleasure owing to the satisfaction of desires—that God may bring about; he cogently argues that sometimes these good states of affairs cannot be brought about without certain evils occurring or its being in the power of some created beings to produce those evils. For example, Swinburne notes that compassion is a good state that requires the existence of the bad state of suffering. Moreover, the unique goodness of compassion may justify God's permission of some degree of suffering in the world. But may it reasonably be thought that the compassion of others for the victims of the Holocaust justifies a loving being's permission of that human tragedy?

Swinburne is aware of this common objection to his theodicy. His critics may agree with him that certain good states require the existence of bad states. They may also agree with him that one should not neglect the intrinsic value of being of help to those who suffer, as well as the intrinsic value of experiencing being helped and comforted. What his critics reject is the idea that these goods require God to permit the extraordinary amount of horrendous suffering that is known to exist in the world. Swinburne's response, "Yet it must be stressed that each evil or possible evil removed takes away one more actual good" (1996, p. 44), may strike many readers as doubtful. Surely, they may say, not every fawn's death by fire serves the good of teaching other deer to avoid fires. And would many great goods have been lost if only four million—

rather than six million—perished in the Holocaust? The connections between evils and goods do not appear to be as fine-tuned as Swinburne takes them to be. In response, Swinburne suggests that the world his critics think God must bring about is a kind of "toy world" where every evil is clearly seen by everyone to directly result in some outweighing good.

See also Evil; Heaven and Hell, Doctrines of.

Bibliography

Adams, Marilyn. *Horrendous Evils and the Goodness of God.* Ithaca, NY: Cornell University Press, 1999.

Adams, Marilyn. "The Problem of Hell: A Problem of Evil for Christians." In *Reasoned Faith: Essays in Philosophical Theology in Honor of Norman Kretzmann*, edited by Eleonore Stump. Ithaca, NY: Cornell University Press, 1993.

Howard-Snyder, Daniel, ed. *The Evidential Problem of Evil.* Bloomington and Indianapolis: Indiana University Press, 1996.

Rowe, William ed. *God and the Problem of Evil.* Malden, MA: Blackwell, 2001.

Swinburne, Richard. *Providence and the Problem of Evil.* Oxford: Clarendon Press, 1998.

Swinburne, Richard. "Some Major Strands of Theodicy." In *The Evidential Argument from Evil*, edited by D. Howard Snyder. Bloomington and Indianapolis: Indiana University Press, 1996.

William L. Rowe (1996, 2005)

EVOLUTION

See *Darwinism*

EVOLUTIONARY ETHICS

Evolutionary theory came of age with the publication of Charles Darwin's *Origin of Species* (1859), in which he argued that all organisms, living and dead, including humans, are the end result of a long, slow, natural process of development from one or a few simple life forms. Believing this new world history to be the death knell of traditional ways of thinking, many were inspired to find evolutionary parallels in other fields, including ethics—in both evolution of appropriate guides for proper human conduct (substantive ethics) as well as the justificatory foundations for all such social behavior (metaethics).

At the substantive level the evolutionary ethicist's usual point of departure was Darwin's own suggested mechanism of change—the "natural selection" of the "fittest" organisms in the struggle for existence—seeking to find an analogue in human conduct. Although this philosophy became known as Social Darwinism, its widespread popularity, especially in America, owed less to Darwin himself and more to the voluminous writings of his countryman Herbert Spencer, a notorious enthusiast for extreme libertarian *laissez-faire* social and economic policies.

In later writings Spencer tempered the harshness of his philosophy, seeing a definite role for cooperation in society, and this ambiguity about his real position led to his followers making contradictory claims, all in the name of the same philosophy. At one end of the spectrum there were supporters like the sociologist J. B. Sumner, who saw a place only for the success of the successful, and at the other end were American Marxists who saw in biology, as interpreted by Spencer, the true rules of moral conduct. Softer and more subtle forms of Social Darwinism tried to combine social responsibility with enlightened capitalism.

In this century the debt to Spencer is ignored and unknown, and the term Social Darwinism, burdened by history, is avoided. Nevertheless, particularly among biologists and politicians, the tradition has continued of seeking rules of conduct in what are believed to be the sound principles of the evolutionary process. At the beginning of the century there was the exiled Russian anarchist, Prince Peter Kropotkin, who argued that all animals are subject to a cooperating tendency toward "mutual aid" and that this can and will function once we dismantle the apparatus of the modern state. Later, the English biologist Julian Huxley became the first director general of UNESCO and based his policies on a biologically oriented religion of humanity directed toward the survival of the human species. And today we have the Harvard entomologist and sociobiologist Edward O. Wilson, who urges the preservation of the rain forests lest humans, who live in symbiotic relation with the rest of nature, fade and die. It is less than obvious, from a historical or conceptual point of view, that some of the more racist ideologies of this century owe much to evolutionary biology. The Nazis, for instance, shrank from the implication that all humans have a common origin, ultimately simian (although they were happy with the idea that within the human species there were biological differences).

Evolutionary ethics has long fallen from favor in philosophical circles, chiefly because of its supposed metaethical inadequacy. In his *Principia Ethica* (1903), G. E. Moore penned the classic critique, complaining that systems like that of Spencer commit the "naturalistic fallacy," trying to define the nonnatural property of goodness in terms of natural properties, in Spencer's case the happiness supposedly produced by the evolutionary process. Psychologically, however, enthusiasts for evolutionary ethics find this critique most unconvincing. It is more effective to point to the earlier attack of Thomas Henry Huxley (Julian's grandfather), who argued that systems deriving morality from evolution invariably rely on the hidden—and dubious—premise that evolution is in some sense progressive and that value is thus increased as one goes up the scale. Recently, with the increased biological interest in the evolution of animal social behavior ("sociobiology"), there has been renewed interest by philosophers in the possibility of fruitful connections between biology and morality. In his influential *A Theory of Justice*, John Rawls suggested that social contract theorists might explore fruitfully the possibility that in real life morality is end result of the evolutionary process rather than the construct of a hypothesized group of rational beings. Rawls drew attention to the similarities between his own beliefs in "justice as fairness" and the results of such sociobiological mechanisms as "reciprocal altruism."

This position taken by Rawls and others is a naturalistic position on ethics. If the science fails, then so does the philosophy. Have we any reason to think that—even if we agree that a Rawlsian type of situation is that which could and would be maintained by selection—that this position would ever come into being? This position of Rawls is an option for intelligent agents rather than beings that are basically under the control of the genes and hence, in crucial respects, might not be planning at all for themselves. There are various ways in which one might start to approach the empirical questions. Much interest has been shown in our close relatives, the chimpanzees. Students of their behavior argue strongly that we do find actions strongly suggestive of cooperation that simulates the moral.

Another naturalistic approach focuses on game theory. Models drawn from game theory are now showing that some kind of justicelike reciprocation can evolve among humans, even when no prior planning is involved. To see this, let us introduce two important concepts. The first is the notion of a Nash equilibrium, which posits that if there are two players in a game who are fighting over a fixed sum, and if they together demand more than the sum, neither will get anything. Given that both players know what the other will do, what is the most rational move for this first player? Suppose, for instance, that there are 100 units to be divided and player 1 knows that player

2 will demand 70 units. Then the most rational demand for player 1 is 30 units. An equilibrium holds if the distribution is 30:70—player 1 cannot do better than this, and could do worse. The second notion is that of an Evolutionarily Stable Strategy, whereby no one mutantation or variation can gain predominate over or eliminate all others in the population. Selection for rarity will lead to such an equilibrium because if the variation gets more common, it will be under heavier selection pressure, and conversely.

Now fairness would seem to demand that the two players agree to divide 50:50, but why should this result evolve given that it could be rational to go 30:70, given the greediness (but not irrationality) of player 2? The philosopher Brian Skyrms has shown that in fact only a 50:50 distribution is an evolutionarily stable situation. His insight is that if anyone coming into a population asked for less than 50 units, where the inhabitants asked for 50 units, then the invaders would do less well. If they asked for more than 50 units in such a population, they would always get nothing. Conversely, if the inhabitants asked for less than 50 units, the invaders asking for 50 units would spread. In his conclusion, where everyone asked for less than 50 units, one would always get less than one might have had. But if one asks for more, then too often one will end up getting nothing at all. So a kind of justice as fairness result comes out of the evolutionary process.

Suppose we grant all of this. You may still complain, legitimately, that we do not have morality. We have beings behaving as if they were moral. Morality, however, involves a sense of moral obligation. At this point, obviously, the Darwinian ethicist supposes—that is, makes an empirical assumption—that this sense of obligation is something put in place by selection to make us work together, to make us altruists who respect fairness. Normally we are self-centered. That is the way that selection has made us. So we look to our own needs when it comes to food and sex and so forth. But we are social animals also, and there are advantages to being social. So we have this moral sentiment that makes us reach beyond ourselves. Morality in this sense is an adaptation, just like any other.

Work is now proceeding at an empirical level showing how moral sentiments emerge in games of strategy. But, at the general level, the most obvious empirical support for the suggestion that ethics (substantive ethics) is an adaptation is that it fits in with the general Darwinian picture. We do have biological inclinations to selfishness—we want food and mates for ourselves—and so, if cooperation is of value, we need adaptations to let us break through the selfishness. A moral sense is just what

is needed. Substantive ethics is a kind of quick and dirty solution to the question of cooperation. It gets you to act quickly, even though (as with quick and dirty solutions) it might not always be the best answer.

Thinking of evolutionary ethics at the metaethical level also, we find that there has been renewed thought. Because the search for foundations seems so misguided – committing what Moore called the "naturalistic fallacy," could it not be that the evolutionist is directed toward some noncognitivist "ethical skepticism," where there simply are no foundations at all? This is the approach taken by Wilson collaborating with the philosopher Michael Ruse. Following up on the thinking of the late John L. Mackie, they suggest that ethics might be simply a collective illusion of our genes, put in place by natural selection to make humans into good cooperators. To this they add that the reason ethics works is that our biology makes us "objectify" our moral sentiments; thus, we are psychologically convinced that morality, despite its lack of real foundation, is more than mere subjective sentiment.

See also Altruism; Darwin, Charles Robert; Darwinism; Human Nature; Huxley, Thomas Henry; Kropotkin, Pëtr Alekseevich; Mackie, John Leslie; Metaethics; Moore, George Edward; Moral Motivation; Rawls, John; Self-Interest; Social Contract; Wilson, Edward O.

Bibliography

Huxley, T. H. *Evolution and Ethics* [1894]. Princeton, NJ, 1989.
Mackie, J. L. "The Law of the Jungle." *Philosophy* 53 (215) (1978), 553–573.
Moore, G. E. *Principia Ethica*. Cambridge, U.K.: Cambridge University Press, 1903.
Richards, R. J. *Darwin and the Emergence of Evolutionary Theories of Mind and Behavior*. Chicago, 1987.
Ruse, M. *Taking Darwin Seriously*. Oxford, 1986.
Ruse, M., and E. O. Wilson. "Moral Philosophy as Applied Science." *Philosophy*, Vol. 61 (1986), 173–192.
Skyrms, B. *Evolution of the Social Contract*. Cambridge, 1996.
Spencer, H. *The Principles of Ethics*. 2 vols. London, 1892.
Wilson, E. O. *On Human Nature*. Cambridge, MA, 1978.
Wright, R. *The Moral Animal*. New York, 1994.

Michael Ruse (1996, 2005)

EVOLUTIONARY PSYCHOLOGY

Human beings are evolved creatures. Our lineage stretches back through the first humans to have evolved roughly 150,000 years ago, through their hominid ancestors, all the way back to the common ancestor we share with all other forms of life on the planet. Many of our traits are the historical results of evolution. This holds as much for psychological traits such as the visual system, emotions, and some behavior-producing mechanisms as for physical traits such as the heart, eye, or hand.

In a broad sense, evolutionary psychology covers any inquiry that uses this fact about our biological heritage to illuminate our human psychology. Historically, Charles Darwin himself pursued this kind of inquiry, as did such disparate figures as Herbert Spencer, John Dewey, and Sigmund Freud. Contemporary scientific fields such as human ethology and evolutionary anthropology are also instances of evolutionary psychology in the broad sense.

More commonly, however, the term evolutionary psychology is used in a narrower sense to refer to a specific research program that deserves to be called a Kuhnian paradigm. This paradigm is most closely associated with the psychologist Leda Cosmides (1957–) and anthropologist John Tooby, who have been among its strongest and most vocal advocates; other prominent figures in this paradigm include David Buss (1953–), Martin Daly (1944–), Steven Pinker (1954–), Donald Symons (1942–), and Margo Wilson (1942–). The manifesto for this group is the 1992 volume *The Adapted Mind*. This specific paradigm has been the most controversial branch of the general evolutionary approach to psychology and is therefore the focus of this entry. Unless otherwise qualified, *evolutionary psychology* will here be used to refer to this specific paradigm. There are four distinctive theoretical commitments in this paradigm of evolutionary psychology.

COMPUTATIONALISM

In keeping with most cognitive science and much contemporary psychology, evolutionary psychology construes the mind as an information-processing machine, which can be described in cognitive and computational terms. What is important about the mind is not what it is made of but what it does, namely, take in information from the environment, operate on internal representations, and produce behavior. The physical properties of the brain, such as its size and the amount of energy it requires, may have played some role in our evolution; but at least as important in evolution is what the mind does, and this is to be characterized functionally.

ADAPTATIONISM

Organisms possess many traits that appear to have been designed to help them survive and reproduce—photo-synthesis in plants, the vertebrate eye, and so on. Such traits increase the fitness of the organism, which essentially means they make it more likely for the organism to transmit its genes to future generations. These traits are adaptive.

Evolution by natural selection is the best explanation for the existence of complex and functionally integrated traits such as the eye. Natural selection works by preserving and modifying heritable mutations that increase their possessors' fitness. Suppose some organism is born with some novel and simple trait (due to random mutation) that gives it a slight fitness advantage over its conspecifics. The next generation will tend to have more such organisms, and so the new trait will spread throughout the population. The more common the trait becomes in the population, the more likely that some new, beneficial mutation will arise in organisms with that trait, in which case organisms with both mutations will become more frequent in the population, and so on. By accumulating many small, beneficial mutations, natural selection can build complex and well-designed traits. Traits that evolved because they increased their bearers' fitness are adaptations.

Two questions can be distinguished about any trait: first, whether it is an adaptation and, second, whether it is currently adaptive. The first is an historical question concerning the role of natural selection in the origin of the trait; the second concerns whether the trait at the present time *fits* the organism to its environment (strictly, whether the trait tends to increase the organism's genetic representation in later generations). Adaptations must have been adaptive when they evolved, but they need not be adaptive now. They may no longer fit the environment if it differs from the environment in which the trait evolved.

Evolutionary psychologists claim that the human mind contains many traits that are adaptations (but may no longer be adaptive in modern environments). The environment in which traits evolved is called the environment of evolutionary adaptedness (EEA). Note that *environment* is construed broadly in evolutionary theory, covering geographical, physical, biological, and social factors. In the case of human psychological evolution, the social environment must have been especially important. According to evolutionary psychologists, the human EEA was the Pleistocene era, which started about 1.8 million years ago and ended 10,000 years ago. They argue that there has not been enough time since then for selection to have produced any significant new adaptations. Adaptations take time to evolve, especially such complex adaptations as psychological traits, and there have not been enough generations since the Pleistocene for new psychological adaptations to evolve.

Throughout the Pleistocene, human beings lived as hunter-gatherers in small-scale groups. Hence our adaptations are equipped to deal with this kind of environment but not necessarily modern environments, which are different in many salient ways. Our food preferences are a commonly cited psychological example. Humans enjoy and seek out foods high in sugar and fat. In the nutrient-poor environment of the Pleistocene, such preferences were adaptive since they helped our ancestors maximize their caloric intake. But they are no longer adaptive in modern environments in the developed world where such foods are all too readily available.

Since the mind/brain is an organ of tremendous complexity and sophistication, evolutionary psychologists argue that it must have evolved by natural selection. More than that, specific psychological mechanisms evolved to solve the suite of adaptive problems faced by our hunter-gatherer ancestors—problems of how to increase their genetic representation in future generations. This fact is crucial to understanding the mind, claim evolutionary psychologists, because it allows researchers to engage in reverse engineering. In an evolutionary functional analysis, evolutionary psychologists try to infer what adaptive problems our ancestors would have faced and what sorts of psychological mechanisms would be required to solve them on the basis of what is known about conditions in the human EEA. Through such an analysis they generate hypotheses about our psychological adaptations and then test for the presence of these adaptations in modern humans.

MODULARITY

The third main theoretical commitment of evolutionary psychology follows naturally from the previous one. The mind is not a single, monolithic adaptation, argue evolutionary psychologists. Rather, the mind is comprised of many functionally distinct units dedicated to solving specific adaptive problems faced in the EEA. These distinct psychological mechanisms are modules.

When Jerry Fodor first developed the notion of a psychological module in *The Modularity of Mind* (1983), he characterized them as sharing a cluster of nine distinctive features. Evolutionary psychologists have focused on only a subset of these. The modules they propose are supposed to operate fast and automatically (without conscious effort). They are more or less informationally encapsulated from other psychological mechanisms—

they do not have full access to all the information stored elsewhere in the mind. Finally, they possess innate information about the adaptive problem they were designed to solve.

Fodor himself believed that modules would only be found at the functional periphery of the mind, handling input processes such as vision. More controversially, evolutionary psychologists claim not only that more central cognitive processes are modular but also that the mind is massively modular. Cosmides and Tooby (1992), for instance, claim that the mind must contain thousands of different modules, each of them dedicated to solving different adaptive problems (and subproblems) in the EEA.

Evolutionary psychologists have offered some general evolutionary arguments for why the mind should be largely comprised of modules rather than domain-general processes. First, the adaptive problems our ancestors faced were many and varied—foraging for food, selecting the best possible mate, avoiding incest with one's kin, and so on—and these require different sorts of solutions. A mind with domain-specific ways to solve these problems is faster, more efficient, and more reliable than a general-reasoning sort of mind. Therefore, modular minds would have been selected over general reasoners in our ancestral lineage, and our own evolved cognitive architecture should be massively modular.

The second argument for massive modularity is that only massively modular minds could have produced adaptive behavior. General reasoners could not have learned by themselves and in their own lifetimes the advantages of avoiding incest or helping kin, especially since what counts as error and success is not the same in all domains. Modular creatures with domain-specific knowledge of what to do and when to do it would have been fitter than general reasoners.

UNIVERSALITY

The last main theoretical commitment of evolutionary psychology is that psychological adaptations are part of our universal human nature, with two exceptions: where a person lacks the adaptation because of mutation, and some cases of sex differences (in particular, adaptations concerning sexual reproduction). Evolutionary psychologists believe this about adaptations in general: Any trait that increases its bearer's fitness will tend to spread to fixation through a population, given enough time. Since our psychological adaptations evolved during the Pleistocene, there was enough time for them to become fixed in the entire human species.

Evolutionary psychologists have several defenses against the obvious rebuttal that human psychological nature looks anything but universal. First, they tend to downplay the massive cultural differences that anthropologists in the early to mid-twentieth century claimed to have found. Second, and a less ad hoc defense, evolutionary psychologists claim only that our psychological adaptations are universal, not that all our psychological traits are universal. Given that they also view complexity as the mark of an adaptation, however, this concession does not really grant the possibility of variation in complex psychological traits.

Their third, most interesting defense is that, even if we grant significant diversity across and between cultures, this diversity may still be produced by a common underlying mechanism. Evolutionary psychologists are interested not in behavior but in the psychological adaptations that produce behavior. An adaptation exposed to one set of environmental cues might produce a different behavior if it were exposed to a different set of cues.

One way a universal mechanism can produce diversity is a common psychological mechanism responding differently to different environmental cues. The linguistic work of Noam Chomsky, himself not an evolutionary psychologist, provides a classic example of this. According to the Chomskian tradition, the world's various languages are all underwritten by a basic universal grammar. All normal humans possess a modular language-acquisition device that enables us to learn the language of our native environment during a certain critical period of development. Although two humans may speak two different languages, they acquired, comprehend, and speak their own language with the same mechanisms.

A second way to get diversity from a universal mechanism is where a common developmental program produces different psychological mechanisms in different environments. For instance, some mechanisms may only develop in the presence of certain environmental cues at certain stages of development. In environments where those cues are lacking, or where different cues are present, the mechanism will not develop. Evolutionary psychologists have proposed both types of explanation of how an underlying common human nature can produce behavioral diversity.

Strictly speaking, then, when evolutionary psychologists claim that our evolved psychology is universal, they mean this in a restricted sense. It is not behaviors, beliefs, or desires that are supposed to be universal but only our psychological adaptations. In some cases even the psychological mechanisms themselves are not universal but only the developmental programs that produce those mechanisms in the appropriate environments.

SPECIFIC ADAPTATIONS PROPOSED BY EVOLUTIONARY PSYCHOLOGISTS

Evolutionary psychologists have proposed too many psychological adaptations to list here, but two examples should suffice. Cosmides and Tooby (in "Cognitive Adaptations for Social Exchange") proposed a module dedicated to detecting cheaters in social exchanges. This module was postulated to explain a puzzling pattern of results on the Wason selection task—a psychological test. Humans tend to perform very badly on this task when it is framed as an abstract logical problem but perform much better when it is framed as a problem for detecting potential social violations. According to Cosmides and Tooby, we should predict that humans have a dedicated cheater-detection module because detecting cheats was a serious adaptive problem for our ancestors in the EEA, and this module is invoked by the second but not the first frame in the Wason task.

The second example of a proposed psychological adaptation is even better known and comes from Buss (particularly in *The Evolution of Desire*). According to Buss, different reproductive strategies would have been successful for men and women in the EEA, and so men and women should have evolved different mating preferences. Men who preferred to mate with younger, more fertile women would have been more reproductively successful than other men. Conversely, women who preferred to mate with high-status men would have been more reproductively successful than other women. In a massive cross-cultural survey, Buss claimed to have shown that these preferences exist to this day.

PROBLEMS WITH EVOLUTIONARY PSYCHOLOGY

Evolutionary psychology has been the subject of much critical scrutiny, from philosophy, psychology, and evolutionary biology. Each of its four main theoretical commitments is contentious, and the empirical case for many of its substantive claims has also been contested.

PROBLEMS WITH COMPUTATIONALISM. It is worth noting briefly that computationalism does have some critics in philosophy of mind. Such critics will thus be skeptical of evolutionary psychology since it assumes that the mind is computational in nature (at least, the parts of the mind of interest to evolutionary psychology). Critics of evolutionary psychology, however, have not tended to challenge its computational assumptions since these are widely shared in cognitive science and contemporary philosophy of mind.

PROBLEMS WITH ADAPTATIONISM. Much more attention has been paid to the adaptationism of evolutionary psychology. Many biologists and philosophers of biology have looked upon adaptationist reasoning with suspicion since the biologists Stephen Jay Gould (1941–2002) and Richard Lewontin (1929–) published their famous critique *The Spandrels of San Marco and the Panglossian Paradigm*. Gould and Lewontin charged that adaptationist hypotheses about ancestral conditions are too speculative, often little more than *just-so* storytelling. Moreover, the dogmatic assumption that every trait must be an adaptation exaggerates the power of selection to overcome constraints imposed by development and population size. Finally, adaptationism neglects the other ways a trait might have evolved, in particular, that a trait might have evolved for one purpose and only later been co-opted for its current use.

For their part, adaptationists have denied the charge of dogmatism; their assumption that any particular trait is an adaptation is a heuristic one, which produces hypotheses about ancestral adaptive problems. These adaptationist hypotheses should be seen as forms of argument to the best explanation and, where possible, can and should be tested against the available empirical evidence.

The appropriateness of adaptationist reasoning is still a much debated question in evolutionary biology. Regardless of the answer to that question, however, the critique of Gould and Lewontin cannot be directly applied to evolutionary psychology. Evolutionary psychologists expressly admit that the original adaptive problem cannot be inferred from the present adaptiveness of a trait. They accept the standard distinction between the historical origin of a trait as an adaptation and its present status as adaptive or otherwise, and they believe that many adaptations are no longer adaptive.

Moreover, the reasoning in evolutionary functional analysis goes in the opposite direction to standard adaptationist reasoning. Adaptationism typically starts with an identifiable biological trait and works backward to hypotheses about the ancestral adaptive problems. By contrast, evolutionary functional analysis starts with hypotheses about the ancestral adaptive problems and predicts traits that should have evolved to solve them. If these traits can then be found in modern populations, the successful prediction corroborates the hypothesis about

ancestral conditions, and we have also made some new discoveries about modern psychology.

This last point, however, highlights a legitimate theoretical concern about the adaptationism of evolutionary psychology. For evolutionary functional analysis to succeed, hypotheses about ancestral conditions must meet two conditions: First, they must be sufficiently likely to be true (or else there is no point in testing predictions derived from them), and secondly, they must be detailed enough to suggest testable predictions.

Evolutionary psychologists can draw on three main sources of evidence when developing hypotheses about ancestral conditions: direct prehistorical evidence of actual conditions in the Pleistocene, the conditions faced by still-extant groups of hunter-gatherers, and our close relatives among the nonhuman primates (primarily the chimpanzee). There is some reason to doubt that any of these sources can provide good enough evidence to meet the two conditions just mentioned, for the prehistorical record is sparse, nonhuman primates have undergone their own evolutionary trajectories since they diverged from our common ancestor, and the lifestyles of extant hunter-gatherer populations have probably changed significantly since the Pleistocene. It is also debatable whether humans in general have stopped accumulating adaptations since the end of the Pleistocene, as evolutionary psychologists claim.

If these concerns are well placed, then our knowledge of ancestral adaptive problems is at too coarse a grain to entail detailed predictions about psychological mechanisms. Granted, we can be sure of very general statements—for instance, that our ancestors faced the ancestral problem of securing a suitable mate—but their very generality robs them of predictive power. All sexually reproducing organisms face this problem, and the adaptations they evolve to solve it vary dramatically. Such coarse adaptive problems cannot provide any predictions about specific psychological solutions in human beings.

Of course evolutionary psychologists deny that the limits to our knowledge of ancestral conditions are so great; hence, a main point of contention is how much skepticism is warranted by these limits. Evolutionary psychologists think it is still possible to produce sufficiently detailed hypotheses even with such limited evidence; their critics claim otherwise.

PROBLEMS WITH MODULARITY. As with adaptationism, the concept of modularity has been the subject of general controversy, this time in psychology. Since Fodor's 1983 book, the notion of a module has been highly influential in cognitive science and psychology. There is broad agreement on the existence of at least some modules, notably, modules for language and for visual processing. The disagreement is over the amount of modularity in the mind as a whole.

Fodor himself from the start denied that the mind could be modular, except at the periphery. He later expanded these arguments into an assault on massive modularity in *The Mind Doesn't Work That Way*. According to Fodor, a massively modular mind would not be able to entertain thoughts with contents that cross the domains of each module—it would be epistemically bounded. For instance, if the mind contained separate modules for thinking about numbers, physical objects, other minds, and so on, it could not entertain a thought about both numbers and objects. A fortiori, it could not integrate information about these various domains in reasoning.

The human mind, however, does not appear to be epistemically bounded in this way, at least for central reasoning processes. Our mind is flexible in the sorts of thoughts it can entertain; moreover, it can use information from different domains flexibly in abduction. Suppose we are trying to predict the outcome of an upcoming election; potentially, information about almost anything might be relevant—facts about geography; meteorology; economics; psychology. Human minds seem able to integrate relevant information from any domain of thought.

At most, however, Fodor's arguments show only that the mind cannot be completely modular. There is need for some central workspace where information from the various modules can be integrated. But this does not show that even central processes might not be substantially modularized. In particular, it fails to show that the mind could not contain modules dedicated to solving specific adaptive problems as well as nonmodular components downstream.

A more pressing criticism is offered by Richard Samuels (in "Evolutionary Psychology and the Massive Modularity Hypothesis") against the evolutionary psychologists' arguments for massive modularity. Samuels distinguishes between two types of module: computational and Chomskian. Computational modules are, so to speak, distinct computers with their own proprietary mental programs. Chomskian modules, by contrast, are mentally represented bodies of innate, domain-specific information that are supposed to underlie our cognitive abilities in various domains. Crucially, Chomskian modules are not computationally isolated but, rather, merely

separate databases of information about the world. Various psychologists have posited the existence of such innate knowledge for domains such as intuitive physics, numbers, intuitive psychology, and universal grammar.

Samuels claims that the arguments from evolutionary psychology show the need for some domain-specific knowledge of the sort contained in Chomskian modules. Perhaps organisms do need substantial amounts of knowledge about the adaptive problems their ancestors faced in order to succeed at reproduction. This does not support the existence of the separate computational modules posited by evolutionary psychologists. All this domain-specific knowledge may be operated on by the same domain-general cognitive processes. It is one thing to argue that the mind must have a vast library of domain-specific information; it is another thing to show that it must also have a vast network of different computers dedicated to using that information.

PROBLEMS WITH UNIVERSALITY. Finally, there is room for debate about the evolutionary psychologists' argument that adaptations will generally be universal. There are known evolutionary mechanisms that can maintain alternative traits in a population, in particular, frequency-dependent selection. Frequency-dependent selection occurs when there is a set of alternative traits, no single one of which is the fittest overall. Rather, the fitness of any one of these traits depends on which traits are present in other organisms in the population and at what frequency. In some cases frequency-dependent selection can maintain polymorphism—that is, the presence of more than one alternative trait in a population—at a stable ratio in which each trait has equal fitness.

Evolutionary psychologists deny that such mechanisms would have produced true genetic polymorphism in humans. Rather than, say, two different sets of genes that produce two alternative traits, there would be a single set of genes that could itself produce the alternative traits (either randomly or in response to environmental cues, where these are available). Selection will favor this kind of adaptive plasticity over polymorphism.

Evolutionary psychologists have not provided a very good argument for this. They claim that sexual reproduction would disrupt complex adaptations unless both partners shared genes for all the adaptive traits in the population. The chief problem with this argument is that it is too strong, for it would disprove the possibility of complex genetic polymorphisms in any sexually reproducing species. Since there are several cases of genetic polymorphisms in different species, the argument cannot be sound.

THE EMPIRICAL CASE FOR EVOLUTIONARY PSYCHOLOGY

All these problems with the theoretical commitments of evolutionary psychology would mean little in the face of good empirical results. If evolutionary psychologists could point to universal psychological adaptations discovered by evolutionary functional analysis, the paradigm could be declared a success, regardless of any theoretical misgivings. Assessing the empirical case for particular evolutionary psychological claims is well beyond the scope of this entry; moreover, any such assessment would be out of date even before it went to print.

What can be said here is that the empirical case remains fiercely contested. Buss has put forth what evolutionary psychologists consider their *textbook cases* in his *Evolutionary Psychology*; David Buller (1959–) challenges the empirical case for three of these putative adaptations in *Adapting Minds*. The empirical terrain here is still up for grabs and will probably continue to be so for some time.

CONCLUSION

There are several reasons to be suspicious of the main theoretical commitments of the Cosmides and Tooby paradigm of evolutionary psychology. These reasons counsel caution about accepting uncritically the various empirical claims put forth by this paradigm. They do not prove that these claims are false, that they have not been adequately empirically supported, or that they will never be supported. To assess the claims of evolutionary psychology, our only recourse is to look to the data.

Finally, it must be stressed that the evolutionary psychology discussed here is only one paradigm within a broader field of inquiry that tries to integrate evolutionary and psychological research. Even if this specific paradigm is not entirely successful, this does not impugn the broader field itself. For human beings have evolved, and surely this fact should be relevant to psychology.

See also Chomsky, Noam; Computationalism; Darwin, Charles Robert; Darwinism; Dewey, John; Evolutionary Theory; Fodor, Jerry A.; Freud, Sigmund; Philosophy of Mind; Psychology.

Bibliography

Barkow, Jerome, Leda Cosmides, and John Tooby, eds. *The Adapted Mind: Evolutionary Psychology and the Generation of Culture*. Oxford: Oxford University Press, 1992.

Buller, David J. *Adapting Minds: Evolutionary Psychology and the Persistent Quest for Human Nature*. Cambridge, MA: MIT Press, 2005.

Buss, David. *Evolutionary Psychology: The New Science of the Mind*. 2nd ed. Boston: Allyn and Bacon, 2003.

Buss, David. *The Evolution of Desire: Strategies of Human Mating*. New York: Basic Books, 1994.

Cosmides, Leda, and John Tooby. "Cognitive Adaptations for Social Exchange." In *The Adapted Mind: Evolutionary Psychology and the Generation of Culture*, edited by Jerome Barkow, Leda Cosmides, and John Tooby. Oxford: Oxford University Press, 1992.

Fodor, Jerry. *The Mind Doesn't Work That Way: The Scope and Limits of Computational Psychology*. Cambridge, MA: MIT Press, 2000.

Fodor, Jerry. *The Modularity of Mind*. Cambridge, MA: MIT Press, 1983.

Gould, Stephen Jay, and Richard C. Lewontin. "The Spandrels of San Marco and the Panglossian Paradigm: A Critique of the Adaptationist Programme." *Proceedings of the Royal Society of London* Series B 205 (1979): 581–592.

Samuels, Richard. "Evolutionary Psychology and the Massive Modularity Hypothesis." *British Journal for the Philosophy of Science* 49 (1998): 575–602.

Kelby Mason (2005)

EVOLUTIONARY THEORY

While the fixity of species was the generally accepted view before Charles Darwin, he was not the first to propose that evolution, understood as the transformation of one species into another, occurred. The ancient Greek philosopher Anaximander maintained that people had evolved from fish, and the zoologist and botanist Jean-Baptiste Lamarck (1744–1829), as well as Darwin's grandfather, Erasmus Darwin (1731–1802), were also proponents of evolution.

Lamarck, for instance, argued, in his *Philosophie Zoologique* (1809), that life resulted from ongoing spontaneous generation and that each lineage, beginning with simple forms, was driven by an inner tendency to complexity and perfection. On his view, more complex creatures belonged to older lineages, with our own the oldest. Adaptation and diversity was explained by the inheritance of acquired characteristics. Different environments caused organisms to have different needs in response to which they would use or not use their various organs: Use would cause an organ to develop, enlarge, and strengthen, whereas disuse would cause it to shrink, deteriorate, and eventually disappear. Lamarck believed that these changes were inherited by offspring, who would in their turn continue to adapt to their environment, thus leading to transformation of the lineage. The term *Lamarckism* (or

Lamarckianism) is now used to refer to the idea that a trait that was not inherited, but was acquired within the life of an individual, could be inherited by that individual's descendants. For the most part, this idea has been discredited, but there are cases in which something that satisfies the description occurs.

DARWIN'S THEORY OF EVOLUTION

Darwin was not persuaded that evolution occurred by any of his evolutionist predecessors. The true history of his development of his ideas is controversial (Sloan 2005), but there were perhaps four main influences on him in this respect.

One was the *Principles of Geology* (1931), written by his mentor and friend, the geologist Charles Lyell (1797–1875), which Darwin read at the start of his famous five-year journey on the *Beagle* (1831–1836). Darwin was profoundly influenced by Lyell's methodological, as well as his factual claims. With respect to the former, Lyell was a uniformitarian. Broadly speaking, uniformitarianism is the view that the laws of nature have always been the same. For Lyell, this meant that geological features are to be explained by natural ("intermediate" not miraculous) processes that can still be observed to be in operation. Since he thought that these tended to bring about only slow and gradual change (e.g., a valley's formation from erosion), Lyell reasoned that the earth must be far older than the biblical 4,000 to 6,000 years. Although not a believer in evolution, Lyell also argued that investigation of the geological layers showed a continual introduction and extinction of species.

A second major influence on Darwin was his observation of the natural world, especially during his journey on the *Beagle*. His extensive collection of living and fossil animals, taken from many diverse parts of the world, and their analysis by experts in the relevant fields, convinced him (and through him, much of the scientific community) that, contra Lyell, neither fossil findings nor the present geographic distribution of species could be adequately explained other than by evolution. The task, as Darwin saw it, was to explain the evolution of species in a manner that was consistent with Lyell's uniformitarian principles.

At least by his own account (Darwin 1876/1958, p. 120) Darwin had help with this from a third major influence, *An Essay on the Principle of Population* (1798), written by the parson and social economist Thomas Robert Malthus (1766–1834). Malthus was no evolutionist; he believed that his understanding of population dynamics supported the view that populations could not change

much. His concern was the possibility of social improvement, but his social theory was driven by an observation that applied to all species: Unchecked increases in population always outrun the means of subsistence. As Malthus says:

> Through the animal and vegetable kingdoms Nature has scattered the seeds of life abroad with the most profuse and liberal hand; but has been comparatively sparing in the room and the nourishment necessary to rear them. The germs of existence contained in this earth, if they could freely develop themselves, would fill millions of worlds in the course of a few thousand years.
>
> (I.I.5, 6TH EDITION)

Malthus's message for the poor was that if they were to reduce their struggle for existence they must reduce their fecundity. According to Darwin, this struggle for existence between members of the same species suggested to him a mechanism by which populations could evolve.

A fourth influence on Darwin that may have been important was his familiarity with the artificial selection of plants and animals for breeding. Such selection showed that differential reproduction could produce a change in the distribution of characteristics in a population. It was believed that this had never produced a new species, and others had used this fact to support the basic fixity of species. However, Darwin argued that if so much change could be produced in the short time since human cultivation began, vastly more change could be produced given vastly more time. Of course, artificial selection involved human intentions; differential reproduction was guided by our choices and design still had a designer. Darwin's task remained that of finding a mechanistic process that could achieve similar, only much more impressive, results.

It is impossible to do justice here to the argument that Darwin assembled in support of his theory, but the main outline of his theory is remarkably simple. It begins with the observation that the individuals of a species vary slightly one from another. Since there are many more offspring born or plants germinated than can possibly survive, there is a struggle for survival within each species. Some of this is direct competition (e.g., for food or mates), but some is indirect (e.g., some individuals are better able to withstand disease or drought). The individuals that have variants that give them an advantage in this struggle will tend to survive longer and leave more offspring. And since offspring tend to resemble their parents, this means that beneficial characteristics will tend to be inherited more frequently than less beneficial characteristics. Over time, this causes a population to be better adapted to its environment and, especially if the environment changes, leads to a gradual change in the character of a population. The relevant periods of time are enormous ("we have almost unlimited time," "millions on millions of generations") so that, eventually, a species can be transformed to such an extent that it would be a new species.

According to Darwin, the main idea for his theory was formed in 1838 when he first read Malthus, but he did not publish his *Origin of Species* until 1859. Even then he was pushed to publish to avoid being preempted by the self-trained naturalist Alfred Russel Wallace, who in 1858 sent Darwin a letter that proposed a similar theory. Darwin's priority is well established, not only by the circle of scientists to whom Darwin had communicated his ideas but also in a summary of his theory sent in 1857 to the Harvard botanist Asa Gray. Darwin was the first to argue that natural selection was the principal cause of the diversity and adaptedness of organisms, and it was his extensive defense of the claim that evolution had occurred and could occur principally by means of natural selection that revolutionized biology.

Darwin's theory differs significantly from Lamarck's, but the views of the men were less distinct than those now attached to their names. Darwin did not believe in an inner tendency to complexity and perfection, and he argued that life had evolved just once or at most a few times. However, while he did not rate it as important as Lamarck did, he agreed that one mechanism of evolution was the inheritance of acquired characteristics.

Notice that Darwin's theory mentions only processes that can still be observed to be in operation. These processes, as he describes them, are also mechanistic: They do not involve a guiding intelligence. There is, as it is nowadays put, design without a designer.

Darwin's theory is also empirical and not, as sometimes alleged, tautological. The tautology problem was raised because the theory tells us that the fit will tend to leave more viable offspring than the unfit, although an individual's fitness is defined in terms of probable reproductive outcome. However, the theory is not tautological. Individuals within a species might not vary, they might not produce more offspring than can survive, and offspring might not tend to resemble their parents. Moreover, these facts might not lead to evolution, since the outcome also depends on any countervailing forces.

THE MODERN SYNTHESIS

In modern terms Darwin's main thesis was that when there is heritable variation in fitness within species, species tend to evolve. While Darwin appealed to natural processes that can still be observed to be in operation, he did not adequately explain all such processes: In particular, he did not adequately explain inheritance or the origin of new variation, both of which are crucial to his theory.

The mechanism of inheritance was a problem for Darwin. His (pangenesis) theory involved the idea, popular at the time, that the material responsible for inheritance was blended in offspring. If that were so, an advantageous new variant would be diluted—a popular metaphor here is that it is like a drop of white paint mixed in a can of red—with the result that its benefit, and selection for it, would probably be dramatically weakened. It was Darwin's concern over this that inclined him in his later years to give more credence to Lamarckian inheritance.

Unfortunately, Darwin never knew of the work of the Austrian monk and botanist Gregor Johann Mendel (1822–1884), which provided experimental support for a particulate theory of inheritance. According to Mendel the material responsible for inheritance consisted of discrete units (now known as genes) that could be passed unchanged from one generation to the next. Mendel's work was mostly ignored during his—and Darwin's—lifetime, and it was not until it was rediscovered in 1900 that this major difficulty with Darwin's theory was removed. The combination of Darwin's theory of evolution by means of natural selection, Mendelian genetics, and mathematical population genetics is often referred to as the modern synthesis. (Some major figures in the development of the modern synthesis were T. H. Morgan, Ronald Fisher, Theodosius Dobzhansky, Julian Huxley, and Ernst Mayr.)

Explaining the origin of variation was also important; without a new source of variation, a population cannot change much beyond a redistribution of already existing characteristics. Biologists now understand how, despite a high degree of fidelity, genes are sometimes altered. Biologists construe the word *gene* in different ways, but a common construal is that a gene is a functional segment of the DNA molecules that constitute chromosomes. Alterations to such genes can occur when there are errors in copying them or when there is a crossing-over of segments of genetic material between matching pairs of chromosomes.

Crucially, the origin of new variation is random, not in the sense that any is as likely to occur as any other, but because whether a given mutation occurs is insensitive to whether it would be adaptive if it occurred. (This leaves open the question of whether there might be selection for an increase in the rate of mutation under some circumstances.) In this sense, mutation is random but selection is not random. Whether there is selection for a characteristic is sensitive to whether or not that characteristic is adaptive. Thus, selection is thought to be mechanistic, but not random or merely a matter of chance.

Darwin's and Mendel's theories form the basis of modern evolutionary theory, but neither has survived without modification. Darwin's support of Lamarckian inheritance has already been mentioned and a number of Mendelian principles have also been revised. For example, Mendel proposed that the units of inheritance were independently sorted during the formation of gametes (sperm and eggs), but it is now known that adjacent genes on a chromosome tend to stay together when gametes are produced (this is known as gene linkage). Since the early twentieth century, however, biology has provided overwhelming confirmation of the dual ideas that evolution occurs by means of (although not exclusively) natural selection and that inheritance involves (although not exclusively) genes that are usually passed unchanged from one generation to the next.

Some developments sometimes touted as radical revisions are better seen as refinements: For example, the theory of punctuated equilibrium, which proposes that long periods of stases in a lineage are punctuated by periods of rapid change, is consistent with Darwin's thesis that evolution occurs primarily through the gradual accretion of small changes: the rapid change of punctuated equilibrium is only rapid relative to the periods of stases: no major saltations are proposed.

PHILOSOPHICAL ISSUES

No sharp line should be drawn between issues in theoretical biology and philosophy of biology. Some issues of interest to philosophers have already been touched on. The following is an outline of a few others of special interest to philosophers.

THE ADAPTATIONISM DEBATE

Biologists agree that natural selection is an important mechanism of evolutionary change, but there has been disagreement over how important it is. The biologists S.J. Gould and Richard Lewontin (1979) accuse some biologists of too readily assuming that every trait has an adaptational explanation (i.e., of assuming that each trait was selected because it was adaptive or contributed to fitness). Although the debate involves certain conceptual issues, and philosophers play a role in clarifying it (e.g., see Sober 1993, chapter 5), it is principally an empirical debate, though with widespread (including methodological) implications.

Evolution (at least genetic evolution) is now said to occur if there is a change in the proportional representation of genes or combinations of genes in a population, counting each individual's genetic makeup just once. Microevolution consists of such change within a species; macroevolution consists of such changes when they result in new species. Biologists agree that much genetic evolution is due to natural selection, but it can also be due to other causes. For example, mutation and migration can bring about a change in frequencies in a population. So can drift.

It is notoriously difficult to define the word *drift*, but the first thing to note is that both zygote (fertilized egg) formation and the selection operating on the resulting individuals are stochastic (probabilistic nor deterministic) processes, and it is this that makes room for drift. Just as a series of tosses of a fair coin can by chance deviate from a fifty-fifty ratio, genetic drift can occur either as a result of a chance disproportionate sampling of genes during fertilization, or as a result of a chance deviation from probable outcomes in survival and reproduction among the resulting individuals.

The potential for drift is increased when the population is small or the force of selection is weak. So it is, for instance, thought to have special importance in allopatric speciation, in which a small portion of a population becomes geographically isolated from the rest, and competition between almost equally or equally adaptive genes or nongene "junk" DNA (neutral selection). While drift is often spoken of as an alternative to selection, it is an aspect of its stochastic nature (Brandon 2005). Nonetheless, if a trait predominates due to drift alone, it is wrong to say that this was because there was selection of the trait, let alone selection for it.

Besides mutation, migration, and drift, there are other ways in which the evolution of a trait can require explanations other than or besides adaptive explanations. For example, even traits that were selected may not have been selected because they were adaptive. They might have been selected because of their special association with adaptive traits. Gene linkage is a way this can happen. Pleiotropy, in which a single gene has multiple phenotypic effects, is another. When a neutral or maladaptive trait has been preserved or proliferated in a population because of its link to a beneficial trait, it is called a piggy-back trait or free rider. There was selection of it, but not selection for it, and only in the latter case are traits considered adaptations (Sober 1984, pp. 97–102).

It is an issue to what extent natural selection has the power to produce ideally adaptive outcomes. How often, for instance, do gene-linked and pleiotropic traits get severed in the long run? To what extent is natural selection playing catch-up with an ever-changing environment? To what extent do developmental and phylogenetic constraints, or the necessity of climbing only local adaptive peaks, restrict its capacity to move around in design-space?

The answers to such questions have interesting methodological implications. Most obviously, if natural selection tends to produce ideally adaptive outcomes, it will be fruitful to try to understand evolutionary products as ideally adaptive solutions to problems posed by a selective regime. In contrast, to the extent that it does not, the fruitfulness of that strategy is more problematic, although the construction of what are known as optimality models could still be useful, for example, in determining to what extent natural selection was involved (Maynard-Smith 1978).

While important questions are engaged in the adaptationism debate, it has often been more rhetorical than substantial. So it is important to stress that behind the heat lays some basic agreement. Contenders agree that natural selection is not the only agent of evolutionary change but they also agree that it is the source of complex adaptive change. As Gould says, when trying to reverse the impression created by his rhetoric:

> May I state for the record that I (along with all other Darwinian pluralists) do not deny the existence and central importance of adaptation, or the production of adaptation by natural selection? Yes, eyes are for seeing and feet are for moving. And, yes, again, I know of no scientific mechanism other than natural selection with the proven power to build structures of such eminently workable design.

(1997, P. 35)

THE SOCIOBIOLOGY DEBATE

The main reason the adaptationism debate has been so heated was its connection with attempts to explain human behavior and psychological characteristics by appeal to evolutionary history. A bitter debate over such attempts, one of the biggest scientific controversies of the twentieth century, began after the publication of *Sociobiology: The New Synthesis* (1975) by the Harvard entomologist Edward O. Wilson, and *The Selfish Gene* (1976/1989) by the English zoologist Richard Dawkins, which together marked the start of or brought into focus a new push by evolutionary theory into the domain of the social sciences.

Wilson's book discusses the social behavior of a wide range of species, beginning with ants and ending with humans. He suggests we should study ourselves as if we were anthropologists from Mars, bearing in mind evolutionary theory in doing so. He also offers bold and (as he acknowledges, speculative) adaptationist hypotheses regarding gender roles, the causes of war, religion, and such like. Dawkins explicitly distances himself from such claims, emphasizing (as Wilson also does to some extent) the significance of culture in our case. However, Dawkins does not refrain from colorful metaphors that undermine this distancing. In a famous passage, having talked about the origin of replicators in the primordial soup, he says:

> Four thousand million years on, what was to be the fate of the ancient replicators? … Now they swarm in huge colonies, safe inside gigantic lumbering robots, sealed off from the outside world, communicating with it by tortuous indirect routes, manipulating it by remote control. They are in you and in me; they created us, body and mind; and their preservation is the ultimate rationale for our existence. They have come a long way, these replicators. Now they go by the name of genes, and we are their survival machines.

(1976/1989, PP. 19–20)

The issues raised relate to what used to be known as the nature versus nurture debate. That debate, put crudely, concerned the extent to which our psychological propensities were due to nature (genes) or nurture (environment). So put, however, the debate is ill conceived, because every trait is necessarily the product of both genes and environment. A better way to understand the debate is that it concerns the extent to which differences among individuals are caused by differences in their genes or in their environments (or both). The suggestion was that we would find psychosocial differences among individuals in our species, as well as between our species and other species, that were due to differences in genes for which there had been selection.

The response was vitriolic. Even sympathizers were often concerned about political implications. Critics blasted Wilson and Dankins—for being adaptationist, for proposing hypotheses that were neither tested nor testable, for being motivated by an ideological defense of the status quo, for being racist and misogynist, and for somehow being against free will and human dignity (e.g., see Rose, Lewontin, and Kamin 1984). They described the application of sociobiology to humans as "biological determinism" and proposed instead a position they called biological potentiality. The latter included the (patently true) claim that all our acts are within our biological potential and, something further, that there are no or virtually no significant task-specific psychological adaptations. On this view, evolution has endowed us with an impressive general-purpose intelligence and a capacity for culture and language, but it has done little else to shape our psychology. The latter is in a way the more absolute position: The claim that some social and psychological characteristics are (let alone may be) genetic adaptations is compatible with the claim that many are not. And those that are in part genetic adaptations might also be shaped by culture.

Evolutionary studies of human social and psychological characteristics now go under other names (e.g., evolutionary psychology). They remain controversial, but universities have increasingly devoted substantial resources to them. Today, the two sides have come together somewhat, with evolutionary theorists stressing the importance of culture, and with less emphasis on the other side on whether certain features are genetic adaptations as opposed to adaptations that can (whatever the basis of their heritability) usefully be understood by means of the concepts and methods developed in the context of evolutionary biology. Gene-culture coevolution has also become an important area of study. There is more discussion of how evolutionary studies should be conducted than whether they should be conducted (for more details, see Laland and Brown 2002). Nonetheless, the criticisms mentioned earlier are still repeated and are worth investigating.

The claim that some sociobiology is unduly adaptationist or inadequately tested is no doubt fair. However, there are poor practitioners in every field. Trivially, one should not too readily assume that a trait is a genetic adaptation, but one should not too readily assume that it is not either. Furthermore, the hypothesis, H1, that a given trait t is a genetic adaptation, competes with the hypothesis, H2, that t is not a genetic adaptation. So if one is not a scientific hypothesis because it cannot be tested, then the same must be true of the other.

Nor does it seem true that we cannot have evidence, one way or another, for such hypotheses. It is hard to assess claims regarding the evolutionary history of social behaviors and psychological characteristics, especially in the human case where ethical considerations constrain experiment more. However, relevant evidence can still be brought to bear. Consider the suggestion that male jealousy is an adaptation to the evolutionary problem posed by fertilization within the female ("Mama's baby, Papa's maybe"). To assess this claim, evolutionary psychologists appeal to analyses of fitness consequences, cross-cultural and cross-species comparisons, and relevant physiological findings (Barkow, Cosmides, and Tooby 1992). All such evidence can be put to poor use but it can also be put to good use. For example, cross-species physiological evidence relating to testes size and sperm competition suggests that human polyandry has been a significant factor. This evidence, while far from conclusive, helps (in combination with other evidence) to confirm rather than disconfirm the hypothesis, since it suggests that, had there been genes that predisposed human males to certain jealous behaviors, (ceteris paribus) there would have been significant selection pressure favoring those genes.

The criticism that sociobiologists are ideologically motivated attacks the scientists rather than the science. People try to fit new information to their preconceived ideas, and scientists are no exception. However, we can ask if, assuming we do not start from a racist or sexist perspective, an evolutionary study of racial or sexual differences will push us in that direction. Here it helps to distinguish between political consequences and logical implications. The former may be worrisome even if the latter are not, and this can muddy discussion. However, what is clear is that attempts to understand certain social and psychological characteristics as evolutionary adaptations need not be used to defend any racist or sexist status quo.

Suppose it were shown, for example, that women tend, on average, to give more priority to their children than to their careers than men do, and that this difference is in part due to a genetic adaptation. Or suppose it were shown that men tend, on average, to be more competitive and aggressive (even violent) in attempting to acquire power and status and that this difference is in part due to a genetic adaptation. It can be argued from this that men will continue to have more power in the public sphere. However, this is a prediction, not a justification, and it is based on an assumption of nonintervention. One could also argue on the basis of such claims that educators need to consider moderating such difference, that there ought to be more work-based childcare, or that the human race would be better served if less aggressive women held more political power. It is not uncommon nowadays to see theorists from the left employ evolutionary theory to make their arguments (Singer 1999).

Finally, the issue of free will is a large one, but philosophers generally agree that it is a confusion to implicate it in this debate. It is a misunderstanding of the nature of the problem of free will to think that free will is enhanced by environmental as opposed to genetic causes of behavior. The problem of free will arises as soon as human choices are viewed in the context of their causes, whatever the nature of those causes. Nor is it right to see sociobiology or its descendants as committed to determinism. In general terms, determinism is the thesis that every event is causally necessitated by preceding conditions and the laws of nature. Neither sociobiology nor its descendants are committed to this or to variants that might plausibly be described as, more specifically, biological determinism. For instance, they are not committed to the view that if a person possesses a gene that was selected because it predisposes individuals to want multiple sexual partners then someone with that gene will be unable to resist the temptation to have multiple sexual partners. Desires need not be more irresistible for being genetic adaptations as opposed to cultural artifacts.

CONCLUDING REMARKS

A general defense of the study of social and psychological characteristics from an evolutionary perspective is not the same as a defense of particular claims about social or psychological adaptation. It is consistent with the claim that such a study will fail to establish that there are any significant social or psychological adaptations. However, many think that this research will provide (and has already provided) valuable insights, relevant to many areas in philosophy. For example, the study of the evolution of altruism and the evolution of emotions are of interest to ethicists, moral psychologists, decision theorists, philosophers of mind, and political philosophers.

Darwinian evolutionary theory has had a profound impact on our understanding of our species and on our worldview, even putting to one side its role in the social sciences. While it is remarkably well confirmed by innumerable findings, and now coheres with our understanding of genetics in innumerable detailed ways, it remains controversial in the public sphere for this reason. Philosophers have played an important role in this debate as well, particularly in discussions of the nature of scientific theories.

This entry has left many issues relating to evolutionary theory untouched. A great many other issues are important as well. For example, what is the role of teleology in Darwinian biology? How does a historical science, like the study of evolution, compare to the other natural sciences? What is the implication of Darwinian evolution for the idea that species are natural kinds? How should living things be classified? How best can the intertwined concepts of selection, fitness, and drift be understood? What is selected in selection? Can memes evolve by means of natural selection? Can cultures? A number of these issues are discussed elsewhere in these volumes.

See also Anaximander; Darwin, Charles Robert; Darwin, Erasmus; Darwinism; Determinism and Freedom; Evolutionary Ethics; Lamarck, Chevalier de; Malthus, Thomas Robert; Paley, William; Philosophy of Biology; Teleological Argument for the Existence of God; Wallace, Alfred Russel; Wilson, Edward O.

Bibliography

Barkow, Jerome H., Leda Cosmides, and John Tooby, eds. *The Adapted Mind: Evolutionary Psychology and the Generation of Culture.* New York: Oxford University Press, 1992.

Brandon, Robert. "Natural Selection." In *The Stanford Encyclopedia of Philosophy*, edited by Edward N. Zalta. Stanford, CA: Metaphysics Research Lab, Stanford University, 2005.

Darwin, Charles. *The Autobiography of Charles Darwin* (1876), edited by Nora Barlow. New York: The Norton Library, 1958.

Darwin, Charles. *The Origin of Species by Means of Natural Selection.* London: John Murray, 1859.

Dawkins, Richard. *The Selfish Gene* (1976). New York: Oxford University Press, 1989.

Gould, Steven J. "The Darwinian Fundamentalist." *New York Review of Books*, 44 (10) (June 12, 1997): 34–37.

Gould, Steven J., and Richard Lewontin. "The Spandrels of San Marco and the Panglossian Paradigm: A Critique of the Adaptationist Programme." In *Proceedings of the Royal Society of London* 205 (1979): 581–598.

Laland, Kevin L., and Gillian R. Brown. *Sense and Nonsense: Evolutionary Perspectives on Human Behavior.* New York: Oxford University Press, 2002.

Malthus, Thomas. *An Essay on the Principle of Populations: A View of Its Past and Present Effects on Human Happiness; with an Inquiry into Our Prospects Respecting the future Removal or Mitigation of the Evils Which It Occasions* (1798). 6th ed. London: John Murray, 1826.

Maynard-Smith, John. "Optimization Theory in Evolution." In *Annual Review of Ecology and Systematics* 9 (1978): 31–56.

Rose, Steven, Richard Lewontin, and L. J. Kamin. *Not in Our Genes: Biology, Ideology, and Human Nature.* New York: Pantheon, 1984.

Singer, Peter. *A Darwinian Left: Politics, Evolution, and Cooperation.* New Haven, CT: Yale University Press, 1999.

Sloan, Phillip. "Evolution." In *The Stanford Encyclopedia of Philosophy*, edited by Edward N. Zalta. Stanford, CA: Metaphysics Research Lab, Stanford University, 2005.

Sober, Elliott. *The Nature of Selection.* Cambridge, MA: MIT Press, 1984.

Sober, Elliott. *Philosophy of Biology.* San Francisco: Westview Press, 1993.

Wilson, Edward, O. *Sociobiology: The New Synthesis.* Cambridge, MA: Harvard University Press, 1975.

Karen Neander (2005)

EXISTENCE

Philosophical discussion of the notion of existence, or being, has centered on two main problems that have not always been very clearly distinguished. First, there is the problem of what we are to say about the existence of fictitious objects, such as centaurs, dragons, and Pegasus; second, there is the problem of what we are to say about the existence of abstract objects, such as qualities, relations, and numbers. Both problems have tempted philosophers to say that there are inferior sorts of existence as well as the ordinary straightforward sort, and they therefore often suggest that we use the word *being* to cover both kinds but restrict "existence" to "being" of the common, nonfictitious, nonabstract sort. (Sometimes the term *reality* is proposed for "existence" or for "being.") The problems of fiction and abstraction are different, however, for there are both real and fictitious abstractions. For example, the integer between two and four is real, but the integer between two and three is fictitious. On the other hand, there are both concrete and abstract fictions; for example, the winged horse of Bellerophon and the integer between two and three. Accordingly, philosophers have often dealt with the two problems in quite different ways and perhaps ought to do so.

While these are the two main problems, there are others, for example, that of what we are to say of the being of objects which have not yet begun, or have now ceased, to exist. The history of this subject, moreover, has been tangled with theological issues, to which it will be necessary to refer at certain points. Most of what follows will concentrate on the question of fictitious existence, with some consideration of past and future existence and with a final section on the being sometimes ascribed to abstractions.

FICTIONS

ANCIENT AND MEDIEVAL. It is clear from Aristotle's earliest works that there was current among the Greeks a sophism to the effect that whatever is thought of must exist in order to be thought of. Countering this, Aristotle distinguished between "to be *A*" (for instance, to be thought of) and "to be" without qualification. He made the same remark about the "being *A*" of that which has "ceased to be"; for instance, from "Homer is a poet" it does not follow that "Homer is." Some such distinction seems necessary, since among the *A*'s that one can be is "dead" or "no longer existent." The Aristotelian view is not simple, however, for elsewhere he suggested that propositions equivalent to "Socrates is ill" and "Socrates is well" imply the plain "Socrates is"; "neither is true if Socrates does not exist at all."

The various facets of the Aristotelian position were reproduced by the Scholastics. They distinguished, for example, between *est secundi adiecti* ("is" added as a second element in a simple sentence, as in "Socrates is"), and *est tertii adiecti* ("is" added as a third element, as in "Socrates is ill"), a distinction made by Aristotle in substantially the same terms; they also had the rule that from "being *A*" we may infer plain "being." But the Scholastics questioned and qualified this rule with the other Aristotelian examples in mind; from *Chimaera est opinabilis,* "The chimera can be thought of," the plain *Chimaera est* does not follow, nor does *Caesar est* follow from *Caesar est mortuus.* Some predicates, they said, presuppose *esse simpliciter,* and some do not. (*Chimaera* itself, incidentally, they put in the first class, and were thereby led to say that even "The chimera is the chimera" is false—the chimera, since it "isn't," isn't anything, even the chimera.) In this connection they sometimes distinguished between "objective" and "formal" being; "objective" not having its modern sense but rather the opposite—for a thing to exist "objectively" it sufficed that it be an object of thought; "formal" being was, as it were, serious being.

Anselm's Ontological Argument for the existence of God hinged on this notion of "objective" being, which he called existence in the mind. The Psalmist's fool who says in his heart that God does not exist must in that very act be thinking of God, so that God exists in his mind. But by definition God is that than which nothing greater can be thought of (if this definition is objected to, we can simply say, "Never mind—that than which nothing greater can be thought of, whether you give this the name "God" or not, can be thought of, and therefore exists in the mind even of one who denies its existence anywhere else"). And to exist outside the mind as well as in it is a greater thing than to exist in the mind only; we can also think of a being that does this, so if it exists in the mind only, the *maximum cogitabile* is not the *maximum cogitabile* at all;

it is therefore self-contradictory to deny real existence to that than which nothing greater can be thought of. "Greater" in this argument means, in part, better, so it is no answer to say that of some things it might be better for them not to exist. If God is by definition everything that a being ought to be, then such a being ought to be, among other things, real; and to think of him as not being real is therefore to think of him as not being all that he ought, and thus is not to be really thinking of God. The thought of an unreal God is internally incoherent, so if God can be thought of at all (and the man who thinks he does not exist does think of him), he must, if we are to be consistent, be thought of as real. But it is clear that this type of argument, if valid, has other than theological applications; as Anselm's opponent Gaunilo pointed out, there would be a similar contradiction in ascribing merely mental existence to the greatest (and best) conceivable island.

The notion of "weak" forms of being entered into another medieval theory, that of the "ampliation," or widening, of the "supposition," or reference, of certain terms in certain contexts. If we say "Some men are running," it is understood that we mean some men now existing; but if we say "Some men were running" or "Some men will be running," it will be enough to verify the former if some formerly existing men were running, and the latter if some men who will then exist will be running; and if we say "Some men are thought of as running," it will do if some merely thought-of men (Sherlock Holmes and Dr. Watson, say) are thought of as running. The pool of objects on which we may draw to verify our statements may in some cases extend to objects whose being is comparatively shadowy yet is substantial enough for them to be genuine subjects of affirmative discourse.

It is noteworthy, however, that at least one medieval thinker, Thomas Aquinas, quite firmly refused to avail himself of the notion of substandard existence at a point where it might have been thought to be helpful: in dealing with objections to the doctrine of creation out of nothing. Creation out of nothing, Thomas insisted, is not creation out of a peculiarly tenuous material; to be created out of nothing is simply not to be created out of anything, and God himself is "created out of nothing" in this sense. But to be created (as God of course is not), yet not created out of anything, is to be given existence; and to what is existence given if there is literally nothing there to give it to? To give existence to nothing, surely, is just not to give existence to anything, and thus not to create at all. That there already are "creatables" whose capacity to exist in the full sense is made actual in their creation is explic-

itly denied; the only power involved is that of God to create, and creating is denied to be a genuine action on an object. All that Thomas could say positively is that the receiver of existence starts to be simultaneously with the giving of that existence—*Deus simul dans esse, producit id quod esse recipit: et sic non oportet quod agat ex aliquo praeexistenti* (*De Potentia Dei,* Q.2, A.1). Leibniz's later talk of God as conferring actual existence upon a selected few of an infinite number of *possibilia,* each with its own eternally complete individuality, seems much less perceptive. Creating out of *possibilia* is not creation out of nothing at all.

EIGHTEENTH AND NINETEENTH CENTURIES. The rejection of halfway points between existence and nonexistence that characterized Thomas's treatment of creation found wider applications in the works of the eighteenth-century philosopher Thomas Reid. In discussing "conception," Reid distinguished this "operation of the mind" from others by the fact that whereas "the powers of sensation, of perception, of memory, and of consciousness [introspection] are all employed solely about objects that do exist, or have existed … conception is often employed about objects that neither do, nor did, nor will exist" (*Essays on the Intellectual Power of Man,* Essay IV). It is important, he said, to "distinguish between that act or operation of the mind, which we call conceiving an object, and the object that we conceive." The former always exists; the latter need not. The notion that it must has led some philosophers to interpose between the act and the object an entity called an idea, which is the "immediate" object of conception and exists even when the "remote" object does not. According to Reid's view, there are no such entities, and "having an idea of" is just a circumlocution for "conceiving."

> The philosopher says, I cannot conceive a centaur without having an idea of it in my mind…. He surely does not mean that I cannot conceive it without conceiving it. This would make me no wiser. What then is this idea? Is it an animal, half horse and half man? No. Then I am certain it is not the thing I conceive…. This one object which I conceive is not the image of an animal— it is an animal. I know what it is to conceive an image of an animal, and what it is to conceive an animal; and I can distinguish the one of these from the other without any danger of mistake. (Ibid.)

Not only is there no reason to believe in the existence of "ideas" (apart from the sheer "prejudice" that all acts of the mind must have existent objects); postulating them does not help, and only gives rise to an infinite regress.

> In every work of design, the work must be conceived before it is executed—that is, before it exists. If a model, consisting of ideas, must exist in the mind, as the object of this conception, that model is a work of design no less than the other, of which it is the model; and therefore, as a work of design, it must have been conceived before it existed. (Ibid.)

The point that the idea or copy theory just does not help seems unanswerable. But Reid's own position has serious difficulties. Every act of conception, he said, "must have an object; for he that conceives must conceive something"; thus, to conceive nothing—not to conceive anything—is not to conceive at all. But if what is conceived—for example, a centaur—does not exist in any sense, is this not simply conceiving without any second term? The object of conception in all cases is something, as Reid claimed; it would therefore seem that "some-things" ("beings," "objects," in a wide sense) are divisible into two sorts, ones with existence over and above their mere objecthood, and ones without. Reid said as much when he spoke of a man as acquiring sufficient judgment to "distinguish things that really exist from things that are only conceived." Reid was trying to slip this statement past as if it were not the theory of weak and strong modes of "being." But if it is not, what is it? He said that men six feet tall and men sixty feet tall are both "things," even if he said it under his breath. The theory of weak and strong being is not easily avoidable, and in the present century it was stated in these terms in Bertrand Russell's early work and in Reid's terms by Alexius Meinong.

There is a rather different strand in postmedieval philosophy, starting perhaps with Pierre Gassendi. Replying to the Cartesian version of Anselm's Ontological Argument, Gassendi said that existence is not a "perfection," not because it is sometimes an undesirable property but because it is not a property at all; it is, rather, a prerequisite for the possession of any properties. In itself this looks like merely accepting one side of Aristotle's dilemma and ignoring the other (must a thing exist in order to possess the property of being thought of?). Later writers, however, took the thought further. David Hume, in particular, held that existence is a nugatory notion. "When after the simple conception of any thing we would conceive it as existent, we in reality make no addition or alteration on our first idea" (*Treatise of Human Nature*, Book I, Part 3, Sec. 7 and note). The notion of an existent God, man, or centaur is simply the notion of a God, a man, or a centaur. The common view of judgment as "the separating or uniting of different ideas" is therefore mistaken; the judgment that God exists, for example, involves only one idea, that of God. The real difference is not that between a God and an existent God but that between conceiving God's existence (which is the same as conceiving God) and believing in his existence; this is a difference in our mode of thought, not in what is thought of. Immanuel Kant made the same point in his treatment of the Ontological Argument; existence, he said, is not a genuine predicate, and the conception of a hundred real dollars has no more "content" than that of a hundred merely possible dollars.

Hume's denial that the object of judgment is necessarily complex was taken further by Franz Brentano. Since the time of Aristotle, logicians had divided propositions or judgments into simple "existential" assertions and denials, of the forms "*X* is" and "*X* is not," and "predicative" ones, of the forms "*X* is *Y*" and "*X* is not *Y*," and had tended, when assimilating the two, to treat existential assertions as a special case of predicative ones—"*X* is" amounts to "*X* is existent" or "*X* is a being." Brentano reversed this, treating the difference between the two types as merely a difference in the complexity of what is asserted or denied to be—"*X* is *Y*" amounts to "*XY* is" and "*X* is not *Y*" to "*XY* is not" (for instance, "Horses don't fly" amounts to "Flying horses do not exist"). He avoided the infinite regress that would appear if "*XY* is" was further transformed into "Existent *XY* is," and "*XY* is not" into "Existent *XY* is not" by denying, with Hume, that existence is a feature of the object of thought. "*X* is" and "*XY* is" simply express the mind's acceptance of the concept *X* or *XY*, as opposed to the mere entertainment of it, and "*X* is not" and "*XY* is not" similarly express the mind's rejection of "*X*" and "*XY*."

An obvious objection to the theories of Hume, Kant, and Brentano is that they are concerned not with the notion of existence but with that of believing in something's existence, and the account given of this latter—that to believe that what is before the mind exists is simply to accept this object—is such that the notion of the object's existence apart from our belief disappears. It is like the account of "believing *X* to be good" that reduces it to "liking *X*"; the notion of *X*'s being good, outside of its being believed to be so, vanishes. However it may be with beliefs about goodness, beliefs about the existence of things are surely true or false; and they are true only if the things in question exist in fact. Brentano's answer was to define what really exists as the object of right affirmative judgment, but this seems to reverse the matter—the judgment that *X* exists is a right one if and only if *X* does exist.

However, the treatment of predicative judgments as complex existential ones can easily be disentangled from Brentano's subjectivism; and it is also found in writers, notably John Venn, whose interests were less in meta-physico-psychological questions than in developing formal logic by algebraic means. If we are to do this, it is natural to write "No *X* is a *Y*" as "*XY* = 0" and to read this as "*XY*'s are nonexistent." Similarly "Some *X* is a *Y*" becomes "*XY* ≠ 0"; "Some *X* is not a *Y*," "*XȲ* ≠ 0" (writing "*Ȳ*" for what is not a *Y*; that is, "non-*Y*"); and "Every *X* is a *Ȳ*," "*XȲ* = 0," or "*X*'s that are not *Y* are nonexistent." This, as Brentano and John Venn observed, has the odd consequence of making both universal forms true of what does not exist, for if there are no *X*'s at all, there are none that are *Y* and none that are not *Y*, so that "No *X* is a *Y*" is true in the sense of "*XY*'s are nonexistent" and "Every *X* is a *Y*" is true in the sense of "*X*'s that are not *Y* are nonexistent." This is sometimes expressed as the dictum that the null (or empty) class is included in every class; the class of centaurs, for example, is included in that of tables because, since there are no centaurs at all, there are no centaurs that are not tables.

This leads to divergences from the scholastic rule that affirmative predications imply the existence of their subject while negative predications do not; and the late nineteenth-century discussions of this problem of the "existential import" of the Aristotelian predicative forms were very elegantly summed up by J. N. Keynes in his *Studies and Exercises in Formal Logic*. The scholastic rule, it should be noted, was subject to qualification in the light of the doctrine of "ampliation" already mentioned; "All centaurs are said to be musical," for example, was not falsified by there being no real centaurs because in this context the reference of "centaur" was extended to centaurs merely spoken of. A nineteenth-century counterpart of this doctrine was the theory of the "universe of discourse." "Existence," according to this theory, always means membership in some collection of objects taken as real for the purposes of the discussion, and this might be either the actual universe or, for instance, the world of Homeric mythology. Taken seriously, this would seem to be a variant of the theory of weak and strong modes of being.

Brentano's account of predicative judgments as complex existential ones is reversed in Alexander Bain's theory that all intelligible assertions of existence have complex subjects and therefore can be restated in the predicative form. For example, "when we say there *exists* a conspiracy for a particular purpose, we mean that at the present time a body of men have formed themselves into a society for a particular object" (*Logic*, Book I, Ch. 3, Sec. 23), and in general, "*XY*'s exist" = "Some *X*'s are *Y*'s." In the present century this view was enlarged upon by John Anderson. According to Anderson, statements are meaningful (and thus true or false) only if all terms occurring in them are real; that is, only if they have objects answering to them. This means, in view of the Bain-Anderson analysis of assertions of existence, that these terms must be implicitly complex and that the statements in which they occur must presuppose other statements in which this implicit complexity is made manifest; these in turn presuppose others, and so on without end. "All *X*'s are *Y*'s" (for instance, "All albinos are short-sighted") is meaningful only if there are *X*'s and *Y*'s (albinos and short-sighted individuals), and this condition is itself meaningful only if "*X*" and "*Y*" are implicitly complex—if an *X*, for example, is an *AB* (an albino is an animal with white hair and pinkish eyes), so that "*X*'s exist" means "Some *A*'s are *B*'s" ("Some animals with white hair have pinkish eyes"); and similarly for these statements in their turn.

The apparent predicate "exists" disappears from this system, without any subjectivism (the plain "*X*'s exist," or at all events "*XY*'s exist," has been given a meaning, and not just "*A* judges that *XY*'s exist"). But the system completely wrecks such simple rules of construction as the one that if "*X*" and "*Y*" can both figure as terms in a meaningful sentence, so can "*XY*" ("what is at once an *X* and a *Y*").

RUSSELL'S THEORY OF DESCRIPTIONS. The most extensive and fruitful discussions of existence in the present century have been those initiated by Russell, in works written after his abandonment of the theory of weak and strong modes of being. On the meaning of "all" and "some" Russell stands squarely in the tradition of Venn: he reads "Some *X*'s are *Y*'s" as "*XY*'s exist" and "All *X*'s are *Y*'s" as "*X*'s that are not *Y*'s do not exist"; but he also insists, in the tradition of Kant, that "exists" is not a genuine predicate. For Russell the fundamental form of prediction is the singular or "atomic" proposition, "*x* φ s," where "*x*" is a proper name of an individual and "φ s" is a genuine predicate or verb. "Lions exist" and "Tame lions exist" (or "Some lions are tame") are respectively analyzed as "For some individual *x*, *x* is a lion" and "For some individual *x*, *x* is a lion and is tame"; the predicates are "is a lion" and "is a lion and is tame"—"exist" has disappeared into the prefix, or "quantifier," "For some individual *x* ... ." To predicate "exists" of an individual directly named is meaningless; but Russell makes a sharp distinction between genuine, or "logically proper," names and spurious ones. A genuine proper name (Russell usually takes the demonstrative "this" as an example) contributes nothing to the meaning of a sentence except the identification of some individual as its subject; in John Stuart Mill's terminology, it "denotes" but does not "connote." Anything it tells us about the individual, if it is being used as a genuine proper name, is no part of what is being said; and if there is no individual that it identifies, then nothing is being said at all. A singular, or "definite," description of the form "the so-and-so," or a grammatical proper name with the sense of such a description (such as "Scott" used to mean "the author of *Waverley*"), is quite a different matter. When analyzed, "the so-and-so," like "some so-and-so" and "every so-and-so," disappears into a complex of predicates and quantifying prefixes; for example, "The present king of France is bald" amounts to "For exactly one individual x, x is now king of France, and for any x, if x is now king of France, x is bald." "The so-and-so exists," unlike "This exists," has a perfectly clear meaning; it means "For exactly one individual x, x is a so-and-so."

This apparatus yields a neat solution to the Aristotelian problem of when "X is Y" entails "X is" and when it does not. When "X" is a genuine proper name, in Russell's view, the question does not arise ("X is" being simply meaningless). But when it is a definite description or has the sense of a definite description, and the predicate is complex, it is often possible to read "X is Y" in different ways; and whether it entails "X is" will depend on how it is read. For example, "The present king of France is not bald" may assert that someone is the present king of France but is not bald, which does entail that someone is the present king of France—that the present king of France exists; but if it means only that it is not the case that someone is the present king of France and is bald, then it does not entail either that there is or that there is not a unique present king of France. Similarly, "The present king of France is believed to be bald" may be read as asserting that someone is the present king of France and it is believed of this person that he is bald, and this does entail the existence of the present king of France; or it might merely mean that it is believed that someone is the present king of France and is bald, and this could be true even if there were in fact no present king of France. Where the whole means something of the form "Someone is the present king of France and …." (the complexity, if any, coming after the "and"), the description "the present king of France" is said to have primary occurrence; where a whole sentence of this form is preceded by

or embedded in some qualifying context, the occurrence of the description is said to be secondary. Only primary occurrences of descriptions entail that there really is something answering to them; that is, that the thing described exists. Russell, incidentally, agrees with Jean Buridan that "The chimera is the chimera" entails "The chimera exists" and thus is false, although where "x" represents a genuine proper name, "x is (identical with) x" is always true.

The Russellian apparatus removes the necessity for postulating weak and strong modes of being, at least where definite descriptions are involved. We do not need to suppose, when we imagine the Hydra, that there is a Hydra that we imagine, even in a weakened sense of "is," or that there is some real thing that we imagine to be the Hydra. Two prefixes, "I imagine that" and "For exactly one individual x," are involved here; and which governs which greatly affects the interpretation. "I imagine that for exactly one individual x, x is a Hydra" makes one assertion, and "For exactly one individual x, I imagine that x is a Hydra" makes quite another; and neither assertion entails that for exactly one individual x, x is a Hydra. The second form, indeed, asserts a relation between me and a certain real individual (the one which I imagine to be the Hydra); but the first form does not assert any relation between me and any individual whatever, real or imaginary—it just asserts that I imagine that there is such a thing as the Hydra.

These forms are sufficient to describe what might be going on; there is no need whatever to suppose that if I imagine that there is a real individual of such and such a sort, then there really must be an "imaginary individual" of whom I imagine these things; that is, there is no need whatever to twist the first form around to "For exactly one imaginary individual x, I imagine that x is the Hydra," or to talk about "imaginary individuals" at all. There is, indeed, a merely imagined state of affairs involved, so that one might say that this solution merely removes the problem one step further. But the existence of states of affairs is part of a different problem, that of the existence of abstract rather than fictitious objects, and is, perhaps, soluble.

Russell's insistence that "exists" has no sense in which it can be a genuine predicate—that is, in which it can attach directly to a genuine proper name—seems a little arbitrary and not at all essential to his position as a whole. As G. E. Moore has pointed out, all that follows from this position is that a sentence like "This exists" is bound to be true; and one like "This does not exist" is bound to be false, if it says anything at all (for if "This exists" were false, "this" would not be picking out any object, and nothing would be being said). Russell's own formal system does in fact contain predicates—for instance, "——is identical with itself"—which have just this property, and he uses such predicates to define the class of individuals, or "things," that is, the "universal" class. He himself, moreover, reads the proposition "For some *x*, *x* is in the universal class" (which follows from "For some *x*, *x* is identical with itself") as "At least one individual exists," and he considers it a defect of *Principia Mathematica* that this proposition is provable in it. Such a proposition is scarcely avoidable in a system which has symbols for logically proper names; and its derivation is not, as some might fear, a revival of the Ontological Argument. "It is necessary that there should be something" does not mean or entail "There is something that 'is' necessarily," any more than "There is bound to be someone who wins" entails "There is someone who is bound to win." Nor can the Ontological Argument arise in its original form even if existence is a predicate, for it is blocked by the illegitimacy of the passage from "I am imagining that God really is" to "There is an imaginary God (a being in the mind) of whom I imagine this."

Nevertheless, there is a genuine problem about contingent and necessary being in this context. One of Moore's arguments for the meaningfulness of "This exists" is that it must have some meaning because "This might not have existed" often does have meaning and in general is true. The suggestion is that "This might not have existed" is analyzable as "It might have been the case that (it is not the case that (this exists))," and this could have no meaning if its innermost component did not. The odd thing, however, is that when it is thus analyzed, the statement does not appear to be true. "It is not the case that this exists" is just "This does not exist," but under what circumstances might this have been true, if "this" is being used as a genuine proper name? Under none at all, it would seem, according to Moore's own argument above.

Some of Russell's followers—Ludwig Wittgenstein in the *Tractatus* and F. P. Ramsey—have argued that in fact the only possible states of affairs alternative to the actual one are ones in which the objects that in fact exist have properties and relations different from those which they in fact have. This is to make all individuals what the Scholastics thought God was, "necessary beings." However, the formulation "This need not have existed," read as "It is not the case that (it is necessary that (this exists))," does not seem open to these difficulties, since its verification does not require that there be states of affairs in

which we could truly say of the object in question "This does not exist"; it is enough if there are states of affairs in which nothing can be said of the object in question at all (for then not all states of affairs will be ones in which we can say of it "This exists," that is, "This exists" will not be a necessary truth). This solution makes a distinction between "possibly not" and "not necessarily," which in most logical systems are equivalent; however, it is possible to develop systems of modal logic in which they are not equivalent.

Russell's distinctions also throw some light on Thomas's problems about creation out of nothing. Thus, P. T. Geach claims that "God has created a man out of something" amounts to "For some *x* (God has brought it about that (*x* is a man))"; but in the case of creation out of nothing we have only "God has brought it about that (for some *x* (*x* is a man))." In the first form, where "For some *x*" governs "God has brought it about that," what is said is that there is an already existing object on which God has so acted as to make it a man; in the second form, where "God has brought it about that" governs "for some *x*," it is not said that there is something that God makes into a man, but only that he brings to pass the state of affairs expressed by "Something is a man." But it is only the creation of something under a certain description ("a man") that could be construed in this latter way; the creation of individuals as such out of nothing (as opposed to their creation out of, say, "possible individuals") still seems impossible, since they have no identity until they are "there," and a divine "Let there be this man" would be senseless before that time.

ABSTRACTIONS

Turning from the supposed existence of fictitious objects to that of abstract ones, it will be useful to make some preliminary grammatical distinctions. Besides the proper names of individuals, most languages contain common nouns, adjectives, and verbs that apply to various individuals without actually naming any of them, and abstract nouns which seem to name the qualities, relations, states, and actions of individuals as if they were themselves individuals of a tenuous sort. We may say that a verb "φs" applies to an individual *x* if in fact *x* φs, that an adjective "*A*" applies to *x* if in fact *x* is *A*, and that a common noun "*C*" applies to *x* if in fact *x* is a *C*. Current logic tends to treat the verb form of a predicate as fundamental and adjectives and common nouns as always implicitly functioning as parts of verbal phrases like "is *A*" or "is a *C*." Where common nouns appear as grammatical subjects, as in "All men are liars," and adjectives as directly qualifying nouns, as in "All white men are liars," a little twisting will usually set the word in the basic verb context ("Whatever is-a-man is-a-liar," "Whatever is-a-man and is-white is-a-liar"). As verbs do not even look like names of objects, there are no very serious problems.

Abstract nouns, however, do look like names of objects, and so do common nouns in certain rather special uses, as in "Man is the noblest of animals" and "Man is a species." The objects which they appear to name are sometimes called universals; here they shall be called abstract objects or abstractions. Numerals also appear to name abstract objects—numbers—and noun clauses like "that Caesar conquered Gaul" and equivalent phrases like "Caesar's conquest of Gaul" also seem to name abstract objects—states of affairs or (in one use of the term) "propositions." Other apparent names frequently used in recent times are phrases of the form "the class of so-and-so's."

Some of these linguistic suggestions were taken very seriously by Plato and others have been taken seriously by other writers, and it is now common to describe as Platonism the view that abstract objects "exist" in a perfectly literal sense as part of the "furniture of the universe" alongside tables and chairs. If the Platonist admits that their being has something peculiar about it, and perhaps calls it subsisting rather than existing, he will nevertheless say that there is a single being which both subsisting and existing objects possess. The opposed Aristotelian tradition is to say that there is no single being which is common to objects of all different categories (things, qualities, relations, etc.), and that they are not just different sorts of beings but rather that they "are" in different but related ("analogous") senses of "are." In the fundamental sense of "are," only substances or things really "are"; qualities "are" also, but only in a secondary sense—their reality consists simply in their qualifying real things; the reality of relations consists similarly in their relating real things, and so on. On the Aristotelian view, one might say there are weaker and stronger senses of "be" but no sense so weak as to cover, unambiguously, the subjects of all the others. The view that there is no necessity to attribute existence in any sense to anything but concrete individuals is generally called nominalism (after the medieval view that "universals" are no more than empty names).

Most abstract nouns have verbs, adjectives, or common nouns related to them in meaning, and the nominalist's problem could be described as that of paraphrasing statements ostensibly about abstract objects in such a way that the abstract nouns disappear into the corresponding verbs or allied forms. Often this can be done quite easily. "Caesar is a member of the class of men" and "Caesar has the attribute of manhood," or "Manhood characterizes Caesar," seem no more than pompous ways of saying that Caesar is human (or human and male). Similarly, "The class of men is included in the class of mortals" and "Manhood is always accompanied by mortality" seem to mean simply that whatever is human is mortal. But other cases are trickier—"Red is a color," for example. This means more than "Whatever is red is colored"; we may presume that all red things, and only red things, occupy a certain set of regions of space (or of space-time), so that it is true that whatever occupies these regions is colored (just as all red things are colored) but not that the occupation of those regions is a color—it is not a color but a location. "Being red is a way of being colored" is more like it, but "being red" and "way of being colored" are as nounlike in form (the one a name of one thing and the other a common noun applying to many) as "red" and "color" themselves. If we write "being red" as "redding" and "being colored" as "coloring," we can perhaps say that "_____ing is a way of _____ing" builds a sentence out of two verbs just as "Whatever _____s, _____s" does and that the suffix "-ing" does not form real names but is an inseparable part of complexes like "_____ing is a way of _____ing." But some might say that rather than be driven to ad hoc solutions such as this last, it is better to admit the existence of abstractions and be done with it.

In comparatively recent history both Platonism and nominalism have run into difficulties of a rather technical sort. Some of these, including special problems about the existence of classes and numbers, are discussed in the entry on Russell, Bertrand Arthur William.

See also Analysis, Philosophical; Anderson, John; Anselm, St.; Aristotle; Bain, Alexander; Brentano, Franz; Correspondence Theory of Truth; Essence and Existence; Existentialism; Gassendi, Pierre; Hume, David; Kant, Immanuel; Moore, George Edward; Ontological Argument for the Existence of God; Plato; Ramsey, Frank Plumpton; Reid, Thomas; Russell, Bertrand Arthur William; Thomas Aquinas, St.; Universals, A Historical Survey; Venn, John.

Bibliography
The key texts in Aristotle are *De Sophistici Elenchis* 167a1 ff.; *De Interpretatione* 19b18 ff. and 21a26 ff.; and *Categories* 13b16 ff. and 29 ff.

Anselm's Ontological Argument is stated in his *Proslogium* and *Monologium,* and Gaunilo's answer is in his *Pro Insipiente*;

Thomas's summary and answer are in his *Summa Theologiae*, 2; Descartes's variant is in his *Meditations*; Gassendi's criticism is in the Objections appended to Descartes's *Meditations*; and Kant's criticism is in his *Critique of Pure Reason*, Transcendental Dialectic, Book II, Ch. 3, Sec. 4. The key passages in Anselm, Descartes, and Kant are included in Charles Hartshorne and William L. Reese, *Philosophers Speak of God* (Chicago: University of Chicago Press, 1953).

For Thomas on creation out of nothing and problems arising out of the notion of "giving existence," see his *De Potentia Dei* Q. 2, A. 1, Objections 2, 7, 11, and 17 and answers. For comments on this, see Antonin Sertillanges, *L'idée de création et ses retentissements en philosophie* (Aubier, 1945), especially pp. 45–48; A. N. Prior, "Identifiable Individuals," in *Review of Metaphysics* 13 (1960): 684–696; and P. T. Geach, "Causality and Creation," in *Sophia* (1962): 1–8. Problems about the identifiability of as yet nonexistent individuals are also acutely discussed in Jonathan Edwards, *Freedom of the Will*, edited by Paul Ramsey (New Haven, CT: Yale University Press, 1957), Part IV, Sec. 8, and in G. E. Moore, *The Commonplace Books*, edited by Casimir Lewy (New York: Humanities Press, 1967), p. 329. Leibniz's solution in terms of preexistent *possibilia* is developed in his correspondence with Arnauld (edited by Geneviève Lewis, Paris, 1952), which arose out of his *Discourse on Metaphysics* (translated and edited by P. G. Lucas and L. Grint, 2nd ed., Manchester, U.K., 1963), and in the dialogue at the end of his *Theodicy* (translated by E. M. Huggard, London and New Haven, CT, 1952).

For Thomas Reid's views, see his *Essays on the Intellectual Powers of Man* (Edinburgh, 1785), Essay IV ("On Conception") and Essay VI ("On Judgment"). For Russell's early position, see *The Principles of Mathematics* (Cambridge, U.K.: Cambridge University Press, 1903), especially pp. 43 and 71. The best and most accessible treatment of Meinong's views is in J. N. Findlay, *Meinong's Theory of Objects* (Oxford, 1933; reprinted with additions, Oxford: Clarendon Press, 1963), Ch. 2.

For Hume, the key passage is in his *Treatise of Human Nature*, Book 1, Part 3, Sec. 7 and note; for Brentano, his *Psychologie vom empirischen Standpunkt* (Leipzig, 1874), Vol. I, Book II, Ch. 7, Sec. 15. J. N. Keynes's discussion of possible responses to the challenge of Brentano and Venn is in his *Studies and Exercises in Formal Logic* (London: Macmillan, 1884; 4th ed., London: Macmillan, 1906), Ch. 8. Bain's views are in his *Logic*, 2nd ed. (London, 1873), Book I, Ch. 3, Sec. 23, and are discussed in a footnote to J. S. Mill's *System of Logic*, 9th ed. (London, 1875), Book I, Ch. 5, Sec. 5.

Russell's later theories are most clearly developed in his 1918 lectures "The Philosophy of Logical Atomism" (included in *Logic and Knowledge*, London: Allen and Unwin, 1956), Lectures V and VI, and in Ch. 16 of his *Introduction to Mathematical Philosophy* (London: Allen and Unwin, 1919). The latter contains, on pp. 168–170, his splendid and rather Reid-like appeal for a "robust sense of reality," G. E. Moore's agreements and disagreements with Russell are in his Aristotelian Society paper "Is Existence a Predicate?," reproduced in his collected *Philosophical Papers* (London: Allen and Unwin, 1959). The same collection contains another relevant Aristotelian Society paper, "Imaginary Objects," which may be compared with pp. 243–245 of Moore's *Commonplace Books*. F. P. Ramsey's development of the consequence that Russell's theory allows for no contingency of existence is in *The Foundations of Mathematics* (London: K. Paul, Trench, Trubner, 1931), p. 285; see also the ingenious argument on p. 155.

On the "grammatical" solution to the problem of universals, see Russell's 1924 essay "Logical Atomism," also included in *Logic and Knowledge*, and Tadeusz Kotarbiński's article "The Fundamental Ideas of Pansomatism," translated by David Rynin, in *Mind* 64 (1955): 488–500.

Much current discussion takes its start from W. V. Quine's paper "On What There Is," included in his *From a Logical Point of View* (Cambridge, MA: Harvard University Press, 1953).

A. N. Prior (1967)

EXISTENCE AND ESSENCE

See *Essence and Existence*

EXISTENTIALISM

Existentialism is not easily definable. Its protagonists have traced it back to Pascal, to St. Augustine, even to Socrates. It has been alleged in our time to be the doctrine of writers as various as Miguel de Unamuno and Norman Mailer. At first sight, characteristics of the doctrine are almost as various. That two writers both claim to be existentialists does not seem to entail their agreement on any one cardinal point. Consequently, to define existentialism by means of a set of philosophical formulas could be very misleading. Any formula sufficiently broad to embrace all the major existentialist tendencies would necessarily be so general and so vague as to be vacuous, for if we refer to a common emphasis upon, for example, the concreteness of individual human existence, we shall discover that in the case of different philosophers this emphasis is placed in contexts so dissimilar that it is put to quite different and incompatible uses. How then is existentialism to be defined?

EXISTENTIALIST THEMES

Existentialism may perhaps be considered most fruitfully as a historical movement in which connections of dependence and influence can be traced from one writer to another. Thus, even if two writers who are both rightly called existentialist differ enormously in doctrine, they can be placed in the same family tree. But this only throws the question of definition one stage back. How do we select our philosophical pedigrees? The answer must be in terms of a number of recurrent themes that are in fact independent of one another but have, as a matter of philosophical history, been associated in a variety of patterns. The key themes are the individual and systems; intentionality; being and absurdity; the nature and significance of choice; the role of extreme experiences; and the nature of communication.

THE INDIVIDUAL AND SYSTEMS. Søren Kierkegaard chose for his own epitaph the words "that individual." The concept of the individual for Kierkegaard was contrasted both with the concept of philosophical system and with the concepts of the stereotype and the mass. Between these contrasts there is a connection. A philosophical system was for Kierkegaard an attempt to understand individual existence within a conceptual scheme of a kind that would exhibit a logically necessary connection between every individual part and the conceptual scheme of the whole universe. People in the mass, or those who live out a stereotyped role, are people who understand themselves in terms of some concept or concepts they happen to embody. In both cases the individual is secondary to the concept it embodies. In fact, however, what exists comes first; concepts are necessarily inadequate attempts to grasp individual existence, which always evades complete conceptualization. One of the difficulties in understanding what Kierkegaard and his later followers have meant by assertions of this kind is that none of their detailed arguments appear to entail their conclusion. Consider two of these arguments.

The first is a revival of Immanuel Kant's argument against the so-called Ontological Proof. Like Kant, Kierkegaard argued that existence is not a property and that no concept of a given object entails the existence of that object. Also, Kierkegaard anticipated some modern writers in arguing that action and choice can be understood only if viewed from the standpoint of the agent rather than from that of the spectator. What is puzzling, however, is that Kierkegaard assumed that the notion of philosophical system is inextricably bound up with the viewpoint of the spectator and the refusal to admit that existence is not a property. In consequence, he concluded that justice can be done to the nature of the individual only if philosophical system building is condemned. The explanation for this particular line of thinking is that Kierkegaard equated the construction of philosophical systems with Hegelianism, and he interpreted Hegelianism as a form of rationalist metaphysics. It is noteworthy that some kind of metaphysical rationalism is almost always the background for existentialism. In countries where empiricism has a long history existentialism does not seem to flourish, even in the form of a reaction to the prevailing moods of thought.

Thus, it is perhaps instructive to regard existentialists as disappointed rationalists. When they announce that reality cannot be comprehended within a conceptual system or, more particularly, that individual existence cannot be so comprehended, they identify the role of a conceptual system with the notion of an all-embracing set of necessary truths derived by deduction from some axiomatic starting point. It may seem, therefore, that existentialists are sometimes doing no more than reformulating the empiricist protest against rationalism (namely, that no matter of fact can be expressed as a necessary truth) in an unnecessary and misleadingly dramatic way. The drama, however, has at least one independent source.

The nineteenth century witnessed a series of very diverse protests against the notion that the universe is a total system, whether one presided over by a Creator God or a purely rational one developing in an evolutionary progress toward higher and higher goals. That the universe does not make sense, that there are no rational patterns discernible in it, is a theme central, for example, to Fëdor Dostoevsky's *Notes from the Underground* (1864). Dostoevsky is often cited as a forerunner of existentialism precisely because in his disillusionment with rationalist humanism he stressed the unpredictable character of the universe and because his individuals appear face to face with pure contingency. Any established connection between things may break down at any minute. Order is a deceptive mask that the universe, especially the social universe, wears. The individual thus confronts the universe with no rational scheme by means of which he can hope to master it. Reason will only lead him to formulate generalizations that will, if he relies upon them, let him down.

Existentialism sometimes gives expression to this kind of view of the limitations of reason. But it is not thereby necessarily committed to irrationalism. At least some existentialist philosophers have been prepared to argue the case for the limits of reason on rational grounds—indeed, on grounds that are partly Kantian. Moreover, when existentialist philosophers speak of the limits of reason they are usually careful to explain that they wish in no way to trespass upon the territory of the natural sciences or of mathematics. Karl Jaspers goes so far as to accept positivism as a valid account of the sciences, illegitimate only when it aspires to give an account of reasoning as such. Moreover, Jaspers would claim that the areas with which existentialism concerns itself are not outside the competence of reason but only demand that reason be understood in new and less restrictive ways.

The claims, therefore, that the individual cannot be comprehended within a rational system and that the universe which the individual confronts is absurd turn out to have a less striking content than might at first sight have appeared. What has led to their exaggeration is perhaps in part an association with two other philosophical traditions, phenomenology and the kind of philosophy that treats ontology as a central philosophical discipline. Each of these provides existentialism with characteristic themes, which will be considered below.

INTENTIONALITY. With the exception of Kierkegaard, existentialist philosophers often make use of a conceptual scheme derived from the phenomenologists Franz Brentano and Edmund Husserl and, through them, from René Descartes. In attempting to answer such questions as What is belief?, What is an emotion?, and What is an act of will? phenomenologists wished to combat the associationist psychology that aspired to explain beliefs and emotions in purely naturalistic terms. In contrast, phenomenology emphasized that belief is always belief that … and anger is always anger about… . The object of belief or of emotion is not an object or a state of affairs in the external world. I may believe what is false or be angry about what did not in fact happen. So the object of belief or emotion is internal to the belief or emotion. It is, in the language of phenomenology, an intentional object.

Brentano concentrated on the isolated individual only in order to describe accurately the central features of believing, feeling, willing, and so on. Husserl treated the individual's consciousness of his own acts as having a primary role not unlike that which Descartes gave it. Among post-Husserl existentialists, notably Jean-Paul Sartre, the doctrine of intentionality is used to underline a fundamental difference between my knowledge of myself and my knowledge of others. Other people, so it is asserted, are viewed not as they are but as intentional objects of my perceptions, my beliefs, my emotions. But to myself I can never be such an object, nor am I in fact an object, and if they regard me as such their view of me is necessarily falsified. The obvious criticism of this is to say that the word *object* has been used as a pun. To say that my beliefs have intentional objects is to say neither that they are necessarily false nor that my beliefs about other people commit me to viewing them as things rather than people. But no existentialist writer is in fact making so simple a mistake. There is always some additional premise to the argument that provides a basis for the existentialist claim that to

make others the object of my perceptions or beliefs is to view them as other than they are. In the writings of Sartre and Simone de Beauvoir, for example, specific theses about the character of love and hate play an important role.

What is clear, however, is that although the doctrine of intentionality need not be understood in an existentialist way, this doctrine does add a dimension to the existentialist concept of the individual. Only through the notion of intentionality could the themes in Kierkegaard (which were partly an inheritance from the individualism of Protestantism and partly a reaction against G. W. F. Hegel) have become in Martin Heidegger part of a theory of knowledge and of a metaphysics.

BEING AND ABSURDITY. Existentialists, believing as they do that reality always evades adequate conceptualization, are especially apt to treat "Being" as a name, the name, in fact, of the realm which we vainly aspire to comprehend. "What the philosophers say about Reality," wrote Kierkegaard, "is often as disappointing as a sign you see in a shop window which reads: Pressing Done Here. If you brought your clothes to be pressed, you would be fooled; for only the sign is for sale" (*Either/Or*, 1843).

In Kierkegaard we get little or no systematic treatment of this kind of theme. In some of his successors, however, we find a systematic ontology, which owes more to the influence of scholastic metaphysics and of rationalism than it does to Kierkegaard. Heidegger took up Gottfried Wilhelm Leibniz's question, Why are there the things that there are rather than nothing? For Leibniz this question could be answered only by producing the Cosmological Argument for the existence of God. For Heidegger the question itself is misleading, because the posing of it relies upon an inadequate analysis of the notions of being and of nothing. Heidegger treats "Being" and "Nothing" as if they were both names, sometimes the names of powers, sometimes the names of realms. It is not that he is entirely unaware of the logical difficulties encountered in so doing. But he treats such difficulties as evidence of the exceptionally elusive character of Being and Nothing rather than as a sign of his own mistakes. He also accepts the fact that scientific thought never uses such concepts or language, but this he treats as a testimony to the inadequacy of science as a method for understanding reality and to the need for poetry and philosophy. He distinguishes Being (*Sein*) from beings (*die Seiende*) and from modes of being. At times his writing is reminiscent of scholastic ontology, but it is more often aphoristic and oracular.

In Sartre, too, there is an implicit relation to metaphysical rationalism of the kind mentioned above. The thesis that existence is absurd, which is especially important in French existentialism, turns out to be a denial of the principle of sufficient reason. There is no ultimate explanation of why things are as they are and not otherwise. What is curious here is that on the one hand the fact that this is so is seen as a flaw in the nature of things. It belongs to what Heidegger calls their "fallenness"; the experience of it arouses in us anxiety and perplexity. Yet on the other hand that it is so is the guarantee of human freedom. Both German and French existentialists distinguish sharply between the beings that exist for themselves (*pour-soi*), which have consciousness and freedom, and the beings that exist in themselves (*en-soi*), which are simply things. Now, for existentialism all the important possibilities of human life are bound up with the fact of human freedom, so that to lament the absurdity of existence is in a way odd. But what this lament does reflect is the ambiguous attitude of existentialists to human freedom.

FREEDOM AND CHOICE. If any single thesis could be said to constitute the doctrine of existentialism, it would be that the possibility of choice is the central fact of human nature. Even the thesis that existence precedes essence often means no more than that people do not have fixed natures that limit or determine their choices, but rather it is their choices that bring whatever nature they have into being. As existentialists develop this thesis, they are involved in at least three separate contentions.

The first is that choice is ubiquitous. All my actions imply choices. Even when I do not choose explicitly, as I may not do in the majority of cases, my action bears witness to an implicit choice. The second contention is that although in many of my actions my choices are governed by criteria, the criteria which I employ are themselves chosen, and there are no rational grounds for such choices. The third is that no causal explanation of my actions can be given.

The first thesis is given varying interpretations. For Kierkegaard a person's actions will always form part of a coherent way of life: the aesthetic, in which pleasure is pursued, or the ethical, in which principles are treated as binding, or the religious, in which God is obeyed. Between these one must choose, and it is in this sense that behind any action there lies a choice. For Sartre it sometimes appears as if each separate action expresses an indi-

vidual choice. Even if I do not choose, I have chosen not to choose.

The second thesis is fundamental to existentialism. But it is plausible to hold that I am free to choose the criteria by which I discriminate true from false beliefs only if this contention is restricted to the field of morals and religions. Kierkegaard sometimes, although not always, allowed for this restriction.

The third thesis, which seems to be logically independent of the others, is often treated by existentialist writers as though it were entailed by the first two. This is less surprising when it is recognized that one of the impulses behind existentialism seems to be a dissatisfaction with the kind of nineteenth-century materialism which held that if human actions can be causally explained, then determinism is true in a sense that excludes the possibility of human agents' being responsible and free. However, instead of denying that causal explanation entails this kind of determinism, the existentialist takes the unnecessary step of denying the probability of causal explanations of human action.

ANXIETY, DREAD, AND DEATH. Kierkegaard argued that in certain psychologically defined moments truths about human nature are grasped. One such moment would be when we realize that we do not just fear specific objects but experience a generalized dread. Of what? Of nothing in particular. What is this nothing, this void we confront? Kierkegaard interpreted it in terms of original sin. Heidegger sees it as an ontological constituent of the universe. Sartre sees it as a confrontation with the fact of freedom, of our unmade future.

The variety of interpretations suggests that perhaps different experiences are being discussed or that the ratio of interpretation to experience may be too high. But stress on the extreme and the exceptional experience is common to all existentialism. Everyday experience, by contrast, is thought of as a conventionalized, predigested aid to complacency, conformity, and self-deception. Heidegger gives a very special place to the continuous awareness of one's own future death; Jaspers lays a more generalized stress on a range of situations in which the fragility of our existence is brought home to us.

THE FORM OF COMMUNICATION. Since the existentialist writer acknowledges the sovereignty of individual choice and the importance of the concrete situation, he cannot address himself to his audience in the manner of traditional philosophy, for ex hypothesi the reader has to make his own choices in the light of his own experiences.

Argument will be powerless unless the reader chooses to agree with the author's premises. As a matter of fact, existentialist writings do commonly argue with the reader. But Kierkegaard, for example, was usually careful to frame his arguments in a hypothetical way: "If you choose this starting point, then that logically follows … ." He was also in the habit of writing different works under different pseudonyms, so that what the reader was confronted with would be a continuing debate between rival standpoints rather than a single argued case.

Later existentialist writers have developed in two differing ways. All the major existentialist philosophers have written systematic treatises. But they have also made large contributions to imaginative literature, and the content of existentialist philosophy makes it clear that dramatic dialogue, whether in plays or in the novel, is probably a form of expression more consistent with the author's intentions than deductive argument would be.

Such, then, are the shared themes of existentialism. But at this point one ought also to stress, even if briefly, the large differences that are compatible with the thematic resemblances between individual authors.

EXISTENTIALIST AUTHORS

Since the major existentialist philosophers are all treated in separate articles, what is delineated here is their interconnections insofar as they influence one another and above all the way in which the same themes recur in quite different social and philosophical contexts.

Søren Aabye Kierkegaard elaborated all his fundamental doctrines in order to expound and to defend what he took to be true Christianity. The philosophers upon whom he drew were Hegel (though only to attack), Kant, Aristotle (purely as understood through the writings of Friedrich Trendelenburg), and the Platonic Socrates. In contrasting philosophy from Plato to Hegel with authentic Christianity, Kierkegaard emphasized the concepts of the individual, of choice, of dread, and of paradox. He thus originated all the fundamental themes of existentialism.

These themes have been put to a quite new use by Karl Jaspers, who is concerned with criticizing positivism rather than Hegelianism. He has undertaken this with a view to defending a generalized spirituality that Christianity shares with other religions, rather than to defending specifically Christian doctrines. Where Kierkegaard spoke of paradox, Jaspers speaks of contradictions, and in this he is influenced as much by Friedrich Nietzsche as by Kierkegaard.

Martin Heidegger, too, has felt the influence of Nietzsche. But St. Augustine and Husserl have also been important for his synthesis of existentialism and phenomenology. As a result of this synthesis Heidegger has outlined a systematic ontology which, as such, stands at the opposite pole to Kierkegaard's enterprise. Heidegger's world is one from which God is absent (in this, too, he contrasts with Kierkegaard), but he has denied that he is therefore an atheist. This has no doubt made it easier for theologians to utilize his writings but makes it all the more surprising that his key concepts should have been so easily integrated into yet another existentialist system, that of Jean-Paul Sartre.

In Sartre the concept of choice, which for Kierkegaard was a decision between fundamentally different ways of life, has become a ubiquitous presence behind every human action, and the being of people, which Heidegger has distinguished from the being of things in terms of the relationship of consciousness in its various modes to the world, is now defined essentially in terms of such choices.

Sartre brings together other threads from the earlier history of existentialism. He employs psychological analyses similar to Kierkegaard's analysis of dread but sets them out in terms borrowed from phenomenology. These analyses are carried through for their own sake in Sartre's philosophical writings but are put to work in his novels and plays. They are employed, too, in the novels of Simone de Beauvoir, whose moral and political writings also use the Sartrian concept of choice.

Of parallel psychological interest are the novels of Albert Camus, but the atheism that for Sartre is a consequence of his views of human nature and the world was basic in the thought of Camus. Human life is represented in the myth of Sisyphus, who was doomed eternally to roll up a hill a vast stone that would always fall back just as he was about to reach the top. The dignity of life derives from humankind's continual perseverance in projects for which the universe affords no foothold or encouragement.

Gabriel Marcel is linked to Sartre and Camus by his critique of their atheism. He is an existentialist in his stress on key experiences and on the impossibility of adequately conceptualizing the important features of human life. But the features upon which he lays stress are those of hope and relationship, and his philosophy derives from Josiah Royce's personal idealism and even from F. H. Bradley, rather than from any existentialist predecessors.

The range of views expressed by existentialist writers has made it all too easy for the most multifarious authors to claim the title and for the most widespread ancestry to be found for existentialism. Someone like Unamuno, whose book on the tragic sense of life belongs to the same climate as Kierkegaard and Dostoevsky, could scarcely for that reason be called an existentialist, but those influenced by him in Spain today might well make use of the term. Karl Heim, the German writer on the philosophy of physics, has defined existentialism so widely that almost everything not strictly in the area of science becomes the subject matter of existentialism. Such examples could be multiplied indefinitely. Therefore, it seems wise now to consider the diffused influence of existentialism in the fields of theology, politics, and psychoanalysis.

EXISTENTIALIST THEOLOGIANS

There is a variety of theological systems which in some way are in debt to existentialism. The multiplicity of conclusions which theological writers have drawn from existentialist premises is perhaps testimony both to the ambiguity of those premises and to an underlying failure to analyze adequately some of the basic concepts involved.

BARTH. The earliest theological developments are to be found in Kierkegaard's thought, not surprisingly, since he was a theologian in his own right. When Karl Barth repudiated the optimistic liberal theologies of pre-1914 Protestantism, he did so in a commentary on the Epistle to the Romans (*Der Römerbrief,* 1919), which draws quite as heavily on Kierkegaard and Dostoevsky as it does on St. Paul. From Kierkegaard, Barth took the view that God is totally other than man. Finite reason cannot hope to grasp or comprehend infinite deity. From both Dostoevsky and Kierkegaard, Barth inherited the thesis that nature and human life are enigmatic, that nothing in the world is reliable.

Barth used these doctrines in two ways. In one direction he repudiated all attempts to find a rational foundation for Christianity, whether in the rational theology of Roman Catholicism or in the philosophical idealism of nineteenth-century Protestantism. In another he used his arguments to revivify the orthodox Protestant theory of the Reformation period. It is worth noting that although Barth repudiates the possibility of any rational ground for revelation, he has, like Kierkegaard, used philosophical argument when it suited his purposes.

TILLICH. Paul Tillich, unlike Barth, used existentialist materials in constructing a system that has analogies with Heidegger's but, in contrast with Heidegger's, reaches theistic conclusions. As with Heidegger, the terms "Being" and "Not-being" or "Nothing" played a key role in his thought. God is Being-itself, but in Tillich's interpretation this characterization of God has a quite different sense from that which the same form of words would bear in medieval theology. For according to Tillich we discover "Being-itself" through self-affirmation; we discover that what we call "God" or "Being-itself" represents our ultimate concern with overcoming doubt and anxiety in the face of nothingness. The message of theology is that we can overcome the meaninglessness of contemporary existence by taking up certain types of attitudes to that meaninglessness. It is pertinent to ask whether Tillich was trying to provide Christian conclusions with a new set of existentialist premises from which they may validly be derived or was trying to provide those Christian conclusions with a new sense, which enabled him to repeat some of the traditional forms of language but gave them a quite unorthodox meaning. Support for the latter alternative can be derived from the fact that Tillich was quite content to admit that the God of traditional theism does not exist. What remains unclear is whether the word *God* is an appropriate name for the concept of Being-itself as it figures in Tillich's thought.

BULTMANN. Rudolf Bultmann, by contrast with Tillich, is avowedly concerned with reconstructing Christianity. Bultmann is a historical critic of the New Testament who believes that in the New Testament a genuinely existentialist message is distorted by being presented in terms of a prescientific cosmology. This cosmology, Gnostic in origin, is a myth from which the kernel of the gospel must be extracted. The Gnostic cosmology pictures a three-tiered universe with human life on the earth occupying a place midway between the divine realm above and the powers of darkness below. The message concealed is that men are poised between the possibility of an "authentic" (Heidegger's term) human existence, in which the individual faces up to the limits of human existence and especially his own death, and the possibility of inauthentic existence, in which the individual retreats from death and Angst and *Sorge* and so becomes their victim. The charge made against Bultmann by orthodox theologians is that he turns Jesus Christ into a mere precursor of Heidegger. Bultmann's reply is that his interpretation of the gospel is still distinctively Christian because of his insistence that the decision in which man chooses between authentic and inauthentic existence is one that the rational man does not have the power to make for himself. But here either Bultmann is bringing in a supernaturalism that he otherwise disowns or he means simply that the choice of authentic existence is an action of which no account can be given in terms of the life of "rational man," of inauthentic existence. But to suppose that the traditional Christian assertion of the need for grace and the necessity of Christ's work is even a disguised version of the Heideggerian account of the choice of authenticity seems highly implausible.

Two of Bultmann's followers, Wilhelm Kamlah and S. N. Ogden, have argued that there is a deep inconsistency between Bultmann's Heideggerian themes and his Christian interpretations. Kamlah has argued that not only belief in the historical Jesus but also belief in a God who intervenes in history is inconsistent with Heidegger and draws atheistic conclusions. Ogden, who remains a Christian, believes that the role of the historical Jesus must be less important than either Bultmann or traditional orthodoxy suggests if justice is to be done to existentialism. It is notable that for all the writers of this kind, existentialism is above all else a characterization of the human condition as such, sharing much of the generality and the theoretical character of the Hegelian doctrines which Kierkegaard condemned.

Bultmann's references to God always appear to be external to his central concerns. When his critics ask him how he justifies belief in and speech about God, he tends to reply in traditional Christian terms that have little to do with existentialism. This perhaps provides some confirmation of the view that existentialism is in fact a theologically neutral doctrine. Its neutrality derives from its stress on ultimate commitment and the unjustifiable character of any particular commitment. If the only justification for *any* belief is, in the last analysis, that I have chosen to believe, then the same justification is equally available for all beliefs, whether theistic or atheistic. But insofar as existentialism is a doctrine about human nature, its themes are very close to those of traditional theology, and it is therefore not surprising, quite apart from any impulses originating from Kierkegaard's special concerns, that most existentialist philosophers have taken up well-defined positions in relation to theology.

An existentialist vocabulary is often used by theological writers who are not in any strong sense existentialists. So the Russian Orthodox thinker Nikolai Berdyaev and some Catholic theologians, in their discussions of anxiety, guilt, and man's relation to God, have used existentialist concepts. But these uses reflect the fashionable character of existentialism rather than any of its philosophical characteristics.

EXISTENTIALISM AND POLITICS

As in theology so also in politics existentialism appears to be compatible with almost every possible standpoint. Kierkegaard was a rigid conservative who viewed with approval the monarchical repression of the popular movements of 1848; Jaspers was a liberal; Heidegger was for a short time a Nazi; and Sartre was over a long period a Communist Party fellow traveler. However, at least three systematic political themes can be discerned in existentialism.

The first is a form of religious humanism designed to counteract what is believed to be an unsatisfactory value system at the basis of modern society. Both Jaspers and Marcel maintained that the growth in technology and bureaucracy was creating in Europe a cult of mediocrity, conformism, and loss of individuality, with the inner life of the individual sacrificed to external forms. Heidegger, too, saw the individual as threatened by impersonality. But although Jaspers and Marcel pleaded for a greater recognition of transcendent and religious values in general, neither had a specific program of social reform to offer.

Second, the existentialist stress on commitment and irrationality of choice has sometimes been used in support of irrationalistic extremism. The most notorious but not the only example is Heidegger's brief excursion into politics. Needless to say, advocates of Nazism tend to ignore the existentialist stress on the importance of the individual.

Commonly, existentialism may be associated with communism, and this is largely due to the influence of Sartre. However, Sartre has occupied more than one position. His prewar writings contain scarcely any reference to politics. During the war and immediately after, his political aims—those of a radical democrat—were expressed in terms that seem largely independent of his existentialism. At that time, in his analysis of political activity he found himself at odds with orthodox Marxism because Marxism offered causal explanations of behavior that Sartre wanted to explain in terms of choices and purposes. But in his later writings he has accepted a Marxist framework for both political theory and political practice and has presented existentialism as merely a corrective to a too rigid and too deterministic Marxism. Yet his account of political life is, in fact, still far more psychological than any a Marxist would give.

EXISTENTIALISM AND PSYCHOANALYTIC TOPICS

There are several points at which existentialism touches on psychiatric themes. Karl Jaspers originally practiced as a psychiatrist, and in *Allgemeine Psychiatrie* (1913) he criticized ordinary scientific psychology and the psychotherapy based upon it. He did so on the ground that what he regards as the positivistic approach of conventional psychotherapy is unnecessarily and misleadingly deterministic. It treats the actual outcome of the patient's life as the inevitable outcome. Jaspers concedes that scientific examination will not reveal the fact of human freedom of choice. The personality available for empirical scrutiny is simply what it is, but the assumption that there is nothing to personality but what empirical scrutiny will reveal is groundless and arbitrary. Behind the empirical self there is, in Jaspers's view, a true self of which we are made aware in what Jaspers calls "boundary-situations"—that is, in situations of an extreme kind where we confront despair, guilt, anxiety, and death. In these moments of awareness we realize our own responsibility for what we are, and the reality of freedom of choice is thrust upon us.

The name "existential psychiatry" has been taken, however, by another tradition of thought, which derives from Heidegger and whose most important exponent is Ludwig Binswanger. Binswanger, who calls his system of analysis *Daseinsanalyse*, criticizes two of Sigmund Freud's central concepts. Freud saw the neurotic symptom of the adult as caused by a past traumatic event, the memory of which has been repressed into the unconscious, from where it exerts its causal power upon present behavior. According to Binswanger, however, the neurotic symptom is to be explained not in terms of the content of the patient's unconscious but in terms of his mode of consciousness, and the key concept involved in the explanation is not that of causality but that of meaning. When an adult reacts to a situation neurotically it is because his consciousness confers upon that situation a meaning he does not recognize as deriving from the nature of his own consciousness. Certainly, past traumatic events are relevant. But they are relevant precisely because in them a like meaning was given to a like situation. Attention is thus focused upon the patient's whole mode of consciousness, the way in which he approaches, attends to, and comprehends the world. The explanation of behavior lies in the present, in the mode of consciousness, not in the past or in the unconscious.

Binswanger's understanding of the different possible modes of consciousness is derived directly from Heidegger. He speaks of "Being-in-the-world" and its modes and

of the contribution of existentialist philosophy to psychiatry as consisting in the a priori analysis of all possible modes of "Being-in-the-world." He very largely discounts the biological determination of human behavior, although he allows it a minor role. But he tends to insist on interpreting behavior, even at the biological level, in terms of the meaning it has for the agent.

This emphasis is reiterated by Sartre, who uses the doctrine of intentionality to criticize all causal theories of emotion and behavior. Sartre attacks both the James-Lange theory of the emotions and the Freudian theory of the unconscious because he holds that they cannot allow for the intentional (in the Husserlian sense) and purposive aspects of emotion and behavior. It has already been suggested that it is unclear why Sartre believes that if emotions, for example, must be understood in terms of their intentional object and aim, they cannot also be explicable in causal terms. Like Binswanger, Sartre approves of much in Freudian technique, and in his writings on Charles-Pierre Baudelaire and Gustave Flaubert he has emphasized the formative experiences of early childhood. Perhaps his most extensive treatment of these themes is his book on Jean Genet (*Saint Genet: Comédien et martyre*, 1952).

Both Sartre's earlier and his later writings have been utilized by R. D. Laing in the study of schizophrenia (*The Divided Self*). Sartre's account of experiencing another person as a free agent for whom one exists only as an object and by whom one is reduced to the status of an object (in *L'être et le néant*, III, 1943) is used by Laing to throw light on case histories of the kind where the decisive actions of another person have resulted in a loss of identity on the part of the patient. Laing's work does, in fact, strongly suggest that Sartre has sometimes offered us not, as he purports to do, a description of what is basic to human consciousness as such but a description of certain abnormal types of consciousness, to which we are all sometimes prone but which become dominant in mental illness. However, Laing himself does not make this criticism of Sartre and has used in the study of normal family life some of the concepts that Sartre elaborates in the *Critique de la raison dialectique* (1960).

CRITICISM AND EXPLANATION

The suggestion that existentialism is a form of disappointed rationalism has already been made. It may now be extended to the charge that existentialism's dissatisfaction with the concepts of traditional rationalist metaphysics has been insufficiently radical. If the thesis that the universe is absurd is simply a denial that the universe

ENCYCLOPEDIA OF PHILOSOPHY
2nd edition

• 507

has a Leibnizian sufficient reason, then it relies as much as Leibniz did on the adequacy of the concept of a sufficient reason. When the existentialist could profitably have questioned the very terms with which the rationalist characterized the world, he has all too often simply taken over the rationalist scheme of concepts and denied what the rationalist affirmed. Moreover, he has mistaken his own denials for a positive characterization of the nature of things.

It has also been suggested that the existentialist often makes the same logical points against rationalism that the empiricist did but invests them with more drama. Perhaps the explanation of this is that the discovery that there are no sufficient reasons or ultimate justifications, of the kind offered by rationalist metaphysics and allied types of theology, is not private to existentialist philosophers. Questions of ultimate justification remain unimportant and unexamined by most people so long as social life is relatively stable and social conflict is not disruptive. When, however, the conventional supports of civilized life are withdrawn, as they have been too often in Europe since 1914, ordinary people are forced to ask questions about justification that normally do not arise for them. The loneliness and self-questioning of a Kierkegaard become far more common. Moreover, people find that their normal responses are put in question; deception and self-deception become pressing topics. What were publicly approved acts with established utilitarian justifications become signals into a darkness where there are no answering lights.

It is a commonplace that it is people living in loneliness and doubt who provide the characters for existentialist novels, but it is less remarked that the existentialist's conceptual psychology rests equally upon examples drawn from extreme situations. How, indeed, could it be otherwise for those who assert that it is only in extreme situations, in what Jaspers calls boundary situations, that authentic human nature is revealed? But existentialist writers remain open to the criticism that they treat the exceptional as the typical. Indeed, because the contrast between the exceptional and the typical has been obliterated, the force of the notion of the boundary situation tends to be lost.

When existentialists come to construct their own systems, the most obvious criticism they are subject to is that they are insensitive to the syntactic and semantic properties of the language they employ. So Kierkegaard spoke of a dread of nothing in particular as though this implied that such dread had an object whose name was "Nothing." So Heidegger hypostatizes Being and Nothing

as substantial entities. So Jaspers discards the traditional framework for metaphysics but writes of "the transcendent" as though this were an expression whose meaning raised few difficulties. A. J. Ayer accused Sartre of a systematic misuse, in his ontology, of the verb "to be."

Ayer suggested that when a philosophical criticism of existentialism has been carried through it is not improper to ask for a sociological explanation of its use and vogue. He himself pointed to the fact that German existentialism followed on the defeat of 1918, whereas French existentialism is a sequel to 1940. But, in fact, Sartre took up all his main existentialist positions before 1939. And the purely philosophical ancestry of later existentialism must be allowed for.

This is not to say that we should look for an account of existentialism only in terms of philosophical antecedents. It would be more illuminating to see existentialism as the fusion of a certain kind of dramatization of social experience with the desire to resolve certain unsolved philosophical problems. The unsolved problems are those of traditional epistemology and metaphysics. In the period between Descartes and Francis Bacon, on the one hand, and Kant and Hegel, on the other, certain philosophical problems were posed but not solved. Within the framework of assumptions in which they were posed they could not, in fact, have been solved. Foremost among these assumptions is that the whole of knowledge has to be reconstructed out of the epistemological resources of the single, isolated knowing subject. Also, there is the search for first principles, based either upon an indubitable, because logically undeniable, proposition or upon an incorrigible set of reports of immediate experience. There is the treatment of the first principles as axioms and their employment as a basis for a deductive model within which all human knowledge is to be set forth. There is the invocation of God or Nature to bridge the gulfs too great for argument on its own.

Hegel abandoned all these assumptions, as Ludwig Wittgenstein did later on. But where Wittgenstein placed epistemological problems in the context of an understanding of language as a social phenomenon Hegel placed them, in the end, in the context of a metaphysical system. Those who rejected his system retreated to the epistemological assumptions of the earlier period, but with this difference: after David Hume and Kant they could no longer believe in guaranteed first principles. So Kierkegaard's choice between the ethical and the aesthetic reproduces the Kantian choice between duty and inclination but lacks its rational basis. More generally, Kierkegaard's individual resembles the Cartesian ego without the *cogito*. Sartre inherited from phenomenology an explicit Cartesianism. In Sartre the individual as the knowing subject is the isolated Cartesian ego; the individual as a moral being is a Kantian man for whom rational first principles have been replaced by criterionless choices. Neither God nor Nature is at hand to render the universe rational and meaningful, and there is no background of socially established and recognized criteria in either knowledge or morals. The individual of existentialism is Descartes's true heir.

According to Marxist critics, especially Georg Lukács, the debased individualism of the existentialist is a symptom of the malaise of the bourgeois intellectual. Bourgeois man can no longer find his values incarnated in the social life that surrounds him; therefore, he makes a fetish of his own inner experience and tries by the fiat of his own choice to legitimate the values that in public life no longer appear to have validity. This theory of Lukács's has two central weaknesses: it appears to suggest a correlation between holding existentialist views in philosophy and having certain highly specific political and social attitudes, and it assimilates all existentialism to one rather restricted model. The suggested correlation is not warranted by the evidence, and the preceding discussion points to the dangers of assimilating different existentialisms too closely to one another.

A more relevant criticism might be phrased as follows. Certain philosophical attitudes are embedded in the matrix of existentialism; in general, existentialism embodies a distrust of metaphysical rationalism. Insofar as existentialist philosophers elaborate conceptual analyses in such fields as ethics and the philosophy of mind, their work can be understood and assessed in the same way as the work of analytical philosophers. Paradoxically, however, when they go beyond conceptual analysis it is usually not only to stress the inevitability of choice or the importance of dread but also to construct systems of the kind that existentialists originally protested against. The outcome of these systems on the whole lends further weight to the protests.

Finally, the doctrine of choice itself stands in need of closer scrutiny than existentialist philosophers have given it. This doctrine depends on the relationship between choice and criteria for judging between true and false and right and wrong. In existentialist writings this relationship remains, on the whole, unscrutinized.

See also Alienation; Augustine, St.; Ayer, Alfred Jules; Bacon, Francis; Barth, Karl; Beauvoir, Simone de; Being; Berdyaev, Nikolai Aleksandrovich; Binswanger, Ludwig; Bradley, Francis Herbert; Bultmann, Rudolf; Camus, Albert; Cartesianism; Cosmological Argument for the Existence of God; Cosmology; Death; Descartes, René; Dostoevsky, Fyodor Mikhailovich; Essence and Existence; Existential Psychoanalysis; Freud, Sigmund; Hegel, Georg Wilhelm Friedrich; Hegelianism; Heidegger, Martin; Heim, Karl; Hume, David; Husserl, Edmund; Jaspers, Karl; Kant, Immanuel; Kierkegaard, Søren Aabye; Leibniz, Gottfried Wilhelm; Lukács, Georg; Marcel, Gabriel; Marxism; Nihilism; Nothing; Pascal, Blaise; Sartre, Jean-Paul; Socrates; Tillich, Paul; Unamuno y Jugo, Miguel de.

Bibliography

Works by individual existentialist philosophers are included only if they contain discussions of existentialism.

Ayer, A. J. "Some Aspects of Existentialism." *Rationalist Annual* (1948).

Barrett, William. *Irrational Man.* New York: Doubleday, 1958.

Binswanger, Ludwig. "Daseinsanalyse und Psychotherapie." *Acta Psychotherapeutica et Psychosomatica* 8 (4) (1960): 258. Translated as "Existential Analysis and Psychotherapy," in *Progress in Psychotherapy*, edited by Frieda Fromm-Reichmann. New York: Grune & Stratton, 1956.

Blackham, H. J. *Six Existentialist Thinkers.* London, 1951; New York: Macmillan, 1952.

Brock, W. *Introduction to Contemporary German Philosophy.* Cambridge, U.K.: Cambridge University Press, 1947.

Bultmann, Rudolf. *Glauben und Verstehen.* Vol II. Tübingen, 1952. Translated as *Essays: Philosophical and Theological.* London: SCM Press, 1955.

Collins, James. *The Existentialists: A Critical Study.* Chicago: H. Regnery, 1952.

Gilson, Étienne, ed. *Existentialisme chrétien.* Paris: Plon, 1947.

Grene, Marjorie. *Introduction to Existentialism.* Chicago: University of Chicago Press, 1959.

Grimsley, R. *Existentialist Thought.* Cardiff, 1960.

Heidegger, Martin. *Existence and Being.* Translated by D. Scott, R. Hull, and A. Crick. Chicago: Regnery, 1949. Translation of *Was ist Metaphysik?; Vom Wesen der Wahrheit; Höderlin und das Wesen der Dichtung*: and *Andenken an den Dichter: "Heimkunft—an die Verwandten."*

Kaufmann, Walter, ed. *Existentialism from Dostoevsky to Sartre.* New York: Meridian, 1956. Selections with introductions.

Kolnai, A. "Existence and Ethics." *PAS*, Supp. Vol. 27 (1963).

Laing, R. D. *The Divided Self.* London: Tavistock, 1960.

Lukács, Georg. *Existentialismus oder Marxismus?* Berlin, 1951.

MacIntyre, Alasdair. "Existentialism." In *A Critical History of Western Philosophy.* London and New York: Free Press, 1964.

Manser, A. "Existence and Ethics." *PAS*, Supp. Vol. 27 (1963).

Marcel, Gabriel. *The Philosophy of Existence.* Translated by Manya Harari. New York: Philosophical Library, 1949. Republished as *Philosophy of Existentialism.* New York, 1961.

Molina, Fernando. *Existentialism as Philosophy.* Englewood Cliffs, NJ: Prentice-Hall, 1962.

Mounier, E. *Introduction aux existentialismes.* Paris, 1947.

Ogden, S. N. *Christ without Myth.* New York: Harper & Brothers, 1961.

Ruggiero, Guido de. *Existentialism.* London: Secker and Warbug, 1946.

Salvan, Jacques. *To Be and Not to Be.* Detroit, MI: Wayne State University Press, 1962.

Sartre, Jean-Paul. *L'existentialisme est un humanisme.* Paris: Nagel, 1946. Translated by P. Mairet as *Existentialism and Humanism.* London: Metheun, 1948.

Sartre, Jean-Paul. "Questions de méthode." In *Critique de la raison dialectique,* Vol. I. Paris: Gallimard, 1960. Translated by Hazel E. Barnes as *The Problem of a Method.* New York, 1963.

Sartre, J.-P., R. Garandy, J.Hyppolite, et al. *Marxisme et existentialisme.* Paris: Plon, 1962.

Tillich, Paul. *The Courage to Be.* London: Nisbet, 1952.

Weigert, E. "Existentialism and Its Relation to Psychotherapy." *Psychiatry* 12 (1949).

Alasdair MacIntyre (1967)

EXISTENTIALISM [ADDENDUM]

The development of "existentialism" in the last years of its leading French proponents, Jean-Paul Sartre and Maurice Merleau-Ponty, occurred in the areas of social philosophy and existential psychoanalysis in the case of Sartre and the philosophy of language and fundamental ontology for Merleau-Ponty. Partly in response to the latter's critiques, but chiefly as a result of his own political commitment, Sartre constructed a social ontology and a theory of history in his *Critique of Dialectical Reason.* Faithful to his existentialist emphasis on the primacy of the individual, but replacing his earlier philosophy of consciousness with one of praxis (roughly, purposive human activity in its historical and socioeconomic context), Sartre formulated a set of concepts, especially praxis, seriality, and the practico-inert, that respected the power of social forces to countermand, deviate, and reverse our undertakings without totally robbing the organic individual of existentialist freedom and responsibility. He allowed far greater play to the force of circumstance in assessing human action and underscored the determining power of family and early childhood experience in his massive existential biography of Gustave Flaubert, *The Family Idiot.* This last, combining the discourse of *Being and Nothingness* with that of the *Critique,* forms a kind of synthesis of Sartre's work.

At the time of his death in 1961 Merleau-Ponty was at work on a manuscript that has come to be known as *The Visible and the Invisible,* a work that some consider his version of Martin Heidegger's "What Is Metaphysics?" It reveals a growing interest in an ontology that avoids the pitfalls of "philosophies of consciousness," with their subject-object relation, which has defined and limited philosophy in the West for centuries. Inspired by the painter's articulation of the world and building on the concepts of chiasm and flesh, introduced in his earlier *The Phenomenology of Perception,* Merleau-Ponty was moving beyond the boundaries of phenomenology to elaborate an "indirect ontology" in which language questioning being questions itself.

See also Existential Psychoanalysis; Heidegger, Martin; Merleau-Ponty, Maurice; Ontology; Phenomenology; Philosophy of Language; Sartre, Jean-Paul.

Thomas R. Flynn (1996)

EXISTENTIAL PSYCHOANALYSIS

"Existential psychoanalysis" is a trend in psychology and psychiatry best understood as a reaction against the theoretical and philosophical presuppositions of the psychologies based on natural science in general and of Freudian psychology in particular. The phenomenology of Edmund Husserl and the existentialism of Martin Heidegger, Jean-Paul Sartre, and Martin Buber, rather than the mechanistic worldview of natural science, are seen by existential psychoanalysts as providing the proper philosophical and methodological route to a more complete understanding of man. In its original form, therefore, existentialist psychoanalysis was not a countermovement to Freudian psychoanalysis, unlike Jungian or Adlerian psychoanalysis, for example. Its criticism always focused on the philosophical theory of man implicit in Sigmund Freud's work, and it offered itself as a philosophical complement to Freud. The main burden of its criticism is that a full understanding of the patient's experience and world is impeded if the patient is approached on terms derived from the hypotheses of natural science rather than on his own specifically human terms.

The pioneer of existential psychoanalysis, Ludwig Binswanger, sought to describe the experiential world of his patients with the help of the conceptual scheme of Heidegger's ontology of man's being. However, his work contained few major differences from Freud in therapeutic technique. Indeed, another existential analyst, Medard Boss, has claimed that existential analysis "enables psychotherapists to understand the meaning of Freud's recommendations for psychoanalytic treatment better than does his own theory" (*Psychoanalysis and Daseinsanalysis*, p. 237). The implication is, of course, that a fuller understanding of the patient will result in more efficacious treatment, but that the methods of treatment will not differ fundamentally from Freud's. The result is to separate Freud's dealings with his patients from the mechanistic scientific constructs by which he sought to explain psychic functioning.

However, those persons in the United States who call themselves or who are called existential psychoanalysts are a very heterogeneous group. Perhaps the most significant change in the United States is that existential psychoanalysis is seen by many practitioners as a substitute for Freudian psychoanalysis. The phenomenological method of describing and hence understanding the patient's world is looked upon as itself a therapeutic measure, something far from the minds of the movement's originators. Certain notions of Sartre or Buber concerning the existential encounter between human beings are taken as replacements for the classical analyst-patient relationship. On this point, Binswanger had simply argued that the full human meaning of the doctor-patient relationship be realized in therapy; he did not seek to eliminate the classical relationship. The result of these changes has been that almost any therapy that departs from the general Freudian mold is called existentialist—particularly those which place emphasis on unusual therapeutic intervention and those which reject the scientific element in psychoanalysis, for good and bad reasons. It is therefore essential to understand the philosophical core of the original movement.

THE SUBJECT-OBJECT SPLIT

The shortcomings attributed to psychoanalysis emanate from the scientific tradition in which psychology has sought to place itself. Natural science since Galileo Galilei can be understood as a mode of approaching the world in which one aspect of the phenomenal world, the aspect of pure corporeality, is given the privileged position of basic substance, of primitive, irreducible fact. The notion of pure corporeality as the reality to which all phenomena are to be reduced is the concomitant of a dictate that the perceiver remove himself as much as possible from the world in the attempt to gain knowledge of that which is perceived. The roots of this dictate lie in the philosophy of René Descartes, which isolates the realm of consciousness from that of the body and the perceived world. Thus, the concept of pure corporeality is the product of a methodological dictate: Keep the self out of its world as it investigates its world.

This famous Cartesian sundering of the world into two isolated regions, *res cogitans* (the thinking substance, the world of consciousness, purpose, telos, will, quality) and *res extensa* (the world of pure extended matter, undifferentiated, quantitative), has been attacked by phenomenologists and existentialists as the most disastrous event in four centuries of Western thought. Nevertheless, this subject-object split had the immeasurable value of disciplining a new kind of human self-awareness, in the air since the Renaissance: man's awareness of his self-sufficiency and his urge to master nature, or the universe, which had revealed itself as a radical other. The split furthered man's alienation from his world, but at the same time it gave him, in the methods and the objective attitude of natural science, the means to bridge the separation in action if not in philosophical comprehension.

But psychology, the most recent child of this attitude, is in a strained position. On the one hand it seeks to be objective, to take its place as one of the natural sciences along with biology, physics, and chemistry. On the other hand it seeks to study that which science since Descartes and Galileo has demanded be ruled out of the field of investigation—the soul, psyche, consciousness. Psychology is thus faced with the apparently self-contradictory task of investigating consciousness as part of the realm of the *res extensa*, although the *res extensa* is that which exists independently of consciousness. To investigate consciousness scientifically, psychology must eliminate from consciousness its essential element. Freud's doctrine of the unconscious can be conceived of as an attempt to overcome this contradiction by viewing the essence of consciousness as that which lies in the realm of *res extensa*. His success is due to the fact that his scientific psychology, unlike others, does not reduce the experienced meanings in the field of consciousness to a level below the level of meaning. In Freudian psychology, meanings are reduced not to physiology or to objectively perceptible spatiotemporal processes, but to another kind of meaning, instinctual meaning.

All explanation involves the reduction of that which is explained to something taken as more basic. The ever-present danger is that that to which the phenomena are reduced may become so alien to the phenomena that there is no returning to them without circularly invoking previous knowledge. Freudian psychoanalysis seems to avoid this danger by focusing on a basic reality, instinctual meaning, which is not totally alien to the phenomena to be explained.

INTENTIONALITY

Existential philosophy denies the subject-object split that defines the whole attitude of natural science. The mind, consciousness, is not a strange and unprecedented thing whose workings are somewhat more puzzling than those of its neighboring objects, the things of this world. Nor is it, as Descartes held, a distant spectator, alien and sufficient unto itself, moving like a ghost on Earth. For existential philosophy, the problem of how the mind reaches over to the object is a pseudo problem that results from the gratuitous and erroneous presupposition that consciousness can be understood independently, apart from that which it intends or is conscious of. Mind, or consciousness, is to be defined as simply this intentionality, this reference-to. Consciousness is not viewed as something that intends an object; consciousness is the intention.

Existentialist-phenomenological psychology maintains, therefore, that the phenomena with which psychoanalysis is concerned are intentional acts, conscious phenomena, not the nonintentional, nonreferring phenomena of the world of objects. Whereas other psychologies, in emulating science, stripped consciousness of that very quality that constitutes its essence, namely intentionality, the minimum level of reduction in psychoanalysis is an intentional act—instinct, a psychic act that intends pleasure.

However, the implications of the definition of consciousness as intentionality militate against the psychoanalytic notion of the unconscious. If consciousness is always consciousness of something, then what appears to consciousness is all of consciousness; there cannot, by definition, be an intentional act below the level of consciousness. To speak of "unconscious" acts is therefore a contradiction if the intentionality of these acts is to be preserved. If intentionality is not to be preserved, there is no contradiction; but then, of course, psychoanalysis would slip below the acceptable level of reduction. Thus Freud, according to existential philosophy, did not avoid the contradiction of placing the *res cogitans* in the *res extensa*, however brilliantly and extensively he refined his definitions of instinctual meaning.

BEING-IN-THE-WORLD

The issue of intentionality springs directly from the work of Husserl, the founder of phenomenology. Husserl, as a pure phenomenologist, did not seek to discover anything about the natural world. He was concerned purely and simply with ascertaining the essence of phenomena as they appear to consciousness. The question whether these phenomena correspond to the natural and real world he left to the explanatory disciplines of philosophy and science. Relations to the real human self he left to psychology. His student Heidegger, however, was interested in that oldest of philosophical questions, the nature of Being. For Heidegger, the essential structure of human being turns out to be an extension of the concept of intentionality. Just as consciousness is defined as consciousness-of, human being is characterized by Heidegger as being-in-the-world. The hyphens are deliberate; they represent an effort to undercut the subject-object split. Just as consciousness is not a separate entity that subsequently relates to objects, so man is not a separate being who then encounters his world. Rather, he is essentially in-the-world, he is his disclosure of world.

One essential that differentiates this basically human mode of being from that of the objectively known world is, for Heidegger, the element of possibility. The essence of man is always his possibilities, which he "has" in a more inclusive sense than the way an object has properties. An account of the factual content of an object can never express the essence of man, because that essence has yet to be his being as his own. Human time and space differ from "objective" time and space in that they are essentially related to man's determination of himself and his world. The essence of man, for Heidegger, is his appropriation of his essence, his making it his own. Thus the categories that describe human being are not qualities, but matrices within which qualities are to be appropriated.

We have noted how psychoanalysis seeks to place the *res cogitans*, or intentionality, into the *res extensa*, or sphere of pure corporeality. Existentialists object to the way in which psychoanalytic theory attempts to give man an essence in the way that an object has an essence. For psychoanalysis instinct, or libido, constitutes a residue that is taken a priori as the irreducible limit of investigation. Man has instinct as an object has its essence. It is not to the credit of psychoanalysis that this instinct is an intentionality of a sort; the existentialists maintain that the whole notion of intentionality is perverted when one particular class of intentional acts is singled out a priori as the basis of all classes. The meaning of psychic acts, intentions, is to be arrived at on their own terms, phenomenologically; they are not to be given meaning, as are the objects of natural science. Since, for the existentialists, human existence precedes essence, the task of an existential psychoanalysis must be, in Sartre's words, to uncover in each individual "a veritable irreducible; that is, an irreducible which would not be presented as the postulate of the psychologist and the result of his refusal or his incapacity to go further…. This demand … is based on the refusal to consider man as capable of being analyzed and reduced to original givens, to determined desires (or 'drives'), supported by the subject as properties [are] by an object" (*Being and Nothingness*, pp. 560–561). The task of existential psychoanalysis is to apprehend the essence of each individual's life and world. If existence precedes essence, the analyst must apprehend the matrix within which essence is yet to be determined in each individual. Sartre calls this matrix the original choice or original project; Binswanger calls it the transcendental category that is the individual's mode of being-in-the-world.

Thus the critique of Freudian theory offered by existential psychoanalysis differs from that of the various revisionists in that it questions the theoretical root of all major movements in contemporary psychology; the assumption that the study of man can be wholly a natural science, that the notion of *homo natura* (man as a creature of nature) most fully expresses the essence of human being. The practical implications for psychiatry involve, among other things, wresting the concepts of mental health and illness away from analogies with purely somatic medicine, and thereby redefining the overall goal of any psychotherapy.

See also Being; Binswanger, Ludwig; Buber, Martin; Cartesianism; Consciousness; Existentialism; Freud, Sigmund; Heidegger, Martin; Husserl, Edmund; Psychoanalysis; Psychoanalytic Theories, Logical Status of; Sartre, Jean-Paul.

Bibliography

SOURCES

Binswanger, Ludwig. *Ausgewahlte Vorträge und Aufsätze*. 2 vols. Bern: Francke, 1947–1955.

Binswanger, Ludwig. *Ausgewählte Werke in vier Bänden*. Heidelberg: R. Asanger Verlag, 2004.

Binswanger, Ludwig. *Drei Formen missglückten Daseins*. Tübingen: Niemeyer, 1956.

Binswanger, Ludwig. *Traum und Existenz* (with an introduction by M. Foucault). Bern: Gachnang & Springer Verlag, 1992.

Binswanger, Ludwig. *Grundformen und Erkenntnis menschlichen Daseins*. Zürich: Niehans, 1942; 2nd ed., 1953.

Binswanger, Ludwig. *Schizophrenie*. Pfullingen, 1957.

Boss, Medard. *The Analysis of Dreams*. Translated by A. J. Pomerans. New York: Philosophical Library, 1958.

Boss, Medard. *Existential Foundations of Medicine and Psychology*. New York and London: Jason Aronson, 1979.

Boss, Medard. *Grundriss der Medizin: Ansze zu einer phänomenologischen Physiologie, Psychologie, Pathologie, Therapie und zu einer daseinsgemässen Präventiv-Medizin in der modernen Industrie-Gesellschaft*. Bern: Benteli, 1971.

Boss, Medard. *Meaning and Content of Sexual Perversions*. Translated by L. L. Abell. New York: Grune and Stratton, 1959.

Boss, Medard. *Psychoanalyse und Daseinsanalytik*. Bern: Huber, 1957. Translated by Ludwig B. Lefebre as *Psychoanalysis and Daseinsanalysis*. New York: Basic, 1963.

Cohn, I. *Existential Thought and Therapeutic Practice*. London: Sage, 1997.

Cohn, I. *Heidegger and the Roots of Existential Theory*. London: Continuum, 2002.

Fromm, Erich. *The Art of Loving*. New York: Harper & Row, 1989.

Keen, E. *A Primer in Phenomenological Psychology*. New York: Holt, Reinhart & Winston, 1975.

May, Rollo. *The Courage to Create*. New York: Bantam, 1984.

May, Rollo. *The Discovery of Being*. New York: W. W. Norton, 1983.

May, Rollo, Ernest Angel, and Henri F. Ellenberger, eds. *Existence*. New York: Basic, 1958. Translations of important works by Binswanger, Erwin Straus, Minkowski, V. E. von Gebsattel, and Kuhn.

Merleau-Ponty, Maurice. *Phénomenologie de la perception*. Paris: Gallimard, 1945. Translated by Colin Smith as *Phenomenology of Perception*. London: Routledge, 1962.

Sartre, Jean-Paul. *Esquisse d'une théorie des émotions*. Paris: Hermann, 1939. Translated by B. Frechtman as *The Emotions*. New York: Philosophical Library, 1948.

Sartre, Jean-Paul. *L'être et le néant*. Paris: Gallimard, 1943. Translated by Hazel Barnes as *Being and Nothingness*. New York: Philosophical Library, 1956.

Sartre, Jean-Paul. *L'imaginaire: Psychologic phénomenologique de l'imagination*. Paris, 1940. Translated by B. Frechtman as *The Psychology of the Imagination*. New York, 1948.

Speigelberg, H. *Phenomenology in Psychology and Psychiatry*. Evanston: Northwestern University Press, 1992.

Straus, Erwin. *The Primary World*. Translated by Jacob Needleman. New York: Free Press of Glencoe, 1963.

Valle R. J., and M. King, eds. *Existential-phenomenological Alternatives for Psychology*. New York: Oxford University Press, 1978.

van Deurzen, Emmy. *Everyday Mysteries—Existential Dimensions of Psychotherapy*. London: Routledge 1997.

Yalom, I. *Existential Psychotherapy*. New York: Basic Books, 1980.

A helpful annotated bibliography is available at http://www.strath.ac.uk/counsunit/features-biblio.html.

CRITICAL STUDIES

Lyons, Joseph. *Psychological Reports*, Monograph Supplement 5. 1959. Extensive bibliography of works in English.

Needleman, Jacob. *Being-in-the-World*. New York: Basic, 1963. The first half is a comparative and interpretive study of Binswanger and Freud.

Sonnemann, Ulrich. *Existence and Therapy*. New York: Grune and Stratton, 1954. A searching presentation, in a difficult prose style, of the issues and their relevance to the several schools of psychology. Bibliography.

Van den Berg, J. H. *The Phenomenological Approach to Psychiatry.* Springfield, IL: Thomas, 1955. A simple, clear, and quite elementary introduction.

Jacob Needleman (1967)
Bibliography updated by Thomas Nenon (2005)

EXISTENTIAL PSYCHOANALYSIS [ADDENDUM]

Toward the conclusion of *Being and Nothingness* Jean-Paul Sartre proposes "existential psychoanalysis" as an alternative to the Freudian version that he had criticized. Respecting individual freedom and responsibility, its basic principle is that "man is a totality and not a collection" of drives and complexes. By a comparative hermeneutic of the complex, multilevel symbolic expressions of an agent's actions it uncovers bad faith and ferrets out that fundamental project that gives unity and direction to our lives. It thereby renders possible "conversion" to an authentic existence, in which one can resist the need to create a substantialized self. Rejecting the hypothesis of an unconscious, this method relies heavily on prereflective consciousness and the distinction between what we prereflectively comprehend and reflectively know. The analyst's empathetic understanding helps bring this comprehension to knowledge. Since all consciousness is practical, for Sartre, this transformation involves a reorientation of one's way of being-in-the-world. Unfortunately, he concedes, "this psychoanalysis has not yet found its Freud."

It has been observed that Sartrean analysis deals with a set of human needs that have nothing to do with Freudian drives, namely "relational needs for holding, mirroring, positive regard, and emotional responsiveness, and needs for the development of a coherent and flexible sense of 'self'" (Cannon 1991, p. 1). Sartre's later work underscores the enabling power of the third to mediate our identity and social efficacy. In social ensembles some third parties objectify and alienate, whereas others generate practical unity and effectiveness. Sartre argues that consciousness is intentional, not only in the traditional phenomenological sense that it constitutes objects, but in the existential sense that it sets goals and strategies to obtain them. Psychoanalytic interpretation unmasks these goals and strategies.

Sartre has been accused of writing as if the human were born adult. But, in trying to understand Flaubert, he claims that "everything took place in childhood" and devotes several volumes of *The Family Idiot* to chart the "spiral of personalization" by which the individual interiorizes and reexteriorizes the structural relations into which it is born (its protohistory), the experiences of infancy and early childhood (its prehistory), and resultant "constitution" of its character and dispositions. At each stage the individual is in process of "making something out of what he or she has been made into." Sartrean metatheory respects the objective possibilities of this individual's situated being as it establishes "the way in which the child lives his or her family relations inside a given society." The approach is familial.

Sartrean psychoanalysis assumed a social orientation in the 1950s and 1960s, as did his thought generally. It became a form of social critique, linked to the thesis that entire societies could suffer from "objective neurosis," making it extremely difficult for its members to live authentic lives. His psychobiographies were prolonged instances of existentialist psychoanalysis conjoined to a kind of historical materialism, which he called the "progressive-regressive method."

Although the concepts of bad faith and authenticity have entered popular discourse, Sartre's psychoanalytic metatheory has yet to be adopted by professionals the way Heideggerian categories have been employed by Ludwig Binswanger, Medard Boss, and others.

See also Bad Faith; Binswanger, Ludwig; Consciousness; Freedom; Freud, Sigmund; Historical Materialism; Psychoanalytic Theories, Logical Status of; Sartre, Jean-Paul; Unconscious.

Bibliography

Bugental, J. F. *The Search for Authenticity: An Existential-Analytic Approach to Psychotherapy.* New York: Irvington, 1981.

Cannon, B. *Sartre and Psychoanalysis: An Existentialist Challenge to Clinical Metatheory.* Lawrence: University Press of Kansas, 1991.

Frankl, V. E. *Psychotherapy and Existentialism: Selected Papers on Logotherapy.* New York, 1985.

Laing, R. D. *The Divided Self.* New York: Routledge, 1999.

Sartre, J.-P. *L'idiot de la famille.* 3 vols. Paris: Gallimard, 1971–1972. Translated by Carol Cosman as *The Family Idiot.* 5 vols. Chicago: University of Chicago Press, 1981–1993.

Van Kaam, A. *Existential Foundations of Psychology.* Garden City, NY: Image, 1969.

Thomas R. Flynn (1996)

EXPERIENCE

As the average person understands the term *experience*, it means no more than familiarity with some matter of practical concern, based on repeated past acquaintance or performance. The experienced doctor or soldier knows his trade, not by the book merely, but by long practice under a variety of circumstances. The older philosophical meaning of the word differs but little from this, denoting as it does the capacity to do something, learned in the habit of doing it and guided rather by rule-of-thumb precept than by theoretical understanding (cf. the well-known passage in Aristotle, *Posterior Analytics* II, 19). It is in this fashion—by retention of individual memories and their gradual hardening into principle—that the craftsman acquires his skill, the scientist his knowledge, and the practical man his wisdom. But (save in the last case, perhaps) it represents at best only a stage on the way to real understanding in terms of universals and is thus by most ancient writers despised as a makeshift and uncertain form of knowledge. The mere empiric cuts, and continues to cut, a poor figure even into the modern period, though by that time associated, rather (as in Francis Bacon), with the trial-and-error experimenter in alchemy or medicine who endeavors by persistence alone to filch Nature's secrets without first gaining insight into its laws. The preference for rational certainty over mere empirical generalization is in fact endemic among philosophers and can be seen not merely in avowed rationalists (such as René Descartes), but also, for example, in those whose uneasiness over the principle of induction has led them to seek ways of validating it as the major premise for a quasi-deductive treatment of science.

The experience from which the empiric draws his conjectures is, of course, the homely and substantial experience of a world of public objects, which forms for all sane and unreflective persons the basis of ordinary life. It has been regularly insisted, however, since the earliest times, that experience in this sense is nothing ultimate: the alleged paradoxes of motion and change and the more familiar facts of perceptual error and illusion are enough (it is thought) to show that it cannot be straightforwardly identified with the real. Hence, in addition to the rejection of habit-learning as a road to knowledge, there arises that further prejudice against the deliverances of the senses and in favor of necessary reasoning from first principles, of which the Parmenidean distinction between the "ways" of truth and opinion is an early and famous example.

THE "GIVEN"

The uncertainty of sense experience leads, by this route, to a further important conclusion. Since perceptual illusion and mistake seem essentially to be the fault of the observer, he must himself contribute something to his experience by way of inference, interpretation, or construction. Experience must, in part at least, be the work of the mind. For all that, the individual certainly does not create or invent his experience and in certain respects is powerless to alter it at will, it seems, therefore, equally undeniable that some part of it is simply "given" and is only thereafter subject to adulteration by its recipient. This given is generally referred to as the object of "bare" or "immediate" experience, in contrast to the more "solid" or developed experience of which it is held to be an essential ingredient. The legitimacy of the contrast is seldom, indeed, disputed, for though immediate experience has often been denounced as a myth, the usual motive for doing so has been to stigmatize it as a mere abstraction got by analysis and not something that could occur, psychologically, by itself. *All* experience, on this view, involves interpretation, and it is thus senseless to suppose any unvarnished, direct acquaintance with the given. But since it would be equally senseless to suppose an interpretation with nothing to interpret, it is commonly admitted that an "epistemic" given must nonetheless be present in experience, though impossible to view independently, since this would ipso facto be to construe it in some fashion under the auspices of thought.

For writers who accept either a psychological or an epistemic given, a number of problems arise. What does it consist of? What marks or features does it exhibit? How is it related to the everyday experience built upon it? And how, once the latter has been derived, is it possible to proceed from there to the realities that presumably underlie, occasion, and explain the whole? The last is essentially a metaphysical question, but the remainder (to which we here confine ourselves) are staple topics of epistemological dispute.

As to the content of immediate experience, there are characteristic differences of opinion. At one extreme lie the theories of direct realism, whose claim is that material objects are immediately given, so that no real difference arises between naked and clothed experience, sensation and perception, or for that matter appearance and reality; apart from perceptual error there is thus no "problem of knowledge" at all. At the opposite pole are the theories of William James and F. H. Bradley, for whom immediate experience presents only an undifferentiated mass of feeling or sensation in which nothing is discriminated or related and in which even the contrast between subject and object has not begun to appear. Of this "blooming, buzzing confusion" (in James's well-known phrase), it is obvious that nothing can be said, even to distinguish its modes. Ex hypothesi, it is merely the residue left after elimination of all processes involving association, memory, judgment, thought, and language; it is free from error because it says nothing; but as such, however indispensable, it has little to contribute to knowledge.

Writers in the empiricist tradition, less anxious to make knowledge the sole work of the mind, have been correspondingly averse to such unstructured versions of the experiential given, though the argument from illusion has equally deterred the majority from claiming direct acquaintance with a world of things. For most of them the given includes at least simple sense-qualities of color, taste, sound, and so on, together with organic sensations, feelings, and images, it being generally assumed that these are presented individually and even as "atomic" cognitive units (impressions, ideas, sense data, etc.) to a consciousness distinct from themselves. Beyond this, however, there is little agreement. Some have asserted, while others have denied, that spatial, temporal, causal, or other relations are given in this fashion. Some have been prepared to admit associative or sign material as part of the given; others have not. Visual impressions, for example, have been held (most notably by George Berkeley) to be initially two-dimensional; but in other writers (for example, H. H. Price) the claim is that they are presented in, or as having, depth. Images, memory impressions, and feelings have all been ascribed to the given, but again it is disputed as to whether all images belong in this category or only those of simple qualities (as with impressions of sense). There is similar contention as to whether the "pastness" of the memory image is intrinsic to it or imputed on the strength of some other feature, and whether, in general, the "inner" and "outer" character of feelings and images, on the one hand, and sense impressions on the other, are marks of the data themselves, or a construction imposed upon them.

CRITERIA OF "GIVENNESS"

The foregoing differences and others like them are not, as they seem, due to want of regard for the facts, nor would closer attention suffice to dispel them. They arise from a failure in agreement as to the formal characteristics of "givenness" itself, and hence as to the criteria for its identification. What are these criteria? The commonest answers seem to be that the given is private; that it is adventitious (in Descartes's sense); that it is simple, as

involving no element of thought or inference; and that it is incorrigible. Too often these tests are also assumed to coincide in yielding the same result or to be sufficient rather than necessary conditions for givenness. Many of the historic uncertainties surrounding the description of the given would appear to have arisen in this way.

Privacy, for example, is inconsistent with simplicity, inasmuch as every variety of thought and feeling, imagery, or sensory seeming is necessarily private, however obvious it may be that it belongs to a sophisticated rather than a primitive level of consciousness. Adventitiousness, as a criterion, would similarly include within the given all phenomena not under the subject's voluntary control, including the appearance and causal behavior of objects, but excluding some part of his thoughts and feelings—though how much it seems impossible to say. In both cases the given seems too generously defined to serve as a foundation for knowledge. If the given is limited to experience uncontaminated by "inference," the difficulty is to know what counts as such and hence where analysis is to stop. Even the lowliest amoeba can react to sensory cues and so "transcend the given," but who is to say if it thinks or not?

The psychological given, on this showing, may well be accounted a myth. The epistemological arguments, however, are harder to put aside. Their main support has been the belief that the data they point to represent the only foundations for knowledge that could be called certain or incorrigible. The judgments of perceptual experience, concerning the existence, properties, and relations of objects, are all (it is said) subject to error, and so open to correction. But reports of what seems merely, of the presence of sense qualities to consciousness, make no such claim about real existence and so run no risk of mistake. The "sense datum" theories popular from 1900 onward, like their eighteenth-century predecessors, attempted to erect on this basis a theory of knowledge more stable and concrete than that underwritten by the necessary truths of rationalism. Their vogue has declined, however, and that for two reasons. On the one hand it has been argued that no sense datum statement, however guarded, can fail (if it says anything at all) to make some conceptual commitment that might later call for retraction; and on the other, that a great many factual statements are quite as certain as those they are alleged to depend on. Given a sufficiently straightforward case of perceptual contact with an object, there is no ground for treating it as a judgment based on the "evidence" of sense data, since it is beyond the power of any future evidence to enforce its withdrawal. It is as certain as anything could be, and nothing is gained, therefore, by an appeal to supposedly more primitive certainties to provide it with support.

ORDINARY EXPERIENCE

The above argument is not beyond question, but it illustrates the difficulties not merely of characterizing the sensory given but even of securing agreement as to its existence. It is more profitable, perhaps, to turn for a moment to those writers who, having accepted a given of some sort from the outset, have occupied themselves with the second stage of the problem, namely, the manner in which this given is elaborated into the fullness of ordinary experience. Here the issue lies chiefly between those who maintain (with John Locke, and still more, with Étienne Bonnot de Condillac) that the concepts employed in the construction of developed experience are themselves derived (by abstraction, association, composition, or induction) from immediate experience, and those who argue (as do all rationalists) that this elaboration depends on principles contributed by the mind a priori, and not first learned from experience itself. The rationalist does not thereby deny the fact of immediate experience any more than does the empiricist. His claim, rather, is that this experience does not make itself intelligible by any natural process and that it is only the logical activity of the mind that brings order and coherence into the result.

The most celebrated statement of this position is doubtless that of Immanuel Kant, for whom the "manifold" of sensory intuition, though spatiotemporally ordered insofar as it is presented at all, is unified into a world of empirical objects only insofar as it is brought under the a priori rules, or categories, of the understanding. Experience in the full sense is thus a synthesis, part given and part made, though in some of Kant's idealist successors the creative aspect is so far emphasized at the expense of the given as to tend toward that extreme of rationalism in which the world of experience is construed as an exclusively mental product, with no element of "brute fact" in it at all. For the modern "logical empiricist" the position is, in effect, reversed, his typical doctrine being (as already noticed) that the content of all empirical propositions can be reduced without remainder to "protocols" recording actual or possible fragments of immediate experience.

But the attempt to reconstitute ordinary experience out of a mixture of sense data and formal logic, though long and ably sustained, has met in the end with little more success than the search for certainty that led to the introduction of these data in the first place. Recent work on the subject has shown signs of impatience with this starting point and seeks to discredit it by attacking the whole distinction between sensation and perception—the two-level theory of experience—and the argument from illusion on which that distinction so largely depends. Whether this rejection of the traditional premises of the problem offers any hope of solving (or dissolving) it is a question that time alone can answer. If experience teaches anything, it is that success is unlikely; but then, even in philosophy (or so philosophy tells us), experience is not always or necessarily a reliable guide.

See also Aesthetic Experience; A Priori and A Posteriori; Aristotle; Bacon, Francis; Berkeley, George; Bradley, Francis Herbert; Consciousness; Descartes, René; Empiricism; Induction; James, William; Kant, Immanuel; Perception; Religious Experience; Sensa.

Bibliography

The literature on this subject is endless. The following is a list of representative works by Anglo-American authors, published in the twentieth and early twenty-first centuries.

Audi, Robert. "Experience and Inference in the Grounding of Theoretical and Practical Reasons: Replies to Professors Fumerton, Marras, and Sinnott-Armstrong." *Philosophy and Phenomenological Research* 67 (1) (2003): 202–221.

Austin, J. L. *Sense and Sensibilia*. Oxford: Oxford University Press, 1962.

Ayer, A. J. *Foundations of Empirical Knowledge*. London: Macmillan, 1940.

Ayer, A. J. *Problem of Knowledge*. London: Macmillan, 1956.

Bonevac, Daniel. "Sellars vs. the Given." *Philosophy and Phenomenological Research* 64 (2002): 1–30.

Brewer, Bill. *Perception and Reason*. Oxford: Clarendon Press, 2002.

Chisholm, Roderick. "The Problem of the Speckled Hen." *Mind* 51 (1942): 368–373.

Crane, T., ed. *The Contents of Experience*. Cambridge, U.K.: Cambridge University Press, 1992.

Hamlyn, D. W. *Sensation and Perception*. London: Routledge and K. Paul, 1961. A history of the problem.

Hirst, R. J. *The Problems of Perception*. London: Allen and Unwin, 1959.

Jackson, Frank. *Perception: A Representative Theory*. Cambridge, U.K.: Cambridge University Press, 1977.

Lewis, C. I. *Analysis of Knowledge and Valuation*. La Salle, IL: Open Court, 1946.

Lewis, C. I. "The Given Element in Empirical Knowledge." *Philosophical Review* 61 (1952): 168–175.

Lewis, C. I. *Mind and the World-Order*. New York: Scribners, 1929.

Moore, G. E. *Philosophical Studies*. London: Routledge, 1922.

Moore, G. E. *Some Main Problems of Philosophy*. London: Allen and Unwin, 1953.

Moser, Paul. "The Given in Epistemology." *Communication and Cognition* 18 (1985): 249–262.

Pasch, A. *Experience and the Analytic*. Chicago: University of Chicago Press, 1958.

Price, H. H. *Perception*. London: Methuen, 1932.

Price, H. H. *Thinking and Experience*. London: Hutchinson, 1953.

Russell, B. A. W. *Our Knowledge of the External World*. Chicago: Open Court, 1914.

Ryle, G. *Concept of Mind*. London: Hutchinson, 1949.

Sellars, Wilfrid. *The Metaphysics of Epistemology*. Atascadero, CA: Ridgeview Press, 1989.

Sosa, Ernest. "Mythology of the Given." *History of Philosophy Quarterly* 14 (1997): 275–286.

Stace, W. T. *Theory of Knowledge and Existence*. Oxford: Clarendon Press, 1932.

Walsh, W. H. *Reason and Experience*. Oxford: Clarendon Press, 1947.

Williams, Michael. "Are There Two Grades of Knowledge? Mythology of the Given: Sosa, Sellars, and the Task of Epistemology." *PAS*, Supp. 77 (2003): 91–112.

Yolton, J. W. *Thinking and Perceiving*. La Salle, IL: Open Court, 1962.

P. L. Heath (1967)
Bibliography updated by Benjamin Fiedor (2005)

EXPERIMENTATION AND INSTRUMENTATION

See Appendix, Vol. 10

EXPLANATION

The three cardinal aims of science are prediction, control, and explanation, but the greatest of these is explanation. It is also the most inscrutable: Prediction aims at truth, and control at happiness, and insofar as one has some independent grasp of these notions, one can evaluate science's strategies of prediction and control from the outside. Explanation, by contrast, aims at scientific understanding, a good intrinsic to science, and therefore something that it seems one can only look to science itself to explicate.

Philosophers have wondered whether science might be better off abandoning the pursuit of explanation. Pierre Duhem (1954), among others, argued that explanatory knowledge would have to be a kind of knowledge so exalted as to be forever beyond the reach of ordinary scientific inquiry: it would have to be knowledge of the essential natures of things, something that neo-Kantians, empiricists, and level-headed practitioners of science could all agree was neither possible nor perhaps even desirable.

Everything changed when Carl Gustav Hempel formulated his deductive-nomological account of explanation. In accordance with the previous observation, that one's only clue to the nature of explanatory knowledge is science's own explanatory practice, Hempel proposed simply to describe what kind of things scientists tendered when they claimed to have an explanation, without asking whether such things were capable of providing true understanding. Since Hempel, the philosophy of scientific explanation has proceeded in this humble vein, seeming more like a sociology of scientific practice than an inquiry into a set of transcendent norms. In keeping with its mission as a branch of philosophy, however, the study of explanation pursues a particular kind of sociological knowledge: It is concerned almost exclusively with the ideal at which scientists take themselves to be aiming, and barely at all with the steps and missteps taken on the way to realizing the ideal.

As Hempel saw it, scientific explanation was of a piece with prediction, requiring the same resources and giving a similar kind of satisfaction. No doubt this modest view of the explanatory enterprise played a part in making the study of explanation acceptable in the climate of postwar empiricism. The story of explanation in decades since Hempel's time, however, is an expansionist one. Over the years philosophers of explanation have gradually required more resources for, and made grander claims for the significance of, explanation's role in science. (For a comprehensive overview of the philosophy of explanation from 1948 to 1988, with a full bibliography, see Wesley C. Salmon [1990].)

THE DEDUCTIVE-NOMOLOGICAL ACCOUNT

Hempel's deductive-nomological (DN) account (Hempel and Oppenheim 1948) is intended to capture the form of any deterministic scientific explanation of an individual event, such as the expansion of a particular metal bar when heated, the extinction of the dinosaurs, or the outbreak of the U.S. Civil War.

According to Hempel such an explanation is always a deductive derivation of the occurrence of the event to be explained from a set of true propositions including at least one statement of a scientific law. (The event to be explained is called the explanandum; the set of explaining statements is sometimes called the explanans.) In other words, a deterministic event explanation is always a sound, law-involving, deductive argument with the conclusion that the explanandum event occurred.

Intuitively, the premises of a DN explanation spell out the relevant initial and background conditions, and the laws governing the behavior of the system in which the explanandum occurred. For example, Hempel cites the following argument as a typical DN explanation of the event of a thermometer's mercury expanding when placed in hot water:

The (cool) sample of mercury was placed in hot water, heating it,

Mercury expands when heated thus

The sample of mercury expanded

Because the law or laws that must be cited in a DN explanation typically cover the pattern of behavior of which the explanandum is an instance, the DN account is sometimes referred to as the covering law account of explanation.

One can see that the DN account is not intended to give the form of probabilistic event explanations; Hempel offers a separate account of probabilistic explanation, which will be discussed later on. The explanation of phenomena other than events is, by contrast, apparently amenable to the DN approach. Hempel suggests that a scientific law can be explained, for example, much like an event, by deducing it from premises including at least one other law. However, he finds himself unable to make good on this proposal, for reasons connected to the relevance problem discussed in the next section.

Many scientific explanations of events and other phenomena undoubtedly have the form proposed by the DN account: They are logical derivations from laws and other information. Hempel does not entirely satisfy himself, however, with answering questions of form. Taking one step beyond sociological humility, he advances a thesis as to why deductive, law-involving arguments should confer understanding, "[A DN explanation] shows that, given the particular circumstances and the laws in question, the occurrence of the phenomenon *was to be expected*; and it is in this sense that the explanation enables us to *understand why* the phenomenon occurred" (1965a, p. 337, emphasis in the original).

Scientific understanding, then, takes the form of retrospective expectation: One might say (loosely) that, whereas prediction is concerned with what one should expect in the future, explanation is concerned with what one should have expected in the past. Explanation is, then, put on a par with prediction and so made safe for empiricist philosophy of science. Hempel even goes so far

as to say that the difference between explanation and prediction is merely pragmatic (Hempel and Oppenheim 1948) though the DN account does not in itself entail such a thesis.

OBJECTIONS TO THE DN ACCOUNT

Three kinds of objections to the DN account have been especially important for the subsequent development of the philosophy of explanation.

The first kind of objection, developed by Henry Kyburg, Salmon, and others, points to the DN theory's inability to account for judgments of explanatory relevance. The paradigm is the following argument, which satisfies all the DN account's criteria for a good explanation of the event of a particular teaspoon of salt's dissolving:

The teaspoon of salt was hexed (meaning that certain hand gestures were made over the salt),

The salt was placed in water,

All hexed salt dissolves when placed in water thus,

The salt dissolved.

The explanation appears to attribute the salt's dissolving in part to its being hexed, when in fact the hexing is irrelevant.

There are various responses to the counterexample that aim to preserve as much of the DN account as possible, for example, holding that the generalization about hexed salt is not a true law or imposing the requirement that a DN explanation use the most general law available.

Salmon's much less conservative reaction is to conclude that Hempel is wrong to think of explanation in terms of expectability, therefore of explanations as kinds of argument. The relation between the factors cited in an explanation and the explanandum itself, Salmon holds, is not epistemic, but ontic; it should be a physical relevance relation—a relation of statistical relevance, he first proposes (1970), or a relation of causal relevance, as he later comes to believe (1984). The faulty explanation of the salt's dissolving is to be discarded, argues Salmon, not because of some formal or logical defect, but because it cites an event, the hexing of the salt, that fails to bear the appropriate relevance relation to the explanandum.

Hempel himself declines (early in his career, at least) to give a DN account of the explanation of laws because of a related problem. Kepler's laws may be derived from a single law that is simply the conjunction of Kepler's laws and Boyle's law. Such a derivation is clearly no explanation of Kepler's laws, writes Hempel, yet it satisfies the DN account's requirements: The premises are true and the argument is valid and law involving (Hempel and Oppenheim 1948).

The second important objection to the DN account is perhaps also the most famous. It shows, most philosophers would agree, that the DN account pays insufficient attention to the explanatory role of causal relations.

The height of a flagpole can be cited, along with the position of the sun and the law that light travels in straight lines, to explain the length of the flagpole's shadow. The DN account is well able to make sense of this explanation: It can be cast in the form of a sound, law-involving argument. However, now take this same argument and switch the premise stating the height of the flagpole with the premise stating the length of the shadow. One now has a sound, law-involving argument for the height of the flagpole that cites, among other things, the length of the shadow—thus, according to the DN account, one has an explanation of the height of the flagpole that cites, as an explainer, the length of the shadow. This consequence of the DN account—that the height of a flagpole can be explained by the length of its shadow—seems obviously wrong, and it is wrong, it seems, because a cause cannot be explained by its own effects.

A further famous example strongly suggests that effects can only be explained by their causes and the laws and background conditions in virtue of which they are causes. Suppose that the arrival of a certain kind of weather front is always followed by a storm and that a certain reading on a barometer is a sure sign that such a front has arrived. Then a barometer reading of this sort is always followed by a storm. The storm cannot be explained, however, by citing the barometer reading and that such readings are always followed by storms, though these two facts together satisfy the requirements of the DN account. A constant, robust correlation is not, it appears, enough for explanation. What is needed, as Salmon eventually concludes, is a causal relation.

At first Hempel resists the suggestion that facts about causation play any special role in explanation (e.g., see 1965a, §2.2). Over the years, however, due in part to the development of sophisticated empiricist accounts of causation, this has become a minority view.

The third class of objections to the DN account focuses on the account's requirements that every explana-tion cite a law and that (except in probabilistic explanation) the law or laws be strong enough to entail, given appropriate boundary conditions, the explanandum. One way to develop the objection is to point to everyday explanations that cite the cause of an event as its explanation, without mentioning any covering law, as when one cites a patch of ice on the road as the cause of a motorcycle accident.

More important for the study of explanation in science are varieties of explanation in which there is no prospect and no need for either the entailment or the probabilification of the explanandum. Perhaps the best example of all is Darwinian explanation, in which a trait T of some species is explained by pointing to the way in which T enhanced, directly or indirectly, the reproductive prospects of its possessor. Attempting to fit Darwinian explanation into the DN framework creates a host of problems, among which the most intractable is perhaps the following (Scriven 1959): For every trait that evolved because it benefited its possessors in some way, there are many other, equally valuable traits that did not evolve, perhaps because the right mutation did not occur, perhaps for more systematic reasons (e.g., the trait's evolution would have required a dramatic reconfiguration of the species' developmental pathways). To have a DN explanation of T, one would have to produce a deductive argument entailing that T, and none of the alternatives, evolved. In other words, one would have to be in a position to show that T had to evolve. Not only does this seem close to impossible but also it seems unnecessary for understanding the appearance of T. One can understand the course of evolution without retrospectively predicting its every twist and turn.

Hempel is aware of the problem with Darwinian explanation. His response is to argue that there is no such thing: Faced with a choice between the DN account and Darwinian explanation, one should opt for the former and consider Darwinian stories to be at best partial explanations of traits (Hempel 1965c). He advocates a similar deflationary treatment of functionalist explanation in sociology and of historical explanations that are not entailments.

THE INDUCTIVE-STATISTICAL ACCOUNT

Hempel's (1965a, §3) account of the probabilistic explanation of events, the inductive-statistical (IS) account, in many ways parallels the DN account of deterministic event explanation. Like a DN explanation, an IS explanation is a law-involving argument giving good reason to expect that the explanandum event occurred. However, whereas a DN explanation is a deductive argument entailing the explanandum, an IS explanation is an inductive argument conferring high probability on the explanandum.

Hempel's example is the explanation of John Jones's swift recovery from a strep infection. The probability of a swift recovery without the administration of penicillin, Hempel supposes, is 0.1, while the probability with penicillin is 0.9. Citing Jones's infection, his treatment with penicillin, and the resulting high probability of recovery, then, confers a high probability on Jones's swift recovery; in the circumstances, one would expect Jones to recover swiftly. This inductive argument is sufficient, in Hempel's view, to explain the swift recovery.

Inductive soundness imposes one additional requirement with no parallel in deductive logic. Suppose one knows that Jones's strain of strep is resistant to penicillin. An inductive argument is said to be sound only if all relevant background knowledge is taken into account; consequently, an inductive argument for Jones's swift recovery must cite the infection's penicillin resistance. But once the new premise is added, the argument will no longer confer a high probability on its conclusion. This is what is wanted: There ought to be no inductive argument for swift recovery—one ought not to expect swift recovery—when the strep is known to be resistant.

Hempel imposes a similar requirement on IS explanations, which he calls the requirement of maximal specificity (for details, see Hempel 1965a, §3.4). In virtue of this requirement, it is not possible to explain Jones's swift recovery by citing treatment with penicillin when the infection is known to be penicillin resistant.

As with the DN account of explanation, a number of objections to the IS account have exerted a strong influence on the subsequent development of the philosophical study of explanation. Versions of both the relevance and the causal objections apply to the IS account as well as to the DN account. Two other important criticisms will be briefly described here.

The first is the complaint that it is too much to ask that explanations confer high probability on their explananda. In many ways, this is the analogue of the third objection to the DN account mentioned earlier; in the same paper that Michael Scriven (1959) expresses doubts about the existence of a DN treatment of Darwinian explanation, he describes the following example, best conceived of as an objection to the IS account. The probability that Jones contracts paresis, a form of tertiary syphilis that attacks the central nervous system, given that he has untreated secondary syphilis, is low. However, only syphilitics contract paresis. It seems reasonable to cite untreated syphilis, then, as explaining Jones's paresis, though the explanation confers only a low probability on the explanandum.

The proponent of the IS account is committed to rejecting such attempts at explanation, as Hempel does, arguing that in such cases one has only a partial explanation of why the patient contracted syphilis. This is perhaps one of the most convincing of Hempel's defenses, but the paresis example is nevertheless widely regarded as posing a serious problem for the expectability approach to explanation.

A second objection to the IS account focuses on the requirement of maximal specificity. The requirement insists that all relevant background knowledge must be included in a probabilistic event explanation, but it does not require that relevant but unknown information be taken into account. In particular, if Jones's infection is penicillin resistant, but this fact is not known to the explainer, then the IS account deems the explainer's appeal to the administration of penicillin as a perfectly good explanation of Jones's swift recovery.

As J. Alberto Coffa (1974) argues, this is surely not correct. If the infection is resistant to penicillin, then the administration of penicillin cannot explain the recovery, regardless of what the explainer does and does not know. The requirement of maximal specificity makes probabilistic explanation relative to the explainer's epistemic situation, then, in a way that it appears not to be. This objection hits right at the heart of the expectability conception of explanation, suggesting that explanation is not an epistemic matter in the least. A third objection that is applicable to many accounts of probabilistic explanation will be raised in the following discussion of the statistical relevance account.

THE STATISTICAL RELEVANCE ACCOUNT

In response to the DN account's relevance problem, Salmon suggests that the factors cited in an explanation must stand in a relation of statistical relevance (SR) to the explanandum. He does not intend this as a friendly amendment to Hempel's account, but as a radical reconceptualization of the nature of explanation: The function of an explanation, Salmon (1970) argues, is not to show that the explanandum was to be expected, but to describe factors—ideally, all the factors—statistically relevant to the occurrence of the explanandum.

From the beginning, statistical relevance is presented as an objective relation, that is, a relation holding independently of the explainer's background knowledge or other context. (Coffa's [1974] critique of the IS account, discussed earlier, discourages relativistic backsliding.) Salmon thus requires an account of probability that is both objective and broad enough to encompass any possible explanandum.

For breadth, he settles on frequentism, the view that the probability of an event type is equal to the frequency with which it occurs in a reference class of outcomes. For objectivity, he develops what he calls a homogeneity constraint on the reference classes that can be used as bases for explanatory probabilities. Such a constraint, he believes, is strong enough to determine a single, observer-independent probability distribution over any set of outcomes of interest. Salmon (1984) summarizes the theory of homogeneity; for further information, see the discussion of the reference class problem in the separate entry on probability and chance.

Statistical relevance is a comparative concept: To say that a factor A is statistically relevant to the occurrence of an event E is to say that the probability of E (or for the frequentist, of events of the same type as E) in the presence of A is greater than the probability of E in the absence of A. Thus, the determination of a relevance relation requires not only a reference class—a class of outcomes all of which occurred in the presence of A—but a contrast class, a class of outcomes all of which occurred in the absence of A. The contrast class is not normally homogeneous. Thus for Salmon, the contrast probability must be a weighted sum of different homogeneous probabilities, each corresponding to a different way that A might have been absent, and giving the probability of E when A is absent in that way.

Perhaps inevitably, if not inescapably, Salmon arrives at the view that a full SR explanation is a complete table of relevance, describing not only factors that are present and statistically relevant to the explanandum but also factors that are absent but would have been statistically relevant if they had been present. He further adds to the table all the alternatives to the explanandum E with respect to which there existed homogeneous probabilities, and a list of all the factors that would have been relevant to these alternatives, if they occurred. Consequently, the information proffered in an SR explanation of an event E not only explains the actual occurrence of E but would also explain any occurrence of an event of the same type, even if different relevant factors were present, as well as the occurrence of any alternative to E.

As something of a corollary to this view, Salmon holds that negatively relevant factors—factors that lower the probability of the explanandum—are as explanatory as positively relevant factors and that all factors should be mentioned regardless of their degree of relevance. Salmon's not discriminating among these factors is perhaps best understood as follows. Seeing that a factor is statistically relevant to the explanandum is an explanatory end in itself. That the factor makes a particular kind of change—positive or negative, large or small—to the total probability of the explanandum would be important only if appreciating the value of the total probability were also an explanatory end. However, it is not; knowing which relevance relations hold is all that matters.

Four objections to the SR account are considered here. First, for all Salmon's justifications, an SR account seems to contain too much information. To explain E when A was absent, why is it necessary to know that, had A been present, it would have been relevant? Why is it further necessary to know what would have been relevant to the occurrence of some alternative to a type E event that did not in fact occur? This information does not appear to be directly relevant to the explanatory task at hand, that of explaining E itself.

Second, the SR account seems vulnerable to the causal objection to the DN account; it seems to hold that A is explanatorily relevant to E whenever A is correlated with E, when in fact it is necessary that A be a cause of E. The barometer reading is statistically relevant to the storm in the example described earlier, but it does not thereby explain the storm.

Salmon is well aware of this problem and proposes that only certain kinds of statistical relevance relations are explanatory, namely, those that survive a screening off test. A factor A that is correlated with E is screened off from E by another factor B if, conditional on B, A makes no difference to the probability of E (just as, for example, conditional on the presence of the front, the barometer reading makes no difference to the probability of the storm), but conditional on A, B does make a difference to the probability of E. When there is some B that screens off A from E, Salmon says that A is not genuinely statistically relevant to E. And A's relevance will indeed disappear in a relevance table that also cites B. Note that Salmon's treatment does not make an explicit appeal to causal facts. Whether all problems concerning the role of causation in explanation can be solved in this way is unclear.

A third objection dogs all the probabilistic accounts of explanation to be considered in this entry. Suppose that I strap a small but unreliable bomb to one wheel of your car. The probability that the bomb detonates is 50 percent, in which case your tire goes flat. The trigger fails, but you drive over a nail and your tire does go flat. The bomb has increased the probability of the flat, but it plays no role in its explanation. (Does the presence of the nail screen off the presence of the bomb? No, if it is assumed that the nail's effect is, like that of the bomb, probabilistic.) Sometimes statistically relevant factors are explanatorily irrelevant. Finally, it is not easy to see how the SR account might be generalized to give an account of the explanation of phenomena other than events.

THE UNIFICATION ACCOUNT

Michael Friedman (1974) suggests that, while the logical empiricists' official account of explanation is the expectability account, they have an unofficial account, too, on which to explain a phenomenon is to see it as an instance of a broad pattern of similar phenomena. Hempel himself occasionally writes in this vein, "The understanding [explanation] conveys lies … in the insight that the explanandum fits into, or can be subsumed under, a system of uniformities represented by empirical laws or theoretical principles" (1965a, p. 488). Friedman formulates what he calls a unification account of explanation, a particularly global version of this conception of explanation as pattern subsumption, on which a phenomenon is explained by the system of subsuming laws that best unifies all the phenomena there are. Philip Kitcher (1981, 1989) amends and extends Friedman's account in various ways.

The unifying power of a theory is proportional, on both Friedman's and Kitcher's accounts, not only to the number of phenomena that can be subsumed under the theory but also to the simplicity of the theory. (Kitcher imposes some additional desiderata.) The theory that best unifies all the phenomena, then, might be said to yield the most for the fewest: The most derivable phenomena for the fewest number of basic principles. It is characteristic of the unificationist position to insist that only the most unifying theory has full explanatory power, but this view does not in itself preclude the possibility of partial explanation by more weakly unifying theories.

Why be a unificationist? Friedman suggests that the virtue of the most unifying theory is that it reduces to a minimum the number of fundamental incomprehensibilities, that is, unexplained explainers. Perhaps a more common justification for unificationism is that suggested by Hempel: To understand something is to fit it into a wider pattern. Add that the wider the pattern, the more

powerful the explanation, and one is well on the way to unificationism.

Many of the virtues of the unification account stem from the great versatility of the pattern subsumption relation. A subsuming pattern need not be exceptionless, so not only probabilistic explanation but also other forms of nondeductive explanation fit the unification mold. Darwinian explanation, for example, can be seen as accounting for a trait by seeing it as part of a widespread pattern of adaptedness in the biological world—though Kitcher (1989, §5), for one, resists this view of evolutionary explanation, and indeed, argues that all explanations can be formulated as deductive arguments. More inclusively, Kitcher argues that unificationism supplies an effective account of mathematical, as well as scientific, explanation. For some further claimed advantages of the unification over the causal approach, see Kitcher (1989, §3).

Unificationism promises to give a powerful and subtle account of explanatory relevance. For example, an explanation of a teaspoon of salt's dissolving that cites the law "all hexed salt dissolves in water" is rejected as insufficiently unifying, because the law is both more complex and covers fewer phenomena than the law "all salt dissolves in water." More interesting, the unificationist can give an account of why many of the low-level details of the implementation of biological, psychological, economic, and social mechanisms seem to be irrelevant to understanding those mechanisms' behavior; the details, however, have yet to be worked out (Kitcher 1984).

Two important classes of objections stand in the way of the unification approach to explanation. First is the familiar question concerning the role of causation in explanation. Can the unification account explain why explanation so often, perhaps always, seems to follow the direction of causation? One might think not: The explanation of a flagpole's height in terms of the length of its shadow seems to cite just as unifying a pattern as the explanation of shadow length in terms of pole height—the same pattern, in fact.

Kitcher (1981) takes up the challenge, arguing that the unification account reproduces the asymmetries in explanation usually put down to something causal. On his view, a unifying pattern is an argument pattern. Since arguments have a direction, the pattern in which the pole height explains the shadow length is distinguished from the pattern in which the length explains the height. The unifying power of each must, therefore, be assessed separately. To solve the problem, the correct comparison is not between the unifying power of these two argument patterns, but between the unifying power of the pattern that wrongly explains pole height in terms of shadow length and that of the pattern one usually cites to explain the height of a flagpole.

Kitcher calls this latter argument pattern an origin and development pattern and claims that it is instantiated by, and so subsumes, every account one gives of the properties of a thing that describes its origin and development, as when, for example, one tells the story of the construction and erection of the flagpole. The pattern is enormously general, then, and so easily wins the right to explain the height of the flagpole. Having argued, in effect, that unificationist explanation tends to proceed in the direction of causation, Kitcher then makes the dramatic claim that it is the order of explanation that determines the order of causation; one's causal beliefs depend on and reflect one's explanatory practice.

The second objection to explanatory unificationism is that it makes explanation an overly global matter. How one phenomenon is to be explained depends, according to the unificationist, on what best unifies all the other phenomena, therefore on what the other phenomena are. To many writers, it seems that finding an explanation does not require, even in principle, knowledge extending to all corners of the universe. A more moderate or local unificationism is possible, of course, but another natural place to look for locality is in the causal approach to explanation.

THE CAUSAL APPROACH

In 1965 Hempel could regard the idea that there is something causal to explanation over and above the exceptionless regularities cited by a DN explanation as lacking a "precise construal" (1965a, p. 353). Since that time philosophers have come to see claims about causal relations as having a rich empirical content that goes far beyond mere regularities and their instantiation (see Spirtes et al. [2000]), though the tradition began well before Hempel made his remark, with Reichenbach [1956]). Even metaphysical empiricists, then, can agree that there is a distinctive causal approach to explanation. Thanks to the development of sophisticated but wholly empiricist accounts of causation (again beginning with Reichenbach), they can go further and in good conscience endorse the causal approach.

Strong arguments suggest that the causal approach is correct. The first and most persuasive is the equation of causal and explanatory direction suggested by the flagpole/shadow and barometer/storm examples. The second is the observation that a requirement of causal relevance

between explainers and the explained will deal with the problem of the hexed salt and similar cases. The third is that one can give a cause for a phenomenon without being able to predict it. In those counterexamples to the DN and IS accounts where grounds insufficient for prediction nevertheless seem to be sufficient for explanation—the explanation of paresis by syphilis and of a trait's evolution by its conferring a certain benefit—the force of the explanation might well be thought to lie in the aptness of the cited cause. The causal approach is now dominant in the philosophy of explanation.

The most important divide within the causal approach concerns the nature of the causal relation called on to do the explanatory work. Salmon (1984) invokes a notion of causation close to fundamental physics and declares the explanation of an event to consist of the sum total of causal influences on the explanandum in this fundamental level sense.

Such an account, however, appears to count far too many events as explanatorily relevant. As Salmon concedes, though a baseball causally influences the window that it shatters, and so rightly counts as a part of the explanation of the shattering, so do the shouts of the ball players, which cause the window to vibrate even as it is struck by the ball. The shouts, too, then, will be counted on Salmon's approach as a part of the explanation of the shattering. However, they are surely (except perhaps in some unusual cases) irrelevant.

A popular response to this worry begins with the observation that, while it is correct to say that the ball caused the window to shatter, it is not correct to say that the shouts caused the window to shatter. Such locutions suggest that there is another kind of causal relation, distinct from Salmon's fundamental physical relation, that holds between the ball and the shattering but not between the shouts and the shattering.

How can it be that Salmon's relation holds between the shouts and the shattering but the new causal relation does not? One response is that Salmon's relation is based on a faulty theory of causation, but this is not the answer normally given. Rather, the new causal relation is understood as relating events at all levels, whereas Salmon's causality relates events only at the lowest level.

The high-level event of the shattering is the event that would have occurred no matter what the physical details of the shattering, that is, no matter which shards of glass flew where. The low-level event is the event individuated by all the shattering's physical details; this event only occurred, then, because the window shattered in exactly the way that it did. (Some writers call high-level events states of affairs or facts and hold that events proper are always low level.)

When one asks for an explanation of the shattering, one is normally asking for an explanation of the fact that the window shattered, not that it shattered in exactly the way it did. Thus, one asks for the causes of the high-level event, not the low-level event. Even though the low- and high-level events are coextensive in space and time, it seems that there are causes of the former that are not among the causes of the latter, namely, the events that determine, given that the shattering occurred, exactly how it occurred. These detail-determining events, because they are not causes of the explanandum, the shattering, do not explain it (for more on the potential for different causal relations between low- and high-level events, see Bennett 1988).

The idea, in short, is that there are many different levels of explananda, corresponding to different levels of eventhood, and different causal relations at all these different levels. Salmon's fundamental physical causation, then, is only one among many different levels of causation. Add this conception of causation as a multilevel relation to the causal approach to explanation, and one gets a theory on which the explainers of an event depend on the level of the event. (This level dependence of the explanation is also characteristic of the DN, IS, and SR accounts.)

The best-known multilevel theory of causation is the counterfactual account. If the shouting had not happened, the high-level shattering event would still have occurred, but because it would have happened in a different way, the low-level shattering event would not have occurred. Thus, the high-level shattering does not, whereas the low-level shattering does, counterfactually depend on the shouting. On a counterfactual approach to causation, this implies that the shouting is a cause of the low-level shattering but not the high-level shattering, and so, taking this multilevel relation as the explanatory causal relation, that the shouting does not explain the high-level shattering, even though—as its causation of the low-level shattering shows—it is connected causally to the shattering in Salmon's sense. For this approach to explanation, but based on a more sophisticated counterfactual account of causation, see David Lewis (1986); for a different though related multilevel approach, see James Woodward (2003).

An alternative to the multilevel approach is a two-factor approach to causal explanation, on which all explainers of an event must causally influence that event at the fundamental physical level, as prescribed by Salmon, but on which they must pass in addition a further test for explanatory relevance. Salmon (1997) himself suggests, late in his career, that the further test might be one of statistical relevance; only the causal influences that change the probability of an event explain the event. Michael Strevens (2004) suggests a different two-factor approach.

An advantage of the two-factor approach is the relatively modest demands it makes of the metaphysics of causation, transferring as it does much of the burden of determining explainers to the further test for relevance. What, then, to say about claims apparently stating the existence of high-level causal relations, such as "The ball's hitting the window, but not the players' shouting, caused the window to shatter"? Strevens (2004) suggests that locutions of this form are in fact causal-explanatory claims, asserting the explanatory relevance of certain causal influences (compare Kitcher's theory of causation mentioned earlier).

Despite the popularity of the causal approach, it is relatively undeveloped. For example, little has been written about the causal explanation of laws; it is usually said that they are explained by describing their underlying mechanisms, but not every law explicitly concerns causes and effects. Equally, not every event explanation appears to involve the delineation of causes. For examples of both kinds of worry, see Kitcher (1989, §3).

Work on the causal approach to probabilistic event explanation is more advanced. Two main currents can be distinguished in the literature. The first springs from the idea that probabilities themselves have the character of dispositions and are able to cause the events to which they are attached. The probability of one-half that a tossed coin lands heads, for example, is interpreted as a statistical disposition that causes the coin (in most cases) to land heads about one-half of the time (Fetzer 1981).

The second current flows from the idea that other events or states of affairs can cause events by making a difference to the probabilities of those events. This view is compatible with the dispositional view of probabilistic causality, but it is compatible also with its rejection. Paul Humphreys writes that "chance is literally nothing" (1989, p. 65) and so cannot cause anything itself, but that events nevertheless cause other events in an indeterministic world by making a difference to their probabilities. Because probability itself is impotent, Humphreys holds that the kind of difference a cause makes to the probability of its effect is irrelevant. It does not matter whether the change in probability is positive or negative, large or small (compare with the SR account). Whatever the change, the factor responsible for the change is a cause and so ought to be cited in an explanation of the effect.

Peter Railton (1978) offers an account of probabilistic explanation that makes room for both conceptions of the relation between probability and causation. On what Railton calls his DNP account, an event is explained by deriving its exact probability from the appropriate initial conditions, background conditions, and laws. Formally, a DNP explanation resembles, as its name suggests, a DN explanation, except that it is the probability of the explanandum, not the explanandum itself, that is deduced. In contrast to Hempel's IS account of probabilistic event explanation, the DNP account does not require a high probability for the explanandum, and because it asks for an accurate derivation of the exact probability, it requires, like the SR account, that an explanation cite all factors probabilistically relevant to the explanandum, whether known or unknown, and (though Railton does not give a criterion for relevance) no irrelevant factors. Perhaps most important of all, the DNP account is, unlike Hempel's various accounts, open to a causal interpretation: The factors that make a difference to the probability, and even the probability itself, can be considered causes of the explanandum, and the explanation successful precisely because it specifies these causes.

An important lacuna in causal accounts of probabilistic explanation is a detailed treatment of probabilistic explanation in sciences such as statistical mechanics and evolutionary biology, where there is some possibility at least that the underlying processes producing the usual explananda are approximately deterministic. The consensus is to regard such explanations as not genuinely probabilistic; Railton (1981) suggests that they can be reinterpreted as reporting on the robustness of the underlying processes with respect to the event to be explained, that is, the processes' tendency to produce the same kind of outcome given a variety of initial and background conditions.

OTHER ISSUES

This entry will conclude with a brief sketch of some issues concerning scientific explanation not mentioned earlier. First is the question of pragmatics in explanation. Most writers hold that pragmatics affects the explanatory enterprise in only one, relatively minor, way: When an explanation is transmitted from one person to another, the act is subject to the usual pragmatics of communication. This position on pragmatics dovetails with the majority view that the explanatory facts are not essentially communicative; explanations exist independently of anyone's intention to explain anything to anyone else.

Both Bas C. van Fraassen (1980, chapter 5) and Peter Achinstein (1983) dissent from this majority, holding that there is no explanation without communication and finding in the pragmatics of communication an account of many facets of explanatory practice. However, this literature has yet to answer the question why science treats explanations as preexisting facts to be discovered, rather than as entities created in the act of communication.

Second, it is an open question whether there is a single standard for evaluating scientific explanations that has remained constant since the beginning of modern science, let alone for the entire history of human explanation. The accounts of explanation in this entry assume, of course, a positive answer, but most work on explanation lacks a substantial historical dimension.

A third issue is idealization in explanation: While almost every account of explanation surveyed earlier requires that explanations contain no false representations of reality, the practice of using idealized models in scientific explanation is widespread. These models deliberately misrepresent the nature of the systems they describe; the ideal gas model, for example, represents gas molecules as having zero volume, but despite this distortion of the facts, it is considered to explain certain behaviors of real gases. Some writers regard idealization as a temporary or practical measure, out of place in a perfected science. Strevens (2004) suggests that on both the unificationist and a certain causal approach to explanation idealizations can be seen as serving a genuine and enduring explanatory role.

See also Causation: Metaphysical Issues; Causation: Philosophical Problems in; Hempel, Carl Gustav; Laws, Scientific.

Bibliography

Achinstein, Peter. *The Nature of Explanation.* New York: Oxford University Press, 1983.

Bennett, Jonathan. *Events and Their Names.* Indianapolis, IN: Hackett, 1988.

Coffa, J. Alberto. "Hempel's Ambiguity." *Synthese* 28 (1974): 141–163.

Duhem, Pierre. *The Aim and Structure of Physical Theory.* Translated by Philip P. Wiener. Princeton, NJ: Princeton University Press, 1954.

Fetzer, James H. *Scientific Knowledge: Causation, Explanation, and Corroboration.* Dordrecht, Netherlands: D. Reidel, 1981.

Friedman, Michael. "Explanation and Scientific Understanding." *Journal of Philosophy* 71 (1974): 5–19.

Hempel, Carl G. "Aspects of Scientific Explanation." In his *Aspects of Scientific Explanation and Other Essays in the Philosophy of Science*, 331–496. New York: Free Press, 1965a.

Hempel, Carl G. *Aspects of Scientific Explanation and Other Essays in the Philosophy of Science*. New York: Free Press, 1965b.

Hempel, Carl G. "The Logic of Functional Analysis." In his *Aspects of Scientific Explanation and Other Essays in the Philosophy of Science*, 297–330. New York: Free Press, 1965c. Revised version of a paper originally published in *Symposium on Sociological Theory*, edited by L. Gross (New York: Harper and Row, 1959).

Hempel, Carl G., and Paul Oppenheim. "Studies in the Logic of Explanation." *Philosophy of Science* 15 (1948): 135–175.

Humphreys, Paul. *The Chances of Explanation: Causal Explanation in the Social, Medical, and Physical Sciences*. Princeton, NJ: Princeton University Press, 1989.

Kitcher, Philip. "Explanatory Unification." *Philosophy of Science* 48 (1981): 507–531.

Kitcher, Philip. "Explanatory Unification and the Causal Structure of the World." In *Minnesota Studies in the Philosophy of Science, vol. 13, Scientific Explanation*, edited by P. Kitcher and Wesley C. Salmon, 410–505. Minneapolis: University of Minnesota Press, 1989.

Kitcher, Philip. "1953 and All That: A Tale of Two Sciences." *Philosophical Review* 93 (1984): 335–373.

Kyburg, Henry Ely. "Comment." *Philosophy of Science* 32 (1965): 147–151.

Lewis, David. "Causal Explanation." In *Philosophical Papers*. Vol. 2, 214–240. New York: Oxford University Press, 1986.

Railton, Peter. "A Deductive-Nomological Model of Probabilistic Explanation." *Philosophy of Science* 45 (1978): 206–226.

Railton, Peter. "Probability, Explanation, and Information." *Synthese* 48 (1981): 233–256.

Reichenbach, Hans. *The Direction of Time*. Edited by Maria Reichenbach. Berkeley: University of California Press, 1956.

Salmon, Wesley C. "Causality and Explanation: A Reply to Two Critiques." *Philosophy of Science* 64 (1997): 461–477.

Salmon, Wesley C. *Explanation and the Causal Structure of the World*. Princeton, NJ: Princeton University Press, 1984.

Salmon, Wesley C. *Four Decades of Scientific Explanation*. Minneapolis: University of Minnesota Press, 1990.

Salmon, Wesley C. "Statistical Explanation." In *Statistical Explanation and Statistical Relevance*, 29–87. Pittsburgh: University of Pittsburgh Press, 1970.

Scriven, Michael. "Explanation and Prediction in Evolutionary Theory." *Science* 30 (1959): 477–482.

Spirtes, Peter, Clark Glymour, and Richard Scheines. *Causation, Prediction, and Search*. 2nd ed. Cambridge, MA: MIT Press, 2000.

Strevens, Michael. "The Causal and Unification Accounts of Explanation Unified—Causally." *Noûs* 38 (2004): 154–176.

Van Fraassen, Bas C. *The Scientific Image*. New York: Oxford University Press, 1980.

Woodward, James. *Making Things Happen: A Theory of Causal Explanation*. New York: Oxford University Press, 2003.

Michael Strevens (2005)

EXTENSION

See *Matter; Primary and Secondary Qualities; Space*

EXTERNAL RELATIONS

See *Relations, Internal and External*

EXTRINSIC AND INTRINSIC PROPERTIES

An "intrinsic property" is one whose possession by an object at a time involves nothing other than the object (and its parts) at that time; an "extrinsic property" is one whose possession at a time involves something else. We might say, therefore, that the properties of being red and round are intrinsic to this ball, but the properties of being in Rhode Island, being less than five feet away from a tree, and having once been owned by my sister are extrinsic to it.

Peter Geach has made a corresponding distinction among changes. There is change whenever "F(*x*) at time *t*" is true and "F(*x*) at time *t'*" is false. Socrates will change when he puts on weight; he will also change when he comes to be shorter than Theaetetus merely in virtue of Theaetetus's growth. Changes of the second kind—intuitively less genuine—Geach calls "mere Cambridge changes," without proposing a rigorous criterion. We might define a mere Cambridge property as a property, change in an object's possession of which is a mere Cambridge change. Mere Cambridge properties are plausibly taken to be the same as extrinsic properties.

The matter is important, among other things, for the clear statement of a Humean view of the world. For a Humean there is in principle a description in intrinsic terms of the state of the world at any one time that is both complete and free of implications for the state of the world at any other time. "Solidity, extension, motion; these qualities are all complete in themselves, and never point out any other event which may result from them" (Hume, *Enquiry*, sec. 8, 1). It is not clear, however, that what Hume says can be true: The motion of an object is hardly free of implications about the state of the world at other times. (If an object at place *p* is said to be moving at time *t*, this is standardly in the sense that, at other times more or less near to *t*, the object is in other places more or less near to *p*.) We may have to decide between complete description and a purely intrinsic one.

Two extreme views are that all properties are really intrinsic and that all properties are really extrinsic. Gottfried Wilhelm Leibniz holds the first: "There are no purely extrinsic denominations." His insistence resulted in the drastic denial of the reality of relations and, most notably, of space and time; it has not been widely accepted. A moderate version of the opposite view, that all properties are really extrinsic, might be held by someone, like Karl Popper, who believes that physical properties are essentially dispositional. Both extremes, in different ways, represent a sense that the nature of one thing cannot be divorced from the nature of others. Confidence in a firm distinction between the intrinsic and the extrinsic, on the other hand, is more characteristic of an optimistic Humean.

It is not easy to give a precise characterization of intrinsic properties, and there may not even be a unique idea, so to speak, waiting to be characterized. We might try saying that extrinsic properties are relational properties and intrinsic properties nonrelational. But many intuitively intrinsic properties still in some way involve a relation—squareness involves a relation among the sides of an object. Can we say that intrinsic properties are those that do not involve a relation to anything that is not a part of the object? This is perhaps the clearest criterion, but it may still be incapable of capturing all our intuitions at once. The power to open locks of kind k, for example, apparently involves a relation to external things of a certain kind—which would seem to make it extrinsic. Yet it is a property that a key can have if it is, so to speak, alone in the world—which would seem to make it intrinsic.

It may be helpful to invoke a distinction between relational descriptions of a property and descriptions of a relational property. But that distinction is itself perplexing. Is "possessing what is actually Jane's favorite intrinsic property" a relational description of a first-order property or a description of second-level relational property?

Philosophers have argued in many cases that apparently intrinsic properties are in fact extrinsic. Terms such as *old, great,* and *imperfect,* John Locke says, "are not looked on to be either relative or so much as external denominations," but they conceal a tacit relation (*Essay*). More worrying are challenges even to the idea that primary qualities, like size and shape, are intrinsic. The size of the ball is, we may think, intrinsic to it. We can describe a scenario where everything else in the universe is twice its actual size while the ball remains the same. But can we properly distinguish this from a scenario where the rest of the world is the same but the ball is half its actual size? Some will argue that length is relational, and the two scenarios make a distinction without a difference: size, after all, is extrinsic. Others will argue instead that even if our descriptions of size are relative, for example, to standard measures, what is described is still an absolute and intrinsic property.

Are any or all of a person's mental properties intrinsic to her? The question is in part about the limitations of methodological solipsism. If Jane could not possess the property of thinking of Bertrand Russell if Russell did not exist, then that property must be extrinsic to her. Some will try to segment referential thought into an internal and an external component; but if that proposal fails, referential thought will typically be extrinsic to the thinker. (Another option is that the thinker, or her mind, extends more widely than her body—and actually includes Russell.) One might argue a similar point with respect to thought about properties as well as about individuals. (A brain that has never been out of a vat does not know what a meter is.) Maybe there are very few mental properties intrinsic to a person; or maybe we should think again about what the notion of the intrinsic is, and what exactly it is supposed to do for us.

See also Hume, David; Internalism versus Externalism; Leibniz, Gottfried Wilhelm; Locke, John; Metaphysics; Popper, Karl Raimund.

Bibliography

Geach, P. T. *God and the Soul.* London: Routledge and Kegan Paul, 1969.

Leibniz, G. W. "Primary Truths" and "Letters to Des Bosses." In *Philosophical Essays,* translated by R. Ariew and D. Garber. Indianapolis: Hackett, 1989. See esp. pp. 32, 203.

Lewis, D. K. "Extrinsic Properties." *Philosophical Studies* 44 (1983): 197–200.

Lewis, D. K. *On the Plurality of Worlds.* Oxford: Blackwell, 1986. Chaps. 1.5, 4.2.

Locke, J. *Essay concerning Human Understanding.* Bk. 2, Chaps. 25, 28.

Popper, K. *The Logic of Scientific Discovery,* 424–425. London: Hutchinson, 1959.

Justin Broackes (1996)

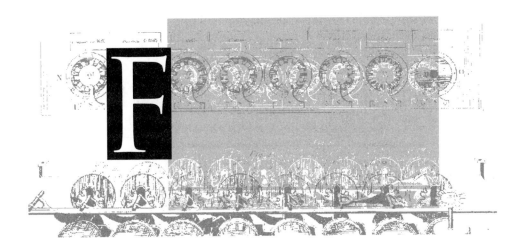

FACTS

See *Analysis, Philosophical; Correspondence Theory of Truth; Propositions*

FAITH

In discourse concerning religion, "faith" has two rather different meanings. As a trusting and confident attitude toward God, faith (*fiducia*) may be compared with trust in one's fellow human beings. As a cognitive act or state whereby men are said to know God or to have knowledge about him, faith (*fides*) may be compared with our perceptual awareness of our material environment or our knowledge of the existence of other persons. This article will deal with the notion of faith as putatively cognitive, as this has operated in Western religious thought.

FAITH IN CLASSIC CATHOLIC AND PROTESTANT THOUGHT

THOMAS AQUINAS. The key thinker for the discussion of faith in Roman Catholicism is Thomas Aquinas, who wrote on the nature of faith in his *Summa Theologiae*. Thomas's main points may be summarized as follows:

(1) Faith is belief in revealed truths. Ultimately the object of faith is God himself, who is not, however, known by the human mind in his divine simplicity but only discursively and by means of propositions. These revealed truths are authoritatively presented in the creeds. Thus, to have faith means to believe the articles of faith summarized in the credal affirmations of the church.

(2) In its degree of certainty, faith stands between knowledge (*scientia*) and opinion. It ranks below knowledge, for although the objective cause of faith—divine truth—is in itself more certain than the product of any human reasoning, yet faith's grasp of its object—since it lacks cogent demonstration—is less certain than rational knowledge. On the other hand, faith ranks above opinion, for while opinion is accompanied by doubt and by fear that the opposite opinion may be true, faith is firm and free from all such hesitations.

(3) The objects of faith on the one hand, and of sight and demonstration on the other, are different: "the object of knowledge [*scientia*] is something seen, whereas the object of faith [*fides*] is the unseen." There can thus be no faith concerning matters that are objects of rational knowledge, for knowledge excludes faith.

However, some truths may be objects of faith to one person and of knowledge to another. In particular, some of the preliminary articles of faith—such as the existence, unity, and incorporeality of God—are capable of being philosophically demonstrated and are revealed as objects of faith only for the sake of those many who are unable to follow the path of abstract reasoning. Those matters that are of faith absolutely are above reason—incapable of being arrived at by human reasoning, however expert.

Thomas's account of the relation between faith and reason is, accordingly, that they apprehend different sets of truths, the truths of faith being above reason. However, this statement must be qualified by adding that there is an area in which faith and reason overlap, since the basic theological propositions—those of natural theology—are held to be both demonstrable and revealed.

(4) Faith is "an act of the intellect assenting to divine truth at the command of the will moved by the grace of God." That is to say, whereas in knowledge the intellect is moved to assent by the object itself, known either directly or by demonstrative reasoning, in faith the intellect is moved to assent "through an act of choice, whereby it turns voluntarily to one side rather than to the other." Faith does not, however, represent an arbitrary or unmotivated decision. It is a response, under the influence of divine grace, to certain external evidences, particularly miracles. As such, it is sufficiently determined by the evidence to be rational and yet sufficiently undetermined and free to be meritorious.

MODERN CATHOLICISM. The doctrine of faith in modern Catholicism is essentially Thomist, although a fuller apologetic context is developed than was necessary in the medieval period. Faith is defined by the first Vatican Council (1870) as "a supernatural virtue, by which, guided and aided by divine grace, we hold as true what God has revealed, not because we have perceived its intrinsic truth by our reason but because of the authority of God who can neither deceive nor be deceived" (*Constitution on Faith*, Ch. 3). Such a definition provokes a query, for faith, characterized as belief in various truths on divine authority, presupposes a knowledge both that God exists and that he has revealed the propositions in question. How is this prior information gained? The question is answered by the doctrine of the *preambula fidei*. The preambles to faith consist in the acceptance of God's existence, established by philosophical proofs, and of the validity of the biblical revelation and the authority of the Catholic church as the divinely appointed guardian of revelation. These latter are authenticated by a variety of

visible signs, such as miracles, fulfillments of prophecy, holy lives, and the growth and durability of the church. The believer's appreciation of the weight of this evidence is not an exercise of faith but of reason: "The use of reason precedes faith and must lead us to it" (Denzinger, *Enchiridion* No. 1626, cf. No. 1651). Thus, the whole structure of belief rests originally upon the historical evidences of miracles and other manifestations of divine activity that do not establish the articles of faith themselves, but rather the fact that the omniscient God has revealed these articles. Although it is denied by Catholic apologists, the comment of John Locke in his *Essay concerning Human Understanding* would still seem pertinent: "Though faith be founded on the testimony of God (who cannot lie) revealing any proposition to us, yet we cannot have an assurance of the truth of its being a divine revelation greater than our own [rationally acquired] knowledge; since the whole strength of the certainty depends upon our knowledge that God revealed it."

It should be noted that in some of the more recent Catholic discussions, such as that by Eugène Joly in the article "Faith" in the *Twentieth Century Encyclopedia of Catholicism* (Paris, 1956), there is a tendency to move beyond a narrowly propositional conception of faith and to be hospitable to the idea of an encounter with God mediated through man's religious experience.

PROTESTANTISM. For Martin Luther (1483–1546), the chief moving spirit of the Reformation, faith was not primarily belief in the church's dogmas but rather a wholehearted trust in the divine grace and love revealed in Jesus Christ. Thus, Luther considered faith as primarily *fiducia* rather than *fides*. Indirectly it included all the fundamental Christian beliefs, but Luther's main emphasis was upon faith as a total reliance upon God's omnipotent goodness. He was not concerned with the logically prior question of our knowledge that God exists. In this he was at one with the biblical writers, who were so vividly conscious of the reality and presence of God that their writings take his existence for granted. In the Bible, as in the thought of Luther, faith is not the belief that God exists, that he is three in one, and so on, but is an attitude of trust and self-commitment to him. In a distinction that Luther himself drew, it is not belief *that* but belief *in*.

John Calvin (1509–1564), the first and greatest systematizer of Reformed theology, gave greater prominence to the cognitive aspect of Christian faith, defining it in the *Institutes* as "a firm and certain knowledge of God's benevolence toward us, founded upon the truth of the freely given promise in Christ, both revealed to our minds and sealed upon our hearts through the Holy Spirit." That to which faith responds is the Bible as the inspired Word of God: "there is a permanent relationship," Calvin says, "between faith and the Word." Thus, in Reformed theology acceptance of the authority of Scripture replaces the *preambula fidei* of Thomism.

The philosophical question raised by this conception of faith is similar to that raised by the Roman Catholic conception: what is the nature of our knowledge that the God whom we are invited to trust in fact exists, and that he has inspired the writings which he is alleged to have inspired?

Two subsequent Protestant contributions to some extent address themselves to this question. In the early nineteenth century Jakob Friedrich Fries, influenced by Friedrich Heinrich Jacobi in the previous century, described faith as *Ahnung* (or *Ahndung*), by which he meant an unconceptualized feeling, hunch, or presentiment as to the reality of the supernatural. Friedrich Schleiermacher also regarded faith as a kind of feeling (*Gefühl*), a sense of absolute dependence upon a higher reality. In a different vein altogether Søren Kierkegaard, the father of modern existentialism, emphasized the objective uncertainty of the religious realm, which can be entered only by a leap of faith. He stressed the tremendous risk involved, like being "out upon the deep, over seventy thousand fathoms of water."

MODERN THEORIES OF FAITH

The Thomist doctrine contains most of the elements that have, in varying proportions, characterized subsequent theories of faith. The Thomist analysis treats faith as (*a*) a form of propositional belief but as (*b*) belief that rests upon weaker evidence than scientific knowledge, and (*c*) regards it as requiring an act of will.

VOLUNTARIST THEORIES. Nearly all subsequent epistemological discussions of faith assume that it is a cognitive attitude directed toward religious propositions. Widespread in modern discussions is the rationalist definition of faith as (to quote a typical formulation) "very firm belief, either unsupported or insufficiently supported by evidence" (C. J. Ducasse, *A Philosophical Scrutiny of Religion,* New York, 1953, p. 74). Some such definition as this is used by a large number of religious philosophers as well as by many of those who reject religious belief.

How, from the believer's point of view, is the evidential gap supposed to be filled? Here the voluntarist theme, first stressed by Thomas, reappears.

Pascal. In the famous Wager passage in his *Pensées* (No. 233) Blaise Pascal (1623–1662) recommends a purely voluntarist route to religious belief, assuming that reason can find no grounds on which to determine whether there is a God. One must decide to believe or to disbelieve; and regarding the decision as a wager, it is prudent to decide to believe. One will then gain eternal life and felicity if God indeed exists and will lose nothing if he does not; whereas if one decides to disbelieve, one will gain nothing if he does not exist but will forfeit eternal life if he does.

William James. The idea briefly adumbrated by Pascal appears in an elaborated form in William James's well-known essay "The Will to Believe" (1895). He points out that there are cases in which we may come into contact with some aspect of reality only by acting, prior to any adequate evidence, as if it existed; in these instances our faith helps to bring its object into being. For example, in the realm of personal relationships faith in an individual's good will or honesty may on occasions elicit these qualities when otherwise they would have been wanting. Precursive faith of this kind is justified by its subsequent verification rather than by prior evidence.

James then proceeds to consider religious faith. Here we have what is for many people a living, momentous, and—James emphasizes—a forced option, for to refuse to say "Yes" to the claim of religion is in effect to say "No" to it. It is to miss the good that follows from believing the religious gospel, if it be true, as decisively as if one had positively rejected it. Therefore we have the right to choose for ourselves between the risk of falling into error by adopting a faith that may turn out to be false, and the risk of missing our highest good by failing to adopt a faith that may turn out to be true.

Furthermore, James adds, the Judeo-Christian religious hypothesis refers specifically to a personal God; and in our dealings with a cosmic Thou, as with our fellow humans, a venture of faith on our part may be necessary if we are to establish any positive relationship. To respond as a person to another person involves showing a certain trustfulness and willingness to "give the benefit of the doubt" and thereby anticipate proof and verification. It may be that God can or will disclose himself only to one who shows such an initial faith and is willing to venture in trust beyond what has been established by scientific proof or philosophical demonstration. In other words, it is possible that in order to gain the religious knowledge upon which our personal good depends, we must give rein to our "passional" desire to believe. Hence, James concludes, we cannot reasonably be required to adopt a methodology that would prohibit us from finding this good: For "a rule of thinking which would absolutely prevent me from acknowledging certain kinds of truth if those kinds of truth were really there, would be an irrational rule."

James's argument has been criticized at a number of points, chief among them being the following:

(1) His basic assumption is that there are no grounds of either reason or evidence which might lead one to accept or reject the "religious hypothesis." There is nothing to make it significantly more probable either that there is or that there is not a God; and in such a situation, says James, we are entitled to follow our desires. But many, both theists and atheists, claim that there are substantial arguments or evidences for (or against) the existence of God, and that we ought to attend to these rather than to our personal predilections. Furthermore, whatever conclusion we arrive at should be held only with the degree of conviction that is warranted by the evidence.

(2) The "precursive faith" that helps to create that in which it believes, although a genuine phenomenon, is irrelevant to belief in the existence of God or in the reality of eternal values; for if these exist, they exist independently of man's belief or lack of belief in them. In the social situations James cites, our willingness to trust someone in advance of proof of his trustworthiness may help to make him trustworthy but does not bring him into existence, and faith in the existence of a divine creator of the universe cannot bring such a being into existence.

(3) James's argument ought not to be applied only to our current live options, since "live option" is a psychological category having no necessary relation to the truth or falsity of hypotheses. We ought to heed equally every momentous and forced option. However, we cannot act upon them all, since they demand incompatible responses. We shall act, then, only upon that which we should most *like* to be true. So stated, the "right to believe" argument stands revealed as an invitation to wishful thinking.

(4) From the side of religion, an unfavorable comparison is made between the kind of faith recommended by James and that already possessed by the religious believer. James presumes a complete absence of grounds for belief and, in this situation, he proposes a prudent gamble. However, the religious believer—as we meet him, for example, in the pages of the Bible—is convinced that he is aware of God acting toward him in and through the events of the world around him, so that at all times he is having to do with God and God with him. His concern is to draw others into this direct awareness of God, rather than to induce them to make James's gamble.

Tennant. F. R. Tennant (1866–1958) has provided the fullest recent voluntarist apologetic for theistic faith. Faith in general, according to Tennant, is the conative element in the acquisition of knowledge. In every advance from sense data to the perception of an ordered world or from the projection of a scientific hypothesis to its observational verification, as in every successful voyage of discovery or in the invention of some new kind of machinery, there must be not only an act of theorizing or of insight but also a sustained effort of will that carries the operation through to completion. In both of these respects religious cognition shares a common structure with knowledge in the sciences and in personal life. First, there is the creation of a hypothesis: Scientific hypotheses satisfy the inclination to explain the structure and order of the universe by quantitative laws, while theological and ethical hypotheses satisfy the inclination toward teleological explanation. Second, there is the volitional investment, the venture of faith, which may eventually be rewarded with a dividend of verified knowledge. The faith venture in secular contexts is continuous in kind with that of the religious prophets and apostles. Thus, faith is the indispensable volitional component within the process of acquiring knowledge, and it plays a basically similar role in both religion and nonreligious life.

However, the kinds of verification that are possible in science and religion are importantly different, although Tennant wavers between stressing their similarity and their dissimilarity. Scientific verification consists in observing that predictions deduced from a hypothesis are fulfilled in the experimenter's observations. Religious verification, on the other hand, consists in the valuable effects of faith in the life of the believer—in strengthening him as a moral agent and in his attainment of heroic life. Thus, while scientific verification leads to objective certainty, or at least to a high degree of objective probability, religious verification leads only to subjective certitude. "Nevertheless," Tennant adds, "verification such as religion claimed for its faith will satisfy most men."

It is noteworthy that the basic features of the classic Thomist analysis of faith reappear, although in a very different setting, in Tennant's theory: (1) Faith, as acceptance of the religious hypothesis, is propositional. (2) Faith is of the same cognitive order as scientific knowledge but is based upon a lower degree of evidence. (3) Faith is not concerned with the material world itself, which is an object of knowledge, but with its teleological meaning. (4) Faith is distinguished by the conative element within it from ordinary belief and knowledge. Whereas the act of will can, in Thomism, appeal for rational justification to such external evidences as miracles and fulfilled prophecies, in Tennant's philosophy it appeals to a comprehensive teleological argument for the existence of God.

This propositional and voluntarist tradition, which has so largely dominated the scene since the time of Thomas, has been criticized on the following grounds: (*a*) Actual religious faith is not, from the believer's point of view, analogous to a scientific hypothesis but with a weaker verification. It is a direct awareness of God, with its own assurance that is not dependent upon philosophical argument. (*b*) As (putatively) a direct awareness of God, faith is not primarily a form of propositional belief; rather, it is a form of religious experience. Theological beliefs naturally grow out of it but are not themselves the primary objects or content of faith.

FAITH AND FREEDOM. A very important connection has long been recognized between faith and what may be called the cognitive freedom of the human mind in its relation to God. The first writer to note this connection was the second-century Christian writer Irenaeus, who said, "And not merely in works, but also in faith, has God preserved the will of man free and under his own control" (*Adversus Haereses*, IV, 37, 5). The theme is continued in Augustine and in Thomas's view that faith is a sufficiently free act to be meritorious. Pascal stated that God's self-revelation in the Incarnation took a deliberately veiled form, so that no one could be compelled to find God in Jesus Christ, and yet so that all who were willing to find God there might do so: "… willing to appear openly to those who seek him with all their hearts, and to be hidden from those who flee from him with all their hearts, he so regulates the knowledge of himself that he has given signs of himself, visible to those who seek him, and not to those who seek him not" (*Pensées*, No. 430). Søren Kierkegaard also spoke of the divine incognito in the Incarnation. The same theme is continued by the twentieth-century Protestant theologian Emil Brunner and by many other writers.

The basic thought behind this emphasis, at any rate in the modern writers, is that God, having created man as personal, always acts toward him in ways that respect and preserve man's freedom and responsibility. For this reason God does not reveal himself to man in his unveiled glory, for in a direct, unmediated awareness of infinite perfection man's frail moral autonomy would be destroyed. Therefore, the divine presence is always mediated through the events and circumstances of a world that God has created to be a relatively independent sphere of interaction with his human creatures. Man's personal autonomy is protected by the fact that he can become conscious of God's activity toward him only by an uncompelled response of faith. Thus, men are not only free to obey or disobey God; they also have the prior and more fundamental freedom to be conscious of God or to refrain from being conscious of him. The human mind displays a natural tendency to interpret its experience religiously, but this tendency acts only as an inclination that can be resisted and inhibited. Man is thus cognitively free in relation to God. Faith is the correlate of freedom and is related to cognition as free will is to conation.

FAITH AS INTERPRETATION. Closely related to this emphasis upon man's cognitive freedom is a contemporary theory that regards faith as the interpretative element in religious experience—that which constitutes it as *religious* experience in distinction from any nonreligious experiencing of the same field of data. Here "interpretation" does not mean intellectual interpretation or theory construction, but something more akin to the interpretative processes which take place in sense perception. From the point of view of epistemology, faith is thus analogous to the phenomenon of "seeing as," which was brought to the attention of philosophers by Ludwig Wittgenstein in his *Philosophical Investigations* (II, xi). We may look at a puzzle picture, seeing it now as a meaningless disarray of lines and now as the outline of, say, a human face. This is an instance of purely visual interpretation. But the concept of "seeing as" can be expanded into that of "experiencing as," referring to the way in which a situation apprehended through our sensory apparatus as a whole is experienced as having some particular kind of significance; that is, as rendering appropriate some particular dispositional response on our part. To cite religious examples, when the Old Testament prophets experienced the events of contemporary Israelite history as mediating the presence and activity of God and as speaking a divine imperative to them, they were undergoing a religious mode of "experiencing as." Again, the apostles whose witness constitutes the message of the New Testament saw, but were not compelled to see, Jesus as the Christ. Indeed, it is always true of the religious mode of "experiencing as" that the data in question are in themselves ambiguous and capable of being responded to either religiously or naturalistically. More strictly, the two types of interpretation are not alternatives on the same level but are different orders of significance found in the same field of data.

The religious significance of events includes and transcends their natural significance. Those events the prophets saw as acts of God can also be seen as having proximate natural or human causes; and the person of Christ, seen by Christian faith as divine, is depicted in the New Testament as being at the same time genuinely human. From a theological point of view, this systematic ambiguity, which is the precondition of faith, serves to protect man's freedom and autonomy as a finite personal being in relation to the infinite God.

See also Atheism; Augustine, St.; Bad Faith; Belief; Brunner, Emil; Calvin, John; Existentialism; Fries, Jakob Friedrich; Jacobi, Friedrich Heinrich; James, William; Kierkegaard, Søren Aabye; Luther, Martin; Miracles; Pascal, Blaise; Teleological Argument for the Existence of God; Tennant, Frederick Robert; Thomas Aquinas, St.; Traditionalism; Truth; Wittgenstein, Ludwig Josef Johann.

Bibliography

The article on πίστις by Rudolf Bultmann and A. Weiser in Vol. VI of Kittel's *Theologisches Wörterbuch zum Neuen Testament* (Stuttgart, 1959) treats authoritatively the various biblical concepts of faith: It was translated by Dorothea M. Barton as *Faith* (London, 1961). Historical treatments of the idea of faith occur in D. M. Baillie, *Faith in God* (Edinburgh, 1927) and W. R. Inge, *Faith* (London, 1909). The distinction between faith as trust and as cognition is developed in Martin Buber, *Zwei Glaubensweisen* (Zürich, 1950), translated by Norman P. Goldhawk as *Two Types of Faith* (London, 1951). The cognitive aspect of Christian faith is defined in John Calvin, *Institutio Christianae Religionis* (Basel, 1536; 5th ed., 1559), translated by F. L. Battles as *Institutes of the Christian Religion*, 2 vols. (London, 1861). Thomas's teaching on the nature of faith occurs in *Summa Theologica* (II–II, 1–7), translated by Anton C. Pegis in *The Basic Writings of Saint Thomas Aquinas,* Vol. II (New York, 1945). Thomas's teaching on the relation between faith and reason is contained in *Summa Contra Gentiles* (I, 3–8), which was translated by Anton C. Pegis as *On the Truth of the Catholic Faith* (Garden City, NY, 1955–1957).

Contemporary Roman Catholic discussions of faith include G. D. Smith, "Faith and Revealed Truth," in *The Teaching of the Catholic Church* (New York, 1956), Vol. I and Eugène Joly, *Qu'est-ce que croire?* (Paris, 1956); the latter was translated by Illtyd Trethowan as *What Is Faith?* (New York, 1956). Also see H. J. D. Denzinger, *Enchiridion Symbolorum* (Freiburg, 1952).

Protestant neoorthodox conceptions of faith are represented by Karl Barth, *Kirchliche Dogmatik* (Zürich, 1932), Vol. I, Part 1, translated by G. T. Thompson as *The Doctrine of the Word of God* (Edinburgh: Clark, 1936); H. F. Lovell Cocks, *By Faith Alone* (London, 1943); and F. Gogarten, *Die Wirklichkeit des Glaubens* (Stuttgart, 1957), translated by Carl Michalson and others as *The Reality of Faith* (Philadelphia, 1959).

The conception of faith as *Ahnung* occurs in F. H. Jacobi, *David Hume über den Glauben, oder Idealismus und Realismus* (1787), in *Werke* (Leipzig, 1815), Vol. II; and J. F. Fries, *Wissen, Glaube und Ahnung* (Jena, 1805), edited by Leonard Nelson (Göttingen, 1905). See also R. Otto, *Kantisch-Fries'sche Religionsphilosophie und ihre Anwendung auf die Theologie* (Tübingen: Mohr, 1909), translated by E. B. Dicker as *The Philosophy of Religion* (London: Williams and Norgate, 1931).

Christian existentialist views of faith occur in Søren Kierkegaard, especially in *Philosophical Fragments*, translated by David F. Swenson (Princeton, NJ, 1936) and *Concluding Unscientific Postscript*, also translated by David F. Swenson (Princeton, NJ, 1941); and in G. Ebeling, *Das Wesen des Christlichen Glaubens* (Tübingen, 1959), translated by Ronald Gregor Smith as *The Nature of Faith* (London, 1961).

The classic attempt to base faith on a moral foundation is in Kant's *Critique of Practical Reason*. W. R. Sorley, *Moral Values and the Idea of God* (Cambridge, U.K., 1918); D. M. Baillie, *Faith in God* (Edinburgh 1927); and J. Baillie, *The Interpretation of Religion* (Edinburgh, 1929) contain more recent endeavors to the same end.

Modern voluntarist theories of faith are found in William James, *The Will to Believe* (New York: Longman, 1897); James Ward, *Essays in Philosophy* (London, 1927); and F. R. Tennant, *Philosophical Theology,* Vol. I (Cambridge, U.K., 1928) and *The Nature of Belief* (London, 1943).

The view that faith operates not only in religion but also in many other spheres of life has an extensive literature, including Arthur Balfour, *The Foundations of Belief* (London, 1885); W. R. Inge, *Faith* (London: Duckworth, 1909); B. H. Streeter, ed., *Adventure: The Faith of Science and the Science of Faith* (London, 1927); Alan Richardson, *Christian Apologetics* (London, 1947); Raphael Demos in the symposium *Academic Freedom, Logic and Religion* (New York, 1953); and H. R. Niebuhr, *Radical Monotheism and Western Culture* (New York: Harper, 1960).

J. H. Newman's Illative Sense theory (*A Grammar of Assent*, London, 1870) is discussed in M. C. D'Arcy, *The Nature of Belief* (London, 1945). Paul Tillich's view of faith as "ultimate concern" occurs in *Dynamics of Faith* (New York: Harper, 1957).

The conception of faith as the interpretative element in religious experience is expounded in J. H. Hick, *Faith and Knowledge* (Ithaca, NY, 1957).

John Hick (1967)

FAITH [ADDENDUM]

This entry focuses on the various ways in which recent philosophers working within or in reaction to the scriptural traditions have construed the relationship between faith in God and the belief in God's existence. The entry will also touch on different views regarding the question of whether faith is, can be, or should be, *rational*. However, a full treatment of the issue of faith and reason is beyond the scope of this entry.

There are several different camps of views regarding the relationship of *faith in God* and *belief in God's existence*. One camp holds that faith is not belief, because it is, so to speak, higher than belief; faith is *knowledge* of God. Thus, Dewey Hoitenga (1991) holds that faith is a knowledge of God that comes through direct acquaintance. According to John Hick (1957), faith is the interpretive element within religious experience that results in an awareness or knowledge of God. On this view, a person who merely believes that God exists does not really have faith at all. And, on this view, faith is rational, in the sense that it is based on a religious experience of a certain sort.

A second camp follows Thomas Aquinas in treating faith in God as basically equivalent to belief in God's existence. In his book *What Is Faith?* (1992), Anthony Kenny recognizes that there are different senses of the term *faith*, but he suggests that in at least one of its senses, faith is equivalent to belief in God's existence. Hence, in discussing the issue of whether faith is rational, Kenny focuses primarily on the question of whether it is rational to believe in God's existence.

A third camp holds that faith in God has nothing to do with belief that God exists. Such philosophers sharply distinguish faith *in* God, from a belief *that* God exists. On this view, faith is a commitment of some sort, such as ultimate concern (Paul Tillich 1958) or hope in some divine end (Louis Pojman 1986). To a large degree, the motivation for such a conception is the claim that what is most crucial about genuine religious devotion is somehow fundamentally noncognitive, or perhaps, "nonpropositional," that is, having nothing to do with the proposition "God exists." On this view, faith is an affective or emotional matter, or a matter of the will; it is not a cognitive or intellectual affair. For Tillich, in some sense the question of the rationality of faith cannot properly arise, because faith is an ultimate commitment that cannot be adjudicated by anything prior or external to itself. And, for Pojman, it can be rational to have faith even if it is *not* rational to believe in God's existence.

In response to this camp, many writers have argued that belief or faith *in* something generally presupposes some kind of *belief that* some proposition is true. In order to commit oneself to God, or to trust God, or to have hope in some divine end, etc., one must have some kind of belief that God exists. Nicholas Wolterstorff (1983) points out that even if it is granted that what is most important about religious devotion is noncognitive, or

even, nonpropositional, it does not follow that religious devotion is altogether noncognitive. Hence, the fourth camp, which holds that although faith is not identical with belief, faith involves or requires at least some kind of belief in God's existence. On this view, the issue of the rationality of faith cannot be completely divorced from the question of whether it is rational to believe in God's existence.

Philosophers within this camp differ on what precisely is involved in faith aside from belief in God's existence, and also on the nature and degree of that belief. Richard Swinburne holds that faith involves doing certain actions to achieve good purposes, whilst relying on the belief that God exists to provide what one wants or needs. For Swinburne, because the evidence that supports the belief in God's existence is strong but inconclusive, it is the role of faith to fill the gap between what the evidence warrants and what the religious believer believes. Paul Helm (2000) agrees that faith involves trust, but he also ascribes to a Lockean view that belief, as well as trust, should be proportionate to the evidence. Thus according to Helm, the more evidence one has that God exists, the greater degree of trust is appropriate.

Still others suggest that faith consists in a kind of practical assumption that God exists. Robert Audi (1991) proposes that to have faith is to assume that God exists as a practical rule for living. According to Audi, one can have this kind of faith so long as one does not actually believe that God does *not* exist. Joshua Golding (1990) proposes that faith be viewed as the pragmatic assumption that God exists, *for purpose of living a religious life*. For Golding, in order to have pragmatic faith, one must at least have the belief that there is at least some live probability that God exists. On either of these latter views, so long as God's existence has not been conclusively refuted or disproved, there might be pragmatic considerations that make it rational or justifiable to have faith. Such pragmatic considerations might include the potential benefits, spiritual, moral, or otherwise, that might accrue to the faithful, especially if it turns out that God does indeed exist.

OTHER VIEWS

Worthy of mention is another view that does not fit neatly into any of the above camps. William Lad Sessions (1994) claims that there is no single substantive concept of faith that applies univocally to everything reasonably labeled "faith" in all religious traditions (or even sometimes within certain traditions). Faith is an "analogical" concept whose various instances resemble one another in various ways, without there being a single feature or set of features common to them all. According to Sessions, it is impossible to pin down what is "faith." However, this is almost a foregone conclusion if one takes under consideration the entire range of world religions. Sessions also concedes that adherents of different religions as well as adherents of the same religion will continue to argue over which sense of faith is the most true to a given tradition or set of texts, as well as over the question of whether faith is rational and if so in what sense. Thus despite Sessions's useful taxonomy, it appears that debates among the above camps are not likely to cease in the near future.

Finally, consider views of faith in Judaism and Islam. The Hebrew word for faith is *emunah*. Interpreting the notion of *emunah* (faith), some Jewish philosophers have emphasized intellectual assent to propositions, whereas other thinkers have emphasized volitional or affective commitment. Perhaps the most well-known discussion of this issue in the twentieth century is by Martin Buber. In his book *Two Types of Faith* (1951), Buber claimed that the Christian view of faith is "an acknowledgement of God's existence," and that the Jewish view is "trust in God." A superficial reading might lead one to think that, for Buber, the Jewish view of faith belongs in the third camp above, namely, that faith has nothing to do with a belief that God exists. However, such a reading is mistaken. While Buber claims that for Judaism the fiduciary aspect of faith is primary, he does not claim that beliefs are irrelevant to faith, or that somehow, one could have trust in God without believing that God exists. Hence, Buber more properly belongs in the fourth camp described above.

Another notable claim made by Buber is that, for Christianity, faith is primarily an *individual* matter; for Judaism, faith is primarily a *communal* matter. Buber argues that for Christianity, a relationship with God is initiated when and if a person decides to adopt Christian faith, that is, to acknowledge God. Of course, there can be a group of Christians who form a Christian community, but the primary act of faith is carried out by individuals. However, in the case of Judaism, God has already established a covenantal relationship with the people of Israel, in which he has made certain commitments to them as a people. Thus the primary act of faith, that is, trust in God, is the Jewish response to God's commitment to the Jewish people. Perhaps Buber's point is borne out by the fact that for centuries the primary liturgical expression of Christian faith has been in the singular, that is, "*credo in unum deo*," which translates as "I believe in one God." In the Jewish liturgy, the primary liturgical expression of faith is in the plural, "*Hear O Israel, the Lord our God, the Lord is One*."

Islam treats faith or *iman* as a religious duty or virtue. According to a well-known *hadith* (Islamic legend), Mohammed made a sharp distinction between *islam* (submission) and *iman* (faith). To accept *islam* is to testify that there is no God but Allah, and that Mohammed is his prophet; to pray, give charity, keep the fasts, and make the pilgrimage. To have *iman* is to believe in God, his angels, his messengers, and the last day of judgment. The Koran itself (49: 14) makes clear that one can be a *muslim* without having *iman*. Merely testifying to God's existence and Mohammed's prophecy makes one a *muslim*, but not one who has *iman*. The implication is that *iman* goes well beyond mere belief in God's existence, and that it involves an active trust in God. Islamic theologians have debated the issue of what kind of belief qualifies a person as a *muslim*. If one believes, but sins, or believes insincerely, does one truly belong in the Muslim community? Over the centuries, different schools of thought adopted different positions on these questions. However, it is difficult to find a discussion among recent Islamic writers directly on the question of what is the precise relationship between *iman* and belief in God's existence.

Bibliography

For a detailed bibliography on discussions of faith, consult William Lad Sessions, *The Concept of Faith*. See below.

Audi, Robert. "Faith, Belief, and Rationality." In *Philosophical Perspectives*. Vol. 5: *Philosophy of Religion*, edited by James E. Tomberlin. Atascerdo, CA: Ridgeview, 1991.

Buber, Martin. *Two Types of Faith*. New York: Macmillan, 1951.

Golding, Joshua L. "Toward a Pragmatic Conception of Religious Faith." Faith and Philosophy 7 (1990): 486–503.

Helm, Paul. *Faith with Reason*. Oxford: Clarendon Press, 2000.

Hick, John. *Faith and Knowledge: A Modern Introduction to the Problem of Religious Knowledge*. New York: Cornell University Press, 1957.

Hoitenga, Dewey. *Faith and Reason from Plato to Plantinga: An Introduction to Reformed Epistemology*. Albany: SUNY Press, 1991.

Kenny, Anthony. *What Is Faith?* Oxford: Oxford University Press, 1992.

Pojman, Louis. "Faith Without Belief." Faith and Philosophy 3 (1986): 157–176.

Sessions, William Lad. *The Concept of Faith: A Philosophical Investigation*. Ithaca, NY: Cornell University Press, 1994.

Swinburne, Richard. *Faith and Reason*. Oxford: Clarendon Press, 1981.

Tillich, Paul. *Dynamics of Faith*. New York: Harper and Row, 1958.

Waines, David. *An Introduction to Islam*. Cambridge, U.K.: Cambridge University Press, 1995. See esp. chap. 4.

Wolterstorff, Nicholas. "Introduction." In *Faith and Rationality: Reason and Belief in God*. Notre Dame: Notre Dame University Press, 1983.

Joshua L. Golding (2005)

FALLACIES

A fallacy, in the strict sense, is an invalid form of argument. Thus fallacy, or unsoundness in reasoning, is distinguished from simple falsity in that a single statement or belief may be false, but what is fallacious is the transition from a set of premises to a conclusion. However, this distinction is often slurred over; and we call other kinds of mistakes or confusion that are more or less closely related to faults in reasoning fallacies, in an extended sense. Indeed, we sometimes give the title of "fallacy" to what is little more than a particular type of false belief. At the same time, we usually count as fallacies only those invalid forms of argument, or related kinds of error, that are plausible and into which people frequently and easily fall. Fallacy is different from sophistry, which is the deliberate use of unsound reasoning or of related errors. A fallacy used with intent to deceive or to win an argument unfairly, to carry conviction without justification, or to defeat proper discussion becomes a sophistic device.

This article will survey and classify the main kinds of fallacies, explaining and illustrating many that have been traditionally recognized and named, and noting especially those that are of particular importance in philosophy; and it will touch on the conditions in which fallacies flourish and the means by which they may be avoided or detected.

In classifying fallacies, we shall take first fallacies in the strict sense, forms of argument in which the conclusion does not follow from the premise or premises. These are divided into formal fallacies, errors in the formal reasoning itself, and informal fallacies, in which the reasoner either argues invalidly without using any precise logical form or goes wrong in putting a thought or an ordinary language statement into logical form or in translating back from logical form into thought or ordinary language. (It is a consequence of this division that if anyone commits an informal fallacy, there would be a formal fallacy somewhere in the argument that would be obtained if his intended premises, conclusion, and intermediate steps were put correctly and consistently into some logical form; but it is useful to distinguish informal fallacies in order to indicate how the mistakes have occurred.)

Next we shall take fallacies in nondeductive reasoning and in observation. We cannot speak accurately of fallacies in this case, since we no longer have strictly valid arguments with which to contrast them; but in a looser way we can contrast good procedures and patterns of reasoning that confirm hypotheses with ones that fail to confirm or are likely to produce errors.

Third, we shall examine fallacies in discourse. Such faults as inconsistency, circularity, prejudice, irrelevance, and unfair interrogation—which include some of the best-known fallacies—are not mistakes in reasoning from premises, or evidence, to a conclusion but are to be condemned on some other ground. Philosophical fallacies do not constitute a special group apart from those already mentioned, but some of these have been singled out for special notice.

FALLACIES IN THE STRICT SENSE

FORMAL FALLACIES. Formal fallacies may be arranged by reference to the logical systems, or parts of a logical system, whose valid argument forms they mimic or distort.

Hypothetical and disjunctive reasoning. Hypothetical and disjunctive reasoning is systematized by the calculus of propositions. The p, q, and other terms in the forms given below stand for variables that range over complete statements or propositions, and the phrases "If … then" and "Either … or" stand either for the corresponding truth operators or for any operators that, with respect to the arguments into which they enter, obey substantially the same calculus. The following fallacies are common in reasoning of this kind.

Asserting the consequent: If p then q, and q, therefore p.

Denying the antecedent: If p then q, and not p, therefore not q.

Converting a conditional: If p then q, therefore if q then p. For example, "If this equation holds, so does that one; therefore, if that equation holds, so does this one."

Negating antecedent and consequent: If p then q, therefore if not p then not q. For example, "If the nations disarm, there will be peace; so if the nations do not disarm, there will not be peace."

These invalid forms of argument are plausible partly because they are distortions of valid forms. The first two are distortions of *modus ponens* (If p then q, and p, therefore q) and *modus tollens* (If p then q, and not q, therefore not *p*). Similarly, the third and fourth both mimic the valid form transposition (If *p* then *q*, therefore if not *q* then not *p*). However, concrete arguments of these invalid forms may also be explained as informal fallacies due to ambiguity (discussed under "Ambiguous Words and Phrases" below). An expression that actually asserts only a proposition of the form "If *p* then *q*" may be wrongly taken as asserting "*q* if and only if *p*," and if each of the conditionals above were replaced by the corresponding biconditional, each fallacy would become a valid form of argument.

It is also easy to fall into these fallacies when one is working in a field in which corresponding statements of the forms "If *p* then *q*" and "If *q* then *p*" are frequently both true or both false. This is the case in certain areas of mathematics, and indeed this fact is used in the procedure for discovering proofs that is sometimes called geometrical analysis. We assume the truth of what we wish to prove, and work out its consequences; if among these we find something that is already known or that can be proved independently, we try to construct a proof by retracing the previous steps. We assume that *p*, we deduce in a series of steps that *q*, we prove independently that *q*, and hence, reversing the previous deduction, that *p*. However, this final proof will be valid only if each of the steps in the analysis is reversible. Geometrical analysis is a useful heuristic procedure because this is often the case, but this utility in many geometric arguments may tempt us to assume, wrongly, that such steps are always reversible and that wherever we have established "If *p* then *q*," we are entitled to infer, from this alone, "If *q* then *p*."

Another common fallacy is that of *asserting an alternative*: Either *p* or *q*, and *p*, therefore not *q*. This is a distortion of the disjunctive syllogism (Either *p* or *q*, and not *p*, therefore *q*). However, concrete examples may also be explained as due to the ambiguity of disjunctive expressions, for if "Either *p* or *q*" were replaced by the strong disjunction "Either *p* or *q* but not both," this would be a valid form of argument.

There are also fallacies that are distortions of De Morgan's rules. Thus, "Not both *p* and *q*" is equivalent to "Either not *p* or not *q*," but we may invalidly infer from it "Both not *p* and not *q*"; and from "Either not *p* or not *q*" we may invalidly infer "Not either *p* or *q*."

Use of arguments. If a conclusion follows validly from a premise or set of premises, we can use this fact correctly in either of two ways. Given that the premises are true, we can infer that the conclusion is true; or, given that the conclusion is false, we can infer that at least one

of the premises is false. However, these correct inferences may be replaced by the following fallacious ones:

(1) The conclusion is true; therefore the premise is true (or therefore all the premises are true).

(2) The premise (or at least one of the premises) is false; therefore the conclusion is false.

The first of these can contribute to confusion between the confirmation of a hypothesis and a proof of it; for when a hypothesis is confirmed, a conclusion drawn from it as a premise is found to be true, and the fallacy would make us infer from this that the hypothesis is itself true.

(3) The conclusion is false; therefore all the premises are false.

We might take as a variant of the above inference a fallacy noted by Aristotle and inappropriately named *non causa pro causa*. In this variant, an assumption is rejected because an argument in which it is used as a premise leads validly to a false or self-contradictory conclusion. This unsatisfactory conclusion is not due to this assumption, however, and would have followed from the other premises used without this assumption. In practice, one may slip into such an improper *reductio ad absurdum* (or *ad falsum*) either through not noticing that other premises besides the assumption are used, or through too easily taking them to be correct.

There are also fallacious ways of using the fact that an argument is invalid, such as:

(4) The argument from this premise (or these premises) to that conclusion is invalid; therefore the conclusion is false.

Examples of the first and fourth fallacies in the use of argument can also be explained in another way. The correct inference in each case is that the conclusion is not supported by the proposed argument, and we may confuse "not supported" with "false." Indeed, where the conclusion is the subject of controversy and we have previously had both arguments tending to show that it is true and arguments tending to show that it is false, the demolition of a supporting argument will shift the balance between the opposing views and will leave our reasons for denying this conclusion relatively stronger than they were before.

Traditional logic. The *simple conversion of an A-proposition* (or universal affirmative) is a common fallacy having the form "all *P* are *Q*, therefore all *Q* are *P*." For example, having agreed that whatever is conceivable is logically possible, we are liable to infer from this that any-

thing that is logically possible is conceivable. An equivalent error is the negating of terms in an A-proposition, that is, arguing from "All *P* are *Q*" to "All not-*P* are not-*Q*": "Whatever is conceivable is logically possible; therefore, anything that is not conceivable is not logically possible."

A similar fallacy is the *conversion of an O-proposition*: "Some *P* are not *Q*, therefore some *Q* are not *P*." An example is "Some states with parliamentary government are not democratic; it follows that there are genuinely democratic states which lack parliamentary government."

We can give a complete list of the possible formal fallacies in the traditional syllogism and sorites because the following set of four rules (one of them in two parts) is such that every argument that has the form of a syllogism or a sorites is valid if it obeys all these rules and is invalid if it breaks any of them.

Rule I. Not more than one premise may be negative.

Rule II. If one premise is negative, the conclusion must be negative, and vice versa.

Rule III. Each middle term must be distributed at least once.

Rule IV. If a term is distributed in the conclusion, it must be distributed in the premise in which it occurs.

In interpreting these rules, we take the subjects of universal propositions and the predicates of negative propositions to be distributed, and the subjects of particular propositions and the predicates of affirmative propositions to be not distributed.

There are, then, the following possible formal fallacies:

Two negative premises.

Negative conclusion with no negative premise.

Negative premise with no negative conclusion.

Undistributed middle. A middle term is not distributed in either of the premises it is meant to connect.

Illicit major. The major term, the predicate of the conclusion, is distributed in the conclusion but not in its premise.

Illicit minor. The minor term, the subject of the conclusion, is distributed in the conclusion but not in its premise.

Fallacies of the last three kinds are the most common and important. The argument "All machines work in accordance with causal laws, and all human beings work in accordance with causal laws; therefore all human beings are machines" commits the fallacy of undistributed middle because the middle term, "things that work causally," is undistributed in each of the premises as the predicate of an affirmative proposition. This fallacy is more plausible if the reasoning is expressed hypothetically: "Machines are causally determined, so if human beings were causally determined, they would be mere machines."

The fallacy becomes yet more plausible if the argument is extended to form a sorites: "Machines are causally determined, and they are not morally responsible for what they do; therefore, if human beings were causally determined, they would be no more morally responsible than machines are." The syllogism "All matters of taste are subjective, and no moral judgments are matters of taste; therefore no moral judgments are subjective" contains the fallacy of illicit major, for the term *subjective* is distributed in the conclusion but not in its premise. The fallacy is not obvious here, and it is still less obvious in the sorites "Matters of taste are subjective, but we do not dispute about matters of taste; since we do dispute about moral judgments, they cannot be subjective." However, the fallacy may be easily seen in an argument of the same form on another subject, such as "All birds are egg-layers; no insects are birds; therefore no insects are egg-layers." Similarly, the argument "All Victorian Gothic buildings have nonfunctional features, and they are all ugly; therefore all buildings with nonfunctional features are ugly" is an example of the fallacy of illicit minor, for the term "buildings with nonfunctional features" is distributed in the conclusion but not in its premise.

There are fallacies that consist in the mishandling of complex (conjunctive and disjunctive) terms. These include distortions of the De Morgan rules for terms, corresponding to fallacies noted above. Thus, it is fallacious to argue from "No policy will both defend freedom and insure peace" (*PeDI*, which is equivalent by obversion to *Pa$\overline{DI}$*) to "Every policy both fails to defend freedom and fails to insure peace" (*Pa$\overline{D}\overline{I}$*).

Two traditionally recognized fallacies are the *fallacy of the accident* and the *converse fallacy of the accident*, which is also called the fallacy *a dicto secundum quid ad dictum simpliciter*. The latter consists in going invalidly from a qualified statement to an unqualified one—for example, in arguing from "It is always wrong to take another person's property without his permission" to "It is always wrong to take another person's property." (It is similarly fallacious to go from a statement qualified in one way to a like statement qualified in another way; both

these errors, when they occur in moral reasoning, amount to neglect of the principle that circumstances alter cases.) Considered formally, the converse fallacy of the accident consists in invalidly dropping a conjoined term, in arguing from "All *PQ* are *R*" to "All *P* are *R*." It is always fallacious to drop a conjunct from a distributed term, and we might therefore extend the traditional name to cover all cases of this sort. But what, then, is the fallacy of which this is the converse? Adding a conjunct to a distributed term is generally valid, but it is always a fallacy to add a conjunct to an undistributed term—for example, to argue from "Some snakes are poisonous" to "Some snakes native to Madagascar are poisonous"—and we may give this fallacy the traditional name of the fallacy of the accident. However, supposed examples of this are often really examples of the converse fallacy.

Parallel with the fallacies of dropping a conjunct from a distributed term and adding a conjunct to an undistributed term are the fallacies of dropping a disjunct from an undistributed term (All *P* are *Q* or *R*, therefore all *P* are *Q*) and adding a disjunct to a distributed term (No *P* are *Q*, therefore no *P* are *Q* or *R*).

Relational arguments. We may recognize certain arguments involving relations as being valid on account of some formal feature of these relations, such as symmetry or transitivity. There will then be a kind of fallacy that consists in treating a certain relation as if it had some formal feature that it does not have. Thus, it is fallacious to argue "Even an experienced doctor may be unable to distinguish diphtheria at an early stage from tonsillitis, or tonsillitis from an ulcerated throat; even an experienced doctor, therefore, may be unable to distinguish diphtheria at an early stage from an ulcerated throat," because the relation "is indistinguishable from" is not transitive. This invalid argument is plausible because this nontransitive relation can be confused with the transitive one "is exactly like."

Multiple and nonextensional operators. In multiply quantified statements, the order of two successive universal quantifiers can be changed. Thus, "Every man is always selfish" (which we can symbolize as ΠmΠtSmt—"For every man, for every time, that man is selfish at that time") is equivalent to "At every time all men are selfish" (ΠtΠmSmt). Similarly, "Someone at some time is selfish" (ΣmΣtSmt) is equivalent to "There is a time at which someone is selfish" (ΣtΣmSmt). However, "Every man is sometimes selfish" (ΠmΣtSmt) is not equivalent to "Sometimes every man is selfish" (ΣtΠmSmt—"There is a time such that every man is selfish at that time"); the latter implies the former but not vice versa. It is, therefore, a

fallacy to change the order of successive quantifiers from universal-particular to particular-universal. Aristotle would have been guilty of this fallacy if he had argued directly from "Every activity aims at some good" to "There is a good at which every activity aims."

There are similarly invalid ways of changing the order of successive operators one or both of which are not quantifiers. "It is certain that someone will win" (which may be symbolized as VΣxWx) does not imply "There is someone who is certain to win" (ΣxVWx), although the invalid inference from the first to the second is facilitated by the fact that "Someone is sure to win" is ambiguous between the two. George Berkeley's central argument (in Section 23 of the *Principles of Human Knowledge* and in the first of the *Three Dialogues*) contains an example of this fallacy. He showed, correctly, that a statement which we can formulate as follows is necessarily false: "There is something which someone truly believes not to be thought of" (ΣmΣmBmNTx). However, he thought he had demonstrated the necessary falsity of the different statement "Someone truly believes that there is something which is not thought of" (ΣmBmΣxNTx). Berkeley argued invalidly from the denial of the former statement to the denial of the latter, and so to the conclusion that it is absurd to maintain that material objects exist unconceived.

We should recognize, then, a *fallacy of rearranging operators*. Indeed, we could bring under this heading many fallacious forms of argument. Thus, the fallacies due to distortions of De Morgan's rules noted above consist in reversing the order of negation and conjunction, or of disjunction and negation. The invalid argument from "You are not obliged to resign" to "You are obliged not to resign" reverses the order of the deontic operator and negation; the fallacious "logical" proof of determinism, "Necessarily either you will go or you will stay; so either you will go necessarily or you will stay necessarily," reverses the order of the modal operator and disjunction; and so on.

Some operators set up nonextensional contexts, contexts in which terms or propositions that are extensionally equivalent cannot be validly substituted for one another. Whereas "Mrs. Jones shot the man in her bedroom," together with the fact that the man in her bedroom was her husband, entails "Mrs. Jones shot her husband," "Mrs. Jones intentionally shot the man in her bedroom" does not similarly entail "Mrs. Jones intentionally shot her husband." And even if "*p*" is logically equivalent to "*q*," "Smith believes that *p*" does not entail "Smith believes that *q*." It is still a matter of dispute how such

contexts should be explained and classified, and what kinds of substitution are valid in each sort of context; however, we can recognize, as a further type of fallacy, *extensional substitution in nonextensional contexts.*

INFORMAL FALLACIES. Many informal fallacies are due to ambiguity or vagueness of expressions used to make statements. If the terms used are vague or ambiguous, the expressions in which they are used will be correspondingly vague or ambiguous. However, the whole expression may be vague or ambiguous even if the terms are not, principally because a sentence form may be indeterminate as to the logical form it represents. We may, therefore, distinguish fallacies that arise from the ambiguity or vagueness of expressions in representing logical form from those that arise from other sorts of ambiguity or vagueness. Ambiguity or vagueness is not in itself a fallacy, but it may lead to fallacy. For example, someone may move invalidly from one assertion to another, but not notice that he has made any move at all because he uses the same ambiguous expression for his premise and for his conclusion. Or he may use an ambiguous expression to assert a premise, and thus infer a conclusion that would follow from one possible sense of that expression but does not follow from the sense he intends to assert. Or, having validly inferred a certain conclusion, he may assert a different conclusion, using an expression ambiguous between the validly derived conclusion and the one asserted.

Indeterminacy of expressions. A sentence such as "Men are unwise" may be ambiguous between "All men are unwise" and "Some men are unwise." It suffers from suppressed quantification. Similarly, if someone says "Courage and wisdom go together" (or "always go together," or "are constantly conjoined"), is he saying that all the courageous are wise, that all the wise are courageous, or both of these? Some philosophical terminology is ambiguous in just this way. If we say that one thing is a criterion of another, do we mean that it is a necessary criterion, a sufficient one, or both? Such indeterminacy may facilitate an invalid move from one meaning to the other, and in actual cases we may be unable to decide whether an arguer has committed the formal fallacy of simply converting an A-proposition or the informal fallacy of going from one sense to the other of an ambiguous expression.

Conditional expressions are often similarly indeterminate. "You will succeed if you make an effort" may say what it would be literally taken as saying ($m \supset s$), but with a different emphasis or in a different context it may mean "You will succeed only if you make an effort" ($s \supset m$), or perhaps the conjunction of these two ($s \equiv m$). Disjunctive expressions, while they are commonly used to express a weak disjunction, can be ambiguous between weak and strong disjunction; but logicians have themselves often fallen into a fallacy in supposing that whenever two disjoined terms are mutually exclusive, either necessarily or as a matter of fact, the disjunction is itself a strong (exclusive) disjunction. The truth is that when the disjoined terms are known to exclude one another, it makes no practical difference whether the disjunction itself is weak or strong.

The name of the *fallacy of division* has been given, by some modern writers, to attempts to argue from the premise that something is true of some whole, or of some class considered collectively, to the conclusion that the same is true of the parts of that whole, or of the class considered distributively (that is, of each of its members); and the name of the *fallacy of composition* has been given to arguments in the reverse direction. Either of these fallacies may be covered by an ambiguity of the word *all* between its collective and its distributive sense. This ambiguity of *all* leads us to commit the fallacy of division when we argue, for example, from the fact that all the citizens are strong enough to resist a tyrant (meaning that the citizen body considered as a whole has sufficient strength to do this) to the conclusion that all the citizens are strong enough to resist a tyrant (meaning that every citizen, considered individually, has sufficient strength to do this). We are in this case arguing from the statement made by a sentence in which "all" is used collectively to the statement made by the same sentence when "all" is used distributively. We are committing the fallacy of composition when we argue from the premise that every man can decide how he will act to the conclusion that the human race can decide how it will act (for example, with regard to the rate of increase of population or the choice between war and peace). In this case we move from the distributive to the collective sense of "all" in "All men can decide on their actions." This, or a similar fallacy, is committed whenever we assume, without adequate reason, that we can speak about groups in the same ways in which we can speak about their members, that we can speak of a nation having a will or interests, or of a society having problems. Of course, it may be possible to do this; there may be predicates applicable (in the same sense) to a group and to its members, but this cannot be assumed without evidence. It may also be possible to introduce a different but useful sense in which a predicate normally applied to individuals may be applied to a group; but if so, the new sense must be explained.

However, what Aristotle called the fallacies of division and composition are different from these. He was speaking about changing the ways in which words are combined; for example, from "John is able-to-write while he is not writing" to "John is able to write-while-he-is-not-writing." In all such cases there is an ambiguity that conceals a fallacy of rearranging operators (the former example may be symbolized as Σ*tKMWatNWat*—"At some time both it is possible that John is writing at that time and John is not writing at that time"—and the latter as *MΣtKWatNWat*—"It is possible that at some time both John is writing at that time and John is not writing at that time"). The ambiguity of "All the men pushed, but could not move the stone" is really of this sort; the first clause is symbolized in one sense as Σ*tΠmPmt*—"There is a time such that every man pushed at that time"—and in another sense as Π*mΣtPmt*—"For every man, there is a time such that the man pushed at that time." There need not be any question of ascribing the activity of pushing to a totality of men. In either case there are only individual pushings; but the statement in one sense says that these were simultaneous and in the other sense it does not. This contrast might also be referred to as a distinction between collective and distributive senses. There are, therefore, at least two distinct pairs of fallacies that have been called fallacies of composition and division, but if we speak about collective and distributive senses we tend to run the two pairs together.

Ordinary language seems to lend itself to ambiguities about operator order. Does "You can fool all of the people some of the time" mean that there are times at which the whole populace can be deceived (Σ*tMΠmDmt*—using *M* for "It is possible that" and *Dmt* for "that man is deceived at that time")? Or that every person is occasionally foolable (Π*mΣtMDmt*)? Does "You can fool some of the people all of the time" mean that some people are capable of being permanently deceived (Σ*mMΠtDmt*), or that at every time it is possible to fool some people (Π*tΣmMDmt* or Π*tMΣmDmt*, these two being perhaps equivalent)?

However, in all the cases considered here, and in some of those to be considered in the next subsection, it may be questioned whether we should say simply that the fallacy is due to ambiguity or vagueness. We may fail to distinguish two kinds (or forms) of situations because we use the same expression to describe them, but it could also be that we use the same expression because we commonly fail to distinguish the two things. Informal falla-

cies, as considered here, are due to confusion as much as to ambiguity. We can conveniently explain them in terms of the ambiguity of various expressions, but we should not assume that the linguistic fact of ambiguity (or vagueness) is the sole or the primary cause of these errors.

Ambiguous words and phrases. Ambiguity is extremely common, but it is likely to lead to fallacy only in cases in which the different meanings of a word or phrase are close enough to be confused. One fallacy that can then arise is that of the *ambiguous middle,* that is, an argument may appear to have the form of a syllogism, but the expression we take as standing for a middle term may have different meanings in the two premises. For example, an authority on theology is more likely than other people to be right about theology, and a learned divine is an authority on theology. Does it follow that a learned divine has a better than ordinary chance of being right about theology? Not if the phrase "an authority on theology" means in the second premise an authority on the body of theological assertions but in the first premise means an authority on that which theological assertions are about. In such cases there is really no term common to the two premises, and therefore there is no genuine syllogism. There are also similar fallacies in which an expression is used in different senses in a premise and in the conclusion. Ambiguity often gives rise to these fallacies when the meaning of a word is fixed by its context, and the two different contexts give the word two different meanings. All these are instances of equivocation.

Some words are systematically ambiguous in a troublesome way. An observation may be either what is observed or the observing of it; a perception may be either a perceiving or what is perceived. There are similar indeterminacies about "experience," "sensation," and "belief." Such ambiguities constantly create difficulties in epistemology, the philosophy of science, and philosophical psychology.

There are also forms of speech that tempt us to confuse what we can say about words with what we can say about the corresponding things. A cause necessarily produces an effect, but only in the sense that it would not be called a cause if it did not. Similarly, murder is necessarily wrong, but not in the sense that there is a necessary connection or a rationally discoverable link between the kind of act called murder and its being wrong.

Sometimes when words are not ordinarily ambiguous, we perversely make them so; for example, by giving a word, in addition to its ordinary meaning, another meaning that is borrowed from a cognate word or a similarly formed word. If John Stuart Mill confused "is desirable" (meaning "ought to be desired") with "can be desired," deriving this second sense from the use of "is visible" to mean "can be seen" and "is audible" to mean "can be heard," he was making a mistake of this kind. Similar results are produced by an idiosyncratic use of language. It is hard to keep to a sense specially assigned to a word, and we are always liable to slip back into some more conventional use. When a psychologist has redefined "learning" in relation to some special procedure by which "learning" can be measured, he or his readers may think that what he then discovers is true also about learning in its ordinary, much broader sense.

Such unwarranted generalization, considered formally, exemplifies the fallacy *a dicto secundum quid*; in practice, however, it is aided by various ambiguities and confusions. Thus, the words *class* and *set* may be confined to finite collections or may embrace infinite ones as well. We are liable to argue from the fact that something holds for all finite classes or sets to the conclusion that it holds for all classes or sets, including infinite ones, partly because the words are ambiguous, partly because we fail to notice that the wider concept is a different one, and partly because we generalize from specimen cases and choose specimens that are more easily visualized but are not fully representative.

As we have noted, errors may arise not only from ambiguity as such but also from the confusing of things that, although similar or related, are different. A classic example of this, of great importance in philosophical discussion, is the confusing of separation with distinction. Thus the distinction between analytic and synthetic statements may be attacked, fallaciously, on the ground that actual statements are difficult to assign, without reservations, to one category or the other. Confusion here is due partly to failure to see what sorts of things are being distinguished—not verbal forms, not sentences, but ways of using sentences to make statements.

When this obscurity is removed, however, we may still have to defend the distinction against the critic who says that because of indeterminacies in the use of component words, every concrete use of a sentence in order to make a statement lies somewhere between being analytic and being synthetic. Even if this critic were right, this would in no way count against the distinction. Indeed, such a status makes it particularly important to draw the distinction, in order to expose the common fallacy of arguing from a statement in which words are so used as to make the statement analytically true to a synthetic statement made by the same words in a different sense (as

might be done with the statement "A change in the moral code means social disintegration").

This confusion can also be used in the opposite way. It may be argued that because two things can be distinguished, they must be separate—for example, to argue that since we can distinguish a motive from a cause, things that have causes cannot have motives, or that a person's having a certain motive cannot be a cause of his action.

FALLACIES IN NONDEDUCTIVE REASONING AND IN OBSERVATION

Outside the sphere of deductive reasoning, we can speak of fallacies only in an extended sense. For example, we can contrast genuine confirmation of hypotheses with something that is mistaken for it, probable arguments that give some support to their conclusions with ones that do not, and, in general, techniques and procedures that tend to give correct results with ones that tend to produce error. However, it would be pointless and misleading to call a piece of inductive reasoning, say, fallacious, merely because its conclusion turned out to be false.

INDUCTION AND CONFIRMATION. We may note two fallacies *about* induction or confirmation: the mistaking of confirmation for proof, and the demanding of proof where no more than confirmation is possible. There are also fallacies *in* induction and confirmation. Where scientific or commonsense reasoning follows the lines of one of the eliminative methods of induction, failure to observe the requirements of that method will count as a fallacy. Thus, in reasoning along the lines of the method of agreement, it will be a fallacy to conclude that there is a causal relation between the phenomenon P and a certain feature A, merely because occurrences of P are repeatedly found to be accompanied or preceded by occurrences of A, without trying to discover other possibly relevant features common to these occurrences of P or, what amounts to the same thing, without trying to find occurrences of P that are as relevantly diverse as possible and then seeing whether A is present in them all. Thus, it is fallacious to conclude that William is allergic to strawberries from the evidence that his allergic symptoms have repeatedly appeared after he has eaten strawberries, if William has eaten strawberries only in one particular house, at a particular sort of gathering, and so on.

Similarly, in reasoning along the lines of the method of difference, it will be a fallacy to conclude that A is even an indispensable part of a sufficient condition for P from a comparison of a case in which *P* and *A* are both present and a case where they are both absent, without checking that the two cases are otherwise relevantly alike, that no likely-to-be-relevant feature except *A* differentiates the case in which *P* occurs from the one in which it does not. In other words, it is fallacious to use a control case that differs from the experimental case in some unwanted respect. Thus, it is fallacious to infer that John's having recovered more rapidly than James is due to a drug that was given only to John, if John was also told that he was having a new treatment and the doctors and nurses all took special care of John because they were interested in the experiment. There can be correspondingly unsound experimental procedures, and corresponding errors in reasoning, in applications of the method of concomitant variation.

Post hoc ergo propter hoc is traditionally listed as a fallacy; but much respectable inductive reasoning would fall under this heading, and it is not to be condemned because it is not deductively valid. We argue, reasonably, that the one likely-to-be-relevant change causes the result that follows. We are, in effect, taking the "before" situation as the control case and the "after" situation as the experimental case. This is a fallacy only if we ignore other likely-to-be-relevant changes.

All such mistakes can be summed up as consisting in failures to test the hypothesis in question—that *A* is (in some sense) the cause of *P*—that is, in failure to look for what, if the hypothesis were false, would be most likely to reveal its falsity. If *A* is not the cause of *P*, we are most likely to reveal this by finding cases of *P* so diverse that *A* is not present in them all, or a control case so like the experimental case that *P* occurs in both, or occurs in neither, in spite of *A*'s being present in one and absent from the other.

Another inductive fallacy is to take a hypothesis as being confirmed by observations to which it is irrelevant, when without this hypothesis our other knowledge and beliefs would explain what is observed equally well. Further, since it is a basic principle of inductive reasoning that alternative hypotheses should be considered, and that to confirm one hypothesis we must eliminate its rivals or show them to be improbable, it is a fallacy to take a hypothesis as being confirmed by observations that are equally well confirmed by an intrinsically more probable alternative hypothesis—for example, to take the Michelson-Morley experiment as confirming the theory of relativity without eliminating the FitzGerald-Lorentz contraction and the emission hypothesis of the velocity of light.

We may add a fallacy of saving hypotheses. It is certainly a fault for a thinker to be so attached to a hypothesis that he notices only evidence that agrees with it and ignores or denies unfavorable evidence. Popular superstitions of all kinds are protected by this fallacy, but it is also common among scientists, historians, and philosophers. It may also be a mistake, when one finds evidence that is prima facie unfavorable, to introduce supplementary ad hoc hypotheses in order to protect the original one from falsification. Carried to an extreme, this procedure constitutes a linguistic change that makes the original hypothesis analytically true, and it can generate the fallacy described above of oscillating between an analytic and a synthetic use of the same expression. In less extreme cases, how can we systematically mark off this error from the respectable procedure of interpreting new observations in the light of an established theory? Perhaps in two ways: first, in the respectable procedure, we are working with a hypothesis that is already well confirmed, but it is a fallacy to "save" a hypothesis for which there is no strong independent support; and second, even if the original hypothesis was well confirmed, it may be appropriate to consider, after it has been "saved" by additional hypotheses (after the new observations have been interpreted in the light of the original hypothesis) or has been modified and qualified in various ways, whether some alternative hypothesis would account better for the whole body of evidence.

ANALOGY. All arguments from analogy are fallacious in the sense that they are not deductively valid. However, we often want further to distinguish weak analogies from strong ones and to suggest that a weak analogy is completely fallacious but that a strong analogy has at least some force. In an analogy we compare two things, *A* and *B*; we find some resemblances, say *X*, *Y*, *Z*, between them; and then we argue that since *A* has some further feature *P*, it is likely that *B* also has this feature. We are inclined to say that if the points of resemblance *X*, *Y*, *Z* are few or trivial, the analogy is weak or far-fetched, but that it is a strong analogy if there are many important points of resemblance. An alternative way of looking at the distinction is that to use this analogy is implicitly to frame and then use the hypothesis that all things that have the features *X*, *Y*, *Z* also have the feature *P*. The analogy will be weak if we already have evidence that falsifies this hypothesis or makes it implausible, but it will be strong if we have no such evidence and what we know about *A* somehow constitutes good inductive evidence for a connection between *X*, *Y*, *Z*, and *P*.

CLASSIFICATION. Faults in classification can in several ways give rise to fallacies in either the strict or the extended sense. If things are classified under headings where they simply do not belong, the classification implicitly asserts false propositions which may be used as premises in arguments that, even if formally valid, will therefore give no real support to their conclusions. If a classification is based on unimportant resemblances, this may give rise to weak analogies and to the framing of unlikely hypotheses, and inductive reasoning that uses such a classification—in the methods of agreement and difference, for example—will give an appearance of support to conclusions that are not really supported by the evidence as a whole. Again, if the division of a class into subclasses is not exhaustive, it may be wrongly taken to be so, and this will provide a false premise for a disjunctive argument. Thus, if we divide trees into conifers and deciduous trees, we may infer that since eucalypts are not conifers, they are deciduous. Similarly, a division that is not exclusive may be wrongly taken to be so; the same division of the class "trees" may lead us to infer that larches, being conifers, are not deciduous.

Two important fallacies concerned with classification arise from the attempt to draw sharp distinctions where the facts show a continuous (or near continuous) gradation. Is a man bald if he has one hair on his head? or two? or three? And so on. Just what degree of mental disorder is to count as insanity? One fallacy consists in assimilating every intermediate case to one or the other of the extremes and is exemplified in the black-and-white thinking that divides people into normal individuals and lunatics or states into peace-loving nations and warmongers. The contrary, and more subtle, fallacy consists in arguing that because there is no break in the gradations, there is no distinction even between the extremes—concluding, for example, that we are all insane—as if the problem about when a man is bald showed that there is no difference between a man with a completely smooth scalp and one with a full head of hair.

STATISTICS. We can deal here only with some elementary mistakes in statistical reasoning. One of these consists in paying attention to simple frequencies or proportions rather than to correlations. If a high proportion of atheists are honest, this in itself does not indicate any sort of causal connection between atheism and honesty; the first thing to discover is whether the proportion of honest people is higher among atheists than among nonatheists. Similarly, the frequency of persons who have both mathematical ability and artistic talent may be small in the population as a whole; but if only one person in ten

has mathematical ability and only one in ten has artistic talent, then only one in a hundred would have both, even if there were no natural opposition between these gifts. Before we conclude that these abilities tend to occur separately, we must find whether artistic talent is more or less common among the mathematically able than among the rest of the population.

Another common statistical fallacy consists in directly inferring a causal connection from a positive correlation: given a positive correlation between cigarette smoking and lung cancer, it is a further question whether this is to be explained by a causal connection between them. An associated fallacy of confusion, which is becoming more common, is simply not to talk about causation but to use the word *correlation* as if it meant causal connection, for example, to infer predictions and practical recommendations directly from correlation statements. Another fallacy is the neglect of the requirements of significance. Essentially, this consists in taking as causally informative, or as representative of a similar correlation in a larger population, a correlation within a sample that could equally well be explained as a chance result. This is, therefore, an instance of the neglect of alternative hypotheses.

Even when there is good statistical evidence for a causal connection between two features A and B, it is a mistake to conclude immediately that one, say A, is the cause of the other without having considered and excluded the possibilities that B may tend to produce A, that A and B may be joint effects of some other cause, and that there may be causation in more than one direction. For example, a positive correlation between poverty and ill health might be due to the fact that poverty causes ill health, to the fact that ill health diminishes earning capacity and wastes resources, to the fact that stupidity, idleness, or drunkenness tends to produce both poverty and ill health, or to a combination of more than one of these causal tendencies.

PROBABILITY. Fallacies in reasoning about probability arise mainly from failure to attend to the fact that a probability is relative to certain evidence and changes as the evidence changes. The best-known is the gambler's fallacy. For example, since it is unlikely that a penny will fall heads up five times in a row, the gambler reasons, when it has fallen heads four times, that it is unlikely to fall heads at the next throw. But although the probability of five heads, relative to the knowledge that an unbiased penny is tossed in a random manner five times, is 1/32, the probability of this result, relative to the conjunction of this knowledge with the knowledge that it has fallen heads on the first four throws, is 1/2.

OBSERVATION. It is questionable whether we should follow Mill and speak of fallacies of observation. Many of the items so described consist of errors in reasoning rather than in observation, and so fall under other headings. We may, however, note the following principles:

First, there are errors of nonobservation, which may be due to deficiency of one's senses or sense apparatus, to carelessness, or to the tendency to see only what we want to see. This may include the nonobservation that is one way of saving hypotheses.

Second, any of the above-mentioned causes may equally produce misobservation.

Third, it is impossible to separate, and difficult even to distinguish, observation from interpretation: we always have some conceptual framework, some expectations that determine how we shall observe what we observe. For example, we expect an object that looks like an adult human being to be between five and six feet tall, and we therefore tend to see any such object as being at a distance that would agree with this. The actual material to which our prior concepts are applied may not conform to them, however, and then we may make wrong judgments through using these concepts. Also, if we do not realize how observation and interpretation are mixed together, we may give the authority of an observed fact to a judgment that really rests on our preconceptions.

Fourth, our perceptual mechanisms automatically allow for factors that have been constant or to which it is inconvenient to attend, and errors arise when allowances are made for what is no longer there; for example, the illusion that the land is moving when we first go ashore after becoming used to the rolling of a ship.

Fifth, we may in perception confuse relations, say of comparison, with intrinsic qualities. This explains the illusions of contrast. For example, if after having had one's left hand in cold water and one's right hand in hot water, one puts both hands into lukewarm water, the lukewarm water feels hot to the left hand and cold to the right hand because it really is *hotter than* the left hand (or than what it has just been feeling) and *colder than* the right hand (or than what it has just been feeling).

Sixth, we may mislocate what we observe. In particular, we have a tendency to project and to treat as objective, as belonging to some external state of affairs, the feeling that the state of affairs arouses in us (the *pathetic fallacy*) or to mistake connections within our thoughts for connections between the corresponding objects. There is no room here for a full discussion of perceptual illusion and observational error, but it seems that many varieties of these can be explained by reference to one or more of these principles.

FALLACIES IN DISCOURSE

INCONSISTENCY. A position or a system of thought cannot be sound if it contains incompatible statements or beliefs, and it is one of the commonest objections to what an opponent says that he is trying to have it both ways. Inconsistency has many possible sources, but one that is of special importance in philosophy is the case in which a thinker, in order to solve one problem or deal with a particular difficulty, denies or qualifies a principle he has previously adopted, although in other contexts he adheres to the principle and uses it without qualification.

Inconsistency is a formal feature and can be formally checked, although it may also be concealed by the use of different expressions with a single meaning. It is not the same as invalidity, however; indeed, any argument with incompatible (or self-contradictory) premises will be formally valid. It is particularly important to detect inconsistencies in a set of premises, for an argument with inconsistent premises, even though valid, gives no support to its conclusion; and using one is not a satisfactory way of establishing anything or of convincing an audience.

On the other hand, it is a formal fallacy to suppose that because your opponent has tried to have it both ways, he cannot have it either way—that every part of an inconsistent position must be false.

PETITIO PRINCIPII. An argument that begs the question, that uses the conclusion as one of the premises, is always formally valid. A conclusion cannot fail to follow from a set of premises that includes it. This is also a fallacy only in the extended sense that such an argument gives no support to its conclusion. One kind of petitio principii consists in arguing in a circle, when one proposition is defended by reference to another, and the second is defended by reference to the first. For example, we may argue that a certain historian is trustworthy because he gives a balanced account of some episode, but also rely on that historian's account in order to decide what actually occurred in this episode, and hence to decide what would be a balanced account of it.

The larger and more complex a circle of argument is, the harder it is to detect the fallacy. One result of circularity is that the propositions that have been proved from one another appear to have been conclusively established, although no empirical evidence has been given for either of them. This can create an illusion that there are synthetic propositions that have no need of empirical support. This may be combined with a fallacy of confusion, of failing to distinguish the coherence or consequential character of a system from its truth—a confusion that has developed into the coherence theory of truth and that is still encouraged by some eccentric uses of the word *true* or of such a phrase as "true within the system."

Circularity is common in moral reasoning, and here, too, it may make us think that moral conclusions can be rationally established without reliance on observations, intuitions, choices, or decisions. The exposure of such circularity compels us to give a more adequate account both of how moral judgments are to be supported and of how they are to be interpreted.

A PRIORI FALLACIES. Under the heading of a priori fallacies Mill listed a number of natural prejudices, including the popular superstition that words have a magical power and such philosophical dogmas as that what is true of our ideas of things must be true of the things themselves; that differences in nature must correspond to our received (linguistic) distinctions; that whatever is, is rationally explicable; that there is no action at a distance; that every phenomenon has a single cause; and that effects must resemble their causes. These are all errors, but we can go further and recognize a general a priorist fallacy, which consists in trying to base knowledge of fundamental synthetic truths on anything other than empirical evidence. These examples illustrate how once we start looking for a priori truths, we are led to try to distill them from language or from our ideas (giving each of these an authority to which it is not entitled), or to confuse continuity with intelligibility and necessity, or to dignify with the title of a priori truths what are no more than sweeping generalizations from the simplest and most familiar observations.

More generally still, we can recognize a fallacy of prejudice, which consists in believing without evidence, in adopting or adhering to views on any subject without any relevant reason. It is worth noting that adopting a method of argument (other than a deductively valid form) is tantamount to adopting an assertion. For example, regularly to judge the rightness of actions by their utility is tantamount to adopting the principle that whatever maximizes utility is right; and, again, regularly to argue that because a statement cannot be verified, it is meaningless is tantamount to adopting a verifiability the-

ory of meaning. This is a particularly easy way of committing the fallacy of prejudice.

IGNORATIO ELENCHI. The fallacy of ignoratio elenchi consists in missing the point, in arguing for something other than what is to be proved. However, we can speak in this way only if the context somehow determines what is to be proved. In the first place, the context may be a discussion between A and B, and B will commit this fallacy if he claims to be replying to what A has said but fails to come to grips with A's argument—for example, if he tries to disprove some proposition that A has not asserted either as a premise or as a conclusion. B is also guilty of this fallacy if he bluntly denies something that A has claimed to prove but does nothing to rebut A's proof. Alternatively, it may be a thinker's general position or some long line of argument that makes it imperative for him to establish some point, and makes him guilty of irrelevance if he establishes something else instead.

There are a number of common and important types of irrelevance in discussion. If the question is whether a certain view is true or false, it is irrelevant to argue that adopting this view will be beneficial or pernicious. Thus, a body of religious doctrine may be irrelevantly defended on the ground that it makes people happier or better behaved. Similarly, the origin of a belief is in general irrelevant to the question of its truth; but if the fact that a belief is widely held has been used as evidence of its truth, then this reasoning may be relevantly rebutted by showing that the belief has come to be held for reasons or from causes that are independent of its truth. The truth of the belief and the account of its origin are in this case alternative explanatory hypotheses. That a view is held by certain people is also in general irrelevant to its truth, so that appeals to authority are usually examples of ignoratio elenchi. Cases in which the authority appealed to can be independently shown to be an authority in the sense of being likely to be well-informed about the point at issue are exceptions. Irrelevancy shades into prejudice; we may readily accept the doctrines of "our party" and reject those of "the enemy." In this, there may also be present a fallacy of confusion, in that we treat factual beliefs as if they were items of another category—principles to which we can adhere or subscribe, or which we can reject, by choice.

Another form of irrelevance is the tu quoque, or "two wrongs" technique. If some action or view of one's own is criticized, one may reply by attacking some action or view of one's critic that is equally hard to defend. The *argumentum ad hominem* is similar—we reject what someone says on the irrelevant ground that he is in no position to say it. However, an *argumentum ad hominem* may quite properly point to an inconsistency, and may validly establish the limited conclusion that this man cannot consistently hold this view—a conclusion that may be of special interest in a moral discussion, where the problem may well be that of finding a policy that is both coherent and acceptable.

Related fallacies of irrelevance have been named *argumentum ad verecundiam* (appeal to authority or to feelings of reverence or respect), *argumentum ad personam* (appeal to personal interest), and *argumentum ad populum* (appeal to popular prejudice). Sometimes an *argumentum ad ignorantiam* or *ad auditores* is grouped with these, but these names seem to refer not to any specific fallacy but to the use of any unsound argument that is likely to deceive the actual audience.

FALLACIES OF INTERROGATION. There are two forms of the *fallacy of many questions*. In one, two or more questions are asked together, and a single answer is demanded to all of them. This is fallacious in that it unfairly prevents the person asked from giving different answers to the different questions. In the second form, the question asked has a presupposition that the answerer may wish to deny but which he would be accepting if he gave anything that would count as an answer. Thus, an answer of either "Yes" or "No" to the question "Have you left the party?" would be an admission of having been a party member, and any answer to the question "Why does such-and-such happen?" presupposes that such-and-such does happen. There is no fallacy, however, in merely asking a question that has a presupposition; the fallacy lies in demanding an answer in the narrow sense, in not permitting or in discouraging a reply that denies the presupposition. Again, it is an instance of the fallacy of prejudice to ask a question that has a presupposition without first investigating whether that presupposition is correct.

FALLACIES IN EXPLANATION AND DEFINITION. Just as a circular argument fails to give support, so a circular explanation fails to explain. There are concealed circularities of explanation; for example, some mental performance is explained by reference to a faculty, but further inquiry shows either that to say that this faculty exists is only to say that such performances occur or that, although more may be meant, there is, apart from such performances, no evidence for the existence of the faculty. Words like "tendency," "power," "disposition," and "capacity" lend themselves to circularities of this sort.

Similarly, a circular definition, in which the term to be defined recurs within the definiens, fails in its task. If it is intended as a stipulative definition, it fails to assign a meaning; and if it is intended as a reportive definition, it fails to inform anyone of the meaning with which the word is used.

Stipulative definitions can create ambiguity when we assign one meaning to a word but also retain another meaning. This amounts to an assertion that the two meanings go together, disguised as the innocent procedure of stipulation. Persuasive definition is an instance of this in which the retained meaning is an emotive one.

It is a fallacy, in the extended sense, to use words without meaning. But it is not a fallacy not to have defined one's terms, provided that they have a meaning that is known to the audience and is precise enough for the purpose in hand. On the contrary, since it is impossible to define all one's terms, it is a fallacy in discourse to demand that in all terms should be defined; a demand for definition can be a sophistic device for preventing the discussion of substantive issues.

PHILOSOPHICAL FALLACIES

THE NATURALISTIC FALLACY. What G. E. Moore called the *naturalistic fallacy* is the identifying of goodness with any natural characteristic, such as pleasantness or being the object of desire. If there is a distinct property, goodness, it will of course be an error to identify it with any other feature, even if the two are coextensive, and this would be an example of the refusal to distinguish what we cannot separate; however, it must first be shown that there is such a property as Moore's goodness. Alternatively, if it is a question of how the word *good* is commonly used, then it would be an error to say that it is used to convey some natural description. However, if the naturalist is not trying to report the ordinary use, but is saying that this ordinary use is somehow unsatisfactory (and also that there is no such property as the one of which Moore speaks) and is therefore proposing a different use, where is his mistake? It is true that if he redefines "good" as the name of some natural characteristic, but still also uses the word in its ordinary evaluative or prescriptive sense, he will be slipping into a fallacy of ambiguity; but a consistent ethical naturalist may be committing no fallacy at all.

ARGUING FROM "IS" TO "OUGHT." An error exposed by David Hume, but still frequently committed, is that of arguing from premises that contain only descriptive terms, and no copula except "is," to a conclusion that contains an "ought." This is a fallacy in the strict sense; arguments of this sort cannot be valid, but they are often made plausible by the ambiguous use of such words as *reasonable, fitting, authority, desirable, beneficial, courageous, temperate, just, right,* and *good* itself, any one of which may be used first in a purely descriptive sense and then interpreted in a sense that is partly descriptive and partly prescriptive. A currently popular version of this fallacy combines it with one or more of the a priori fallacies. Since our concept of, say, courage or our ordinary use of the word *courage* combines a certain natural description with a certain prescription or evaluation, it is concluded that behavior that conforms to this natural description must be recommended or valued in just this way; that is, the move from *is* to *ought* is covered by an appeal to the supposed authority of our language or our ideas.

CONFUSING RELATIONS WITH THINGS OR QUALITIES.

A group of philosophical errors that is less well known than the two just mentioned but at least as widespread and harmful consists in identifying a quality with a relation, in treating a relation as if it were an intrinsic quality of one of its terms, or in constructing fictitious entities out of relational situations. Presented linguistically, this means that a term is treated as standing both for a thing or a quality and for a relation, and this, like other ambiguities, can make synthetic connections appear necessary. Thus, an idea or a sense datum is supposed to be an object of which someone can be aware and to have this relation—someone's being aware of it—as part of its nature. This conflation generates a supposed matter of fact about which one can have infallible knowledge and thus gives rise to the pseudo problem of bridging the gap between this direct and infallible knowledge and ordinary fallible knowledge of objects that do not have being known built into their natures. Similarly, minds (or consciousness) have been treated as things that have as part of their nature the relation of being aware of something, and this generates difficulties in philosophical psychology. Also, errors that the naturalistic fallacy was meant to cover are better dealt with in this category. Goodness may be both treated as an intrinsic quality (natural or nonnatural) of, say, states of affairs and identified with or taken as logically including the relation of being pursued, aimed at, or recommended; indeed, it seems that it is just such a conflation of features that makes a quality nonnatural. Similarly, beauty may be both treated as an intrinsic quality and identified with or taken as logically including such relations as pleasing or being admired.

CATEGORY MISTAKES.

Philosophers now carefully distinguish different uses of language, different "language games"; the contrasting error is to confuse different ways of using words, to treat a term that belongs to one category as if it belonged to another. However, the concept of a *use* of language is itself ambiguous. In distinguishing uses, we may be noting differences that lie within language, differences in the relations between words and things, differences in the things to which our expressions apply; and it will be a mistake to confuse one kind of distinction with another. There is also a tendency to think that, at least in philosophy, we cannot employ this distinction between words and things; this view is supported by a variant of Berkeley's fallacy: Since we cannot talk about something except by using words in relation to it, it is supposed that we cannot talk about things as they are, apart from relations to words.

AVOIDANCE AND DETECTION OF FALLACIES

Popular discussions of fallacies rightly lay great stress on the psychological or emotional aspect of fallacious arguments. Under the influence of violent passions, thinking becomes more purely associative and less consequential, and we are more than usually ready not only to employ arguments, however unsound, that appear to support whatever cause we espouse but also to extend our favor to anything linked, however loosely, with what we already like, respect, or admire, and to extend our hostility to anything linked with what we already dislike, despise, or fear. Ridicule can also be used to brush aside relevant considerations and to condemn a person or a view without a hearing. All sorts of attachments, passions, and emotional prejudices can foster fallacies, and one of the chief means for the avoidance or detection of fallacies is to consider a problem calmly.

Precise formal statement often helps in the detection not only of fallacies in the strict sense but also of inconsistency, circularity, and irrelevance. However, since it is too laborious a task to state all our reasonings formally, we can use this device only when we already have reason to suspect a fallacy. Also, in cases involving equivocation or a category mistake, there is a danger that inaccurate formulation will conceal the fallacy instead of exposing it.

As Richard Whately remarked, "a very *long* discussion is one of the most effective veils of Fallacy; … a Fallacy which when stated barely … would not deceive a child, may deceive half the world if *diluted* in a quarto volume" (*Elements of Logic*, p. 151). Consequently, an important weapon against fallacy is condensation, extracting the substance of an argument from a mass of verbiage. But this device too has its dangers; it may produce oversimplification, that is, the fallacy *a dicto secundum quid*, of dropping relevant qualifications. When we suspect a fallacy, our aim must be to discover exactly what the argument is; and in general the way to do this is first to pick out its main outlines and then to take into account any relevant subtleties or qualifications.

See also Aristotle; Bentham, Jeremy; Berkeley, George; Conditionals; Definition; Hume, David; Induction; Logical Terms, Glossary of; Mill, John Stuart; Mill's Methods of Induction; Moore, George Edward; Probability; Truth and Falsity in Indian Philosophy; Whately, Richard.

Bibliography

The pioneer work on fallacies is the *De Sophisticis Elenchis* of Aristotle. Medieval and later logicians followed and expanded his account. Many textbooks on logic include a chapter on fallacies. Jeremy Bentham, throughout his writings, paid much attention to fallacious reasonings by which views that he opposed were supported, and he collected many of them in *The Book of Fallacies,* which is in Vol. II of his *Works,* edited by J. Bowring (Edinburgh, 1843). Richard Whately, in Ch. 3 of his *Elements of Logic* (London, 1826), gave a much improved classification and analysis of fallacies. John Stuart Mill devoted Book V of *A System of Logic* (London, 1843) to an account of fallacies, developing a new classification and concentrating on a priori fallacies (prejudices) and mistakes in observation and generalization.

Augustus De Morgan, in Ch. 13 of *Formal Logic* (London, 1847), rejected the attempt to list all possible ways of going wrong but gave a penetrating and well-illustrated analysis of many of the traditionally listed fallacies. Arthur Schopenhauer, in "The Art of Controversy," in *Essays from the Parerga and Paralipomena,* translated by T. B. Saunders (London, 1951), described stratagems that may be used in disputes, that is, both sophistic devices and ways of countering them. H. W. B. Joseph included in *An Introduction to Logic* (London, 1906) an appendix on fallacies based on the Aristotelian account.

M. R. Cohen and Ernest Nagel, in Ch. 19 of *An Introduction to Logic and Scientific Method* (New York, 1934), emphasized abuses of scientific method. R. H. Thouless in *Straight and Crooked Thinking* (London, 1930), Susan Stebbing in *Thinking to Some Purpose* (Harmondsworth, U.K., 1939), and W. W. Fearnside and W. B. Holther in *Fallacy—The Counterfeit of Argument* (Englewood Cliffs, NJ, 1959), gave lively and readable accounts, illustrated with many examples of popular errors and of sophistry in practice, concentrating on political and social debate and propaganda, and stressing the emotional basis of a great deal of fallacy.

J. L. Mackie (1967)

FARABI, AL

See *al-Fārābī*

FARADAY, MICHAEL
(1791–1867)

Michael Faraday, the British chemist and physicist, came from a poor family and had no formal schooling beyond the elementary level. While a bookbinder's apprentice, he became interested in chemistry and electricity. Faraday took notes on a series of lectures given by Sir Humphry Davy, the leading British chemist, presented them to Davy, and soon afterward, at the age of twenty-one, was appointed laboratory assistant to Davy at the Royal Institution (London). He became director of the laboratory in 1825 and Fullerian professor of chemistry at the institution in 1833. His early scientific work in chemistry included the discovery of several new compounds and the liquefaction of chlorine and other gases. In 1831, Faraday discovered electromagnetic induction, or the creation of electric currents in a conductor by changing currents or moving magnets in the vicinity; this phenomenon is the basis of the electrical generator. This was followed by a series of investigations demonstrating with greater certainty than had been previously achieved the identity of the nature of the electricity generated by friction, voltaic cells, electromagnetic induction, and other means. Extensive experiments in electrochemistry led Faraday to the enunciation of his laws of electrolytic decomposition in 1833. The source of the power of the voltaic pile, or battery, was the object of his subsequent research. He investigated the electrical properties of insulators, or dielectrics, in 1837. In 1845 he discovered that the plane of polarization of light was rotated on passing through a transparent diamagnetic substance in the direction of externally applied lines of magnetic force. At the same time he began his investigation of diamagnetism. In his last years he suffered from loss of memory, and he ceased his researches in 1855. He was a member of a small Christian sect, the Sandemanians, and was noted for his gentleness of character.

Faraday is generally regarded as one of the greatest of all experimental scientists. The truth of this, adequately attested to in the three-thousand-odd paragraphs of the *Experimental Researches in Electricity,* should not be allowed to obscure the fertility of his imagination and conceptualizing powers and the guiding role of theoretical principles in sustaining his persistent research. His most important contribution to physics is probably the concept of lines of force, which was the beginning of the development of field theory. The accepted approach to electrodynamical phenomena at the time was to express the forces between charges mathematically as direct actions at a distance, an approach that was to prove unfruitful. Faraday was not trained in the mathematics necessary for this tradition. In order to represent the action of electromagnetic induction, he envisaged the space surrounding magnets to be filled with lines of magnetic force representing everywhere the direction of the force that would be experienced by a magnetic pole introduced from outside in the manner of the lines formed by iron filings sprinkled on a paper resting on a magnet. The lines of magnetic force have not only direction but also sense—that is, a north magnetic pole is pushed one way along them, and a south pole is pushed in the opposite sense; furthermore, their concentration near a given point represents the intensity of the magnetic force at that point. Each such line forms a closed loop, beginning or ending nowhere, but in the case of a magnet passing through its substance from one pole to the other. In these terms the law of electromagnetic induction may be expressed: "The quantity of electricity thrown into a current is directly as the amount of curves intersected" (*Experimental Researches in Electricity*). In James Clerk Maxwell's famous words:

> Faraday, in his mind's eye, saw lines of force traversing all space where the mathematicians saw centres of force attracting at a distance: Faraday saw a medium where they saw nothing but distance: Faraday sought the seat of the phenomena in real actions going on in the medium, they were satisfied that they had found it in a power of action at a distance impressed on the electric fluids. (Preface to the first edition of the *Treatise on Electricity and Magnetism*)

In most of Faraday's researches the concept of lines of force was used merely as a "representative aid" and was not meant to include "any idea of the nature of the physical cause of the phenomena." This cautiousness was a mark of Faraday's methods; in the choice of terminology to describe new phenomena, for example, he carefully attempted to avoid suggesting anything more than they warranted. However, at times Faraday allowed himself to speculate, and in 1852 he considered "the possible and probable *physical existence* of such lines" ("On the Physical Lines of Magnetic Force"). On the basis of arguments that can be characterized only as suggestive (such as that the magnetic lines are curved), he hypothesized that magnetic lines of force have physical existence and contrasted this with gravitation, where there was no evidence that the lines of force are anything but abstract and ideal. In a charming talk published in 1846 ("Thoughts on Ray-Vibrations") Faraday speculated that the atoms of matter might be simply point centers of force, as Roger Joseph Boscovich had suggested in the eighteenth century, or, in Faraday's terms, points from which lines of force spread into space. The extension of the atom may be identified with the extent of these lines, so that each atom would occupy all space and atoms would be mutually penetrable. Light might consist of vibrations in these lines, possibly obviating the need for an ethereal medium for its propagation; on the other hand, he suggested elsewhere that the lines might represent a condition of the ether, "for it is not at all unlikely that, if there be an ether, it should have other uses than simply the conveyance of radiations."

Faraday's geometric-intuitive representation was in particular rejected by the Continental electrodynamicists, and in 1846 Wilhelm Weber developed a theory of forces acting directly at a distance between charges that included the phenomena of electromagnetic induction. The validity of the lines of force concept was vindicated by the theoretical researches of William Thomson and particularly of Maxwell, who regarded his task to be putting Faraday's ideas into mathematical notation. It was with this motive that Maxwell developed his electromagnetic field theory, which, reinterpreted in quantum terms, remains the accepted theory of electromagnetic action and which was the prototype of all the field theories that dominate physics today. Maxwell's early representation of the lines of magnetic force as vortexes in the ether spinning about these lines as axes was in part suggested by Faraday's discovery of the magnetic rotation of the plane of polarization of light. The existence of this magnetic effect upon light had confirmed others in their speculations that light was some sort of propagated electromagnetic phenomenon, and the rotation of the plane of polarization suggested to Thomson and Maxwell that magnetism was in some way a rotatory effect, or, in contemporary terminology, the magnetic field is a pseudovector field.

Faraday was one among many who gave adumbrations of the generalized principle of conservation of energy, the clear expression of which is credited to Julius Mayer, James Joule, and Hermann von Helmholtz. His convictions regarding the interconvertibility of forces led him, from Hans Christian Ørsted's generation of magnetism by an electric current, to seek that generation of a current from magnetism that he found. In a lecture of 1834, Faraday spoke explicitly of this mutual convertibility, but he did not proceed further to specify how he conceived of the "forces" or "powers" that might be conserved or to discover quantitative relations. In connection with his investigations in 1840 of the source of the action of the voltaic pile he cited this principle against the contact theory, according to which the mere contact of two metals was the source of the current so that there would be a "creation of power" out of nothing, and in favor of the chemical theory, which found the source in the chemical actions occurring in the pile.

See also Boscovich, Roger Joseph; Chemistry, Philosophy of; Dynamism; Energy; Helmholtz, Hermann Ludwig von; Maxwell, James Clerk.

Bibliography

Faraday's work in electricity, including electrochemistry, is to be found in his *Experimental Researches in Electricity,* 3 vols. (London: R. and J. E. Taylor, 1839, 1844, 1855); his chemical work is collected in *Experimental Researches in Chemistry and Physics* (London: R. Taylor and W. Francis, 1859). Of particular interest are the speculative papers "Thoughts on Ray-Vibrations," in *Philosophical Magazine* 28 (1846): 345–350, reprinted in the *Experimental Researches in Electricity,* Vol. III, pp. 447–452, and "On the Physical Lines of Magnetic Force," in *Royal Institution Proceedings* June 11, 1852, reprinted in *Experimental Researches,* pp. 438–443. The standard biography is H. Bence-Jones, *The Life and Letters of Faraday,* 2 vols. (London: Longmans, Green, 1870). See also L. P. Williams, *Michael Faraday* (New York: Basic, 1965). A brief and lucid treatment of the development of his researches is given by John Tyndall in *Faraday as a Discoverer* (London: Longmans, Green, 1868).

Arthur E. Woodruff (1967)

FARIAS BRITO, RAIMUNDO DE
(1862–1917)

Raimundo de Farias Brito was the philosophic forerunner of Brazilian modernism. A profound sense of crisis underlies the work of Farias Brito. Individual existence is a precarious struggle against despair and death, and social order is threatened by moral disintegration and anarchy. Knowledge of man's role in his world is necessary to confront this crisis. Intellectual pursuit of the truth is the primary ethical obligation. Lacking certainty, man establishes a relative morality through conviction, involving both philosophy and religion. Metaphysics attempts to embrace the truth theoretically through formulation of worldviews; religion embraces the truth practically through acceptance and appropriation of a given worldview. This free acceptance of common convictions creates community, informing and giving thrust to the total culture of which it serves as a focus. The theoretical task is a permanent activity of the human spirit; the practical task, a permanent necessity. Convinced that modern philosophy was not adequate to its task, largely because of its predominantly skeptical mood grounded in phenomenalism, Farias Brito hoped to establish a new dogmatism capable of providing convictions that could give both courage for withstanding suffering and despair and the bases for reestablishing social order and direction. There was a transition in his thought from an early attempt to provide grounds for a naturalistic religion, inspired by German monism, to the articulation of his philosophy of spirit, influenced by French spiritualism. The naturalism is expressed in an incomplete series of volumes titled *A finalidade do mundo* (1895–1905). The new series, *Filosofia do espírito* (1912–1914), was initiated after Farias Brito had moved to Rio de Janeiro in 1909 to accept the chair in logic at Colégio Pedro II.

The spirit, "a live principle of action, capable of modifying … the order of nature; … of dominating itself; … of exercising dominion over things" is the "foundation of all reality and the basis of all experience." Psychological data are therefore indispensable to the metaphysician. Physiological psychology deals solely with the physical base of spirit; psychology proper ought to be concerned with subjective psychic phenomena. Its method is introspective, direct introspection supplemented by indirect introspection, a study of the manifestations of consciousness through which men achieve expression and communication. "Transcendent psychology" is the method employed for utilizing psychological data in metaphysics. From the felt fact of human existence, it is possible to rise to the level of transcendence, seeking knowledge concerning essence. The introspective operation of the individual consciousness reveals two facets of experience—consciousness itself and that which is presented to consciousness; both constitute existential reality. Through abstraction and analysis of each, pure consciousness is seen to have priority. Understanding man as essentially conscious spirit, the method of "transcendent psychology," leads to the postulation of divine spirit.

See also Introspection; Latin American Philosophy; Logic, History of; Naturalism.

Bibliography
Other works by Farias Brito are *Verdade como regra das acões* (Truth as the rule of action; Rio de Janeiro, 1905), *Base física do espírito* (Physical base of truth; Rio de Janeiro, 1912), and *Mundo interior* (Inner world; Rio de Janeiro, 1912).
For a study on Farias Brito, see Fred Gillette Sturm, "Farias Brito: Brasilian Philosopher of the Spirit," in *Revista interamericana de bibliografía* 13 (1963): 176–204.

Fred Gillette Sturm (1967)

FASCISM

"Fascism" was the ideology of the movement that, under the leadership of Benito Mussolini, seized power in Italy in 1922 and held power until the Allied invasion of Italy in World War II. Mussolini was a socialist until 1915, and fascism is a paradoxical but potent mixture of extreme socialist, or syndicalist, notions with a Hegelian or idealist theory of the state.

An attempt to provide fascism with a fully articulated theory was made by an Italian neo-Hegelian philosopher of some distinction, Giovanni Gentile, who was converted to fascism after Mussolini's coup. But as a former liberal and collaborator of Benedetto Croce, Gentile was opposed by the anti-intellectual wing of the Fascist Party, and his draft for a manifesto of fascist ideology was rewritten by Mussolini himself and published in 1932 in the *Enciclopedia italiana* as *La dottrina del fascismo*. However, no adequate conception of fascism could be derived from these theoretical sources alone; the actual behavior of the Italian fascists during their twenty years of power must also be taken into account.

The word *fascism* is often used, especially by left-wing writers, not only for the Italian doctrine but also for the similar, if more fanatic, national socialism of Adolf Hitler and for the altogether less coherent ideologies of Francisco Franco, Juan Perón, Ion Antonescu, and other such dictators. But however justifiable the wider and looser use of the word, the present article is confined to the system and ideology that called itself *Fascismo* and that flourished in Italy under Mussolini.

Gentile in his two books *Che cosa è il fascismo* (1925) and *Origini e dottrina del fascismo* (1929) stressed, as one might expect, the Hegelian elements in fascism. He argued that fascism was essentially idealistic and spiritual. Whereas liberalism, socialism, democracy, and the other progressive movements of the nineteenth century had asserted the rights of man, the selfish claims of the individual, fascism sought, instead, to uphold the moral integrity and higher collective purpose of the nation. And

whereas liberalism saw the state simply as an institution created to protect men's rights, fascism looked on the state as an organic entity that embodied in itself all the noblest spiritual reality of the people as a whole. Fascism opposed the laissez-faire economics of capitalism and the bourgeois ethos that went with it. But fascism equally opposed socialism, which preached class war and trade unionism and thus served only to divide the nation. Fascism could tolerate no organized sectional groups that stood outside the state, for such groups pressed the supposed interests of some against the true interests of all. Hence, in place of trade unions, employers' federations, and similar organizations, fascism set up corporations that were designed to integrate the interests of particular trades, industries, professions, and the like into the wider harmony of the state.

Fascism, said Gentile, understood all the defects of bourgeois capitalism that had led to the rise of socialism, but fascism revolutionized society in such a way that the socialist critique was no longer relevant. For fascism replaced the old, competitive, hedonistic ethos of liberalism with an austere, stern, rigorous patriotic morality in which "the heroic values of service, sacrifice, indeed death itself were once more respected." Fascism did not deny liberty, but the liberty it upheld was not the right of each man to do what he pleased but "the liberty of a whole people freely accepting the rule of a state which they had interiorised, and made the guiding principle of all their conduct."

Fascism was proud of its comprehensive nature, of its totalitarian scope. For fascism, Gentile argued, was not just a method of government; it was a philosophy that permeated the whole will, thought, and feeling of the nation. "The authority of the state," Gentile wrote, "is absolute. It does not compromise, it does not bargain, it does not surrender any portion of its field to other moral or religious principles which may interfere with the individual conscience. But, on the other hand the state becomes a reality only in the consciousness of individuals." The state was "an idea made actual."

When Mussolini revised Gentile's draft for his *La dottrina del fascismo*, he retained most of the neo-Hegelian idealistic talk about the ideal nature of the state, but he had more to say about fascism's debts to the more extreme and fanatic elements of the nineteenth-century left wing. Mussolini named Georges Sorel, Charles Péguy, and Hubert Lagardelle as "sources of the river of Fascism." From these theorists, especially from Sorel, Mussolini derived the idea that "action is more important than thought"; by "action" he meant, as Sorel meant, violence. The extremists of the anarchist movement in the nineteenth century were obsessed by what they called *la propagande par le fait* (propaganda by deed); this "deed" tended to take the form of undiscriminating acts of revolutionary violence, such as throwing bombs into crowded cafés. The exhilaration of this policy soon blinded several of its champions to the end they were supposed to be pursuing—overthrowing the state—so that anarchism produced a movement of revolutionary disciplinarianism that Mussolini recognized as the source of his own inspiration.

Fascism was thus a movement that not only accepted, but also rejoiced in, violence. It had no patience with parliamentary or democratic methods of changing society. Indeed, Mussolini believed that the violent seizure of power, such as his own movement accomplished when it marched on Rome in 1922, was a necessary part of the moral rejuvenation of the nation; it was needed in order to create that "epic state of mind" (a phrase of Sorel's) that fascism prized so highly. Thus rejoicing in violence, fascism was, as Mussolini explained, hostile to all forms of pacifism, universalism, and disarmament. Fascism frankly acknowledged that "war alone keys up all human energies to their maximum tension, and sets a seal of nobility on those persons who have the courage to fight and die." The fascist state would have nothing to do with "universal embraces"; it "looked its neighbour proudly in the face, always armed, always vigilant, always ready to defend its integrity." Schemes such as that of the League of Nations were anathema to fascism.

With some reason Mussolini also claimed that fascism derived historically from the nationalistic movement of the nineteenth century. Nationalism, he insisted, owed nothing to the left. The German nation was not unified by liberals but by a man of iron, Otto von Bismarck. The nation of Italy, too, had been created by such men as Giuseppe Garibaldi, a man of revolutionary violence; the first great prophet of Italian unity was Niccolò Machiavelli, the archenemy of liberal, pacifist scruples. Mussolini had the highest regard for the author of *The Prince*. Machiavelli's desire to rekindle in modern Italy all the military virtues and military glory of ancient Rome was also Mussolini's ambition, but Mussolini's version of Machiavelli's dream was a much more vulgar one, and his achievements would have struck Machiavelli as tawdry, shabby, and corrupt.

Mussolini argued that it was the Italian state that had created the Italian nation. Indeed, it was the state, as the expression of a universal ethical will, which created the right to national existence and independence. Mussolini rejected the racism that was so central a feature of Nazi teaching in Germany. "The people," he wrote, "is not a race, but a people historically perpetuating itself; a multitude united by an idea." It must be recorded in favor of fascism that it never taught race hatred, and even when Mussolini entered the war on Hitler's side and introduced anti-Semitic legislation to please his ally, the Italian fascists were far from zealous in the enforcement of the laws against Jews.

Indeed, Mussolini's glorification of war and violence had never more than a limited success with the Italian people. Accustomed to rhetoric and appreciative of any kind of display, the Italians accepted the showier side of fascism more readily than the "austere, heroic way of life" that it demanded. Slow to conquer the backward Ethiopians in Mussolini's colonialist war against Abyssinia in 1935, the average Italian conscript soldier was even less eager to meet the Allied forces in World War II. Likewise, despite the cruelty of Mussolini's henchmen to his numerous political prisoners, there was never in Italy anything approaching the genocide that was faithfully enacted by Hitler's followers in Germany; even at its worst fascism never robbed the Italians of their humanity.

Mussolini earned a reputation, even among critical foreign observers, for the "efficiency" of his administration; he was popularly supposed abroad "to have made the Italian trains run on time." This achievement was largely mythical, for economic growth was minimal, but Mussolini was able, by forbidding strikes and subordinating industries to his state corporations, to prevent any of the more easily discernible manifestations of economic disorder. In any case his rule was never a mere personal dictatorship. He built up a powerful party with an elaborate hierarchy of command that served him much as the Soviet Communist Party served Joseph Stalin. Fascism was in a very real sense the dictatorship of a party, and the effectiveness of the party organization in a country by no means notable for good organization was one secret of fascism's twenty years of success.

See also Anarchism; Croce, Benedetto; Democracy; Gentile, Giovanni; Machiavelli, Niccolò; Marxist Philosophy; Nationalism; Political Philosophy, History of; Socialism; Sorel, Georges; Violence.

Bibliography

Ambrosini, G. *Il partito fascista e lo stato*. Rome: Instituto Nazionale Fascista di Cultura, 1934.

De Felice, Renzo. *Interpretations of Fascism.* Translated by Brenda Huff Everett. Cambridge, MA: Harvard University Press, 1977.

De Grand, Alexander J. *Fascist Italy and Nazi Germany: The "Fascist" Style of Rule.* London: Routledge, 1995.

Eatwell, Roger. *Fascism: A History.* New York: Allen Lane, 1996.

Finer, Herman. *Mussolini's Italy.* New York, 1935.

Gentile, Giovanni. *Genesi e struttura della società.* Florence: Sansoni, 1946.

Gentile, Giovanni. *Origins and Doctrine of Fascism: With Selections from Other Works.* Translated and edited by James Gregor. New Brunswick, NJ: Transaction, 2002.

Germino, Dante L. *The Italian Fascist Party in Power: A Study in Totalitarian Rule.* Minneapolis: University of Minnesota Press, 1959.

Gregor, James A. *The Ideology of Fascism: The Rationale of Totalitarianism.* New York: Free Press, 1969.

Griffin, Roger, ed. *Fascism.* Oxford: Oxford University Press, 1995.

Landini, Pietro. *La dottrina del fascismo.* Florence: Nuova Italia, 1936.

Larsen, Stein Ugelvik, Bernt Hagtvet, and Jan Petter Myklebust, eds. *Who Were the Fascists: Social Roots of European Fascism.* Bergen: Universitetsförlaget, 1980.

Lion, Aline. *The Pedigree of Fascism.* London: Sheed and Ward, 1927.

Mussolini, Benito. "The Doctrine of Fascism." In *Social and Political Doctrines of Contemporary Europe,* edited by Michael Oakeshott, 2nd ed. New York: Macmillan, 1942.

Mussolini, Benito. *Scritti e discorsi,* 12 vols. Milan, 1934–1939.

Pitigliani, Fausto. *The Italian Corporative State.* London: King, 1933.

Rocco, Alfredo. *Political Doctrine of Fascism: Recent Legislation in Italy.* New York: Carnegie Endowment for International Peace, Division of Intercourse and Education, 1926.

Salvatorelli, Luigi. *Storia del fascismo.* Rome: Edizioni di Novissima, 1952.

Salvemini, Gaetano. *Under the Axe of Fascism.* New York: Viking Press, 1936.

Spencer, H. R. *The Government and Politics of Italy.* Yonkers, NY: World Book, 1932.

Maurice Cranston (1967)
Bibliography updated by Philip Reed (2005)

FATHERS OF THE CHURCH

See *Patristic Philosophy*

FECHNER, GUSTAV THEODOR
(1801–1887)

Gustav Theodor Fechner, the German philosopher, was the founder of psychophysics, and a pioneer in experimental psychology. He was born in Gross-Saerchen, Prussia, and studied medicine at the University of Leipzig, where he passed his examinations at the age of twenty-one. His interests, however, led him into physics, and by 1830 he had published more than forty papers in this field. He also wrote a number of poems and satirical works under the pseudonym of "Dr. Mises," which he also used for some of his later metaphysical speculations. A paper on the quantitative measurement of electrical currents (1831) led to his appointment as professor of physics at Leipzig. Fechner's incipient interest in psychology is shown in papers of 1838 and 1840 on the perception of complementary colors and on subjective afterimages. His experiments on afterimages, however, had tragic consequences. As a result of gazing at the sun he sustained an eye injury, and his subsequent blindness led to a serious emotional crisis. Fechner resigned his professorship in 1839 and virtually retired from the world.

A seemingly miraculous recovery, three years later, stimulated Fechner's interest in philosophy, particularly in regard to the question of the soul and the possibility of refuting materialistic metaphysics. In a work titled *Nanna oder das Seelenleben der Pflanzen* (Nanna, or the soul-life of plants; Leipzig, 1848) he defended the idea that even plants have a mental life. This book is indicative of the panpsychistic bent of Fechner's thought, which was the major cause of the direction taken by his further work.

PSYCHOPHYSICS

In 1848 Fechner returned to the University of Leipzig as professor of philosophy. His desire to substantiate empirically the metaphysical thesis that mind and matter are simply alternative ways of construing one and the same reality was the main motivation for his pioneering work in experimental psychology. His *Elemente der Psychophysik* (Leipzig, 1860) was intended to be an outline of an exact science of the functional relations between bodily and mental phenomena, with a view to showing that one and the same phenomenon could be characterized in two ways. Fechner divided his new science of psychophysics into two disciplines: inner psychophysics, which studies the relation between sensation and nerve excitation; and outer psychophysics, to which Fechner's own experimental work was devoted and which studies the relation between sensation and physical stimulus. Psychophysics became one of the dominant fields within experimental psychology.

Fechner's work on the relation between physical stimuli and sensations led to a mathematical formulation that he called the law of intensity, which states that the intensity of a sensation increases as the logarithm of the stimulus, that is, by diminishing increments. When Fechner realized that his principle corresponded to the findings of E. H. Weber (1795–1878), he called it Weber's law, a name now reserved for the vaguer statement that a barely noticeable difference in stimulus has a constant ratio to the stimulus. Fechner's studies in psychophysics included a number of classical experiments on the perception of weight, visual brightness, and distance.

PANPSYCHISM

Fechner's psychological studies were meant to confirm his theory of panpsychism. He maintained that the whole universe is spiritual in character, the phenomenal world of physics being merely the external manifestation of this spiritual reality. That which *to itself* is psychical is *to others* physical. In his *Atomenlehre* he argued that physics requires us to regard atoms only as centers of force or energy, as Gottfried Wilhelm Leibniz had argued; it is not necessary to suppose them to be material or extended. These atoms are only the simplest elements in a spiritual hierarchy leading up to God. Each level of this hierarchy includes all those levels beneath it, so that God contains the totality of spirits. Consciousness is an essential feature of all that exists, but this assertion does not mean, as Leibniz had supposed, that every physical entity or phenomenon has its own soul. Only certain systems, namely, organic wholes, give evidence of possessing souls, and those bodies that do not are only the constituents of besouled bodies. The evidences of soul are the systematic coherence and conformity to law exhibited in the behavior of organic wholes. Fechner regarded Earth, "our mother," as such an organic besouled whole. The stars and the physical universe as a whole are also bodies of this kind. God is the soul of the universe; He is to the system of nature as that system is *to itself.*

To regard the whole material universe as inwardly alive and conscious is to take what Fechner called the "daylight view" (*Tagesansicht*). To regard it as inert matter, lacking in any teleological significance, is to take what he called the "night view" (*Nachtansicht*). Fechner ardently advocated the daylight view and hoped that it could be supported inductively by means of his psychophysical experiments. But he also argued for the daylight view on pragmatic grounds, offering the sort of arguments that William James later found highly congenial. Fechner urged that any hypothesis that cannot be positively proved but that does not contradict scientific findings be accepted if it makes us happy. The antimate-

rialistic daylight view is such a hypothesis. Fechner also defended his theory by means of analogical arguments. When certain qualities are found to be present in several types of objects, we are justified in assuming hypothetically that these objects share other, undetected qualities. Entities which exhibit the sort of order that our own bodies do may therefore be assumed to be alive and inwardly spiritual as we are.

IMMORTALITY

Fechner's argument for immortality is based on the observation that many individual experiences that are forgotten or unnoticed may later be recalled into consciousness. If the soul as a whole is treated on the analogy of its individual experiences, then, since these do not vanish utterly but often return in the form of memory, the soul itself may likewise continue to exist in God's memory. Mind and body are not parallel aspects of some third substance, as in Benedict (Baruch) de Spinoza; they are identical. The persistence of mind is therefore no more difficult to entertain than the persistence of the material universe itself, which is only the outward manifestation of an all-inclusive soul.

AESTHETICS

Between 1865 and 1876 Fechner turned his attention to aesthetics. He published a paper on the golden section, the supposedly ideal proportion, and several papers on the controversy over two Hans Holbein paintings of the Madonna. These two paintings, one in Dresden, the other in Darmstadt, were the subject of serious debate among art critics and aestheticians. Fechner hoped to settle the question of their relative excellence by means of a public preference poll when the paintings were exhibited together.

The desire to put aesthetics on an empirical, scientific footing and to bring philosophical speculation into some sort of accord with experimental science is shown further in Fechner's *Vorschule der Aesthetik* (Propaedentic to aesthetic; Leipzig, 1876), a work of considerable significance for the history of experimental aesthetics. In the preface to this work Fechner stated that previous aestheticians such as Friedrich Schelling and G. W. F. Hegel had theorized "downward" from universal principles to particulars. Fechner proposed to reverse this procedure, to build aesthetic theory "from below," on a foundation of empirical evidence. The word *beauty*, he maintained, denotes the approximate subject matter of aesthetics. It is a word applicable to everything that has the property of arousing pleasure directly and immediately. (Pleasure aroused by thoughts of the consequences of an object is nonaesthetic.) Our experiences of aesthetic pleasure are simple, unanalyzable psychic atoms. The aim of an experimental aesthetics is to discover the objects that produce such atoms, that is, the causal laws connecting aesthetic experiences with the characteristics of outer objects.

EXPERIMENTAL METHODS. Fechner suggested three experimental methods for carrying out this program: the method of selection or choice, the method of production or construction, and the method of measuring common objects. The first of these methods is illustrated by Fechner's experiments with rectangles. Ten rectangles of varying dimensions but equal areas were spread at random on a table. The subject was asked to make a selection, ranking the rectangles in the order of his aesthetic pleasure and displeasure. A record was kept of his responses, with allowance being made for variation in hesitation of response. Fechner's results seemed to support the hypothesis that there exist certain ratios of length to width that possess specific aesthetic value. Most of the people tested tended to reject as unpleasant both the square or nearly square and the extremely elongated figures, with the largest number of favorable responses going to the rectangle whose proportions were 34:21. Fechner took this as empirical confirmation of the special aesthetic status of the golden section.

In the second of Fechner's methods, the subject was confronted, for example, with four vertical lines of various lengths and asked to place a dot over each line at the distance that seemed to him most aesthetically pleasing. The results were that the average distance was proportional to the length of the line. This experiment was referred to as the "inquiry into the letter 'i.'" Fechner's third experimental method involved measuring such objects as books, visiting cards, and so on, and here too he found the ratio of the golden section in a large percentage of cases.

LAWS OF PSYCHOLOGICAL AESTHETICS. A number of psychological laws formulated by Fechner are relevant to aesthetic experience. His principle of aesthetic threshold states that a stimulus must acquire a certain intensity before it can produce pleasure or pain. The effect will then increase gradually until it reaches a maximum point, whereupon it will decrease to the point of indifference. In the case of pleasure but not in that of pain, the effect may, after the maximum is reached, change to its opposite. Aesthetic reinforcement refers to the fact that several conditions of pleasure may, when combined, produce a total satisfaction greater than the sum of these conditions taken separately, for example, melody and harmony in music, meaning and rhythm in poetry. The principle of "uniform connection within the manifold" states that we prefer objects which are both unified and complex over objects which are homogeneous or excessively diverse. The principle of "absence of contradiction" claims that harmony and truth are aesthetically preferable to disagreement, contradiction, or error. Vagueness and ambiguity are aesthetically displeasing, as the principle of "clarity" announces. The recollection of an event portrayed in some aesthetic object may bring pleasure or displeasure, depending on whether the event reminds us of something pleasant or unpleasant: the principle of "aesthetic association." The principle of "minimum effort" states that pleasure is derived from the smallest possible expenditure of energy relative to a given end in view and not simply from the minimum expenditure of energy as such.

CONCLUSION

These "laws of the mind" illustrate the spirit of Fechner's philosophizing. He was one of the most versatile thinkers of the nineteenth century, laboring to reconcile an idealistic view of reality with the methodology of modern science and, in so doing, providing some of the groundwork for further developments in a number of areas of experimental psychology. His somewhat fantastic metaphysical speculations disclose a mind of poetic sensitivity, whose visions, however, he insisted on subjecting to scientific scrutiny.

See also Aesthetic Experience; Aesthetics, History of; German Philosophy; Hegel, Georg Wilhelm Friedrich; Immortality; James, William; Leibniz, Gottfried Wilhelm; Mind-Body Problem; Panpsychism; Psychology; Schelling, Friedrich Wilhelm Joseph von; Spinoza, Benedict (Baruch) de.

Bibliography

ADDITIONAL WORKS BY FECHNER

Büchlein vom Leben nach dem Tod. Dresden, 1936. Translated by John Erskine as *Life after Death*. New York, 1943.

Zend-Avesta oder über die Dinge des Himmels und des Jenseits (Zend-Avesta, or concerning matters of heaven and the world to come). 3 vols. Leipzig, 1851.

Über die physikalische und philosophische Atomenlehre (On physical and philosophical atomic theory). Leipzig, 1850.

Über die Seelenfrage. Ein Gang durch die sichtbare Welt, um die Unsichtbare zu finden (On the question of the soul: a path through the visible world in order to find the invisible). Leipzig, 1861.

Die Tagesansicht gegenüber der Nachtansicht (The daylight view as opposed to the night view). Leipzig, 1879.

Die drei Motive und Grunde des Glaubens (The three motives and grounds of faith). Leipzig: Breitkopf and Härtel, 1863.

Elements of Psychophysics. Edited by Davis H. Howes and Edwin Garrigues. New York: Holt, Rinehart and Winston, 1966.

Zur experimentellen Aesthetik. Vorschule der Aesthetik. Hildesheim; New York: G. Olms, 1978, 1925.

Fix, Ulla, Irene Altmann, and Gustav Theodor Fechner. *Fechner und die Folgen ausserhalb der Naturwissenschaften: interdisziplinäres Kolloquium zum 200. Geburtstag gustav Theodor Fechners.* Tübingen: Niemeyer, 2003.

Tagebücher 1828 bis 1879. Leipzig: Verlag der Sächsischen Akademie der Wissenschaften zu Leipzig; Stuttgart: In Kommission bei F. Steiner, 2004.

Note: A bibliography of 175 of Fechner's writings can be found in *Elemente der Psychophysik.* 2nd ed. (Leipzig, 1889. Vol. 1).

WORKS ON FECHNER

In English

Boring, E. G. *History of Experimental Psychology.* New York: Century, 1929 and 1950. Ch. 14.

James, William. *A Pluralistic Universe.* New York: Longman, 1909. Lecture 4.

James, William. *Principles of Psychology.* New York: Holt, 1890. Vol. 1, pp. 553–549.

Külpe, O. *Die Philosophie der Gegenwart in Deutschland.* Leipzig, 1902. Translated by M. L. Patrick and G. T. W. Patrick as *The Philosophy of the Present in Germany.* London: G. Allen, 1913. Pp. 147–160.

Murphy, G. *Historical Introduction to Modern Psychology.* New York: Harcourt Brace, 1949. Pp. 82–94.

Perry, R. B. *Philosophy of the Recent Past.* New York: Scribners, 1926. Pp. 82–86.

In German

Hermann, J. *Gustav Theodor Fechner.* Munich, 1926.

Kuntze, J. E. *Gustav Theodor Fechner.* Leipzig, 1882.

Lasswitz, K. *Gustav Theodor Fechner.* Stuttgart: F. Frommann, 1896.

Meyer, F. A. E. *Philosophische Metaphysik und Christliche Glaube bei Gustav Theodor Fechner.* Goettingen, 1937.

Arnulf Zweig (1967)
Bibliography updated by Michael Farmer (2005)

FËDOROV, NIKOLAI FËDOROVICH

(1829–1903)

Nikolai Fëdorovich Fëdorov was a Russian religious philosopher. From 1854 to 1868 he taught history and geography at district schools in Russia. From 1869 to 1872 he worked at the Chertkovskaia Library in Moscow, and from 1874 to 1898 he worked at the libraries of the Moscow Public and Rumiantsev Museums. For a quarter of a century he defined the spiritual atmosphere of this latter library, infusing it, in the words of his contemporaries, with the traditions of the "philosophical school." Many talented men of Russian science and culture used to gather in the catalogue room of the library where Fëdorov served to converse with the "Moscow Socrates." In the 1880s and 1890s Fëdorov met with Vladimir Sergeevich Solov'ëv, who called Fëdorov's teaching "the first progress the human spirit has made on the way of Christ." In that time period Fëdorov also carried on his religio-philosophical dialogue and debate with Lev (Leo) Nikolaevich Tolstoy.

Starting in 1851 Fëdorov expounded his ideas first orally, and then, starting in the second half of the 1870s, in large works and articles. After Fëdorov's death, his disciples V. A. Kozhevnikov and N. P. Peterson prepared for publication a three-volume collection of the philosopher's works under the title *Filosoviia obshchego dela* (The Philosophy of the common cause; the first two volumes were published in 1906 and 1913, respectively; the third volume remained unpublished).

In the evolutionary process Fëdorov discerned a tendency to the birth of consciousness and reason, which, beginning with man, were called to become the instruments, no longer of an unconscious, but of a conscious and morally and spiritually oriented perfecting of the world. "In us, nature begins not only to be conscious of itself but also to control itself." Man is both the crown of evolution and its agent; the labor of the cosmicization of being lies on his shoulders. In opposition to the existing parasitical and exploitative relation of man to the natural environment, which is leading civilization to the brink of catastrophe ("A civilization that exploits but does not restore can have no other result than its own end"), Fëdorov advanced the idea of the *regulation of nature*, which unfolds in a series of tasks. This series comprises the prevention of natural disasters (earthquakes, floods, droughts, etc.), the regulation of climate, the control of cosmic processes, labor directed at the conquest of death, and—as the climax of this regulation of nature, the focus of all of its efforts—the return to a new transfigured life of all those who have departed into nonbeing, infinite creative work in a renewed Universe.

Fëdorov gave his teaching both a natural-scientific and a religious foundation. Basing his thought on the patristic tradition (St. Basil the Great, St. Gregory the Theologian, and Gregory of Nyssa), he developed an actively Christian anthropology: God, in creating man in His image and likeness, acts in the world first and foremost through man, and through him He will realize the central ontological promises of the Christian faith, such as the raising of the dead, the transfiguration of their nature, and the entry into the immortal, creative eon of being, the Kingdom of Heaven. He propounded the idea of divine humanity, the collaboration of the divine and human energies in the work of salvation, and argued that the prophecies of the Revelation have only a conditional significance. Will the end of history be catastrophic, leading to the Last Judgment with the consequent division of humankind into a handful of the saved and a vast multitude of the eternally damned? Or will it be radiant, where all will be saved (the apocatastasis)? This depends on people themselves, on whether the world's movement will continue on its false, antidivine vector or whether it will redirect itself to the ways of God.

Fëdorov also gave the idea of the regulation of nature a religious interpretation. Based on the sense of the profound moral responsibility of man for the fate of the entire earth, of the entire cosmos, and of the entire creation, regulation represents the fulfillment of the biblical commandment that man be lord of the earth. "Restoration of the world to that splendid beauty of incorruption that it possessed before the Fall"—that is how the philosopher of the universal task defines God's assignment to the "sons of men."

A successful outcome of history, which becomes a "work of salvation," presupposes, according to Fëdorov, the necessity of a new fundamental choice that is associated with the imperative of the evolutionary ascent of humanity. He exposes the defects of a one-sided technological development that improves machines and mechanisms but that leaves man's nature untouched and vulnerable, entirely at the mercy of the vagaries of the external environment. As an alternative, he advances the idea of organic progress that is oriented toward the transformation of the physical substance of conscious beings. As a result of this transformation, man himself, without the aid of technology, will be able to fly, to see far and deep, to build his tissues from elementary materials of the environment like plants under the effect of sunlight (here, Fëdorov anticipates what V. I. Vernadskii would later call *autotrophism*), and to create necessary organs for himself or change his existing organs as a function of the medium of his habitation and action (the notion of "fullness of organs"). According to Fëdorov the body, the receptacle of the soul, must be made wholly subordinate to the consciousness; the body must be regulated and spiritualized. Spirit must achieve total power over matter, leading to a state where the forces of decay, corruption, and death are limited and finally expelled from being.

Fëdorov envisaged a radical change in philosophy. This change would consist in the rejection of abstract thought and passive contemplation, in a transition toward the definition of the values of the necessary order of things, toward the development of a plan for humanity's transformative activity. He proclaimed the inseparability of ontology and deontology ("truth is only the path to the good") and the necessity of a projective thought (the project connects the ideal and reality and seeks ways toward a practical realization of the supreme idea). He advanced the principle of the integrity and universality of knowledge ("all people must be knowers and all things must be an object of knowledge"), and he spoke of the transformation of gnoseology into *gnoseo-urgy*. He called his system *supramoralism*, establishing the foundations of a "mature," "filial" morality ("we are all brothers according to love for the fathers").

Here, he did not limit the laws of ethics to the sphere of human relationships, indicating the dependence of the moral principle in man and in society on the material and natural order of things. Unkindred and unbrotherly attitudes, he emphasized, are rooted in the depths of postlapsarian, mortal being, which is based on the law of the succession of generations, with mutual devouring, expulsion, and struggle. And therefore only one thing can guarantee the attainment of "universal kinship": the conquest of the forces of death in the external world (by means of natural-cosmic regulation) and in man himself (by means of psycho-physiological regulation). Convinced of the incompleteness of altruistic morality (where the self-sacrifice of some presupposes the eternal egotism of others), Fëdorov offers the formula, "[N]ot for oneself and not for others, but with all and for all." He resolved the antinomy of individualism and collectivism through the principle of sobornost (communalism or all-togetherness), affirming the latter as the foundation of the perfect social organization (society "according to the type of the Trinity").

Fëdorov also interpreted the meaning of culture in the light of the idea of immortality and the raising of the dead. He viewed culture as an attempt at an "imaginary raising from the dead," as an impulse to preserve the memory of that which had lived in the past. He put a high value on museums and libraries as centers of the universal human memory. He dreamed of a radical expansion of the activity of museums and libraries, of their transformation into centers of collection, investigation, education, and training, around which associations of scholars would be grouped, associations of "specialists in all domains of human knowledge." By becoming an instrument of the universal task, the museum, according to Fëdorov, was to animate knowledge with a heartfelt feeling of kinship, with a spirit of love for fathers and ancestors, thus serving the restoration of the brotherly connection of people.

Fëdorov's philosophy is at the origin of the Russian religio-philosophical renaissance and helps to define the fundamental themes of the latter. His philosophy is the source of the actively evolutionary noospheric thought of the twentieth century (N. A. Umov, V. I. Vernadskii, and A. L. Chizhevskii). Various talented representatives of Russian literature were influenced, at different times and to different degrees, by *The Philosophy of the Common Task*: Fëdor Mikhailovich Dostoevsky and Tolstoy, Valerii Briusov and Vladimir Maiakovskii, Nikolai Kliuev and Velimir Khlebnikov, Mikhail Prishvin and Maksim Gorky, Andrei Platonov and Boris Pasternak. Fëdorov's theurgic aesthetics (the transition from an "art of imitations" to the creative work of life to the liturgical synthesis of the arts) exerted an influence on the philosophical-aesthetic quests at the end of the nineteenth century and the beginning of the twentieth century (Solov'ëv, Belyi, Viacheslav Ivanovich Ivanov, V. Chekrygin, P. Filonov, and others).

See also Aesthetics, History of; Consciousness; Darwinism; Dostoevsky, Fyodor Mikhailovich; Gregory of Nyssa; Patristic Philosophy; Reason; Russian Philosophy; Solov'ëv (Solovyov), Vladimir Sergeevich; Tolstoy, Lev Nikolaevich.

Bibliography

WORKS BY FËDOROV

Sochineniia (Works). Moscow, 1982.

Sobranie sochinenii (Collected works). Vols. 1–4. Moscow, 1995–1999.

What Was Man Created For? The Philosophy of the Common Task: Selected Works, edited by E. Kontaissoff and M. Minto. Lausanne, Switzerland: Henyglen/L'Age d'Homme, 1990.

WORKS ON FËDOROV

Kozhevnikov, V. A. *Nikolai Fedorovich Fedorov*. Part 1. Moscow, 1908.

Gorsky, A. K. *Nikolai Fedorovich Fedorov i sovremennost'* (Nikolai Fëdorovich Fëdorov and the present time). Issues 1–4. Harbin, 1928–1933.

Hagemeister, Michael. *Nikolaj Fedorov: Studien zu Leben, Werk, und Wirkung*. Munich: Sagner, 1989.

Koehler, L. *N. F. Fedorov: The Philosophy of Action*. Pittsburgh, PA, 1979.

Lukashevich, Stephen. *N. F. Fedorov (1828–1903): A Study in Russian Eupsychian and Utopian Thought*. Newark: University of Delaware Press, 1977.

Semenova, S. G. *Filosof budushchego veka Nikolai Fedorov* (Philosopher of the future age, Nikolai Fëdorov). Moscow, 2004.

Semenova, S. G. *Nikolai Fedorov: Tvorchestvo zhizni* (Nikolai Fëdorov: The creativity of life). Moscow, 1990.

Young, George M., Jr. *Nikolai F. Fedorov: An Introduction*. Belmont, MA: Nordland, 1979.

S. G. Semenova (2005)
Translated by Boris Jakim (2005)

FEELING

See *Emotion*

FEINBERG, JOEL
(1926–2004)

Joel Feinberg was a noted moral, social, political, and legal philosopher. He was born in Detroit, Michigan. After his military service in World War II, Feinberg earned bachelor's, master's, and doctoral degrees at the University of Michigan (Ann Arbor). His doctoral dissertation was titled "Naturalism and Liberalism in the Philosophy of Ralph Barton Perry" (1957).

It was not until 1960, when Feinberg was thirty-three years old, that he published his first philosophical essay. During the next four decades, while Feinberg taught at Brown, Princeton, UCLA, Rockefeller, and Arizona, his scholarly output was prodigious. Within a few years of his arrival at the University of Arizona, the philosophy department there attracted several other prominent philosophers and become one of the most highly regarded programs in the United States. Feinberg was honored by his philosophical peers in 1981 by being elected president of the Pacific Division of the American Philosophical Association. In 1988, he was one of the first individuals to be designated Regents Professor at the University of Arizona.

Liberalism was Feinberg's focus throughout his long and distinguished career. During the 1980s, he wrote his *magnum opus*, the four-volume, 1,397-page *Moral Limits of the Criminal Law*. Feinberg's aim in this work (which he called his "tetralogy") was "to make the best possible case for liberalism" with respect to the moral limits of the criminal law (*Harm to Others*, p. 15). He thought of himself as "vindicat[ing] the traditional liberalism derived from [John Stuart] Mill's *On Liberty* [1859]" (ibid.). Although Feinberg had no legal credentials (other than having been a Liberal Arts Fellow at Harvard Law School in 1963–1964), he has already influenced American law. At least one state supreme court has cited him as a persuasive authority. (See *Armstrong v. Montana*, 296 Mont. 361, 989 P.2d 364 [1999] [holding that a Montana statute prohibiting physician assistants from performing abortions violated the privacy, equal-protection, and bill-of-attainder provisions of the Montana constitution].)

Feinberg begins his tetralogy with what he calls a presumption in favor of (individual) liberty. This presumption means that "[l]iberty should be the norm; coercion always needs some special justification" (*Harm to Others*, p. 9). He then sketches a number of "liberty-limiting principles," each of which states a reason—but not a necessary or a sufficient condition—for coercing individuals. The question he sets for himself is which of these principles, if any, are valid. Here, for example, is the harm principle:

> It is always a good reason in support of penal legislation that it would probably be effective in preventing (eliminating, reducing) harm to persons other than the actor (the one prohibited from acting) and there is probably no other means that is equally effective at no greater cost to other values. (*Harm to Others*, p. 26 [italics in original; footnote omitted])

Feinberg endorses two liberty-limiting principles: the harm principle and the offense principle. He rejects two others: legal paternalism and legal moralism. Volume one of his tetralogy, *Harm to Others*, elaborates and defends the harm principle. Volume two, *Offense to Others*, elaborates and defends the offense principle. Volume three, *Harm to Self*, elaborates and rejects legal paternalism. Volume four, *Harmless Wrongdoing*, elaborates and rejects legal moralism.

Legislators who are guided by Feinberg's liberalism, with its normative commitments to individual liberty and personal autonomy, would prohibit and punish only harmful or seriously offensive conduct (but not necessarily *all* of such conduct). An example of seriously offensive conduct would be a pornographic billboard that individuals cannot reasonably avoid. Feinbergian (ideal) legislators would not punish conduct solely on the ground that it is harmful to the actor. That is legal paternalism, which is an affront to personal autonomy. Nor would they punish conduct solely on the ground that it is immoral. That is legal moralism. It is important to understand that Feinberg's rejection of legal moralism does not rest on moral skepticism, nihilism, relativism, or subjectivism. One can be a moral objectivist—a believer in objective moral values—and still hold that it is improper for legislators to

enforce a single "true" morality. Feinberg's aim is practical: to "guide the legislator by locating the moral constraints that limit his options" (*Harm to Others*, p. 4). It is "a quest not for useful policies but for valid principles" (*Harm to Others*, p. 4).

The four volumes together make a powerful case for "the liberal position" on the moral limits of the criminal law. Feinberg does not argue for liberalism directly by appealing to "moral primitives" or "self-evident truths" (*Harm to Others*, p. 17). Instead, he adopts the *argumentum ad hominem* technique. This type of argument consists in appealing to values, beliefs, and convictions his readers are presumed to have or to judgments they are presumed to make. Feinberg's objective is to persuade these readers that the liberal position on the moral limits of the criminal law systematizes their values, beliefs, convictions, and judgments better than any alternative. It is a search for coherence, not foundations. In effect, he is trying to show his readers that they are—already, unwittingly—liberals.

Among the areas in applied or practical ethics to which Feinberg made important contributions are abortion and animal rights. In his influential 1979 essay "Abortion," he sought to structure the debate over the morality and legality of abortion by (as he later put it) "locating crucial but implicit presuppositions, centrally affected interests, critical distinctions, and so on" (*Freedom and Fulfillment*, p. viii). In an essay published in 1971, four years before Peter Singer's celebrated *Animal Liberation* appeared, Feinberg argued that animals are "among the sorts of beings of whom rights can meaningfully be predicated and denied" (*Rights, Justice, and the Bounds of Liberty*, p. 166). Feinberg was not arguing that animals do in fact have rights. He was arguing that it is not incoherent—as many people had thought—to ascribe rights to them. This was an important step in what became a powerful case for including nonhuman animals in the moral community. By clarifying the concept of a right, Feinberg was able to show that certain denials of rights were ill-founded. To Feinberg, "[c]onceptual clarification is the most distinctively philosophical of enterprises" (*Harm to Others*, p. 17). Clear thought leads to or is an indispensable part of sound moral judgment.

Feinberg's work, taken as a whole, is best characterized as social philosophy—interpreted broadly to include moral, political, and legal philosophy. In addition to the moral limits of the criminal law, he was interested in and made original contributions to the understanding of responsibility, punishment, desert, mental illness, rights, justice, liberty, civil disobedience, freedom of expression, paternalism, autonomy, and fulfillment. His textbook *Reason and Responsibility: Readings in Some Basic Problems of Philosophy*, which appeared in 1965 (the twelfth edition was published in 2005), is among the best-selling philosophy textbooks of all time. Feinberg proved that original, important philosophical work is compatible with textbook writing. He was ever the teacher. Late in life, he published a delightful little book entitled *Doing Philosophy: A Guide to the Writing of Philosophy Papers* (1997).

It is fitting that Feinberg wrote a book on writing, for his writing style is justly famous and much emulated. His writing is clear, simple, and penetrating—at times even beautiful—despite the complexity of the issues and concepts with which he grappled. Several generations of philosophers have admired and learned from Feinberg, both substantively and stylistically. Many of his students went on to prominent careers of their own, in law or philosophy or both. In 1994, one of his most accomplished students, Jules Coleman, and a former colleague, Allen Buchanan, published an aptly titled collection of critical essays devoted to Feinberg's work: *In Harm's Way: Essays in Honor of Joel Feinberg*.

Bibliography

WORKS BY FEINBERG

Doing and Deserving: Essays in the Theory of Responsibility. Princeton, NJ: Princeton University Press, 1970. This volume collects essays published between 1960 and 1969 (inclusive). The essays concern such concepts as act, cause, harm, punishment, desert, and blame. Feinberg thought of these essays as "straddling ethics, philosophy of mind, and philosophy of law."

Social Philosophy. Foundations of Philosophy Series, edited by Elizabeth Beardsley and Monroe Beardsley. Englewood Cliffs, NJ: Prentice-Hall, 1973. This highly regarded monograph concerns itself with "philosophical questions about social relations." Among the concepts investigated are freedom, coercion, legal rights, human rights, and social justice. This book is where Feinberg introduced the concept of a liberty-limiting principle that figured so prominently in his later work.

Rights, Justice, and the Bounds of Liberty: Essays in Social Philosophy. Princeton, NJ: Princeton University Press, 1980. This volume collects essays published between 1964 and 1978 (inclusive). The essays concern such concepts as liberty, harm, offense, legal paternalism, and rights. Feinberg thought of these essays as dealing with "hard cases for the application of the concept of a right."

The Moral Limits of the Criminal Law, Vol. 1: *Harm to Others*. New York: Oxford University Press, 1984. This is the first volume of Feinberg's "account of the moral constraints on legislative action." Feinberg discusses the concept of harm; its relation to such concepts as interests, wants, hurts,

offenses, rights, and consent; hard cases for application of the concept of harm; and various problems involved in assessing, comparing, and imputing harms.

The Moral Limits of the Criminal Law, Vol. 2: *Offense to Others*. New York: Oxford University Press, 1985. Feinberg discusses the concept of offense (as a mental state distinct from harm) and some of its applications, including pornography, obscenity, and "dirty words."

The Moral Limits of the Criminal Law, Vol. 3: *Harm to Self*. New York: Oxford University Press, 1986. Feinberg discusses legal paternalism, personal autonomy, and the concept of voluntariness.

The Moral Limits of the Criminal Law, Vol. 4: *Harmless Wrongdoing*. New York: Oxford University Press, 1988. Feinberg discusses legal moralism: the view that "[i]t can be morally legitimate to prohibit conduct on the ground that it is inherently immoral, even though it causes neither harm nor offense to the actor or to others."

Freedom and Fulfillment: Philosophical Essays. Princeton, NJ: Princeton University Press, 1992. This volume collects essays published between 1975 and 1991 (inclusive). The essays concern such concepts as wrongful life, abortion, freedom of expression, bad samaritanism, moral rights, and absurd self-fulfillment. Despite the title, Feinberg thought of these essays as dealing with "problems about rights."

Doing Philosophy: A Guide to the Writing of Philosophy Papers. Belmont, CA: Wadsworth, 1997.

Problems at the Roots of Law: Essays in Legal and Political Theory. Oxford: Oxford University Press, 2003. This volume collects essays published between 1992 and 2003 (inclusive). The essays concern such concepts as natural law, moral rights, entrapment, criminal attempts, government subsidies for the arts, and evil. As the title implies, Feinberg thought of these essays as dealing with "basic questions" in the philosophy of law.

Works on Feinberg

Coleman, Jules L., and Allen Buchanan, eds. *In Harm's Way: Essays in Honor of Joel Feinberg*. Cambridge, U.K.: Cambridge University Press, 1994. This volume contains critical essays by Allen Buchanan, Shelly Kagan, Richard J. Arneson, David Lyons, David A. J. Richards, Thomas Morawetz, Jules L. Coleman, Jean Hampton, John Martin Fischer and Mark Ravizza, Jeffrie G. Murphy, Joan McGregor, Robert F. Schopp, Sanford H. Kadish, Holly M. Smith, and Hyman Gross.

Keith Burgess-Jackson (2005)

FEMINISM AND CONTINENTAL PHILOSOPHY

Continental philosophy has been a significant force in the development of contemporary feminist thought. Many feminists have turned to the work of continental philosophers because the topics explored by these philosophers are germane to the kinds of questions feminists pursue.

Since Hegel continental philosophy has been concerned with questions of ethics, metaphysics, consciousness, and experience. Continental philosophy has occupied a prominent position in contemporary feminist philosophy because it examines these issues so central to feminist concerns.

EXISTENTIALISM AND PHENOMENOLOGY

The publication of Simone de Beauvoir's *The Second Sex* in 1949 marks the beginning of the contemporary feminist movement. De Beauvoir's work is rooted in two prominent continental philosophies, existentialism and phenomenology. The theme of her book is summarized in her famous statement that one is not born a woman, one becomes one. This statement and the analyses ensuing from it reveal the influence of both existentialism and phenomenology at the very beginning of the contemporary feminist movement. Existentialists such as Jean-Paul Sartre emphasized the ontological complexity of our existence as consciousness in bodies. Existential philosophers explored the themes of freedom and oppression, objectification, and the social construction of consciousness. Feminists such as de Beauvoir adapted these themes to the analysis of the situation of women in society. Existential feminists have described female bodily experience as socially constructed. They have analyzed the structures of society that perpetuate patriarchy and the oppression of women.

The influence of phenomenological thought has also been decisive. Husserl's phenomenological philosophy was rooted in an examination of how phenomena appear to consciousness. The phenomenological approach of Husserl, Heidegger, and Merleau-Ponty grounded philosophy in lived experience. For feminists this approach has provided a means of challenging a conception of objectivity that many theorists believe grounds Western philosophical thought and that many feminist philosophers identify as masculinist. It has fostered the development of feminist theory that arises from the distinctive lived experiences of women. Feminist phenomenologists explore how living in a female body in modern society produces a consciousness unique to women. They emphasize human subjectivity and the role of language in creating social reality. Their goal is to develop a feminist consciousness of oppression (Bartky 1990). Exploring the boundaries of that consciousness is the hallmark of feminist phenomenology.

In contemporary feminist thought the approaches of phenomenology and existentialism have merged in feminist analyses of the body. Feminist philosophers such as Iris Marion Young (1990) examine the phenomenon of the female body in patriarchal society. Young explores aspects of women's lived experience—pregnancy, for example—that are unique to women. Her point is that women's bodily experience is different from that of men and that this difference effects women's consciousness under patriarchy. Young argues that existential phenomenology exhibits an adherence to the subject/object dualism. Young's goal is to replace this dualism with an understanding that erases the difference between the inner and the outer. She wants to develop a position that corrects this error without abandoning the advantages of existential phenomenology.

MARXISM

In the 1960s many feminists were attracted to Marxist philosophy as a vehicle for feminist theory. There were several reasons for the convergence of feminism and Marxism. First, Marxism was the oppositional philosophy of the time; to be opposed to the status quo in this time period almost necessarily entailed a Marxist stance. Second, Marxism, like feminism, was concerned with oppression. Although Marx was not himself concerned with the oppression of women, his theory of the oppression of the proletariat seemed to many feminists to have much to contribute to the attempt to develop a theory of the oppression of women.

The aspect of Marx's theory that became most influential in feminist thought was his theory of the standpoint. Marx argues that the standpoint of the proletariat in capitalism affords it a privileged understanding of its social structure; in his view the proletariat's position as the oppressed class allows it to see the true reality of capitalism. As a social determinist, Marx asserts that knowledge is governed by the subject's historical/material position. Yet he also claims that the knowledge produced by those in the oppressed class is the only true knowledge; the knowledge of other classes, in contrast, is "partial and perverse."

Feminists such as Nancy Hartsock (1983) and Dorothy Smith (1987) have used Marx's theory of the standpoint to analyze the position of women in society. They argue, first, that women, like the proletariat, are an oppressed class. Their thesis is that the bourgeoisie's oppression of the proletariat parallels men's oppression of women. Patriarchy, like captialism, is a system of oppression in which the dominant class, men, hold the oppressed class, women, in subjection. Second, feminist-standpoint theorists argue that the activity of women in society—child-rearing, child-bearing, and housework—creates a particular reality for women. Like Marx, they argue that the social actor's activity creates her knowledge. Finally, they contend that the knowledge produced by the standpoint of women is truer than that produced by men. Following Marx, they argue that the knowledge of the oppressed class of women reveals the truth of patriarchy, whereas that of the ruling class of men is partial and perverse.

Feminist standpoint theory has been a major component of contemporary feminist thought. Hartsock's *Money, Sex, and Power* (1983) advanced the thesis that the distinctive activity of women in society provides them with a privileged access to reality. Her analysis of how the feminist standpoint is produced through the practices distinctive of women in society became the basis for extensive analyses of that standpoint. Dorothy Smith's analysis of the "lifeworld" of women extends the concept of the standpoint into an analysis of the everyday life of women. Combining standpoint theory with a phenomenological approach, Smith argues for an analysis of the everyday life of women as constitutive of their social reality.

But feminist standpoint theory has also raised questions for feminist thought. As feminists moved from a consideration of the difference between men and women to the differences among women, the concept of the feminist standpoint became problematic. Feminists questioned how one feminist standpoint could account for the variety of women's experiences. Feminists also began to question the epistemology of the standpoint. If, as Marx claims, all knowledge is perspectival, then how can one perspective be "truer" than another? Standpoint theorists have difficulty answering either of these questions.

POSTMODERNISM AND POSTSTRUCTURALISM

Since the 1990s one of the principal influences in feminist thought has come from the predominantly French philosophies of postmodernism and poststructuralism. Inspired by the work of Friedrich Nietzsche, postmodern and poststructuralist philosophers have questioned not just aspects of Western thought but its very foundation. Rejecting the Cartesian subject and the pursuit of universal knowledge, these thinkers have fundamentally altered the project of philosophy. Many feminists have been attracted to these theories because they provide a radically new way to understand the feminine and its place in Western philosophy. Postmodernism and poststructuralism, by redefining truth as plural rather than universal,

provide the possibility of overcoming the inferiority of women that has pervaded Western thought.

The widely acknowledged inspiration for postmodern thought is the work of Nietzsche. The object of Nietzsche's attack is the tradition of Western thought beginning with the Greeks. Two aspects of his thought have been particularly relevant to feminism. First, truth, for Nietzsche, is relational and perspectival. It is a "mobile army of metaphors" that is harnessed for use by those in power. Second, Nietzsche questions the centerpiece of modern Western philosophy, the subject. By undermining the subject/object dualism that provides the grounding for the subject, Nietzsche calls into question the autonomy of the subject and its place in the constitution of knowledge.

The radical quality of Nietzsche's thought has resonated with many feminists. For those feminist philosophers claiming that the "man of reason" informing Western thought has excluded women from the pursuit of truth, Nietzsche's approach provided a mean of further articulating this claim and of exploring an alternative.

Two theorists whose work is rooted in that of Nietzsche have played a significant role in contemporary feminist philosophy. The work of Michel Foucault, although controversial, has had a significant impact on contemporary feminism. Like Nietzsche, Foucault takes on the two pillars of Western thought: truth and the subject. For Foucault truth is constituted through discourses; it is specific to the discourse in which it operates. It follows that the universal truth of the Western tradition is a fiction created, itself, by a particular discourse. For Foucault standards for what constitutes truth are not universal but, rather, internal to particular discourses. The most radical element of Foucault's thought, however, is his declaration of "the death of man." Foucault argues that the autonomous, constituting subject of modern philosophy (the Cartesian subject) is a creation of a particular discourse at a particular time and, most significantly, is now in eclipse. For Foucault discourses create specific kinds of subjects; there is no universal subject but only the subjects constituted by particular discourses.

Feminists have found Foucault's work extremely useful. His theory of the death of man has obvious feminist implications even if Foucault did not explore them. "Man"— the rational, autonomous, self-constituting subject—has been a problem for many feminists. Exposing this concept as the product of historically located discourses and thus vulnerable to change eliminates these problems. Feminists have also used Foucault's work to explicate how the subject "woman" is created by the dis-

ENCYCLOPEDIA OF PHILOSOPHY
2nd edition

courses of patriarchal society. In the highly influential *Gender Trouble* (1990), Judith Butler uses a postmodern approach to explicate how the identity "woman" is constituted. Butler argues that this identity is a fiction created by the actions of women who perform that identity. She advocates a feminist politics that eschews the identity "woman" and instead creates "gender trouble," the destabilization of the gender structures of society. Feminists have also used Foucault's thought to challenge the "truth" about woman, enshrined in Western philosophy and science. Using a Foucaultian approach, feminists have explicated how truths are established and sedimented into their discursive foundation.

The work of Jacques Derrida has also provided the basis for feminist philosophical investigations. Derrida's "deconstructive" approach, like that of Nietzsche and Foucault, constitutes a fundamental critique of Western rationalism. Derrida's strategy of deconstruction focuses on language and its construction of a monolithic reign of truth. Derrida attacks what he calls the "metaphysics of presence," the presuppositions informing the tradition of Western philosophy. His goal is to examine the elements of Western rationalism and expose them as an elaborate construction rather than as absolute truth. He does so by "deconstructing" its basic concepts—that is, examining the presuppositions that inform those concepts and the consequences that flow from them.

Feminist philosophers such as Luce Irigaray, Julia Kristeva, and Helene Cixous have employed a Derridean perspective to deconstruct the dualisms that found Western philosophy. Questioning the masculine definitions of rationality and truth on which Western thought is grounded, these feminist philosophers have argued for a distinctively feminine way of writing as a counterweight to the norms of male-dominated discourse. If, as Derrida claims, we are constituted by language, then we need another language to resist this constitution. The goal of these philosophers is to redefine "woman" and the feminine in ways that are not structured by Western dualisms.

Postmodern and poststructuralist philosophy have provided a rich addition to feminist philosophy. They have allowed feminists to examine the relationship between language and the status of women in radically different ways. But postmodern feminism has also been strongly criticized within the feminist community. Its critics have argued that postmodernism, by rejecting absolute truth, is a form of relativism, even nihilism. Without some conception of truth, these critics claim, feminists cannot proclaim the truth of the oppression of women. They further argue that postmodernism deprives

feminism of a political stance, a necessary component of feminism. The defenders of postmodern feminism counter that their outlook does not preclude politics but, rather, offers a different understanding of the political. They point to the revolutionary force implicit in Derrida's deconstruction and the "local" rather than universal resistance advocated by Foucault. But the controversies over postmodernism and feminism show no signs of abating.

CRITICAL THEORY AND HERMENEUTICS

Although they do not represent as pervasive an influence as postmodernism, both critical theory and hermeneutics have also found a following among feminist philosophers. The work of Jurgen Habermas has influenced the writings of both Nancy Fraser and Seyla Benhabib. These theorists find Habermas's philosophy attractive because, although it is critical of Enlightenment rationalism, it nevertheless provides a normative basis for an alternative conception. Partly inspired by Marxism, Habermas's approach entails both a critique of social norms and an alternative vision of a society without oppression. Focusing on the communicative basis of society, Habermas envisions a polity characterized by undistorted communication. Feminists who embrace this view argue that it provides an appropriate basis for feminist politics.

The hermeneutics of Hans-Georg Gadamer has also attracted feminist attention. Although Gadamer is usually viewed as a conservative, some feminists drawn on his writings. Like Habermas, Gadamer attacks the Enlightenment conception of a single path to truth, arguing that there are many paths other than that of reason and logic. Gadamer also challenges the hegemony of the autonomous, rational subject, emphasizing instead the way in which languages create the "horizon of meaning" in which we live. For Gadamer, "horizons" are perspectives in which we are all located, positions from which we understand the world. Like other approaches rooted in language, Gadamer's approach has allowed feminists to analyze the linguistic constitution of social reality, and, in particular, the historical context that informs that reality. Linda Alcoff (1996) and Lorraine Code, for example, argue that feminists can employ Gadamer's approach to articulate an understanding of knowledge that is engaged, situated, and feminist.

See also Beauvoir, Simone de; Cixous, Helene; Code, Lorraine; Continental Philosophy; Critical Theory; Derrida, Jacques; Enlightenment; Feminist Epistemology;

Feminist Metaphysics; Feminist Philosophy; Foucault, Michel; Gadamer, Hans-Georg; Habermas, Jürgen; Hegel, Georg Wilhelm Friedrich; Heidegger, Martin; Hermeneutics; Husserl, Edmund; Irigaray, Luce; Kristeva, Julia; Marx, Karl; Marxist Philosophy; Merleau-Ponty, Maurice; Nietzsche, Friedrich; Postmodernism; Rationalism; Sartre, Jean-Paul; Structuralism and Poststructuralism.

Bibliography

Alcoff, Linda. *Real Knowing*. Ithaca: Cornell University Press, 1996.

Bartky, Sandra. *Femininity and Domination: Studies in the Phenomenology of Oppression*. New York: Routledge, 1990.

Butler, Judith. *Gender Trouble*. New York: Routledge, 1990.

Cahill, Ann, and Jennifer Hansen. *Continental Feminism Reader*. Lanham, MD: Rowman and Littlefield, 2003.

De Beauvoir, Simone. *The Second Sex*. Hammondsworth: Penguin, 1972.

Hartsock, Nancy. *Money, Sex, and Power*. New York: Longman, 1983.

Hekman, Susan. *Gender and Knowledge: Elements of a Postmodern Feminism*. Cambridge: Polity, 1990.

Nicholson, Linda, ed. *Feminism/Postmodernism*. New York: Routledge, 1990.

Smith, Dorothy. *The Everyday World as Problematic: A Feminist Sociology*. Boston: Northeastern University Press, 1987.

Young, Iris Marion. *Throwing Like a Girl and Other Essays in Feminist Philosophy and Social Theory*. Bloomington: Indiana University Press, 1990.

Susan Hekman (2005)

FEMINISM AND PRAGMATISM

Pragmatist feminists hold some or all the following conceptual commitments, which are rooted in classical pragmatism:

(1) A rejection of foundationalist and essentialist notions of reality and truth, in favor of an understanding of reality as the result of mutually constitutive transactions between agents and their environments and of truth as good knowing that it enables an inquiry to grow

(2) A recognition that chance and uncertainty are parts of one's world, not (necessarily) signs of one's incomplete understanding of that world

(3) A rejection of sharp dichotomies separating theory from practice, self from world, mind from body, fact from value, and reason from emotion

(4) A view of inquiry as experiential and experimental: Inquiry springs from experience, and its findings must have the capacity to improve on experience, for the individual or for society

(5) Respect for the philosophical value of ordinary, everyday experience—including experiences that characterize women's lives

(6) Cognizance that the community of inquirers plays a central role in inquiry and a commitment to improving the goodness of inquiry by actively increasing the perspectives represented in the community

(7) An understanding of ends, aims, and values as experimental: subject to revision in light of new experiences

(8) A recognition that democracy provides a model of intellectual and moral growth for society and the individual possessing the greatest capacity to promote justice

Feminist strands of pragmatism stand in the somewhat unusual position of having been part of their parent tradition virtually since that tradition emerged in the late nineteenth century. However, only in the 1980s did an explicitly, self-consciously pragmatist feminist philosophical movement emerge.

EARLY FIGURES

The pragmatist movement counted women and feminists among its members from the early days; many were associated with the classical pragmatist John Dewey as his colleagues and as his students. These theorists worked almost exclusively at the margins of academic philosophy, as educators and school administrators, policy makers, and social activists. While their outsider status was not always chosen, their decisions to work in the community as teachers, policy makers, and community workers nevertheless embody a pragmatist commitment to creating philosophy that works to ameliorate the problems of everyday life—not simply the problems of philosophy.

Among women who contributed to the emergence of pragmatist thought in explicitly feminist ways, perhaps none exerted greater influence on subsequent pragmatist feminism than Jane Addams (1860–1935), a social activist, theorist, and founder of the Hull House settlement. Her choice to theorize with, rather than about, the people of the neighborhoods surrounding Hull House embodied a pragmatist understanding that inquiry transforms both inquirer and inquired; she and the other residents of Hull House produced both theory and public policy that began in, and returned to, the problems of the people of their community. Addams's feminism was rooted in her understanding that women are, by enculturation if not by nature, different from men, and that such differences constitute actual assets—in city government, for instance. There, women's experiences as homemakers and mothers directly prepare them for the associated tasks of running a city. Addams's long association with Dewey significantly shaped the intellectual development of both theorists, particularly in the areas of democracy and education.

Charlotte Perkins Gilman (1860–1935), a contemporary of Dewey and an acquaintance of Addams, shared with them a debt to the evolutionary theory of Charles Darwin. All three understood evolutionary theory to assert that humans have both a capacity and an obligation to improve the conditions of their world through reflection on concrete experience; they also understood that value concepts like improvement, progress, and the good themselves evolve as a result of reflection and action; they are not fixed and timeless. Gilman's *Women and Economics* (1998) offers an evolutionary account of human social development that argues for the necessity (indeed, inevitability) of women's evolution as workers and public figures; only as women so develop will humans realize their social and intellectual potential. Gilman argued for transformations of domestic life to enable women to take their place in the world of work: public kitchens and day care centers, for instance. She saw these proposals echoed in organizations and programs for working women developed at Hull House.

Several early women pragmatists worked as educators. Ella Flagg Young (1845–1918), Elsie Ripley Clapp (1879–1965), and Lucy Sprague Mitchell (1878–1967) studied with Dewey—in some cases, when they were already mature thinkers who exerted an influence on him. All three worked actively to develop pragmatist models of education that emphasized experiential, student-oriented, community-based learning: Young, as general supervisor of the Laboratory School at the University of Chicago; Mitchell, as a researcher and founder of the Bank Street School in New York; and Clapp, as the head of a community school system in Arthurdale, West Virginia, the first New Deal community in the United States.

CONTEMPORARY THEORISTS

Contemporary pragmatist feminists, like feminists working in other traditions, have undertaken two separate but related projects: reclaiming forgotten or neglected work of early women/feminist pragmatists and advancing pragmatist thought by developing new, explicitly feminist versions of it. In the first category, *Pragmatism and Feminism* (1996), by Charlene Haddock Seigfried, presents a systematic exposition of the contributions of early women pragmatists, documenting the lines of influence running among Addams, Clapp, Mitchell, Young, and Dewey. As Seigfried points out, such recovery work transforms both the history of pragmatist philosophy (restoring important voices that were lost) and its conceptual frameworks (engendering a reconceptualization of pragmatist positions that incorporates feminist contributions) (p. 6). Illustrative of this transformation is the work of Marilyn Fischer and Judy D. Whipps (2003), who elucidate the importance of Addams's work for the pragmatist tradition in their edited collection of her writings on peace.

Theorists working on the second task—developing feminist versions of pragmatist thought—draw on the (implicitly and explicitly) feminist and antiracist thought of several earlier pragmatist thinkers, including Addams, Dewey, W. E. B. Du Bois (1868–1963), and Alain Locke (1886–1954). Seigfried's *Pragmatism and Feminism* also marks the most significant early contribution to this project; it lays out a broad, flexible research agenda in epistemology, ethics, and sociopolitical philosophy to be undertaken by pragmatists and feminists using "a pragmatic hermaneutics of cooperation" and aimed at "changing the theoretical analyses and concrete practices of both" (1996, p. 4).

Much pragmatist feminist development has been in the area of feminist epistemology. Theorists here ground their work in the pragmatist emphasis on the primacy of experience and the experiential nature of knowing. Inquiry begins in the problems of ordinary life and possesses a melioristic function; this naturalistic epistemology is grounded in pragmatist thinkers such as Dewey and should not be conflated with Willard Van Orman Quine's naturalized epistemology.

Pragmatist feminist theorists also emphasize the pragmatist commitment to undermine or dissolve traditional dualisms between self and world, mind and body, and theory and practice. Shannon Sullivan challenges the self-world dichotomy to develop a Deweyan feminist understanding of humans as "transactional," where transaction is understood as "an active and dynamic relationship between things such that those things are co-constitutive of each other" (2001, p. 12). This gives rise to a conception of truth as "transactional flourishing":

truth and objectivity are conceived not in terms of transparency to reality, but as characteristics of transactions that enable both humans and their environments to flourish.

Pragmatist feminists have developed conceptions of reason, rationality, and objectivity that recognize the inherently collective, relational nature of these concepts—and that thus acknowledge their ethical, social, and political dimensions along with the epistemological. Lisa Heldke (1990) conceives a "coresponsible model" of objectivity grounded in responsibility to the inquiry community; on this model, inquiry becomes more objective as it acknowledges, fulfills, and expands responsibility to an increasingly pluralistic community. Reflecting the pragmatist commitment to problems of ordinary life, she develops the model through an analysis of food making, conceived as a "thoughtful practice"—a categorization that eschews the traditional division drawn between theoretical and practical activity.

Another significant body of work has developed in social and political philosophy. Theorists here utilize pragmatist understandings that social and moral ends are themselves subject to revision in light of new experience and that intelligent inquiry has melioristic potential and the pragmatist commitment to democracy, understood as a way of living emphasizing collective experimentation to transform current social realities. In *The Task of Utopia* (2001) Erin McKenna develops a pragmatist feminist concept of utopia, which understands it not as a fixed state, but as a characteristic of a (democratic) community's collective inquiry and education process. Such a utopia is necessarily open-ended, its aims always in principle subject to revision.

Pragmatist feminists deepen classical pragmatist notions of community, which emphasize the importance of pluralism for democracy and inquiry; and of personhood, which reject liberal notions of the individual in favor of a relational, transactional model. Feminists show why the perspectives of marginalized persons must be explicitly sought, if people's democratic communities are to continue to grow, promote justice, and create more reliable understandings of social reality. Whipps (2004) draws from Addams a form of communitarianism that rejects the radical individualism characteristic of its contemporary forms and recognizes the (messy, multiplicitous) ways selves are constituted through the interactions of daily life in the diverse community. And in *Deep Democracy* (1999) Judith Green creates a model of democratic practice as experimental. Her "radical critical pragmatism ... engage[s] with liberalism, communitari-

anism, postmodernism, critical theory, feminism, and cultural pluralism" (p. x), not simply to identify the weaknesses of these other traditions, but also to draw on these expanded resources to address concrete problems of democracy, most notably racial, economic, and sexual injustice.

See also Feminist Epistemology; Feminist Philosophy; Feminist Philosophy of Science.

Bibliography

Addams, Jane. *Democracy and Social Ethics*. Introduction by Charlene Haddock Seigfried. Urbana: University of Illinois Press, 2002.

Addams, Jane. *Jane Addams's Writings on Peace*. 4 vols., edited by Marilyn Fischer and Judy D. Whipps. Bristol, U.K.: Thoemmes Press, 2003.

Gilman, Charlotte Perkins. *Women and Economics: A Study of the Economic Relation between Men and Women as a Factor in Social Evolution*. Minneola, NY: Dover, 1998.

Green, Judith. *Deep Democracy: Community, Diversity, and Transformation*. Lanham, MA: Rowman and Littlefield, 1999.

Heldke, Lisa. "Foodmaking as a Thoughtful Practice" and "Recipes for Theory Making." In *Cooking, Eating, Thinking: Transformative Philosophies of Food*, edited by Deane Curtin and Lisa Heldke. Bloomington: Indiana University Press, 1990.

McKenna, Erin. *The Task of Utopia: A Pragmatist and Feminist Perspective*. Lanham, MA: Rowman and Littlefield, 2001.

Rorty, Richard. "Feminism and Pragmatism." *Michigan Quarterly Review* 30 (1991): 231–258.

Seigfried, Charlene Haddock, ed. *Feminist Interpretations of John Dewey*. University Park: Pennsylvania State University Press, 2002.

Seigfried, Charlene Haddock. *Pragmatism and Feminism: Reweaving the Social Fabric*. Chicago: University of Chicago Press, 1996.

Seigfried, Charlene Haddock, ed. "Special Issue on Feminism and Pragmatism." *Hypatia* 8 (2) (1993).

Sullivan, Shannon. *Living across and through Skins: Transactional Bodies, Pragmatism, and Feminism*. Bloomington: Indiana University Press, 2001.

Whipps, Judy D. "Jane Addams's Social Thought as a Model for a Pragmatist-Feminist Communitarianism." *Hypatia* 19 (3) (2004): 118–133.

Whipps, Judy D. "Pragmatist Feminism." In *Stanford Encyclopedia of Philosophy*, edited by Edward N. Zalta. Stanford, CA: Metaphysics Research Lab, Stanford University, 2004.

Lisa Heldke (2005)

FEMINISM AND THE HISTORY OF PHILOSOPHY

The beginning of the twenty-first century was witness to an emergent transformation of the history of philosophy. While still the subject of intense debate within philosophy, the dominance of the image of the history of philosophy as a succession of "master thinkers" whose texts provide the historical background to contemporary philosophical debates has begun to wane. As philosophers come to embrace the historiography of philosophy and accept that attention to the past is not a simple process of reading past masters, methodological issues have become central to the history of philosophy and questions are being raised concerning the canonization of both theorists and texts, the conceptual role of history in philosophy, the accessibility of the past, and the role of interpretation.

Feminist history of philosophy has played a significant role in this transformation. From its outset, feminist historians of philosophy have raised issues of canon formation and have developed new and productive reading strategies in their efforts to attend both to women and to the role of the feminine in the history of philosophy. These efforts to understand the apparent absence or denigration of women and of the feminine have led to interpretive strategies that have value beyond feminist concerns and have contributed to the transformation of contemporary history of philosophy.

Feminist attention to gender in the history of philosophy has led to the recovery of lost or silenced women philosophers, as well as having called into question models of philosophy and philosophical concepts emerging from a privileging of the masculine. As feminists came to understand the extent to which privileged concepts such as reason and justice revolve around the denigration of so-called "feminine" traits, they began not only to question the division between reason, emotion, and imagination in the history of philosophy, but also to search for and develop interpretive strategies that would not perpetuate such divisions.

ATTENTION TO WOMEN

Feminist attention to women in the history of philosophy has raised issues concerning canon formation. Until the mid- to late twentieth century, much of contemporary history of philosophy proceeded along a model of "master thinkers" in which only the truly great minds of philosophy are considered worthy of attention. Admittedly there has been significant debate within the various tra-

ditions of philosophy as well as between different historical periods concerning which philosophers are indeed worthy. In addition, even when there is general agreement about the canonization of such philosophers as René Descartes, David Hume, Immanuel Kant, and Plato, there remains significant contestation concerning which aspects of their corpus are most central, with Descartes's *Meditations*, for example, receiving far more attention than his *Passions of the Soul* in twentieth-century analytic history of philosophy.

As feminist philosophers of history contest the "great man" model of history, they have begun to demonstrate the importance of a richer approach to the history of philosophy. The recovery of women philosophers like Elisabeth of the Palatine, Jane Addams, Mary Astell, Sor Juana Inés de la Cruz, Jacqueline Pascal, Anna Maria van Schurman, and Mary Wollstonecraft has begun to transform modern prejudices about the history of philosophy. Since there were hundreds of women who contributed to philosophy, their absence from contemporary histories brings to the foreground the complex values that inform the narratives of philosophy and determine which questions and styles count as philosophical and whose voices are sufficiently influential to be chronicled. Feminist historians of philosophy have demonstrated, for example, how the nineteenth century move to excise from the canon work judged to be motivated by religious faith resulted in numerous philosophical schools and philosophical styles, and with them the work of many women, being excluded from the domain of philosophy. Feminists have also pointed out that if we limit our definition of philosophy to that work done only in the academy and the seminary, then we will exclude those locations, such as the convent and the salon, where women are most likely to be found in certain historical periods.

These investigations of the roles of women in philosophy have led to an enriched appreciation of the workings of the canon. For instance, feminist attention to the philosophy of Princess Elisabeth and the impact of her philosophical influence on Descartes has led to a renewed appreciation not only of *Passions of the Soul*, but of Elisabeth's philosophy in its own right and of her influence on Descartes's philosophy. Such feminist work details Elisabeth's efforts to develop a unique philosophical position that does not divorce reason from the body, but defends a rich interaction between the body and the mind without reducing one to the other or denying Descartes's intuition that thought is not determined by extension. Thanks to such work feminist historians of philosophy have been able to uncover lines of influence between Elisabeth's thought and Descartes's *Passions*, arguing for a subtle yet important shift in his ideas concerning the role of embodiment upon the mind resulting from their correspondence. In this way, recovery of the work of women philosophers and the feminist desire to undo the denigration of faculties and traits (such as the body) that have been associated with the feminine go hand-in-hand with a rereading of the canon.

Feminist attention to women has also included a chronicling of philosophers' perceptions of woman. Through this lens feminists have uncovered a systematic perception of woman and the feminine as inferior and man and the masculine as the true form. This has led philosophers of sexual difference such as Luce Irigaray to argue that woman has been defined not in terms of true difference, but in terms of lack according to an A (male) / -A (female) logic, a logic well illustrated by Hegel's claim that women while educable, are not capable of activities like science or philosophy that demand a universal faculty. In such a schema, woman and the feminine receive no positive definition, no true difference, but are merely an inferior inversion of the masculine. These investigations have led to the contention that the very concepts of philosophy—reason, justice, virtue—have themselves been inscribed by this conception of man and thereby by the masculine as the true form.

PHILOSOPHICAL IMAGINARY

Feminist attention to gender thus presents as an issue central to philosophical investigation the question of whether the central categories of philosophy are formed through an exclusion or denigration of the feminine. Genevieve Lloyd's early study of the "maleness" of reason demonstrated that conceptions of rationality have privileged traits historically associated with masculinity and required control or transcendence of those traits historically associated with the feminine such as the body, the emotions, and the passions. Michèle Le Dœuff has referred to the often unacknowledged linkage of concepts, images, and metaphors in philosophical texts as the philosophical imaginary. She argues that this imaginary often inscribes values historically associated with masculinity onto dominant philosophical conceptions of reason and argues that this is not an instance of an individual philosopher's sexism that can be ignored or excised for it is at the core of the values from which the category emerges.

This scholarship has led to various efforts to identify and refigure the role of "the feminine" in the texts of canonized philosophers and to examine the specifically feminine sites of philosophy. These reading strategies are diverse. Some, like Annette Baier's work on Hume or Barbara Herman's analysis of Kant, return to the canonical texts to tease out new or overlooked resources for revaluing the role of embodiment, imagination, and the affective life. Others turn to the work of "recovered" women philosophers to trace alternatives to dominant models of philosophy. Catherine Villanueva Gardner, for example, argues that a complex notion of sensibility and a rhetorical style that exemplifies sensibility can be found in the work of women philosophers such as Wollstonecraft, Catharine Macaulay, Christine De Pisan, George Eliot, and Mechthild of Magdeburg that provide a rich conception of the role the passions play in moral philosophy. Another reading strategy is to provide correctives to histories of philosophy that have ignored topics like the emotions or the imagination as does Susan James (1997) in her account of the passions in seventeenth-century philosophy. Yet another style of feminist reading can be found in the work of Luce Irigaray who focuses on the moments of instability in philosophical texts caused by the contradictory effort to achieve universality through a denial of sexual difference. It is her goal to open the historical texts of philosophy to contemporary feminist concerns not simply to confront what has been repressed, but to rethink it.

Feminist attention to the philosophical imaginary and the lessons learned from the canonization of particular philosophical styles, has led to sensitivity to the rhetorical dimensions of philosophical writings, as well as to an appreciation of their affective dimensions. But such attention to style also means a rich situating of the history of philosophy and a realization that the writings of the past are not transparent. The meanings and affective resonance of philosophical texts are neither in the control of the author nor the contemporary interpreter of the text, but involve a complex interplay between the author's cultural context and the concerns of the contemporary reader. In this way, mainstream efforts to excise the figural in order to uncover the literal truth of canonical texts give way in feminist rereadings to an appreciation of the role of imagination in philosophy and better understanding of how reason, imagination, and emotion are interwoven in the practice of philosophy. This attention to rhetoric and affect is another dimension of the feminist rejection of conceptions of reason divorced from the "feminine."

In such attention to neglected aspects of historical texts, feminists are motivated by our own feminist wonder at the relation between reason and emotion in the play of the canon and a feminist inspired desire to find a place in-between mind and body. In this sense, our desires are enacted in our reading strategies.

See also Astell, Mary; Baier, Annette; Descartes, René Eliot, George; Elisabeth, Princess of Bohemia; Feminist Philosophy; History and Historiography of Philosophy; Hume, David; Irigaray, Luce; Kant, Immanuel; Plato; Wollstonecraft, Mary; Women in the History of Philosophy.

Bibliography

Atherton, Margaret, ed. *Women Philosophers of the Early Modern Period*. Indianapolis, IN: Hackett, 1994.

Baier, Annette. *A Progress of Sentiments: Reflections on Hume's Treatise*. Cambridge, MA: Harvard University Press, 1991.

Bordo, Susan. *The Flight to Objectivity: Essays on Cartesianism and Culture*. Albany: State University of New York Press, 1987.

Conley, John J. *The Suspicion of Virtue: Women Philosophers in Neoclassical France*. Ithaca, NY: Cornell University Press, 2002.

Deutscher, Penelope. *Yielding Gender: Feminism, Deconstructionism, and the History of Philosophy*. London and New York: Routledge, 1997.

Dykeman, Therese Boos, ed. *The Neglected Canon: Nine Women Philosophers First to the Twentieth Century*. Boston and London: Kluwer Academic Publishers, 1999.

Gardner, Catherine Villanueva. *Rediscovering Women Philosophers: Philosophical Genre and the Boundaries of Philosophy*. Boulder: Westview Press, 2000.

Herman, Barbara. *The Practice of Moral Judgment*. Cambridge, MA: Harvard University Press, 1993.

Irigaray, Luce. *An Ethics of Sexual Difference*. Translated by Carolyn Burke and Gillian C. Gill. Ithaca, NY: Cornell University Press, 1993.

Irigaray, Luce. *Speculum of the Other Woman*. Translated by Gillian C. Gill. Ithaca, NY: Cornell University Press, 1985.

James, Susan. *Passions and Action: The Emotions in Seventeenth-Century Philosophy*. Oxford: Clarendon Press, 1997.

Kofman, Sarah. *Socrates: Fictions of a Philosopher*. Translated by Catherine Porter. Ithaca, NY: Cornell University Press, 1998.

Le Dœuff, Michèle. *The Philosophical Imaginary*. Translated by C. Gordon. Stanford, CA: Stanford University Press, 1989.

Lloyd, Genevieve. *Feminism and the History of Philosophy*. New York: Oxford University Press, 2002.

Lloyd, Genevieve. *The Man of Reason: "Male" and "Female" in Western Philosophy*. Minneapolis: University of Minnesota Press, 1984.

Nye, Andrea. *The Princess and the Philosopher: Letters of Elisabeth of Palatine to René Descartes*. Lanham, MD: Rowman and Littlefield, 1999.

Oliver, Kelly. *Womanizing Nietzsche: Philosophy's Relation to "The Feminine."* New York: Routledge, 1995.

O'Neill, Eileen. *Women Philosophers of the Seventeenth and Eighteenth Centuries: A Collection of Primary Sources*. Oxford: Oxford University Press, 1998.

Schott, Robin. *Cognition and Eros: A Critique of the Kantian Paradigm*. Boston: Beacon Press, 1988.

Tougas, Cecile T., and Sara Ebenrick, eds. *Presenting Women Philosophers*. Philadelphia: Temple University Press, 2000.

Tuana, Nancy, series ed. *Re-Reading the Canon*. 26 vols. University Park: Pennsylvania State University Press, 1994–2005.

Tuana, Nancy. *Woman and the History of Philosophy*. New York: Paragon Press, 1992.

Waithe, Mary Ellen, ed. *A History of Women Philosophers*. Vols. 1–4. Boston and London: Kluwer Academic Publishers, 1987–1995.

Nancy Tuana (2005)

FEMINIST AESTHETICS AND CRITICISM

As artists in the late 1960s and early 1970s started to produce explicitly feminist works, critics and historians of the various arts began to examine a previously unnoticed gender bias in the Western artistic tradition. Feminists discern this bias on two levels.

First, feminist critics charge that canonical artworks represent women and men in markedly different ways, a difference evident in the organization and scenarios of the works themselves. Whereas men are typically portrayed as strong, active, heroic, and playing important historical roles, women are nearly always shown as weak, inert, and vulnerable; in domestic or nurturing roles; identified with nature; and as sexually available for men's needs. This is perhaps most evident in the visual arts where representations of passive, anonymous, and vulnerable female nudes dominate many historical periods. Drawing on semiotics, psychoanalysis, and Marxist theory, feminists sought to expose and analyze manifestations of gender bias in structural features of traditionally admired artworks. One of the most influential concepts developed in this early period of criticism is the notion of "the male gaze" (Mulvey 1975). Although it is sometimes mistaken for an empirical description of individuals' actual viewing practices, "the male gaze" in fact refers to the viewpoint that many pictures adopt toward women, portraying women as passive objects of sexual desire.

Second, feminists argue that fully addressing gender inequality in the arts also requires questioning the canon; that is, those works traditionally deemed artistically excellent that form the core of a given discipline. Feminists are skeptical of the canon for two reasons. First, although women make up roughly half of the population, they are almost entirely absent from the pantheon of great artists. Second, the kinds of artifacts traditionally produced by women—for example, quilts, pottery, needlework, and weaving—have not been taken seriously as art but rather have been relegated to the diminished categories of "decorative arts" or "crafts." The coincidence of pervasive gender inequality in the world with the exclusion of women's artifacts from the canon suggests that the canon might be shaped by more than purely aesthetic concerns. But what exactly is the relationship between unequal social relations and women's lack of representation in the canon? What explains the paucity of great women artists and the underestimation of artifacts customarily produced by women?

Some feminists, most notably Linda Nochlin (1971), argue that social, economic, and institutional barriers have prevented women from making art. For instance, in much of Europe in the nineteenth century women were not allowed to attend life-drawing classes and so lacked the training and practice necessary to adequately represent the human form. Although such obstacles and lack of opportunity surely contributed to the canon's one-sided configuration, this explanation has difficulty accounting for two facts: First, despite these adverse conditions, some women have been making oil paintings, sculptures, and the like for centuries, yet none number among the canon of great artists, and second, women still encounter discrimination in the contemporary art world (Guerilla Girls 1998). The historical explanation also has trouble accounting for the exclusion of *kinds* of artifacts conventionally produced by women.

Such questions prompt a need to examine traditional understandings of art. Might the prevailing standards of artistic excellence be tainted by biases that help explain why women and the artifacts they customarily produce have been excluded from the ranks of artistic greatness? At this point feminist philosophers and theoreticians enter the conversation to scrutinize the philosophical canon itself and analyze established theories of art, artistic talent, and aesthetic experience and value.

In their critical examination of the Western philosophical tradition feminists uncover and analyze previously unnoticed gender biases in theories of art from Plato onward. Some contend, for instance, that central aesthetic concepts such as "genius" and "masterpiece" have been traditionally gendered male (Battersby 1989). Others argue that influential theories of aesthetic perception implicitly take men's experience as their model by favoring sight and hearing, which customarily play a

prominent role in men's lives, and by underestimating the aesthetic importance of those senses integral to the social roles assigned to women, namely touch, smell, and taste (Korsmeyer 2004). Finally, many feminist philosophers are critical of a cluster of theories and concepts that assume or attempt to justify the autonomy of art and of aesthetic appreciation and evaluation (for an overview, see Devereaux 1998). For example, some maintain that the common insistence on art's segregation from practical concerns results in the art-craft distinction and hence in the systematic depreciation of the sorts of artifacts customarily produced by women. Others make the case that the related doctrine of aesthetic formalism, which restricts artistic value to a work's formal features, departs in practice from purely formal concerns by reflecting masculine preferences for particular themes (such as the female nude). In these ways feminists argue that the presumed disinterestedness and universality of aesthetic judgment in theories following Immanuel Kant mask standards of evaluation that are partial to men's experience, preferences, and sensibilities.

Once the sources of this undervaluation of women's artistic efforts have been uncovered and analyzed, feminists then aim to delineate the positive means to overcome it. Besides providing women with opportunities in the art world, the prevailing conceptions of art and standards of artistic excellence must be revised. On this point most agree, yet several different solutions can be distinguished.

PERSPECTIVISM

One approach calls for the outright abandonment of the problematic concepts, methods, and categorizations of traditional aesthetics. Artistic autonomy, aesthetic formalism, the art-craft distinction, presumptions of a disinterested aesthetic attitude, and concepts of talent or genius are all to be rejected in favor of a perspectivism that embraces a pluralistic conception of art and artistic value (Hein and Lauter 1993). This approach eschews all pretension to universal standards of aesthetic excellence, leaving no standpoint from which to adjudicate between differing understandings of art and aesthetic experience. In practice this has led some art historians and critics to reject the notion of artistic canons altogether and to replace talk of art with that of visual or material culture (Pollock 1999).

One concern is that this perspectival approach risks rendering any notion of artistic value meaningless, a result that is particularly unwelcome given feminists' efforts to demonstrate the artistic merit of women's artifactual efforts. Another worry is that one ought not mistake the discriminatory and faulty use of concepts such as genius or of methods like formalism for inherent features of these concepts, methods, or standards themselves. It does not follow from the fact that the so-called universal voice of aesthetic judgment has surreptitiously been biased toward masculine concerns that the very ideal of universality in aesthetic judgment is inherently gender biased. Indeed, that traditional theories of art have been criticized for their *bias* is evidence of feminism's reliance on the notion of impartial standards of artistic excellence.

REVISIONISM

Some feminists warn against the assumption that all of aesthetic theory has been tainted by gender bias (Felski 1998) and point to developments in philosophical aesthetics, such as the critique of disinterestedness, that are continuous with feminism's aims (Silvers 1998). Others show how at least aspects of certain ideals such as artistic autonomy are actually useful for feminism (Devereaux 1998). These developments suggest that feminism might be compatible with traditional theories of art and aesthetic experience, provided that these theories are purged of their masculine biases. This could motivate revaluation of those canonical works that cater to male-defined assumptions about women, on the one hand, and would allow these theories and their central concepts to be adapted to the kinds of objects customarily produced by women, on the other hand. In practical terms this approach would mean integrating women's artistic efforts into the canon, a process that some historians and critics have already begun (Guerilla Girls 1998).

DIFFERENCE AESTHETICS

Still, some insist, incorporating women into the canon misses what is distinctive about their art. Likewise, they contend, traditional aesthetic theories cannot be adequately modified to capture the uniqueness of women's experience, preferences, values, sensibilities, and modes of expression. Instead, a variety of alternative aesthetic concepts and theories of art indigenous to women is proposed (Battersby 1989, Frueh 1998, Robinson 2001, Barwell 1993, Donovan 1993, French 1993, Lorraine 1993). Some French feminists like Irigaray and Kristeva, for instance, argue that women imagine, express themselves, and experience art somatically or experimentally, and that these distinctive methods require standards, concepts, and definitions of art that differ radically from the traditional ones (See Korsmeyer, 2004, Chapter 6, for

an overview). In practical terms, this could lead to the formation of separate women's canons in each of the arts.

Critics charge that this approach rests on false essentialist assumptions about woman's nature and overlooks important differences between women such as ethnicity, race, class, sexual orientation, ability, and age, to name only a few (Felski 1998). Some also worry that separate principles and criteria of artistic excellence and aesthetic experience risk leaving the canon with its biases in tact while ghettoizing women's art (Nochlin 1971, Pollock 1999).

The debate about how to deal with gender bias in artworks, canon formation, and traditional theories of art is lively and ongoing. Many of the disputes rest on the question of how, if at all, gender matters to the production, appreciation, and evaluation of art. Besides these unresolved questions, all approaches face new challenges such as the insistence that one cannot divorce feminist struggles from those of other disenfranchised groups. For these reasons, feminist aesthetics does not involve a particular stance or methodological commitment but, rather, unites a variety of approaches toward the common goal of ending women's subordination in the arts and discourses about the arts.

See also Aesthetics, History of; Feminism and Continental Philosophy; Feminist Philosophy.

Bibliography

Barwell, Ismay. "Feminine Perspectives and Narrative Points of View." In *Aesthetics in Feminist Perspective*, edited by Hilde Hein and Carolyn Korsmeyer, 93–104. Bloomington: Indiana University Press, 1993.

Battersby, Christine. *Gender and Genius: Towards a Feminist Aesthetics*. Bloomington: Indiana University Press, 1989.

Brand, Peg Zeglin, and Mary Devereaux. "Women, Art, and Aesthetics." *Hypatia: A Journal of Feminist Philosophy* (Special Issue) 18 (4) (2003).

Brand, Peg Zeglin, and Carolyn Korsmeyer, eds. *Feminism and Tradition in Aesthetics*. University Park: Pennsylvania State University Press, 1995.

Devereaux, Mary. "Autonomy and Its Feminist Critics." In *Encyclopedia of Aesthetics*. Vol. 1, edited by Michael Kelly, 178–182. New York: Oxford University Press, 1998.

Donovan, Josephine. "Everyday Use and Moments of Being: Toward a Nondominative Aesthetic." In *Aesthetics in Feminist Perspective*, edited by Hilde Hein and Carolyn Korsmeyer, 53–67. Bloomington: Indiana University Press, 1993.

Felski, Rita. "Feminism: Critique of Feminist Aesthetics." In *Encyclopedia of Aesthetics*, edited by Michael Kelly, 170–172. New York: Oxford University Press, 1998.

French, Marilyn. "Is There a Feminist Aesthetic?" In *Aesthetics in Feminist Perspective*, edited by Hilde Hein and Carolyn

Korsmeyer, 68–76. Bloomington: Indiana University Press, 1993.

Frueh, Joanna. "Towards a Feminist Theory of Art Criticism." In *Feminist Art Criticism: An Anthology*, edited by Arlene Raven, Cassandra L. Langer, and Joanna Frueh, 153–165. Ann Arbor, MI: UMI Research Press, 1998.

Guerilla Girls. *The Guerilla Girls' Bedside Companion to the History of Western Art*. New York: Penguin Books, 1998.

Hein, Hilde, and Carolyn Korsmeyer, eds. *Aesthetics in Feminist Perspective*. Bloomington: Indiana University Press, 1993.

Hein, Hilde, and Estella Lauter. "Re-enfranchising Art: Feminist Interventions in the Theory of Art." In *Aesthetics in Feminist Perspective*, edited by Hilde Hein and Carolyn Korsmeyer, 21–34. Bloomington: Indiana University Press, 1993.

Korsmeyer, Carolyn. *Gender and Aesthetics: An Introduction*. New York: Routledge, 2004.

Lorraine, Renée. "A Gynecentric Aesthetic." In *Aesthetics in Feminist Perspective*, edited by Hilde Hein and Carolyn Korsmeyer, 35–52. Bloomington: Indiana University Press, 1993.

Mulvey, Laura. "Visual Pleasure and Narrative Cinema." *Screen* 16 (3) (1975): 6–18.

Nochlin, Linda. "Why Have There Been No Great Women Artists?" *ARTnews* 69 (9) (1971): 22–39.

Parker, Rozsika, and Griselda Pollock. *Old Mistresses: Women, Art, and Ideology*. New York: Pantheon Press, 1981.

Pollock, Griselda. *Differencing the Canon: Feminist Desire and the Writing of Art's Histories*. London: Routledge, 1999.

Robinson, Hilary, ed. *Feminism—Art—Theory: An Anthology, 1968–2000*. Malden, MA: Blackwell, 2001.

Silvers, Anita. "Feminism: An Overview." In *Encyclopedia of Aesthetics*. Vol. 2, edited by Michael Kelly, 161–167. New York: Oxford University Press, 1998.

A. W. Eaton (2005)

FEMINIST EPISTEMOLOGY

Feminist epistemology emerges from reflection on feminist inquiry. Core themes in feminist epistemology can be understood by considering a prima facie tension between two distinct strands of feminist research, one critical and one constructive. The critical strand aims to expose male bias in research while the positive strand aims to construct theories that are avowedly feminist and that bring women's experiences and interests to the center of inquiry. Most disciplines have come under critical scrutiny for male bias. Forms of bias identified include:

(1) Marginalizing women or women's interests. For example, economic theory is charged with making women's economic contributions invisible, political theory with overlooking power relations in the family, and evolutionary theory and anthropology with privileging male activities.

(2) Producing theories that naturalize and thus reinforce oppressive gender relations. Primatology and sociobiology are among the disciplines that have been charged with such bias.

(3) Embedding gendered metaphors that bias theory selection.

(4) Presupposing cognitive styles that arise from male psychosocial development. This charge is laid against philosophy, scientific method, and theories of moral development.

A puzzle immediately arises, however: If such research is bad because biased, then how can the constructive strand of feminist research escape a similar charge of bias and hence of epistemic fault? The puzzle deepens still further: Epistemic norms, including norms of objectivity, have themselves been charged with male bias. A charge of bias seems, however, to require a commitment to the value of objectivity. This puzzle is called "the bias paradox" (Antony 1993, pp. 114–115) and provides the context in which core themes in feminist epistemology can be understood. These are: the ideological role of epistemic norms; the importance of situated knowledge; the role of values in inquiry; and the nature of objectivity.

THE IDEOLOGICAL ROLE OF EPISTEMIC NORMS

Feminists have charged epistemic norms with being male biased. MacKinnon's analysis of the stance of objectivity as involving two components—distance and aperspectivity—is representative: "To perceive reality accurately, one must be distant from what one is looking at and view it from no place and at no time in particular, hence from all places and times at once" (MacKinnon 1989, p. 97).

To the extent that a putative knowledge claim can be shown to be the product of the inquirer's social situation, that claim is undercut as knowledge: "If social knowledge can be interpreted in terms of the social determinates of the knower, it is caused. Therefore its truth value, in this definition of the test for truth, is undercut. If it has a time or place—or gender—it becomes doubtful because situated" (MacKinnon 1989, p. 98).

Aperspectivity is alleged to be a "strategy of male hegemony" (MacKinnon 1982, p. 57) that maintains gender relations in three ways: by being implicated in the objectification of women, by masking malebias in research, and by deauthorizing women as knowers. According to MacKinnon, aperspectivity lends support to the (false) belief that women are by nature fitted to the position of eroticized subordination prescribed by current gender relations. Men project onto women the qualities (e.g., docility and submissiveness) that they desire women have. When such projection is accompanied by the social power to make women behave as desired and to silence contesting conceptions of social reality, women come to have the properties men ascribe to them. The stance of objectivity allows men to assume that the regularities they observe are objective and to overlook the exercise of power that produced them. In this way, aperspectivity masks the fundamentally prescriptive nature of gender norms and thus lends stability to the oppressive relations constitutive of gender.

Aperspectivity also enables mainstream research to evade critical scrutiny. Even though, given the theory-dependence of method, all research requires presuppositions, mainstream theoretical presuppositions will typically not need to be articulated and defended. Since the beliefs that feminists contest are relatively entrenched, it will tend to be feminists and not mainstream researchers who are called on to defend the presuppositions of their research. Thus, credibility is differentially apportioned between feminist and mainstream views on gender.

In addition, norms that disparage knowledge claims that can be explained as the result of the inquirer's social location are incompatible with feminist method, including the method of consciousness raising. While the formats of consciousness-raising groups—a grass-roots phenomenon chiefly of the 1960s and 1970s—differed, they focused on recounting women's day-to-day experiences, especially of intimate relationships, and on their emotional responses to those experiences. In women's often-inchoate responses to their day-to-day experiences were found the resources with which to understand women's social position. Given that this method starts out from a detailed examination of women's lived experience an experience both available because of and constitutive of women's gender subordination, it finds social location to be an epistemic asset rather than a liability. Different epistemic frameworks offer different accounts of when and how social location is an epistemic asset. This is the subject of the next section.

SITUATED KNOWLEDGE

Feminist standpoint theory begins from the Marxist assumption that material life shapes consciousness, and it draws an analogy between the position of the proletariat under capitalism and women under patriarchy. Just as the proletariat has a privileged standpoint from which to understand the nature of capitalist social relations, there is an epistemically privileged *standpoint* from which to understand the nature of patriarchal social relations. The basis of this standpoint lies in the sexual division of labor. Key features of women's relation to material life that Hartsock argues provide the grounds for the feminist standpoint are women's domestic labor and their role in childbearing and rearing; the experience of female embodment, including pregnancy and lactation; and the relational self-conception that object relations theorists argue is the result of girls being raised by mothers with whom they can share gender identification. The standpoint is identified as feminist rather than as women's standpoint to signal that the understanding it embodies must be struggled for and does not arise simply in virtue of occupying a subordinated social position.

Patricia Collins defends a black feminist standpoint, which she argues generates its own epistemology that emphasizes experience over book learning, dialogue in assessing knowledge claims, and relations of care and personal accountability. She finds the grounds for a black feminist standpoint in black women's experience of multiple oppressions.

Standpoint theorists reject any conception of objectivity that disparages beliefs that are to be explained by the social location of the believer as merely caused and hence as not truth tracking. They thus resolve the bias paradox by claiming that feminist perspectives provide insight into social relations that are obfuscated by dominant nonfeminist perspectives.

Standpoint theory is charged with valorizing oppression, with being unable to explain which standpoints have epistemic privilege without circularity, and with presupposing an overly simple and exclusionary conception of gender. Feminist postmodern charges standpoint theory with essentialism; that is with making false and exclusionary generalizations about women and their experiences. Feminist postmodernism challenges the stability of the category of woman: One is never simply a woman, but always a woman of some particular race, ethnicity, class, sexuality or historical and national location. Gender is constructed differently at each of these intersectional nodes of identity: One cannot extract from these complex and shifting social categories the single variable *gender*. Destabilizing the category *woman* undercuts the possibility of *a* feminist standpoint; moreover, given there is no in principle limit to the fragmentation of social categories, positing a black feminist standpoint likewise risks making false and exclusionary generalizations about black women.

The epistemic resources and liabilities of social location and other aspects of situated epistemic agency (embodiment, specifically human cognitive architecture, and so on) can be recognized without embracing the notion of epistemic privilege characteristic of standpoint theory in its initial formulations. Sandra Harding argues for multiple standpoints and views, each as a source of questions rather than a source of privileged answers. Lorraine Code calls for an epistemology that takes subjectivity into account; that is, for an epistemology that studies the psychology, interests, and social–cultural locations of inquirers. Likewise, feminists influenced by naturalized epistemology call for the empirical study of those features of our situated epistemic agency that enable one to truth-track and those that prevent one from doing so. Naturalized epistemologists view epistemology as the empirical study of knowers; thus, instead of offering a priori defenses of epistemic norms, they defend a posteriori norms of inquiry designed to help human agents—that is, finite embodied, social, agents—reliably to truth track. These tailored epistemic norms might be different for dominants and for subordinates. Whether and when such norms must recommend insulating political values from inquiry is a question to be settled empirically.

VALUES AND INQUIRY

Values and interests are recognized as influencing the choice of research questions, as contributing to the ways knowledge is applied, and as constraining research methods, especially those used in research involving human subjects. There is, however, widespread skepticism about according values and interests any role in *justification*. Inquiry aims at the truth and, the skeptic presses, nonepistemic considerations can only distract from this truth-seeking goal. Permitting moral and political values to influence theory choice leads to wishful thinking and totalitarian constraint on free inquiry.

Feminist epistemologists respond that it is a mistake to see epistemic and nonepistemic values as in competition so that inquiry must be governed *either* by epistemic values *or* by nonepistemic values. Given the underdetermination of theory by evidence, so that a body of evidence counts in support of a theory only given background assumptions, and given the pragmatics of inquiry, which aims not just for truth but for *significant* truth (where significance is a function of the interests motivating the research question), inquiry will be porous to nonepistemic values. These can enter into choice of background assumptions, of explanatory concepts, and of methodological frameworks. What matters is whether the

values and interests that enter contribute to the goal of discovering significant truths and whether they are themselves defensible.

Because of their commitment to transforming gender relations, feminists are alert to background assumptions about gender that shape inference from a body of data and that shape choice of explanatory categories (e.g., the use of *dominance* to name a unified trait in primate research). This awareness has provided the platform from which to mount successful critiques of sociobiology, among other disciplines. Helen Longino argues for framework assumptions, including preference for models that allow for ontological heterogeneity and for complex multifaceted interaction over linear relations because only such models can allow one to represent complex human potentialities. This is no defense of wishful thinking: The claim being made is not that humanist political commitments determine which of two equally empirically supported theories to accept but, rather, that these commitments enjoin one to have models that enable such potentialities to be represented *if* they exist.

OBJECTIVITY REVISITED

Even though it is generally accepted that the concept of objectivity has functioned ideologically to deauthorize women as knowers, feminist epistemologists are unwilling to abandon the notion. Some argue that the conception of objectivity found in mainstream epistemology must be radically overhauled and others that mainstream epistemology has the resources to develop a conception of objectivity that is fully compatible with feminist epistemological projects both critical and constructive. A number of alternative feminist accounts of objectivity have been developed in the literature.

Naturalized epistemology rejects any conception of objectivity as requiring presupposition or bias-free inquiry. Given the theory-dependence of method, the success of inquiry depends on presuppositions. Thus, not only is the injunction to eliminate bias impossible to meet, inquiry without presuppositions would get nowhere. Inquiry based on presuppositions can yet be objective: One needs to distinguish the good biases from the bad: Good biases enable one to truth-track; bad biases prevent one from doing so. Presupposition-rich methods can yield knowledge just in case the presuppositions are approximately true.

Working within standpoint theory, Harding (1993) defends "strong objectivity" based on the notion of reflexivity: Subjects of knowledge must themselves become objects of inquiry. Their interests and social positions must be acknowledged and the presuppositions that flow from them investigated. Communities of inquiry must be made democratic for *epistemic* as well as political reasons. Drawing on postmodernist perspectives, Sandra Haraway reaches similar conclusions claiming that "feminist objectivity means quite simply "situated knowledges" (Haraway 1991, p. 188). Only situated knowers who acknowledge the partiality of their perspectives and their responsibility in adopting them can be held accountable for their knowledge claims. To achieve objectivity, Haraway advocates combining these partial located perspectives though power-sensitive conversation and through a politics of solidarity.

Longino argues that objectivity is not a property of individuals and their methods of inquiry but, rather, of communities and their structure. A community of inquiry is objective just in case it facilitates transformative criticism. In order to do this, the community must be democratically structured: It must have publicly recognized forums for critique and change in response to that critique; it must have publicly recognized standards for evaluating theories and standards that respect both cognitive and social values; and it must be characterized by equality of intellectual authority. Longino's account is procedural: Communities structured in the right way generate knowledge. She claims that this enables her to avoid begging the question about which standpoints are privileged and to avoid the naturalized epistemologist's assumption that some knowledge claims can be taken for granted. It is controversial, however, whether an account of equality of intellectual authority can, without presupposing the truth of at least some contested claims, simultaneously rule out those holding "irrelevant positions"—Longino cites New Age "crystallology" and creationism (1993, p. 118)—recognize the legitimate authority of expertise and not exclude those whose expertise has been denied for economic and political reasons.

All four accounts of objectivity recognize the importance of social relations and institutions in the production of knowledge; thus, feminist epistemology makes an important contribution to social epistemology—that family of theories that investigates epistemic dependencies and the role of social factors in knowledge and justification—by drawing critical attention to the political dimensions of the social.

See also Feminism and Continental Philosophy; Feminist Metaphysics; Feminist Philosophy; Feminist Philosophy of Science.

Bibliography

Alcoff, Linda, and Elizabeth Potter, eds. *Feminist Epistemologies*. New York: Routledge, 1993.

Anderson, Elizabeth. "Knowledge, Human Interests, and Objectivity in Feminist Epistemology." *Philosophical Topics* 23 (1995): 27–58.

Antony, Louise. "Quine as Feminist: The Radical Import of Naturalized Epistemology." In *A Mind of One's Own: Feminist Essays on Reason and Objectivity*, edited by L. Antony and C. Witt. Boulder, CO: Westview Press, (1993): 185–225.

Antony, Louise. "Sisters, Please, I'd Rather Do It Myself: A Defense of Individualism in Feminist Epistemology." *Philosophical Topics* 23 (2) (1995): 59–94.

Bar On, Bat-Ami. "Marginality and Epistemic Privilege." In *Feminist Epistemologies*, edited by Linda Alcoff and Elizabeth Potter. New York: Routledge, (1993): 83–100.

Bleier, Ruth. *Feminist Approaches to Science*. New York: Pergamon Press, 1986.

Bordo, Susan. *The Flight to Objectivity*. Albany: State University of New York Press, 1987.

Boyd, Richard. "On the Current Status of the Issue of Scientific Realism." *Erkenntnis* 19 (1983): 45–90.

Butler, Judith. *Gender Trouble*. New York: Routledge, 1990.

Chodorow, Nancy. *The Reproduction of Mothering*. Berkeley: California University Press, 1977.

Code, Lorraine. *Rhetorical Spaces: Essays on Gendered Locations*. New York: Routledge, 1995.

Code, Lorraine. *What Can She Know?* Ithaca, NY: Cornell University Press, 1991.

Collins, Patricia Hill. *Black Feminist Thought*. Boston: Unwin, 1990.

Flax, Jane. "Political Philosophy and the Patriarchal Unconscious: A Psychoanalytic Perspective on Epistemology and Metaphysics." In *Discovering Reality: Feminist Perspectives on Epistemology, Metaphysics, Methodology, and the Philosophy of Science*, edited by Sandra Harding and Merrill B. Hintikka. Dordrecht, Holland: Reidel, (1983): 245–282.

Gilligan, Carol. *In A Different Voice*. Cambridge MA: Harvard University Press, 1982.

Goldman, Alvin. *Knowledge in a Social World*. Oxford: Oxford University Press, 1999.

Haack, Susan. "Knowledge and Propaganda: Reflections of an Old Feminist." *Partisan Review* 60 (1994): 556–564.

Haraway, Donna. *Primate Visions*. New York: Routledge, 1989.

Harding, Sandra. "Rethinking Standpoint Epistemology: What is Strong Objectivity"? In *Feminist Epistemologies*, edited by Linda Alcoff and Elizabeth Potter. New York: Routledge, (1993): 49-82.

Harding, Sandra. *The Science Question in Feminism?* Ithaca: Cornell University Press, 1986.

Harding, Sandra. *Whose Science? Whose Knowledge?* Ithaca NY: Cornell University Press, 1991.

Hartsock, Nancy. "The Feminist Standpoint: A Specifically Feminist Historical Materialism." In *Discovering Reality: Feminist Perspectives on Epistemology, Metaphysics, Methodology, and the Philosophy of Science*, edited by Sanadra Harding and Merrill B. Hintikka. Dordrecht, Holland: Reidel, (1983): 283–310.

Hrdy, Sarah. *The Woman that Never Evolved*. Cambridge, MA: Harvard University Press, 1981.

Haslanger, Sally. "On Being Objective and Being Objectified." In *A Mind of One's Own: Feminist Essays on Reason and Objectivity*, edited by L. Anthony and C. Witt. Boulder, CO: Westview Press, 1993.

Keller, Evelyn Fox, and Helen E. Longino, eds. *Feminism and Science*. Oxford: Oxford University Press, 1996.

Keller, Evelyn Fox. *Reflections on Gender and Science*. New Haven: Yale University Press, 1985.

Lloyd, Genevieve. *The Man of Reason*. 2nd ed. Minneapolis: University of Minnesota Press, 1993.

Longino, Helen. *Science as Social Knowledge*. Princeton, NJ: Princeton University Press, 1990.

Longino, Helen. "Subjects, Power, and Knowledge: Description and Prescription in Feminist Philosophy of Science." In *Feminist Epistemologies*, edited by Linda Alcoff and Elizabeth Potter. New York: Routledge, (1993) 101–120.

Lugones, Maria, and Elizabeth Spelman. "Have We Got a Theory for You! Feminist Theory, Cultural Imperialism, and the Demand for 'The Woman's Voice.'" *Women's Studies International Forum* 6 (1983): 573–581.

MacKinnon, Catherine. "Feminism, Marxism, Method, and the State: An Agenda for Theory." *Signs* 7 (3) (1982): 515–544.

MacKinnon, Catherine. *Towards a Feminist Theory of the State*. Cambridge MA: Harvard University Press, 1989.

Martin, Emily. "The Egg and the Sperm: How Science has Constructed a Romance Based on Stereotypical Male–Female Roles." In *Feminism and Science*, edited by Evelyn Fox Keller and Helen E. Longino. Oxford: Oxford University Press, (1996): 103–117.

Nelson, Lynn Hankinson. *Who Knows*. Philadelphia: Temple University Press, 1990.

Okin, Susan. *Justice, Gender, and the Family*. New York: Basic Books, 1989.

Spelman, Elizabeth. *Inessential Woman: Problems of Exclusion in Feminist Thought*. Boston: Beacon Press, 1988.

Waring, Marilyn. *If Women Counted*. San Francisco: Harper Collins, 1990.

Karen Jones (2005)

FEMINIST ETHICS

Feminist ethics is a diverse and growing body of philosophical work, initially based in the recognition that most canonical accounts of morality neglected, distorted, and/or trivialized women's moral perspectives while either ignoring or defending unjust power imbalances between women and men. Feminist ethicists have largely agreed that women's invisibility in canonical ethical theories—even leaving aside the overtly misogynist statements that also litter the tradition—is not only morally objectionable in and of itself, but also profoundly distorts many of the arguments and conclusions therein. Perhaps the most nearly unanimous claim of feminist ethicists has been that what passes for a human ideal in much of mainstream philosophical ethics is in fact a male or masculine ideal—and that such bias leads us into error not simply about women, but about morality itself.

In general, feminist ethicists suspect that, in ethical theory as in other disciplines of thought and research, what has been portrayed as the human experience is in fact (at least in significant part) the distillation of a very specific experience—namely, that of highly privileged white men who relied on the exploited labor of others (typically men and women of lower economic classes and/or of despised ethnicities, as well as women of their own class and ethnicity) to enable them to pursue higher inquiry. These relationships of unjust privilege and group-based oppression, although they need not characterize human experience, in fact have done so throughout the period of time (including the present) during which Western moral philosophers have developed and refined their theories. These oppressive conditions shape people's moral beliefs, values, priorities, and characters at deep levels.

The task of feminist ethicists is to try to correct for existing biases in moral theory while also developing new theories, concepts, and strategies that will forge a path away from oppression and toward more just and humane social relationships. Bringing a feminist perspective to moral philosophy has included critiquing and reinterpreting both canonical male authors (such as Immanuel Kant, Plato, Friedrich Nietzsche, Aristotle, and David Hume) as well as reclaiming underappreciated female and/or feminist foremothers (including Simone Weil, Iris Murdoch, and Simone de Beauvoir). An early emphasis on criticizing sexist biases in traditional moral theories has given way to the formulation of new theories which, though their degree of engagement and continuity with canonical theories varies widely, all share an understanding of both gender oppression and women's perspectives as fundamental to human experience.

For feminist ethicists, where one stands in a social world pervasively structured by oppression always matters in understanding and evaluating one's moral beliefs and responsibilities. Such analysis is rendered more complex by the fact that gender is only one of many bases for oppression and privilege. Many feminist ethicists (again, like feminists in other disciplines) have devoted significant attention to the intersections among different forms of oppression, including but not limited to oppression on the basis of race, of economic class, of age, of physical and mental ability, and of sexual orientation. A central question for feminist ethicists is *how* one's positions within these and other oppressive systems—especially the kinds and degrees of power, authority, privilege, and entitlement that these positions afford one in various particular contexts—shape both one's moral character and one's moral responsibilities. This focus on power relationships and on their effects on moral life means that the boundary between feminist ethics and feminist social and political philosophy is often a fluid one.

CARE, RELATIONSHIP, AND WOMEN'S LABOR

One vital step toward remedying any masculinist bias in moral theory is to investigate and understand women's points of view. The research of educational psychologist Carol Gilligan (1982) was an important early inspiration for feminist ethicists' efforts to take seriously and learn from women's moral perception and reasoning. Based on her research interviewing males and females about moral dilemmas (both real and imagined), Gilligan argued that there are two distinct moral perspectives (or "voices") loosely associated with men and women respectively.

The justice perspective begins with a conception of persons as separate individuals who need moral rules to govern their interactions with each other, and in particular to safeguard a realm of autonomy within which each individual may act and make decisions without undue interference from others. Moral decision making is most centrally a matter of impartially adjudicating conflicts between individual rights and interests, and of seeing to it that one's actions conform to certain universal rules of conduct. According to Gilligan, the justice perspective is more prominent in the moral voices of males than in those of females.

The care perspective, in contrast, begins with a conception of persons as embedded in social relationships in which they bear different and sometimes conflicting responsibilities to one another. Here, the priority is on creating and preserving connections and on avoiding and ending suffering. One's primary responsibility is to respond to the needs of individuals located in concrete, particular situations, often by strengthening the relationships that support those individuals. Gilligan found that the care perspective is expressed most prominently and most frequently by women and girls, and urged that theorists pay due attention and respect to this perspective, rather than seeing it as an inferior and immature form of moral reasoning.

Since the 1990s, an early tendency to identify feminist ethics with care ethics has receded as feminist ethics itself grows more diverse and wide-ranging. Nonetheless, some of the themes that Gilligan highlighted continue to occupy a central place in the thinking of many feminist ethicists. One such theme is what is sometimes called a relational conception of the person. Annette Baier (1985) usefully captures this concept by describing persons as essentially "second persons"; that is, beings whose subjectivities are formed and maintained in and through connections with others. Feminist ethicists typically focus on persons as participants in relationships both public and intimate, as inhabitants and co-constructors of social roles and identities. Many have sought to reconceive and expand vital moral concepts such as autonomy, rights, respect, responsibility, and equality in ways that centrally incorporate such a relational understanding of persons.

When theorizing begins with a vision of persons as inextricably located in and shaped by relationships, the fact that many of those relationships are oppressive ones naturally comes to play an important role in the theorizing. Feminist ethicists have emphasized not only how people ought ideally to behave, but also the personal, social, and political conditions that would enable people to develop their characters and behave responsibly—and in particular, to how relations of oppression can cripple and distort the moral capacities of persons (both those who suffer from oppression and those who benefit from it). Identifying and possibly repairing the moral damage of oppression has been an important theme in feminist ethics; in such work, a key challenge is always to distinguish the important (and often neglected) values and insights of oppressed people from the moral damage of oppression itself.

The centrality of relationship, the importance of valuing women's perspectives, and the question of oppression's moral damage all converge in feminist ethicists' discussions of the labor that has most centrally characterized women's experience over the centuries. This might be called the work of relationship itself—of caring and nurturance, of tending to others' intimate emotional and physical needs (including for love, food, cleanliness, clothing, and the like) both inside the home as wives and mothers and outside of the home in professions such as nursing and teaching. Thus, in feminist ethics, due respect for the role of emotion in moral reasoning has been supplemented by attention to emotional labor: its importance to human well-being, its invisibility in some received ethical theories, and its disproportionate and often exploitative allocation to women (Bartky 1990, Calhoun 1992).

Sara Ruddick's influential *Maternal Thinking* (1989) attempted to reclaim the work of mothers as involving particular forms of moral reasoning that are vital not only to the work of raising children, but to efforts to create and sustain a just and livable world. Virginia Held argued in *Feminist Morality* (1993) that the relationship between mother (or "mothering person") and child—rather than contractual relations or market transactions—should be considered the central or paradigmatic human experience and the basis for a feminist account of morality. While other feminists have been more wary of taking mothering either as paradigmatic of women's experience or as a model for morality itself, most feminist ethicists grant that having primary responsibility for the intimate care and nurturing of children seems likely to shape women's moral perspectives in deep and pervasive ways that are worthy of philosophical attention.

Peta Bowden (1997) argues against attempts to formulate universal principles to govern caring. Instead, care must be understood and elaborated through detailed attention to examples; she discusses motherhood, nursing, friendship, and citizenship as substantively different caring practices. In contrast to the canon's highly idealized emphasis on relations among persons considered as equal in freedom and power, another area of feminist analysis in care-based ethics is the dependencies that accompany certain stages and conditions of life, including childhood, illness, old age, and various physical and mental disabilities. Feminist discussions of such dependencies (such as that of Kittay 1999) focus attention on the ineluctable facts of human vulnerability and interdependence, as well as on inequalities both between caregivers (or "dependency workers") and those for whom they care, and between caregivers and non-caregivers in various communities.

Feminist ethicists have also drawn on women's experiences challenging, or at least moving outside of, traditional feminine roles as nurturers of children and men. Important forms of ethical insight and practice emerge from alternative or resistant female lives, particularly from the bonding of women with each other in friendship (Friedman 1993) and/or love (Card 1995, Calhoun 2002) and from feminist networks and communities. Work in this vein tends to ask what values, virtues, and capacities are necessary for women to maintain their own well-being under patriarchy as well as to challenge and resist oppressive structures. While Marilyn Frye (1983, 1992) would likely resist a characterization of her work as part of ethics, her work on vital concepts such as arrogance, loving perception, whiteness and racism, oppression, humanism, and lesbianism has been enormously influential for many who are working to articulate resistant feminist moral values and practices.

ISSUES, CONCEPTS, AND METHODOLOGIES

Feminist ethicists have extensively discussed concrete normative issues that are clearly gender-related: abortion, rape and sexual consent, sexual harassment, marriage, pornography and hate speech, prostitution, surrogate or contracted motherhood, reproductive technologies, homophobia and heterosexism, domestic labor and intrafamilial justice, and welfare policy, to name only a few. These discussions have often focused not only on whether or not the practice in question is morally legitimate but also—for instance, in the case of rape and other forms of misogynist violence—on exposing its role in maintaining women's political subordination and in forming women's and men's moral subjectivities. They have also brought a feminist perspective to bear on other concepts and attitudes that are less obviously gender-related, but for which an understanding of gender and power is illuminating. These include gratitude (Card 1996), shame (Bartky 1990), trust (Baier 1994), paternalism (Sherwin 1992), self-respect (Dillon 1997), guilt (Bartky 2002), and evil (Card 2002).

The feminist ethics lexicon also includes novel concepts developed specifically as part of the project of analyzing and finding ways to move beyond oppression and privilege—for example, María Lugones's (1987) concept of "world-traveling," which she recommends to feminists and others who seek to replace arrogance with love, identification, and loyalty in their relations to women who occupy different social "worlds." Finally, feminist ethicists have developed ambitious new conceptions of morality's nature, purposes, and sources of authority, such as Margaret Urban Walker's (1998) "expressive-collaborative" model of morality (as distinct from the "theoretical-juridical" model that she thinks more typical of mainstream moral theory).

Whatever the specific topic at hand, certain methodological approaches and themes cut across much of what goes under the rubric of feminist ethics. Feminist ethics is typically characterized by a resistance to excessive idealizing in moral theory, especially to idealizing that obscures the pervasive relationships of dependence and of unequal freedom and power that moral life calls upon us to navigate responsibly. As Claudia Card puts it, feminist ethics generally errs on the side of "peeling back rather than donning veils of ignorance" (1991, p. 25). Relatedly, many (though certainly not all) feminist ethicists are wary of attempts to formulate universal and highly articulable rules or principles in ethical theory, tending instead to draw more limited conclusions based on detailed analyses of particular socially located experiences. Particularly since the 1990s, feminist ethics has developed a fairly consistent focus on the *practices* of morality, on how moral concepts are actually used and deployed in various contexts: what we do with rights, how we take and assign responsibility, for what and to whom we hold ourselves and others accountable.

Not surprisingly, then, many feminist ethicists emphasize the necessity of ongoing real (rather than hypothetical or idealized) conversation and dialogue as important to revealing, justifying, and/or challenging people's moral practices and agreements. What matters is not only what is said, but who is thought to be entitled to say it: As Margaret Urban Walker puts it, "Feminist ethics pursues questions about *authority, credibility,* and *representation* in moral life and in the practice of moral theorizing itself" (1998, p. 54).

Some longstanding themes in feminist ethics continue to be refined and taken in new directions. Some feminist ethicists, like Joan Tronto (1993), have continued to develop and refine a care-based approach. In *Moral Boundaries,* Tronto urges that we renegotiate the boundary between morality and politics and endorse care not as a form of "women's morality," but rather as a political virtue that can aid in redistributing power and transforming the public sphere. Several themes—a relational conception of persons, the need to repair oppression's moral damage and to articulate practical modes of resistance—combine in Hilde Lindemann Nelson's (2001) discussion of identities as narratively constructed. Nelson argues for the importance of oppressed people developing "counterstories" that can resist and ultimately replace the damaging and undermining stories told about them by dominant groups. Such "narrative repair" is especially vital, in Nelson's view, because who one takes oneself to be, and who others take one to be, affects how freely one can act. Perhaps reflecting the maturation of the field itself, as well as its longstanding focus on persons as embodied beings proceeding through a life cycle, some feminist ethicists (Walker 1999, Bartky 2002) have turned their attention to aging—particularly to the strengths, natural and humanly arranged vulnerabilities, and specific forms of inequality that confront elderly women.

Finally, a global focus in feminist ethics, already well underway in the work of such feminists as Uma Narayan (1997) and Martha Nussbaum (2000), also finds expression in Alison Jaggar's (1998) attempt to enlarge the possibilities for egalitarian and inclusive global feminist dialogue. In discussing the challenges facing feminists who would respectfully communicate and cooperate with each other across vast global divisions of power, resources, and accorded authority, Jaggar exemplifies and develops several ongoing themes in feminist ethics. Among these are a suspicion of idealization (in Jaggar's case, of "romanticizing discursive utopias"), a corrective emphasis on actual dialogue and on questions of authority and silencing therein, and a relentless attention to the effects of power dynamics on women variously located in multiple matrices of domination.

See also Applied Ethics; Aristotle; Baier, Annette; Beauvoir, Simone de; Ethics; Feminist Legal Theory; Feminist Philosophy; Feminist Social and Political Philosophy; Hume, David; Kant, Immanuel; Murdoch, Iris; Nietzsche, Friedrich; Nussbaum, Martha; Plato; Weil, Simone.

Bibliography

Baier, Annette. *Moral Prejudices*. Cambridge, MA: Harvard University Press, 1994.

Baier, Annette. *Postures of the Mind*. Minneapolis: University of Minnesota Press, 1985.

Bartky, Sandra. *Femininity and Domination: Studies in the Phenomenology of Oppression*. New York: Routledge, 1990.

Bartky, Sandra. *Sympathy and Solidarity and Other Essays*. Lanham, MD: Rowman and Littlefield, 2002.

Bowden, Peta. *Caring: Gender-Sensitive Ethics*. New York: Routledge, 1997.

Calhoun, Cheshire. "Emotional Work." In *Explorations in Feminist Ethics: Theory and Practice*, edited by Eve Browning Cole and Susan Coultrap-McQuin. Bloomington: Indiana University Press, 1992.

Calhoun, Cheshire. *Feminism, the Family, and the Politics of the Closet: Lesbian and Gay Displacement*. Oxford: Oxford University Press, 2002.

Card, Claudia. *The Atrocity Paradigm: A Theory of Evil*. Oxford: Oxford University Press, 2002.

Card, Claudia, ed. *Feminist Ethics*. Lawrence: University of Kansas Press, 1991.

Card, Claudia. *Lesbian Choices*. New York: Columbia University Press, 1995.

DesAutels, Peggy, and Joanne Waugh, eds. *Feminists Doing Ethics*. Lanham, MD: Rowman and Littlefield, 2001.

Dillon, Robin. "Self-Respect: Moral, Emotional, Political." *Ethics* 107 (1997): 226–249.

Friedman, Marilyn. *What are Friends For? Feminist Perspectives on Personal Relationships and Moral Theory*. Ithaca, NY: Cornell University Press, 1993.

Frye, Marilyn. *The Politics of Reality: Essays in Feminist Theory*. Freedom, CA: Crossing Press, 1983.

Frye, Marilyn. *Willful Virgin: Essays in Feminism*. Freedom, CA: Crossing Press, 1992.

Gilligan, Carol. *In a Different Voice: Psychological Theory and Women's Development.* Cambridge, MA: Harvard University Press, 1982.

Held, Virginia. *Feminist Morality: Transforming Culture, Society, and Politics.* Chicago: University of Chicago Press, 1993.

Held, Virginia, ed. *Justice and Care: Essential Readings in Feminist Ethics.* Boulder, CO: Westview, 1995.

Jaggar, Alison. "Globalizing Feminist Ethics." *Hypatia* 13 (2) (1998): 7–31.

Kittay, Eva Feder. *Love's Labor: Essays on Women, Equality, and Dependency.* New York: Routledge, 1999.

Lugones, Maria. "Playfulness, 'World'-Travelling, and Loving Perception." *Hypatia* 2 (1987): 3–19.

Mackenzie, Catriona, and Natalie Stoljar, eds. *Relational Autonomy: Feminist Perspectives on Autonomy, Agency, and the Social Self.* New York: Oxford University Press, 2000.

May, Larry. *Masculinity and Morality.* Ithaca, NY: Cornell University Press, 1998.

Narayan, Uma. *Dislocating Cultures: Identities, Traditions, and Third World Feminism.* New York: Routledge, 1997.

Nelson, Hilde Lindemann. *Damaged Identities, Narrative Repair.* Ithaca, NY: Cornell University Press, 2001.

Nussbaum, Martha. *Women and Human Development: The Capabilities Approach.* Cambridge, U.K.: Cambridge University Press, 2000.

Ruddick, Sara. *Maternal Thinking: Toward a Politics of Peace.* Boston: Beacon Press, 1989.

Sherwin, Susan. *No Longer Patient: Feminist Ethics and Health Care.* Philadelphia: Temple University Press, 1992.

Tronto, Joan. *Moral Boundaries: A Political Argument for an Ethic of Care.* New York: Routledge, 1993.

Walker, Margaret Urban. *Moral Understandings: A Feminist Study in Ethics.* New York: Routledge, 1998.

Walker, Margaret Urban. *Mother Time: Women, Aging, and Ethics.* Lanham, MD: Rowman and Littlefield, 1999.

Rebecca Whisnant (2005)

FEMINIST LEGAL THEORY

Feminist legal theory is the study of the philosophical foundations of law and justice; informed by women's experiences, its goal is to transform the legal system and the understanding of it to improve the quality of jurisprudence and women's lives. Feminists working in law share the convictions that the historical and continuing exclusions of women from the law's protective domain have injured women and that the exclusion of women from the study of law has limited both the understanding of law and it ethical compass. Feminists have accordingly sought to transform the rules and principles governing particular areas of law—torts, criminal law, constitutional law—so as to make them more responsive to women's needs and more reflective of women's perspectives. Feminist legal theorists examine the conse-quences—both for women and for jurisprudence—of the exclusion of women's input into our shared understanding of the law's philosophical foundations. Toward that end feminists have examined competing philosophical understandings of the nature of law, have attempted to show how they fail to reflect women's perspectives, and have attempted in each case to reinvigorate them by centralizing rather than marginalizing women's experiences.

Some feminist legal theorists—sometimes called liberal feminist scholars—argue that women's lives will be most improved by simply extending to women what are widely regarded as two of the central promises of law in a liberal regime: first, the promise of "formal equality," the idea that the state's legal institutions will "treat like causes alike"; and second, the promise to each individual of a wide a sphere of individual autonomy. Women, liberal feminists argue, are "like men" in all the ways that should matter to the state and accordingly should be treated, wherever possible, in precisely the same way as men by the law. Women and men are the same in their abilities: Women, like men, can engage in the professions and trades, wage war, fairly serve on juries, administer estates, and vote responsibly, and the law must accordingly not discriminate on the basis of a false claim of difference and must also forbid discrimination against women in the private sector on the basis of such false claims (Williams 1984).

Similarly, women and men are the same in their needs: Women, like men, need protection against violence, meaningful work and civic participation, and, most important, the freedom to develop their individual life plans. The law should therefore extend to women the same protection against private violence and the same sphere of autonomy it extends to men (McClain 1992). By pursuing the logic of these applications of fundamental liberal principles to the law's treatment of women, liberal feminist legal theorists have contributed to widespread changes in the relations of women, men, and the state, ranging from the institution of bans on private and state discrimination on the basis of gender to the expansion of women's reproductive freedom and choices so as to maximize their social and political autonomy.

As critics of liberal feminism have pointed out, however, women are not "like men" in all ways, and as a consequence a rigid application of liberal premises to the sometimes distinctive situation of women will often backfire. Where women are unlike men, the blanket insistence on equal treatment will sometimes impoverish actual women, albeit toward the admirable end of a gender-blind utopian society (Becker 1987). Equal distribution of property at the time of divorce, for example, will impoverish the majority of divorcing women who have less earning potential than their husbands. The equal refusal of an employer to grant maternity or parental leave upon the birth of a child will disproportionately hurt female workers, who, because of their greater biological role in the process of reproduction, will need more time out of the workplace than will men if they are to enjoy the same rights as men to be both workers and parents (Littleton 1987). The refusal of the state to extend the protection of social security to career homemakers treats women and men similarly but disproportionately harms women because women are disproportionately represented in the ranks of unpaid domestic labor.

At the professional level, tenure policies and partnership tracks, equally applied, hurt women more than men, because of the differing reproductive cycles of the two sexes. To take an extreme and only partly hypothetical example, a state that failed altogether to criminalize rape would on one level treat men and women similarly and thereby abide by the liberal mandate of equal treatment, but women would obviously be disproportionately harmed by such a regime. In all of these cases, the evenhanded application of legal rules harms women because of the very real differences in women and men's economic, political, and social conditions.

Partly in response to the perceived theoretical and practical inadequacies of liberal feminist legal theory and partly as a response to work in other fields on the differences between men and women's psychological lives, a number of feminists in legal studies, sometimes called difference or cultural feminists, have sought to place at the center of inquiry not the many ways in which women and men are the same or similar but, rather the ways in which women and men are different. This focus on difference has in turn led to three promising areas of inquiry. First, difference feminists in legal studies have put forward a modified or quasi-liberal theory of equality sometimes called an acceptance theory (Littleton 1987). According to this view, the state's moral (and constitutional) obligation to treat citizens equally entails the state's obligation not only to provide equal treatment of the sexes wherever the sexes are similarly situated but also to provide different treatment wherever necessary to ensure an equal acceptance of differences, so that those differences, whatever their origin, do not cause women harm. Because women (but not men) get pregnant, bear children, and lactate, for example, the law must fashion rules of employment and civic engagement that will facilitate the acceptance of those differences in the public and economic spheres, whether or not that in turn requires different or similar treatment of the sexes in various legal regimes. Since women engage in more unpaid domestic labor, the liberal mandate of equality demands that family law, divorce law, and social security law should develop in ways that will render that difference harmless.

Other difference feminists have put forward a related critique of liberalism itself, sometimes called the "dependency critique" (Kittay 1999, Fineman 1995). The conception of human nature on which liberal norms of justice and equality (and the vast bodies of law they imply) typically rests is that citizens of a liberal polity should be treated as fundamentally independent and autonomous. But this conception of our nature is transparently and badly flawed: All human beings are dependent upon caregivers for their very lives for a good part of their early childhood and continue to require care throughout adolescence so as to become the autonomous citizens, independent entrepreneurs, moral agents, and free individuals so valued by various strands of liberalism and so vigorously protected by our fundamental, constitutional law. Further, all of us require care when we are elderly, likewise undercutting the dominant understanding of the independent individual at the heart of liberal theory. Almost all women and many men spend a very high percentage of their adult lives providing this care, in private and for no compensation when done within the family, or for very low wages when done through labor markets.

The disproportionately greater amount of caregiving labor done by women throughout history tends to be invisible within a liberalism that steadfastly insists on individual autonomy; hence, legal regimes that depend upon or aspire to those liberal values are often irrelevant or harmful to women and to the children and elders that depend upon them. The result in practical terms is often the impoverishment of women and dependents; the jurisprudential and philosophical result is a set of moral ideals for law and legal justice that badly undercuts the aspirations and needs of much of the world's populations (West 1996). A liberalism enriched with a feminist regard for the centrality of caregiving labor, for the moral and ethical perspectives such labor both demands and partly produces, and a fuller understanding of the dependencies and interdependencies of our social and biological lives would enhance women's well-being and the strength of both legal and political philosophy (McClain 1992).

Difference feminists have tried to explicate the distinctive harms women suffer that have little or no correlate in men's lives, on the assumption that by virtue of their difference, among other things, the harms that women suffer often go unnoticed as well as unaddressed (West 1996). Women suffer from sexual assault, sexual harassment, and sexual violence in greater numbers and in different ways than men do. Women suffer unwanted and nonconsensual pregnancies; men do not. Whatever the reason, women world-over are more engaged in childraising, and consequently are more harmed than men by the loss of children in custody disputes and are more vulnerable than men to the threat of such loss, which significantly weakens their economic bargaining position both in the family and at the point of divorce. If women are to enjoy legal protection against these and other gender-specific harms, the laws governing the social interactions that occasion these harms must be responsive to the existence and the different nature of the harms that women differentially and distinctively experience.

Radical feminist legal theory, sometimes called dominance feminism, is also an attempt to fashion a feminist theory of law that avoids the pitfalls of liberal feminist legal theory, but it does so in a different way. The central question for feminists working in law, according to radical feminist theorists, is not whether women and men are fundamentally alike or different but how the state might foster the greater empowerment of women. Women are unlike men in one significant respect: women as a group lack power (MacKinnon 1989). Liberal feminists are wrong to downplay or disregard that difference, and difference feminists are wrong to focus on any other differences. A focus on the differential treatment of women by the state, whether with the liberal feminists' aim of eradicating those differences, expanding upon them, as difference feminists wish, will be at best distracting. Disempowerment, not discrimination, and not difference, is the source of the problem, and patriarchy, not law, is the source of women's disempowerment. Law reflects patriarchal influences, but patriarchy also exists independent of law. Consequently, law can be and should be employed to end it.

Loosely reflecting the logic of critical legal scholars' Gramscian analysis of the relation of law and market capitalism, radical feminists have sought to highlight the nonlegal ways in which patriarchal power is created and reinforced in culture and then legitimated by legal rules and institutions. Women are disempowered, for example, by the violence done them through rape, sexual harassment, and street hassling as well as other forms of sexual assault. That disempowerment is then underscored through the distorting messages and the attacks on women's self-esteem occasioned by pornography, the culture of romance, and other societal influences, all of which aim to render that disempowerment in some sense voluntary and all of which render problematic the liberal feminist insistence on expanding individual autonomy as a means for improving women's well-being. Absent feminist intervention, the law's role in this process of disempowerment and cooptation is largely to legitimate those harms: The constitutional doctrine of privacy, laws governing and only partially regulating rape and domestic violence, and the constitutional protection accorded to even extremely damaging assaultive speech all trivialize or render invisible the harms women sustain and reinforce the tendencies that cause them. Law does not itself cause these harms, but it contributes to a culture that tolerates them.

There is, however, nothing necessary about the handmaidenlike role of law in sustaining patriarchy; it only reflects current distributions of sexual and gendered power. Arguably, all of these forms of patriarchal power, and certainly those employing violence, can and should be prohibited by law. The law legitimates a good bit of the disempowerment occasioned by rape by underregulating it, but that can be changed: Rape laws can be expanded, and enforcement of those laws strengthened; to do both would go a long way toward undermining patriarchy. The goal of radical feminist theory is to employ the law in precisely this utterly conventional way toward the unconventional goal of first prohibiting and then eradicating the violence that sustains a patriarchal cultural regime.

Finally, a number of feminists engaged in legal theory have sought to appropriate the tools of postmodern analysis to free liberal, difference, and radical feminist legal theory from the presumed dangers of their essentialist premises. Two distinct projects have emerged from this effort, one critical and one reconstructive. First, postmodernists have joined with African-American, lesbian, and other arguably marginalized feminist legal scholars in an attempt to criticize the consciously or unconsciously racist or heterosexist assumptions in feminist legal theory, thus laying the groundwork for the emergence of a feminist jurisprudence strengthened by its recognition of women's racial, sexual, ethnic, and cultural differences (Harris1990). Critical-race feminist legal theorists have contributed the most to this project. Theoretical and empirical scholarship has accordingly shown the ways in which, for example, feminist writing on rape and rape law has failed to attend to the experiences of African American women, whose understanding of rape is informed by a history of the use of rape law as an instrument of terror by the white state and by rape as an instrument of terror by men. These critics also point to the ways in which feminist writing on difference, care, and caregiving has failed to attend to the extent to which African American women have provided such care to whites for no or little pay. Likewise, critical-race theorists and writers in the civil rights traditions fail to attend to the different experiences of women and men in communities of color: for example, the communal censoring of African American women who try to theorize or even describe experiences of domestic violence or sexual violence in communities of color. Feminist race scholars writing in law have urged the adoption of the perspective of persons at the "intersection" of various "axes of subordination" to best understand the ways in which these modes of social interaction injure those most vulnerable to multiple forms of marginalization (Crenshaw 1991).

Second, postmodernist feminists have joined with cultural critics and "queer theorists" from other disciplines in an attempt to highlight the ways in which perceived differences between the genders and between sexual orientations are themselves socially constructed rather than biologically mandated (J. Williams 1989, Halley 2002). The aim has been partly to free feminism from false and essentialist stories or metanarratives of women's disempowerment and partly to redirect feminist legal reforms. Postmodern feminists, for example, have been attempting to redirect the law of sexual harassment, largely a product of radical feminism theorizing, away from its current focus on sexuality and toward a more pluralistic understanding of the various harms, whether sexualized or not, that women and men suffer in the workplace (Shultz 1998). This is in part in response to the postmodern complaint that radical feminism and hence sexual harassment law have wrongly relied on a grand metanarrative of women's sexual disempowerment by men and in part a response to a concern that sexual-harassment law may encourage or rest on homophobic responses to what might be harmless socio-sexual gestures in workplaces (Halley 2002).

Both projects—the enrichment of traditional feminist theory with the perspectives of African American and other ethnic minority women, and the challenge to the narratives of female sexual disempowerment at the heart of sexual harassment law and radical feminism—both resonate with long-standing feminist (as well as postmodernist) goals: the first in its insistence on respecting and honoring the voices of outsiders, including those women who find themselves "outside" mainstream feminist discourse, and the second in its insistence on locating within culture, rather than nature, the causes of women's oppression and the key to ending it.

See also Feminist Ethics; Feminist Philosophy; Feminist Social and Political Philosophy; Gramsci, Antonio; Justice; Philosophy of Law.

Bibliography

Becker, Mary. "Prince Charming: Abstract Equality." *Supreme Court Review* 5 (1987): 201–247.

Crenshaw, Kimberlé Williams. "Mapping the Margins: Intersectionality, Identity Politics, and Violence Against Women of Color." *Stanford Law Review* 43 (1991): 1241–1299.

Fineman, Martha Albertson. *The Neutered Mother, The Sexual Family and Other Twentieth Century Tragedies*. NY: Routledge, 1995.

Fineman, Martha Albertson. *The Autonomy Myth: A Theory of Dependency*. NY: New Press: 2004.

Halley, Janet. "Sexuality Harassment." In *Left Legalism/Left Critique*, edited by Wendy Brown and Janet Halley. Durham: Duke University Press: 2002.

Harris, Angela. "Race and Essentialism in Feminist Legal Theory." *Stanford Law Review* 42 (1990): 581–616.

Kittay, Eva. *Love's Labor: Essays on Women, Equality, and Dependency*. NY: Routledge, 1998.

Littleton, Christine. "Reconstructing Sexual Equality." *California Law Review* (1987): 1279–1337.

MacKinnon, Catherine. *Toward a Feminist Theory of the State*. Cambridge, MA: Harvard University Press, 1989.

McClain, Linda. "Atomistic Man Revisited: Liberalism, Connection, and Feminist Jurisprudence." *Southern California Law Review* (1992): 1171–1264.

McClain, Linda. "Care as a Public Value: Linking Responsibility, Resources, and Republicanism." *Chicago-Kent Law Review* (2001): 1673–1731.

Shultz, Vicki. "Reconceptualizing Sexual Harassment." *Yale Law Journal* 107 (1998): 1683–1805.

West, Robin. *Caring for Justice* NY: NYU Press, 1996.

Williams, Joan. "Deconstructing Gender." *Michigan Law Review* 1989: 797–845.

Williams, W. "Notes From A First Generation." *University of Chicago Legal Forum* 1989: 99–113.

Robin L. West (2005)

FEMINIST METAPHYSICS

Metaphysics seems to be one of the least relevant, most foreign, and inhospitable disciplines of philosophy in relation to feminist projects and concerns. Traditional metaphysicians have tried to answer questions about the basic structure of reality, about what kinds of beings exist, about the nature of time and causation, and they have probed difficulties like free will and determinism, the nature of universals and particulars and the like. None of these issues seems directly pertinent to feminism, and their abstract formulation and universalist perspective strike some feminists as deeply suspect. Nonetheless feminist metaphysics has emerged as a distinct and lively field in feminist theory. And there are important connections between feminist work on certain metaphysical issues and mainstream metaphysics.

Feminist metaphysics revolves around three core issues: essentialism and anti-essentialism about sex/gender, theories of the self or the subject, and realism versus social constructionism (a version of the realism/anti-realism controversy in mainstream philosophy). Each of these issues is central to Simone de Beauvoir's *The Second Sex*, which is rightly seen as the primary intellectual source for twentieth-century developments in continental and analytic feminist theory. Beauvoir oriented her pioneering work toward ontology and essentialism by defining woman as the Other (in relation to man). At the same time she sketched out the first detailed and comprehensive social constructionist account of gender. And she was centrally concerned to retrieve the possibility of subjectivity, agency, and transcendence for women.

Beauvoir's legacy has been developed in two major directions. In broad strokes continental feminist theory is anti-essentialist about sex and gender, and skeptical about the unity and coherence of the self or subject. Continental feminist theory tends to derive both anti-essentialism and anti-realism about sex/gender from a social constructionist view of sex/gender. In contrast analytic feminist theory tends to distinguish among these positions, holding, for example, that socially constructed categories and entities are real, and perhaps even constituted by essential properties. Analytic feminist theory is more hospitable to essentialism about sex and gender, and open to the possibility of non-androcentric theories of the self. These are generalizations, however, as we can see by considering the fact that Luce Irigaray, a pioneer of continental feminist theory, has developed an essentialist theory of sexual difference.

Feminist preoccupation with the questions of essentialism and the nature of the self rather than other metaphysical topics is neither coincidental nor arbitrary. Both of these issues are directly relevant to feminist politics because of their implications regarding the possibility of individual agency and effective shared activity toward political change. For example, Naomi Zack (1997, 2005) points out the consequences of anti-essentialism about gender for collective agency on behalf of women. If women share nothing in common as a group, then on

what basis can they forge a group identity, and on what basis can they find common goals? Other feminists, like Diana Meyers (1997, 2002), are troubled by the claim that there is no self or subject because of the implications of that position for the possibility of individual resistance to patriarchal norms, and for collective political agency. Similarly the feminist debate concerning social constructionist and realism/anti-realism is intended to reveal the arbitrariness and contingency of oppressive social and political structures in order to allow for the possibility of political change and an end to oppression. This entry explores the development of feminist metaphysical thinking about sex/gender essentialism, the self or the subject, and social constructionism and realism.

ESSENTIALISM AND ANTI-ESSENTIALISM IN FEMINIST THEORY

The feminist discussion of essentialism usually begins with a distinction between sex differences, which are the biological markers that distinguish females from males, and gender differences, which are the cultural or psychological features that distinguish women from men. Some feminists question the distinction between biology (or nature) and culture underlying the sex/gender distinction. They argue that there is cultural intervention in the production of two sexes from a more complex biological reality. In making this argument, they reject an essentialist account of sex because there are no biological features that demarcate human beings into just two kinds that correspond to female and male. See the discussion in Anne Fausto-Sterling (2000), and the essentialist account of sex differences by Linda Alcoff (2005). In addition, Sally Haslanger (2000) has argued that a major project of feminist metaphysics is the unmasking of putatively natural categories or properties as social.

A similar argument is made against gender essentialism; namely, that there are no biological, psychological, or cultural properties that are common to all women and not shared by any men. Let's call this the commonality problem. Moreover, women of color (and others) have pointed out that the psychological and cultural properties that some feminists propose as essential to all women in fact exclude many women. Let's call this the exclusion problem. Elizabeth Spelman (1998) and bell hooks (1981) made important contributions in articulating these problems. The doctrine of intersectionality was developed by Kimberle Crenshaw (1991) to respond to both the commonality problem and the exclusion problem. Intersectionality is the idea that feminists need to attend to the multiplicity of identities that can and do characterize individuals (race, class, and sexual orientation) in order to avoid the problems of exclusion and commonality. However, the concept of intersectionality is problematic to the extent that it fractures the unity of women, and leads to skepticism concerning whether any useful program for political change can reflect the interests of a heterogeneous collection of individuals.

Feminists have responded to anti-essentialist arguments by developing approaches to essentialism that respect the problems of commonality and exclusion without fracturing the unity of women. There are two basic approaches. A materialist approach to gender essentialism, developed in different ways by Haslanger and Monique Wittig (1997), among others, begins with the body, and the way that bodies are hierarchically ordered in and by patriarchal (and racist, ageist) societies. Gender is a material, embodied state and bodies are classified by societies into hierarchical relations. Being gendered is a relational property because gender categorization is dependent upon how bodies are perceived by others rather than upon the possession of any intrinsic biological or psychological property. Being gendered is also a political property in the sense that it carries with it a position in a hierarchical social structure. The materialist approach meshes with the intersectionality perspective because it allows that bodies can be classified in multiple ways according to overlapping social hierarchies; for example, racialized bodies that are men occupy a different social niche from racialized bodies that are women. Able-bodied women occupy a different position from disabled women and so on. On this approach the identities of being a woman and being a man necessarily have positions in a hierarchical grid of social power relations; if patriarchy did not exist then neither would women and men.

Alternatively Natalie Stoljar (1995) makes the case for understanding woman as a cluster concept rather than an Aristotelian universal. In a related development Naomi Zack (1997) argues that that being a woman is a relational, disjunctive property shared by all women. Like the materialist approach these accounts emphasize the features common to all women, but select features that are sensitive to the problem of exclusion. Unlike the materialist approach to gender essentialism these views do not make oppression intrinsic to being a woman. They also do not provide a conceptual grid for other identities like race, or sexual orientation as the materialist approach does. Tracing the similarities and dissimilarities between gender and other social categories and identities, like race and sexual orientation, is a major theme in feminist writing on essentialism and anti-essentialism. Although the question of gender essentialism remains contested within feminist theory, dogmatic anti-essentialism is no longer a criterion for adequate feminist theorizing.

Finally, some philosophers frame the discussion of gender essentialism in terms different from those we have been considering. Rather than try to determine whether or not there are any properties common to all women, we might wonder whether or not being gendered is essential to the identity of individual women and men. Essentialism in this sense is not about kind membership but rather concerns the issue of whether or not any of an individual's properties constitutes her as the individual she is, and if so, whether or not being a woman is one of an individual's constitutive properties. In different ways, Anthony Appiah (1990) and Charlotte Witt (1992, 1995) explore essentialist theories of gender by focusing on the relationship between an individual's identity and his or her gender rather than the question of what all women or all men have in common.

As mentioned in the introductory text of this entry, one reason for the persistence of the issue of essentialism in feminist theory is the political requirement that women be identifiable as a group with common interests, and who suffer shared injustices. Group identity is politically necessary; mere strategic essentialism does not seem to be sufficient as a basis for political change. For similar reasons the issue of the subject or the self is central to feminist metaphysical thinking. Despite the shortcomings of traditional accounts of subjectivity, it is hard to conceptualize a politically adequate view of agency without some account of the subject who acts.

FEMINIST ACCOUNTS OF SUBJECTIVITY

Traditionally to be an agent one must be a self or a subject, and not a thing or an object that is acted upon. But feminists have catalogued serious deficiencies with the way in which traditional philosophers have described the self. These deficiencies include the tendency to identify the self or subject with reason in contrast with the emotions and the body; the tendency to associate agency with autonomous individuals rather than connected, relational selves, and the characterization of the subject as unified and coherent. The last criticism is the most radical as it rejects the very notion of a consistent self or subject rather than pointing out deficiencies with traditional characterizations of unified subjects.

The rejection of the unified and coherent subject or self is related to one strand of anti-essentialist argument as we see in Judith Butler's work. Not only does Butler (1990) reject all forms of sex/gender essentialism, but also she does so as part of a rejection of the metaphysics of substance. And the rejection of the metaphysics of substance, the denial that individual, persisting beings exist entails the rejection of subjects in so far as they are characterized as unified individuals that persist through time. Some feminists find the dissolution of stable subjectivities liberating because of the possibilities for innovation, creativity, and performance that this view endorses. Other feminists find the rejections of stable subjects inadequate to the requirements of political resistance and change. Recall that the possibility of agency is based upon the existence of subjects who are agents. Agents can resist patriarchal norms, and can band together to effect political change.

However even those feminists who accept the importance of unified and coherent subjects criticize traditional notions of the self. For example, Susan Babbitt (1996) is critical of the philosophical tradition that centers subjectivity on reason, and defines reason as exclusive of emotions, imagination, perception, and other faculties associated with the body. And theories of the subject, which are mentalistic, also have come under feminist scrutiny. In response feminists like Moira Gatens (1996) have worked to define a bodily notion of subjectivity, which is more adequate to feminist understanding of the importance of embodiment in explaining human agency. Feminists have also developed a relational theory of the self, which interprets agents as constituted by their relations to others, and as embedded in concrete historical and cultural horizons.

The idea of the subject as relationally constituted and historically embedded is more adequate to feminist projects than the traditional idea of subjectivity. However, it is also problematic in relation to the idea of autonomy, which is an important constituent of many theories of moral and political agency. Moral and political subjects or agents act autonomously in some sense of the term. There appears to be tension between the requirement of autonomy on the one hand, and the feminist notion of a relational and embedded subject. If subjects are formed in and by particular cultures, and if their being is determined by their relations to other subjects and also in and by their relations to cultural and historical institutions, then in what sense do they choose and act autonomously?

Feminists like Diana Meyers (1997, 2002) have worked to specify criteria for a notion of autonomy that both recognizes the concrete causal formations of subjectivity, and carves out a reasonable zone for autonomous

decision making. In this way, feminists have absorbed the lessons of contingency from social constructionism without giving up the important ethical and political norm of autonomy. Other feminists like Marilyn Frye (1983, 1989, 1996, 2000, 2005) question whether the ideas of individual choice, individual autonomy and individual selves are the central notions that feminists need to understand the structures of patriarchy. They argue against the focus on individual subjectivity and choice not because there are no individual subjects but because focus on the individual subject and her choices obscures the horizon of oppression against which and within which choice operates. It reflects a political commitment to individualism, which does not provide an adequate framework for feminist politics.

GENDER, SOCIAL CONSTRUCTIONISM, AND REALISM

Most feminists reject a biological, deterministic conception of gender. Instead they see gender as constituted and defined by social norms, practices and institutions. Since social norms, practices and institutions vary in different cultures, and also differ in the same culture at different historical periods, it seems to follow that gender is indeterminate and variable rather than fixed and stable. As we have seen some feminists think that the social construction of gender, in itself, rules out the possibility of gender essentialism because of the variety of cultural norms and their fluctuations through history. We have seen that not all feminists agree with that position. A related issue concerns the reality of gender, which can be understood as a local dispute within the realism/anti-realism debate in the philosophy of science.

Some feminists, influenced by postmodernism and continental philosophy, hold that gender is not a real and determinate category, but a designation whose meaning is indeterminate and unstable. Both Butler (1990) and Drucilla Cornell (1993) have developed views along these lines. An antirealist view of gender has the positive attribute of allowing for immediate liberation for both individuals and groups through novel and creative performances of gender. If you think that gender is performed, enacted, created through behavior in unstable patterns and novel directions, then there is no difficulty in rejecting oppressive structures and stereotypes. Even those who choose to enact conventionally appropriate gender roles can miss the mark and fail to do so exactly. One tension in this position concerns the appropriate understanding of the subject, the agent who enacts liberatory behavior, since anti-realists about gender tend to also reject the notion of the unified, coherent subject.

Other feminists accept the social constructionist thesis about gender, but do not conclude that gender categories are unreal, unstable or indeterminate in meaning. The division between natural entities and artificial or social entities (however we might wish to draw this distinction, and indeed even if we reject it) does not require us to place only natural entities on the side of reality. On the contrary, socially constructed identities like gender and race are fully determinate and very real in their effects on individuals and communities. One tension in this position concerns the autonomy of individuals who are the product of very real social norms and institutions. If we are constructed causally as women and men, then how can we act autonomously to resist patriarchal norms? One response to this issue is to distinguish between the social construction claim interpreted as making a causal claim (which raises the specter of determinism) and the social construction claim interpreted as a view about the social constitution of gender norms (which does not have any implications for determinism). Gender norms are socially constituted through cultural practices and social institutions, but it is up to the individual to accept or to resist them.

Feminist metaphysics is a robust field within feminist philosophy that also contributes in important ways to recent work in feminist social and political theory. Feminist metaphysics also contributes to mainstream metaphysical thought especially in the topics of subjectivity, autonomy and agency; and social ontology, social constructionism and essentialism.

See also Beauvoir, Simone de; Feminism and Continental Philosophy; Feminist Epistemology; Feminist Philosophy; Feminist Philosophy of Science; Irigaray, Luce; Metaphysics; Postmodernism; Social Constructionism.

Bibliography

Alcoff, Linda. "The Metaphysics of Gender and Sexual Difference." In *Feminist Interventions in Ethics and Politics*, edited by Barbara S. Andrew, Jean Keller, and Lisa H. Schwartzman. Lanham, MD: Rowman and Littlefield, 2005.

Appiah, Anthony K. "'But Would That Still Be Me?': Notes On Gender, 'Race,' Ethnicity, As Sources of 'Identity.'" *Journal of Philosophy* 87 (10) (1990).

Babbitt, Susan E. *Impossible Dreams: Rationality, Integrity, and Moral Imagination*. Boulder, CO: Westview Press, 1996.

Beauvoir, Simone de. *The Second Sex*, edited and translated by H. M. Parshly. New York: Alfred A. Knopf, 1993.

Butler, Judith. *Gender Trouble: Feminism and the Subversion of Identity*. New York: Routledge, 1990.

Cornell, Drucilla. *Transformations*. New York: Routledge, 1993.

Crenshaw, Kimberle. "Mapping the Margins: Intersectionality, Identity Politics, and Violence Against Women." *Stanford Law Review* 43 (6) (1991).

Dupre, John. "Sex, Gender, and Essence." In *Midwest Studies in Philosophy*, Vol. 11, edited by Peter A. French, Theordore E. Uehling, Jr., and Howard K. Wettstein, Minneapolis: University of Minnesota Press, 1986.

Fausto-Sterling, Anne. *Sexing the Body: Gender Politics and the Construction of Sexuality*. New York: Basic Books, 2000.

Frye, Marilyn. "Categories and Dichotomies." In *Encyclopedia of Feminist Theories*, edited by Loraine Code. New York: Routledge, 2000.

Frye, Marilyn. "Categories in Distress." In *Feminist Interventions in Ethics and Politics*, edited by Barbara Andrew, Jean Keller, and Lisa Schwartzman. Lanham, MD: Rowman and Littlefield, 2005.

Frye, Marilyn. "Essentialism/Ethnocentrism: The Failure of the Ontological Cure." In *Is Academic Feminism Dead? Theory in Practice*, edited by the Center for Advanced Feminist Studies at the University of Minnesota. New York: New York University Press, 2000.

Frye, Marilyn. "The Necessity of Differences: Constructing a Positive Category of Women." *SIGNS: Journal of Women in Culture and Society* 21 (3) (1996).

Frye, Marilyn. *The Politics of Reality: Essays in Feminist Theory*. Trumansburg, NY: Crossing Press, 1983.

Fuss, Diana. *Essentially Speaking: Feminism, Nature, and Difference*. New York: Routledge, 1989.

Garry, Ann, and Marilyn Pearsall. *Women, Knowledge and Reality*. 2nd ed. New York: Routledge, 1996.

Gatens, Moira. *Imaginary Bodies: Ethics, Power, and Corporeality*. New York: Routledge, 1996.

Haslanger, Sally. "Feminism and Metaphysics: Negotiating the Natural." In *The Cambridge Companion to Feminism in Philosophy*, edited by Miranda Fricker and Jennifer Hornsby. Cambridge, U.K.: Cambridge University Press, 2000.

Haslanger, Sally. "Gender and Race: (What) Are They? (What) Do We Want Them To Be?" *Nous* 34 (1) (2000).

Haslanger, Sally. "Ontology and Social Construction." *Philosophical Topics: Feminist Perspectives on Language, Knowledge and Reality* 23 (2) (1995).

hooks, bell. *Ain't I a Women? Black Women and Feminism*. Boston: South End, 1981.

Meyers, Diana Tietjens, ed. *Feminists Rethink the Self*. Boulder, CO: Westview Press, 1997.

Meyers, Diana Tietjens. *Gender in the Mirror: Cultural Imagery and Women's Agency*. New York: Oxford University Press, 2002.

Spelman, Elizabeth V. *Inessential Woman: Problems of Exclusion in Feminist Thought*. Boston: Beacon Press, 1988.

Stoljar Natalie. "Essence, Identity and the Concept of Woman." *Philosophical Topics: Feminist Perspectives on Language, Knowledge and Reality* 23 (2) (1995).

Witt, Charlotte. "Anti-Essentialism in Feminist Theory." *Philosophical Topics: Feminist Perspectives on Language, Knowledge and Reality* 23 (2) (1995).

Witt, Charlotte. "Feminist Metaphysics." In *A Mind of One's Own: Feminist Essays on Reason and Objectivity*, edited by

Louise Antony and Charlotte Witt. Boulder, CO: Westview Press, 1992.

Wittig, Monique. "One is Not Born a Woman." In *The Second Wave: A Reader in Feminist Theory*, edited by Linda Nicholson. New York: Routledge, 1997.

Zack, Naomi. *Inclusive Feminism: A Third Wave Theory of Women's Commonality*. Lanham, MD: Rowman and Littlefield, 2005.

Zack, Naomi, ed. *Race/Sex: Their Sameness, Difference, and Interplay*. New York: Routledge, 1997.

Charlotte Witt (2005)

FEMINIST PHILOSOPHY

The rubric "feminist philosophy" applies to work in many philosophical subareas, often spanning several disciplines. The work is united by its authors' commitment to feminism in some form and by their belief that an engagement between feminism and philosophy will have both theoretical and practical benefits for everyone.

Some work in feminist philosophy focuses on philosophical issues that have arisen in the course of feminist political activism. Not surprisingly, much of this work is in political philosophy or ethics. Some work in feminist political philosophy consists of the articulation and defense of feminist theory, whereas other work examines the relationships between feminist political theory and other more general political theories, like liberalism and socialism. Much early work in feminist ethics dealt with issues in practical ethics that were of particular concern to women, such as abortion and affirmative action.

Throughout the 1980s and 1990s, however, feminist philosophers increasingly drew from other areas of philosophy to gain clarity about basic concepts in feminist theory and abstract foundational issues. Feminist work in metaphysics, for example, takes up such issues as the ontological status of categories like "gender" and "race," the basis of personal and cultural identity, the nature of truth, and the nature of freedom and autonomy. Feminist work in epistemology has been concerned, inter alia, with the relationship between practical and theoretical knowledge, the nature of intuition, the role of trust and other emotions in the achievement of knowledge, the social construction of expertise, and the nature of objectivity. Feminist philosophers of science ask such questions as why science has so often been enlisted on the side of sexism, and why so few women enter scientific fields, even today. Other burgeoning fields of feminist philosophy are feminist legal theory and feminist aesthetics.

Feminist philosophers have also been interested in understanding the ramifications of the historical exclusion of women from the discipline of philosophy. This exclusion has several forms: First, women have had very little opportunity, until very recently, to engage in systematic philosophical study; second, women and gender relations have received very little philosophical attention from the male authors who dominate the philosophical canon; and third, when women are discussed in the canonical literature, they are almost with exception represented as intellectually and morally inferior to men. Feminist philosophers have been concerned to document, analyze, and explain these various exclusions. Some feminist philosophers, including, prominently, many feminist philosophers of science, have concluded the methods and central concepts of traditional Western philosophy have been corrupted by an "androcentric" bias—a pervasive presumption that distinctively male characteristics and experiences provide appropriate normative standards for the whole human race. Other feminist philosophers argue the problem is a matter of grossly false assertions about women that can be excised without affecting traditional methods or concepts. Feminist historians of philosophy have also been engaged in the "uncovery" of female philosophers not properly recognized either in their own times or in the present.

As a result of these sorts of investigations, many feminist philosophers have concluded that there is a need for distinctively feminist methodologies and have been engaged, along with feminist theorists in other disciplines, in developing such methodologies. Typically, these methodologies focus on ways of knowing that have been denigrated or excluded by mainstream philosophy and thus emphasize the cognitive value of the emotions, of practical experience, and of social interaction.

Feminist philosophers come from a wide variety of intellectual backgrounds and invoke a variety of figures and texts. While feminist philosophers do not all agree about how deeply sexist the field is, they do agree that there is much in the institutional culture of academic philosophy that is inimical to women. Feminist philosophers work for reforms individually and collectively through informal professional networks and through such organizations as the American Philosophical Association's Committee on the Status of Women and the Society for Women in Philosophy.

See also Analytical Feminism; Feminism and Continental Philosophy; Feminism and Pragmatism; Feminism and the History of Philosophy; Feminist Aesthetics and Criticism; Feminist Epistemology; Feminist Ethics;

Feminist Legal Theory; Feminist Metaphysics; Feminist Philosophy of Science; Feminist Social and Political Philosophy.

Bibliography

Cudd, Ann, and Robin Andreasen, eds. *Feminist Theory: A Philosophical Anthology.* Oxford: Blackwell, 2005.

Fricker, Miranda, and Jennifer Hornsby, eds. *The Cambridge Companion to Feminism in Philosophy.* Cambridge, U.K.: Cambridge University Press, 2000.

Jaggar, Alison M., and Iris Marion Young, eds. *A Companion to Feminist Philosophy.* Oxford: Blackwell, 2000.

Kourany, Janet A., ed. *Philosophy in a Feminist Voice.* Princeton, NJ: Princeton University Press, 1998.

Kourany, Janet A., James Sterba, and Rosemarie Tong, eds. *Feminist Philosophies.* 2nd ed. Upper Saddle River, NJ: Prentice Hall, 1999.

Louise M. Antony (2005)

FEMINIST PHILOSOPHY OF SCIENCE

Feminist philosophy of science arises at the intersection of feminist interests in science and philosophical studies of science. Feminists have taken an active interest in the sciences both as a key resource in understanding and contesting sexist institutions and systems of belief, and as an important locus of gender inequality and source of legitimation for this inequality. Feminist practitioners in many sciences, especially in the life and social sciences, typically engage two lines of critique: They document inequalities in the training, representation, and recognition of women in the sciences, and they identify myriad ways in which, far from eliminating the contextual biases of a pervasively sexist society, standard scientific methodologies frequently reproduce them in the content of even the most credible and well-established scientific theories.

The work of feminist philosophers of science is continuous with these critiques. Some feminist philosophers contribute to the analysis of androcentrism in the content and practice of particular sciences, in some cases linking these to inequities in the role played by women in science. The form these analyses take necessarily varies with the type of science in question. Critiques of disciplines concerned with an overtly gendered subject matter—the social and behavioral sciences and some branches of the life sciences—draw attention to ways in which unexamined, often stereotypic, assumptions about gender roles, relations, and identities delimit the subject of inquiry, define categories of analysis and description, shape

assessments of plausibility that define the range of hypotheses to be taken seriously (e.g., in comparative evaluation), and inform judgments about the bearing of evidence on these hypotheses. Women may be simply left out of account; behaviors, patterns of practice or development, and values and roles associated with men may be treated as normative for the population as a whole; where women diverge from male-defined norms they may be treated as deviant, immature, or anomalous; gender differences may be assumed irrelevant or, alternatively, taken as a given, a parameter for analysis rather than a variable; and the description and analysis of gendered subjects may be structured by conceptual categories that embody highly specific (enthnocentric) assumptions about the form that gender roles, identities, institutions, and values may take. In short, critiques in these domains call attention to ways in which the social and behavioral sciences (including ethology) are pervasively androcentric in content (see Bleier 1986, Haraway 1989, contributions to Harding and Hintikka 1983, Longino and Doell 1983, Tuana 1989, Wylie et al. 1990).

When the subject domain of a science is not overtly gendered, as in the case of most natural and life sciences, it may be projectively gendered, as when gendered categories are used to describe natural phenomena or when scientific categories have (gendered) social meanings (Potter 1988). And even when the subject is not characterized in gendered terms, feminist critics find that the enterprise and practice of science may be conceptualized in gendered terms, metaphorically characterized as the domain of men or as exemplifying masculine qualities of intellect and disposition (see Keller 1985). Whether or not these metaphors directly shape the content of science or, indeed, accurately characterize the practice of a majority of scientists, they do articulate and reinforce a conception of scientific inquiry that aligns it with attributes that are valorized as masculine (see Martin 1988).

The philosophical significance of these discipline-specific critiques lies in the questions they raise for our understanding of science, specifically, its objectivity, the role of values and interests in science, the status of scientific evidence and of extant methodologies for developing and evaluating scientific theory. If androcentrism is pervasive in much that is accepted as 'good,' even exemplary, science—if it is by no means limited to examples of manifestly "bad" science (from Harding 1986)—then feminist critiques of science challenge us to rethink the relationship between what Longino has described as "contextual" and "constitutive" values (these correspond roughly to standard distinctions between cognitive or epistemic considerations "internal" to science and the noncognitive, sociopolitical factors that many believe are properly "external" to science).

In taking up these questions the interests of feminist philosophers of science intersect with themes central to postpositivist philosophy of science. Feminist critiques of specific sciences illustrate, and draw attention to the implications of, central antifoundationalist claims about the complexity and contingency of scientific practice. If scientific theories are routinely (indeed, perhaps, necessarily) underdetermined by all available evidence, and if hypotheses are never evaluated independently of one another and the evidence supporting (or refuting) them is always itself richly interpreted (the theses of holism and the theory-ladenness of evidence), then it seem unavoidable that nonevidential values and interests, features of the "external" context of science, must play a role not only in the formulation but also in the evaluation of hypotheses. The contribution of discipline-specific feminist critiques is the insight that these contextual factors may include gendered interest, values, and social structures.

Although feminist philosophers are sometimes charged with advocating an untenable, "cynical," and self-defeating relativism (Haack 1993) because of their insistence that social factors such as gender shape the practice and results of science, in fact neither feminist critics within the sciences nor feminist philosophers of science show much sympathy for extreme forms of social constructivism or contextualism on which epistemic considerations are reduced to social, political factors. Harding's (1986) discussions of a "postmodern" epistemic stance and some of Haraway's (1989) reflections on hybrid constructions of nature may be seen to move in this direction. But Harding was explicitly "ambivalent" about postmodern options at the time she proposed them and has since elaborated a thesis of "strong objectivity" according to which an understanding of the standpoint (the social location, interests, values) of epistemic agents serves as a resource in producing and evaluating "less partial and less distorted" knowledge claims (1991). Haraway has likewise elaborated the concept of "situated knowledges" with the aim of capturing the sense in which it is reasonable to require "a no-nonsense commitment to faithful accounts of a 'real' world" while yet acknowledging the radical historical and social contingency of all knowledge production (1991).

In a similar vein, while Keller reaffirms the value of psychodynamic analyses of the masculine orientation of science (e.g., as elaborated in Keller 1985), she distances herself from strong sociological theses and argues the need for feminist analyses of science that attend to "logical and empirical constraints" and account for the "technological prowess" that makes scientific claims so compelling for scientists and for the world at large (1992, p. 3). The central preoccupation of feminist philosophers of science who elaborate a positive account of scientific inquiry is to understand the ways in which the (gendered) standpoint of epistemic agents and epistemic communities shapes inquiry while yet making sense of constraints imposed by constitutive values such as the standard requirements of epistemic adequacy, reliability, internal coherence, and consistency.

A number of positions have been explored in this connection. Feminist standpoint theory is one such approach. Harding's (1991) formulation draws on the earlier proposals of feminists, such as Hartsock (1983), who are influenced both by Marxist-derived epistemologies and by psychoanalytic theory, and on the work of black and minority feminist theorists who draw attention to the insights afforded by subdominant status (Collins 1991, Narayan 1988). The central thesis of standpoint theory, as developed by feminist theorists, is that the empirical evidence to which epistemic agents have access, their powers of discernment and breadth of understanding, may be both enhanced and limited by their social location and associated experience, values, and interests. For example, those who must understand a dominant world of privilege from which they are excluded as well as the subdominant world(s) of which they are members may well be better situated to understand both worlds, in empirical detail and with critical precision, than those who are beneficiaries of systemic privilege. The epistemic partiality and authority of knowledge claims, and therefore the effective assessment of their epistemic adequacy, is thus contingent on understanding the conditions under which they are produced and authorized, the standpoint of epistemic agents and communities.

A number of feminist philosophers of science have argued that the social dimensions of scientific practice (including but not limited to its gendered dimensions) can be understood in terms compatible with a modified empiricism. Longino's (1990) carefully worked distinction between contextual and constitutive values provides a framework for identifying the various points at which epistemic considerations leave room for the play of social factors, institutional context, political commitment, and personal interests in the formulation of descriptive categories, the interpretation of data as evidence, and the evaluation of hypotheses against evidence. At the same time she accords constitutive (epistemic) values a central role, arguing that standards of rational acceptability can be identified that are independent of individual interests and that the social nature of science (e.g., institutional structures that encourage rigorous critical scrutiny of knowledge claims) serves as much to protect scientific knowledge from idiosyncratic bias as to render it vulnerable to such bias.

In a similar vein Nelson (1990) argues that an empiricist theory, which grounds knowledge in evidence and construes evidence in experiential terms, is compatible with a feminist reconceptualization of the agents of inquiry as communities, not abstract individuals, which are historically situated and of socially specified form. Sophisticated feminist empiricisms offer an account of epistemic virtues that transcend standpoint-specific interests—the virtues of empirical adequacy, reliability, scope of applicability, and explanatory power, which different standpoints help or inhibit us from realizing—without invoking an untenable (asocial) foundationalism.

Despite significant philosophical differences between proponents of these positions, feminist philosophers of science share an ambition to develop an account of science that resolves (or circumvents) the polarized debate between objectivists and rationalists on one hand and constructivists and relativists on the other. This is conceived both as a contribution to postpositivist philosophy of science, in which the terms of debate are most clearly articulated, and to feminist theory, where questions about the proper grounds for evaluating knowledge claims are a matter of immediate practical concern.

See also Feminist Epistemology; Feminist Metaphysics; Feminist Philosophy; Feminist Philosophy of Science: Contemporary Perspectives; Philosophy of Science; Sexism.

Bibliography

Bleier, Ruth. *Feminist Approaches to Science.* New York: Pergamon Press, 1986.

Collins, P. H. "Learning from the Outsider Within." In *Beyond Methodology: Feminist Scholarship as Lived Research*, edited by Mary M. Fonow and J.A. Cook. Bloomington: Indiana University Press, 1991.

Haack, S. "Knowledge and Propaganda: Reflections of an Old Feminist." *Partisan Review* 60 (1993): 556–564.

Haraway, Donna Jean. *Primate Visions: Gender, Race and Nature in the World of Modern Science.* New York: Routledge, 1989.

Haraway, Donna Jean. "Situated Knowledges: The Science Question in Feminism and the Privilege of Partial Perspective." In *Simians, Cyborgs, and Women: The Reinvention of Nature.* New York: Routledge, 1991.

Harding, Sandra G. *The Science Question in Feminism.* Ithaca, NY: Cornell University Press, 1986.

Harding, Sandra G. *Whose Science? Whose Knowledge? Thinking from Women's Lives.* Ithaca, NY: Cornell University Press, 1991.

Harding, Sandra G., and Merrill B. Hintikka, eds. *Discovering Reality: Feminist Perspectives on Epistemology, Metaphysics, Methodology, and Philosophy of Science.* Boston: D. Reidel, 1983. 2nd ed., Boston: Kluwer, 2003.

Hartsock, N. "The Feminist Standpoint." In *Discovering Reality*, edited by Sandra G. Harding and Merrill B. Hintikka. Boston: D. Reidel, 1983.

Keller, Evelyn Fox. *Reflections on Gender and Science.* New Haven, CT: Yale University Press, 1985.

Keller, Evelyn Fox. *Secrets of Life, Secrets of Death: Essays on Language, Gender, and Science.* New York: Routledge, 1992.

Longino, Helen E. *Science as Social Knowledge: Values and Objectivity in Scientific Inquiry.* Princeton, NJ: Princeton University Press, 1990.

Longino, Helen E., and R. Doell. "Body, Bias, and Behavior: A Comparative Analysis of Reasoning in Two Areas of Biological Science." *Signs* 9 (1983): 206–227.

Martin, J. "Science in a Different Style." *American Philosophical Quarterly* 25 (1988): 129–140.

Narayan, U. "Working Together across Difference." *Hypatia* 32 (1988): 31–48.

Nelson, Lynn Hankinson. *Who Knows: From Quine to a Feminist Empiricism.* Philadelphia: Temple University Press, 1990.

Potter, E. "Modeling the Gender Politics in Science." *Hypatia* 3 (1988): 19–35.

Tuana, Nancy, ed. *Feminism and Science.* Bloomington: Indiana University Press, 1989. 2nd ed., with Evelyn Fox Keller, New York: Oxford Unviersity Press, 1996.

Wylie, A., K. Okruhlik, L. Thielen-Wilson, and S. Morton, "Philosophical Feminism: A Bibliographic Guide to Critiques of Science." *Resources for Feminist Research* 19 (1990): 2–36.

Alison Wylie (1996)

FEMINIST PHILOSOPHY OF SCIENCE: CONTEMPORARY PERSPECTIVES

Feminists are a very diverse lot, but one thing they all share is a commitment to gender equality and a determination to bring it about. Feminist philosophers of science, along with feminist historians and sociologists of science and feminist scientists themselves, have focused especially on science, investigating both the ways science has helped to perpetuate gender inequality (their critical investigations) and the ways science can now help to eliminate it (their constructive investigations).

CRITICAL INVESTIGATIONS

Feminists' critical investigations have dealt with fields as diverse as primatology and molecular biology, economics and medical research, and their claims have been jarring. For example, feminists have documented a history of misogyny in both psychology and biology. In psychology, a dominant theme has been the inferiority—the intellectual, social, sexual, and even moral inferiority—of women to men (Marecek 1995, Wilkinson 1997). In biology, a host of research projects have aimed to "explain" the origins and manifestations of these presumed inferiorities in terms of what is largely unchangeable: genes, brain structure, and hormonal structure (Schiebinger 1989, Fausto-Sterling 1992, 2000). Feminists have argued that other sciences, as well, have supported this view of women's inferiority: for example, the historical sciences (such as archaeology), with their modes of representation of the past, modes of representation marked by heroic exploits and spectacular accomplishments of men counterpoised with lackluster doings or outright invisibility of women (Conkey and Williams 1991). And they have argued that still other scientific fields have perpetuated or added to the problems of inequality women confront, but in different ways than by documenting women's inferiority. Neglecting women's needs and priorities in the employment and household sectors in economic model-building, they have claimed, has had dire effects on public policy relating to women (Waring 1992, Ferber and Nelson 1993, Nelson 1996). And neglecting women in both basic and clinical research until well into the 1990s, they have added, has had dire effects on women's health care (Rosser 1994, Weisman and Cassard 1994, Schiebinger 1999). Other scientific fields that have figured prominently in feminists' critical investigations are anthropology, sociology, and political science, and even—with regard to their past and sometimes even present exclusionary practices—the physical sciences and mathematics (Kramarae and Spender 1992, Stanton and Stewart 1995, Schiebinger 1999, Kourany 2002).

CONSTRUCTIVE INVESTIGATIONS

Feminists' constructive investigations have been the site of considerable controversy, far more so than their critical investigations. It is agreed all around that science will aid the cause of equality for women if science works to replace prevailing ignorance and prejudice and misinformation about women with more adequate perspectives. But just how is this to be done?

THE METHODOLOGICAL APPROACH. Many feminist scientists have pointed out that a great deal of sexist science is, by the lights of traditional scientific methodology, simply *bad* science. Thus, they have taken to task mainstream authors of androcentric and sexist scientific work for failing to abide by accepted standards of concept formation, experimental design, interpretation of data, and the like (Bleier 1984, Hubbard 1990, Fausto-Sterling 1992). If such standards were rigorously followed, they have suggested, the problem of sexism and androcentrism in science would be, at the very least, much reduced. Feminist health researchers, for example, have pointed out that until the 1990s diseases such as heart disease that affect both sexes were defined as "male diseases," studied primarily in white, middle-aged, middle-class males, and clinically handled accordingly. As a result, heart disease in women (who, as it turns out, differ from men in symptoms, patterns of disease development, and reactions to treatment) was often not detected and not properly managed when it was detected. Such problems could be—and ultimately were—handled simply by following accepted methodological procedures such as designing clinical studies with groups of subjects that were more nearly representative of the patient population at large (see, for example, Rosser 1994 and the special report on "Women's Health Research" in *Science* 1995).

Other feminist scientists have explored ways of reforming traditional scientific methodology. Margrit Eichler (1988 and 1980), for example, has developed batteries of detailed sex- and gender-related guidelines concerning such aspects of research as concept formation, research design and instrumentation, and data interpretation to help scientists screen sexism and androcentrism out of their research, and the Biology and Gender Study Group (1988) conceptualizes such procedures as a new kind of experimental control to deal with gender bias. Feminist scientists have also explored new pedagogies to reform scientists themselves: for example, cooperative rather than competitive pedagogical methods and ones that take full note of the experiences of women and the contributions of women scientists (Rosser 1995).

All of these suggestions can be rationalized by appeal to the ideal of value-free science. According to this ideal, scientific investigations must be kept strictly free of ethical or political commitments. Since sexism and androcentrism embody social values, they simply do not belong in science. Indeed, they bias science and thereby jeopardize science as an impartial resource in the struggle for social justice. On this view of science, the *only* legitimate strategy for eliminating sexist and androcentric bias is to press for stricter adherence to the canons of scientific inquiry on the part of individual scientists. This view, that good method will yield science undistorted by sexism or androcentrism, can be called the methodological approach.

THE SOCIAL APPROACH. Few feminist philosophers of science accept the individualistic and formalistic conception of science implicit in the methodological approach. Some of them, along with some feminist scientists, have opted instead for a social approach unallied with the ideal of value-free science. They argue that no scientific method, however rigorous and however rigorously applied, can be guaranteed to screen out the various values and interests that scientists from their different social locations (race, gender, class, and so on) bring to their research. Scientists' values and interests can and do determine which questions they investigate and which they ignore, can and do motivate the background assumptions they accept and those they reject, can and do influence the observational or experimental data they select to study and the way they interpret those data, and so on. As a result, changes must be sought in the communities that generate our scientific knowledge if the knowledge generated is to aid the cause of equality for women. After all, scientific communities have historically been dominated by men—men who have been raised within sexist and androcentric societies and trained within sexist and androcentric scientific traditions; men who, moreover, profit from this sexism and androcentrism. Small wonder, then, that sexist and androcentric values have shaped the scientific knowledge generated by these communities.

But if changes should be made in the communities that generate our scientific knowledge, exactly what should be the nature of these changes? Here advocates of the social approach differ. Feminist-standpoint theorists argue that women—who also have been raised within sexist and androcentric societies and trained within sexist and androcentric scientific traditions—are still in a better position than their male counterparts to uncover and critique sexist and androcentric scientific perspectives and replace them with more adequate perspectives (are still in a better position, for example, to uncover and critique sexist assumptions about the sexual division of labor in prehistory made by male archaeologists and replace them with questions and hypothetical answers suggestive of new lines of research). "They have less to lose by distancing themselves from the social order; thus, the perspective from their lives can more easily generate fresh and critical analyses" (Harding 1991, p. 126, and cf. 1986). The upshot is that women's perspectives should

not only be welcomed into scientific communities, but they should also be privileged over men's perspectives, at least in gender-relevant areas of research, if the knowledge generated by those communities is to be an adequate basis for social justice.

Feminist empiricists such as Helen Longino and her followers, on the other hand, argue that standpoint theorists fail to take note of the diversity of perspectives of both women and men. There are women, for example, who have participated in research that is damaging to women, and there are men who have done just the opposite (see, for example, the diversity of perspectives in the special report on "Women's Health Research" in *Science* 1995). As a matter of empirical fact there simply is no one standpoint shared by all and only women, and hence, no "women's standpoint" especially conducive to uncovering and correcting prevailing ignorance and prejudice and misinformation about women. If science is to provide us with more adequate views about women, Longino urges, scientific communities must finally be made into inclusive places where women and feminist perspectives are given an equal though not a privileged hearing. More specifically, scientific communities will have to have public venues for criticism, publicly recognized standards by reference to which criticism can be made, "uptake" of such criticism (that is, the criticism will have to be taken seriously and responded to), and "tempered equality" of intellectual authority among all parties to the debate, among whom "all relevant perspectives are represented" (Longino 2002, pp. 128–135; and cf. 1990). Only if scientific communities are organized in these ways, says Longino, will the necessary "transformative criticism" of our current views of women be possible. But Longino gives us no reason to believe—and certainly no empirical evidence to suggest—that organizing scientific communities in these ways *will* issue in that transformative criticism, that is, will dispel the ignorance and prejudice and misinformation about women of which we are now possessed.

THE POLITICAL APPROACH. This motivates yet another approach different from both the methodological and social approaches—what might be called the political approach. Like the methodological approach, the political approach recognizes that sexism and androcentrism must be rooted out of science if science is to replace prevailing ignorance and prejudice and misinformation about women with more adequate perspectives, but unlike the methodological approach, the political approach also recognizes that rooting sexism and androcentrism out of science is tantamount to implanting egalitarian social values into science. Again, like the social approach, the political approach recognizes that social values inevitably enter into science, but unlike the social approach, the political approach recognizes that we as a society have a definite say—through funding priorities and restrictions, for example—as to what these social values will be. Indeed, given that science is both a profound shaper of society and a profound beneficiary of society, these social values should be chosen so as to meet the needs of society, including the justice-related needs of society.

Under the political approach, in short, our scientific views (and hence, ultimately, our generally accepted knowledge) of women would no longer be plagued by sexism or androcentrism simply because those would be the morally justified political conditions under which scientific research would be conducted (Kourany 2003, Anderson 1995, 2004). But would this political structure for science jeopardize science's objectivity? That is to say, would it render science's resultant "knowledge of women" not genuine knowledge at all?

THE NATURALIST APPROACH. Feminist naturalists provide a possible answer. A naturalist approach to the philosophy of science rejects a priori prescriptions about the conduct of inquiry or the composition of scientific communities. This approach advocates instead a close look at successful scientific practice in order to identify those of its features that contribute to and explain its success (Antony 1993, 1995). Such observation shows, feminist naturalists point out, that egalitarian social values need not compromise the objectivity of science any more than do other features of scientific communities such as competitiveness, deference to authority, or the desire for credit for one's accomplishments.

Indeed, such observation shows, feminist naturalists point out, that egalitarian social values can be *aids* in the acquisition of objective knowledge: when these values are allowed to influence science (for example, by motivating particular lines of research or the maintenance of particular social structures), that science can actually be more developed and more empirically adequate than before (Wylie and Nelson 1998, Campbell 2001). And when we reflect on the effects of feminism in science during the last three decades—the wide-ranging critiques of traditional science in such fields as psychology, sociology, economics, political science, archaeology, anthropology, biology, and medical research, and the new research directions and results forged in the wake of these critiques—when we reflect on the effects of feminism in sci-

ence during the last three decades, the claims of these feminist naturalists seem especially convincing. Egalitarian social values in these cases have seemed to yield better rather than worse science, more objective rather than contaminated science (Schiebinger 1999; Creager, Lunbeck, and Schiebinger 2001).

Feminist naturalism, however, faces at least one large problem, one that stems from a problem for naturalized epistemology in general: It threatens to eliminate the normative in favor of the descriptive, and in doing so, eliminate the grounds for normative critique. It is impossible, after all, to say a priori which values will be aids and which will be hindrances to the acquisition of objective knowledge. Racism and sexism and egalitarian social values, all are possible aids or hindrances to the acquisition of objective knowledge, and all must be empirically tested to see which they are. There is at least the suggestion, therefore, that any of them will do if only they can prove their mettle in scientific research. So if, for example, a close comparative study of German science before, during, and after the Third Reich discloses that Nazi social values produced the best scientific results, the most abundant and most empirically successful science, then Nazi social values would be "good" values and should therefore be welcomed into science. Or if such a study discloses that Nazi social values produced a science just as good as the others, but no better, then it should be a matter of complete indifference whether Nazi social values or the other sciences' values should find their way into science. In short, feminist naturalists do not tell us what considerations, other than empirical adequacy, ought to govern our choice of social values. Some feminist naturalists emphasize that social values are empirically tested by an interrelated *system* of facts and values (Nelson 1990, 1993; Anderson 1995, 2004; Campbell 1998), but it is unclear whether this move is sufficient to address the general problem.

THE CONTRIBUTION TO PHILOSOPHY OF SCIENCE

Feminists have pursued still other approaches in their constructive investigations of science, but what do they, or the critical investigations that preceded them, have finally to do with *philosophy of science*?

Nearly a half-century ago, Thomas Kuhn, Paul Feyerabend, Stephen Toulmin, Norwood Russell Hanson, and others issued a challenge to philosophers of science to make their field more relevant to actual science. That challenge, over time, has elicited a number of useful responses: first, efforts to "historicize" philosophy of science, to make philosophy of science relevant to the actual development of science, both past and present; and second, efforts to "socialize" philosophy of science, to make philosophy of science relevant not only to science's conceptual products but also to the actual knowledge-productive social practices that have led to those products. But very few efforts have thus far been made to "societize" philosophy of science, to make philosophy of science relevant to the ways in which science interacts with the wider society in which it occurs, the ways in which science both shapes and is shaped by that society. The unit of analysis for philosophy of science has tended to remain (an historical, social) science-in-a-vacuum. Feminist philosophers of science, in collaboration with feminist historians and sociologists of science and feminist scientists themselves, provide philosophers of science with a start to a societized philosophy of science.

First, feminists *have* situated science within its wider social context when philosophizing about science. Indeed, feminists have been especially concerned with the social consequences of science—in particular, the ways science has all too frequently perpetuated and added to the problems of inequality women confront. This concern with science's social consequences has led feminists to scrutinize those features of science that help to shape its social consequences—not only the research strategies of scientists but also their social location and training, the social as well as epistemic values that inform their practice, and the funding priorities that direct their research. What's more, in all this feminists have been motivated, not only by the need and desire for understanding, but also by the need and desire for social change, and they have explored social/political/epistemic initiatives intended to bring about that change—new funding priorities for science, for example, or new kinds of recruitment or training programs, or new social or epistemic values.

In short, feminist philosophers of science, in collaboration with feminist historians and sociologists of science and feminist scientists themselves, have been pursuing a comprehensive analysis of science-in-society and a comprehensive plan of action to bring about needed change in both science and society. This is the first way in which feminists have given us a start to a societized philosophy of science—by giving us a ready-made example of such philosophizing.

In addition, the ready-made example of societized philosophy of science that feminists have given us can be generalized—this is the second way in which feminists have given us a start to a societized philosophy of science.

Indeed, science has all too frequently perpetuated and added to other kinds of inequality besides gender inequality—inequality relating to race and sexual orientation and physical ability and disability, for example. And science has all too frequently perpetuated and added to other kinds of social problems besides those relating to inequality—problems relating to the environment, for example, and problems relating to the inability to achieve peaceful coexistence among nations. What's more, with different kinds of funding priorities, or different kinds of recruitment or training programs, or different kinds of social or epistemic values, or the like, science can not only cease to put obstacles in the way of solutions to these problems, but more effectively help to bring those solutions about. So there is much descriptive and normative philosophical work to be done on many fronts, philosophical work that can, at least in part, be modeled on the work already done by feminists.

Finally, the work done by feminists provides not only a generalizable example of societized philosophy of science, but it provides important additional resources as well—insights concerning the relations between epistemic values and social values and the place of social values in science, for example, insights concerning what makes for scientific objectivity and what threatens it, insights concerning the ultimate goals of science and the methods that are appropriate to them, and the like. This is the third way in which feminists have given us a start to a societized philosophy of science.

See also Feminist Epistemology; Feminist Metaphysics; Feminist Philosophy; Feminist Philosophy of Science; Philosophy of Science; Sexism.

Bibliography

Anderson, Elizabeth. *Hypatia* 19 (2004): 1–24.

Anderson, Elizabeth. "Knowledge, Human Interests, and Objectivity in Feminist Epistemology." *Philosophical Topics* 23 (1995): 27–58.

Antony, Louise. "Quine as Feminist: The Radical Import of Naturalized Epistemology." In *A Mind of One's Own: Feminist Essays on Reason and Objectivity*, edited by Louise Antony and Charlotte Witt, 110–153. Boulder, CO: Westview, 1993.

Antony, Louise. "Sisters, Please, I'd Rather Do It Myself: A Defense of Individualism in Feminist Epistemology." *Philosophical Topics* 23 (1995): 59–94.

Biology and Gender Study Group. "The Importance of Feminist Critique for Contemporary Cell Biology." *Hypatia* 3 (1988): 61–76.

Bleier, Ruth. *Sex and Gender*. New York: Pergamon Press, 1984.

Campbell, Richmond. "The Bias Paradox in Feminist Epistemology." In *Engendering Rationalities*, edited by Nancy

Tuana and Sandra Morgen. Albany: State University of New York Press, 2001.

Campbell, Richmond. *Illusions of Paradox: A Feminist Epistemology Naturalized*. Maryland and Oxford: Rowman and Littlefield, 1998.

Conkey, Margaret W., and Sarah H. Williams. "Original Narratives: The Political Economy of Gender in Archaeology." In *Gender at the Crossroads of Knowledge: Feminist Anthropology in the Postmodern Era*, edited by Micaela di Leonardo, 102–139. Berkeley and Los Angeles: University of California Press, 1991.

Creager, Angela N., Elizabeth Lunbeck, and Londa Schiebinger, eds. *Feminism in Twentieth-Century Science, Technology, and Medicine*. Chicago: University of Chicago Press, 2001.

Eichler, Margrit. *The Double Standard: A Feminist Critique of Feminist Social Science*. New York: St. Martin's Press, 1980.

Eichler, Margrit. *Nonsexist Research Methods: A Practical Guide*. Boston: Allen & Unwin, 1988.

Fausto-Sterling, Anne. *Myths of Gender*. 2nd ed. New York: Basic Books, 1992.

Fausto-Sterling, Anne. *Sexing the Body: Gender Politics and the Construction of Sexuality*. New York: Basic Books, 2000.

Ferber, Marianne A., and Julie A. Nelson, eds. *Beyond Economic Man: Feminist Theory and Economics*. Chicago: University of Chicago Press, 1993.

Harding, Sandra. *The Science Question in Feminism*. Ithaca, NY: Cornell University Press, 1986.

Harding, Sandra. *Whose Science? Whose Knowledge?* Ithaca, NY: Cornell University Press, 1991.

Hubbard, Ruth. *The Politics of Women's Biology*. New Brunswick, NJ: Rutgers University Press, 1990.

Kourany, Janet A., ed. *The Gender of Science*. Upper Saddle River, NJ: Prentice Hall, 2002.

Kourany, Janet A. "A Philosophy of Science for the Twenty-First Century" and "Reply to Giere." *Philosophy of Science* 70 (2003): 1–14, 22–26.

Kramarae, Cheris, and Dale Spender, eds. *The Knowledge Explosion*. New York and London: Teachers College Press, 1992.

Longino, Helen. *The Fate of Knowledge*. Princeton, NJ: Princeton University Press, 2002.

Longino, Helen. *Science as Social Knowledge: Values and Objectivity in Scientific Inquiry*. Princeton, NJ: Princeton University Press, 1990.

Marecek, Jeanne. "Psychology and Feminism: Can This Relationship Be Saved?" In *Feminisms in the Academy*, edited by Domna C. Stanton and Abigail J. Stewart, 101–132. Ann Arbor: University of Michigan Press, 1995.

Nelson, Julie A. *Feminism, Objectivity and Economics*. London and New York: Routledge, 1996.

Nelson, Lynn Hankinson. "Epistemological Communities." In *Feminist Epistemologies*, edited by Linda Alcoff and Elizabeth Potter. New York: Routledge, 1993.

Nelson, Lynn Hankinson. *Who Knows: From Quine to a Feminist Empiricism*. Philadelphia: Temple University Press, 1990.

Rosser, Sue, ed. *Women's Health—Missing from U.S. Medicine*. Bloomington and Indianapolis: Indiana University Press, 1994.

Rosser, Sue, ed. *Teaching the Majority: Breaking the Gender Barrier in Science, Mathematics, and Engineering*. New York: Teachers College, Columbia University, 1995.

Schiebinger, Londa. *Has Feminism Changed Science?* Cambridge, MA: Harvard University Press, 1999.

Schiebinger, Londa. *The Mind Has No Sex?* Cambridge, MA.: Harvard University Press, 1989.

Stanton, Domna C., and Abigail J. Stewart, eds. *Feminisms in the Academy*. Ann Arbor: University of Michigan Press, 1995.

Waring, Marilyn J. "Economics." In *The Knowledge Explosion*, edited by Cheris Kramarae and Dale Spender, 303–309. New York and London: Teachers College Press, 1992.

Weisman, Carol S., and Sandra D. Cassard. "Health Consequences of Exclusion or Underrepresentation of Women in Clinical Studies (I)." In *Women and Health Research*. Vol. 2, edited by Anna C. Mastroianni, Ruth Faden, and Daniel Federman, 35–40. Washington, DC: National Academy Press, 1994.

Wilkinson, Sue. "Still Seeking Transformation: Feminist Challenges to Psychology." In *Knowing Feminisms: On Academic Borders, Territories and Tribes*, edited by Liz Stanley, 97–108. London: Sage Publications, 1997.

"Women's Health Research." *Science* 269 (1995): 765–801.

Wylie, Alison, and Lynn Hankinson Nelson. "Coming to Terms with the Value(s) of Science: Insights from Feminist Science Scholarship." Paper delivered at the Workshop on Science and Values, Center for Philosophy of Science, University of Pittsburgh, 1998.

Janet A. Kourany (2005)

FEMINIST SOCIAL AND POLITICAL PHILOSOPHY

Within the enormously varied and fluid field of feminist social/political philosophy and political theory, several foci can be identified: analyses of women's oppression; explorations of differences among women and their implications for feminism; critiques of political philosophers and retrieval of little-known women philosophers; reanalyses of central concepts in political philosophy; analyses and recommendations on practical political issues.

A COMMON THEORETICAL BASIS FOR FEMINISM?

Whether there is anything that cuts across these different areas of work and the varieties of theoretical perspectives is not entirely clear. If feminism is to have a common basis it would seem necessary to say that whatever the disagreements, all agree that women are oppressed, or at least subordinated to men, and that to eliminate this requires not only legal changes of a kind that have mostly been achieved in the developed world, but more profound changes in society and consciousness. However, even these modest generalizations are suspect to postmodernist feminists who eschew talk of "women" because the term conceals so many differences among women, and who are skeptical of claims to truth and objectivity.

Indeed, the question of differences—both between women and men, and among women—has been a consuming issue throughout the history of feminism. In first-wave feminism, whether women and men had distinct natures (beyond the biological) was the dominant theoretical question, with early feminists like Mary Wollstonecraft and Harriet Taylor basing their call for women's rights on the claim that women had the same capacity for reason as men. Utopian socialists and Marxists agreed, deepening the critique of naturalistic justifications of the hierarchy between women and men, with a call to end class inequality as well. By the time of second-wave feminism, most educated people agreed that whatever differences exist between women and men were largely social in origin and certainly not sufficient to explain women's subordination. Even among feminists, however, this view was not universal and for a period this disagreement consumed considerable attention. Nevertheless, the question of "differences" that dominated second-wave feminism and beyond was differences among women and how they affected the feminist project.

The issue was not discussed directly in those terms at first. Feminists assumed that women could all be said to be treated unfairly, or to be oppressed, the particular word chosen reflecting different political theoretical perspectives, but most shared an optimistic assumption of commonality expressed in slogans like Sisterhood Is Powerful. The issue of differences among women emerged implicitly, however, in debates regarding how to understand women's subordination. The standard labels for the competing political and philosophical perspectives on the roots of oppression and how to end it, best explicated by Alison Jaggar, are liberal feminism, Marxist feminism, radical feminism, and socialist feminism. There has also been much rich discussion of how to conceive oppression that is independent of these labels, by Iris Young, for example.

CRITIQUES AND REVISIONS OF LIBERALISM

Liberal feminism is liberal theory as adapted by criticisms that women had been left out. By and large, liberal feminists in the United States and Western Europe accept the terms of the dominant political discourse such as methodological individualism, the centrality of the values of individual freedom and choice, the focus on legal and political change, such as securing the legal right to abortion and the passage of an Equal Rights Amendment, and a faith in education to eradicate prejudice. They believe that the dominant political and economic system, that is, capitalism, is compatible with equal opportunities for women, but that many existing social arrangements need to be changed. In particular, they argue that it is unjust that the care of children should be exclusively women's responsibility and they call for arrangements to make possible sharing of childcare, like part-time work. Liberal feminists accept sexual freedom as a matter of individual right, but it is not central to their concerns, nor are differences among women along the lines of race/ethnicity, class, or sexuality.

The extension of the concept of justice from the public sphere to the family, traditionally understood as private, is one of the most distinctive features of feminist thought. While feminists differ on the importance of the notion of privacy, they point out that what counts as the private depends on the public, that is, legislation, and question many aspects of this fundamental distinction. Independence is another central concept and value that feminists question, pointing out that humans are all interdependent and that some people's independence is actually dependent on the invisible or undervalued labor of others, usually women. Feminists have also reconceived the concepts of autonomy and obligation in more relational terms, have debated the adequacy of rights talk for feminist concerns, have proposed that rights be extended to groups, and have explored positive and negative dimensions of power. The social contract tradition within liberalism, particularly Thomas Hobbes, has been radically reconceived by Carole Pateman as in actuality a sexual contract.

Most of these criticisms of liberal political philosophy are still within liberal feminism, but a broader sense of liberalism that encompasses social-welfare liberalism. Since it is these latter types of liberalism that have been influential in East and Central Europe, along with strains of liberalism that recognize collective goods like the family and the nation, many of the Western feminist critiques of liberalism do not apply there. As Nanette Funk shows, in those contexts feminists have needed to insist on individual rights versus the common good and neutral universalistic rights versus gendered and nationalistic conceptions. Western European and American feminists have also disagreed on these issues because they have disagreed about the source and centrality to political theory of differences between women and men.

In the 1980s and 1990s, an approach known as "difference feminism" was very influential, according to which universalistic gender neutral ideals and policies did not do justice to women's specific roles and capacities. Some went so far as to hold that these differences between women and men were biologically based, but most accepted a psychoanalytic approach to understanding the origins of psychological sex differences rooted in the fact that women are the primary caretakers of children; they paid little attention to class, race/ethnic and historic variations among women and men. Given male/female differences, whatever the source, they held that citizenship should be reconceived and accommodations for women should be made in law and public policy, such as pregnancy and maternity leave. Other feminists favored gender neutral policies such as disability and parenting leave.

Feminist philosophers have brought to light little known women philosophers such as Christine Di Pisan who had the idea of the body politic before Hobbes, and have examined classic and contemporary political philosophers with feminist eyes. Their purpose is not simply to expose sexist assumptions but to explore how central these are to the theory. Sexism is seen as inelimiinable from the political theories of Aristotle, Jean-Jacques Rousseau, and Georg Hegel, for example. John Locke is credited by some with opening the door to feminism, but others, such as Lorene Clark, argue that Locke's theory is fundamentally inconsistent; while political obligation is said to rest on free, equal, and rational individuals consenting to a limited government, Locke's theory requires that women be subordinate in the family and society in order to guarantee his other aim, the preservation of private property. Hence, Locke's theory cannot be rewritten in universal terms. Not all feminist critiques of political philosophers have been so devastating. For example, according to Susan Moller Okin, though Rawls assumed the traditional sexual division of labor in his theory of justice, and did not extend the sphere of justice into the family, his theory does not depend on this sexist limitation and would be stronger without it.

MARXIST, RADICAL AND SOCIALIST FEMINIST PERSPECTIVES

Many feminists, particularly outside the United States, have found Marxism a useful tool for understanding women's oppression. Although focused on economic exploitation, Marxism does not deny other forms of oppression, like sexism or racism, or reduce them to the economic, (except for the crudest of "Marxists"), but it gives them less explanatory primacy. According to Marx-

ism each exploitative mode of production, such as feudalism or capitalism, is distinctive in its mode of exploitation and each gives rise to certain distinctive forms of government, religion, culture, and family. Thus relations between women and men will vary in different modes of production. While women's lot in life is better in capitalism than in feudalism or slave societies, Marxist feminists generally maintain that sexism has certain benefits for capitalism, such as allowing socially necessary caring labor to be unpaid, and hiding the (un)(der)employment of women. They have debated the relations between sexism and capitalism, such as whether housework is exploited in a Marxist sense, whether women can be said to constitute a class and how domination and alienation at work contribute to the hierarchical construction of gender. For a sample, see the debate between Wally Secombe and Margaret Coulson et al. in the *New Left Review* (1975). Some feminist uses of Marxism involve quite significant revisions of Marxism, and in Europe some call this radical feminism.

Implicit in a Marxist approach is that women share certain common interests, but that women of different economic classes also have fundamentally different interests; and, moreover, that these are likely to be most important to them. For example, all women need the legal right to birth control and abortion, but poor women need public funding to exercise this right. The greatest problem facing women around the world is extreme poverty, according to the World Health Organization, but women capitalists profit directly from this poverty, while many others benefit from poor women's cheap labor. The political and strategic implications are that all women should unite to secure their common cross-class interests, but that working class women need to work with working class men to secure their specific economic interests, and that ultimately the elimination of women's oppression requires the end of capitalism.

Radical feminism, the youngest and most fluid of feminist theoretical perspectives, was developed by feminists who saw liberalism's goal of equality for women as not nearly radical enough and Marxism's focus on the economic as blind to the specific oppression of women by men of all classes. The very notion of politics, they held, must be radically reconceived. "The personal is political," they proclaimed. Some radical feminists like Catherine MacKinnon attempted to develop a theory in which sex replaced class as the primary category with which to understand history and current societies, seeing most societies as profoundly misogynist. Whether they share this overarching theory or not, radical feminists see differences among women such as race/ethnicity, class or nationality as less important than what unites them — oppression by men, particularly sexual violence, focusing attention on the outrageous prevalence of rape and its use as a weapon of war, on trafficking and sexual slavery, and on pornography, Andrea Dworkin's work being the most notable on the latter. Most radical feminists are deeply skeptical about the pleasures of sexual liberation for women, focusing instead on the dangers and coercion of heterosexual sex in a male dominated universe, although some sexual liberationists might also fall within the radical feminist camp. Many have connected violence against women to violence against other species and nature, universally associated with women, and some have evolved into "difference feminists," echoing those first-wave feminists who argued for women's suffrage on the grounds that women were more moral than men.

"Socialist," as distinct from Marxist, feminism is best understood as a synthesis of Marxism and radical feminism. Maintaining that women's oppression in capitalist society is a function of both the economic system, capitalism, and the sex/gender system, which they called patriarchy, socialist feminists like Heidi Hartman refused to give primacy to one over the other. Many saw as sexist the Marxist emphasis on wage labor rather than on all kinds of labor, especially women's unpaid caring labor, and on the relations of production, rather than on what they called the "relations of reproduction" (sexuality and parenting). To correct this deficiency Ann Ferguson proposed a concept of "sex-affective production." While its synthesis is attractive, the theory gives rise to questions as to whether the oppression of women requires a "system" (patriarchy) to explain it, and if so, why doesn't racism or heterosexism, require a system to explain them, and what exactly a "system" means anyway. Some socialist feminists tried to accommodate racism by adding a race/ethnicity system, but questions remain regarding the meaning of "system," how the systems are related, and how the theory differs from simple pluralism.

In the twenty-first century, as Nancy Holmstrom explains, "socialist feminism" is often used more broadly to refer to any theory that tries to integrate class and sex, as well as other aspects of identity such as race/ethnicity in a coherent way, however exactly they are related. On this broad definition, it would encompass perspectives that either go by other names such as materialist feminism, womanism and black feminism or that have no theoretical labels of any kind. Which term a feminist uses to describe herself indicates where she wishes to position herself within certain debates or else signals certain com-

mitments, but is not necessarily a "grand theory" in competition with liberal, Marxist/socialist or radical feminism. Although "materialist feminism" was introduced by Christine Delphy and Colette Guillaumin as a competing grand theory, and the label has recently been used by feminists wishing to engage with postmodernism, it fits within this broad definition. "Womanist" was introduced initially by some women of color who felt that "feminism" is too one-dimensional and who wished to indicate solidarity with men of color as well as women. "Black feminist," particularly as developed by Patricia Hill Collins, is a position whose insights stem from the particular experiences of African-American women.

RETREAT FROM GRAND THEORY

Most feminists in the early twenty-first century, especially in the United States, eschew the word socialist, both because of negative associations and because of an antitheoretical mood brought on by postmodern criticisms of "totalizing narratives." Instead of one overarching feminist theory, feminists prefer to rest on the concept of intersectionality, to use Kimberle Crenshaw's useful descriptive term. Racism, sexism, classism, and heterosexism are seen as overlapping forms of oppression, similar in some ways, different in others, none of which is more important politically or theoretically than the others. But if being a woman cannot be separated from being a particular kind of woman, black or white or gay or working class, then this seems to imply that there can be no theory of women's oppression as such. And this suggests there is no basis for feminism, a theory and political movement for all women, but rather only for particular kinds of women, for example for black women. Moreover, the same logic can be carried further. Black women are also of a particular nationality, class, sexual orientation, (dis)ability. Thus, this seems to lead to a dead-end theoretically.

A hopeful assumption widespread among twenty-first-century feminists is that while commonalities cannot be assumed, they can be found, unity can be forged, despite the differences among women, but only with strong political commitment and efforts to seek commonalities. It entails accepting, negotiating and transcending differences and first of all, it means really listening. Implicit in this approach is the assumption that the various kinds of differences—"identities"—are on a par: race/ethnic, class, sexual orientation, (dis)ability. To give any order of importance is mistaken and oppressive.

This sounds promising for feminist political philosophy in that it could provide a common basis for feminism, without denying differences. However, whether this approach to overcoming or at least bridging differences is applicable to all the different kinds of difference depends on whether or not they are inherently antagonistic. A plausible example is sexuality. Despite what social conservatives say, heterosexuality is not threatened by homosexuality. Neither the existence of heterosexuals nor their happiness is compromised by acceptance of different kinds of sexual and emotional desire. On the other hand, class differences are more problematic. Imagine a conversation between two women, a sweatshop owner and her employee. However much they talk and negotiate and understand each other's position, how is the difference between them to be overcome? Since classes are socially constituted by their antagonistic relationship of interest and power, those relations between members of different classes will persist.

Other feminist philosophers have been more involved with ethical theory, particularly care ethics, than with wholesale analyses of oppression, assuming that sufficient commonalities exist among women to justify their analyses and policy recommendations. Nel Nodding's approach starts with a characterization of the best of familial relations and then applies the lessons learned there to broad social policies regarding welfare, education, and criminal justice. Especially since the September 11, 2001, terrorist attacks, issues of war, peace, and terrorism have received a lot of attention, but Sara Ruddick connected mothering to peace politics early on. Many feminist philosophers have turned their attention in recent years to global gender issues, and have debated whether human rights, capabilities, or a care ethics is the most fruitful approach. Postcolonial feminists like Chandra Mohanty pay particular attention to the ways in which colonialism and imperialism work together with patriarchal structures and ideology to subordinate women. Within global feminism, differences among women are again a problematic issue, as the controversy around Okin's critique of multiculturalism attests.

See also Aristotle; Feminism and Pragmatism; Feminist Ethics; Feminist Metaphysics; Feminist Philosophy; Ferguson, Ann; Hegel, Georg Wilhelm Friedrich; Heterosexism; Hobbes, Thomas; Locke, John; Marxist Philosophy; Racism; Rawls, John; Rousseau, Jean-Jacques; Social and Political Philosophy; Wollstonecraft, Mary.

Bibliography

Butler, Judith, and Joan Scott, eds. *Feminists Theorize the Political*. New York: Routledge, 1992.

Clark, Lorenne M. G., and Lynda Lange. *The Sexism of Social and Political Philosophy*. Toronto: University of Toronto Press, 1979.

Collins, Patricia Hill. *Black Feminist Thought*. 2nd ed. New York: Routledge, 2000.

Coulson, Margaret, Branka Magas, and Hilary Wainwright. "The Housewife and Her Labour Under Capitalism." *New Left Review* 89 (1975).

Crenshaw, Kimberle. *Demarginalizing the Intersectionality of Race and Sex: A Black Feminist Critique of Anti-Discrimination Doctrine, Feminist Theory and Antiracist Politics*. Chicago: University of Chicago Legal Forum, 1989.

Daly, Mary. *Gyn/Ecology: A Metaethics of Radical Feminism*. Boston: Beacon, 1978.

Davis, Angela. *Women, Race and Class*. New York: Random House, 1983.

Delphy, Christine, and Diane Leone. *Close to Home: A Materialist Analysis of Women's Oppression*. New York: Harper-Collins, 1984.

Dworkin, Andrea. *Pornography: Men Possessing Women*. New York: Perigee, 1981.

Funk, Nanette. "Feminist Critiques of Liberalism, Can They Travel East." *Signs* 29 (3) (2004).

Ferguson, Ann. *Sexual Democracy: Women, Oppression, and Revolution*. Boulder, CO: Westview Press, 1991.

Guillaumin, Colette. *Racism, Sexism, Power and Ideology*. New York: Routledge, 1995.

Hartmann, Heidi. "The Unhappy Marriage of Marxism and Feminism: Toward a More Progressive Union." In *Women and Revolution*, edited by Lydia Sargent. Boston: South End Press, 1981.

Held, Virginia. *Rights and Goods: Justifying Social Action*. Chicago: University of Chicago Press, 1984.

Holmstrom, Nancy. *The Socialist Feminist Project: A Reader in Theory and Politics*. New York: Monthly Review Press, 2002.

Jaggar, Alison. *Feminist Politics and Human Nature*. Totowa, NJ: Rowman and Allanheld, 1983.

MacKinnon, Catherine A. *Toward a Feminist Theory of the State*. Cambridge, MA: Harvard University Press, 1989.

Mohanty, Chandra Talpade. *Feminism without Borders: Decolonizing Theory, Practicing Solidarity*. Durham, NC: Duke University Press, 2003.

Noddings, Nel. *Starting at Home*. Berkeley: University of California Press, 2002.

Nussbaum, Martha, and Jonathan Glover, eds. *Women, Culture and Development: A Study of Human Capabilities*. Oxford: Oxford University Press, 1995.

Okin, Susan Moller, *Is Multiculturalism Bad for Women?* Princeton, NJ: Princeton University Press, 1999.

Okin, Susan Moller. *Justice, Gender and the Family*. New York: Basic Books, 1989.

Pateman, Carole. *The Sexual Contract*. Stanford, CA: Stanford University Press, 1997.

Peters, Julie, and Andrea Wolper. *Women's Rights, Human Rights: International Feminist Perspectives*. New York: Routledge, 1995.

Ruddick, Sara. *Maternal Thinking: Toward a Politics of Peace*. Boston: Beacon Press, 1989.

Sargent, Lydia, ed. *Women and Revolution*. Boston: South End Press, 1981.

Secombe, Wally. "The Housewife and Her Labour Under Capitalism." *New Left Review* 83 (1973).

Shanley, Mary Lyndon, and Carole Pateman. *Feminist Interpretations and Political Theory.* University Park, PA: Penn State University Press, 1991.

Shanley, Mary Lyndon, and Uma Narayan. *Reconstructing Political Theory: Feminist Perspectives.* University Park, PA: Penn State University Press, 1997.

Waters, Kristin. *Women and Men Political Theorists: Enlightened Conversations.* Oxford: Blackwell Press, 2000.

Young, Iris Marion. *Justice and the Politics of Difference.* Princeton, NJ: Princeton University Press, 1990.

Nancy Holmstrom (2005)

FÉNELON, FRANÇOIS DE SALIGNAC DE LA MOTHE
(1651–1715)

François de Salignac de la Mothe Fénelon, the French bishop and author, was born in Périgord of an ancient noble but impoverished family. He received his education in Cahors and then in Paris, where he entered the seminary of Saint-Sulpice and was ordained priest about 1675. First in Paris and then in Saintonge he was made responsible for securing the conversion of Protestants, and in this, especially after the revocation of the Edict of Nantes (1685), he had to offset the effects of brutal military repression. He was certainly firm and successful, but opinions vary on how gentle he was. By 1689 he enjoyed the favor of Bishop Jacques Bénigne Bossuet and Mme. de Maintenon and had been appointed tutor to Louis XIV's grandson, the duc de Bourgogne.

Fénelon's association with Mme. Guyon, the exponent of quietism, dramatically changed his career. In 1694, mainly on Bossuet's initiative, she was censured by an official inquiry and temporarily put under his supervision at Meaux. Both Fénelon and Mme. de Maintenon were implicated with Mme. Guyon in a devotional group, but when Bossuet consecrated Fénelon archbishop of Cambrai in 1695 it seemed that he had averted potential scandal by using promotion as a pretext for removal. Fénelon, however, had become personally committed to mysticism and the doctrine of pure love (the disinterested love of God, divorced from any act of will, or even concern for one's salvation). Learning that Bossuet planned a crushing (and unfair) attack on Mme. Guyon and, through her, on all mysticism, Fénelon tried to forestall him by publishing a reasoned defense of mystical spirituality, *Les maximes des saints* (1679). Bossuet then embarked on a campaign of slander, falsification, and corruption, which resulted in Fénelon's banishment from the court (1697) and his condemnation by the pope (1699). Fénelon, who had always been fragile in health, remained in exile at Cambrai, conscientiously ruling his war-ravaged diocese, earning a reputation for sanctity, and pursuing a relentless, and ultimately successful, struggle against Jansenism in high places.

Though he owed much of his early success to Bossuet, whom he had at first admired, Fénelon was by temperament so different that a subsequent breach was inevitable. In his attitude to the theater Fénelon had a breadth and humanity of outlook that led him to praise Jean Racine and even Molière, who had been mercilessly attacked by Bossuet (*Lettre à l'Académie*, 1714). Fénelon had been deeply influenced by Greek culture, and much of his thinking bore the mark of Plato. He combined sensitivity and idealism with a strong vein of practicality, but he echoed neither the authoritarianism nor the moral grimness of Bossuet.

In philosophy Fénelon was enthusiastic rather than original. In 1687 he undertook for Bossuet a *Réfutation du système de la nature et de la grâce* against Nicolas Malebranche, but he soon espoused a form of Cartesianism—best represented in his *Traité de l'existence de Dieu* (1712 and 1718)—that came very close to Malebranche's position. Fénelon also wrote *Lettres sur divers sujets de métaphysique et de religion* (1718).

His early *Traité de l'education des filles* (1687) is humane and sensible, arguing that to neglect the education of one half of the human race can only have adverse effects on the other. Basing his system firmly on Christian teaching, he emphasized the need for a moral education deriving from love of virtue, rather than from fear of punishment. In addition to general literacy and elocution, Fénelon advocated the teaching of such practical matters as sufficient knowledge of law to enable women to protect their much-abused interests.

Fénelon's principle of developing rather than repressing character appears in *Télémaque*, written for his pupil about 1694 and semiofficially condemned on publication (1699). The transparent veil of Homeric legend does nothing to conceal the author's detestation of royal absolutism in its contemporary manifestations. Wars of aggression fought in the name of national prestige, territorial aggrandizement and extravagant luxury at court are condemned, not only for the misery they cause for impoverished subjects, but also as evils in themselves. For Fénelon a good king is one whose people enjoy prosperity based on industry and commerce and who accepts the duty of ensuring not only their material but also, through his example, their moral welfare. Fénelon's fundamental political axiom was that kings and their policies are subject to and judged by the moral law, as embodied in Christian teaching, and that the true interests of a state can never conflict with this law. Similar views occur in the *Dialogues des morts*. Had it not been for the premature death of the duc de Bourgogne (1712), Fénelon's teaching, so contrary to Louis XIV's practice, might well have become official policy.

See also Bossuet, Jacques Bénigne.

Bibliography

WORKS BY FÉNELON

Oeuvres complètes. 10 vols, edited by J. Gosselin. Paris, 1848–1852.

Numerous editions of separate works.

WORKS ON FÉNELON

Adam, A. *Histoire de la littérature française au XVIIᵉ siècle.* Vol. V, Ch. 5. Paris, 1956. Excellent chapter on Fénelon.

Bremond, H. *Apologie pour Fénelon.* Paris, 1910.

Carcassonne, E. *Fénelon, l'homme et l'oeuvre.* Paris: Boivin, 1946.

Goré, Jeanne-L. *L'itinéraire de Fénelon.* Paris, 1957.

Hazard, P. *La crise de la consciense européenne.* 2nd ed. Paris, 1961. Translated by J. L. May as *The European Mind.* London: Hollis and Carter, 1953; Harmondsworth, U.K. (paperback), 1964.

Kearns, Edward J. *Ideas in Seventeenth Century France.* New York: St. Martin's Press, 1979.

A. J. Krailsheimer (1967)
Bibliography updated by Tamra Frei (2005)

FERGUSON, ADAM
(1723–1816)

Born in Logierait, Scotland, to a parish minister, Adam Ferguson was educated first at the local parish school, then at grammar school in Perth, then at St. Andrews (MA 1742), and finally studied divinity at the University of Edinburgh (1743–1745). In Edinburgh he befriended many leading figures in moderate circles, including fellow divinity students Alexander Carlyle (1722–1805), William Robertson (1721–1793), and Hugh Blair (1718–1800) and older members of the Select Society including his close friend, David Hume. In 1745 he cut his studies short, was ordained, and became deputy chaplain (eventually chaplain) preaching in Gaelic to the Highland Black Watch Regiment. He returned to secular nonmilitary life in 1754 and became a mainstay of the Edinburgh intelligentsia, succeeding Hume as the librarian of the

Faculty of Advocates (1758–1759), then (also with Hume's assistance) became professor of natural philosophy at the University of Edinburgh (1759–1764) and finally professor of pneumatics and moral philosophy (1764–1785).

Ferguson's international reputation was secured with the publication of his masterpiece, *An Essay on the History of Civil Society* in 1767. The *Essay* was quickly followed by the *Institutes of Moral Philosophy* (1769), a popular textbook used in moral philosophy curricula in America, Germany, and Russia. Now famous, Ferguson traveled extensively and engaged vigorously with the philosophical and political issues of his day, particularly the American Revolution, which he criticized in its revolutionary practice in a pamphlet against Richard Price (*Observations on the Nature of Civil Liberty* [1776]) and the settlement of which he sought as secretary to the Carlisle Commission (1778). Ferguson continued his publishing successes with the philosophical history *History of the Progress and Termination of the Roman Republic* (1783) and later, after his retirement from Edinburgh, the *Principles of Moral and Political Science* (1792). His intellectual engagements hardly dampened until his death, and in addition to his books he published a significant number of pamphlets.

His contemporaries were impressed by his intelligence and his distinctive temperament. Carlyle described Ferguson as having "a dignified reserve" in conversation filled with "dark allusions," and as jealous yet with a "boundless sense of humor" in private company. A nineteenth-century biographer nicknamed Ferguson the "the Scottish Cato" due to these qualities of character appropriate to the Scots advocate of republican Stoical virtue.

Like many of his contemporaries, Ferguson brought a wide range of scientific, anthropological, and historical resources to bear on moral and politics in a characteristically Scottish fusion of mid- and late Stoicism, natural law theory, history, natural science, and the natural sciences of man (including pneumatics or the physical history of mind). His *Essay on Civil Society* was built on a stadial theory that divided human societies according to their means of subsistence, social organization, and equality (among other variables). At the same time, Ferguson stressed that although morals should be fully informed by natural science and social history, it had a special provenance: what one ought to do in regard to good and evil and virtue and vice.

So far, nothing in Ferguson's theory was unique and he drew on many of his Scottish contemporaries—

notably Hume, Adam Smith, and Thomas Reid—for his arguments. What was distinctive was how Ferguson used this framework to think about the relation between morals and politics. For Ferguson virtue was thoroughly intertwined with political *virtù* in the tradition of Niccolò Machiavelli and Baron de Montesquieu. Francis Hutcheson had stressed the civic and social character of morality, but Ferguson drew on Montesquieu's arguments in *Spirit of the Laws* (1748), that laws and social institutions create a virtuous citizenry, and on his definition of political liberty as virtuous action in and through good laws, to interweave civic morality with the new sciences of man. For Ferguson, like Montesquieu, the growth of virtue was neither isomorphic with material progress nor necessarily antithetical to it: Virtue can be found in different times and places. But unlike Montesquieu and like Smith, John Millar, and numerous other Scots, he always assumed in the background a theory of historical stages, not as linear progress but as a means to analyze nations and peoples both synchronically and diachronically, and as a species of conjectural history to be used as an analytic framework for comparing progress, wealth, equality, virtue, and other variables. On the one hand, the optimal setting for virtue and equality was a small, republican meritocracy of social and political equals actively contributing to the common good. On the other hand, Ferguson also stressed that ancient, simple military societies tended to be impoverished, violent, and "rude," lacking many of the sociable virtues admired in a commercial society. The problem was, then, given the different forces that can affect a nation morally—its size, its prosperity, its historical stage, and its laws—how to maximize virtue and minimize vice?

Ferguson's diagnosed this problem as endemic to his contemporaries thinking about morals and politics. Hume (and later Smith and Millar) argued that commerce was a fundamental civilizing force and gave rise to a liberal progressive society superior to societies that preceded it. Still, Hume recognized the virtue of small, egalitarian societies. Ferguson thought that Hume and Smith confused material prosperity with wealth and this showed in their moral recommendations. Obviously, material prosperity was desirable, and once attained it was difficult to forego, but prosperous nations are often corrupt and there was no guarantee from the progress of history that they would not become luxurious and despotic. The focus should be on a broader conception of wealth that included moral and political virtue.

So what sorts of laws and civic institutions prevent moral corruption and reinforce virtue in large, wealthy societies? Ferguson focused throughout his career in his books and pamphlets on the importance of citizens' militias, that is, defense by ordinary citizenry as opposed to professional soldiers. His service in the Black Watch during the Jacobite uprising of 1745–1746 made him aware firsthand of the difficulties a standing army in a commercial society had in quelling rude but fierce Highland militias. Most of the Edinburgh intelligentsia—including Smith and Hume—supported a Scottish militia. Ferguson thought that the issue was philosophically pivotal and that Smith's lukewarm support for the militia was a symptom of the conflict in his theory between virtue and wealth. He believed that militias are paradigmatic egalitarian, socially activist institutions. Any soldier can rise in a militia through merit, and military and social virtue are rewarded and reinforced in local organizations where citizenry know one another, rely on one another, and are responsible for their actions. Complex, prosperous societies need such invigorating, egalitarian social institutions to be wealthy in a broader sense, to avoid moral corruption, and so to be vigilant against tyranny. They also are a bulwark against the deadening effect of the division of labor, which is driven forward by commerce but not morality. Active social institutions allow the moral vigor of rude society, above all the early Roman republic, to be infused in commercial societies when people cannot, or even do not want to, return to a prior state.

Ferguson's works were particularly popular in Italy, France, and Germany and influenced, among others, Gottfried Lessing, Christian Garve, and Friedrich Schiller. He also influenced Karl Marx in particular (with his criticisms of progressivism and the division of labor) and modern sociology in general, above all through the proliferation of the idea of civil society.

See also Garve, Christian; Hume, David; Hutcheson, Francis; Lessing, Gotthold Ephraim; Machiavelli, Niccolò; Marx, Karl; Montesquieu, Baron de; Natural Law; Price, Richard; Reid, Thomas; Schiller, Friedrich; Smith, Adam; Stoicism.

Bibliography

Oz-Salzberger, Fania. *Translating the Enlightenment: Scottish Civic Discourse in Eighteenth-Century Germany.* New York: Oxford University Press, 1995.

WORKS BY ADAM FERGUSON

The Correspondence of Adam Ferguson, edited by Vincenzo Merolle. Brookfield, VT: William Pickering, 1995a.

An Essay on the History of Civil Society (1767), edited by Fania Oz-Salzberger. New York: Cambridge University Press, 1995b.

Collection of Essays, edited by Yasua Amoh. Kyōto, Japan: Rinsen Books, 1996.

WORKS ABOUT ADAM FERGUSON

Burton, John Hill, ed. *The Autobiography of Dr. Alexander Carlyle of Inveresk: 1722–1805*. London: T. N. Foulis, 1910.

Kettler, David. *The Social and Political Thought of Adam Ferguson*. Columbus: Ohio State University Press, 1965.

Oz-Salzberger, Fania. "Adam Ferguson." In *Dictionary of National Biography*. New York: Oxford University Press, 2004.

Sher, Richard B. "Adam Ferguson, Adam Smith, and the Problem of National Defense." *Journal of Modern History* 61 (1989): 240–268.

Aaron Garrett (2005)

FERGUSON, ANN
(1938–)

Ann Ferguson, a socialist-feminist philosopher (PhD, Brown University, 1965; BA, Swarthmore College, 1959) teaches philosophy and women's studies at the University of Massachusetts at Amherst. Her political support for a democratic socialism grew out of sustained involvement with the civil-rights movement, the anti–Vietnam War movement, the new left, and the women's liberation movement in the United States.

Ferguson is best known for her critique of male dominance and her formulation of the concept of sex/affective production (1989). She contends that Marxist accounts of class oppression and radical feminist accounts of heterosexist exploitation do not properly account for (a) the social energies involved in parenting, sexuality, and affective bonding and (b) the unequal, exploitative production and exchange of services between men and women in a patriarchal society (1991). Critiquing Sigmund Freud, Ferguson claims that affective bonding and sexual desires aim primarily not at biological reproduction but rather at connecting with other humans, queer or straight.

In early work, Ferguson highlighted women's potential as a revolutionary class. In *Sexual Democracy* (1991), she developed a materialist-feminist multisystems theory of oppression: that race, class, and gender function as dominant, semi-independent categories, and thus that the ideal of sisterhood is obstructed by race, caste, class, and sexual identities. Her advocacy of "gynandry" (1991), a play on "androgyny" (1977), not only critiques the ideology of the theory that gender roles naturally complement each other, but also calls for revaluing feminine strengths and for building a society free of patriarchal

oppression. In her vision, the feminine is not a fixed gender trait. In her important aspect theory of the self, Ferguson noted that it is misguided to speak of one essential core self; it is more helpful to note that "one's sense of self and … values" are context-dependent (1991, p. 105).

Expanding on her aspect theory of the self, Ferguson (1996) proposed building bridge identities as a strategy to counter positive- and essentialist-identity politics. Bridge identities "attempt to refuse the fixed identities given us by gender, race, class, and sexual differences" (1998a, p. 207) and reconstitute identities politically (1998b). For instance, when a feminist researcher from the global North wishes to network with people in the global South who are relatively disadvantaged, by self-questioning she can put her privileged position in check even to the point of destabilizing her identity. But by building a bridge identity, she can begin to recognize participants as *subjects* of resistance rather than as *objects* of knowledge (1998b). Ferguson (1998a) argues for a transitional feminist morality in which prostitution is defined as a morally risky practice, rather than, as most feminists define it, as a morally forbidden practice. In formulating a viable feminist ethico-politics, she affirms the political stance of subjects of resistance: sex workers who demand unionization and decriminalization. With a bridge-identity politics that refuses fixed identities of race, gender, etc., a feminist coalition could consistently support sex workers' rights locally and oppose trafficking in women internationally.

Ferguson exudes a passion for feminist coalitional and solidarity work with people who face marginalization due to capitalist, racist, or patriarchal forces. Her work is informed par excellence by the rich dialectical interplay of theory and practice.

See also Feminist Philosophy; Feminist Social and Political Philosophy; Marxist Philosophy; Social and Political Philosophy.

Bibliography

WORKS BY FERGUSON

"Androgyny as an Ideal for Human Development." In *Feminism and Philosophy*, edited by Mary Vetterling-Braggin, Frederick Elliston, and Jane English. Totowa, NJ: Rowman and Allanheld, 1977.

Blood at the Root: Motherhood, Sexuality, and Male Dominance. London: Pandora, 1989.

Sexual Democracy: Women, Oppression, and Revolution. Boulder, CO: Westview Press, 1991.

"Bridge Identity Politics: A Feminist Integrative Ethics of International Development." *Organization* 3(4) (1996): 571–587.

"Prostitution as a Morally Risky Practice." In *Daring to Be Good: Feminist Essays in Ethico-politics*, edited by Bat-Ami Bar On and Ann Ferguson. New York: Routledge, 1998a.

"Resisting the Veil of Privilege: Building Bridge Identities as an Ethico-politics of Global Feminism." *Hypatia* 13 (3) (1998b): 95–113.

Mechthild Nagel (2005)

FERRARA, FRANCIS SYLVESTER OF

See *Sylvester of Ferrara, Francis*

FERRI, LUIGI
(1826–1895)

Luigi Ferri, the Italian epistemologist and historian of philosophy, was born in Bologna. He studied at Paris and was professor of the history of philosophy at Florence and at Rome. A self-styled disciple of Terenzio Mamiani, Ferri contributed to Mamiani's journal, *La filosofia delle scuole italiana*, and continued editing the journal, under the title *Rivista italiana di filosofia*, from the death of Mamiani in 1885 until his own death in Rome in 1895.

Ferri's philosophizing moved within the framework of Italian ontologism, which saw in man the capacity for a direct and "intuitive" relationship with the Absolute (Being or God), but his interest focused principally on the psychological conditions in which this relationship takes shape. His investigations, therefore, had as their object man's interior experience, the "inner (or intimate) sense" of which Maine de Biran spoke. To the latter Ferri owed his basic inspirations. Reproving associationist psychology for reducing the spirit, or self, to an associative mechanism that takes no account of the activity of consciousness, Ferri tried to bring to light the function of this activity. He saw this activity as a kind of force or energy that "by making itself its own object, determines its modes according to rules proper to itself, proposes goals, directs and oversees its own work, and frees itself finally from the influence of sensation and emotive impressions so as to find truth with the intellect and to reproduce in itself, with ideas and the evidence of experience, the world of phenomena."

Ferri used the term *dynamism* to refer to the conception that the substance of both the physical and the spiritual worlds is energy and that in both of these worlds energy is regulated by the same laws of conservation. Thus there is a "permanence in the quantity, quality, and relationships of the spiritual world" just as there is a permanence in the amount of matter and energy. Ferri also held that only the energy regulating the spiritual world is known or immediately given to man in the act of consciousness; the actions of energy operating in the external world are known to man only indirectly, that is, by the effects they have upon this act through sense perception. The unity of the universal energy is, however, the sole theme of metaphysics.

See also Absolute, The; Energy; History and Historiography of Philosophy; Italian Philosophy; Maine de Biran; Ontology.

Bibliography

WORKS BY FERRI

Essai sur l'histoire de la philosophie en Italie au dix-neuvième siècle, 2 vols. Paris, 1869. Traces the development of Italian philosophy from the sensationalism of the eighteenth century to the ontologism or idealism of the nineteenth, represented by Rosmini, Gioberti, and Mamiani.

La psicologia di Pietro Pomponazzi. Rome, 1877. Contains a previously unpublished commentary by Pomponazzi on Aristotle's *De Anima*.

La psychologie de l'association depuis Hobbes jusqu'à nos jours, histoire et critique. Paris, 1883.

In the *Atti dell'Academia dei Lincei*, of which Ferri was a member: *Analisi del concetto di sostanza e sue relazione con i concetti di essenza, di causa, e di forza; contributo al dinamismo filosofico* (1885); *Il fenomeno sensibile e la percezione esteriore ossia i fondamenti del realismo* (1886); *Dell'idea del vero e sue relazione con l'idea dell'essere* (1887); *Dell'idea dell'essere* (1888).

WORKS ON FERRI

Barzellotti, G. "Luigi Ferri." *Nuova Antologia* (1895).

Gentile, G. *Le origini della filosofia contemporanea in Italia*, Vol. 1, pp. 215–233. Messina, 1917.

Nicola Abbagnano (1967)
Translated by Nino Langiulli

FERRIER, JAMES FREDERICK
(1808–1864)

James Frederick Ferrier, the Scottish metaphysician, was born in Edinburgh into a wealthy family of lawyers. After studying at the universities of Edinburgh and Oxford, he spent some months in Germany. He settled in Edinburgh in 1832 as an advocate, becoming active in the intellectual circle of Sir William Hamilton, which included Thomas De Quincey and "Christopher North" of *Blackwood's Magazine.* Under this stimulus Ferrier contributed to *Blackwood's* between 1838 and 1843 the eleven long articles that fill most of the second volume of his *Lectures and Remains* (2 vols., Edinburgh and London, 1866). In 1845 he was appointed professor of moral philosophy and political economy at the University of St. Andrews. Ferrier issued a drastically revised version of his philosophy in the *Institutes of Metaphysic* (Edinburgh and London, 1854; 2nd ed., 1856). The *Institutes* was to some extent affected by Ferrier's commitments in the political and ecclesiastical struggles that then divided Scotland. This social influence is still more marked in the pamphlet defending his position, *Scottish Philosophy, the Old and the New* (Edinburgh, 1856). Meanwhile, Ferrier elaborated, until incapacitated in 1861, on an impressive series of lectures on Greek philosophy, posthumously published as Volume I of *Lectures and Remains.*

The first seven *Blackwood's* articles constitute a unitary work on the philosophy of consciousness. Its starting point is a critique of Thomas Brown's doctrine that it is wrong to regard states of mind, such as emotions, as objects of consciousness. Brown argued that to speak of being conscious of feeling angry is the same thing as to speak of feeling angry. Ferrier pointed out that there is a marked difference between speaking of someone as boiling with rage and speaking of him as being conscious of the boiling rage within him. In the latter case, instead of looking outward at the injustice and brooding on the affront, he looks inward at the consequent irritation in his heart and ceases to brood.

Thus far Ferrier was merely making an intelligent use of the doctrine of the inverse variation of feeling and knowledge proposed by his friend Sir William Hamilton. But as Hamilton noted with approval, Ferrier then went beyond the customary limits of British philosophy by asking what is involved in the shift from unself-conscious anger to self-conscious anger. This self-knowledge does not arise straightforwardly out of ordinary experience. The use of the first personal pronoun, which is the mark of self-knowledge in the proper sense, is something that cannot be learned from the experience of other people and their talk in the same imitative way as the use of a word like *table* can. The indubitability of self-knowledge arises just because it is not based on observation in the same way that our knowledge of mountains is. Therefore, Ferrier concluded, there is something anomalous about the foundations of self-knowledge. What is it?

In his four *Blackwood's* articles on the subject of sense perception, contributed between 1841 and 1843, Ferrier gave his problem a definite form by limiting it. To gain light on the nature of self-knowledge he looked into the foundations of the ordinary distinction between act of sense and object of sense. Ferrier's discussion is brilliantly original. The key to the difficulty is that as long as we view each sense field in isolation, no proper distinction can be drawn between the act and the object of sense. Within the visual field alone vision does not stand out as empirically separable from the colors seen; within the tactual field the effort of feeling presents itself as indistinguishable from the solids felt. But when the sense fields are viewed in correlation with one another, seeing separates itself from the colors seen as being connected with something tangible but not visible: the eye. Similarly, feeling distinguishes itself from solidity by being vested in an organ of touch revealed by vision rather than by touch. Ferrier thus argued that the key to self-experience is the peculiar experience of appropriating one's own body in the sense of correlating one's own sense organs. This is reminiscent of Maurice Merleau-Ponty and Jean-Paul Sartre. Like them, Ferrier developed the theme of human freedom, first by reference to the contrast between reflective experience and prereflective experience, then by reference to the contrast between the experience of one's own body and the experience of foreign bodies.

Ferrier was stimulated by Friedrich Schelling and G. W. F. Hegel, but there is a distinctive originality to his position in his attempt to give life and definiteness to their ideas by viewing them in terms of the problems of philosophy posed by Hamilton and Thomas Brown. As De Quincey said, Ferrier's philosophy is "German philosophy refracted through a Scottish medium."

Ferrier's highly original early efforts have been overshadowed for posterity by the respectable academic contributions of his later life. In his *Institutes of Metaphysic* he moved from a "phenomenological" standpoint, inherited from Thomas Reid by way of Hamilton and Victor Cousin, to a narrowly a priori point of view which, distinguishing sharply between necessary and contingent truth, would restrict philosophy to necessary truth. As a result, the *Institutes of Metaphysic* omits the analysis of self-knowledge and the experience of one's own body that distinguishes the *Blackwood's* articles, confining itself to well-worn doctrines that can be expounded in an a priori way, such as the Cartesian *cogito* and a verifiability principle not unlike that of modern positivism. But Ferrier's later work should not be underestimated. It contains remarkably illuminating discussions of the relations of universals and particulars (rather like that in Henry Mansel), which is carried further in the *Lectures on Greek Philosophy*. In this work there is also an extremely impressive analysis of the experience of change and movement that in one way anticipates Henri Bergson and in another way looks back to Hegel.

Ferrier's later work was very influential in the late nineteenth century in the English-speaking world and to some extent in France. In particular, the *Institutes of Metaphysic* provided Shadworth Hodgson with his starting point and most of his leading ideas. Ferrier's early work, unfortunately, escaped notice in the nineteenth century, but a reevaluation of it has begun.

See also Bergson, Henri; British Philosophy; Brown, Thomas; Cousin, Victor; Hamilton, William; Hegel, Georg Wilhelm Friedrich; Hodgson, Shadworth Holloway; Hume, David; Mansel, Henry Longueville; Merleau-Ponty, Maurice; Sartre, Jean-Paul; Schelling, Friedrich Wilhelm Joseph von; Verifiability Principle.

Bibliography

WORKS BY FERRIER

Ferrier's works are collected in the three-volume *Philosophical Works* (Edinburgh: Blackwood, 1875).

WORKS ON FERRIER

Arthur Thomson's article "The Philosophy of J. F. Ferrier," in *Philosophy* 39 (1964): 46–62, reevaluates Ferrier's early work. There is a short biography by E. S. Haldane, *James Frederick Ferrier* (Edinburgh, 1894). See also *The Democratic Intellect*, by G. E. Davie (Edinburgh: Edinburgh University Press, 1961).

George E. Davie (1967)

FEUERBACH, LUDWIG ANDREAS

(1804–1872)

Ludwig Andreas Feuerbach, the German philosopher, theologian, and moralist, was born in Landshut, Bavaria. He studied theology at Heidelberg and Berlin and then, in 1825, under the influence of G. W. F. Hegel, transferred to the faculty of philosophy. He received his doctorate in 1828 at Erlangen, where he remained to teach as docent until 1832. In 1830 he published anonymously at Nuremberg a work—*Gedanken über Tod und Unsterblichkeit*—that created a minor scandal by interpreting Christianity as an egoistic and inhumane religion. When his authorship of this book became known, he was dismissed from the faculty. In 1836 he retired to Bruckberg, where he lived on a modest pension from the Bavarian government, income from his writings, and revenue provided by his wife's interest in a pottery factory.

Between 1836 and 1843 he collaborated with Arnold Ruge on Ruge's *Hallische Jahrbücher für deutsche Wissenschaft und Kunst*, in which many of Feuerbach's most important early writings on religion and philosophy first appeared. He broke with Ruge when the latter began collaboration with Karl Marx on the *Deutsch-Französische Jahrbücher*, although he contributed to the one issue of that journal. He reappeared briefly in academic life in 1848–1849, lecturing to audiences of intellectuals and workers at Heidelberg at the request of students, for whom he had become a symbol of liberal thought.

With the failure of the Frankfurt Assembly and the defeat of liberalism in Germany, Feuerbach retired once more to Bruckberg, where he devoted himself to the study of the natural sciences, the composition of a monumental *Theogonie* (Leipzig, 1857), and a voluminous correspondence with friends and admirers all over Europe. In 1860 his wife's pottery factory failed, and Feuerbach removed his family to Nuremberg, where he was forced to live off the generosity of his friends. In 1867 he suffered the first of a number of strokes that finally killed him.

WORKS

Feuerbach's most important works—"Zur Kritik der Hegelschen Philosophie" (in the *Hallische Jahrbücher*, 1839), *Das Wesen des Christentums* (Leipzig, 1841; translated by M. Evans [George Eliot], London, 1854), *Grundsätze der Philosophie der Zukunft* (Zürich and Winterthur, 1843), and *Das Wesen der Religion* (Leipzig, 1846)—were produced in his early years. They were meant to expose the contradictions in Hegelian philosophy, to establish the "illusionistic" character of all religious belief, and to plead for a "new philosophy," based on anthropology and physiology, that would provide the foundation of a naturalistic-humanistic ethic. His criticism of Hegelianism served as the point of departure for the so-called left Hegelians, of whom Marx and Friedrich Engels were the most important representatives.

CRITICISM OF HEGELIANISM. Feuerbach's critique of Hegelianism proceeded not from sympathy for "obtuse materialism," under which term he grouped Newtonian science, empiricism, and positivism alike, but rather from his discovery of contradictions in Hegel's own system. The resolution of these contradictions would, he believed, allow the establishment of a "new philosophy," which, while remaining thoroughly materialistic, would accommodate those insights into the operations of human consciousness that constituted Hegelianism's definitive contribution to human self-knowledge.

Feuerbach viewed Hegelianism as the culmination of modern rationalism, and he believed that "the secret of Hegel," as of all rationalism, lay in an essentially religious spirit concealed beneath an apparent denial of all transcendence. This hidden religious element accounted for the degradation of the material world, of man, and of the senses that was characteristic of Hegel's metaphysics, ethics, and epistemology, respectively. In Hegel's thought, however, the means were provided for finally transcending all of the religious residues in modern philosophy. For Hegel's attempt to sustain simultaneously the primacy of intellect and the necessity of reason's realizing itself in matter results in the negation of the Hegelian system itself in the interest of a materialistic metaphysics, a humanistic ethics, and a sensible (*sinnliche*) epistemology, the bases of the "philosophy of the future."

DEVELOPMENT OF MODERN PHILOSOPHY. Feuerbach believed that modern philosophy had followed a pattern of development set by theology. The attempt of theology to establish the relationship between the sensible attributes of God and the extrasensible sphere in which he exists necessarily led to pantheism, which makes matter an attribute of God or defines God (as did Benedict de Spinoza) as "extended essence" and thus ends by deifying matter itself. In fact, pantheism is "theological atheism," the discovery by theology that matter is the sole reality, and hence it foreshadows the ultimate self-dissolution of religion.

Empiricism had already discovered that matter was the sole reality, but only in a practical, not in a theoretical, sense, for in making "mere" matter the sole reality it was unable to deal with the data of human consciousness. Rationalism, however, of which idealism was the necessary outcome, underwent a secularized development from theism as a divinization of spirit to pantheism as the self-dissolution of spirit. Idealism was nothing but an attempt to salvage God by vesting full epistemic authority in consciousness, intellect, or reason at the expense of the senses. Yet because it was overtly secularist, rationalism had to account for the world discovered by the senses. It could do this only by affirming, as Immanuel Kant did, an absolute hiatus between the world of intellect, to which it ascribed all truth, and the world of sense, to which it granted reality. Hegel tried to close this gap between truth

and reality, but he could do so only by extending the Cartesian divinization of Reason to the world as a whole. The result was a transition from Kantian "rational theism, theism rationalized" to Hegelian "pantheistic idealism."

REASON IN HEGEL. In affirming the rationality of the real and the reality of the rational, Hegel, according to Feuerbach, elevated reason to the status of "absolute essence." Then, to account for the existence of the spatiotemporal world, he had to hold simultaneously that matter is the negation of thought and that thought can only "realize itself" by becoming matter. To Feuerbach this showed that on Hegel's own terms "thought presupposes, without being aware of it, that truth is reality, sensibility independent of thought." On the one hand Hegel viewed sensibility as "an attribute of the idea," whereas on the other he maintained that it is "an attribute without which thought has no truth"; that is, he had to hold that it is "at one and the same time central and marginal, essence and accident."

According to Feuerbach, idealism knew implicitly that "truth, reality, and sensibility are identical," but it suppressed this truth in order to subordinate the sensible world to an absolute being endowed with the attributes of the human ego, that is, with consciousness and reason. This led idealism to assert that the thinking of the absolute being is real, whereas that of the finite sensible being, man, is not. According to Hegel, human reason is nothing but the self-revelation of the absolute being to itself. Thus, Feuerbach exclaimed, Hegel "alienates and expropriates from man his typical essence and activity!"

PRIMACY OF HUMAN CONSCIOUSNESS. Feuerbach's own "new philosophy" began with the axiom "Only a sensible being is a real, true being," standing the Hegelian position on its feet so that its truth could be seen aright. "The true relation of thought to being is only this," he wrote in the *Vorläufige Thesen*: "being is the subject, thought the predicate. Thought is a product of being, not being of thought. … The essence of being as being is the essence of nature." The consciousness deified by Hegel, like the reason deified by René Descartes and Kant and the Matter deified by Spinoza, "is our ego, our intellect, our essence: and this God is no God in itself, but only the appearance of ourselves to ourselves." Hence, the lasting contribution of idealism to philosophy is its analysis, under the aspect of an examination of the absolute being, of the operations of human consciousness, the reality of which is denied by simple empiricism. Hegelianism, like all metaphysics, is nothing but "esoteric psychology."

MATERIALISM AND IDEALISM. Unlike conventional materialism the new philosophy granted ontological and epistemological status to consciousness and intellect, and unlike idealism it accorded reality to matter. But it deified neither matter nor consciousness. For according to Feuerbach, it is wrong to say, with the materialist, that "man is distinguished from the brute *only* by consciousness"; in fact, "in a being which awakes to consciousness, there takes place a qualitative change, a differentiation of the entire nature." Yet this "qualitative change" in no way justifies the idealist contention that man is consciousness alone, "for as man belongs to the essence of Nature,—in opposition to common materialism; so Nature belongs to the essence of man,—in opposition to subjective idealism."

MAN. Every attempt to specify the essence of man by deriving his material from his spiritual nature, or vice versa, is therefore mistaken, in Feuerbach's view. The task of philosophy is to encounter man in his situation, as that part of nature endowed with consciousness which seeks to realize its own peculiar essence through specific kinds of relationships with the rest of nature and with other members of its species. Feuerbach's philosophy assumed only that "I am a real, sensible essence: the body is constituted of my essence; indeed the body in its totality is my ego, my existence itself." It recognized that man's essence reveals itself quintessentially in the impulse toward union with other men: "The essence of man is contained only in community, in the unity of man with man—a unity which however is founded only on the reality of the differences between I and thou." To comprehend human action and thought one must take account of man's capacity to transcend the limited responses of the lower animals to their environment.

Philosophy, properly studied, then, is "the complete, coherent, and absolute resolution of theology into anthropology.... "It takes man as the culmination of the natural process and defines him as "universal essence" and then concentrates on the study of the totality of his responses to the rest of the world. Among these responses will be found the passions, especially the emotion of love, the impulse toward "union" with the "other" that is peculiar to man. The capacity to create communities of shared emotive contents is the secret of man and therefore the secret of all thought and action; for what men are really seeking in every imagined absolute is nothing but the "unity of I and thou."

RELIGION. All of this is assumed in Feuerbach's studies of religion and lies at the base of his "unmasking" of Christian beliefs in *Das Wesen des Christentums*, his most celebrated work.

Feuerbach regarded religion as one of the forms of human thought and action by which man raised himself above the animal. Beginning with the assumption of D. F. Strauss that religion, myth, ritual, and dogma tell us more about the inner lives of individual people than about their presumed object of worship, Feuerbach tried to determine the purely human significance of all mythological thought. He professed to be a uniformitarian in religious matters—that is, he denied that past religious experiences differ from those that can be observed in the present—thus anticipating the approach to religious experience of both William James and Sigmund Freud. Like them, he claimed to be rigidly empirical in method. "I found my ideas on materials which can be appropriated through the senses," he wrote in the 1843 preface to *Das Wesen des Christentums*; "I do not generate the object from the thought, but the thought from the object; and I hold that alone to be a proper object which has an existence beyond one's brain.... I am nothing but a natural philosopher in the domain of the mind."

His study led him to conclude that religion is a form of the projective spirit in man, the means by which man "projects his being into objectivity, and then again makes himself an object to this projected image of himself thus converted into a subject; he thinks of himself not as an object to himself but as an object of an object, of another being than himself." Thus, religion is "the dream of the human mind"; properly understood, it is a dream of human, not divine, development: "it is and can be nothing else than the consciousness which man has of his own—not finite and limited—but infinite nature." Man, then, unlike the animal, is self-transcending, and religion is one of man's means of objectifying his own essence in ideal terms, of spinning out visions of what he might be. For example, the Christian idea of the Incarnation is nothing but a reflection of the dream of man to become God and the realization that this can be achieved only through a transcendent love of one's fellow man.

Religious feelings thus depend on an alienation of man from himself. Religion generates belief in an objective "other" in which all of man's best qualities are vested, his worst qualities being designated as the true human essence. Philosophy must therefore "destroy an illusion" that deprives man of the power of a free life as well as a genuine sense of truth and virtue, "for even love, in itself the deepest, truest emotion, becomes by means of religiousness merely ostensible, illusory, since religious love gives itself to man only for God's sake, so that it is given only in appearance to man, but in reality to God." In short, for Feuerbach religion is the uncontrolled and unconscious exercise of a human faculty that with the aid of the sciences of anthropology, physiology, and psychology can be controlled, raised to consciousness, and turned toward the attainment of genuine health, well-being, and community here on earth. For "the consciousness of God is nothing but the consciousness of the species."

INFLUENCE

Feuerbach was little concerned with political polemics, for which Marx and Engels vehemently criticized him, but his work served as an inspiration for those who were trying to work out a realistic program of reform in Germany during the middle decades of the century. Many of his dicta became dogmata for the radical movement, as for example the 1850 statement: "The doctrine of foods is of great ethical and political significance. Food becomes blood, blood becomes heart and brain, thoughts and mind-stuff. Human fare is the foundation of human culture and thought. Would you improve a nation? Give it, instead of declamations against sin, better food. Man is what he eats" (quoted in Höffding, *History of Modern Philosophy*, London, 1900, Vol. II, p. 281). But his main concern remained the mystery of the transformation of "human fare" into human thought. This mystery was the basis of his naturalistic humanism, which Marx and Engels regarded as merely a vestige of the old idealism. According to Marx's "Theses on Feuerbach," Feuerbach resolved "the essence of religion into the essence of *man*," and Marx protested that "the essence of man is no abstraction inherent in each separate individual. In its reality it is the ensemble of social relations." The judgment was basically correct. Feuerbach, though he resolved Hegelianism into psychology, made of consciousness itself a mystery, if not a miracle.

By 1850 Feuerbach's star had already set. The future of materialism in Germany lay with mechanists such as Ludwig Büchner on the one hand and with Marx on the other. Engels was right in saying, "With one blow, [Feuerbach] pulverized the contradiction [of idealism] and without circumlocutions … placed materialism on the throne again." But he was also right in noting that Feuerbach "stopped halfway; the lower half of him was materialist, the upper half idealist." Feuerbach's "destruction" of Hegelianism was less important than the way he carried it out, since this destruction was the sport of almost every significant thinker in the Germany of his day. But because he generated materialism out of Hegel himself, Feuerbach

provided the means by which German thought could become "scientific" while still indulging its overriding interest in historical processes. Thus, his work inspired both Marx and Engels, but it also laid the foundation for that phenomenological anthropology that has made him a source of information and insights for such modern philosophers as Martin Heidegger, Jean-Paul Sartre, and Karl Barth.

See also Alienation; Barth, Karl; Büchner, Ludwig; Empiricism; Engels, Friedrich; Freud, Sigmund; Hegel, Georg Wilhelm Friedrich; Hegelianism; Heidegger, Martin; Idealism; James, William; Kant, Immanuel; Marx, Karl; Materialism; Pantheism; Philosophical Anthropology; Rationalism; Sartre, Jean-Paul; Spinoza, Benedict (Baruch) de; Strauss, David Friedrich.

Bibliography

WORKS BY FEUERBACH

Ludwig Feuerbach Sämtliche Werke. 10 vols., edited by Wilhelm Bolin and Friedrich Jodl. Stuttgart: Frommann, 1903–1910. New and augmented ed., 12 vols. Stuttgart, 1959–1960. The complete works of Feuerbach, accompanied by a full *apparatus criticus* and biographical and bibliographical information on writings both by and about him.

The Essence of Christianity, translated by M. Evans. New ed. New York: Harper, 1957. Contains a chapter on Feuerbach from Barth's *Theologie und die Kirche.*

WORKS ON FEUERBACH

Barth, K. *Die protestantische Theologie im 19. Jahrhundert.* Zürich, 1952. Translated by Brian Cozens as *Protestant Thought from Rousseau to Ritschl.* New York: Harper, 1959.

Barth, K. *Die Theologie und die Kirche.* Vol. II, pp. 212–239. Zürich, 1928. Translated by L. P. Smith as *Theology and Church.* London: SCM Press, 1962.

Chamberlain, W. B. *Heaven Wasn't His Destination: The Philosophy of Ludwig Feuerbach.* London: Allen and Unwin, 1941.

Cornu, A. *Moses Hess et la gauche hégélienne.* Paris, 1934.

Engels, F. *Ludwig Feuerbach und der Ausgang der klassischen deutschen Philosophie.* Stuttgart, 1888. Translated as *Ludwig Feuerbach and the Outcome of Classical German Philosophy,* edited by C. P. Dutt. New York: International, 1934.

Grégoire, F. *Aux Sources de la pensée de Marx.* Paris, 1947.

Grün, K. *Ludwig Feuerbach in seinem Briefwechsel und Nachlasse.* 2 vols. Leipzig, 1874.

Hook, S. *From Hegel to Marx.* New York: Reynal and Hitchcock, 1936.

Jodl, F. *Ludwig Feuerbach.* Stuttgart: Frommans, 1904.

Lévy, A. *La philosophie de Feuerbach.* Paris, 1904.

Löwith, K. *Von Hegel zu Nietzsche.* Stuttgart, 1941.

Marcuse, H. *Reason and Revolution.* London: Oxford University Press, 1941.

Nüdling, Gregor. "Die Auflosung des Gott-Menschenverhältnis bei Ludwig Feuerbach." In *Der Mensch vor Gott.* Düsseldorf, 1948.

Nüdling, Gregor. *Ludwig Feuerbachs Religionsphilosophie.* Paderborn, Germany, 1936.

Rawidowicz, S. *Ludwig Feuerbachs Philosophie.* Berlin: Reuther and Reichard, 1931.

Tucker, R. *Philosophy and Myth in Karl Marx.* Cambridge, U.K.: Cambridge University Press, 1961.

OTHER RECOMMENDED WORKS

Amengual, Gabriel. *Crítica de la religión y antropología en Ludwig Feuerbach: La reducción antropológica de la teología como paso del idealismo al materialismo.* Barcelona: Laia, 1980.

Barata-Moura, José, and Viriato Susamenho Marques. *Pensar Feuerbach: Colóquio comemorativo dos 150 anos da publicação de "A essência do Cristianismo (1841–1991).* Lisboa: Edições Colibri, 1993.

Braun, Hans-Jürg. *Ludwig Feuerbach und die Philosophie der Zukunft: Internationale Arbeitsgemeinschaft am ZIF der Universität Bielefeld 1989.* Berlin: Akademie-Verlag, 1990.

Cabada Castro, Manuel. *El humanismo premarxista de Ludwig Feuerbach.* Madrid: La Editorial Católica, 1975.

Feuerbach, Ludwig. *Anthropologischer Materialismus. Ausgewählte Schriften.* Edited by Alfred Schmidt. Wien: Europa Verlag, 1967.

Feuerbach, Ludwig. *The Essence of Faith According to Luther.* New York: Harper & Row, 1967.

Feuerbach, Ludwig. *The Fiery Brook; Selected Writings of Ludwig Feuerbach.* Garden City, NY: Anchor Books, 1972.

Feuerbach, Ludwig. *Geschichte der neueren Philosophie: Von Bacon von Verulam bis Benedikt Spinoza.* Frankfurt am Main: Röderberg-Verlag, 1976.

Feuerbach, Ludwig. *Grundsätze der Philosophie der Zukunft.* Frankfurt am Main: Vittorio Klostermann, 1983.

Feuerbach, Ludwig. *Kleine Schriften.* Frankfurt am Main: Suhrkamp, 1966.

Feuerbach, Ludwig. *Lectures on the Essence of Religion.* New York: Harper & Row, 1967.

Feuerbach, Ludwig. *Philosophische Kritiken und Grundsätze.* Leipsig: Reclam, 1969.

Feuerbach, Ludwig. *Principles of the Philosophy of the Future.* Indianapolis, IN: Hackett, 1986,.

Feuerbach, Ludwig. *Principles of the Philosophy of the Future.* Translated, with an introduction, by Manfred H. Vogel. Indianapolis, IN: Bobbs-Merrill, 1966.

Feuerbach, Ludwig. *Schriften aus dem Nachlass.* Darmstadt: Wissenschaftliche Buchgesellschaft, 1974-1976.

Feuerbach, Ludwig. *Thoughts on Death and Immortality: From the Papers of a Thinker, along with an Appendix of Theological-satirical Epigrams.* Berkeley: University of California Press, 1980.

Feuerbach, Ludwig. *Werke* Frankfurt am Main: Suhrkamp, 1975-.

Harvey, Van Austin. *Feuerbach and the Interpretation of Religion.* Cambridge U.K.; New York: Cambridge University Press, 1995.

Kamenka, Eugene. *The Philosophy of Ludwig Feuerbach.* New York: Praeger, 1970.

Ludwig Feuerbach e la natura non umana: ricostruzione genetica dell'Essenza della religione con pubblicazione degli inediti. Firenze: La Nuova Italia, 1986.

Solidarität oder Egoismus: Studien zu einer Ethik bei und nach Ludwig Feuerbach: Sowie kritisch revidierte Edition "Zur Moralphilosophie" (1868) besorgt von W. Schuffenhauer. Braun, Hans-Jürg, 1927; Schuffenhauer, Werner; Feuerbach, Ludwig; Zur Moralphilosophie. Berlin: Akademie Verlag, 1994.

Wartofsky, Marx W. *Feuerbach.* Cambridge, U.K.; New York: Cambridge University Press, 1977.

Hayden V. White (1967)
Bibliography updated by Michael J. Farmer (2005)

FICHTE, JOHANN GOTTLIEB
(1762–1814)

Johann Gottlieb Fichte was a German philosopher. The most original and most influential thinker among the immediate successors of Immanuel Kant, Fichte was the first exponent of German idealism. He set the agenda for the philosophical work of the generation of Friedrich Wilhelm Joseph Schelling and Georg Wilhelm Friedrich Hegel and exerted tremendous influence on German cultural life in the final decade of the eighteenth century and the first decade of the nineteenth century. Fichte undertook pioneering philosophical work on a number of topics, including the primacy of the practical over the theoretical, the nature and development of self-consciousness, the status and function of one's own body, the original discovery of the other person, the integration of freedom and nature, and the separation of law and morality.

LIFE

Fichte was born on May 19, 1762, in the village of Rammenau in Saxony (in today's eastern Germany). Through the support of local benefactors, he received an education that would have been beyond the means of his family, who were ribbon weavers. He attended the Princely Latin School at Porta (Schulpforta) (1774–1780), studied theology and law at the universities of Jena, Wittenberg, and Leipzig under difficult financial circumstances and without taking a degree (1780–1784), and served as a private tutor in Leipzig, Eastern Prussia, and Zurich (1785–1793).

In 1790, upon studying Kant's *Critique of Pure Reason* (1781) and *Critique of Practical Reason* (1788), he became an enthusiastic adherent and supporter of Kant's critical philosophy. When Fichte's first publication, *Attempt at a Critique of All Revelation* (1792), appeared, in part, anonymously, it was widely assumed to be a work by Kant, whose public clarification of the authorship launched Fichte's meteoric philosophical career. He was offered a professorship in philosophy at the University of Jena, where he began teaching in the summer semester of 1794. Fichte's widely attended lecture courses and the publications based on them turned German academic philosophy for a brief period into a world-historical movement on a par with the French Revolution and literary Romanticism.

In 1799 Fichte lost his professorship in Jena over charges of atheism, based on his published view that God was nothing but the moral order of the world. He spent most of the remaining years of his life in Berlin where he initially supported himself by giving private and public lecture courses and later received a professorship at the newly founded university (1810–1814), at which he also served as Dean (1810) and Rector (1811–1812). Between 1804 and 1808 Fichte gave several popular lecture series in Berlin, that were also published, in which he presented a scathing diagnosis of the cultural and moral ails of his time along with a fervent call for spiritual and political renewal. The most famous of these works, the *Addresses to the German Nation* (1807–1808, published in 1808), arose as an act of public resistance against the Napoleonic occupation of Prussia, Fichte's adopted homeland. The work's call for autochthonous culture and politics was repeatedly instrumentalized in the nineteenth and twentieth centuries for nationalist and socialist thought and politics. Fichte died on January 29, 1814, from hospital fever, which he had contracted from his wife of twenty years, who had been working as a nurse during the uprising against Napoleon.

"THE FIRST SYSTEM OF FREEDOM"

From his chance rise out of poverty and obscurity and his vehement early support of the French Revolution, which brought him a reputation as a Jacobin, through his daring breakaway from academic and religious traditions, to his eloquent agitation for liberation from Napoleonic rule, Fichte struggled all his life for freedom from tutelage of all kinds and for radical self-determination. The theoretical counterpart to this unrelenting project of self-liberation is what Fichte himself termed *the first system of freedom*—a comprehensive account of natural and cultural reality in which the concept of freedom serves to ground and integrate the key aspects of human existence (cognition and volition) as well as their corresponding worlds (the sensible or the natural and the supersensible or the spiritual). Unlike Kant, who had correlated and connected nature and freedom as different but comple-

mentary domains, each with its own principles, Fichte subordinates all of nature to freedom, turning the material world into nothing but the arena for the exercise of free self-determination under self-given laws of acting. With nature relegated to a merely instrumental status, the conditions and principles of social and cultural life receive primary consideration. Fichte's systematic treatment of law, morality, religion, history, and politics as the main spheres for the actualization of freedom is grounded in a detailed account of the deep structure of the human subject.

Throughout, Fichte follows Kant's transcendental or Copernican turn. But he deepens as well as widens his predecessor's dual focus on the conditions of the possibility of experience and the conditions of the possibility of morality into a highly integrated inquiry into the structural requirements of consciousness of all kinds and of all kinds of objects. In order to stress both the rigorous scientific character of his investigations and their merely preparatory status for everyone's own practice of freedom, Fichte abandons the traditional designation, *philosophy* or *love of wisdom*, replacing it with the coinage *Wissenschaftslehre*, or *Science of Knowledge*. The term is not a reference to epistemology in the modern sense but to the protoscience that is to achieve a metaknowledge of the conditions of the possibility of all object-knowledge and that then refers everyone to their own experience for the contingent content of such formally functioning consciousness. In a wider sense all parts of Fichte's projected and partially executed philosophical system are termed *Science of Knowledge*. But Fichte preferentially employs the term for his various presentations of the *first philosophy*, which contains only the basic principles of all knowledge and its objects.

Insisting on the freedom of genuine philosophical thought from any fixed letter and on the need for direct, oral philosophical communication, Fichte worked out some fifteen different presentations of his core philosophy over a period of twenty years, of which he himself published only the first one. As a result of this unique practice of continued production but discontinued publication of his main philosophical work, the full extent and content of Fichte's thinking after 1800 remained, for the most part, unknown to his contemporaries and was recognized and became influential only with the partial publication of Fichte's literary remains in the nineteenth century and their integral edition by the Bavarian Academy of Sciences over almost half a century starting in the early 1960s.

THE "I" AS THE PRINCIPLE OF PHILOSOPHY

In the early presentations of the Science of Knowledge, dating from 1794 through 1799, Fichte terms the unitary unconditional ground of theoretical and practical knowledge and of its object domains, *the I*. The nominalized first person pronoun serves to designate the principle for the derivation (*deduction*) of the basic features of the subject and its world or worlds. Fichte's strategy is to elucidate the necessary conditions under which the subject is able to achieve consciousness of itself, or self-consciousness. Among those conditions are the application of a set of categorial concepts (such as cause and effect) that assure the law-governed structure of the objects in space and time and the individuation of the subject as an intelligent being among other such beings. In particular, Fichte aims to show that the subject's practical relation to the world by way of volition and action is a necessary condition, even for its theoretical relation to the world through thinking and knowing. Fichte's defense of the systematic primacy of practice over theory is counterbalanced by the recognition that all practice in turn stands in need of some guidance through the cognition of the ends to be pursued.

In the original presentation of the Science of Knowledge from 1794–1795 (*Science of Knowledge with the First and Second Introductions*), the basic distinctions between the subject and the object and between the theoretical and the practical are generated by means of a transcendental dialectic involving the progressive but never completely achieved elimination of the contradictions to be found among the three chief capacities of the I as absolute I, theoretical I, and practical I.

As absolute I, the I is the unconditional ground of everything in the I and for the I, including everything that is not I (Not-I). Fichte employs the term *positing* for the generic, preconscious, and spontaneous activity of the I in bringing about the most basic structure of the subject as well as the object. He distinguishes the threefold absolute activity of the I's positing itself, positing its other (the Not-I), and positing the mutual determination of I and Not-I. As theoretical I, or as subject of cognition, the I posits itself as determined through the Not-I. The subject thereby conceives of itself as bound by the properties of the object to be cognized. The contradiction between the active nature of the absolutely positing I and the passive nature of the I of theoretical cognition is resolved through the I's third capacity as practical I, which consists in the I's striving to completely determine the Not-I and to have all determination of the I be the I's self-determi-

nation. To be sure, for Fichte, the striving of the practical I toward the status of the absolute I—to determine everything and to be determined only by itself—is an infinite process in which the absolute I serves as an unobtainable ideal (*idea*).

In Fichte's reconstruction of the principal constitutive features of consciousness, the key factors of Kant's transcendental philosophy (apperception, space, time, categories, imagination, ideas of reason) are gathered into a *history of consciousness* that stretches from minimal self-awareness in undifferentiated feeling through the workings of the imagination in theoretical understanding to the practical self-consciousness of striving reason. Fichte's completion of Kant's transcendental idealism does away with the existence of unknowable things in themselves and provides a maximally internalist account of the determination and self-determination of the I. The only remaining externalist concession is the appeal to the I's inexplicable experience of being held in *check* by what is subsequently objectified, according to the I's own laws, as a world of things seemingly existing independently of the theoretical I.

When his initial transcendental account of the I was widely mistaken for referring to an individual person rather than to the set of structural requirements for personhood, Fichte provided important methodological clarifications and doctrinal expansions in his *New Presentation of the Science of Knowledge* (*Foundations of Transcendental Philosophy [Wissenschaftslehre] nova methodo*; 1796–1799). In particular, he stressed the difference between the transcendental, supraindividual I of the Science of Knowledge and the empirical, individual I of ordinary cognition and life; he argued for the reconstructive, experimental, and hence artificial nature of the transcendental account of the I; and he maintained that the ultimate evidence for the transcendental–idealist reduction of everything to the I's clandestine absolute activity was the fundamental, extraphilosophical belief that absolute freedom from all foreign reality and complete self-determination were the essence and end of human existence.

Among the doctrinal additions of Fichte's alternative presentation of the Science of Knowledge are the systematically prominent position of the will and the foundational role accorded to interpersonal relations (intersubjectivity) in the constitution of the subject and its relation to the world. Fichte's transcendental philosophy of the I now presents itself as a theory of the principal forms and conditions of practical activity (willing and doing), into which the main features of cognitive activity and the world of objects to be cognized are integrated. More specifically, Fichte argues that the mutual requirement of willing and knowing threatens to involve the I's theoretical–practical double nature (*duplicity*) in a vicious circle: Willing an end requires prior cognition of the object to be willed while knowing an object requires a prior engagement of the will in the course of which objects first come into view. Fichte resolves the circle by postulating a nonempirical, prepersonal, and hence predeliberative willing that comes with its own knowledge of what do—a type of willing modeled on Kant's notion of pure practical reason in which knowing the morally good and willing it are supposed to coincide. This move transposes the I from its embeddedness in the natural world into the moral realm of the pure will and entails its individuation among a community of finite rational agents.

The grounding of the I's theoretical as well as practical activities in original, self-determined volition points to the strictly moral core of human subjectivity in Fichte. What lends reality and objectivity to the I's pervasive activity of positing and determining is not some external physical or metaphysical entity but the I's own unconditional laws for the exercise of its spontaneity and freedom. In Fichte's ethical idealism the physical world has reality as the sphere for the exercise of our moral obligations.

In his most popular and accessible work, *The Vocation of Man* (1800), Fichte summarizes his philosophy of freedom in a dramatic portrayal of the course of human insight: from initial doubt about how to reconcile the competing claims of freedom and determination in human affairs through the intermediary stage of (merely theoretical) knowledge, for which everything and everyone is but a product of the I, to the concluding stage of practical knowledge and the faith associated with it, which reconciles freedom and determination by reconceiving the latter as moral self-determination.

THE I AND THE ABSOLUTE

Fichte's subsequent popular lectures and publications in the philosophy of history, culture, and religion (1804–1808) continued to stress the practical and specifically the moral dimension of human existence. In his continuing work on the Science of Knowledge (1801–1814) Fichte explored in ever-new attempts and with changing terminological and conceptual means the possibilities as well as the limitations of human knowledge and human freedom. In critical distance to the contemporary turn toward an affirmative philosophy of the absolute in philosophers such as Friedrich Heinrich

Jacobi, Schelling, and Hegel, Fichte stressed the epistemological strictures of any ascent from the transcendental to the metaphysical. While de-emphasizing the self-sufficiency of the I and abandoning much of his earlier terminology of the I, he nevertheless insisted on the close linkage—and the ultimate identity—of the absolute and the absolute I and on the I's function as the basic mode (*I form*) of theoretical and practical subjectivity.

For the later Fichte, the absolute is not some higher being apart from our self-determined existence as knowers and doers but that which sustains and animates our theoretical and practical activities as the unfathomable ground of their dynamics and laws. In order to avoid any objectivist misunderstanding of the subject's origination in the absolute, Fichte replaces the latter's appellation as *being* with that of *life*, understood as sheer activity, without a distinct bearer and a resultant product. For the later Fichte, human existence—more specifically, its normative accomplishment of knowledge of what there is and ought to be—is the one and only manifestation (*appearance* or *image*) of the absolute while everything else has being only secondarily, as possible object of cognition and volition. Moreover, the authentic manifestation of the absolute is the absolute's self-manifestation as such. The ultimate knowledge to be achieved is the philosophical or metaknowledge that knowledge is but the appearance of the absolute and that the absolute appears only as knowledge.

For Fichte this ultimate insight, which completes the Science of Knowledge, involves at once the self-limitation of knowledge over and against the absolute, of which knowledge is but an image, and the self-affirmation of knowledge as being the absolute itself in the latter's external mode (*existence*). Accordingly, the insight achieved by the Science of Knowledge is not some abstract, rare cognition but results from the lived identification of the subject with its absolute ground and results in a manner of thinking and acting animated by the inner presence of the absolute. Moreover, on Fichte's account, the thinking and acting in light of the absolute does not occur automatically but depends on the subject's free decision and sustained effort to radical reflection and its decision and effort to engage in conduct corresponding to the insight achieved. Thus, the speculative efforts of the Science of Knowledge aim beyond science and knowledge at practical wisdom and at the moral activity resulting from it—an ultimate confirmation of the intellectual and moral freedom of the subject.

Despite some appearances to the contrary, which are due to occasional metaphysically charged terminology

(*God, being*), the late presentations of the Science of Knowledge, when considered in their entirety, show Fichte arguing for the essentially practical nature of the absolute as absolute will and as the animating principle of the moral order. Thus, the later Fichte exhibits a striking continuity with the ethical orientation of his earlier speculative philosophy and, beyond that, with the moral agenda of Kant's critical philosophy.

PHILOSOPHY OF LAW AND ETHICS

Given its unique combination of systematic rigor, argumentative concentration, and freely varied presentation, Fichte's foundational work on the Science of Knowledge initially met with incomprehension; soon became marginalized by the work of his followers, Schelling and Hegel; and even in the early twenty-first century, in the context of detailed historical scholarship and extensive textual analysis, defies summary assessment and doctrinal reconstruction. By contrast, Fichte's work on the applied part of the Science of Knowledge, which consists of the philosophy of law and ethics, has always been more widely appreciated and quite influential.

Fichte's *Foundations of Natural Law* (1796–1797) integrates the theory of right and political authority into a systematic account of the I's individuation and socialization. Fichte argues that a subject can only possess self-consciousness if a number of conditions are met that take the form of the subject's implicit self-ascription (*positing*) of increasingly specific nonrelational and relational properties. To begin with, the subject has to ascribe to itself the faculty of free efficacy along with a sphere of objects, the world of sense, in which the efficacy can be exercised by bringing about change in the objects. Moreover, the subject's practical activity in the world of sense requires its self-ascription of a material object (*body*), by means of which it can act upon the material word.

In a crucial and highly original next step, Fichte argues that a further requirement for the subject's self-conscious, practical activity in the empirical world is its initiation into the rational standards of knowing and doing, which in turn leads to the presupposition of another, already fully functioning, subject and specifically to the latter's influencing the first subject to discover and engage its potential for theoretical–practical rationality. Moreover, the required influence has to be such that the constitutive freedom of the subject to be influenced is not infringed upon but rather called upon and made to emerge. The required influence is not physical but a *determination to self-determination* or the encouraging appeal (*summons* or *solicitation*) to act freely and rationally.

Fichte terms the soliciting subject's attitude of acknowledgment and respect toward the solicited subject's full human potential an act of *recognition* and moves on to inquire into the necessary condition for the possibility of continued mutual recognition between individual subjects. This condition is the *relationship of law*, in which each subject freely limits the exercise of its free efficacy in the world of sense through the concept of the possible freedom of the other individual subject—under the condition that the latter does the same.

Unlike Kant, Fichte does not subordinate the sphere of law under that of morals but defends a strict separation of law and morality. To be sure, for Fichte, the concept of law—the concept of the mutual recognition of free agency—represents a necessary condition of self-consciousness. But becoming part of a political state and following its laws is not an unconditional command of practical reason, as in the "Metaphysical First Principles of the Doctrine of Right" in Kant's *Metaphysics of Morals* (Immanuel Kant, *Practical Philosophy*. Translated and edited by Mary J. Gregor. General introduction by Allen Wood. Cambridge, U.K.: Cambridge University Press, 1996: 455–456.), which was published only after Fichte's work (1797). In Fichte, the validity of the law and that of its subsequent specifications as state law, family law, and cosmopolitan law is contingent upon the agreed-upon and continued practice of recognitional conduct on the part of all individual subjects involved. Accordingly, Fichte's account of the powers of the state is designed to assure the continued observance of mutual recognitional conduct.

With the philosophy of law and its postulation of the transcendental conditions of sociality relegated to an extension of theoretical philosophy, practical philosophy in Fichte completely coincides with ethics or the doctrine of our unconditional moral duties as opposed to our contingent legal obligations. Moreover, Fichte's ethics, published as *The System of Ethics* in 1798, differs widely in scope and structure from the "Metaphysical First Principles of the Doctrine of Virtue" of Kant's *Metaphysics of Morals* published in the preceding year. While Kant had focused on the systematic presentation of particular duties and had limited more general considerations to comparatively brief introductory sections, Fichte provides a detailed derivation of the principle of morality along with the basic conditions of its application. The treatment of ethics in the narrow sense, or the presentation of particular duties, is limited to the work's brief concluding section.

Fichte's chief ambition in practical philosophy is to overcome what he perceives to be the emptiness and formalism inherent in a Kantian ethics focusing on the moral criterion (*categorical imperative*) of the possible universality of subjective principles of action (*maxims*). By contrast, Fichte integrates the formation and execution of moral willing into the overall structure of practical subjectivity. The factual starting point of Fichte's real or material ethics is the subject's original self-experience as willing or as engaged in conceptually mediated efficacy in the world of sense. Its normative end point is the absolute freedom of the subject or radical self-determination. Under conditions of human finitude, this goal can only be approximated. Morality provides the direction and the motivation of the finite subject toward its infinite destination.

In his effort to lend content and specificity to moral obligation, Fichte positions the free will of the practical subject under the influence of a unitary but twofold *drive*: the *pure drive* that represents the claims of pure practical reason to radical self-determination and the *natural drive* that represents the demands of our nonrational nature. Fichte considers the *moral drive* to be a mixed drive in which the natural drive provides the content and the pure drive contributes the impetus for acting or the motivation. Fichte further argues for a pre-established harmony of sorts between the natural drive and the pure drive such that in each and every situation there is one and only one action that is both proposed by the natural drive and sanctioned by the pure drive. According to Fichte, the specific duties are detected by a non-sensory feeling of immediate practical certainty (*conscience*). The principle of morality can therefore be put into the following formula, which is empty by itself and refers everyone to their own conscience for its completion: Do in each case your duty and do it for duty's sake.

PHILOSOPHY OF HISTORY, EDUCATION, AND RELIGION

Compared with the unprecedented systematic rigor and highly abstract reasoning pervading the presentations of the Science of Knowledge in its foundational as well as applied parts, Fichte's historically influential contributions to the philosophy of history, education, and religion are popular works conceived and executed with the explicit intent of exercising moral and political influence on listeners and readers—whose abilities, preconceptions, and contemporary experiences have therefore entered into the design of these works. Accordingly, Fichte's popular works call not only for philosophical

analysis but also for historical knowledge and exegetical skill in assessing the complex relation between their claims and their contexts.

Fichte's philosophy of history, presented in the *Characteristics of the Present Age* (1804–1805, published in 1806) and supplemented by the *Addresses to the German Nation* (1807–1808), constructs the ideal course of history as a linear progress in the governance of humankind in five stages: from blind but clandestinely rational instinct through irrational authority to anarchical intellectual, moral and political freedom—the *present age*, according to Fichte—on to incipient, freely exercised rationality, and finally to the complete reign of rational freedom. The transition from the present age of *complete sinfulness* to genuine freedom and true enlightenment is to be brought about by education and specifically by educational reform at all levels—from instituting compulsory public primary schools to a structural and curricular reform of the university, of which Fichte was a major theoretician and practitioner. Fichte's high regard for public education is also reflected in the three lecture courses that he gave on the moral and political role of the public intellectual (*vocation of the scholar*) at the beginning, toward the middle, and toward the end of his academic career (1794, 1805, 1811).

Fichte's philosophy of religion, presented as *The Way Towards the Blessed Life* (1806), recasts the speculative core of the Science of Knowledge in the form of a popular ontology identifying life with love and bliss. Fichte distinguishes five world views, each correlated to a specific standpoint and associated with a specific affect: the standpoint of sensibility and its enjoyments: that of objective legality (merely formal morality) and its love of formal freedom; that of higher morality and the self-satisfaction it affords; that of religion and the blessed life it entails: and that of science (viz., the Science of Knowledge), which adds no viewpoint of its own but unites the preceding ones by lending them clarity and by transforming the mere faith in the absolute into envisioning it through the self-immersion of reflection into the absolute.

ASSESSMENT

The immediate, immense, but short-lived influence that Fichte had on the course of German culture and philosophy around 1800 is augmented by the long-term and more clandestine effects that his original thinking on the nature of subjectivity and the relation between theory and practice exercised on such diverse philosophers as Arthur Schopenhauer, Karl Marx, Martin Heidegger, and

Jürgen Habermas. With several of his later works only now available for the first time, Fichte is very much a philosopher still to be discovered. His early work on the system of freedom is a tour de force in radicalized Kantianism while his later work on the absolute and its appearance as knowledge and will is a serious competitor to Schelling's and Hegel's claims of having brought to completion German idealist philosophy.

See also Copernicus, Nicolas; Epistemology; Hegel, Georg Wilhelm Friedrich; Habermas, Jürgen; Heidegger, Martin; Jacobi, Friedrich Heinrich; Kant, Immanuel; Marx, Karl; Schelling, Friedrich Wilhelm Joseph; Schopenhauer, Arthur.

Bibliography

WORKS BY FICHTE: GERMAN EDITIONS

Johann Gottlieb Fichte's nachgelassene Schriften. 3 vols. Edited by Immanuel Hermann Fichte. Bonn: Adolph-Marcus 1834–1835. Reprinted as *Fichtes Werke*. 11 vols. (vols. 9–11). Berlin: de Gruyter, 1971.

Johann Gottlieb Fichte's sämmtliche Werke. 8 vols. Edited by Immanuel Hermann Fichte. Berlin: Veit, 1845–1846. Reprinted as *Fichtes Werke*, 11 vols. (vols. 1–8). Berlin: de Gruyter, 1971.

J. G. Fichte-Gesamtausgabe der Bayerischen Akademie der Wissenschaften. Edited by Reinhard Lauth and Hans Gliwitzky. Stuttgart-Bad Cannstatt: Frommann-Holzboog: 1962– (40 vols. planned; to be completed by 2010). Series I: *Published Works*; series II: *Unpublished Works*; series III: *Correspondence*; series IV: *Lecture Transcripts*.

Fichte im Gespräch: Berichte der Zeitgenossen. 6 vols. Edited by Erich Fuchs. Stuttgart-Bad Cannstatt: Frommann-Holzboog, 1978–1992.

Fichte in zeitgenössischen Rezensionen. 4 vols. Edited by Erich Fuchs, Wilhelm G. Jacobs, and Walter Schieche. Stuttgart-Bad Cannstatt: Frommann-Holzboog, 1995.

Ultima Inquirenda. J. G. Fichtes letzte Bearbeitungen der Wissenschaftslehre Ende 1813/Angang 1814. Edited by Reinhard Lauth. Stuttgart-Bad Cannstatt: Frommann-Holzboog, 2001.

WORKS BY FICHTE: ENGLISH TRANSLATIONS

The Popular Works of Johann Gottlieb Fichte. 2 vols. Translated by William Smith. London: Trübner, 1889; 4th ed, introduction by Daniel Breazeale. Sterling, VA: Thoemmes, 1999. (Contains *The Vocation of the Scholar, The Nature of the Scholar, The Vocation of Man, The Characteristics of the Present Age, The Way towards the Blessed Life or the Doctrine of Religion*, and *Outlines of the Doctrine of Knowledge*.)

Addresses to the German Nation. Translated by R. F. Jones and G. H. Turnbull. Chicago: University of Chicago Press, 1922. Reprinted, edited by George Armstrong Kelly. New York: Harper, 1968.

"The Science of Knowledge in Its General Outline." Translated by Walter E. Wright. *Idealistic Studies* 6 (1976): 106–117.

Attempt at a Critique of All Revelation. Translated by Garrett Green. Cambridge, U.K.: Cambridge University Press, 1978.

Science of Knowledge with the First and Second Introductions. Translated by Peter Heath and John Lachs. Cambridge, U.K.: Cambridge University Press, 1982.

"Some Lectures Concerning the Scholar." Translated by Daniel Breazeale. In *Philosophy of German Idealism*. Edited by Ernst Behler, 4–38. New York. Continuum 1987.

The Vocation of Man. Translated by Peter Preuss. Indianapolis, IN: Hackett, 1987.

"A Crystal Clear Report to the General Public Concerning the Actual Essence of the Newest Philosophy. An Attempt to Force the Reader to Understand." Translated by John Botterman and William Rash. In *Philosophy of German Idealism*. Edited by Ernst Behler, 39–115. New York: Continuum, 1987.

Early Philosophical Writings. Edited and translated by Daniel Breazeale. Ithaca, NY: Cornell University Press, 1988.

Foundations of Transcendental Philosophy (Wissenschaftslehre) nova methodo 1796–1799. Edited and translated by Daniel Breazeale. Ithaca, NY: Cornell University Press, 1992.

"Reclamation of the Freedom of Thought from the Princes of Europe, Who Have Oppressed It Until Now." Translated by Thomas E. Wartenberg. In *What Is Enlightenment? Eighteenth-Century Answers and Twentieth-Century Questions*. Edited by James Schmidt, 225–232. Berkeley: University of California Press, 1996.

Introductions to the Wissenschaftslehre and Other Writings. Edited and translated by Daniel Breazeale. Indianapolis, IN: Hackett, 1994.

Foundations of Natural Right. Edited by Frederick Neuhouser and translated by Michael Baur. Cambridge, U.K.: Cambridge University Press, 2000.

"Annotated Translation J. G. Fichte's Review of L. Creuzer's *Skeptical Reflections on the Freedom of the Will* (1793)." Translated and edited by Daniel Breazeale. *Philosophical Forum* 32 (2001): 289–296.

"Annotated Translation of J. G. Fichte's Review of F. H. Gebhard's *On Ethical Goodness as Disinterested Benevolence* (1793)." Translated and edited by Daniel Breazeale. *Philosophical Forum* 32 (2001): 297–310.

"Annotated Translation of J. G. Fichte Review of I. Kant's *Perpetual Peace* (1796)." Translated and edited by Daniel Breazeale. *Philosophical Forum* 32 (2001): 311–321.

The Science of Knowing. J. G. Fichte's 1804 Lectures on the Wissenschaftslehre. Edited and translated by Walter E. Wright. Albany: State University of New York Press, 2005.

The System of Ethics. Edited and translated by Daniel Breazeale and Günter Zöller. Cambridge, U.K.: Cambridge University Press, 2005.

WORKS ON FICHTE

Breazeale, Daniel, and Tom Rockmore, eds. *Fichte. Historical Contexts/Contemporary Controversies*. Atlantic Heights, NJ: Humanities Press, 1994.

Breazeale, Daniel. "Check or Checkmate? On the Finitude of the Fichtean Self." In *The Modern Subject. Conceptions of the Self in Classical German Philosophy*. Edited by Karl Ameriks and Dieter Sturm, 87–114. Albany: State University of New York Press, 1995.

Breazeale, Daniel, and Tom Rockmore, eds. *New Essays on Fichte.* Atlantic Heights, NJ: Humanities Press, 1996.

Breazeale, Daniel, and Tom Rockmore, eds. *New Essays in Fichte's "Foundation of the Entire Doctrine of Scientific Knowledge."* New York: Humanity Books, 2001.

Breazeale, Daniel, and Tom Rockmore, eds. *New Essays on Fichte's Later Jena "Wissenschaftslehre."* Evanston, Ill.: Northwestern University Press, 2002.

Breazeale, Daniel, and Tom Rockmore, eds. *Rights, Bodies, and Recognition. New Essays on Fichte's Foundations of Natural Right.* Aldershot, U.K.: Ashgate, 2005.

Henrich, Dieter. "Fichte's Original Insight." *Contemporary German Philosophy* 1 (1982): 15–53.

Horstmann, Rolf-Peter. "The Early Philosophy of Fichte and Schelling." In *The Cambridge Companion to German Idealism.* Edited by Karl Ameriks, 117–140. Cambridge, U.K.: Cambridge University Press, 2000.

La Vopa, Anthony J. Fichte. *The Self and the Calling of Philosophy, 1762–1799.* Cambridge, U.K.: Cambridge University Press, 2001.

Martin, Wayne. *Idealism and Objectivity. Understanding Fichte's Jena Project.* Stanford, CT: Stanford University Press, 1997.

Neuhouser, Frederick. *Fichte's Theory of Subjectivity.* Cambridge, U.K.: Cambridge University Press, 1990.

Pippin, Robert. "Fichte's Contribution." *Philosophical Forum* 19 (1988): 74–96.

Williams, Robert. *Recognition. Fichte and Hegel on the Other.* Albany: State University of New York Press, 1992.

Wood, Allen W. "Fichte's Philosophical Revolution." *Philosophical Topics* 19 (1992): 1–28.

Zöller, Günter, ed. *The Cambridge Companion to Fichte.* Cambridge, U.K.: Cambridge University Press (in preparation).

Zöller, Günter. *Fichte's Transcendental Philosophy. The Original Duplicity of Intelligence and Will.* Cambridge, U.K.: Cambridge University Press, 1998.

Zöller, Günter. "German Realism: The Self-Limitation of Idealist Thinking in Fichte, Schelling and Schopenhauer." In *The Cambridge Companion to German Idealism.* Edited by Karl Ameriks, 200–218. Cambridge, U.K.: Cambridge University Press, 2000.

Zöller, Günter, "The Unpopularity of Transcendental Philosophy: Fichte's Controversy with Reinhold (1799–1801)." *PLI: The Warwick Journal of Philosophy* 10 (2000): 50–76.

Günter Zöller (2005)

FICINO, MARSILIO
(1433–1499)

Marsilio Ficino, the founder of the Florentine Academy, was born the eldest son of a physician in Figline, near Florence. He studied the humanities, philosophy, and medicine in Florence but apparently did not obtain an academic degree. About 1456 he began to study Greek. In 1462 he received from Cosimo de' Medici a house in Careggi, near Florence, and several Greek manuscripts; this is regarded as the date the Platonic Academy of Florence was founded. Having earlier taken minor orders, Ficino was ordained in 1473; he held several ecclesiastic benefices and became a canon of Florence Cathedral in 1487. After the expulsion of the Medicis from Florence in 1494, Ficino, who had been closely associated with several generations of the family, apparently retired to the country. He was honored after his death in a funeral oration delivered by a chancellor of the republic of Florence.

Ficino became interested in Platonist philosophy at an early age, presumably through studying Augustine. His earliest extant writings also show familiarity with Aristotle and his commentators and with Lucretius. Among Ficino's Latin translations from the Greek, the first that attained a wide circulation was his version (1463) of the works attributed to Hermes Trismegistus. Ficino's translation of Plato, the first complete rendering of all his dialogues in any Western language, was begun in 1463, probably completed in 1469, subsequently revised, and first printed in 1484. His influential commentary on Plato's *Symposium* was written in 1469; the other Platonic commentaries, some of them extensive, belong to different periods of Ficino's life. The translation of and commentary on Plotinus was begun in 1484 and printed in 1492. Translations of Porphyry, Iamblichus, Proclus, and other philosophers appeared in 1497. Ficino's chief philosophical work, *Theologica Platonica de Immoralitate Animarum* (Platonic theology—on the immortality of the souls) was written between 1469 and 1474 and was printed in 1482. Aside from this work and his commentaries, the most important source for Ficino's philosophy is his letters, which he began to collect around 1473 and finally published in 1495. Important also are his apologetic treatise *De Christiana Religione* (1474) and his work on medicine and astrology, *De Vita Libri Tres* (1489), which is often wrongly referred to as *De Vita Triplici.*

Ficino's work as a translator of and commentator on Plato and the Neoplatonists, and his avowed intention of reviving Platonism, led many older historians to treat his doctrine merely as a repetition of ancient Neoplatonism. More recently, however, a closer study of his known and unpublished works has shown that in restating the doctrines of Plato and his ancient followers, Ficino showed a good deal of originality. In addition, his writings show the influence of medieval and Byzantine Platonism, early Italian humanism, and also the tradition of scholastic Aristotelianism, which had a strong impact upon his terminology and method. He was familiar with Dante

Alighieri and other Italian poets and wrote or rewrote several of his own works in the Tuscan vernacular.

Ficino was the founder and for many years the head and guiding spirit of the Platonic Academy of Florence, which has remained famous as a symbol and institutional center of Renaissance Platonism. The academy was not a firmly established institution in the manner of later academies but a rather loosely organized spiritual community of friends. We hear of informal discussions between the older members of the circle and of philosophical banquets celebrated on Plato's birthday. There were recitals of edifying orations before a small audience, private readings of Plato and other texts given by one or a few younger disciples, and public lectures on Plato and Plotinus delivered in a church or auditorium. Distinguished visitors from other Italian cities and abroad called upon Ficino or participated in the meetings, and Ficino's correspondence served as a vehicle both for maintaining contact with the members of the academy and for arousing the interest of strangers in the academy's activities. The catalog of his pupils, which he gives in one of his letters, and the list of the persons with whom he was in correspondence, whom he mentions, or who owned the manuscripts and printed editions of his writings are ample evidence of the wide influence he exerted during his lifetime.

Ficino's writings present a highly complex system of ideas, embroidered with similes, allegories, and lengthy quotations from his favorite authors. We can mention but a few of his more important and influential doctrines.

HIERARCHY

In his description of the universe, Ficino took from Neoplatonic and medieval sources the conception of a great hierarchy in which each being occupies its place and has its degree of perfection, beginning with God at the top and descending through the orders of the angels and souls, the celestial and elementary spheres, the various species of animals, plants, and minerals, down to qualityless prime matter. In spite of Ficino's indebtedness to earlier schemes, it appears on closer examination that his hierarchy differs in significant details from those of his predecessors. It is arranged in a final scheme of five basic substances: God, the angelic mind, the rational soul, quality, and body. This scheme comes fairly close to that of Plotinus but differs from it in various ways. Above all, quality did not constitute a separate level of being for Plotinus, who instead assigned separate places to the sensitive and vegetative faculties of the soul. It can be shown that Ficino intentionally revised the Plotinian scheme,

partly to make it more symmetrical and partly to assign the privileged place in its center to the human soul, thus giving a kind of metaphysical setting and sanction to the doctrine of the dignity of man, which he had inherited from his humanist predecessors. The soul is truly the mean of all things created by God, Ficino tells us. It is in the middle between higher and lower beings, sharing some of its attributes with the former and some with the latter.

Ficino was not satisfied with a static hierarchy in which each degree merely stands beside the others and in which the relationship of degrees consists only in a continuous gradation of attributes. He was also convinced that the universe must have a dynamic unity and that its various parts and degrees are held together by active forces and affinities. For this reason, he revived the Neoplatonic doctrine of the world soul and made astrology part of a natural system of mutual influences. Since thought for Ficino has an active influence upon its objects, since love is an active force that binds all things together (as in Plato's *Symposium*), and since the human soul extends its thought and love to all things, from the highest to the lowest, in Ficino's writing the soul becomes once more and in a new sense the center of the universe. The soul is the greatest of all miracles in nature because it combines all things, it is the center of all things, and possesses the forces of all things. Therefore the soul may rightly be called the center of nature, the middle term of all things, the bond and juncture of the universe.

CONTEMPLATION

Ficino's cosmology, which was very influential during the sixteenth century, offers some points of intrinsic interest; however, it constitutes only one side of his thought. The other and even more profound component is his analysis, based on direct inner experience, of the spiritual or contemplative life, and analysis that links him with some of the medieval mystics and, again, with Neoplatonism. In the face of ordinary daily experiences, the mind finds itself in a state of continuous unrest and dissatisfaction, but it is capable of turning away from the body and the external world and of concentrating upon its own inner substance. Thus purifying itself of things external, the soul enters the contemplative life and attains a higher knowledge, discovering the incorporeal world that is closed to it while it is engaged in ordinary experience and in the troubles of the external life. Ficino interpreted this contemplative life as a gradual ascent of the soul toward always higher degrees of truth and being, an ascent that finally culminates in the immediate knowledge and vision of God. This knowledge of God represents the ultimate goal of human life and existence—in it alone the unrest of our mind is satisfied—and all other modes and degrees of human life and knowledge must be understood as more or less direct and conscious preparations for this end. In accordance with Plotinus, Ficino was convinced that this highest experience could be attained during the present life, at least by a few privileged persons and for a short while, although he never explicitly claimed to have attained this state himself.

In describing the various states and the ultimate goal of inner experience, Ficino used a twofold terminology, and in this he was influenced by St. Augustine and by the medieval philosophers. The ascent of the soul toward God is accomplished with the help of two wings, the intellect and the will; accordingly, the knowledge of God is accompanied and paralleled on each level by the love of God; and the ultimate vision, by an act of enjoyment. Ficino also considered the question of whether intellect and knowledge or will and love are more important in this process, and although he seemed to come to different conclusions in different parts of his writings, in general he leaned toward the superiority of will and love over intellect and knowledge. Yet the question was not so important for him as might be expected, since he regarded the knowledge of God and the love of God as merely two different aspects or interpretations of the same basic experience—namely, the contemplative ascent of the soul toward its ultimate goal.

This experience and the manner in which it is interpreted hold the key to both Ficino's metaphysics and his ethics. It is the inner ascent of contemplation, through which the reality of incorporeal things—of the ideas and of God himself—is discovered and verified. Since this inner ascent constitutes the basic task of human existence, Ficino was not interested in specific moral precepts or in casuistry, but only in the general identification of the human good and man's moral excellence with the inner life. His whole moral doctrine, as expressed in his letters, may be said to be a reduction of all specific moral rules to a praise of the contemplative life. He who has attained this life is exempt from the blows of fortune; and, animated by his inner certainty and insight, he will know and do the right thing under any given circumstance.

Intimately related to the doctrine of the contemplative life are two other theories of Ficino's, both of great historical importance: his theory of the immortality of the soul and his theory of Platonic love.

IMMORTALITY

Ficino's main work, *Theologia Platonica de Immortalitate Animarum,* consists for the most part of a series of arguments in support of the soul's immortality. It appears from a famous passage twice repeated in Ficino's writings that, in direct contrast with the teachings of the Aristotelian philosophers of his time, he considered this doctrine the central tenet of his Platonism. It is true that the immortality of the soul had been defended by Plato and Plotinus, by Augustine and many other Christian writers, and that Ficino borrowed many specific arguments from them. It may also be granted that Averroes's doctrine of the unity of the intellect in all people, which had been widely discussed and often accepted by Aristotelian philosophers from the thirteenth to the fifteenth century, made a defense of individual immortality imperative. In addition, the humanists had attached great importance to the individual human being, his experiences, and his opinions; and the belief in personal immortality was, as it were, a metaphysical counterpart of this individualism and an extension of it into another dimension.

Yet it seems evident that for Ficino the doctrine of immortality was a necessary complement and consequence of his interpretation of human existence and of the goal of human life. If it is our basic task to ascend, through a series of degrees, to the immediate vision and enjoyment of God, we must postulate that this ultimate goal will be attained, not merely by a few persons and for a short while but by a great number of human beings and forever. Otherwise, man's effort to attain this ultimate end would be in vain, and the very end for which he had been destined would remain without fulfillment. Thus, man would be unhappier than the animals, which do attain their natural ends, and this would be inconsistent with the dignity of the place man occupies in the universe. Moreover, if a natural end corresponding to a natural desire implanted in all men could not be attained, this would contradict the perfection of the order of nature and the wisdom of God, who created that order. In his "Platonic Theology," and in other parts of his writings, Ficino never tired of repeating these and similar arguments. It seems obvious that they reflect the real intent and motivation of his thought, for his whole interpretation of human life as a contemplative ascent toward God would lose its meaning unless this ascent were to find its permanent fulfillment in the eternal afterlife of the immortal soul. This alone would explain why the doctrine of immortality assumed such a central place for him. All other arguments are merely auxiliary to this central one.

Ficino's doctrine of immortality, and his arguments for it, made a profound impression on many thinkers of the sixteenth century; and it may very well be due to his indirect influence that the immortality of the soul was formally pronounced a dogma of the Catholic Church at the Lateran Council of 1512.

THEORY OF LOVE

Of equal historical importance, although different in character, is Ficino's doctrine of human love. In this doctrine, as in many of his others, Ficino combined elements from several different sources and traditions. He took over and reinterpreted Plato's theory of love as expressed in the *Symposium* and *Phaedrus,* and combined it with other ancient theories of friendship that were known to him primarily through Aristotle and Cicero; he also tried to identify it with the Christian love (*caritas*) praised by St. Paul. He even added some touches from the tradition of medieval courtly love as it was known to him through Guido Cavalcanti, Dante, and other early Tuscan poets. This doctrine of love, which exercised a tremendous influence during the sixteenth century, and for which Ficino himself coined the terms *Platonic love* and *Socratic love,* was first expressed by him in his commentary on Plato's *Symposium* and further developed in many of his letters and other writings. The term *Platonic love* means love as described by Plato, according to Ficino's interpretation; more frequently, he spoke of it as divine love. The basic point is that he regarded love for another human being as merely a preparation, more or less conscious, for the love of God, which constitutes the real goal and true content of human desire and which is turned toward persons and things by virtue of the reflected splendor of divine goodness and beauty that may appear in them. Ficino insisted that true love or friendship is always mutual. A genuine relationship between two people is a communion founded on what is essential in man, that is, it is based in each of them on his original love for God. There can never be only two friends; there must always be three—two human beings and one God. God alone is the indissoluble bond and perpetual guardian of any true friendship for a true lover loves the other person solely for the sake of God. True love and friendship between several persons is derived from the love of the individual for God; it is thus reduced to the basic phenomenon of the inner ascent, which constitutes the core of Ficino's philosophy.

It appears from Ficino's letters that he considered true friendship in this sense to be the bond that united the members of his academy with each other and with himself, their common master, and that he liked to think of the academy not merely as a school but as a community of friends. This conception of Platonic love was to exercise a strong influence on Italian and European literature throughout the sixteenth century. Many lyric poets spoke of their love in terms that reflected the influence of Ficino, as well as that of the old Tuscan poets and Petrarch; and there was a large body of treatises and lectures on love that derived much of their inspiration, directly or indirectly, from Ficino's commentary on the *Symposium.* In this literature the concept of Platonic love was separated from the philosophical context in which it had originated with Ficino, and so it became more and more diluted and trivial. For this reason, the notion of Platonic love has acquired a slightly ridiculous connotation for the modern reader. Yet we should try to recapture its original meaning, remembering that the true meaning of an idea is best understood in the context of the thought in which it originated and which, in a sense, made its formulation necessary. If we trace Platonic love back to its origin in Ficino—back to the context of an individual's love of God—it may still seem a strange and remote concept, but we shall at least understand that it had a serious content and that it was related to the central ideas of his philosophy.

A further aspect of Ficino's thought that requires mention is his conception of religion and of its relationship to philosophy. Ficino was a priest and a canon of Florence Cathedral; he had an adequate knowledge of Christian theology; and he even wrote an apologetic treatise on the Christian religion as well as several other theological works. There is not the slightest doubt that he intended to be orthodox, although some of his doctrines may seem to have dubious implications and although he was in danger of an ecclesiastical condemnation for the views on astrology and magic expressed in his work *De Vita* (1489). He insisted on his Christian faith and submitted to the judgment of the church. He was even willing to abandon the opinions of his favorite Platonist philosophers when they seemed to contradict Christian doctrine. Thus, we are not surprised to find that he regarded Christianity as the most perfect of all religions.

At the same time, he saw some merit in the variety of religions and insisted that any religion, however primitive, is related indirectly to the one true God. In his implicit tolerance toward other religions, Ficino came very close to a concept of natural religion, a position that made him a forerunner of Herbert of Cherbury, the deists, and other advocates of a universal religion. Divine worship, he said, is almost as natural for men as neighing is for horses or barking is for dogs. A common religion of all nations, having one God for its object, is natural to the human species. This religion, which is again based on man's primary knowledge and love of God, is not shared by the animals but is peculiar to man, a part of his dignity and excellence and a compensation for the many defects and weaknesses of his nature.

As to the relation between religion and philosophy, Ficino was convinced that true religion (that is, Christianity) and true philosophy (that is, Platonism) are in basic harmony with each other; and he was inclined to treat them as sisters instead of trying to make one subservient to the other. He believed that it is the task of Platonic reason to confirm and support Christian faith and authority, and he even considered it his own mission, assigned to him by divine providence, to revive true philosophy for the benefit of true religion. He believed that those who will not be guided by faith alone can be guided toward truth only through reason and the most perfect philosophy.

In the light of this relationship, the continuity of the Platonic tradition assumed a new significance for Ficino. Since this tradition was thought by him to go back to Hermes and Zoroaster, whose apocryphal writings Ficino treated as venerable witnesses of early pagan theology and philosophy, he considered the tradition to be as old as the religious tradition of the Hebrews. Thus, the religious tradition of the Hebrews and Christians, and the philosophical tradition of the Hermetics and Platonists, seemed to run a parallel course in human history from the early beginnings through antiquity and the Middle Ages down to the modern period. It is in accordance with this view of Ficino's that Augustinus Steuchus, a Catholic theologian of the sixteenth century, wrote his *De Philosophia Perenni* (On the perennial philosophy; 1542).

INFLUENCE

Ficino's influence was considerable, both during his lifetime and for a long time afterward. As a metaphysician in the proper sense of the word, Ficino added an element to Florentine culture that had been largely absent from it before and left a new imprint on that culture that was to last for several generations. Among his associates and pupils we find Cristoforo Landino, author of the *Camaldulensian Disputations* and of an influential commentary on Dante's *Commedia,* and Lorenzo de' Medici, famous not only as a statesman but also as one of the best Italian poets of his century. Whereas Giovanni Pico della Mirandola developed an independent position, another pupil, Francesco da Diacceto, carried the Platonic tradition of

Ficino into the first decades of the sixteenth century; and later in that century, Platonic philosophy was cultivated both at the new Florentine Academy of 1540 and at the University of Pisa. This Platonist climate of opinion in Florence and Pisa accounts for some of the opinions and preconceptions of Galileo Galilei. In the rest of Italy, poets and prose writers drew on Ficino's theory of love, and theologians and philosophers upon his doctrine of immortality as well as some of his other ideas. His influence appears in the works of such leading philosophers as Francesco Patrizi and Giordano Bruno: Even thinkers who opposed his views, such as Pietro Pomponazzi, were impressed with his learning and acumen.

During his lifetime, Ficino's influence was already growing, through his correspondence and through the circulation of his writings, in most European countries. His admirers included Johannes Reuchlin and John Colet, Gaguin and Jacques Lefèvre d'Étaples. During the sixteenth century his writings were reprinted, collected, read, and quoted all over Europe. His medical and astrological treatises were especially popular in Germany. In France, he was repeatedly quoted and plagiarized by Symphorien Champier, and admired in the circles of Queen Marguerite of Navarre and of the Pléïade. There, some of his writings and his Latin translations of Plato were translated into French. Elements of his Platonism appear in Carolus Bovillus and Postel, and not so much in Peter Ramus as in his mortal enemy Jacques Charpentier. Even in René Descartes there are strong elements of Platonism. Outside of France, Desiderius Erasmus, Thomas More, Sebastian Fox Morcillo, Paracelsus, Cornelius Agrippa, and finally Johannes Kepler exemplify the importance of Platonism in sixteenth-century thought, an importance that is closely linked with the writings, translations, and commentaries of Ficino.

In the seventeenth century, after Galileo and Descartes, the speculative cosmology of the Renaissance was no longer possible within the framework of a natural science based on experiments and mathematical formulas. The influence of Platonism persisted, however, in the metaphysics and epistemology of Benedict de Spinoza and Gottfried Wilhelm Leibniz, Nicolas Malebranche and George Berkeley; and it gained a new life in the school of Cambridge Platonists. And, since the authority of Plato himself remained a powerful force with many thinkers, we find even in Immanuel Kant and Johann Wolfgang von Goethe several theories associated with the name and prestige of Plato (and Plotinus) that actually belong to his Florentine translator and commentator. Samuel Taylor Coleridge wrote in his autobiography that as a youth he read Plato and Plotinus, together with the commentaries and the *Theologia Platonica* of the illustrious Florentine. It was only in the nineteenth century that Ficino lost even this anonymous or pseudonymous influence, after a new school of philological and historical criticism had begun to make a rigorous distinction between the genuine thought of Plato and that of his successors and commentators in late antiquity and during the Renaissance. On the basis of this distinction, it has become possible again to understand Ficino's thought in its own right—to appreciate its indebtedness to sources other than Plato, its close connection with the thought and scholarship, art and literature of its time, and its own peculiar style and originality.

See also Florentine Academy.

Bibliography

Of Ficino's main works, only the commentary on Plato's *Symposium* has been reprinted in modern editions. See *Marsilio Ficino's Commentary on Plato's Symposium,* translated and edited by Sears R. Jayne, Vol. XIX, No. 1, in The University of Missouri Studies (Columbia, MO, 1944), and *Commentaire sur le Banquet de Platon,* edited by Raymond Marcel (Paris, 1956). For the others, the Basel editions of his collected works, *Opera Omnia,* 2 vols. (1561 and 1576), are still the only source; the second edition is slightly more complete and has been reprinted more recently (Turin, 1959). Also see *Supplementum Ficinianum,* edited by Paul Oskar Kristeller, 2 vols. (Florence, 1937), with lists of manuscripts and editions and a chronology of Ficino's works, and P. O. Kristeller, *Studies in Ficino's Thought and Letters* (Rome, 1956), with a number of papers discussing Ficino's life, sources, influence, and thought. Aside from the commentary on the *Symposium,* only the short *Five Questions concerning the Mind* (from Ficino's *Letters*) has been translated into English, by Josephine L. Burroughs, in *The Renaissance Philosophy of Man,* edited by Ernst Cassirer and others (Chicago: University of Chicago Press, 1948), pp. 193–212.

For Ficino's life and the history of the Platonic Academy, see Arnaldo Della Torre, *Storia dell'Accademia platonica di Firenze* (Florence, 1902), which is still indispensable, and Raymond Marcel, *Marsile Ficin* (Paris, 1958).

For discussions of Ficino's philosophy, see Giuseppe Saitta, *La filosofia di Marsilio Ficino* (Messina: Principato, 1923; 3rd ed., Bologna: Fiammenghi and Nanni, 1954); Sears R. Jayne, *John Colet and Marsilio Ficino* (London: Oxford University Press, 1963); Paul O. Kristeller, *Il pensiero filosofico di Marsilio Ficino* (Florence: Sansoni, 1953), translated by Virginia Conant as *The Philosophy of Marsilio Ficino* (New York: Columbia University Press, 1943)—the Italian edition is superior because of its additional indexes and original text quotations.

Also see Michele Schiavone, *Problemi filosofici in Marsilio Ficino* (Milan, 1957), and Ernst Cassirer, *Individuum und Kosmos in der Philosophie der Renaissance* (Berlin and Leipzig: Teubner, 1927; reprinted Darmstadt, 1962), translated by Mario Domandi as *The Individual and the Cosmos in Renaissance Philosophy* (New York: Harper and Row, 1963).

Ficino's influence on the theory and iconography of Renaissance art has been discussed by Erwin Panofsky— *Idea* (Leipzig and Berlin: Teubner, 1924; 2nd ed., Berlin: Hessling, 1960) and *Studies in Iconology* (New York: Oxford University Press, 1939; reprinted, New York: Harper and Row, 1962)—and by E. H. Gombrich and others; see especially André Chastel, *Marsile Ficin et l'art* (Geneva: Droz, 1954). For a discussion of Ficino and magic, see D. P. Walker, *Spiritual and Demonic Magic from Ficino to Campanella* (London: Warburg Institute, University of London, 1958).

Literature on the influence of Ficino's theory of love includes A. M. J. Festugière, *La philosophie de l'amour de Marsile Ficin et son influence sur la littérature française du XVIe siècle* (Paris: Vrin, 1941); John C. Nelson, *Renaissance Theory of Love* (New York: Columbia University Press, 1958). See also Nesca A. Robb, *Neoplatonism of the Italian Renaissance* (London: Allen and Unwin, 1935), and Raymond Klibansky, *The Continuity of the Platonic Tradition during the Middle Ages* (London: Warburg Institute, 1939 and 1950).

OTHER RECOMMENDED TITLES

Allen, Michael J. B. "The Absent Angel in Ficino's Philosophy." *Journal of the History of Ideas* 36 (1975): 219–240.

Allen, Michael J. B. "The Ficinian Timaeus and Renaissance Science." In *Plato's Timaeus as Cultural Icon,* edited by Gretchen Reydams-Schils. Notre Dame, IN: University of Notre Dame Press, 2003.

Allen, Michael J. B. "Marsilio Ficino on Significatio." *Midwest Studies in Philosophy* 26 (2002): 30–43.

Allen, Michael J. B. *The Platonism of Marsilio Ficino: A Study of His Phaedrus Commentary, Its Sources and Genesis.* Berkeley: University of California Press, 1984.

Collins, Ardis B. "Love and Natural Desire in Ficino's Platonic Theology." *Journal of the History of Philosophy* 9 (1971): 435–442.

Collins, Ardis B. "The Secular Is Sacred: Platonism and Thomism in Marsilio Ficino's *Platonic Theology.*" The Hague: Nijhoff, 1974.

Devereux, James A. "The Object of Love in the Philosophy of Marsilio Ficino." *Journal of the History of Ideas* 30 (1969): 161–170.

Fogarty, Anne. "Mystical Modernism: Yeats, Ficino and Neoplatonic Philosophy." *Accademia* 3 (2001): 131–147.

Gandillac, Maurice de. "Neoplatonism and Christian Thought in the Fifteenth Century." In *Neoplatonism and Christian Thought,* edited by Dominic J. O'Meara. Norfolk, VA: International Society for Neoplatonic Studies, 1981.

Hendrix, John. *Platonic Architectonic: Platonic Philosophies and the Visual Arts.* New York: Peter Lang, 2004.

Jacob, Alexander. "Henry More's 'Psychodia Platonica' and Its Relationship to Marsilio Ficino's 'Theologia Platonica.'" *Journal of the History of Ideas* 46 (1985): 503–522.

Kuczyanska, Alicja. "The Third World of Marsilio Ficino." *Dialectics and Humanism* 15 (1988): 157–171.

Mojsisch, Burkhard. "The Epistemology of Humanism." *Bochumer Philosophisches Jahrbuch* 1 (1996): 127–152.

O'Rourke Boyle, Marjorie. "Pure of Heart: From Ancient Rites to Renaissance Plato." *Journal of the History of Ideas* 63 (1) (2002): 41–62.

Paul Oskar Kristeller (1967)
Bibliography updated by Tamra Frei (2005)

FICTIONALISM

A fictionalist is one who aims to secure the benefits of talking *as if* certain kinds of things exist—numbers, moral properties, possible worlds, composite objects, or whatever—while avoiding commitment to believing in their existence. This understanding of fictionalism is broad and ecumenical, and it should be noted that *fictionalism* is frequently used in the recent literature to refer to one or other of the more specific doctrines that this entry discusses.

1. FICTIONALISM AND FICTIONS

Consider paradigm cases of works of fiction such as J. R. R. Tolkein's *Lord of the Rings* or Charles Dickens's *Christmas Carol*. On some occasions, such works of fiction are taken as the object of philosophical enquiry and explanation. In that case, as one would expect, there are competing philosophical accounts of the nature of fiction—competing answers to such questions as the following: whether hobbits exist; whether it is true that Ebenezer Scrooge was visited by Marley; how, or why, people come to rejoice in Scrooge's redemption, or whether *Lord of the Rings* might have existed if Tolkien had not. On other occasions, however, works of fiction (in general) are invoked to explain (by analogy) various philosophically interesting discourses that are not obviously works of fiction or intended to be. In that case, certain answers to questions about the ontology and language of works of fiction are taken as given, and the workings of other discourses are accounted for by analogy with works of fiction so construed—hence the use of the term *fictionalism* to describe accounts of this sort. Fictionalists need not explicitly propose an analogy with works of fiction. The link between works of fiction and fictionalism is best forged as follows.

There are three natural and plausible theses about fictions that fictionalists typically wish to transfer to the discourses that are the targets of their explanations. Firstly, a thesis of vindication: Fictional discourses do not call for elimination or rejection, nor may they be simply ignored. We should neither discourage novelists from writing stories nor prohibit literary critics from dis-

cussing fictional characters: Fiction fulfills some function in our lives and calls for a philosophical account that acknowledges that function. Secondly, an ontological attitude: We should not accept the existence of characters and kinds that are paradigmatically fictional. For instance, we should not believe in the existence of hobbits or Ebenezer Scrooge. Thirdly, a semantic thesis: It is not the case that any sentence that appears to be about fictional entities both (a) entails the existence of a fictional entity and (b) is literally true. This thesis is particularly important in the case of those sentences of the fictional narrative that are paradigmatically correct or true according to the fiction—for example, "Some hobbits live underground" and "Scrooge is the employer of Bob Cratchit." These sentences appear to entail the existence of fictionalia such as hobbits and Scrooge, and they appear to be true, so that anyone who accepts both these appearances will seemingly be committed to believing in the existence of hobbits and of Scrooge.

Fictionalists turn these theses about fiction into claims about the discourse for which they are accounting. Characterizing fictionalism this way enables us to distinguish fictionalism about a discourse (*F*-talk, say) from the most eminent rival approaches to interpretation and ontology—namely, eliminativism, realism, and reductionism. Firstly, the fictionalist's thesis of vindication says that we are well motivated in persisting in our use of *F*-talk because it serves some characteristic function or purpose that cannot effectively or efficiently be replicated if we abstain from *F*-talk. In contrast, the *eliminativist* characteristically denies that *F*-talk is so vindicated and proposes to abstain from its use. Secondly, the fictionalist's ontological attitude is that we ought not to accept the existence of *F*s. Thus the fictionalist is no *realist*—assuming that realists about *F*-discourse must believe in *F*s. We should also expect the realist to reject the characteristic semantic thesis of fictionalism and so to insist that there are *F*-sentences that both (a) entail the existence of *F*s and (b) are literally true. Thirdly, the fictionalist does not accept the existence of *F*s and so, a fortiori, does not accept the conjunctive thesis that the *F*s exist and (for some *G*) are identical with the *G*s. This separates the fictionalist from ontological reductionists, who assert this conjunctive thesis.

2. FICTIONALIST STRATEGIES OF INTERPRETATION

As has been seen, the fictionalist wishes to exploit the thesis that no sentence of fictional discourse both (a) entails the existence of any fictional entity and (b) is literally true. Different general strategies of fictionalist interpretation correspond to different ways of rejecting (a) or of rejecting (b). To spell out these strategies, let us focus on the kind of sentence that may look like a counterexample to the view of fiction on which the fictionalist is drawing—one that appears to entail the existence of a fictional entity:

(1) Some hobbits live underground.

The first kind of fictionalist strategy proceeds from denial of the entailment component (a) of the thesis. It claims that the sentences do not have the existential consequences that they appear to have. If this claim is secured, then in order to avoid unwanted existential commitment, the fictionalist need not deny that the sentences in question are true. This entry distinguishes three versions of this strategy, modeled on different accounts of the nature of fiction:

(A1) NONFACTUALISM (RELATED TERMS: NONCOGNITIVISM, EXPRESSIVISM, INSTRUMENTALISM). The sentences of the fictional narrative are not used with the kind of illocutionary force or intent that is required in order for them to state a propositional, genuinely truth-evaluable content. The proper use of the sentence is in a kind of illocutionary act that precludes assertion or presenting the content of a belief. Accordingly, sentences so used are not truth-apt and lack the kinds of content that can be, or properly entail, any existential proposition. In fictional narratives, perhaps the crucial illocutionary act is that of fictionalizing or pretending. The nonfactualist strategy of interpretation is familiar from the moral and aesthetic cases, where fact-stating is contrasted with evaluating or attitude-expressing, but is also applied in certain instrumentalist approaches to (portions of) mathematics and science. The locus classicus of ethical nonfactualism is the emotivism of A. J. Ayer (1936, ch. 6). For an instrumentalism about infinitary portions of mathematics see David Hilbert's article "On the Infinite" (1983). Simon Blackburn presents a list of nonfactualist (expressivist) suggestions about a further range of discourses as background to his own nonfactualism (quasi-realism) about morals and modals (1984, chs. 5–6).

(A2) NONEISM (RELATED TERM: MEINONGIANISM). Sentences such as (1) may be used assertorically, they have propositional content, but they do not entail the existence of hobbits because, generally, propositions of particular quantification (some As are Bs) do not entail the existence of those things over which they quantify. On this view, it is consistent to hold, in general, that there are some things that do not exist and, in particular, that

among some of the things that do not exist are hobbits that live underground, or infinitely many prime numbers or worlds that have talking donkeys as parts. A comprehensive, noneist fictionalism would treat all apparently existential quantification in the true propositions of the discourse as particular quantification, and would treat all such particular quantification as quantification that is not existentially committing. The locus classicus of noneism is Richard Routley (1980; see also McGinn 2000, ch. 2).

(A3) PARAPHRASIS. Sentences of the fictional narrative are elliptical expressions of propositions that do not entail the existence of fictionalia; correspondingly, sentences of F-discourse do not entail the existence of Fs. One prominent development of this thought has it that sentences such as (1) express propositions in which nonfactive operators take position of widest scope—operators of modality, conditionalization, or consequence operators invoking a story (or theory). For example:

(1*) According to the Tolkein stories, some hobbits live underground;

or,

(1**) The Tolkein stories entail that some hobbits live underground.

The modal fictionalist introduced in Gideon Rosen's article "Modal Fictionalism" (1990) claims that one can have all the benefits of talking about possible worlds without the ontological costs by interpreting apparently existential claims about a plurality of worlds as claims about what is the case according to the plurality of worlds hypothesis advanced by David Lewis (1986). (Armstrong 1989 puts forward a related view; for discussion, see Lycan 1993). In the philosophy of mathematics, Geoffrey Hellman's (1989) modal structuralism is a proposal to treat apparently existential claims about numbers as claims about what would follow from the hypothesis that certain structures are instantiated. The presentism of A. N. Prior (1957) incorporates a proposal to paraphrase away apparent reference to past and future times by translation into a medium of tensed operators.

The second kind of fictionalist strategy proceeds from refusal to accept the component thesis (b)—that the sentences in question are literally true. A choice then presents itself. One might proceed by multiplying kinds of truth and make out the case that there is a feature of nonliteral truth or relativized truth that can be attributed to the "correct" sentences of the discourse. Thus, it might be held that (1) is fictively true or (in a metalinguistic analogue of an earlier proposal) is true-in-the-Tolkein-stories but not literally true or true simpliciter. Going the other way, one might stick with only one univocal notion of (literal) truth but refuse to ascribe (univocal) truth to (1) or any other correct existential sentence of the fiction. Here only the latter, better-charted path will be explored. If the fictionalist refrains from holding that any existential sentence is true, she may treat those sentences as expressing the existential propositions that they appear to express without having immediate cause to worry that unwanted existential commitment will ensue. Three versions of this strategy are as follows:

(B1) PRESUPPOSITIONISM. When sentences containing special fictional terms occur outside the scope of a story operator ("According to T ...") they simply lack a truth-value. This view might be supported by the contention that in order for some such sentences to be true or false, the existential presuppositions invoked by the use of the narrative—presupposition of the existence of hobbits and other kinds of things—would have to be fulfilled. For such a view of sentences involving predications to empty definite descriptions see P. F. Strawson's essay "On Referring" (1971).

(B2) AGNOSTICISM. The problematic existential sentences of the discourse may properly be used to assert the existence of Fs and do have a determinate truth-value. But people are not, and perhaps cannot be, in a position to judge what that truth-value is, and certainly not in a position to assert any such sentence. The most famous agnostic fictionalism is that of Bas C. Van Fraassen (1980) on the unobservables of microphysical theory. Rosen and Cian Dorr (2002) proposed agnosticism about the existence of the composite objects—entities that have other entities as parts—which people's ordinary talk is about.

(B3) ERROR THEORY. The problematic existential sentences are assertoric of the existence of Fs and do have determinate truth-value, and one is justified in holding that these sentences are systematically false. J. L. Mackie (1977) famously reads Locke as an error-theorist about secondary properties and develops a parallel error theory of morals. Mackie interprets ordinary moral judgements as requiring the existence of "objective prescriptivity"—states of affairs that give reasons for action independently of the agent's motivations—and thus as systematically false. However, Mackie goes on to recommend that one persevere with moral discourse in order to secure the benefits of social cooperation. The moral fictionalism of Richard Joyce (2001) develops this position, suggesting that people should cease to believe moral claims while continuing to utter sentences such as "Kicking babies is wrong," provided they do not do so with assertoric force.

Error theories about mathematics abound. Hartry Field (1989) construes the existential sentences of mathematical theories as entailing the existence of abstract objects. On epistemological grounds one should hold these sentences false. But, Field maintains, because reference to mathematical entities can be removed from the best physical theories, one is entitled to continue using theories that contain mathematics and is motivated to do so because it offers significant shortcuts in inference and calculation. Other mathematical error theorists develop positions that are not committed to such dispensability of quantification over abstract entities. Joseph Melia (2000) claims that mathematical sentences can convey useful information about the concrete part of the world, even though they are often false through entailing the existence of abstract objects.

When the fictionalist proceeds along any of the (b)-route strategies, she will typically offer as an alternative to truth some other subsidiary norm that the "correct" sentences satisfy and in terms of which the success or characteristic function of the discourse is to be explained. What the norm is will differ from discourse to discourse. For example, Van Fraassen's refusal to hold true the existential sentences of microphysical theory, and the theories that entail them, is combined with the views that the good theories in which they feature are good because they are empirically adequate and that one can explain their success without ascribing truth to them. Similarly, Field holds that mathematical "goodness" is not truth but membership of a nominalistically conservative theory (compare Rosen and Dorr 2002 on the atomistic adequacy of ordinary composite object talk). However, the fictionalist who proceeds along the (b)-route in withholding the ascription of truth may not feel compelled to appeal to any norm other than truth. The alternative is to maintain that the discourse could still fulfill its function if people limited themselves to believing or holding true only its *nonexistential* claims.

It is not the case that all versions of fictionalism are presented explicitly as versions of these strategies. Often other explanatory resources are prominent (e.g., quasi-assertion, games of make-believe, and metaphor. See Yablo 2001, Walton 1990). However, it is suspected that in order to avoid relevant ontological commitment, fictionalists must eventually commit to one of the semantic strategies presented here.

3. ISSUES FOR THE FICTIONALIST STRATEGIES OF INTERPRETATION

A fictionalist strategy of interpretation will succeed only if:

(1) It avoids the ontological commitments that it is intended to avoid;

(2) it secures the benefits that motivate persistence with use of the discourse; and

(3) it makes intelligible whatever distinctive semantic devices that it invokes in orderto escape ontological commitment.

Nonfactualist fictionalism faces its primary challenges over points (2) and (3). In particular, if apparently existential sentences do not, at bottom, state propositions, then how are nonfactualists to square whatever linguistic properties they ascribe to those sentences with the role of the sentences as premises in inferences? This point bites hard when the target discourse is one that functions as an inferential medium as, notably, portions of mathematics and scientific theory do with respect to observation statements.

Noneist fictionalism faces the sharpest challenge of all under point (3), for it has been held that the pivotal claim of noneism—that there are things that do not exist—is unintelligible. Moreover, there is a particular methodological challenge to be faced by all fictionalists that the noneist in particular seems to invite. Suppose that a fictionalist succeeds in avoiding commitment to some problematic realm of objects. It would smack of absurdity if their strategy could be applied globally, to free everyone of all ontological commitments whatsoever—even in cases where those commitments were not undesirable. The fictionalist who holds that some but not all discourses can be treated fictionally needs a principled way of drawing the line.

Paraphrastic fictionalists who invoke nonfactive operators immediately face a dilemma over point (3). If the operators in question are taken as primitive, that is at least an ideological cost of the theory; but if the (modal, consequence, or conditional) operators in question are interpreted in standard ways, then they may generate commitment to entities such as models (sets) or possible worlds. But these semantically induced entities may either be, or share problematic features with, the entities that the fictionalist is trying to avoid—thus contravening (1). For example, a fictionalist about numbers who is suspicious of abstract objects had better not end up invoking other abstract objects in order to explain what "according to standard arithmetic" means. Along the first horn of the dilemma the question arises again, as it did for the non-factualist, of how to account for the (perhaps crucial) inferential role of the sentences. Often it seems that one could do so if the existential sentences were interpreted as existence-entailing; the paraphrastic fictionalist has to demonstrate that her alternative construal can do the same work.

Another difficulty arises when the nonfactive operator chosen is of the sort "According to T," where T is a philosophical theory the fictionalist holds to be false. (Rosen-style modal fictionalism is an example of a fictionalist theory that invokes such an operator.) It seems reasonable to ask the fictionalist why any philosophical theory—especially one the fictionalist holds to be false—should play such a central role in her account of the discourse. In addition, it may be asked why the fictionalist chooses to use the particular theory that she does. What distinguishes that theory from other philosophical falsehoods?

The various route (b) strategies that withhold ascription of literal truth face their most immediate difficulty over (2). Can the characteristic function of the discourse really be secured if all of the intuitively correct sentences are held to have some feature that is weaker than truth or if only the nonexistential intuitively correct sentences are held to be true? A question that lies just beyond this one is whether proper strictures of charitable interpretation will permit an interpretation of the discourse that ascribes such powerful existential entailments and then sets the standard of truth so high (and so distinct from the operating standards of correctness) that the users of the discourse systematically fail to meet them.

4. HISTORICAL POSTSCRIPT

These contemporary fictionalist views have many historical antecedents. The phenomenalist strand of empiricist thought, as represented, for example, in John Stuart Mill's *An Examination of Sir William Hamilton's Philosophy* (1979 [1865]) is paraphrastically fictionalist when it suggests the translation of ordinary material object talk into counterfactual claims about sensations. The nonfactualist strand of empiricist thought, which is often discerned in Hume (1978), can be viewed as suggesting fictionalism about a wide range of cases from the external world to the self. More specifically the notion of paraphrase, and its function in avoiding ontological commitment, is prominent in the thought of Jeremy Bentham in the nineteenth century and in that of W. V. Quine in the twentieth century. Arguably, this style of fictionalism also surfaces in Bertrand Russell's doctrine that classes are "logical fictions," eliminable through contextual definition, and in his famous general treatment of definite descriptions (1956). Finally, in the early twentieth century, Hans Vaihinger (1924) proposes that one should accept atomic theory, theology, and many other discourses, without believing them. Vaihinger presents his views as a reading of Kant, though recent commentators have stressed his affinities with pragmatist thought.

See also Agnosticism; Ayer, Alfred Jules; Eliminative Materialism, Eliminativism; Error Theory of Ethics; Field, Hartry; Hilbert, David; Hume, David; Kant, Immanuel; Lewis, David; Literature, Philosophy of; Locke, John; Mackie, John Leslie; Mill, John Stuart; Noncognitivism; Prior, Arthur Norman; Propositions; Quine, Willard Van Orman; Strawson, Peter Frederick; Vaihinger, Hans; Van Fraassen, Bas.

Bibliography

Armstrong, D. M. *A Combinatorial Theory of Possibility.* Cambridge, U.K.: Cambridge University Press, 1989.

Ayer, A. J. *Language, Truth and Logic.* London: Gollancz, 1936.

Blackburn, Simon. *Spreading The Word: Groundings in the Philosophy of Language.* Oxford: Clarendon Press, 1984.

Field, Hartry. *Realism, Mathematics, and Modality.* Oxford: Blackwell, 1989.

Hellman, Geoffrey. *Mathematics without Numbers: Towards a Modal-Structural Interpretation.* Oxford: Oxford University Press, 1989.

Hilbert, David. "On the Infinite." In *Philosophy of Mathematics: Selected Readings.* 2nd ed., edited by Paul Benacerraf and Hilary Putnam. Cambridge, U.K.: Cambridge University Press, 1983.

Hume, David. *A Treatise of Human Nature.* 2nd ed., edited by L. A. Selby-Bigge. Oxford: Oxford University Press, 1978.

Joyce, Richard. *The Myth of Morality.* Cambridge, U.K.: Cambridge University Press, 2001.

Lewis, David. *On The Plurality of Worlds.* Oxford: Blackwell, 1986.

Lycan, William G. "Armstrong's New Combinatorialist Theory of Modality." In *Ontology, Causality, and Mind: Essays in Honour of D. M. Armstrong,* edited by John Bacon, Keith Campbell, and Lloyd Reinhardt. Cambridge, U.K.: Cambridge University Press, 1993.

Mackie, J. L. *Ethics: Inventing Right and Wrong.* Harmondsworth, U.K.: Penguin, 1977.

McGinn, Colin. *Logical Properties: Identity, Existence, Predication, Necessity, Truth.* Oxford: Clarendon Press, 2000.

Melia, Joseph. "Weaseling away the Indispensability Argument." *Mind* 109 (2000): 455–479.

Mill, John Stuart. *An Examination of Sir William Hamilton's Philosophy* (1865), edited by J. M. Robson. London: Routledge, 1979.

Ogden, C. K. *Bentham's Theory of Fictions.* London: Kegan Paul, Trench, Trubner, 1932.

Prior, A. N. *Time and Modality.* Oxford: Oxford University Press, 1957.

Quine, W. V. "Existence and Quantification." In his *Ontological Relativity, and Other Essays.* New York: Columbia University Press, 1969.

Rosen, Gideon. "Modal Fictionalism." *Mind* 99 (1990): 327–354.

Rosen, Gideon, and Cian Dorr. "Composition as a Fiction." In *The Blackwell Guide to Metaphysics,* edited by Richard M. Gale. Oxford: Blackwell, 2002.

Routley (Sylvan), Richard. *Exploring Meinong's Jungle and Beyond: An Investigation of Noneism and the Theory of Items.* Canberra, Australia: Research School of Social Sciences, Australian National University, 1980.

Russell, Bertrand. "The Philosophy of Logical Atomism." In *Logic and Knowledge,* edited by R. C. Marsh. London: Allen and Unwin, 1956.

Strawson, P. F. "On Referring." In his *Logico-Linguistic Papers.* London: Methuen, 1971.

Vaihinger, Hans. *The Philosophy of "As If": A System of the Theoretical, Practical and Religious Fictions of Mankind.* Translated by C. K. Ogden. London: Kegan Paul, Trench, Trubner, 1924.

van Fraassen, Bas C. *The Scientific Image.* Oxford: Clarendon Press, 1980.

Walton, Kendall. *Mimesis as Make-Believe: On the Foundations of the Representational Arts.* Cambridge, MA: Harvard University Press, 1990.

Yablo, Stephen. "Go Figure: A Path through Fictionalism." *Midwest Studies in Philosophy* 25 (2001): 72–102.

John Divers (2005)
David Liggins (2005)

FICTIONALISM, MATHEMATICAL

See *Nominalism, Modern*

FIDEISM

Fideism is the view that truth in religion is ultimately based on faith rather than on reasoning or evidence. This claim has been presented in many forms by theologians from St. Paul to contemporary neoorthodox, antirationalist writers, usually as a way of asserting that the fundamental tenets of religion cannot be established by proofs or by empirical evidence but must be accepted on faith. Some forms of fideism denigrate or deny the value of reason and science, and these amount to a kind of irrationalism, as indicated in David Hume's ironic statement at the end of his essay "Of Miracles":

> [The] *Christian Religion* not only was at first attended with miracles, but even to this day can-

not be believed by any reasonable person without them. Mere reason is not sufficient to convince us of its veracity; and whoever is moved by *Faith* to assent to it, is conscious of a continued miracle in his own person, which subverts all the principles of his understanding, and gives him a determination to believe what is most contrary to custom and experience. (*Essay concerning Human Understanding,* edited by L. A. Selby-Bigge, Oxford, 1951, p. 131)

EXTREME FIDEISM

Extreme fideists such as J. G. Hamann and Søren Kierkegaard have praised Hume's formulation as a proper characterization of religious orthodoxy.

Starting with St. Paul's contention that the central doctrine of Christianity was nonsensical by Greek philosophical standards and with Tertullian's announcement *credo quia absurdum* (I believe that which is absurd), there have been theologians who have insisted that religious truths are contrary to those that might be supported or justified by reasonable evidence and that rational activities are not proper means to arrive at such truths. Some have insisted that there are suprarational or extrarational ways, such as mystical or revelatory experiences that provide the "knowledge" of fundamental truths. Such writers have tended to ignore rational arguments or standards, and often, as St. John of the Cross did, they have offered means by which one could train oneself to escape the confines of rationality in order to intensify religious experience and belief.

Others have tried to show the inability of reason to establish any fundamental or absolutely certain truth. Usually employing skeptical arguments, they have contended that ultimate principles are open to question or rational standards, and also that these standards can themselves be questioned. In view of this, they have contended, basic truths are to be accepted on faith. Michel Eyquem de Montaigne, Pierre Charron, and other so-called Christian skeptics set forth this form of fideism.

Others, such as Pierre Bayle, Kierkegaard, Félicité Robert de Lamennais, and Lev Isaakovich Shestov, went further and asserted that religious truths were of such a nature that they were contrary to the kinds of assertions that were probable, plausible, or even possible on rational or reasonable standards and that such truths could therefore be believed or accepted only on faith. Bayle insisted that religious tenets were not only above and beyond reason but also in opposition to it and that the strongest faith was that which denied the truths based on natural

light and embraced those most incomprehensible to or contrary to reason. Kierkegaard first accepted the type of skepticism developed by Bayle and Hume about rational knowledge and then insisted that the fundamental tenet of Christianity, the Incarnation, is not only contrary to rational evidence but even a self-contradiction on rational standards: "No knowledge can have for its object the absurdity that the eternal is the historical" (*Philosophical Fragments, or A Fragment of Philosophy,* p. 50). Kierkegaard held Hamann's view that Hume had summed up the nature of religious belief—that it really is contrary to reason, custom, and experience. For Kierkegaard the very absurdity of the Christian claim makes it worthy of belief, and it is only by total commitment, or "the leap into faith," that it can be accepted. There can be no reasons for the leap, no justification for it. In the words of Bayle's opponent, Pierre Jurieu (also an irrationalist), all the believer can say is, "I believe it because I want to believe it."

In the twentieth century, among the fideists who advanced Kierkegaard's view, one of the most striking was the Russian Orthodox theologian Shestov, who insisted that the rejection of all rational standards is a part of true belief. In a commentary on Fëdor Dostoevsky he contended that the refusal to accept that 2 + 2 = 4 and the ability to believe that 2 + 2 = 5 are intimately connected with attaining religious truth.

MODERATE FIDEISM

In contrast to irrationalist or antirationalist fideism, a more moderate kind has developed, especially within the Christian Augustinian tradition. Rather than insisting that all ultimate certitude rests on faith in contrast to reason, this tradition has admitted that faith precedes reason in establishing certain fundamental truths but that reason and evidence can play some role both in the search for these truths and in the explanation and comprehension of them. The Augustinian slogan, *credo ut intelligam* (I believe in order to know), places the primary emphasis on faith. However, as Augustine's philosophical dialogues show, the recognition of the basic fideistic element may be (and perhaps must be) preceded by a rational search for truth. Once rational inquiry has revealed the need to accept some fundamental principles or beliefs on faith, then it may be possible to show that these commitments are reasonable, probable, or plausible. Purported proofs of the existence of God, metaphysical systems interpreting what is accepted on faith, and historical and psychological evidences about the nature of religion and its effects on believers can all be offered as rational explanations or even justifications of what has already been accepted on faith.

Blaise Pascal's presentation in the *Pensées* illustrates this form of fideism. He forcefully argued that the natural capacities of man are inadequate to lead him to any completely certain truth. A man can show that it is unreasonable or unwise to be an atheist but not that it is reasonable to be a theist. Once one has realized the human predicament—man's fundamental need for ultimate truths and his inability to find them—then one is ready to hear God and to accept his revealed Word on faith alone. Once one has faith, one can see the force of the apologetic and psychological evidence for the truth of the Christian religion. Such evidence might then constitute "good reasons" for believing what one has already accepted fideistically.

FIDEISM IN PHILOSOPHY

A nonreligious analogue of moderate fideism appears in various skeptical philosophical views, such as those of Hume, Bertrand Russell, and George Santayana. Hume's contention that it is belief that "peoples the world," and that everybody lives within his own private belief system, could be considered as a kind of fideism. The ultimate presuppositions by which we live cannot be justified by reason or evidence and are accepted not on religious faith but (to use Santayana's term) on "animal faith." Russell, in his *Human Knowledge,* insisted (on the basis of Hume's arguments) that the fundamental assumptions of science cannot be justified but must be accepted on faith. However, even if one has the mystical skeptical experience Santayana described, of seeing all in doubt, it is still rational investigation that led Hume and his successors to the recognition of the belief factor involved in rational activities. Having discovered this, Hume then showed that one can study the causes of beliefs and that beliefs can be explained even though they can never be justified; working from the basis of a set of "reasonable" beliefs, one can evaluate other beliefs in terms of psychological factors. The philosophical tradition emanating from Hume, then, can be considered as a kind of fideism, sharing some of the characteristics of the moderate fideism of the Augustinian tradition.

CONTEMPORARY DEVELOPMENTS

At present irrationalistic fideism, especially of the Kierkegaardian variety, is extremely popular, especially among Protestant theologians (partly in reaction to liberal, rationalistic theological tendencies of the nineteenth century). Many theologians have been concerned with man's apparent inability to find any ultimate answers through science, secular political movements, and so forth, and his need to base his ultimate commitment on faith alone. The existentialist stress on the fundamental absurdity of man's world is part of this movement. The official Catholic position from the time of the Council of Trent to the present remains opposed to the central fideistic thesis, that ultimate beliefs can be established not by reason or evidence but only by faith. However, in a world in which so many optimistic, "reasonable," scientifically supported views have been undermined by the cataclysmic events of the twentieth century, fideism may provide one of the main avenues to some kind of significant belief for the present age. William James's analysis, in his "Will to Believe," of the psychological need for commitment and belief despite the lack of evidence may represent much of the present mood. The religious fideists, however, find James's own faith too tepid, and they seem to be moving more and more to the irrationalist fideism of Kierkegaard, Dostoevsky, and Shestov.

See also Atheism; Augustine, St.; Bayle, Pierre; Charron, Pierre; Dostoevsky, Fyodor Mikhailovich; Faith; Hamann, Johann Georg; Hume, David; James, William; John of the Cross, St.; Kierkegaard, Søren Aabye; Lamennais, Hugues Félicité Robert de; Montaigne, Michel Eyquem de; Pascal, Blaise; Russell, Bertrand Arthur William; Santayana, George; Shestov, Lev Isaakovich; Skepticism; Tertullian, Quintus Septimius Florens.

Bibliography

Bartley, William W. *Retreat to Commitment.* New York: Knopf, 1962. A critique of some contemporary fideistic views.

Bayle, Pierre. *Historical and Critical Dictionary, Selections.* Translated by R. H. Popkin. Indianapolis: Bobbs-Merrill, 1965. "Pyrrho" and the "Third Clarification" deal especially with fideism.

Evans, C. Stephen. *Faith beyond Reason: A Kierkegaardian Account.* Grand Rapids, MI: Eerdmans, 1998.

Geivett, R. Douglas, and Brendan Sweetman, eds. *Contemporary Perspectives on Religious Epistemology.* Oxford: Oxford University Press, 1992.

Harent, S. "Foi." In *Dictionnaire de théologie catholique,* Vol. VI, cols. 55–514. Paris, 1920.

Herberg, Will. *Four Existentialist Theologians: A Reader from the Works of Jacques Maritain, Nicolas Berdyaev, Martin Buber and Paul Tillich.* Garden City, NY: Doubleday, 1958.

Herberg, Will. *Judaism and Modern Man.* New York: Farrar, Straus, 1951.

Kierkegaard, Søren. *A Kierkegaard Anthology.* Edited by Robert Bretall. New York: Modern Library, 1959.

Kierkegaard, Søren. *Philosophical Fragments, or A Fragment of Philosophy.* Translated by David F. Swenson. Princeton, NJ: Princeton University Press, 1936.

Penelhum, Terrence. *God and Skepticism: A Study in Skepticism and Fideism.* New York: Kluwer Academic Publishers, 1983.

Pojman, Louis P. *Religious Belief and the Will.* London: Routledge and Kegan Paul, 1986.

Popkin, Richard H. "Kierkegaard and Scepticism." *Algemeen Nederlands Tijdschrift Voor Wijsbegeerte en Psychologie* 51 (1959): 123–141.

Popkin, Richard H. "Theological and Religious Scepticism." *Christian Scholar* 39 (1956): 150–158.

Santayana, George. *Scepticism and Animal Faith.* New York: Dover, 1955.

Sauvage, G. M. "Fideism." In *Catholic Encyclopedia,* Vol. V, 68–69. New York, 1909.

Shestov, Lev I. *In Job's Balances.* Translated by Camilla Coventry and C. A. Macartney. London: Dent, 1932.

Shestov, Lev I. *Kierkegaard et la philosophie existentielle.* Translated by T. Rageot and Boris de Schloezer. Paris: Vrin, 1936.

Swinburne, Richard. *Faith and Reason.* Oxford: Oxford University Press, 1984.

Tillich, Paul. *Dynamics of Faith.* New York: Harper, 1957.

Richard H. Popkin (1967)
Bibliography updated by Christian B. Miller (2005)

FIELD, HARTRY
(1956–)

Hartry H. Field was born in Boston. He received his BA in Mathematics at the University of Wisconsin (1967) and his Ph.D. at Harvard (1972) working under Hilary Putnam and Richard Boyd. He has taught at Princeton, USC, CUNY Graduate Center, and NYU, where he is currently Silver Professor of Philosophy. Field is the recipient of, among other awards, a Guggenheim Foundation Fellowship (1979–1980) and the Lakatos prize (1986) for his book *Science without Numbers* (1980). He was elected in 2003 to the American Academy of Arts and Sciences.

Field has made significant contributions in a number of areas. He is best known for his work in philosophy of mathematics and on a variety of issues connected with realism and with the notion of truth. In philosophy of mathematics, Field has defended a version of fictionalism: a view according to which mathematics, which he takes at face value as asserting the existence of numbers, pure sets, and so on, is literally false and cannot be interpreted via a nonliteral reading in such a way that it works out true. Field sees the central argument in favor of realism about mathematics to be its indispensability for formulating and making use of scientific theories, and he proposes to answer this argument by giving an account of the use of mathematics in the sciences that does not require that the mathematics be true: If T is a nominalistic physical theory (roughly, one that makes no mention of mathematical entities), and M is a mathematical theory used to derive consequences from T (an example of such a theory might be a version of set theory that allows

one to treat the objects of T as urelements and that allows the vocabulary of T to appear in the comprehension axioms) then M is said to be conservative over T if any such consequences, if entirely stated in the vocabulary of T, are already (semantic) consequences of T—that is, true in any model of T.

Field points out that people have always expected mathematics to be conservative over physical theories, and that in fact there is good reason to believe it is. The importance of this observation is the following. Suppose P is a physical theory that, like most such theories, is not nominalistic. It may be possible to find a nominalistic theory N, from which one can derive P via definitions and mathematics. It will then follow that P and mathematics are jointly conservative over N. This at least suggests that N captures all the physical content of P, and that the mathematics (together with P itself) is simply a convenient device for drawing out the consequences of N. Following (and significantly extending) techniques familiar to decision theorists and others under the title of "measurement theory," Field succeeded in constructing a natural nominalistic N for the case where P is a form of Newtonian gravitation theory.

Field's project of extending this result to all of physics has stimulated widespread interest in a number of issues. To name just one, Newtonian gravitation, and any theory remotely like it, requires an N that quantifies over sets of points, which may be identified with regions of space; the sense of consequence in which anything about N provable in P + mathematics is already a consequence of N is second-order consequence, thought of as the complete logic of the part-whole relation. This raises interesting questions, both about the extent to which first-order approximations to Field's result are available or convincing, and about whether one can speak about second-order consequence while continuing to be a fictionalist about mathematics. Indeed, the latter question arises for first-order consequence, despite that it is coextensive with a syntactic notion—because a fictionalist about mathematics ought to be a fictionalist about, for example, the claim that a given theory is syntactically consistent. Field has responded to this question with an interesting theory of (purely) logical necessity as a sui generis kind of necessity, one that is not explained in terms of models or possible worlds.

Field's earliest work on truth, the essay "Tarski's Theory of Truth" (1972), appeared at a time when Putnam and others were trying to argue for a form of scientific realism that stressed, as against, for example, Thomas Kuhn, the continuity of reference across changing scientific theories. Integral to this view was a conception of reference that made it a nontrivial question how use of the word "water" brings it about that "water" refers to the particular chemical compound it does, and thereby a nontrivial question, what brings it about that "Water tastes good," as uttered by an American, is true (beyond the fact that it does taste good). This conception, which sometimes goes (as do many other views) under the name "correspondence theory" (of reference or of truth), contrasts with the "deflationist" idea according to which "'water' refers to water (in English)" is nothing more than a straightforward consequence of a natural definition of "refers in English." In this paper and later related essays, Field forcefully articulated what has turned out to be the most persuasive argument in favor of the need for a correspondence theory: namely, that human success in interacting with the world using language requires a systematic explanation of a kind a deflationist is unable to supply.

It turns out that deflationists have some at least initially plausible responses to this argument, and in fact Field has been increasingly sympathetic to deflationism. One topic he has addressed is what the theory of meaning looks like from a deflationist perspective, given that deflationism needs to sever the apparently intimate connections between meaning and reference. Another has been what a deflationist (or anyone else—but the problem is particularly pressing for deflationists) is to make of situations where it seems correct to say that "there is no fact of the matter"; these include not only areas where philosophers have traditionally debated about realism, but also in borderline cases involving vague expressions like "bald." Field has presented an appealing picture in which one both abandons excluded middle, and introduces a "determinately" operator into the language. The "determinately" operator is not given a semantics; it is rather understood both through its connections with degrees of belief, and through its relations to a natural non-truth-functional conditional. Field shows that such a language allows one consistently (despite the presence of the "determinately" operator) to introduce a truth predicate T such that the Tarski sentences (written using the new conditional) work out to be theorems; in fact "T(A)" is everywhere substitutable for "A."

See also Mathematics, Foundations of.

Bibliography

The fictionalist approach to mathematics was first set out in Field's *Science without Numbers: A Defence of Nominalism* (Princeton, NJ: Princeton University Press, 1980). Many of Field's papers can be found in the collections *Realism, Mathematics, and Modality* (Oxford: Blackwell, 1989; rev. ed.

1991) and *Truth and the Absence of Fact* (New York: Oxford University Press, 2001).

For the recent work on vagueness and the liar, see "A Revenge-Immune Solution to the Semantic Paradoxes," in *Journal of Philosophical Logic* 72 (2003): 139–177; and "No Fact of the Matter," in *Australian Journal of Philosophy* 81 (2003): 457–480. Some recommended papers not in the collections, and on topics not mentioned in this entry, are "Logic, Meaning and Conceptual Role," in *Journal of Philosophy* 74 (1977): 379–409; "A Note on Jeffrey Conditionalization," in *Philosophy of Science* 45 (1978): 361–367; "The A Prioricity of Logic" *Proceedings of the Aristotelian Society* 96 (1996): 359–379; and "Causation in a Physical World," in *The Oxford Handbook of Metaphysics*, edited by M. Loux and D. Zimmerman, 435–460 (Oxford: Oxford University Press, 2003; reprinted in *The Philosopher's Annual* 26 (2003), edited by P. Grim, K. Baynes, and G. Mar). See also "Tarski's Theory of Truth," *Journal of Philosophy* 69 (13) (July 1972): 347–375.

Stephen Leeds (2005)

FIELDS AND PARTICLES

Broadly speaking, a field is a collection of properties ascribed to regions of space (one might also speak of the region itself as being "the field"); if the properties are quantifiable then the field is a mathematical function of spatial coordinates, $\Phi(x,y,z)$. Examples include the temperature at each point of a room, the velocity at each point of a fluid, the gravitational potential, and the electromagnetic field. In contrast—and broadly speaking—particles are entities of which positions are ascribed (and which lack any relevant internal structure). While these will do as broad characterizations, they are inadequate in a number of ways.

CLASSICAL FIELDS

For instance, one could say that a field theory ascribes positions (and field strengths) to the parts of a field, as a particle theory treats particles. Worse, one can reformulate particle theories (e.g., Isaac Newton, 1642–1727, and Immanuel Kant, 1724–1804) as theories that ascribe mobile particle-sized regions of repulsion to space: as a field theory according to the intuitive distinction. Hence a useful formal characterization adopts the practice of physicists and takes the difference between field and particle theories to be that the former associates infinitely many "degrees of freedom" (kinematically independent variables—the values of Φ at each point) with finite regions of space, but the latter only finitely many (the positions and momenta of a finite number of particles in a finite region).

The problem with the broad and formal characterizations of the field is that they ignore historically important distinctions. For instance, Aristotle's (384–322 BCE) plenum (i.e., space full of matter, with no vacuum) ascribes different properties—gravity here, levity there—to regions of space, but one would like to distinguish the modern concept of a field from the ancient plenum. Newton's (1687) gravitational field ascribes to every point of space a quantitative disposition for bodies to move (absent other bodies, if a body were at a point a distance r from a body of mass M then it would have acceleration proportional to M/r^2), which distinguishes it from the ancient plenum. But understood literally, Newtonian gravity is a force that acts at a distance without mediation, hence Newton took it as a purely mathematical, "effective" description of some unknown underlying physics (which he sought in vain; in the early twenty-first century it is believed to be general relativity). Indeed, arguably the modern conception of the field is of something physical that mediates the long-range interactions between bodies. If so, Michael Faraday's (mid-nineteenth-century) arguments for the reality of the electromagnetic field are crucial. For instance, he distinguished physical from merely mathematical fields according to whether changes propagate at a finite speed or not (i.e., "through" the medium or not).

The atomists (especially Democritus, 460–370 BCE) rejected the plenum, arguing that the physical world could be understood in terms of atoms moving in the void. However, general rejection of the vacuum meant that this idea did not become the foundation of useful science until Descartes (1596–1650); and while he believed in the plenum, he envisioned it to be composed of particles of varying sizes. Although Descartes failed to derive quantitative consequences from atomism, his successors, up to the present, have found it one of the most fruitful ideas in physics.

QUANTUM FIELDS AND QUANTUM PARTICLES

In the twentieth century, quantum field theory (henceforth "QFT") was developed, and experimentally tested with unprecedented accuracy, particularly in particle accelerators. Classical fields can be decomposed into a sum of waves of different amplitudes (as a chord can be decomposed into different notes), which means, intuitively speaking, that quantum fields can be decomposed into a sum of waves with quantized (i.e, whole number) amplitudes. In quantum mechanics a wave(-function) represents a particle (its probability distribution in space), so there is a natural equivalence of a quantum field with a system of quantum particles, with the whole number amplitude of a wave in the decomposition representing the number of particles with that wavefunction. Thus because amplitudes become quantized, QFT is the best theory of both fields and subatomic particles.

However, the particle interpretation is only approximate: The field-particle distinction does not really dissolve in QFT. First, quantum mechanical superposition means that a quantum field may contain an indeterminate number of particles (e.g., two with some probability and three with another), which conflicts with the intuitive idea of a particle. Second, an accelerating observer will decompose a field into waves differently from a nonaccelerating observer; in particular, when the nonaccelerating observer says the field contains no particles, the accelerating observer will say that it does (these are known as "Rindler" particles). There is no contradiction, because if the accelerating observer captures a particle, he or she thereby changes the field to a state that all observers agree contains particles. All the same, the concept of a "particle" does not allow for the absence or presence of particles to be frame-dependent. Finally, there is a theorem that in relativistic QFT it is impossible to localize particles to any finite region; if so, they don't fit the intuitive idea of a particle at all.

According to formal definitions, QFT is a field, not particle theory, because it involves infinitely many degrees of freedom—a fact with profound consequences in quantum mechanics, which are obscured by the particle interpretation. Infinite degrees of freedom mean that there are many quantum versions of a field, some of which may not allow a particle decomposition at all (technically, there are unitarily inequivalent representations of the canonical commutation relations). One might think that observations of particles in the world show that the particle version is the correct one, but because of the Haag-Hall-Whiteman theorem there are reasons to think that realistic fields have no particle formulation (technically, there may be no Fock representation of an interacting field). If so, the appearance of particles is presumably explained by the correct version suitably approximating a system of particles. Specifically, there are field states arbitrarily close to states of particles infinitely far apart.

Quantum mechanics can also treat a system of particles, which is (modulo the previous discussion) a field for which the particle content is always definite. Beyond the fact that quantum particles are represented by wavefunctions, there are important differences in the "identities" of classical and quantum particles that the following analogies illustrate. Classical particles are like badges with different pictures on them; the pictures make them distinguishable entities. Some quantum particles—bosons—are like money in the bank: Nothing distinguishes two of the dollars in an account from each other. Other particles—fermions—are like memberships in a particular club: Like money, one membership isn't any different from another; but unlike dollars, one can only have a single membership. (Technically, fermions satisfy the "exclusion principle": there can be at most one particle in any state.) To distinguish bosons and fermions, they are called "quanta"; however, these analogies fail to reveal that quantum mechanics allows other kinds of particles—"quarticles"—that differ from both quanta and classical particles.

See also Aristotle; Descartes, René; Faraday, Michael; Kant, Immanuel; Leucippus and Democritus; Newton, Isaac; Philosophy of Physics; Quantum Mechanics; Space.

Bibliography

Earman, John, and Doreen Fraser. "Haag's Theorem and Its Implications for the Foundations of Quantum Field Theory." Forthcoming.

Hesse, Mary. *Forces and Fields*. London: Greenwood, 1962.

Huggett, Nick. "Philosophical Foundations of Quantum Field Theory." *British Journal for the Philosophy of Science* 51 (2000): 617–638. Reprinted in *Philosophy of Science Today*, edited by Peter Clark and Katherine Hawley. Oxford: Oxford University Press, 2003.

Lange, Marc. *An Introduction to the Philosophy of Physics: Locality, Fields, Energy and Mass*. Oxford: Blackwell Publishers, 2002.

McMullin, Ernan. "The Origins of the Field Concept in Physics." *Physics in Perspective* 4 (2002): 13–39.

Pullman, Bernard. *The Atom in the History of Human Thought*. Translated by Axel R. Reisinger. Oxford: Oxford University Press, 2002.

Teller, Paul. *An Interpretive Introduction to Quantum Field Theory*. Princeton, NJ: Princeton University Press, 1995.

Nick Huggett (2005)

FILMER, ROBERT
(c. 1588–1653)

Robert Filmer, the English political writer and theorist of the divine right of kings, was an early expositor of the patriarchal account of the state and of society. He was a country gentleman of the county of Kent but also belonged to the intellectual society of London and had some connection with the Court. He was an associate of prominent lawyers and historians, such as John Selden and Sir Henry Spelman, of the orthodox clergy, and of the Jacobean poets and literati too, including George Herbert and possibly John Donne. His absolutist views on political matters may have been acquired while he was at Trinity College, Cambridge, or at the Inns of Court and were developed well before the outbreak of the Civil War between the king and Parliament in 1642. In this he resembles Thomas Hobbes, his contemporary, but Filmer wrote his works for circulation in manuscript among his London acquaintances and the manor houses of Kent rather than for publication in print. Although his family was engaged on the side of the king in the struggle with Parliament in the 1640s and although he himself suffered considerable losses, Sir Robert never actually fought with the royalist forces and even pleaded neutrality, which has since been looked upon as inconsistency in the conduct of an extreme defender of royalist claims. His neutrality did not prevent his being sent to prison for a time.

Filmer's importance in the history of thought rests almost entirely on the fact that John Locke's work on political theory, the famous *Two Treatises of Government*, was directed against him, though it was not published until 1689, nearly forty years after Filmer's death. It has only recently been shown how extensive was Locke's preoccupation with Filmer, in the second of his treatises as well as in the first. But the social theorists of the present day are also interested in Filmer's thinking as an expression of traditional patriarchal attitudes toward authority and social structure. The relationship between Locke and Filmer has become the classic example of a rationalist-critical political system (the Lockean) confronting an ideological-determinist outlook (the Filmer view).

It has not been possible, however, to see in Filmer simply a "codifier of unconscious prejudice," as he has been called. He was remarkably enlightened in some of his views, especially as to witchcraft, and wrote with surprising urbanity rather as a critical reviewer of the political works current in his time than as the solemn expositor of outraged orthodoxy. Those of his works he himself had printed, mainly reviews of Aristotle, John Milton, Hugo Grotius, and Hobbes, are brief and pointed, and it is, perhaps, significant that he refused to publish the only concerted exposition of his political theory, the famous *Patriarcha; or the Natural Power of Kings* (London, 1680), from which all the others derive. He may have thought his political theory too extreme in its earlier, positive form.

Patriarcha, which was composed for the gentry of Kent in the 1630s, asserts that every individual is absolutely bound to obey the political authority established in his country because that authority enjoys by divine decree the powers originally conferred on Adam at the creation over his wife, his children, and their descendants eternally. From this view of the Old Testament it follows that males are always superior to females, the elder to the younger, and that all humans are naturally—physiologically—related to each other. Society is a family, descended from one single male individual. All men are born, and always remain, unfree and unequal, and consent is irrelevant to political association. Political society is also universal, for there are no humans who are not descended from Adam. A prepolitical state of nature makes no sense at all, nor does any idea of a contract to replace such a condition by political society. Property as well as political power is distributed according to God's patriarchal decrees and belongs absolutely to the person who inherits it or to whom it has been given.

These social and political doctrines are original only in the sense that Filmer combined together many positions held by his predecessors, notably those of the French legal theorist Jean Bodin, those of the bishops of the Anglican Church, and especially those of its royal head, King James I. These views are acceptable only to a naively fundamentalist believer in the Christian scriptures, and Locke had no difficulty in demolishing all the "glib nonsense," as he called it, about the kingship of Adam and its descent to the Stuart kings, to the usurper Oliver Cromwell, to any man or group lucky enough to seize power. Nevertheless, there was rather more to Filmer's "rope of sand" than Locke wished to admit, and in Filmer's shrewd remarks about the historical absurdities of a state of nature and in his very acute analysis of majority rule he raised difficulties that Locke never satisfactorily overcame.

Filmer demanded to know how an assembly convened for the purpose of making a universal contract could ever proceed to a valid vote of everyone with the right to vote. There would be bound to be absentees, and when it came to original multitudes voting to set up a government, the rights of some individuals would inevitably be overrun. What about servants, women, children, and the sick? Locke blandly responded by dogmatically asserting that in "one Body Politick the Majority have the Right to act and conclude the rest" (*Second Treatise,* 95). Filmer's doctrine of property seems to have impelled Locke into the formulation of the labor theory

of value, with all its enormous consequences in social thinking.

Filmer's doctrines by no means disappeared with the Glorious Revolution of 1688 and the victory of Lockean rationalism. His arguments were persuasively restated by Jonathan Boucher in championship of the Tories at the American Revolution, and again by George Fitzhugh in defense of the South in the 1850s. Filmer remains the most valuable literary source for traditional European preindustrial patriarchal political attitudes.

See also Aristotle; Bodin, Jean; Determinism, A Historical Survey; Grotius, Hugo; Hobbes, Thomas; Ideology; Locke, John; Milton, John; Political Philosophy, History of; Political Philosophy, Nature of; Social Contract.

Bibliography

PRIMARY WORK

Patriarcha and Other Writings. Edited by Johann P. Somerville. Cambridge, U.K.: Cambridge University Press, 1991.

SECONDARY WORKS

Daly, James. *Sir Robert Filmer and English Political Thought.* Toronto: University of Toronto Press, 1979.

Fitzhugh, George. *Cannibals All, or, Slaves without Masters.* Edited by C. Vann Woodward. Cambridge, MA: Belknap Press, 1960.

Laslett, Peter, ed. *Patriarcha and the Other Political Works of Sir Robert Filmer.* Oxford: Blackwell, 1949.

Schochet, Gordon J. *Patriarchalism in Political Thought.* New York: Basic, 1975.

Peter Laslett (1967)
Bibliography updated by Philip Reed (2005)

FINK, EUGEN
(1905–1975)

Eugen Fink was born and first educated in Konstanz, where his reading in philosophic classics (Giordano Bruno, Kant, and Nietzsche) began in the Gymnasium. He took up the formal study of philosophy at Freiburg in 1925 during a period of extraordinary richness: Edmund Husserl, in the chair previously held by Wilhelm Windelband and Heinrich Rickert, was at his peak in both philosophic labor and renown when he retired in 1928; he was succeeded by Martin Heidegger—Husserl's own choice—after several years at Marburg. Fink's dissertation under Husserl was completed in December 1929 with Heidegger as coevaluator (*Korreferent*), at a point in time when a long-smoldering break between Husserl and Heidegger was fully manifest.

On Husserl's retirement he chose Fink as second research assistant, alongside Ludwig Landgrebe—who had been Husserl's assistant since 1923. As Landgrebe turned to his Habilitation, he relinquished his assistantship with Husserl (March 1930), and Fink, who was just then entering more closely into Husserl's regimen of work, became not only sole assistant with Husserl in his retirement, but indispensable. Their daily walks in the hillside park near Husserl's residence and the tasks Husserl had Fink take up in furthering and consolidating Husserl's manuscript studies made for a unique philosophic collaboration. Husserl drove himself to produce manuscript after manuscript in an effort to present new work to the public to demonstrate the breadth, solidity, and relevance of his phenomenology in the face of Heidegger's ascendancy, and Fink worked at projects of integration, critique, and recasting so as to bring Husserl's massive output to coherence and philosophic clarity. In particular, he was able—as Husserl was not—to come to terms in phenomenology with Heidegger's thinking, along with that of others such as Hegel and Nietzsche, who had not really figured into Husserl's consideration. At the same time, Fink worked on writings that would counter two misperceptions: that transcendental phenomenology was a brand of idealism not much different from neo-Kantianism, and that Husserl's logic-driven abstractness was incapable of dealing with the existential trenchancy of actual life in the world.

Fink's essay in *Kantstudien* (1933), "The Phenomenological Philosophy of Edmund Husserl and Contemporary Criticism" (Elveton 2003), attempted to counter the first misperception, and was widely influential upon the French grasp of Husserl's phenomenology, most notably in the work of Gaston Berger and Maurice Merleau-Ponty. Unfortunately National Socialism's taking power in January of 1933 cut short Fink's providing a similar defense against the second misperception, influentially expressed in Georg Misch's *Lebensphilosophie und Phänomenologie: eine Auseinandersetzung der Diltheyschen Richtung mit Heidegger und Husserl* (1931). At the same time, Fink's Habilitation project, "Sixth Cartesian Meditation: The Idea of a Transcendental Theory of Method," was prevented from being pursued in that it purveyed "Jewish" philosophy, namely Husserl's. Fink recounts that, as he was not of Jewish background, Nazi authorities tried to get him to abandon his work

with Husserl. He would not, and as a result lost all prospects for an academic future in Germany. He remained with Husserl until Husserl's death in April 1938. During that time he managed to get but two articles published, the *Kantstudien* essay, appearing just as that journal was being "coordinated" to Nazi policy, and "What Does the Phenomenology of Edmund Husserl Want to Accomplish?" in *Die Tatwelt* (1934), a cultural review edited by one of the few resistance circles in Freiburg around the well-known political economist Walter Eucken. It was only in 1939, after Fink emigrated to Belgium subsequent to Husserl's death, that he was again able to publish his work; but that was not to last long.

Nevertheless, it was Fink's contribution to the ongoing final development of Husserl's phenomenological program that must be noted. The unpublished "Sixth Meditation" was read and reread by Husserl, bringing home to him the need to be theoretically self-critical about the status and character of transcendental assertions. More concretely, Fink's drafts of projects he was involved in with Husserl—paradigmatically exemplified in the two-volume German edition of the "Sixth Meditation" (Fink 1988)—showed how earlier formulations of transcendental phenomenology needed radical recasting in order for their philosophic sense to stand forth in coherence and relevance. Here one can see Fink's ability both to develop an integrative perspective on Husserl's work and to make the critical moves that would express the philosophic core of transcendental phenomenology, an ability for which Husserl valued Fink's "cophilosophizing" so highly.

Upon Husserl's death in 1938, the visit of the Belgian Franciscan, Herman Leo Van Breda, in search of materials for his dissertation, led to Van Breda's finding a way to move out of Germany all Husserl's manuscripts as well as his entire library. Van Breda also arranged for Malvine Husserl, now widowed, as well as Fink and Landgrebe, to emigrate to Louvain. This was accomplished by the spring of 1939, and the Husserl Archives were born; and, as it happened, Maurice Merleau-Ponty became the first visitor to consult Husserl's manuscript materials in its new home at the University of Louvain (April 1–6, 1939). Here Fink finally began university lecturing, and the work of transcribing and interpreting Husserl's shorthand manuscripts began anew, only to be ended in May 1940 with Germany's attack upon the Low Countries and the onset of a Europe-wide world war. By the end of that year, Fink and Landgrebe were back in Germany, excluded from university involvement.

After the war's end in 1946 Fink was given a beginner's position as lecturer at Freiburg University, and in 1948 finally took up there a newly established chair in *Philosophie und Erziehungswissenschaft*. Fink's work after the war was unlike that of others influenced by Husserl. Rather than explicate Husserl's writings, in the books of his own thinking he turned to developing the dimension of the phenomenological program that he found Husserl had left too implicit and unrealized, what he termed the "speculative" component of the program, the overarching philosophical sense of its findings (Fink 1957, 1958, 1960). He did, however, occasionally present essays on Husserl (Fink 1976) that were highly respected and accorded high authority—given his intimacy with Husserl's thinking; but these papers stood in some contrast to dominant interpretations other scholars made of phenomenology. Ultimately in his writings and lecturing Fink dedicated himself to ways of awakening listeners to philosophical questioning. Rather than establishing definitive theses, it was the ever-increasing radicality of realizing what lay in philosophical problems, what was at issue in them, that mattered most. He kept apart from the various postwar philosophical currents and avoided fostering a following of disciples. Heidegger was one who especially appreciated discussions with him, and his closest philosophical comrade was Jan Patočka, of unique renown and importance for his underground seminars in Prague under Communist rule.

See also Husserl, Edmund; Phenomenology.

Bibliography

WORKS BY FINK, INCLUDING THE ONLY TRANSLATIONS OF HIS WRITINGS INTO ENGLISH

VI. Cartesianische Meditation, Teil 1: Die Idee einer transzendentalen Methodenlehre, edited by Hans Ebeling, Jann Holl, and Guy van Kerckhoven. *Teil 2: Ergänzungsband*, edited by Guy van Kerckhoven, Husserliana Dokumenta II/1-2, Dordrecht: Kluwer, 1988.

Sixth Cartesian Meditation: The Idea of a Transcendental Theory of Method. Translated by Ronald Bruzina. Bloomington: Indiana University Press, 1995.

Nähe und Distanz: Phänomenolgische Vorträge und Aufsätze, edited by Franz-Anton Schwarz. Freiburg, Germany: Karl Alber, 1976.

"Operative Concepts in Husserl's Phenomenology." Translated by William McKenna. In *A priori and World: European Contributions to Husserlian Phenomenology*, edited by William McKenna, Robert M. Harlan, and Laurence E. Winters. The Hague: Martinus Nijhoff, 1981.

Sein, Wahrheit, Welt: Vor-Fragen zum Problem des Phänomen-Begriffs. The Hague: Martinus Nijhoff, 1958.

Spiel als Weltsymbol. Stuttgart: W. Kohlammer, 1960.

"The Phenomenological Philosophy of Edmund Husserl and Contemporary Criticism." In *The Phenomenology of Husserl, Selected Critical Readings*, edited by Roy Elveton. Chicago: Quadrangle Books, 2003.

"The Problem of the Phenomenology of Edmund Husserl." Translated by Robert M. Harlan. In *A Priori and World: European Contributions to Husserlian Phenomenology*, edited by William McKenna, Robert M. Harlan, and Laurence E. Winters. The Hague: Martinus Nijhoff, 1981.

"What Does the Phenomenology of Edmund Husserl Want to Accomplish?" Translated by Arthur Grugan. *Research in Phenomenology* 7 (1972): 5–27.

Zur Ontologischen Frühgeschichte von Raum-Zeit-Bewegung. The Hague: Martinus Nijhoff, 1957.

Ronald Bruzina (2005)

FIRST-ORDER LOGIC

First-order logic is a bag of tools for studying the validity of arguments. At base it consists of a family of mathematically defined languages called *first-order languages*. Because these languages are constructed to be "logically perfect" (in Gottlob Frege's phrase), we can guarantee from their grammatical form that certain arguments written in these languages are valid. Separately from this we can study how arguments in English or any other natural language can be translated into an appropriate first-order language. It was Gottfried Wilhelm Leibniz who in the 1680s first proposed to divide the study of arguments into a mathematical part and a translational part, though his notion of mathematical languages was barely adequate for the purpose. First-order languages first came to light in the work of Charles S. Peirce in the 1880s; his name for them was "first-intentional logic of relatives." It took some time to develop a satisfactory mathematical description of these languages. David Hilbert achieved this in his lectures at Göttingen in 1917–1922, which appeared in an edited form in his book *Grundzüge der Theoretischen Logik* with Wilhelm Ackermann. Many logicians reckon that the appearance of this book in 1928 marked the true birth of first-order logic.

LOGIC AND ARGUMENTS

For purposes of this article an argument consists of one or more sentences of English, then the word "Therefore," and then a sentence. The sentences before "Therefore" are called the *premises* of the argument and the sentence at the end is called its *conclusion*. We say that the argument is *valid* if the conclusion follows from the premises, and *invalid* otherwise. Logic is the study of valid arguments. Typical questions of logic are: Which arguments are valid and which are invalid? How can we construct valid arguments?

We shall study these questions with the help of first-order languages. First-order languages differ from natural languages in several ways. One is that their vocabulary and grammar are precisely defined. A second and equally important difference is that they contain expressions that we can interpret in a range of possible ways, and the range is determined by the grammatical form of the expressions.

Take for example the first-order sentence

(1) $\qquad\qquad \forall x\,(P(x) \to Q(x)).$

The part in brackets,

(2) $\qquad\qquad (P(x) \to Q(x)),$

is read "If $P(x)$ then $Q(x)$" and for the moment we can read "$\forall x$" as "Whatever x may be." Here there is no object named "x." Rather, "x" is a variable ranging over a class of possible objects. We call this class the *domain of quantification*, or more briefly the *domain*. The domain is not supplied with the sentence itself; when somebody uses the sentence to make a statement, we have to be told what domain the user of the sentence intended.

We also have to be told how the expressions "$P(x)$" and "$Q(x)$" are interpreted. For the whole sentence (1) to make sense, each of these expressions must translate into a *predicate*, that is, an English sentence with the variable "x" standing where we could have put a name; for example

(3) $\qquad\qquad x$ is a town in Italy.

(4) $\qquad\qquad$ The number $5 + 3$ is equal to x.

(5) $\qquad\qquad$ The father of x is a pianist.

But there is a further requirement. It must be possible to paraphrase the predicate into the form

(6) $\qquad\qquad x$ is a member of S

where S names a particular class of objects in the domain. For example the sentences (3)–(5) paraphrase as follows:

(3)' x is a member of the class of towns in Italy.

(4)' x is a member of the class of numbers that $5 + 3$ is equal to.

(5)' x is a member of the class of individuals whose fathers are pianists.

To see why this restriction is needed, consider my father-in-law Marcus Ward, who was born on July 4th. He used to reason:

(7) Americans celebrate July 4th. July 4th is the birthday of Marcus Ward. Therefore: Americans celebrate the birthday of Marcus Ward.

This conclusion gave him constant pleasure. Unfortunately the argument is unsound. The predicate

(8) $\qquad\qquad$ Americans celebrate x

allows two paraphrases into class form:

(9) x is in the class of events celebrated by Americans.

(10) x is in the class of days of the year celebrated by Americans.

On the first paraphrase, the second premise of the argument breaks down; the event that the Americans celebrate is not Marcus Ward's birthday. On the second paraphrase, the conclusion holds but not in the sense that pleased my father-in-law. Requiring a translation into classes is very effective for detecting ambiguities in arguments.

Returning to the sentence (1) we can interpret "$P(x)$" and "$Q(x)$" by saying what the classes in question are. So in an obvious notation, here is an interpretation of the first-order sentence above:

(11)

domain	the class of people now living
P	the class of pianists
Q	the class of musicians

On this interpretation the sentence (1) expresses that among all people now living, the pianists are musicians. Under this interpretation the sentence is true. Another possible interpretation is

(12)

domain	the class of people now living
P	the class of musicians
Q	the class of pianists

Under this second interpretation the sentence (1) is false; there are musicians who are not pianists. A crucial fact about first-order languages is that their sentences may change from true to false, or vice versa, when their interpretation is changed.

There are many first-order languages. Their common core consists of the following symbols, known as the *logical symbols*.

(13) symbol	¬	∧	∨	→
read as	'not'	'and'	'or'	'if…then'
alternative	~	&		⊃

(symbol)	↔	∀x	∃x	=
(read as)	'if and only if'	'for all x'	'there is x'	'equals'
(alternative)	≡	(x), ∧x	(Ex), ∨x	

The third row of the table lists the commonest alternative notations, though in this entry we will use only the symbols on the top row.

Besides the logical symbols, each first-order language has its own collection of *nonlogical symbols*, sometimes known as *primitives*. These are symbols such as "P" and "Q" above. The nonlogical symbols need to be interpreted, and the language carries a rule specifying what kinds of interpretation are allowed. The set of all nonlogical symbols of a language, together with the information what kinds of interpretation are allowed, is called the *signature* of the language. An *interpretation* of the language consists of a domain and allowed interpretations of all the symbols in the signature of the language.

Below we shall see what kinds of nonlogical symbol a first-order language can have. But before we do that, we shall define a notion that brings us back to the difference between valid and invalid arguments.

Suppose L is a first-order language and $\phi_1, \ldots, \phi_n, \psi$ are sentences of L. Then the expression

(14) $$\phi_1, \ldots, \phi_n \models \psi$$

means that if I is any interpretation of L and all of $\phi_1, \ldots, \phi_n$ are true under I, then ψ is also true under I. We call the expression (14) a *semantic sequent*, or for short a *sequent*. We say that (14) is *valid* if it is true, and *invalid* otherwise. The sentences $\phi_1, \ldots, \phi_n$ are called the *premises* of the sequent, and ψ is called its *conclusion*.

An example of a valid sequent, using the kinds of symbol that we have already seen, is

(15) $$\forall x(P(x) \to Q(x)), \forall x(Q(x) \to R(x)) \models$$
$$\forall x(P(x) \to R(x)).$$

In any interpretation I, the first sentence of (15) expresses that the class assigned to "P" is a subclass of the class

assigned to "Q," and the second sentence expresses that the class assigned to "Q" is a subclass of the class assigned to "R." If these two sentences are true then it follows that the class assigned to "P" is a subclass of the class assigned to "R," and hence the conclusion of (15) is true under interpretation I. So (15) is valid.

Now suppose we have an argument written or spoken in English. Suppose also that we can find a suitable first-order language L, sentences $\phi_1, \ldots, \phi_n$ of L and an interpretation I of L, such that under the interpretation I the sentences $\phi_1, \ldots, \phi_n$ are translations of the premises of the English argument and ψ is a translation of its conclusion. Suppose finally that we have a proof that

(16) $$\phi_1, \ldots, \phi_n \models \psi.$$

is a valid sequent. Then via the translation from English to L our proof shows that if the premises of the argument are true, its conclusion must also be true. In short we have shown that the English argument is valid.

The following example appears as an exercise in Richard Whately's logic textbook of 1826:

(17) A negro is a man; therefore he who murders a negro murders a man.

This argument seems to defy the logical tools available in 1826; in fact some years later Augustus De Morgan challenged the logicians of his age to develop a logic that does recognize such arguments. There is no record of how Whately expected his students to solve (17), but at least for first-order logic it is straightforward. The main step is to introduce symbols whose interpretations are predicates with two variables:

(18) domain	the class of living beings (for example)
$N(x)$	x is a negro
$M(x)$	x is a man
$R(x, y)$	x murders y

(We need the variables on the left side of (18) to distinguish between "x murders y" and "y murders x.") Again we insist that there is a translation into classes. For example we can paraphrase "x murders y" by

(19) The pair of objects (x,y) lies in the class of all ordered pairs of objects such that the first murders the second.

Classes of this kind, whose members are ordered pairs, are called *relations*. Now Whately's argument translates into first-order sentences as follows:

(20) $\forall x(N(x) \rightarrow M(x)) \vDash \forall x(\exists y(N(y) \wedge R(x,y)) \rightarrow \exists y(M(y) \wedge R(x,y)))$.

Here the premise has a form that we have already considered. We can read "$\exists y$" as "There is something, call it y, such that," and we can read "$\wedge$" as "and." So the conclusion says: For every living being x, if there is a negro y such that x murders y, then there is a man y such that x murders y. Now one can show that under every interpretation if the premise of (20) is true then the conclusion is true. So Whately's argument is valid.

If we fail to find a translation of an English argument into a valid first-order sequent, this does not prove that the original argument was invalid. It could be that the argument is valid but a more powerful language than first-order is needed to show this. It could be that there is a suitable first-order sequent but we simply failed to find it.

PROPOSITIONAL LOGIC

Before we define the languages of first-order logic, we should examine a simpler logic called *propositional logic* or *sentential logic*. It uses the symbols $\neg$, $\wedge$, $\vee$, $\rightarrow$ and $\leftrightarrow$ but not $\forall$ or $\exists$ or $=$.

In "classical" propositional logic we consider meaningful sentences that are either true or false. We say that their *truth value* is Truth (T for short) if they are true, and Falsehood (F for short) if they are false. There are also "many-valued" propositional logics that allow three or more truth values; we shall not consider these.

If ϕ is any sentence, we can form a new sentence $\neg\phi$ by writing the negation sign "$\neg$" immediately in front of ϕ. We stipulate that $\neg\phi$ is true if ϕ is false, and false if ϕ is true. For example

(21) $\neg$ Today is Tuesday.

expresses

(22) It is not true that today is Tuesday.

We read the symbol "$\neg$" as "not," and $\neg\phi$ is called the *negation* of ϕ. Likewise if ϕ and ψ are sentences, we can form a sentence $(\phi \wedge \psi)$, and we stipulate that $(\phi \wedge \psi)$ is true if and only if both ϕ and ψ are true. For example we can form

(23) (Today is Tuesday $\wedge$ The paper is not yet finished),

and this sentence expresses

(24) Today is Tuesday and the paper is not yet finished.

The sentence $(\phi \wedge \psi)$ is called the *conjunction* of ϕ and ψ, and the sentences ϕ and ψ are its *conjuncts*. We read the symbol "$\wedge$" as 'and.'

The remaining logical symbols of propositional logic have similar explanations. They all form new sentences from old ones, and in each case we stipulate the truth value of the new sentence in terms of the truth values of the old ones. The following table records these stipulations:

(25)	ϕ	ψ	$\neg\phi$	$(\phi \wedge \psi)$	$(\phi \vee \psi)$	$(\phi \rightarrow \psi)$	$(\phi \leftrightarrow \psi)$
(i)	T	T	F	T	T	T	T
(ii)	T	F		F	T	F	F
(iii)	F	T	T	F	T	T	F
(iv)	F	F		F	F	T	T

We read the table as follows. Suppose for example that ϕ is the sentence "Today is Tuesday" and ψ is the sentence "The paper is not yet finished." If ϕ is true and ψ is false, then we are in row (ii) of the table. In this row there is F below $(\phi \wedge \psi)$, and this tells us that the sentence

(26) (Today is Tuesday $\wedge$ The paper is not yet finished)

is false. Likewise for the other rows and formulas.

We call $(\phi \vee \psi)$ the *disjunction* of ϕ and ψ; the sentences ϕ and ψ are its *disjuncts*. The symbol '$\vee$' can be read as 'or.' But notice that $(\phi \vee \psi)$ is true when both ϕ and ψ are true; so in some circumstances a safer reading of $(\phi \vee \psi)$ is 'Either ϕ or ψ, or both.'

The symbol "$\leftrightarrow$" can be read safely as "if and only if."

There remains the symbol "$\rightarrow$," sometimes known as *material implication*. The one case where $(\phi \rightarrow \psi)$ is false is where ϕ is true and ψ is false, and this suggests reading $(\phi \rightarrow \psi)$ as "If ϕ then ψ." In mathematical contexts this reading generally works well. But note that we also have T in the bottom two rows of the table below $(\phi \rightarrow \psi)$, so that this sentence counts as true whenever ϕ is false, whether or not there is any connection between ϕ and ψ. For example the following sentence is true on any day of the week:

(27) (Three plus three is two $\rightarrow$ Today is Tuesday)

Likewise $(\phi \to \psi)$ is true whenever ψ is true, and so the following sentence is also true on any day of the week:

(28)   (Today is Tuesday $\to$ Three plus three is six)

These properties of " $\to$ " are sometimes referred to as the *paradoxes of material implication*—though really they are not so much paradoxes as puzzles about how to translate " $\to$ " into English.

The symbols "$\neg$," "$\wedge$," "$\vee$," "$\to$," and "$\leftrightarrow$" are known as the *propositional operators*. We can build up complex sentences by using the propositional operators any number of times. But first it is helpful to introduce so-called *propositional symbols*

(29) $p, q, r, p_0, p_1, p_2, \ldots$

which can stand as abbreviations of any sentence. Thus we can form sentences

(30) $\neg p, ((p \to q) \wedge r), (p \vee \neg q), \neg\neg p_2$

and so on. The *sentences of propositional logic* are the propositional symbols and all the complex sentences that can be built up from them using the propositional operators. The table (25) tells us when each of these sentences is true, as soon as we know what truth values to assign to the propositional symbols in them. Take $((p \to q) \wedge r)$, for example. It uses three propositional symbols. Each of these three symbols could stand for a true sentence or a false one, and so there are eight possible cases that we can list as follows.

(31)

p	q	r
T	T	T
T	T	F
T	F	T
T	F	F
F	T	T
F	T	F
F	F	T
F	F	F

For each row we can evaluate the truth value of $((p \to q) \wedge r)$ by starting at the propositional symbols and working

upwards to more complex sentences, reading values from the table (25). Thus:

(32)

p	q	r	$($	$(p$	$\to$	q	$\wedge$	$r)$
T	T	T		T	T	T	T	T
T	T	F		T	T	T	F	F
T	F	T		T	F	F	F	T
T	F	F		T	F	F	F	F
F	T	T		F	T	T	T	T
F	T	F		F	T	T	F	F
F	F	T		F	T	F	T	T
F	F	F		T	T	F	F	F
				(i)	(iv)	(ii)	(v)	(iii)

On the right the columns below the propositional symbols copy the truth values from the left side of the table. The column below a propositional operator gives the truth values of the sentence formed by introducing this operator; for example the table below " $\to$ " gives the truth values of $(p \to q)$. The numbers at the bottom of the table show a possible order for working out the columns. The final column calculated, number (v), gives the truth value of the whole sentence in each of the eight cases listed on the left. The table

(33)

p	q	r	$((p \to q) \wedge r)$
T	T	T	T
T	T	F	F
T	F	T	F
T	F	F	F
F	T	T	T
F	T	F	F
F	F	T	T
F	F	F	F

is called the *truth table* of the sentence $((p \rightarrow q) \wedge r)$.

We say that a sentence of propositional logic is a *tautology* if its truth table has T in every row, and a *contradiction* if its truth table has F in every row.

Suppose ϕ is a tautology and suppose also that we replace each propositional symbol in ϕ by an English sentence (the same English sentence for each occurrence of the same propositional symbol), creating a sentence S. Then S must be true since the truth values of the English sentences will indicate a particular row of the truth table, and we know that the value in this row must be T since ϕ has T in every row. Generally S will be a mixture of English and propositional operators. But we can translate S into a sentence S' of English, for example translating the propositional operators as suggested above but with due caution. Since S' is a translation of S, it has the same truth value, and we saw that this value has to be Truth. In short S' will be a necessary truth in English.

Here are some tautologies.

(34) $((p \wedge q) \rightarrow p)$

$((p \wedge q) \rightarrow q)$

$(p \rightarrow (p \vee q))$

$(q \rightarrow (p \vee q))$

$(p \rightarrow (q \rightarrow p))$

$((p \rightarrow q) \rightarrow ((q \rightarrow r) \rightarrow (p \rightarrow r)))$.

$(((p \rightarrow q) \wedge p) \rightarrow q)$

$((p \leftrightarrow q) \rightarrow (p \rightarrow q))$

$(\neg\neg p \rightarrow p)$

$((p \wedge \neg p) \rightarrow q)$

$(((p \rightarrow q) \rightarrow p) \rightarrow p)$

A possible translation of the first of these tautologies into English is "If the light is broken and the switch is on, the light is broken." This sentence has to be true in any situation in which each of the sentences "The light is broken" and "The switch is on" has a truth value, regardless of what these truth values are.

Suppose ϕ, ψ and χ are sentences of propositional logic. As above, the expression

(35) $$\phi, \psi \vDash \chi$$

is called a (semantic) *sequent*. We say that it is *valid* if in every case where ϕ and ψ are true, χ is also true. It's easy to calculate from the truth tables of ϕ, ψ and χ whether or not the sequent (35) is valid. As with tautologies we can

translate the sentences ϕ, ψ and χ simultaneously into sentences of English, by choosing sentences to replace the propositional symbols and then paraphrasing to remove the propositional operators. The result is an English argument, if we write "Therefore" in place of $\vDash$. Suppose we have a proof that the sequent (35) is valid (for example, by truth tables). Then this proof shows that if the premises of the English argument are true, its conclusion must be true too. In this way we justify the English argument.

For example we can justify the English argument

(36) If sending abusive e-mails is an offense, then Smith has just committed an offense. Sending abusive e-mails is an offense. Therefore: Smith has just committed an offence.

by proving that the following sequent is valid:

(37) $$(p \rightarrow q), p \vDash q$$

In fact it is valid, as truth tables quickly show. Since this sequent corresponds to indefinitely many other English arguments too, we should think of it as a rule of argument rather than an argument in itself. Logicians sometimes express this point by saying that in logic we study forms of argument rather than individual arguments.

TRANSLATING BETWEEN ENGLISH AND FIRST-ORDER LOGIC

Translations from first-order logic to English are generally straightforward; the problem is to make the English version digestible. But for assessing English arguments we need translation in the other direction, and this can be hazardous.

NOUN PHRASES. Proper names with singular meaning can go over into constants. For example the interpretation

(38)

a	the Pyrenees range
b	France
c	Spain
$R(x_1, x_2, x_3)$	x_1 is between x_2 and x_3

(with any suitable domain supplied) allows us to make the translation

(39)   The Pyrenees lie between France and Spain.

$$R(a, b, c)$$

Complex singular noun phrases such as "my father" are in general more complicated to translate. In first-order logic we are allowed to use function symbols, as F in the interpretation and translation

(40)

a	Lloyd George
b	me
$F(x_1)$	the father of x_1
$R(x_1, x_2)$	x_1 knew x_2

(41)   Lloyd George knew my father.

$$R(a, F(b))$$

But there is a catch. The requirement that first-order languages should be "logically perfect" implies that if "a" names any element of the domain of an interpretation, the expression $F(a)$ should also name an element of the domain. So the domain to be supplied for (40) above must contain not only me but my father, my father's father, my father's father's father, and so on. Worse still, to adapt an example from Frege, if for any reason the domain contains the moon, it must also contain the father of the moon!

For such reasons, one hardly ever meets function symbols in first-order logic outside mathematical contexts. Even there caution is needed. For example in studying number fields one would like to have a "multiplicative inverse" function taking 2 to 1/2, 3 to 1/3, and so on; but 1/0 is undefined.

A common solution is to use, instead of a function symbol, a relation symbol with one more argument place:

(42)

a	Lloyd George
b	me
$P(x_1, x_2)$	x_1 the father of x_2
$R(x_1, x_2)$	x_1 knew x_2

(43)   Lloyd George knew my father.

$$\exists x(P(x, b) \land R(a, x))$$

This raises a further problem: If the implication that I have exactly one father plays any role in an argument using this sentence, then our translation by (42) fails to convey this implication. Here we need to call in Bertrand Russell's analysis of definite descriptions.

According to Russell's analysis, a sentence of the form "The X is a Y" paraphrases as

(44) At least one thing is an X, at most one thing is an X, and everything that is an X is a Y.

We can translate this directly into first-order symbols, but the following paraphrase is neater:

(45) $\exists z(\forall x\,(x \text{ is an X} \leftrightarrow x = z) \land z \text{ is a Y}).$

A major problem with Russell's analysis is that it assumes we can choose the domain of the interpretation in such a way that it contains a unique x. But there are other requirements on the domain; all the quantifiers in the first-order sentence range over it. These requirements may clash. In everyday English we use the phrase "the X" in situations in which there is one "salient" X (see for example David Lewis), and to do justice to this in a first-order translation we need to make explicit what makes a certain individual "salient."

NOUN PHRASES THAT CONTAIN QUANTIFIER WORDS LIKE "EVERY." We can handle some cases by paraphrasing:

(46)

P	the class of prime numbers greater than two
Q	the class of odd numbers

(47) Every prime number greater than two is odd.

Every object, if it is a prime number greater than two, is an odd number.

$$\forall x(P(x) \rightarrow Q(x))$$

(48) Some prime numbers greater than two are odd.

$$\exists x(P(x) \land Q(x)).$$

If we wanted "some" to imply "more than one" in this example, we would need a longer paraphrase using " = ":

(49) $\exists x \exists y(P(x) \land Q(x) \land P(y) \land Q(y) \land x \neq y)$

("$x \neq y$" is a standard abbreviation for "$\neg(x = y)$.") Likewise we can express that there are at least three odd numbers:

(50) $\exists x_1 \exists x_2 \exists x_3 \ (x_1 \neq x_2 \wedge x_1 \neq x_3 \wedge x_2 \neq x_3 \wedge Q(x_1) \wedge$
$$Q(x_2) \wedge Q(x_3))$$

Using " = " in analogous ways, first-order logic is equipped to express things like "There are exactly ten million Xs."

CONDITIONALS. The nub of the paradoxes of material implication may be that in real life as opposed to mathematics, sentences play many roles besides being true or false. Paul Grice argued that when we make the appropriate distinction between "what is said" and "what is implicated," there remains no difference in meaning between 'If ϕ then ψ' and ($\phi \rightarrow \psi$). On the other side, Dorothy Edgington pointed out that

(51) $$((p \rightarrow q) \vee (\neg p \rightarrow q))$$

is a tautology, and drew the following consequence of reading " $\rightarrow$ " as "If … then":

(52) … if I reject the conditional "If the Conservatives lose, Thatcher [the leader of the Conservative party] will resign," I am committed to accepting "If the Conservatives win, Thatcher will resign"!

She found this consequence implausible.

ADVERBS. Consider the argument

(53) Nadia accidentally poisoned her father. Therefore: Nadia poisoned her father.

The obvious first-order translations of "Nadia poisoned her father" don't allow us to add further information like "accidentally" or "last Wednesday" or "with strychnine." Peirce in 1892 suggested a way around this problem, namely to talk explicitly about actions. Thus:

(54)

n	Nadia
f	Nadia's father
$A(x_1, x_2)$	x_1 is an action that was performed by x_2
$P(x_1, x_2)$	x_1 is an action of poisoning x_2
$U(x_1)$	x_1 is accidental

(55) $\exists x \ (A(x,n) \wedge P(x,f) \wedge U(x)) \models \exists x \ (A(x,n) \wedge P(x,f))$

Donald Davidson and others have independently revived Peirce's suggestion in connection with the semantics of natural languages.

Peirce comments that his translation consists in "catching one of the transient elements of thought upon the wing and converting it into one of the resting places of the mind." This is more than idle whimsy. Peirce's point is that in order to formalize arguments like (53), we sometimes need to introduce abstract objects—in his case, actions—into the domain.

A different kind of example to illustrate Peirce's point is the sentence

(56) For every drop of rain that falls a flower grows.

(George Boolos.) Taken literally, this statement implies that there at least as many flowers as raindrops. If we wanted to make this explicit in order to draw out consequences in an argument, we would need to incorporate some set-theoretic apparatus for talking about cardinalities.

Arguments about past, present and future are another example of the same general point. Since sentences of first-order logic lack tense, the normal way to handle such arguments in first-order logic is to add points of time (or sometimes intervals of time) to the domain. Then in general we need to add to the premises of an argument some basic facts about time, for example that the ordering of time into earlier and later is a linear ordering. (One can use the axioms for linear ordering, (76) below.)

NON-INDICATIVE SENTENCES. Sentences of first-order logic are all in the indicative. They are not designed for giving instructions or asking questions. One place where this matters is the formalization of mathematical reasoning. Mathematicians often use imperatives:

(57) "Draw a triangle ABC and consider the midpoint of the side AB."

"Assume there is a greatest prime."

"Let x be a number between 0 and 5."

First-order logic has no straightforward way of expressing these instructions. In 1926 Jan Łukasiewicz suggested we should regard such instructions as moves in a proof. For example the instruction "Assume ϕ" is an indication that we are going to prove the sequent (84) below by proving the sequent (83).

Most English sentences can be translated into first-order sentences in many different ways. The translation that we choose should be guided by the arguments that we are trying to formalize. Some philosophers have speculated that for each unambiguous English sentence S there is a first-order translation ϕ that expresses the correct analysis of S into its most primitive components. If we knew these translations we could use them to formalize in first-order sentences any valid argument in English. A difficulty with this thesis is that (as we saw) analyses of English sentences for the purpose of justifying arguments may need to bring in whole ontologies of abstract objects: Sets, actions, points of time and space. Some philosophers would add possible worlds.

Most of the starred textbooks in the bibliography below give further advice about translating from English into first-order sentences.

FIRST-ORDER SYNTAX

The signature of a first-order language consists of symbols of four kinds, though not every first-order language has all four kinds. The kinds are as follows:

(i) *Propositional symbols* as in section "Propositional Logic."

(ii) *Relation symbols*, usually

$$P, Q, R, R_0, R_1, R_2, \dots.$$

(iii) *Individual constant symbols*, or more briefly *constants*, usually

$$a, b, c, c_0, c_1, c_2, \dots.$$

(iv) *Function symbols*, usually symbols such as

$$F, G, H, F_0, F_1, F_2, \dots.$$

Each relation symbol and each function symbol has an *arity*, which is a positive integer. One normally requires that no symbol occurs in more than one of these kinds, and that no relation or function symbol occurs with more than one arity. If a function or relation symbol has arity n, we describe the symbol as *n-ary*. *Binary* means 2-ary.

A first-order language also has an infinite set of symbols called *variables*. Variables are usually chosen as lower case letters near the end of the alphabet:

(58) $u, v, w, x, y, z, v_0, v_1, \dots.$

The variables are not in the signature.

Given any signature σ, we define a first-order language $L(\sigma)$ in terms of σ. We begin with the terms of $L(\sigma)$.

(a) Every constant of σ is a term of $L(\sigma)$.

(b) Every variable of L is a term of $L(\sigma)$.

(c) Suppose F is a function symbol of σ, n is the arity of F, and $t_1, \dots, t_n$ are terms of $L(\sigma)$. Then the expression

$$F(t_1, \dots, t_n)$$

is a term of $L(\sigma)$.

(d) $L(\sigma)$ has no terms except as given by (a)–(c).

This definition is an *inductive definition*. Clauses (a) and (b) together form its *base clause*; they say outright that certain expressions are terms. Clause (c) is the *inductive clause*; it says that if certain expressions are terms then certain other expressions are terms too. Clause (d) tells us that if t is a term of $L(\sigma)$ then t can be generated in a finite number of steps by using the base and inductive clauses.

A *metatheorem* of first-order logic is a theorem about first-order logic (as opposed to a theorem proved by means of first-order logic).

METATHEOREM 1 (UNIQUE PARSING OF TERMS). *If t is a term of $L(\sigma)$ then exactly one of the following holds:*

(1) t is a constant of σ.

(2) t is a variable.

(3) t is $F(t_1, \dots, t_n)$ where F is a function symbol of σ, n is the arity of F and $t_1, \dots, t_n$ are terms of $L(\sigma)$.

Moreover in case (3) if t is also $G(s_1, \dots, s_m)$ where G is a function symbol of σ and $s_1, \dots, s_m$ are terms of $L(\sigma)$, then F is G and n is m and t_1 is s_1 and $\dots$ and t_n is s_n.

See Stephen Kleene §17 for the proof. Thanks to unique parsing, we can distinguish three types of term. The first two types are the constants and the variables, and together they form the *atomic* terms of L. The third type of term consists of those of the form $F(t_1, \dots, t_n)$; these are said to be *compound* terms. Broadly speaking the terms of $L(\sigma)$ correspond grammatically to the singular definite noun phrases of a natural language.

The unique parsing lemma is used to justify certain types of definition and proof by induction. For example we can define, for each term t, the set $V(t)$ of variables that occur in t, as follows:

(a) If t is a constant then $V(t)$ is $\emptyset$ (the empty set).

(b) If t is a variable then $V(t)$ is the set $\{t\}$.

(c) If t is $F(t_1, \dots, t_n)$ then $V(t)$ is the union

$$V(t_1) \cup \dots \cup V(t_n).$$

(This is the set of objects that are in at least one of $V(t_1), \ldots, V(t_n)$.) We say that a term is *closed* if it contains no variables.

Along similar lines we can define $t(s_1, \ldots, x_n/v_1, \ldots, v_n)$, which is the term got by taking the term t and putting the term s_1 in place of each occurrence of the variable v_1 in t, s_2 in place of each occurrence of v_2 and so on; the replacements should be made simultaneously. For example if t is $F(x,G(y))$ and s is $G(z)$, then $t(s/x)$ is $F(G(z),G(y))$ and $t(y,t/x,y)$ is $F(y,G(F(x,G(y))))$.

Having defined the terms of $L(\sigma)$, we define the formulas of $L(\sigma)$ as follows.

(a) Every propositional symbol of σ is a formula of $L(\sigma)$.

(b) If R is a relation symbol of σ, n is the arity of R and $t_1, \ldots, t_n$ are terms of $L(\sigma)$, then the expression

$$R(t_1, \ldots, t_n)$$

is a formula of $L(\sigma)$.

(c) If s and t are terms of $L(\sigma)$ then the expression

$$(s = t)$$

is a formula of $L(\sigma)$.

(d) If ϕ is a formula of $L(\sigma)$ then the expression

$$\neg\phi$$

is a formula of $L(\sigma)$.

(e) If ϕ and ψ are formulas of $L(\sigma)$ then the four expressions

$$(\phi \wedge \psi), (\phi \vee \psi), (\phi \rightarrow \psi), (\phi \leftrightarrow \psi)$$

are formulas of $L(\sigma)$.

(f) If ϕ is a formula of $L(\sigma)$ and v is a variable of $L(\sigma)$, then the two expressions

$$\forall v\phi, \exists v\phi$$

are formulas of $L(\sigma)$. ($\forall v$ is called a *universal quantifier* and $\exists v$ is an *existential quantifier*.)

(g) Nothing is a formula of $L(\sigma)$ except as given by clauses (a)–(f) above.

The obvious counterpart to Metatheorem 1 is true for formulas. It allows us to say that a formula is *atomic* if it comes from clauses (a)–(c) and *compound* if has one of the forms described in clauses (d)–(f). Also no expression of $L(\sigma)$ is both a term and a formula.

The next definition will get its full motivation when we come to discuss satisfaction of formulas. Roughly speaking, a variable x can serve to name an object, unless it appears in one of the contexts "For all objects x, … x …" and "There is an object x such that … x …." (Here we recall that in first-order logic, 'for all objects x' is written $\forall x$ and "there is an object x such that" is written $\exists x$.) An occurrence of a variable in one of these contexts is said to be *bound*; an occurrence that is not bound is *free*. We say a variable is *free in* ϕ if it has a free occurrence in ϕ. A definition by induction of the set $FV(\phi)$ of variables free in the formula ϕ runs as follows:

(a) If ϕ is atomic then $FV(\phi)$ is the set of all variables that occur in ϕ.

(b) $FV(\neg\phi)$ is $FV(\phi)$.

(c) $FV((\phi \wedge \psi))$, $FV((\phi \vee \psi))$, $FV((\phi \rightarrow \psi))$ and $FV((\phi \leftrightarrow \psi))$ are all equal to

$$FV(\phi) \cup FV(\psi).$$

(d) If ϕ is a formula and v is a variable, then $FV(\forall v\phi)$ and $FV(\exists v \phi)$ are both the set

$$FV(\phi) \setminus \{v\}$$

of all the variables that are in $FV(\phi)$ and are not v.

A formula ϕ is said to be a *sentence* if $FV(\phi)$ is empty, in other words, if no variable is free in ϕ. For example $\forall x (P(x) \rightarrow Q(x))$ is a sentence, but $(P(x) \rightarrow Q(x))$ is not a sentence since x has two free occurrences in it.

Unique parsing also allows us to define by induction the *complexity* of a formula ϕ, comp(ϕ), as follows:

(1) If ϕ is an atomic formula then comp(ϕ) = 0.

(2) For every formula ϕ, comp($\neg\phi$) = comp(ϕ) + 1.

(3) If ϕ and ψ are formulas and n is the maximum of comp(ϕ) and comp(ψ), then comp($(\phi \wedge \psi)$), comp($(\phi \vee \psi)$), comp($(\phi \rightarrow \psi)$) and comp($(\phi \leftrightarrow \psi)$) are all equal to $n + 1$.

(4) If ϕ is a formula and v is a variable then comp($\forall v\phi$) = comp($\exists v\phi$) = comp(ϕ) + 1.

There is a similar definition for the complexity of terms. The chief use of complexity is in *proofs by induction on complexity*, which run as follows. We want to show that all formulas of a first-order language have a certain property P. So we show first that all atomic formulas have the property P, and then we show that for every positive integer n, if all formulas of complexity $<n$ have P then every formula of complexity n has P too.

One speaks of the *subformulas* of a formula ϕ in two senses. First a subformula of ϕ is a segment of ϕ that is a formula in its own right. Second a subformula of ϕ is a formula that occurs as a subformula of ϕ in the first sense. For example the formula $(P(x) \leftrightarrow P(x))$ has two subformulas of the form $P(x)$ in the first sense, but only one in the second sense. It is easy to give a formal definition of the set of subformulas of ϕ in the second sense, by induction on the complexity of ϕ. Metatheorem 12 below uses subformulas in the first sense.

There are several useful conventions about how to write first-order formulas. For example

(59) $$\phi \wedge \psi \wedge \chi$$

is strictly not a first-order formula, but we count it as an abbreviation of

(60) $$((\phi \wedge \psi) \wedge \chi).$$

In the same spirit the conjunction

(61) $$(\phi_1 \wedge \phi_2 \wedge \ldots \wedge \phi_n)$$

is an abbreviation for

(62) $$(\ldots(\phi_1 \wedge \phi_2) \wedge \ldots \wedge \phi_n),$$

and the disjunction

(63) $$(\phi_1 \vee \phi_2 \vee \ldots \vee \phi_n)$$

is an abbreviation for

(64) $$(\ldots(\phi_1 \vee \phi_2) \vee \ldots \vee \phi_n).$$

We count "$\wedge$" and "$\vee$" as binding tighter than "$\rightarrow$" or "$\leftrightarrow$," in the sense that

(65) $$(\phi \wedge \psi \leftrightarrow \chi), (\phi \rightarrow \psi \vee \chi)$$

are respectively abbreviations for

$$((\phi \wedge \psi) \leftrightarrow \chi), (\phi \rightarrow (\psi \vee \chi)).$$

Other useful abbreviations are

(66) $$(x \neq y) \text{ for } \neg(x = y),$$

$$\forall x_1 \ldots x_n \, \phi \text{ for } \forall x_1 \ldots \forall x_n \, \phi,$$

$$\exists x_1 \ldots x_n \, \phi \text{ for } \exists x_1 \ldots \exists x_n \, \phi.$$

Also we allow ourselves to leave out a pair of brackets when they stand at the opposite ends of a formula.

Another useful convention is based on mathematical notation for functions. If ϕ is a formula and all the variables free in ϕ are included in the list $v_1, \ldots, v_n$, we introduce ϕ as $\phi(v_1, \ldots, v_n)$. Then if $t_1, \ldots, t_n$ are terms, we write

(67) $$\phi(t_1, \ldots, t_n)$$

for $\phi(t_1, \ldots, t_n/v_1, \ldots, v_n)$, which is the result of putting t_i in place of each free occurrence of v_i in ϕ, simultaneously for all i from 1 to n. (We shall revise this definition later.)

INTERPRETATIONS OF FIRST-ORDER LANGUAGES

A first-order language is a language $L(\sigma)$ for some signature σ. The signature σ determines the language $L(\sigma)$, but equally if we know the formulas of $L(\sigma)$ we can recover σ. So if L is the language $L(\sigma)$, we could equally well say "formula of σ" or "formula of L." Likewise σ-structures, which we are about to define, can equally well be called L-structures.

We recall some set theory. If X is a set and n a positive integer, then an *n-tuple* from X is an ordered list $(a_1, \ldots, a_n)$ where $a_1, \ldots, a_n$ are members of X. We write X^n for the set of all n-tuples from X. An n-ary *relation* on X is a subset of X^n. An n-ary *function* on X is a function $f: X^n \rightarrow Y$, for some set Y, which assigns to each n-tuple $(a_1, \ldots, a_n)$ from X an element $f(a_1, \ldots, a_n)$ of Y.

Suppose σ is a signature. A σ-*structure* is a set-theoretic interpretation for the symbols in σ. More precisely a σ-structure A has the following ingredients:

(a) A set (usually required to be nonempty) which is the domain of a, in symbols dom (A).

(b) For each propositional symbol p of σ, a truth value (T or F) which we write as p_A.

(c) For each constant c of σ, an element c_A of dom (A).

(d) For each relation symbol R of σ, an n-ary relation R_A on dom $(A)^n$, where n is the arity of R.

(e) For each function symbol F of σ, an n-ary function $F_A: \text{dom}(A)^n \rightarrow \text{dom}(A)$, where n is the arity of F.

EXAMPLE 1 (ARITHMETIC AND ITS LANGUAGE). For talking about the natural numbers

(68) $$0, 1, 2, \ldots,$$

we use a first-order language called the *language of arithmetic*. Its signature $\sigma_{\mathbb{N}}$ consists of one constant symbol $\underline{0}$, two function symbols $+$ and $\cdot$ of arity 2, a function symbol S of arity 1 and a relation symbol $<$ of arity 2. The number structure $\mathbb{N}$ is the following $\sigma_{\mathbb{N}}$-structure. The domain is the set of natural numbers. The constant $\underline{0}$ stands for the number zero (i.e. , $\underline{0}_{\mathbb{N}} = 0$). The function symbols $+$ and $\cdot$ stand for addition and multiplication of natural numbers, and S stands for the function "plus one." The binary relation symbol $<$ stands for the relation "less than" (i.e. , $<_{\mathbb{N}}$ is the set of all ordered pairs of natural numbers (m, n) with $m < n$). Following normal mathematical usage we write $+ (x, y)$, $\cdot (x, y)$ and $< (x, y)$ as $x + y$, $x \cdot y$ and $x < y$ respectively.

The structure $\mathbb{N}$ interprets the closed terms of $L(\sigma_{\mathbb{N}})$ as names of numbers. For example the term $S(\underline{0})$ stands for the number 1, the term $S(S(\underline{0}))$ stands for the number 2, and so on; we write these terms as $\underline{0}, \underline{1}, \underline{2}$ and so on. Likewise the closed term $\underline{2} + \underline{3}$ names the number 5.

We can use our earlier explanations of the first-order symbols in order to read any sentence of $L(\sigma_{\mathbb{N}})$ as making a statement about $\mathbb{N}$. The following sentences are all true in $\mathbb{N}$:

(69)   PA1. $\forall x\ (Sx \neq \underline{0})$.

PA2. $\forall x \forall y\ (S(x) = S(y) \to x = y)$.

PA3. $\forall x\ (x + \underline{0} = x)$.

PA4. $\forall x \forall y\ (x + S(y) = S(x + y))$.

PA5. $\forall x\ (x \cdot \underline{0} = \underline{0})$.

PA6. $\forall x \forall y\ (x \cdot S(y) = (x \cdot y) + x)$.

PA7. $\forall x \neg (x < \underline{0})$.

PA8. $\forall x \forall y\ (x < Sy \leftrightarrow x < y \vee x = y)$.

The following *induction axiom* is also true in $\mathbb{N}$, though it is not a first-order sentence because the variable 'X' ranges over sets rather than numbers.

(70)   For every set X of numbers,
$((0 \in X) \wedge \forall x\ (x \in X \to S(x) \in X \to \forall x\ (x \in X))$.

Within $L(\sigma_{\mathbb{N}})$ the closest we can come to this axiom is to give a separate axiom for each set X defined by a first-order formula. Namely let $\phi(x, y_1, \ldots, y_n)$ be any formula of $L(\sigma_{\mathbb{N}})$. Then we write the sentence

(PA.9)

$\forall y_1 \ldots \forall y_n\ (\phi(\underline{0}, y_1, \ldots, y_n)$
$\qquad \wedge \forall x\ (\phi(x, y_1, \ldots, y_n) \to \phi(S(x), y_1, \ldots, y_n)$
$\qquad \to \forall x\ \phi(x, y_1, \ldots, y_n))$.

The sentences of the form PA9 constitute the *first-order induction schema for arithmetic*. The infinite set of sentences PA1–PA9 is called *first-order Peano arithmetic*, or PA for short.

The situation with $\mathbb{N}$ is typical. Given any signature σ, any σ-structure A and any sentence ϕ of $L(\sigma)$, we can read ϕ as making a statement about A. If this statement is true we say that A is a *model* of ϕ, and we express this fact by writing

(71) $A \vDash \phi$.

If ϕ is false in a we write $A \nvDash \phi$. It is an unfortunate fact of history that we use the symbol "$\vDash$" both in (71) (which is not a sequent) and in semantic sequents such as (16) above and (72) below. One can avoid confusion by noting that in (71) there is a structure to the left of "$\vDash$," whereas in sequents the space to the left of "$\vDash$" is empty or contains sentences.

THEORIES AND THEIR MODELS

Let L be a first-order language. A set of sentences of L is called a *theory*. An L-structure A is called a *model* of T if it is a model of every sentence in T. The semantic sequent

(72) $T \vDash \psi$

states that every model of T is a model of ψ; when this holds, we say the sequent is *valid* and that ψ is a *(logical) consequence* of T. When T is a finite set, say $\{\phi_1, \ldots, \phi_n\}$, we write the sequent (72) as

(73) $\phi_1, \ldots, \phi_n \vDash \psi$.

When T is empty, we also write the sequent as

(74) $\vDash \psi$.

(74) says that ψ is true in every L-structure; when it holds, we say that the sentence ψ is *valid*, and that it is a *theorem*. Finally the sequent

(75) $T \vDash$

expresses that T has no models.

We say that T is *consistent* if it has models, in other words if $T \nvDash$. We say that T is *complete* if for every sentence ϕ of L, at least one of ϕ and $\neg\phi$ is a consequence of

T. So T is consistent and complete if and only if for every sentence φ of L, exactly one of φ and ¬φ is a consequence of T.

Since a sentence of $L(\sigma)$ is also a sentence of $L(\tau)$ whenever τ includes σ, we should check that the validity of a sequent depends only on the sentences in it, and not on the signature—otherwise our notation for sequents would need to mention the signature. The following metatheorem assures this. (It requires that every structure has nonempty domain. In a structure with empty domain, $\exists x\ (x = x)$ is false; but adding a constant to the signature automatically excludes structures with empty domains and hence makes $\exists x\ (x = x)$ a theorem.)

METATHEOREM 2. *If* T *and* ψ *are a theory and a sentence of* L(σ), *and* τ *is a signature extending* σ, *then (72) is valid for* σ-*structures if and only if it is valid for* τ-*structures.*

A theory T is said to be *deductively closed* if T contains all its consequences. If S is any theory then the set T of all consequences of S is deductively closed and contains S; we call T the *deductive closure* of S. When T is the deductive closure of S we say also that S is a *set of axioms* for T.

First-order theories commonly arise in one of two ways.

In the first way we have a first-order language L and an L-structure A, and we want to list the facts that we know about A. By the *complete theory* of A we mean the set T of all sentences of L that have A as a model. This set T is always deductively closed, consistent and complete. If we have a set S of sentences that are all true in A, then certainly S is consistent; if it is also complete, then S is a set of axioms for the complete theory of A. An ambition for logicians is to give sets of axioms for the complete theories of various mathematical structures. For many cases this is achieved. But in 1931 Kurt Gödel gave an indirect but astonishingly insightful proof that PA is not complete, so that it doesn't axiomatise the complete first-order theory of ℕ. (See entry on "Gödel's Theorem.")

The second common source of first-order theories is the definitions of classes of mathematical structures. For example a linearly ordered set is a structure in a signature containing a binary relation symbol <, which is a model of the three sentences:

$$(76) \qquad \forall x\forall y\forall z\ (x < y \land y < z \rightarrow x < z)$$

$$\forall x\neg\ (x < x)$$

$$\forall x\forall y\ (x < y \lor y < x \lor x = y)$$

The structure ℕ forms a linear ordering, since all of (76) is true in ℕ. This theory (76) is a direct translation into first-order notation of the usual informal definition of linear orderings.

FORMULAS AND SATISFACTION

The formula $x < \underline{3}$ is neither true nor false in ℕ, because the variable x lacks an interpretation. The interpretations of the symbols of $\sigma_{\mathbb{N}}$ are fixed in ℕ, but the interpretations of the variables are not. The same holds for any first-order language L, any L-structure A and any formula φ of L in which some variables are free.

By an *assignment in* the structure A we mean a function α whose domain is a set of variables and which assigns to each variable in its domain an element of A. If t is a term and α is an assignment in A whose domain includes all the variables in t, then A and α together tell us how to treat t as the name of an element of A, and we write this element $t_A[\alpha]$. For example if A is ℕ and α is an assignment in ℕ with $\alpha(x) = 4$, and t is the term $x + \underline{5}$, then $t_{\mathbb{N}}[\alpha]$ is $4 + 5$, in other words 9.

When t is a closed term, $t_A[\alpha]$ is independent of α and we write it simply as t_A.

Similarly we can use assignments to interpret the free occurrences of variables in a formula. (The bound occurrences need no interpretation; they are part of the apparatus of quantification.) For example in ℕ, any assignment α with $\alpha(x) = 4$ interprets the formula $x < \underline{5}$ as making the statement that 4 is less than 5, which is true. We express the fact that this statement is true by writing

$$(77) \qquad \mathbb{N} \vDash (x < \underline{5})[\alpha].$$

More generally if α is an assignment in A which makes assignments to all the variables free in φ, then

$$(78) \qquad A \vDash \phi[\alpha]$$

states that φ, interpreted in A by means of α, is true. When (78) holds we say that α *satisfies* φ in A. We write

$$(79) \qquad A \nvDash \phi[\alpha]$$

if α fails to satisfy φ in A.

There are two reasons for introducing the notion of "satisfying." The first is that it allows us to use formulas with free variables in order to express properties of individual elements or sequences of elements in a structure. For this application another notation is helpful. Suppose $\phi(x_1, \ldots, x_n)$ is a formula of L and α is an assignment that assigns elements to at least the variables $x_1, \ldots, x_n$. Write a_i for $\alpha(x_i)$. Then instead of "$A \vDash \phi[\alpha]$" we also write

(80) $A \vDash \phi[a_1, \ldots, a_n].$

We read this statement as "$a_1, \ldots, a_n$ satisfy ϕ in A."

The second reason for introducing satisfaction is that (as Alfred Tarski pointed out) it allows us to give a fully precise mathematical definition of the relation "$A \vDash \phi$," by first defining the relation "$A \vDash \phi[\alpha]$." The first step of the definition is to define $t_A[\alpha]$ by induction on the complexity of t; we omit details. This done, the definition of "$A \vDash \phi[\alpha]$" goes by induction on the complexity of ϕ. We give some typical cases and leave the remainder to the reader.

(a) For every propositional symbol p,

$$A \vDash p \text{ if and only if } p_A \text{ is T.}$$

(b) If R is a relation symbol of arity n and ϕ has the form $R(t_1, \ldots, t_n)$, then

$$A \vDash \phi[\alpha] \text{ if and only if } ((t_1)_A[\alpha], \ldots, (t_n)_A[\alpha]) \text{ is in } R_A.$$

(c) $A \vDash (\phi \wedge \psi)[\alpha]$ if and only if $A \vDash \phi[\alpha]$ and $A \vDash \psi[\alpha]$.

The clauses for quantifiers need some further notation. Suppose α is an assignment whose domain includes all the variables free in ϕ except perhaps v, and a is an element of the structure A. Then we write $\alpha(a/v)$ for the assignment β whose domain is the domain of α together with v, and such that for each variable x in the domain of β,

(81)
$$\beta(x) = \begin{cases} \alpha(x) & \text{if } x \text{ is not } v, \\ a & \text{if } x \text{ is } v. \end{cases}$$

(d) $A \vDash \forall v \phi[\alpha]$ if and only if for every element a of $\mathrm{dom}(A)$, $A \vDash \phi[\alpha(a/v)]$.

(e) $A \vDash \exists v \phi[\alpha]$ if and only if there is an element a of $\mathrm{dom}(A)$ such that $A \vDash \phi[\alpha(a/v)]$.

Tarski's definition of "$A \vDash \phi[\alpha]$" goes by induction on the complexity of formulas, as above. But by standard set-theoretic methods we can convert it to an explicit set-theoretic definition and hence prove the following metatheorem:

METATHEOREM 3. *There is a formula θ of set theory such that*

$$\theta(\sigma, A, \phi, \alpha)$$

is true in the universe of sets if and only if σ is a signature, A is a σ-structure, ϕ is a formula of $L(\sigma)$ and $A \vDash \phi[\alpha]$.

We would like to know that $\phi(y/x)$ says the same thing about an object y as $\phi(x)$ says about an object x. More precisely, we would like to know the following:

METATHEOREM 4. *Suppose $\phi(x)$ is a formula of the first-order language L, $t(y)$ is a term of L, α is an assignment whose domain includes y, and β is an assignment with $\beta(x) = t_A[\alpha]$. Then*

$$A \vDash \phi(t/x)[\alpha] \text{ if and only if } A \vDash \phi[\beta].$$

Unfortunately this metatheorem is false unless we make certain adjustments. For example let $\phi(x)$ be the formula $\exists y\,(x \neq y)$ which says that there is something else besides x, and let t be the variable y. Then $\phi(t/x)$ is the everywhere false sentence $\exists y\,(y \neq y)$, not a formula saying that there is something else besides y. The quantifier $\exists y$ has captured the variable y when we substituted t for x in $\phi(t/x)$.

There is a remedy. Given any formula ϕ and any term t, we define $\phi(t//x)$ as follows. For each variable v occurring in the term t, choose another variable v' that doesn't occur in either t or ϕ, taking different variables v' for different v. Form the formula ϕ' by replacing each bound occurrence of each variable v in ϕ by an occurrence of v'. Finally take $\phi(t//x)$ to be $\phi'(t/x)$. (A more precise account would say how we choose the variables v' and would explain the relevance of the logical equivalence (90)(i) below.) Then $\phi(t//x)$ is said to come from ϕ by substituting t for x "without clash of variables." For simplicity of notation we now redefine $\phi(t/x)$ to mean $\phi(t//x)$, thus throwing away the ladder we climbed up. After this redefinition, Metatheorem 4 is true.

Some authors avoid this redefinition by forbidding the use of $\phi(t/x)$ when ϕ contains a quantifier that captures a variable in t.

SOME METATHEOREMS OF FIRST-ORDER LOGIC

The metatheorems in this section are mostly immediate from the definitions. We state them because they have useful applications.

METATHEOREM 5. *If ϕ is a first-order sentence then the sequent $\phi \vDash \phi$ is valid.*

METATHEOREM 6 (MONOTONICITY). *If ψ is a sentence and T a theory in a first-order language, and U is a subset of T such that the sequent $U \vDash \psi$ is valid, then the sequent $T \vDash \psi$ is valid.*

METATHEOREM 7 (CUT). *If T is a theory and ϕ, ψ are sentences, all in a first-order language, and the sequents*

$$(82) \qquad T \vDash \phi, \quad T \cup \{\phi\} \vDash \psi$$

are both valid, then the sequent $T \vDash \psi$ is valid. (The sentence ϕ is "cut.")

There are a number of metatheorems expressing properties of particular logical operators. The three below are only a sample.

METATHEOREM 8. *Suppose T is a first-order theory and ϕ is a first-order sentence. Then the sequent $T \vDash \phi$ is valid if and only if the sequent $T \cup \{\neg\phi\} \vDash$ is valid.*

METATHEOREM 9. *Suppose T is a first-order theory and ϕ and ψ are first-order sentences. If*

$$(83) \qquad T \cup \{\phi\} \vDash \psi$$

is valid, then

$$(84) \qquad T \vDash (\phi \to \psi)$$

is valid. Also if

$$(85) \qquad T \vDash \phi, \quad T \vDash (\phi \to \psi)$$

are both valid then

$$(86) \qquad T \vDash \psi$$

is valid.

The first half of Metatheorem 9 is sometimes called the Deduction Theorem. The second half is one form of a rule traditionally called Modus Ponens.

METATHEOREM 10. *Suppose T is a first-order theory, $\phi(x_1, \ldots, x_n)$ is a first-order formula and $c_1, \ldots, c_n$ are n distinct constants that occur nowhere in either T or ϕ. Then if either of the following sequents is valid, so is the other:*

$$T \vDash \phi(c_1, \ldots, c_n).$$

$$T \vDash \forall x_1, \ldots \forall x_n \phi.$$

Our remaining metatheorems describe important properties of first-order logic as a whole.

METATHEOREM 11. *Let L be a first-order language and $\phi(v_1, \ldots, v_n)$ and $\psi(v_1, \ldots, v_n)$ formulas of L. Then the following are equivalent:*

(a) For every σ-structure A and all elements $a_1, \ldots, a_n$ of the domain of A,

$$A \vDash \phi[a_1, \ldots, a_n] \text{ if and only if } A \vDash \psi[a_1, \ldots, a_n].$$

(b) $\vDash \forall v_1 \ldots \forall v_n (\phi(v_1, \ldots, v_n) \leftrightarrow \psi(v_1, \ldots, v_n)).$

When these conditions (a) and (b) hold, we say that ϕ and ψ are logically equivalent, *and we write this as $\phi \equiv \psi$.*

Logical equivalence is an equivalence relation on formulas. Here are some logically equivalent pairs:

(87)			
(a)	$(\phi \vee \psi)$	$\equiv$	$\neg(\neg\phi \wedge \neg\psi)$
(b)	$\neg(\phi \wedge \psi)$	$\equiv$	$(\neg\phi \vee \neg\psi)$
(c)	$\neg(\phi \vee \psi)$	$\equiv$	$(\neg\phi \wedge \neg\psi)$
(d)	$(\phi \wedge (\psi \vee \chi))$	$\equiv$	$((\phi \wedge \psi) \vee (\phi \wedge \chi))$
(e)	$(\phi \to \psi)$	$\equiv$	$(\neg\phi \vee \psi)$
(f)	$(\phi \leftrightarrow \psi)$	$\equiv$	$((\phi \wedge \psi) \vee (\neg\phi \wedge \neg\psi))$

Equivalences (a), (b) and (c) are examples of a group of equivalences that go by the name of *De Morgan's Laws*.

METATHEOREM 12. *Let L be a first-order language and suppose ϕ and ϕ' are logically equivalent formulas of L. Let ψ be a formula of L, and let ψ' come from ψ by replacing a subformula of ψ of the form ϕ by a copy of ϕ'. Then ψ' is logically equivalent to ψ.*

Metatheorem 12 together with equivalences (a), (e), and (f) tells us that, given any first-order formula ϕ, we can remove all occurrences of the symbol "$\leftrightarrow$", and then all occurrences of the symbols "$\vee$" and "$\to$," and so find a formula logically equivalent to ϕ in which none of these symbols occurs. So there would be no loss of expressive power if we removed these symbols from the language. By a similar argument we could make do with "$\vee$" and "$\neg$," discarding "$\wedge$," "$\to$" and "$\leftrightarrow$."

Other choices of symbol are open to us. For example we can introduce the symbol "$\bot$" as an atomic formula; since it has no variables it is a sentence, and we stipulate that its truth value is F in all structures. This symbol "$\bot$" is logically equivalent to $\neg\forall x(x = x)$, or more generally to $\neg\phi$ where ϕ is any valid sentence. We pronounce "$\bot$" as "absurdity"; some computer scientists read it as "bottom." Given the logical equivalences

(88)
$$\neg\phi \equiv (\phi \rightarrow \bot)$$
$$(\phi \wedge \psi) \equiv \neg(\phi \rightarrow \neg\psi)$$

we see that in the presence of "$\bot$" and "$\rightarrow$" we can drop "$\neg$," "$\wedge$," "$\vee$," "$\leftrightarrow$" from the language.

A formula with no quantifiers is said to be *quantifier-free*. By a *literal* we mean a formula that is either atomic or the negation of an atomic formula. By a *basic conjunction* we mean either a literal or a conjunction of literals; likewise a *basic disjunction* is a literal or a disjunction of literals. A quantifier-free formula is said to be in *disjunctive normal form* if it is a basic conjunction or a disjunction of basic conjunctions; it is in *conjunctive normal form* if it is a basic disjunction or a conjunction of basic disjunctions.

METATHEOREM 13. *Every quantifier-free formula $\phi(x_1, \ldots, x_n)$ is logically equivalent to a quantifier-free formula $\phi^{dnf}(x_1, \ldots, x_n)$ in disjunctive normal form, and to a quantifier-free formula $\phi^{cnf}(x_1, \ldots, x_n)$ in conjunctive normal form.*

We illustrate Metatheorem 13:

(89)

$\neg(p \leftrightarrow q)$	$\equiv$ (by (f))
$\neg((p \wedge q) \vee (\neg p \wedge \neg q))$	$\equiv$ (by (c))
$\neg(p \wedge q) \wedge \neg(\neg q \wedge \neg q)$	$\equiv$ (by (b))
$(\neg p \vee \neg q) \wedge (p \vee q)$	$\equiv$ (by (d))
$((\neg p \vee \neg q) \wedge p) \vee ((\neg p \vee \neg q) \wedge q)$	$\equiv$ (similarly)
$(\neg p \wedge p) \vee (\neg q \wedge p) \vee (\neg p \wedge q) \vee (\neg q \wedge q) \equiv$	
$(\neg q \wedge p) \vee (\neg p \wedge q)$	

Here follow some important logical equivalences involving quantifiers.

(90)

(g) $\forall x \phi$	$\equiv \neg\exists x \neg\phi$
(h) $\exists x \phi$	$\equiv \neg\forall x \neg\phi$
(i) $\forall x \phi$	$\equiv \forall y \phi'$ if y doesn't occur in ϕ and ϕ' comes from ϕ by replacing x by y everywhere
(j) $(\forall x \phi \wedge \psi)$	$\equiv \forall x(\phi \wedge \psi)$ if x is not free in ψ
(k) $(\forall x \phi \vee \psi)$	$\equiv \forall x(\phi \vee \psi)$ if x is not free in ψ

A formula is said to be *prenex* if it is quantifier-free or consists of a string of quantifiers followed by a quantifier-free formula. The (possibly empty) string of quantifiers at the front of a prenex formula is called its *quantifier prefix*.

METATHEOREM 14 (PRENEX FORM THEOREM). *Let L be a first-order language and $\phi(x_1, \ldots, x_n)$ a formula of L. Then there is a prenex formula $\psi(x_1, \ldots, x_n)$ of L that is logically equivalent to ϕ.*

To prove the prenex form theorem, one establishes ways of moving a quantifier in a formula "outwards." Equivalences (j) and (k) above are typical examples, and there are corresponding equivalences with $\exists$. If the variable x does occur free in ψ, we first use equivalence (i) to change x to another variable not occurring in ψ.

CONSTRUCTION OF MODELS

One way to show that a theory T is consistent is to build a model of T. Depending on what T is, this can call for a good deal of ingenuity. A number of logicians have studied how, by analysing T itself, we can make the process more systematic. The approach described below follows suggestions of Jaakko Hintikka.

Let L be a first-order language and T a set of sentences of L. For simplicity we assume L doesn't have $\vee$, $\rightarrow$ or $\leftrightarrow$. We say that T is a *Hintikka set* if it has the following properties:

(H1) If $(\phi \wedge \psi)$ is in T then both ϕ and ψ are in T; if $\neg(\phi \wedge \psi)$ is in T then at least one of $\neg\phi$ and $\neg\psi$ is in T.

(H2) If $\neg\neg\phi$ is in T then ϕ is in T.

(H3) For every closed term t, $(t = t)$ is in T.

(H4) If $(s = t)$ and $\phi(s/x)$ are both in T then $\phi(t/x)$ is in T.

(H5) If $\exists x \phi(x)$ is in T then for some constant c, $\phi(c)$ is in T; if $\neg\exists x \phi(x)$ is in T then $\neg\phi(t)$ is in T for every closed term t.

(H6) If $\forall x \phi(x)$ is in T then $\phi(t)$ is in T for every closed term t; if $\neg\forall x \phi(x)$ is in T then for some constant c, $\neg\phi(c)$ is in T.

(H7) If ϕ is an atomic sentence then ϕ and $\neg\phi$ are not both in T.

METATHEOREM 15. *If L is a first-order language, A is an L-structure and every element of A is named by a constant, then the set of all sentences of L that are true in A is a Hintikka set.*

METATHEOREM 16. *If the first-order language L has at least one constant and T is a Hintikka set in L then T has a model.*

We sketch the proof of Metatheorem 16. Let C be the set of all closed terms of L. Define a relation $\sim$ on C by: $s \sim t$ if and only if $(s = t)$ is in T. Then we can show, using (H3) and (H4), that $\sim$ is an equivalence relation on C. Write $t^{\sim}$ for the equivalence class of the closed term t, and $C^{\sim}$ for the set of equivalence classes $t^{\sim}$. Since L has at least one constant, $C^{\sim}$ is not empty. We shall build an L-structure A whose domain is $C^{\sim}$. For each constant c we take c_A to be $c^{\sim}$. If F is a function symbol of arity n and $t_1, \dots, t_n$ are closed terms, we define $F_A(t_1^{\sim}, \dots, t_n^{\sim})$ to be the equivalence class

(91) $$F(t_1, \dots, t_n)^{\sim}.$$

We can use (H4) to justify this definition. An argument by induction on complexity shows that for each closed term t of L, t_A is $t^{\sim}$. If R is a relation symbol of arity n and $t_1, \dots, t_n$ are closed terms, we define

(92) $(t_1^{\sim}, \dots, t_n^{\sim})$ is in R_A if and only if $R(t_1, \dots, t_n)$ is in T.

Again this definition is justified by an argument involving (H4). This completes the definition of the structure A.

Now we prove, by induction on the complexity of ψ, that for every sentence ψ of L, if ψ is in T then $A \vDash \psi$, and if $\neg\psi$ is in T then $A \vDash \neg\psi$. A typical clause is where ψ is $\exists x\, \phi(x)$. If ψ is in T then by (H5) there is a constant c such that $\phi(c)$ is in T. Since $\phi(c)$ has lower complexity than $\exists x\, \phi(x)$, the induction hypothesis shows that $A \vDash \phi(c)$. So $A \vDash \exists x\, \phi(x)$. On the other hand if $\neg\exists x\, \phi(x)$ is in T, then by (H5) again and induction hypothesis, $A \vDash \neg\phi(t)$ for every closed term t, so that $A \vDash \neg\phi[t_A]$. Since all elements of A are of the form t_A, this shows that $A \vDash \neg\exists x\, \phi(x)$. Thus A is a model of every sentence in T, proving the metatheorem.

As an example we shall show that the sequent

(93) $\forall x \,\neg(P(x) \wedge \neg Q(x)), \forall x \,\neg(Q(x) \wedge \neg R(x)) \vDash \forall x$
$\neg(R(x) \wedge \neg P(x))$

is not valid. ((93) is the sequent (15) but with the conclusion reversed and " $\rightarrow$ " removed in favour of " $\neg$ " and " $\wedge$.") We begin by noting that by Metatheorem 8, the sequent is valid if and only if the theory consisting of the sentences

(94) $\forall x \,\neg(P(x) \wedge \neg Q(x)), \forall x \,\neg(Q(x) \wedge \neg R(x)), \neg\forall x$
$\neg(R(x) \wedge \neg P(x))$

is inconsistent. So we can show the invalidity of (93) by constructing a model of these three sentences. We aim to build a Hintikka set that contains the sentences.

Property (H5) of Hintikka sets and the hypothesis of Metatheorem 16 alert us that we may need to call on constants. Maybe L has no constants; maybe it has constants, but they are all used in sentences of T that make their use for (H5) and (H6) impossible. So as a first step we allow ourselves to add new constant symbols to the language when needed. Metatheorem 2 tells us that this expansion of L makes no difference to the consistency of T. The added constants are called *witnesses*, since in (H5) the sentence $\phi(c)$ serves as a witness to the truth of $\exists x\phi$.

We begin by writing the sentences (94):

(95) $$\forall x \,\neg(P(x) \wedge \neg Q(x))$$
$$\forall x \,\neg(Q(x) \wedge \neg R(x))$$
$$\neg\forall x \,\neg(R(x) \wedge \neg P(x))$$

At this point we apply the second part of (H6) to the third sentence. This requires us to introduce a witness, say c. A Hintikka set containing $\neg\forall x \,\neg(R(x) \wedge \neg P(x))$ needs to contain $\neg\neg(R(c) \wedge \neg P(c))$, so we add this to the diagram. We notice that by (H2) a Hintikka set containing this new sentence must also contain $(R(c) \wedge \neg P(c))$, so we add this too. Next (H1) tells us that a Hintikka set containing $(R(c) \wedge \neg P(c))$ must also contain $R(c)$ and $\neg P(c)$, so we add these below. Then by the first part of (H6) we also need to add $\neg(P(c) \wedge \neg Q(c))$ and $\neg(Q(c) \wedge \neg R(c))$, so we add them.

(96)
$$\forall x \,\neg(P(x) \wedge \neg Q(x))$$
$$\forall x \,\neg(Q(x) \wedge \neg R(x))$$
$$\neg\forall x \,\neg(R(x) \wedge \neg P(x))$$
$$|$$
$$\neg\neg(R(c) \wedge \neg P(c))$$
$$(R(c) \wedge \neg P(c))$$
$$|$$
$$R(c)$$
$$\neg P(c)$$
$$|$$
$$\neg(P(c) \wedge \neg Q(c))$$
$$\neg(Q(c) \wedge \neg R(c))$$

Here we meet a problem. The Hintikka set that we are constructing contains $\neg(P(c) \wedge \neg Q(c))$, so by the second part of (H1) it must contain either $\neg P(c)$ or $\neg\neg Q(c)$. But we don't yet know which will work; so we try both possibilities. The diagram will branch. To the left we try to construct a Hintikka set containing $\neg P(c)$, and to the right, a Hintikka set containing $\neg\neg Q(c)$ (and hence also $Q(c)$ by (H2)). The same rule (H1) applies to the sentence $\neg(Q(c) \wedge \neg R(c))$, and tells us to add either $\neg Q(c)$ or $\neg\neg R(c)$. We must try each of these choices in each branch, so we have a double branching. At this point we notice that the third branch from the left contains both the atomic sentence $Q(c)$ and its negation $\neg Q(c)$; so by (H7) there is no hope of extending this branch to a Hintikka set, and we close it with a horizontal line across the bottom.

(97)
$$\forall x \neg (P(x) \wedge \neg Q(x))$$
$$\forall x \neg (Q(x) \wedge \neg R(x))$$
$$\neg \forall x \neg (R(x) \wedge \neg P(x))$$
$$|$$
$$\neg\neg(R(c) \wedge \neg P(c))$$
$$(R(c) \wedge \neg P(c))$$
$$|$$
$$(R(c)$$
$$\neg P(c)$$
$$|$$
$$\neg(P(c) \wedge \neg Q(c))$$
$$\neg(Q(c) \wedge \neg R(c))$$

(diagram with branches)
$\neg(P(c))$ ... $\neg\neg(Q(c))$
$Q(c)$
$\neg Q(c)$ ... $\neg\neg R(c)$
$R(c)$ ... $\neg(Q(c))$ ... $\neg\neg(R(c))$
$R(c)$

The first, second, and fourth branches are still open. Inspection shows that all that is needed to turn the contents of each of these branches into a Hintikka set is to add the equation $(c = c)$; so we do that. Now choose one of the open branches, say the first. Since its contents (reckoning from the top of the diagram) form a Hintikka set, it has a model, and this model is a model of the first three sentences in particular. So we have shown that the sequent (93) is not valid.

What would happen if we replaced the conclusion of (93) by $\forall x \neg (P(x) \wedge \neg R(x))$? The resulting sequent is a paraphrase of (15) from section 1, and we claimed that that sequent was valid. Here is the tree for the revised sequent:

(98)
$$\forall x \neg (P(x) \wedge \neg Q(x))$$
$$\forall x \neg (Q(x) \wedge \neg R(x))$$
$$\neg \forall x \neg (P(x) \wedge \neg R(x))$$
$$|$$
$$\neg\neg(P(c) \wedge \neg R(c))$$
$$(P(c) \wedge \neg R(c))$$
$$|$$
$$(P(c)$$
$$\neg R(c)$$
$$|$$
$$\neg(P(c) \wedge \neg Q(c))$$
$$\neg(Q(c) \wedge \neg R(c))$$

(diagram with branches)
$\neg(P(c))$ ... $\neg\neg(Q(c))$
$Q(c)$
$\neg(Q(c))$ ... $\neg\neg(R(c))$
$R(c)$

Here every branch contains an atomic sentence together with its negation, so they all close and we say that the diagram is *closed*. This closed diagram shows that there is no Hintikka set containing the top three sentences. Hence by Metatheorem 15 they have no model, and this shows that our revised sequent is valid, giving a formal justification of (15).

PROOF CALCULI

A proof calculus is a mathematical device for proving the validity of sequents. In any proof calculus a central notion is that of a *formal proof of a sequent*. For most proof calculi a formal proof is an array of symbols that can be written on a page. But some calculi are for use by computers and their formal proofs are not meant for visual inspection. On the other hand the proof calculus *Hyperproof* (Jon Barwise and John Etchemendy) allows formal proofs that consist of sequences of labelled pictures.

If a proof calculus $\mathscr{C}$ contains a formal proof of the sequent

(99)
$$\phi_1, \ldots, \phi_n \vDash \psi,$$

we express this fact by writing

(100)
$$\phi_1, \ldots, \phi_n \vdash_{\mathscr{C}} \psi.$$

The expression (100) is called a *syntactic sequent*. When we are discussing a particular proof calculus $\mathscr{C}$, we can drop the subscript from $\vdash_{\mathscr{C}}$ and write simply $\vdash$; the symbol "$\vdash$" is read as "turnstile."

In many proof calculi a formal proof of a sequent is a formalisation of an argument that one might use in order to persuade someone that the sequent is valid. For example the *natural deduction* calculus proposed by Gerhard Gentzen in 1934 is designed to make the same moves as are used in "natural" mathematical arguments. But in general a formal proof need not have any visible connection with arguments. The main requirements on a proof calculus $\mathscr{C}$ are as follows.

(a) Whenever a syntactic sequent (100) holds, the corresponding semantic sequent (99) is valid. A proof calculus satisfying this condition is said to be *sound*.

(b) Whenever a semantic sequent (99) is valid, the corresponding syntactic sequent (100) holds. A proof calculus satisfying this condition is said to be *complete*.

(c) A computer can identify those arrays of symbols that are formal proofs in $\mathscr{C}$, and for each formal proof and each finite semantic sequent, the computer can calculate whether or not the proof is a formal proof of the sequent.

Soundness says that $\mathscr{C}$ doesn't prove any sequent that it ought not to; completeness says that $\mathscr{C}$ does prove any sequent that it ought to.

All the proof calculi commonly taught to undergraduates are both sound and complete. There is one main exception: the resolution calculus is limited to proofs of sequents of the form

$$(101) \qquad \forall x_1 \ldots \forall x_m \, \phi \vDash$$

where ϕ is quantifier-free and in conjunctive normal form. Computer science students who study this calculus also learn how to reduce more general proof problems to this form. Also some Hilbert-style calculi are only able to prove sequents of the form $\vDash \psi$.

If a proof calculus $\mathscr{C}$ is sound and complete, then finite sequents with $\vDash$ are valid if and only if the corresponding sequents with $\vdash_{\mathscr{C}}$ are also valid. It follows that all the metatheorems of section 8 using $\vDash$ remain true when they are stated with $\vdash_{\mathscr{C}}$. But the versions with $\vdash_{\mathscr{C}}$ generally have direct proofs using syntactic properties of the proof calculus $\mathscr{C}$. Sometimes these direct proofs (particularly proofs of the Deduction Theorem) play a role in

proving that $\mathscr{C}$ is complete. One deathtrap for unwary teachers is the Cut rule, Metatheorem 7. This is very easy to prove directly for some calculi, for example natural deduction. But for the truth tree calculus below, the truth of the Cut rule is a deep fact equivalent to Gentzen's cut elimination theorem; a syntactic proof of it is a major enterprise.

The entry "Proof Theory" contains much more information about proof calculi. For example it discusses how one can translate proofs in one proof calculus into proofs in another. If two proof calculi translate into each other in this way, then clearly soundness and completeness theorems for one calculus carry over to the other calculus too. This is probably the main reason why logicians often talk about "the completeness theorem" as if there was a single theorem for all proof calculi, when strictly each complete proof calculus has its own completeness theorem.

We introduced a kind of proof calculus when we discussed the construction of models. Suppose we have a tree diagram in the style of that section, showing that there is no Hintikka set containing the sentences

$$(102) \qquad \phi_1, \ldots, \phi_n, \neg\psi.$$

Then in view of Metatheorem 8 we count this diagram as a formal proof of the sequent

$$(103) \qquad \phi_1, \ldots, \phi_n \vDash \psi.$$

The proof calculus based on Hintikka sets in this way is called *truth trees*.

The truth tree calculus is sound by Metatheorem 15. In order to establish that the calculus is complete, we must show the following: If it is not possible to construct a closed truth tree in a finite number of steps starting from $\phi_1, \ldots, \phi_n, \neg\psi$, then it is possible to construct a truth tree starting with these sentences, in which one branch forms a Hintikka set (so that it has a model by Metatheorem 16). We have to bear in mind that a branch might go on forever. In fact if L has infinitely many closed terms, then (H3) implies that every Hintikka set in L must be infinite. In this case the conditions (H1)–(H7) impose infinitely many separate requirements on a Hintikka set, and we have to be sure that we construct our branches in such a way that each of these requirements will eventually be faced and met if possible. This can be arranged.

DECIDABILITY

When the signature σ is finite, we can assign natural number values to the symbols of $L(\sigma)$ and thereby express each formula of $L(\sigma)$ as a finite sequence of natural numbers. (In fact this is possible, though less tidy, when σ is countably infinite.) Hence it makes sense to apply notions of computability theory to $L(\sigma)$. Thus we say that a set X of finite sequences of numbers is *computably enumerable* (abbreviated to *c.e.*) if a computer can be programmed to output all and only the sequences in X. Also we say that X is *computable* if a computer can be programmed to output Yes if a sequence in X is input, and No if a sequence not in X is input. These notions carry over immediately to theories in $L(\sigma)$. We say also that a theory T is *decidable* if the set of its logical consequences is computable. A procedure for computing whether any given sentence is a consequence of T is called a *decision procedure* for T.

Now suppose we have a proof calculus $\mathscr{C}$ for L that meets the conditions (a), (b) and (c) of section 10. Then $\mathscr{C}$ is sound and complete, so that we have the equivalence

(104) ϕ is a consequence of T if and only if:

There is a finite subset U of T and there is P such that

$[P$ is a formal proof in $\mathscr{C}$ of the sequent $U \vDash \phi]$.

By property (c) of $\mathscr{C}$, the relation in square brackets is computable. It follows that if T is computably enumerable, we can program a computer so that it (i) lists all possible finite subsets U of T, all sentences ϕ of $L(\sigma)$ and all formal proofs P in $\mathscr{C}$, (ii) tests, for each U, ϕ and P, whether or not P is a proof of $U \vDash \phi$, and (iii) outputs ϕ whenever the answer to (ii) is Yes. This computer will output all and only the logical consequences of T. We have shown:

METATHEOREM 17. *If T is a c.e. theory in a first-order language with finite signature, then the set of consequences of T is also c.e.*

An important corollary is:

METATHEOREM 18. *Suppose T is a complete, consistent, and c.e. theory in a first-order language with finite signature. Then T is decidable.*

To compute whether ϕ is a consequence of T, list all the consequences of T; eventually either ϕ or $\neg\phi$ will appear in the list. This is not a practical method. But when this abstract argument shows that T is decidable, one can usually find a much better decision procedure.

An important case is to determine whether a given sentence ϕ is a consequence of the empty theory, that is, whether ϕ is a theorem of first-order logic. By a result proved by Alonzo Church in 1936, the set of theorems of

first-order logic (say, in a signature with at least one relation symbol of arity at least 2) is not computable. But if we restrict ϕ to come from some appropriate class of sentences, the picture changes. Suppose for example that ϕ is in propositional logic. Then we can construct a truth tree to determine whether $\neg\phi$ has a model, and after a finite number of steps the truth tree will have ground to a halt in the sense that there are no new sentences that we can add to it. If all its branches are closed, there is no model of $\neg\phi$; if at least one branch remains open, it gives us a Hintikka set and hence a model of $\neg\phi$. This provides a decision procedure for propositional sentences.

In fact the truth tree procedure allows us to test for theoremhood every first-order sentence of the form $Q_1Q_2\phi$ where Q_1 is a string of universal quantifiers, Q_2 is a string of existential quantifiers and ϕ is a quantifier-free formula with no function symbols.

A formula is said to be *universal* if it is quantifier-free or consists of a string of universal quantifiers followed by a quantifier-free formula. Thoralf Skolem proved that the problem of determining whether a given first-order sentence has a model can always be reduced to the problem of determining whether a certain universal first-order sentence has a model:

METATHEOREM 19. *Let L be a first-order language with finite signature σ. There is a computational procedure which, given any sentence ϕ, will find a universal first-order sentence ϕ^{sk} with the following properties:*

(a) ϕ^{sk} is in a signature got by adding function symbols and constants to σ.

(b) Every model of ϕ^{sk} is a model of ϕ.

(c) Every σ-structure that is a model of ϕ can be made into a model of ϕ^{sk} by adding suitable interpretations for the new function symbols and constants.

In particular ϕ has a model if and only if ϕ^{sk} has a model.

We can illustrate Skolem's idea. Let ϕ be the sentence

(105) $\forall x \, \exists y \forall z \exists w \, R(x,y,z,w)$.

Then for ϕ^{sk} we can take the sentence

(106) $\forall x \, \forall z \, R(x,F(x),z,G(x,z))$.

The function symbols F and G, and the functions they represent in a model of ϕ^{sk}, are called *Skolem functions*.

Thus if we want to determine whether ϕ is a first-order theorem, one way to proceed is to find $(\neg\phi)^{sk}$ and determine whether it has a model or not. There is no guarantee that this approach will settle the question; the importance of Skolem's theorem is mainly theoretical.

See also Church, Alonzo; Conditionals; Davidson, Donald; De Morgan, Augustus; Frege, Gottlob; Hilbert, David; Hintikka, Jaakko; Leibniz, Gottfried Wilhelm; Lewis, David; Logic, History of; Logic, Non-Classical; Łukasiewicz, Jan; Mathematics, Foundations of; Peirce, Charles Sanders; Proof Theory; Russell, Bertrand Arthur William; Second-Order Logic; Tarski, Alfred; Whately, Richard.

Bibliography

In the citations below, modern introductory texts not requiring mathematical sophistication are marked with an *.

*Barwise, Jon, and John Etchemendy. *Hyperproof*. Stanford, CA: CSLI, 1994.

*Bergmann, Merrie, James Moor, and Jack Nelson. *The Logic Book*. New York: McGraw-Hill, 1997.

Boolos, George. "For Every A There is a B." *Linguistic Inquiry* 12 (1981): 465–466.

Church, Alonzo. *Introduction to Mathematical Logic, Volume 1*. Princeton, NJ: Princeton University Press, 1956.

Dalen, Dirk van. *Logic and Structure*. Berlin: Springer, 1980.

Davidson, Donald. "The Logical Form of Action Sentences." In *Essays on Actions and Events*, edited by Donald Davidson, 105–148. Oxford: Clarendon Press, 2001.

Edgington, Dorothy. "Do Conditionals Have Truth-Conditions?" *Critica* xviii, 52 (1986): 3–30. Reprinted in *Conditionals*, edited by Frank Jackson. Oxford: Oxford University Press, 1991.

*Forbes, Graeme. *Modern Logic: A Text in Elementary Symbolic Logic*. New York: Oxford University Press, 1994.

*Gabbay, Dov. *Elementary Logics: A Procedural Perspective*. Hemel Hempstead: Prentice Hall Europe, 1998.

Grice, Paul. *Studies in the Way of Words*. Cambridge, MA: Harvard University Press, 1989.

Hilbert, David, and Wilhelm Ackermann. *Principles of Mathematical Logic*. Translated from the second edition of *Grundzüge der Theoretischen Logik*. New York: Chelsea, 1950.

Hintikka, Jaakko. "Form and Content in Quantification Theory." *Acta Philosophica Fennica* 8 (1955): 11–55.

Hodges, Wilfrid. "Elementary Predicate Logic." In *Handbook of Philosophical Logic*. 2nd ed., vol. 1, edited by Dov Gabbay and Franz Guenthner. Dordrecht: Kluwer, 2001.

*Hodges, Wilfrid. *Logic*. 2nd ed. London: Penguin, 2001.

*Jeffrey, Richard C. *Formal Logic: Its Scope and Limits*. New York: McGraw-Hill, 1994.

Kalish, Donald, and Richard Montague. *Logic, Techniques of Formal Reasoning*. New York: Harcourt Brace, 1964.

Kleene, Stephen Cole. *Introduction to Metamathematics*. Amsterdam, North-Holland, 1964.

Lewis, David. "Scorekeeping in a Language Game." *Journal of Philosophical Logic* 8 (1979): 339–359.

*Mates, Benson. *Elementary Logic*. New York: Oxford University Press, 1965.

Mendelson, Elliott. *Introduction to Mathematical Logic*. 3rd ed. Belmont, CA: Wadsworth and Brooks/Cole, 1987.

Peirce, Charles S. "On the Algebra of Logic: A Contribution to the Philosophy of Notation." *American Journal of Mathematics* 7 (1885): 180–202.

Peirce, Charles S. "The Reader Is Introduced to Relatives." *The Open Court* 6 (1892): 3416–3418.

*Quine, Willard Van Orman. *Methods of Logic*. London: Routledge and Kegan Paul, 1952.

Shapiro, Stewart. "Classical Logic." *Stanford Encyclopedia of Philosophy*. Available at http://plato.stanford.edu.

Shoenfield, Joseph R. *Mathematical Logic*. Reading, MA: Addison-Wesley, 1967. Republished Urbana, IL: Association for Symbolic Logic and A. K. Peters, 2001.

Smullyan, Raymond M. *First-Order Logic*. New York: Dover Publications, 1995.

*Suppes, Patrick. *Introduction to Logic*. Princeton, NJ: Van Nostrand, 1957.

Velleman, Daniel J. *How To Prove It*. Cambridge, U.K.: Cambridge University Press, 1994.

Whately, Richard. *Elements of Logic*. London: Mawman, 1826. Reprinted Bologna: Editrice CLUEB, 1987.

Wilfrid Hodges (2005)

FISCHER, KUNO
(1824–1907)

Kuno Fischer, the German philosopher and historian of philosophy, was born at Sandewalde in Silesia. He studied philology at Leipzig and theology and philosophy at Halle. In 1850 Fischer was appointed *Privatdozent* in philosophy at the University of Heidelberg, but his pantheistic views caused his dismissal three years later. In 1856 he qualified as *Privatdozent* at the University of Berlin, and in the same year he was invited to Jena as professor of philosophy. In 1872 he returned to Heidelberg, where he taught with great success until 1903.

Fischer's major work is his *Geschichte der neueren Philosophie* (1852–1877). This widely reprinted history of modern philosophy owed its success in large part to Fischer's splendid gift for exposition. Endowed with a remarkable capacity for sympathetic understanding, Fischer was able to reproduce the great philosophical systems in a literary form of exemplary brilliance and clarity, as well as to unravel their basic themes and subtlest ramifications and to illuminate and reconstruct them systematically. At the same time, he sought to place these systems in their larger cultural and historical context and thus to understand the historical development of philosophy as the progressive self-knowledge of the human mind.

Fischer was the author of the first large German monograph on Immanuel Kant, *Kants Leben und die*

Grundlagen seine Lehre (Mannheim, 1860), and it is from Fischer that Neo-Kantianism received its decisive impulse.

Apart from Kant, G. W. F. Hegel was the chief object of his interest. In its equating of logic and metaphysics, Fischer's *System der Logik und Metaphysik oder Wissenschaftslehre* (Stuttgart, 1852) exhibited the strong influence of Hegel. In this work an attempt was also made to bring Hegel's principle of dialectical development into harmony with modern evolutionism in the sense of a teleological idealism. Fischer held that the dialectical development ran from Being through Essence to purpose. The system of logical and, at the same time, metaphysical categories that he outlined culminated in the idea of finality, which guaranteed a purposeful development that goes beyond the merely given. In the second edition (Stuttgart, 1865), Fischer attempted to mediate between Kant and Hegel and to do justice not only to Hegelianism but also to Kantianism and empiricism.

Arthur Schopenhauer also influenced Fischer. In the study *Das Verhältnis zwischen Willen und Verstand im Menschen* (Heidelberg, 1896), Fischer distinguished between the will that is guided by knowledge and the unconscious volition that precedes all knowledge and conscious behavior. He also claimed that just as the essence of nature is "force," so the essence of man is "will" and the essence of the body is the manifestation of volition.

Fischer was also an extremely productive literary aesthetician. His conception of art is to be found in his early publication *Diotima: Die Idee des Schönen* (Diotima: the idea of the beautiful; Pforzheim, 1849). In this work Fischer defined the aesthetic attitude as one of "playing," characterized by a concentration and uniting of all our faculties. He devoted later works to the origin and development of humor and to the classical poetry of William Shakespeare, Gotthold Ephraim Lessing, Johann Wolfgang von Goethe, and Friedrich Schiller.

See also Aesthetic Attitude; Empiricism; Goethe, Johann Wolfgang von; Hegel, Georg Wilhelm Friedrich; Hegelianism; History and Historiography of Philosophy; Humor; Kant, Immanuel; Lessing, Gotthold Ephraim; Neo-Kantianism; Schiller, Friedrich; Schopenhauer, Arthur.

Bibliography

ADDITIONAL WORKS BY FISCHER

Fischer's chief work is the *Geschichte der neueren Philosophie* (Stuttgart, Mannheim, and Heidelberg, 1852–1877).

Originally published in six volumes (on René Descartes, Benedict de Spinoza, Gottfried Wilhelm Leibniz, Kant, Johann Gottlieb Fichte, and Friedrich Schelling), it was later extended to ten volumes, with a second volume on Kant, one on Schopenhauer (1893), and one on Hegel (1901); and it also included Fischer's early work on Francis Bacon and his school (Leipzig, 1856). Other writings include *Kleine Schriften*, 8 vols. (Heidelberg, 1888–1898), which contains *Über den Witz* (On humor), *Über die menschliche Freiheit* (On human freedom), *Das Verhältnis zwischen Willen und Verstand* (The relationship between will and understanding), and other essays. See also *Philosophische Schriften* (Philosophical writings), 6 vols. (Heidelberg, 1891–1892; 6th ed., 1908–1909).

English translations of Fischer's works include the following: J. Oxenford, *Francis Bacon* (London, 1857); J. P. Mahaffy, *A Commentary on Kant's "Critick of the Pure Reason"* (London and Dublin, 1866); F. Schmidt, *Benedict Spinoza* (Edinburgh, 1882); J. P. Gordy, *Descartes and His School* (New York, 1887); W. S. Hough, *A Critique of Kant* (London: S. Sonnenschein, 1888).

WORKS ON FISCHER

For literature on Fischer, see Hugo Falkenheim, *Kuno Fischer und die literarhistorische Methode* (Berlin, 1892); Wilhelm Windelband, *Kuno Fischer* (Heidelberg, 1907), a memorial address; and Ernst Hoffmann, *Kuno Fischer* (Heidelberg, 1924).

Franz Austeda (1967)
Translated by Albert E. Blumberg

FISHER, R. A.
(1890–1962)

Ronald Aylmer Fisher was a titan who bestrode two signature disciplines of twentieth-century science: population genetics (or the mathematical theory of evolution), of which he was a cofounder and principal architect, and mathematical statistics, in which he played a pivotal role. On the one hand, he led a revolution that replaced the Bayesian approach of inverse probability with one based solely on direct probabilities (i.e., probabilities of outcomes conditional on hypotheses). On the other hand, he unequivocally rejected the conception of statistics as decision making under uncertainty that his own work inspired. This rift in the new statistical orthodoxy has never healed. Thus, Fisher's conception of probability was at once frequentist and epistemic, his approach to statistics at once inferential and non-Bayesian, and the chief question his life's work poses is whether a consistent theory can be built along these lines.

After excelling in mathematics at the secondary level, Fisher won a scholarship to Cambridge University in 1909 and graduated in 1912 as a Wrangler (i.e., with honors) in the Mathematical Tripos, then spent another year at Cambridge studying statistical mechanics and quantum theory under the astronomer James Jeans. In the 1911 paper (unpublished at the time) "Mendelism and Biometry," he pointed the way to a synthesis of Mendelian genetics and Darwinian evolution.

Fisher received two important job offers in 1919: one as chief statistician under Karl Pearson at the Galton Laboratory of University College, London, and the other a temporary position at the Rothamsted (Agricultural) Experimental Station. Fisher was already on famously bad terms with Pearson, so he accepted the Rothamsted offer, leaving him free to develop his own non-Bayesian approach to statistics free of Pearson's supervision. Over the next fifteen years Fisher developed a world renowned Department of Statistics at Rothamsted that became a training ground for many statisticians who disseminated his new methods far and wide. Fisher's "golden age of invention" at Rothamsted ended in 1933 when Karl Pearson retired and his department was split into a Department of Statistics, with Egon S. Pearson (Karl's son) as head, and a Department of Eugenics, with Fisher as head. Relations between the two departments were never cordial. Further details may be found in the biography by Fisher's daughter, Joan Fisher Box (1978), who gives excellent sketches of his many and varied contributions as well as his side of the many protracted debates in which he engaged.

FISHER AND THE BAYESIANS

Although weaned on inverse probability at school (Fisher 1950, 27.248), Fisher came to regard Bayesian solutions as vitiated by the arbitrary and subjective character of prior distributions not squarely based on frequency data. Replying to criticism by Karl Pearson of a Bayesian solution he had proposed in his earliest published paper, he noted that the solution favored by Pearson "depends almost wholly upon the preconceived opinions of the computer and scarcely at all upon the actual data" (Fisher 1971–1974, 14.17). This led him to emphasize the need to "allow the data to speak for themselves," an injunction some of his followers carry to the extreme of deliberately ignoring, for example, all prior information bearing on the efficacy of a new medical treatment. To the Bayesians' palliative that whatever errors of estimation arise from use of an inappropriate prior will become negligible with accumulating data, he retorts that "it appears more natural to infer that it should be possible to draw valid conclusions from the data alone and without *a priori* assumptions." Then he adds, "we may question whether

the whole difficulty has not arisen in an attempt to express in terms of the single concept of mathematical probability, a form of reasoning which requires for its exact statement different though equally well-defined concepts" (Fisher 1950, 24.287).

Of the alternative measures suitable for "supplying a natural order of preference" among competing estimates or hypotheses, Fisher recommended the likelihood function (LF) or the data distribution qua function of the unknown parameter(s) of one's model. Or, when the LF is undefined (i.e., when the probability of the observed outcome conditional on the alternative hypotheses cannot be computed from the model), significance tests are in order. Now the LF provides only relative probabilities and is nonadditive, but the logarithm of the LF is additive and this allows one to combine evidence from different (independent) sources. The value of the unknown parameter that maximizes the LF—the so-called maximum likelihood estimate (MLE)—when it exists and is unique, must then be the best supported value. Fisher's first task was to provide a rationale for this evidential use of the LF, which Pierre Simon de Laplace and Carl Gauss had drawn as a corollary of Bayesian conditioning, but that, from Fisher's perspective, "has no real connection with inverse probability" (*Statistical Methods for Research Workers* in Fisher 2003, p. 22).

THEORY OF ESTIMATION

The first thing that struck him is that, unlike the uniform prior Thomas Bayes and Laplace seemed to conger out of ignorance, the MLE is invariant. That is, if a problem is reparametrized as $\zeta = g(\theta)$, then the MLE of the new parameter, ζ, is $g(\hat{\theta})$, writing $(\hat{\theta})$ (throughout) for the MLE of θ (De Groot 1986, p. 348). At the same time, he noted, unbiased estimators—those whose mean is equal to θ—are noninvariant, an unbiased estimator of θ being a biased estimator of θ^2 or θ^{-1}. His requirement of invariance is, in reality, a requirement of consistency, namely, that one's estimates and inferences do not depend on which of several equivalent forms of a problem one adopts. This already brings Fisher closer to the position of his protagonist, Harold Jeffreys, or that of Jeffreys's worthy successor, Edwin T. Jaynes. Nor did it ever occur to Fisher, as it did to Jeffreys and Jaynes, to use an invariant prior to represent, not pure ignorance, but a state of knowledge that is unaltered by a specifiable group of transformations. Knowing, for example, no more than that θ is a scale parameter, a suitable prior—the Jeffreys prior—would be one invariant under changes of scale.

However, Fisher was not satisfied with this justification of MLEs, but insisted that "the reliance to be placed" on one "must depend on its frequency distribution." (Fisher 1950, 10.327) Thus, Gauss had shown that the arithmetic average (or sample mean) of a set of normally distributed errors of known variance, $\frac{\sigma^2}{n}$, is itself normally distributed about the population mean, μ, with variance μ^2/n. Since a normal distribution is determined by its location parameter, μ, which locates the bell-shaped density curve along the x-axis, and its scale parameter, σ^2, which measures the spread, the variance presents itself as the uniquely suitable measure of the concentration of any estimator whose distribution is normal or asymptotically normal about the estimated parameter. What Fisher claimed to show in his seminal 1922 paper, "On the Mathematical Foundations of Theoretical Statistics" (Fisher 1971–1974: paper 18; Fisher 1950, paper 10), is that MLEs are the most concentrated. He dubbed such estimators of (asymptotically) smallest variance efficient.

One source of tension in Fisher is that his use of likelihood implies the irrelevance of outcomes that might have been but were not observed, and, at various places, he explicitly endorses this implication (*Statistical Methods and Scientific Inference* in Fisher 2003, pp. 71, 91; hereafter *SMSI*). For if as he says "the whole of the information supplied by a sample … is comprised in the likelihood" (p. 73), the LF of the outcome actually observed, all other points of the sample space must be irrelevant. However, the sampling (or frequency) distribution of an estimator, T, depends on the whole sample space, and its use to compare estimators therefore violates this likelihood principle.

In the course of his investigation of the large-sample properties of MLEs, Fisher uncovered a class of statistics a knowledge of which renders all other statistics irrelevant for inferences about θ, and so he termed them *sufficient* for θ. In the classic 1922 paper, he showed that sufficient estimators are asymptotically efficient, thus linking a purely logico-informational requirement—that of utilizing all the information supplied by the data—with a performance characteristic—that of having maximal precision. In fact, he virtually equated the property of not wasting information with efficiency. Then he could describe the statistician's job succinctly in purely cognitive terms as that of effecting the maximum information-preserving reduction of the data (Fisher 1950, 26.366). Such a maximal reduction is called a minimal sufficient statistic and is mathematically a function of every other sufficient statistic. Philosophers will recognize sufficiency as a close relative of Rudolf Carnap's requirement of total

evidence, and Fisher remarks that "our conclusions must be warranted by the whole of the data, since less than the whole may be to any degree misleading" (Fisher 1950, 26.54).

Fisher's claim that maximal likelihood estimation is "unequivocally superior" to all other methods (Fisher 1950, 24.287) would then be vindicated, at least for large samples, by showing that MLEs are sufficient (hence, asymptotically efficient). His proof of this in the 1922 paper was less than rigorous, as he candidly admitted (Fisher 1950, 10.323), and he offered improved versions in sequels to that paper. In the 1934 paper "On Two New Properties of Mathematical Likelihood," CMS paper #.24, he presented a new criterion of sufficiency, namely, that the LF factors as

(1) $$p(x|\theta) = g(T, \theta)h(x)$$

which allows one to recognize a sufficient statistic at sight. This was of great importance because the property of utilizing all the information in one's data can be applied to estimators based on small samples. And Fisher's experimental work in genetics and agronomy (at Rothamsted) had impressed on him the great practical importance of statistical methods applicable to small samples, and, hence, of exact tests or estimates based on exact, as opposed to approximate, sampling distributions. In this he was also strongly influenced by W. S. Gossett's 1908 discovery of the exact distribution of the statistic,

$$n^{1/2}(\overline{x} - \theta)/s$$

where

$$s^2 = (n-1)^1 \sum_{i=1}^{n} (x_i - \overline{x})^2$$

is the sample variance, which could then be used to test hypotheses about normal means using a small sample when the variance of the measurements is unknown. Thus, he came to view large sample theory, concerned with the never-never world of asymptotic behavior, as a mere preliminary to the study of small samples (*SMSI*, p. 163).

To facilitate the study of small samples, he introduced a quantitative measure of information. His leading idea was to measure the information an experiment with outcome variate X conveys about an unknown parameter θ by the precision (or inverse variance) of an MLE of θ. Earlier work of Karl Pearson and Francis Ysidro Edgeworth, the two leading figures of the British school of statisticians of the generation preceding Fisher's, had linked the precision of an estimator to the second derivative of the logarithm of the LF, $\ln p(x|\theta)$, where $x = (x_1, \ldots, x_n)$, which one denotes $L(x|\theta)$, or even by $L(\theta)$. For example, to find the MLE of a binomial parameter, p, noting that the LF and its logarithm have the same maxima, one solves the likelihood equation,

$$0 = L'(p) = \frac{x}{p} - \frac{n-x}{1-p},$$

the observed relative frequency of successes. Taking the second derivative, one finds:

$$L''(p) = -\left(\frac{x}{p^2} + \frac{n-x}{(1-p)^2}\right)$$

whereupon replacing x by its mean, np, reduces this to:

$$-E[L''(p)] = \frac{np}{p^2} + \frac{n(1-p)}{(1-p)^2} = \frac{n}{p(1-p)}$$

the variance of p. "This formula," he declares, "supplies the most direct way known to me of finding the probable error of statistics," adding (with critical reference to Pearson) that "the above proof [not shown here] applies only to statistics obtained by the method of maximum likelihood" (Fisher 1950, 10.329).

Now one might hope to show that the Fisher information, defined by

(2) $$I_n(\theta) = -E[L''(x|\theta)]$$

imposes an upper limit on the precision of any estimator of θ for any given sample size n. To make a long tangled story short, Edgeworth proved special cases of this using the Schwarz inequality and Fisher extended his results (see Hald 1998, pp. 703–707, 716–719, 724–726, 734), offering a proof (again less than rigorous) that $V(T) \geq 1/I_n(\theta)$. The first rigorous proofs came in the 1940s (Cramer 1946, p. 475; De Groot 1986, p. 425) and a general form of this so-called Cramer-Rao inequality reads:

(3) $$\text{var}(T) \geq m'(\theta)^2/I_n(\theta)$$

where $m(\theta) = E(T) = \int T(x)p(x|\theta)dx$. One's assumptions are that the density is defined for a nondegenerate interval that does not depend on θ and has (finite) moments up to second order. When $m(\theta) = \theta$, so that T is unbiased, (3) simplifies to $\text{var}(T) \geq 1/I_n(\theta)$, as anticipated by Edgeworth and Fisher. Estimators that achieve this minimum variance bound are called MVB estimators, and this con-

dition effectively replaces asymptotic efficiency since it applies to samples of all sizes. Cramer then proved (1946, pp. 499ff) that if an efficient (or MVB) estimator T of θ exists, then the likelihood equation has a unique solution given by T, and that if a sufficient estimator of θ exists, any solution of the likelihood equation will be a function of that estimator. These results round out Fisher's small sample theory of estimation.

Fisher used his factorization criterion (1) for sufficient statistics to show that the distributions admitting a sufficient statistic are precisely those of the form:

(4) $$p(x|\theta) = F(x)G(\theta)\exp[u(x)v(\theta)]$$

provided that the range of X does not depend on θ, as it does for the uniform distribution on $[0, \theta]$ with θ unknown. Called the exponential class, (4) includes almost all the other distributions that figure prominently in applied probability and statistics, including the normal, Poisson, beta, gamma, and chi-squared distributions (and there is also a multiparameter form of (4)). Thus, the class (4) occupies a position of central importance, akin to that of the central limit theorem. Using a clever change of variable in the condition for equality in (3), Jaynes (2003, p. 519) shows that the exponential class is also the class of maxent distributions, those yielded by the principle of maximizing the (Shannon) entropy subject to one or more given mean value constraints. Thus, as Jaynes proclaims, "if we use the maximum entropy principle to assign sampling distributions, this automatically generates the distributions with the most desirable properties from the standpoint of … sampling theory (because the sampling variance of an estimator is then the minimum possible value)" (520). Once again, the fruits of Fisher's own investigations drew him closer to the objectivist Bayesian position that he so vigorously opposed. Indeed, the maximum entropy formalism can be used to generate either data distributions or prior distributions and is supported by the kinds of consistency properties Fisher also endorsed. Mathematics makes strange bedfellows!

Fisher information defined by (2), or, equivalently, by $I_n(\theta) = E[L'(x|\theta)^2] = \text{var}[L'(x|\theta)$, also plays a prominent role, as one would expect, in Fisher's theory of experimental design. Given multinomial data with category counts $a_1, \ldots, a_k$ and category probabilities $p_1(\theta), \ldots, p_k(\theta)$ that depend on a parameter θ, the Fisher information for a sample of one is:

(5) $$I(\theta) = \sum \frac{1}{p_i}\left(\frac{dp_i}{d\theta}\right)^2$$

Examples arise in genetics, especially linkage. For example, one may wish to compare the information about the linkage parameter θ (the recombination fraction) yielded by a double backcross, $AB/ab \times ab/ab$, with that given by a single backcross, $Abab \times Abab$. Under the former mating, the genotypes AB/ab, Ab/ab, aB/ab, ab/ab occur among the offspring with probabilities $\frac{1}{2}(1 - \theta)$, $\frac{1}{2}(\theta)$, $\frac{1}{2}(\theta)$, and $\frac{1}{2}(1 - \theta)$, and so

$$I(\theta) = \frac{2}{1-\theta}\left(-\frac{1}{2}\right)^2 + \frac{2}{\theta}\left(\frac{1}{2}\right)^2 + \frac{2}{\theta}\left(\frac{1}{2}\right)^2 + \frac{2}{1-\theta}\left(-\frac{1}{2}\right)^2$$

$$= \frac{1}{\theta(1-\theta)}$$

while for the single backcross one similarly finds $I(\theta) = 1/2\theta(1 - \theta)$, or half the information yielded by the double backcross. Further refinements arise when there is dominance in one or both factors (see Edwards 1992, pp. 148–149). For more examples, see chapter 11 of *The Design of Experiments* (in Fisher 2003; hereafter *DE*) and Kenneth Mather's *The Measurement of Linkage in Heredity* (1938).

SIGNIFICANCE TESTS

One comes, at last, to Fisher's second important measure for ordering hypotheses, namely, significance tests. The earliest significance tests were aimed at distinguishing a hypothesis of chance from one of cause or design (Hald 1998, §4.1). For example, is the perfect agreement of the wrong answers of two students on a multiple choice test due to collusion or a mere coincidence? In the usage of Laplace, one compares the probability of such agreement on the two hypotheses and when this probability is "incomparably greater" on the hypothesis of design, "we are led," he says, "to disbelieve" that of chance. Laplace readily extended this reasoning to the separation of "real" from "spurious" physical causes, as when he concluded that "the actual disposition of our planetary system," by which he meant that all six planets and their satellites move in the same direction as the earth and have inclinations to the ecliptic within a small neighborhood of zero, "would be infinitely small if it were due to chance" and so indicates a "regular cause" (§4.4). In the same vein, Gustav Kirkhoff concluded that the perfect coincidence of the sixty dark lines in the solar spectrum of iron with sixty bright lines of the spectrum obtained by heating iron filings in a Bunsen burner could not be due to chance but indicated the presence of iron in the sun.

In such cases, the probability of agreement on the hypothesis of design may be only qualitatively defined, but the logic is essentially that of a likelihood ratio test. Nor did Laplace speak in terms of rejecting the hypothesis of chance or prescribe a threshold of improbability beyond which belief gives way (or should give way) to disbelief. He took as his test criterion the tail area probability, that is, the probability of a deviation at least as large as that observed (Hald 1998, p. 25). Moreover, a low probability of observing so large a deviation by chance points to some alternative explanation that, however, need not be formulated beforehand. Rather, "by letting the remarkable feature [of the data] determine the statistic used in the test, we concentrate implicitly on an alternative hypothesis" (p. 67).

Fisher embraced most but not all these features. The *locus classicus* of his account is the famous treatment of the tea-tasting lady who claims to be able to tell whether milk or tea was added first to a mixture of the two (*DE*, chapter 2). Every serious student of inductive reasoning should read and reread this chapter with infinite care. Of great importance, too, is the fourth chapter of *SMSI*, "Some Misapprehensions about Tests of Significance."

To begin with, a significance test is, emphatically, not a decision rule (*DE*, §12.1; *SMSI*, §4.1], the differences between them being characterized as "many and wide" (*SMSI*, p. 80). Thus opens Fisher's trenchant critique of the Neyman-Pearson theory of testing. In choosing a test statistic, "the experimenter will rightly consider all points on which, in the light of current knowledge, the hypothesis may be imperfectly accurate, and will select tests … sensitive to these possible faults, rather than to others" (p. 50).

However, Fisher is clear that the hypothesis one chooses to test may be suggested by one's data (p. 82). Thus, in tossing a coin, the outcome may lead one to test the hypothesis that the coin is fair, that the trials are independent, or that the same coin was tossed each time. Each test will require a different reference set and a different measure of deviation from the null hypothesis. This point is further illustrated by examples from genetics, where departures from posited 9:3:3:1 Mendelian ratios for a hybrid cross may be due to linkage, partial dominance in one of the factors, linked lethals, or other causes. In such cases, the partitioning of the chi-squared statistic into orthogonal components allows one to pinpoint the source(s) of such a discrepancy (for illustrations of this method, see Mather 1938, chapter 4). This practice is markedly at odds with the Neyman-Pearsonite insistence on predesignating all the elements of a test. Fisher goes on to draw three more such contrasts between significance testing and the acceptance sampling paradigm that informs the Neyman-Pearsonite theory.

First, in acceptance sampling, the population of lots from which one is sampling is well defined and one has a real sequence of repeated trials, "whereas the only populations that can be referred to in a test of significance have no objective reality, being exclusively the product of the statistician's imagination through the hypothesis which he has decided to test" (*SMSI*, p. 81). Thus, a test is possible where no repetition of one's experiment is contemplated. However, Fisher's hypothetically infinite populations lead a shadowy existence and, as Jaynes (2003) remarks, it is hard to see how such imaginings can confer greater objectivity on one's methods.

Second, decisions are final, and conclusions are provisional. And, third, "in the field of pure research, no assessment of the cost of wrong conclusions … can conceivably be more than a pretence, and in any case … would be inadmissible and irrelevant in judging the state of scientific evidence" (*DE*, pp. 25–26; also see *SMSI*, pp. 106–107). Still, Fisher could easily have admitted the relevance of cost functions to the planning of an experiment and still deny their relevance to the weighing of the evidence that results.

The main thrust of Fisher's critique of the Neyman-Pearsonite theory, however, was to deny that the significance level, which measures the strength of the evidence against the null hypothesis of no difference, can be identified with the frequency with which the null hypothesis is erroneously rejected—with the Neyman-Pearsonite's "type I error probability" (*SMSI*, pp. 93–96). Varying Fisher's more complicated example, J. G. Kalbfleisch and D. A. Sprott (1976, p. 262) consider the composite hypothesis H that at least one of m coins is fair ($m > 1$). Each coin is tossed ten times, and if each shows 0, 1, 9, or 10 heads (with at least one showing 1 or 9), one can quote an exact significance level of $22 \times 2^{-10} = 0.0215$ against the fairness of each coin, hence evidence no stronger than this against H. (Intuitively, the evidence that all the coins are biased can be no stronger than the evidence that any particular one of them is biased.) However, the frequency of rejecting H using this criterion, even when H is "truest" (i.e., when all the coins are fair) is only $.0215^m$, which, even for moderately large m, is much smaller than $.0215$. This leads Kalbfleisch and Sprott to conclude, with Fisher, that "the frequency with which a true hypothesis would be rejected by a test in repetitions of the experiment will not necessarily be indicative of the strength of the evidence against H" (p. 263). More generally, it may be

nearly impossible to obtain strong evidence simultaneously ruling out all the simple constituents of a composite hypothesis (*SMSI*, p. 93), which prompts Fisher to conclude that "the infrequency with which, in particular circumstances, decisive evidence is obtained, should not be confused with the force, or cogency, of such evidence" (p. 96).

Fisher, like Laplace, refrains from imposing a universal critical level of significance and almost always reports exact significance levels or tail area probabilities, but, unlike Laplace, he does speak of rejecting hypotheses, even though in most instances this is just shorthand for "regard the data as discordant or inconsistent with the hypothesis." Nevertheless, this language invited confusion with the different decision theoretic approach of Jerzy Neyman and Egon Pearson, and, in fact, misled generations of textbook writers, who regularly graft the Neyman-Pearson account of testing onto Fisher's and paper over the many and wide differences between them.

Fisher's crucial departure from Laplace is to construe significance levels as evidence against the null hypothesis. Like Karl Popper, he steadfastly refuses to concede that evidence sufficient to reject the null hypothesis at a stringent level of significance is evidence for the alternative hypothesis of interest. However, his own practice belies his precept. In testing for genetic linkage, rejection of the hypothesis of independent assortment is routinely followed by estimation of the recombination fraction, that is, the degree of association. And in the example of the tea-tasting lady, his language is that the lady "makes good her claim" when she classifies all the cups presented to her correctly (*DE*, p. 14). The reason he gives for denying that an experiment can do more than disprove the null hypothesis (p. 16) is that the alternative hypothesis that the lady can discriminate "is ineligible as a null hypothesis to be tested by experiment, because it is inexact." That reason is rather question-begging. The real reason, one suspects, is that Fisher wanted to be able to disprove a null hypothesis without providing evidence for any alternative hypothesis. The possibility of such purely negative significance tests has been at the heart of the controversies that have swirled about this topic (see Royall 1997, chapter 3, especially §3.9).

For Laplace, as it was seen, significance tests are extensions of likelihood ratio tests to rather amorphous ill-defined alternatives. And for Fisher, too, they come into play when the LF is unavailable—a point that seems to have been lost on Neyman and Pearson, whose methodology assumes that outcome probabilities conditional on the alternative hypotheses can be computed from the model. However, for Fisher, the logic of a test is a probabilistic form of *modus tollens*. A hypothesis is rejected when the outcome it entails does not occur; similarly, it is rejected at a stringent level of significance when an outcome it predicts with high probability does not occur. And this eliminativist logic applies whether or not alternative hypotheses have entered the arena.

Kalbfleisch and Sprott (1976) also strongly insist that the alternative to, say, a null hypothesis of homogeneity may be too amorphous to admit specification. Significance tests allow one to postpone the hard work of formulating such an alternative until a significance test has demonstrated the need for one. No doubt, there are strong arguments on both sides and the issue may be considered unresolved. An interesting case in point is provided by the maximum entropy method wherein the signs and magnitudes of the deviations from expected values indicate a new mean value constraint that then leads to a new maxent distribution. The presence of such an additional constraint is indicated when the entropy of the current maxent distribution lies sufficiently far below the maximum allowed by the current mean value constraints. Ultimately, however, one must agree with Gossett (see Royall 1997, p. 68) that one cannot securely reject a hypothesis or a model unless or until one has a better fitting one to put in its place (compare de Groot 1986, p. 523).

Critics of significance testing have also questioned the use of tail areas, which as Fisher admits, "is not very defensible save as an approximation" (*SMSI*, p. 71), for it appears to make the import of what was observed depend on possible outcomes that were not observed. Actually, in cases where the measure of deviation is a continuous variate, like Pearson's chi square or Gossett's $n^{1/2}(\bar{x} - \mu)/s$, the probability of a deviation exactly as large as that observed is nil and so one has no choice but to use a tail area. However, more to the point, tail areas give (approximately) the proportion of possible outcomes that agree with the hypothesis of cause, design, or efficacy as well as that observed, and this provides a sort of absolute standard of comparison, one that even allows one to compare the strength of the evidence in favor of hypotheses in disparate fields. In any case, the Laplacean logic of significance testing, which views such a test as an index of the evidence in favor of some hypothesis of design, averts a host of interpretive difficulties and fits well with a form of argument—the piling up of improbabilities—that occurs across a broad spectrum of the sciences.

CONCLUSION

No article of reasonable length could hope to touch on more than a fraction of Fisher's vast output and the many thorny issues raised therein. Nothing has been said here, for example, about Fisher's notorious third measure of uncertainty, namely, fiducial probabilities. A good place to start is with the example of Gossett's t-test (*SMSI*, pp. 84–86). Turn next to the critique of the fiducial argument by A. W. F. Edwards (1992, §10.5), and then to the excellent papers by Teddy Seidenfeld (1992) and Sandy L. Zabell (1992). Oscar Kempthorne somewhere remarked that it would require at least ten years of preliminary study before attempting a definitive account of Fisher's work in statistics alone, but the effort would be well repaid. The same may be said of his work in genetics and evolution.

One may view Fisher as a "foiled circuitous wanderer," for his heroic attempts to construct a comprehensive alternative to the Bayesian account of inductive reasoning drew him ever more firmly back into the Bayesian position he started from and then rejected. The question one must address, however, is not whether Fisher would ultimately have returned to the Bayesian fold had he lived, say, another decade, but whether the consistency requirements he endorsed force one "back to Bayes." As it has been seen, his position is close to the objectivist Bayesianism of Laplace, Jeffreys, and Jaynes at many points (see Zabell 1992, p. 381 and notes 42 and 56). At the same time, it has to be admitted that Fisher created almost single-handedly the conceptual framework and technical vocabulary all statisticians, whether Bayesian or non-Bayesian, utilize. For sheer fertility of invention, Fisher has few equals in the history of the mathematical sciences.

See also Information Theory; Statistics, Foundations of.

Bibliography

Cramer, Harald. *Mathematical Methods of Statistics*. Princeton, NJ: Princeton University Press, 1946.

De Groot, Morris. *Probability and Statistics*. Reading, MA: Addison-Wesley, 1986.

Edwards, A. W. F. *Likelihood*. 2nd ed. Baltimore, MD: Johns Hopkins University Press, 1992.

Hald, Anders. *A History of Mathematical Statistics from 1750 to 1930*. New York: Wiley, 1998.

Jaynes, Edwin T. *Probability Theory: The Logic of Science*. Edited by G. Larry Bretthorst. New York: Cambridge University Press, 2003.

Kalbfleisch, J. G., and D. A. Sprott. "On Tests of Significance." In *Foundations of Probability Theory, Statistical Inference, and Statistical Theories of Science*. Vol. 2, edited by W. L.

Harper and C. A. Hooker. Dordrecht, Netherlands: D. Reidel, 1976.

Mather, Kenneth. *The Measurement of Linkage in Heredity.* London: Metheun, 1938.

Royall, Richard. *Statistical Evidence: A Likelihood Paradigm.* London: Chapman-Hall, 1997.

WORKS BY FISHER

Contributions to Mathematical Statistics. New York: Wiley, 1950.

Collected Papers of R. A. Fisher, 5 vols, edited by J. H. Bennett. Adelaide, Australia: University of Adelaide, 1971–1974.

Statistical Inference and Analysis: Selected Correspondence of R. A. Fisher. Edited by J. H. Bennett. Oxford, U.K.: Clarendon Press, 1990.

Statistical Methods, Experimental Design, and Scientific Inference. New York: Oxford University Press, 2003. Reprints of the latest editions of Fisher's three books, *Statistical Methods for Research Workers*, *The Design of Experiments*, and *Statistical Methods and Scientific Inference.* All page references are to this edition.

WORKS ABOUT FISHER

Box, Joan Fisher. *R. A. Fisher: The Life of a Scientist.* New York: Wiley, 1978.

Seidenfeld, Teddy. *Philosophical Problems of Statistical Inference: Learning from R. A. Fisher.* Dordrecht, Netherlands: D. Reidel, 1979.

Seidenfeld, Teddy. "R. A. Fisher's Fiducial Argument." *Statistical Science* 7 (1992): 358–368.

Zabell, Sandy L. "R. A. Fisher and the Fiducial Argument." *Statistical Science* 7 (1992): 369–387.

Roger D. Rosenkrantz (2005)

FISKE, JOHN
(1842–1901)

John Fiske, the American philosopher and advocate of evolutionary theory, was born in Hartford, Connecticut, and baptized Edmund Fisk Green. He changed his name to John Fisk shortly after his mother remarried in 1855 (the *e* was added in 1860). He grew up in Middletown and attended the Congregational Church, but he became dissatisfied with orthodox Christianity and found himself drawn to the philosophical and theological implications of modern science. He early declared himself an "infidel," meaning by the word "non-Christian" rather than atheist. While he was a student at Harvard, he was punished by the college faculty for reading Auguste Comte in church.

Fiske's main philosophical work, *Outlines of Cosmic Philosophy*, developed from lectures given at Harvard in 1869 and 1871, and was completed in London during 1873 and 1874. In it he acknowledged himself a disciple and expositor of the philosophy of Herbert Spencer, the importance of which, he believed, would in time be seen to surpass that of Isaac Newton. This judgment did not appear extravagant to Fiske, since Spencer's law of evolution was "the first generalization concerning the concrete universe as a whole." According to Fiske's formulation of this law, "The integration of matter and concomitant dissipation of motion, which primarily constitutes Evolution, is attended by a continuous change from indefinite, incoherent homogeneity to definite, coherent heterogeneity of structure and function, through successive differentiations and integrations." He illustrated the law's operation at great length with examples drawn from organic processes, the nebular origin of the solar system, comparative philology, and the development of civilization.

Fiske maintained that at some time in the past, human evolution had reached a stage in which man's brain alone continued to evolve; ultimately, a level was achieved at which the individual's brain continued to develop after his birth. This process, which necessitated a period of prolonged infancy accompanied by the evolution of strong parental affection, provided the physical setting for the evolution of the resulting family into clans and society; for the origin of morality in the altruism demanded by family care; and for cultural progress, through the enhanced receptivity of yet developing minds. Prolonged infancy was the cornerstone of an evolutionary explanation of civilization; indeed, Fiske believed that this theory was his most important contribution to philosophy.

Fiske aimed to show the unity of all knowledge, the inevitability of progress, and the ultimate harmony of science and religion. He appealed to the law of evolution to accomplish the first two aims and to "Berkeleian idealism" to accomplish the third. All knowledge is "relative" in the sense that it consists only of classifying and discovering regularities among phenomena. What underlies and creates our experience or phenomena Fiske calls the "Unknowable," "Deity," and "Absolute Power." This "Deity" is the only proper concern of religion, while the regularities discoverable among the phenomena in which Deity manifests itself are the scientist's laws of nature. Thus Fiske's "cosmic theism" reconciles religion and science. Religious dogmas that intrude upon the scientist's world of phenomena are vestiges of primitive, anthropomorphic stages of religious development. Miracles must therefore be rejected, and the doctrine of special creation must give way to Charles Darwin's theory of natural selection. Pantheism, which according to Fiske identifies Deity with the phenomenal world, is rejected, since Fiske's Deity is an "unconditioned existence" which is "something more than the universe." He rejects Comte's Religion of Humanity as a mere conceit. Materialism is rejected because it is at least conceivable that matter is reducible to mind or feeling, but inconceivable that feeling should evolve from matter; thus, the view that Deity is "Spirit" is plausible.

The major difference between Fiske and Spencer is Fiske's greater emphasis on the religious implications of evolutionary philosophy. Whereas Spencer was guarded, Fiske was unambiguous in calling what lay behind the phenomenal world "Spirit," and he took pains to prove that it was a plausible object of earnest religious contemplation. A further difference between the two thinkers is that Fiske, unlike Spencer, brought evolutionary philosophy to the defense of social conservatism, in the belief that inevitable progress obviated the need for radical social and religious change.

Fiske greatly enjoyed living in Cambridge, Massachusetts, and as late as 1878 he retained the hope of gaining a permanent position at Harvard in either the department of history or that of philosophy. He declined job offers from other universities, but at Harvard he could obtain only temporary positions as a lecturer and as assistant librarian of the college. Early in life Fiske sought to make a living from his writing. Later he was always short of money and tried to make ends meet by going on the lecture circuit; however, he achieved genuine popularity both as a writer and lecturer only in the last decade of his life.

Throughout his life Fiske retained an earnest religious attitude, which he expressed in his later popular lectures in terms were more and more conciliatory toward New England Protestantism. Thus "The Unseen World" (1876), the title essay of his first collection of essays, merely urged that science could not refute the immortality of the soul and that "a simple act of trust" in immortality was not unreasonable. In "The Destiny of Man" (1884), another title essay, Fiske said that the human soul was not merely the end product, but the goal of the great evolutionary process contrived by God. Finally, in *Through Nature to God* (1899), Fiske argued, in reply to T. H. Huxley's Romanes lecture "Evolution and Ethics" (1893), that nature is not morally indifferent but, on the contrary, that evolution "exists purely for the sake of moral ends." He also argued that science offered confirmation of the existence of God and of immortality.

After 1887 Fiske wrote nearly twenty volumes on American history. He was never an original philosopher, but through his clear writing and well-phrased public lectures he helped to advance American religious liberalism.

He was a competent popularizer of Darwin's theory of evolution at a time when most religious writers were attacking evolution with frenzy.

See also Comte, Auguste; Cosmos; Darwin, Charles Robert; Darwinism; Evolutionary Theory; Huxley, Thomas Henry; Newton, Isaac.

Bibliography

Fiske's more philosophical works include *Outlines of Cosmic Philosophy; Based on the Doctrine of Evolution, with Criticisms on the Positive Philosophy*, 2 vols. (Boston: Houghton Mifflin, 1874); *The Unseen World, and Other Essays* (Boston: J. R. Osgood, 1876); *Darwinism, and Other Essays* (London and New York: Macmillan, 1879); *The Destiny of Man Viewed in the Light of His Origin* (Boston: Houghton Mifflin, 1884); *Excursions of an Evolutionist* (Boston: Houghton Mifflin, 1884); *The Idea of God as Affected by Modern Knowledge* (Boston: Houghton Mifflin, 1886); *A Century of Science, and Other Essays* (Boston: Houghton Mifflin, 1899); and *Through Nature to God* (Boston: Houghton Mifflin, 1899). Josiah Royce examines Fiske's philosophy in the introduction to the 1902 edition of *Cosmic Philosophy*. Milton Berman's *John Fiske: The Evolution of a Popularizer* (Cambridge, MA: Harvard University Press, 1961) includes an extensive bibliography.

Andrew Oldenquist (1967)

FITNESS

See *Evolutionary Theory; Philosophy of Biology*

FLORENSKII, PAVEL ALEKSANDROVICH
(1882–1937)

Pavel Aleksandrovich Florenskii was a Russian philosopher, theologian, art theoretician, and scientist-polymath. He was born January 22, 1882, of a Russian father and Armenian mother, and died on December 8, 1937. Florenskii lived in the Caucasus, mainly in Tiflis (Tbilissi), Georgia, until 1898, when he entered the Department of Physics and Mathematics of Moscow University. Endowed with many talents, he was invited to stay at the university after graduation for further studies in mathematics, but declined and instead entered Moscow Theological Academy in 1904. By then he was already known as an active member of the Russian Symbolist movement; he published poetry, essays, and philosophical articles, and he corresponded with Andrey Bely—a leading Symbolist poet and theorist—regarding basic theoretical problems of Symbolism. In 1908 Florenskii graduated from the Academy and stayed there as a professor of philosophy. In 1911 he was ordained a priest. Between 1906 and 1914 he wrote his magnum opus, *The Pillar and Ground of the Truth*, that became one of the principal texts of Russian religious philosophy. It is also a very unusual text, a modernist masterpiece that is at once a theological treatise (bearing the subtitle *An Essay of Orthodox Theodicy*), an exposition of a new philosophical system, a cycle of lyrical letters to a friend (it is divided into "Letters," not chapters, with each letter accompanied by a period engraving with a motto), and an endless chain of digressive studies on all kinds of subjects. Essentially, *An Essay of Orthodox Theodicy* is an itinerary of a spiritual journey; and because the journey is undertaken by a philosopher, it includes the creation of a philosophy.

FLORENSKII'S EARLY PHILOSOPHY: SOPHIOLOGY

The philosophy that is expounded in the book is a system of metaphysics of All-Unity. In Russian philosophy this kind of metaphysics was introduced by Vladimir Solov'ev. Its basic concept represents a specific transrational principle of inner form that ensures a perfect unity of a manifold such that any part of the latter is identical to the whole. The principle is an ancient aporetic philosophical paradigm that originated in pre-Socratics, was later articulated in Neoplatonism, and then carefully elaborated by Nicolas of Cusa. It made its last appearance in Western metaphysics in Schelling's thought. Solov'ev's contribution to this philosophical tradition consisted in making the concept of All-Unity the guiding principle of a comprehensive philosophical system. The main new element introduced by Solov'ev was the linking of All-Unity with the biblical and Gnostic mythologem of Sophia, the Wisdom of God. As a result, Solov'ev's metaphysics of All-Unity was articulated as a metaphysics of Sophia (sophiology). Florenskii accepts the connection between Sophia and All-Unity but otherwise does not follow Solov'ev and hardly ever mentions him. *The Pillar* presents a new, different kind of sophiology.

One may single out two lines in the history of the mythological Sophia, both deriving from the Wisdom books of the Bible. One included Gnostic and later Western mystical doctrines, with Valentine, Heinrich Seuse, Jacob Boehme, and Emmanuel Swedenborg as the chief exponents; whereas the other, found in Eastern Christianity, manifested itself in cultic forms, such as consecration of churches to Sophia and icon-painting. Solov'ev drew upon the Western tradition, whereas Florenskii upon the Eastern one. Further elaboration, turning Wisdom of God into a metaphysical concept, is also independent of Solov'ev. The association of All-Unity with Sophia is based on the fact that, ontologically, they both are intermediate realities between God and the empirical world. Such reality was traditionally conceived as "the world in God" or, according to Greek patristic writings, the system of divine logoi (ideas, designs) of all created things.

Florenskii made this conception of Christian Platonism still more Christian by linking each human person to God's love of this person. This love further coincides with the divine logos or God's idea of this person, and represents a monad of Liebnitzian type; thus there is a noumenal love-idea-monad corresponding to each person and implementing his or her connection to God. Love also connects all these love-idea-monads with one another, and taken together, they form a loving and *eo ipso* living being. Sophia is this noumenal, meta-empirical, living and loving being. Analyzing love, Florenskii finds that it means a certain kind of identity of lovers, their "consubstantiality in God." Thus any two monads belonging to Sophia are consubstantial by virtue of their love, which implies that all parts of Sophia are identical both to one another and to the whole, while at the same time retaining their individual differences. This means in turn that Sophia is the perfect unity of a manifold—that is, All-Unity.

The concept of Sophia as a noumenal loving being and community of monads connected by love forms the basis of the Platonist ontology in Florenskii's early philosophy. Florenskii's epistemology is also Platonist at this stage. The key to the epistemology of *The Pillar* is given in the epigraph of the book, which is a quotation from St. Gregory of Nyssa: "Knowledge is achieved by love." As in Florenskii's ontology, the main principle here is love: Cognition is a kind of communion of the knower and the known, it implies building up their unity and consubstantiality, and this implies, in turn, that genuine cognition is achieved only in love and by love. Such treatment, integrating epistemology into ontology, is opposite to the mainstream of Western metaphysics and especially to Kantian and post-Kantian philosophy that insisted on the primacy of epistemology and subsumed ontology under it. Accentuating this opposition to the extreme, Florenskii depicts the entire history of European thought as a dramatic conflict between Platonism and Kantianism.

FLORENSKII'S LATE PHILOSOPHY: "CONCRETE METAPHYSICS"

The Pillar and Ground of the Truth made Florenskii famous, but it was a milestone rather than an exhaustive treatment of his ideas. In it he tried to follow strictly the Church doctrine and thus had to put aside many themes that were important for him, above all, his ideas of the symbol and its role. Florenskii considered symbol as a constitutive element and building block of reality, and invariably defined his outlook as symbolist. He began to develop this view already in his early texts and returned to it after the publication of *The Pillar*. He conceives and nearly completes a broad project of symbolistic philosophy called *concrete metaphysics*, a kind of all-embracing synthesis resulting in a detailed symbolist picture of Being and the Universe. Originally, symbol was conceived by Florenskii in the classical Platonic and Schellingian way, as an inseparable union of the phenomenal (sensuous) and noumenal (intelligible), joined in perfect mutual expression (the Schellingian *Einbildung*).

In Florenskii's concrete metaphysics the concept of symbol acquired new features—along with his entire worldview that should now be described as Christian Neoplatonism. Firstly, the structure of symbol became layered, as a set of concentric spheres, with the one in the center corresponding to the perfect union of the symbol's phenomenal and noumenal components, whereas the outer spheres represented increasingly imperfect expressions of the noumenon in the phenomenon. Secondly, the inner mechanism of symbol was now seen as a dynamic union of phenomenal and noumenal energies. Energy became the basic new element in Florenskii's late philosophy, which he treated in unwavering Neoplatonist terms.

Concrete Metaphysics was intended to provide a systematic description of reality as formed by symbols of various kinds. In many aspects it resembles Ernst Cassirer's contemporaneous theory of symbolic forms. The description had to consist of studies devoted to definite kinds of symbols. Its basic criteria for distributing symbols into types or classes are anthropological and correspond to human perceptive modalities; the main classes of symbols analyzed by Florenskii are visual (spatial) and acoustic (verbal). The study of visual symbols includes, first of all, a specific model of the Cosmos. In this model, the physical Universe is complemented by a noumenal yet equally spatial world; contacts and transitions between the two worlds include death as well as phenomena of religious and mystical experience, and the boundary between the two worlds is regulated by the cult. Another

vast domain of visual symbols is provided by the plastic arts. Florenskii made detailed studies of this domain; he developed a theory of reverse perspective used in icons and then more general theory of space as it figures in works of art; from 1921 to 1924 he expounded these theories in lecture courses in Vkhutemas, one of the main centers of the Russian avant-garde art of 1920s. As for the studies of acoustic symbols, they include mainly Florenskii's philosophy of language, a specific feature of which is the idea of occult energies present in the word. Other parts of Concrete Metaphysics that merit mention are the outlines of the philosophy of technics, based on the idea of the projection of human organs.

Florenskii's late philosophy is presented in numerous works, nearly all of which were created in the decade from 1914 to 1924. Many of the studies planned were not completed. After 1917 the Theological Academy was closed, and Florenskii started working in applied physics and engineering. As he never relinquished his Christian faith, he was persecuted, being arrested in 1928 and again in 1933. After the second arrest he was sent first to the Far East and then, in 1934, to the concentration camp in the Solovetsky islands in the White Sea. In 1937, in the campaign of mass murders, he was shot. Most of his works written after 1917 remained unpublished until the 1980s and 1990s; when they gradually became known, it was discovered that they contain pioneering ideas in many fields—for example, in semiotics—and some bold previsions, such as the existence of the genetic code.

See also Metaphysics; Philosophy of Religion; Russian Philosophy; Sophia.

Bibliography

FLORENSKII'S WORKS

Beyond Vision: Essays on the Perception of Art. Translated by Wendy Salmond. London: Reaktion, 2002.

Detyam moim. Vospominanya proshlykh dnei. Genealogicheskie issledovaniya. Iz solovetskikh pisem. Zaveshchanie. Moscow: Moskovskii rabochii, 1992.

Iconostasis. Translated by Donald Sheehan and Olga Andreev. Crestwood, NY: St. Vladimir Seminary Press, 1966.

The Pillar and Ground of the Truth. Translated by Boris Jakim. Princeton, NJ: Princeton University Press, 1997.

Sobranie sochinenii. Filosofiya kul'ta (opyt pravoslavnoi antropoditsei). Moscow: Mysl', 2004.

Sobranie sochinenii. Stat'i i issledovaniya po istorii i filosofii iskusstva i arkheologii. Moscow: Mysl', 2000.

Sobranie sochinenii v chetyrekh tomakh, Tt.1–4. Moscow: Mysl', 1994–1998.

OTHER WORKS

Franz, Norbert, Michael Hagemeister, and Frank Haney, eds. *Pavel Florenskij—Tradition und Moderne: Beitraege zum Internationalen Symposium an der Universitaet Potsdam, 5. bis 9. April 2000.* New York: Peter Lang, 2001.

Hagemeister, Michael, and Nina Kauchtschischwili, eds. *P. A. Florenskii i kul'tura ego vremeni.* Atti del Convegno Internazionale, Università degli Studi di Bergamo, 10–14 gennaio 1988. Marburg, Germany: Blaue Hoerner Verlag, 1995.

Khoruzhii, Sergei S. *Mirosozertsanie Florenskogo.* Tomsk, Russia: Vodolei, 1999.

Sergey Horujy (2005)

FLORENTINE ACADEMY

"Florentine Academy," or Platonic Academy of Florence, is the name usually applied to the circle of philosophers and other scholars who gathered around Marsilio Ficino, under the auspices of the Medici, in Careggi, near Florence, between 1462 and 1494. These scholars were engaged in the study and discussion of the works of Plato and his followers and of Platonic philosophy. The name "academy" was adopted in memory of Plato. There is no direct link between this Platonic Academy and other academies active in Florence at a later date.

According to Ficino, the academy was founded by Cosimo de' Medici because his enthusiasm for Plato had been aroused by the lectures of Gemistus Pletho at the time of the Council of Florence (1438). In 1462 Cosimo placed a villa in Careggi at the disposal of Ficino, the promising young son of his physician, and lent him several Greek manuscripts of Plato and other ancient philosophers, assigning him the task of studying, translating, and interpreting these writings. This event may be considered the founding of the Florentine Academy. Unlike most later academies, Ficino's Platonic Academy had no formal organization, charter, or fixed membership, and its activities must be inferred from contemporary sources, mainly the letters and other works of Ficino and his associates.

The chief products of the academy are the numerous writings of Ficino and his associates. Whether the public lectures given by Ficino on Plato, Plotinus, and St. Paul were considered part of the work of the academy we do not know. Its activities probably included some regular readings of the Platonic texts and some lectures about them, and surely Ficino gave individual instruction to some of his pupils. On many occasions he addressed edifying sermonlike speeches to his gathered friends and pupils, and this fact, along with a few others, suggests a link between the academy and some of the lay religious associations of the same period. The most famous events of the academy are the banquets celebrated on Plato's reputed birthday, November 7, in 1468 and in 1473, and perhaps in other years. The banquet of 1468 provided the setting for Ficino's commentary on Plato's *Symposium.* The academy also held discussions on philosophical and other subjects on numerous occasions, and it was customary for learned or otherwise distinguished visitors to Florence to attend some of the meetings. The study in which Ficino talked to his pupils contained a painting that represented the globe, with the crying Heraclitus and the laughing Democritus on either side. The often repeated story that Ficino kept an ever-burning lamp before a bust of Plato must be rejected as a legend.

There is no philosophical doctrine common to the Florentine Academy distinct from that of Ficino, but the thought of all its members was influenced to a greater or lesser degree by his teachings. The circle included such philosophers as Giovanni Pico della Mirandola and Francesco Cattani da Diacceto, and such philosophically inclined scholars and poets as Cristoforo Landino, Lorenzo de' Medici, Angelo Poliziano, and Girolamo Benivieni, to mention only some of the better-known members whose writing showed the impact of the academy. The meetings of the academy became famous during its own time, and its intellectual influence, through its visitors and through Ficino's correspondence, spread to the rest of Italy and Europe. Thus, in spite of its informal and fluctuating character, the academy became, and has remained in history and tradition, the most tangible center of Renaissance Platonism.

There is a close link between Ficino's philosophical doctrine and the structure of the academy as he conceived it. Following the model of the ancient philosophical schools, Ficino considered the academy as a community of friends, and his philosophy included an elaborate theory of friendship that he identified with Platonic love. The members of the academy were, he felt, linked with each other and with their master through a "divine" friendship that was based on their common concern with the contemplative life and with the spiritual ascent toward the knowledge and enjoyment of God.

The goal of the academy was philosophical and, in a broader sense, spiritual and cultural rather than political. Although Ficino and the academy were closely identified with four generations of Medici rulers, it cannot be proved that he was their political tool or that his personal and scholarly attachments were limited to their partisans. Nonetheless, although Ficino lived until 1499 and remained active as a scholar throughout his later years, we hear next to nothing of the activities of the academy after 1494, the year in which the Medici were expelled from Florence, Poliziano and Pico died, and Ficino's published correspondence stopped. There is no direct evidence that the meetings of the academy were discontinued, but it is easy to understand that the illness and old age of its leader, the death of some of its most prominent members, and the political and religious climate that prevailed in Florence after 1494 must have put an end to the academy or at least reduced its activities to a strictly private character.

See also Ficino, Marsilio.

Bibliography

Barzman, Karen-edis. *The Florentine Academy and the Early Modern State: The Discipline of Disegno.* New York: Cambridge University Press, 2000.

De Gaetano, Armand L. *Giambattista Gelli and the Florentine Academy: The Rebellion against Latin.* Florence: L.S. Olschki, 1976.

Della Torre, Arnaldo. *Storia dell'Accademia Platonica di Firenze.* Florence, 1902. This work is still indispensable.

Kristeller, Paul Oskar. "The Platonic Academy of Florence." *Renaissance News* 14 (1961): 147–159. Reprinted in Kristeller's *Renaissance Thought II,* 89–101. New York: Harper and Row, 1965.

Marcel, Raymond. *Marsile Ficin.* Paris, 1958.

Wallach, John R. "The Platonic Academy and Democracy." *Polis* 19 (1–2) (2002): 7–27.

Paul Oskar Kristeller (1967)
Bibliography updated by Tamra Frei (2005)

FLOROVSKII, GEORGII VASIL'EVICH
(1893–1979)

Georgii Vasil'evich Florovskii was a Russian clergyman, theologian, patrologist, and historian of culture. A descendant of several generations of Orthodox priests, Florovskii graduated from the Department of History and Philology of Novorossiyskii University in Odessa (1916), and taught in Odessa until January 1920, when he emigrated to Sofia, Bulgaria. There he became a member of a group of five Russian émigrés who, in 1920 and 1921, founded the so-called Eurasianism. The Eurasian doctrine was first presented in the collective work "Exodus to the East," for which Florovskii wrote three articles.

"Exodus to the East" presented what was essentially a cultural morphology of Oswald Spengler's type (i.e., the botanized view of history as a process of development and interaction of ethnic and cultural organisms) and a geopolitical theory stating that, because Europe had exhausted its spiritual energies, Russia should break with it and cultivate cultural and political ties with Asia. Eurasianists sharply criticized European civilization and argued that in all principal aspects Russia belongs neither to the European nor to the Asian world; rather, it occupies its own continent "Eurasia" and has its own type of culture that borrowed much from the Mongols in the thirteenth to the fifteenth centuries—when Russia was their vassal state. In politics, they propounded the principle of *ideocracy,* very close to that of the one-party rule in Bolshevik Russia.

During the next several years, Eurasianism became popular among young Russian émigrés, evolving from a cultural theory into a political movement that had a pro-Soviet orientation and engaged in secret activities. Florovskii made a significant contribution to the initial form of the Eurasianist doctrine that gravitated toward philosophy of history and philosophy of culture. However, as early as 1923 he began to object strongly to his fellow Eurasianists' growing tendency toward ethnic and geopolitical concerns, favoring instead the opposite orientation toward Orthodox Christianity. This line was rejected by other Eurasianist leaders and, as a result, Florovskii left the movement. In 1928 he published the article "The Eurasian Temptation," in which he presented a profound critical analysis of Eurasianism, and in later years he invariably minimized the scale of the Eurasian episode in his biography.

NEOPATRISTIC SYNTHESIS

From 1922 to 1926 Florovskii lived in Prague, where he received a doctorate in philosophy for his study on Alexander Ivanovich Herzen's philosophy of history and wrote a number of essays on Russian cultural history, including works on Fyodor Dostoyevsky, Fyodor Tytchev, and Mikhail Gershenzon. In September 1926 he moved to Paris to become Professor of Patristics at the St. Sergius of Radonezh Theological Institute that was founded in 1925 and developed quickly into the leading Orthodox theological school. Though a self-taught theologian, Florovskii found in patristics his true calling. He focused on the Greek Fathers of the Church and developed brilliant survey courses, marked by a pioneering presentation of the subject. The teachings of the Greek Fathers also became the cornerstone of the theories that he started to develop in philosophy of culture, theology, and ecclesiology.

At the core of these theories was the concept of *Neopatristic Synthesis*. According to its main thesis, a permanent creative renewal of ties with patristic thought is a necessary condition for Christian culture; in fact, such a renewal defines the mode of the latter's existence. This thesis has manifold implications. Firstly, it is a restatement of the basic tenet of the Orthodox doctrine that establishes a permanent and all-embracing normative role of the Tradition of Fathers. Secondly, it is a polemic reformulation of the claim that Greek philosophy—rather than theology—is an eternal source for all subsequent philosophical thought, so that keeping ties with it is necessary for philosophy of all ages. And thirdly, it is a viable premise for constructing a new philosophy or theology of culture of the archeological type—that is, one based on the permanent generating and productive role of a certain source. Florovskii's theory stated that Greek patristics made Hellenism not simply Christian or Christianized, but "ecclesianised" (*votserkovlenny*)—integrated into the life of the Church with all its mystical and sacramental dimensions. This new transfigured Hellenism replaces the old pagan one and should serve as the generating source of a new "ecclesianised," Christocentric culture. The principle of this culture is a sui generis creative traditionalism, which is open to all contemporary problems and tries to solve them, drawing upon Fathers not for ready answers, but for the mental, cultural, and spiritual attitudes required to meet the challenge.

Seeing in the concept of Neopatristic Synthesis an original and universal criterion, Florovskii applies it to many cultural phenomena. He elaborates a critique of German Idealism and of the mainstream European metaphysical tradition in general, charging them with gnosticism and a mere continuation of the primordial pagan, untransfigured Hellenism. This critique of European thought (likened by himself and others to the philosophy of Charles Renouvier) did not gain much popularity.

By contrast, Florovskii's discussion of the Russian intellectual tradition in the *Ways of Russian Theology* (1937)—which he described as an "attempt at an historical synthesis"—became a widely acknowledged masterpiece. The book is a systematic and enormously erudite exposition of Russia's cultural and spiritual evolution from the fifteenth century until the Bolshevik revolution; many of its sections are of independent value as brilliant critical essays. In his conceptual analyses Florovskii strictly applies the criterion of Neopatristic Synthesis, which renders most of his assessments mercilessly critical. In particular, Russian religious-philosophical renaissance and its main figures—such as Pavel Aleksandrovich Florensky and Nikolai Aleksandrovich Berdyaev—are severely reprimanded. Another such figure, Fr. Sergius Bulgakov, the dean of St. Sergius Institute and author of a controversial teaching about Sophia Divine Wisdom, became Florovskii's target during the so-called "Dispute over Sophia," a heated debate over Bulgakov's teaching in émigré theological circles in the mid-1930s.

THE ECUMENTICAL MOVEMENT

Another important dimension of Florovskii's work was his participation in the Ecumenical Movement. During his Paris period, he was ordained as a priest and took an active part in inter-religious contacts. Beginning with the Edinburgh Conference of 1937, he was a member of various ruling bodies of the Movement, playing a significant role in its formative period and recognized as a leading Orthodox voice in theological discussions. In connection with this activity, he produced a significant number of texts on the Church, its nature and tasks. Taken together, these texts form a self-consistent ecclesiology that eventually became widely known and influential. In September of 1948 Florovskii moved from Paris to the United States to take up the position of Professor of Dogmatic Theology and Patristics at St. Vladimir's Orthodox Theological Seminary in Crestwood, New York. The concluding American period of his biography is chiefly that of brilliant teaching career: at St Vladimir's (until 1955), Columbia University (1951–1956), Harvard University Divinity School (1956–1964), and Princeton University (1964–1972). During these years, his reputation as a theologian and church historian reached its peak. Although Florovskii was not a founder of a school, his numerous disciples include many prominent personalities—and not only from the Orthodox world. He can be considered as the most influential Orthodox theologian of the last decades of the twentieth century.

See also Eurasianism; Philosophy of Religion; Religion; Russian Philosophy.

Bibliography

Blane, Andrew, ed. *Georges Florovsky: Russian Intellectual and Orthodox Churchman*. Crestwood, NY: St. Vladimir's Seminary Press, 1993.

Florovsky, Georges. *Collected Works of Georges Florovsy*, Vols. 1–5. Belmont, MA: Nordland, 1972–1979.

Florovsky, Georges. *Collected Works. Vols. V–XIV*. Vaduz (Lichtenstein), Germany: Academic Books, 1987–1992.

Florovsky, Georges. *Ways of Russian Theology*, edited by Richard S. Haugh, translated by Robert L. Nichols. Belmont, MA: Nordland, 1979.

Horuzhy, Sergey S. "Neo-Patristic Synthesis and Russian Philosophy." *St. Vladimir's Theological Quarterly* 44 (3–4) (2000): 309–328.

Sergey Horujy (2005)

FLUDD, ROBERT
(1574–1637)

Robert Fludd, or Flud, also known as Robertus de Fluctibus, was an English physician, author, and occultist. The son of Sir Thomas Fludd, paymaster to Queen Elizabeth I's forces in France and the Low Countries, Fludd was born at Milgate House, Bearsted, Kent. At the age of seventeen he entered St. John's College, Oxford, then a center of high Anglicanism. After taking his M.A. degree in 1598, Fludd spent some years abroad, studying medicine. On returning to Oxford, he entered Christ Church. He took the degrees of MB and MD in 1605, but had considerable difficulty obtaining from the College of Physicians the right to practice medicine, which was not granted until 1606. It was alleged that he had spoken with contempt of Galen. Nevertheless, he was admitted as a fellow of the College of Physicians in 1609.

As a London doctor Fludd prospered; he was able to provide himself with an amanuensis, to whom he dictated his numerous treatises. His first book, *Apologia Compendiaria Fraternitatem de Rosea Cruce* (1616), was a defense of the ideas of the "Fraternity of the Rosy Cross." About the origins and character of the Rosicrucian Fraternity there is considerable dispute. Although allegedly introduced into Europe in the fifteenth century, Rosicrucian ideas, in fact, derive from two anonymously published tracts written by the Lutheran theologian Johann Valentin Andreä in the early seventeenth century. These, for motives that are somewhat obscure, purported to be of fifteenth-century origin. Whether, even in the seventeenth century, there actually was a Rosicrucian Society as described by Andreä remains a matter of dispute. But these tracts provided a common point of reference for like-minded occultists.

It is impossible to take Fludd seriously as a philosopher; however, he did give expression to a system of ideas that was very influential in the seventeenth century. This can most succinctly be described as an attempt to uphold allegorical interpretation of the Bible, and the established pseudosciences—astrology, chiromancy, alchemy, and sympathetic magic—against the scientific spirit.

Fludd attacked scientific inquiry mainly in its Greek form, as represented in Aristotle and Galen, but certainly with an eye on what was happening around him. His point of departure was St. Paul's attack upon philosophers who try to discover the truth by their own efforts rather than by the interpretation of what God has chosen to reveal. Fludd's criticism of science can be summed up in the familiar phrase: "What is true isn't new; what is new isn't true." He argued that so far as science has any truth in it, it teaches doctrines that careful interpretation will reveal in Genesis (Like Henry More, Fludd was greatly influenced by cabalistic writings). For the most part, however, the teachings of science have to be rejected. Fludd attacked Aristotle's meteorological writings, for example, because Aristotle gives a naturalistic account of lightning and thunder; whereas lightning, according to Fludd, "is a fire burning from the face and presence of Jehovah."

Yet, strangely enough, there is a good deal of contemporary science incorporated into Fludd's work. His contemporaries, he complained, demanded "ocular demonstrations" of divine truths and he used the thermometer—the invention of which is sometimes ascribed to him—and the lodestone for that purpose. Like many of his fellow occultists, Fludd had a passion for diagrams, and some of his optical diagrams remained in physics textbooks up to the twentieth century.

His general approach, however, is cosmogonical, in the manner of the mythmaker, rather than cosmological, in the manner of the scientist. His ideas are most fully presented in *Utriusque Cosmi, Maioris Scilicet et Minoris, Metaphysica, Physica atque Technica Historia* (An account, metaphysical, physical, and technical, of both worlds, greater and lesser), which was published as a series of volumes from 1617 to 1621, and was even then left unfinished. Fludd makes great play with the general concepts of light (heat) and darkness (cold)—hence his interest in optics; rarefaction and condensation—hence the thermometer; sympathy and antipathy—hence the lodestone. His theory can be described in this way: in the beginning God created a void by withdrawing into himself (contraction), and the void appeared as darkness because God is light. Expanding again as light into the void, God created all the substances of the world. Thus, the world we live in is ruled partly by light (God) and partly by darkness (the kingdom of the devil). Since everything is of the same nature—that is, a mixture of light and darkness—there are secret sympathies and secret antipathies everywhere, marked by signs that the adept can discover with God's help. The practice of medicine depends entirely on understanding these forces, as do the practices of chiromancy and astrology.

Fludd's works were published in Latin, and circulated on the Continent, where they attracted a considerable amount of attention. In 1623 Marin Mersenne attacked Fludd as an "evil magician"; and when Fludd replied, Pierre Gassendi, at Mersenne's request, criticized his occultism at length. Fludd also engaged in controversy with Johannes Kepler, who had criticized Fludd in the appendix to his *Harmonice Mundi* (1619).

See also Aristotle; Cosmology; Galen; Gassendi, Pierre; Kabbalah; Kepler, Johannes; Mersenne, Marin; More, Henry; Philosophy of Medicine.

Bibliography

Fludd's works were brought together as *Opera* (Gouda, 1638); *Philosophia Moysaica* appeared posthumously in an English version—Fludd's own—in London (1659); his short alchemical essay "Truth's Golden Harrow" was published in *Ambix*, Vol. III, Nos. 3 and 4 (April 1949), 91–150, with an introduction by C. H. Josten.

James Brown Craven, in *Doctor Robert Fludd, the English Rosicrucian* (Kirkwell, U.K., 1902) summarizes Fludd's works enthusiastically, but without much insight. Craven's book includes details of the Fludd–Mersenne–Gassendi controversy.

Other writings on Fludd include Serge Hutin, *Robert Fludd: Le Rosicrucien* (Paris, 1953) with a bibliography; Walter Pagel, "Religious Motives in the Medical Biology of the Seventeenth-Century," in *Bulletin of the Institute of the History of Medicine* 3 (4) (1935): 265–312; Robert Theodore Gunther, *Early Science in Oxford,* Vol. XI (Oxford, 1937); Sherwood Taylor, "The Origins of the Thermometer," in *Annals of Science* 5 (2) (December 1942): 129–156; Lynn Thorndike, *History of Magic and Experimental Science,* Vols. VII and VIII (New York: Macmillan, 1958). See also Denis Saurat, *Milton: Man and Thinker* (London: Dent, 1944), Ch. 3, pp. 248–267.

John Passmore (1967)

FODOR, JERRY A.
(1935–)

Jerry Fodor is the most significant philosopher of mind in the last fifty years. A student of Hilary Putnam, he joined him, Noam Chomsky, and others at MIT in the early 1960s and became the philosopher most responsible for the "cognitive revolution" that replaced the behaviorism that had dominated much of philosophy and psychology since the 1920s, replacing it with a computational approach derived from the work of Alan Turing. In this way he hoped to provide a basis for a naturalist and realist account of mental processes that rendered them amenable to scientific study. Indeed, he is one of the few philosophers who has combined philosophical and empirical psychological research, publishing work in both domains, and developing at least two theories that have become highly influential in each: a computational/representational theory of thought processes ("CRTT") and a "modularity" theory of perception and linguistic processing.

CRTT is an effort to salvage what Fodor (1975) regards as essential to the familiar "belief/desire," or "(propositional) attitude" psychology with which people routinely explain each other's behavior, as when one explains someone's crossing a road in terms of a desire to meet a colleague. As the name emphasizes, the theory has two parts. According to the computational part, each attitude involves a computationally specifiable relation to a syntactically specifiable representation in a "language of thought" entokened in the agent's brain. For example, *judgment* might be the output of perceptual and reasoning systems that serves as the input to decision making. For the "representational" part, Fodor (1998) argues at length against popular "prototype," "conceptual role" and "holistic" theories of content, and defends instead an "atomistic," "informational," "asymmetric dependency" theory according to which, (i) *ceteris paribus*, tokenings of symbols causally co-vary with phenomena that they thereby mean; and (ii) tokenings caused by phenomena they don't mean *depend* upon (i), but (i) doesn't depend upon them. For example, "horse" means *horse* if (i) it's a *ceteris paribus* law that "horse" tokens are caused by horses, and (ii) nonhorses (e.g., distant cows) causing "horse" tokens depends on horses doing so, but not *vice versa* (1991). Thus, Jones's judgment that horses fly might consist in a sentence, "Horses fly," playing the aforementioned judging role in her brain, where "Horses" and "flies" are each asymmetrically dependent upon the respective phenomena in the world. In this way Fodor hopes to defend intentional realism, in contrast to the widespread eliminativism about the mental, and mere instrumentalism about psychology, that renders psychological ascription a matter of mere "interpretation," such as one finds in the work of Willard Quine, Donald Davidson, Daniel Dennett, and Paul and Patricia Churchland. (Fodor's [1983, 1998] account of representation also leads him to claim that virtually all concepts expressed by single morphemes in natural language are innate, rejecting the empiricism also associated with these figures.)

CRTT is a species of functionalism, or the view, due originally to Putnam, that mental states are to be individuated by their causal relations, for example, to inputs, outputs, external phenomena, and each other, in ways analogous to the individuation of a program in a computer (1968). Since different physical phenomena can realize these relations, functionalism naturally gives rise to cross-classificatory *layers* of explanation: one level of causal relations may be "multiply realized" by different mechanisms at lower levels (1968, 1975). Specifically, the *intentional level* of a cognitive psychology may be implemented at a lower level by various computational *syntactic* processes, which in turn may be implemented by different physical mechanisms—brains in the case of people, transistors in the case of machines. For this reason, intentional psychology enjoys a considerable "autonomy" from levels of explanation closer to the brain, for example, neurophysiology. However, although the laws and explanations at the intentional level are not *reducible* to laws and explanations at the lower levels, Fodor presumes that they "*supervene*" on them.

One of Fodor's (1986) main arguments for CRTT is that it promises to account for the sensitivity of human beings to indefinitely many properties that are not "transducible" by sense organs, in particular, to arbitrary nonphysical and/or nonlocal properties, such as being a morpheme or a noun phrase, a crumpled shirt, a grieving widow, or a collapsing star. These sensitivities are particularly impressive given that they seem to be (i) *productive* and (ii) *systematic* (1987): that is, people seem capable of discriminating stimuli of indefinite logical complexity, such as *being a crumpled shirt that was worn by the thief who stole the cat that chased the rat* ...; and anyone capable of thinking one logical form is capable of thinking logical permutations of it: for example, one can think *John loves Mary* if and only if one can think *Mary loves John* (1987). Fodor (1968, 1987, 1988) argues that non-CRTT accounts, such as behaviorism, Gibsonianism, and purely connectionist accounts are either vacuous or empirically inadequate for this task. What one needs is a system that can exploit internal processes of logical combination, inference and hypothesis confirmation, which presuppose at the least the resources of a CRTT.

However, Fodor (1983) has also been a critic of the "New Look" theories of perception, such as one finds in the work of Jerome Bruner, Thomas Kuhn, and Nelson Goodman, which emphasize how people's background expectations color their perceptions. Against this view, Fodor calls attention to the fact that the very perceptual illusions that New Look theorists prize actually tell against their case: for many of these illusions do not disappear even when one knows better, suggesting, along lines developed by Zenon Pylyshyn, that visual perception occurs in a "cognitively impenetrable module," that

is "informationally encapsulated" from the "central" system whereby we reason and fix our beliefs. Fodor argues for a similar view of linguistic perception.

By contrast, the central system is "Quinian" (i.e., computed over the totality of beliefs, as when people settle on a theory that is, for example, simplest and most conservative overall) and "isotropic" (every belief is potentially relevant to the confirmation of every other, as when radio waves confirm the age of the universe). This leads Fodor (1983, 1999) to somewhat pessimistic conclusions regarding the tractability of central reasoning to a Turing-style CRTT, which depends upon exploiting *local* syntactic features of representations. Although CRTT is necessary for an adequate theory of mind, it may not be sufficient.

See also Behaviorism; Chomsky, Noam; Computationalism; Content, Mental; Davidson, Donald; Dennett, Daniel C.; Functionalism; Goodman, Nelson; Kuhn, Thomas; Language of Thought; Mental Representation; Putnam, Hilary; Quine, Willard Van Orman; Turing, Alan.

Bibliography

WORKS BY FODOR

For a full bibliography of Fodor's work up until 1991, see B. Loewer and G. Rey, *Meaning in Mind: Fodor and his Critics* (Oxford: Blackwell, 1991), which also contains a long introduction to his work and critical essays by a number of prominent philosophers and cognitive scientists.

Psychological Explanation. New York: Random House, 1968.

The Language of Thought. New York: Thomas Y. Crowell Co., 1975.

"How Direct is Visual Perception? Some Reflections on Gibson's 'Ecological Approach.'" With Z. Pylyshyn. *Cognition* 9 (1981): 139–96.

Representations: Essays on the Foundations of Cognitive Science. Cambridge, MA: MIT Press, 1981.

The Modularity of Mind: An Essay on Faculty Psychology. Cambridge, MA: MIT Press, 1983.

"Why Paramecia Don't Have Mental Representations." In *Midwest Studies in Philosophy*, vol. 10, edited by P. French, T Uehling, Jr., and H. Wettstein. Minneapolis: University of Minnesotta Press, 1986.

Psychosemantics. Cambridge, MA: MIT Press, 1987.

"Connectionism and Cognitive Architecture." With Z Pylyshyn. *Cognition* 28 (1–2) (1988): 3–71.

A Theory of Content and other Essays. Cambridge, MA: MIT Press, 1990,

Holism: A Shopper's Guide. With E. Lepore. Oxford: Blackwell, 1992.

Concepts: Where Cognitive Psychology Went Wrong, Oxford: Oxford University Press, 1998.

The Mind Doesn't Work That Way: The Scope and Limits of Computational Psychology. Cambridge, MA: MIT Press, 2000.

Georges Rey (2005)

FOLK PSYCHOLOGY

Among the more remarkable qualities of human beings is that they describe and explain their own minds and behavior. People are self-explainers and self-understanders. By and large, though not invariably, of course, people's efforts to understand themselves are couched in a familiar language: the language of belief, desire, intention, hope, and so forth—the language of intentional mental states. Perhaps just as remarkable is that people are "mindreaders" (Nichols and Stich 2003). In everyday commerce people attribute—sometimes unself-consciously, sometimes painfully and with great difficulty—to others intentional mental states.

Humans are social creatures—competitive and cooperative—and the practice of attributing intentional mental states is, by and large, the vehicle whereby they come to understand others and others come to understand them, and so, this practice is fundamental to efforts to navigate the social world. One is often able to anticipate or to predict what another will do via the command of what one takes the other person to believe and to desire. Whether the arena is chess or rock-paper-scissors, arms negotiations or freeway driving, the human capacity to characterize others in terms of such intentional mental states is often what determines whether plans succeed or fail. Not surprisingly, this scheme of intentional characterization is applied retrospectively in the explanation of the behavior of others and in the explanation and, often, the justification of one's own behavior to others. So, for example, why did Achilles, after earlier refusing to return to the battle, suddenly rejoin it? One may say that Achilles wants desperately to avenge the death of Patroklos, and he believes that killing Hektor, and so reentering the fray, is the best way to accomplish this aim. In less lofty instances, one can explain why the dog lover ran upon seeing Fido (the dog lover believed the dog was rabid), and why a dear friend refused to return repeated phone calls (the dear friend is angry and wants to stew a bit longer). This commonsense framework of mentalistic understanding, this scheme of intentional description, explanation, and prediction, among many other uses, has come to be termed *folk psychology*.

UNDERSTANDING FOLK PSYCHOLOGY

An intuitively compelling and seductive understanding of the nature of folk psychology might be seen to be offered by René Descartes. At the end of the *Second Meditation*, he famously writes, "I know plainly that I can achieve an easier and more evident perception of my own mind than of anything else" (1988, p. 86). In short, nothing is more easily known by or to the mind than itself. Just by looking within, and by, as we say, introspecting, I can know that I believe certain things to be the case, that I desire this or that to be so, and that I behaved as I did because I believed and desired as I did. This mentalistic characterization, made manifest to me in the first person, is then applied to the characterization of the minds and behavior of others. One upshot of such a view is that the description and understanding of the mental and intentional action are unlike the efforts to understand other natural phenomena.

This view of the human capacity to describe and to understand the mental has proved exceedingly unpopular with both philosophers and psychologists over the past six decades or so. Wilfrid Sellars (1956) pioneered an alternative account of the mentalistic talk of human beings. Sellars tells a story, a *myth*, he terms it, according to which at a time in human prehistory people understood their conspecifics in purely behavioral or observational terms and without appeal to the language of intentional mental states. Then, something of a savant, named "Jones," came to posit unobservable theoretical entities that served to explain the behavior of others. *Belief*, *desire*, and *intention*, are explicitly introduced as theoretical terms to explain why it is that, for example, Tom is behaving as he is. Finally, this theory came to be applied in the first person, to oneself. The point of the myth is not, of course, that it is historically accurate; rather, the point is that people's mentalistic talk needn't be viewed, as it was on the Cartesian model, as picking out entities or states to which people have some special, privileged, access.

This Sellarsian picture has produced a conception of folk psychology that has come to be extremely influential: the "theory-theory" account of folk psychology. In part the result of dominance of functionalist accounts of the mental, the "theory-theory" has it that folk psychology is an empirical theory of mind and behavior (Lewis 1972, Morton 1980, Churchland 1981). And, in this way, folk psychology is "protoscience" (Rudder Baker 1999). *Belief*, *desire*, and *intention* are theoretical terms whose meaning and reference are secured by their place in a vast network of implicit folk psychological laws. One such law might be stated as follows: If S desires or intends that v, and believes that k is necessary for v, then, ceteris paribus, S tries to bring it about that k. Another such law might be: If S believes that p and believes that if p then q, then, ceteris paribus, S comes to believe that q. (The entry thus far has emphasized intentional mental states, but it should be noted that qualitative states—pains, itches, visual imaginings—fall within the purview of folk psychology.) The human capacity to engage in folk psychologizing points, then, to a constellation of psychological laws that relate behavior, internal states, and stimuli. Belief, desire, intention and the rest of the mentalist vocabulary are theoretical posits of a folk theory of mind.

In an important essay, "What Is Folk Psychology?" (1994) Stephen Stich and Ian Ravenscroft point out that there is a good deal of ambiguity in discussions of folk psychology. They characterize a sense of "folk psychology" according to which that term picks out a theory that is implicit in the everyday talk about the mental. This sense they term an "external account" of folk psychology, because such a view (largely the conception described above) carries with it no commitment to the claim that folk psychology is "an internally represented knowledge structure or body of information" (1994, p. 460). Folk psychology in this sense "ain't in the head" (p. 460), and so is not implicated in an informative account of just how it is that people in fact have the capacities to predict, to explain, or to describe the minds and behavior of their fellows. A second account of folk psychology Stich and Ravenscroft term *internal*. In this sense of "folk psychology," it is an internally represented theory that explains how it is that people predict, describe, and explain in the psychological realm. Stich and Ravenscroft go on to muster powerful arguments for the claim that this distinction has important implications for the eliminativist-vindicationist debate.

THE ELIMINATIVIST CHALLENGE

Historically, many of the chief philosophical issues surrounding folk psychology have been engaged in the effort to characterize the nature and status of folk-psychological explanation. For it is one immediate consequence of the theory-theory that folk psychology might be false in the way that any empirical theory might be false. Vindicationists argue that folk psychology is, in broad terms at least, a correct theory of mind and behavior. Eliminativists argue that folk psychology is plausibly a false theory. As a causal explanatory account of mind and behavior, folk psychology awaits replacement by some

nonintentional robustly scientific account of behavior (Churchland 1981, Stich 1983). The theory of mind and behavior implicit in one's everyday talk is just false, the eliminativist alleges.

Thus the eliminativist-vindicationist debate hinges upon the anticipated relationship between folk psychology and scientific psychology/neuroscience. Because both of these aim to explain what is intuitively—though, controversially—the same class of explananda, if people are to regard folk psychology as, by and large, a correct account of human behavior, then they are presumably committed to thinking that the cognitive sciences will, in some way, serve to vindicate the ontology and explanations of folk psychology (Kim 1989).

A notable advocate of this brand of vindicationism, Jerry Fodor (1987), has argued that a scientific psychology will count as vindicating folk psychology just in case it postulates states that (1) are semantically evaluable; (2) have causal powers; and (3) are found to conform to the tacit laws of folk psychology. Each of these has given rise to eliminativist complaint.

Insofar as intentional content figures essentially in folk psychological explanation, it may seem a quick matter to demonstrate that such explanations are not respectable:

(1) The causes of behavior supervene upon the current, internal, physical states of the organism.

(2) Intentional mental content does not supervene upon such states.

(3) The science of psychology is concerned to discover the causes of behavior.

(4) Therefore a causal explanatory psychology will not trade in the intentional idiom.

If this argument were correct, folk psychological explanations would be deeply suspect, because appeal to such explanations would be irrelevant to the causal explanation of behavior. The argument is, however, suspect on many fronts. One might dispute the sense of "behavior" in (1) and with it the notion the respectable explanation must be "individualistic" (Burge 1986). In addition, one might grant that whereas truth-evaluable content is "wide," and so fails to supervene upon internal states of the subject, there is a kind of content, "narrow content," that respects individualist scruples.

Content-based objections such as those above focus upon the puzzling status of intentional properties in a physical universe; many theorists point to the allegedly irreducible nature of intentional mental content as a way of undermining the integrity of folk psychology (Churchland 1986). Another family of eliminativist worries points to matters structural. It is, for example, claimed that if certain connectionist models of humans' cognitive architecture are correct, then there will literally be no states or events that play the causal role intentional mental states are understood to play in folk psychology. Folk psychology appears committed to the view that mental states are "functionally discrete" internal states with a certain causal profile (Ramsey, Stich, and Garon 1991). Yet, on connectionist models there are no such discrete internal states with the causal roles that belief, desire, and so on are presumed to play in folk psychology.

If these objections are given some taste of the eliminativist assault, they serve as well to highlight an assumption held by many vindicationists and eliminativists alike: folk psychology possesses, in Fodor's terminology, "causal depth" (1987, p. 6). It posits unobservable states and events in aid of the causal explanation of observed phenomena. The explanations of folk psychology are, then, structurally informative insofar as they aim to offer information about the structure of causal relations that hold between behavior, stimuli, and unobservable internal states. Only on such a supposition is it plausible to suggest that folk psychological states and events will go the way of caloric and phlogiston. And this is why many vindicationists hold that the survival of folk psychology demands that there be some scientific level of the description of human cognitive architecture that mirrors the folk psychological one.

Much hinges upon the resolution of this dispute. If the eliminativist is correct, there are no beliefs and desires, and so no intentional actions. It is, for example, just false that human beings often intend to do what they most desire. Nothing would appear to remain of people's conception of themselves as deliberators and actors. While this may strike one as incredible, the eliminativist will insist that this is but another case in which what the folk have taken to be patently obvious turns out to be radically false.

Even so it has been argued that, more than incredible, eliminativism is self-refuting or pragmatically incoherent (Rudder Baker 1987). The charge here is not that the eliminativist thesis is self-contradictory or internally inconsistent. Rather the claim is that there is no perspective from which the doctrine can be coherently put forth. For if eliminativism is true, there are no actions. Yet the eliminativist asserts the truth of eliminativism, and assertion is certainly an action. Moreover, the eliminativist asserts eliminativism because she takes it to be a correct or true thesis, one amply supported by available evidence. But what sense can be made of the notion of justification or even truth without the intentional framework of folk psychology? This argument is sometimes developed in concert with the suggestion that folk psychological principles are not contingent regularities but are, rather, normative principles that are true a priori.

FOLK PSYCHOLOGY STRIKES BACK

Whatever the merits of the foregoing lines of argument, the prima facie oddity that attaches to eliminativism suggests that whereas it is one thing to assert that intentional mental states will not figure in the ontology of some ideal cognitive science, it is another to assert that there are no intentional mental states. In hopes of saving the folk psychological phenomena, an alternative conception of the nature of folk psychology rejects the assumption that folk psychology does offer such informative causal explanations. Rather, folk psychological explanations are silent about the internal mechanisms and processes of cognition and behavior. Because its explanations are not informative in the ways that a cognitive science aims to be informative, folk psychological explanation is not in competition with a scientific psychology, and so folk psychology might be regarded as immunized against scientific advances.

In an extremely influential series of papers, Daniel Dennett (1987) advocates something like this view. According to him, folk psychological explanation and prediction proceeds via the assumption of rationality. When one predicts what an agent will do in various circumstances, the question asked amounts to: What is it rational for her to do, given that she believes and desires as she does? To be, in Dennett's terminology, an "intentional system"—to be such as to have beliefs truly attributable to one—is to be a system whose behavior is so predictable. Folk psychological description, then, does not aim at the description of internal processes and mechanisms. And, whereas an empirically informative cognitive science will reject the intentional idiom, folk psychological explanation is adequate in its own preserve. Even so, it is not easy to see how this brand of instrumentalism about the intentional makes folk psychological description anything more than a façon de parler.

Other philosophers who offer various versions of this approach emphasize that many of the folk explanations that people regard as true bear no easy relationship to science (Chastain 1988, Horgan and Woodward 1985, Horgan and Graham 1991). One may, for example, explain why Ajax slipped by the ramparts by pointing out that the ground was slimy. In such a case, one is in command of a tacit law to the effect that slimy surfaces are apt to produce slippings. But sliminess and slipperiness are certainly not scientific kinds; it seems likely that no science will make appeal to such kinds. Still, it would be mad to insist that such explanations are false, and that the description of surfaces as slimy is no more than a colorful way of speaking.

Such explanations can survive most any developments in the sciences. People, moreover, are likely to regard the more informative scientific account of the phenomena as a way of spelling out and so vindicating the folk "slimy/slippery" account. With such folk explanations all that is demanded is that there be some more basic account of the properties/processes one characterizes in terms of "sliminess" and "slipperiness." The source of the robustness of such explanations is precisely their relative uninformativenss. Indeed, folk recognize that sliminess and slipperiness do not play any deep or informative role in the causal explanations in which they figure. Rather, their role would appear to be something like the following: There's *something* about the surface picked out as "slimy" that causes events picked out as "slippings." So, just by virtue of their offering scant information about the relevant causal processes, they are insulated from any serious threat of elimination posed by developments in the sciences.

It is, then, urged that we adopt a similar position as to the status of folk psychological explanation. Just as there are slimy things, there are beliefs and desires. And just as it is true that Ajax slipped because the ground was slimy, so it is true that Achilles behaved so because he believed and desired as he did. It should, nonetheless, be noted that this appealing conclusion has been secured at some considerable price: folk psychological explanations, though serviceable for everyday purposes, are about as superficial as causal explanations can be. It is not all apparent that, for example, people's conception of ourselves as reasoners and actors—a conception that appears to implicate certain views as to the nature of mental processes—can withstand so deflationary a reading. One might well conclude that this gives everything to the eliminativist but what she wants.

Finally, Michael Bishop and Stephen Stitch argue that both eliminativists and vindicationists, in developing their arguments, make use of favored theories of reference to establish the conclusion that the terms of folk psychology either do or do not refer, and from this they draw the further conclusion that beliefs do or do not exist. Bishop and Stitch point out that neither the elimi-

nativist nor vindicationist bothers to defend the claim that his or her favored theory of reference is the correct account, one that would sanction a transition from a claim about reference to a claim about existence or nonexistence. The upshot of this argument is that neither eliminativists not vindicationists have a right to make claims about the existence or nonexistence of folk psychological states and entities on the basis of the considerations they adduce.

SIMULATION VERSUS THEORY

In response to the unpalatable alternatives described above (folk psychology is gravely at risk of elimination, or folk psychology is exceedingly unlikely to be eliminated by virtue of its uninformativeness) some have suggested that it is the theory-theory account of folk psychology itself that demands reevaluation. This reevaluation of the nature and status of folk psychology can assume a number of different forms. By far the most influential of these accounts is the simulation account of folk psychology. Jane Heal (1986), Robert Gordon (1986), and Alvin Goldman (1989) have resuscitated the view that people's folk psychological capacities are mediated by the simulation of others. In the effort to understand others, people make adjustments for their cognitive and affective constitutions and, then, using these as inputs, allow their own psychological mechanisms to run "offline." In prediction, simulated beliefs and desires are attributed to the psychological subject of interest.

Advocates of the account claim that simulation is a far simpler and more psychologically plausible account of folk psychologizing. In this way, simulation is, in the language of Sitch and Ravenscroft, a response to an internal theory-theory account. What explains, according to simulationists, the human capacity to describe, explain, and predict the mental states and behavior of others is not an internally represented theory, but rather just the capacity to engage in simulation. In this regard, it is important to note the much of the original impetus behind the development of a competing simulation account of folk psychology was to blunt the force of eliminativist argument. For if psychology is not a theory it cannot be a false theory. So, it seems that on a simulationist account the eliminativist worry cannot be raised. But, as Stich and Ravenscroft (1994) point out, even if human folk psychological capacities may not be subserved by an internally represented theory, it may nonetheless be that eliminativism threatens folk psychology on an external reading.

See also Simulation Theory.

Bibliography

Bishop, Michael, and Stephen Stich. "The Flight to Reference." *Philosophy of Science* 65 (1998): 33–49.

Burge, Tyler. "Individualism and Psychology." *The Philosophical Review* 45 (1986): 3–45.

Chastain, Charles. "Comments on Baker." In *Contents of Thought*, edited by R. Grimm and D. Merrill. Tucson, AZ: University of Arizona Press, 1988.

Churchland, Patricia S. *Neurophilosophy*. Cambridge, MA: MIT Press, 1986.

Churchland, Paul. "Eliminative Materialism and the Propositional Attitudes." *Journal of Philosophy* 78 (1981): 67–90.

Dennett, Daniel. *The Intentional Stance*. Cambridge, MA: Bradford Books, 1987.

Descartes, René. *Descartes: Selected Philosophical Writings*, translated by John Cottingham, Robert Stoothoff, and Dugald Murdoch. Cambridge, U.K.: Cambridge University Press, 1988.

Fodor, Jerry. *Psychosemantics*. Cambridge, MA: Bradford/MIT Press, 1987.

Goldman, Alvin. "Interpretation Psychologized." *Mind and Language* 4 (1989): 161–185.

Gordon, Robert. "Folk Psychology as Simulation." *Mind and Language* 1 (1986): 158–171.

Heal Jane. "Replication and Functionalism." In *Language, Mind and Logic*, edited by J. Butterfield. Cambridge, U.K.: Cambridge University Press, 1986.

Horgan, Terrence, and George Graham. "In Defense of Southern Fundamentalism." *Philosophical Studies* 62 (1991): 107–134.

Horgan, Terrence, and James Woodward. "Folk Psychology is Here to Stay." *The Philosophical Review* 44 (1985): 197–226.

Kim, Jaegwon. "Mechanism, Purpose, and Explanatory Exclusion." In *Philosophical Perspectives*, edited by James Tomberlin. Atascadero, CA: Ridgeview Publishing Company, 1989.

Lewis, David. "Psychophysical and Theoretical Identifications." *Australasian Journal of Philosophy* 50 (1972): 249–258.

Morton, Adam. *Frames of Mind*. Oxford: Oxford University Press, 1980.

Nichols, Shaun, and Stephen Stich. *Mindreading*. Oxford: Clarendon Press, 2003.

Ramsey, William, Stephen Stich, and William Garon. "Connectionism, Eliminativism, and the Future of Folk Psychology." In *The Future of Folk Psychology*, edited by John Greenwood. Cambridge, U.K.: Cambridge University Press, 1991.

Rudder Baker, Lynne. *Explaining Attitudes*. Cambridge, U.K.: Cambridge University Press, 1995.

Rudder Baker, Lynne. *Saving Belief*. Princeton, NJ: Princeton University Press, 1987.

Rudder Baker, Lynne. "What Is This Thing Called 'Folk-Psychology.'" *Philosophical Explorations* 2 (1999): 3–19.

Ryle, Gilbert. *The Concept of Mind*. London: Hutchinson, 1949.

Sellars, Wilfrid. "Empiricism and the Philosophy of Mind." In *Minnesota Studies in the Philosophy of Science*, edited by H. Feigl and M. Scriven. Minneapolis: University of Minnesota Press, 1956.

Stich, Stephen. *From Folk Psychology to Cognitive Science.* Cambridge, MA: Bradford Books/MIT Press: 1983.

Stich, Stephen, and Ian Ravenscroft. "What Is Folk Psychology?" *Cognition* 50 (1994): 447–468.

Dion Scott-Kakures (1996, 2005)

FONSECA, PETER
(1528–1599)

Peter Fonseca, the neo-Scholastic Aristotelian philosopher, was born at Proença-a-Nova, Portugal, and died at Lisbon. He entered the Society of Jesus at the age of twenty, completed philosophical and theological studies in that order, and spent most of his life as a professor of philosophy at Coimbra, where he was the leader of a group of scholars who produced a famous series of textbooks (*Cursus Conimbricensis*). Fonseca has been called the Aristotle of Portugal. His *Institutionum Dialecticarum* (Eight Books on Logic; Lisbon, 1564), was widely used as a textbook throughout Europe, and in 1625 it was in its thirty-fourth printing.

Basically an interpreter of the philosophy of Aristotle, Fonseca corrected the Aristotelian text then in use, using Greek manuscripts, and started the process of improving the Renaissance Latin versions. His logic is the traditional syllogistic which continued to be taught in Europe until J. S. Mill and the nineteenth-century mathematicians broadened the scope of the subject. As a student Fonseca had, of course, been taught a modified form of Thomism, but he showed a great deal of independence on specific questions. In theory of knowledge he maintained that a singular thing is directly known by the human intellect (contrary to Thomas Aquinas), and he seems to have felt (with the later Ockhamists) that the theory of intelligible species as intellectual determinants of the process of conceptualization is useless.

Fonseca placed great emphasis on the unity of the formal concept of being (influencing Francisco Suárez) and taught that this concept is univocal and not analogical in its reference to individual realities. However, he approximated the Thomistic real distinction of essence and existence by treating essence as an ultimate intrinsic mode of the nature of a thing and existence as a contingent addition to this nature. He is, then, partly responsible for the introduction of the terminology of modes into early modern metaphysics. Fonseca abandoned Thomism in denying that matter is pure potency and in rejecting quantified matter as the principle of individuation in bodies. He explained individuation as due to a positive difference (*differentia*) added to the essence of a thing, a theory reminiscent of John Duns Scotus.

See also Aristotelianism; Aristotle; Being; Duns Scotus, John; Mill, John Stuart; Ockhamism; Scotism; Suárez, Francisco; Thomas Aquinas, St.; Thomism.

Bibliography

WORKS BY FONSECA

Commentariorum in Libros Metaphysicorum Tomi IV (Commentary on Aristotle's Metaphysics). Vols. I and II, Rome, 1577–1589; Vol. III, Evora, 1604; Vol. IV, Lyons, 1612.

Isagoge Philosophica (Introduction to philosophy). Lisbon, 1591.

WORKS ON FONSECA

Ashworth, Earline J. "Petrus Fonseca and Material Implication." *Notre Dame Journal of Formal Logic* 9 (1968): 227–228.

Ashworth, Earline J. "Petrus Fonseca on Objective Concepts and the Analogy of Being." In *Logic and the Workings of the Mind*, edited by Patricia A. Easton. Atascadero, CA: Ridgeview, 1997.

Coombs, Jeffrey. "The Ontological Source of Logical Possibility in Catholic Second Scholasticism." In *The Medieval Heritage in Early Modern Metaphysics and Modal Theory, 1400–1700*, edited by Russell L. Friedman. Dordrecht: Kluwer Academic, 2003.

Giacon, C. *La seconda scolastica*. Vol. II, 31–66. Milan: Fratelli Bocca, 1946.

Gomes, Joaquim F. "Pedro Da-Fonseca, Sixteenth Century Portuguese Philosopher." *International Philosophical Quarterly* 6 (1966): 632–644.

Nedelhofen, M. *Die Logik des Petrus Fonseca*. Bonn, 1916.

Vernon J. Bourke (1967)
Bibliography updated by Tamra Frei (2005)

FONTENELLE, BERNARD LE BOVIER DE
(1657–1757)

Bernard Le Bovier de Fontenelle, the French author, forerunner of the Enlightenment, was born in Rouen and died in Paris, having lived one month short of a century. Schooled by the Jesuits, he also studied law, but soon abandoned the career of advocate to follow in the literary footsteps of his uncles, Pierre and Thomas Corneille. Neither then nor later was he to distinguish himself as a poet or dramatist but, in 1683, with the appearance of the *Dialogues des morts* (*Dialogues of the Dead*), he achieved immediate success as a man of letters. The witty paradoxes and sparkling conversations in these imaginary dialogues of illustrious and notorious figures of the past

confirmed the reputation of their twenty-six-year-old author as a seventeenth-century *belesprit*; more important, they revealed him as a singularly independent thinker, skeptical of traditional values and, as such, a potential enemy of seventeenth-century orthodoxy. Judging his literary fame firmly established, Fontenelle turned to the study of mathematics, physics, and astronomy and published *Entretiens sur la pluralité des mondes* (*Conversations on the Plurality of Worlds*, 1686), a brilliantly successful popularization of the Copernican system which, until that time, had achieved very limited acceptance.

The following year his *Histoire des Oracles*, ingeniously adapted from the ponderous Latin of A. van Dale, appeared anonymously. Ostensibly an exposure of imposture and charlatanism in religious practices of pagan antiquity, the work was soon recognized for what it really was: a bold attack on credulity and superstition in all ages. Equally daring was *De l'origine des fables* (The Origin of Fables), composed by Fontenelle before 1680, but fear of persecution invited prudence, and it was not published until 1724. One of the first modern studies in the field of comparative religion, it based early man's belief in the supernatural on his ignorance of natural phenomena. But it was obvious that the criticism was intended to apply equally as well to Christianity and other revealed religions.

The quarrel over the relative literary merits of the Ancients and Moderns had been raging for some years when, in 1688, Fontenelle entered the fray with his *Digression sur les Anciens et les Modernes*, His thesis was that since the question also included the problem of man's progress, the recent accumulation, organization, and dissemination of scientific knowledge proved the superiority of the Moderns. Because of his position in the dispute, entry into the French Academy was denied him on four occasions; and he was not elected a member until 1691.

In 1697 Fontenelle was elected to the Academy of Science, and two years later he became its secretary. His clarity and intelligence, the cool impartiality of his judgment, his wide range of scientific knowledge, and his gift for expression made Fontenelle ideally suited for the post, and he came to be considered as spokesman for his fellow academicians. He contributed a great deal to the widespread popularization of the scientific spirit at home and abroad with his remarkable series of *Éloges* for departed academy members, written over a period of forty years. These essays provided an impressive, constantly renewed picture of accomplishments in science on various fronts, written with the same lucidity and ease of expression that marked all of Fontenelle's serious writing. They were admirably complemented by the *Histoire de l'Académie royale des sciences* that alone, with its masterful preface and original views, would have assured Fontenelle's reputation throughout eighteenth-century Europe as one of the great historians of the philosophy of science.

In the field of mathematics, Fontenelle was particularly interested in the differential calculus of Isaac Newton and Gottfried Wilhelm Leibniz and the analytical geometry of René Descartes. One of his own mathematical treatises is the *Préface des éléments de la géométrie de l'infini* (Elements of Infinitesimal Calculus; 1727). The last book he wrote was also scientific in nature. Titled *Théorie des tourbillons cartésiens* (The Theory of Cartesian Vortices; 1752), it showed him to be a disciple of Descartes in physics, if not in metaphysics.

Concerning Descartes, Fontenelle said that he should be held in esteem at all times but followed only now and then. Nevertheless, Fontenelle can be considered a Cartesian in two respects. First, his own skepticism was closely bound up with Descartes's principle of methodical doubt. Second, as a stout believer in the purely mechanical philosophy of nature, he found the Cartesian theory of vortices far closer to reality than Newton's laws of attraction, according to which it was necessary to hold that some invisible, seemingly supernatural force operated across vast stretches of space.

Among a number of audaciously conceived, anonymous works on religion and metaphysics ascribed to Fontenelle is the *Traité de la liberté*, which appeared in 1745 together with four other pamphlets under the title of *Nouvelles Libertés de penser*, The work, a few copies of which escaped police seizure, purports to reconcile divine foreknowledge with human free will, but, in fact, casts doubt on the existence of either.

Immediately following Fontenelle's death in January 1757, the general opinion of his accomplishments was summed up by Frédéric-Melchior Grimm: "The philosophic spirit, today so much in evidence, owes its beginnings to M. de Fontenelle" (*Correspondance littéraire*, February 1, 1757).

Although there were serious lapses in Fontenelle's knowledge and, hence, in his scientific judgment, his works nevertheless served as the single most important bond between the philosophico-scientific revolution in progress during his life and the *philosophe* movement just getting under way. He was one of the great forerunners of the French Enlightenment, and no small part of his success in this role lay in the fact that he exploited, as had never been done before, a technique for the popularization of science that was still to have its effects some two centuries later.

See also Cartesianism; Clandestine Philosophical Literature in France; Descartes, René; Enlightenment; Leibniz, Gottfried Wilhelm; Newton, Isaac; Philosophy of Science, History of.

Bibliography

PRINCIPAL WORKS BY FONTENELLE
Oeuvres. 3 vols, edited by G.-B. Depping. Paris, 1818.
Entretiens sur la pluralité des mondes; Digression sur les Anciens et les Modernes, edited by Robert Shackleton. Oxford: Clarendon Press, 1955.

WORKS ON FONTENELLE
Adkins, Gregory M. "When Ideas Matter: The Moral Philosophy of Fontenelle." *Journal of the History of Ideas* 61 (3) (2000): 433–452.
Carré, J.-R. *La philosophie de Fontenelle ou le sourire de la raison*, Paris: Alcan, 1932.
Cohen, Bernard I. "The Eighteenth-Century Origins of the Concept of Scientific Revolution." *Journal of the History of Ideas* 37 (1976): 257–288.
Cosentini, John W. *Fontenelle's Art of Dialogue*, New York: King's Crown Press, 1952.
Kearns, Edward J. *Ideas in Seventeenth Century France*, New York: St. Martin's Press, 1979.
Maigron, Louis. *Fontenelle, l'homme, l'oeuvre, l'influence*, Paris: Librairie Plon, Plon-Nourrit, 1906.
Marsak, Leonard M. "Bernard de Fontenelle, the Idea of Science in the French Enlightenment." *Transactions of the American Philosophical Society*, n.s., 49 (7) (1959): 64.
Riley, Patrick. "The General Will before Rousseau." *Political Theory* 6 (1978): 485–516.
Vartanian, Aram. *Science and Humanism in the French Enlightenment*, Charlottesville, VA: Rookwood Press, 1999.
White, Reginald J. *The Anti-Philosophers: A Study of the Philosophes in Eighteenth-Century France*, London: Macmillan, 1970.

Otis Fellows (1967)
Bibliography updated by Tamra Frei (2005)

FOOT, PHILIPPA
(1920–)

In the last half of the twentieth century, few philosophers figured as prominently and persistently in the central debates of English-speaking moral philosophy as Philippa Foot. Née Philippa Ruth Bosanquet, she was born in 1920 in Owston Ferry, Lincolnshire, in the United Kingdom. She studied for the PPE (philosophy, political science, and economics) at Somerville College, Oxford, from 1939 to 1942. After receiving an MA in 1947, she became the Sommerville's first philosophy tutorial fellow in 1949 and vice principal in 1967. Moving to the United States, she held positions at Cornell University, the University of California at Berkeley, the Massachusetts Institute of Technology, Princeton University, New York University, and Stanford University. She settled at the University of California at Los Angeles in 1976 and became the first holder of the Gloria and Paul Griffin Chair in Philosophy in 1988, which she held until her retirement in 1991. A founder of Oxfam, she has been instrumental in bringing philosophy to bear on practical issues.

Although her work on such practical topics as abortion and euthanasia has been widely and justly influential, Foot's fundamental contributions are to the foundational questions of moral theory. Her publications in moral theory concentrate on three interlocking themes: the notion that virtue is central to morality, naturalism in ethics, and the place of practical reason in the moral life. These themes are pursued in a set of forcefully argued, original essays, most of which are collected in Foot 2002 and 2003. Foot's thoughts on these topics culminated in her book *Natural Goodness* (2001).

Although these themes are a constant preoccupation of her writings, Foot's positions evolve in significant and unexpected ways. This evolution can usefully be divided into an early, middle, and late period (for an excellent discussion of the first two periods, see Lawrence 1995). In several early papers (notably 1958–1959/2002 and 1961/2002), Foot set herself in opposition to a dominant trend in moral philosophy toward noncognitivism, as represented by the emotivism of Charles L. Stevenson (1947) and the prescriptivism of R. M. Hare (1952). According to these philosophers, evaluative language, and moral language in particular, has a distinctive function or meaning that sets it sharply apart from empirical or factual discourse. On this view, the primary function of a moral utterance is not to describe human actions and choices but rather to express the speaker's attitudes or stances (e.g., emotions or commitments) regarding them. Hence moral judgment is not objective, because it is not answerable to the nature or properties of its subject matter.

Foot strenuously opposed this trend, arguing that the concept of morality concerns what is necessary for human flourishing, and therefore that the truth of moral judgments is fixed by facts about the needs of human beings in relation to one another. This naturalism is intimately linked to Foot's view that "a sound moral philosophy should start from a theory of the virtues and vices" (2002, p. xi). The ultimate standard of choosing and acting well is the natural needs of human beings. And the virtues are those traits that enable us to do so.

This virtue-centered naturalism, which Foot has never abandoned, reaches back to the ethics of Aristotle (1998), and sparked a resurgence of interest in virtue ethics in the last two decades of the twentieth century. Yet her naturalism was in tension with two further views to which she was drawn. If possessing and acting on the virtues is necessary for human flourishing, she thought, then having and acting on the virtues benefits their possessor. But common experience shows that in the case of at least some virtues, notably justice, acting virtuously might not benefit the agent, for justice restricts us from advancing our interests in certain ways. So either justice is not a virtue, or virtues are not necessarily good for us. In that case (as Thrasymachus was made to argue in Plato's *Republic*), we cannot honestly recommend justice as a virtue, and we have to concede that not everyone has reason to act justly.

Foot's initial response (1958–1959/2002) was to take Thrasymachus's challenge seriously, arguing, in effect, that the potential costs of committing injustice, and of being the kind of person who would commit injustice, are too steep to be worth it, that being unjust does not pay. But this response, Foot came to think, rested on a mistaken assumption. Justice is indeed a virtue because of its essential role in human happiness, but the mistake is to think (as Foot had tended to do) that the only way that virtues can serve well-being is by advancing the interests of those who possess them. Justice is concerned with the *common* good. Human life goes badly when individuals are prepared to cheat, lie, and steal. In this way, a deep connection between virtue and human well-being is retained, but it does not follow that every individual who acts contrary to justice disadvantages himself. This recantation (2002, pp. xii–xiii) marks Foot's transition to her middle period.

This reply to Thrasymachus prompted Foot to reconsider an orthodoxy to which she had previously been inclined to subscribe: that "moral judgments give reason for acting to each and every man" (1958–1959/2002, n. 6). One has reason to do something, Foot had argued, only if doing so contributes to one's ends or good. Since acting as justice or loyalty or charity does not necessarily promote my interests or ends, I do not necessarily have a reason to act in these ways. Foot concludes that the allegiance to morality derives not from the authority of practical reason (as followers of

Immanuel Kant (1998) argue) but from contingent attachments and devotions, such as love of the common good and hatred of cruelty. In this sense, Foot argues in a famous essay (1972/2002), moral reasons are "hypothetical," not categorical.

Although this provocative thesis deeply shaped the ensuing philosophical literature on the connection between morality and practical reason, Foot eventually rejected it. This rejection signaled the third period of her work, in which she sets forth an entirely novel conception of practical reason. A vice like injustice is a kind of natural defect, she comes to argue, analogous to the defect in a lioness who neglects her cubs. What makes it a moral defect is that it concerns the will, in a broad sense: the ways in which the individual recognizes and responds to reasons. The virtues are a form of goodness in choosing, that is, in taking certain considerations as reasons for acting and desiring.

This way of linking the concept of the virtues to that of practical reason stands the traditional account on its head. Traditionally, it was supposed that we could develop a robust theory of practical reason independent of an account of virtue, and then we could see how morality measures up by that standard of rationality. This is an error, Foot argues in *Natural Goodness* (2001), for practical rationality is reasoning well in matters of action, and that cannot be specified without a general conception of what it is to function well as a human being. The theory of practical reason thus depends on a naturalistic understanding of virtue and vice.

Whether this understanding can be developed without relying on an unconvincing Aristotelian conception of human function is a disputed question. One major challenge is to spell out the sense in which goodness is natural. Foot recognizes that assertions about what is and is not rational cannot be settled by the methods of the natural sciences. (For reflections on this challenge, see Thompson 1995.) A related challenge is to understand the role that culture plays in morality. Culture is, of course, natural to human beings, but particular cultures obviously shape the content and understanding of morality by their members. It remains to be seen how these points can be accommodated within a contemporary Aristotelian theory.

See also Abortion; Aristotelianism; Aristotle; Ethical Naturalism; Ethics, History of; Euthanasia; Hare, Richard M.; Kant, Immanuel; Metaethics; Plato; Stevenson, Charles L.; Virtue Ethics.

Bibliography

WORKS BY FOOT

"Moral Beliefs" (1958–1959). In her *"Virtues and Vices" and Other Essays in Moral Philosophy*. Oxford, U.K.: Oxford University Press, 2002.

"Goodness and Choice" (1961). In her *"Virtues and Vices" and Other Essays in Moral Philosophy*. Oxford, U.K.: Oxford University Press, 2002.

"Morality as a System of Hypothetical Imperatives" (1972). In her *"Virtues and Vices" and Other Essays in Moral Philosophy*. Oxford, U.K.: Oxford University Press, 2002.

Natural Goodness. Oxford, U.K.: Clarendon Press, 2001.

"Virtues and Vices" and Other Essays in Moral Philosophy. Oxford, U.K.: Oxford University Press, 2002.

Moral Dilemmas and Other Topics in Moral Philosophy. Oxford: Oxford University Press, 2003.

OTHER WORKS

Aristotle. *Nicomachean Ethics*. Translated by David Ross; revised by J. L. Ackrill and J. O. Urmson. Oxford, U.K.: Oxford University Press, 1998.

Crisp, Roger, and Michael Slote, eds. *Virtue Ethics*. Oxford, U.K.: Oxford University Press, 1997.

Darwall, Stephen, ed. *Virtue Ethics*. Oxford, U.K.: Blackwell Publishing, 2003.

Darwall, Stephen, Allan Gibbard, and Peter Railton. *Moral Discourse and Practice: Some Philosophical Approaches*. Oxford, U.K.: Oxford University Press, 1997.

Hare, R. M. *The Language of Morals*. Oxford, U.K.: Oxford University Press, 1952.

Hursthouse, Rosalind. *On Virtue Ethics*. Oxford, U.K.: Oxford University Press, 1999.

Hursthouse, Rosalind, Galvin Lawrence, and Warren Quinn, eds. 1995. *Virtues and Reasons: Philippa Foot and Moral Theory*. Oxford, U.K.: Oxford University Press.

Kant, Immanuel. *Groundwork for the Metaphysics of Morals*. Translated by Allen W. Wood. New Haven, CT: Yale University Press, 2002.

Lawrence, Gavin. "The Rationality of Morality." In *Virtues and Reasons: Philippa Foot and Moral Theory*, edited by Rosalind Hursthouse, Galvin Lawrence, and Warren Quinn. Oxford, U.K.: Oxford University Press, 1995.

MacIntyre, Alasdair. *After Virtue*. South Bend, IN: University of Notre Dame Press, 1985.

McDowell, John. "Two Sorts of Naturalism." In *Virtues and Reasons: Philippa Foot and Moral Theory*, edited by Rosalind Hursthouse, Galvin Lawrence, and Warren Quinn. Oxford, U.K.: Oxford University Press, 1995.

Stevenson, Charles L. *Ethics and Language*. New Haven, CT: Yale University Press, 1947.

Thompson, Michael. "The Representation of Life." In *Virtues and Reasons: Philippa Foot and Moral Theory*, edited by Rosalind Hursthouse, Galvin Lawrence, and Warren Quinn. Oxford, U.K.: Oxford University Press, 1995.

Gary Watson (2005)

FORCE

In the most general sense, force denotes the faculty of action or the power to overcome a resistance. In the physical sciences it is that entity that changes, or tends to change, the state of rest or of motion of a body. Consequently, it may also be defined as the cause of motion, or more precisely—assuming the validity of the principle of inertia, according to which unaccelerated motion and rest are dynamically and causally equivalent and correspond merely to different choices of the reference systems—as the cause of acceleration.

The metric unit of force in science is the *dyne,* which is the force necessary in order to give a mass of one gram an acceleration (increase of velocity) of one centimeter per second in each second. The British unit of force is the *poundal,* which is the force necessary to give a mass of one pound an acceleration of one foot per second each second. The practical unit is the *gram force,* that is, the force Earth exerts on one gram of mass at sea level and 45° latitude; it equals 980.616 dynes. Another common unit is the *newton,* which is the force necessary in order to give a mass of one kilogram an acceleration of one meter per second each second, and is therefore equivalent to 10^5 dynes.

Apart from being used in a figurative sense, such as "force of habit," "police force," or "economic forces," the word *force,* especially in the natural philosophy of the eighteenth and nineteenth centuries and in the early writings on the principle of conservation of energy (R. Mayer, H. von Helmholtz) signified action and energy. This homonymic use caused considerable confusion at the time.

Originally taken as an analogy to human will power, muscular effort, and spiritual influence, the concept early became projected into inanimate objects and played an important role in ancient thaumaturgy, occultism, and medieval sorcery.

CONCEPT OF FORCE IN ANCIENT PHILOSOPHY

The early Greek hylozoism of the Milesian school (Thales, Anaximander, Anaximenes) conceived nature as a living, animated, and self-moving being, and consequently did not see a problem in the origin of motion. The concept of force gained prominence only with Heraclitus's doctrine of opposing tensions, according to which force is a primary constituent of physical reality and a regulative element in the universe. In Empedocles's philosophy of love (*philia*) and strife (*neikos*), forces, although still conceived in analogy to human affections, became efficient causes of change and motion. In spite of the fact that Plato's natural philosophy relegates the principle of motion ultimately to the existence of a world soul and corresponds in this respect to early hylozoism rather than to the dynamistic teachings of Empedocles and Anaxagoras, the term *dynamis,* signifying not only transitive activity but also passive susceptibility or receptibility, plays an important role in his doctrine. Although Aristotle, in his conception of nature as "physis," still recognized the Platonic notion of force as something inherent in matter, in *De Caelo* he also approached the formulation of a more mechanical conception of force as a physical emanation from one substance to another: through push and pull, bodies affect each other and generate motion in extraneous objects. This Aristotelian notion of emanating kinematic effects, although restricted to contiguous modes of action, is the first instance of the modern dynamical conception of force. In his *Physics* Aristotle subjected this cause of compulsory motion to a quantitative investigation: A force A that moves a mobile B through a distance D during the time T could move half the mobile ($\frac{1}{2}B$) through twice the distance ($2D$) during the same time (T), or could move half the mobile ($\frac{1}{2}B$) through the distance D during half the time ($\frac{1}{2}T$), and so forth. In modern terminology Aristotle's dynamical law of motion may be stated as follows: The velocity of a mobile is proportional to the ratio of the motive force and the resistance of the medium. Nowhere did Aristotle employ units in which these quantities were to be measured. Although it is fairly obvious that forces were practically measured in terms of weight (the early use of the balance is an evidence of this), Aristotle's conception of weight as a manifestation of natural motion and not as a cause of compulsory motion precluded, on theoretical grounds, the possibility of using the units of weight as units of force. Since, according to Aristotle, contiguity between the motor and the mobile was an indispensable prerequisite for the occurrence of dynamical action, force as an action at a distance had no place in his conceptual scheme. Hence, an explanation of planetary motion required the assumption of an external agent or astral intelligence as a "motor" attached to the star, unless the star was thought to be endowed with a life of its own.

With Posidonius's investigations at Gades of the connection between the tides and the movements of the sun and the moon and his doctrine of a universal tension, the concept of force was generalized as something able to pervade all space. Stoic philosophy thus abandoned the Aristotelian restriction of an immediate linkage between the mover and the moved, and conceived force as a

ENCYCLOPEDIA OF PHILOSOPHY
2nd edition

mutual correspondence of action between objects, even when the objects were separated in space. In fact, the Stoics were probably the first to formulate the idea of a field of forces and to regard the universe as a vast system ruled by the interaction of forces.

MEDIEVAL PHILOSOPHY

Arabian and Christian medieval philosophy, in general, adhered to the Aristotelian conception of force. The exceptions were mostly inspired by Neoplatonic ideas. Thus, in Abū-Yūsuf Yaʿqūb ibn Ishāq al-Kindī's treatise *On the Tides* (*Fi-l-madd wal-jazr*), his notion of force is wholly Aristotelian except that he holds that force can be propagated by means of optical rays, a theory conducive to astrological exploitation. Roger Bacon's conception of forces as "species"—isolated entities, detached from their subject and spreading through space in accordance with specific laws of propagation—showed similar features.

The Aristotelian law of motion, already criticized by John Philoponus in the sixth century CE and by Avempace in the twelfth century, was shown by Thomas Bradwardine in the middle of the fourteenth century to contradict experience in the case of equality between the motive force and the resistance, so that the ratio is one but the velocity zero. Bradwardine consequently modified the law, claiming that the velocity, in modern terms, depends on the logarithm of the ratio between motive force and resistance.

In the fourteenth century the Stoic conception of a field of forces was also revived, probably independently of the ancient school. In his *Quaestiones Super Libris Quattuor de Caelo et Mundo* (Questions on the four books of the heaven and the Earth) John Buridan postulates a celestial force that permeates all space and exerts its influence on physical bodies, in contrast to the Peripatetic dictum, *Causa agens est simul cum suo effectu proximo et immediato*. However, the revolutions of celestial bodies, according to Buridan, are not the result of a constant activity of special intelligences, but rather of an original rotational impetus communicated to these bodies by the Creator at the beginning of time.

KEPLER

A decisive stage in the development of the concept of force was reached in Johannes Kepler's search for a quantitative determination of dynamic activity. In his early writings, such as the *Mysterium Cosmographicum* (1596), Kepler still refers to force as a soul animating the celestial bodies. His correspondence, however, and particularly his letters addressed to David Fabricius, show clearly that his use of the term *anima* ("soul") in his writings was merely a metaphor to express the immateriality of the principle that governs the mutual movements of celestial bodies. In 1605 Kepler was already convinced that the force of attraction could be subjected to a mathematical formalism. In the third part of his *Astronomia Nova* (1609), Kepler discusses the causes of planetary motion and insists for the first time on a mathematical definition of force, even if it is not a push or pull. "For we see that these motions take place in space and time and this virtue emanates and diffuses through the space of the universe, which are all mathematical conceptions. From this it follows that this virtue is subject also to other mathematical necessities." Having discovered that the planets move in their orbits with velocities that vary with the distance from the sun, Kepler inquired into the physical cause of this mathematical relation and was thus led to assume the existence of a regulative force whose magnitude decreases with the distance. However, attraction was not yet seen as a radial force, but rather as a tangential drag, and Kepler, under the influence of William Gilbert's *De Magnete* (1600), suggested an analogy with magnetism. But in spite of this, Kepler's conception of a gravitational force of attraction is a typical example of the fact that the existence of forces is, and has to be, inferred from the phenomenological aspects of regularities in the variations of motion. It also exemplifies the fact that the postulation of forces as causes of motions and their kinematic variations is a methodological process that finds its philosophical justification in the reduction of numerous cases of functional dependence to one single agency. Kepler's procedure thus became the prototype for the introduction of forces in the various branches of physics: gravitational, elastic, electromagnetic, nuclear forces, and so forth.

NEWTON

Isaac Newton's conception of force can be traced to two originally disparate classes of mechanical or dynamical phenomena which, however, finally found their logical unification in his *Principia* (1687), through its very definitions of force and mass. Documentary evidence seems to show that his earliest conception of force originated from the study of impact phenomena. Thus Newton's "Waste Book 1664" (Ms. Add. 4004, Portsmouth Collection, University Library, Cambridge, U.K.) starts with a definition of the quantity of motion of a body as the product of its "quantity" (mass) and its velocity, and continues: "Hence it appears how & why amongst bodys moved some require a more potent or efficacious cause others a lesse to hinder or helpe their velocity. And ye power of this cause is usually called force. And as this cause useth or applyeth its power or force to hinder or change ye perseverance of bodys in theire state, it is said to Indeavour to change their perseverance." In another document (Ms. Add. 3965, Portsmouth Collection), force is implicitly defined by the statement: "The alteration of motion is ever proportional to ye force by wch it is altered." Considering the exact text of Newton's second law of motion in the *Principia*, "The change of motion is proportional to the motive force impressed," one is led to the conclusion that "force" in these statements denotes more or less what we mean today by "impulse" (which, in fact, is equal to the change of momentum). Newton's original conception of force was consequently that of a thrust, a kick, or a push, as exhibited in collision phenomena, which at that time were the subject of extensive studies by Galileo Galilei, Marcus Marci, John Wallis, and Christian Huygens. On the other hand, in his search for a derivation of the phenomenological aspects of planetary motions from the hypothesis of an inverse-square law, Newton needed the time rate of change of momentum as the primitive notion, and thus identified the change of momentum with its rate of change for astronomical applications. Later commentators, therefore, interpreted Newton as stating that force is measured by the product of mass and acceleration, a product that for constant mass equals the time rate of change of momentum. Thus, although not rigorously impeccable, Newton's definition of force led to a unified treatment of terrestrial and celestial mechanics, and the notion of force became a fundamental concept of physics. Whereas Newton's first law of motion or law of inertia, according to which every body, unaffected by a force, persists in a state of rest or of uniform motion, may be regarded as a qualitative definition of force (namely, as change of state of motion), the second law quantified the concept and provided a meaning for the notion of mass. The Newtonian characterization of force is completed with the third law, which states, in essence, that every force manifests itself invariably in a dual aspect: It has a mirror-image twin. For it claims that if A acts on B, then B acts on A with equal magnitude in the opposite direction; or in other words, to every action there is always opposed an equal reaction. Forces, consequently, arise only as the result of a combined interaction of at least two entities. In a universe composed of only one body, no forces are conceivable.

Having thus explored the quantitative aspects of force, and of gravitational force in particular, Newton does not specify the metaphysical nature of force; as far as physical science is concerned, force is an ultimately irreducible notion. Newton's contribution may thus be regarded as the culmination of a conceptual development in a search for a quantitative determination of an otherwise obscure and indiscernible, yet necessary, notion—a development whose philosophical necessity had already been stressed by Bacon, Thomas Hobbes, and even René Descartes.

The scientific legitimacy of a force such as gravitation, which could act at a distance without the intermediacy of an intervening medium, was early called into question. Newton himself, particularly in his *Opticks* (1704), referred to certain speculations, primarily to the notion of an ether, in order to reduce such actions at a distance to contiguous effects compatible with the corpuscular-kinetic theory prevalent at that and later times. Yet, in spite of early opposition (as voiced particularly by Gottfried Wilhelm Leibniz, who rejected action at a distance as a scholastic obscure quality), the notion of force as conceived by Newton became the basic concept of classical theoretical mechanics. Pierre de Laplace, in his *Mécanique céleste* (1799–1805), considered the reduction of all mechanical phenomena to forces acting at a distance as the ultimate objective of the physical sciences, and Joseph Louis Lagrange's *Mécanique analytique* (1788), the highlight of classical mechanics, was written in the same spirit. The mechanics of action at a distance gained further support through its successful applications by Laplace, Siméon Denis Poisson, and Wilhelm Weber in the classical theories of electricity and magnetism. Even capillary phenomena—contact phenomena par excellence—were treated by Laplace and Karl Gauss as subject to actions at a distance.

CRITICISM OF ACTION AT A DISTANCE

The great mathematical success of these theories of force as an action at a distance did not suppress doubts as to the philosophical legitimacy of such conceptions, and alternative mechanistic or kinetic-corpuscular theories, especially for gravitation, were proposed in great number. One of the earliest attempts in this direction, George Louis Lesage's theory of "ultramundane particles" (1747), was typical of similar hypotheses that gained great popularity in the nineteenth century. Particles were assumed to move in all directions through space and to be rebounded by macroscopic bodies; the resulting screening effects were supposed to produce the mutual "attractions" of "gravitating" bodies. The main criticism of the Newtonian conception of force from the philosophical point of view, however, was directed against the hypostatization of force as a metaphysical entity of an autonomous ontological status. George Berkeley, in his *De Motu* (On motion; 1721) opposed this approach and viewed the notion of force as a convenient auxiliary fiction with which to work; for the notion had the same status in science as the concept of epicycle has in astronomy. Such terms as *force, gravity,* and *attraction,* he admitted, are convenient for purposes of reasoning or computation; for an understanding of the nature of motion itself, however, Berkeley regards them as wholly irrelevant. They should not lead us to the fallacy that they could throw any light on the real efficient causes of motion, for the only objective of physical science is the establishment of the regularities and uniformities of natural phenomena; to account for particular phenomena means "reducing them under, and shewing their conformity to, such general rules" (*Siris,* 1744). David Hume, Pierre de Maupertuis, and especially the early proponents of modern positivism (Gustav Kirchhoff, Heinrich Hertz, Ernst Mach) followed Berkeley in asserting that force is merely a construct in the conceptual scheme of physics and that it should not be confounded with metaphysical causality. Most radical in this respect was Mach's antimetaphysical attitude, in accordance with which he tried to divest mechanics of all conceptions of cause and force and to adopt a purely functional point of view. Following Kirchhoff's *Lectures on Mechanics* (*Vorlesungen über Meckanik,* 1874–1876), Mach, in his *Science of Mechanics* (*Die Mechanik in ihrer Entwicklung, historisch-kritisch dargestellt,* 1883), identified force with the product of mass and acceleration and thus reduced it to a purely mathematical expression relating certain measurements of space and time.

But even after this process of purification and divestment of all causal or teleological implications, the concept of force was not eliminated from the conceptual scheme of physics. Its methodological justification lies in the fact that it enables us to discuss the general laws of motion irrespective of the particular physical situation with which these motions are associated. In contemporary physics the concept plays somewhat the same role as does the middle term in the traditional syllogism; it is a methodological intermediate in terms of which we can study the kinematical behavior of a physical body independent of the particular configuration in which it is found.

PSYCHOLOGICAL ORIGINS OF THE CONCEPT OF FORCE

The advancement of the critical attitude toward the concept of force, initiated by Berkeley and Hume and culminating in the logical and metaphysical point of view held by Kirchhoff and Mach, brought in its wake a study of the psychological origin of the notion. The first to deal at length with this problem was Thomas Reid, Hume's immediate successor and founder of the Scottish school. He derived the concept of force from the consciousness we have of the operations of our own mind, and especially from the consciousness of our voluntary exertions in producing effects. Reid concluded that if we were not conscious of such exertions, we would not have formed any conception of force and consequently would not have projected this notion into nature and the changes in it that we observe. Immanuel Kant's younger contemporary, Maine de Biran, whose personalistic philosophy has many points in common with Reid's empirical intuitionalism, considered our own will as the source of the notion of force; in his view, the resistance to muscular effort felt in the case of voluntary activity makes us aware that certain actions are not involuntary acts, but the results of our ego as a source of force. From the twofold nature of the ego as an individual source of action and as inseparably united to a resisting organism, we acquire the universal and necessary notion of force. While the Berkeley-Hume criticism led almost to the exclusion of the concept of force from science and natural philosophy, at the same time it supplied to the more psychologically and physiologically oriented philosophy important arguments to oppose such elimination. For it was claimed that the concept of force stands in the same relation to the sensation of muscular effort as the concept of motion to visual perception, and science without the concept of motion is inconceivable. Moreover, if one kind of sensation is to be preferred to the others, it should certainly be muscular sensation, the nearest to the psychological experience of volition. Even William James, who, in "The Feeling of Effort," in *Collected Essays and Reviews* (1920), rejected the so-called feeling of innervation and opposed the view that the resistance to our muscular effort is the only sense that brings us into close contact with reality, contended that reality reveals itself in the form of a force like the force of effort we exert ourselves. The concept of force, according to James, thus remains "one of those universal ideas which belong of necessity to the intellectual furniture of every human mind."

See also al-Kindī, Abū-Yūsuf Yaʿqūb ibn Isḥāq; Anaximander; Anaximenes; Aristotle; Bacon, Roger; Berkeley, George; Bradwardine, Thomas; Buridan, John; Descartes, René; Empedocles; Energy; Galileo Galilei; Heraclitus of Ephesus; Hertz, Heinrich Rudolf; Hobbes, Thomas; Hume, David; Ibn Bājja; James, William; Kant, Immanuel; Kepler, Johannes; Kirchhoff,

Gustav Robert; Laplace, Pierre Simon de; Laws, Scientific; Leibniz, Gottfried Wilhelm; Mach, Ernst; Maine de Biran; Mass; Matter; Medieval Philosophy; Neoplatonism; Newtonian Mechanics and Mechanical Explanation; Newton, Isaac; Panpsychism; Philoponus, John; Plato; Power; Reid, Thomas; Stoicism; Thales of Miletus.

Bibliography

Ellis, Brian D. "Newton's Concept of Motive Force." *Journal of the History of Ideas* 23 (1962): 273–278.

Hesse, Mary B. *Forces and Fields.* London: Nelson, 1961.

James, William. "The Feeling of Effort." In *Collected Essays and Reviews.* New York: Longman, 1920.

Jammer, Max. *Concepts of Force (A Study in the Foundations of Dynamics).* Cambridge, MA: Harvard University Press, 1957; reprinted in paperback, New York, 1962.

Mach, Ernst. *Die Mechanik in Ihrer Entwicklung, historisch-kritisch dargestellt.* Leipzig, 1883. Translated by T. J. McCormack as *Science of Mechanics.* La Salle, IL: Open Court, 1960. With introduction by Karl Menger.

Margenau, Henry. *The Nature of Physical Reality.* New York: McGraw-Hill, 1950. Ch. 12.

Röhr, Julius. *Der Okkulte Kraftbegriff im Altertum.* Leipzig, 1923.

Weyl, Hermann. *Philosophy of Mathematics and Natural Science.* Princeton, NJ: Princeton University Press, 1949. Pp. 148ff.

M. Jammer (1967)

FORCE [ADDENDUM]

Forces, understood as pushes or pulls that are exerted (in the first instance) by particulars and that cause motions, have received little philosophical attention in recent decades, reflecting both that forces no longer play a role in fundamental physical theory and that even where they do play a role (e.g., in Newtonian mechanics), it has seemed advisable (following Jammer, above) to give them a purely instrumentalist interpretation. What attention has been paid however indicates that various aspects of the notion of force (or notions; see below) deserve further philosophical consideration.

One such aspect concerns the ontological status of forces. Jammer's deflationary account of force as a mere "methodological intermediate," enabling the kinematical behavior of particulars to be studied independent of the details of specific configurations, but not to be taken with ontological seriousness, was motivated by traditional empiricist concerns with forces as purely theoretical entities (of the sort that exercised Berkeley); such concerns

also figure in van Fraassen's instrumentalist agnosticism about forces. Another source of concern about forces lies in the redundancy argument (of which Mill was an early proponent), according to which forces are not needed to explain motions (the usual non-force causes and effects being sufficient unto the task) and hence should (by Ockham's razor) be eliminated.

There are however ways of resisting or responding to such concerns. Hesse rejects Jammer's instrumentalism as inappropriately eliminating "the metaphysical, a priori, intuitive and anthropomorphic elements" of the classical notion of force. More straightforwardly one can deny that forces are purely theoretical on grounds that these are experienced in the course of ordinary events (of, for instance, liftings, pushings), in which case instrumentalist concerns with force are misguided. And in response to the redundancy argument, Bigelow et al. note that the appropriate application of Ockham's razor involves a ceteris paribus clause: Other things being equal, forces should be eliminated. But, they argue, other things are not equal: In particular, physics without forces does not explanatorily unify phenomena (in particular, motions) as well as does physics with forces. Indeed, one might maintain that, even if other entities unify motions, so long as forces unify these in a distinctive fashion (as they appear to do) Ockham's razor can be resisted.

It remains the case that forces do not play the role in contemporary physics that they once were thought to do. Even within the domain of classical (slow-moving, non-quantum) entities, Newton's force-based formulation of mechanics has been superseded for most explanatory and practical purposes by energy-based (e.g., Lagrangian and Hamiltonian) formulations. And while forces and Newton's laws (the third law being understood as a statement of conservation of momentum) are recognizably present in the relativistic extension of Newtonian mechanics, quantum indeterminacy appears to prevent Newton's theory (which presupposes that bodies have a determinate position and momentum) from being extended to treat quantum phenomena. (This is so, assuming the incorrectness of Bohm's deterministic, force-based interpretation of quantum theory, developed in Bohm and Hiley 1993, on which indeterminacy is given an epistemological spin, as uncertainty.) By way of contrast the concepts and operative principles of energy-based theories (energy, Hamilton's principle of stationary action) straightforwardly extend to both quantum and relativistic contexts. Moreover, in the General Theory of Relativity (GTR), the concept of force disappears altogether:

geometry plus inertial motion, rather than forces, guide motions due to gravity.

Upon closer examination however the above considerations do not show that the concept of force is ontologically obsolete. Concerning the classical domain: Force-based and energy-based formulations of mechanics are not only compatible but are also interderivable (under assumptions generally in place); as Feynman notes, Newtonian and Lagrangian dynamics are "exactly equivalent." This equivalence reflects, among other things, the fact that both potential and kinetic energies are initially defined in terms of the work done by a force; more generally, it appears that force-based and energy-based mechanics are, from a theoretical point of view, mutually supporting, compatible perspectives on the same phenomena. (Such a take is reflected in an intuitive ontological conception of the relation between forces and potentials or potential energies, according to which the latter are dispositions of which forces are the manifestations.) Moreover the restricted application of Newtonian mechanics needn't imply that forces don't exist—at least supposing that the similarly restricted application of special sciences such as chemistry and biology doesn't impugn the existence of their subject matters.

The question remains whether the posit of force is compatible with more fundamental theories. As mentioned, quantum indeterminacy poses a barrier to taking forces, as traditionally conceived, to exist at the quantum level; but if forces are special science entities, this is no surprise (plants don't exist at the quantum level, either). Compatibility might rather be indicated by noting that the deep connection between forces and energies persists in quantum theory, albeit at an analogical level; as Jammer says, "No one has ever directly demonstrated the force of attraction between, say, a proton and an electron. And yet, in writing Schrödinger's equation for such a system, we use the term e^2/r [associated with inverse-square attraction] for the potential energy, carrying it over, so to say, from classical dynamics as a generalization ultimately based on the concept of force." More to the ontological point, one might take the fact that quantum interactions involve exchanges of momentum to suggest that forces are constituted by quantum particle exchanges.

A greater difficulty from the perspective of common applications of force-based mechanics is GTR's denial of gravitational forces. It appears that *if* GTR is the correct theory of gravity, then the posit of gravitational forces cannot be maintained. For GTR and Newtonian mechanics agree that inertial motion does not involve forces; hence there is no way of arguing that an object's inertial

motion along a geodesic "constitutes" the occurrence of gravitational forces. It is presently unclear, however, whether GTR is the correct treatment of gravity. In response to well-known problems in incompatibility between GTR and quantum theories, various attempts are underway to quantize gravity, which if successful might allow for gravitational forces after all.

Philosophers who agree that forces exist may yet disagree over metaphysical details. It remains unclear for example whether forces are independent intermediaries between non-force causes and effects (as Bigelow et al. suggest), or are rather dependent aspects of the latter entities. What (considered) ontological category do forces fall under—are they properties, manifested dispositions, relations, causal relations, sui generis? Another question concerns the status of component vs. resultant forces. In cases in which phenomena involve more than one sort of force (e.g., both an electromagnetic and a gravitational force—supposing the latter exist), do the associated component forces (whose occurrence is expressed by Coulomb's law and Newton's law of gravitation, respectively) exist alongside the resultant force input into Newton's second law? Cartwright maintains that only the resultant force exists, while the component forces are mere mathematical fictions; Creary argues that the need to explain by composition of causes (here, forces) indicates that it is better to keep component and reject resultant forces.

Besides what might be called "Newtonian forces," a distinct but related scientific notion of force also deserves philosophical attention: that of a "fundamental force" or interaction. Paradigmatic fundamental forces/interactions (electromagnetic, gravitational, nuclear) come in many of the same varieties as paradigmatic Newtonian forces; and as already indicated, there are interesting open questions here concerning the relationship between (e.g., electromagnetic) Newtonian forces and the lower-level mechanisms operative in the field-theoretic treatments of the corresponding fundamental forces/interactions. Besides these general metaphysical concerns, fundamental forces/interactions may shed new light on old metaphysical debates. For example, an appeal to fundamental forces/interactions provides what is arguably the best way of formulating physicalism and emergentism as viably contrasting views: With this approach, physicalists maintain that all phenomena are grounded solely in fundamental physical forces/interactions, whereas emergentists maintain that, at certain complex levels of organization (notably, those involved in the having of mental states), a new fundamental force/interaction comes into play.

See also Bohm, David; Cartwright, Nancy; Maxwell, James Clerk; Newtonian Mechanics and Mechanical Explanation; Relativity Theory; Schrödinger, Erwin.

Bibliography

Berkeley, George. "De Motu." In *The Works of George Berkeley,* edited by A. A. Luce and T. E. Jessop. London: Nelson.

Bigelow, John, John Ellis, and Robert Pargetter. "Forces." *Philosophy of Science* (1988): 614–630.

Bohm, David, and B. J. Hiley. *The Undivided Universe: An Ontological Interpretation of Quantum Theory.* London: Routledge, 1993.

Cartwright, Nancy. "Do the Laws of Physics State the Facts?" *Pacific Philosophical Quarterly* 61 (1980): 75–84.

Creary, Lewis. "Causal Explanation and the Reality of Natural Component Forces." *Pacific Philosophical Quarterly* 62 (1981): 148–157.

Feynman, Richard. *The Character of Physical Law.* Cambridge, MA: MIT Press, 1965.

Goldstein, Herbert, Charles Poole, and John Safko. *Classical Mechanics.* San Francisco, CA: Addison Wesley, 2002.

Hesse, Mary. "Review of Concepts of Force." *The British Journal for the Philosophy of Science* 10 (1960): 69–73.

Jammer, Max. *Concepts of Force.* Cambridge, MA: Harvard University Press, 1957.

Mill, John S. *A System of Logic.* London: Longmans, Green, Reader, and Dyer, 1843.

van Fraassen, Bas. *The Scientific Image.* Oxford: Oxford University Press, 1980.

Jessica Wilson (2005)

FOREKNOWLEDGE

See *Precognition*

FOREKNOWLEDGE AND FREEDOM, THEOLOGICAL PROBLEM OF

Divine foreknowledge, like the other classical theistic attributes, raises philosophical problems of at least three kinds. First, there are problems with understanding the attribute itself. How should it be construed (assuming that it is even coherent)? And how might God come by such knowledge? (Are future events all present in their causes? Does God arrive at foreknowledge by inference from "middle knowledge"? Does he *see* the future as through a "time telescope"? Or does he just know it?) Second, there are questions about how this attribute can be compatible with the other divine attributes. As the creator, sustainer, and providential overseer of the world, for

example, God is supposed to be the supreme agent—but how can God approach the future as an active agent if his foreknowledge presents to him everything, including his own decisions and engagements with the world, as a fait accompli?

Finally, there are problems reconciling God's possession of this attribute with other things that appear undeniable. Of these, the most important is surely human freedom. If God knows before a person is even born exactly what that person will do throughout life, how could this person nevertheless retain the power to do otherwise, as free agency apparently requires? This is the classic foreknowledge problem; efforts to solve it are often what drive proposed solutions to the other two problems.

HISTORICAL BACKGROUND

In *De Interpretatione*, Aristotle worried that accepting the truth of future contingents would result in a necessitarianism incompatible with human freedom; for if it is true either that there will be a sea battle tomorrow or that there will not be a sea battle tomorrow, the admiral on whose decision this event depends either cannot issue the requisite order (if there will not be a sea battle) or cannot refrain from issuing the order (if there will be a sea battle). A similar worry was later elaborated into the influential "Master Argument" of Diodorus Cronus, discussed by the Stoics. Because this threat to human freedom rests solely on logical principles, like the Law of Excluded Middle, it is often called "logical fatalism" in contrast to the "theological fatalism" generated by divine foreknowledge.

The subtheistic nature of the ancient divinities and the pluralism of pagan theology made the problem of theological fatalism avoidable, but this was to change with the advent of Christianity. Augustine provides a classic early exposition of the problem in *On Free Choice of the Will* (III.3):

> How is it that these two propositions are not contradictory and inconsistent: (1) God has foreknowledge of everything in the future; and (2) We sin by the will, not by necessity? For ... if God foreknows that someone is going to sin, then it is necessary that he sin. But if it is necessary, the will has no choice about whether to sin .... [So:] either we draw the heretical conclusion that God does not foreknow everything in the future; or ... we must admit that sin happens by necessity and not by will.

Augustine went on to offer his own solution to this problem; his medieval successors added further solutions and contributed enormously to the understanding of the problem, especially its modal character. Recent interest in the problem, sparked by a 1965 article by Nelson Pike, is probably as strong as it has been since the problem's heyday in the Middle Ages.

FORMULATING THE PROBLEM

As Augustine notes, the argument for theological fatalism is designed to show that a certain assumption about God is incompatible with a certain assumption about free will, so that one of them must be rejected.

THE GOD ASSUMPTION. The theological assumptions that play an actual role in the argument concern God's existence and cognitive excellence. It is assumed in the first place that God knows all truths, or

(i) God is omniscient.

Moreover, God believes *only* truths; indeed, he not only *does* not but *could* not believe any falsehoods. So

(ii) God is essentially inerrant, that is, infallible.

The final assumption about God is

(iii) God exists "from eternity."

The phrase *from eternity* is purposely ambiguous, straddling the view of God as an everlasting temporal being existing at all points in time (sempiternity) and the view of God as an atemporal being whose existence transcends time altogether (eternity proper). If (iii) is read, "There is no time such that the proposition *God exists*, if asserted at that time, would be false," then both views are accommodated. This allows for disambiguation, if necessary, to occur in the argument itself.

THE FREEDOM ASSUMPTION. The assumption with which the God Assumption is supposed to be incompatible is simply this:

Someone sometime does something freely.

Freely should be understood here in whatever sense is required for morally responsible agency, but otherwise pretheoretically—that way the theory of freedom under which it is allegedly incompatible with the God Assumption can emerge as a premise in the argument, and rejection of that premise can count as a solution to the problem.

THE ARGUMENT. Suppose someone X performs an action A at a time T3. Let T2 be a time prior to X's birth and T1 any time prior to T2. Then

(1) It is true at T1 that X will do A at T3.

The principle underwriting this claim, sometimes called the omnitemporality of truth, is that a statement true at any time is (suitably modified) true at every time. This does not imply, in the case of (1), that anyone can know at T1 what X will do at T3, let alone that there are conditions at T1 sufficient for X's future action; it only says that, since X's doing A at T3 is an assumption of the argument, it is, at T1, *true* that X will do A at T3.

According to clauses (i) and (iii) of the God Assumption, an omniscient God who exists "from eternity" must know at T1 whatever is true at T1. So

(2) God knows at T1 that X will do A at T3.

And if (2) is true, then so is

(3); God believes at T1 that X will do A at T3.

This follows from the standard analysis of knowledge, according to which knowledge entails belief.

Once God holds this belief, it becomes part of the fixed past that he held that belief. It is no longer possible for him not to have held this belief. This is an instance of the "necessity of the past," conveyed in such maxims as "what's done is done." This is not logical necessity, since there are logically possible worlds with a different past; but it is arguably stronger than natural or causal necessity. Aristotle notes that "this alone is lacking even to God, to make undone things that have once been done" (*Nicomachean Ethics* VI.2.1139b10–11), and Aquinas comments, "As such it is more impossible than the raising of the dead to life, which implies no contradiction, and is called impossible only according to natural power" (*Summa Theologiae* I.25.4). Because what is necessary when past might have been nonnecessary or accidental when future, it is often called accidental necessity. The next step in the argument can therefore be stated this way:

(4) It is accidentally necessary at T2 that God believed at T1 that X will do A at T3.

Since T1 is past relative to T2, (4) is true, given (3).

Though accidental necessity was introduced as a modality characteristic of the past, it is more general in scope. For a proposition *p* to be accidentally necessary at a time T is for *p* to be true no matter how the world continues after T. The past is then accidentally necessary by default; but the future can also qualify as accidentally necessary if entailed by accidentally necessary facts about the past. One such fact is the following:

(5) It is accidentally necessary at T2 that X will do A at T3.

This follows from (4) combined with clause (ii) of the God Assumption, according to which God's believing that X will do A at T3 entails that X will do A at T3.

Since T2 is a time prior to X's birth, X comes into existence with it already being the case that he must do A at T3. It is therefore too late for X to bring it about that he fails to do A at T3—that is,

(6) X cannot refrain from doing A at T3.

But if X cannot refrain from doing A at T3, then

(7) X does not do A at T3 *freely*.

This last inference is sanctioned by a "freedom version" of the so-called Principle of Alternate Possibilities, according to which a person is morally responsible for performing an action only if the person could have refrained from performing it. If a person is not morally responsible, owing to an inability to refrain, this person is not free in the sense required for moral responsibility. This is precisely the sense of "free" that is relevant to the Freedom Assumption.

The foregoing argument does not turn on any peculiar features of X, A, or T3; the same argument can be given for any agent, action, and time. So no one ever does anything freely. If the God Assumption is true, the Freedom Assumption is false.

SOME COMMENTS ON THE ARGUMENT

Before canvassing possible responses to this argument, some explanatory remarks are in order.

First, some versions of the argument bypass (4), inferring the necessity of X's future action from (3) and divine infallibility alone. Such versions might succeed if clause (ii) of the God Assumption could be parsed this way:

(iia) If God believes that p, then necessarily p.

Unfortunately, the correct analysis of divine infallibility is

(iib) Necessarily, if God believes that p, then p.

And all that follows from (iib), given simply that God believes that X will do A at T3, is that X will do A at T3 (and will do so in any world in which God holds this belief). For the action to be necessary, based on (iib), God's belief must be necessary. The illusion that (5) can be derived without reliance on (4) is produced by an equivocation between (iia) and (iib). Boethius, who called the necessity in (iia) "simple necessity" and the necessity in (iib) "conditional necessity," and Aquinas, who termed these "the necessity of the consequent" and "the necessity of the consequence" respectively, diagnosed the problem accurately and rightly insisted on the ineliminability of (4).

Second, step (4) does not rest on the simplistic principle that all true statements indexed to the past through tense or temporal references like "at T1" are accidentally necessary. This principle is in fact false. Confident of victory in tomorrow's election, the candidate proclaims, "My campaign for President began two years before its successful completion." Having just been fooled, I vow, "That was the last time I'm falling for that trick!" Suppose these declarations are in fact true. Though both assert something about the past, neither one is accidentally necessary, since either could (though ex hypothesi it won't) turn out false: The candidate might lose, I might get fooled again. Statements like these, which are not *genuinely* and *strictly* about the past, are called "soft facts" about the past as opposed to the "hard facts" to which the necessity of the past is applicable. What justifies (4), then, is that (3) looks like a *hard* fact about the past. (Certainly there is little question about the human analogue: If Joe believed yesterday that he will shave tomorrow, it is a hard fact, and therefore accidentally necessary, today that he held this belief yesterday.) This also explains the apparently trivial move from (2) to (3). To say of God's cognition in (2) that it constitutes knowledge is to say, in part, that it is true; but its truth depends on how things go at T3. So (2) is not strictly about the past; unlike (3), it is not a hard fact relative to T2.

Third, some critics point out that the future-truth argument for logical fatalism also begins with (1), but then moves directly to (4') It is accidentally necessary at T2 that it was true at T1 that X will do A at T3, and thence to (5). Their claim is that the argument for theological fatalism is just a needlessly complicated version of this argument, and is equally fallacious. The problem with this critique is that (1) is a paradigmatic soft fact relative to T2, undermining the inference to (4'), whereas routing the argument through the theological premises (2) and (3) allows (4) to follow from a prima facie hard fact about the past. This gives the argument for theological fatalism a clear logical advantage.

RESPONSES

If the argument succeeds, either the God Assumption or the Freedom Assumption must be rejected. Those who deny the Freedom Assumption in response to the argument are "theological fatalists." There appear to be very few theological fatalists in this sense. Calvinists would qualify if anyone would. But most Calvinists are compatibilists and would therefore affirm the Freedom Assumption, while those who do reject the Freedom Assumption tend to do so on grounds other than the argument for theological fatalism.

Denying the God Assumption does not entail atheism unless the falsity of just one of the three clauses constituting the God Assumption is sufficient for there being no God. Some theists, indeed, deny that clause (i) is essential to theism when omniscience includes future contingents. If the argument succeeds, such truths are logically unknowable and should be excluded from divine omniscience, just as the logically impossible is excluded from divine omnipotence. "Open Theists" sometimes take this position, maintaining that God willingly limits his foreknowledge to make space for human freedom. There are, however, a number of reasons for thinking that the argument does not succeed.

THE ARISTOTELIAN SOLUTION. Step (1) has been rejected on the grounds that a statement about the future is not (yet) either true or false; it acquires a truth value only when what is now future becomes present. This seems to have been the position Aristotle adopted in response to the "future truth" argument for logical fatalism. It is also the favored position of Open Theists who prefer not to deny the God Assumption: If future contingents lack truth value, a deity who fails to foreknow them will not thereby lack anything necessary to omniscience. Critics, however, have pointed to serious logical costs associated with this move.

THE BOETHIAN SOLUTION. Step (2) follows from (1) only if God exists at T1. But if God does not exist in time, a view famously associated with Boethius, (2) is false; what is true instead is:

(2*) God (timelessly) knows that X will do A at T3.

Two questions may be raised here. The first is whether this view of God is coherent: Though it is the classical view, it has come in for increasing criticism in recent years. The second question is whether a timeless deity might succumb to a modified version of the argument. It has been claimed, for example, that (2) can be replaced by:

(2#) It is true at T1 that God (timelessly) knows that X does A at T3.

(3) and (4) can be similarly modified, and (5) will then follow as before. It has also been claimed that what is fixed in eternity may be no less accidentally necessary than what is fixed in the past, so that (2*) leads to:

(4*) It is accidentally necessary at T2 that God (timelessly) believes that X will do A at T3.

and thence again to (5). But intuitions are a fragile guide here, and the viability of the Boethian solution remains open.

THE OCKHAMIST SOLUTION. The most popular solution in the contemporary debate is the denial of (4). A radical critique might challenge the very idea of accidental necessity as a modality characteristic of the past; but this extreme position runs counter to deep intuitions about the necessity of the past. The principal assault has come from those who accept the necessity of the past but argue, following William Ockham, that (3) is really a soft fact about the past.

In his treatise *Predestination, God's Foreknowledge and Future Contingents*, Ockham distinguishes hard and soft facts this way: "Some propositions are about the [past] as regards both their wording and their subject matter. ... Other propositions are about the [past] as regards their wording only and are equivalently about the future, since their truth depends on the truth of propositions about the future." Ockham's modern followers have cited at least four grounds for placing (3) among the latter propositions.

First, God's belief that X will do A at T3 is counterfactually dependent on X's doing A at T3; if X were to do otherwise, God would have believed otherwise. Unfortunately, this counterfactual dependence can obtain even if X *cannot* do otherwise; hence it provides no reason to think that God can still believe otherwise.

Second, one might develop necessary and sufficient conditions for hard facthood and show that (3) does not qualify. If this is done in terms of an "entailment criterion," it appears that (3) is a soft fact after all, since it entails the future fact that X will do A at T3. But analyses of the hard/soft distinction, most employing entailment criteria, have grown mind-numbingly complex in response to counterexamples, and none has won consensus. This strategy has fallen into disfavor.

Third, one might approach the question from the side of the divine beliefs. How should divine cognition be construed so that (3) can be a soft fact relative to T2? Perhaps the "narrow content" of God's belief is a hard fact about the past, but its "wide content" is determined by the way the future actually unfolds—that the belief counts as the belief *that p* might then be a soft fact about the past. Or perhaps God's beliefs about future contingents are dispositional rather than occurrent in nature, and this makes a difference to their status as hard or soft; then God might be (dispositionally) omniscient at the same time as future contingents remain contingent. Or perhaps, as William Alston (1986) argues, God does not even have beliefs—a position which Linda Zagzebski (1991) terms Thomistic Ockhamism. Even if coherent, such proposals appear to make God's foreknowledge unavailable to him for action-guidance.

Fourth, one might finesse the difficulties of the above approaches with a direct demonstration that (3) is a soft fact, as suggested by Alvin Plantinga (1986) and (in another form) Ted Warfield (1997). If God exists necessarily, then (3) is true in all and only the worlds in which (1) is true, making (3) logically equivalent to (1). Since (1) is a paradigmatic soft fact relative to T2, (3) must be a soft fact as well, and (4) no longer follows. Critics, however, have charged this argument with question-begging.

THE SCOTIST SOLUTION. The inference from (4) to (5) has this form:

(4) It is accidentally necessary that M

(iib) Necessarily, if M, then N

Therefore:

(5) It is accidentally necessary that N

This is a so-called *transfer principle*, since it transfers necessity from one proposition to another. Whether the inference is valid depends on the logic of accidental necessity. The parallel inference for logical necessity is certainly valid; if accidental-necessity-at-T can be modeled as truth in all of some subset of logically possible worlds—for example, the set of all worlds that share the same past up to T—then the above inference should be valid as well. Nevertheless, some types of necessity appear not to work like this, and similar transfer principles, like Peter Van Inwagen's (1983) "rule β," have been disputed.

THE EDWARDSIAN SOLUTION. A compatibilist about free will and causal determinism will not agree that (5) is a reason for endorsing (6). The case for (and against) compatibilism is too large a subject to be broached here and is best pursued in connection with the problem of freedom vs. determinism, where it has received its most sophisticated development. Among theists who come to compatibilism from theological rather than causal deter-

minism, Jonathan Edwards is notable for rejecting step (6).

THE AUGUSTINIAN SOLUTION. Augustine seems to have argued that the agent might remain free even if divine foreknowledge closes all alternatives, so long as the agent's action is self-initiated and God's foreknowledge does not cause, compel, or otherwise explain the action. (How this fits with what Augustine says about divine grace, sovereignty, and predestination is another question.) The moral Augustine draws from foreknowledge cases is arguably the same moral that Harry Frankfurt (1969) draws from cases in which a mechanism eliminates an agent's alternatives without interfering with the agent's actual course of action; indeed, when divine foreknowledge is the mechanism, the result appears to be a perfect "Frankfurt-type counterexample" to the Principle of Alternate Possibilities, on which step (7) rests. If, however, only a predetermined future can be foreknown, even by God, then this solution fails.

THE NATURE OF THE PROBLEM

There are a number of philosophical problems in the neighborhood of this one that can be approached simply as thought experiments, without regard to whether the world is arranged as the problem presupposes. These include Newcomb's puzzle, the paradoxes of time travel and retrocausation, and perhaps even causal determinism itself. The problem of theological fatalism might be one of these; if it is, certain solutions become irrelevant. If someone reflecting on Zeno's paradoxes of motion is puzzled about how Achilles could fail to pass the tortoise, the puzzlement is not addressed by denying Achilles' existence or by reconceiving his attributes (for example, by making him a cripple or supposing he is in a coma). Likewise, someone reflecting on the argument for theological fatalism might be puzzled about how a paradigmatic candidate for free agency might be rendered unfree simply by adding infallible foreknowledge to the situation. Reconceiving God or denying God's existence outright simply removes God from complicity in this puzzle; it does not solve the puzzle. The purely theological solutions—the Boethian and the third and fourth of the Ockhamist responses—fail to address this deeper puzzle, assuming that it is genuine.

See also Alston, William; Aristotle; Augustine, St.; Boethius, Anicius Manlius Severinus; Diodorus Cronus; Duns Scotus, John; Edwards, Jonathan; Frankfurt, Harry; Freedom; Plantinga, Alvin; Precognition; Stoicism; Thomas Aquinas, St.; William of Ockham.

Bibliography

Adams, Marilyn McCord. "Is the Existence of God a 'Hard' Fact?" *Philosophical Review* 76 (1967): 492–503.

Alston, William P. "Does God Have Beliefs?" *Religious Studies* 22 (1986): 287–306.

Craig, William Lane. *The Only Wise God*. Grand Rapids, MI: Baker Book House, 1987.

Fischer, John Martin. "Freedom and Foreknowledge." *Philosophical Review* 92 (1983): 67–79.

Fischer, John Martin, ed. *God, Foreknowledge, and Freedom*. Introduction by John Martin Fischer. Stanford, CA: Stanford University Press, 1989.

Fischer, John Martin. "Scotism." *Mind* 94 (1985): 231–243.

Frankfurt, Harry. "Alternate Possibilities and Moral Responsibility." *Journal of Philosophy* 46 (1969): 828–839.

Freddoso, Alfred J. "Accidental Necessity and Logical Determinism." *Journal of Philosophy* 80 (1983): 257–278.

Haack, Susan. "On a Theological Argument for Fatalism." *Philosophical Quarterly* 24 (1974): 156–159.

Hasker, William. *God, Time, and Knowledge*. Ithaca, NY: Cornell University Press, 1989.

Hunt, David P. "The Compatibility of Divine Determinism and Human Freedom: A Modest Proposal." *Faith and Philosophy* 19 (2002): 485–502.

Hunt, David P. "Dispositional Omniscience." *Philosophical Studies* 80 (1995): 243–278.

Hunt, David P. "On Augustine's Way Out." *Faith and Philosophy* 16 (1999): 3–26.

Hunt, David P. "What *Is* the Problem of Theological Fatalism?" *International Philosophical Quarterly* 38 (1998): 17–30.

Kvanvig, Jonathan. *The Possibility of an All–Knowing God*. New York: St. Martin's Press, 1986.

Pike, Nelson. "Divine Omniscience and Voluntary Action." *Philosophical Review* 74 (1965): 27–46.

Plantinga, Alvin. "On Ockham's Way Out." *Faith and Philosophy* 3 (1986): 235–269.

Purtill, Richard L. "Fatalism and the Omnitemporality of Truth." *Faith and Philosophy* 5 (1988): 185–192.

Stump, Eleonore, and Norman Kretzmann. "Eternity." *Journal of Philosophy* 78 (1981): 429–458.

Van Inwagen, Peter. *An Essay on Free Will*. Oxford: Clarendon Press, 1983.

Warfield, Ted. "Divine Foreknowledge and Human Freedom Are Compatible." *Nous* 31 (1997): 80–86.

Widerker, David. "Troubles with Ockhamism." *Journal of Philosophy* 87 (1990): 462–480.

Widerker, David. "Two Forms of Fatalism." In *God, Foreknowledge, and Freedom*, edited by J. M. Fischer, 97–110. Stanford, CA: Stanford University Press, 1989.

Zagzebski, Linda. *The Dilemma of Freedom and Foreknowledge*. New York: Oxford University Press, 1991.

Zemach, Eddy, and David Widerker. "Facts, Freedom, and Foreknowledge." *Religious Studies* 23 (1988): 19–28.

David P. Hunt (2005)

FORGIVENESS

Through the mid-twentieth century, academic treatments of forgiveness were largely theologically based. The latter part of the century saw the start of a secular discussion of forgiveness within analytic philosophy. The topic provides rich ground for philosophical reflection.

Participants in the discussion often focus on three issues: what forgiveness is, how it is accomplished, and when it is justified. Regarding the first, many appropriate Bishop Butler's claim that forgiveness is the overcoming of resentment. It is widely thought to be accomplished through compassion, perhaps by an imaginative process. The question of justification raises interesting issues about whether forgiveness can be required or whether it is always supererogatory.

There is, however, a prior question of considerable philosophical interest: How is forgiveness, so understood, even possible? Most would agree that not just any elimination of resentment counts as forgiving. You could not forgive by simply taking a pill that rendered you incapable of resentment. Nor does simply forgetting count as forgiving. Forgiveness requires overcoming resentment in the right way. However, it is not merely hard to say what that way is; it is unclear whether there could be such a way.

To keep forgiveness distinct from other responses, such as excuse or contempt, the forgiver must not deny (a) the seriousness of the wrong, (b) the moral standing of the wrongdoer, or (c) his or her own moral standing. Overcoming resentment by denying either the seriousness of the wrong or one's own claim against being wronged is excusing. Overcoming resentment by denying the standing of the wrongdoer is showing contempt for the wrongdoer, excluding him or her from the class of persons whose actions matter. To forgive, one must affirm the seriousness of the wrong and the importance of both oneself and the wrongdoer. Forgiveness must be uncompromising. The difficulty is that the three claims that forgiveness must not deny seem sufficient to ground the resentment that forgiveness must overcome. How, then, is forgiveness possible?

If resentment were necessarily vengeful or malicious, one could overcome it without compromise by achieving compassion. But resentment—that anger over a wrong that is incompatible with forgiveness—is not necessarily vengeful or malicious. One can empathize with the plight of the wrongdoer, have no desire to see him or her harmed, and still resent the wrong. Thus, in contrast with a widely held view, compassion will not secure forgiveness.

If the three most obvious ways to overcome resentment—to discount the wrong, the wrongdoer, or oneself—were the only ways to overcome it, then forgiveness would be impossible. In order to understand an overcoming of resentment as a case of forgiveness, it needs to be distinguished from compromise. Here, then, lies a task for philosophy: to provide an articulate account of the way in which the overcoming of resentment can count as forgiveness. With that task completed, discussion can turn to how forgiveness is accomplished and when it is justified.

See also Moral Sentiments.

Bibliography

Butler, Bishop Joseph. *Sermons*. Boston: Hilliard and Brown, 1827.

Grover, Trudy. *Forgiveness and Revenge*. London: Routledge, 2002.

Hieronymi, Pamela. "Articulating an Uncompromising Forgiveness." *Philosophy and Phenomenological Research* 62 (2001): 529–555.

Murphy, Jeffrie G., and Jean Hampton. *Forgiveness and Mercy*. Cambridge Studies in Philosophy and Law. Cambridge, U.K.: Cambridge University Press, 1988.

Pamela Hieronymi (2005)

FORM

See *Medieval Philosophy; Plato; Universals, A Historical Survey*

FORM, AESTHETIC

See *Aesthetics, History of; Aesthetics, Problems of*

FORMALISM IN MATHEMATICS

See *Mathematics, Foundations of*

FOUCAULT, MICHEL
(1926–1984)

Michel Foucault, though trained in philosophy, never considered himself a professional philosopher. Still, his research into the historical formation of truth, power relations, and modes of recognition regarded as self-evident in various disciplines—most notoriously the figure of man—is an important contribution to philosophy and is itself strikingly original philosophical thought. Born in Poitiers, France, Foucault studied at the École Normale Supérieure under Maurice Merleau-Ponty, Jean Beaufret (1907–1982)—Martin Heidegger's major interpreter in France—and Louis Althusser (1918–1990). Foucault earned his License de philosophie in 1948 and Diplôme de psycho-pathologie in 1952. He taught in Sweden, Poland, and Germany before his appointment as the head of the philosophy department at the University of Clermont-Ferrand. After two years in Tangiers following the publication of *Les mots et les choses* (*The Order of Things*) in 1966, Foucault returned to France and the university at Vincennes, France, just after the anti-authoritarian protests of May 1968. Foucault was elected to the Collège de France in the fall of 1970. Though he grew more engaged in political struggles in the late 1960s and early 1970s, his resistance to humanism made him an uneasy participant in organized movements. Still, his activism and writing earned him attention in the United States, where he became a popular lecturer. Foucault contracted AIDS at the outset of the epidemic and died of complications from the disease in June 1984.

Foucault's work is often divided into three periods, the earliest marked by his archaeological approach, the middle by a genealogy of the modern subject and the relation between power and knowledge, and the late identified with his turn to ethics and the "care of the self." This chronology is controversial: though it orients much of the secondary literature about Foucault, its value lies in its convenience more than in its philosophical or conceptual importance. Taken together, Foucault's works pursue critical inquiry into formative, elementary dimensions of knowledge, autonomy, and experience and are an important contribution to a process of critical engagement with the emergence and limitations of dominant forms of power and knowledge. His goal was to analyze the conditions under which forms of self-relation are created or modified so far as these relations constitute possible knowledge of oneself when such knowledge is referred to something other than an essential identity. Through a historical or genealogical approach to these conditions, Foucault challenges the traditional philosophical model of the subject as having a nature or essence associated with ahistorical capabilities.

ARCHAEOLOGY

Folie et déraison (*Madness and Civilization*; 1965) is the first of Foucault's archaeological works. At the time it was published, Foucault's thinking ranged from psychology and the human sciences (in relation to Ludwig Binswanger, Gaston Bachelard, and Georges Canguilhem [1904–1995]) to Friedrich Nietzsche and avant-garde literature. The book is therefore a powerful introduction to the challenge posed to traditional philosophical practice (and the dominance of phenomenology and existentialism in France) by the growing interest in structuralism, psychoanalysis, and postmodernism. Combining a materialist historical approach associated with the Annales group (Ernst Bloch, Henri Lefebvre [1901–1991], and Fernand Braudel [1902–1985]) and an ontology of the subject derived from his engagement with literature and his critical approach to psychoanalysis, *Madness and Civilization* established Foucault as an important philosopher and social critic in France.

THE ASYLUM AND THE CLINIC

Madness and Civilization traces the emergence of a form of reason in reason's encounter with indications of its limits in unreason (in the Renaissance) and later in madness (in the classical age—the mid-seventeenth century to the beginning of the nineteenth century). Reason encountered its limits in the course of a transformation—at once administrative, moral, and epistemological—in which the exclusion of madness at the margins of community gave way to its confinement in hospitals and then in asylums. This confinement produced new objects of study—excluded populations marked by an inability to work, moral weakness, and disorder—displayed and subjected to emerging forms of knowledge and techniques for the disciplining of disorder and the cure of insanity. On the basis of these practices scientific psychology established the limits of the "normal," themselves a product of a moral, medical, and juridical synthesis made possible by an ascendant administrative capacity to confine populations marked by unreason.

Madness and Civilization comprises an examination of the historical a priori conditions of the emergence of classical reason and an imaginative account of the formation of an experience of reason that defines not only the classical age (particularly René Descartes) but also contemporary thought. Its archaeological approach supposes that discursive formations—statements that delimit and condition what can sensibly be said of madness—are governed by rules that are not reducible to subjective intentions or consciousness and that also govern what can be said or known. *Madness and Civilization* can also be understood as a preface to an analysis of discursive practices that produce relations of knowledge and power. It thus introduces readers to themes that traverse Foucault's work: the exclusion of difference in institutional contexts, the formation of knowledge of subjects on the basis of that exclusion, the relationship between knowledge and power, and the possibility of achieving distance from one's judgments, commitments, and philosophical prejudices through critique. Thus, these works are critical in the Kantian sense as Foucault understood it: they allow one to examine and transform the conditions through which the subject becomes an object of possible knowledge.

Foucault pursues a similar archaeological project in *Naissance de la clinique* (*The Birth of the Clinic*; 1963), an account of the formation of a mode of perception that makes possible medical knowledge of the body. Foucault shows that modern knowledge of disease is dependent on changing structures of perception and language that are sustained by practices and powers that inhabit the space of the clinic. Where standard histories of medicine portray medical knowledge as derived from an unstructured gaze and converging on objectivity, Foucault shows that accepted medical practices have their origins in something other than necessities of medical reason (e.g., the practice of the "round") or inference and pure observation in the context of steadily improving methods. The philosophical importance of the book is its analysis of the merging of clinical language and ways of seeing—a contingent form of a gaze and its links to institutional powers that sustain it—with the language of rationality.

WORDS AND THINGS

The most significant work of Foucault's archaeological period is *Order of Things*, in which Foucault again unearths and articulates the historical conditions for the possibility of knowledge in the human sciences in a given period: those knowledges associated with labor, life, and language. At the same time, *Order of Things* is a genealogy in an important sense: it traces the emergence of Foucault's own commitments and of the privileges and imperatives that accompany his own discourse. Thus, some critics accuse Foucault of engaging in criticism that leaves him with no standpoint from which to judge structures of power and knowledge that are evidently in question in his work, undermining his own ground and promulgating relativism. Foucault called this charge "intellectual blackmail."

Order of Things is a genealogy of the Same, of the rules and conditions that make possible the perception and knowledge of order. It proceeds by way of an account of two profound breaks in the coherence of knowledge about man and of the way those breaks affect modern knowledge and give it resources with which to freely think new possibilities. The first break occurred between the Renaissance and the classical epistemes. Foucault uses the word *episteme* to designate the regularities that account for the coherence of knowledge in a given period. The Renaissance episteme was coherent—one could speak truly about nature and link one's speech to the world—because of its dependence on resemblance and similitude for the organization of what counted as knowledge and true perception. But this understanding of the relationship between language and the world, between the signifier and the signified, is ultimately broken—similitude becomes deceptive. The subsequent Renaissance episteme is oriented around the primacy of representation: the capacity of language to mirror the world and to correspond to it in a truthful way by virtue of its capacity to organize the multiplicity of identities and differences in a table or grid, making possible a new recognition of sameness. This is the first of two breaks.

Foucault's primary concern, though, is to document the second break, the "profound upheaval" that led to the disintegration of representation at the end of the eighteenth century. This disintegration was prompted in various domains by a growing recognition of the limits of representation, particularly of its ability to account for the act of representing itself and to adequately represent the being who represents. As a result of this disintegration, knowledge in the human sciences becomes an "Analytic of Finitude." Man appears for the first time as both the object of knowledge and the one who knows, an "empirico-transcendental doublet" understood in terms of his labor that can be alienated, his organism that is part of an evolutionary history, or his speaking a language that is no longer controlled by a representing subject but that has its own historicity, rules, and organic structures, while being utterly internal. Knowledge of man as this doublet is thus dependent on being able to account for man's being in those places or regions in which man is absent. One of the consequences of this analysis is that the centrality of the figure man is itself subject to questioning and overcoming, which Foucault hoped his work would both reflect and generate. This project is to a large extent shared by Nietzsche, Heidegger, and Sigmund Freud.

L'archéologie du savoir (*The Archaeology of Knowledge*; 1969) attempts to give a systematic account of his methodological assumptions and procedures in his archaeological works, formulating the rules that operate within a discourse "at a superficial level" and that constitute a discourse's coherence as a "game of truth." Foucault's work after *Archaeology of Knowledge* is usually understood as genealogical in scope and approach.

GENEALOGY

The word *genealogy* is associated with Nietzsche and is understood as a patient tracing of the descent of authoritative discursive practices that structure the application of power to bodies and subjects (e.g., in the school, the hospital, and the prison). Foucault studies *dispositifs*, practices that exclude and construct forms of experience as abnormal in various ways (e.g., criminality, madness, and sexual deviancy) and that construct forms of subjectivity on the basis of knowledge of normalcy (e.g., the soldier, the student, the guard, or the attendant). He examines practices and texts that are no longer part of received knowledge but that nevertheless were important in the formation of a practice or the exclusion of a form of experience, where genealogy is an attempt to remember those lost experiences and complicated formations. The genealogy of various formations of subjectivation led Foucault to the identification and articulation of forms of power, most importantly the power of surveillance—a "microphysics of power"—in *Surveiller et punir* (*Discipline and Punish*; 1975).

Discipline and Punish concerns the emergence of the modern power to punish in the prison and of the way in which the prison, through observation, examination, and normalizing judgment, produces the conditions for the recognition of delinquency. Thus, it is a genealogy of the way in which power divides the "normal" from the "incarcerated" and of the formation of self-relation around the axes of normalcy, lawfulness, and the careful monitoring of one's own excesses. Modern power encourages one to correct one's own deviance. The notion of power at work in *Discipline and Punish* applies to the practices and techniques that operate inside and outside of the prison that discipline subjects who show signs of disorder (e.g., children, soldiers, students, crowds, criminals, and workers). Those techniques aim to produce a moral subject capable of self-discipline and of being aware of the virtues of obedience.

On this conception of power there are no agents in whom power is concentrated, but only techniques, regimens, regulations, and measures that divide the normal or average from the pathological or criminal. This power is not in the service or control of a dominant interest, class, or group, but dispersed throughout the social body and concentrated in various institutions that are simultaneously carceral and clinical. This dispersion makes resistance to power difficult, but Foucault thought resistance was possible by intensifying one's recognition of the intolerability of specific forms of power by attention to voices or discourses that cannot be adequately heard from within dominant regimes. He conceived of his work as tools for use in the strategic interruption of dominant discourses and practices.

ETHICS

While working on his genealogies and occasional politically incendiary essays in the 1970s (including lecture courses on the contemporaneous emergence of psychiatry and racism in *Abnormal* [2003a] and on discourse of and as war in *Society Must Be Defended* [2003b]), Foucault assembled his three-part *Histoire de la sexualité* (*History of Sexuality*). *La volonté de savoir* (*An Introduction*; 1976), the first volume, was an analysis of the "repressive hypothesis," the idea that sexual expression went through a period of repression in the Victorian era and subsequently was liberated by an increasing awareness of the naturalness of sex. Foucault argues instead that sex was an important and much discussed issue for the Victorians and that discourses of sexuality and techniques of sexual control and expression are important avenues through which power operates on the body (by encouraging subjects to work on themselves) and are not reducible to a single repressive power. To examine what he called subjectivizing practices at work on the formation of sexuality, he constructs a genealogy of the experience of sexuality. On Foucault's terms sexuality is not a constant, natural feature of human beings, but takes historically singular forms, the emergence of which can be traced through a genealogical account.

L'usage des plaisirs (*The Use of Pleasure*; 1984) and *Le souci de soi* (*Care of the Self*; 1984), the second and third volumes of the *History of Sexuality*, respectively, were published eight years after the first volume and after considerable revision of his overall project. Foucault turns his attention from relatively recent formations of sexuality in the eighteenth and nineteenth centuries to the problem of desire and the desiring subject in ancient Greek and Hellenic thought, though always in relation to the present. He conducts a genealogy of the problematizations—the ways in which certain practices and forms of knowledge become a matter of concern—and practices surrounding

the formation of the subjects who can recognize and understand themselves in terms of the techniques, ethical concerns, and political relations that form around men who desire. *Use of Pleasure* focuses on the ways in which pleasure was a matter of concern for the Greeks and how it played a crucial role in the command that one "know thyself." Foucault then traces a change from a focus on pleasure and its use to a focus on desire and how to protect oneself from its dangers before the emergence of the Christian problematic of pleasure, desire, and ethics. The third volume is a genealogy of the emergence of the modern subject in Hellenic and Roman practices of self-control and asceticism.

Foucault made important contributions to discreet areas of philosophical research, including feminist philosophy and gender theory, social, political and legal philosophy, the philosophy of science, aesthetics, theories of knowledge, and especially ethics, which is a constant concern throughout Foucault's works. While Foucault resisted moral theory and insisted on its danger, and while he resisted the articulation of a solid moral stance on which one could found commitment or advocacy, he nevertheless insisted on the ethical value of his genealogical work. Through the investigation of the conditions under which subjects are formed and modes of recognition are validated or legitimated, Foucault intensified awareness of the subjugating powers that invest the practices and discourses that structure one's understanding of oneself and others and turned that awareness back on itself to promote the exploration of new and singular modes of self-relation.

See also Archaeology; Binswanger, Ludwig; Bloch, Ernst; Descartes, René; Feminist Philosophy; Freud, Sigmund; Heidegger, Martin; Merleau-Ponty, Maurice; Nietzsche, Friedrich; Renaissance; Structuralism and Post-structuralism; Subject.

Bibliography

WORKS BY FOUCAULT

Mental Illness and Psychology. Translated by Alan Sheridan. New York: Harper and Row, 1976. Originally published under the title *Maladie mentale et psychologie* in 1962.

Birth of the Clinic. Translated by A. M. Sheridan Smith. New York: Pantheon, 1973. Originally published under the title *Naissance de la clinique* in 1963.

Madness and Civilization. Translated by Richard Howard. New York: Pantheon, 1965. Originally published under the title *Folie et déraison* in 1966.

The Order of Things: An Archaeology of the Human Sciences. New York: Pantheon, 1970. Originally published under the title *Les mots et les choses* in 1966.

The Archaeology of Knowledge. Translated by A. M. Sheridan Smith. New York: Pantheon, 1972. Originally published under the title *L'archéologie du savoir* in 1969.

Discipline and Punish: The Birth of the Prison. Translated by Alan Sheridan. New York: Pantheon, 1977. Originally published under the title *Surveiller et punir* in 1975.

The History of Sexuality. 3 vols. Translated by Robert Hurley. New York: Pantheon, 1978–1986. Originally published in three volumes under the title *Histoire de la sexualité* in 1976 and 1984.

The Essential Works of Foucault, 1954–1984. 3 vols. Translated by Robert Hurley. New York: New Press, 1997–2000.

Fearless Speech. Edited by Joseph Pearson. Los Angeles: Semiotext(e), 2001.

Abnormal: Lectures at the Collège de France, 1974–1975. Translated by Graham Burchell; edited by Valerio Marchetti and Antonella Salomoni. New York: Picador, 2003a.

Society Must be Defended : Lectures at the Collège de France, 1975–1976. Translated by David Macey; edited by Mauro Bertani and Alessandro Fontana. New York: Picador, 2003b.

The Hermeneutics of the Subject: Lectures at the Collège de France, 1981–1982. Translated by Graham Burchell; edited by Frédéric Gros. New York: Palgrave-Macmillan , 2004.

WORKS ABOUT FOUCAULT

Bernauer, James W. *Michel Foucault's Force of Flight: Toward an Ethics for Thought.* Atlantic Highlands, NJ: Humanities Press International, 1990.

Eribon, Didier. *Michel Foucault.* Translated by Betsy Wing. Cambridge, MA: Harvard University Press, 1991.

Davidson, Arnold I., ed. *Foucault and His Interlocutors.* Chicago: University of Chicago Press, 1997.

Deleuze, Gilles. *Foucault.* Minneapolis: University of Minnesota Press, 1988.

Dreyfus, Hubert L., and Paul Rabinow. *Michel Foucault: Beyond Structuralism and Hermeneutics.* Chicago: University of Chicago Press, 1982.

Foucault.Info (May 2005), http://www.foucault.info.

Foucault Resources (May 2005), http://www.qut.edu.au/edu/cpol/foucault/.

Gutting, Gary. *Michel Foucault's Archaeology of Scientific Reason.* New York: Cambridge University Press, 1989.

Han, Béatrice. *Foucault's Critical Project: Between the Transcendental and the Historical.* Translated by Edward Pile. Stanford, CA: Stanford University Press, 2002.

Macey, David. *The Lives of Michel Foucault: A Biography.* New York: Pantheon, 1993.

McWhorter, Ladelle. *Bodies and Pleasures: Foucault and the Politics of Sexual Normalization.* Bloomington: Indiana University Press, 1999.

Sawicki, Jana. *Disciplining Foucault: Feminism, Power, and the Body.* New York: Routledge, 1991.

Visker, Rudi. *Michel Foucault: Genealogy as Critique.* Translated by Chris Turner. New York: Verso, 1995.

Benjamin Pryor (2005)

FOUCHER, SIMON
(1644–1696)

Simon Foucher was one of the foremost critics of Cartesian philosophy. He was born in Dijon, France, where, after taking orders, he was made honorary canon of the Sainte Chapelle. He took a bachelor's degree in theology at the Sorbonne and spent his adult life as a chaplain in Paris, where he died. His first published work is a long didactic poem commemorating the death of Anne of Austria (1601–1666). In another long poem he defends the compatibility of Greek and Christian moral principles. In Paris he attended the lectures on Cartesian physics given by Jacques Rohault, which inspired him to make original experiments in the science of hygrometry (humidity of the atmosphere) on which he published two pioneering works in 1672 and 1686. He also produced three major dissertations concerning the value of Academic skepticism in the search for truth. He was the first to publish criticisms of both Nicolas Malebranche's occasionalism and Gottfried Wilhelm Leibniz's monadism, and it is for these critiques that he is best known.

ACADEMIC METHOD

Foucher considered himself to be the reviver of Academic philosophy, by which he means Socratic ignorance combined with the reasonable doubt of Philo of Larissa and Antiochus of Ascalon, who say that they know some things and are ignorant of others; he argues that this is the middle way between dogmatism and Pyrrhonism. The primary maxim of his Academic philosophy is to recognize only *vérité evident* as a rule of truth. The Academic laws are:

(1) To proceed only by demonstrations in philosophy

(2) To avoid unanswerable questions

(3) To admit when one does not know

(4) To distinguish what one knows from what one does not know

(5) Always to seek after knowledge

There are three important axioms:

(1) True knowledge cannot come from sense experience

(2) Opinion is not knowledge

(3) Words must presuppose concepts

ENCYCLOPEDIA OF PHILOSOPHY
2nd edition

Foucher argues that the goal of philosophy is to find a criterion of truth with which to avoid error in judgment. The criterion can be used to obtain knowledge of the essence of things and to put this knowledge into a necessary order. But no criterion of truth can be adequate for attaining the absolute certainty that René Descartes seeks. Truth is basically human and fallible.

Foucher builds no system of his own; his talents are primarily critical. His method is that of the traditional skeptic: he assumes the suppositions of the system under analysis and then reasons by *reductio ad absurdum* to contradictory conclusions. But unlike the Pyrrhonian skeptics who wish to confute all knowledge claims, Foucher's Academic skepticism is meant to advance probable science and knowledge.

CRITICISMS OF MALEBRANCHE AND CARTESIANISM

Foucher claims that Descartes, to his credit, takes his rules of method from the Academics but that it is a major mistake on Descartes's part to assert that clear and distinct ideas can be certain and that they represent things external to one. Foucher follows Aristotle in professing that he cannot understand how one can have knowledge of the external world if no such knowledge comes through the senses. He further insists that both Descartes's claim that the knowledge of the essence of matter is innate and that knowledge of the properties of extension comes only through the reason, and not the senses, are unintelligible. Beyond this, Foucher makes four basic criticisms of Cartesianism.

First, Foucher argues that if mind and matter differ in essence, this allows no possibility of essential likeness between the two substances, which is necessary for causal interaction. Therefore, Cartesian mind and matter cannot interact.

Second, interaction between mind and matter obviously takes place, yet this interaction cannot be accounted for by Cartesian principles. Consequently, the Cartesians cannot know the true essences of mind and matter. The principle that likeness is necessary between cause and effect is self-evident, Foucher says, so mind and matter cannot be essentially different.

The third criticism concerns the ontological similarity between sensations and conceptual ideas, both of which are said by the Cartesians to be modifications of the mind. Both also are caused by the interaction of the mind with material things. However, ideas are said to represent objects external to the mind, whereas sensations do not. Foucher argues that if ideas are mental modifications representative of the material things that cause them, then why cannot sensations, which are also modifications of the mind, represent the material things that cause them? Or conversely, if sensations cannot represent material things, then how can ideas do so? This objection of Foucher's seems to be based on the Cartesian dictum that the cause of an idea must have at least as much formal or eminent reality as the idea has objective reality. Foucher argues that this means that it is necessary for there to be a likeness between the formal or eminent reality of the material thing and the objective reality of its idea. Because of this likeness, the material thing can cause the idea to resemble it and, hence, to represent it. Since sensations are caused by the same objects that cause ideas, why would sensations not also be like their causes, and hence representative of them? In this criticism Foucher basically ignores the Cartesian implication that conceptual ideas represent through description, not through resemblance, as sensations are ordinarily thought to do (although not by Descartes).

Fourth, if mind and matter are substances that differ in essence, then there can be no similarity or resemblance between them or their respective modifications. And, Foucher claims, it is obvious that if there is no resemblance, there can be no representation. Unextended ideas cannot represent extended material things or material modifications because ideas are mental modifications that can in no way resemble material things or material modifications. Hence, Cartesian ontology precludes an intelligible epistemology.

Such Cartesians as Rohault, Pierre-Sylvain Régis, Robert Desgabets, Louis de La Forge (1632–1666), and Antoine Le Grand (1629–1699) deny that ontological likeness or resemblance is necessary for an idea to represent its object. Foucher persists in asking for an explication of this nonresembling representation that is as intelligible as the notion that representation depends on resemblance, but he receives little more in reply than that God assures it. Foucher is himself a faithful Christian, but he insists against the Cartesians and Malebranche that declarations of faith in God's power and wisdom cannot be used as principles in philosophy.

Foucher takes Malebranche, as well as Descartes, to be saying that both sensations and ideas are modifications of the soul, which is a substance differing in essence from body. Malebranche denies that his ideas are mental modifications, but holds rather that they are beings in the mind of God. Foucher argues that Malebranchian ideas external to the mind, even if they are in the mind of God, would be as difficult to know as are material objects external to the mind. Despite Malebranche's derision and that Foucher never takes him to be anything but a Cartesian, Foucher's criticisms bear on a vital point in Malebranche's system as well as in the systems of nonoccasionalist Cartesians. The epistemological failure of Cartesianism stems from the inability of Cartesians to give an explication of how ideas represent material things that is compatible with their dualist ontology.

CORRESPONDENCE WITH LEIBNIZ

In a correspondence noteworthy for the clearness with which each philosopher states his views, Leibniz agrees with Foucher that Academic principles are useful and that once in a lifetime a philosopher should follow his suppositions to their foundations. But Foucher insists that philosophy is primarily the examination and establishment of first principles, whereas Leibniz contends that very few philosophers are needed for this task; the important work is to follow out consequences in the development of knowledge. Foucher agrees that mathematics and hypothetical systems based on propositions of identity allow the deduction of truths internal to coherent systems, but he is concerned with the correspondence relation of these conceptual systems to the external world. Before a deductive natural philosophy is possible, it must be determined that the physical world is truly represented by one's concepts, axioms, and systems.

Extracts from the correspondence appear in the *Journal des Sçavans* from 1692 to 1696. In these Leibniz first places his new system before the public and Foucher gives it its first published critique. Foucher sees Leibniz's new system as little more than preestablished Malebranchian occasionalism, and he asks why God should go to such trouble to make it appear that mind and body interact if they really do not. Leibniz objects to occasionalism on the grounds that God should not continually be involved in making adjustments; Foucher argues that preestablished harmony, with all adjustments made at once, is no better. He says that Leibniz, like Malebranche, retains matter that is useless in his system because everyone experiences the interaction between mind and body. The task is to explain how interaction does take place, not merely how it seems to take place and how one can talk as though it does. For this, a monistic ontology in which mind and matter are metaphysically similar is required.

Foucher thus approves of Leibniz's denial of the Cartesian contention that extension is the essence of matter and his development of a monism of monads. The closest Foucher himself comes to outlining a monistic ontology is his suggestion to Leibniz that he should develop his ontology of monads to this end. Leibniz does not do this.

Foucher is not assured that any first principles apply to the world, and he criticizes Leibniz for building a system on uncertain foundations. Foucher reiterates that Descartes's criterion of certainty, clarity, and distinctness is useless and that the infallible mark of truth has not yet been discovered.

Foucher is important in the history of modern philosophy as a skeptic who originated epistemological criticisms that are fatal to the Cartesian way of ideas. Foucher's arguments against the distinction between ideas and sensations—that both are modifications of mind—were utilized by Pierre Bayle (*Dictionnaire historique et critique*, 5th ed. 1740, "Pyrrhon," Remark B), George Berkeley (*A Treatise concerning the Principles of Human Knowledge* 1710, 8–15; *Three Dialogues Between Hylas and Philonous* 1710, I), and David Hume (*A Treatise of Human Nature* 1739, I, IV, iv) to destroy the distinction between the primary qualities of size, shape, and position that John Locke says actually modify material bodies and the secondary qualities of sensible visual imagery, touch, taste, sound, and smell that Locke says do not modify bodies but are merely caused by them. The argument is that all these qualities are equally sensible.

See also Antiochus of Ascalon; Aristotle; Bayle, Pierre; Berkeley, George; Cartesianism; Descartes, René; Desgabets, Robert; Hume, David; Leibniz, Gottfried Wilhelm; Locke, John; Malebranche, Nicolas; Philo of Larissa; Pyrrhonian Problematic, The; Régis, Pierre-Sylvain; Rohault, Jacques.

Bibliography

WORKS BY FOUCHER

Critique la recherche de la vérité, 1675.

De la sagesse des anciens, 1682.

Dissertation sur la reserche de la vérité, 1687.

GENERAL

Armour, Leslie. "Simon Foucher, Knowledge, and Idealism: Philo of Larissa and the Enigmas of a French 'Skeptic.'" In *Cartesian Views: Papers Presented to Richard A. Watson*, edited by Thomas M. Lennon, 97–115. Leiden, Netherlands: Brill, 2003.

Lennon, Thomas M. "Foucher, Huet, and the Downfall of Cartesianism." In *Cartesian Views: Papers Presented to Richard A. Watson*, edited by Thomas M. Lennon, pp. 117–128. Leiden, Netherlands: Brill, 2003.

Maia Neto, Jose R. "Foucher's Academic Cartesianism." In *Cartesian Views: Papers Presented to Richard A. Watson*, edited by Thomas M. Lennon, 71–95. Leiden, Netherlands: Brill, 2003.

Popkin, Richard H. *The History of Scepticism: From Savonarola to Bayle*. Rev. ed. New York: Oxford University Press, 2003.

Schmaltz, Tad M. *Radical Cartesianism: The French Reception of Descartes*. New York: Cambridge University Press, 2002.

Watson, Richard A. *The Downfall of Cartesianism, 1673–1712: A Study of Epistemological Issues in Late Seventeenth Century Cartesianism*. The Hague: Nijhoff, 1965.

Watson, Richard A. "Foucher's Mistake and Malebranche's Break: Ideas, Intelligible Extension, and the End of Ontology." In *Nicolas Malebranche: His Philosophical Critics and Successors*, edited by Stuart Brown, 22–34. Assen/Maastricht, Netherlands: Van Gorcum, 1991.

Watson, Richard A. Introduction to *Critique de la recherche de la vérité* by Simon Foucher. New York: Johnson Reprint Corporation, 1969.

Watson, Richard A. "Introduction and Translation of Simon Foucher's *Critique [of Nicolas Malebranche's] of the Search for Truth*." In *Malebranche's First and Last Critics: Simon Foucher and Dortous de Mairan*, edited by Richard A. Watson and Marjorie Grene, 1–57. Carbondale: Southern Illinois University Press, 1995.

Richard A. Watson (1967, 2005)

FOUILLÉE, ALFRED
(1838–1912)

Alfred Fouillée, the French philosopher and sociologist, was a prolific writer, especially on political, social, and historical subjects. He was a lecturer in lycées at Douai and Montpellier, at the University of Bordeaux, and finally, from 1872 to 1875, at the École Normale in Paris. When he had to retire because of ill health, he devoted his time to his writings. Through most of his varied output there ran a common thread. This was a concern to reconcile the values of traditionally metaphysical or spiritualistic philosophy—above all, liberty and free will—with the deterministic and antimetaphysical findings of contemporary work in the natural sciences: a concern, that is, to reconcile philosophical idealism with scientific naturalism. Fouillée, who was not closely identified with any formal school of thought, thus represented a further step in the direction indicated before him by some of the later disciples of the spiritualistic school of Victor Cousin, such as Paul Janet and Étienne Vacherot, who aimed at absorbing or coming to terms with, rather than combating, the rising power of natural science and scientific philosophy.

Fouillée's outstanding and most original contribution to this enterprise was the idea that thought could lead to action, which he embodied in his concept of *idée-force,* or "thought force." This concept contains in itself the essence of Fouillée's consciously eclectic, conciliatory method and aim, for it borrows the notion of "force" from contemporary physical science and applies it to mental states, to consciousness. Force, defined as a tendency to action, becomes a universal fact of consciousness; conversely, every idea is a force that has a potential for realizing itself in action. Thus ideas, whether or not they are themselves caused, are causes; and since ideas are mental phenomena, mind is an efficient cause of physical action. The *idées-forces* are intermediaries between the private existence of consciousness and the objective existence of things. They enabled Fouillée to preserve spiritual values within the conditions imposed by natural science by developing what has been called a "positive metaphysics," that is, a metaphysics within the limits of the physically conceivable. Thus he undertook to refute the central tenet of materialism that mind or consciousness is merely an epiphenomenon. Specifically taking up the crucial concept of liberty, Fouillée argued that the consciousness of liberty amounts to the existence of liberty, since it gives rise to ideas formulated in terms of freedom of choice and since these ideas can in fact exert an effect on the outside world.

Fouillée's system is based primarily on psychological analysis, resembling, again, the spiritualism of the school of Cousin. This orientation was indicated by Fouillée himself when in his last work he labeled his philosophy "voluntaristic idealism." The will is the most immediate reality of consciousness, although not sharply separated from the intelligence or reason; ideas in Fouillée seem scarcely distinguishable from intentions. Yet, since he was attempting a comprehensive philosophical synthesis, Fouillée also constructed ontological categories on his psychological foundations. Causation, for instance, was established as an objective reality because it is one of the conditions necessary for the exercise of will, for the efficacy of the *idées-forces.* In like manner he developed an ethics with a strong social orientation. Consciousness, he taught, is aware not only of its own existence but of the consciousness of others (in this connection he suggested the emendation of René Descartes's famous dictum to read *Cogito ergo sumus*). Altruism is a necessity, since isolation is impossible; moral choice is explained in terms of the attractive or repulsive power of *idées-forces* in the form of ideals; and ethical conduct is defined in terms of social beneficence.

It is doubtful whether a system like Fouillée's, developed from a defensive posture, could ever prove generally acceptable. The concept of *idées-forces* is suggestive and useful as a tool of psychological analysis, but dubious if elevated to the status of ontological reality. It is ultimately a merely verbal concept or device, seeking to bridge the gap between internal or mental processes and physical actions by, as it were, inserting a hyphen between them. But it will not bear the weight it is meant to carry, and as a result, the system as a whole remains merely suspended between idealism and naturalism. Though he struck a responsive chord and was widely read in his day, Fouillée had, in the end, few if any important followers.

See also Cousin, Victor; Descartes, René; Determinism and Freedom; Force; Idealism; Liberty; Naturalism.

Bibliography

Among the most important of Fouillée's works are *La liberté et le déterminisme* (Paris: Ladrange, 1872); *La science sociale contemporaine* (Paris: Hachette, 1880); *L'évolutionnisme des idées-forces* (Paris: F. Alcan, 1890); *Critique des systèmes de morale contemporains* (Paris: G. Baillière, 1883); *L'avenir de la métaphysique* (Paris: F. Alcan, 1889); *Psychologie des idées-forces*, 2 vols. (Paris, 1893), perhaps the central work; *Le mouvement idéaliste et la réaction contre la science positive* (Paris: F. Alcan, 1896); *Les éléments sociologiques de la morale* (Paris, 1905); *Morale des idées-forces* (Paris, 1908); *La pensée et les nouvelles écoles anti-intellectualistes* (Paris, 1911); *Esquisse d'une interprétation du monde* (Paris, 1913).

For literature on Fouillée, consult Augustin Guyau, *La philosophie et la sociologie d'Alfred Fouillée* (Paris, 1913), a laudatory view; Harald Höffding, *Moderne Filosofer* (Aarhus, 1904), translated by Alfred C. Mason as *Modern Philosophers*, pp. 82–88 (London, 1915); D. Parodi, *La philosophie contemporaine en France*, pp. 40–48 (Paris, 1919); and Elisabeth Ganne de Beaucoudrey, *La psychologie et la métaphysique des idées-forces chez Alfred Fouillée* (Paris: J. Vrin, 1936), a massive and judicious work.

W. M. Simon (1967)

FOUNDATIONALISM

See *Classical Foundationalism*

FOURIER, FRANÇOIS MARIE CHARLES
(1772–1837)

François Marie Charles Fourier, the French social critic, utopian socialist, and eccentric, was born into a merchant family in Besançon. Except during the French Revolution, Charles Fourier led a quiet and isolated life as a minor business employee and bachelor in Paris, Lyons, Rouen,

and elsewhere in France, with occasional trips abroad. Shortly after the turn of the nineteenth century, Fourier began to develop his doctrine, publishing his first major work, *Théorie des quatres mouvements et des destinées générales,* in 1808. He continued throughout his life to elaborate and propagate his views with a single-minded devotion, acquired some followers, and was able to dedicate his last years entirely to his self-appointed task.

After a superficial classical secondary education in a Jesuit school in Besançon, Fourier was entirely self-taught. His reading was confined largely to contemporary periodicals and often apparently to bits of articles or merely to headlines. His views reflect many ideas of the Enlightenment and of the early nineteenth century, with strong Rousseauistic and physiocratic strains.

Fourier believed that, because the world had been created by a benevolent deity and yet wallowed in misery, men had obviously failed to carry out the divine plan. The plan was discovered by Fourier, and it had to be translated into practice. Happiness would then replace misery, unity would replace division, Harmony would replace Civilization. The transformation would occur through the release of man's thirteen passions, instilled by God but repressed in Civilization: the five senses; the four "group," or social, passions of ambition, friendship, love, and family feeling; the three "series," or distributive, passions, that is, the "cabalist," or passion for intrigue, the *papillone* (butterfly), or passion for diversification, and the "composite," or passion for combining pleasures; and, finally, the passion for harmony, which synthesizes all the others. With the passions released, existence would become intense joy, and a lifetime would seem but a moment.

To accomplish the release of the passions, humanity would have to be organized into phalanxes of about eighteen hundred men, women, and children. In each phalanx different characters and inclinations would be scientifically combined in a complex and finely graded system of groups and series so that each person could give full expression, in his work and in his other activities, to all his passions, tastes, and capacities, and avoid everything that did not suit him. The economies accomplished by communal work and living and by finding the right place for every talent, and the enormous enthusiasms and energies mobilized by the new order, would make phalanxes extremely successful economically as well as in terms of human happiness. Indeed, a single trial phalanx would prove its absolute superiority within a few weeks or, at the most, months and, through imitation, abolish Civilization in a year or two. Moreover, the savages and barbarians who had stubbornly resisted Civilization would eagerly join Harmony. The result would be one world of happy phalanxes, linked vaguely by a hierarchy of monarchs and more effectively by temporary industrial armies for special tasks and similar touring bands of poets, actors, and musicians. Fourier's life became a constant search for the means to establish a trial phalanx, and his political, social, and other preferences were all subordinated to this one great purpose. Fourier believed his main enemies to be the *philosophes* of all sorts, with their "400,000 false volumes."

Fourier's ideas for transforming society were linked to peculiar views on man's past and to strange cosmological beliefs and "analogical" methods (Fourier argued "by analogy" in dealing with all elements of the cosmos). Because the world was one, the coming of Harmony would lead to new, beneficial creations on earth and would result in the appearance of new satellites, in the regaining of health by our planet, and in more distant desirable cosmic repercussions. At the moment, however, earth remained deplorably behind other planets, and Fourier hoped that sufficiently powerful telescopes would enable men to observe the system of Harmony as practiced by the Solarians or the inhabitants of Jupiter. Fantastic details of many kinds abound in Fourier's writings, and the very form of the writings is frequently bizarre.

In addition to giving rise to Fourierist communal experiments and anticipating cooperatives, Fourier has exercised a broad general influence as social critic, early socialist, and man of many insights, especially psychological ones. Fourier's criticism, appreciated by Karl Marx and Friedrich Engels among others, is notable for its fundamental character, its incisiveness, its richness, and its lack of compromise or nuance. It ranges from magnificent denunciations of exploitation and sham in family, society, church, and state, through striking discussions of fraudulent business practices (in particular of fraud in commerce, Fourier's bête noire), and of the appalling conditions of the masses, to a listing of dozens of different kinds of cuckoldry. Fourier was a moralist and believed that Harmony would establish truth as well as happiness among men, for truth rather than deception and hypocrisy would then become the profitable and accepted way of life.

Fourier's socialism is sui generis; he would have retained some private property, and he regarded inequality and discord as necessary for the construction of graded series and groups and the exercise of all passions. He stressed gastrosophy (the science of cuisine), opera, and horticulture rather than large-scale agriculture or industry. Far from desiring to mold man to a social purpose, he essayed to create a society where every individual whim would be satisfied. But Fourier did define man in social terms (the natural unit for lions, he said, is the couple, and for man, a phalanx, for only in a phalanx could man truly be man); and he charted an extremely complicated and interdependent socialist society, in which men own property, work, and live in common, in their specially built phalansteries, one for each phalanx.

This vision, together with his criticism of the existing system and many of his specific doctrines, places Fourier as one of the most inspired preachers and prophets of modern socialism. Fourier's remarkable psychological insights, such as his championing of brief sessions and variety in work, his quickness to see oppression no matter how veiled, and his at times penetrating concern with different character formations and problems, link him, for instance, to modern pedagogy, the emancipation of women, and personnel management. Fourier can also be described as a brilliant exponent of the idea of alienation or as a premature theoretician of the affluent society. Especially notable are his emphasis on the repression of passions as the source of all evil, as well as the foundation of Civilization, and his vision of that insane world of repressed passions.

See also Enlightenment; Philosophy of Social Sciences; Social and Political Philosophy; Socialism; Society.

Bibliography

PRIMARY WORKS

Théorie des quatre mouvements et des destinées générales, 2 vols. Lyons, France, 1808.

Théorie de l'unité universelle. Paris, 1822.

Le nouveau monde industriel et sociétaire. Paris: Bossange, 1829.

La fausse industrie morcelée, répugnante, mensongère, et l'antidote: l'industrie naturelle, combinée, attrayante, véridique, donnant quadruple produit, 2 vols. Paris: Bossange, 1835–1836.

Oeuvres Complètes de Charles Fourier, 12 vols. Paris: Anthropos, 1966–1968.

Utopian Vision of Charles Fourier; Selected Texts on Work, Love, and Passionate Attraction. Translated and edited by Jonathan Beecher and Richard Bienvenu. Boston: Beacon, 1971.

The Theory of the Four Movements. Edited by Gareth Stedman Jones and Ian Patterson. Cambridge, U.K.: Cambridge University Press, 1996.

SECONDARY WORKS

Beecher, Jonathan. *Charles Fourier: The Visionary and His World.* Berkeley: University of California Press, 1986.

Bourgin, Hubert. *Fourier Contribution à l'étude du socialisme français.* Paris: Société Nouvelle de Librairie et d'Édition, 1905.

Manuel, Frank E. *The Prophets of Paris.* Cambridge, MA: Harvard University Press, 1962.

Poulat, Émil. *Les cahiers manuscrits de Fourier.* Paris: Entente Communautaire, 1957.

Riasanovsky, Nicholas V. *The Teaching of Charles Fourier.* Berkeley: University of California Press, 1969.

Zilberfarb, I. I. *Sotsialnaia Filosofiia Sharlia Fure i Ee Mesto v Istorii Sotsialisticheskoi Mysli Pervoi Poloviny XIX Veka.* Moscow, 1964.

Nicholas V. Riasanovsky (1967)
Bibliography updated by Philip Reed (2005)

FRAME PROBLEM

A conundrum known as the frame problem within artificial intelligence concerns the application of knowledge about the past to draw inferences about the future. It requires distinguishing those properties that change across time against a background of those properties that do not, which thus constitute a frame (Charniak and McDermott 1985). From the point of view of philosophy it appears to be a special case of the problem of induction, which requests justification for drawing inferences about the future based on knowledge of the past. David Hume, in particular, suggested that one's expectations about the future are no more than habits of the mind and doubted that knowledge relating the future to the past was possible.

Bertrand Russell, a twentieth-century student of Hume's eighteenth-century problem, observed that this problem cannot be resolved merely by stipulation or by postulating that the future will be like the past. That the future will be like the past in every respect may be significant but it is also false. That the future will be like the past in some respect may be true but it is also trivial. The problem is to discover those specific respects in which the future will be like the past that provide justification for inferences to some outcomes rather than others, under the same initial conditions. That in turn suggests that the frame problem, like the problem of induction, depends for its solution on a defensible theory of natural laws that supplies a basis for linking the future to the past.

BACKGROUND

The first mention of a problem by this name was by John McCarthy and Patrick J. Hayes, who advanced a solution—the situational calculus—that depends on making assumptions about "the complete state of the universe at an instant of time," where "the laws of motion determine, given a situation, all future situations" (1969, p. 477). The reference to time raises concerns with relativity but, more important, not every feature of the universe makes a difference to every other feature at a later time. If one draws a distinction between global and local situations, where *global* concerns the complete state of the universe at a time and *local* only specific parts thereof, then local situations may prove tractable even if global situations should prove to be intractable.

Other characterizations of the problem include keeping track of the consequences of an action, including changes that they entail for representations of the world (Hayes 1973), and as a process of updating databases in response to changes that occur in the world (Barr and Feigenbaum 1981). Some claim it is not the problem of justifying inferences but of finding appropriate ways to express them (Hayes 1991), while others discuss the importance of the problem in relation to robots (Dennett 1984). As Robert Hadley notices, researchers in artificial intelligence tend to adopt narrower definitions of the problem, while philosophers tend to take the frame problem "to include any problem whose solution is *presupposed* by a solution to the narrow problem" (1988, p. 34). Some authors characterize the problem as less about knowledge than about knowledge representation.

WORLDS OF ROBOTS

The connection between actions, representations, and the problem of change arises in part from the desire to provide artificial human beings (or robots) with the directional capabilities to navigate their way around the world. If those robots act on the basis of maps—where the term is being used as a generic characterization for internal representations—then it becomes important to distinguish between permanent and transient features of those maps, which makes database updating important. And because robots may bring about changes in their environment through interaction, it becomes important to revise those maps to reflect those changes, to maintain the current relevance of those internal representations, where these concerns converge.

The same connections, however, also obtain for human beings as other things that act on the basis of beliefs as their internal representations of the world. When those beliefs are sufficiently accurate and complete, actions taken based on them may be expected to be more appropriate and less likely to fail than would otherwise be the case. Insofar as the frame problem revolves around knowledge of when things are going to change and when they are not going to change, it possesses general significance for natural humans and for artificial humans alike. Beliefs are true when they correspond to reality (as the way things are or as everything that is the case), and when they correspond to reality they provide an appropriate foundation for human action as well as for robotic behavior.

The suggestion has been made that the frame problem concerns common sense as a product of everyday experience in interacting with the world, based on the fact that often the course of events conforms to one's expectations (Hayes 1991, p. 72). The existence of habits of the mind, however, does not resolve the problem with respect to justifying those habits on the basis of experience in the past nor explain how one's beliefs about the future ought to be represented. Presumably, the problem of knowledge must be resolved to have knowledge to represent. The kind of knowledge that holds promise for solving these problems derives from studying those features of the world that remain constant across time as the objects of scientific inquiries rather than as the products of common sense. These properties are known as the laws of nature.

LAWS OF NATURE

Laws of nature, unlike laws of society, cannot be violated or changed and require no enforcement. They must be distinguished from what are called accidental generalizations, which may be true as correlations that describe the history of the world but which could be violated and changed. If every Ferrari during the world's history happened to be red, then the generalization "all Ferraris are red" would be true, but it would not be a law, since there are processes and procedures, such as repainting a Ferrari, that would render it false. For a generalization to be lawlike, its falsity must be logically possible but not physically possible, precisely because there are no processes or procedures that could separate an attribute from its reference property, even though the possession of that attribute is not true merely as a matter of definition.

There appear to be several species of natural laws, including simple laws of nomic form and causal laws of different kinds (Fetzer 1981, 1990). That gold is malleable and that matches are ignitable are examples of simple laws, provided that those attributes are permanent. The selling price of gold, by comparison, at $500 an ounce, for example, is a transient attribute. These laws characterize properties that are possessed at one and the same time and do not explicitly imply changes across time. If the property of being malleable is a permanent property of

gold, however, then gold has the causal properties that define *malleability*, including assuming different shapes at subsequent times as an effect of different forces at prior times. Thus, simple laws entail causal counterparts.

CAUSAL KINDS

The conception advanced by McCarthy and Hayes (1969), according to which complete states of the universe determine subsequent complete states according to laws of motion, presumes that those laws are exclusively deterministic, where given a complete state of the universe S1 at time t1, one and only one complete successor state S2 is physically possible at t2. Gottfried Wilhelm Leibniz and Pierre Simon de Laplace advanced similar conceptions. However, if any of the parts of the world are governed by causal processes that are indeterministic (or probabilistic), more than one successor state, S2, S3, … , Sn may be physically possible at time t2. Simple examples may include flips of coins, tosses of dice, and draws of cards from decks, but that depends on the specificity of the conditions attending those events.

Draws of cards from decks, for example, are ontically deterministic in the sense that, given specific arrangements of the cards in the deck, one and only one specific card can be drawn. These draws are epistemically indeterministic in the sense that, as long as one adheres to the rules of the game, one does not know the specific arrangements and is consequently unable to predict the outcome. The situation is different with the laws of radioactive decay, however. For example, an atom of polonium-218 has a half-life of 3.05 minutes, which means that, during any specific 3.05 minute interval, it has a probability of decay of one-half. This implies that, for collections of polonium atoms, one can expect that, during any 3.05-minute interval, about half will decay without knowing which ones.

TYPES OF SYSTEMS

Atoms of polonium-218 are closed systems for which there are no other properties that make any difference to their probability of decay than the length of temporal interval. Neither the weather, the day of the week, the presence or absence of observers—none of these factors affect the strength of this probability. In the case of flips of coins, tosses of dice, and draws of cards from decks there are other properties, such as the precise angular momentum imparted to a coin when flipped, which make it predictable with greater and greater precision, where condition F is relevant to outcome O under conditions C when it makes a difference to the probability outcome O, given C. Increasingly precise specifications of the relevant conditions that affect outcomes thus allow instances of epistemic indeterminism to be established as ontically deterministic.

The probabilities of outcome depend on and vary with the complete sets of factors that are present on any specific occasion. When coins are bent, dice are loaded, or decks are stacked, the probabilities of various outcomes are no longer what they would have been under normal conditions. It follows that the truth of a lawlike sentence depends on taking into account the presence or absence of every property whose presence or absence makes a difference to the outcome on any specific occasion, which has been called the requirement of maximal specificity (Fetzer 1981, 1990). Closed systems are systems that satisfy this requirement, which is why their behavior across time can be systematically anticipated on the basis of corresponding maximally specific causal laws.

PREDICTION

For closed systems, it is therefore possible to predict—either invariably or probabilistically—precisely how that system will behave over an interval of time t to t* (when those properties are instantiated at time t and the outcome occurs at t*), so long as the laws of systems of that kind are known. When either (1) the laws of systems of that kind are not known or (2) the description available for that system is not closed, however, then precisely how that system would behave over a corresponding interval of time t to t* cannot be predicted with—invariable or probabilistic—confidence, because essential information remains unknown. In those cases the frame problem cannot be solved; but, even given knowledge of those kinds, the representation problem remains.

Indeed, there are at least two dimensions to the problem, where the first concerns whether the system under consideration qualifies as an open or as a closed system in relation to the outcome of interest. In either case, one needs to have predicates in one's language to describe each of its relevant properties. The second concerns whether or not the system under consideration, even if it happens to be a closed system, requires a finite or an infinite set of predicates for its complete description. When the complete description of states of the universe requires infinitely many predicates, for example, because infinitely many properties need to be described relative to successive states of the universe, there are no solutions to frame problems for global situations. Those are restricted to closed systems appropriately describable by finite sets of predicates.

SEMANTIC ISSUES

McCarthy and Hayes (1969) consider hypothetical situations that concern what would happen if specific events were to occur (such as the situation that would arise if Mr. Smith sold his car to Mrs. Jones, who has offered $250 for it). These situations are properly represented by subjunctive conditionals (concerning what would be the case, if something were the case) and counterfactuals (as subjunctive conditionals with false antecedents). However, this implies that, even envisioned primarily as a problem of representation, the solution to the frame problem entails solving some of thorniest issues in philosophical logic concerning intensional conditionals and possible-world semantics. A plausible solution involves distinguishing ordinary-language subjunctives from scientific conditionals elaborated in recent research (Nute 1975; Fetzer and Nute 1979, 1980).

The semantics that appears most appropriate for scientific conditionals and lawlike sentences is a form of maximal-change semantics rather than one of the varieties of minimal-change semantics proposed by Robert Stalnaker (1968) and by David Lewis (1979). Thus, while their semantics depend on assuming that possible worlds that differ from the actual world are as similar to the actual world as they could be, apart from the specific features being varied, the semantics assumed here—for the sake of exploring representational aspects of the frame problem—permits possible worlds to differ from the actual world in all respects except those specified by their maximally specific reference-property descriptions and the permanent properties that attend them. Subjunctives are true provided that, in every world in which their antecedents are true, their consequents are also true or would be true with constant probabilities.

LOGICAL FORM

An intensional calculus for the representation of lawlike sentences and causal conditionals of deterministic and probabilistic strength affords a possible framework for resolving the problem of representation (Fetzer and Nute 1979, 1980). Suppose that matches of kinds defined by chemical composition M are such that, when they are dry D, struck in fashion S, in the presence of oxygen O, then they light L. That could justify the lawlike claim, for every match x of kind M that is D and O, S-ing x at t1 would invariably bring about its L-ing at t2. That maximally specific antecedent could equally well be represented by various alternative formulations that included the same complete sets of relevant conditions, since adding oxygen when the other properties were present, for example, would bring about the outcome just as the striking of the match, when those other properties were present, would bring it about.

Employing the double arrow, ___ ⇒ ... , as the subjunctive conditional sign and the causal double arrow, ___ n⇒ ... , as the (probabilistic) causal conditional sign—where values of n range over u for deterministic cases and p (from zero to one) for probabilistic cases—then these lawlike relations could be formalized by means of a generalized conditional, $(x)(t)[(Mxt \& Dxt \& Oxt) \Rightarrow (Sxt\ u\Rightarrow Lxt^*)]$, which would be read, "For all x and all t, if x were M and D and O at t, then S-ing x at t would bring about (invariably) L-ing x at t*" (where t* is a specific interval after t). An instance of this generalization for a specific object c at a specific time t1 would have the following logical form, $(Mct1 \& Dct1 \& Oct1) \Rightarrow (Sct1\ u\Rightarrow Lct2)$, which would have logically equivalent variations, such as $(Mct1 \& Dct1 \& Sct1) \Rightarrow (Oct1\ u\Rightarrow Lct2)$, and so on.

SCOREKEEPING

The conception of conversational scorekeeping was introduced by Lewis (1973) as a helpful technique for keeping track of assumptions that have been made within the context of an ordinary conversation. Donald Nute (1980), for example, discusses its application relative to conditionals that occur during ordinary language conversations. Suppose, for example, that, at one point in their conversation, Bill and Hillary agree that either she will run for the Senate (again) or she will run for president. If they later conclude that she is not going to run for the presidency, they are entitled to infer that she is going to run for the Senate, even if that conversation occurs weeks later, assuming the premise has not been withdrawn.

Analogously, for a computerized system with the capacity for the representation of conditionals, such as LISP or Prolog, for example, developing programs that reflect the laws of systems that interest project managers should be relatively straightforward. No matter when specific data enters the program and regardless of the specific order in which it is received, once the antecedent of the conditional has been satisfied, the program draws the inference with deterministic certainty or probabilistic confidence that an outcome of kind O either has occurred or may be expected to occur, given the temporal parameters that apply. The function **cond** in LISP, for example, appears to be appropriately adaptable for this purpose (Wilensky 1984, Fetzer 1991). Hayes (1991) raises the objection that **cond** supports inferences of the form

modus ponens but not of the form *modus tollens*, but that is sufficient for deriving predictions.

IMPLEMENTATION

It appears to be the case that the frame problem can be solved, at least in principle, for closed systems involving only finite sets of relevant properties. Whether or not it can be solved in practice, of course, depends on the state of science and one's knowledge of systems and laws of the kind under consideration. The solution that has been presented here, of course, presupposes an account of the nature of laws of which Hume would not have approved. Hume adopted an epistemic principle that precluded inference to the existence of properties and relations, including lawful and causal connections, that are not directly accessible to experience. His narrow form of inductivism cannot justify inferences to the existence of laws by contrast with mere correlations. Fortunately, a more robust epistemology based on inference to the best explanation accommodates the discovery of natural laws, where hypotheses are empirically testable by means of severe attempts to refute them (Fetzer 1981, 1990).

In spite of his emphasis on the representational aspect of the frame problem, even Hayes (1991) acknowledges that a theory of causation is a necessary condition for its solution. During the course of their review of a recent collection of studies of the frame problem, Selmer Bringsjord and Chris Welty (1994) suggest that the frame problem presupposes a solution to the problem of induction, which agrees with the position presented here. Whether or not the frame problem can be solved depends on whether or not the problem of induction can be solved, which in turn depends on deep issues in ontology and epistemology. If the considerations outlined earlier are well founded, however, then the problem of induction and the frame problem are both capable of successful resolution, even including its representational dimensions.

See also Artificial Intelligence; Computationalism; Connectionism; Induction; Laws of Nature.

Bibliography

Barr, Avron, and Edward A. Feigenbaum. *The Handbook of Artificial Intelligence.* Vol. 1. Reading, MA: Addison-Wesley, 1981.

Bringsjord, Selmer, and Chris Welty. "Navigating through the Frame Problem." *AI Magazine* (Spring 1994): 69–72.

Charniak, Eugene, and Drew McDermott. *Introduction to Artificial Intelligence.* Reading, MA: Addison-Wesley, 1985.

Dennett, Daniel. "Cognitive Wheels: The Frame Problem in AI." In *Minds, Machines, and Evolution*, edited by

Christopher Hookaway, 129–151. New York: Cambridge University Press, 1984.

Fetzer, James H. *Artificial Intelligence: Its Scope and Limits.* Dordrecht, Netherlands: Kluwer Academic, 1990.

Fetzer, James H. "The Frame Problem: Artificial Intelligence Meets David Hume." In *Reasoning Agents in a Dynamic World: The Frame Problem*, edited by Kenneth M. Ford and Patrick J. Hayes, 55–69. Greenwich, CT: JAI Press, 1991.

Fetzer, James H. *Scientific Knowledge.* Dordrecht, Netherlands: D. Reidel, 1981.

Fetzer, James H., and Donald Nute. "A Probabilistic Causal Calculus: Conflicting Conceptions." *Synthese* 44 (1980): 241–246.

Fetzer, James H., and Donald Nute. "Syntax, Semantics, and Ontology: A Probabilistic Causal Calculus." *Synthese* 40 (1979): 453–495.

Hadley, Robert. Review of *The Robot's Dilemma: The Frame Problem in Artificial Intelligence*, edited by Z. Pylyshyn. *Canadian Philosophical Reviews* 8 (1988): 33–36.

Hayes, Patrick J. "Commentary on 'The Frame Problem': Artificial Intelligence Meets David Hume." In *Reasoning Agents in a Dynamic World: The Frame Problem*, edited by Kenneth M. Ford and Patrick J. Hayes, 71–76. Greenwich, CT: JAI Press, 1991.

Hayes, Patrick J. "The Frame Problem and Related Problems in Artificial Intelligence." In *Artificial and Human Thinking*, edited by Alick Elithorn and David Jones, 45–59. New York: Elsevier, 1973.

Lewis, David. "Scorekeeping in a Language Game." *Journal of Philosophical Logic* 8 (1979): 339–359.

McCarthy, John, and Patrick J. Hayes. "Some Philosophical Problems from the Standpoint of Artificial Intelligence." In *Machine Intelligence 4*, edited by Bernard Meltzer and Donald Michie, 463–502. New York: American Elsevier, 1969.

Nute, Donald. "Conversational Scorekeeping and Conditionals." *Journal of Philosophical Logic* 9 (1980): 153–166.

Nute, Donald. "Counterfactuals and the Similarity of Worlds." *Journal of Philosophy* 72 (1975): 773–778.

Pylyshyn, Zenon W., ed. *The Robot's Dilemma: The Frame Problem in Artificial Intelligence.* Norwood, NJ: Ablex, 1987.

Stalnaker, Robert. "A Theory of Conditionals." In *American Philosophical Quarterly Supplementary Monograph No. 2*, 98–112. Oxford, U.K.: Basil Blackwell, 1968.

Wilensky, Robert. *LISPcraft.* New York: Norton, 1984.

James H. Fetzer (2005)

FRANCK, SEBASTIAN
(1499–1542)

Sebastian Franck, also known as Franck von Word, was an outstanding figure among the spiritualists of the Reformation. His basic spiritualist concept of the conflict in each human being and in the world between the Inner Word (Son of God; eternal, invisible Christ), which is ultimate reality, and the outer word (law, flesh, selfishness), which is only appearance, shadow or phantom, was developed in all his philosophical, theological, historical, and cosmographical works. Franck was born in Donauwörth, Germany, and died in Basel. After studying at the University of Ingolstadt, Franck entered the Dominican Bethlehem College in Heidelberg in 1518. As a priest he officiated in the diocese of Augsburg. He turned to the Lutheran faith about 1526 and became Lutheran pastor in Buchenbach near Ansbach and then in Gustenfelden near Nürnberg. Franck resigned his pastorate in 1528 or early 1529 to become an independent writer and lived in Nürnberg until 1529 or early 1530.

Nürnberg, a cultural center, offered ample literary resources and personal contacts, especially with Theophrastus Paracelsus and the many followers of Hans Denck. Among Denck's followers were Albrecht Dürer's famous pupils the brothers Hans Sebald and Barthel Beham, whose sister Ottilie became Franck's wife. When Franck left Nürnberg, three of his controversial books were already written. Two of them were free translations from Latin into German (with many of his own unorthodox ideas injected) of Andreas Althamer's *Diallage* (1528), a Lutheran attack against Anabaptism, and of an unknown author's *Chronica und beschreibung der Türkey mit yhrem begriff* (Nürnberg, 1530), in which his ideas on the invisible church were already outlined. The first book wholly his own, *Von dem grewlichen laster der trunckenheyt* (1528), is a notable contribution to the literature on alcoholism.

From Nürnberg he moved to Strassburg, where he had occasion to meet Johann Buenderlin, Caspar Schwenckfeld, Melchior Hofmann, Jacob Ziegler, Michael Servetus, Johann Campanus, and, again, Paracelsus. There he wrote a universal history, extending from the creation of the world to the reign of Emperor Charles V and of Pope Clement VII, titled *Chronica, Zeytbuch und geschycht bibel* (Strassburg, 1531), famous for its numerous penetrating spiritualistic comments on many ecclesiastical and secular personalities and events. Its chronicle of heretics included Erasmus of Rotterdam as a Roman heretic. Because of this and his adverse remarks about Charles V, Franck was arrested and banned from Strassburg in 1531.

After living in Esslingen, Franck settled in Ulm as a printer and wrote most of his books there. His spiritualistic interpretation of the Scriptures can be found in his *Paradoxa ducenta octoginta …* (Ulm, 1534), *Die guldin Arch …* (Augsburg, 1538), and *Das verbütschiert mit sieben Siegeln verschlossen Buch* (Basel, 1539). *Die vier*

Kronbüchlein (Ulm, 1534) contains Erasmus's *Das thèur und kunstlich Buochlein Morie Encomion, das ist, ein Lob der Thorhait* and Cornelius Agrippa's *Von der Heylosigkeit Eitelkeit und ungewissheit aller Menschlichen Kunst und Weissheit* (both of which he freely translated from the original Latin texts), *Vom Baum des Wissens Guts and Böss …*, in which he tries to prove that awareness of good and evil can impair one's goodness, and *Encomion, ein Lob des Thorechten Gottlichen Worts …*. His *Weltbuch, Spiegel un bildtniss des gantzen Erdbodens …* (Tübingen, 1534), a cosmography with one of the first German descriptions of America and with one chapter dealing with the different religious movements of his time, which initiated systematic comparison of religion on Reformation soil, became one of his most popular books. His *Germaniae Chronicon* (Augsburg, 1538) has been used as an important source for historical research. In his *Das Krieg büchlein des Friedens …* (1539) Franck tried to prove that war not only contradicts Christ's teaching but is also "a devilish, inhuman thing, an abhorrent plague … an open door for all vices and sins and destruction of land, soul, body and honor." Most of these works made Franck the defendant in a trial before the city council that was instigated by Martin Frecht, main preacher in the cathedral of Ulm, Philipp Melanchthon, Martin Butzer, and Landgrave Philip of Hesse. It resulted in his expulsion from Ulm.

Franck, his wife, and their six children went to Basel in July 1539. There, after the death of his wife, he married Barbara Beck of Strassburg. His famous collection, with his interpretation, of *Sprichwörter …* (Frankfurt, 1541) was partially republished by G. E. Lessing. The last years of his life were devoted mostly to his Latin paraphrase of the *Deutsche Theologie*, which was never published, and to several posthumously published tractates (*Van het Ryke Christi*, Gouda, 1611; *Een Stichtelijck Tractaet van de Werelt des Duyvels Rijck*, Gouda, 1618; and *Sanctorum Communio*, Gouda, 1618), all of which survive only in the Dutch translations. They prove that dualism of God and world fully dominated his thoughts before his death.

Franck's worldview is primarily panentheistic, with heterogeneous elements drawn from Lutheranism, medieval mysticism, Neoplatonism, Renaissance speculation, humanism, Anabaptism, and rationalism, with ample citation of the Church Fathers and non-Christian philosophers. This comprehensive syncretism makes Franck an almost unique figure in the Reformation era and therefore a major figure in the history of ideas. As a religious philosopher he will be remembered for his radical spiritualistic tendency to replace exterior authority with inner illumination by God's spirit. The deep spiritual meaning of the Bible (outer word)—which is allegorical, not historical but typological, full of contradictions and merely testimonial to the eternal truth—can be comprehended only by those who have already accepted the Inner Word: "Unless we listen to the word of God within ourselves, we can make nothing of Scripture … for everything can be decked and defended with texts" (*Das verbütschiert mit sieben Siegeln verschlossen Buch*). In the light of his spiritualism none of the churches and sects, with their outgrown external disciplines, dogmas, sacraments, ceremonies, and festivals can be the true church. The true church is his *ecclesia spiritualis*, where only inward enlightenment is sufficient; it is the universal invisible church of the spirit, to which even those non-Christians who without knowledge of the incarnate Word have accepted the Inner Word can belong: "I love any man whom I can help and I call him brother, whether he be Jew or Samaritan … I cannot belong to any separate sect" (ibid.).

As a historian Franck placed the Reformation in the stream of historical development and thus relativized it. He is credited with recognizing the historic force that externalizes the spiritual ("The world must have a papacy even if it has to steal it."). He also observed the typical recurrent rise and fall of kingdoms and peoples, and by recognizing this change of fortune as God's punishment for disobedience of his Inner Word, saw history as interaction between God and the world, as the struggle between the spirit and the forces which resist it.

As one of the most ardent advocates of religious liberty in the sixteenth century, Franck insisted on toleration not only among the individual members of the different churches and sects in Christendom but also toward Jews, Muslims, heathens, and even heretics, since all men, created by God, descended from Adam, and accessible to the Holy Spirit, are equal.

Martin Luther, Philipp Melanchthon, and Martin Butzer were especially aware of the danger of Franck's unorthodox thoughts to the new Protestant position. Luther called him "the devil's most cherished slanderous mouth." The convention of Protestant theologians at Schmalkalden in 1540 issued a resolution of condemnation of both Franck and Schwenckfeld, which the latter called a (Protestant) papal bull.

Franck's extraordinarily well written books had a great influence on German prose style. They were widely read in German, Dutch, Swiss, and even English editions until the end of the seventeenth century. There exist at least ten editions of his *Chronica* and as many of his

Sprichwörter. His *Weltbuch* went through at least six editions, as did his *Vier Kronbüchlein* or parts of it.

While Franck's specific traceable influence was restricted in Germany to Valentin Weigel and Gottfried Arnold, and in Basel to Sebastian Castellio, his spirit and ideas found ardent followers in Holland (Dirk Volkerts Coonhert, Menno Simons, David Joris, and the Franckists or Sebastianists). Although he had strong roots in the late Middle Ages, much of Franck's thought carried the seed of what was to become important in modern thinking. Wilhelm Dilthey rightly testifies that "the ideas of Franck flow toward modern times in a hundred streamlets."

See also Dilthey, Wilhelm; Emanationism; Humanism; Ideas; Lessing, Gotthold Ephraim; Luther, Martin; Medieval Philosophy; Melanchthon, Philipp; Neoplatonism; Paracelsus; Reformation; Servetus, Michael; Toleration.

Bibliography

ADDITIONAL WORKS BY FRANCK

Klagbrieff oder supplication der armen dürftigen in Englandt an den könig daselbst gestellt wider die reychen geystlichen Bettler. Strassburg, 1529.

Dass Gott das einig ain und höchstes Gut sey …. Ulm, 1534.

Sechshundertdreyzehn Gebot und Verbot der Juden. Ulm, 1537.

Des Grossen Nothelffers und Weltheiligen Sant Gelts oder S. Pfennings lobgesang …. Ulm, 1537.

Was gesagt sei: Der Glaub tuts alles: Und warumb im die Rechtfertigung alleyn werde zugeschriben …. Ulm, 1539.

Schrifftliche und gantz grundtliche ausslegung des LXIIII Psalm. …. Ulm, 1539.

Handbüchlein Siben Haubtpunken aus der Bibel gezogen und zusammengebracht, darin angezeigt ist leben und todt, Himmel und Hell … durch Sebastian Franck gemacht. …. Frankfurt, 1539.

"A Letter to John Campanus by Sebastian Franck, Strassburg, 1531." Translated by G. H. Williams, in *Spiritual and Anabaptist Writers.* Library of Christian Classics, Vol. XXV. Philadelphia: Westminster Press, 1957.

WORKS ON FRANCK

Bainton, R. H. "Concerning Heretics (Castellio)." In *Records of Civilization XXV,* 93–104. New York, 1935. Republished New York, 1966.

Barbers, Meinulf. *Toleranz bei Sebastian Franck.* Bonn: Röhrscheid, 1964.

Becker, Bruno. "Nicolai's Inlasshing over de Franckisten." *Nederlandsch Archief voor Kerkgeschiedenes,* n.s. 18 (1925): 286–296.

Dilthey, Wilhelm. "Auffassung und Analyse des Menschen im 15. und 16. Jahrhundert." In his *Gesammelte Schriften,* Vol. II. Stuttgart and Göttingen, 1957.

Gritsch, E. W. "The Authority of the Inner Word. A Special Study of the Major German Spiritual Reformers in the 16th Century." Dissertation. Yale University, 1959.

Hayden-Roy, Patrick. *The Inner Word and the Outer World: A Biography of Sebastian Franck.* New York: Peter Lang, 1994.

Hegler, Alfred. "Beitrage zur Geschichte der Mystik in der Reformationszeit," in *Archiv für Reformationsgeschichte,* Vol. I. Berlin, 1906.

Hegler, Alfred. *Geist und Schrift bei Sebastian Franck.* Freiburg im Breisgau, 1892. The most important work on Franck.

Hegler, Alfred. *Sebastian Francks lateinische Paraphrase der deutschen Theologia und sein holländisch erhaltenen Traktate.* Tübingen, 1901.

Jones, R. M. *Spiritual Reformers in the 16th and 17th Centuries,* 46–64. London: Macmillan, 1914. Republished, Boston: Beacon, 1959.

Kaczerowsky, Klaus. *Sebastian Franck: Bibliographie.* Wiesbaden, Germany: G. Pressler, 1976.

Koyré, Alexandre. *Mystiques, spirituels, alchimists du XVIᵉ siècle allemand,* 22–43. Paris, 1955.

Krahn, Cornelius, and N. van der Zijpp. "Sebastian Franck." In *The Mennonite Encyclopedia,* Vol. II, 363–367. Scottdale, PA, 1956.

Muller, Jan. *Sebastian Franck, 1499–1542.* Wiesbaden, Germany: Otto Harrassowitz, 1993.

Oncken, Hermann. "Sebastian Franck als Historiker." In *Historisch-Politische Aufsätze und Reden,* Vol. I, 273–319. Munich and Berlin: Oldenbourg, 1914.

Peuckert, W. E. *Sebastian Franck, ein deutscher Sucher.* Munich: Piper, 1943. The only recent interpretation of all aspects of Franck's thought.

Quast, Bruno. *Sebastian Francks 'Kriegbüchlin des Frides': Studien zum radikalreformatorischen Spiritualismus.* Tübingen, Germany: Francke, 1993.

Racber, K. *Studien zur Geschichtsbibel Sebastian Francks.* Basel: Helbing and Lichtenhahn, 1952.

Raumer, Kurt von. *Ewiger Friede,* 23–60, 249. Freiburg im Breisgau: Alber, 1953.

Rieber, Doris. "Sebastian Franck (1499–1542)." *Bibliothèque d'humanisme et Renaissance* 21 (1959): 190–204.

Schottenloher, Karl. *Bibliographie zur deutschen Geschichte im Zeitalter der Glaubensspaltung,* Vol. I, 263–266. Leipzig: Hiersemann, 1933. Lists all books on Franck to 1932.

Teufel, Eberhard. "Die 'Deutsche Theologie' und Sebastian Franck im Lichte der neueren Forschung." *Theologische Rundschau,* n.s. 11 (1939): 304–319, and 12 (1940): 99–129.

Teufel, Eberhard. *Landraümig; Sebastian Franck, ein Wanderer an Donau, Rhein und Neckar.* Neustadt an der Aich: Degener, 1954.

Teufel, Eberhard. "Luther und Luthertum im Urteile Sebastian Francks." In *Festgabe für D. Dr. Karl Müller zum 70. Geburtstag dargebracht von Fachgenossen und Freunden,* 132–144. Tübingen, 1922.

Troeltsch, Ernst. *The Social Teaching of the Christian Churches,* Vols. I and II. Republished, London: Allen and Unwin, 1956.

Weigelt, Horst. *Sebastian Franck und die lutherische Reformation.* Gütersloh, Germany: Gerd Mohn, 1972.

Williams, G. H. *The Radical Reformation.* Philadelphia: Westminster Press, 1962.

Jacques J. Whitfield (1967)
Bibliography updated by Christian B. Miller (2005)

FRANK, ERICH
(1883–1949)

Erich Frank studied philology and classics at the universities of Vienna, Freiburg, and Berlin. In 1907 he turned to philosophy, which he studied in Heidelberg under Heinrich Rickert and Wilhelm Windelband. His philosophical career in Germany was brief but distinguished. In 1923 he became professor at Heidelberg, and five years later he was appointed Martin Heidegger's successor in Marburg. Three years after his dismissal from Marburg in 1936, he came to Harvard on a research fellowship and made America his second home. Almost all of Frank's works reflect his double interest in philosophy and history and his efforts to combine historical knowledge and philosophical thought: *Plato und die sogennanten Pythagoreer* (Halle, 1923); *Wissen, Wollen, Glauben* (Knowledge, will, belief), a collection of English and German historical and speculative essays, edited with an appreciation by Ludwig Edelstein (Zürich, 1955), of which the title essay represents Frank's most original contribution to philosophy; *Philosophical Understanding and Religious Truth* (New York, 1945).

As a student, Frank felt dissatisfied with current attempts to model philosophy on science and to eliminate the traditional questions of metaphysics, ontology, and religion. Nor was he long satisfied with the post-Kantian idealism that was offered as an alternative and which for a time attracted him. When in 1914 he discovered Søren Kierkegaard, at that time almost unknown in philosophical circles, he thought he had found the beginning of a new and fruitful approach to the problem of the subject-object dialectic. He shared his discovery with Karl Jaspers, and five years later, with the publication of Frank's essay *Wissen, Wollen, Glauben* and Jaspers's *Psychologie der Weltanschauungen* the foundations of German existentialism were laid. The major theme of Frank's essay is that the unity of the subject in self-consciousness is achieved not in the act of knowing or in the act of willing, but only in the act of faith. This knowledge of the self is logically unprovable but is also incontrovertible. The act of faith is neither blind belief nor a "will to believe," but arises out of the immediate awareness both of oneself as free and of a transcendence of oneself. Faith is thus both the condition and the result of the subject's freedom, and all theoretical and practical activity has its source in this freedom. Frank believed he had found in the act of faith the unity of the subject that Immanuel Kant sought but could not find in the act of judging.

Later Frank came to question the subjective direction in which existentialist philosophy was developing. In his review of Jaspers's *Philosophie* (1933) he not only criticized what he called the "*atheistischer Nihilismus*" (atheistic nihilism) of Heidegger, but also pointed out the insufficiency of Jaspers's existential ontology (the *Chiffre*), which, he claimed, bears no analogical relation to Being. Existentialism, he argued, has not succeeded in combining existential concerns with metaphysical objectivity. The freedom of the subject is not threatened by his encounter with the objective. Indeed, that freedom which does not express, historically and analogically, a truth concerning objective Being, is an empty, irrational freedom.

In *Philosophical Understanding and Religious Truth*, which grew out of the Flexner Lectures he gave at Bryn Mawr in 1943, Frank considered the question of analogical terms through which alone, in his view, philosophy could adequately express the subjective, existential experience of objective reality. All philosophical truth, he argued, is analogical in that it recounts, in and for each historical period, the relation of man to Being. Philosophical analogy is possible only because there is an objective reality to which our thinking bears a relation. Just as in *Knowledge, Will, Belief* Frank argued that the freedom of the subject always presupposes a transcendence of it, so he now maintained that philosophical thought presupposes an object beyond itself that is its content and its substance. Thus, philosophy shares with religion the belief that there is an objective reality to be known; the task of philosophy is, in part, the rational elucidation of religious truths. However, philosophy must not take the place of the revealed mystery of religion. In every historical period philosophical truths have a different starting point and find a different expression, but their content—Being—is eternal. Philosophical analogy is possible only because there is Being; and Being becomes part of our thinking only in analogy. The purpose of philosophy is to present in rational terms the existential dialectic of the subjective and the objective, the temporal and the eternal.

See also Being; Existentialism; Faith; Heidegger, Martin; History and Historiography of Philosophy; Jaspers, Karl; Kierkegaard, Søren Aabye; Rickert, Heinrich; Windelband, Wilhelm.

Bibliography
In addition to the works cited above, the reader may wish to consult Frank's "Das Prinzip der dialektischen Synthese und die Kantische Philosophie," in *Kant-Studien*, Ergänzungsheft

No. 21 (1911), and his "Mathematik und Musik und der griechische Geist," in *Logos* 9 (2) (1920): 222–259. See also his editions of Fichte's *Die Anweisung zum seligen Leben* (Jena, 1910) and of the so-called *Nachtwachen von Bonaventura* by Clemens Brentano (Heidelberg, 1912), and his literary and philological studies of Schelling and Brentano in *Sitzungsberichte der Heidelberger Akademie der Wissenschaften, Philosophische–Historische Klasse*, 1 Abh. (1912); and *Germanisch–Romanische Monatsschrift* 4 (1912): 417–440.

Eva Gossman (1967)

FRANK, SEMËN LIUDVIGOVICH
(1877–1950)

Semën Liudvigovich Frank, the Russian philosopher and religious thinker, was trained in law at Moscow University (1894–1898) and in economies and philosophy at the universities of Berlin and Munich (1899–1902). As a student in Moscow he was a member of a Marxist group headed by P. B. Struve; his first published work was a critique of Karl Marx's theory of value (1900). Between 1902 and 1905 (during which years he moved back and forth between Moscow and Germany) he was a principal contributor to Struve's journal *Osvobozhdenie* (Liberation), published in Stuttgart.

Frank joined a number of other young ex-Marxist intellectuals—among them Struve, Nikolai Berdiaev, and Sergei Bulgakov—in publishing three important symposium volumes: *Problemy idealizma* (Problems of Idealism; Moscow, 1903); *Vekhi* (Signposts; Moscow, 1909); and *Iz glubiny* (De profundis; Moscow, 1918). This last work was printed but because of Soviet censorship was never released.

In 1906 Frank settled in St. Petersburg; in 1912 he joined the Russian Orthodox Church and began to teach philosophy at St. Petersburg University. In 1915 (at St. Petersburg) he published, and in 1916 defended, his master's thesis, *Predmet znaniia* (The object of knowledge); in 1917 he published his doctoral dissertation, *Dusha cheloveka: Opyt vvedeniia v filosofskuyu psikhologiyu* (Man's soul: An introductory essay in philosophical psychology; Moscow), but was unable to defend it because of political events. From 1917 to 1921 Frank was professor of philosophy and dean of the newly organized faculty of history and philosophy at Saratov University. In 1921 he was named professor of philosophy at Moscow University. He was among the group of non-Marxist intellectuals expelled from the Soviet Union in the summer of 1922.

He settled in Berlin, where he gave university lectures (in German) on Russian literature and culture. In 1937, forced to leave Germany, he moved to France. In 1945 he moved to London, where he died.

From Vladimir Solov'ëv—and ultimately from Plotinus—Frank took his central doctrine of positive "total-unity" (*vseedinstvo*). His epistemological intuitivism was close to that of his older colleague Nikolai Losskii. His characteristic emphasis on the "metalogical unity" of the real, and its transcendence of the Aristotelian laws of thought, was drawn mainly from Nicholas of Cusa. Frank always identified himself as a Platonist.

Although Frank's thought exhibits many Hegelian strands, and although he regularly used terms like *moment* (*das Moment*) in G. W. F. Hegel's special sense (as "dialectical phase" or "component of a totality"), he employed one crucial pair of terms in a very un-Hegelian way. To the absoluteness of *real'nost'* (reality) he opposed the relativity of *deistvitel'nost'*, not "actuality" in the sense of Hegel's *Wirklichkeit* (the common meaning of *deistvitel'nost'* in Russian philosophy) but the merely empirical or factual. Frank distinguished between conceptualizable and objectifiable "factuality" and the non-conceptualizable, metalogical "dual-unity" (*dvuedinstvo*) of "reality." The real is fully related and concrete; the factual is isolated and abstract: "Being is a total-unity, in which everything particular exists and is conceivable only in its relation to something else" (*Nepostizhimoe* [The unknowable], p. 51). We apprehend reality as a "mono-dual" coincidence of opposites, as both "distinct from all particular determinate contents" of knowledge and as "containing and permeating" every such content (*Real'nost' i chelovek* [Reality and man], pp. 93–94). The real is both "transdefinite" and "transfinite"; and in both respects it eludes conceptualization. "Everything finite," Frank declared, "is given against a background of infinity. … The knowable world is surrounded on all sides by the dark abyss of the unfathomable" (*Nepostizhimoe*, pp. 29, 35).

Frank agreed with René Descartes that, although the term *finite* is prior and positive in meaning, and the term *infinite* is derived from it by negation, "it is precisely the infinite as the 'fullness of all' that is given as primary and positive, while the concept of finitude is formed by negation of that fullness" (*Real'nost' i chelovek*, p. 57).

Forms, or "ideal elements," are determinate aspects of factuality. The totality of such determinations is grounded in what Frank, following Solov'ëv, called the primordial unity or total-unity of the real. Although reality is unfathomable, it is not hidden; rather, it is "entirely evident, being mysterious only in the sense that it is inexplicable, irreducible to anything else, and inaccessible to logically analytic thought. It is what Johann Wolfgang von Goethe called *ein offenes Geheimnis*" (*Real'nost' i chelovek*, p. 78). "Objective factuality" is something alienated and abstract, a "rationalized, i.e., logically crystallized, part of reality." Like a nut's shell, it forms a "hard and relatively distinct outer layer, produced by the inner saps and energies of a living organism" (pp. 106ff.).

Reality in its wholeness is graspable only in the integral intuition of "living knowledge" (*zhivoe znanie*), of which conceptual knowledge is only a derivative product or superstructure: "All particular knowledge is partial knowledge of a whole."

The "I" of the Cartesian *cogito* is a "reality in which subject and object coincide—a "self-revealing" and "self-transparent being-for-itself," accessible to "living knowledge." Sounding rather like Martin Heidegger, whose general position he repudiated, Frank wrote, "We are conscious of ourselves only as a self-revelation of [being] in us" (*Nepostizhimoe*, p. 93). He also offered a more emphatic version of Heidegger's doctrine of *Mitsein*: "No finished 'I' exists prior to the encounter with the 'thou.' … It is in this encounter … that the 'I' in a genuine sense first comes into being" (pp. 148, 154). Frank also suggested Heidegger's category of impersonal "itness" (*das Man*): "The 'we' appears in the form of an 'it' … which constitutes the basis and first source of objective being" (p. 177). Although there can be no "I" apart from its relation to a "thou," "every 'I' has a special root of its own, lying in secret depths inaccessible to others" and "the most essential part of me remains solitary and inexpressible." The more one is aware of oneself as a person, the more one withdraws into "metaphysical solitude," for "we are wholly open only to ourselves and to God" (*Real'nost' i chelovek*, pp. 127, 129).

In religious—and especially mystical—experience, "I encounter God as a 'thou' for me, only in … that ultimate and essentially solitary stratum of my 'I' in which I am … inaccessible to everyone except myself—and God (as Kierkegaard rightly insisted). I encounter God in the utter solitude in which I encounter death" (pp. 215f.).

Like Solov'ëv, Frank generalized the notion of "Godmanhood" (Solov'ëv's term was *Bogochelovechestvo*; Frank's somewhat more abstract term, *Bogochelovechnost'*) beyond its Christian context. Its primary reference is not to the Incarnation, but to the basic ontological category of "divine-human reality." In Frank's words, "The dual-unity of Godmanhood is logically prior to the conceptions of both God and man" (p. 249).

See also Berdyaev, Nikolai Aleksandrovich; Bulgakov, Sergei Nikolaevich; Descartes, René; Goethe, Johann Wolfgang von; Hegel, Georg Wilhelm Friedrich; Hegelianism; Heidegger, Martin; Kierkegaard, Søren Aabye; Losskii, Nikolai Onufrievich; Marx, Karl; Nicholas of Cusa; Platonism and the Platonic Tradition; Plotinus; Russian Philosophy; Solov'ëv (Solovyov), Vladimir Sergeevich.

Bibliography

WORKS BY FRANK

Man's Soul: An Introductory Essay in Philosophical Psychology. Translated by Boris Jakim. Athens: Ohio University Press, 1993.

Reality and Man: An Essay in the Metaphysics of Human Nature. Translated by Natalie Duddington. London: Faber and Faber, 1965.

The Spiritual Foundations of Society: An Introduction to Social Philosophy. Translated by Boris Jakim. Athens, Ohio: Ohio University Press, 1987.

The Unknowable: An Ontological Introduction to the Philosophy of Religion. Translated by Boris Jakim. Athens, Ohio: Ohio University Press, 1983.

WORKS ON FRANK

Boll, M. M. *The Social and Political Philosophy of Semen L. Frank: A Study in Prerevolutionary Twentieth-Century Russian Liberalism.* Madison, WI: author, 1970.

Boobbyer, P. *S. L. Frank: The Life and Work of a Russian Philosopher, 1877–1950.* Athens, OH: Ohio University Press, 1995.

Lossky, N. O. *History of Russian Philosophy.* New York: International Universities Press, 1951. Pp. 266–292.

Nazarova, O. *Ontologicehskoe obosnovanie intuitivizma v filosofii S. L. Franka* (The ontological grounding of intuitivism in S. L. Frank's philosophy). Moscow: Ideia-Press, 2003.

Swoboda, P. *The Philosophical Thought of S. L. Frank.* Ph.D. Diss., University of Columbia, 1992.

Zenkovsky, V. V., *Istoriya Russkoi Filosofii.* 2 vols. Paris, 1948, 1950. Translated by G. L. Kline as *A History of Russian Philosophy.* 2 vols. London and New York: Columbia University Press, 1953. Pp. 852–872.

Zenkovsky, V. V., ed., *Sbornik Pamyati Semëna Lyudvigovicha Franka* (A collection of essays in memory of Simon Ludvigovich Frank). Munich, 1954. Reminiscences and critical essays by Zenkovsky and others. Contains a bibliography of Frank's writings, compiled by L. A. Zander, on pp. 177–192.

BIBLIOGRAPHY

Frank, V. *Bibliographie des oeuvres de Simon Frank.* Paris: Institut d'études slaves, 1980.

George L. Kline (1967)
Bibliography updated by Vladimir Marchenkov (2005)

FRANK, SIMON LYUDVIGOVICH

See *Frank, Semën Liudvigovich*

FRANKFURT, HARRY
(1929–)

Harry Frankfurt grew up in Brooklyn, New York, and Baltimore, Maryland. He received his PhD in philosophy from Johns Hopkins University in 1954, and he taught in the philosophy departments at Ohio State University; State University of New York, Binghamton; Rockefeller University; Yale University; and Princeton University.

Frankfurt has made original and important contributions to various fields in philosophy, including history of modern philosophy (primarily René Descartes), philosophical psychology, and moral philosophy. He has explored such issues as the relationship between moral responsibility and free will, the nature of the self, the role of necessitation or inevitability in both constraining and constituting persons, and central phenomena such as care, love, and truth. His work has exerted a significant influence on philosophers working in these areas, and some of his writings (especially on the role of love and truth in our lives) have been read by a wide audience. It is perhaps not surprising that Frankfurt's work has been appreciated beyond the walls of academia, as it is both penetrating and elegant.

In one of his most influential papers, "Alternate Possibilities and Moral Responsibility," Frankfurt argued that moral responsibility does not require the sort of free will that entails *alternative possibilities* or genuine freedom to do otherwise. He offered a template for a kind of example that calls into question the *Principle of Alternative Possibilities*, (PAP), according to which moral responsibility requires alternative possibilities. The *Frankfurt-Style Counterexamples* (to PAP) have a distinctive structure that involves *preemptive overdetermination*, that is, the existence of a fail-safe device that plays no role in the causal sequence that issues in the relevant behavior, but which renders that behavior inevitable.

The examples can be seen to be extensions of an example presented by John Locke. Locke discussed a man who is transported into a room while asleep. When he awakens, the man considers whether to leave the room, but stays for his own reasons. Unbeknownst to him, the door was locked and thus he could not have successfully left the room. According to Locke, the man stayed in the room voluntarily although he could not have left the room.

Now it might be pointed out that although the man in Locke's example lacked a certain alternative possibility (the power to leave the room), he nevertheless had various important options available, including choosing to leave, trying to leave, turning the knob, and so forth. Frankfurt's distinctive contribution is the addition of a component to this sort of example which, as it were, *brings the locked door into the agent's brain*. That is, Frankfurt asks us to imagine someone who can secretly monitor an agent, even his brain activities; as things happen, no intervention by this kind of shadowy *counterfactual intervener* occurs. But if the agent were about to choose to do otherwise, this would trigger some process by which the intervener—say, a *nefarious neurosurgeon*—could ensure that the agent choose and behave as he actually does. Thus, Frankfurt has provided a more sophisticated version of Locke's example, one in which it is at least plausible to suppose that the agent in question chooses and acts freely and could legitimately be held morally responsible even though the agent literally could not have chosen otherwise and could not have done otherwise.

Frankfurt thus denied PAP. One who agrees with Frankfurt can thus contend that one of the main objections to compatibilism about causal determinism and moral responsibility can be blocked. That is, it is traditionally supposed that causal determinism threatens moral responsibility because it rules out the sort of free will that involves alternative possibilities; but if this sort of free will is not required for moral responsibility, then at least this sort of objection to compatibilism is rendered irrelevant. Of course, there may be other reasons to reject compatibilism. Frankfurt himself is officially agnostic about compatibilism, saying that we cannot be confident that causal determinism is compatible with being *active*, and thus we cannot be confident in the truth of the compatibility of causal determinism and moral responsibility.

In another seminal paper, "Freedom of the Will and the Concept of a Person," Frankfurt suggested that the distinctive feature of persons is a certain characteristic structure in their motivational states. We share preferences, beliefs, and so forth with mere animals. But we are unique in that we can step back from our preferences and form *second-order* preferences—preferences about our first-order preferences. Some of these second-order preferences are what Frankfurt called *second-order volitions*—the preference that a certain first-order preference lead one to act. According to Frankfurt it is not crucial what the basis for the second-order reflection is; it need not be moral deliberation, for example. On his view, persons are distinctive in that they have the capacity to form second-order volitions; thus, they are the sort of entities for which freedom of the will can be a problem.

For Frankfurt, it is important to distinguish such notions of freedom to choose otherwise and freedom to do otherwise, on the one hand, from notions such as choosing freely and acting freely, on the other. The former involve alternative possibilities whereas the latter do not. In "Freedom of the Will and the Concept of a Person," Frankfurt gives an account of acting freely in terms of the hierarchical account of the structure of human motivation. When one acts freely, one acts on the preference one really wants to have as one's *will* (roughly, the actually motivating preference). In Frankfurt's terminology when one acts freely, one *identifies* with one's will, that is, one identifies with the first-order desire that actually motivates one to act. In contrast, one does not act freely when one does not identify with one's will—one acts (say, smokes another cigarette or eats another piece of chocolate cake) despite identifying with other first-order desires). Frankfurt suggests, additionally, that identification consists in forming the relevant second-order volition; he suggests that one identifies with a first-order desire insofar as one forms a second-order preference to be motivated by that first-order desire. So, acting freely consists in a kind of *mesh* or harmony in the hierarchical structure of one's mental economy. Of course, the existence of this synchronization of levels is entirely compatible with the agent's lacking alternative possibilities.

In further work Frankfurt has refined the analysis of the crucial notion of identification in light of various problems. Additionally, whereas the early papers were primarily addressed to issues pertaining to freedom, determinism, and moral responsibility, the later papers exhibit an evolution toward questions about the *true self*. In "Identification and Wholeheartedness," Frankfurt concedes that mere formation of the relevant second-order volition is not sufficient for identification, and he provides a more refined analysis, including the important notion of *decisive commitment* or *decision*. In a later paper, "The Faintest Passion," Frankfurt adds the component of *satisfaction* to the analysis of identification. The notion of identification is important both to the account of acting freely and the true self, and it is interesting to ask whether the same notion can play the required roles in both accounts.

Not only is a certain sort of inevitability (lack of alternative possibilities) compatible with moral responsibility, Frankfurt contends that certain *volitional necessi-* ties—things we simply cannot bring ourselves to will—help to constitute the boundaries of our true selves. In a series of papers Frankfurt explores the way in which our selves are formed through the process of caring, identification, and volitional constraints. In "The Importance of What We Care About," Frankfurt identifies *caring* as a distinctive kind of motivation importantly different from morality. He denies that all-things-considered rationality needs to coincide with the deliverances of morality. In later work Frankfurt has built on his work on caring to give a nuanced account of the nature of love. For Frankfurt, love is central to the foundations of morality as well as to the formation of our selves.

Central themes in Frankfurt's work are as follows: the compatibility of moral responsibility, caring, and love with certain sorts of necessity or inevitability and the contention that morality, normativity, or rationality should not be *built into* our analyses of human motivation at the very foundational level. For Frankfurt, caring and love are more central or, perhaps, more fundamental notions than rationality and morality.

See also Descartes, René; Determinism and Freedom; Ethics, History of; Locke, John; Love; Responsibility, Moral and Legal; Truth.

Bibliography

Buss, S., L. and Overton, eds. *Contours of Agency: Essays on Themes from Harry Frankfurt.* Cambridge, MA: MIT Press, 2002.

WORKS BY FRANKFURT

"Alternate Possibilities and Moral Responsibility." *Journal of Philosophy* 66 (1969): 829–839.

Demons, Dreamers, and Madmen. Indianapolis, IN: Bobbs-Merrill, 1970.

"Freedom of the Will and the Concept of a Person." *Journal of Philosophy* 68 (1971): 5–20.

"The Importance of What We Care About." *Synthese* 53 (1982): 257–272.

"Identification and Wholeheartedness." In *Responsibility, Character, and the Emotions*, edited by F. Schoeman, 27–45. New York: Cambridge University Press, 1987.

The Importance of What We Care About. New York: Cambridge University Press, 1988.

"The Faintest Passion." *Proceedings of the American Philosophical Association* 66 (1992): 5–16.

Necessity, Volition, and Love. New York: Cambridge University Press, 1999.

The Reasons of Love. Princeton, NJ: Princeton University Press, 2004.

On Bullshit. Princeton, NJ: Princeton University Press, 2005.

John Martin Fischer (2005)

FRANKLIN, BENJAMIN
(1706–1790)

Benjamin Franklin, the U.S. statesman, scientist, and author, was born in Boston, where he attended school for less than a year. He learned the printer's trade, and at seventeen he ran away to Philadelphia. After two years in England (1724–1726) he returned to Pennsylvania, where, prospering in his trade, he began publishing the *Pennsylvania Gazette* in 1729 and *Poor Richard's Almanack* in 1732. He had already formed a tradesman's self-improvement club, the Junto, and soon began civic and educational promotions, including the founding of the American Philosophical Society.

Franklin retired from business in 1748, turned to science, and in 1751 published *Experiments and Observations on Electricity*. The same year he entered the Pennsylvania Assembly, where he was a leader in opposing the influence of Proprietor Thomas Penn and in advocating colonial union. In 1757, as agent for the assembly, he went to England, where, except for eighteen months, he lived until 1775, enjoying English society and the friendship of David Hume, Henry Home (Lord Kames), Richard Price, and other British philosophers. At first he worked loyally for the expansion of the British Empire and sought to exchange proprietary for royal government in Pennsylvania, but after 1765 he became the leading colonial spokesman in resisting British measures in North America. Although he opposed every act of oppression, he sought until the very end to reconcile differences; but in 1775 he returned home, signed the Declaration of Independence, and worked for a united war effort. In 1776 he went to France, where he signed the French Alliance (1778), secured loans and supplies for the Revolutionary War, and helped negotiate the Treaty of Paris (1783).

He was lionized by Voltaire, Madame Helvétius, Marquis de Condorcet, La Rochefoucauld d'Enville, and other *philosophes*, and returned home in 1785. He served for three years as president of the Pennsylvania Executive Council, attended the Constitutional Convention of 1787, sought the abolition of slavery, and worked on his *Autobiography* in the five years preceding his death.

Franklin's greatest popular fame is as a moralist. The aphorisms of Poor Richard and the example of his *Autobiography* have served as a philosophy of life for millions. In these two works Franklin sought deliberately to set down the rules of conduct that would enable anyone, however humbly born, to prosper and live more meaningfully. The emphasis was unashamedly on the mundane virtues: thrift, hard work, diligence, prudence, moderation, honesty, and shrewdness. For this, Franklin has been denounced by D. H. Lawrence and others as a "snuff-colored man" who impoverished life by "fencing it in" with a stifling, despiritualizing morality. In fact, Franklin knew the precepts of Poor Richard were but a partial philosophy; in his own career and in his other writings he showed abundantly how full and imaginative human life can be.

Like many deists of his day, Franklin believed "in one God, Creator of the Universe, that he governs it by his Providence … [and] that the soul of Man is immortal" (letter to Ezra Stiles, March 9, 1790).

As a scientist, Franklin formulated important and influential laws concerning the nature of electricity. By proving that lightning is an electrical discharge, he placed electricity beside heat, light, and gravity as one of the primordial forces in the universe and hypothesized a new dimension or quality possessed in some measure by all matter. Characteristically, Franklin turned readily from electrical theory to a useful invention, the lightning rod. His scientific attitude is summarized in the statement "Let the experiment be made," and in the observation that electrical experiments would "help to make a vain man humble."

As a public philosopher, Franklin assumed that the traditional personal values have political relevance. He shared the Aristotelian belief that government exists for the sake of the good life and that its powers can be used to that end. A good citizen, guided by the virtues Franklin encouraged in *Poor Richard's Almanack* and in his *Autobiography*, would undertake civic improvement and participate disinterestedly in government. In an expanding country filled with opportunity, Franklin saw individual initiative as the essential engine of progress, but he did not hesitate to seek whatever seemed required for the public good through government. His confidence in the virtue of the citizens of the United States caused him to favor government by consent, but he was not a simple democrat who believed majority will should be omnipotent. He accepted democracy because he thought it would yield good government; if it did not, he readily rejected it.

Franklin thought freedom's dynamism would cause its spread around the world, and therefore that the United States, as a leading free nation, would be influential without being predatory. At the same time he understood the anarchic character of international relations and counseled the nation to maintain its strength, protect its national interest, and act to maintain a balance between France and Great Britain. His essential faith was that, from tradesmen's juntos to the court of Versailles, good men working together could improve the condition of humankind.

See also Aristotelianism; Condorcet, Marquis de; Deism; Home, Henry; La Rochefoucauld, Duc François de; Price, Richard; Voltaire, François-Marie Arouet de.

Bibliography

For Franklin's writings, see L. W. Labaree and others, eds., *The Papers of Benjamin Franklin*, 37 vols. (New Haven, CT: Yale University Press, 1959–) and *The Autobiography of Benjamin Franklin* (New Haven, CT: Yale University Press, 1964); and A. H. Smyth, ed., *The Writings of Benjamin Franklin*, 10 vols. (New York: Macmillan, 1905–1907).

For his life and thought, see Carl Van Doren, *Benjamin Franklin* (New York: Viking Press, 1938); Carl Becker, *Benjamin Franklin* (Ithaca, NY: Cornell University Press, 1946); and R. L. Ketcham, *Benjamin Franklin* (New York: Washington Square Press, 1965).

On his scientific thought, see I. B. Cohen, *Franklin and Newton, an Inquiry into Speculative Newtonian Experimental Science and Franklin's Work in Electricity as an Example Thereof* (Philadelphia: American Philosophical Society, 1956). For his political thought, see R. L. Ketcham, ed., *The Political Thought of Benjamin Franklin* (Indianapolis: Bobbs-Merrill, 1965). For his place as an Enlightenment philosopher, see Frank L. Mott and Chester E. Jorgenson, eds., introduction in *Representative Selections* (New York: American, 1936).

C. L. Sanford, ed., *Benjamin Franklin and the American Character* (Boston: Heath, 1955), reprints a good collection of critical essays on Franklin.

OTHER RECOMMENDED WORKS

Aldridge, Alfred Owen. *Benjamin Franklin and Nature's God*. Durham, NC: Duke University Press, 1967.

Lemay, J. A. Leo. *The Oldest Revolutionary: Essays on Benjamin Franklin*. Philadelphia: University of Pennsylvania Press, 1976.

Wright, Esmond. *Franklin of Philadelphia*. Cambridge, MA: Belknap Press of Harvard University Press, 1986.

Ralph Ketcham (1967)
Bibliography updated by Michael J. Farmer (2005)

FREEDOM

In the history of philosophical and social thought "freedom" has a specific use as a moral and a social concept—to refer either to circumstances that arise in the relations of man to man or to specific conditions of social life. Even when so restricted, important differences of usage are possible, and most of the political or philosophical argument about the meaning or the nature of freedom is concerned with the legitimacy or convenience of particular applications of the term.

ABSENCE OF CONSTRAINT OR COERCION

It is best to start from a conception of freedom that has been central in the tradition of European individualism and liberalism. According to this conception, freedom refers primarily to a condition characterized by the absence of coercion or constraint imposed by another person; a man is said to be free to the extent that he can choose his own goals or course of conduct, can choose between alternatives available to him, and is not compelled to act as he would not himself choose to act, or prevented from acting as he would otherwise choose to act, by the will of another man, of the state, or of any other authority. Freedom in the sense of not being coerced or constrained by another is sometimes called negative freedom (or "freedom from"); it refers to an area of conduct within which each man chooses his own course and is protected from compulsion or restraint. J. S. Mill's essay *On Liberty* is perhaps the best-known expression in English of this individualistic and liberal conception of freedom.

Some writers take the view that the absence of coercion is the sufficient and necessary condition for defining freedom; so long as a man acts of his own volition and is not coerced in what he does, he is free. Other writers wish to widen the concept in one or both of two ways. They argue that natural conditions, and not only the will or the power of other men, impose obstructions and restraints on our capacity to choose between alternatives and that therefore the growth of knowledge or anything else that increases our capacity to employ natural conditions for the achievement of our purposes ipso facto enlarges our freedom. They also sometimes argue that whether or not it is the will of other men or natural obstacles that are considered as limiting or constraining our actions, we cannot truly be said to be free to choose some preferred alternative unless we have the means or the power to achieve it, and thus the absence of means or power to do X is equivalent to absence of freedom to do it. For those who take this view the necessary conditions for the existence of freedom would be (*a*) the absence of human coercion or restraint preventing one from choosing alternatives he would wish to choose; (*b*) the absence of natural conditions preventing one from achieving a chosen objective; (*c*) the possession of the means or the power to achieve the objective one chooses of one's own volition. Many of the assertions frequently made about liberty in recent political thought assume that possession of the means or power to realize preferred objectives is part of what it means to be free. For example, the contention that men who suffer from poverty or have a low level of education cannot really be free, or that they cannot be as free as the well-to-do and the well educated, relies on the assumption that "to be free to do X" includes within its meaning "to be able," "to have the means," and "to have the power" to do X.

What are the objections to thus connecting "being free to" with "having the capacity or the power to"? It can be said that, at least in many cases, equating freedom with possession of power will involve a distortion of ordinary language. If I ask, "Am I free to walk into the Pentagon?" the question will be clearly understood; but if I ask, "Am I free to walk across the Atlantic Ocean?" the appropriate answer will be "You are free to, if you can." This suggests the main argument: The linking of "being free to" with "having the capacity or power" deprives the word *free* of its essential and unequivocal function, which is to refer to a situation or state of affairs in which a man's choice of how he acts is not deliberately forced or restrained by another man. As Bertrand de Jouvenel points out, if we say that to be free to achieve chosen ends requires the possession of the power and the social means necessary for their achievement, then the problem of freedom coincides with (or becomes confused with) the quite different problem of how satisfactions are to be maximized. It may be true to say that the poor man is as free to spend his holidays in Monte Carlo as the rich man is, and true also to say that he cannot afford to do so. These two statements, it is argued, refer to two distinct states of affairs, and nothing is gained by amalgamating them.

MEANING OF "COERCION"

Even if we confine ourselves to saying that a man is free insofar as his action is not coerced by another, it is evident that the concept of coercion itself requires some consideration. An important point may be made by examining Bertrand Russell's often-quoted sentence: "Freedom in general may be defined as the absence of obstacles to the realization of desires." This hardly goes far enough. Let us imagine an authoritarian society in which rulers have for years been so successful in controlling and manipulating what members of the community read and what views they encounter, and in which the educators have been able so subtly and skillfully to mold the minds and dispositions of the very young, that almost all citizens naturally desire what their rulers desire them to desire, without its ever occurring to them that there are alternatives to what

they are accustomed to or that their freedom to choose has been in any way circumscribed. They are not conscious of any obstructions to the satisfaction of desire and, indeed, no obstructions may exist to the satisfaction of any desires they experience. This is a limiting case, but it points to conditions that exist more or less in all societies. We would scarcely concede that the members of such a society enjoyed any or much freedom. The society described may be one in which coercion in the usual sense does not occur and has in fact become unnecessary.

Two important points follow from this. First, if absence of coercion is a necessary condition of being free, coercion must be understood as including not only the direct forms—commands or prohibitions backed by sanctions or superior power—but also the many indirect forms—molding and manipulation or, more generally, forms of control that are indirect because they involve control by certain persons of the conditions that determine or affect the alternatives available to others. This is an important extension of the notion of coercion. Second, if liberty means the right of individual choice between alternatives, then this right in turn implies that the alternatives can be known by those who are to choose; that individuals have the opportunity to understand the character of available alternatives and can make a deliberate or informed choice. The freedom that members of a society enjoy will be connected, therefore, with the extent to which competing opinions, objectives, modes of behavior, ways of living, and so on are, so to speak, on display; on how freely they can be recommended, criticized and examined; and thus on the ease with which men can make a deliberate choice between them.

For this reason, since literacy or education enlarges the capacity or faculty of choice and decision, it is an important precondition of the existence of freedom: knowledge extends the capacity for acting freely. Similarly, not only suppression but also distortion and misrepresentation, any kind of dishonest propaganda that gains its effect from privileged control over sources of publicity, may restrict the freedom of others; insofar as it succeeds in concealing or misrepresenting the character of certain of the available alternatives, it will tend to restrict or manipulate the range of choice no less effectively than direct coercion or constraint may; and thus it will also tend to limit the exercise of freedom in a particular society. It is not sufficient to consider only the presence or absence of coercion in the more literal and direct sense. Freedom in its positive aspect is the activity or process of choosing for oneself and acting on one's own initiative, and choice can be manipulated as readily as it can be coerced.

Does it follow from this that the extent of freedom is related to the number of available alternatives, in that the more alternatives there are for choice, the freer a man is? Clearly there can be no simple or direct relationship between the range of available alternatives and the extent of freedom. However numerous the alternatives between which a man may choose, he will not admit himself to be free if the one alternative that he would most prefer is the one that is excluded. In a society that forbids the preaching of Catholic doctrine and the practice of Catholic forms of worship, Catholics will not concede that they are free just because they are still free to be either Anglicans, Methodists, or Buddhists. In certain circumstances the extent of the range of available alternatives may be relevant to a judgment of the extent of freedom; but in general we can talk profitably about both the existence and the extent of freedom in a particular society only by taking into account the individual and social interests, the capacities, the modes of behavior, and the ways of living on behalf of which freedom is claimed.

KINDS OF FREEDOM

When men speak of their being free or claim freedom for themselves, they are referring not only to the absence of coercion and restraint imposed by others (freedom *from*) but also to that on behalf of which freedom is being claimed (what they are claiming freedom *for*). This is another sense in which we can speak about a positive aspect of freedom. In political and social discussion a claim to freedom is almost invariably (albeit usually implicitly) a claim to a particular liberty, a claim to freedom for or in the exercise of some particular interest or form of activity. Although Russell says that freedom is the absence of obstacles to the satisfaction of desire, probably no serious philosophical or social thinker has defended freedom in the sense of absence of obstacles to the satisfaction of *any* desire; what has been defended, and what freedom has been identified with, is the absence of obstacles to the exercise and satisfaction of specific interests and forms of activity that are accepted as possessing special moral and social significance.

Thus, freedom in the abstract is a class comprising many species—freedom of thought and speech, freedom of association, freedom of assembly, freedom of worship, freedom of movement, freedom in the use or disposal of one's property, freedom in the choice of one's employer or occupation, and so on. In every case there is, of course, a reference to the absence of coercion or interference and

to an area within which one can choose or act on one's own initiative; not to an abstract or indeterminate possibility of choosing but instead to a specific sphere of individual or social activity within which the right to make one's own choices and decisions, to follow one's own course, is regarded as being of particular importance in the moral life of the individual. This seems to be one way in which positive notions of freedom (as contrasted with the more abstract idea of bare immunity from coercion or interference by others) have emerged, namely, in the attempt to identify (and thus to identify with freedom) those specific spheres of human activity within which what Mill calls individuality, the right and capacity for individual choice and initiative, really matter.

Some of the particular freedoms that have been much emphasized in recent times (freedom from want and freedom from fear are important examples) seem at first sight to refer neither to the absence of coercion nor to any specific interest or form of activity for which freedom is being claimed. It might appear that what *is* being claimed is, rather, the institution of political and economic arrangements by means of which men may be made immune from feelings and circumstances that they find to be evil. If this is all that is meant, then this is to employ freedom in a sense different from the one we have been discussing; this is shown by the fact that freedom from want and fear could conceivably be attained by the setting up of political and social arrangements under which the amplitude of choice within important spheres of activity would be drastically restricted and under which there might be a considerable measure of coercion and constraint; in other words, freedom from want and freedom from fear might well be compatible with a very authoritarian regime, just as in contemporary China freedom from flies is said to have been achieved by very authoritarian methods. Thus, if "freedom from want" and "freedom from fear" are taken simply in that way, the freedom involved is logically and socially distinct from that which has so far been taken as being central and fundamental in the tradition of liberal thinking. However, this may be to interpret these two freedoms superficially. For a more sympathetic interpretation we must return to what has been said about manipulation.

FREEDOM AND POWER

In modern societies manipulation in various forms is at least as important as the processes we normally identify as coercive. It is well known that, within a society, a group of men may enjoy such control over property or the means of production, or over an educational system or the media of communication, that they are able to determine within a fairly narrow range the alternatives between which their fellow citizens can choose. It is not only true that less privileged men often lack the means or the power to attain their preferred alternative but also that others can exploit their lack of power in order to prevent them from attaining what they would wish to attain; sometimes the less powerful can even be prevented from knowing what alternatives there are and from knowing that some of them might be capable or worthy of being pursued. It is this argument that can justify notions like "freedom from want" or "freedom from economic insecurity" and that links them with what has been taken to be the central sense of freedom, the absence of constraint. Even though we refuse to conclude that the mere absence of the means or the power to attain a preferred alternative goal is equivalent to not being *free* to pursue it, it is a different situation when means and power are controlled and manipulated by others in order to secure compliance with their demands. Thus, if "want" and "insecurity" describe a condition in which there is unequal control over the means and conditions of choice and action, in consequence of which some men can manipulate the range of choice available to others, then freedom from want and insecurity belongs with freedom from coercion; in that case, freedom from want and insecurity is the condition of the ability to act on one's own initiative, which is the positive side of liberty.

There is, then, this connection between freedom and power: When there is conflict between individuals and groups for possession or control of scarce means and conditions of action, control over means is a condition of the availability of alternatives, and hence of choice and freedom. It follows, therefore, that when men have unequal power, this will often mean that they will also be unequal with respect to the freedom they enjoy—not merely in the sense that the man who is better off has the means to choose more widely and live more abundantly than his poorer brother (although this is also true) but in the more relevant sense that the more powerful man can restrict the range of choice and the freedom of the less powerful in order to satisfy his own interests more fully. Obviously this relation between inequality of power and inequality of freedom provides one of the connections that exist between liberty and democracy. If we define democracy as being a form of political organization in which all adult members of the community share in making decisions about the common arrangements of the society (including those decisions about the use and distribution of the resources that affect the choices of acting available to men), then the right to participate in the

making of these decisions is a liberty that will affect (or at least may very substantially affect) the range and character of the alternatives that are available in very important areas of social and private life.

POLITICAL PARTICIPATION. Thus, we may say that political participation, or sharing in the process of government, will enter into the meaning of "liberty" in society in at least two different ways. First, political activity and participation in government is an interest and mode of activity to which many men attach great importance, and thus the existence of the right and opportunity to engage in this form of activity is one of the liberties that some men cherish highly. Second, it is in addition a liberty that forms part of a wider structure of liberties because the extent to which this liberty is accorded and exercised will usually also affect the extent to which liberty is available in other areas of social life. This is not to say, of course, that the more democratic a society is (the less men are restrained or restricted in their participation in the activity of government), the more freedom there will be in other areas of social life; it is possible for democracies to be exceptionally coercive, restrictive, or intolerant in certain areas of living and, apart from this, it is also true that expansion of particular liberties (or of liberty in particular areas) often entails the curtailment of others. The point is, rather, that political liberty in the sense specified forms part of a more complex system of liberties in any developed society; both logically and causally, political liberty is connected with the liberties that are established in other spheres of individual activity.

FREEDOM AND CHOICE

We have seen that liberty has its negative and its positive sides—"negative" referring to the absence of obstructions, interference, coercion, or indirect control; "positive," to the processes of choosing and acting on one's own initiative, and more concretely and less formally to the general types of human interests or forms of activity for the expression and exercise of which liberty is claimed. Some writers, concentrating particularly on the positive aspect, have been inclined to assert that a man is being free only when he is actually choosing, exercising initiative, and acting deliberately or responsibly. Mill, in what he says in *On Liberty* about "individuality," "individual spontaneity," the "despotism of custom," and related matters, comes very close to asserting this, although he never quite does so. The same kind of view is hinted at in Graham Wallas's "Freedom is the capacity for continuous initiative," but it would be difficult to accept

ENCYCLOPEDIA OF PHILOSOPHY
2nd edition

this as a general position. For the devotee of a religious faith, the religious freedom he claims and believes himself to enjoy may be no more than the freedom to practice unmolested a form of worship he has inherited and which he has never felt the faintest temptation to question; in such a case it is a fiction to speak of a process of choice. The same can be said of the man who is content to follow narrowly, uncritically, and unadventurously the established customs and conventions of his society. Even though there may be a sense in which we can intelligibly talk of such men as being slaves to customs, habits, or orthodoxies, it would still be straining the point to maintain that they are not free.

On the other hand, the man who has been so molded and manipulated that he always wants what his ruler or superior wants him to want is scarcely free. This case suggests that freedom will exist only where there exists the *possibility* of choice, and the possibility of choice in turn implies not only the absence of direct coercion and compulsion but also that the availability and the characteristics of alternatives must be capable of being known. Thus, whatever the situation of any particular individual may be, it is most likely that there will be a large measure of individual freedom within a society when there exists what Mill calls a variety of conditions—where a wide variety of beliefs are in fact expressed and where there is a considerable diversity of tastes and pursuits, customs and codes of conduct, ways and styles of living. And, because of the connection between inequality of power and inequality with respect to the enjoyment of freedom, a society in which power is widely distributed is also likely to be the one characterized by the existence of wide possibilities for choice and individual initiative.

See also Authority; Censorship; Democracy; Determinism and Freedom; Liberalism; Liberty; Mill, John Stuart; Power; Rights; Russell, Bertrand Arthur William.

Bibliography

Adler, M. J. *The Idea of Freedom,* 2 vols. New York, 1958–1961; Westport, CT: Greenwood, 1973.

Bay, Christian. *The Structure of Freedom.* Stanford, CA: Stanford University Press, 1958.

Berlin, Isaiah. *Two Concepts of Liberty.* Oxford: Clarendon Press, 1958.

Cranston, Maurice. *Freedom: A New Analysis.* London: Longmans, Green, 1953.

Friedrich, C. J. *Man and His Government.* New York: McGraw-Hill, 1963.

Fuller, Lon. "Freedom: A Suggested Analysis." *Harvard Law Review* 68 (1955): 1305–1325.

Hayek, F. A. *The Constitution of Liberty.* London, 1960.

Jouvenel, Bertrand de. *Sovereignty: An Inquiry into the Political Good.* Chicago: University of Chicago Press, 1957.

Knight, Frank. *Freedom and Reform.* New York: Harper, 1947.

Malinowski, Bronislaw. *Freedom and Civilisation.* London: Allen and Unwin, 1947; Westport, CT: Greenwood, 1976.

Mill, J. S. *On Liberty.* London: Parker, 1859.

Oppenheim, F. E. *Dimensions of Freedom.* New York: St. Martin's, 1961.

Russell, Bertrand. "Freedom and Government." In *Freedom: Its Meaning,* edited by Ruth N. Anshen. New York: Harcourt Brace, 1940.

P. H. Partridge (1967)

FREE WILL

See *Determinism and Freedom*

FREGE, GOTTLOB
(1848–1925)

LIFE

After studying mathematics, physics, chemistry, and philosophy at the universities of Jena and Göttingen, the German mathematician, logician, and philosopher Gottlob Frege obtained his mathematical doctorate in Göttingen (1873) and his mathematical *habilitation* in Jena (1874). From 1874 to 1879 he taught mathematics at the University of Jena as a lecturer; in 1879 he was promoted to adjunct professor, and in 1896 to associate professor. Frege never obtained a full professorship. He retired from teaching in 1917 because of illness, becoming emeritus in 1918.

While he received little professional recognition during his lifetime, Frege is widely regarded in the early twenty-first century as the greatest logician since Aristotle, one of the most profound philosophers of mathematics of all times, and a principal progenitor of analytic philosophy. His writing exhibits a level of rigor and precision that was not reached by other logicians until well after Frege's death.

MAIN WORKS

In the monograph *Begriffsschrift* (1879) Frege introduces his most powerful technical invention, nowadays known as predicate logic. In his second book, *Die Grundlagen der Arithmetik* (1884), he discusses the philosophical foundations of the notion of number and provides an informal argument to the effect that arithmetic is a part of logic (a thesis later known under the epithet *logicism*). The pamphlet *Funktion und Begriff* (1891) is an elucidation of Frege's fundamental ontological distinction between functions (with concepts as a special case) and objects; certain difficulties with the views expressed therein are discussed in the essay "Über Begriff und Gegenstand" (1892). Frege's most celebrated achievement in the philosophy of language, the distinction between the sense and the reference of an expression, is expounded in his landmark essay "Über Sinn und Bedeutung" (1892). *Grundgesetze der Arithmetik* (volume 1, 1893; volume 2, 1903), his magnum opus, constitutes his abortive (because of Bertrand Arthur William Russell's antinomy) attempt at rigorously proving the logicist thesis. The essay "Der Gedanke: Eine logische Untersuchung" (1918) is a conceptual investigation of truth and that with respect to which the question of truth arises (called thoughts by Frege).

FREGE'S LOGIC

By replacing the traditional subject-predicate analysis of judgments with the function-argument paradigm of mathematics and inventing the powerful quantifier-variable mechanism, Frege was able to overcome the limitations of Aristotelian syllogistics and created the first system of (higher-order) predicate logic. He thereby devised a formal logical language adequate for the formalization of mathematical propositions, especially through the possibility of expressing multiply general statements such as "*for every* prime number, *there is* a greater one."

The first presentation of his *begriffsschrift* (concept script—Frege's logical formula language) is contained in the 1879 monograph by the same name. At this time, the linguistic and philosophical underpinnings of begriffsschrift, as well as the description of the language itself, are still somewhat imprecise. There are, for instance, no formation rules given for the formulas of the language; functions seem to be identified with functional expressions; the meanings of the propositional connectives are specified in terms of assertion and denial rather than truth and falsity; and although Frege officially countenances only one inference rule, namely, *modus ponens*, he tacitly uses an instantiation rule for the universal quantifier as well. The first volume of *Grundgesetze*, however, presents a mature and amazingly rigorous version of the system, taking into account the various insights Frege had developed since the publication of *Begriffsschrift*. Unless otherwise noted, the following discussion pertains to this later

system; for the time being, one should ignore the course-of-values operator, which is discussed later on in connection with Russell's antinomy.

The primitive symbols of Frege's begriffsschrift are then those for equality, negation, the material conditional, and the first- and higher-order universal quantifiers. In addition, there are gothic letters serving as bound variables (of first and higher orders), as well as Latin letters, whose role one would today characterize as that of free variables (again, of various orders). Disjunction, conjunction, and the existential quantifier are neither primitive, nor are they introduced as abbreviations, as would be customary today; rather, Frege notes that they can be simulated by means of the existing primitives.

Frege carefully distinguishes between basic laws (axioms) on the one hand, and inference rules on the other hand. With respect to a specified set of basic laws and rules of inference, he comes close to a rigorous definition of derivations in the predicate calculus.

The logical connectives, as well as the quantifiers, are taken to be denoting expressions, having as references the requisite truth functions and higher-order functions, respectively. Equality undergoes a radical change in interpretation between the time of *Begriffsschrift* and that of *Grundgesetze*. In the earlier system, assuming that the expression A refers to the object a, and the expression B to object b, Frege construes identities of the form $A = B$ metalinguistically, taking them to mean that the expressions A and B are coreferential, rather than that a and b are the same object. In *Grundgesetze*, however, identity is conceived of as a binary relation between objects, much as is standard today (this change in interpretation is, incidentally, accompanied by a switch in notation from the triple bar $\equiv$ to the now customary double bar $=$). Arguably, there is an analogous shift in the understanding of the universal quantifier; the formulations in *Begriffsschrift* suggest that it is to be interpreted substitutionally, whereas it is fairly clear in *Grundgesetze* that an objectual interpretation is intended. But the issue is difficult to judge, not only because the language of the earlier work is rather imprecise but also because it is not clear whether Frege was aware of the significance of the distinction between objectual and substitutional quantification.

Frege's perhaps most impressive achievement in pure logic is his celebrated definition (with the proof of its adequacy) of the ancestral (or transitive closure) R^* of a binary relation R with the help of second-order quantification, already contained in *Begriffsschrift* and central to the logicist enterprise. Informally, an object a bears the ancestral R^* of a relation R to an object b if b can be reached from a in a finite (nonzero) number of R-steps. That is, whenever there are objects $a_1, a_2, \ldots, a_n$ ($n > 1$) such that $a_1Ra_2, a_2Ra_3, \ldots, a_{n-1}Ra_n$, then a_1 bears R^* to a_n. For example, if R is the parenting relation (so that xRy holds if and only if x is a parent of y), then R^* is the ancestor relation (i.e., xR^*y holds if and only if x is an ancestor of y), because x is an ancestor of y if y is a child of x, or a child of a child of x, or a child of a child of a child of x, and so on. Frege's idea is to define R^* from R as follows: a stands in the relation R^* to b if and only if b has every property F such that (1) all objects to which a bears R have F, and (2) F is hereditary with respect to the relation R (meaning that, whenever something x has the property F, and x bears R to some y, then y also has F). Note that this definition employs second-order quantification (over all R-hereditary properties F).

It is clear that, if b can be reached from a in a finite nonzero number of R-steps, then Frege's definition correctly implies that aR^*b, for if F is any property and b can be reached from a in one step, then by clause (1) of the definition b must have F, and if b can be reached from a by some number of R-steps greater than 1, one must have passed through an object to which a bears R, and which thus has F by clause (1), and every further object through which one has passed, including the last object b, must have F by clause (2). On the contrary, if b cannot be reached from a in a finite nonzero number of R-steps, then b lacks just that property of being reachable from a in a finite number of R-steps (a property that fulfills conditions [1] and [2]). In modern notation Frege's formal definition is as follows:

$$aR^*b : \leftrightarrow \forall F((\forall x(aRx \rightarrow Fx) \,\&\, \forall x\forall y \,(Fx \,\&\, xRy \rightarrow Fy)) \rightarrow Fb).$$

It should be noted, finally, that Frege did not regard the sentences of his begriffsschrift as mere forms, open to arbitrary interpretation. Rather, he took them to express definite thoughts (i.e., propositions). This is manifest in the presence of a special symbol, the vertical judgment stroke, whose occurrence before a begriffsschrift formula indicates that the formula's content is actually asserted (and not talked about or simply entertained without judgment as to truth and falsity). While Frege did discuss the formal character of logic in terms of preservation of consequence on substituting nonlogical expressions for others (witness his correspondence with David Hilbert and the 1906 essay series "Über die Grundlagen der Geometrie"), he showed little inclination to pursue such investigations himself. Frege also has little to say about the characterization of propositions as logical truths; there is no indication that he had anything like Alfred

Tarski's model-theoretic criterion in mind. He occasionally remarks that logical axioms are required to be "obvious," but generally takes it for granted that the specific basic laws he lays down are in fact logical truths.

FREGE'S ONTOLOGY AND PHILOSOPHY OF LANGUAGE

Frege's mature ontology is characterized by the fundamental dichotomy between saturated entities or objects (Gegenstände) on the one hand, and unsaturated entities or functions on the other hand. Functions are unsaturated or incomplete in the sense that they carry argument places that need to be filled; an object is anything that is not a function. Concepts are special functions, namely, functions whose values are always one of the two truth-values: the True and the False (which Frege takes to be objects, as will be explained). The realm of functions is stratified: Unary functions mapping objects to objects are first level, unary functions mapping first-level functions to objects are second level (an instance being the concept denoted by the first-level existential quantifier, which maps every first-level concept under which some object falls to the True, and all other first-level concepts to the False), and so on. The stratification becomes more complicated with functions of more than one argument, since there exist, for instance, functions of two arguments with one argument place for unary first-level functions and one argument place for objects (an instance being the application function, which maps a unary first-level function f and an object a to the result $f(a)$ of applying f to a), and so on.

The saturated-unsaturated dichotomy has, for Frege, a parallel in the linguistic realm. Singular terms, such as proper names and definite descriptions, are (linguistically) saturated (or complete) and refer to objects; predicate and functional expressions are incomplete and refer to functions. In determining the ontological status of certain entities Frege often proceeds by analyzing the expressions used to refer to them and takes the saturated or unsaturated nature of the expressions as a reliable guide to their ontological saturation status.

Now since the expression "the concept horse" is grammatically a singular term, Frege takes it to refer to an object, which commits him to the paradoxical claim that the concept horse is not a concept (compare to "Über Begriff und Gegenstand"). In an attempt to resolve this predicament Frege proposes that with every concept F is associated a certain (proxy) object that serves as the referent of "the concept F" (some commentators believe that Frege intended the extension of F to be this proxy object, but the interpretive issue remains contentious). There remains a fundamental problem, however, for on the one hand, objects and concepts belong to distinct ontological categories, so that no predicate can be meaningfully applied to both a concept and an object; but on the other hand, Frege's explanation of this categorial distinction requires him to use the predicates "is an object" and "is a concept" in just this way—as contrasting (nonempty) predicates that can be applied to the same items. This creates some famous difficulties, some of which are discussed in the essay "Über Begriff und Gegenstand," because singular terms such as "the concept *horse*" cannot, according to Frege, refer to concepts, but refer to certain (proxy) objects instead.

Frege's most famous invention is perhaps his distinction between the sense (*Sinn*) and the reference (*Bedeutung*) of a linguistic expression, first introduced in his short 1891 booklet *Funktion und Begriff*, and expounded in detail in the 1892 essay "Über Sinn und Bedeutung." In the case of a singular term its reference is the object denoted by the term, whereas its sense is determined by the way that object is presented through the expression (its mode of presentation). Frege conceives of complete (declarative) sentences, perhaps infelicitously, as peculiar singular terms, so that their references, the special logical objects the True and the False, respectively, are objects. The thought expressed by a sentence is then defined by Frege to be the sentence's sense. The sense of a sentence is thus the mode of presentation of its truth-value; that is, on a natural reading, the sentence's truth-conditions. In the case of incomplete expressions, such as predicates and functional expressions, the references are of course the corresponding unsaturated concepts and functions.

While not explicitly discussed in "Über Sinn und Bedeutung," it becomes clear from the Frege-Husserl correspondence that Frege intended the notion of sense to apply to predicates as well. Scholarly discussion continues whether Frege considered the senses of unsaturated expressions to be functions, or whether he regarded all senses as objects (a stance suggested by the fact that every sense can be referred to by means of a singular nominal phrase of the form "the sense of the expression X"). In the essay "Der Gedanke" Frege expounds a Platonistic view of senses as inhabitants of a "third realm" of nonperceptible, objective entities, as opposed to the (perceptible) objects of the external world and the subjective contents (ideas) of humans' minds.

Frege was motivated to introduce the sense-reference distinction to solve certain puzzles, chief among them (1) the apparent impossibility of informative identity state-

ments and (2) the apparent failure of substitutivity in contexts of propositional attitudes. As for (1), Frege argued that the statements "the morning start is the evening star" and "the morning star is the morning star" obviously differ in cognitive value (*Erkenntniswert*), which would be impossible if the object designated constituted the only meaning of a singular term. The sense-reference distinction allows one to attribute different cognitive values to these identity statements if the senses of the terms flanking the identity sign differ, while still allowing the objects denoted to be one and the same.

Regarding (2), Frege noticed that the sentences "John believes that the morning star is a body illuminated by the sun" and "John believes that the evening star is a body illuminated by the sun" may have different truth-values, although the one is obtained from the other by substitution of a coreferential term. He argued that, in contexts of propositional attitudes, expressions do not have their usual reference, but refer to their ordinary senses (which thus become their indirect references); then since "the morning star" and "the evening star" differ in ordinary sense, they are not, in the context at hand, coreferential, having distinct indirect references. Debate continues as to Frege's intentions concerning indirect senses of expressions, in particular whether iterated propositional attitude contexts give rise to an infinite hierarchy of indirect senses.

In the introduction to *Grundlagen* Frege enunciates "three fundamental principles" for his investigations. The first of these is an admonition to separate the logical from the psychological (a motif that runs through all of Frege's works); the third demands observance of the concept-object distinction. But it is the second of these principles that has drawn most attention and interpretation: "never to ask for the meaning of a word in isolation, but only in the context of a proposition." Other (not obviously equivalent) formulations of the principle occur in sections 60, 62, and 106 of *Grundlagen*; some authors take Frege to express a precursor of this principle in section 9 of *Begriffsschrift*, and some see an echo of it in *Grundgesetze*, volume 1, section 29.

The proper interpretation of the context principle continues to be contentious. While some philosophers regard it as being of the utmost importance to an understanding of Frege's philosophy, others view it as a rather ill-conceived and incoherent doctrine that he appears to have given up in later works. Those who take the context principle seriously mostly take it to claim some sort of epistemological priority of sentences (or perhaps the thoughts expressed by such) over subsentential linguistic items (or perhaps their senses). It is easy to see why one might have misgivings about such an interpretation; after all, it at least appears to conflict with another Fregean principle, namely, that of compositionality (according to which the sense/reference of a compound expression is determined by the senses/references of its constituent expressions), which he held in high regard throughout his life.

FREGE'S PHILOSOPHY OF MATHEMATICS

Frege was, first and foremost, a philosopher of mathematics. While he followed Immanuel Kant in taking the truths of (Euclidean) geometry to be synthetic and knowable *a priori* (forcefully defending this view against Hilbert's axiomatic method in geometry), he vigorously argued, against Kant, for the logicist thesis, that is, the claim that the arithmetic truths, presumably including real and complex analysis, are analytic. In comparing Frege's views with Kant's it is however important to keep in mind that Frege was operating with his own technical definitions of analyticity and syntheticity, which are not obviously equivalent to Kant's: According to Frege (*Grundlagen* §3), a mathematical truth is analytic if it is derivable by means of logical inference rules from the general logical laws (and definitions) alone, whereas it is synthetic if it cannot be proved without recourse to truths belonging to a particular area of knowledge. Thus, analyticity and syntheticity are, for Frege, logico-epistemic notions, while Kant took them to be part semantic (analytic judgments are those whose predicate is contained in the subject, they are true by virtue of the meanings of their terms) and part epistemic (synthetic judgments extend one's knowledge, analytic ones do not).

In the preface to *Begriffsschrift* Frege makes it clear that it was the question of the epistemic status of arithmetic truths that prompted him to develop his new logic. At this time, Frege still avoids outright endorsement of the logicist thesis, stating only that he intends to investigate how far one may get in arithmetic with logical inferences alone. But there can be little doubt that he already envisages a definite path along which the ultimate proof of logicism is to proceed. Thus, he notes in part 3 of this work that mathematical induction rests on the *Begriffsschrift* theorem that, if an object *x* bears the transitive closure $R^\star$ of a binary relation R to an object *y*, and if *x* has a property F that is inherited along R, then *y* has F as well. It therefore seems clear that Frege already understood the possibility of logically proving the mathematical induction principle once the number 0 and the successor rela-

tion among natural numbers had been suitably defined, for the natural numbers could then be given as just those objects following 0 in the transitive closure of the successor relation.

By the time of *Grundlagen* the doctrine of logicism is firmly in place. Having vigorously criticized a selection of philosophical views about the notion of number (notably John Stuart Mill's empiricist and Kant's transcendentalist views), Frege, in the second part of that work, provides an informal, yet rigorous outline of how the reduction of arithmetic to logic may actually be carried out. He begins this endeavor by insisting that (1) ascriptions of number involve assertions about concepts and (2) the numbers themselves must be construed as objects. Frege argues for (1) by noting first that certain statements, like universal categoricals such as "all whales are mammals" and existential statements such as "there are books on the shelf," predicate something of concepts (rather than individuals). The first example statement is clearly not about any individual whale, but says of the concept *whale* that it is subsumed under the concept *mammal*; the second example predicates nonemptiness of the concept *book on the shelf*. The point is even clearer with respect to negated existential statements; "there are no Venus moons" is obviously not about any moon of Venus (if the statement is true, there are none), but denies that something falls under the concept *Venus moon*. Indeed, Frege notes, saying that there are no Venus moons amounts to the same thing as ascribing the number zero to the concept *Venus moon*. And just as in these examples, the numerical statement "there are four books on the shelf" clearly does not predicate anything of any particular book; instead, it, too, is a statement about the concept *book on the shelf*.

The thesis that ascriptions of number are best understood, in analogy with these examples, as assertions about concepts, is further bolstered by the observation that everyday numerical statements invariably involve common nouns or predicates, which, according to Frege, refer to concepts. Moreover, faced with the fact that one may with equal justice say "there is one deck of cards on the table," "there are fifty-two cards on the table," and "there are four suits of cards on the table," one is led to the recognition that there are different standards of unit involved in these assertions, and it seems perfectly natural to identify the respective concepts as these standards of unit. Thesis (2) is a consequence of Frege's view that the ontological category of an entity may be read off reliably from the linguistic category of expression that denotes the entity: According to Frege number terms typically appear as singular terms in natural languages, for example, as "*the* number of cards on the table" or "*the* number four." Furthermore, pure arithmetic number terms typically flank the equality symbol, positions that, in Frege's view, are reserved for singular terms. Hence, Frege concludes, numbers must be objects.

Thus on the one hand, numbers, qua properties of concepts, would seem to be (higher-order) concepts; yet on the other hand, they must be construed as objects. Frege solves this apparent difficulty by suggesting that attributive uses of number words, as in "Jupiter has four moons," can always be paraphrased away, as in "the number of moons of Jupiter is four" (or, even more explicitly, "the number belonging to the concept *moon of Jupiter* is four"). In the latter statement, Frege claims, the *is* must denote identity and cannot function merely as a copula, since *four* is a singular term, and singular terms cannot follow the *is* of predication. The paradigmatic ascription of number then has the form "the number belonging to *F* = *x*," where *F* represents a predicate and *x* a singular term. Thus, the number term only forms part of the (higher-order) property ascribed to the concept, so that the objectual nature of number and the attributive character of ascriptions of number are compatible after all.

Frege next identifies a constraint that his reconstruction of arithmetic will have to abide by. Of fundamental importance for arithmetic are judgments of recognition, that is, identities, and so the definitions of the number-theoretic notions required for a proof of the logicist thesis must ensure that, in particular, identities of the form "the number belonging to *F* = the number belonging to *G*" receive the proper truth conditions. For this special type of identity statement, the truth conditions can readily be formulated in (dyadic second-order) logical terms, namely, the number belonging to *F* is the same as the number belonging to *G* if and only if there exists a binary relation *R* that correlates the objects that are *F* one-one and onto with the objects that are *G*. Since Frege quotes a somewhat obscure passage from David Hume at this point in *Grundlagen*, the principle has, perhaps infelicitously, come to be known as Hume's principle (HP).

Frege rejects HP as a definition of "the number belonging to *F*" on the grounds that it fails to specify truth conditions for contexts of the form "the number belonging to *F* = *x*," where *x* is a term that does not have the form "the number belonging to *G*," for example, when *x* is an individual variable. (This objection is now usually referred to as the Caesar problem—somewhat inaccurately, as Frege uses Julius Caesar as an example in arguing against a slightly different proposal for a definition). Some commentators maintain that Frege's only point in

bringing up this objection is to show how HP is inadequate as a definition of *number* as described earlier. Other commentators see Frege as struggling here to arrive at adequacy conditions for the introduction of new sortal concepts into a language. On such a reading, however, it is difficult to see why Frege was not troubled by the obvious analogous problem arising for extensions of concepts in the *Grundgesetze*.

In any case Frege proposes an explicit definition of "the number belonging to *F*" that in effect amounts to taking this number to be the equivalence class of *F* under the equivalence relation of equinumerosity (which is explained in terms of the existence of a one-one and onto correlation): the number belonging to *F*, Frege stipulates, is the extension of the concept "concept equinumerous with *F*." Frege relies on a naive understanding of the notion of extension (later, in *Grundgesetze*, extensions themselves would be governed by an axiom that was to prove fatal for Frege's project). Frege then defines an object *a* to be a (cardinal) number if there exists a concept *F* such that *a* is the number belonging to *F*.

From the explicit definition of the number belonging to a concept, Frege proceeds to show that HP becomes derivable by means of pure logic and defines 0 as the number belonging to the concept "is an object not identical with itself" and 1 as the number belonging to the concept "is an object identical with 0." The successor relation among cardinal numbers is defined as follows: *n* succeeds *m* if *n* is the number belonging to some concept *F* under which some object *a* falls, and *m* is the number belonging to the concept "is an object falling under *F*, but not identical to *a*." Without proof Frege mentions the theorems that every number has at most one successor and one predecessor, and that every number except 0 succeeds some number. Making use of his definition of the ancestral (transitive closure) of a binary relation (as developed in *Begriffsschrift*), he defines the finite or natural numbers as those objects standing to 0 in the transitive reflexive closure of the successor relation, that is, informally, as those numbers than can be reached from 0 by taking successors finitely many times. Frege observes that this definition allows for a rather straightforward proof of the mathematical induction principle for natural numbers.

At this point, he has effectively recovered all the axioms of (second-order) Peano arithmetic from his definitions, except the one requiring every natural number to have a successor. Frege sketches a proof for this remaining axiom, which ultimately consists in showing by means of induction that, for any natural number *n*, the number belonging to the concept "object to which *n* bears the transitive reflexive closure of the successor relation" (i.e., informally, "natural number being less than or equal to n") succeeds n (a fully detailed proof is carried out in *Grundgesetze*, although it is not entirely clear whether this is the same proof Frege intended in *Grundlagen*).

While the exposition of *Grundlagen* is entirely informal, *Grundgesetze*, which Frege hoped to be the final word on the logical nature of arithmetic, carries out the earlier sketch with full rigor, containing pages and pages of formal deductions in begriffsschrift notation. The crucial element added in *Grundgesetze* is the rigorous treatment of extensions of concepts (more precisely, of courses-of-values of functions, of which concept extensions are a special case). These are governed by Frege's basic law V, whose special case for concepts says that the extensions of concepts F and G coincide if and only if the same objects fall under F as fall under G. The use of extensions allows for the technique of type-lowering: First-level concepts can be simulated by their extensions, second-level concepts H can be simulated by the first-level concepts under which fall precisely the extensions of concepts falling under H, and so on. Frege makes extensive use of this technique; in particular, instead of defining the number belonging to F as the extension of the second-level concept "concept equinumerous with F," he is now able to take numbers to be extensions of first-level concepts. Otherwise, he follows the sketch of *Grundlagen* closely.

As Russell pointed out in a letter to Frege in 1902, the theory expounded in *Grundgesetze* is inconsistent, since it allows for the derivation of Russell's antinomy: Letting R be the first-level concept "x is the extension of some concept under which x does not fall," and r its extension, it follows easily from Frege's rules of inference, together with basic law V, that r both does and does not fall under R. Frege immediately realized that the antinomy threatened to undermine his life's work. While the second volume of *Grundgesetze* was in press, he hastily devised a quick fix that has come to be known as Frege's way out and added an appendix to the book, expressing both confidence that the revised system would prove capable of reconstructing arithmetic and worries about the philosophical underpinning of his revised basic law V. Frege's way out proved not to be a way out, since it was inconsistent with the existence of more than one object. The genesis of the antinomy in Frege's system is by now well understood; it arises through interplay of two principles that are individually consistent, namely, basic law V as mentioned earlier and *impredicative* second-order comprehension (roughly, statements to the effect that there

exists a concept with a certain property, where that property is itself specified with the help of quantification over concepts); Frege's system with basic law V but only predicative instances of comprehension is now known to be consistent, but too weak to allow for a reconstruction of substantial mathematics.

Frege's work on the logical foundation of real analysis remained fragmentary; the second volume of *Grundgesetze* contains only preliminary definitions and theorems. Presumably he had planned a third volume, which, however, never appeared. Toward the end of his life, Frege seems to have abandoned logicism altogether, suggesting that arithmetic was instead based entirely on geometry, and hence synthetic, as Kant had held. His ideas on how such a claim might be proved were, however, never worked out.

NEO-FREGEANISM

Frege himself, and generations of philosophers and logicians after him, considered the mathematical content of *Grundlagen* and *Grundgesetze* largely obsolete because of the inconsistency of Frege's theory of extensions of concepts. In the 1980s, however, it began to be recognized that Frege had indeed hit on an exciting fact: If one takes the framework of Frege's theory to be essentially second-order predicate logic and adopts HP (with a primitive operator "the number belonging to," attaching to concept expressions) as an axiom, all of second-order Peano arithmetic becomes derivable, using the exact definitions and proofs employed by Frege (who used the explicit definition of "the number of F" only to prove HP from it, obtaining all further results directly from HP). This fact has become known as Frege's theorem. Importantly, it was soon observed that Frege arithmetic (i.e., full axiomatic second-order logic plus HP) is consistent, in contradistinction to the system of *Grundgesetze* (indeed, consistent relative to second-order Peano arithmetic).

It is still being debated whether, and to what extent, these discoveries have any bearing on the validity of the logicist thesis (restricted to arithmetic proper). While no one has seriously suggested that HP could be regarded as a principle of logic, some argue that it nevertheless enjoys some privileged epistemological status akin to analyticity, the principle being, in some sense, "analytic *of*" number. There are, however, serious difficulties in defending Frege arithmetic as being analytic. To start with, there is the familiar problem about the status of second-order logic itself, quite independently of HP. But even granting that second-order logic may count as logic in the requisite sense, further objections apply to HP. First, the principle is not ontologically innocent, since it requires the first-order domain to be infinite, which is usually taken to be incompatible with analyticity. Second, any attempt to ground a privileged logical status of HP on its logical form (of an abstraction principle) runs afoul of the "bad company objection": There are abstraction principles of the same general logical form as HP that are inconsistent (such as Frege's basic law V). What is more, there are abstraction principles (like Boolos's parity principle) that hold only in finite domains, which makes them incompatible with HP, and hence it cannot be the logical form of an abstraction principle alone that could make HP analytic. Research on abstraction principles has increased significantly as a consequence of this discussion, as has work on the general logical and mathematical features of Frege's systems.

FREGE'S INFLUENCE

Through his publications, as well as through personal correspondence, Frege exerted a profound influence on Russell, who appears to have been the first major thinker to appreciate Frege's achievements in logic. Russell took over the logicist torch from Frege, and although Alfred North Whitehead and Russell's *Principia Mathematica* differs in many ways from Frege's work (it is much wider in scope, considerably less rigorous, and, in view of Russell's antinomy, takes a different approach to classes), it is clearly also heavily influenced by Frege (e.g., in imposing a structure of levels, or types, on the underlying ontology, and in the definition of number, nowadays often referred to as the Frege-Russell definition of cardinal number). It is known that Russell had read "Über Sinn und Bedeutung" and at least parts of *Grundgesetze* when he developed his celebrated theory of descriptions; and while there is no direct evidence for such a claim, it seems plausible to assume that Frege's discussion of definite descriptions in these works (especially the fully worked out formal theory of *Grundgesetze*) provided a helpful foil for Russell's own theory.

The degree to which Frege influenced Edmund Husserl is a more contentious matter. It is known that Husserl read all of Frege's major works and that the two corresponded extensively (except in the aftermath of Frege's rather hostile review [1894] of Husserl's *Philosophie der Arithmetik* [1891]). It seems fair to say that Frege (in particular, through the aforementioned review, as well as the preface to the first volume of *Grundgesetze*) is at least partly responsible for Husserl's antipsychologistic turn.

While Frege met neither Russell nor Husserl in person, he did have personal interactions with both Rudolf Carnap and Ludwig Josef Johann Wittgenstein. As a student, Carnap enrolled in various classes on begriffsschrift taught by Frege in Jena between 1910 and 1914; surely it was Frege who instilled in Carnap the idea that mathematics was reducible to logic, a view that was to become central to the Vienna Circle's philosophy. More generally, Frege shaped Carnap's whole attitude toward philosophy. After his immigration to the United States, Carnap, with Alonzo Church, was instrumental in keeping Fregean ideas in logic alive in the United States (where they came to flourish, for instance, in the work in semantics of David Kaplan and Richard Montague). Wittgenstein first visited Frege in Jena in 1911, and then at least two more times, in 1912 and 1913, while he was Russell's student in Cambridge. In addition, the two corresponded rather extensively from 1911 to 1920; it is clear from this correspondence that Frege and Wittgenstein thought highly of each other (the end of the correspondence is marked by an exchange of rather critical remarks by Frege on the *Tractatus* and by Wittgenstein on "Der Gedanke"). Fregean themes pervade the work of both the early and the late Wittgenstein, and it appears that Wittgenstein's intellectual respect for Frege never subsided.

In spite of this illustrious group of correspondents, Frege was for many years regarded as a somewhat obscure and ultimately failed predecessor of Russell's, possibly because few philosophers fully acknowledged Frege's influence on them (of course, the extent of this influence may not have been clear to them at the time). In the 1930s Heinrich Scholz and his school in Münster, Germany, rediscovered Frege and began work on an edition of his works, but that never materialized. The situation changed somewhat in the wake of John Langshaw Austin's English translation of the *Grundlagen*, which appeared in 1950; Frege was read, at that time, mainly as a philosopher of language, and as such influenced, among others, the British philosopher Peter Geach. The originality and independence of Frege's work (especially from Russell's), as well as his important role as a progenitor of analytic philosophy, was brought to prominence through the writings of Michael Dummett in the 1970s, who was himself heavily influenced by Frege's methodology and interests. In the United States, besides those mentioned earlier, Donald Davidson's work also revived discussion of Fregean themes. Crispin Wright's neologicism, especially as subsequently articulated and criticized by George S. Boolos and others, caused a veritable renaissance of interest in Frege's logical and mathematical work, beginning in the 1980s and continuing to this day.

See also Analytic and Synthetic Statements; Analyticity; Aristotle; Austin, John Langshaw; Carnap, Rudolf; Categories; Church, Alonzo; Davidson, Donald; Dummett, Michael Anthony Eardley; Geometry; Hilbert, David; Hume, David; Husserl, Edmund; Identity; Kant, Immanuel; Kaplan, David; Logic, History of; Logical Positivism; Mathematics, Foundations of; Mill, John Stuart; Montague, Richard; Peano, Giuseppe; Propositions; Russell, Bertrand Arthur William; Scholz, Heinrich; Whitehead, Alfred North; Wittgenstein, Ludwig Josef Johann.

Bibliography

ABBREVIATIONS

CP

Collected Papers on Mathematics, Logic, and Philosophy. Translated by Max Black et. al; edited by Brian McGuinness. New York: Blackwell, 1984.

PW

Posthumous Writings. Translated by Peter Long and Roger White; edited by Hans Hermes, Friedrich Kambartel, and Friedrich Kaulbach. Chicago: University of Chicago Press, 1979.

TPW

Translations from the Philosophical Writings of Gottlob Frege. 3rd ed, edited by Peter Geach and Max Black. Totowa, NJ: Rowman & Littlefield, 1980.

FR

The Frege Reader, edited by Michael Beaney. Cambridge, MA: Blackwell, 1997.

KS

Kleine Schriften, edited by Ignacio Angelelli. Hildesheim, Germany: Georg Olms, 1967.

FBB

Funktion, Begriff, Bedeutung: Fünf logische Studien, edited by Günther Patzig. Göttingen, Germany: Vandenhoeck and Ruprecht, 1962.

LU

Logische Untersuchungen, edited by Günther Patzig. Göttingen, Germany: Vandenhoeck and Ruprecht, 1966.

WORKS BY FREGE

Ueber eine geometrische Darstellung der imaginären Gebilde in der Ebene. Inaugural-Dissertation der philosophischen Facultät zu Göttingen zur Erlangung der Doctorwürde vorgelegt von G. Frege aus Wismar. Jena: A. Neuenhahn, 1873. Reprinted in *KS*, tr. as "On a Geometrical Representation of Imaginary Forms in the Plane," in *CP*, pp. 1–55.

Rechnungsmethoden, die sich auf eine Erweiterung des Größenbegriffes gründen. Dissertation zur Erlangung der Venia Docendi bei der Philosophischen Facultät in Jena von Dr. Gottlob Frege (1874). Reprinted in *KS*, tr. as "Methods of Calculation based on an Extension of the Concept of Quantity [Magnitude]," in *CP*, pp. 56–92.

Review of H. Seeger, *Die Elemente der Arithmetik, für den Schulunterricht bearbeitet. Jenaer Literaturzeitung* 1 (46) (1874): 722. Reprinted in *KS*, tr. as "Review of H. Seeger, *Die Elemente der Arithmetik,*" in *CP*, pp. 93–94.

Review of A. v. Gall and Ed. Winter, *die analytische Geometrie des Punktes und der Geraden und ihre Anwendung auf Aufgaben. Jenaer Literaturzeitung* 4 (9) (1877): 133–134. Reprinted in *KS*, tr. as "Review of A. von Gall and E. Winter, *Die analytische Geometrie des Punktes und der Geraden und ihre Anwendung auf Aufgaben,*" in *CP*, pp. 95–97.

Review of J. Thomae, *Sammlung von Formeln welche bei Anwendung der elliptischen und Rosenhain'schen Funktionen gebraucht werden. Jenaer Literaturzeitung* 4 (30) (1877): 472. Reprinted in *KS*, tr. as "Review of J. Thomae, *Sammlung von Formeln, welche bei Anwendung der elliptischen und Rosenhainschen Funktionen gebraucht werden,*" in *CP*, p. 98.

"Über eine Weise, die Gestalt eines Dreiecks als complexe Grösse aufzufassen," *Jenaische Zeitschrift für Naturwissenschaft* 12 (1878) Supplement, p. XVIII. Reprinted in *KS*, tr. as "Lecture on a Way of Conceiving the Shape of a Triangle as a Complex Quantity," in *CP*, pp. 99–100.

Begriffsschrift, eine der arithmetischen nachgebildete Formelsprache des reinen Denkens. Halle: L. Nebert, 1879. Reprinted in *Conceptual Notation and Related Articles,* tr. and ed. by T. W. Bynum (OUP, 1972), pp. 101–203. Also in *From Frege to Gödel: A Source Book in Mathematical Logic, 1879–1931* ed. J. van Heijenoort, tr. S. Bauer-Mengelberg (Harvard University Press, 1967), pp. 5–82. §1–12 in *TPW*, pp. 1–20, and in *FR*, pp. 47–78.

"Anwendungen der Begriffsschrift," *Jenaische Zeitschrift für Naturwissenschaft* 13 (1879) Supplement II, pp. 29–33. Reproduced in *Begriffsschrift und andere Aufsätze,* ed. I. Angelelli (Hildesheim: Georg Olms, 1964), tr. as "Applications of the 'Conceptual Notation,'" (1879), in *Conceptual Notation and Related Articles,* tr. and ed. by T. W. Bynum (OUP, 1972), pp. 204–208.

Review of Hoppe, *Lehrbuch der analytischen Geometrie, Deutsche Literaturzeitung* 1 (6) (1880). Reprinted in *KS*, tr. as "Review of Hoppe, *Lehrbuch der analytischen Geometrie I,*" in *CP*, pp. 101–102.

"Ueber die wissenschaftliche Berechtigung einer Begriffsschrift," *Zeitschrift für Philosophie und philosophische Kritik* 81 (1882), pp. 48–56. Reprinted in *KS*, tr. as "On the Scientific Justification of a Conceptual Notation," in *Conceptual Notation and Related Articles,* tr. and ed. by T. W. Bynum (OUP, 1972), pp. 83–89, and tr. by J. M. Bartlett as "On the Scientific Justification of a Conceptual Notation," *Mind* 73 (1964), pp. 155–160.

"Über den Zweck der Begriffsschrift," *Jenaische Zeitschrift für Naturwissenschaft* 16 (1883) Supplement, pp. 1–10. Reprinted in *Begriffsschrift und andere Aufsätze,* ed. I. Angelelli (Hildesheim: Georg Olms, 1964), tr. as "On the Aim of the 'Conceptual Notation,'" in *Conceptual Notation and Related Articles,* tr. and ed. by T. W. Bynum (OUP, 1972), pp. 90–100. Also tr. by V. Dudman as "On the Purpose of the Begriffsschrift," *The Australasian Journal of Philosophy* 46 (1968), pp. 89–97.

"Geometrie der Punktpaare in der Ebene," *Jenaische Zeitschrift für Naturwissenschaft* 17 (1884) Supplement, pp. 98–102.

Reprinted in *KS*, tr. as "Lecture on the Geometry of Pairs of Points in the Plane," in *CP*, pp. 103–107.

Die Grundlagen der Arithmetik, eine logisch-mathematische Untersuchung über den Begriff der Zahl. Breslau: W. Koebner, 1884; reprints Breslau: M. & H. Marcus, 1934, Hildesheim: G. Olms, 1961, and Darmstadt: Wissenschaftliche Buchgesellschaft, 1961. Tr. as *The Foundations of Arithmetic* by J. L. Austin, with German text, 2nd edition (Blackwell, 1953). §55–91, 106–109 also tr. M. S. Mahoney, in *Philosophy of Mathematics: Selected Readings*, 2nd edition, eds. P. Benacerraf and H. Putnam (CUP, 1983) pp. 130–159. Introduction, §1–4, 45–69, 87–91, 104–9 with summaries of remaining sections also in *FR*, pp. 84–129. Also reprinted as *Die Grundlagen der Arithmetik*, German centenary critical edition, ed. C. Thiel (Hamburg: Felix Meiner, 1986).

Review of H. Cohen: *Das Princip der Infinitesimal-Methode und seine Geschichte, Zeitschrift für Philosophie und philosophische Kritik* 87 (1885), pp. 324–329. Reprinted in *KS*, tr. as "Review of H. Cohen, *Das Prinzip der Infinitesimal-Methode und seine Geschichte*," in *CP*, pp. 108–111.

"Erwiderung," *Deutsche Literaturzeitung* 6 (28) (1885): 1030. Reprinted in *KS*, tr. as "Reply to Cantor's Review of *Grundlagen der Arithmetik*," in *CP*, p. 122.

"Über formale Theorien der Arithmetik," *Jenaische Zeitschrift für Naturwissenschaft* 19 (1886) Supplement, pp. 94–104. Reprinted in *KS*, tr. as "On Formal Theories of Arithmetic," in *CP*, pp. 112–121.

"Über das Trägheitsgesetz," *Zeitschrift für Philosophie und philosophische Kritik* 98 (1891). Reprinted in *KS*, tr. as "On the Law of Inertia," in *CP*, pp. 123–136, and tr. by R. Rand as "About the Law of Inertia" in *Synthese* 13 (1961), pp. 350–363.

Function und Begriff. Vortrag, gehalten in der Sitzung vom 9. Januar 1891 der Jenaischen Gesellschaft für Medicin und Naturwissenschaft. Jena: H. Pohle, 1891. Reprinted in *FBB*. Tr. as "Function and Concept," in *TPW*, pp. 21–41, also in *CP*, pp. 137–156, and *FR*, pp. 151–171.

"Über Sinn und Bedeutung," *Zeitschrift für Philosophie und philosophische Kritik*, NF 100 (1892): 25–50. Reprinted in *FBB* and *KS*. Tr. by H. Feigl as "On Sense and Nominatum," in H. Feigl and W. Sellars, eds., *Readings in Philosophical Analysis* (New York: Appleton-Century-Croft 1949), as "On Sense and Reference," in *TPW*, pp. 56–78, also in *CP*, pp. 157–77, and *The Philosophical Review* 57 (1948), pp. 207–230, and as "On Sinn and Bedeutung" in *FR*, pp. 151–71.

"Ueber Begriff und Gegenstand," *Vierteljahrsschrift für wissenschaftliche Philosophie* 16 (1892): 192–205. Reprinted in *FBB* and *KS*. Tr. as "On concept and Object," in *TPW*, pp. 42–55, also in *PW*, pp. 87–117, in *CP*, pp. 182–94, *Mind* 60 (1951): 168–180 and in *FR*, pp. 181–193.

Review of Georg Cantor: *Zur Lehre vom Transfiniten. Gesammelte Abhandlungen aus der Zeitschrift für Philosophie und philosophische Kritik. Erste Abteilung. Zeitschrift für Philosophie und philosophische Kritik* 100 (1892): 269–272. Reprinted in *KS*, tr. as "Review of Cantor's *Zur Lehre vom Transfiniten*," in *CP*, pp. 178–81.

Grundgesetze der Arithmetik. Begriffsschriftlich abgeleitet. Jena: H. Pohle, Band I: 1893, Band II: 1903. Repr. together, Hildesheim: Georg Olms, 1962, 1998; and Darmstadt: Wissenschaftliche Buchgesellschaft, 1962. Preface,

introduction and §1–52 of Vol. I tr. as *The Basic Laws of Arithmetic: Exposition of the System*, tr. and ed. by M. Furth (University of California Press, 1964). Selections from both vols. also tr. in *TPW*, and in *FR*, pp. 194–233, 258–289. Selections also tr. by J. Stachelroth and P. Jourdain as "A Formal System of Logic and Mathematics" in *Readings on Logic*, eds. I. Copi and J. Gould (New York: Macmillan, 1964).

Review of Dr. E. G. Husserl: *Philosophie der Arithmetik. Psychologische und logische Untersuchung. Zeitschrift für Philosophie und philosophische Kritik* 103 (1894): 313–332. Reprinted in *KS*, tr. as "Review of E. G. Husserl, *Philosophie der Arithmetik I*," in *CP*, pp. 195–209. Extracts in *TPW*, pp. 79–85, and *FR*, pp. 224–226.

"Kritische Beleuchtung einiger Punkte in E. Schöders Vorlesungen über die Algebra der Logik," *Archiv für systematische Philosophie* 1 (1895): 433–456. Reprinted in *LU*, also in *KS*, tr. as "A Critical Elucidation of Some Points in E. Schröder, *Vorlesungen über die Algebra der Logik*," in *CP*, pp. 210–228, also in *TPW*, pp. 86–106.

"Le nombre entier," *Revue de Métaphysique et de Morale* 3 (1895): 73–78. Reprinted in *KS*, tr. as "Whole Numbers," in *CP*, pp. 229–233.

"Lettera del sig. G. Frege all'Editore," *Revue de Mathématiques (Rivista di Matematica)* 6 (1896–1899): 53–59. Reprinted in Giuseppe Peano. *Opere scelte, II* (Rome: Cremonese, 1958), also in *KS*.

"Über die Begriffsschrift des Herrn Peano und meine eigene," *Berichte über die Verhandlungen der Königlich Sächsischen Gesellschaft der Wissenschaften zu Leipzig. Mathematisch-Physische Klasse* 48 (1897): 361–378. Reprinted in *FBB*, tr. as "On Mr. Peano's Conceptual Notation and My Own," in *CP*, pp. 234–248.

Über die Zahlen des Herrn H. Schubert. Jena: H. Pohle, 1899. Reprinted in *LU*, also in *KS*, tr. as "On Mr. H. Schubert's Numbers," in *CP*, pp. 249–72.

"Über die Grundlagen der Geometrie." *Jahresbericht der Deutschen Mathematiker-Vereinigung* 12 (1903): 319–324. Reprinted in *KS*, tr. in "On the Foundations of Geometry: First Series," in *CP*, pp. 273–284, also in *On the Foundations of Geometry and Formal Theories of Arithmetic*, tr. by Eike-Henner W. Kluge (Yale University Press, 1971), pp. 22–37, and as "The Foundations of Geometry," *The Philosophical Review* 69 (1960), pp. 3–17.

"Über die Grundlagen der Geometrie II." *Jahresbericht der Deutschen Mathematiker-Vereinigung* 12 (1903): 368–375. Reprinted in *KS*, tr. in "On the Foundations of Geometry: First Series," in *CP*, pp. 273–284, also in *On the Foundations of Geometry and Formal Theories of Arithmetic*, tr. by Eike-Henner W. Kluge (Yale University Press, 1971), pp. 22–37, and as "The Foundations of Geometry," *The Philosophical Review* 69 (1960), pp. 3–17.

"Was ist eine Funktion?" In: *Festschrift Ludwig Boltzmann gewidmet zum sechzigsten Geburstage, 20. Feb. 1904* (Leipzig: J. A. Barth, 1904), pp. 656–666. Reprinted in *FBB* and *KS*, tr. as "What is a Function?" in *TPW*, pp. 107–16, also in *CP*, pp. 285–92.

"Über die Grundlagen der Geometrie I." *Jahresbericht der Deutschen Mathematiker-Vereinigung* 15 (1906): 293–309. Reprinted in *KS*, tr. in "On the Foundations of Geometry: Second Series," in *CP*, pp. 293–340, also in *On the*

Foundations of Geometry and Formal Theories of Arithmetic, tr. by Eike-Henner W. Kluge (Yale University Press, 1971), pp. 49–112.

"Über die Grundlagen der Geometrie (Fortsetzung) II." *Jahresbericht der Deutschen Mathematiker-Vereinigung* 15 (1906): 377–403. Reprinted in *KS,* tr. in "On the Foundations of Geometry: Second Series," in *CP,* pp. 293–340, also in *On the Foundations of Geometry and Formal Theories of Arithmetic,* tr. by Eike-Henner W. Kluge (Yale University Press, 1971), pp. 49–112.

"Über die Grundlagen der Geometrie (Schluß) III," *Jahresbericht der Deutschen Mathematiker-Vereinigung* 15 (1906): 423–430. Reprinted in *KS,* tr. in "On the Foundations of Geometry: Second Series," in *CP,* pp. 293–340, also in *On the Foundations of Geometry and Formal Theories of Arithmetic,* tr. by Eike-Henner W. Kluge (Yale University Press, 1971), pp. 49–112.

"Antwort auf die Ferienplauderei des Herrn Thomae." *Jahresbericht der Deutschen Mathematiker-Vereinigung* 15 (1906): 586–590. Reprinted in *KS,* tr. as "Reply to Mr. Thomae's Holiday *Causerie,*" in *CP,* pp. 341–345.

"Die Unmöglichkeit der Thomaeschen formalen Arithmetik aufs Neue nachgewiesen." *Jahresbericht der Deutschen Mathematiker-Vereinigung* 17 (1908): 52–55. Reprinted in *KS,* tr. as "Renewed Proof of the Impossibility of Mr. Thomae's Formal Arithmetic," in *CP,* pp. 346–350.

Notes to Jourdain, Philip E. B., "The Development of the Theories of Mathematical Logic and the Principles of Mathematics." *Quarterly Journal of Pure and Applied Mathematics* XLIII (1912): 237–269.

"Der Gedanke: Eine logische Untersuchung." *Beiträge zur Philosophie des deutschen Idealismus* 1 (1918): 58–77. Reprinted in *LU* and *KS,* tr. as "Thought," Part I of *Logical Investigations,* ed. P. T. Geach, tr. P. T. Geach and R. Stoothoff (Blackwell, 1977), included in *CP,* pp. 351–372, and in *FR,* pp. 325–345. Also as "The Thought: A Logical Inquiry," in *Mind* 65 (1956): 289–311, tr. by A. M. and Marcelle Quinton.

"Die Verneinung. Eine logische Untersuchung." *Beiträge zur Philosophie des deutschen Idealismus* 1 (1918): 143–157. Reprinted in *LU* and *KS,* tr. as "Negation," Part II of *Logical Investigations,* ed. P. T. Geach, tr. P. T. Geach and R. Stoothoff (Blackwell, 1977), included in *CP,* pp. 373–389, and in *FR,* pp. 346–361.

"Logische Untersuchungen. Dritter Teil: Gedankengefüge." *Beiträge zur Philosophie des deutschen Idealismus* 3 (1923): 36–51. Reprinted in *LU, KS,* tr. as "Compound Thoughts," Part III of *Logical Investigations,* ed. P. T. Geach, tr. P. T. Geach and R. Stoothoff (Blackwell, 1977), included in *CP,* pp. 390–406, and *Mind* 72 (1963): 1–17.

UNPUBLISHED WORKS BY FREGE

Wissenschaftlicher Briefwechsel. Edited by Gottfried Gabriel et al. Hamburg, Germany: Felix Meiner, 1976, abridged for English edition by Brian McGuinness and translated by Hans Kaal as *Philosophical and Mathematical Correspondence.* Chicago: University Press of Chicago, 1980.

WORKS ABOUT FREGE

Antonelli, G. Aldo, and Robert May. "Frege's New Science." *Notre Dame Journal of Formal Logic* 41 (3) (2000): 242–270.

Beaney, Michael, and Erich H. Reck, eds. *Gottlob Frege: Critical Assessments of Leading Philosophers.* 4 vols. London: Routledge, 2005.

Blanchette, Patricia. "Frege and Hilbert on Consistency." *Journal of Philosophy* 93 (1996): 317–336.

Boolos, George S. *Logic, Logic, and Logic,* edited by Richard Jeffrey. Cambridge, MA: Harvard University Press, 1998.

Burge, Tyler. "Frege on Knowing the Foundations." *Mind* 107 (1998): 305–347.

Burgess, John P. *Fixing Frege.* Princeton, NJ: Princeton University Press, 2005.

Demopoulos, William, ed. *Frege's Philosophy of Mathematics.* Cambridge, MA: Harvard University Press, 1995.

Demopoulos, William. "The Philosophical Basis of Our Knowledge of Number." *Noûs* 32 (1998): 481–503.

Dummett, Michael. *Frege and Other Philosophers.* New York: Oxford University Press, 1991.

Dummett, Michael. *Frege: Philosophy of Language.* 2nd ed. Cambridge, MA: Harvard University Press, 1981.

Dummett, Michael. *Frege: Philosophy of Mathematics.* Cambridge, MA: Harvard University Press, 1991.

Dummett, Michael. *The Interpretation of Frege's Philosophy.* Cambridge, MA: Harvard University Press, 1981.

Ferreira, Fernando, and Kai F. Wehmeier. "On the Consistency of the (11 -CA Fragment of Frege's *Grundgesetze.*" *Journal of Philosophical Logic* 31 (2002): 301–311.

Goldfarb, Warren. "Frege's Conception of Logic." In *Future Pasts: The Analytic Tradition in Twentieth Century Philosophy,* edited by Juliet Floyd and Sanford Shieh. New York: Oxford University Press, 2001.

Hale, Bob, and Crispin Wright. *The Reason's Proper Study: Essays towards a Neo-Fregean Philosophy of Mathematics.* New York: Oxford University Press, 2001.

Heck, Richard G., Jr. "The Consistency of Predicative Fragments of Frege's Grundgesetze der Arithmetik." *History and Philosophy of Logic* 17 (1996): 209–220.

Heck, Richard G., Jr., ed. *Language, Thought, and Logic: Essays in Honour of Michael Dummett.* New York: Oxford University Press, 1997.

Heijenoort, Jean van. "Logic as Calculus and Logic as Language." *Synthese* 17 (1967): 324–330.

Hodes, Harold. "Logicism and the Ontological Commitments of Arithmetic." *Journal of Philosophy* 81 (3) (1984): 123–149.

McFarlane, John. "Frege, Kant, and the Logic in Logicism." *Philosophical Review* 111 (2002): 25–65.

Quine, Willard Van Orman. "On Frege's Way Out." *Mind* 64 (1955): 145–159.

Reck, Erich H., ed. *From Frege to Wittgenstein: Perspectives on Early Analytic Philosophy.* New York: Oxford University Press, 2002.

Resnik, Michael D. *Frege and the Philosophy of Mathematics.* Ithaca, NY: Cornell University Press, 1980.

Ricketts, Thomas. "Frege's 1906 Foray into Metalogic." *Philosophical Topics* 25 (2) (1997): 169–187.

Sluga, Hans D. *Gottlob Frege.* Boston: Routledge and Kegan Paul, 1980.

Stepanians, Markus S. *Frege und Husserl über Urteilen und Denken.* Paderborn, Germany: Schöningh, 1998.

Tait, William W., ed. *Early Analytic Philosophy—Frege, Russell, Wittgenstein: Essays in Honor of Leonard Linsky*. Chicago: Open Court, 1997.

Tappenden, Jamie. "Metatheory and Mathematical Practice in Frege." *Philosophical Topics* 25 (2) (1997): 213–264.

Thiel, Christian. *Sense and Reference in Frege's Logic*. Translated by T. J. Blakeley. Dordrecht, Netherlands: D. Reidel, 1968.

Weiner, Joan. *Frege in Perspective*. Ithaca, NY: Cornell University Press, 1990.

Wright, Crispin. *Frege's Conception of Numbers as Objects*. Aberdeen, Scotland: Aberdeen University Press, 1983.

Zalta, Edward N. "Frege's Logic, Theorem, and Foundations for Arithmetic." In *The Stanford Encyclopedia of Philosophy*, edited by Edward N. Zalta. Stanford, CA: Metaphysics Research Lab, Center for the Study of Language and Information, Stanford University, 2005.

Zalta, Edward N. "Gottlob Frege." In *The Stanford Encyclopedia of Philosophy*, edited by Edward N. Zalta. Stanford, CA: Metaphysics Research Lab, Center for the Study of Language and Information, Stanford University, 2005.

Kai F. Wehmeier (2005)

FRENCH ENCYCLOPEDIA, THE

See *Encyclopédie*

FRENCH PHILOSOPHICAL LITERATURE

See *Clandestine Philosophical Literature in France; Encyclopédie*

FREUD, SIGMUND
(1856–1939)

Sigmund Freud was the father of psychoanalysis, but—contrary to much apocryphal lore that dies hard—certainly not the originator of the hypothesis that unconscious ideation is essential to explain much of human overt behavior.

The generic doctrine of an unconscious domain of the mind has a venerable, long pre-Freudian history. Indeed, many of the most important doctrines commonly credited to Freud as his creations were tenets of his intellectual patrimony. Thus, as we recall from Plato's dialogue *The Meno*, Plato was concerned to understand how an ignorant slave boy could have arrived at geometric truths under mere questioning by an interlocutor with reference to a diagram. Plato argued that the slave boy had not acquired such geometric knowledge during his life. Instead, he explained, the boy was tapping prenatal but unconsciously stored knowledge, and restoring it to his conscious memory.

At the turn of the eighteenth century, Gottfried W. Leibniz gave psychological arguments for the occurrence of subthreshold sensory perceptions and for the existence of unconscious mental contents or motives that manifest themselves in our behavior (Ellenberger 1970). Moreover, in his *New Essays on Human Understanding* (1981), Leibniz pointed out that when the contents of some forgotten experiences subsequently emerge in our consciousness, we may misidentify them as new experiences, rather than recognize them as having been unconsciously stored in our memory.

Historically, it is more significant that Freud also had other precursors who anticipated some of his key ideas with impressive specificity. As he himself acknowledged ([the abbreviation "S.E." will be used to refer to the Standard Edition of Freud's complete psychological works in English] S.E., 1914, 14:15–16), Arthur Schopenhauer and Friedrich Nietzsche had speculatively propounded major psychoanalytic doctrines that he himself reportedly developed independently from his clinical observations only thereafter. Indeed, in a 1995 German book, *Die Flucht ins Vergessen: Die Anfänge der Psychoanalyse Freuds bei Schopenhaeur*, the Swiss psychologist Marcel Zentner traces the foundations of psychoanalysis to the philosophy of Schopenhauer.

But, as Freud then pointed out illuminatingly, it is one of the greatest threats to human self-esteem to face that "*the [human conscious] ego is not master in its own house*" (S.E., 1917, 17:143; emphasis in original). On the other hand, it is evasive to dismiss substantive criticisms of Freudian theory as being due to fears induced by psychoanalytic accounts of presumed unconscious motivations. Such a dismissal does not address the merits of the strictures directed against psychoanalysis.

Freud was born in Freiberg, Moravia, then part of the Austro-Hungarian Empire, in 1856. But when he was three years old, his family moved to Vienna, where he entered the University of Vienna in 1873 to study medicine. He lived there until he was expelled by the Nazis, when he moved to London, where he died in 1939.

It is important to distinguish between the validity of Freud's work qua psychoanalytic theoretician, and the merits of his earlier work. The zealous Freudian partisan

Mark Solms has edited and translated a presumably forthcoming four-volume series, *The Complete Neuroscientific Works of Sigmund Freud*. One focus of these writings is the neurological representation of mental functioning; another is Freud's supposed discovery of the essential morphological and physiological unity of the nerve cell and fiber.

They also contain contributions to the histology of the nerve cell, neuronal function, and neurophysiology. As a clinical neurologist, Freud wrote a monograph on aphasia (Solms and Saling, 1990). As Solms claims furthermore in his preview *An Introduction to the Neuro-Scientific Works of Sigmund Freud* (unpublished), Freud wrote major papers on cerebral palsy that earned him the status of a world authority. And he was a distinguished pediatric neurologist in the field of the movement disorders of childhood. Besides, Freud did scientific work on the properties of cocaine that benefited perhaps from his own use of that drug. Alas, that elating intake may well also account for some of the abandon featured by the more bizarre and grandiose of his psychoanalytic forays.

In 1880, he published a (free) translation of some of John Stuart Mill's philosophical writings. Yet, as Paul-Laurent Assoun notes in his 1995 *Freud, La Philosophie, et les Philosophes*, Freud was often disdainful of philosophy, despite clearly being indebted to the Viennese philosopher Franz Brentano, from whom he had taken several courses. The marks of Brentano's quondam representationalist and intentionalist account of the mental in the 1995 edition of his *Psychology from an Empirical Standpoint* are clearly discernible in Freud's conception of ideation. And the arguments for the existence of God championed by the quondam Roman Catholic priest Brentano further solidified the thoroughgoing atheism of Freud, who has been called a "*godless Jew*" (Gay, 1987, pp. 3–4; Grünbaum, 1993, ch. 7).

PSYCHOANALYSIS

The most basic ideas of psychoanalytic theory were initially enunciated in Josef Breuer and Sigmund Freud's *Preliminary Communication* of 1893, which introduced their *Studies on Hysteria*. But the first published use of the word *psychoanalysis* occurred in Freud's 1896 French paper on *Heredity and the Aetiology of the Neuroses* (S.E., 1896, 3:151). Therein Freud designated Breuer's method of clinical investigation as "a new method of psychoanalysis." Astonishingly, the coauthored 1893 prolegomenon, which lays bare the logical foundation of the cornerstone theory of repression, has been overlooked

and untutoredly neglected in the literature, both psychoanalytic and philosophical. Breuer used hypnosis to revive and articulate a patient's unhappy memory of a supposedly repressed traumatic experience. The repression of that painful experience had occasioned the first appearance of a particular hysterical symptom, such as a phobic aversion to drinking water. Thus, Freud's mentor also induced the release of the suppressed emotional distress originally felt from the trauma. Thereby Breuer's method provided a catharsis for the patient.

The cathartic lifting of the repression yielded relief from the particular hysterical symptom. Breuer and Freud (1893) believed that they could therefore hypothesize that the repression, coupled with affective suppression, was the crucial cause for the development of the patient's psychoneurosis (S.E., 1893, 2:6–7; 3:29–31).

Having reasoned in this way, they concluded, in Freud's later words: "Thus one and the same procedure served simultaneously the purposes of [causally] investigating and of getting rid of the ailment; and this unusual conjunction was later retained in psycho-analysis" (S.E., 1924, 19:194).

In his 1924 historical retrospect, Freud acknowledged the pioneering role of Breuer's cathartic method: "The cathartic method was the immediate precursor of psychoanalysis; and, in spite of every extension of experience and of every modification of theory, is still contained within it as its nucleus" (S.E., 1924, 19:194).

Yet Freud was careful to highlight the contribution he made himself after the termination of his collaboration with Breuer. Referring to himself in the third person, he tells us: "Freud devoted himself to the further perfection of the instrument left over to him by his elder collaborator. The technical novelties which he introduced and the discoveries he made changed the cathartic method into psycho-analysis" (S.E. 1924, 19:195). Later on, Freud regarded repressed wishes rather than forgotten traumata as the principal pathogens of neuroses. These extensive elaborations have earned him the mantle of being the father of psychoanalysis.

It is important to recognize that there are major differences between the unconscious processes hypothesized by current cognitive psychology, on the one hand, and the unconscious contents of the mind claimed by psychoanalytic psychology, on the other (Eagle, 1987). These divergences are such that the existence of the cognitive unconscious clearly fails to support, if not impugns, the existence of Freud's "dynamic" unconscious.

His so-called dynamic unconscious is the supposed repository of repressed forbidden wishes of a sexual or aggressive nature, whose reentry or initial entry into consciousness is prevented by the defensive operations of the ego-agency of the mind. Though socially unacceptable, these instinctual desires are so imperious and peremptory that they recklessly seek immediate gratification, independently of the constraints of external reality.

But, in the cognitive unconscious, there is great rationality in the ubiquitous computational and associative problem-solving processes required by memory, perception, judgment, and attention. By contrast, as Freud emphasized, the wish-content of the dynamic unconscious makes it operate in a highly illogical way.

Having populated the dynamic unconscious with repressions, Freud reasoned that the use of his new technique of free association could lift these repressions of instinctual wishes, and could thereby bring the banished ideas back to consciousness unchanged. But in the case of the cognitive unconscious, we typically cannot bring to phenomenal consciousness the intellectual processes that are presumed to occur in it, although we can describe them theoretically. For example, even if his/her life depended on it, a student of czarist history simply could not bring into his/her phenomenal conscious experience the elaborate scanning or search process by which he/she rapidly comes up with the name of the Russian czarina's confidant G.Y. Rasputin, when asked for it. In sum, the presumed psychoanalytic unconscious as such cannot derive any credibility from the hypothesized cognitive unconscious.

PSYCHOANALYSIS AND WESTERN CULTURE

The poet W.H. Auden claimed that psychoanalysis is a whole climate of opinion. And indeed, it has been argued dubiously that the supposed pervasive influence of Freudian ideas in our culture vouches for the validity of the psychoanalytic enterprise. But even the premise that Freudian theory has become part of the intellectual ethos and folklore of Western culture cannot be taken at face value. As the distinguished Swiss scholar Henri Ellenberger stressed in his major historical work of 1970 *The Discovery of the Unconscious*, the prevalence of vulgarized pseudo-Freudian concepts makes it very difficult to determine reliably the extent to which genuine psychoanalytic hypotheses have actually become influential in our culture at large.

For example, any slip of the tongue or other bungled action (parapraxis) is typically yet incorrectly called a *Freudian slip*. But, as Freud himself pointed out, what is required for a slip or so-called parapraxis to qualify technically as Freudian is that it be motivationally opaque rather than transparent, precisely because its psychological motive is repressed (S.E., 1916–1917, 15: 41). Once it is clear what is meant by a bona fide Freudian slip, we need to ask whether there actually exist any such slips at all, that is, slips that appear to be psychologically unmotivated but are actually caused by repressed, unpleasant ideas. It is very important to appreciate how difficult it is to provide cogent evidence for such causation, as shown by strenuous attempts to furnish it experimentally.

Thus, as long as good empirical support for the Freudian scenario is unavailable, we actually do not know whether any bona fide Freudian slips exist at all. Just this lack of evidence serves to undermine the thesis that cultural influence is a criterion of validity. After all, if we have no cogent evidence for the existence of genuinely Freudian slips, then Freud's theory of bungled actions (parapraxes) might well be false. And if so, it would not contribute one iota to its validity even if our entire culture unanimously believed in it and made extensive explanatory use of it: When an ill-supported theory is used to provide explanations, they run the grave risk of being bogus, and its purported insights may well be pseudo-insights.

THE CORNERSTONE OF PSYCHOANALYSIS

In his 1914 *On the History of the Psychoanalytic Movement*, Freud wrote: "The theory of repression is the cornerstone on which the whole structure of psychoanalysis rests. It is the most essential part of it" (S.E., 1914, 14:16) The pillars of the avowed cornerstone of Freud's theoretical edifice comprise several major theses: (1) Distressing mental states induce the operation of a psychic mechanism of repression, which consists in the banishment from consciousness of unpleasurable psychic states (S.E., 1915, 14:147); (2) once repression is operative (more or less fully), it not only banishes such negatively charged ideas from consciousness, but plays a further crucial multiple causal role: It is causally necessary for the pathogenesis of neuroses, the production of our dreams, and the generation of our various sorts of slips (bungled actions); and (3) the method of free association can identify and lift (undo) the patient's repressions; by doing so, it can identify the pathogens of the neuroses, and the generators of our dreams, as well as the causes of our motivationally opaque slips; moreover, by lifting the pathogenic repressions, free association also functions therapeutically, rather than only investigatively.

Freud provided two sorts of arguments for his cardinal etiologic doctrine that repressions are the pathogens of the neuroses: His earlier one, which goes back to his original collaboration with Josef Breuer, relies on purported therapeutic successes from lifting repressions; the later one, designed to show that the pathogenic repressions are sexual, is drawn from presumed reenactments (transferences) of infantile episodes in the adult patient's interactions with the analyst during psychoanalytic treatment. The process of repression, which consists in the banishment of ideas from consciousness or in denying them entry into it, is itself presumed to be unconscious (S.E., 1915, 14:147). In Freud's view, our neurotic symptoms, the manifest contents of our dreams, and the slips we commit are each constructed as "compromises between the demands of a repressed impulse and the resistances of a censoring force in the ego" (S.E., 1925, 20:45; and 1916–1917, 16:301).

By being only such compromises, rather than fulfillments of the instinctual impulses, these products of the unconscious afford only substitutive gratifications or outlets. For brevity, one can say, therefore, that Freud has offered a unifying compromise model of neuroses, dreams, and parapraxes. Since the repressed impulse made a compromise with the repressing ego, compromise-formations are products of *unsuccessful* repressions!

But what, in the first place, is the motive or cause that initiates and sustains the operation of the unconscious mechanism of repression before it produces its own later effects? Apparently, Freud assumes axiomatically that distressing mental states, such as forbidden wishes, traumata, disgust, anxiety, anger, shame, hate, guilt, and sadness—all of which are unpleasurable—almost always actuate, and then fuel, forgetting to the point of repression. Thus, repression regulates pleasure and so called "unpleasure" or displeasure by defending our consciousness against various sorts of negative affect. Indeed, Freud claimed perennially that repression is the paragon among our defense mechanisms. As he put it dogmatically: "The tendency to forget what is disagreeable seems to me to be a quite universal one" (S.E., 1901, 6:144), and "The recollection of distressing impressions and the occurrence of distressing thoughts are opposed by a resistance" (S.E., 1901, 6:146).

Freud tries to disarm an important objection to his thesis that "distressing memories succumb especially easily to motivated forgetting". He says:

The assumption that a defensive trend of this kind exists cannot be objected to on the ground that one often enough finds it impossible, on the contrary, to get rid of distressing memories that pursue one, and to banish distressing affective impulses like remorse and the pangs of conscience. For we are not asserting that this defensive trend is able to put itself into effect *in every case.*

(S.E., 1901, 6:147, ITALICS ADDED).

He acknowledges as "also a true fact" that "distressing things are particularly hard to forget" (S.E., 1916–1917, 15:76–77).

Indeed, Freud himself told us as an adult that he "can remember very clearly," from age seven or eight, how his father rebuked him for having relieved himself in the presence of his parents in their bedroom. In a frightful blow to the boy's ego, his father said: "The boy will come to nothing" (S.E., 1900, 4:216).

But Freud's attempt here to uphold his thesis of motivated forgetting is evasive and unavailing: Since some painful mental states are vividly remembered, while others are forgotten or even repressed, it appears that factors different from their painfulness determine whether they are remembered or forgotten. For example, personality dispositions or situational variables may in fact be causally relevant. To the great detriment of his theory, Freud never came to grips with the unfavorable bearing of this key fact about the mnemonic effects of painfulness on the tenability of the following pillar of his theory of repression: When painful or forbidden experiences are forgotten, the forgetting is tantamount to their repression due to their negative affect, and thereby produces neurotic symptoms or other compromise formations.

The numerous and familiar occurrences of vivid and even obsessive recall of negative experiences pose a fundamental statistical and explanatory challenge to Freud that neither he nor his followers have ever met. Astonishingly, Freud thinks he can parry this basic statistical and explanatory challenge by an evasive dictum, as follows: "Mental life is the arena and battle-ground for mutually opposing purposes [of forgetting and remembering] (S.E. 1916–1917, 15:76) …; there is room for both. It is only a question … of what effects are produced by the one and the other" (S.E., 1916–1917, 15: 77). Indeed, just that question cries out for an answer from Freud if he is to make his case. Instead, he cavalierly left it to dangle epistemologically in limbo.

Freud's argument here is an evasive attempt to neutralize the ubiquitous refuting instances undermining his aforecited claim (S.E., 1901, 6:144) that "The tendency to forget what is disagreeable seems to me to be a quite universal one." And he tries to do so by peremptorily inventing ad hoc an opposing tendency to remember negatively charged experiences. But since this gambit clearly fails, he has forfeited his basis for his pivotal etiologic scenario that forbidden or aversive states of mind are usually repressed and thereby cause compromise formations, such as neurotic symptoms.

UNSUCCESSFUL REPRESSIONS AS PATHOGENS OF THE PSYCHONEUROSES

Let us articulate and scrutinize Breuer and Freud's 1893 argument, in their foundational *Preliminary Communication*, for the pathogenicity of unsuccessful repressions. There they wrote:

> For we found, to our great surprise at first, that each individual hysterical symptom immediately and permanently disappeared when we had succeeded in bringing clearly to light the memory of the event by which it was provoked and in arousing its accompanying affect, and when the patient had described that event in the greatest possible detail and had put the affect into words. Recollection without affect almost invariably produces no result. The psychical process which originally took place must be repeated as vividly as possible; it must be brought back to its status nascendi and then given verbal utterance.
>
> (S.E., 1893, 2:6–7).

Breuer and Freud make an important comment on their construal of this therapeutic finding:

> It is plausible to suppose that it is a question here of unconscious suggestion: the patient expects to be relieved of his sufferings by this procedure, and it is this expectation, and not the verbal utterance, which is the operative factor. This, however, is not so. (S.E., 1893, 2:7)

And their avowed reason is that, in 1881, that is, in the "'pre-suggestion' era," the cathartic method was used to remove separately distinct symptoms, "which sprang from separate causes" such that any one symptom disappeared only after the cathartic (abreactive) lifting of a particular repression. But Breuer and Freud do not tell us why the likelihood of a placebo effect should be deemed to be lower when several symptoms are wiped out seriatim, than in the case of getting rid of only one symptom. Thus, as is pointed out in Grünbaum (1993), to discredit the hypothesis of placebo effect, it would have been essential to have comparisons with treatment outcome from a suitable control group whose repressions are not lifted. If that control group were to fare equally well, treatment gains from psychoanalysis would then be placebo effects after all.

In sum, Breuer and Freud inferred that the therapeutic removal of neurotic symptoms was produced by the cathartic lifting of the patient's previously ongoing repression of the pertinent traumatic memory, not by the therapist's suggestion or some other placebo factor (see Grünbaum 1993). This claim can be codified as follows:

> *T. Therapeutic Hypothesis*: Lifting repressions of traumatic memories cathartically is causally relevant to the disappearance of neuroses.

As we saw, Breuer and Freud (S.E., 1893, 2:6) reported the immediate and permanent disappearance of each hysterical symptom after they cathartically lifted the repression of the memory of the trauma that occasioned the given symptom. They adduce this "evidence" to draw an epoch-making inductive etiologic inference, which postulates "a causal relation between the determining [repression of the memory of the] psychical trauma and the hysterical phenomenon" (S.E., 1893, 2:6). Citing the old scholastic dictum *Cessante causa cessat effectus* (When the cause ceases, its effect ceases), they invoke its contrapositive (S.E., 1893, 2:7), which states that as long as the effect (symptom) persists, so does its cause (the repressed memory of the psychical trauma). And they declare just that to be the pattern of the pathogenic action of the repressed psychical trauma. This trauma, we learn, is not a mere precipitating cause. Such a mere "agent provocateur" just releases the symptom, "which thereafter leads an independent existence." Instead, "the [repressed] memory of the trauma … acts like a foreign body which long after its entry must continue to be regarded as an agent that is still at work" (S.E., 1893, 2:6).

The upshot of their account is that their observations of positive therapeutic outcome from the abreactive lifting of repressions, which they interpret in the sense of their therapeutic hypothesis, spelled a paramount etiologic moral as follows:

> *E. Etiologic Hypothesis*: An ongoing repression accompanied by affective suppression is causally necessary for the initial pathogenesis and persistence of a neurosis.

Clearly, this etiologic hypothesis *E* permits the valid deduction of the therapeutic finding reported by Breuer and Freud as codified in their therapeutic hypothesis *T*: The cathartic lifting of the repressions of traumatic memories of events that occasion symptoms engendered the disappearance of the symptoms. And, as they told us explicitly (S.E., 1893, 2:6), this therapeutic finding is their evidence for their cardinal etiologic hypothesis *E*.

But this inductive argument is vitiated by what might be called the fallacy of crude hypothetico-deductive (H-D) pseudo-confirmation. Thus, note that the remedial action of aspirin consumption for tension headaches does not lend H-D support to the outlandish etiologic hypothesis that a hematolytic aspirin deficiency is a causal sine qua non for having tension headaches, although such remedial action is validly deducible from that bizarre hypothesis.

Wesley Salmon called attention to the fallacy of inductive causal inference from mere valid H-D deducibility by giving an example in which a deductively valid pseudo-explanation of a man's avoiding pregnancy can readily give rise to an H-D pseudo-confirmation of the addle-brained attribution of his nonpregnancy to his consumption of birth control pills. Salmon, in his coauthored 1971 book *Statistical Explanation and Statistical Relevance*, states the fatuous pseudo-explanation:

> John Jones avoided becoming pregnant during the past year, for he had taken his wife's birth control pills regularly, and every man who regularly takes birth control pills avoids pregnancy. (p. 34)

Plainly, this deducibility of John Jones's recent failure to become pregnant from the stated premises does not lend any credence at all to the zany hypothesis that this absence of pregnancy is causally attributable to his consumption of birth control pills. Yet it is even true that any men who consume such pills in fact never do become pregnant. Patently, as Salmon notes, the fly in the ointment is that men just do not become pregnant, whether they take birth control pills or not.

His example shows that neither the empirical truth of the deductively inferred conclusion and of the pertinent initial condition concerning Jones nor the deductive validity of the inference can provide bona fide confirmation of the causal hypothesis that male consumption of birth control pills prevents male pregnancy: That hypothesis would first have to meet other epistemic requirements, which it manifestly cannot do.

Crude H-D confirmationism is a paradise of spurious causal inferences, as illustrated by Breuer and Freud's unsound etiologic inference. Thus, psychoanalytic narratives are replete with the belief that a hypothesized etiologic scenario embedded in a psychoanalytic narrative of an analysand's affliction is made credible merely because the postulated etiology then permits the logical deduction or probabilistic inference of the neurotic symptoms to be explained.

THE PSYCHOANALYTIC METHOD OF CLINICAL INVESTIGATION BY FREE ASSOCIATION: IS IT BOTH INVESTIGATIVE AND THERAPEUTIC?

This method, the so-called "Fundamental Rule" of clinical investigation in the setting of psychoanalytic treatment, is the supposed microscope, and even X-ray tomograph, as it were, of the human mind. Freud devised it, when he became dissatisfied with the use of hypnosis, which Breuer and he had employed theretofore as their probe.

The rule of free association directs the patient to tell the analyst without reservation whatever comes to mind. Thus, it serves as the fundamental method of clinical investigation. We are told that by using this technique to unlock the floodgates of the unconscious, Freud was able to show that neuroses, dreams, and slips are caused by repressed motives. Just as in Breuer's cathartic use of hypnosis, it is a cardinal thesis of Freud's entire psychoanalytic enterprise that his method of free association has a twofold major capability, which is both investigative and therapeutic: (1) It can identify the unconscious causes of human thoughts and behavior, both abnormal and normal; and (2) by overcoming resistances and lifting repressions, it can remove the unconscious pathogens of neuroses and thus provide therapy for an important class of mental disorders.

But on what grounds did Freud assert that free association has the stunning investigative capability to be causally probative for etiologic research in psychopathology? Is it not too good to be true that one can put a psychologically disturbed person on the couch and fathom the etiology of her or his affliction by free association? As compared to fathoming the causation of major somatic diseases, that seems almost miraculous, if true at all. Freud tells us very clearly (S.E., 1900, 5:528) that his argument for his investigative tribute to free association as a means of uncovering the causation of neuroses is, at bottom, a therapeutic one going back to the cathartic method of treating hysteria.

In a nutshell, his argument for claiming that free associations are causally probative for etiologic research in psychopathology, as well as vehicles of therapy, is as follows: (1) As he and Breuer had contended, unsuccessful repressions are the pathogens of the psychoneuroses; (2) The supposedly free associations departing from the patient's neurotic symptoms uncover the pertinent repressions; (3) Hence the method of free associations can identify the pathogenic repressions, and in so doing, it lifts them and thereby provides therapy for the neurosis and its symptoms. But it behooves us to expand this argument with a view to then seeing why it fails in several respects, no matter how revealing the associative contents may otherwise be in regard to the patient's psychological preoccupations and personality dispositions.

Drawing on his joint work with Breuer, Freud first inferred that the therapeutic disappearance of the neurotic symptoms is causally attributable to the cathartic lifting of repressions by means of the method of free association. Relying on this key therapeutic hypothesis, he then drew two further major theoretical inferences: (1) The seeming removal of the neurosis by means of cathartically lifting repressions is good inductive evidence for postulating that repressions accompanied by affective suppression are themselves causally necessary for the very existence of a neurosis (S.E., 1893, 2:6–7), and (2) granted that such repressions are thus the essential causes of neurosis, and that the method of free association is uniquely capable of uncovering these repressions, this method is uniquely competent to identify the causes or pathogens of the neuroses.

But the argument fails for the following several reasons. In the first place, the durable therapeutic success on which it was predicated did not materialize, as Freud was driven to admit both relatively early and very late in his career (S.E., 1925, 20:27; 1937, 23:216–253). And indeed, over a century later, three currently practicing English psychoanalysts, (Fonagy et al., 2005, p. 367) conceded ruefully: "Notwithstanding a history of over 100 years, psychoanalytically informed psychological therapies have a poor evidence base." But even insofar as Freud achieved transitory therapeutic gain, it will be recalled that he had failed to rule out a rival hypothesis which undermines his attribution of such gain to the lifting of repressions by free association: the ominous rival hypothesis of placebo effect, which asserts that treatment ingredients other than insight into the patient's repressions—such as the mobilization of the patient's hope by the therapist—are responsible for any resulting improvement. (For a detailed account of the placebo concept in both psychiatry and medicine, see Grünbaum, 1993, chap. 3). Nor have other analysts ruled out the placebo hypothesis during the past century.

Last, but not least, the repression etiology is inductively ill-founded, as will be recalled, and will now be seen further. It is unavailing to the purported etiologic probativeness of free associations that they may lift repressions, because Freud failed to show that the latter are pathogenic. In sum, Freud's argument has forfeited its premises.

Long after the *Preliminary Communication* of 1893, Freud (S.E., 1914, 14:12) offered an argument in his theory of "Transference" for the pathogenic role of repressions, hailing that argument as the most unshakable proof for his sexual etiology of the neuroses. It is a commonplace that many, if not all, adults carry over (transfer) to their adult interactions with other people attitudes and notions that they had acquired in (early) childhood. In this vein, Freud elaborates on this phenomenon in the context of the interpersonal transactions between the psychoanalyst and the patient. Thus, we learn, the patient transfers onto his or her psychoanalyst feelings and thoughts that originally pertained to important figures in his or her earlier life. In this important sense, the fantasies woven around the psychoanalyst by the analysand, and quite generally the latter's conduct toward his or her doctor, are hypothesized to be thematically recapitulatory of childhood episodes. And by thus being recapitulatory, the patient's behavior during treatment can be said to exhibit a thematic kinship to such very early episodes. Therefore, when the analyst interprets these supposed reenactments, the ensuing interpretations are called transference interpretations.

Freud and his followers have traditionally drawn the following highly questionable causal inference: Precisely in virtue of being thematically recapitulated in the patient-doctor interaction, the hypothesized earlier scenario in the patient's life can cogently be held to have originally been a pathogenic factor in the patient's affliction. For example, in his 1909 case history of the "Rat-Man," Freud infers that a certain emotional conflict had originally been the precipitating cause of the patient's inability to work, merely because this conflict had been thematically reenacted in a fantasy the "Rat-Man" had woven around Freud during treatment.

Thus, in the context of Freud's transference interpretations, the thematic reenactment is claimed to show that the early scenario had originally been pathogenic. According to this major etiologic conclusion, the patient's thematic reenactment in the treatment setting is also asserted to be pathogenically recapitulatory by being pathogenic in the adult patient's here and now, rather than only thematically recapitulatory. Freud extols this dubious etiologic transference argument in his *On the History of the Psycho-Analytic Movement* (S.E., 1914, 14:12).

On the contrary, the patient's thematically recapitulatory behavior toward his or her doctor does not show that it is also pathogenically recapitulatory. The etiologic belief that it does so commits the "thematic affinity fallacy" (Grünbaum, 1993, p. 129; 2002, p. 134). How, for example, does the reenactment, during treatment, of a patient's early conflict show at all that the original conflict had been pathogenic in the first place? Indeed, it is epistemologically circular to infer the occurrence of infantile episodes from the adult patient's reports, and then to claim that these early episodes are thematically recapitulated in the adult analysand's conduct toward the analyst. Quite generally, how do transference phenomena focusing on the analyst show that a presumed current replica of a past event is pathogenic in the here and now?

Freud went on to build on the quicksand of his etiologic transference argument. It inspired two of his further fundamental tenets: first, the investigative thesis that the psychoanalytic dissection of the patient's behavior toward the analyst can reliably identify the original pathogens of his or her long-term neurosis; second, the cardinal therapeutic doctrine that the working through of the analysand's so-called transference neurosis is the key to overcoming his or her perennial problems.

THE PSYCHOANALYTIC THEORY OF DREAMING

As we learn from Freud's opening pages on his method of dream interpretation, he extrapolated the presumed causally probative role of free associations from being only a method of etiologic inquiry aimed at therapy, to serving likewise as an avenue for finding the purported unconscious causes of dreams (S.E., 1900, 4:100–101; 5:528). And in the same breath, he reports that when patients told him about their dreams while associating freely to their symptoms, he extrapolated his compromise model from neurotic symptoms to manifest dream contents. A year later, he carried out the same twofold extrapolation to include slips or bungled actions.

But what do free associations tell us about our dreams? Whatever the manifest content of dreams, they are purportedly wish-fulfilling in at least two logically distinct ways: For every dream D, there exists at least one normally unconscious infantile wish W such that: (1) W is the motivational cause of D; and (2) the manifest content of D graphically displays, more or less disguisedly, the state of affairs desired by W. As Freud opined: "When the latent dream-thoughts that are revealed by the analysis [via free association] of a dream are examined, one of them is found to stand out from among the rest … the isolated thought is found to be a wishful impulse" (S.E., 1925, 20:44). But as Clark Glymour (1983) has emphasized, Freud manipulated and doctored the free associations to yield a distinguished wish motive. Thus, Freud had declared with categorical universality (S.E. 1900, 4:134) "there cannot be any dreams but wishful [i. e., wish-generated] dreams"

Quite independently of Freud's abortive therapeutic argument for the causal probativeness of free association, he offered his analysis of his 1895 *Specimen Irma Dream* as a nontherapeutic argument for the method of free association as a cogent means of identifying hypothesized hidden, forbidden wishes to be motives of our dreams. But, in a detailed critique of that unjustly celebrated Irma Dream, it has been shown that Freud's account there is, alas, no more than a piece of false advertising for the following reasons:

- It does not deliver at all the promised vindication of the probativeness of free association.

- It does nothing toward warranting his foolhardy dogma that all dreams are wish-fulfilling in his stated sense.

- It does not even pretend that his alleged "Specimen Dream" is evidence for his compromise model of manifest-dream content.

- The inveterate and continuing celebration of Freud's analysis of his "Irma Dream" in the psychoanalytic literature as the paragon of dream interpretation is completely unwarranted, because it is mere salesmanship (Grünbaum 1984, pp. 216–239).

Moreover, careful studies have shown that the so-called free associations are not free but are strongly influenced by the psychoanalyst's subtle promptings to the patient (Grünbaum 1984). And recent memory research has shown further how patients and others can be induced to generate pseudo-memories, which are false but deemed veridical by the patients themselves (Goleman 1994). As a corollary of the latter epistemological defects of the method of free association, it appears that such associations cannot reliably vouch for the contents of presumed past repressions that are lifted by them.

Once Freud had clearly chained himself gratuitously to the universal wish monopoly of dream generation, his interpretations of dreams were constrained to reconcile wish-contravening dreams with the decreed universality of wish fulfillment. Such reconciliation demanded imperiously that all other parts and details of his dream theory be obligingly tailored to the governing wish dogma so as to sustain it. Yet Freud artfully obscured this dynamic of theorizing, while begging the methodological question (S.E., 1900, 4:135). Wish-contravening dreams include anxiety dreams, nightmares, and the so-called counter-wish dreams (S.E., 1900, 4:157). As an example of the latter, Freud reports a trial attorney's dream that he had lost all of his court cases (S.E., 1900, 4:152).

His initial 1900 statement of his dual wish fulfillment in a dream had been: "Thus, its content was the fulfillment of a wish and its motive was a wish" (S.E., 1900, 4:119). But the sense in which dreams are wish fulfilling overall is purportedly threefold rather than only twofold: One supposed motivating cause is the universal preconscious wish to sleep, which allegedly provides a generic causal explanation of dreaming as such and, in turn, makes dreaming the guardian of sleep (S.E., 1900, 4:234; 5:680); another is the individualized repressed infantile wish, which is activated by the day's residue and explains the particular manifest content of a given dream; furthermore, as already noted, that manifest content of the dream graphically displays, more or less disguisedly, the state of affairs desired by the unconscious wish. The disguise is supposedly effected by the defensive operation of the dream distortion of the content of forbidden unconscious wishes.

But this theorized distortion of the hypothesized latent content must not be identified with the very familiar phenomenological bizarreness of the manifest dream content! By achieving a compromise with the repressed wishes, the postulated distortion makes "plausible that even dreams with a distressing content are to be construed as wish fulfillments" (S.E., 1900, 4:159). Accordingly, Freud concedes: "The fact that dreams really have a secret meaning which represents the fulfillment of a wish must be proved afresh in each particular case by analysis" (S.E., 1900, 4:146).

THE HERMENEUTIC RECONSTRUCTION OF PSYCHOANALYSIS

In concert with the so-called hermeneutic German philosophers Karl Jaspers and Jürgen Habermas, the French philosopher Paul Ricoeur believed that victory can be snatched from the jaws of the scientific failings of Freud's theory by abjuring his scientific aspirations as misguided. Claiming pejoratively that Freud himself had "scientistically" misunderstood his own theoretical achievement, some hermeneuts misconstrue it as a semantic accomplishment by trading on the multiply ambiguous word *meaning* (Grünbaum 1999, 2002).

In Freud's theory, an overt symptom manifests one or more underlying unconscious causes and gives evidence for its cause(s), so that the sense or meaning of the symptom is constituted by its latent motivational cause(s). But this notion of meaning is different from the one appropriate to the context of communication, in which linguistic symbols acquire semantic meaning by being used deliberately to designate their referents. Clearly, the relation of being a manifestation, which the symptom bears to its cause, differs from the semantic relation of designation, which a linguistic symbol bears to its object.

The hermeneutic reconstruction of psychoanalysis slides illicitly from one of two familiar senses of the term "meaning" encountered in ordinary discourse to another. When a pediatrician says that a child's spots on the skin mean measles, the meaning of the symptom is constituted by one of its causes, much as in the Freudian case. Yet, when speaking of Freud's making sense of a patient's symptoms, the analyst Anthony Storr (1986) conflates the fathoming of the etiologic sense or meaning of a symptom with the activity of making semantic sense of a text, preposterously transmogrifying Freud into a semanticist: "Freud was a man of genius whose expertise lay in semantics" (p. 260). And Ricoeur even wrongly credits Freud's theory of repression with having provided, *malgré lui*, a veritable semantics of desire.

Relatedly, John R. Searle has noted illuminatingly in his 1990 book *Intentionality* that, unlike many mental states, language is not intrinsically intentional in Brentano's directed sense; instead, the intentionality (aboutness) of language is extrinsically imposed on it by deliberately decreeing it to function referentially. Searle points out that the mental states of some animals and of pre-linguistic very young children do have intrinsic intentionality but no linguistic referentiality.

Thus, it is a fundamental hermeneuticist error to slide illicitly from the intrinsic, non-semantic intentionality of (many, but not all) mental states to the imposed, semantic sort possessed by language. Moreover, some of the neurotic symptoms of concern to psychoanalysts, such as diffuse depression and manic, undirected elation even lack Brentano intentionality.

Yet some version of a hermeneutic reconstruction of the psychoanalytic enterprise has been embraced with alacrity by a considerable number of analysts no less than by professors in humanities departments of universities. Its psychoanalytic adherents see it as buying absolution for their theory and therapy from the criteria of validation mandatory for causal hypotheses in the empirical sciences, although psychoanalysis is replete with just such hypotheses. This form of escape from accountability also augurs ill for the future of psychoanalysis, because the methods of the champions of the hermeneutic reconstruction of psychoanalysis have not spawned a single new important hypothesis. Instead, their reconstruction is a negativistic ideological battle cry whose disavowal of Freud's scientific aspirations presages the death of his legacy from sheer sterility, at least among those who demand the validation of theories by cogent evidence.

FREUD ON THEISTIC RELIGION

In his 1933 essay *The Question of a Weltanschauung*, Freud appraised theism under the label of *religion* and wrote:

Religion is an attempt to master the sensory world in which we are situated by means of the wished world which we have developed within us as a result of biological and psychological necessities. But religion cannot achieve this. Its doctrines bear the imprint of the times in which they arose, the ignorant times of the childhood of humanity. Its consolations deserve no trust. Experience teaches us that the world is no nursery.

(S.E., 1933, 22:168).

And in his 1927 critique of theism entitled *The Future of an Illusion*, he stresses the logical priority of his atheism vis-à-vis his psychology of theism:

Nothing that I have said here against the truth-value of religions needed the support of psychoanalysis; it had been said by others long before analysis came into existence. If the application of the psycho-analytic method makes it possible to find a new argument against the truths of religion, tant pis [so much the worse] for religion; but defenders of religion will by the same right make use of psycho-analysis in order to give full value to the affective significance of religious doctrines.

(S.E., 1927, 21:37).

This avowed entitlement of religious partisans is presumably an allusion to Freud's friend Oskar Pfister, a Lutheran clergyman and avid champion of the use of psychoanalysis in pastoral work. Relatedly, though, like Freud, also a committed atheist, Karl Marx had expressed sympathy for the quest for solace in the face of the trials and tribulations of life. Marx wrote:

"Religion … is … the protest against real distress. Religion is the sigh of the oppressed creature, the heart of a heartless world, just as it is the spirit of an unspiritual situation. It is the opium of the people."

(FEUER 1959, P. 523).

Marx's use of the term *opium* here to characterize the consoling function of religion is descriptive rather than pejorative: In his time, opium was a commonly used anodyne, available without prescription.

Freud maintained that religious beliefs are engendered by the synergism of three significantly different sorts of powerful, relentless wishes. And for each of this trio of wishes, he conjectures a distinct scenario that specifies their content and mode of operation.

As he points out, the first set of these psychogenetic assumptions features wish motives that are largely conscious or manifest, instead of being the repressed wishes postulated by psychoanalytic theory. Accordingly, this component of Freud's triadic psychology of religion does not rely on any of his technical psychoanalytic teachings. But what are the relevant archaic conscious wishes? He explains eloquently in his 1927 book *The Future of an Illusion*:

… the terrifying impression of helplessness in childhood aroused the need for protection—for protection through love—which is provided by the father; and the recognition that this helplessness lasts throughout life made it necessary to cling to the existence of a father, but this time a more powerful one. Thus the benevolent rule of a divine Providence allays our fear of the dangers of life; the establishment of a moral world-order ensures the fulfillment of the demands of justice, which have so often remained unfulfilled in human civilization; and the prolongation of earthly existence in a future life provides the local and temporal framework in which these wish-fulfillments shall take place. Answers to the riddles that tempt the curiosity of man, such as how the universe began or what the relation is between body and mind, are developed in conformity with the underlying assumptions of this system

(S.E., 1927, 21:30).

Understandably, therefore, the protector, creator, and lawgiver are all rolled into one. No wonder, says Freud

(S.E., 1933, 22:163–164), that in one and the same breath, Immanuel Kant coupled the starry heavens above, and the moral law within as both being awe-inspiring. After all, Freud asks rhetorically, "what have the heavenly bodies to do with the question of whether one human creature loves another or kills him?" And he answers: "The same father (or parental agency) which gave the child life and guarded him against its perils, taught him as well what he might do and what he must leave undone" (S.E., 1933, 22:164).

Insofar as Freud's psychogenetic portrayal of religion depicts it as the product of conscious wishes, his account draws, not only on Ludwig A. Feuerbach, but also on commonsense psychology. After all, at least prima facie, it is rather a commonplace that people seek to avoid anxiety, and that they therefore tend to welcome the replacement of threatening beliefs by reassuring ones. Hence, for brevity, this component of Freud's triadic psychology of religion can be designated as the "*commonsense hypothesis*," which is not to say, however, that it is obviously true. Each of the other two components of this trinity is a set of psychoanalytic claims, asserting the operation of repressed motives. And yet they differ from each other, because one of them relies on Freud's theory of the psychosexual development of the human individual, while the other consists of ethnopsychological and psychohistorical averrals pertaining to the evolution of our species as a whole. Accordingly, the former psychoanalytic assumptions can be dubbed *ontogenetic*, while the latter can be labeled *phylogenetic*.

The legitimacy of any psychogenetic portrait of religious creeds depends on the evidential merit of the explanatory psychological hypotheses adduced by it. Even the commonsense component of Freud's triad is subject to this caveat. Invoking the criticisms of his great predecessors, he took it for granted that there is no cogency in any of the arguments for the existence of God offered by believers. But he coupled this philosophical judgment with the daring motivational claim that the faithful who nonetheless adduce such proofs had not, in fact, themselves been decisively moved by them, when giving assent to theism. Instead, he maintained, psychologically this assent is emotional or affective in origin.

Thus he is telling us that motivationally, the dialectical excogitations offered as existence proofs are post hoc rationalizations in which an elaborate intellectual façade takes the place of the deep-seated wishes that actually persuaded the theologians. Speaking epigrammatically in another context, Freud quotes Shakespeare's Falstaff as saying that reasons are "as plenty as blackberries" (S.E., 1914, 14:24).

It would seem to be basically a matter of empirical psychological fact whether the commonsense constituent of Freud's psychogenetic portrait of religion is sound. Yet, it is not clear how to design a cogent test even of this hypothesis. For note that the required design needs to have two epistemic capabilities as follows: (1) It needs to yield evidence bearing on the validity of the functional explanation of religious belief as being anxiety-reducing; presumably this explanation postulates some kind of stabilizing psychic servomechanism that reacts homeostatically to psychological threat; and, furthermore, (2) the required test needs to be at least able to rank-order the intensity of the wish to escape from anxiety, as compared to the motivational persuasiveness of the theological existence proofs. Perhaps oscillating anxieties of believers who went through cycles of doubt and belief have already gone some way toward meeting the first condition by Mill's method of concomitant variations. In any case, it would seem that an explicitly fideist belief in the existence of God—which avowedly is not based on any arguments—calls for psychological explanation in terms of wish motives!

The second requirement, however, seems to be a tall order indeed, although it does not warrant putting a cap on the ingenuity of potential empirical investigators. It, too, must be met, because of Freud's bold claim that even the best of the arguments for the existence of God would not have convinced the great minds who advanced them, unless stronger tacit wishes had carried the day, or had prompted these intellects to prevaricate. But note that, so far, Freud's portrayal of the motives for religious belief has studiously refrained from claiming that this belief is false, although he does avow its falsity later, after arguing that it is delusional. Hence whatever the empirical difficulties of validating his psychogenetic portrait, they are hardly tantamount to his commission of the hackneyed genetic fallacy, a mode of inference that he had explicitly rejected by means of disclaimers and qualifications.

In accord with his diagnosis of religion as an unwholesome childish fixation, Freud did advocate—as an experiment worth making—that children be given an irreligious education. But he took pains to say at once: "Should the experiment prove unsatisfactory I am ready to give up the reform and to return to my earlier, purely descriptive judgment that man is a creature of weak intelligence who is ruled by his instinctual wishes" (S.E., 1927, 21:48–49).

The two psychoanalytic components of Freud's triadic psychology of theism—its ontogeny and phylogeny—even more than its pre-psychoanalytic commonsense constituent, exigently require evidence for the existence of the two different sorts of wishes postulated by them. Insofar as even the very existence of these hidden desires is questionable, one remains less than convinced, when told that they contributed significantly to the initial genesis and later persistence of religious creeds. It is a corollary of the evidential scrutiny of the pertinent hypotheses that the psychoanalytic ontogeny of theism still lacks cogent evidential warrant (Grunbaum 1984, 1993).

But Freud was not content to confine himself to explanatory reliance on the conscious quest for anxiety reduction, and on his ontogeny of theism. Rather, he went on to develop a psychoanalytic phylogeny of theism (S.E., 1913, 13:100). In his view, this historical ethnopsychology is a valid extension of psychoanalysis.

As he sees it, by combining ethnography with psychoanalysis, he has discerned a third set of strong wishes that unite synergistically with the other two classes of this triad, and make the psychogenesis of belief in God the Father the more imperative. Therefore he proclaimed: "We now observe that the store of religious ideas includes not only wish-fulfillments but important historical recollections. This concurrent influence of past and present must give religion a truly incomparable wealth of power" (S.E., 1927, 21:42).

Daring and ingenious though it is, Freud's psychoanalytic phylogeny of theism is dubious, if only because it assumes a Lamarckian inheritance of repressed racial memories. Furthermore, contrary to the uniform evolution of religions required by his account, more recent historical scholarship seems to call for developmental pluriformity, as pointed out by Hans Küng in his 1979 book *Freud and the Problem of God* (p. 67).

Professor Edward Erwin's essay *Psychoanalysis: Theory, Therapy, and Method of Inquiry Created by Sigmund Freud (1856–1939)* herein covers the post Freudians.

See also Atheism; Brentano, Franz; Common Consent Arguments for the Existence of God; Dreams; Egoism and Altruism; Existential Psychoanalysis; Feuerbach, Ludwig Andreas; Habermas, Jürgen; Hermeneutics; Intentionality; Jaspers, Karl; Kant, Immanuel; Leibniz, Gottfried Wilhelm; Marx, Karl; Mill, John Stuart; Nietzsche, Friedrich; Philosophy of Religion; Plato; Popular Arguments for the Existence of God; Psychoanalysis; Psychoanalytic Theories, Logical Status of; Ricoeur, Paul; Salmon, Wesley; Schopenhauer, Arthur; Searle, John; Unconscious.

Bibliography

PRIMARY WORKS BY FREUD

Breuer, Josef, and Sigmund Freud. "On the Psychical Mechanism of Hysterical Phenomena: Preliminary Communication" (1893). In *The Standard Edition of the Works of Sigmund Freud*, Vol. 2, edited and translated by J. Strachey. London: Hogarth Press, 1953–1974.

"On the Psychical Mechanism of Hysterical Phenomena: A Lecture" (1893). In J. Strachey, *The Standard Edition of the Works of Sigmund Freud*, Vol. 3, edited and translated by J. Strachey. London: Hogarth Press, 1953–1974.

"Heredity and the Aetiology of the Neuroses" (1896). In *The Standard Edition of the Works of Sigmund Freud*, Vol. 3, edited and translated by J. Strachey. London: Hogarth Press, 1953–1974.

"The Interpretation of Dreams" (1900). In *The Standard Edition of the Works of Sigmund Freud*, Vols. 4 (Part I) and 5 (Part II), edited and translated by J. Strachey. London: Hogarth Press, 1953–1974.

"The Psychopathology of Everyday Life" (1901). In *The Standard Edition of the Works of Sigmund Freud*, Vol. 6, edited and translated by J. Strachey. London: Hogarth Press, 1953–1974.

"The Claims of Psycho-Analysis to Scientific Interest" (1913). In *The Standard Edition of the Works of Sigmund Freud*, Vol. 13, edited and translated by J. Strachey. London: Hogarth Press, 1953–1974.

"The Return of Totemism in Childhood" (1913). In *The Standard Edition of the Works of Sigmund Freud*, Vol. 13, edited and translated by J. Strachey. London: Hogarth Press, 1953–1974.

"On the History of the Psycho-Analytic Movement" (1914). In *The Standard Edition of the Works of Sigmund Freud*, Vol. 14, edited and translated by J. Strachey. London: Hogarth Press, 1953–1974.

"Repression" (1915). In *The Standard Edition of the Works of Sigmund Freud*, Vol. 14, edited and translated by J. Strachey. London: Hogarth Press, 1953–1974.

"Introductory Lectures on Psycho-Analysis" (1915–1917). In *The Standard Edition of the Works of Sigmund Freud*, Vol. 15 (Parts I and II) and Vol. 16 (Part III), edited and translated by J. Strachey. London: Hogarth Press, 1953–1974.

"A Difficulty in the Path of Psycho-Analysis" (1917). In *The Standard Edition of the Works of Sigmund Freud*, Vol. 17, edited and translated by J. Strachey. London: Hogarth Press, 1953–1974.

"A Short Account of Psychoanalysis" (1924). In *The Standard Edition of the Works of Sigmund Freud*, Vol. 19, edited and translated by J. Strachey. London: Hogarth Press, 1953–1974.

"An Autobiographical Study" (1925). In *The Standard Edition of the Works of Sigmund Freud*, Vol. 20, edited and translated by J. Strachey. London: Hogarth Press, 1953–1974.

"The Future of an Illusion" (1927). In *The Standard Edition of the Works of Sigmund Freud*, Vol. 21, edited and translated by J. Strachey. London: Hogarth Press, 1953–1974.

"New Introductory Lectures on Psychoanalysis" (1933). In *The Standard Edition of the Works of Sigmund Freud*, Vol. 22, edited and translated by J. Strachey. London: Hogarth Press, 1933.

"Analysis Terminable and Interminable" (1937). In *The Standard Edition of the Works of Sigmund Freud*, Vol. 23, edited and translated by J. Strachey. London: Hogarth Press, 1953–1974.

SECONDARY WORKS

Assoun, Paul-Laurent. *Freud, La Philosophie, et les Philosophes*. Paris: Presses Universitaires de France, 1995.

Brentano, Franz. *Psychology from an Empirical Standpoint*. New York: Routledge and Kegan Paul, 1995.

Eagle, Morris N. "The Psychoanalytic and the Cognitive Unconscious." In *Theories of the Unconscious and Theories of the Self*, edited by R. Stern. Hillsdale, NJ: Analytic Press, 1987.

Ellenberger, Henri. *The Discovery of the Unconscious*. New York: Basic Books, 1970.

Fonagy, Peter. "The Outcome of Psychodynamic Psychotherapy for Psychological Disorders." *Clinical Neuroscience Research* 40 (2005): 367.

Gay, Peter. *A Godless Jew: Freud, Atheism, and the Making of Psychoanalysis*. New Haven, CT.: Yale University Press, 1987.

Glymour, Clark. "The Theory of Your Dreams." In *Physics, Philosophy, and Psychoanalysis: Essays in Honor of Adolf Grünbaum*, edited by R.S. Cohen and L. Laudan. Dordrecht, Netherlands: Reidel, 1983.

Goleman, Daniel. "Miscoding Is Seen as the Root of False Memories." *New York Times* May 31 (1994): C1 and C8.

Grünbaum, Adolf. "Critique of Psychoanalysis." In *The Freud Encyclopedia, Theory, Therapy, and Culture*, edited by E. Erwin. New York; London: Routledge, 2002.

Grünbaum, Adolf. *The Foundations of Psychoanalysis: A Philosophical Critique*. Berkeley: University of California Press, 1984.

Grünbaum, Adolf. "The Hermeneutic Versus the Scientific Conception of Psychoanalysis: An Unsuccessful Effort to Chart A Via Media for the Human Sciences." In *Einstein Meets Magritte, An Interdisciplinary Reflection: The White Book of Einstein Meets Magritte*, edited by D. Aerts. Dordrecht, Netherlands: Kluwer Academic, 1999.

Grünbaum, Adolf. *Validation in the Clinical Theory of Psychoanalysis: A Study in the Philosophy of Psychoanalysis*. Madison, CT: International Universities Press, 1993.

Küng, Hans. *Freud and the Problem of God*. New Haven, CT: Yale University Press, 1979.

Leibniz, Gottfried W. *New Essays on Human Understanding* (1705). Translated by P. Remnant and J. Bennett. Cambridge, U.K.: Cambridge University Press, 1981.

Salmon, Wesley. *Statistical Explanation and Statistical Relevance*. Pittsburgh, PA: University of Pittsburgh Press, 1971.

Searle, John R. *Intentionality*. New York: Cambridge University Press, 1990.

Solms, Mark, and Michael Saling. *A Moment of Transition: Two Neuroscientific Articles by Sigmund Freud*. New York: Karnac Books, 1990.

Storr, Anthony. "Human Understanding and Scientific Validation." *Behavioral and Brain Sciences* 9 (1986): 259–260.

Zentner, Marcel. *Die Flucht ins Vergessen: Die Anfänge der Psychoanalyse Freuds bei Schopenhauer*. Darmstadt, Germany: Wissenschaftliche Buchgessellschaft, 1995.

Adolf Grünbaum (2005)

FRIENDSHIP

FRIENDSHIP AND ITS PLACE IN THE MORAL DEBATE

Friendship is a central theme in ancient ethics, most notably in Aristotelian ethics, with two of the ten books of Aristotle's *Nicomachean Ethics* (Books VIII and IX) (1985) devoted to the subject. But modern moral philosophy (from the mid-eighteenth century to the later part of the twentieth century) largely overlooked the role of friendship in moral life, in part because of the dominance of the impartialist stance of utilitarian and Kantian moral theory. Those theories also influenced the study of Aristotelian ethics. In the late 1970s and early 1980s, this trend shifted, in part due to a confluence of causes—renewed interest in Aristotelian ethics for its own sake, the development of modern *virtue ethics*, and the rise of feminist ethical theory. A seminal article by John Cooper on Aristotelian friendship (1977) helped to make Aristotle's account accessible, and especially emphasized the role of friendship in a morally reflective life. Aristotle's account remains the *locus classicus* for understanding the nature of friendship and its place in the moral life; however, before turning to that account, some background is important for understanding its resuscitation in the contemporary moral debate.

THE NEGLECT OF FRIENDSHIP IN MODERN MORAL PHILOSOPHY

From a classical utilitarian view, in the broad tradition of Jeremy Bentham (1748–1832), an agent is obligated to do that which promotes maximally desired outcomes for the greatest number of people, irrespective of standing commitments to friends and family or other personal projects and pursuits. One is to view oneself as a causal lever, Bernard Williams (1963) charged, of optimal outcomes. Thus, if one can save one's spouse or the next inventor of a cure for AIDS, one may be obligated, on a strict utility theory, to save the latter over the former. Rule utilitarians try to counter the unwelcome result, arguing that a general *rule* or *practice* of taking care of kith and kin is an overall best way of promoting general welfare. But a strict act utilitarian (that is, one committed to assessing the overall good consequences produced by discrete acts) cannot consistently make this response.

From a Kantian view, drawn primarily from Immanuel Kant's early work *The Groundwork from the Metaphysic of Morals* (1785), motives of friendship may be acted upon in morally permissible ways when properly constrained by the impartial point of view of the Categorical Imperative. But even then, such motives, like those of sympathy or other inclinations, lack intrinsic moral worth of their own. So, to adapt a well-known example from Michael Stocker (1976) on a Kantian view, one acts in a morally worthy way when one visits a hospitalized friend not out of friendship, but out of duty. In later writings, Kant seems to soften his view, arguing that acting from friendship may be an important way of realizing the more general, obligatory end of beneficence. Still, Kant is ever wary that intimacy can undermine mutual respect; thus, friendship, is a constant teeter-totter between getting close and keeping at bay: "For we can regard love as attraction and respect as repulsion, and if the principle of love commands friends to come together, the principle of respect requires them to keep each other at a proper distance" (1976, p. 470).

The difficulty of fitting friendship squarely into modern moral theory led many to return to Aristotle's account. This renewal of interest coincides with a feminist push to take seriously the role of interpersonal relationships and caring in a moral point of view. In particular, the influential work by psychologist Carol Gilligan (1982) galvanized philosophers of various stripes to begin to look at friendship and attachment relations as important arenas of moral agency and moral development. Thus, in a sense, the renewed interest in friendship brought with it a rediscovery of the kind of moral psychology that is an integral part of ancient ethics.

FRIENDSHIP IN ARISTOTELIAN ETHICS

The framing question of Aristotelian ethics, like that of most ancient ethics, is what constitutes flourishing or happiness (*eudaimonia*) for human beings? Aristotle's answer is that happiness is a composite of virtuous activity and external goods; chief among those external goods is the relational good of friendship, or *philia*. Humans are by nature "social creatures," Aristotle says, and self-sufficiency is always relational. Even if it turned out that the kind of virtuous or excellent activity most fitting for humans was contemplative and not civic or practical,

people would still contemplate best in the company of others (*NE* 1177a33).

According to Aristotle's definition, *philia* is a mutually acknowledged reciprocation of affection and good will on the basis of some ongoing specific interest, such as pleasure, utility, or virtue. Chosen friendship grounded in virtue or good character is the paradigmatic and most stable form of friendship. It is a friendship dedicated to the whole person and committed to the joint project of good living. The best sort of friends "live together" and "spend their days together," not as cattle grazing the same pasture, but "by sharing in argument and thought" (*NE* 1170b11–12). Given the intensity of these ideal friendships, one can reasonably expect to cultivate only a few at a given time. There is much good sense in these views: People are attracted to others on the basis of common pursuits and affinities and show mutual practical concern and good will within the context of the friendship. Were the friendship to dissolve, so, too, would the degree and nature of practical concern for the other.

Aristotle has sometimes been criticized for viewing friendship as a kind of mutual admiration society, and this, in part, because of his remark that a friend is "another self" or a "second self" (*NE* 1170b7). But in the context of his larger discussion, his claim is that people can rely on the best sort of friends to critically see themselves. Friends, he insists, are essential for the process of self-knowledge and for sustaining activities with a kind of zest and zeal that would be hard to muster individually (*NE* 1170a4–6). The best kind of friendship, he insists, is a sphere for moral growth and learning throughout life. And it is so, he concedes, even if friendship, as a kind of external good, exposes the individual to risk of loss and vulnerability. Kant's later worry that intimacy might erode self-sufficiency or autonomy is not Aristotle's concern. People's lives would lack luster without friends and loved ones. One misunderstands the nature of human happiness if one arms against the losses that attachments bring.

EMPATHY AND FRIENDSHIP

However, there is an aspect of friendship that Aristotle never fully articulates, though it is central to a viable conception of friendship. And this is the notion of empathy, or better, mutual empathy. Part of the craving of friendship is to be in synchrony with another. People want their closest friends to track their hearts and minds. They want to know that another can feel their joy or anguish and share concerns and wishes in a way that is psychologically deeper than just formally sharing ends or activities. They want to know that without too much struggle, a friend can be on the same page and convey that fact in a way that makes it clear that they are understood.

Empathy is an early-twentieth-century psychology word, a Greco translation (from *empatheia*) of the German *Einfülhlung*, to feel one's way into another. A century and a half earlier, the Scottish moral sentiment theorists David Hume and Adam Smith used the term sympathy to mean something similar. For Hume sympathy is a kind of vicarious arousal, a congruent feeling that allows access into others' minds. His model is mechanical: One is connected as if by a cord. A tug at one end causes a reverberation at the other. In this way, one "catches" another's feelings, as if by contagion. Adam Smithproposed a more cognitive account: Feeling another's pain or anguish through an act of imagination; to trade "places in fancy" (1968, p. 4). And this requires some analogical reasoning. As he puts it, one brings another's experiences "home" to oneself; bring the case back to one's own "breast" (1968, p. 4-5). More precisely, one conjures up in one's own mind, through associations and memories, what it would be like to stand in the other's shoes. The process, while cognitive, is not emotionally flat. One must feel something of what the other is feeling, "beat time" with the other, as Smith says (1968, p. 140,146,167). Moreover, to really understand the other's mind, it is not enough for imagination to transport *oneself* into *the other's* shoes. One may have to become *the other* in *the other's* shoes. As Smith puts it in one point, one has to "become in some measure same person with him" (1968, p. 4).

Whether one thinks of empathy as congruent feeling or imaginative transport, one expects close friendship to have some degree of attunement of this sort. The demand is not for a friend to be a mind reader of one's most concealed thoughts; that would be both psychologically implausible and, moreover, an invasion of privacy and autonomy. The point is that one wants some sense of being in sync, of being understood by another in a way that truly makes a life shared. Granted, this can become narcissistic—reminiscent of what an infant demands of a parent and what a parent offers an infant as part of the basic formation of the parent-child bond. Thus, shared eye gaze and reciprocal smiling are part of the early moments of learning mutuality. But a touch of this is what most people still wish for into their adult years. The craving seems a reasonable part of close friendship.

See also Aristotle; Bentham, Jeremy; Hume, David; Kant, Immanuel; Love; Loyalty; Smith, Adam; Virtue Ethics; Williams, Bernard.

Bibliography

Aristotle. *Nicomachean Ethics*, translated by W. D. Ross, rev. J. O. Urmson. In *The Complete Works of Aristotle: The Revised Oxford Translation*, Vol. 2, Bks. VIII, IX, edited by Jonathan Barnes. Princeton: Princeton University Press, 1985. From the same set by Oxford, also see Aristotle's *Eudemian Ethics*. Translated by J. Solomon. VII. 1–2; *Magna Moralia*. Translated by St. G. Stock, II.16; *Rhetoric*, translated by W. R. Roberts, II.4.

Badhwar, N. K., ed. *Friendship: A Philosophical Reader*. Ithaca, NY: Cornell University Press, 1993.

Blum, Lawrence. *Friendship, Altruism, and Morality*. Boston: Routledge & Kegan Paul, 1980.

Cicero, Marcus Tullius. *De amicitia*. Translated by W. A. Falconer. London: Heinemann, 1923.

Cooper, John M. "Aristotle on the Forms of Friendship." *Review of Metaphysics* 30 (1977): 618–648. A revised and condensed version of both original articles appears as "Aristotle on Friendship" in *Essays on Aristotle's Ethics*, edited by A. O. Rorty. Berkeley: University of California Press, 1980.

Cooper, John M. "Friendship and the Good in Aristotle." *Philosophical Review* 86 (1977): 290–315. Reprinted in *Aristotle's Ethics: Critical Essays*, edited by Nancy Sherman. Lanham, MD: Rowman and Littlefield, 1999.

Friedman, Marilyn. *What are Friends For? Feminist Perspectives on Personal Relationships and Moral Theory*. Ithaca: Cornell University Press: 1993.

Gilligan, Carol. *In a Different Voice: Psychological Theory and Women's Development*. Cambridge, MA: Harvard University Press, 1982.

Hume, David. *A Treatise of Human Nature*, edited by L.A. Selby-Bigge. Oxford: Oxford University Press, 1968 (1739).

Pakaluk, Michael. *Other Selves: Philosophers on Friendship*. Indianapolis, IN: Hackett, 1991.

Kant, Immanuel. *Doctrine of Virtue*. Part II of *The Metaphysic of Morals*. Translated by Mary J. Gregor. Philadelphia: University of Pennsylvania Press, 1964 (1797).

Kant, Immanuel. *Groundwork of the Metaphysics of Morals*. Translated by H.J. Paton. New York: Harper and Row, 1964 (1785).

Sherman, Nancy. "Empathy and Imagination." In *Philosophy of Emotions*. Edited by Peter French and Howard Wettstein. Midwest Studies in Philosophy, Vol. 22. Notre Dame, IN: University of Notre Dame Press, 1998, p. 82–199.

Sherman, Nancy. "The Shared Life." Chap. 4 in *Fabric of Character* Oxford: Oxford University Press, 1989, p. 118–157; *Philosophy and Phenomenological Research* 47 (1987): 589–613.

Sherman, Nancy. "The Shared Voyage." Chap. 5 in *Making a Necessity of Virtue: Aristotle and Kant on Virtue*. Cambridge, MA: Cambridge University Press, 1997, 187–238.

Smart, J. J. C., and Bernard Williams. *Utilitarianism, For and Against*. Cambridge, U.K.: Cambridge University Press, 1973.

Smith, Adam. *The Theory of Moral Sentiments*. New York: Prome Thesus Books, 2000 (1759).

Stocker, Michael. "The Schizophrenia of Modern Ethical Theories." *Journal of Philosophy* 73 (1976): 453–466.

Stocker, Michael. "Values and Purposes: The Limits of Teleology and the Ends of Friendship." *Journal of Philosophy*

78 (1981): 747–765. Reprinted in *Friendship: A Philosophical Reader*, edited by N. K. Badhwar. Ithaca, NY: Cornell University Press, 1993.

Telfer, E. "Friendship." *Proceedings of the Aristotelian Society* Supp. (1970–1971): 223–241.

Nancy Sherman (2005)

FRIES, JAKOB FRIEDRICH
(1773–1843)

Jakob Friedrich Fries, the German critical philosopher, was born in Barby, Saxony. An avowed follower and elaborator of Immanuel Kant's philosophy, Fries emphasized the analytical, descriptive, and methodological aspects of the critical philosophy as against the constructive and speculative idealism of such contemporaries as K. L. Reinhold, Johann Gottlieb Fichte, Friedrich Schelling, and G. W. F. Hegel. He received his secondary and college education at the Moravian Academy in Niesky. From his Pietistic Moravian background Fries preserved a conviction of the importance of "pure feeling" as a manifestation of "the infinite in the finite." At Niesky he was given a thorough grounding in mathematics and in the natural sciences. There he was also introduced to a version of Kant's philosophy based on Reinhold's, which he early sought to correct and supplement by secretly reading in Kant's own writings. In 1795 he went to Leipzig, where he studied under the philosopher-physician Ernst Plattner.

The influence of Plattner and of F. H. Jacobi accounts for Fries's emphasis on the concept of self-observation. From 1797 on, Fries continued his studies in mathematics and physics at Jena, where he also attended Fichte's lectures. "I listened to Fichte, took notes, then rushed home and wrote rebuttals," he later recalled. These critical notes were incorporated into his polemical writings. As early as 1798, in the article "Über das Verhältniss der empirischen Psychologie zur Metaphysik" (On the relation of empirical psychology to metaphysics; in *Erhard Schmids Psychologische Magazin*, Vol. 3), he argued that the task of philosophy is essentially descriptive rather than speculative.

Following his studies at Jena, Fries served as a private tutor in Switzerland, then returned to Jena as a docent in 1801, submitting a habilitation thesis on intellectual intuition. The polemical tract *Reinhold, Fichte und Schelling* (Leipzig, 1803) established his reputation as a critic of the romantic orthodoxy in German philosophy. From Jena he was called to a professorship in philosophy and mathematics at Heidelberg. That year he published *Wissen,*

Glaube und Ahndung (Knowing, faith and presage; Jena, 1805), a popular exposition of his doctrine of a threefold approach to reality. This was followed, during the years 1806–1807, by his chief work, the three-volume *Neue Kritik der Vernunft* (New critique of reason; Heidelberg, 1807; 2nd ed., *Neue oder anthropologische Kritik der Vernunft*, Heidelberg, 1828–1831), in which he attempted to correct and restate the Kantian critique of speculative and practical reason as a program of psychological self-observation or "anthropology."

PROGRESSIVE POLITICAL VIEWS

A decisive shift in Fries's career occurred in 1816, when he returned to Jena to a professorship in theoretical philosophy. Under the tolerant and liberal regime of Duke Karl August, he published his *Ethik* (Heidelberg, 1818), a work in which he stressed the ideal of individual liberty and political equality as a consequence of the Kantian doctrine of the dignity proper to a human being. In pamphlets and lectures and at student gatherings during this period, Fries argued for constitutional and representative government, extolled the political wisdom of the "people," opposed the conservatism of student secret societies, and advocated German unification. This activity, climaxed by his participation in the Wartburg Festival of October 18, 1817—a demonstration by student liberals that included a ceremonial burning of "reactionary" books—inevitably incurred the wrath of the Austrian and Prussian governments. It also elicited scornful comments from the politically more orthodox Hegel, who in his *Philosophy of Right* (translated by J. M. Knox, Oxford, 1942) downgraded Fries as "a ringleader of those hosts of superficiality, of these self-styled 'philosophers,'" and attacked his Wartburg speech as "the quintessence of shallow thinking … a broth of 'heart, friendship, and inspiration.'" By 1819 the conservative opposition had prevailed upon Karl August, and Fries was suspended from his position at Jena. He had earlier lost hope that he would be offered the chair of philosophy at Berlin, which in 1818 went to Hegel.

Although Fries was eventually allowed to resume teaching at Jena (he taught science from 1824 and philosophy from 1825 on) and held this post until his death, the 1819 suspension was the final turn in his estrangement and isolation from the intellectual currents of the period. From then on, supported by a small following, he devoted his life to studies of mathematics, physics, and psychology, to systematization of his metaphysics and ethics, and to a rewriting of the history of philosophy on the theme of "progress in scientific development." To this period belong *Die mathematische Naturphilosophie* (Heidelberg, 1822); *System der Metaphysik* (Heidelberg, 1824); *Handbuch der psychischen Anthropologie* (2 vols., Jena, 1820 and 1821); and *Die Geschichte der Philosophie* (2 vols., Halle, 1837–1840).

APPROACHES TO REALITY

Fries followed Immanuel Kant in the overall architectonic of his philosophy and in specific doctrines. Corresponding to Kant's three Critiques, he distinguished three approaches or attitudes toward reality—knowing, faith, and presage, or presentiment (*Ahndung*). We know things only as appearances to a peculiarly human sensibility and understanding. But we have faith in the reality of a world of real moral agents under eternal moral laws. Our understanding is aware of this world only negatively, as a limitation of the empirical world, through the Ideas of Reason. Finally, through presage or presentiment, a pure and disinterested feeling akin to the experience of the beautiful and the sublime, we are given the assurance that the world of appearances and the real world are not two worlds but one, and that the former is a manifestation of the latter—a finite projection of the infinite into the finite.

TYPES OF KNOWLEDGE

Within the sphere of knowing, Fries distinguished two levels: original or immediate knowledge, and reflective or mediate knowledge. The types of mediate knowledge are given in the Kantian forms of judgment: analytic, synthetic a posteriori, and synthetic a priori. We must also distinguish three types of immediate knowledge. An empirical intuition is a direct awareness of the sensory given; a pure intuition is a direct awareness of space and time as empty containers of sensible entities; and an immediate metaphysical cognition is the direct but nonintuitive awareness of principles involving the categories of the understanding (for example, the principle of causality or the principle of the permanence of substance). No attempt to reduce cognitions of the second and third types to cognitions of the first type can ever succeed. Space and time are the forms of our empirical intuitions; the categories are the forms of human understanding. Fries thus shared with Kant the critical solution of the problem of a priori knowledge. He also shared with Kant the rejection of both the empiricist and the intellectual intuitionist solutions of the problem.

METAPHYSICAL KNOWLEDGE

Fries departed from Kant, however, in his interpretation of the basis for the critical solution in the case of a priori metaphysical knowledge. Fries found inconsistency and circularity in Kant's attempt to validate categories and to "prove" the principles of the understanding by referring them to "the possibility of experience." If these are indeed principles, no proof could be required and none would be sufficient. Kant succumbed, in Fries's judgment, to the ancient rationalist prejudice that everything can be proved and that all truths can be reduced to a single principle—in Kant's case, the concept of possible experience. All that is possible, Fries objected, is to display the status of certain cognitions *as* a priori and necessary. "I do not prove," he explained, "that all substance is permanent; rather I point to the fact that the principle of the permanence of substance lies in every finite mind" (*Neue oder anthropologische Kritik der Vernunft*, 2nd ed., Vol. I). In Kant's language, only a "metaphysical deduction" (the answer to the question, "What is the case?") is possible.

DISCOVERY OF METAPHYSICAL PRINCIPLES

The regression to metaphysical principles is not an easy task, for unlike empirical and pure intuitions, which are clear and readily available to consciousness, metaphysical principles lie "concealed and obscure" in the depths of human reason. Fries described this regression as a process of self-observation or "psychic anthropology," and likened it to experimental physics insofar as the latter aims to discover the general law involved in specific physical phenomena. Kant, accordingly, misunderstood the function of critical philosophy and the status of the judgments that constitute it, for whereas the truths that critical philosophy aims to uncover are nonempirical and necessary, the critique itself is empirical and fallible. Fries admired the long "subjective" deductions of the categories in the first edition of Kant's *Critique of Pure Reason* but was skeptical of the short "objective" deductions of the second edition.

PROOF

A complete theory of proof must, therefore, distinguish three kinds: (1) demonstration, or the reduction of a "reflective" or "mediate" cognition to an intuition (pure or empirical); (2) proof, or the reduction of one mediate cognition to another; and (3) deduction, or a regressive analysis that traces a given cognition to its ground in immediate metaphysical knowledge. Just as in the case of demonstration, in which no question can arise concerning the validity of the intuitions themselves, so too, in the case of deduction, no question can possibly arise as to the validity of our immediate metaphysical knowledge. A deduction is, of course, something fallible; closer scrutiny may later reveal a disparity between a given cognition and its supposed ground. But the same danger exists for demonstration—in this case minimally.

TRUTH

Truth is a matter of correspondence between thought and object, but the object is not something transcendent; it is simply an immediate cognition. Truth is a relation between two levels of cognition. With regard to immediate knowledge itself we must accept the principle of "Reason's self-reliance" (*Selbstvertrauen der Vernunft*), that is, that we possess such knowledge and that it is intrinsically valid.

FRIES'S "PSYCHOLOGISM"

Fries's restatement of the Kantian deduction has often been attacked as psychologism. If psychologism is understood as the attempt to find the validity of human beliefs in their psychological causes and in the laws of association, the charge is unfair. Fries was not a proponent of psychologism in that sense: For him, the validity of immediate knowledge lay in its logical character, universality, and necessity, not in its causal origins. Indeed, Fries wrote critically against such contemporary advocates of psychologism as Friedrich Eduard Beneke, with whom he was sometimes mistakenly compared. At the same time, he did seem to suggest that logical character can be gathered from mere psychological observation of our mental processes. And in this connection he has been justly criticized for confusing a mental act with its logical content. Certainly the process that Fries described as "anthropology" would be more accurately described today as "logical" or "phenomenological" analysis. Fries was perhaps misled by the analogy between a logical regress to presuppositions in philosophy and the heuristic regress (induction) to general hypotheses and theories in physics.

SCIENCE AND MATHEMATICS

In the fields of mathematics, physics, and psychology, Fries's thought was highly original and expertly worked out. He had a clear conception of a philosophy of mathematics and physics as an independent discipline, and anticipated the modern distinction between a theory and a metatheory. In his theory of nature he attacked Kant's concessions to teleology and argued for a thoroughgoing mechanism that would also encompass the biological sciences. His psychological investigations extended into the study of pathological phenomena. He took note of the distinction between inherited and acquired, as well as between continuous and periodic, mental disorders and argued for the physiological basis of mental illness—concepts that were by no means as current in Fries's time as they are in ours and that were unfortunately ignored by the psychiatric practitioners of his day.

FRIES'S INFLUENCE

Fries was succeeded at Jena by his pupil E. F. Apelt, who published a masterly textbook of Friesian metaphysics and in 1847 established the journal *Abhandlungen der Fries'schen Schule*, which served for two years as a forum for critical, scientifically oriented philosophy. There was a revival of interest in Fries and in his approach to Kant in the years preceding and immediately following World War I, centering about Leonard Nelson at Göttingen, who shared Fries's scientific outlook and reacted to the idealist Neo-Kantian orthodoxy in the German universities of his time much as Fries had reacted to Fichte, Schelling, and Hegel. The theologian Rudolf Otto, an early associate of Nelson, developed Fries's concept of "presage" in his influential book *Das Heilige* (*The Idea of the Holy*, Gotha, 1917). In 1904 Nelson established a new series of the *Abhandlungen der Fries'schen Schule* of which six volumes appeared before publication was discontinued in 1937. National Socialism proved itself as inimical to Nelson's school as Klemens von Metternich's political reaction had been to Fries's. In 1958 Julius Kraft, a student of Nelson's, founded the philosophical journal *Ratio* as a continuation of the *Abhandlungen*.

Although Fries's influence was and remains limited, part of the interest that his philosophy holds for the modern reader lies in its analogues with, and anticipations of, positions and problems that were central in twentieth-century thought, especially in England and the United States. There is, first, an obvious but quite unexplored analogy between Fries's psychological method and Edmund Husserl's phenomenology. Moreover, the view that metaphysical principles can only be exhibited as such but not proved has been variously defended by R. G. Collingwood and by representatives of the Oxford school of linguistic analysis. There are also apparent counterparts of Fries's "self-reliance of Reason" in G. E. Moore's appeal to common sense, in the positivists' appeal to a level of incorrigible knowledge, and in Ludwig Wittgenstein's famous dictum that "the propositions of our ordinary language are in perfect order." Indeed, the question of the status of the propositions employed by the critical or analytical philosopher, which was first raised by Fries, has come under much discussion in recent years, under the heading "the problem of analysis."

See also Collingwood, Robin George; Faith; Fichte, Johann Gottlieb; Hegel, Georg Wilhelm Friedrich; Husserl, Edmund; Jacobi, Friedrich Heinrich; Kant, Immanuel; Knowledge, A Priori; Moore, George Edward; Nelson, Leonard; Neo-Kantianism; Otto, Rudolf; Psychologism; Reinhold, Karl Leonhard; Schelling, Friedrich Wilhelm Joseph von; Wittgenstein, Ludwig Josef Johann.

Bibliography

WORKS BY FRIES

A list of all Fries's writings will be found in *Abhandlungen der Fries'schen Schule*, n.s., 6 (1937): 473–495.

With G. König and Lutz Geldsetzer. *Sämtliche Schriften.* Aalen: Scientia Verlag, 1967.

With D. Z. Phillips. *Dialogues on Morality and Religion.* Totowa, NJ: Barnes & Noble, 1982.

With Frederick Gregory. *Knowledge, Belief, and Aesthetic Sense.* Köln: Jürgen Dinter, Verlag für Philosophie, 1989.

On Fries's life and writings, the fundamental work remains E. L. T. Henke, *Jakob Friedrich Fries* (Leipzig, 1867). The last detailed study of Fries's theory of knowledge is in Alfred Kastil, *Fries' Lehre von der Unmittelbaren Erkenntnis*, a monograph that constitutes *Abhandlungen der Fries'schen Schule* 4 (1912). For a short critical assessment of the same subject, see Ernst Cassirer, *Das Erkenntnissproblem in der Philosophie und Wissenschaft der neueren Zeit* (Berlin, 1923), Vol. III, Ch. 7. A stimulating but partisan account of Fries's philosophy will be found in Leonard Nelson, *Fortschritte und Rückschritte der Philosophie* (Frankfurt, 1962). In connection with Fries's theory of law and religion, especially interesting are Julius Kraft, *Die Methode der Rechtstheorie in der Schule von Kant und Fries* (Berlin, 1924) and Rudolf Otto, *Kantisch-Fries'che Religionsphilosophie und ihre Anwendung auf die Theologie* (Tübingen: Mohr, 1909), translated by E. B. Dicker as *The Philosophy of Religion Based on Kant and Fries* (London: Williams and Norgate, 1931).

Alexander P. D. Mourelatos (1967)
Bibliography updated by Michael Farmer (2005)

FROEBEL, FRIEDRICH
(1782–1852)

Friedrich Froebel, the German philosopher of education, was born at Oberweissbach in Thuringia. He studied forestry and related fields at the University of Jena, came in contact with Johann Heinrich Pestalozzi in 1808, and participated as a volunteer in the war of liberation against Napoleon Bonaparte. In 1816 he established a school, which soon was moved from Griesheim to Keilhau, and in 1837 he founded his first kindergarten at Blankenburg in Thuringia, which became the model of many similar institutions. However, these institutions had to be closed in Prussia in 1851 because the government, as well as the clergy, suspected Froebel of liberal political and religious leanings. The prohibition lasted for ten years, but afterward the kindergarten movement spread rapidly throughout the European countries.

Froebel's whole educational theory and practice was determined by his conviction of the ultimate oneness of life, of nature and spirit. According to him it is the destiny of all things to unfold their divine essence and to reveal God in their transient being.

As Froebel's autobiography shows, he was, as a child, deeply troubled by the contrast between "spirit" and "the flesh" in the Christian supernaturalism and moralistic dualism of his father, a pastor, until he discovered the pervasive beauty of nature and the mystery of sex life in the whole creation. His conviction about the inner unity of the cosmos was confirmed by his scientific studies, his reading of the Zend-Avesta, and his acquaintance with Friedrich Schelling's philosophy of identity.

In conformity with his metaphysics, Froebel conceived of education as a continuation of the world's unceasing evolution on the level of consciousness, with the child's play being the first sign of life's urge toward purposeful activity. Thus, he wrote in *The Education of Man* (pp. 1ff.), "Education consists in leading man, as a thinking, intelligent being, growing into self-consciousness, to a pure, unsullied, conscious and free representation of the inner law of divine unity, and in teaching him means thereto." Out of respect for the "inner law of unity" or for life as an "unbroken whole in all its operations and phenomena" (*The Education of Man*, p. 238), the educator should organize the instructional process in such a way that the order of the subjects to be taught supports the learner's inner development, while the whole program of studies should help the student to realize the reflection of the unity of life in the unity of knowledge.

Froebel's educational principles may be summarized as follows:

(1) That the development of nature reveals itself in the development of the individual mind should be demonstrated in the teaching of science, the humanities, and religion.

(2) Education should be structured to harmonize with the natural inner development of the pupil.

(3) Education should unfold the whole man in each person. Religion should be taught in order to cultivate the emotions, nature should be studied because it is the self-revelation of God, and mathematics should be appreciated as the symbol of universal order. Language, too, connects man with the order and rhythm of things and should therefore take its part in education.

(4) The arts should be taught, for art is a general human talent and conducive to the harmonious unfolding of a person's inner life.

The central theme in Froebel's educational work is most evident in *The Education of Man,* which presents a unique attempt to provide an ontological explanation of the process of human learning.

Historically, Froebel must be understood as being in the tradition of John Comenius, Jean-Jacques Rousseau, and Pestalozzi. His ideas have been criticized for many and sometimes contradictory reasons: for their pantheistic naturalism, their romanticism, their individualism and neglect of discipline, their sentimentality and their one-sided emphasis on early childhood. But there can be no doubt that the work with which his name is mainly connected, the kindergarten, has been an inestimable blessing to humankind, and many of his psychological insights, like those of Pestalozzi, have been increasingly confirmed by modern psychology.

See also Art, Value in; Comenius, John Amos; German Philosophy; Pestalozzi, Johann Heinrich; Schelling, Friedrich Wilhelm Joseph von; Philosophy of Education, History of; Rousseau, Jean-Jacques.

Bibliography

Froebel's *Gesammelte pädagogische Schriften* was edited by Richard Lange (Berlin, 1862–1874). Of the many translations of this work, the following are most important: *Froebel's Chief Writings on Education,* translated by S. S. F. Fletcher and J. Walton (New York, 1912); *Education by Development,* translated by J. Jarvis (New York: Appleton, 1899); and *The Education of Man,* translated by W. N. Hailmann (New York: Appleton, 1887).

For literature on Froebel, see Robert Ulich, *History of Educational Thought* (New York: American Book, 1950), and his *Three Thousand Years of Educational Wisdom* (Cambridge, MA: Harvard University Press, 1954).

Robert Ulich (1967)

FRYE, MARILYN
(1941–)

Marilyn Frye, American feminist philosopher, was born in Tulsa, Oklahoma. She earned her bachelor's degree in philosophy from Stanford University in 1963, and her doctorate in philosophy at Cornell University in 1969, where she worked under the supervision of the analytic philosopher Max Black. She taught at the University of Pittsburgh, the University of Michigan, and the University of Washington before taking up a position at Michigan State University, where she was tenured in 1978, promoted to professor in 1983, and named University Distinguished Professor in 2003, the position she currently holds. Frye has held fellowships at the Center for the Study of Women in Society at the University of Oregon, the Center for Advanced Feminist Studies at the University of Minnesota, and the National Humanities Center in North Carolina. In 2001 she was awarded the Distinguished Woman Philosopher Award by the Society for Women in Philosophy.

Frye's writings reflect the analytic philosophical style of conceptual analysis and display clear, concise, jargon-free writing, though she applies this to subjects beyond the pale of the narrow world of analytic philosophy. Frye's dissertation, "Meaning and Illocutionary Force," and her first several articles in philosophy were on topics in philosophy of language. Subsequently she turned to topics in feminist philosophy, especially sexism, lesbianism, and racism, and it is in this field that she has made her most important contributions to philosophy. Frye expresses unusual commitment to bringing about social change through her writings. Moreover, she expresses herself with a pragmatic urgency frequently lacking in most professional philosophy, and she also makes exceptionally clear the time-bound and culture-bound nature of such change.

Frye's book *The Politics of Reality* (1983) begins with one of her most important and most often reprinted essays: "Oppression." In this essay she seeks to clarify the term "oppression" and how women can be said to be oppressed. Oppression, on her analysis, is a network of (often microscopic) forces that bind and confine certain social groups within a defined place so as to benefit a privileged social group. She analogizes oppression to a birdcage, which is macroscopic and visible, even though each of the wires of the cage is itself small and seemingly inconsequential in itself. Frye describes two characteristic features of women's oppression. First, women hold positions that simultaneously make them responsible yet powerless to effect decisions to carry out their responsibilities successfully. Second, women internalize and self-police their limitations and restrictions. While men also face social restrictions (e.g., they cannot cry in front of other men), their restrictions are a part of a system that oppresses women and privileges men. In her essay "Sexism," Frye defines "sexism" as an institutional term characterizing social structures that "create and enforce the elaborate and rigid patterns of sex-marking and sex-announcing which divide the species, along the line of sex, into dominators and subordinates" (1983, p. 38). She uses the term "male-chauvinism" to describe the personal relations that men engage in as dominators with women as subordinates. Most of the essays of the book are devoted to illuminating the social and personal relations that serve to oppress women.

In her writings, Frye illuminates the oppression of sexual minorities by heterosexuals and the oppression of minority races, and she connects these to the project of feminism. In two essays in her first book and in the majority of the essays of her book *Willful Virgin: Essays in Feminism* (1992), Frye takes up the theme of heterosexism as manifested in feminism and society at large. She carefully describes and analyzes the myriad ways in which heterosexuality is taken to be normative. In her essay "Willful Virgin, or Do You Have to Be a Lesbian to Be a Feminist," Frye argues, "The central constitutive dynamic and key mechanism of the global phenomenon of male domination, oppression and exploitation of females is near-universal female heterosexuality" (1992, p. 129). By the term "female heterosexism" she refers not to a preference to engage in heterosexual sex, but rather to the worship of men and maleness that heterosexuality has traditionally required of women. That is, sexism exists because most women willingly tolerate being subordinate to and serving men. Furthermore, because women are subordinate to "their" men, they often comply with whatever other oppression their men perpetrate, such as racism, classism, and ethnic oppression. Thus, not participating in the patriarchal institution of female heterosexuality is an important kind of resistance to oppression generally.

Frye also devotes particular attention to the struggle against racism. She notes that acting White is a way of being privileged, yet for women, acting White consists largely of conformity to white men's expectations of chastity, obedience, and decorum, does not offer any solace to white women, and serves only to separate them from other women. Thus for Frye, Whiteness, heterosexuality, and sexism are bound together in ways that institute and enforce patriarchy.

See also Feminist Philosophy.

Bibliography

WORKS BY FRYE

"Inscriptions and Indirect Discourse." *Journal of Philosophy* 61 (24) (1964): 767–772.

"Force and Meaning." *Journal of Philosophy* 70 (1974): 281–294.

The Politics of Reality: Essays in Feminist Theory. Trumansburg, NY: Crossing Press, 1983.

Willful Virgin: Essays in Feminism, 1976–1992. Freedom, CA: Crossing Press, 1992.

"The Necessity of Differences: Constructing a Positive Category of Women." *Signs: Journal of Women in Culture and Society* 21 (3) (1996): 991–1010.

Ann E. Cudd (2005)

FUNCTIONALISM

"Functionalism" is one of the major proposals that have been offered as solutions to the mind-body problem. Solutions to the mind-body problem usually try to answer questions such as: What is the ultimate nature of the mental? At the most general level, what makes a mental state mental? Or more specifically, what do thoughts have in common in virtue of which they are thoughts? That is, what makes a thought a thought? What makes a pain a pain? Cartesian dualism said the ultimate nature of the mental was to be found in a special mental substance. Behaviorism identified mental states with behavioral dispositions; physicalism, in its most influential version, identifies mental states with brain states. Functionalism says that mental states are constituted by their causal relations to one another and to sensory inputs and behavioral outputs. Functionalism is one of the major theoretical developments of twentieth-century analytic philosophy, and provides the conceptual underpinnings of much work in cognitive science.

Functionalism has three distinct sources. First, Hilary Putnam and Jerry Fodor saw mental states in terms of an empirical computational theory of the mind. Second, John Jamieson Carswell Smart's "topic neutral" analyses led David M. Armstrong and David Lewis to a functionalist analysis of mental concepts. Third, Ludwig Wittgenstein's idea of meaning as use led to a version of functionalism as a theory of meaning, further developed by Wilfrid Sellars and later Gilbert Harman.

One motivation behind functionalism can be appreciated by attention to artifact concepts such as *carburetor*, and biological concepts such as *kidney*. What it is for something to be a carburetor is for it to mix fuel and air in an internal combustion engine—*carburetor* is a functional concept. In the case of the kidney, the *scientific* concept is functional—defined in terms of a role in filtering the blood and maintaining certain chemical balances.

The kind of function relevant to the mind can be introduced via the parity-detecting automaton illustrated in the following figure, which tells us whether it has seen an odd or even number of "1"s. This automaton has two states, S_1 and S_2; one input, "1" (though its input can be nothing) and two outputs, it utters either the word "Odd" or "Even." The table describes two functions, one from input and state to output, and another from input and state to next state. Each square encodes two conditionals specifying the output and next state given both the current state and input. The left box says that if the machine is in S_1 and sees a "1," it says "odd" (indicating that it has seen an odd number of "1"s) and goes to S_2. The right box says, similarly, that if the machine is in S_2 and sees a "1," it says "even" and goes back to S_1.

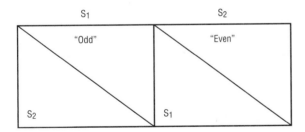

Now suppose we ask the question: "What is S_1?" The answer is that the nature of S_1 is entirely relational, and entirely captured by the table. We could give an explicit characterization of "S_1," as follows:

Being in S_1 = being in the first of two states that are related to one another and to inputs and outputs as follows: Being in one of the states and getting a "1" input results in going into the second state and emitting "Odd"; and being in the second of the two states and getting a "1" input results in going into the first and emitting "Even."

Making the quantification over states more explicit:

Being in S_1 = Being an x such that $\exists P \exists Q$[If x is in P and gets a "1" input, then it goes into Q and emits "Odd"; if x is in Q and gets a "1" input it gets into P and emits "Even" & x is in P] (Note: Read "$\exists P$" as "There is a property *P*.")

This illustration can be used to make a number of points. (1) According to functionalism, the nature of a mental state is just like the nature of an automaton state: constituted by its relations to other states and to inputs and outputs. All there is to S_1 is that being in it and getting a "1" input results in such and such, and so forth. According to functionalism, all there is to being in pain is that it disposes you to say "ouch," wonder whether you are ill, it distracts you, and so forth. (2) Because mental states are like automaton states in this regard, the illustrated method for defining automaton states is supposed to work for mental states as well. Mental states can be totally characterized in terms that involve only logicomathematical language and terms for input signals and behavioral outputs. Thus functionalism satisfies one of the desiderata of behaviorism, characterizing the mental in entirely nonmental language.

(3) S_1 is a second-order state in that it consists in having other properties, say mechanical or hydraulic or electronic properties, that have certain relations to one another. These other properties, the ones quantified over in the definitions just given, are said to be the realizations of the functional properties. So, although functionalism characterizes the mental in nonmental terms, it does so only by quantifying over realizations of mental states, which would not have delighted behaviorists. (4) One functional state can be realized in different ways. For example, an actual metal and plastic machine satisfying the machine table might be made of gears, wheels, pulleys and the like, in which case the realization of S_1 would be a mechanical state; or the realization of S_1 might be an electronic state, and so forth.

(5) Just as one functional state can be realized in different ways, one physical state can realize different functional states in different machines. This could happen, for example, if a single type of transistor were used to do different things in different machines. (6) Since S_1 can be realized in many ways, a claim that S_1 is a mechanical state would be false (at least arguably), as would a claim that S_1 is an electronic state. For this reason, there is a strong case that functionalism shows physicalism is false: If a creature without a brain can think, thinking cannot be a brain state. (But see the section on functionalism and physicalism below.)

The notion of a realization deserves further discussion. In the early days of functionalism, a first-order property was often said to realize a functional property in virtue of a 1-1 correspondence between the two realms of properties. But such a definition of realization produces far too many realizations. Suppose, for example, that at t_1

we shout "one" at a bucket of water, and then at t_2 we shout "one" again. We can regard the bucket as a parity-detecting automaton by pairing the physical configuration of the bucket at t_1 with S_1 and the heat emitted or absorbed by the bucket at t_1 with "odd"; by pairing the physical configuration of the bucket at t_2 with S_2 and the heat exchanged with the environment at t_2 with "even"; and so on. What is left out by the post hoc correlation way of thinking of realization is that a true realization must satisfy the *counterfactuals* implicit in the table. To be a realization of S_1, it is not enough to lead to a certain output and state given that the input is a "1"; it is also required that had the input been a "0," the S_1 realization would have led to the other output and state. Satisfaction of the relevant counterfactuals is built into the notion of realization mentioned in (3) above.

Suppose we have a theory of mental states that specifies all the causal relations among the states, sensory inputs, and behavioral outputs. Focusing on pain as a sample mental state, it might say, among other things, that sitting on a tack causes pain, and that pain causes anxiety and saying "ouch." Agreeing for the sake of the example to go along with this moronic theory, functionalism would then say that we could define "pain" as follows: being in pain = being in the first of two states, the first of which is caused by sitting on tacks, which in turn causes the other state and emitting "ouch." More symbolically

Being in pain = Being an x such that $\exists P \exists Q$[sitting on a tack causes P & P causes both Q and emitting "ouch" & x is in P]

More generally, if T is a psychological theory with n mental terms of which the 17th is "pain," we can define "pain" relative to T as follows (the "F_1" ... "F_n" are variables that replace the n mental terms, and i_1, etc. And o_1, etc. indicates):

Being in pain = Being an x such that $\exists F_1...\exists Fn$ [$T(F_1...F_n, i_1$, etc., o_1, etc.) & x is in F_{17}]

In this way, functionalism characterizes the mental in nonmental terms, in terms that involve quantification over realizations of mental states but no explicit mention of them; thus functionalism characterizes the mental in terms of structures that are tacked down to reality only at the inputs and outputs.

The psychological theory T just mentioned can be either an empirical psychological theory or else a commonsense "folk" theory, and the resulting functionalisms are very different. In the latter case, conceptual functionalism, the functional definitions are aimed at capturing our ordinary mental concepts. In the former case, "psychofunctionalism," the functional definitions are not supposed to capture ordinary concepts but are only supposed to fix the extensions of mental terms. The idea of psychofunctionalism is that the scientific nature of the mental consists not in anything biological, but in something "organizational," analogous to computational structure. Conceptual functionalism, by contrast, can be thought of as a development of logical behaviorism. Logical behaviorists thought that pain was a disposition to pain behavior. But as Peter Geach and Roderick Chisholm pointed out, what counts as pain behavior depends on the agent's beliefs and desires. Conceptual functionalists avoid this problem by defining each mental state in terms of its contribution to dispositions to behave—and have other mental states.

FUNCTIONALISM AND PHYSICALISM

Theories of the mind prior to functionalism have been concerned both with (1) what there is, and (2) what gives each type of mental state its own identity, for example what pains have in common in virtue of which they are pains. Stretching these terms a bit, we might say that (1) is a matter of ontology and (2) of metaphysics. Here are the ontological claims: Dualism told us that there are both mental and physical substances, whereas behaviorism and physicalism are monistic, claiming that there are only physical substances. Here are the metaphysical claims: Behaviorism tells us that what pains (for example) have in common in virtue of which they are pains is something behavioral; dualism gave a nonphysical answer to this question, and physicalism gives a physical answer to this question.

Turning now to functionalism, it answers the metaphysical question without answering the ontological question. Functionalism tells us that what pains have in common—what makes them pains—is their function; but functionalism does not tell us whether the beings that have pains have any nonphysical parts. This point can be seen in terms of the automaton described above. In order to be an automaton of the type described, an actual concrete machine need only have states related to one another and to inputs and outputs in the way described. The machine description does not tell us how the machine works or what it is made of, and in particular it does not rule out a machine which is operated by an immaterial soul, so long as the soul is willing to operate in the deterministic manner specified in the table.

In thinking about the relation between functionalism and physicalism, it is useful to distinguish two categories of physicalist theses: One version of physicalism competes with functionalism, making a metaphysical claim about the physical nature of mental state properties or types (and is thus often called "type" physicalism). As mentioned above, on one point of view, functionalism shows that type of physicalism is false.

However, there are more modest physicalisms whose thrusts are ontological rather than metaphysical. Such physicalistic claims are not at all incompatible with functionalism. Consider, for example, a physicalism that says that every actual thing is made up entirely of particles of the sort that compose inorganic matter. In this sense of physicalism, most functionalists have been physicalists. Further, functionalism can be modified in a physicalistic direction, for example, by requiring that all properties quantified over in a functional definition by physical properties. Type physicalism is often contrasted with token physicalism. (The word *teeth* in this sentence has five letter tokens of three letter types.) Token physicalism says that each pain (for example) is a physical state, but token physicalism allows that there may be nothing physical that all pains share, nothing physical that makes a pain a pain.

It is a peculiarity of the literature on functionalism and physicalism that while some functionalists say functionalism shows physicalism is false, others say functionalism shows physicalism is true. In Lewis's case, the issue is partly terminological. Lewis is a conceptual functionalist about "having pain." Having pain on Lewis's regimentation could be said to be a rigid designator of a functional property. (A rigid designator names the same thing in each possible world. "The color of the sky" is nonrigid, since it names red in worlds in which the sky is red. "Blue" is rigid, since it names blue even in worlds in which the sky is red.) "Pain," by contrast, is a nonrigid designator conceptually equivalent to a definite description of the form "the state with such and such a causal role." The referent of this phrase in us, Lewis holds, is a certain brain state, though the referent of this phrase in a robot might be a circuit state, and the referent in an angel would be a nonphysical state. Similarly, "the winning number" picks out "17" in one lottery and "596" in another. So Lewis is a functionalist (indeed a conceptual functionalist) about having pain.

In terms of the metaphysical issue described above—what do pains have in common in virtue of which they are pains—Lewis is a functionalist, not a physicalist. What a person's pains and the robot's pains share is a causal role, not anything physical. Just as there is no numerical similarity between 17 and 596 relevant to their being winning numbers, there is no physical similarity between human and Martian pain that makes them pains. And there is no physical similarity of any kind between human pains and angel pains. However, on the issue of the scientific nature of pain, Lewis is a physicalist. What is in common to human and Martian pain in his view is something conceptual, not something scientific.

FUNCTIONALISM AND PROPOSITIONAL ATTITUDES

The discussion of functional characterization given above assumes a psychological theory with a finite number of mental state terms. In the case of monadic states like pain, the sensation of red, and so forth, it does seem a theoretical option simply to list the states and their relations to other states, inputs and outputs. But for a number of reasons, this is not a sensible theoretical option for belief-states, desire-states, and other propositional attitude states. For one thing, the list would be too long to be represented without combinatorial methods. Indeed, there is arguably no upper bound on the number of propositions, any one of which could in principle be an object of thought. For another thing, there are systematic relations among beliefs: for example, the belief that John loves Mary and the belief that Mary loves John. These belief states represent the same objects as related to each other in converse ways. But a theory of the nature of beliefs can hardly just leave out such an important feature of them. We cannot treat "believes-that-grass-is-green," "believes-that-grass-is-blue," and so forth, as unrelated primitive predicates. So we will need a more sophisticated theory, one that involves some sort of combinatorial apparatus.

The most promising candidates are those that treat belief as a relation. But a relation to what? There are two distinct issues here. One issue is how to state the functional theory in a detailed way. A second issue is what types of states could possibly realize the relational propositional attitude states. Hartry Field and Fodor argue that to explain the productivity of propositional attitude states, there is no alternative to postulating a language of thought, a system of syntactically structured objects in the brain that express the propositions in propositional attitudes. In later work, Fodor has stressed the systematicity of propositional attitudes mentioned above. Fodor points out that the beliefs whose contents are systematically related exhibit the following sort of empirical relation: If one is capable of believing that Mary loves John, one is also capable of believing that John loves Mary. Fodor argues that only a language of thought in the brain could explain this fact.

EXTERNALISM

The upshot of the famous "twin earth" arguments has been that meaning and content are in part in the world and in the language community. Functionalists have responded in a variety of ways. One reaction is to think of the inputs and outputs of a functional theory as long-arm as including the objects that one sees and manipulates. Another reaction is to stick with short-arm inputs and outputs that stop at the surfaces of the body, thinking of the intentional contents thereby characterized as narrow—supervening on the nonrelational physical properties of the body. There has been no widely recognized account of what narrow content is, nor is there any agreement as to whether there is any burden of proof on the advocates of narrow content to characterize it.

MEANING

Functionalism says that understanding the meaning of the word *momentum* is a functional state. On one version of the view, the functional state can be seen in terms of the role of the word *momentum* itself in thinking, problem solving, planning, and so forth. But if understanding the meaning of *momentum* is this word's having a certain function, then there is a very close relation between the meaning of a word and its function, and a natural proposal is to regard the close relation as simply identity, that is, the meaning of the word just *is* that function. Thus functionalism about content leads to functionalism about meaning, a theory that purports to tell us the metaphysical nature of meaning. This theory is popular in cognitive science, where in one version it is often known as procedural semantics, as well as in philosophy where it is often known as conceptual role semantics. The theory has been criticized (along with other versions of functionalism) by Putnam, Fodor, and E. LePore.

HOLISM

Ned Block and Fodor noted the "damn/darn" problem. Functional theories must make reference to any difference in stimuli or responses that can be mentally significant. The difference between saying "damn" and "darn" when you stub your toe can, in some circumstances, be mentally significant. So the different functionalized theories appropriate to the two responses will affect the individuation of every state connected to those utterances, and for the same reason, every state connected to those states, and so on. His pains lead to "darn," hers to "damn," so their pains are functionally different, and likewise their desires to avoid pain, their beliefs that interact with those desires, and so on. Plausible assumptions lead to the con-

clusion that two individuals who differ in this way share almost nothing in the way of mental states. The upshot is that the functionalist needs a way of individuating mental states that is less fine-grained than appeal to the whole theory, a molecularist characterization. Even if one is optimistic about solving this problem in the case of pain by finding something functional in common to all pains, one cannot assume that success will transfer to beliefs or meanings, for success in the case of meaning and belief may involve an analytic/synthetic distinction.

QUALIA

Recall the parity-detecting automaton described at the beginning of this entry. It could be instantiated by two people, each of whom is in charge of the function specified by a single box. Similarly, the much more complex functional organization of a human mind could "in principle" be instantiated by a vast army of people. We would have to think of the army as connected to a robot body, acting as the brain of that body, and the body would be like a person in its reactions to inputs. But would such an army really instantiate a mind? More pointedly, could such an army have pain, or the experience of red? If functionalism ascribes minds to things that do not have them, it is too liberal. W. G. Lycan suggests that we include much of human physiology in our theory to be functionalized to avoid liberalism; that is, the theory T in the definition described earlier would be a psychological theory plus a physiological theory. But that makes the opposite problem, chauvinism, worse. The resulting functional description will not apply to intelligent Martians whose physiologies are different from ours. Further, it seems easy to imagine a simple pain-feeling organism that shares little in the way of functional organization with us. The functionalized physiological theory of this organism will be hopelessly different from the corresponding theory of us. Indeed, even if one does not adopt Lycan's tactic, it is not clear how pain could be characterized functionally so as to be common to us and the simple organism.

Much of the force of the problems just mentioned derives from attention to phenomenal states like the look of red. Phenomenal properties would seem to be intrinsic to (nonrelational properties of) the states that have them, and thus phenomenal properties seem independent of the relations among states, inputs and outputs that define functional states. Consider, for example, the fact that lobotomy patients often say that they continue to have pains that feel the same as before, but that the pains do not bother them. If the concept of pain is a functional concept, what these patients say is contradictory or incoherent—but it seems to many of us that it is intelligible.

The chauvinism/liberalism problem affects the characterization of inputs and outputs. If we characterize inputs and outputs in a way appropriate to our bodies, we chauvinistically exclude creatures whose interface with the world is very different from ours—for example, creatures whose limbs end in wheels or, turning to a bigger difference, gaseous creatures who can manipulate and sense gases but for whom all solids and liquids are alike. The obvious alternative of characterizing inputs and outputs themselves functionally would appear to yield an abstract structure that might be satisfied by, for example, the economy of Bolivia under manipulation by a wealthy eccentric, and would thus fall to the opposite problem of liberalism.

It is tempting to respond to the chauvinism problem by supposing that the same functional theory that applies to a person also applies to the creatures with wheels. If they thought they had feet, they would try to act like us, and if we thought we had wheels, we would try to act like them. But notice that the functional definitions have to have some specifications of output organs in them. To be neutral among all the types of bodies that sentient beings could have would just be to adopt the liberal alternative of specifying the inputs and outputs themselves functionally.

TELEOLOGY

Many philosophers propose that we avoid liberalism by characterizing functional roles teleologically. We exclude the armies and economies mentioned because their states are not for the right things. A major problem for this point of view is the lack of an acceptable teleological account. Accounts based on evolution smack up against the swamp-grandparents problem. Suppose you find out that your grandparents were formed from particles from the swamp that came together by chance. So, as it happens, you do not have any evolutionary history to speak of. If evolutionary accounts of the teleology underpinnings of content are right, your states do not have any content. A theory with such a consequence should be rejected.

CAUSATION

Functionalism dictates that mental properties are second-order properties, properties that consist in having other properties that have certain relations to one another. But there is at least a prima facie problem about how such second-order properties could be causal and explanatory

in a way appropriate to the mental. Consider, for example, provocativeness, the second-order property that consists in having some first-order property (say redness) that causes bulls to be angry. The cape's redness provokes the bull, but does the cape's provocativeness provoke the bull? The cape's provocativeness might provoke an animal protection society, but is not the bull too stupid to be provoked by it?

Functionalism continues to be a lively and fluid point of view. Positive developments in recent years include enhanced prospects for conceptual functionalism and the articulation of the teleological point of view. Critical developments include problems with causality and holism, and continuing controversy over chauvinism and liberalism.

See also Armstrong, David M.; Behaviorism; Causation: Metaphysical Issues; Causation: Philosophy of Science; Chisholm, Roderick; Cognitive Science; Computationalism; Harman, Gilbert; Language of Thought; Lewis, David; Materialism; Meaning; Metaphysics; Mind-Body Problem; Ontology; Philosophy of Mind; Physicalism; Propositional Attitudes: Issues in Philosophy of Mind and Psychology; Propositional Attitudes: Issues in Semantics; Putnam, Hilary; Qualia; Sellars, Wilfrid; Smart, John Jamieson Carswell; Wittgenstein, Ludwig Josef Johann.

Bibliography

Ben-Yami, H. "An Argument against Functionalism." *Australasian Journal of Philosophy* 77 (1999): 320–324.

Block, N. "The Mind as the Software of the Brain." In *An Invitation to Cognitive Science*, edited by D. Osherton, et al. Cambridge, MA: MIT Press, 1995.

Braddon-Mitchell, D., and F. Jackson. *Philosophy of Mind and Cognition*. Oxford: Blackwell, 1997.

Crane, T. *Mechanical Mind: A Philosophical Introduction to Minds, Machines, and Mental Representation*. London: Routledge, 2003.

David, M. "Kim's Functionalism." *Philosophical Perspectives* 11 (1997): 133–148.

Melnyk, A. *A Physicalist Manifesto*. Cambridge, U.K.: Cambridge University Press, 2003.

Polger, T. *Natural Minds*. Cambridge, MA: MIT Press, 2004.

Shoemaker, S. "Realization and Mental Causation." In *Physicalism and Its Discontents*, edited by C. Gillett and B. Loewer. Cambridge, U.K.: Cambridge University Press, 2001.

Ned Block (1996)
Bibliography updated by Alyssa Ney (2005)

FUNCTIONALISM IN SOCIOLOGY

In sociology and social anthropology the term "functional analysis" is used not only in the mathematical sense, where a function expresses a correspondence between two variables such that for every value of the one there are one or more determinate values of the other, and the second, or dependent, variable is, in a less technical use of the term, said to be a function of the first. Sociologists, of course, like all scientists, are interested in establishing such dependencies. The term "functional analysis" in their work also has a special connotation analogous to the use of the notion of "function" in describing biological systems or such artifacts as are self-organizing systems—for example, a heat engine with a thermostat. Such a system can be considered as a unitary whole; it is differentiated into elements, and the function of the elements can be said to be the part they play in maintaining the system in a persisting state or (in the case of artifacts) in maintaining the efficiency of the system for the purpose for which it has been set up. There are, however, differences between the use of the notion in sociology and the use as applied to biological and artificial systems, and these have become more apparent as sociologists have worked with and reflected on "functional methods." The differences hinge on the questions of whether a society should be taken to be a single integrated system or whether it may be so diversified that what is "functional" for one part may not be so for others, and whether the only "end" to which an element of a social system should be shown to contribute is the maintenance of the system as a whole in its environment.

FUNCTION AND CULTURAL FACTS

Functional notions were used by the pioneers of modern social anthropology and sociology, Émile Durkheim and W. Robertson Smith. The term *functionalism,* however, was first put forward as the name of a special method and approach by Bronislaw Malinowski in the article "Anthropology" in the *Encyclopaedia Britannica* (13th ed., supp. I). The article reads as something of a manifesto, in which functionalism is said to be "the right method" in social anthropology. Functional analysis is said to be "explanation of … facts … by the part they play within the integral system of culture, by the manner in which they are related to each other within the system, and by the manner in which this system is related to the physical surroundings. … The functional view … insists therefore upon the principle that in every type of civilisation, every

custom, material object, idea and belief fulfils some vital function, has some task to accomplish, represents an indispensable part within a working whole" (ibid., pp. 132–133). Thus, the function of magic is said to consist in its being "a remedy for specific maladjustments and mental conflicts, which culture creates in allowing man to transcend his biological equipment" (ibid., p. 136), and myth is said to perform an "indispensable function" in strengthening the traditions on which a cultural life depends.

These claims for the "functional method" were both vague and grandiose. Later exponents and critics of a functional method in the social sciences have been concerned to state more precisely what it does and what it does not claim to assert. (See especially Merton, 1957, and Nagel, 1956.) Malinowski's account left the notion of the "needs" to which a function was said to be related insufficiently clear; his use of the word *indispensable* left it uncertain whether the "needs" themselves were indispensable to the society in question or whether the particular cultural item held to be the means of satisfying them was indispensable in the sense of not admitting of a substitute.

Malinowski's statement of the method was also far more than a recommendation to anthropologists to look for functions; it was a dogmatic assertion that "an object … appears as 'inessential,' 'arbitrary,' 'devoid of function' only as long as we do not understand the function of that detailed feature or object" (ibid., pp. 138–139). It also implied that every cultural item was necessary to the working of the social system as a whole. Of course, if the social system is defined as the total complex of all its cultural items, this becomes tautological. Malinowski avoided this by speaking of "vital needs" that the elements in the system are held to fulfill. But the notion of "needs," interpreted biologically and psychologically, is so extremely general that it is not shown why they can be fulfilled only by particular cultural arrangements.

FUNCTION AND SOCIAL STRUCTURE

The next leading anthropologist to use and also to write about "functional methods" was A. R. Radcliffe-Brown. (See especially his *Structure and Function in Primitive Society.*) Radcliffe-Brown worked with an even more "organic" notion of a society than did Malinowski, since the latter held that practices in a society should be seen as functional for the biological and psychological needs of its *members,* while Radcliffe-Brown was interested in seeing the function of a particular social usage as the contribution it makes to the *total social life,* which is unified as

ENCYCLOPEDIA OF PHILOSOPHY
2nd edition

a social system. Radcliffe-Brown regarded a social system as a set of interconnected features of social life, while he defined a social structure as "an arrangement of persons in institutionally controlled and defined relations." This definition appears insufficiently abstract: "Social structure" surely should not be used to refer to persons in relationships, but to the distinguishable pattern of recurrent sets of relationships described by social roles. But Radcliffe-Brown's account helped to link the notion of function with that of structure; that is, the uses studied were not those of separate cultural items, but of persistent forms of social relations, such as those shown in marriage arrangements.

The linking of function with structure helps to strengthen the biological, organic analogy behind this way of thinking. Thus, Radcliffe-Brown spoke of a social system as though it were a unitary whole in which every part is internally related to every other, and where it is possible to speak, by analogy with a biological organism, of the structure as serving a "total life." Following this analogy, the use so served is seen as the survival of the total society as an ongoing concern. This way of looking on a society was no doubt made more plausible by the fact that the societies so studied were small-scale primitive ones, where the society might seem to be a whole of integrated parts that, it was thought, could be exhaustively enumerated. It becomes much less plausible when applied to larger, more flexible societies comprising a number of subgroups that often are hostile to one another. This may also explain why it appeared that the "function" served was the survival of the society in its traditional given form and why, therefore, functional theory has been held to support a conservative ideology.

THE CONTEXT OF A FUNCTION

That functional theory need not be conservative was shown by Thomas Merton, who defined its central orientation as "the practice of interpreting data by establishing their consequences for larger structures in which they are implicated." Merton pointed out that although the notion of function is related to that of some end or need served, this end may not be the perpetuation of the existing social system. Subgroups may have radical interests served by certain social practices that would thus be functional within the context of those interests. Hence, it is not meaningful to speak of a cultural element or institutional practice simply as "functional." It must be shown to be functional in some specific context and in some specific respect; that is, it must have designated consequences for designated properties of designated units, but these

units need not be "the society as a whole." However, the notion does presuppose some complex context in which it is possible to show how certain elements have certain consequences contributing to the complex being maintained in a certain state or to the furthering of some interest to which one "function" is related. That an element has such a function relative to such a context or interest can be stated as a matter of descriptive fact, and it need have no ethical implication to the effect that the interest itself (or the function) is thereby commended. Still less need it imply that persons or groups in a society are of consequence only because of such alleged functions.

EXPLANATIONS AND DESCRIPTIONS

How far can the direction of attention to consequences be a form not only of description but also of explanation? Malinowski spoke of such functional analyses as "explanations," though he also remarked that explanation, to the scientific thinker, is nothing but the most adequate description of a complex fact (*A Scientific Theory of Culture*, New York, 1944, p. 117). Whether or not this is a satisfactory view of scientific explanation, there remains the question of whether a functional analysis is the most adequate description of a complex fact *tout court*, or rather a description of the effects of certain elements in the complex on certain other elements; that is, a partial description from the point of view of a particular interest. Merton indeed used the word *interpretation*, which is presumably weaker than "explanation," and he spoke throughout his work of "functional analyses."

A functional analysis would be an explanation only if the answer to the question "What is the effect of x in context a, b, c?" could also be seen as an answer to the question "Why does x occur?" or "Why does x have the character it has?" It could be so put if the effect of x is the intended effect of an intentional action (the effect of my turning the key is to unlock the door, and the reason I turn the key is to unlock the door); that is, if the explanation is explicitly teleological, so that it is said that x occurs in order to produce the effect y.

The interest of sociologists is, however, largely directed to detecting the unintended and unanticipated consequences of actions (what Merton called their "latent" as distinct from their "manifest" functions). In such cases, can an effect y be cited as an explanation, or partial explanation, answering the question "Why does x occur?" Can functional statements in contexts where conscious purpose is presumably absent be looked on as explanations? Jonathan Cohen has defined a functional explanation as one in which the fact to be explained, for example, the beating of the heart, is a necessary condition for that which is cited as explaining it, for example, "to circulate the blood" ("Teleological Explanation," *PAS* 51 [1950–1951]: 255–292; cf. D. M. Emmet, *Function, Purpose and Powers,* pp. 48ff.)

This definition describes the form of a functional statement, but does it show that it is a different kind of explanation from a causal one? Ernest Nagel claimed that the factual content of such functional statements can be exhaustively translated into causal terms (*Logic without Metaphysics,* pp. 250–251); for example, "the beating of the heart is a necessary condition for maintaining the circulation of the blood." Similarly Kingsley Davis, in "The Myth of Functional Analysis as a Special Method in Sociology and Anthropology," maintained that such statements simply assert that certain phenomena have certain consequences. To direct attention to consequences, especially unintended but interconnected consequences, is, he held, the distinctive approach of sociologists. "Functional" analysis is therefore not a special method in sociology, but just sociological method; and the name "functionalism," as supposedly that of a special movement or school, had better be dropped.

From this it would appear that functional statements can be explanations where they can be interpreted teleologically in terms of purpose; that is, where to say an element in a system has a function is to say that it is as it is because it has been so designed with reference to a purpose for which the system has been set up. Where this reference to purpose cannot be made, functional statements would be a form of causal statement in which the interest is directed not to the cause of a phenomenon itself, but to its effects considered as causes within a wider context. However, the reference to a wider context and the need for this to be a context within which some systematic interconnections can be shown distinguish such statements from those presenting unilinear sequences of cause and effect.

SELF-REGULATING SYSTEM

Functional statements are also particularly appropriate in those systematic contexts in which "return effects" on the cause itself can be shown; that is, where some of its consequences react back on it, so that the consequences can be invoked to explain, in part at any rate, why it is as it is. Thus, Nagel held that functional statements are most appropriately used in describing self-maintaining or self-regulating systems. His formulation for such systems can be briefly summarized as follows: Let S be a system and E its environment, and let S be functional, self-maintaining,

or directively organized with respect to a trait (property, state, process), G. Let S undergo a series of alterations terminating in G. Let there then be some fairly extensive class of changes either in E or in certain parts of S. Then, unless S contains some mechanism that produces effects compensating for these changes, S will cease to exhibit G or the tendency to acquire G.

The system S must be specified to show how its parts are causally relevant to the state G, and if the "function" of a part in maintaining G against changes is to be cited as a cause of the state of S, the return effects of this part on other parts of S must be specified. The instantaneous values of the state coordinates must be independent at any given time, although the values of one set at one time will not be independent of those of another set at another given time (that is, the values in one set will change according to previous changes in another set). Nagel held that the relations between the elements in a functional system need to be thus precisely specified, and that very few "functional analyses" in sociology satisfy these requirements.

LATENT AND MANIFEST FUNCTIONS

Nevertheless, sociologists may be said to produce analyses in which they seek to approximate this model even if they do not entirely satisfy it. This is true particularly where the data studied are shown to have consequences in some larger context, and the consequences are return effects upon the data themselves, so that there is a mutual reinforcement. For instance, Malinowski claimed that the "function" of myths was to strengthen the traditions that help to maintain a social way of life. This may not have been the original reason for the creation of the myth (whatever this may have been, it was said by Malinowski to be sociologically unimportant). But it may be the case that the fact that the myth now performs this perhaps originally unintended function strengthens people's interest in the myth and its hold upon them, and so serves to perpetuate it. Perhaps in some cases what was a "latent" function of some activity, such as recounting a myth, can thus be made the "manifest" function, the explicit purpose of the activity, without disturbing the disposition of its practitioners to go on doing it. But in some cases this may not be true. When, for instance, Malinowski said that "the function of religion is to relieve anxiety," or others (such as Radcliffe-Brown) said that the function of religious ritual is to strengthen the will to maintain the common values on which the society depends, it is at least open to question whether the adherents of a religion would be able to go on practicing it if they came to look on these functions as the "real reason" for doing so. Thus in some cases the change of a latent into a manifest function will be self-frustrating.

Certain conclusions can be drawn. First, it is misleading to speak of *the* function of a practice, belief, or institution *tout court*. It may have *a* function in relation to a certain interest in a certain context, and this itself may be a disfunction in relation to other interests. Thus, the fact that religion can sometimes relieve anxiety might be a disadvantage in contexts where interest lay in religion as a challenge to complacency.

Further, if such statements of "function" are to do more than merely describe consequences, it should be possible to show that the alleged function also reinforces the practice of the activity. But this must not be taken to imply that this is the sole or "real" reason for the practice. Thus, it may well be that, because of the complexity of human motivation, religious practices sometimes (not necessarily or always) relieve anxieties or promote loyalty to common values; if so, this can strengthen inducements to perform them.

The fact that activities performed with one interest in view can have unanticipated consequences in satisfying other interests can add to the survival value of these activities. Thus, Max Weber's well-known view that there was a nexus between the Calvinistic ethic and the pursuit of capitalist enterprise should not be taken to imply that "the function" of Calvinistic religion was to promote moneymaking (or vice versa), still less that the pursuit of the former was a hypocritical cloak for the latter. Rather, Weber's view implies that a particular kind of moral outlook, stressing diligence, thrift, and abstinence, was appropriate to the furtherance of capitalist enterprise, so that two independent and strong human interests, the religious and the economic, reinforced each other and thus helped to establish a way of life with considerable survival value. (It is worth noticing that this particular nexus could probably become established only under social and environmental conditions where there were opportunities for the entrepreneur who could save capital. But this is not to interpret these probably necessary conditions as sufficient conditions for explaining the Calvinistic way of life.)

A functional approach in sociology can therefore be taken not as the assumption that every cultural item has a function, but as a directive to watch for "functions," particularly in the unintended consequences of a form of social action, above all for those functions that react back on the form of social action itself, so as to produce a mutually reinforcing nexus. But the analogy with biolog-

ical or with self-organizing systems must not be pressed too far, since behind forms of social activity are persons or groups capable of entertaining a variety of values and interests. Functional statements in sociology, even if they are not themselves teleological, carry an indirect teleological implication in that if something is said to have a function it has one in relation to some value, interest, or purpose held by some person or group within the society (though not necessarily by the sociologist himself, who may simply be reporting the fact that some form of activity promotes this value). Where no value is stated, the presumption tends to be that what is served is the preservation of the society as an ongoing concern. That it is desirable to preserve the society (though not necessarily just in its existing form) is taken for granted by almost everyone. Thus, when something is said to have a "function" in maintaining the society, although the point is not always recognized, one ingredient in the complex notion of function is a value judgment.

See also Durkheim, Émile; Functionalism; Nagel, Ernest; Sociology of Knowledge; Weber, Max.

Bibliography

There is an extensive literature discussing functional methods in sociology. Most of it is surveyed by Robert K. Merton, "Manifest and Latent Functions," in his *Social Theory and Social Structure* (Glencoe, IL: Free Press, 1949; revised and enlarged, 1957), pp. 19–84.

Discussions of the use of functionalism in anthropology up to 1954 are considered by Raymond Firth, "Function," in *Year Book of Anthropology* (Glencoe, IL, 1956).

See especially Bronislaw Malinowski, "Anthropology," in *Encyclopaedia Britannica,* 13th ed., supplement I (Chicago, 1926); A. R. Radcliffe-Brown, *Structure and Function in Primitive Society* (London: Cohen and West, 1952), which contains some papers and addresses written some 20 years before publication; and Talcott Parsons, *Essays in Sociological Theory, Pure and Applied* (Glencoe, IL: Free Press, 1957).

Other discussions include Ernest Nagel, "Formalization of Functionalism," in his *Logic without Metaphysics* (Glencoe, IL: Free Press, 1957), pp. 247–283, and *The Structure of Science* (New York: Harcourt Brace, 1961), pp. 520–535; D. M. Emmet, *Function, Purpose and Powers* (London, 1957); Kingsley Davis, "The Myth of Functional Analysis as a Special Method in Sociology and Anthropology," in *American Sociological Review* 24 (1959): 757ff.; C. G. Hempel, "The Logic of Functional Analysis," in *Symposium on Sociological Theory,* edited by Llewellyn Gross (Evanston, IL: Row, Peterson, 1959).

Dorothy M. Emmet (1967)

FUZZY LOGIC

"Fuzzy logics" are multivalued logics intended to model human reasoning with certain types of imprecision. The field of fuzzy logic originated with a 1965 paper by Lotfi Zadeh, a professor of engineering at the University of California, Berkeley. It is significant that the inventor of fuzzy logic was neither a philosopher nor a linguist. Since 1965 research in fuzzy logic has always had an engineering and mathematical bent, while the philosophical foundations of fuzzy logic have always been under attack.

Many different formal systems have been proposed under the general name of fuzzy logic, but there is wide acceptance that the fundamental principles of fuzzy logic are

(1) $$t(A \wedge B) = \min\{t(A), t(B)\}$$

(2) $$t(A \vee B) = \max\{t(A), t(B)\}$$

(3) $$t(\neg A) = 1 - t(A).$$

In these axioms A and B represent arbitrary propositions. The truth value of A, a real number between 0 and 1, is denoted $t(A)$. The first axiom above says that the truth value of $A \wedge B$ is the lesser of the truth value of A and the truth value of B. The second and third axioms concerning disjunction and negation are to be understood similarly.

At the same time that Zadeh introduced fuzzy logic, he also introduced fuzzy set theory, a variant of naive set theory (i.e., everyday set theory as opposed to a foundational set theory such as the Zermelo-Fraenkel axioms) with the basic axioms

(1) $$\mu(x \in P \cap Q) = \min\{\mu(x \in P), \mu(x \in Q)\}$$

(2) $$\mu(x \in P \cup Q) = \max\{\mu(x \in P), \mu(x \in Q)\}$$

(3) $$\mu(x \in P^c) = 1 - \mu(x \in P).$$

Here $\mu\,(x \in P)$ denotes the degree to which x is a member of the set P. Since 1965 many branches of mathematics have been generalized along fuzzy set theory lines.

There are two fundamental differences between fuzzy logics and conventional logics such as classical predicate calculus or modal logics. Although these differences are technical, they are of considerable philosophical significance. First, conventional logics (except intuitionistic logics) require for every proposition that either it or its negation be true, that is, that $t(A \vee \neg A) = 1$ in fuzzy logic notation. In fuzzy logics this "law of the excluded middle" does not hold. Second, there is no consensus about a semantics for fuzzy logic that is well-defined independently of its proof theory, that is, the inferential axioms given above. In contrast, conventional logics have well-accepted semantics, for example Tarskian model theory for predicate calculus, and Kripkean possible worlds semantics for modal logics.

Fuzzy logics are claimed to be capable of representing the meanings of intrinsically imprecise natural language sentences, such as "Many Texans are rich," for which the law of excluded middle fails. There is disagreement as to whether fuzzy methods successfully represent the complexities of concepts such as "many" and "rich." What is clear is that the rules of fuzzy logic cannot be used for reasoning about frequentist or subjective types of uncertainty, whose properties are captured by standard probability theory. The central issue here is that the probability of a compound proposition such as $A \wedge B$ is not a function just of the probabilities of the propositions A and B: The probability of $A \wedge B$ also depends on the relationship between the propositions A and B, in particular on their independence or correlation.

The tolerance for ambiguity found in fuzzy logic, and specifically the rejection of the law of the excluded middle, is a revolutionary idea in mathematical logic. Some advocates of fuzzy logic claim that tolerance for ambiguity is also revolutionary philosophically, since Western philosophy, from Plato through René Descartes, has supposedly been an intrinsically dualistic tradition. According to this argument, fuzzy logic has been better received in Japan and other Asian countries than in the West because of the holistic, subtle nature of the Eastern intellectual tradition. Apart from the dualistic oversimplification of the distinction between "Western" and "Eastern" thought, this claim also ignores the continuous holistic tradition in European philosophical thought, from Zeno through Blaise Pascal to Martin Heidegger and Ludwig Wittgenstein.

There has been much artificial intelligence research on using fuzzy logic for representing real-world knowledge, and there has been some recent convergence between this work and parallel work by a distinct research community on knowledge representation using classical logics, nonmonotonic logics, and probability theory. So far this research has remained almost exclusively theoretical. In contrast, engineering work on using fuzzy logic for controlling complex machines heuristically has been highly successful in practice.

A fuzzy controller is a device, usually implemented as software for an embedded microprocessor, that continually monitors readings from sensors, and makes decisions about actuator settings. For example, a controller for the automatic transmission of a car monitors road speed, the position of the accelerator pedal, and other factors, and decides whether to shift gears down or up, or not to shift. The knowledge possessed by a fuzzy controller is typically represented as rules such as

$$\mu(speed, \text{MODERATE}) \wedge \mu(pedal, \text{FULL-DOWN}) \rightarrow$$
$$\mu(shift, \text{DOWN})$$

Here *speed* and *pedal* are sensory readings, *shift* is a possible actuator setting, and MODERATE, FULL-DOWN, and DOWN are fuzzy sets. Through inference rules for the fuzzy connectives $\wedge$ and $\rightarrow$, the degree of membership of *speed* in MODERATE and of *pedal* in FULL-DOWN determines the desired degree of membership of *shift* in DOWN. Given a set of rules, a fuzzy controller continually computes the degree to which the antecedents of each rule are satisfied, and selects a conclusion that is the weighted average of the conclusion of each rule, where rules are weighted using these degrees.

Fuzzy controllers are widely used for two basic reasons. First, since the action chosen at each instant is typically the result of interpolating several rules, their behavior is smooth. Second, fuzzy controller rule sets are easy for humans to read and understand intuitively, hence easy to construct by trial and error.

See also Artificial Intelligence; Descartes, René; Heidegger, Martin; Kripke, Saul; Logic, History of; Mathematics, Foundation of; Modal Logic; Model Theory; Pascal, Blaise; Plato; Probability and Chance; Proof Theory; Quantum Mechanics; Semantics; Set Theory; Tarski, Alfred; Wittgenstein, Ludwig Josef Johann; Zeno of Elea.

Bibliography

Elkan, C. "The Paradoxical Success of Fuzzy Logic." *IEEE Expert* 6 (August 1994): 3–8.

Mamdani, E. H. "Application of Fuzzy Algorithms for Control of Simple Dynamic Plant." *Proceedings of the Institution of Electrical Engineers* 121 (1974): 1585–1588.

Zadeh, L. A. "Fuzzy Sets." *Information and Control* 8 (1965): 338–353.

Zimmermann, H.-J. *Fuzzy Set Theory—And Its Applications.* Boston: Kluwer Academic, 1991.

Charles Elkan (1996)